J APAN

19th E it on

WI   Stay and Eat
for   dgets

Mu   e Sights
an   al Secrets

---

a You Can Trust

Fodor's Travel Publications   New York, Toronto, London, Sydney, Auckland
www.fodors.com

FODOR'S JAPAN
Editors: Stephanie E. Butler, Alexis C. Kelly

Editorial Contributor: Mark Sullivan

Writers: Joshua Bisker, Brett Bull, Nicholas Coldicott, Maruan El Mahgiub, James Hadfield, Amanda Harlow, Misha Janette, Kaya Laterman, Kevin Mcgue, Robert Morel, and John Malloy Quinn

Production Editor: Carrie Parker
Maps & Illustrations: David Lindroth, *cartographer*; Bob Blake, Rebecca Baer, *map editors*; William Wu, *information graphics*
Design: Fabrizio La Rocca, *creative director*; Guido Caroti, Siobhan O'Hare, *art directors*; Tina Malaney, Chie Ushio, Ann McBride, Jessica Walsh, *designers*; Melanie Marin, *senior picture editor*
Cover Photo: Cherry blossoms, Tokyo: Corbis
Production Manager: Angela L. McLean

19th Edition

ISBN 978-1-4000-0827-8

ISSN 0736-9956

SPECIAL SALES
This book is available at special discounts for bulk purchases for sales promotions or premiums. Special editions, including personalized covers, excerpts of existing books, and corporate imprints, can be created in large quantities for special needs. For more information, write to Special Markets/Premium Sales, 1745 Broadway, MD 6-2, New York, New York 10019, or e-mail specialmarkets@randomhouse.com.

AN IMPORTANT TIP & AN INVITATION
Although all prices, opening times, and other details in this book are based on information supplied to us at press time, changes occur all the time in the travel world, and Fodor's cannot accept responsibility for facts that become outdated or for inadvertent errors or omissions. So **always confirm information when it matters**, especially if you're making a detour to visit a specific place. Your experiences—positive and negative—matter to us. If we have missed or misstated something, **please write to us.** We follow up on all suggestions. Contact the Japan editor at editors@fodors.com or c/o Fodor's at 1745 Broadway, New York, NY 10019.

PRINTED IN THE UNITED STATES OF AMERICA

10 9 8 7 6 5 4 3 2 1

Be a Fodor's Correspondent

Share your trip with Fodor's

Our latest guidebook to Japan owes its success to travelers like you. Sprinkled throughout this guide you'll find "Word of Mouth" features, which include tips, suggestions, and experiences shared by our community of travelers on Fodors.com. Also, the guide's opening chapter is devoted to helping you determine the kind of trip you'd like to take. Picture yourself in the photos that appear throughout this chapter. Several were submitted by members of Fodors.com in the "Show Us Your . . . Japan" photo contest. We gratefully acknowledge the Japan National Tourism Organization, whose sponsorship of the contest made the inclusion of these photos possible. On page 10 you'll find the winning photograph, taken by Fodors.com member Jay Sottolano.

No other guide to Japan is as up to date or has as much practical planning information. If you feel inspired and can plan a better trip because of what you find here, we've done our job.

Now we invite you to join the conversation: Your opinion matters to us and to your fellow travelers. Come to Fodors.com to plan your trip, share your experience, ask a question, submit a photograph, post a review, or write a trip report. Please tell our editors about your trip to—what went well and how we can make this guide even better—by sending us feedback at our website (*www.fodors.com/feedback*) or sending an email to *editors@fodors.com* with the subject heading "Japan Editor." You may find your comments published in a future Fodor's guide. We look forward to hearing from you.

Itterasshai! (Happy Traveling!)

Tim Jarrell, Publisher

CONTENTS

CONTENTS

ABOUT
THIS BOOK

Our Ratings

Sometimes you find terrific travel experiences and sometimes they just find you. But usually the burden is on you to select the right combination of experiences. That's where our ratings come in.

As travelers we've all discovered a place so wonderful that its worthiness is obvious. And sometimes that place is so experiential that superlatives don't do it justice: you just have to be there to know. These sights, properties, and experiences get our highest rating, **Fodor's Choice,** indicated by orange stars throughout this book.

Black stars highlight sights and properties we deem **Highly Recommended,** places that our writers, editors, and readers praise again and again for consistency and excellence.

By default, there's another category: any place we include in this book is by definition worth your time, unless we say otherwise. And we will.

Disagree with any of our choices? Care to nominate a place or suggest that we rate one more highly? Visit our feedback center at www.fodors.com/feedback.

Budget Well

Hotel and restaurant price categories from ¢ to $$$$ are defined in the opening pages of each chapter. For attractions, we always give standard adult admission fees; reductions are usually available for children, students, and senior citizens. Want to pay with plastic? **AE, D, DC, MC, V** following restaurant and hotel listings indicate if American Express, Discover, Diners Club, MasterCard, and Visa are accepted.

Restaurants

Unless we state otherwise, restaurants are open for lunch and dinner daily. We mention dress only when there's a specific requirement and reservations only when they're essential or not accepted—it's always best to book ahead.

Hotels

Hotels have private bath, phone, TV, and air-conditioning and operate on the European Plan (aka EP, meaning without meals), unless we specify that they use the Continental Plan (CP, with a continental breakfast), Breakfast Plan (BP, with a full breakfast), or Modified American Plan (MAP, with breakfast and dinner), or are all-inclusive (AI, including all meals and most activities). We

always list facilities but not whether you'll be charged an extra fee to use them, so when pricing accommodations, find out what's included.

Many Listings
★ Fodor's Choice
★ Highly recommended
⊠ Physical address
✢ Directions
⌂ Mailing address
☎ Telephone
🖷 Fax
⊕ On the Web
✑ E-mail
🎫 Admission fee
☉ Open/closed times
Ⓜ Metro stations
🖃 Credit cards

Hotels & Restaurants
🏨 Hotel
🛏 Number of rooms
⚲ Facilities
🍽 Meal plans
✗ Restaurant
🖉 Reservations
⚲ Smoking
🍷 BYOB
✗🏨 Hotel with restaurant that warrants a visit

Outdoors
⛳ Golf
⛺ Camping

Other
☾ Family-friendly
⇨ See also
⊠ Branch address
☞ Take note

1

Experience Japan

WORD OF MOUTH

"Look into getting a goodwill guide. Many of the larger cities have Web sites where you make contact to arrange it. They are local residents who will personalize a tour of their town for you at no cost, but you do have to pay for any entrance fees and expect to pay for their lunch. The opportunity to simply be able to converse and get to know a lot more about Japanese life is priceless."

—shandy

WHAT'S WHERE

The following numbers refer to chapters.

2 Tōkyō. Tōkyō, home to 10% of Japan's population, would take a lifetime to fully explore. Rather than any coherent center there is a mosaic of colorful neighborhoods—Shibuya, Asakusa, Ginza, Tsukiji, Shinjuku, and dozens more—each with its own texture.

3 Side Trips from Tōkyō. A quick train ride to Nikkō or Kamakura will provide of all your shrine and temple viewings. Hakone is home to Mount Fuji and numerous lakes. In Hase, the 37-foot Daibutsu—the Great Buddha—has sat for seven centuries, gazing inward.

4 Nagoya, Ise-Shima, and the Kii Peninsula. Ise Jingū (Grand Shrines of Ise)—the most important site in Japan's national religion—is found in Ise-Shima National Park. To the south, Kii Peninsula has magnificent coastal scenery and fishing villages. Inland, the mountain monastery of Kōya-san looms mythically with 120 temples.

5 The Japan Alps and the North Chūbu Coast. Soaring mountains, slices of old Japan, famed lacquerware and superb hiking, skiing, and *onsen* soaking are found here. In Kanazawa is Kenroku Garden, one of the three finest in the country.

6 Kyōto. Kyōto, Japan's ancient capital, represents 12 centuries worth of history and tradition in its beautiful gardens, castles, museums, and nearly 2,000 temples and shrines—Kinkaku-ji and Kiyomizu-dera top most itineraries. Here you'll also see geisha and sample *kaiseki ryōri*, an elegant meal.

7 Nara. Nara may not match Kyōto's abundance of sacred sites, but its coherently arranged shrines and parks count among Japan's finest. Head for Nara Kōen, a splendid park with about 1,200 tame deer, and to the Kasuga Taisha temple complex. Near the park is the Daibutsuden, which houses a 53-foot bronze Buddha.

8 Ōsaka. Ōsaka dazzles with bright lights rather than tradition. However, Ōsaka-jō is a match for any castle in the country. Sumō wrestle at the Ōsaka Furitsu Taiikukaikan while Bunraku puppet masters ply a gentler art. For nightlife, visit Dōtombori-dōri and dine among the unreserved, food-loving locals.

9 Kōbe. For a break from traditional Japan, try Kōbe. European and Japanese influences have long mingled here, resulting in Kitano-chō, a beautiful neighborhood with old Western-style homes.

0   50 miles
0   75 km

Tsushima

Hagi

Iki Island   Yamaguchi

Fukuoka

Goto Islands

Nagasaki

Mt. Nakadake   Beppu

Aso   Ōit

Amakusa Islands   Kumamoto

Shimo-Koshiki Island

Kagoshima   Miyazak

KYŪSHŪ

Kuchinoerabu Island   Yaku Island   Tanega Island

HOKKAIDŌ
(see inset)

Hakodate

Tsugaru
Peninsula

Shimoki
Peninsu.

Aomori

NIHON–KAI
(Sea of Japan)

Akita

Morioka

Kakunodate

Tono

Tsuruoka

Sado
Island

Niigata

Yamagata

Matsushima

Sendai

Wajima

Noto
Peninsula

Noto-Hantō

Fukushima

Oki
Islands

Yudanaka

Kanazawa

Toyama

Nikkō

Matsue

Fukui

Nagano

Utsunomiya

Tottori

Matsumoto

Oyama

Tsuwano

Takayama

Maebashi

Mito

Maibara

Kofu

Hiroshima

Okayama

Gifu

Tōkyō

Kurashiki

Kōbe

Kyōto

Nagoya

Fuji-san

Chiba

Bizen

Takamatsu

Awaji
Island

Ōsaka

Tsu

Shizuoka

Yokohama

Hakone

Kamakura

Matsuyama

Nara

Hase

Tokushima

Wakayama

Izu

Uwajima

Kōchi

Kōya-san

Ise

Peninsula

Oshima

Kii
Peninsula

SHIKOKU

Shingu

H O N S H Ū

TAIHEIYŌ
(Pacific Ocean)

WHAT'S WHERE

Shopping is one of Kōbe's strong points, and at the Tasaki Shinju company you can learn how pearls get from mollusk to necklace. You can also dine on world-famous Kōbe beef.

10 Western Honshū. Mountains divide this region into an urban south and a rural north. Hiroshima is the modern stronghold, where the sobering remnants of the charred A-Bomb Dome testify to darker times. Offshore at Miyajima, the famous Ō-torii appears to float on the water. Bizen masters craft the famous local pottery.

11 Shikoku. Thanks to its isolation, this southern island has held on to its traditions and staved off the industry that blights parts of Japan. There's great hiking, dramatic scenery, some of the country's freshest seafood, and the can't-miss Awa Odori festival in Tokushima.

12 Kyūshū. Rich in history and blessed with a balmy climate, lush Kyūshū is the southernmost of Japan's four main islands. At Aso National Park you can look into the steaming caldera of Mt. Nakadake, an active volcano. With its quiet hills and street-cars, Nagasaki is often called the San Francisco of Japan, a testament to the city's

resurrection from the second atomic bomb.

13 Okinawa. Okinawa is known as the Hawaii of Japan. Relaxation and water sports are the main attractions of this archipelago that stretches for some 435 mi south of Kyūshū. A paradise for snorkelers and scuba divers, the islands teem with reefs, canyons, and shelves of coral.

14 Tōhoku. Zaō-san draws skiers, while tourists clamor for a look at the *juhyō*, snow-covered fir trees that resemble fairy-tale monsters. Sendai is a good base for trips to Zaō-san and Matsu-shima, a bay studded with 250 pine-clad islands. Make time for the traditional town of Kakuno-date and Japan's deepest lake Tazawa-ko.

15 Hokkaidō. Japan's northernmost island is also its last frontier. Glorious landscapes, hiking, and skiing adventures await. In February, the Sapporo Snow Festival dazzles with huge ice sculptures. To the south are the famous hot springs of Noboribetsu Onsen and Jigoku-dani (Valley of Hell), a volcanic crater that belches boiling water and sulfurous vapors.

HOKKAIDŌ

HOKKAIDŌ
(see inset)

Monbetsu

Shiretoko
Peninsula

Abashiri

Kunashiri
Island

Kushiro

NIHON–KAI
(Sea of Japan)

Hakodate

Tsugaru
Peninsula

Shimoki
Peninsu

Aomori

Akita

Morioka

Kakunodate

Tono

Tsuruoka

Sado
Island

14

Niigata

Yamagata

Matsushima

Sendai

Wajima

Noto
Peninsula

Noto-Hantō

Fukushima

Oki
Islands

Kanazawa

Toyama

Yudanaka

Nikkō

Nagano

Utsunomiya

Matsue

Fukui

Matsumoto

Maebashi

Oyama

Mito

Tsuwano

Tottori

Takayama

Kōfu

10

Maibara

Gifu

Tōkyō

Hiroshima

Okayama

Kyōto

Nagoya

Fuji-san

Chiba

Kurashiki

Bizen

Yokohama

Takamatsu

Awaji
Island

Ōsaka

Tsu

Shizuoka

Hakone

Kamakura

Matsuyama

Tokushima

Nara

Hase

Izu
Peninsula

Oshima

11

Kōchi

Wakayama

Ise

Uwajima

Kōya-san

Kii
Peninsula

HONSHU

SHIKOKU

Shingu

TAIHEIYŌ
(Pacific Ocean)

JAPAN PLANNER

When to Go

Pleasant temperatures arrive with spring, which along with fall is one of the best times to visit. *Sakura* (cherry blossoms) bloom in Kyūshū in March, reaching Tōkyō by early April. Early summer is rainy, but July and August are hot and humid except in Hokkaidō. Fall is cool and typhoons may occur. Winter is chilly, but heavy snowfalls are limited to the mountain regions, Hokkaidō, and the Japan Sea coast. ■TIP➔ **Seasons are the same in Japan as they are in North America.** Travel is not advised during the three holiday periods: the few days before and after New Year's; Golden Week in early May; and the mid-August week of Obon.

Mark Your Calendar

Grass Burning: The vegetation atop Mt. Wakakusayama in Nara is set ablaze on the second Sunday evening of January.

Sapporo Snow Festival: Snow sculptures line Sapporo's central park for a week in early February.

Hiroshima Peace Memorial Ceremony: On August 6, a ceremony commemorates the dropping of the atomic bomb.

Choosing the Right Hotel

Japan's lodging options are varied and include both Japanese and Western styles.

The *ryokan*, a traditional Japanese inn, provides the most unique experience. Rooms are outfitted with Japanese-style interiors—tatami flooring, paper (*shoji*) blinds, a low table for tea service, and pillows. A futon is rolled out for sleeping. Meals are offered in the evening and at breakfast, and often include small Japanese dishes of various seafood and regional specialties. Lodges usually offer the use of an *onsen* (hot spring bath). Average per-person rates are ¥10,000–¥30,000 per night.

Similar to the ryokan, *minshuku* are Japanese-style bed-and-breakfasts. Usually family-run, these inns feature Japanese-style rooms and meals for roughly ¥8,000.

Western digs are found in business hotels; basic and small, these are ideal for one night and are usually close to major transportation hubs. Rates run ¥5,000–¥10,000. Big cities like Tōkyō and Ōsaka feature hotels with ritzy spas, fully equipped gyms, and some of Japan's better restaurants. Room rates range ¥20,000–¥40,000.

On the flip side, hostels—¥3,000 per night—are perfect for the budget conscious. Shared and solo rooms are usually available, as are affordable meals—usually less than ¥1,000.

Capsule hotels—generally men-only—are the most spartan accommodations around, providing a chamber that you slide your body into laterally, much like a coffin. No frills here, but the price is right: roughly ¥3,000 per night. Areas for television viewing and socializing and lockers for valuables and luggage come standard.

The often garish love hotel is not really a lodging option but more of a place for couples to relax in private. Overnight stays are possible (¥8,000) but two-hour stopovers are more common (¥4,000). Most have an ostentatious theme, like "Christmas" or "Medieval Europe," reflected in the decor.

Hot spring areas, such as Hakone, near Tōkyō, are for those seeking a dip in an onsen. Resorts in these parts focus their services and amenities on relaxation—either while naked or in a swimsuit.

Getting Around by Train

Trains are grouped into five categories: Local, Rapid, Express, Limited Express, and Super Express. The Shinkansen bullet trains are Super Express trains.

There are two seat classes offered on JR trains: ordinary and green. Most local trains only have ordinary cars. Green cars, or first class, are about 50% more expensive, but are less crowded and more comfortable. Super Express and Limited Express train have nonreserved and reserved seats; some only have reserved. On most local, rapid, and express trains seats will be nonreserved. Seat reservations are included in the JR Pass.

Smoking and no-smoking cars are available on a few long distance trains; otherwise it's not permitted.

Regional Trains: About 70% of Japan's railways are owned by Japan Railways (JR Group); the other 30% is owned by private companies. When it comes to service or experience, there's no real difference between the two, however, private lines can be less expensive. Japan Railways serves the entire country with its six regional railway companies—JR Hokkaido, JR East (Tōkyō), JR Central (Nagoya), JR West (Ōsaka), JR Shikoku, and JR Kyūshū. Private railways operate in major metropolitan areas like Tōkyō, Chubu, Kanto, and Kyūshū. Some consist of one line, while others are full-fledged networks.

Subways: The easiest way to exploring a city's center is via its subway. In Tōkyō, you have a choice between Tōkyō Metro and Toei. These are separate entities so separate fares must be paid. It's cheaper to stay with one company.

Commuter Trains: Typically, lines are in operation every day between 5 AM and 1 AM. At stations on some of the busier city-bound routes, keep an eye out for the white-gloved station staff that can be seen forcibly pushing morning commuters into the jammed cars.

Purchasing Tickets

Within cities, basic fares (train or subway) are between ¥110 and ¥310. Tickets can be purchased from machines that take coins or cash near the gates. Maps above each machine—usually in Japanese and English—give destinations. ■TIP→ **Navigating through the various lines can be confusing. If you're unsure about something, buy the lowest priced ticket and adjust the fare upon arrival.** Fare adjustment machines can be found at each exit. Simply slide your ticket into the slot by the blinking light and pay the requested sum (bills or coins).

JR Pass

Japan Railways offers the Japan Rail Pass, an affordable way to see the country. It can be used on all JR railways, buses, and ferryboats including the Shinkansen "bullet" trains—the exception being seats on Nozomi trains on the Tokaido and Sanyo lines. Hikari or Kodama trains, however, serve these same routes and are included. Passes must be purchased before your trip and are available for 7-, 14-, or 21-day periods. Activate them upon arrival at a major rail station or Narita and Kansai airports. A "first-class" version allows access to the Shinkansen Green Cars.

Prepaid Cards

JR East offers Suica, a rechargeable debit card, in major cities. JR West has Icoca for the Kansai region (Kōbe, Kyōto, Ōsaka), and JR Central has Toica in Nagoya and Shizuoka.

Use PiTaPa on buses and non-JR train systems in Kansai. PASMO, another prepaid card, can be used on non-JR and JR trains in Tōkyō.

The one-day Holiday Pass works in the entire Tōkyō–JR network on holidays, weekends, and the summer holiday period (July 20–August 31). Tōkyō's other one-day passes include the Tokunai Pass for JR lines and the Tōkyō Free Kippu, which also covers subways and buses.

JAPAN
TOP ATTRACTIONS

Mt. Fuji

(A) Mt. Fuji, the nation's highest peak, rises 3,376 m. One of Japan's most famous symbols, the symmetrical Fuji-san inspires artists and commoners alike. The dormant volcano sits between Yamanashi and Shizuoka prefectures. During nice weather, it can be viewed from Tōkyō and Yokohama. For a closer peek, climb it during the summer or see it from the Shinkansen train between Tōkyō and Ōsaka.

Imperial Palace East Gardens

(B) Open to the public, the gardens are all that remain of the former innermost circle of defense for Edo Castle, the residence of the Tokugawa shogun between 1603 and 1867. The gardens are accessed by three gates: Hirakawa-mon, Otemon, and Kitahanebashi-mon. Sculpted, rolling greenery surround stone walls, moats, and guardhouses.

Grand Shrines of Ise

(C) Located in Mie Prefecture, the Ise-Jingū Shrine is arguably Japan's most revered shrine complex. Often referred to simply as Jingū, or "The Shrine," it includes more than 100 small Shintō shrines and two main shrines, Naikū and Gekū. Naikū, the Inner Shrine, houses the sun goddess Amaterasu ōmikami. The Outer Shrine, Gekū, is home to the deity for industry and agriculture, Toyouke no ōmikami.

The Temples of Kyōto

(D) The former capital of Japan, Kyōto, is known for its grand, historic structures. Two of the famous Buddhist temples are the Ginkaku-ji (1474), the "Temple of the Silver Pavilion," which features the Kannon Hall and a rock and gravel Japanese garden, and Kinkaku-ji (1397), its golden sister that includes a gold-leaf adorned hall. Each is fronted by a spectacular lake.

Den Den Town

(E) Ōsaka's version of Akihabara in Tōkyō, Den Den offers all the wired gear and fantasy products that a geek could want. The area's filled with small (and often grungy) mom-and-pop shops peddling electronic parts, computers, anime and manga, and numerous gadgets. Many shops expect customers to bargain, so go ahead.

Peace Memorial Park

(F) Hiroshima's Peace Memorial Park, dedicated to those killed following the atomic bomb attack, is the city's most famous tourist attraction. Inside is the Peace Memorial Museum, which provides a history of the bomb. Also in the park is the A-Bomb Dome (the former Prefectural Industrial Promotion Hall), whose curved roof stands partly intact and serves as a symbol of peace.

Maehama Beach

This spectacular 7-km stretch of sand is on the island of Niijima, a volcanic island under the jurisdiction of Tōkyō. Located 163 km south of the capital (accessible by boat or ferry), the beach offers water recreation opportunities and camping. The beach also provides a view of Mt. Fuji on occasion and is the starting point for the Miyako Triathlon.

Nibutani Ainu Culture Museum

(G) Located in Hokkaidō, the Nibutani Ainu Culture Museum preserves the history and traditions of the Ainu, an ethnic group indigenous to this northern island. The museum has three themes: "Ainu (Human being)," "Kamui (Gods)," and "Moshiri (the blessings of nature)." On display are examples of woven items, carvings, and canoes. Be warned that descriptions are only in Japanese.

TOP EXPERIENCES

Sumo

Sumo pits two extremely large athletes against one another in a ring (*dohyo*). A wrestler who breaches the ring's boundary or touches the ground with a body part (other than the sole of his foot) loses. Originally intended as entertainment for Shinto gods, single bouts usually last less than a minute. Tournaments, running 15 days, are held three times a year in Tōkyō and once a year in Ōsaka, Nagoya, and Fukuoka. Novice wrestlers (*jonokuchi*) compete in the morning and top athletes (*yokozuna*) wrestle in the late afternoon. Crowds get pretty boisterous, especially for the later matches.

Ryokan

The *ryokan,* or traditional Japanese inn, offers rooms outfitted with Japanese-style interiors, such as tatami flooring and paper (*shoji*) blinds. For in-room tea service pillows and small tables make sitting very comfortable. Futons are rolled out onto the tatami at bedtime. Meals, usually included in the room rate, are breakfast and dinner, both of which contain small Japanese dishes of various seafood and regional specialties. The tourist areas of Kyōto and Hakone, near Tōkyō, are home to a wonderful selection of these inns.

Japanese Gardens

Gardens in the traditional Japanese style appear in parks, on castle grounds, and in front of shrines and temples. Featuring stone lanterns, rocks, ponds, a pavilion, and rolling hedges, many of the principles that influence Japanese garden design come from religion. Shintoism, Taoism, and Buddhism all stress the contemplation and re-creation of nature as part of the process of achieving understanding and enlightenment. Jisho-ji Garden and Nijō Castle Ninomaru Garden in Kyōto and Hamarikyu Gardens in Tōkyō are some of Japan's more prominent gardens to visit.

Karaoke

Karaoke is a Japanese institution whose rabid popularity cannot be understated. Often used as an after-work recreation, the activity is enjoyed by millions and involves the singing of a popular song into a microphone as the instrumental track plays on the in-room sound system and its lyrics roll across a monitor. Rooms, referred to as karaoke boxes, can be rented by the hour and seat between 2 and 10 customers. Drinks and light snacks can be downed as song selection books are studied.

Baseball

Yakyū (baseball) is often said to epitomize the Japanese character. Players are subject to punishing preseason training regimes that test their stamina and will. In contrast to the American style of play, the sacrifice bunt is a routine tactic, often employed in the early innings. The prized quality of group harmony is evident as ballparks reverberate to repetitive theme songs created for each batter, with the fans of the Hiroshima Carp going through perhaps the most elaborate routines. Following the final out of the Japan Series, fans of the winner crowd into city streets for a night—or, if its Ōsaka's Hanshin Tigers, jump from a bridge into a river—and hit the victory sales at local stores the next morning.

Seafood and Sushi

As might be expected of a nation consisting of 3,000 islands, Japan is synonymous with the fruits of the sea. Sashimi and sushi have gained popularity with restaurant goers around the world, but it's hard to imagine some other so-called delicacies catching on. The northern island

of Hokkaidō boasts of the quality of its *uni* (sea urchin), while Akita Prefecture is famous for *shiokara* (raw squid intestines). Domestic tourism and television schedules are dominated by food, and city dwellers travel the length and breadth of the country on weekend excursions to taste regional specialties.

Depato

Department stores (*depato*) are towering palaces that cater to the whims of the kings and queens of global consumerism. From the ultrapolite elevator attendants to the expert package wrapper, the attention to detail is extraordinary. Established stores follow a convenient pattern in their layout. In the basement is an expansive array of elaborately presented food, ranging from handmade sweets to bentō boxes. The first floor has cosmetics, and the next floors offer the latest in female fashion. Farther up you will find designer suits for men, ornate stationery, and refined home decorations. Finally, on the top floor, often with excellent urban views, is a restaurant area.

Tea Ceremony

The tea ceremony is a precisely choreographed program that started more than 1,000 years ago with Zen monks. The ritual begins as the server prepares a cup of tea for the first guest. This process involves a strictly determined series of movements and actions, including the cleansing of each utensil to be used. One by one, the participants slurp up their bowl of tea and then eat a sweet confectionary served with it. In Tōkyō, the teahouse at Hamarikyu Park offers a wonderful chance to enjoy this tradition.

Kampai!

Whether you're out with friends, clients, or belting out a tune at the local karaoke bar, you're sure to have a drink at least once during your stay. Rice-based sake, pronounced *sa*-kay, is Japan's number one alcoholic beverage, with more than 2,000 different brands available. The sake bar Amanogawa, in the basement of the Keio Plaza Hotel in Tōkyō, provides a wonderful opportunity to sample different varieties. *Shōchū* is made from grain and is served either on the rocks or mixed with juice or water. As to beer, Asahi and Kirin are the two heavyweights, constantly battling for the coveted title of Japan's leading brewer, but many beer fans rate Suntory's Malts brand and Sapporo's Yebisu brand as the tastiest brews in the land.

The Performing Arts

The performing arts date back hundreds of years but are still practiced in theaters across Japan. *Noh* is a minimalist dance drama where a masked actor performs very stylized moves accompanied by instrumental music. Often in conjunction with noh are *kyogen* performances, which are comedic plays known for their down-to-earth humor. Kabuki is theater performed by adult males that also portray the female roles. Fans of puppet theater may enjoy a *Bunraku* performance, in which large puppets are manipulated to the accompaniment of narrators and stringed instruments.

IF YOU LIKE

Nightlife

Cocktails with pizzazz or chicken on a stick, dreamy jazz or thumping techno beats—you'll find it all under urban Japan's neon-soaked night sky. Walking the bar-and-club crazy streets at night is a great way to discover a city's character. Tipping is not customary, but upscale establishments may have extra service charges ranging from a few hundred yen to a few thousand. Karaoke clubs and *izakaya,* traditional watering holes, are ubiquitous and a great way to mix with locals. All-night revelers might want to consider the likes of Roppongi in Tōkyō or Dōtombori in Ōsaka, while the more culturally inclined will find theaters and cinemas in every major city.

Susukino, Sapporo. Wander this northern city's entertainment district for a taste of how many Japanese wind down after work. Bars, clubs, restaurants, and karaoke joints abound.

Kabuki-za, Ginza, Tōkyō. There's no better place to catch a Kabuki performance than at this theater.

Sweet Basil 139, Roppongi, Tōkyō. Come for dinner or just a drink at this upscale club featuring a variety of musical performances.

Metro, Kyōto. A wide range of events and guest DJs make this one of Kansai's top clubs.

Bears, Ōsaka. This live venue features the best of Japan's underground music.

Garden Life

Gardens are an obsession in Japan. Many urban homes have a couple of topiary trees, and Buddhist temples nationwide have immaculately maintained grounds. The best Japanese gardens are like the canvasses of master painters, in which nature is ingeniously manipulated and represented in subtly rearranged forms. Some re-create entire landscapes in miniature, and are designed for viewing from one optimal position. Others skillfully integrate immense backdrops of mountains or forest, always managing to add to the innate beauty of the natural environment. Kyōto is home to Zen gardens, minimalist affairs of raked sand, moss, and meaningfully arranged rocks.

Imperial Palace East Garden, Tōkyō. An oasis of tree-lined paths, rhododendrons, and water features that provides great views of the Imperial Palace buildings.

Kenrokuen, Kanazawa. Originally landscaped in 1676, 25-acre Kenrokuen looks good all year round thanks to a wide variety of seasonal plants and trees.

Koinzan Saihō-ji, Kyōto. Escape the modern city by losing yourself in this remarkable world of verdant green and blue created by more than 120 species of moss planted on a number of levels.

Suizenji Kōen, Kumamoto. Part of this garden re-creates the 53 stations of the old Tōkaidō post road that was immortalized by Hiroshiga Ando in a series of woodblock prints.

Outdoor Adventure

For many people modern Japan conjures images of the concrete, neon-lighted urban jungles of Kantō and Kansai. The country's wealth of natural attractions is easily overlooked, but outdoor enthusiasts will find their every whim catered to. In winter generous snowfall makes Hokkaidō and Nagano ideal destinations for skiers and snowboarders. The Japan Alps mountain range that stretches along the north side of Honshu offers excellent hiking trails, and Shikoku is well suited to cyclists. To the south, Okinawa boasts tropical temperatures for much of the year, and its clear waters are excellent for scuba diving and snorkeling.

Niseko, Hokkaidō. Australians in the know head here by the tens of thousands each winter for arguably the best skiing in Japan.

Kamikōchi, Nagano. En route to this small mountain village you pass though some stunning scenery, and upon arrival a series of trails provides access to the upper reaches of the surrounding peaks.

Shikoku. The best way to enjoy this picturesque island in the Inland Sea is from the seat of a bicycle. Slow down to the local pace and spend time exploring unexpected diversions.

Manta Way, Okinawa. From April to June divers can observe rarely seen manta feeding on plankton in this strait between Iriomote and Kohama islands.

Holy Sites

Most modern Japanese would not express an affiliation with one religion, and both Shintōism and Buddhism play important roles in many people's lives. Shintō architecture, with the exception of Nikko's colorful shrines, tends to be plain and simple, like the style of the nation's most sacred site at Ise, emphasizing natural materials such as wood and thatch. Temples run the gamut from austere to gaudy, both in color and design. Kyōto boasts many of the finest examples of religious architecture, while in mountain areas the act of pilgrimage and supplication to the elements is almost as important as the shrines and temples themselves.

Sensō-ji, Asakusa, Tōkyō. Proof positive that even Japan's largest metropolis can preserve tradition. Sensō-ji has a tangible Old Tōkyō atmosphere from the first entrance gate, with its immense red lantern, through the narrow pedestrian streets to the huge incense burners of the temple.

Ise-jingū, Mie prefecture. Home of Shintoism, the national religion, the Grand Shrines of Ise are majestic thatched wooden buildings concealed in expansive forested grounds.

Tōdai-ji, Nara. This temple's Daibutsu-den (Hall of the Great Buddha) is the largest wooden building in the world, and houses Japan's biggest Buddha figure, cast in bronze.

Kiyomizu-dera, Kyōto. The Golden Pavilion of Kinkaku-ji may feature on more postcards, but this temple's large-scale wood construction is stunning. The steep approach to Kiyomizu-dera is lined with hundreds of craft, souvenir, and food shops.

GREAT ITINERARIES

7 DAYS IN TŌKYŌ

Day 1

Start *very* early (5 AM) with a visit to the **Tōkyō Central Wholesale Market** (Tōkyō Chūō Oroshiuri Ichiba) in the Tsukiji district to have the finest, freshest sushi for breakfast. Direct train service starts around 5 AM from Shinjuku (Toei Oedo line) or Roppongi (Hibiya subway line) and gets you to Tsukuji or Tsukujishijo station respectively in under 20 minutes. Or take a taxi. Then use the rest of the day for a tour of the **Imperial Palace** and environs.

Day 2

Spend the morning at **Sensō-ji** and adjacent **Asakusa Jinja** in Asakusa. If you're looking for souvenir gifts—sacred or secular—allow time and tote space for the abundant selection local vendors have to offer. From there go to **Ueno** for an afternoon of museums, vistas, and historic sites.

Day 3

Take a morning stroll through **Ginza** to explore its fabled shops and *depāto* (department stores). Then hit a chic restaurant or café for lunch (more reasonably priced ones are found on the upper floor of most department stores). In the afternoon see the Shintō shrine, **Meiji Jingū** and walk through the nearby Harajuku and Omotesandō fashion districts to the **Nezu Institute of Fine Arts**.

Day 4

Spend the morning browsing in **Akihabara**, Tōkyō's electronics quarter, and see the nearby Shintō shrine **Kanda Myōjin**. Spend the afternoon on the west side of **Shinjuku**, Tōkyō's 21st-century model city; and savor the view from the observation deck of architect Kenzō Tange's monumental **Tōkyō Metropolitan Government Office;** cap off the day visiting **Shinjuku Gyo-en National Garden.**

Day 5

Fill in the missing pieces: see the Buddhist temple, **Sengaku-ji** in Shinagawa; the remarkable **Edo-Tōkyō Hakubutsukan** in **Ryōgoku;** a tea ceremony; Kabuki play; or a sumō tournament, if one is in town. Or visit the **Kokugikan,** National Sumō Arena, in the Ryōgoku district, and some of the sumō stables in the neighborhood.

Days 6 and 7

You can make Tōkyō your home base for a series of side trips *(⇨Chapter 3).* Take a train out to **Yokohama,** with its scenic port and Chinatown. A bit farther is **Kamakura,** the 13th-century military capital of Japan. The **Great Buddha** (Daibutsu) of the **Kōtoku-in** in nearby Hase is among the many National Treasures of art and architecture that draw millions of visitors a year.

Still farther off, but again an easy train trip, is **Nikkō,** where the founder of the Tokugawa Shogun dynasty is enshrined. **Tōshō-gū** is a monument unlike any other in Japan, and the picturesque **Lake Chūzen-ji** is in a forest above the shrine. Two full days, with an overnight stay, allows you an ideal, leisurely exploration of both. Yet another option is a trip to **Hakone,** where you can soak in a traditional onsen or climb to the summit of **Fuji-san** (Mt. Fuji).

HIGHLIGHTS OF CENTRAL JAPAN

Yes, Japan is a modern country with its skyscrapers, lightning-fast train service, and neon. But it's also rich in history, culture, and tradition. Japan is perhaps most fascinating when you see these two faces at once: a 17th-century shrine sitting defiantly by a tower of steel and glass and a geisha chatting on a cell phone.

Day 1: Ise and Koya-san
Ise-jingū (Grand Shrines of Ise), with their harmonious architecture and cypress-forest setting, provide one of Japan's most spiritual experiences.

Day 2: Kōya-san
More than 100 temples belonging to the Shingon sect of Buddhism stand on one of Japan's holiest mountains, 30 mi south of Ōsaka. An exploration of the atmospheric cemetery of **Okuno-in** takes you past headstone art and 300-year-old cedar trees.

Day 3: Nara
During the 8th century Nara was the capital of Japan, and many cultural relics of that period, including some of the world's oldest wooden structures, still stand among forested hills and parkland. Be sure to visit Nara's 53-foot-high, 1,300-year-old bronze Daibutsu (Great Buddha) in **Tōdai-ji** temple and to make friends with the deer of **Nara Kōen.**

Days 4–6: Kyōto
For many visitors **Kyōto** *is* Japan, and few leave disappointed. Wander in and out of temple precincts like **Ginkaku-ji,** spot geisha strolling about **Gion,** and dine on *kaiseki ryōri,* an elegant culinary event that engages all the senses. Outside the city center, day-trip to hillside **Arashiyama,** the gardens of the Katsura Rikyū, and the temple of Enryaku-ji atop **Hiei-zan.** With nearly 2,000 temples and shrines, exquisite crafts, and serene gardens, Kyōto embodies traditional Japan.

Day 7: Ōsaka
Although by no means picturesque, **Ōsaka** provides a taste of urban Japan outside the capital, along with a few traditional sights. The handsome castle **Ōsaka-jo** nestles among skyscrapers, and the neon of **Dōtombori** flashes around the local Kabuki theater. Ōsakans are passionate about food, and you'll find some of the finest in the country here.

Day 8: Kōbe
Kōbe has recovered from the dark day in 1995 when it was struck by an earthquake that killed more than 5,000 people. Some of the first foreigners to live in Japan after the Meiji Restoration built homes in **Kitano-chō,** near the station, and the area retains an interesting mix of architectural styles.

Day 9: Himeji
The Western Honshū city's most famous sight, **Himeji-jō,** also known as the White Egret Castle (Shirasagi-jō), dominates the skyline. The castle takes only an afternoon to see, but museums near the train station are worthy examples of Japan's modern architecture. Kenzō Tange designed the informative **Hyōgo Prefectural Museum of History,** and boxer-turned-architect Tadao Andō is responsible for the **Himeji Museum of Literature,** which is celebrated more for its unique minimalist exterior than for its exhibits inside.

GREAT ITINERARIES

HIGHLIGHTS OF SOUTHERN JAPAN

South and west of the tourist centers of Kyōto and Nara, Japan takes on a different feel. The farther you go, the more relaxed people become. Shikoku is a side step from Honshū in more ways than one, with a character very much its own. Behind the historical significance of Hiroshima lies one of the Japan's more attractive large cities, and nearby Miyajima is almost a theme park of mountains and shrines. Kyūshū boasts some of the most interactive scenery in the country, with active volcanoes, hot-sand baths, and steaming geysers. Hundreds of kilometers from Japan's main islands, the stark divide between the tropical beaches of Okinawa and Honshū's concrete metropolises is reflected in a different culture and cuisine.

Days 1 and 2: Shikoku

The **Iya Valley** may be slightly difficult to access, but it offers untouched, deep canyons, the best river rafting in Japan, and good walking trails. For a break from Japan—and the rest of the world—visit the **Chichu Art Museum.** This experimental project on Naoshima Island, near Takamatsu, integrates art works into everyday locations, often with inspiring results.

Day 3: Kurashiki

This rustic town, an important trading port in centuries past, retains its picturesque 17th-century buildings. The 1930s classical-style **Ōhara Art Museum** houses a fine collection of European art. The **Kurashiki Craft Museum** displays crafts from around the world, including pottery from nearby Bizen.

Days 4 and 5: Hiroshima

A quick glance at the busy, attractive city of Hiroshima gives no clue to the events of August 6, 1945. Only the city's **Peace Memorial Park** (Heiwa Kinen Kōen)—with its memorial museum and its **A-Bomb Dome** (Gembaku Dōmu), a twisted, half-shattered structural ruin—serves as a reminder of the atomic bomb. From Hiroshima, make a quick trip to the island of **Miyajima** to see the famous floating torii of **Itsukushima Jinja,** a shrine built on stilts above a tidal flat.

Days 6 and 7: Yufuin and Mt. Aso

You don't need to be shaken by an earthquake to realize that Japan is seismically active. One of the locals' favorite pastimes is relaxing in an *onsen* (hot spring), and in the artsy little spa town of Yufuin, on the southernmost island of Kyūshū, you can soak in mineral water or bubbling mud. Nearby, five volcanic cones combine to create Japan's largest caldera at **Mt. Aso.** An immense 18 km (11 mi) by 24 km (15 mi), the stark volcanic peak contrasts vividly with the surrounding green hills. One crater, **Nakadake,** is still active, and reaching it on foot or via cable car affords views of a bubbling, steaming lake.

Days 8 and 9: Okinawa

Check out cosmopolitan **Naha,** which gives a feel for how Okinawan culture and cuisine differ from those of "mainland" Japan. Take a boat to one of the smaller **Kerama** islands to relax on uncrowded, unspoiled beaches. And to truly appreciate the beauty of the ocean, get into the water—there are plenty of scuba diving and snorkeling centers, with **Nishibama Beach** on **Aka-jima** highly rated.

HIGHLIGHTS OF NORTHERN JAPAN

With 80% of Japan's surface covered by mountains, the country is a dream for hikers and lovers of the great outdoors. Unfortunately, even rural areas are often spoiled by the nation's obsession with concrete, but the wilds of Hokkaidō, quietly impressive Tōhoku, and the vertiginous Japan Alps frequently reward exploration with spectacular scenery and experiences of traditional Japanese culture that have long-since been lost from urban areas.

Days 1 and 2: Sapporo

Sapporo is a pleasant and accessible city that serves as a good base for exploring the dramatic landscape of Hokkaidō. Mountains encircle Sapporo, drawing Japanese and increasing numbers of Australian skiers in winter. Take day trips out to **Tōya-ko** or **Shikotsu-ko,** picturesque caldera lakes where you can boat or fish, and the excellent **Nibutani Ainu Culture Museum** for an insight into the island's original inhabitants.

Days 3 and 4: Daisetsu-zan National Park

Japan's largest National Park, **Daisetsu-zan** is one of the nation's most popular spots for hiking and skiing, and reflects the essence of Hokkaidō: soaring mountain peaks, hidden gorges, cascading waterfalls, forests, and hot springs. Sheer cliff walls and stone spires make for a stunning drive through the **Sōun-kyō** ravine. Take a cable car up to the top of Hokkaidō's tallest mountain, **Asahi-dake**; hike or ski for a couple of hours, then unwind at a hot spring below.

Days 5 and 6: Haguro-san

This mountain, the most accessible of the Dewa-san range, a trio of sacred mountains in Tōhoku, is worth the trip not only for the lovely climb past cedars, waterfalls, and shrines but also for the thatched shrine at the top. You may even happen upon one of the many festivals and celebrations that take place at the shrine throughout the year. The rigorous climb itself, up 2,446 stone steps to the summit, is the main draw; however, it's possible to take a bus up or down the mountain.

Days 7–9: Japan Alps and North Chubu Coast

Nagano Prefecture, host of the 2000 Winter Olympics, is home to the backbone of the Japan Alps. Visit **Zenkō-ji** temple in Nagano City before heading to the hot springs of **Yudanaka Onsen** or **Kusatsu.** Alternatively, **Kamikōchi** allows you to really get away from it all—no cars are allowed into this mountain retreat. Farther west the cities of **Kanazawa** and **Takayama** offer some of the best-preserved traditional architecture in Japan, including old samurai family houses and sake breweries. Between the two is **Shirakawa-go,** where steep-roofed thatched farmhouses sit snugly in a mountain valley. Stay a night to see the buildings at their best while sharing a meal around an *irori* fireplace with your fellow guests.

JAPANESE ETIQUETTE

Many Japanese expect foreigners to behave differently and are tolerant of faux pas, but they are pleasantly surprised when people acknowledge and observe their customs. The easiest way to ingratiate yourself with the Japanese is to take time to learn and respect Japanese ways.

General Tips

■ Bow upon meeting someone.

■ Japanese will often point at their nose (not chest) when referring to themselves.

■ Pointing at someone is considered rude. To make reference to someone or something, wave your hand up and down in his or her direction.

■ Direct expression of opinions isn't encouraged. It's more common for people to gently suggest something.

■ Avoid physical contact. A slap on the back or hand on the shoulder would be uncomfortable for a Japanese person.

■ Avoid too much eye contact when speaking. Direct eye contact is a show of spite and rudeness.

At Someone's Home

■ Most entertaining is done in restaurants and bars; don't be offended if you're not invited to someone's home.

■ Should an invitation be extended, a small gift—perhaps a bottle of alcohol or box of sweets—should be presented.

■ At the entryway, remove your shoes and put on the provided slippers. Remove your slippers if you enter a room with tatami flooring. Before entering the bathroom, remove your house slippers and switch to those found near the bathroom doorway.

■ Stick to neutral subjects in conversation. The weather doesn't have to be your only topic, but you should take care not to be too nosy.

■ It's not customary for Japanese businessmen to bring wives along. If you're traveling with your spouse, don't assume that an invitation includes both of you. If you want to bring your spouse, ask in a way that eliminates the need for a direct refusal.

In Business Meetings

■ For business meetings, *meishi* (business cards) are highly recommended. Remember to place those you have received in front of you; don't shove them in your pocket. It's also good to have one side of your business card printed in Japanese.

■ Japanese position their employees based upon rank within the company. Don't be surprised if the proceedings seem perfunctory—many major decisions were made behind the scenes before the meeting started.

■ Stick to last names and use the honorific -san after the name, as in Tanaka-san (Mr. or Mrs. Tanaka). Also, respect the hierarchy, and as much as possible address yourself to the most senior person in the room.

■ Many Japanese businessmen still don't know how to interact with Western businesswomen. Be patient, and, if the need arises, gently remind them that, professionally, you expect to be treated as any man would be.

At Lodgings and Ryokan

■ When you arrive at a minshuku or ryokan, put on the slippers that are provided and make your way to your room. Remember to remove your slippers before entering your room; never step on the tatami (straw mats) with shoes or slippers.

■ Before entering a thermal pool, make sure you wash and rinse off entirely before getting into the water. Do not get soap in the tub. Other guests will be using the same bathwater, so it is important to observe this custom. After your bath, change into the yukata provided in your room. Don't worry about walking around in it—other guests will be doing the same.
⇨ *For more tips on Ryokan behavior, see the box in Chapter 6.*

At Restaurants

■ *Oshibori* is a small hot towel provided in Japanese restaurants. This is to wipe your hands but not your face. If you must use it on your face, wipe your face first, then your hands, and never toss it on the table: fold or roll it up.

■ When eating with chopsticks, don't use the part that has entered your mouth to pick up food from communal dishes. Instead, use the end that you've been holding in your hand. Always rest chopsticks on the edge of the tray, bowl, or plate; sticking them upright in your food is reminiscent of how rice is arranged at funerals.

■ There's no taboo against slurping your noodle soup, though women are generally less boisterous about it than men.

■ Pick up the soup bowl and drink directly from it, rather than leaning over the table to sip it. Eat the fish or vegetables with your chopsticks.

■ When drinking with a friend, never serve yourself. Always pour for the other person, who will in turn pour for you. If you would rather not drink, don't refuse a refill, just sip, keeping your glass at least half full.

■ It's considered gauche to eat as you walk along a public street.

While Shopping

■ After entering a store, the staff will greet you with *irasshaimase*, which is a welcoming phrase. A simple smile's an appropriate acknowledgment. After that, polite requests to view an item or try on a piece of clothing should be followed as anywhere in the West. Bargaining is common at flea markets, but not so in conventional stores.

■ There's usually a plastic tray at the register for you to place your money or credit card. Your change and receipt however, will be placed in your hand. It should be noted that many small shops do not accept credit cards.

Giving Gifts

■ Gift giving is a year-round national pastime, peaking during summer's *ochugen* and the year-end *oseibo*. Common gifts between friends, family, and associates include elegantly wrapped packages of fruit, noodles, or beer.

■ On Valentine's Day women give men chocolate, but on White Day in March the roles are reversed.

■ For weddings and funerals, cash gifts are the norm. Convenience stores carry special envelopes in which the money (always crisp, new bills) should be inserted.

JAPANESE CUISINE

Eating and dining in Japan can be quite a culture shock for the first time traveler. Beyond the raw fish, the incredible variety of vegetation used in Japanese cooking surprises most Western palates: *take-no-ko* (bamboo shoots), *renkon* (lotus root), and the treasured *matsutake* mushrooms, to name a few. But fear not, with some simple phrases and basic cuisine knowledge (and a sense of adventure), you can dine quite successfully and maybe even try something new.

On the Menu

Sushi and tempura are the best-known Japanese dishes, but they aren't the only ones. **Sashimi,** very fresh, thinly sliced seafood, is served with soy sauce, wasabi paste, thinly sliced ginger root, *ponzu* (a citrus-based sauce), and/or a simple garnish like shredded daikon radish. Though most seafood is raw, some sashimi ingredients, like octopus, can be cooked.

Sukiyaki, a popular beef dish sautéed with vegetables, is cooked and served in an iron skillet at the table. The best sukiyaki houses often run their own butcher shops.

Shabu-shabu is more popular with tourists than with the Japanese. Similar to sukiyaki, it's prepared at the table with a combination of vegetables, but it's cooked in boiling water.

Nabemono, or one-pot dishes, are less familiar to Westerners. Simmered in a light, fish-based broth, these stews can be made of almost anything: chicken (*tori-nabe*), oysters (*kaki-nabe*), or the sumō wrestler's favorite—the hearty *chanko-nabe,* which is chock full of chicken, fish, tofu, and vegetables.

Regional Differences

Every island in the Japanese archipelago has its specialty, and within each island every province has its own *meibutsu*

ryōri, or specialty dish. Foods in the Kansai district (including Kyōto, Nara, Ōsaka, and Kōbe) tend to be lighter, the sauces less spicy, and the soups not as hardy as those of the Kantō district, which includes Tōkyō. Foodies go to Kyōto for the delicate and formal kaiseki and to Tōkyō for sushi.

Nigiri zushi—slices of raw fish on bite-size balls of rice (the form of sushi with which most Westerners are familiar)—originated in the seaside Kantō district. **Saba zushi,** the forerunner of nigiri zushi, is the specialty of landlocked Kyōto. It's made by pressing salt-preserved mackerel on a bed of rice into a mold.

In Nagasaki, on Kyūshū, try **shippoku-ryōri,** a banquet-style feast of different dishes that culminates with a large fish mousse topped with shrimp. Shikoku's main city, Kōchi, specializes in **sawachi-ryōri,** an extravaganza of elaborately prepared platters of fresh fish dishes. On Hokkaidō, where salmon dishes are the local specialty, try **ishikari-nabe,** a hearty salmon-and-vegetable stew.

Dining Like a Japanese Royal

The formula for the basic Japanese meal was derived from the rules governing formal *kaiseki* dining—not too large a portion, just enough; not too spicy, but perhaps with a savory sprig of trefoil to offset the bland tofu. It follows a specific order: soup, raw fish, an entrée (grilled, steamed, simmered, or fried fish, chicken, or vegetables), then rice and pickles, fresh fruit for dessert, and a cup of green tea.

Despite this formality, the principles behind a traditional Japanese meal are deceptively simple. Absolute freshness is key. Fish must be brought in from the sea that morning (not yesterday) and vegetables are from the earth (not the hothouse).

Simplicity is next. Japanese chefs prefer flavors that enhance, not elaborate, accent rather than conceal. Fish is permitted a degree of natural fishiness—a garnish of fresh red ginger offsets the flavor rather than disguising it.

Finally beauty is considered. Simple, natural foods must appeal to the eye and the palate. Examples inclue green peppers on a vermilion dish or an egg custard in a blue bowl. The visual harmony is as vital as the balance and variety of the foods' flavors.

An excellent way to experience the upper echelon of Japanese cuisine on a budget is to visit a kaiseki restaurant at lunchtime. Many of them offer *kaiseki bentō* lunches at a fraction of the dinner price, exquisitely presented in lacquered boxes.

Feasting on a Budget

Many restaurants provide excellent meals that won't empty your wallet. To find them though, you might have to venture outside your hotel or try a spot with no English menu; be prepared to use the point-and-order method. Many restaurants post menus out front that clearly state the full price (some add a 10% tax, and possibly a service charge, so ask in advance).

The traditional and extremely portable **bentō,** or Japanese box lunch, is available everywhere. Rice, pickles, grilled fish or meat, and vegetables are included in an almost limitless variety of combinations to suit the season.

Soba and Udon dishes are lifesaving treats for stomachs unaccustomed to exotic flavors. Small shops serving soba (thin, brown, buckwheat noodles) and udon (thick, white-wheat noodles) dishes can be found all over the country.

Perhaps the most expensive of the inexpensive options is the **robatayaki** (grill).

Platters of fish, vegetables, tofu, and other ingredients are lined up in front of the chef: just point at the fixings you want and he'll throw your concoction on the griddle. Popular choices are *yaki-zakana* (grilled fish), particularly *karei-shio-yaki* (salted and grilled flounder) and *asari saka-mushi* (clams simmered in sake).

Somewhat misleadingly called the Japanese pancake, **okonomiyaki** is actually a mixture of vegetables, meat, and seafood in an egg-and-flour batter grilled at your table. This is frequently do-it-yourself cooking but many places also have a counter where a chef will make the pancakes for you.

A popular drinking snack is **kushi-age,** skewered bits of meat, seafood, and vegetables dipped in bread crumbs, and deep-fried.

Oden—an inexpensive winter favorite that includes a variety of meats and vegetables slowly simmered in vats of soy-flavored *dashi* (cooking stock)—goes well with a beer or sake.

RITUAL AND RELIGION

There's a saying in Japan that you're Shintō at birth (marked with a Shintō ceremony), Christian when you marry (in a Western-style wedding), and Buddhist when you die (honored with a Buddhist funeral). The Japanese take a utilitarian view of religion and use each as suits the occasion.

Today, a trip to Japan will almost certainly bring you into contact with ancient Buddhist and Shintō structures. Each has a storied past.

Buddhism

More than 90 million Japanese are Buddhist. Originating in 6th-century BC India, Buddhism spread through China, Korea, and Japan; it states that the only way to be free of the suffering caused by human desire is to realize your true "Buddha Nature." All Buddhists believe in reincarnation, with the eventual goal of reaching nirvana (the Buddhist equivalent of heaven) in the afterlife. Every conscious being (ant to aardvark) has Buddha Nature and is on this same path. That's why many strict Buddhists are vegetarians.

Karma, good and bad, determines your spiritual journey, and can speed your accent to nirvana or doom you to innumerable lifetimes on earth. Doing good deeds and adhering to tenets like love and compassion help you accumulate good karma. Selfishness, anger, and greed garner bad karma. Bodhisattvas—beings that have achieved nirvana but choose to return to earth to guide others—can appear in any form and offer simple, momentary advice or lifelong guidance.

Japan's nobility welcomed Buddhism, but commoners rejected its complex structure and theories. Different sects evolved making Buddhism more accessible—Pure Land Buddhism, Zen Buddhism, and Nichiren Buddhism—through good works, meditation, and traditional arts like calligraphy and karate. Zen even helped shape Bushido, the samurai warrior code.

Shintōism

Shintō translates as the "kami way;" kami means god or spirit. Followers believe that all things—sun, animals, spirits of the dead, stones, trees, mountains, waterfalls, even the Japanese islands—contain representative spirits. These spirits are honored and worshipped in myriad shrines.

This ancient and indigenous faith relates directly to the creation of the islands and lineage of the emperor. Shintō mythology outlines creation with numerous kamis. Of these, three were the most important—the sun goddess (Amaterasu-o-Mikami); her brother in charge of the Earth (Susano-o-no-mikoto); and the Moon Goddess (Tsuki yomi no mikoto) who ruled the realm of darkness.

The grandson of the sun goddess (Ninigi-no-mikoto) was instructed to rule Japan with three divine treasures—a mirror, a sword, and a string of jewels. His great-grandson, Emperor Jimmu Tennō (literally "Jimmu of heaven") assumed human form, and all subsequent emperors of Japan have claimed descent from this divine being.

Shintō has evolved to include strange symbolism, exotic rites and ceremonies, colorful festivals, and a mystical atmosphere in its shrines.

How to Spot Temples and Shrines

A gate marks the entrance to Buddhist temples and sometimes additional gates lead to the main one. Depictions of guardian gods on either side usually wear scowls meant to repel evil. Upon entering, you'll most likely see a pagoda—a Japan-specific structure that's three or

five tiered—that stores the remains of the Buddha. Next, the main hall holds sacred statues and images of the Buddha. At the back is the lecture hall, where Buddhist scripture is allowed. While layouts and buildings vary, these main elements can be found at most temples. The grounds might also hold a lavish garden for reflective thinking.

See it: Among Japan's most noted temples are Kinkakuji, in Kyōto, which is covered in gold; Sanjusangendo, also in Kyōto, which contains 1,000 life-size statues; and the Todaiji Temple, in Nara, home to a huge Buddha statue.

Shintō shrines are erected on sites where some manifestation of the local kami has been observed. Shrines are fronted by a *torii* (gateway), which marks a divine space, and *komainu* (stone guard dogs). Near the entrance is the *chōzuya*, a water trough for cleansing before praying. In the main hall, there's usually an inner compartment where the kami dwells, with a space in front for offerings adorned with a *gohei* (zigzag) pattern. People place offerings of salt, rice, water, fruit, flowers, and sake on tables. You'll likely see lucky charms scattered throughout the shrine area, and souvenir stands sell *omikuji*—papers with a fortune and blessings.

See it: Some of Japan's most important shrines include Nikko's Toshogu Shrine, an ornate mausoleum for Tokugawa Ieyasu; Kyōto's Fushimi Inari Shrine, featuring a series of elaborate torii gates; and Miyajima's Itsukushima Shrine, fronted by a torii gate that rises up from the sea.

SHRINE AND TEMPLE ETIQUETTE

When visiting a temple or shrine, a good rule of thumb is to follow the behavior of the Japanese visitors. These simple steps will help you avoid committing a faux pas:

■ Stay out of roped-off areas. Some areas are accessible to monks and priests only.

■ At most Shintō shrines, a purification fountain will be at the entrance. Wash your hands and mouth. Spit the water on the ground rather than swallowing it.

■ Bow, facing the main altar or shrine area, before entering and leaving.

■ Before entering a building, remove your shoes. Put on a pair of slippers at the entrance; they are there for your use.

■ When standing before the altar, make some sort of offering. In most Buddhist temples light incense (*osenko*) and place it in the censer. Wave the smoke toward you to capture its healing powers. At Shintō shrines ring the bell, clap your hands twice, and drop a few coins in the offering box.

■ At a Shinto shrine, after reading your *omikuji*, tie the fortune to a pine tree in the compound.

■ Don't take flash photographs without asking permission. Many shrines and temples house ancient scrolls or icons.

■ Avoid loud and disrespectful behavior. Behave as if you're in a museum or cathedral.

BUDGET TRAVEL TIPS

Travelers posting in the Travel Talk Forums at Fodors.com recommend the following budget saving tips.

Lodging

"A hotel's own Japanese Web site usually gives the best rates and choices—some guarantee they beat any other online quotation!"—Alec

"If there are four of you traveling together, youth hostels can be an attractive budget option. Rooms are often set up for four people, so no sharing with strangers! We've found them to be very clean and usually well located." —lcuy

"Forget the word 'hotel' (unless it is preceded by 'business') and learn the word 'minshuku'. Big hotel chains (Western or Japanese) can be expensive, but Japan also has 'business hotels' that provide small basic hotel rooms at reasonable prices; a minshuku is a type of budget lodging." —mrwunrfl

Transportation

"Not only will the JR Pass get you on the Shinkansen, but it'll also get you on JR sleeper trains. Your pass entitles you to a small enclosed space (not private though), and for a surcharge you can get a private cabin. You can save one night's accommodation by traveling overnight."—Sydney2K

"Use frequent flyer miles to get around Japan. The award levels are low, just 15K or 20K miles. Once, I flew from Tōkyō to Sapporo, poked around Hokkaido a bit with JR Pass, and then flew from Sapporo to Hiroshima. Then I used my JR Pass to get back to Tōkyō, after a couple of stops."—mrwunrfl

"An overnight voyage by ferry from Kōbe or Ōsaka to Shikoku or Kyūshū is an experience worth having. Not only is it the cheapest way to travel, but the real payoff is that your ticket provides sleeping space so you save hotel expenses too. Ferries reflect the usual incomparable Japanese care in planning, scheduling, and organization. Decidedly a more-for-less travel opportunity."—WillJame

Food

"Eating takeout from department store basement food halls is an excellent way to save money. You will save even more if you wait until an hour before closing when many prepared foods are marked down 25% to 50%. Makes for nice inexpensive dinners."—mjs

"Choose those cheap set meals which come with a bowl of rice or order oyakadon (fried egg and chicken on a big bowl of rice) which is cheap and delicious and will keep you full for some hours."—Cilla_Tey

Entertainment

"The flea market at Kitano Tenmangu Shrine in Kyōto is held on the 25th of each month. Great to see the locals poking around, plenty of street food and seeing old fashioned sideshow alley games for the kids. Prices for souvenirs are very cheap as it's a market for locals not tourists. The temple itself is very good as well. All free."—shandy

"On the main page of the JNTO Web site they have a link to a list of events for the month. Festivals are listed, of course, but there also are some performances. Many of these are free."—mrwunrfl

Tōkyō

WORD OF MOUTH

"Go to Tokyo Tower at night! It is stunning to see the view from up there and all the lights. And there are interactive maps at the top level observatory where you push a button on a map in front of you and it tells you what area you are seeing out the windows."

—emd

Updated by
Brett Bull,
Kevin Mcgue,
Nicholas Col-
dicott, Misha
Janette

The 2003 film *Lost in Translation*, by Sophia Coppola, was for many the first chance to see beyond Tōkyō's historic temples and sushi to the modern, pulsating metropolis it is today. But don't think that the temples and sushi stands have gone away. This is a city of old and new, where opposites attract and new trends come and go like the tide, but history and tradition continue to be held in utmost respect.

The city is also the center of design and cutting-edge fashion. One step into the hip neighborhoods of Harajuku and Shibuya and you'll know what we mean. Dining is also a study in contrasts. People can dine at a Michelin-starred restaurant one night, and then belly up to the counter at the local ramen joint the next. And the people are as varied as their city. Residents of Aoyama may wear European designer fashion and drive fancy imports but those residing in Asakusa prefer the decidedly less flashy, including the subway system. Stop in a bar in Ginza and one might find groups of salarymen, flush with large expense accounts, entertaining clients, but down the Hibiya Line in Ebisu many of the cheap watering holes are filled with young office professionals.

Even the landscape is varied. The metropolis hosts some of the most unsightly and vast sprawls of concrete housing—extending for miles in all four directions—in the world. But it's also home to some tall buildings. In Roppongi, you'll find the city's tallest building, Tōkyō Midtown (248 meters [814 feet]), and the 200-meter (656-foot) Grand Tōkyō North Tower at Tōkyō Station.

Whether you're gazing at the glow of Tōkyō's evening lights or the green expanse of its parks or a plate of the freshest sushi imaginable or dramatically dressed people, this is a city of astonishing and intriguing beauty. If you're a foodie, artist, design lover, or cultural adventurer, then Tōkyō, a city of inspiration and ideas, is for you.

ORIENTATION AND PLANNING

GETTING ORIENTED

Greater Tōkyō incorporates 23 wards, 26 smaller cities, seven towns, and eight villages—altogether sprawling 88 km (55 mi) from east to west and 24 km (15 mi) from north to south with a population of 35 million people. The wards alone enclose an area of 590 square km (228 square mi), which comprise the city center and house 8 million residents. Chiyoda-ku, Chūō-ku, Shinjuku-ku, and Minato-ku are the four central business districts.

Imperial Palace District. Kōkyo, the Imperial Palace, is the center of Tōkyō, where Edo Castle once stood. Although the imperial residence is only open two days a year, you can explore the palace grounds and gardens

TOP REASONS TO GO

2

■ **A City Oasis.** Located in the middle of the city, the Imperial Palace East Gardens is a wonderful place to escape the hustle and bustle of the city.

■ **Hello Master.** At maid cafés, an Akihabara phenomenon, waitresses dress in maid costumes, address patrons as *master*, and cater to the festishes of Japanese *otaku* (nerds).

■ **Dancing in the Streets.** A visit during May must include the Kanda Festival—one of Tōkyō's major street celebrations. More than 200 portable shrines are carried in a parade toward the ground of the Kanda Jinja Shrine.

■ **Shining Shrine.** Dating back to 1627, the Tōshō-gū Shrine is a national treasure that houses a priceless collection of historical art and is one of the few remaining early-Edo-period buildings in Tōkyō—it survived the 1868 revolt, the 1923 earthquake, and the 1945 bombings.

■ **Make a Wish.** Visit the Asakusa Jinja where the souls of the three men who built Sensō-ji are enshrined. If you have a special wish, purchase a wooden placard, write your message on it, and leave it for the gods.

■ **A Japanese Party.** Half-naked drunken people? Loud crowds? Brilliant colors? It's all part of the Sanja Festival, which happens every May in the streets of Asakusa.

■ **Don't Eat That!** Discover the delight of Japanese plastic food in Kappabashi.

■ **Shop 'Til You Drop.** Looking for trinkets or gifts to bring home? Visit more than 80 shops on Nakamise-dōri that sell everything from rice crackers to *kiriko* (traditionally cut and colored glassware whose style was developed in the Edo period).

■ **Got Fish?** You'll dine on the freshest sushi in the world at Tsukiji fish market.

■ **Off the Beaten Path.** Discover the local charm of old sushi and sashimi restaurants, and small markets in the backstreets of Tsukiji.

■ **Japanese Impressions.** Go to the Bridgestone Museum of Art, one of Japan's best private collections of French impressionist art and sculpture and of post-Meiji Japanese painting in Western styles by such artists as Shigeru Aoki and Tsuguji Fujita.

■ **A Leisurely Stroll.** On weekends, the main roads of Ginza are closed off for pedestrians, so you can see the historical Wako department store, and explore the small side streets of this old shopping district without fearing the crazy drivers.

■ **Feeding Frenzy.** Check out the basement food halls in Mitsukoshi department store, in Nihombashi and Ginza, where you will find hundreds of delicious desserts and prepared foods of many varieties.

■ **Trendy Togs and Tots.** Observe the trendy Japanese youth street fashions of **Takeshita Street**.

■ **On a Clear Day.** The observation deck of Tōkyō Metropolitan Government Office has a great view of Mt. Fuji, and the complex hosts open-air concerts and exhibitions.

■ **Priceless Art.** The Seiji Tōgō Memorial Sompo Japan Museum of Art has van Gogh's *Sunflowers*, and the work of Japanese painter Seiji Tōgō.

■ **Fun in the Sun.** Decks Tōkyō Beach has shopping, arcades, and great Chinese food, while Odaiba Kaihin Kōen offers a sandy beach, a small knockoff of the Statue of Liberty, and a view of the Rainbow Bridge.

■ **Buff Bathing.** Odaiba's Hot Spring Theme Park is a memorable onsen experience in Edo-era surroundings; that is, if you don't mind being naked in a crowd.

at your leisure. Nearby are museums, Yasukuni Jinja shrine, the Japanese parliament and supreme court buildings, the National Theater, and Tōkyō station.

Akihabara and Jimbō-chō. Akihabara and Jimbō-chō are northeast of the Imperial Palace. Akihabara's famed for its electronics stores and manga memorabilia shops and cafés. The theme's more cerebral in Jimbō-chō, which is filled with booksellers hawking anything printed including antique wood-block books, scrolls, and current literature.

Ueno. Ueno Park, directly north of Akihabara, is home to three superb national museums, a university of fine arts, and a zoo. A stone's-throw south is Ameyoko market. The area's geared towards locals looking for legit Western wares.

Asakusa. The sacred merges with secular and ancient tradition meets modernity in Asakusa. The area's home to Tōkyō's oldest temple, the 13th-century Sensō-ji, as well as the Asakusa Jinja shrine. It's also home to artists, hipsters, and generations of locals fiercely proud of and loyal to their neighborhood.

Tsukiji and Shiodome. Tsukiji, in southeastern Tōkyō on the Sumida-gawa River, is home to the famed sumō stables and what's purportedly the world's largest fish market—The Central Wholesale Market, home to nearly 1,000 vendors hawking some 2,000 metric tons of fish and seafood a day. Shiodome, a bit farther inland, is a massive development zone, with plenty of fashionable shops and restaurants. Most of the area was built after 2000 and includes the Nippon Television Tower and the replica of the Shinbashi railway station.

Nihombashi, Ginza, and Yūraku-chō. Nihombashi, east of the Imperial Palace, lays claim to the geographical and financial center of Tōkyō. Follow the money slightly south to Ginza, where you'll find Tōkyō's traditional high-end stores and art galleries. Yūraku-chō, between Ginza and the Outer Garden of the Imperial Palace, known for its countless izakayas, or traditional watering holes, underneath the train tracks.

Aoyama, Harajuku, and Shibuya. Aoyama and Harajuku, west of the Imperial Palace, are chic neighborhoods saturated with designer and chain stores, independent boutiques, and malls where high fashion is the name of the game. To the south is Shibuya, which is more than a major transportation hub: it's an urban teen's dream. This loud, sprawling, neon jungle's packed with people, hip shops, megachain stores, and eateries.

Roppongi and Azabu Juban. Southeast of Shibuya is Roppongi, with a rich and sometimes sordid history of catering to foreign nightlife; here you'll find the massive Roppongi Hills development. Azabu Juban, a prestigious residential district with many embassies, is located just south of Roppongi.

Shinjuku. Northeast of Roppongi, Shinjuku's home to the city's government and what is said to be the busiest train station in the world. The station's adjacent to Takashimaya Times Square, a towering mall that includes department stores, shops, and restaurants. When the sun sets the area lights up with bars, clubs, and the famed red-light district.

Shinjuku's also home to the towering Tōkyō Tochō complex, whose observation platforms provide sweeping views.

Odaiba. Odaiba, an artificial island south of the city's center and in Tokyo Bay, is a mecca of shops, restaurants, clubs, and anything hip.

PLANNING

Tōkyō is a state-of-the-art financial marketplace, where billions of dollars are whisked electronically around the globe at the blink of an eye. However, most ATMs in the city shut down by 9 PM, so be sure to get enough cash when you find one. Most Citibank, Shinsei Bank (in some subway stations), and Japan Post ATMs allow international bank card transactions, but they are not always accessible. Tōkyō is a safe city, so you may carry cash without fear of street crime.

WHEN TO GO
Spring and fall are the best times to visit. Sakura (cherry blossoms) begin blooming in Tōkyō by early April. Fall has clear blue skies, though occasional typhoons occur. June brings an intense rainy season. July and August bring high temperatures and stifling humidity. Winter's gray and chilly, with Tōkyō and other areas along the Pacific Coast receiving very little snow.

GETTING HERE AND AROUND
AIR TRAVEL
Flying time to Tōkyō is 13¾ hours from New York, 12¾ hours from Chicago, and 9½ hours from Los Angeles. Your trip east, because of tailwinds, can be about 45 minutes shorter.

You can fly nonstop to Tōkyō from Chicago, Detroit, New York, Los Angeles, San Francisco, Portland (OR), Seattle, Minneapolis, and Washington, D.C.

Tōkyō's Narita Airport (NRT) lies 80 km (50 mi) northeast of the city. It takes about 90 minutes—a time very dependent on city traffic—and costs around $20. If you are arriving with a Japan Rail Pass and staying in Tōkyō for a few days it's best to pay for the transfer into the city and activate the Rail Pass for travel beyond Tōkyō.

Tōkyō Narita's Terminal 2 has two adjoining wings, north and south. When you arrive, your first task should be to convert your money into yen; you need it for transportation into Tōkyō. In both wings ATMs and money-exchange counters are in the wall between the customs inspection area and the arrival lobby. Both terminals have a Japan National Tourist Organization tourist information center, where you can get free maps, brochures, and other visitor information. Directly across from the customs-area exits at both terminals are the ticket counters for airport limousine buses to Tōkyō. Buses leave from platforms just outside terminal exits, exactly on schedule; the departure time is on the ticket. The Friendly Airport Limousine offers the only shuttle-bus service from Narita to Tōkyō.

Japan Railways trains stop at both Narita Airport terminals. The fastest and most comfortable is the Narita Limited Express (NEX), which makes 23 runs a day in each direction. Trains from the airport go directly to the central Tōkyō station in just under an hour, then continue to Yokohama and Ōfuna. Daily departures begin at 7:43 AM; the last train is at 9:43 PM. The one-way fare is ¥2,940 (¥4,980 for the first-class Green Car and ¥5,380 per person for a private compartment that seats four). All seats are reserved, and you'll need to reserve in advance, as this train fills quickly.

The Keisei Skyliner train runs every 20–30 minutes between the airport terminals and Keisei-Ueno station. The trip takes 57 minutes and costs ¥1,920 ($17). The first Skyliner leaves Narita for Ueno at 9:21 AM, the last at 9:59 PM. There's also an early train from the airport, called the Morning Liner, which leaves at 7:49 AM and costs ¥1,400. From Ueno to Narita the first Skyliner is at 6:32 AM, the last at 5:21 PM.

Airport Information Haneda Airport (HND) (☎ 03/5757–8111 ⊕ www. tokyo-airport-bldg.co.jp/en). **Narita Airport (NRT)** (☎ 0476/34–5000 ⊕ www. narita-airport.jp/en/index.html).

Bus Contacts Airport Transport Service Co (☎ 03/3665–7232 in Tōkyō, 0476/ 32–8080 for Terminal 1, 0476/34–6311 for Terminal 2). **IAE Co** (☎ 0476/32–7954 for Terminal 1, 0476/34–6886 for Terminal 2). **Japan Railways** (☎ 03/3423–0111 for JR East InfoLine ☉ Weekdays 10–6). **Keisei Railway** (☎ 03/3831–0131 for Ueno information counter, 0476/32–8505 at Narita Airport).

BOAT TRAVEL

Ferries connect most of the islands of Japan. Some of the more popular routes are from Tōkyō to Tomakomai or Kushiro in Hokkaidō; from Tōkyō to Shikoku; and from Tōkyō or Ōsaka to Kyūshū. You can purchase ferry tickets in advance from travel agencies or before boarding. The ferries are inexpensive and are a pleasant, if slow, way of traveling. Private cabins are available, but it's more fun to travel in the economy class, where everyone sleeps on the carpeted floor in one large room. Passengers eat, drink, and enjoy themselves in a convivial atmosphere.

Contacts Hankyu Ferry (⊕ www.han9f.co.jp). **Meimon Taiyo Ferry** (⊕ www.city line.co.jp/english).

CAR TRAVEL

There is little on-street parking in Tōkyō. Parking is usually in staffed parking lots or in parking towers within buildings. Expect to pay upwards of $3 per hour. Parking regulations are strictly enforced, and illegally parked vehicles are towed away. Recovery fees start at $300 and increase hourly.

MOTORCYCLE TRAVEL

With its super-narrow roads and alleyways, a fantastic way to tool around Tōkyō is with a scooter, while the rest of the country—with its rolling hills, mountains, and shoreline—is really great to see via motorcycle. There are many bikers in Japan, so highways, rest stops, and campgrounds are all equipped to handle whatever bike you choose to tour with. Japan Bike Rentals is the only bike-rental place that is run by a gaijin (foreigner) so you can drop your dictionaries and do all the paperwork in English—and online. All riders will need a passport, a valid unrestricted motorcycle license from their own country, and an

International Driving Permit. Japan Bike Rentals is open seven days a week, but you will need to make your booking online first, whether to rent a bike, a GPS for a self-guided tour, or join a guided tour. It's closed in January and February. SCS Motorcycle is one of the largest Japanese motorcycle rental chains, but finding an English-speaking staff member to help you may be difficult. It has several branches around Tōkyō, but its head rental office is in Hakusan, near the Tōkyō Dome.

Contacts Japan Bike Rentals (☎ *03/3584–5185* ⊕ *www.japanbikerentals.com*). **SCS Motorcycle** (☎ *03/3815–6221*).

TRAIN TRAVEL

The Shinkansen (bullet train), one of the fastest trains in the world, connects major cities north and south of Tōkyō. It's only slightly less expensive than flying, but is in many ways more convenient because train stations are more centrally located than airports (and, if you have a Japan Rail Pass, it's extremely affordable).

Other trains, though not as fast as the Shinkansen, are just as convenient and substantially cheaper. There are three types of train services: *futsū* (local service), *tokkyū* (limited express service), and *kyūkō* (express service). Both the tokkyū and the kyūkō offer a first-class compartment known as the Green Car. Smoking is allowed only in designated carriages on long-distance and Shinkansen trains. Local and commuter trains are entirely no-smoking.

MONEY-SAVING TIPS

If you plan on visiting a lot of the city's sites, purchasing a **GRUTTO Pass** (⊕ *www.museum.or.jp/grutto*) is the way to go. The pass, which is only ¥2,000, gives visitors free or discounted admission to 61 sites throughout the city including museums, zoos, aquariums, and parks. Passes can be purchased at all participating sites, as well as the Tōkyō Tourist Information Center, or Family Mart and 7-Eleven convenience stores. Keep in mind that passes expire two months after date of purchase.

VISITOR INFORMATION

The Japan National Tourist Organization (JNTO) has offices in Tōkyō. Look for the sign showing a red question mark and the word "information" at train stations and city centers. Need help on the move? For recorded information 24 hours a day, call the Teletourist service. The Tōkyō Convention and Visitors Bureau regularly updates its Web site with details about the city's events, lodging, and more.

Teletourist Service Tōkyō (☎ *03/3201–2911*).

Tourist Information Centers (TIC) Tōkyō International Forum B1 (✉ *3-5-1 Marunouchi, Chiyoda-ku, Tōkyō* ☎ *03/3201–3331*).

EXPLORING TŌKYŌ

IMPERIAL PALACE AND GOVERNMENT DISTRICT 皇居近辺

This district is the core of Japan's government. It is primarily comprised of *Nagata-chō,* the Imperial Palace (*Kōkyo-gaien*), the Diet (national parliament building), the Prime Minister's residence (*Kantei*), and the Supreme Court. The Imperial Palace and the Diet are both important to see, but the Supreme Court is nondescript. Unfortunately, the Prime Minister's residence is only viewable from afar, hidden behind fortified walls and trees.

The Imperial Palace was built by the order of Ieyasu Tokugawa, who chose the site for his castle in 1590. The castle had 99 gates (36 in the outer wall), 21 watchtowers (of which three are still standing), and 28 armories. The outer defenses stretched from present-day Shimbashi Station to Kanda. Completed in 1640 (and later expanded), it was at the time the largest castle in the world. The Japanese Imperial Family resides in heavily blockaded sections of the palace grounds. Tours are conducted by reservation only, and restricted to designated outdoor sections, namely, the palace grounds and the East Gardens. The grounds are open to the general public only twice a year, on January 2 and December 23 (the Emperor's birthday), when thousands of people assemble under the balcony to offer their good wishes to the Imperial Family.

Numbers in the margin correspond to the Imperial Palace and Government District map.

ORIENTATION AND PLANNING
ORIENTATION
The Imperial Palace is located in the heart of central Tōkyō, and the city's other neighborhoods branch out from here. The palace, in which the Imperial Family still resides, is surrounded by a moat that connects through canals to Tōkyō Bay and Sumida river (*Sumida-gawa*) to the east. Outside the moat, large four-lane roads trace its outline, as if the city expanded from this primary location.

PLANNING
The best way to discover the Imperial Palace is to take part in one of the free tours offered by the **Imperial Household Agency** (☎*03/3213–1111* ⊕*www.kunaicho.go.jp*), which manages matters of the state. There are four different tours: Imperial Palace Grounds, the East Gardens (*Higashi Gyo-en*), Sannomaru Shōzōkan, and Gagaku Performance (in autumn only). All tours require registration a day in advance and hours change according to the season.

If you are exploring on your own, allow at least an hour for the East Garden and Outer Garden of the palace itself. Plan to visit Yasukuni Jinja after lunch and spend at least an hour there. The Yūshūkan (at Yasukuni Jinja) and Kōgeikan museums are both small and should engage you for no more than a half hour each, but the modern art museum requires a more leisurely visit—particularly if there's a special exhibit. The best time to visit is during the spring when the *sakura* (cherry tree blossoms) are in bloom between late March and early April, or during the Yasukuni Spring festival (April 21–23), which pays homage to the war dead and shrine deities.

■TIP➜ Avoid visiting the Imperial Palace on Monday, when the East Garden and museums are closed; the East Garden is also closed Friday. In July and August, heat will make the palace walk grueling—bring a hat and bottled water.

GETTING HERE AND AROUND

The best way to get to the Imperial Palace is by subway. Take the Chiyoda line to Nijūbashimae station (Exit 6) or the JR lines to Tōkyō station (Marunouchi Central Exit). There are three entrance gates—Ōte-mon, Hirakawa-mon, and Kita-hane-bashi-mon. You can also easily get to any of the three from the Ōte-machi or Takebashi subway stations.

TOP ATTRACTIONS

❷ Chidorigafuchi National Memorial Garden 千鳥ヶ淵戦没者墓苑. High on the edge of the Imperial Palace moat, this park is famous for its cherry tree blossoms, which appear in spring. The most popular activity in this garden is renting rowboats on the moat at the **Chidorigafuchi Boathouse.** The entrance to the garden is near Yasukuni Jinja. ⊠ *2 Sanbanchō, Chiyoda-ku* ☎ *03/3234–1948* ⊠ *Park free, boat rental ¥500 for 30 min during regular season, and ¥ 800 for 30 min during cherry blossom season* ☺ *Park daily sunrise–sunset; boathouse late Mar.–early Apr., daily 9:30–4, usually closed Mon.* Ⓜ *Hanzō-mon and Shinjuku subway lines, Kudanshita Station (Exit 2).*

❸ Imperial Palace East Garden 皇居東御苑 *(Kōkyo Higashi Gyo-en).* The entrance to the East Garden is the *Ōte-mon,* once the main gate of Ieyasu Tokugawa's castle. Here, you will come across the National Police Agency *dōjō* (martial arts hall) and the Ōte Rest House, where for ¥100 you can buy a simple map of the garden.

The **Hundred-Man Guardhouse** was once defended by four shifts of 100 soldiers each. Past it is the entrance to what was once the *ni-no-maru,* the "second circle" of the fortress. It's now a grove and garden. At the far end is the **Suwa Tea Pavilion,** an early-19th-century building relocated here from another part of the castle grounds.

The steep stone walls of the **hon-maru** (the "inner circle"), with the Moat of Swans below, dominate the west side of the garden. Halfway along is **Shio-mi-zaka,** which translates roughly as "Briny View Hill," so named because in the Edo period the ocean could be seen from here.

Head to the wooded paths around the garden's edges for shade, quiet, and benches to rest your weary feet. In the southwest corner is the Fujimi Yagura, the only surviving watchtower of the hon-maru; farther along the path, on the west side, is the **Fujimi Tamon,** one of the two remaining armories.

The odd-looking octagonal tower is the **Tōkagakudo Concert Hall.** Its mosaic tile facade was built in honor of Empress Kōjun in 1966. ⊠ *Chiyoda-ku* ⊠ *Free* ☺ *Apr.–Aug., weekends and Tues.–Thurs. 9–5; Sept.–Mar., weekends and Tues.–Thurs. 9–4:30* Ⓜ *Tōzai, Marunouchi, and Chiyoda subway lines, Ōte-machi Station (Exit C13b).*

FodorśChoice
★

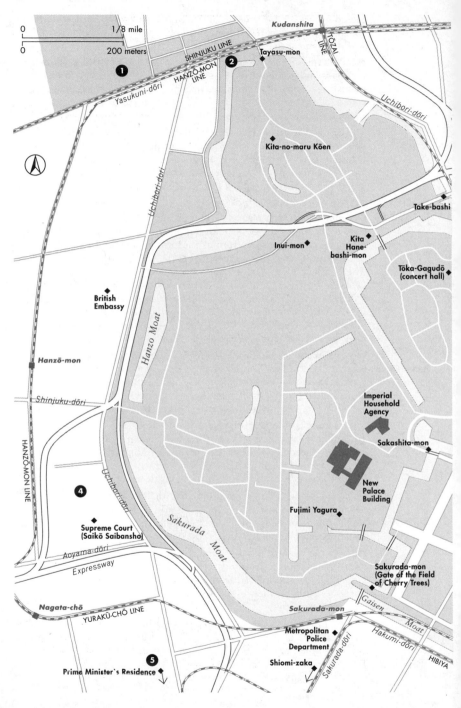

0 | 1/8 mile
0 | 200 meters

Kudanshita

SHINJUKU LINE
HANZŌ-MON LINE
TŌZAI LINE

Yasukuni-dōri

1

2 Tayasu-mon

Uchibori-dōri

Kita-no-maru Kōen

Take-bashi

Inui-mon

Kita Hane-bashi-mon

Tōka-Gagudō (concert hall)

British Embassy

Hanzo Moat

Hanzō-mon

Shinjuku-dōri

Uchibori-dōri

Imperial Household Agency

Sakashita-mon

4

HANZŌ-MON LINE

Supreme Court (Saikō Saibansho)

New Palace Building

Sakurada Moat

Fujimi Yagura

Aoyama-dōri

Expressway

Sakurada-mon (Gate of the Field of Cherry Trees)

Nagata-chō

YURAKŪ-CHŌ LINE

Sakurada-mon

Gaisen

Moat

Hakumi-dōri

HIBIYA

Metropolitan Police Department

Sakurada-dōri

5 Prime Minister's Residence

Shiomi-zaka

Imperial Palace and Government District

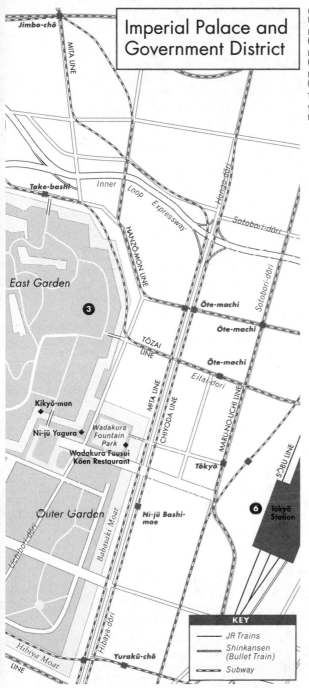

Jimbo-chō

MITA LINE

Take-bashi

Inner Loop Expressway

HANZŌ-MON LINE

Hongo-dōri

Sotobori-dōri

Sotobori-dōri

East Garden

3

TŌZAI LINE

Ōte-machi

Ōte-machi

Ōte-machi

Eitai-dōri

MARU-NO-UCHI LINE

MITA LINE

CHIYODA LINE

SŌBU LINE

Kikyō-mon

Ni-jū Yagura

Wadakura Fountain Park

Wadakura Fuusui Kōen Restaurant

Tōkyō

Outer Garden

Ni-jū Bashi-mae

6 Tōkyō Station

Babasaki Moat

Uchibori-dōri

Hibiya Moat

Hibiya-dōri

Yurakū-chō

LINE

KEY

——	JR Trains
====	Shinkansen (Bullet Train)
- - -	Subway

⑤ National Diet Building 国会議事堂 *(Kokkai-Gijidō).* This building, which houses the Japanese parliament, is the perfect example of post–World War II Japanese architecture; on a gloomy day it seems as if it might have sprung from the screen of a German Expressionist movie. Started in 1920, construction took 17 years to complete. The Prime Minister's residence, Kantei, is across the street. ⊠*1–7–1 Nagata-chō, Chiyoda-ku* Ⓜ*Marunouchi subway line, Kokkai-Gijidō-mae Station (Exit 2).*

④ National Theater 国立劇場 *(Kokuritsu Gekijō).* Architect Hiroyuki Iwamoto's winning entry in the design competition for the National Theater building (1966) is a rendition in concrete of the ancient *azekura* (storehouse) style, invoking the 8th-century Shōsōin Imperial Repository in Nara. The large hall seats 1,746 and presents primarily Kabuki theater, ancient court music, and dance. The small hall seats 630 and is used mainly for Bunraku puppet theater and traditional music. The building is worth a look, but all performances are in Japanese, so it can be difficult to sit through an entire show. ⊠*4–1 Hayabusa-chō, Chiyoda-ku* ☎*03/3265–7411* ✉*Varies depending on performance* Ⓜ*Hanzō-mon subway line, Hanzō-mon Station (Exit 1).*

⑥ Tōkyō Station 東京駅. The work of Kingo Tatsuno, one of Japan's first modern architects, Tōkyō Station was completed in 1914. Tatsuno modeled his creation on the railway station of Amsterdam. The building lost its original top story in the air raids of 1945, but was promptly repaired. In the late 1990s, a plan to demolish the station was impeded by public outcry. Inside, it has been deepened and tunneled and redesigned any number of times to accommodate new commuter lines, but the lovely old redbrick facade remains untouched. Since the hotel has now closed, one of the better attractions is the Gran Tōkyō North Tower, which opened in 2007. The 200-meter-tall (656-foot-tall) glass-and-steel office building includes a branch of the high-end department store chain Daimaru. ⊠*1–9–1 Marunouchi, Chiyoda-ku* ☎*03/3212-8011* ⊕*www.grantokyo-nt.com* Ⓜ*Marunouchi subway line and JR lines.*

① Yasukuni Jinja 靖国神社 *(Shrine of Peace for the Nation).* This shrine is ★ not as impressive as Asakusa Shrine and Meiji Jingū, so if you much choose between the three, visit the latter. Founded in 1869, this shrine is dedicated to approximately 2.5 million Japanese, Taiwanese, and Koreans who have died since then in war or military service. Since 1945 Yasukuni has been a center of stubborn political debate given that the Japanese constitution expressly renounces both militarism and state sponsorship of religion. Several prime ministers have visited the shrine since 1979, causing a political chill between Japan and its close neighbors, Korea and China—who suffered under Japanese colonialism. Despite all this, hundreds of thousands of Japanese come here every year, simply to pray for the repose of friends and relatives they have lost. These pilgrimages are most frenzied on August 15, the anniversary of the conclusion of World War II, when former soldiers and ultra-right-wing groups descend upon the shrine's grounds en masse.

The shrine is not one structure but a complex of buildings that include the **Main Hall** and the **Hall of Worship**—both built in the simple, unadorned style of the ancient Shintō shrines at Ise—and the **Yūshūkan,** a museum of documents and war memorabilia. Also here are a Nō theater and, in the far western corner, a sumō-wrestling ring. Sumō matches are held at Yasukuni in April, during the first of its three annual festivals. You can pick up a pamphlet and simplified map of the shrine, both in English, just inside the grounds.

Refurbished in 2002, the Yūshūkan presents Japan at its most ambivalent—if not unrepentant—about its more recent militaristic past. Critics charge that the newer exhibits glorify the nation's role in the Pacific War as a noble struggle for independence; certainly there's an agenda here that's hard to reconcile with Japan's firm postwar rejection of militarism as an instrument of national policy. Many Japanese visitors are moved by such displays as the last letters and photographs of young kamikaze pilots; visitors from other countries tend to find the Yūshūkan a cautionary, rather than uplifting, experience.

Although some of the exhibits have English labels and notes, the English is not very helpful; most objects, however, speak clearly enough for themselves. Rooms on the second floor house an especially fine collection of medieval swords and armor. Perhaps the most bizarre exhibit is the *kaiten* (human torpedo) on the first floor. ⊠ *3–1–1 Kudankita, Chiyoda-ku* ☎ *03/3261–8326* ⊕ *www.yasukuni.or.jp* ≈ *¥800* ⊙ *Grounds daily, usually 9–9. Museum Mar.–Oct., daily 9–5; Nov.–Feb., daily 9–4:30* Ⓜ *Hanzō-mon and Shinjuku subway lines, Kudanshita Station (Exit 1).*

AKIHABARA 秋葉原 AND JIMBŌ-CHŌ 神保町

Akihabara is techno-geek heaven. Also known as Akihabara Electric Town, this district, which was once all about electronics, is becoming a wacky fetish district where *otaku* (nerds) can indulge in Japanese anime computer-game fantasies, hang out in kinky cafés, and buy anime comics. Visitors don't just come here to buy digital cameras, but to observe the bizarre subculture of this tech-savvy country.

If you're looking for something a little more cerebral, head to Jimbō-chō where family-run specialty bookstores of every genre abound including rare antiquarian and Japanese manga. The area is also home to Meiji University and Nihon University.

Numbers in the margin correspond to the Akihabara and Jimbō-chō map.

ORIENTATION AND PLANNING
ORIENTATION

Akihabara is east of the Imperial Palace, right below Ueno and Asakusa. Akihabara Station is located north of Tōkyō Station, on the JR Yamanote line, Hibiya line, and Tsukuba line. It's right below Asakusa and Ueno districts.

Located just to the west of Akihabara, Jimbō-chō should be a very short stopover either before or after an excursion to Akihabara. The best way to get there is by taxi, which should cost about ¥800 to or from Akihabara station.

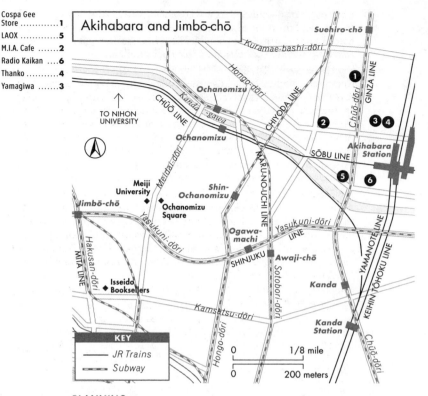

PLANNING

This is a rougher part of Tōkyō, so mind your bags and wallets. Credit cards are accepted at all major electronics superstores, but bring enough cash to get around, because ATMs are difficult to find. Keep in mind that most stores in Akihabara do not open until 10 AM. Weekends draw hordes of shoppers, especially on Sunday, when the four central blocks of Chūō-dōri are closed to traffic and become a pedestrian mall. That's when the geeks come out.

GETTING HERE AND AROUND

Take the train to Akihabara Station on the JR Yamanote line. Akihabara is a 30- to 40-minute ride from most tourist hotels in Shinjuku or Minato-ku.

TOP ATTRACTIONS

1 **Cospa Gee Store.** Fans of anime will enjoy this zany Japanese costume-shop experience. It's like no other in the world and a good place to pick up an original costume for Halloween. ✉ *2F MN Bldg., 3–15–5 Soto-Kanda, Chiyoda-ku* ☎ *03/3526–6877* ⊙ *Daily 11–7* Ⓜ *JR Yamanote line, Akihabara station (Akihabara Electric Town Exit 2).*

5 **LAOX** ラオックス**.** Of all the discount stores in Akihabara, LAOX has the largest and most comprehensive selection, with four buildings in this area—one exclusively for musical instruments, another for duty-free appliances—and outlets in Yokohama and Narita. This is a good place to find the latest in digital cameras, watches, and games. ✉*1–2–9 Soto-Kanda, Chiyoda-ku* ☎*03/3253–7111* ⊙*Mon.–Sat.* *10–9* Ⓜ*JR Akihabara Station (Akihabara Electric Town Exit).*

➋ **Maid in Angels' (M.I.A.) Cafe** ミアカフェ. This maid café is not exceptional by any standards, but it's a glimpse inside the world of the otaku. Waitresses in frilly dresses serve beer, juice, tea, pasta, curries, and desserts at simple wood tables and booths. Check the event board outside the front door for special café happenings, like when the girls change costumes based on the holidays. Santa suits anyone? ✉ *1F Meiji Bldg., 3–1–2 Soto-Kanda, Chiyoda-ku* ☎*03/5294–0078* ⊕*www.cos-cafe.com* ⊙*Weekdays noon–10, weekends 11–10* Ⓜ*JR Yamanote line, Akihabara station (Akihabara Electric Town Exit).*

➏ **Radio Kaikan** ラジオ会館. Eight floors featuring a variety of vendors selling mini-spy cameras, cell phones disguised stun guns, anime comics, adult toys, gadgets, and oddball hobby supplies is a shopping mecca for otaku and visitors alike. Start browsing from the top floor and work your way down. ✉*1–15–16 Soto-Kanda, Chiyoda-ku* ☎*03/5298–6300* ⊙*Daily 11–7* Ⓜ*JR Yamanote line, Akihabara station (Akihabara Electric Town Exit).*

➍ **Thanko** サンコー. As the recent king of wacky electronics from Japan, Thanko sells everything from recording binoculars to a smokeless ashtray to a flower pot with a speaker mounted on its side. This showroom is a must-see for gadget geeks. ✉*1F Machida Bldg., 3–9–10 Soto-Kanda, Chiyoda-ku* ☎*03/3526–5472* ⊕*www.thanko.jp* ⊙*Mon.–Sat. 11–8, Sun. 11–7* Ⓜ*JR Yamanote line, Akihabara station (Akihabara Electric Town Exit).*

➌ **Yamagiwa** ヤマギワ. This superstore is for die-hard electronic shoppers. Entire floors of this discount electronics giant are devoted to computer hardware and software, fax machines, and copiers. Yamagiwa has a particularly good selection of lighting fixtures, most of them 220 volts, but the annex has export models of the most popular appliances and devices, plus an English speaking staff to assist you with selections. You should be able to bargain prices down a bit—especially if you're buying more than one big-ticket item. ✉*1–5–10 Soto-Kanda, Chiyoda-ku* ☎*03/3253–5111* ⊕*www.yamagiwa.co.jp* ⊙*Weekdays 11–7:30, weekends 10:30–7:30* Ⓜ*JR Akihabara Station (Akihabara Electric Town Exit).*

UENO 上野

JR Ueno Station is Tōkyō's version of the Gare du Nord: the gateway to and from Japan's northeast provinces. Since its completion in 1883, the station has served as a terminus in the great migration to the city by villagers in pursuit of a better life.

Ueno was a place of prominence long before the coming of the railroad. Since Ieyasu Tokugawa established his capital here in 1603, 36 subsidiary temples were erected surrounding the Main Hall, and the city of Edo itself expanded to the foot of the hill where Kan-ei-ji's main gate once stood.

The Meiji government turned Ueno Hill into one of the nation's first public parks. It would serve as the site of trade and industrial expositions; it would have a national museum, a library, a university of fine arts, and a zoo. The modernization of Ueno still continues, but the park is more than the sum of its museums. The Shōgitai failed to take everything with them: some of the most important buildings in the temple complex survived or were restored and should not be missed.

Numbers in the margin correspond to the Ueno map.

ORIENTATION AND PLANNING

ORIENTATION

Ueno and Asakusa make up the historical enclave of Tōkyō. Traditional architecture and way of life are preserved here at the northeastern reaches of the city. Both areas can be explored in a single day, though if you have the time, it's also a good idea to devote an entire day to this place to fully appreciate its many museum exhibits and shrines.

PLANNING

Exploring Ueno can be one excursion or two: an afternoon of cultural browsing or a full day of discoveries in one of the great centers of the city. ■TIP→ Avoid Monday, when most of the museums are closed. Ueno out of doors is no fun at all in February or the rainy season (late June–mid-July); mid-August can be brutally hot and muggy. In April, the cherry blossoms of Ueno Kōen are glorious.

GETTING HERE AND AROUND

Ueno Station can be accessed by train on the Hibiya line, Ginza line, and JR Yamanote line (Kōen Entrance). Be sure to avoid morning (8–9) and evening rush hour (6–9) and bring plenty of cash for admission fees to museums and food for the day; there are no ATMs. To purchase souvenirs, museum stores accept many major credit cards.

TOP ATTRACTIONS

❼ Ame-ya Yoko-chō Market アメヤ横丁. Not much besides Ueno Station survived the bombings of World War II, and anyone who could make it here from the countryside with rice and other small supplies of food could sell them at exorbitant black-market prices. Sugar was a commodity that couldn't be found at any price in postwar Tōkyō. Before long, there were hundreds of stalls in the black market selling various kinds of *ame* (confections), most made from sweet potatoes. These stalls gave the market its name, Ame-ya Yoko-chō (often shortened to Ameyoko), which means "Confectioners' Alley." Shortly before the Korean War, the market was legalized, and soon the stalls were carrying watches, chocolate, ballpoint pens, blue jeans, and T-shirts that had somehow been "liberated" from American PXs. In years to come the merchants of Ameyoko diversified still further—to fine Swiss timepieces and fake designer luggage, cosmetics, jewelry, fresh fruit, and fish. The market became especially famous for the traditional prepared foods of the New Year, and, during the last few days of December, as many as half a million people crowd into the narrow alleys under the railroad tracks to stock up for the holiday. ✉ *Ueno 4-chōme, Taitō-ku* ☉ *Most shops and stalls daily 10–7* Ⓜ *JR Ueno Station (Hirokō-ji Exit).*

⑤ Benzaiten 弁財天. Perched in the middle of Shinobazu Pond, this shrine is dedicated to the goddess Benten, one of the Seven Gods of Good Luck that evolved from a combination of Indian, Chinese, and Japanese mythology. As matron goddess of the arts, she is depicted holding a lutelike musical instrument called a *biwa*. The shrine, which was built by Abbot Tenkai, was destroyed in the bombings of 1945; the present version, with its distinctive octagonal roof, is a faithful copy. You can rent rowboats and pedal boats at a nearby boathouse. ✉ *Taitō-ku* ☎ *03/3828–9502 for boathouse* 🚣 *Rowboats ¥600 for 1 hr, pedal boats ¥600 for 30 min, swan boats ¥700 for 30 min* 🕙 *Boathouse daily 10–5:30* Ⓜ *JR Ueno Station (Kōen-guchi/Park Exit); Keisei private rail line, Keisei-Ueno Station (Ikenohata Exit).*

④ Kannon Hall 観音堂 *(Kiyomizu Kannon-dō).* This National Treasure was a part of Abbot Tenkai's attempt to build a copy of Kyōto's magnificent Kiyomizu-dera in Ueno. His attempt was honorable, but failed to be as impressive as the original. The principal Buddhist image of worship here is the Senjū Kannon (Thousand-Armed Goddess of Mercy). Another figure, however, receives greater homage. This is the Kosodate Kannon, who is believed to answer the prayers of women having difficulty conceiving children. If their prayers are answered, they return to Kiyomizu and leave a doll, as both an offering of thanks and a prayer for the child's health. In a ceremony held every September 25, the dolls that have accumulated during the year are burned in a bonfire. ✉ *1–29 Ueno Kōen, Taitō-ku* ☎ *03/3821–4749* 🆓 *Free* 🕙 *Daily 7–5* Ⓜ *JR Ueno Station (Kōen-guchi/Park Exit).*

⑥ Shinobazu Pond 不忍池. Shinobazu was once an inlet of Tōkyō Bay. When the area was reclaimed, it became a freshwater pond. Abbot Tenkai, founder of Kan-ei-ji on the hill above the pond, had an island made in the middle of it, which he built for *Benzaiten,* the goddess of the arts. Later improvements included a causeway to the island, embankments, and even a racecourse (1884–93). Today the pond is in three sections. The first, with its famous lotus plants, is a wildlife sanctuary. Some 5,000 wild ducks migrate here from as far away as Siberia, sticking around from September to April. The second section, to the north, belongs to Ueno Zoo; the third, to the west, is a small lake for boating. ✉ *Shinobazu-dōri, Taitō-ku* 🆓 *Free* 🕙 *Daily sunrise–sunset* Ⓜ *JR Ueno Station (Kōen-guchi/Park Exit); Keisei private rail line, Keisei-Ueno Station (Higashi-guchi/East Exit).*

NEED A BREAK?

Hasumi Teahouse, a charming Japanese teahouse located on the bank of the pond, is only open during the summer, when the lotus flowers cover Shinobazu Pond. It's an open, airy café that offers perfect views of the lotus flowers in bloom and serves lunch and dinner sets: for lunch, you can get a set of tea and snacks for ¥900; for dinner you can get a set of cold beer and snacks for ¥1,000. English is not spoken, but sets are displayed in plastic models at the entrance to make ordering easier. ✉ Shinobazu-dōri, Taitō-ku ☎ 03/3833–0030 (Mon.–Sat.) 🕙 June 17–Aug., daily noon–4 and 5–9 Ⓜ Toei Oedo line, Ueno-Okachimachi Station (Exit 2), JR Yamanote line, Ueno Station (Exit 6).

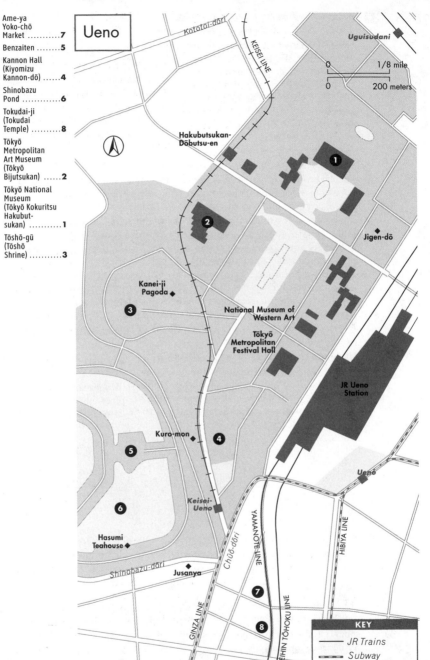

8 **Tokudai-ji** 徳大寺 *(Tokudai Temple).* This is a curiosity in a neighborhood of curiosities: a temple on the second floor of a supermarket. Two deities are worshipped here. One is the bodhisattva Jizō, and the act of washing this statue is believed to safeguard your health. The other is of the Indian goddess Marici, a daughter of Brahma; she is believed to help worshippers overcome difficulties and succeed in business.

> **JUNE JOYS**
>
> During the first week of June, a path along the Shinobazu Pond is lined with the stalls of the annual All-Japan Azalea Fair, a spectacular display of flowering bonsai shrubs and trees. Gardeners in *happi* (work coats) sell plants, seedlings, bonsai vessels, and ornamental stones.

✉4–6–2 Ueno, Taitō-ku ☎03/3831–7926 Ⓜ*JR Yamanote and Keihintōhoku lines, Okachi-machi Station (Higashi-guchi/East Exit) or Ueno Station (Hirokō-ji Exit).*

2 **Tōkyō Metropolitan Art Museum** 東京都美術館 *(Tōkyō-to Bijutsukan).* The museum displays its own collection of modern Japanese art on the lower level and rents out the remaining two floors to various art institutes and organizations. At any given time, there can be a variety of exhibits in the building: international exhibitions, work by local young painters, or new forms and materials in sculpture or modern calligraphy. ✉8–36 Ueno Kōen, Taitō-ku ☎03/3823–6921 ⊕*www.tobikan.jp* ✉*Permanent collection free; fees vary for other exhibits (usually ¥800–¥1,400)* ⊘*Daily 9–5; closed 3rd Mon. of month* Ⓜ*JR Ueno Station (Kōenguchi/Park Exit).*

1 **Tōkyō National Museum** 東京国立博物館 *(Tōkyō Kokuritsu Hakubutsukan).* This complex of four buildings grouped around a courtyard is one of the world's great repositories of East Asian art and archaeology. Altogether, the museum has some 87,000 objects in its permanent collection, with several thousand more on loan from shrines, temples, and private owners.

Fodor'sChoice
★

The Western-style building on the left (if you're standing at the main gate), with bronze cupolas, is the **Hyōkeikan.** Built in 1909, it was devoted to archaeological exhibits; aside from the occasional special exhibition, the building is closed today. The larger **Heiseikan,** behind the Hyōkeikan, was built to commemorate the wedding of crown prince Naruhito in 1993 and now houses Japanese archaeological exhibits. The second floor is used for special exhibitions.

In 1878, the 7th-century Hōryū-ji (Hōryū Temple) in Nara presented 319 works of art in its possession—sculpture, scrolls, masks, and other objects—to the Imperial Household. These were transferred to the National Museum in 2000 and now reside in the **Hōryū-ji Hōmotsukan** (Gallery of Hōryū-ji Treasures), which was designed by Yoshio Taniguchi. There's a useful guide to the collection in English, and the exhibits are well explained. Don't miss the hall of carved wooden *gigaku* (Buddhist processional) masks.

The central building in the complex, the 1937 **Honkan,** houses Japanese art exclusively: paintings, calligraphy, sculpture, textiles, ceramics, swords, and armor. Also here are 84 objects designated by the government as National Treasures. The Honkan rotates the works on display several times during the year. It also hosts two special exhibitions annually (April and May or June, and October and November), which feature important collections from both Japanese and foreign museums. These, unfortunately, can be an ordeal to take in: the lighting in the Honkan is not particularly good, the explanations in English are sketchy at best, and the hordes of visitors make it impossible to linger over a work you especially want to study. The more attractive **Tōyōkan**, to the right of the Honkan, completed in 1968, is devoted to the art and antiquities of China, Korea, Southeast Asia, India, the Middle East, and Egypt. ⊠*13–9 Ueno Kōen, Taitō-ku* ☎*03/3822–1111* ⊕*www. tnm.go.jp* ⊠*Regular exhibits ¥600, special exhibits approx. ¥1,500* ⊗*Tues.–Sun. 9:30–5, times vary during special exhibitions* Ⓜ*JR Ueno Station (Kōen-guchi/Park Exit).*

❸ **Tōshō-gū** 東照宮 *(Tōshō Shrine).* This shrine, built in 1627, is dedicated
★ to Ieyasu, the first Tokugawa shōgun. It miraculously survived all major disasters that destroyed most of Tōkyō's historical structures—the fires, the 1868 revolt, the 1923 earthquake, the 1945 bombings—making it one of the only early-Edo-period buildings left in Tōkyō. The shrine and most of its art are designated National Treasures.

Two hundred *ishidōrō* (stone lanterns) line the path from the stone entry arch to the shrine itself. One of them, just outside the arch to the left, is more than 18 feet high, called *obaketōrō* (ghost lantern). Legend has it that one night a samurai on guard duty slashed at a ghost (*obake*) that was believed to haunt the lantern. His sword was so strong, it left a nick in the stone, which can be seen today.

The first room inside the shrine is the **Hall of Worship;** the four paintings in gold on wooden panels are by Tan'yū, a member of the famous Kano family of artists, dating from the 15th century. Behind the Hall of Worship, connected by a passage called the *haiden,* is the sanctuary, where the spirit of Ieyasu is said to be enshrined.

The real glory of Tōshō-gū is its so-called **Chinese Gate,** at the end of the building, and the fence on either side that has intricate carvings of birds, animals, fish, and shells of every description. The two long panels of the gate, with their dragons carved in relief, are attributed to Hidari Jingoro—a brilliant sculptor of the early Edo period whose real name is unknown (*hidari* means "left"; Jingoro was reportedly left-handed). The lifelike appearance of his dragons has inspired a legend. Every morning they were found mysteriously dripping with water and it was believed that the dragons were sneaking out at night to drink from the nearby Shinobazu Pond. Wire cages were put up to curtail this disquieting habit. ⊠*9–88 Ueno Kōen, Taitō-ku* ☎*03/3822–3455* ⊠*¥200* ⊗*Daily 9–5* Ⓜ*JR Ueno Station (Kōen-guchi/Park Exit).*

ASAKUSA 浅草

Historically, Asakusa has been the hub of the city's entertainment. The area blossomed when Ieyasu Tokugawa made Edo his capital and it became the 14th-century city that never slept. For the next 300 years it was the wellspring of almost everything we associate with Japanese

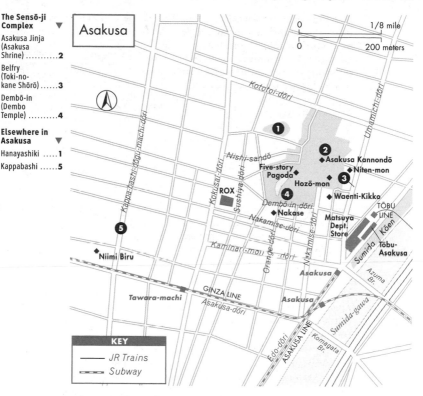

culture. In the mid-1600s, it became a pleasure quarter in its own right with stalls selling toys, souvenirs, and sweets; acrobats, jugglers and strolling musicians; and sake shops and teahouses—where the waitresses often provided more than tea. Then, in 1841, the Kabuki theaters moved to Asakusa.

The theaters were here for a short time, but it was enough to establish Asakusa as *the* entertainment quarter of the city—a reputation it held unchallenged until World War II, when most of the area was destroyed. Though it never fully recovered as an entertainment district, the area today is home to artisans and small entrepreneurs, children and grandmothers, hipsters, hucksters, and priests. If you have any time to spend in Tōkyō, make sure you devote at least a day to exploring Asakusa.

Numbers in the margin correspond to the Asakusa map.

ORIENTATION AND PLANNING
ORIENTATION
Rich in history and traditional culture, this northeastern area of Tōkyō should be top on your list of destinations. Asakusa is a border city ward that separates central Tōkyō from suburban areas beyond. It's a unique spiritual and commercial, tourist and residential area, where locals walk their dogs on the Asakusa Jinja grounds or give offerings and pray at Kannon Temple. Life in this area is slow-paced and uncomplicated.

Asakusa's just east of Ueno and can be explored thoroughly in a half day, whether you go straight from Ueno or on a separate excursion.

PLANNING
Unlike most of the other areas to explore on foot in Tōkyō, Sensō-ji is admirably compact. You can easily see the temple and environs in a morning. The garden at Dembō-in is worth a half hour. If you decide to include Kappabashi, allow yourself an hour more for the tour. Some of the shopping arcades in this area are covered, but Asakusa is essentially an outdoor experience. Be prepared for rain in June and heat and humidity in July and August.

> **THREE WISE MEN**
>
> The Sanja Festival, held annually over the third weekend of May, is said to be the biggest, loudest, wildest party in Tōkyō. Each of the neighborhoods under Sanja Sama's protection has its own mikoshi, and, on the second day of the festival, are paraded through the streets of Asakusa to the shrine. Many of the "parishioners" take part naked to the waist, or with the sleeves of their tunics rolled up, to expose fantastic red-and-black tattoo patterns that sometimes cover their entire backs and shoulders. These are the markings of the Japanese underworld.

The Asakusa Tourist Information Center (Asakusa Bunka Kankō Center) is across the street from Kaminari-mon. A volunteer with some English knowledge is on duty here daily 10–5 and will happily load you down with maps and brochures.

GETTING HERE AND AROUND
Getting here by subway from Ueno Station (Ginza line, Ueno Station to Asakusa Station, ¥160) or taxi (approximately ¥900) is most convenient. Asakusa is the last stop (eastbound) on the Ginza subway line.

Another way get to Asakusa is by river bus ferry from Hinode Pier, which stops at the southwest corner of Sumida Kōen.

TOP ATTRACTIONS
THE SENSŌ-JI COMPLEX 浅草寺
Fodor'sChoice ★ Dedicated to the goddess Kannon, the **Sensō-ji Complex** is the heart and soul of Asakusa. Come for its local and historical importance, its garden, its 17th-century Shintō shrine, and the wild Sanja Festival in May. ⊠ *2–3–1 Asakusa, Taitō-ku* ☎ *03/3842–0181* 🎫 *Free* ⏱ *Temple grounds daily 6–sunset* Ⓜ *Ginza subway line, Asakusa Station (Exit 1/ Kaminari-mon Exit).*

② **Asakusa Jinja** 浅草神社 *(Asakusa Shrine)*. Several structures in the temple complex survived the bombings of 1945. The largest, to the right of the Main Hall, is this Shintō shrine to the Hikonuma brothers and their master, Naji-no-Nakamoto—the putative founders of Sensō-ji. In Japan, Buddhism and Shintōism have enjoyed a comfortable coexistence since the former arrived from China in the 6th century. The shrine, built in 1649, is also known as Sanja Sama (Shrine of the Three Guardians). Near the entrance to Asakusa Shrine is another survivor of World War II: the east gate to the temple grounds, **Niten-mon,** built in 1618 for a shrine to Ieyasu Tokugawa and designated by the government as an Important Cultural Property. ⊠ *Taitō-ku* ☎ *03/3844–1575* ⊕ *www. asakusajinja.jp.*

❸ Belfry 時の鐘鐘楼 *(Toki-no-kane Shōrō)*. The tiny hillock Benten-yama, with its shrine to the goddess of good fortune, is the site of this 17th-century belfry. The bell here used to toll the hours for the people of the district, and it was said that you could hear it anywhere within a radius of some 6 km (4 mi). The bell still sounds at 6 AM every day, when the temple grounds open. It also rings on New Year's Eve—108 strokes in all, beginning just before midnight, to "ring out" the 108 sins and frailties of humankind and make a clean start for the coming year. Benten-yama and the belfry are at the beginning of the narrow street that parallels Nakamise-dōri. ⊠ *Taitō-ku.*

NEED A BREAK?

Originally a teahouse, **Waenti-Kikko** 和えん亭 吉幸 is now a cozy, country-style Japanese restaurant and bar. The owner, Fukui Kodai, is a traditional Japanese *Tsugaru Shamisen* (string instrument) musician, who performs at scheduled times throughout the day. Narrow your field of vision, shut out the world outside, and you could be back in the waning days of Meiji-period Japan. This pub specializes in premium sake, with set courses of food and drink for lunch (¥1,890 to ¥3,500) and dinner (¥6,300 to ¥12,600). There's a 10% service charge for dinner. ⊠ *2-2-13 Asakusa, Taitō-ku* ☎ *03/5828-8833* ⊕ *www.waentei-kikko.com* ⊗ *Daily 11:30-2 and 5-10* Ⓜ *Ginza subway line, Asakusa Station (Exit 1/Kaminari-mon Exit).*

❹ Dembō-in 伝法院 *(Dembō Temple)*. Believed to have been made in the 17th century by Kōbori Enshū, the genius of Zen landscape design, the garden of Dembō-in, part of the living quarters of the abbot of Sensō-ji, is the best-kept secret in Asakusa. The garden of Dembō-in is usually empty and always utterly serene, an island of privacy in a sea of pilgrims. Spring, when the wisteria blooms, is the ideal time to be here.

A sign—you'll find the sign about 150 yards west of the intersection with Naka-mise-dōri—in English on Dembō-in-dōri leads you to the entrance, which is a side door to a large wooden gate. ■ TIP→ For permission to see the abbot's garden, you must first apply at the temple administration building, between Hōzō-mon and the Five-Story Pagoda, in the far corner. ⊠ *2-3-1 Asakusa, Taitō-ku* ☎ *03/3842-0181 for reservations* ⊠ *Free* ⊗ *Daily 9-4; may be closed if abbot has guests* Ⓜ *Ginza subway line, Asakusa Station (Exit 1/Kaminari-mon Exit).*

NEED A BREAK?

Nakase 中瀬 is a lovely retreat from the overbearing crowds at Asakusa Kannon. The building, which is 130 years old, lends to a truly authentic Japanese experience: food is served in lacquerware bento boxes and there are an interior garden and pond, which is filled with carp and goldfish. Across Orange-dōri from the redbrick Asakusa Public Hall, Nakase is expensive (lunch at the tables inside starts at ¥3,000; more elaborate meals by the garden start at ¥7,000), but the experience is worth it. ⊠ *1-39-13 Asakusa, Taitō-ku* ☎ *03/3841-4015* ▭ *No credit cards* ⊗ *Wed.-Mon. 11-3 and 5-8* Ⓜ *Ginza subway line, Asakusa Station (Exit 1/Kaminari-mon Exit).*

Is That Edible?

The custom of putting models of the food served in the restaurant's windows dates back to the Meiji Restoration period, but the food wasn't always plastic. In fact, the idea first came to Japan from the wax models that were used as anatomical teaching aids in the new schools of Western medicine. A businessman from Nara decided that wax models would also make good point-of-purchase advertising for restaurants. He was right: the industry grew in a modest way at first, making models mostly of Japanese food. In the boom years after 1960, restaurants began to serve all sorts of dishes most people had never seen before, and the models provided much-needed reassurance: "So *that's* a cheeseburger. It doesn't look as bad as it sounds. Let's go in and try one." By the mid-1970s, the makers of plastic food were turning out creations of astonishing virtuosity and realism. If you're looking for what some have deemed a form of pop art, then head to Kappabashi.

ELSEWHERE IN ASAKUSA

❶ ★ **Hanayashiki** 花やしき. Dubbing itself as "the old park with a smile," Hanayashiki, established in 1853, is Tōkyō's premier retro amusement park—think Coney Island. A haunted house, Ferris wheel, and merry-go-round await the kids who will likely be a little tired of Asakusa's historic areas. ⊠*2–28–1 Asakusa, Taitō-ku* ☎*03/3842–8780* ⊕*www.hanayashiki.net* ⊠*¥900–¥2,200* ⊗*10–6, but check schedule for later closing times* Ⓜ*Ginza subway line, Asakusa Station (Exit 1/Kaminari-mon Exit)*.

❺ ★ **Kappabashi** かっぱ橋. In the 19th century, according to local legend, a river ran through the present-day Kappabashi district. The surrounding area was poorly drained and was often flooded. A local shopkeeper began a project to improve the drainage, investing all his own money, but met with little success until a troupe of *kappa*—mischievous green water sprites—emerged from the river to help him. A more prosaic explanation for the name of the district points out that the lower-ranking retainers of the local lord used to earn extra money by making straw raincoats, also called *kappa*, that they spread to dry on the bridge.

Today, Kappabashi's more than 200 wholesale dealers sell everything the city's restaurant and bar trade could possibly need to do business, from paper supplies and steam tables to the main attraction, plastic food. It is baffling to most Japanese that Kappabashi is a hot tourist attraction. ⊠*Nishi-Asakusa 1-chōme and 2-chōme, Taitō-ku* ⊗*Most shops daily 9–6* Ⓜ*Ginza subway line, Tawara-machi Station (Exit 1)*.

TSUKIJI 築地 AND SHIODOME 汐留

Although it's best known today as the site of the largest wholesale fish market in the world, Tsukiji is also a reminder of the awesome disaster of the great fire of 1657. In the space of two days, it killed more than 100,000 people and leveled almost 70% of Ieyasu Tokugawa's new capital. Ieyasu was not a man to be discouraged by mere catastrophe, however; he took it as an opportunity to plan an even bigger and better city, one that would incorporate the marshes east of his castle. Tsukiji, in fact, means "reclaimed land," and a substantial block of land it was, laboriously drained and filled, from present-day Ginza to the bay. The common people of the tenements and alleys, who had suffered most in the great fire, did not benefit from this land project as it was first allotted to feudal lords and temples. After 1853, when Japan opened its doors to the outside world, Tsukiji became Tōkyō's first foreign settlement—the site of the American delegation and an elegant two-story brick hotel, and home to missionaries, teachers, and doctors.

To the west of Tsukiji lie Shiodome and Shimbashi. In the period after the Meiji Restoration, Shimbashi was one of the most famous geisha districts of the new capital. Its reputation as a pleasure quarter is even older. In the Edo period, when there was a network of canals and waterways here, it was the height of luxury to charter a covered boat (called a *yakata-bune*) from one of the Shimbashi boathouses for a cruise on the river; a local restaurant would cater the excursion, and a local geisha house would provide companionship. Almost nothing remains in Shimbashi to recall that golden age, but as its luster has faded, adjacent Shiodome has risen—literally—in its place as one of the most ambitious redevelopment projects of 21st-century Tōkyō.

Shiodome (literally "where the tide stops") was an area of saltwater flats on which in 1872 the Meiji government built the Tōkyō terminal—the original Shimbashi Station—on Japan's first railway line, which ran for 29 km (18 mi) to nearby Yokohama. The area eventually became Japan Rail's (JR) most notorious white elephant: a staggeringly valuable hunk of real estate, smack in the middle of the world's most expensive city that JR no longer needed and couldn't seem to sell. By 1997 a bewildering succession of receivers, public development corporations, and zoning commissions had evolved an urban renewal plan for the area, and the land was auctioned off. Among the buyers were Nippon Television and Dentsū, the largest advertising agency in Asia and the fourth largest in the world.

In 2002 Dentsū consolidated its scattered offices into the centerpiece of the Shiodome project: a 47-story tower and annex designed by Jean Nouvel. With the annex, known as the Caretta Shiodome, Dentsū aspired not just to a new corporate address, but an "investment in community": a complex of cultural facilities, shops, and restaurants that has turned Shiodome into one of the most fashionable places in the city to see and be seen. The 1,200-seat Dentsū Shiki Theater SEA here has become one of Tōkyō's major venues for live performances; its resident repertory company regularly brings long-running Broadway hits like *Wicked* to eager Japanese audiences.

Numbers in the margin correspond to the Tsukiji and Shiodome map.

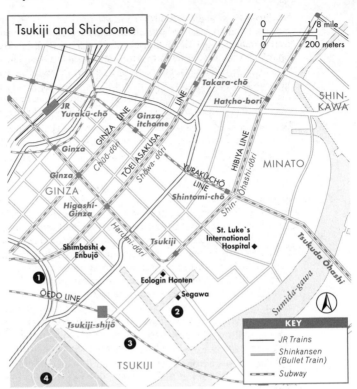

ORIENTATION AND PLANNING

ORIENTATION

Shiodome is the southeastern transportation hub of central Tōkyō.
Tsukiji is a sushi-lover's dream. Perhaps getting up at 5 AM to eat fish at
the market isn't your idea of breakfast, but this is definitely an excellent
place taste the freshest sushi on earth, located just east of Shiodome.

PLANNING

Tsukiji has few places to spend time *in*; getting from point to point,
however, can consume most of a morning. The backstreet shops will
probably require no more than an hour. Allow yourself about an hour
to explore the fish market; if fish in all its diversity holds a special fascination for you, take two hours. Remember that in order to see the fish
auction in action, you need to get to the market before 6:30 AM; by 9
AM the business of the market is largely finished for the day. Sushi and
sashimi will be cheaper here than in other parts of Tōkyō, with sushi
sets at most sushi stalls costing between ¥1,000 to ¥2,100.

This part of the city can be brutally hot and muggy in August; during
the O-bon holiday, in the middle of the month, Tsukiji is comparatively
lifeless. Mid-April and early October are best for strolls in the Hama
Rikyū Tei-en.

GETTING HERE AND AROUND

Shidome's easily accessed by public transport: JR Yurikome Line Shim-bashi Station, Toei-Ōedo Shiodome Line Station, Toei-Asakusa Line Shimbashi Station, and Ginza Line Shimbashi Station. The connection station to the Yuikamome Monorail, a scenic ride that takes you to Odaiba in approximately 30 minutes, is also here. You can also get around quite easily on foot. There are sophisticated walkways in the sky that connect all the major buildings and subway and train stations.

To visit the fish market, take the subway to Tsukiji Station, which will always be the more dependable and cost-efficient option. To take the train there and back (depending on where you are staying), it will cost between ¥160 and ¥600.

TOP ATTRACTIONS

❶ Advertising Museum Tōkyō アド・ミュージアム東京. ADMT puts the unique Japanese gift for graphic and commercial design into historical perspective, from the sponsored "placements" in 18th-century wood-block prints to the postmodern visions of fashion photographers and video directors. The museum is maintained by a foundation established in honor of Hideo Yoshida, fourth president of the mammoth Dentsū Advertising Company, and includes a digital library of some 130,000 entries on everything you ever wanted to know about hype. There are no explanatory panels in English—but this in itself is a testament to how well the visual vocabulary of consumer media can communicate across cultures. ✉1–8–2 Higashi-Shimbashi, Caretta Shiodome B1F–B2F, Chūō-ku ☎03/6218–2500 ⊕www.admt.jp ☞Free ☉Tues.–Fri. 11–6:30, Sat. 11–4:30 Ⓜ Ōedo subway line, Shiodome Station (Exit 7); JR (Shiodome Exit) and Asakusa and Ginza lines (Exit 4), Shim-bashi Station.

❷ Backstreet shops of Tsukiji 築地6丁目. Tōkyō's markets provide a vital **Fodor's Choice** counterpoint to the museums and monuments of conventional sight- **★** seeing: they let you see how people really live in the city. If you have time for only one market, this is the one to see. The three square blocks between the Tōkyō Central Wholesale Market and Harumi-dōri have, naturally enough, scores of fishmongers, but also shops and restaurants. Stores sell pickles, tea, crackers and snacks, cutlery (what better place to pick up a professional sushi knife?), baskets, and kitchenware. Hole-in-the-wall sushi bars here have set menus ranging from ¥1,000 to ¥2,100; look for the plastic models of food in glass cases out front. The area includes the row of little counter restaurants, barely more than street stalls, under the arcade along the east side of Shin-Ōhashi-dōri, each with its specialty. If you haven't had breakfast by this point in your walk, stop at **Segawa** for *maguro donburi*—a bowl of fresh raw tuna slices served over rice and garnished with bits of dried seaweed (Segawa is in the middle of the arcade, but without any distinguishing features or English signage; your best bet is to ask someone). ▉TIP➔ **Some 100 of the small retailers and restaurants in this area are members of the Tsukiji Meiten-kai (Association of Notable Shops) and promote themselves by selling illustrated maps of the area for ¥50; the maps are all in Japanese, but with proper frames they make great souvenirs.** ✉Tsukiji 4-chōme, Chūō-

ku Ⓜ *Ōedo subway line, Tsukiji-shijō Station (Exit A1); Hibiya subway line, Tsukiji Station (Exit 1).*

❹ **Hama Rikyū Tei-en** 浜離宮庭園 *(Detached Palace Garden).* Like a tiny
★ sanctuary of Japanese tradition and nature that's surrounded by towering glass buildings, this garden is worth a visit. The land here was originally owned by the Owari branch of the Tokugawa family from Nagoya, and it extended to part of what is now the fish market. When one of the family became shōgun in 1709, his residence was turned into a shōgunal palace—with pavilions, ornamental gardens, pine and cherry groves, and duck ponds. The garden became a public park in 1945, although a good portion of it is fenced off as a nature preserve. None of the original buildings have survived, but on the island in the large pond is a reproduction of the pavilion where former U.S. president Ulysses S. Grant and Mrs. Grant had an audience with the emperor Meiji in 1879. The building can now be rented for parties. The path to the left as you enter the garden leads to the "river bus" ferry landing, from which you can leave this excursion and begin another: up the Sumida-gawa to Asakusa. ⚠ **Note that you must pay the admission to the garden even if you're just using the ferry.** ✉ *1–1 Hamarikyū–Teien, Chūō-ku* ☎ *03/3541–0200* ✑ *¥300* 🕐 *Daily 9–4:30* Ⓜ *Ōedo subway line, Shiodome Station (Exit 8).*

❸ **Tōkyō Central Wholesale Market** 東京都中央卸売市場 *(Tōkyō Chūō Oroshi-*
★ *uri Ichiba).* The city's fish market used to be farther uptown, in Nihombashi. It was moved to Tsukiji after the Great Kantō Earthquake of 1923, and it occupies the site of what was once Japan's first naval training academy. Today the market sprawls over some 54 acres of reclaimed land and employs approximately 15,000 people, making it the largest fish market in the world. Its warren of buildings houses about 1,200 wholesale shops, supplying 90% of the seafood consumed in Tōkyō every day—some 2,400 tons of it. Most of the seafood sold in Tsukiji comes in by truck, arriving through the night from fishing ports all over the country. ✉ *5–2–1 Tsukiji, Chūō-ku* ☎ *03/3542–1111* ⊕ *www. shijou.metro.Tokyo.jp* ✑ *Free* 🕐 *Business hrs Mon.–Sat. (except 2nd and 4th Wed. of month) 5* AM*–3* PM Ⓜ *Ōedo subway line, Tsukiji-shijō Station (Exit A1); Hibiya subway line, Tsukiji Station (Exit 1).*

NIHOMBASHI日本橋, GINZA 銀座, AND YŪRAKU-CHŌ 有楽町

Tōkyō is a city of many centers. The municipal administrative center is in Shinjuku. The national government center is in Kasumigaseki. Nihombashi is the center of banking and finance, and Ginza is the center of commerce.

When Ieyasu Tokugawa had the first bridge constructed at Nihombashi, he designated it the starting point for the five great roads leading out of his city, the point from which all distances were to be measured. His decree is still in force: the black pole on the present bridge, erected in 1911, is the Zero Kilometer marker for all the national highways and is considered the true center of Tōkyō.

The early millionaires of Edo built their homes in the Nihombashi area. Some, like the legendary timber magnate Bunzaemon Kinokuniya, spent

CLOSE UP

Fishmongers Wanted

Why go to the Tsukiji fish market? Quite simply, because of how the fish is sold—at auction. The catch—more than 100 varieties of fish in all, including whole frozen tuna, Styrofoam cases of shrimp and squid, and crates of crabs—is laid out in the long covered area between the river and the main building. Then the bidding begins. Only members of the wholesalers' association can take part. Wearing license numbers fastened to the front of their caps, they register their bids in a kind of sign language, shouting to draw the attention of the auctioneer and making furious combinations in the air with their fingers. The auctioneer keeps the action moving in a hoarse croak that sounds like no known language, and spot quotations change too fast for ordinary mortals to follow.

Different fish are auctioned off at different times and locations, and by 6:30 AM or so, this part of the day's business is over, and the wholesalers fetch their purchases back into the market in barrows. Restaurant owners and retailers arrive about 7, making the rounds of favorite suppliers for their requirements.

Chaos seems to reign, but everybody here knows everybody else, and they all have it down to a system.

⚠ The 52,000 or so buyers, wholesalers, and shippers who work at the market may realize that they are at the center of one of Tōkyō's top tourist attractions, but their priority is with the business at hand. They're in the fish business, moving more than 600,000 tons of it a year to retailers and restaurants all over the city, and this is their busiest time of day. The cheerful banter they use with each other can turn snappish if you get in their way. Also bear in mind that you are not allowed to take photographs while the auctions are under way (flashes are a distraction). Tourists are also required to remain behind roped-off areas. The market's kept spotlessly clean, which means the water hoses are running all the time. Boots are helpful, but if you don't want to carry them, bring a pair of heavy-duty trash bags to slip over your shoes and secure them above your ankles with rubber bands.

everything they made in the pleasure quarters of Yoshiwara and died penniless. Others founded the great trading houses of today—Mitsui, Mitsubishi, Sumitomo—which still have warehouses nearby.

When Japan's first corporations were created and the Meiji government developed a modern system of capital formation, the Tōkyō Stock Exchange (Shōken Torihikijo) was established on the west bank of the Nihombashi-gawa (Nihombashi River). The home offices of most of the country's major securities companies are only a stone's throw from the exchange.

In the Edo period there were three types of currency in circulation: gold, silver, and copper. Ieyasu Tokugawa started minting his own silver coins in 1598 in his home province of Suruga, even before he became shōgun. In 1601 he established a gold mint; the building was only a few hundred yards from Nihombashi, on the site of what is now the Bank of Japan. In 1612 he relocated the Suruga plant to a patch of reclaimed land west of his castle. The area soon came to be known informally as Ginza (Silver Mint).

Currency values fluctuated during this time and eventually businesses fell under the control of a few large merchant houses. One of the most successful of these merchants was a man named Takatoshi Mitsui, who by the end of the 17th century created a commercial empire—in retailing, banking, and trading—known today as the Mitsui Group. Not far from the site of Echigo-ya stands its direct descendant: Mitsukoshi department store.

The district called Yūraku-chō—the Pleasure (*yūraku*) Quarter (*chō*)—lies west of Ginza's Sukiya-bashi, stretching from Sotobori-dōri to Hibiya Kōen and the Outer Garden of the Imperial Palace. The "pleasures" associated with this district in the early postwar period stemmed from a number of the buildings that survived the air raids of 1945 and were requisitioned by the Allied forces. Yūraku-chō quickly became the haunt of the so-called *pan-pan* women, who kept the GIs company. Because it was so close to the military post exchange in Ginza, the area under the railroad tracks became one of the city's largest black markets. Later, the black market gave way to clusters of cheap restaurants, most of them little more than a counter and a few stools, serving yakitori and beer. Office workers on meager budgets and journalists from the nearby *Mainichi, Asahi,* and *Yomiuri* newspaper headquarters would gather here at night. Yūraku-chō-under-the-tracks was smoky, loud, and friendly—a kind of open-air substitute for the local taproom. The area has long since become upscale, and no more than a handful of the yakitori stalls remain.

Numbers in the margin correspond to the Nihombashi, Ginza, and Yūraku-chō map.

ORIENTATION AND PLANNING

ORIENTATION

The combined areas of Yūraku-chō, Ginza, and Nihombashi are located beside the Imperial Palace district, to the southeast of central Tōkyō. Yūraku-chō lies west of Ginza's Sukiya-bashi, stretching from Sotobori-dōri to Hibiya Kōen and the Outer Garden of the Imperial Palace.

PLANNING

There's something about this part of Tōkyō—the traffic, the number of people, the way it urges you to keep moving—that can make you feel you've covered a lot more ground than you really have. Attack this area early in the morning but avoid rush hour (8–9) if you plan on taking the subway. None of the area's sites, with the possible exception of the Bridgestone and Idemitsu museums, should take you more than 45 minutes. The time you spend shopping, of course, is up to you. In summer make a point of starting early or in the late afternoon, because by midday the heat and humidity can be brutal. Make sure to carry bottled water. On weekend afternoons (October–March, Saturday 3–5 and Sunday noon–5; April–September, Saturday 2–6 and Sunday noon–6), Chūō-dōri is closed to traffic from Shimbashi all the way to Kyō-bashi and becomes a pedestrian mall with tables and chairs set out along the street. Keep in mind that some of the museums and other sights in the area close on Sunday.

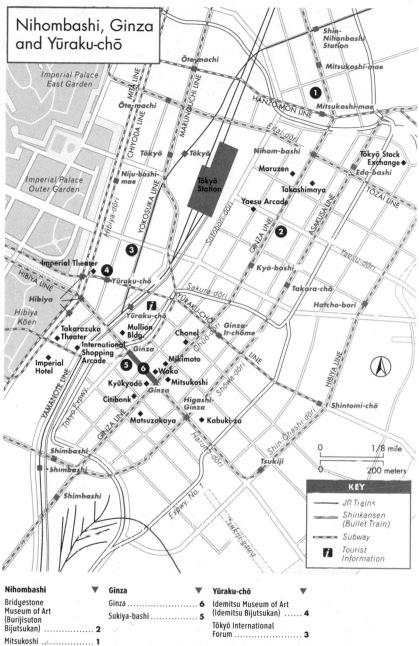

Nihombashi, Ginza and Yūraku-chō

TOP ATTRACTIONS

② **Bridgestone Museum of Art** ブリヂストン美術館 *(Burijisuton Bijutsukan)*. This is one of Japan's best private collections of French impressionist art and sculpture and of post-Meiji Japanese painting in Western styles by such artists as Shigeru Aoki and Tsuguji Fujita. The collection, assembled by Bridgestone Tire Company founder Shōjiro Ishibashi, also includes works by Rembrandt, Picasso, Utrillo, and Modigliani. The small gallery devoted to ancient art has a breathtaking Egyptian cat sculpture dating to between 950 and 660 BC. The Bridgestone also puts on major exhibits from private collections and museums abroad. ✉ *1–10–1 Kyō-bashi, Chūo-ku* ☎ *03/3563–0241* ⊕ *www.bridgestone-museum. gr.jp* 🎫 *¥800* ⊙ *Tues.–Sat. 10–8, Sun. 10–6 (entrance up to 30 min before closing)* Ⓜ *Ginza subway line, Kyō-bashi Station (Meijiya Exit) or Nihombashi Station (Takashimaya Exit).*

⑥ **Ginza** 銀座. With more history as a shopping district than trendier Omotesandō and Harajuku, Ginza is where high-end shopping first took root in Japan and now it's where Japanese "ladies who lunch" shop. But this area didn't always have the cachet of wealth and style. In fact, it wasn't until a fire in 1872 destroyed most of the old houses here that the area was rebuilt as a Western quarter. It had two-story brick houses with balconies, the nation's first sidewalks and horse-drawn streetcars, gaslights, and, later, telephone poles. Before the turn of the 20th century, Ginza was home to the great mercantile establishments that still define its character. The **Wako** department store, for example, on the northwest corner of the 4-chōme intersection, established itself here as Hattori, purveyors of clocks and watches. The clock on the present building was first installed in the Hattori clock tower, a Ginza landmark, in 1894.

Many of the nearby shops have lineages almost as old, or older, than Wako's. A few steps north of the intersection, on Chūo-dōri, **Mikimoto** sells the famous cultured pearls first developed by Kōkichi Mikimoto in 1883. His first shop in Tōkyō dates to 1899. South of the intersection, next door to the San-ai Building, **Kyūkyodō** carries a variety of handmade Japanese papers and traditional stationery goods. Kyūkyodō has been in business since 1663 and on Ginza since 1880. Across the street and one block south is the **Matsuzakaya** department store, which began as a kimono shop in Nagoya in 1611. And connected to the Ginza line Ginza Station is the **Mistukoshi** department store, where the basement food markets are a real attraction.

There's even a name for browsing this area: Gin-bura, or "Ginza wandering." The best times to wander here are Saturday afternoons and Sunday from noon to 5 or 6 (depending on the season), when Chūo-dōri is closed to traffic between Shimbashi and Kyō-bashi. ✉ *Chūo-ku* Ⓜ *Ginza and Hibiya subway lines, Ginza Station.*

④ **Idemitsu Museum of Art** 出光美術館 *(Idemitsu Bijutsukan)*. The strength
★ of the collection in these four spacious, well-designed rooms lies in the Tang- and Song-dynasty Chinese porcelain and in the Japanese ceramics—including works by Nonomura Ninsei and Ogata Kenzan. On display are masterpieces of Old Seto, Oribe, Old Kutani, Karatsu,

and Kakiemon ware. The museum also houses outstanding examples of Zen painting and calligraphy, wood-block prints, and genre paintings of the Edo period. Of special interest to scholars is the resource collection of shards from virtually every pottery-making culture of the ancient world. The museum is on the ninth floor of the Teikoku Gekijō building. ✉ *3–1–1 Marunouchi, Chiyoda-ku* ☎ *03/3213–9402* ⊕ *www.idemitsu.co.jp/museum* 💴 *¥800* 🕙 *Tues.–Sun. 10–4:30* Ⓜ *Yūraku-chō subway line, Yūraku-chō Station (Exit A1).*

❶ ★ **Mitsukoshi** 三越. Takatoshi Mitsui made his fortune by revolutionizing the retail system for kimono fabrics. The emergence of Mitsukoshi as Tōkyō's first *depāto* (department store), also called *hyakkaten* (hundred-kinds-of-goods emporium), actually dates to 1908, with the construction of a three-story Western building modeled on Harrods of London. This was replaced in 1914 by a five-story structure with Japan's first escalator. The present flagship store is vintage 1935. Even if you don't plan to shop, this branch merits a visit. Two bronze lions, modeled on those at London's Trafalgar Square, flank the main entrance and serve as one of Tōkyō's best-known meeting places. Inside, a sublime statue of Magokoro, a Japanese goddess of sincerity, rises four stories through the store's central atrium. Check out the basement floors for a taste of the food-market culture of Japanese department stores and grab a quick meal-to-go while you're there. Delicious local and international prepared food is sold here at premium prices: intricately designed *mochi* (sweet red bean) cakes, Japanese bento boxes, sushi sets, and square watermelons all sell for approximately ¥10,000. ✉ *1–4–1 Nihombashi Muro-machi, Chūō-ku* ☎ *03/3241–3311* ⊕ *www.mitsukoshi.co.jp* 🕙 *Daily 10–8* Ⓜ *Ginza and Hanzō-mon subway lines, Mitsukoshi-mae Station (Exits A3 and A5).*

❺ **Sukiya-bashi** 数寄屋橋. The side streets of the Sukiya-bashi area are full of art galleries, which operate a bit differently here than they do in most of the world's art markets. A few, like the venerable **Nichidō** (5–3–16 Ginza), **Gekkōsō** (7–2–8 Ginza), **Yōseidō** (5–5–15 Ginza), and **Kabuto-ya** (8–8–7 Ginza), actually function as dealers, representing particular artists, as well as acquiring and selling art. The majority, however, are rental spaces. Artists or groups pay for the gallery by the week, publicize their shows themselves, and in some cases even hang their own work. You might suspect, and with good reason, that some of these shows are vanity exhibitions by amateurs with money to spare, even in a prestigious venue like Ginza; thankfully, that's not always the case. ✉ *Chiyoda-ku* Ⓜ *Ginza, Hibiya, and Marunouchi subway lines, Ginza Station (Exit C4).*

❸ ★ **Tōkyō International Forum** 東京国際フォーラム. This postmodern masterpiece, the work of Uruguay-born American architect Raphael Viñoly, is the first major convention and art center of its kind in Tōkyō. Viñoly's design was selected in a 1989 competition that drew nearly 400 entries from 50 countries. The plaza of the Forum is that rarest of Tōkyō rarities: civilized open space. There's a long central courtyard with comfortable benches shaded by trees. Freestanding sculpture, triumphant architecture, and people strolling are all here. The first and third Sundays of each month feature an antiques flea market in the plaza's courtyard. The Forum itself is actually two buildings. On the east side of the plaza is Glass Hall, the main exhibition space, and the west building has six halls for international conferences, exhibitions, receptions, and concert performances. ✉ *3–5–1 Marunouchi, Chiyoda-ku* ☎ *03/5221–9000* ⊕ *www.t-i-forum.co.jp* Ⓜ *Yūraku-chō subway line, Yūraku-chō Station (Exit A-4B).*

NEED A BREAK?

Amid all of Tōkyō's bustle and crush, you actually can catch your breath in the Tōkyō International Forum—cafés and Italian, Japanese, and French restaurants are located throughout the complex. A reasonably priced and delicious Kyoto-style vegetarian restaurant to try is **Tsuruhan**. Lunch sets start at ¥1,000 and dinner ¥3,000. Maps are available, so pick and choose. There are also ATM machines on the third floor. ✉ *3–5–1 Marunouchi, Chiyoda-ku* ☎ *03/3214–2260* ⊕ *www.t-i-forum.co.jp.*

AOYAMA 青山, HARAJUKU 原宿, AND SHIBUYA 渋谷

Who would have known? As late as 1960, this was as unlikely a candidate as any area in Tōkyō to develop into the chic capital of Tōkyō. Between Meiji shrine and the Aoyama Cemetery to the east, the area was so boring that the municipal government zoned a chunk of it for low-cost public housing. Another chunk, called Washington Heights, was being used by U.S. occupation forces who spent their money elsewhere. The few young Japanese people in Harajuku and Aoyama were either hanging around Washington Heights to practice their English or attending the Methodist-founded Aoyama University—seeking entertainment farther south in Shibuya.

When Tōkyō won its bid to host the 1964 Olympics, Washington Heights was turned over to the city for the construction of Olympic Village. Aoyama-dōri, the avenue through the center of the area, was renovated and the Ginza and Hanzō-mon subway lines were built under it. Suddenly, Aoyama became attractive for its Western-style fashion houses, boutiques, and design studios. By the 1980s the area was positively *smart*. Today, most of the low-cost public housing along Omotesandō are long gone, and in its place are the glass-and-marble emporia of *the* preeminent fashion houses of Europe: Louis Vuitton, Chanel, Armani, and Prada. Their showrooms here are cash cows of their worldwide empires. Superb shops, restaurants, and amusements in this area target a population of university students, wealthy socialites, young professionals, and people who like to see and be seen.

Numbers in the margin correspond to the Aoyama, Harajuku, and Shibuya map.

ORIENTATION AND PLANNING

ORIENTATION

Aoyama, Omotesandō, and Harajuku, west of the Imperial Palace and just north of Roppongi, are the trendsetting areas of youth culture and fashion. Omotesandō and Aoyama contain a laundry list of European fashion houses' flagship stores. Harajuku is a bohemian and younger fashion district that inspired Gwen Stefani to write a hit song, "Harajuku Girls," and create a "Harajuku Lovers" fashion line in 2005.

Just north of Omotesandō and Aoyama, in front of the Harajuku JR Station, is Harajuku's Meiji Jingū, which is a famous hangout for dressed-up teens and crowds of onlookers.

Because it's the entertainment district for Japanese youth, Shibuya is not as clean or sophisticated as Tōkyō's other neighborhoods. Rarely will you see an elderly person on the streets. Shops, cheap restaurants, karaoke lounges, bars, theaters, concert halls, and nightclubs are everywhere. With Shibuya station connecting thousands of passengers from the suburbs into the heart of the city, it is the western frontier of central Tōkyō, and the last stop of the Ginza Line.

PLANNING

Trying to explore Aoyama and Harajuku together will take a long time because there is a lot of area to cover. Ideally, you should devote an entire day here, giving yourself plenty of time to browse in shops. You can see Meiji Shrine in less than an hour; the Nezu Institute warrants a leisurely two-hour visit. Spring is the best time of year for the Meiji Jingū Inner Garden. Just like everywhere else in this city, June's rainy season is horrendous, and the humid heat of midsummer can quickly drain your energy and add hours to the time you need to comfortably explore. The best way to enjoy this area is to explore the tiny shops, restaurants, and cafés in the backstreets.

Shibuya seems chaotic and intimidating at first, but it is fairly compact, so you can easily cover it in about two hours. Be prepared for huge crowds and some shoulder bumping. Shibuya crossing is one of the busiest crossings in the world and at one light change, hundreds rush to reach the other side. Unless you switch into shopping mode, no particular stop along the way should occupy you for more than a half hour; allow a full hour for the NHK Broadcasting Center, however, if you decide to take the guided tour. Spring is the best time of year for Yoyogi Kōen, and Sunday is the best day. The area will be crowded, but Sunday affords the best opportunity to observe Japan's younger generation on display. Two subway lines, three private railways, the JR Yamanote line, and two bus terminals move about a million people a day through Shibuya.

TOP ATTRACTIONS

⑤ **Japanese Sword Museum** 刀剣博物館 *(Tōken Hakubutsukan)*. It's said that
★ in the late 16th century, before Japan closed its doors to the West, the Spanish tried to establish a trade here in weapons made from famous Toledo steel. The Japanese were politely uninterested; they had been making blades of incomparably better quality for more than 600 years. At one time there were some 200 schools of sword making in Japan; swords were prized not only for their effectiveness in battle but for the beauty of the blades and fittings and as symbols of the higher spirituality of the warrior caste. There are few inheritors of this art today. ⊠*4–25–10 Yoyogi, Shibuya-ku* ☎*03/3379–1386* ⊕*www.touken. co.jp* ⊠*¥525* ⊙*Tues.–Sun. 10–4:30* Ⓜ*Odakyū private rail line, Sangū-bashi Station.*

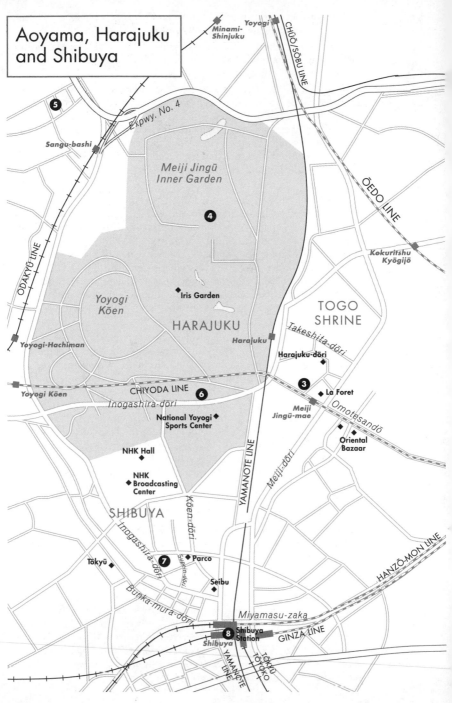

Aoyama, Harajuku and Shibuya

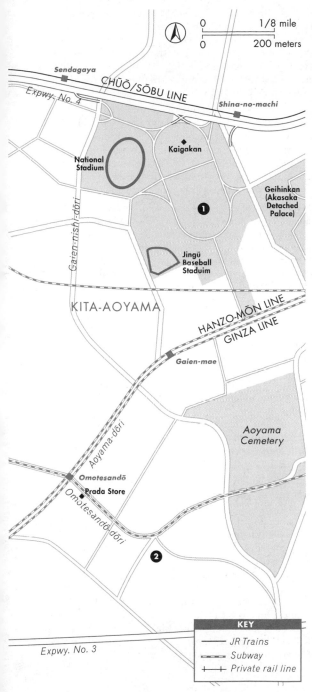

❹ **Meiji Shrine** 明治神宮 *(Meiji Jingū)*. The Meiji Shrine honors the spirits of
★ Emperor Meiji, who died in 1912, and Empress Shōken. It was established by a resolution of the Imperial Diet the year after the emperor's
death to commemorate his role in ending the long isolation of Japan
under the Tokugawa Shōgunate and setting the country on the road to
modernization. Completed in 1920 and virtually destroyed in an air
raid in 1945, it was rebuilt in 1958.

A wonderful spot for photos, the mammoth entrance gates *(torii)*, rising
40 feet high, are made from 1,700-year-old cypress trees from Mt. Ari
in Taiwan; the crosspieces are 56 feet long. Torii are meant to symbolize
the separation of the everyday secular world from the spiritual world
of the Shintō shrine. The buildings in the shrine complex, with their
curving, green, copper roofs, are also made of cypress wood. The surrounding gardens have some 100,000 flowering shrubs and trees.

An annual festival at the shrine takes place on November 3, Emperor
Meiji's birthday, which is a national holiday. On the festival and New
Year's Day, as many as 1 million people come to offer prayers and pay
their respects. Several other festivals and ceremonial events are held
here throughout the year; check by phone or on the shrine Web site to
see what's scheduled during your visit. Even on a normal weekend the
shrine draws thousands of visitors, but this seldom disturbs its mood
of quiet serenity.

The peaceful **Inner Garden** (Jingū Nai-en), where the irises are in full
bloom in the latter half of June, is on the left as you walk in from
the main gates, before you reach the shrine. Beyond the shrine is the
Treasure House, a repository for the personal effects and clothes of
Emperor and Empress Meiji—perhaps of less interest to foreign visitors than to the Japanese. ✉*1–1 Kamizono-chō, Yoyogi, Shibuya-ku*
☎*03/3379–9222* ⊕*www.meijijingu.or.jp* ✉*Shrine free, Inner Garden*
¥500, Treasure House ¥500 ◯*Shrine daily sunrise–sunset; Inner Garden Mar.–Nov., daily 9–4; Treasure House daily 10–4; Closed 3rd Fri.
of month* Ⓜ*Chiyoda subway line, Meiji-jingū-mae Station; JR Yamanote line, Harajuku Station (Exit 2).*

❶ **Meiji Shrine Outer Gardens** 明治神宮外苑 *(Meiji Jingū Gai-en).* This rare
expanse of open space is devoted to outdoor sports of all sorts. The
Yakult Swallows play at **Jingū Baseball Stadium** (✉*13 Kasumigaoka,
Shinjuku-ku* ☎*03/3404–8999*); the Japanese baseball season runs
from April to October. The main venue of the 1964 Summer Olympics,
National Stadium (✉*10 Kasumigaoka, Shinjuku-ku* ☎*03/3403–1151*)
now hosts soccer matches. Some of the major World Cup matches
were played here when Japan cohosted the event with Korea in autumn
2002. The **Meiji Memorial Picture Gallery** *(Kaigakan* ✉*1–1 Kasumigaoka,
Shinjuku-ku, Aoyama* ☎*03/3401–5179*), across the street from the
National Stadium, doesn't hold much interest unless you're a fan of
Emperor Meiji and don't want to miss some 80 otherwise undistin-
guished paintings depicting events in his life. It's open daily 9–5 and
costs ¥500. ✉*Shinjuku-ku*⊕ *www.meijijingugaien.jp* Ⓜ*Ginza and
Hanzō-mon subway lines, Gai-en-mae Station (Exit 2); JR Chūō line,
Shina-no-machi Station.*

8 **Myth of Tomorrow.** This once-lost
Fodor'sChoice mural by avant-garde artist Taro
★ Okamoto has been restored and
mounted inside Shibuya Station.
Often compared to Picasso's *Guernica*, the 14 colorful panels depict
the moment of an atomic bomb
detonation. The painting was discovered in 2003 in Mexico City,
where in the late '60s it was originally set to be displayed in a hotel
but wound up misplaced following
the bankruptcy of the developer.
Walk up to the Inokashira Line
entrance; the mural is mounted
along the hallway that overlooks
Hachikō plaza. ⊠ *JR Shibuya Station, Hachikō Exit, Shibuya-ku.*

2 **Nezu Institute of Fine Arts**
Fodor'sChoice 根津美術館 *(Nezu Bijutsukan).* This
★ museum houses the private art collection of Meiji-period railroad magnate and politician Kaichirō Nezu.
The permanent display in the main building and the annex includes
superb examples of Japanese painting, calligraphy, and ceramics—some
of which are registered as National Treasures—plus Chinese bronzes,
sculpture, and lacquerware. The institute also has one of Tōkyō's finest
gardens, with more than 5 acres of shade trees and flowering shrubs,
ponds, and waterfalls, as well as seven tea pavilions. ⊠ *6–5–1 Minami-Aoyama, Minato-ku* ☏ *03/3400–2536* ⊕ *www.nezu-muse.or.jp*
⊠ *¥1,000* ☉ *Tues.–Sun. 9–4* Ⓜ *Ginza and Hanzō-mon subway lines,
Omotesandō Station (Exit A5).*

3 **Ōta Memorial Museum of Art** 太田記念美術館 *(Ōta Kinen Bijutsukan).*
★ The gift of former Tōhō Mutual Life Insurance chairman Seizō Ōta,
this is probably the city's finest private collection of ukiyo-e, traditional
Edo-period wood-block prints. *Ukiyo-e* (pictures of the floating world)
flourished in the 18th and 19th centuries. The works on display are
selected and changed periodically from the 12,000 prints in the collection, which include some extremely rare work by artists such as Hiroshige, Hokusai, Sharaku, and Utamaro. Be sure to verify opening hours
on its official Web site or call ahead. ⊠ *1–10–10 Jingū-mae, Shibuya-ku* ☏ *03/3403–0880* ⊕ *www.ukiyoe-ota-muse.jp* ⊠ *¥700–¥1,000,
depending on exhibit* ☉ *Tues.–Sun. 10:30–5:30; closed from the 26th
or 27th to the last day of each month.*

7 **Tōkyū Hands** 東急ハンズ. This is a hobbyist's fantasy store. Everything
★ anyone would ever need, and plenty of things we don't, is here: tools
for woodworking, painting, do-it-yourself home improvement, travel
accessories, and jewelry making. Its slogan is "creative life store," and
it truly is: seven floors of cool stuff that can take two hours at least
to fully browse. This superstore is worth a visit, especially for souve-

> **TEENYBOPPER
> SHOPPERS HARAJUKU**
>
> On weekends the heart of Harajuku, particularly the street called
> Takeshita-dōri, belongs to high
> school and junior high school
> shoppers, who flock there for the
> latest trends. Entire industries give
> themselves convulsions just trying
> to keep up with adolescent styles.
> Stroll through Harajuku—with its
> outdoor cafés, designer-ice-cream
> and Belgian-waffle stands, profusion of stores with names like A
> Bathing Ape and Chicago—and you
> may find it impossible to believe
> that Japan's the most rapidly aging
> society in the industrial world.

nir shopping. ⊠ *12–18 Udagawacho, Shibuya-ku* ☎*03/5489-5111* ⊙*Daily 10–8:30.*

❻ Yoyogi Kōen 代々木公園 *(Yoyogi Park).* This is the perfect spot to have
☾ a picnic on a sunny day. On Sunday, people come here to play music,
practice martial arts, and ride bicycles on the bike path (rentals are
available). Be sure to look out for a legendary group of dancing Elvis
impersonators, who meet at the entrance every Sunday and dance to
classic rock 'n' roll music. There is also a community of homeless people who live in orderly, clean camps along the periphery. Sunday and
holidays there's a flea market along the main thoroughfare that runs
through the park, opposite the National Yoyogi Sports Center. ⊠*Jinnan
2-chōme, Shibuya-ku* Ⓜ*Chiyoda subway line, Meiji Jingū-mae Station
(Exit 2); JR Yamanote line, Harajuku Station (Omotesandō Exit).*

ROPPONGI 六本木 AND AZABU JŪBAN 麻布十番

During the last quarter of the 20th century, Roppongi was a better-
heeled, better-behaved version of Shinjuku or Shibuya, without the
shopping: not much happens by day, but by night the area is an irresistible draw for young clubbers with foreign sports cars and wads of
disposable income.

Today, this area has become an entertainment capital, attracting tourists
to its bustling bar, restaurant, and nightclub scenes; English is spoken
at most restaurants and shops. Ritzy developments like Roppongi Hills
and Tōkyō Midtown have revitalized the area. However, some of the
shine has recently been taken off Mori Tower, once the main building in
Roppongi Hills, as it recently lost some of its high-rolling tenants—the
now-defunct Lehman Brothers Japan and Livedoor, founded by dis-
graced renegade businessman Takafumi Horie. Tōkyō Midtown, which
opened in 2007, is home to the headquarters of Yahoo! Japan, Cisco
Japan, and game maker Konami. Further separating Roppongi from
its wild ways is "Art Triangle Roppongi," a promotion campaign for
three of the area's museums: The National Art Center, Tōkyō; Mori Art
Museum; and Suntory Museum of Art.

Azabu Jūban is a prestigious residential district with many embassies in
Minato-ku. Before the fire raids of 1945, Azabu Jūban, like Roppongi,
was a famous entertainment district with department stores, a red-light
quarter, and theaters. The fires destroyed the entire neighborhood, and
it was reborn as a residential area. Though the apartments may be small
and dilapidated, this is one of the most expensive areas of the city and
many celebrities, artists, and businesspeople reside here.

*Numbers in the margin correspond to the Roppongi and Azabu Jūban
map.*

ORIENTATION AND PLANNING
ORIENTATION
Roppongi is located just east of Shibuya and Aoyama, and south of the
Imperial Palace. Azabu Jūban is located just south of Roppongi, within
seven-minute walking distance from Roppongi Hills, or a short subway
ride on the Toei Ōedo line to Azabu Jūban station.

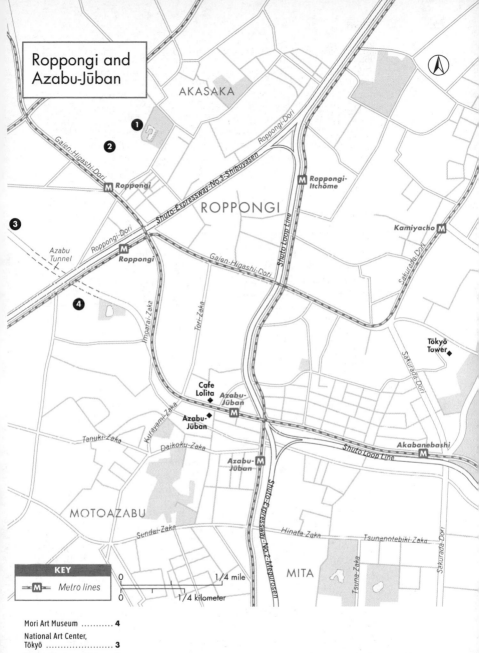

Roppongi and Azabu-Jūban

AKASAKA

Gaien-Higashi-Dori

Roppongi-Dori

M Roppongi

Shuto-Expressway-No-3-Shibuyasen

ROPPONGI

M Roppongi-Itchōme

Shuto Loop Line

Kamiyacho **M**

3

Azabu Tunnel

Roppongi-Dori

M Roppongi

Gaien-Higashi-Dori

Sakurada-Dori

4

Imoarai-Zaka

Tori-Zaka

Tōkyō Tower ◆

Sakurada-Dori

Cafe Lolita ◆

Azabu-Jūban

Azabu-Jūban **M**

Kurayami-Zaka

Azabu-Jūban ◆

Tanuki-Zaka

Daikoku-Zaka

Azabu-**M** Jūban

Akabanebashi **M**

Shuto Loop Line

MOTOAZABU

Sendai-Zaka

Shuto-Expressway-No-2-Meguroscn

Hinata-Zaka

Tsunanotebiki-Zaka

Sakurada-Dori

MITA

Tsuna-Zaka

KEY

=M= Metro lines

0 ————————— 1/4 mile

0 ————————— 1/4 kilometer

PLANNING

There are ATMs and currency exchange services at Roppongi Hills and Tōkyō Midtown, as well as family- and kid-friendly activities, such as small parks and sculpture.

Azabu Jūban is a quick visit, and a good place to sit in a café and people-watch. The best time to visit is in August, during the **Azabu-Jūban Summer Festival,** one of the biggest festivals in Minato-ku. The streets, which are closed to car traffic, are lined with food vendors selling delicious international fare and drinks. Everyone wears their nicest summer kimonos and watches live performances. Check the online *Minato Monthly* newsletter (⊕ *www.city.minato.tokyo.jp*) in August for a list of summer festivals.

GETTING HERE AND AROUND

The best way to get to Roppongi is by subway, and there are two lines that'll take you to Roppongi Station: the Hibiya line, which takes you right into the complex of Roppongi Hills, or the Toei Ōedo line, with exits convenient to Tōkyō Midtown.

Azabu Jūban is only a short 10-minute walk from Roppongi. You can also take the Toei Ōedo line from Roppongi to Azabu Jūban Station (Exit 5), just one stop away, for ¥160.

TOP ATTRACTIONS

④ Mori Art Museum. Occupying the 52nd and 53rd floors of sparkling Mori Tower, Mori Art Museum is one of the leading contemporary art showcases in Tōkyō. Though lacking a permanent collection, the space is well designed (by American architect Richard Gluckman), intelligently curated, diverse in its media, and hospitable to big crowds. The nine galleries occupy 2,875 square meters for exhibits that rotate every few months and tend to focus on contemporary architecture (Le Corbusier), fashion, design, and photography. ⊠ *Minato-ku* ☎ *03/5777–8600* ⊕ *mori.art.museum/jp* 🖼 *Admission fees vary with each exhibit* ☉ *Wed.–Mon. 10–10, Tues. 10–5* Ⓜ *Hibiya subway line, Roppongi Station (Exit 1C).*

③ National Art Center, Tōkyō 国立新美術館. Tōkyō's nightlife-happy Roppongi neighborhood has never been an art lover's destination—until now. The debut of the National Art Center adds to this town's newly burgeoning intellectual heft. Architect Kishō Kurokawa's stunning facade shimmers in undulating waves of glass. The cavernous 171,000-square-foot space houses seven exhibition areas; a library; restaurant Brasserie Paul Bocuse Le Musée, offering fine French dishes; and a museum shop. The Center features traveling exhibitions that focus on modern and contemporary art. ⊠ *7–22–2 Roppongi, Minato-ku* ☎ *03/5777–8600* ⊕ *www.nact.jp* ☉ *Closed Tues. Open late Fri.* 🖼 *Admission per exhibition* Ⓜ *Toei Ōedo and Hibiya lines, Roppongi Station (Exit 7).*

① Suntory Museum of Art. Based on the principle of dividing profits three ways, Suntory, Japan's beverage giant, has committed a third of its profits to what it feels is its corporate and social responsibility to provide the public with art, education, and environmental conservation. The establishment of the Suntory Art Museum in 1961 was just one of the fruits of this initiative. The museum's new home at Tōkyō Midtown

Gardenside is a beautiful place to view some of Tōkyō's finest fine art exhibitions. Past displays have included everything from works by Picasso and Toulouse-Lautrec to fine kimonos from the Edo Period. ⊠ *Tōkyō Midtown Gardenside, 9–7–4 Akasaka, Minato-ku* ☎*03/3479–8600* ⊕ *www.suntory.com/culture-sports/sma* ⊙ *Wed.–Fri. 10–8, Sun. and Mon. 10–6* ⊠ *Around ¥1,300 but varies by exhibition* Ⓜ *Toei Ōedo Line, Roppongi Station; Hibiya Line, Roppongi Station.*

2 **Tōkyō Midtown.** The trend toward luxury, minicity development projects, which started with Roppongi Hills in 2003, is changing the dynamic of the city. With Tōkyō Midtown, Mitsui Fudōsan created the tallest building in Tōkyō—the 248-meter main tower rises 10 meters higher than Mori Tower at Roppongi Hills. Office, residential, and retail spaces fill out the development. Inside the complex's park is architect Tadao Ando's slope-roofed design center 21_21 Design Sight, a gallery and exhibition space that covers 1,700 square meters. ⊠ *9 Akasaka, Minato-ku* ⊕ *www.tokyo-midtown.com* Ⓜ *Toei Ōedo Line, Roppongi Station; Hibiya Line, Roppongi Station.*

NEED A BREAK? A popular local hangout in Azabu-Jūban at all hours of the day, **Café Lolita** カフェロリータ is open until 4 AM. The multiple reflective wall decorations and chrome piping give a retro feel, and street-level seating allows perfect people-watching vantage points while you enjoy well-prepared pasta dishes (less than ¥1,000) and draft beer (Japanese or German). ⊠ *1F, Mademoiselle Bldg.* ⊠ *1-4-8 Azabu-Jūban, Minato-ku* ☎ *03/3586–8422* ⊙ *Daily 11–4.*

SHINJUKU 新宿

If you have a certain sort of love for big cities, you're bound to love Shinjuku. Come here, and for the first time Tōkyō begins to seem *real*: all the celebrated virtues of Japanese society—its safety and order, its grace and beauty, its cleanliness and civility—fray at the edges.

To be fair, the area has been on the fringes of respectability for centuries. When Ieyasu, the first Tokugawa shōgun, made Edo his capital, Shinjuku was at the junction of two important arteries leading into the city from the west. It became a thriving post station, where travelers would rest and refresh themselves for the last leg of their journey; the appeal of this suburban pit stop was its "teahouses," where the waitresses dispensed a good bit more than sympathy with the tea.

When the Tokugawa dynasty collapsed in 1868, 16-year-old Emperor Meiji moved his capital to Edo, renaming it Tōkyō, and modern Shinjuku became the railhead connecting it to Japan's western provinces. As the haunt of artists, writers, and students, it remained on the fringes of respectability; in the 1930s Shinjuku was Tōkyō's bohemian quarter. The area was virtually leveled during the firebombings of 1945—a blank slate on which developers could write, as Tōkyō surged west after the war. By the 1970s property values in Shinjuku were the nation's highest, outstripping even those of Ginza.

After the Great Kantō Earthquake of 1923, Nishi-Shinjuku was virtually the only part of Tōkyō left standing; the whims of nature had given this one small area a gift of better bedrock. That priceless geological stability remained largely unexploited until the late 1960s, when technological advances in engineering gave architects the freedom to soar. Some 20 skyscrapers have been built here since then, including the Tōkyō Metropolitan Government Office complex, and Nishi-Shinjuku has become Tōkyō's 21st-century administrative center.

By day the quarter east of Shinjuku Station is an astonishing concentration of retail stores, vertical malls, and discounters of every stripe and description. By night it's an equally astonishing collection of bars and clubs, strip joints, hole-in-the-wall restaurants, pachinko parlors (Japanese version of pinball), and peep shows—just about anything that amuses, arouses, alters, or intoxicates is for sale in Higashi-Shinjuku. Recent crackdowns by police have limited this sort of adult activity but whatever you are after is probably still there if you know where to look.

Numbers in the margin correspond to the Shinjuku map.

ORIENTATION AND PLANNING
ORIENTATION
By day, Shinjuku is a bustling center of business and government where office workers move in droves during rush hour. By night, people are inundated with flashing signs, and a darker side of Tōkyō emerges, where drunken hordes leave their offices to go out for drinks, food, and sometimes, sex. Perhaps this is a rougher side of town, but Shinjuku is a fascinating place to discover at night.

PLANNING
Every day four subways, seven railway lines, and more than 3 million commuters converge on Shinjuku Station, making this the city's busiest and most heavily populated commercial center. The hub at Shinjuku—a vast, interconnected complex of tracks and terminals, department stores and shops—divides the area into two distinctly different subcities, Nishi-Shinjuku (West Shinjuku) and Higashi-Shinjuku (East Shinjuku).

Plan at least a full day for Shinjuku if you want to see both the east and west sides. Subway rides can save you time and energy as you're exploring, but don't rule out walking. The Shinjuku Gyo-en National Garden is worth at least an hour, especially if you come in early April during *sakura* (cherry blossom) season. The Tōkyō Metropolitan Government Office complex can take longer than you might expect; lines for the elevators to the observation decks are often excruciatingly long. Sunday, when shopping streets are closed to traffic, is the best time to tramp around Higashi-Shinjuku. The rainy season in late June and the sweltering heat of August are best avoided.

TOP ATTRACTIONS
❺ **Hanazono Jinja** 花園神社 *(Hanazono Shrine)*. Constructed in the early Edo period, Hanazono is not among Tōkyō's most imposing shrines, but it does have one of the longest histories. Prayers offered here are believed to bring prosperity in business. The shrine is a five-minute walk north on Meiji-dōri from the Shinjuku-san-chōme subway station. The shrine grounds are at their most lively during the spring and autumn festivals. The block just to the west (5-chōme 1) has the last, embattled,

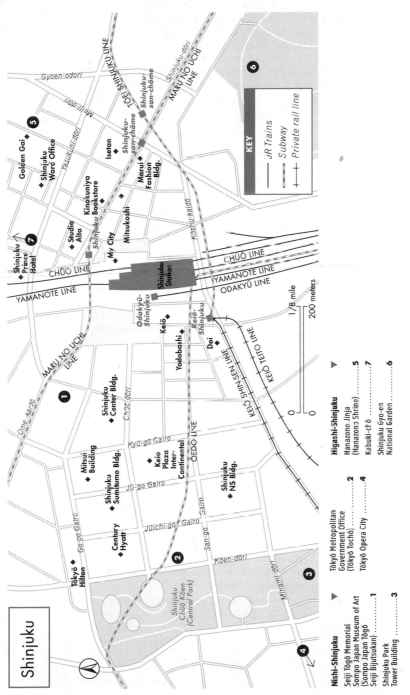

Shinjuku

KEY
— JR Trains
— Subway
+‑+ Private rail line

Gyoen-odori
Meiji-dōri
Yasukuni-dōri
Shinjuku-dōri
Kōshū-kaidō

TŌEI SHINJUKU LINE
MARU NO UCHI LINE
CHŪŌ LINE
YAMANOTE LINE
ODAKYŪ LINE
MARU NO UCHI LINE
ŌEDO LINE
KEIŌ SHIN-SEN LINE
KEIŌ TEITO LINE

Golden Gai ❺
Shinjuku Ward Office
Isetan
Shinjuku-san-chōme
Shinjuku-san-chōme
Marui Fashion Bldg.
Kinokuniya Bookstore
Studio Alta
Mitsukoshi
My City
Shinjuku City
Shinjuku Prince Hotel ❼
Shinjuku Station
Odakyū-Shinjuku
Keiō
Keiō-Shinjuku
Doi
Yodobashi
Shinjuku Center Bldg. ❶
Mitsui Building
Shinjuku Sumitomo Bldg.
Keio Plaza Inter-Continental
Shinjuku NS Bldg.
Century Hyatt
Tōkyō Hilton
Shinjuku Chūō Kōen (Central Park)
❷ ❸ ❹

Chūō-dōri
Ōme-kaidō
Go-gō Gairo
Jū-gō Gairo
Jūichi-gō Gairo
Jū-san-gō Gairo
Kyū-gō Gairo
Kōen-dōri
Minami-dōri

1/8 mile
200 meters
0

Nishi-Shinjuku
Seiji Tōgō Memorial
Sompo Japan Museum of Art
(Sompo Japan Tōgō
Seiji Bijutsukan) **1**
Shinjuku Park
Tower Building **3**
Tōkyō Metropolitan
Government Office
(Tōkyō Tōchō) **2**
Tōkyō Opera City **4**

Higashi-Shinjuku
Hanazono Jinja
(Hanazono Shrine) **5**
Kabuki-chō **7**
Shinjuku Gyo-en
National Garden **6**

remaining bars of the "Golden-Gai": ⇨*See Golden Gai in "Nightlife"*, a district of tiny, unpretentious, even seedy, *nomiya* (bars) that in the '60s and '70s commanded the fierce loyalty of fiction writers, artists, freelance journalists, and expat Japanophiles—the city's hard-core outsiders. ⊠*5–17–3 Shinjuku, Shinjuku-ku* ☎*03/3209–5265* ✉*Free* ⊙*Daily sunrise–sunset* Ⓜ*Marunouchi and Fukutoshin subway lines, Shinjuku-san-chōme Station (Exits B2 and B3).*

> **HE SAID WHAT?**
>
> Yasuda Fire & Marine Insurance Company (now Sompo Japan Insurance) CEO Yasuo Gotō acquired *Sunflowers* in 1987 for ¥5.3 billion—at the time the highest price ever paid at auction for a work of art. He later created considerable stir in the media with the ill-considered remark that he'd like the painting cremated with him when he died.

❼ **Kabuki-chō** 歌舞伎町. In 1872 the Tokugawa-period formalities governing geisha entertainment were dissolved, and Kabuki-chō became Japan's largest center of prostitution. Later, when vice laws got stricter, prostitution just went a bit deeper underground, where it remains—widely tolerated. ⚠ **In spite of recent crackdowns by police on sex shops and hostess clubs, Kabuki-chō remains Japan's most vast adult entertainment quarter. Neon signs flash; shills proclaim the pleasures of the places you particularly want to shun. Even when a place looks respectable, ask about prices first:** *bottakuri*— **overcharging for food and drink—is indeed a possibility, and watered-down drinks can set you back ¥5,000 or more in a hostess or host club.** You needn't be intimidated by the area though. Stop in to a street-level bar (that clearly indicates its pricing) and watch out the window as the hosts, hostesses, and local denizens shuffle on past. In an attempt to change the area's image after World War II, plans were made to replace Ginza's fire-gutted Kabuki-za with a new one in Shinjuku. The plans were never realized, however, as the old theater was rebuilt. But the project gave the area its present name.

▐ NEED A BREAK? Need a break from the sensory overload? At the **Humax Pavilion** (⊠*1–20–1 Kabuki-chō, Shinjuku-ku* ☎*03/3200–2213* ⊕ *www.humax.co.jp*), you can see a movie, hit the bowling lanes, relax in a karaoke box, or sharpen your skills at Grand Theft Auto. This multifloor entertainment center is smack dab in the middle of Kabuki-chō's chaos. ⊠*Shinjuku-ku* Ⓜ*JR (Higashi-guchi/East Exit) and Marunouchi subway line (Exits B10, B11, B12, and B13), Shinjuku Station.*

❶ **Seiji Tōgō Memorial Sompo Japan Museum of Art** 東郷青児美術館 *(Sompo Japan Tōgō Seiji Bijutsukan)*. The painter Seiji Tōgō (1897–1978) was a master of putting on canvas the grace and charm of young maidens. More than 100 of his works from the museum collection are on display here at any given time, along with works by other Japanese and Western artists. The museum also houses van Gogh's *Sunflowers*. The gallery has an especially good view of the old part of Shinjuku. ⊠*Sompo Japan Headquarters Bldg., 42nd fl., 1–26–1 Nishi-Shinjuku, Shinjuku-ku* ☎*03/3349–3591* ⊕*www.sompo-japan.co.jp/museum* ✉*¥1,000;*

additional fees for special exhibits ⊘ *10–6* Ⓜ *Marunouchi and Shinjuku subway lines, JR rail lines; Shinjuku Station (Exit A18 for subway lines, Nishi-guchi/West Exit or Exit N4 from the underground passageway for all others).*

⑥ Shinjuku Gyo-en National Garden 新宿御苑. This lovely 150-acre park was once the estate of the powerful Naitō family of feudal lords, who were among the most trusted retainers of the Tokugawa shōguns. After World War II, the grounds were finally opened to the public. It's a perfect place for leisurely walks: paths wind past ponds and bridges, artificial hills, thoughtfully placed stone lanterns, and more than 3,000 kinds of plants, shrubs, and trees. There are different gardens in Japanese, French, and English styles, as well as a greenhouse (the nation's first, built in 1885) filled with tropical plants. ■**TIP→ The best times to visit are April, when 75 different species of cherry trees—some 1,500 trees in all—are in bloom, and the first two weeks of November, during the chrysanthemum exhibition.** ⊠ *11 Naitō-chō, Shinjuku-ku* ☎ *03/3350–0151* ⌚¥*200* ⊘ *Tues.–Sun. 9–4; also open Mon. 9–4 in cherry-blossom season (late Mar. to early Apr.)* Ⓜ *Marunouchi subway line, Shinjuku Gyo-en-mae Station (Exit 1).*

❸ Shinjuku Park Tower Building 新宿パークタワー. Kenzō Tange's Shinjuku Park Tower has in some ways the most arrogant, hard-edged design of any of the skyscrapers in Nishi-Shinjuku, but it does provide any number of opportunities to rest and refuel. Some days there are free chamber-music concerts in the atrium. There are many restaurants to choose from in the building, with a variety of international and Japanese restaurants. Take a ride up to the skylighted bamboo garden of the Peak Lounge on the 41st floor of the **Park Hyatt Hotel** (☎ *03/5322–1234*), which was the set location of the Oscar-winning film *Lost in Translation.* Order a Suntory whiskey at the New York Bar 11 floors above, and you might feel a little like Bill Murray's character in the movie. Also come for brunch at Giranole, a French brasserie with a fantastic view of the city. ⊠ *3–7–1 Nishi-Shinjuku, Shinjuku-ku* Ⓜ *JR Shinjuku Station (Nishi-guchi/West Exit).*

❷ Tōkyō Metropolitan Government Office 東京都庁 *(Tōkyō Tochō).* Dominating the western Shinjuku skyline and built at a cost of ¥157 billion, this Kenzō Tange–designed, grandiose, city-hall complex is clearly meant to remind observers that Tōkyō's annual budget is bigger than that of the average developing country. The late-20th-century complex consists of a main office building, an annex, the Metropolitan Assembly building, and a huge central courtyard, often the venue of open-air concerts and exhibitions. The building design has raised some debate: Tōkyōites either love it or hate it. On a clear day, from the observation decks on the 45th floors of both towers, you can see all the way to Mt. Fuji and to the Bōsō Peninsula in Chiba Prefecture. Several other skyscrapers in the area have free observation floors—among them the Shinjuku Center Building, the Shinjuku Nomura Building, and the Shinjuku Sumitomo Building—but city hall is the best of the lot. The Metropolitan Government Web site, incidentally, is an excellent source of information on sightseeing and current events in Tōkyō. ⊠ *2–8–1 Nishi-Shinjuku, Shinjuku-ku* ☎ *03/5321–1111* ⊕ *www.metro.tokyo.*

jp ⬛*Free* ⊙*North observation deck daily 9:30* AM–*10:30* PM; *south observation deck daily 9:30–5:30* Ⓜ*Marunouchi and Shinjuku subway lines, JR, Keiō Shin-sen and Teitō private rail lines; Shinjuku Station (Nishi-guchi/West Exit).*

❹ **Tōkyō Opera City** 東京オペラシティ. Completed in 1997, this is certain to be the last major cultural project in Tōkyō for the foreseeable future. The west side of the complex is the New National Theater (Shin Kokuritsu Gekijō), consisting of the 1,810-seat opera house, the 1,038-seat playhouse, and an intimate performance space called the Pit, with seating for 468. Architect Helmut Jacoby's design for this building, with its reflecting pools, galleries, and granite planes of wall, deserves real plaudits.

The east side of the complex consists of a 54-story office tower flanked by a sunken garden and art museum on one side and a concert hall on the other. The museum focuses rather narrowly on post–World War II Japanese abstract painting. The 1,632-seat concert hall is arguably the most impressive classical-music venue in Tōkyō, with tiers of polished-oak panels, and excellent acoustics despite the venue's daring vertical design. ✉*3–20–2 Nishi-Shinjuku, Shinjuku-ku* ☎*03/5353–0700 concert hall, 03/5351–3011 New National Theater* ⊕*www.tokyoopera city.co.jp* Ⓜ*Keiō private rail line, Hatsudai Station (Higashi-guchi/East Exit).*

ODAIBA お台場

Tōkyō's "offshore" leisure and commercial-development complex rises on more than 1,000 acres of landfill, connected to the city by the Yurikamome monorail from Shimbashi. People come here for the arcades, shopping malls, and museums, as well as the city's longest (albeit artificial) stretch of sand beach, along the boat harbor—swimming is not recommended because of high levels of pollution. There's also a large Ferris wheel—a neon phantasmagoric beacon for anyone driving into the city across the Rainbow Bridge. With hotels and apartment buildings as well, this is arguably the most successful of the megaprojects on Tōkyō Bay.

Numbers in the margin correspond to the Odaiba map.

ORIENTATION AND PLANNING
ORIENTATION
Located on the southernmost point of Tōkyō, this is a popular weekend destination for families. The lack of historical monuments or buildings in Odaiba separates it from Tōkyō's other districts.

PLANNING
If you can, visit Odaiba during the week, as weekends are frenzied and crammed with families.

GETTING HERE AND AROUND
The best way to get here is by monorail, which will also be packed on weekends. From Shimbashi Station you can take the JR, Karasumori Exit; Asakusa subway line, Exit A2; or the Ginza subway line, Exit 4—follow the blue seagull signs to the monorail. You can pick up a map

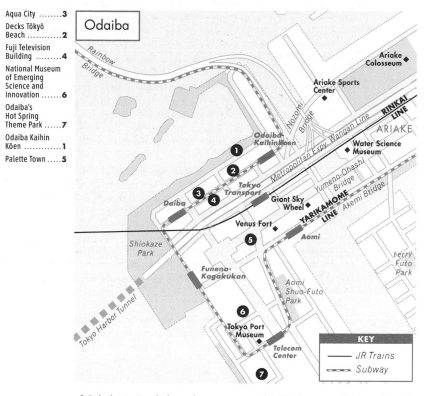

of Odaiba in English at the entrance. The Yurikamome Line makes 10 stops between Shimbashi and the terminus at Ariake; fares range from ¥310 to ¥370, but the best strategy is to buy a ¥1,000 prepaid card that allows you to make multiple stops at different points in Odaiba. The monorail runs every three to five minutes.

TOP ATTRACTIONS

❸ Aqua City アクアシティお台場. This massive shopping complex has six floors of boutiques, cafés, and eateries—including a branch of the hamburger chain Kua' Aina on the fourth level and the excellent noodle house Beninomama two floors above. ✉*1–7–1 Daiba, Minato-ku* ☎*03/3599–4700* ⊕*www.aquacity.jp* Ⓜ*Rinkai line, Tokyo Teleport Station; Yurikamome line, Daiba Station.*

❷ Decks Tōkyō Beach デックス東京ビーチ. Overlooking the harbor, this seven-story complex of shops, restaurants, and boardwalks is really two connected malls: Island Mall and Seaside Mall. Daiba Little Hong Kong, on the sixth and seventh floors of the Island Mall, has a collection of Cantonese restaurants and dim sum joints on neon-lighted "streets" designed to evoke the real Hong Kong. At the Seaside Mall, a table by the window in any of the restaurants affords a delightful view of the harbor, especially at sunset, when the *yakatabune* (traditional-roofed pleasure boats) drift down the Sumida-gawa from Yanagibashi and Ryōgoku. ✉ *1–6–1 Daiba, Minato-ku* ☎ *03/3599–6500* ⊕ *www. odaiba-decks.com* Ⓜ *Rinkai line, Tokyo Teleport Station; Yurikamome line, Odaiba-kaihin Kōen Station.*

❹ **Fuji Television Building** フジテレビ. Architecture buffs should make time for Daiba if only to contemplate this futuristic building. From its fifth-floor Studio Promenade, you can watch programs being produced. The observation deck on the 25th floor affords a spectacular view of the bay and the graceful curve of the Rainbow Bridge. ✉ *2–4–8 Daiba, Minato-ku* ☎ *03/5500–8888* ⊕ *www.fujitv.co.jp* ✎ *¥500* ⊗ *Daily 10–8* Ⓜ *Rinkai line, Tokyo Teleport Station; Yurikamome line, Odaiba-kaihin Kōen Station.*

❻ **National Museum of Emerging Science and Innovation** 日本科学未来館 *(Nihon Gagaku Miraikan)*. Make sure to stop by the third floor of this museum (known locally as Miraikan), where you will meet the most famous intelligent robot in the world, ASIMO, and a host of other experimental robots in development. This museum has four different themes: "Earth Environment and Frontiers," "Innovation and the Future," "Information Science and Technology for Society," and "Life Science." The rest of the museum is what the Japanese call ō-*majime* (deeply sincere)—five floors of thematic displays on environment-friendly technologies, life sciences, and the like with high seriousness and not much fun. The director of this facility, Dr. Mamoru Mohri, was Japan's first astronaut, who in 1992 logged some 460 hours in space aboard the NASA Spacelab-J *Endeavor*. Some of the exhibits have English-language explanations. It's a short walk here from the Museum of Maritime Science. ✉ *2–41 Aomi, Kōtō-ku* ☎ *03/3570–9151* ⊕ *www.miraikan.jst.go.jp* ✎ *¥500* ⊗ *Wed.– Mon. 10–5* Ⓜ *Yurikamome line, Funeno-Kagakukan Station.*

❼ **Odaiba's Hot Spring Theme Park** 大江戸温泉物語 *(Ōedo Onsen Monogatari)*. Once upon a time, when bathtubs in private homes were a rarity, the great defining social institution of Japanese urban life was the *sentō*: the local public bath. At the end of a hard day of work, there was no pleasure like sinking to your neck in hot water with your friends and neighbors, soaking your cares away, and sitting around afterward for soba, beer, and gossip. And if the sentō was also an *onsen*—a thermal spring—with waters drawn from some mineral-rich underground supply, the delight was even greater. No more than a handful of such places survive in Tōkyō, but the Ōedo Onsen managed to tap a source some 4,600 feet below the bay. A two-minute walk south from the Telecom Center, visitors can choose from several indoor and outdoor pools, each with different temperatures and motifs—but remember that you must soap up and rinse off (including your hair) before you enter any of them. Follow your soak with a massage and a stroll through the food court—modeled after a street in Yoshiwara, the licensed red-light district of the Edo period—for sushi or noodles and beer. Charges include the rental of a yukata and a towel. ✉ *2–57 Aomi, Kōtō-ku* ☎ *03/5500–1126* ⊕ *www.ooedoonsen.jp* ✎ *¥2,900; ¥1,600 (children); surcharge for entrance after midnight* ⊗ *Daily 11 AM–8 AM; front desk closes at 2 AM* Ⓜ *Rinkai line, Tokyo Teleport Station; Yurikamome line, Odaiba-kaihin Kōen Stations.*

❶ **Odaiba Kaihin Kōen** お台場海浜公園. This artificial beach and its board-walk are home to a small replica of the Statue of Liberty and, for many strolling couples, a wonderful evening view of the Rainbow Bridge. Ⓜ *Yurikamome line, Odaiba-kaihin Kōen Station.*

❺ **Palette Town.** This complex of malls and amusements is located at the east end of the island. The uncontested landmark here is the the 377-foot-high Palette Town Ferris Wheel, one of the world's largest. It was modeled after the London Eye; it's open daily 10–10 and costs ¥900. Just opposite is Mega Web, a complex of rides and multimedia amusements that's also a showcase for the Toyota Motor Corporation. You can ride a car (hands off—the ride is electronically controlled) over a 1-km (½-mi) course configured like a roller coaster but moving at a stately pace. You can drive any car you want, of course, as long as it's a Toyota. The shopping mall **Venus Fort** (✉ *Palette Town 1-chōme, Aomi, Kōtō-ku* ☎ *03/3599–0700*) at Aomi consists of galleries designed to suggest an Italian Renaissance palazzo, with arches and cupolas, marble fountains and statuary, and painted vault ceilings. The mall is chock-full of boutiques by the likes of Jean Paul Gaultier, Calvin Klein, Ralph Lauren, and all the other usual suspects. Ⓜ *Yurikamome line, Odaiba-kaihin Kōen Station.*

ELSEWHERE IN TŌKYŌ

The sheer size of the city and the diversity of its institutions make it impossible to fit all of Tōkyō's interesting sights into neighborhoods. Plenty of worthy places—from Tōkyō Disneyland to sumō stables to the old Ōji district—fall outside the city's neighborhood repertoire. Yet no guide to Tōkyō would be complete without them.

AMUSEMENT CENTERS

☺ **Kasai Seaside Park** 葛西臨海公園. With two artificial beaches, a bird sanctuary, and the ⇨ *Tōkyō Sea Life Park* aquarium spread over a stretch of landfill between the Arakawa and the Kyū-Edogawa rivers, Kasai Seaside Park is one of the major landmarks in the vast effort to transform Tōkyō Bay into Fun City. The **Diamonds and Flowers Ferris Wheel** (*Daia to Hana no Dai-kanransha*) takes passengers on a 17-minute ride to the apex, 384 feet above the ground, for a spectacular view of the city. One rotation takes 70 minutes. On a clear day you can see all the way to Mt. Fuji; at night, if you're lucky, you reach the top just in time for a bird's-eye view of the fireworks over the Magic Kingdom, across the river. To get here, take the JR Keiyo line local train from Tōkyō Station to Kasai Rinkai Kōen Station; the park is a five-minute walk from the south exit. ✉ *6–2 Rinkai-chō, Edogawa-ku* ☎ *03/3686–6911* 🎟 *Free, Ferris wheel ¥700* ⊙ *Ferris wheel Sept.–July, Tues.–Fri. 10–8, weekends 10–9; Aug., weekdays 10–8, weekends 10–9.*

☺ **Tōkyō Disneyland** 東京ディズニーランド. At Tōkyō Disneyland, Mickey-san and his coterie of Disney characters entertain just the way they do in the California and Florida Disney parks. When the park was built in 1983 it was much smaller than its counterparts in the United States, but the construction in 2001 of the adjacent DisneySea, with its seven "Ports of Call" with different nautical themes and rides, added more than 100 acres to this multifaceted Magic Kingdom.

There are several types of admission tickets. Most people buy the One-Day Passport (¥5,800), which gives you unlimited access to the attractions and shows at one or the other of the two parks; also available are a weekday after–6 PM pass, at ¥3,100, and a weekend (and national holiday) after–3 PM pass, at ¥4,700 (check online for updates). There's also a two-day pass, good for both parks, for ¥10,000. You can buy tickets in advance in Tōkyō Station, near the Yaesu North Exit—look for red-jacketed attendants standing outside the booth—or from any local travel agency, such as the Japan Travel Bureau (JTB).

The simplest way to get to Disneyland is by JR Keiyō Line from Tōkyō Station to Maihama; the park is just a few steps from the station exit. From Nihombashi you can also take the Tōzai subway line to Urayasu and walk over to the Tōkyō Disneyland Bus Terminal for the 25-minute ride, which costs ¥230. ✉ *1–1 Maihama, Urayasu-shi* ☎*0570/05-1118 information, 045/683-3333 reservations* ⊕*www.tokyodisneyresort. co.jp* ⊗*Daily 9* AM*–10* PM; *seasonal closings in Dec. and Jan. may vary, so check before you go.*

♻ **Tōkyō Dome City** 東京ドームシティ. The Kōrakuen stop on the Marunouchi subway line, about 10 minutes from Tōkyō Station, lets you out in front of the Tōkyō Dome, Japan's first air-supported indoor stadium, built in 1988 and home to the Tōkyō Yomiuri Giants baseball team. Across from the stadium is Tōkyō Dome City, a combination of family amusement park, shopping mall, restaurants, and a natural-spring spa. **Baseball Hall of Fame and Museum** 野球体育博物館 (✉ *¥500* ⊗*Mar.–Sept., daily 10–6; Oct.–Feb., daily 10–5*) offers a chance to see some of the bats, balls, and gloves of the legends that made Japanese Pro Baseball the game it is today. **LaQua Amusement Park** (✉*Roller-coaster rides ¥600–¥1,000* ⊗*10–10*) has three stomach-churning roller coasters, a haunted house, and a merry-go-round. The **LaQua Shopping Center** (⊗*Shops daily 11* AM*–9* PM; *restaurants daily 11* AM*–11* PM) holds 70 shops and restaurants. **LaQua Spa** (✉*¥2,565; ¥315 more on holidays; and ¥1,890 surcharge midnight–6* AM; *¥525 surcharge for Healing Room* ⊗*Daily 11* AM*–9* AM) is a natural hot spring for adults, more like an amusement park in itself. There are four floors of pampering and hot springs with high concentrations of sodium chloride, which is believed to increase blood circulation. ✉*1–3–61 Kōraku, Bunkyō-ku* ☎*03/5800–9999* ⊕*www.tokyo-dome.co.jp.*

♻ **Tōkyō Tower** 東京タワー. In 1958 Tōkyō's fledgling TV networks needed a tall antenna array to transmit signals. Trying to emerge from the devastation of World War II, the nation's capital was also hungry for a landmark—a symbol for the aspirations of a city still without a skyline. The result was the 1,093-foot-high Tōkyō Tower, an unabashed knockoff of Paris's Eiffel Tower, but with great views of the city. The Grand Observation Platform, at an elevation of 492 feet, and the Special Observation Platform, at an elevation of 820 feet, quickly became major tourist attractions; they still draw some 3 million visitors a year,

2

the vast majority of them Japanese youngsters on their first trip to the big city. A modest art gallery, Guinness Book of World Records Museum Tokyo, and a wax museum round out the tower's appeal as an amusement complex. Enjoy live music and stunning views on the main observation-floor café during **Club 333** (⊙ *Wed. and Thurs. 7–9* PM *, Fri. 7–9:30* PM), an in-house radio show, featuring live jazz, R&B, and bossa nova performances at no extra charge. ⊠*4–2–8 Shiba-Kōen, Minato-ku* ☎*03/3433–5111* ☞*Main Observation Platform ¥820, Special Observation Platform ¥600 extra; art gallery ¥400; wax museum ¥500; Guinness Museum ¥700* ⊙*Tower, daily 9* AM*–10* PM*. Museums and art gallery, daily 10–9* ⊕*www.tokyotower.co.jp* Ⓜ*Hibiya subway line, Kamiyachō Station (Exit 2).*

⊙ **Toshima-en** としまえん. This large, well-equipped amusement park in the northwestern part of Tōkyō has four roller coasters, a haunted house, and seven swimming pools. What makes it special is the authentic Coney Island carousel—left to rot in a New York warehouse, discovered and rescued by a Japanese entrepreneur, and lovingly restored down to the last gilded curlicue on the last prancing unicorn. From Shinjuku, the Ōedo subway line goes directly to the park. ⊠*3–25–1 Koyama, Nerima-ku* ☎*03/3990–3131* ⊕*www.toshimaen.co.jp* ☞*Day pass ¥3,900* ⊙*Thurs.–Mon. 10–6* Ⓜ *Seibu Ikebukuro Line, Toshimaen Station.*

ZOO AND AQUARIUMS

⊙ **Shinagawa Aquarium** 品川水族館 *(Shinagawa Suizokukan).* The fun part of this aquarium in southwestern Tōkyō is walking through an underwater glass tunnel while some 450 species of fish swim around and above you. There are no pamphlets or explanation panels in English, however, and do your best to avoid Sunday, when the dolphin and sea lion shows draw crowds in impossible numbers. Take the local Keihin-Kyūkō private rail line from Shinagawa to Ōmori-kaigan Station. Turn left as you exit the station and follow the ceramic fish on the sidewalk to the first traffic light; then turn right. You can also take the JR Tōkaidō Line to Oimachi Station; board a free shuttle to the aquarium from the No. 6 platform at the bus terminal just outside Oimachi Station. ⊠*3–2–1 Katsushima, Shinagawa-ku* ☎*03/3762–3431* ☞*¥1,100* ⊙*Wed.–Mon. 10–5; dolphin and sea lion shows 3 times daily, on varying schedule* Ⓜ*Keihin Kyuko line, Omori Kaigan Station.*

⊙ **Sunshine International Aquarium** サンシャイン国際水族館. This aquarium has some 750 kinds of sea creatures on display, plus sea lion performances four times a day (except when it rains). An English-language pamphlet is available, and most of the exhibits have some English explanation. If you get tired of the sea life, head to the newly refurbished Sunshine Starlight Dome planetarium, where you can see 400,000 stars. And if that still isn't enough to keep you occupied, head to the 60th floor observatory to take in some great views of the city. To get there, take the JR Yamanote Line to Ikebukuro Station (Exit 35) and walk about eight minutes west to the Sunshine City complex. You can also take the Yūraku-chō subway to Higashi-Ikebukuro Station (Exit 2); Sunshine City and the aquarium are about a three-minute walk north.

✉*3–1–3 Higashi-Ikebukuro, Toshima-ku* ☎*03/3989–3331* ⊕*www. sunshinecity.co.jp* ⊠*Aquarium ¥1,800; planetarium ¥900; observatory ¥620; tickets may be purchased in combination* ⊙*Aquarium open weekdays 10–6, weekends 10–6:30; Planetarium open daily 11–7; Observation deck open daily 10–9:30* Ⓜ*Yurakucho subway line, Ikebukuro Station (Exit 35).*

🕙 **Tama Zoo** 多摩動物園 *(Tama Dōbutsu Kōen).* More a wildlife park than a zoo, this facility in western Tōkyō gives animals room to roam; moats typically separate them from you. You can ride through the Lion Park in a minibus. To get here, take a Keiō Line train toward Takao from Shinjuku Station and transfer at Takahata-Fudō Station for the one-stop branch line that serves the park. ✉*7–1–1 Hodokubo, Hino-shi* ☎*0425/91–1611* ⊠*¥600* ⊙*Thurs.–Tues. 9:30–5* Ⓜ *From JR Tachikawa Station, take the Tama Monorail, and get off at Tama Dobutsu Kōen Station.*

OFF THE BEATEN PATH

Asakura Sculpture Gallery 朝倉彫刻館. Outsiders have long since discovered the Nezu and Yanaka areas of Shitamachi—much to the dismay of the handful of foreigners who have lived for years in this charming, inexpensive section of the city. Part of the areas' appeal lie in the fact that some of the giants of modern Japanese culture lived and died here, including novelists Ōgai Mori, Sōseki Natsume, and Ryūnosuke Akutagawa; scholar Tenshin Okakura, who founded the Japan Art Institute; painter Taikan Yokoyama; and sculptors Kōun Takamura and Fumio Asakura. If there's one single attraction here, it's probably Asakura's home and studio, which was converted into a gallery after his death in 1964 and now houses many of his most famous pieces. The tearoom on the opposite side of the courtyard is a quiet place from which to contemplate his garden.

From the north wing (Nishi-guchi/West Exit) of JR Nippori Station, walk west—Tennō-ji temple will be on the left side of the street—until you reach a police box. Turn right, then right again at the end of the street. The museum is a three-story black building on the right, a few hundred yards from the corner. ✉*7–18–10 Yanaka, Taitō-ku* ☎*03/3821–4549* ⊠*¥400* ⊙*Tues.–Thurs. and weekends 9:30–4:30* Ⓜ *JR Yamanote Line, Nippori Station.*

Ōji. Want to take a trip back in time? Take the JR Yamanote Line to Ōtsuka, cross the street in front of the station, and change to the Toden Arakawa Line—Tōkyō's last surviving trolley. Heading east, for ¥160 one way, the trolley takes you through the back gardens of old neighborhoods on its way to Ōji—once the site of Japan's first Western-style paper mill, built in 1875 by Ōji Paper Company, the nation's oldest joint-stock company. The mill is long gone, but the memory lingers on at the **Asuka-yama Ōji Paper Museum** (✉*1–1–3 Ōji, Kita-ku* ☎*03/3916–2320* ⊕*www.papermuseum.jp* ⊠*¥300* ⊙*Tues.–Sun. 10–5*). Some exhibits here show the process of milling paper from pulp. Others illustrate the astonishing variety of products that can be made from paper. The museum is a minute's walk from the trolley stop at

Asuka-yama Kōen; you can also get here from the JR Ōji Station (Minami-guchi/South Exit) on the Keihin–Tōhoku Line, or the Nishigahara Station (Asuka-yama Exit) on the Namboku subway line.

Fodor's Choice
★

Ryōgoku 両国. Two things make this working-class Shitamachi neighborhood worth a special trip: this is the center of the world of sumō wrestling as well as the site of the extraordinary Edo-Tōkyō Museum. Five minutes from Akihabara on the JR Sōbu Line, Ryōgoku is easy to get to, and if you've budgeted a leisurely stay in the city, it's well worth a morning's expedition.

The **Edo-Tōkyō Museum** (⊠ *1–4–1 Yokoami, Sumida-ku* ☎ *03/3626–9974* ⊕ *www.edo-tokyo-museum.or.jp* ✉ *¥600; additional fees for special exhibits* ⊙ *Tues.–Sun. 9:30–5:30, Fri. 9:30–7:30)* opened in 1993, more or less coinciding with the collapse of the economic bubble that had made the project possible. Money was no object in those days; much of the large museum site is open plaza—an unthinkably lavish use of space. From the plaza the museum rises on massive pillars to the permanent exhibit areas on the fifth and sixth floors. The escalator takes you directly to the sixth floor—and back in time 300 years. You cross a replica of the Edo-period Nihombashi Bridge into a truly remarkable collection of dioramas, scale models, cutaway rooms, and even whole buildings: an intimate and convincing experience of everyday life in the capital of the Tokugawa shōguns. Equally elaborate are the fifth-floor re-creations of early modern Tōkyō, the "enlightenment" of Japan's headlong embrace of the West, and the twin devastations of the Great Kantō Earthquake and World War II. If you only visit one non-art museum in Tōkyō, make this it.

To get to the museum, leave Ryōgoku Station by the west exit, immediately turn right, and follow the signs. The moving sidewalk and the stairs bring you to the plaza on the third level; to request an English-speaking volunteer guide, use the entrance to the left of the stairs instead, and ask at the General Information counter in front of the first floor Special Exhibition Gallery. Walk straight out to the main street in front of the west exit of Ryogoku station, turn right, and you come almost at once to the Kokugikan (National Sumō Arena), with its distinctive copper-green roof.

If you can't attend one of the Tōkyō sumō tournaments, you may want to at least pay a short visit to the **Sumō Museum** (⊠ *1–3–28 Yokoami, Sumida-ku* ☎ *03/3622–0366* ✉ *Free* ⊙ *Weekdays 10–4:30)*, in the south wing of the arena. There are no explanations in English, but the museum's collection of sumō-related wood-block prints, paintings, and illustrated scrolls includes some outstanding examples of traditional Japanese fine art.

★ **Sengaku-ji** 泉岳寺 *(Sengaku Temple).* In 1701, a young provincial baron named Asano Takumi-no-Kami attacked and seriously wounded a courtier named Yoshinaka Kira. Asano, for daring to draw his sword in the confines of Edo Castle, was ordered to commit suicide, so his family line was abolished and his fief confiscated. Forty-seven of Asano's loyal retainers vowed revenge; the death of their leader made them *rōnin*—masterless samurai. On the night of December 14, 1702, Asano's rōnin stormed Kira's villa in Edo, cut off his head, and brought

A Mostly Naked Free-For-All

Sumō wrestling dates back some 1,500 years. Originally a religious rite performed at shrines to entertain the harvest gods, a match may seem like a fleshy free-for-all to the casual spectator, but to the trained eye, it's a refined battle. Two wrestlers square off in a dirt ring about 15 feet in diameter and charge straight at each other in nothing but silk loincloths. There are various techniques of pushing, gripping, and throwing, but the rules are simple: except for hitting below the belt, grabbing your opponent by the hair (which would certainly upset the hairdresser who accompanies every sumō ringside), or striking with a closed fist, almost anything goes. If you're thrown down or forced out of the ring, you lose. There are no weight divisions and a runt of merely 250 pounds can find himself facing an opponent twice his size.

You must belong to one of the 30 *heya* (stables) based in Tōkyō to compete. Stables are run by retired wrestlers who have purchased the right from the Japan Sumō Association. Hierarchy and formality rule in the sumō world. Youngsters recruited into the sport live in the stable dormitory, do all the community chores, and wait on their seniors. When they rise high enough in tournament rankings, they acquire their own servant-apprentices.

Most of the stables are concentrated on both sides of the Sumida-gawa near the Kokugikan. Wander this area when the wrestlers are in town (January, May, and September) and you're more than likely to see some of them on the streets, in their wood clogs and kimonos. Come 7 AM–11 AM, and you can peer through the doors and windows of the stables to watch them in practice sessions. One of the easiest to find is the **Tatsunami Stable** (⊠ *3-26-2 Ryōgoku*),

only a few steps from the west end of Ryōgoku Station (turn left when you go through the turnstile and left again as you come out on the street; then walk along the station building to the second street on the right). Another, a few blocks farther south, where the Shuto Expressway passes overhead, is the **Izutsu Stable** (⊠ *2-2-7 Ryōgoku*).

When: Of the six Grand Sumō Tournaments (called *basho*) that take place during the year, Tōkyō hosts three: in early January, mid-May, and mid-September. Matches go from early afternoon, when the novices wrestle, to the titanic clashes of the upper ranks at around 6 PM.

Where: Tournaments are held in the Kokugikan, the National Sumō Arena, in Ryōgoku, a district in Sumida-ku also famed for its clothing shops and eateries that cater to sumō sizes and tastes. ⊠ *1–3–28 Yokoami, Sumida-ku* ☎ *03/3623–5111* ⊕ *www.sumo. or.jp* Ⓜ *JR Sōbu Line, Ryōgoku Station (West Exit).*

How: The most expensive seats, closest to the ring, are tatami-carpeted loges for four people, called *sajiki*. The loges are terribly cramped, but the cost (¥9,200–¥11,300 per person) includes all sorts of food and drink and souvenirs, brought to you by traditionally clad attendants. Cheap seats cost ¥3,600 for advance sales, ¥2,100 for same-day box office sales. For same-day box office sales you should line up an hour before the tournament. You can also get tickets through **Playguide** (☎ *03/5802–9999*) or at 7-Eleven, Family Mart, or Lawson convenience stores.

it in triumph to Asano's tomb at Sengaku-ji, the family temple. The rōnin were sentenced to commit suicide—which they accepted as the reward, not the price, of their honorable vendetta—and were buried in the temple graveyard with their lord.

Through the centuries this story has become a national epic and the last word on the subject of loyalty and sacrifice, celebrated in every medium from Kabuki to film. The temple still stands, and the graveyard is wreathed in smoke from the bundles of incense that visitors still lay reverently on the tombstones. There is a collection of weapons and other memorabilia from the event in the temple's small museum. One of the items dispels forever the myth of Japanese vagueness and indirection in the matter of contracts and formal documents. Kira's family, naturally, wanted to give him a proper burial, but the law insisted this could not be done without his head. They asked for it back, and Ōishi—mirror of chivalry that he was—agreed. He entrusted it to the temple, and the priests wrote him a receipt, which survives even now in the corner of a dusty glass case. "Item," it begins, "One head."

Take the Asakusa subway line to Sengaku-ji Station (Exit A2), turn right when you come to street level, and walk up the hill. The temple is past the first traffic light, on the left. ⊠ *2–11–1 Takanawa, Minato-ku* ☎ *03/3441–5560* ✉ *Temple and grounds free, museum ¥200* ☺ *Temple Apr.–Sept., daily 7–6; Oct.–Mar., daily 7–5. Museum daily 9–4* Ⓜ *Toei Asakusa subway line, Sengakuji Station (Exit A2).*

Sōgetsu Ikebana School 草月会館 *(Sōgetsu Kaikan).* The schools of *Ikebana,* like those of other traditional arts, are highly stratified organizations. Students rise through levels of proficiency, paying handsomely for lessons and certifications as they go, until they can become teachers themselves. At the top of the hierarchy is the *iemoto,* the head of the school, a title usually held within a family for generations. The Sōgetsu school of flower arrangement is a relative newcomer to all this. It was founded by Sōfū Teshigahara in 1927, and, compared to the older schools, it espouses a style flamboyant, free-form, and even radical. Introductory lessons in flower arrangement are given in English on Monday from 10 to noon. Reservations must be made a day in advance. The main hall of the Sōgetsu Kaikan, created by the late Isamu Noguchi, one of the masters of modern sculpture, is well worth a visit. Sōgetsu Kaikan is a 10-minute walk west on Aoyama-dōri from the Akasaka-mitsuke intersection or east from the Aoyama-itchōme subway stop. ⊠ *7-2–21 Akasaka, Minato-ku* ☎ *03/3408–1151* ⊕ *www.sogetsu.or.jp* Ⓜ *Ginza and Marunouchi subway lines, Akasaka-mitsuke Station; Ginza and Hanzō-mon subway lines, Aoyama-itchōme Station (Exit 4).*

WHERE TO EAT

Though Tōkyō is still stubbornly provincial in many ways, whatever the rest of the world has pronounced good in the realm of dining has made its way here. And, at last count, there were more than 200,000 bars and restaurants in the city.

Restaurants in Japan naturally expect most of their clients to be Japanese, and the Japanese are the world's champion modifiers. Only the most serious restaurateurs refrain from editing some of the authenticity out of foreign cuisines; in areas like Shibuya, Harajuku, and Shinjuku, all too many of the foreign restaurants cater to students and young office workers who come mainly for the *fun'iki*

(atmosphere). Choose a French bistro or Italian trattoria in these areas carefully, and expect to pay dearly for the real thing. That said, you can count on the fact that the city's best foreign cuisine is world-class. Several of France's two- and three-star restaurants, for example, have established branches and joint ventures in Tōkyō, and they regularly send their chefs over to supervise. The style almost everywhere is nouvelle cuisine: small portions, with picture-perfect garnishes and light sauces. More and more, you find interesting fusions of French and Japanese culinary traditions served in poetically beautiful presentations. Recipes make imaginative use of fresh Japanese ingredients, like *shimeji* mushrooms and local wild vegetables.

Tōkyō has also embraced the range and virtuosity of Italian cuisine; chances are good that the finer trattorias here will measure up to even Tuscan standards. Indian food is also consistently good—and relatively inexpensive. Chinese food is the most consistently modified; it can be very good, but it pales in comparison to fare in Hong Kong or Beijing.

A few pointers are in order on the geography of food and drink. The farther "downtown" you go—into Shitamachi—the less likely you are to find the real thing in foreign (that is, non-Japanese) cuisine. There's superb Japanese food all over the city, but aficionados of sushi swear (with excellent reason) by Tsukiji, where the fish market supplies the neighborhood's restaurants with the freshest ingredients; the restaurants in turn serve the biggest portions and charge the most reasonable prices. Asakusa takes pride in its tempura restaurants, but tempura is reliable almost everywhere, especially at branches of the well-established, city-wide chains like Tenya and Tsunahachi.

Tōkyōites love to wine and dine at first-rate establishments, some of which are grotesquely expensive. But have no fear: the city has a fair number of bargains, too—good cooking of all sorts that you can enjoy on even a modest budget. Every department store and skyscraper office building devotes at least one floor to restaurants; none of them stand out, but all are inexpensive and quite passable places to lunch. Food and drink, even at street stalls, are safe wherever you go. ■ TIP➔ **When in doubt, note that Tōkyō's top-rated international hotels also have some of the city's best places to eat and drink.**

DRESS

Dining out in Tōkyō does not ordinarily demand a great deal in the way of formal attire. If it's a business meal, of course, and your hosts or guests are Japanese, dress conservatively: for men, a suit and tie; for women, a dress or suit in a basic color and a minimum of jewelry. On your own, follow the unspoken dress codes you'd observe at home and you won't go wrong. We mention dress only when men are required to wear a jacket or a jacket and tie.

For Japanese-style dining on tatami floors, keep two things in mind: wear shoes that slip on and off easily and presentable socks, and choose clothing you'll be comfortable in for a few hours with your legs gathered under you.

QUICK BITES

If you're in a hurry, a visit to one branch of the MOS Burger, Freshness Burger, or First Kitchen will fit the bill. These nationwide chains offer familiar hamburgers, but they also have local variations. Yoshinoya is another popular chain, serving grilled salmon, rice, and miso soup for breakfast (until 10), and then hearty portions of rice and beef for the rest of the day.

PRICES

Eating at hotels and famous restaurants is costly; however, you can eat well and reasonably at standard restaurants that may not have signs in English. Many less expensive restaurants display in their front windows plastic replicas of the dishes they serve, so you can always point to what you want if the language barrier is insurmountable. Good places to look for moderately priced dining spots are in the restaurant concourses of department stores, usually on the first and/or second basement levels and the top floors.

All restaurants charge 5% tax, and by law, the price on the menu includes tax. Izakaya often charge a flat table charge (around ¥500 per person), which technically pays for the tiny appetizer that's served to all guests. Some restaurants add a service charge of 10% on large parties, which is usually indicated at the bottom of menus.

The restaurants we list are the cream of the crop in each price category. Price-category estimates are based on the cost of a main course at dinner, excluding drinks, taxes, and service charges. Japanese-style restaurants often serve set meals, which may include rice, soup, and pickled vegetables in addition to the main course—this can drive up the cost. You can sometimes request the main dish without the sides, but then you'd be missing out on the beauty and harmony of a Japanese meal.

WHAT IT COSTS IN YEN					
	¢	$	$$	$$$	$$$$
AT DINNER	under ¥800	¥800–¥1,000	¥1,000–¥2,000	¥2,000–¥3,000	over ¥3,000

Prices are per person for a main course.

BEST BETS FOR TŌKYŌ DINING

With hundreds of restaurants to choose from, how will you decide where to eat? Fodor's writers and editors have selected their favorite restaurants by price, cuisine, and experience in the Best Bets lists below. In the first column, Fodor's Choice properties represent the "best of the best" in every price category. You can also search by neighborhood for excellent eats—just peruse our reviews on the following pages.

Fodor'sChoice ★

Aoi-Marushin, p. 97
Ganchan, p. 105
Inakaya, p. 106
Robata, p. 112
Tableaux, p. 99
Ume no Hana, p. 97

Best By Price

$

Takeno, p. 110
Afuri, p. 99
Homeworks, p. 98

$$

Heiroku-zushi, p. 101
Maisen, p. 96
Mist, p. 102
Sakuratei, p. 103

$$$

Jidaiya, p. 106
Sasashū, p. 103

$$$$

Chez Inno, p. 104
Aquavit, p. 101
Le Papillon de Paris, p. 102
Chez Matsuo, p. 109

Best By Experience

BEST SUSHI

Takeno, p. 110
Edo-gin, p. 110
Heiroku-zushi, p. 101

BEST RAMEN

Afuri, p. 99
Mist, p. 102
Suzuran, p. 107
Kohmen, p. 106
Darumaya, p. 96

HOTEL DINING

Attore, p. 104
Gordon Ramsay, p. 99
Toh-Ka-Lin, p. 110

GREAT VIEW

Wa no Mori Sumika, p. 100
T. Y. Harbor Brewery, p. 108
Montoak, p. 102
Gordon Ramsay, p. 99

BEST BRUNCH

Good Honest Grub, p. 107
Fujimamas, p. 101
Ben's Café, p. 108

LATE NIGHT DINING

Kushinobo, p. 109
Sawanoi, p. 96
Tableaux, p. 99

MOST ROMANTIC

Red Pepper, p. 102
Aquavit, p. 101
Chez Inno, p. 104

LUNCH PRIX-FIXE

Pizza Salvatore Cuomo, p. 93
Aquavit, p. 101
Tenmatsu, p. 107
Mist, p. 102

CHILD-FRIENDLY

Tony Roma's, p. 107
Ninja, p. 93
Pizza Salvatore Cuomo, p. 93

AMERICAN

Roti, p. 107
Tony Roma's, p. 107
Homeworks, p. 98
T.Y. Harbor Brewery, p. 108

SOUTH ASIAN

Moti, p. 93
Tonki, p. 104
Sankō-en, p. 98

AKASAKA 赤坂

$$$
JAPANESE

✕ **Jidaiya** 時代屋. Like the Jidaiya in Roppongi, these two Akasaka branches serve various prix-fixe courses, including shabu-shabu, tempura, sushi, and steamed rice with seafood. The food isn't fancy, but it's delicious and filling. ✉ *Naritaya Bldg. 1F, Akasaka 3–14–3, Minato-ku* ☎ *03/3588–0489* ▤ *AE, DC, MC, V* ◷ *No lunch weekends* Ⓜ *Ginza and Marunouchi subway lines, Akasaka-mitsuke Station (Belle Vie Akasaka Exit)* ✉ *Isomura Bldg. B1, Akasaka 5–1–4, Minato-ku* ☎ *03/3224–1505* ▤ *AE, DC, MC, V* Ⓜ *Chiyoda subway line, Akasaka Station (Exit 1A).*

$$$$
JAPANESE

✕ **Kisoji** 木曽路. The specialty here is shabu-shabu: thin slices of beef cooked in boiling water at your table and dipped in sauce. Normally this is an informal, if pricey, sort of meal; after all, you do get to play with your food a bit. Kisoji, however, adds a dimension of posh to the experience, with all the tasteful appointments of a traditional *ryōtei*—private dining rooms with tatami seating (at a 10% surcharge), elegant little rock gardens, and alcoves with flower arrangements. ✉ *3–10–4 Akasaka, Minato-ku* ☎ *03/3588–0071* ▤ *AE, MC, V* Ⓜ *Ginza and Marunouchi subway lines, Akasaka-mitsuke Station (Belle Vie Akasaka Exit).*

$$
INDIAN
★

✕ **Moti** モティ. Vegetarian dishes at Moti, especially the lentil and eggplant curries, are very good; so is the chicken masala, cooked in butter and spices. The chefs here are recruited from India by a family member who runs a restaurant in Delhi. As its reputation for reasonably priced North Indian cuisine grew, Moti established branches in nearby Akasaka-mitsuke, Roppongi, and farther away in Yokohama. They all have the inevitable Indian friezes, copper bowls, and white elephants, but this one—popular at lunch with the office crowd from the nearby Tōkyō Broadcasting System headquarters—puts the least into decor. ✉ *Kimpa Bldg., 3rd fl., 2–14–31 Akasaka, Minato-ku* ☎ *03/3584–6640* ▤ *AE, DC, MC, V* Ⓜ *Chiyoda subway line, Akasaka Station (Exit 2).*

AKASAKA-MITSUKE 赤坂見附

$$$–$$$$
JAPANESE

✕ **Ninja** 忍者. In keeping with the air of mystery you'd expect from a ninja-theme restaurant, a ninja-costumed waiter leads you through a dark underground maze to your table in an artificial cave. The menu has more than 100 choices, including some elaborate set courses that are extravagant in both proportion and price. Among the impressively presented dishes are "jack-in-the-box" seafood salad—a lacquerware box overflowing with seasonal seafood and garnished with mustard, avocado tartar, and miso paste—and the life-size bonsai-tree dessert made from cookies and green-tea ice cream. Magical tricks are performed at your table during dinner—it's slightly kitschy but entertaining nonetheless. ✉ *Akasaka Tōkyū Plaza, 2–14–3 Nagata-chō, Minato-ku* ☎ *03/5157–3936* ✍ *Reservations essential* ▤ *AE, MC, V* Ⓜ *Ginza and Marunouchi subway lines, Akasaka-mitsuke Station (Tōkyū Plaza Exit).*

$$–$$$
ITALIAN

✕ **Pizza Salvatore Cuomo** ピッツァサルヴァトーレクオモ. Visitors to Pizza Salvatore Cuomo instantly catch the rich aroma of the wood-burning

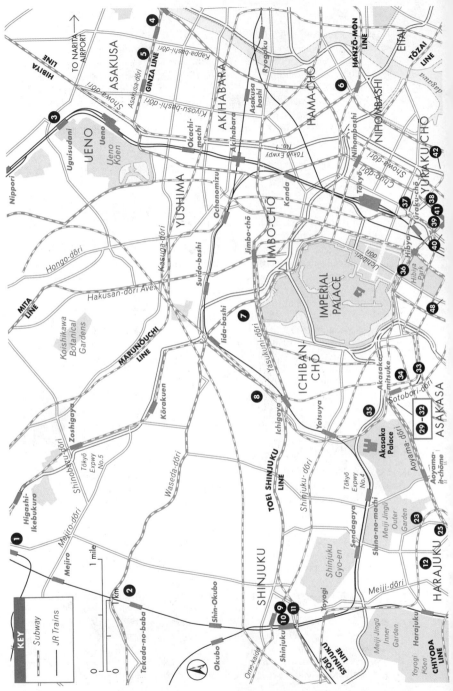

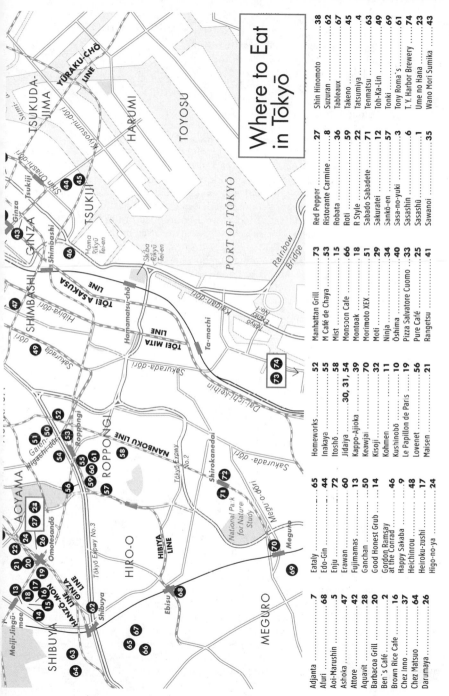

Where to Eat in Tōkyō

oven that is the centerpiece of this homey, spacious restaurant. Chef Salvatore Cuomo adheres to traditional Neapolitan methods, while updating recipes with dough infused with spinach, herbs, and even squid ink. Lunch courses are filling, affordable, and quick. For

dinner, classic antipasto dishes such as caprese make for an authentic Italian meal. ⊠ *Prudential Plaza Bldg., 2–13–10 Nagata-chō, Chiyoda-ku* ☎*03/3500–5700* ⊟*AE, DC, MC, V* Ⓜ*Chiyoda and Marunouchi subway lines, Akasaka-mitsuke Station.*

$–$$
JAPANESE

✗**Sawanoi** 澤乃井. The homemade udon noodles, served in a broth with seafood, vegetables, or chicken, make a perfect light meal or midnight snack. Try the *inaka* (country-style) udon, which has bonito, seaweed flakes, radish shavings, and a raw egg dropped in to cook in the hot broth. For a heartier meal, chose the *tenkama* set: hot udon and shrimp tempura with a delicate soy-based sauce. A bit run-down, Sawanoi is one of the last remaining neighborhood shops in what is now an upscale business and entertainment district. It stays open until 3 AM, and a menu is available in English. ⊠*Shimpo Bldg., 1st fl., 3–7–13 Akasaka, Minato-ku* ☎*03/3582–2080* ⊟*No credit cards* ⊗*Closed Sun.* Ⓜ*Ginza and Marunouchi subway lines, Akasaka-mitsuke Station (Belle Vie Akasaka Exit).*

AOYAMA 青山

$–$$
JAPANESE

✗**Darumaya** だるまや. While the classic bowl of ramen is topped with slices of pork, Darumaya, in the fashion district of Omotesandō, offers a slightly different take, topping its noodles with grilled vegetables. ⊠*1F Murayama Bldg., 5–9–5 Minami-Aoyama, Minato-ku* ☎*03/3499–6295* ⊟*No credit cards.*

$$$
JAPANESE

✗**Higo-no-ya** 肥後の屋. The specialty of the house is *kushi-yaki*: small servings of meat, fish, and vegetables cut into bits and grilled on bamboo skewers. There's nothing ceremonious or elegant about kushi-yaki; it resembles the more familiar yakitori, with somewhat more variety to the ingredients. Higo-no-ya's helpful English menu guides you to other delicacies like shiitake mushrooms stuffed with minced chicken; bacon-wrapped scallops; and bonito, shrimp, and eggplant with ginger. The restaurant is a postmodern–traditional cross, with wood beams painted black, paper lanterns, and sliding paper screens. There's tatami, table, and counter seating. ⊠*AG Bldg. B1, 3–18–17 Minami-Aoyama, Minato-ku* ☎*03/3423–4461* ⊟*AE, DC, MC, V* ⊗*No lunch* Ⓜ*Ginza, Chiyoda, and Hanzō-mon subway lines, Omotesandō Station (Exit A4).*

$$–$$$
JAPANESE

✗**Maisen** まい泉. Converted from a *sentō* (public bathhouse), Maisen still has the old high ceiling (built for ventilation) and the original signs instructing bathers where to change. Bouquets of seasonal flowers help transform the large, airy space into a pleasant dining room. Maisen's specialty is the *tonkatsu* set: tender, juicy, deep-fried pork cutlets served with a spicy sauce, shredded cabbage, miso soup, and rice. A popular alternative is the *Suruga-zen* set, a main course of fried fish served

The Quintessential Japanese Restaurant

Most often walled off from the outside world, a *ryōtei* is like a villa that has been divided into several small, private dining rooms. These rooms are traditional in style, with tatami-mat floors, low tables, and a hanging scroll or a flower arrangement in the alcove. Servers are assigned to each room to present the meal's many dishes (which likely contain foods you've never seen before), pour sake, and provide light conversation. Think of this as an encounter with the centuries-old graceful, almost ritualized, style of meal service unique to Japan. Many parts of the city are renowned for their ryōtei; the top houses tend to be in Akasaka, Tsukiji, Asakusa, and nearby Yanagi-bashi and Shimbashi.

with sashimi, soup, and rice. There are no-smoking rooms upstairs. ⊠*4–8–5 Jingū-mae, Shibuya-ku* ☎*03/3470–0071* ⊟*AE, DC, MC, V* Ⓜ*Ginza, Chiyoda, and Hanzō-mon subway lines, Omotesandō Station (Exit A2).*

$–$$
JAPANESE
Fodor'sChoice
★

✕**Ume no Hana** 梅の花. The exclusive specialty here is tofu, prepared in more ways than you can imagine—boiled, steamed, stir-fried with minced crabmeat, served in a custard, wrapped in thin layers around a delicate whitefish paste. Tofu is touted as the perfect high-protein, low-calorie health food; at Ume no Hana it's raised to the elegance of haute cuisine. Remove your shoes when you step up to the main room of the elegant restaurant. Latticed wood screens separate the tables, and private dining rooms with tatami seating are available. Prix-fixe meals include a complimentary aperitif. ⊠*2F Aoyama M's Tower, 2–27–18 Minami-Aoyama, Minato-ku* ☎*03/5412–0855* ⊟*AE, DC, MC, V* ⦰*No smoking except in private rooms* Ⓜ*Ginza Line, Gaien-mae Station (Exit 1A).*

ASAKUSA 浅草

$$
JAPANESE
Fodor'sChoice
★

✕**Aoi-Marushin** 葵丸進. This large and historic tempura restaurant, founded in 1946, has six floors of table and tatami seating and English menus. This is a family restaurant. Don't expect much in the way of decor—just lots of food at very reasonable prices. Asakusa is a must on any itinerary, and tempura *teishoku* (an assortment of delicate batter-fried fish, seafood, and fresh vegetables) is the specialty of the district. Aoi-Marushin's location, just a few minutes' walk from the entrance to Sensō-ji temple, makes it an obvious choice after a visit to the temple. ⊠*1–4–4 Asakusa, Taitō-ku* ☎*03/3841–0110* ⊟*AE, DC, MC, V* Ⓜ*Ginza and Asakusa subway lines, Asakusa Station (Exit 1).*

$$
JAPANESE

✕**Tatsumiya** たつみや. Here's a restaurant that's run like a formal ryōtei but has the feel of a rough-cut *izakaya* (Japanese pub). Neither inaccessible nor outrageously expensive, Tatsumiya is adorned—nay, cluttered—with antique chests, braziers, clocks, lanterns, bowls, utensils, and craft work, some of it for sale. The evening meal is in the *kaiseki* style, with seven courses: tradition demands that the meal include something raw, something boiled, something vinegary, and something grilled. The kaiseki dinner is served only until 8:30, and you must reserve ahead for it. Tatsumiya also serves a light lunch, plus a variety of *nabe* (one-pot seafood and vegetable stews, prepared at your table) until 10. The pork nabe is the house specialty. ✉*1–33–5 Asakusa, Taitō-ku* ☏*03/3842–7373* ▣*MC, V* Ⓜ*Ginza and Asakusa subway lines, Asakusa Station (Exits 1 and 3).*

AZABU-JŪBAN 麻布十番

$–$$
AMERICAN/
CASUAL

✗**Homeworks** ホームワークス. Every so often, even on alien shores, you've got to have a burger. When the urge strikes, the Swiss-and-bacon special at Homeworks is an incomparably better choice than anything you can get at one of the global chains. Hamburgers come in three sizes on white or wheat buns, with a variety of toppings. There are also hot teriyaki chicken sandwiches, pastrami sandwiches, and vegetarian options like a soybean veggie burger or a tofu sandwich. Desserts, alas, are so-so. With its hardwood banquettes and French doors open to the street in good weather, Homeworks is a pleasant place to linger over lunch. There's also a branch in Hiro-o. ✉*Vesta Bldg. 1F, 1–5–8 Azabu-jūban, Minato-ku* ☏*03/3405–9884* ▣*AE, MC, V* Ⓜ*Namboku and Ōedo subway lines, Azabu-Jūban Station (Exit 4).*

$$–$$$
KOREAN

✗**Sankō-en** 三幸園. With the embassy of South Korea a few blocks away, Sankō-en stands out in a neighborhood thick with Korean-barbecue joints. Customers—not just from the neighborhood but from nearby trendy Roppongi as well—line up at all hours (from 11:30 AM to midnight) to get in. Korean barbecue is a smoky affair; you cook your own food, usually thin slices of beef and vegetables, on a gas grill at your table. The *karubi* (brisket), which is accompanied by a great salad, is the best choice on the menu. If you like kimchi (spicy pickled cabbage), Sankō-en's is considered by some to be the best in town. ✉*1–8–7 Azabu-Jūban, Minato-ku* ☏*03/3585–6306* ⚘*Reservations not accepted* ▣*MC, V* ☾*Closed Wed.* Ⓜ*Namboku and Ōedo subway lines, Azabu-Jūban Station (Exit 4).*

DAIKANYAMA 代官山

$$$–$$$$
ITALIAN

✗**Eataly** イータリー. The Italian luxury supermarket chain that originated in Turin has come to Tōkyō. The complex, the first of its kind in Japan, is dedicated to all things Italian. In addition to shopping, there is a gelato and cake bar with outdoor seating, casual pasta and pizza restaurants open for lunch and dinner, and Guido, an elegant "slow food" dinner restaurant. ✉*20–23 Daikanyama-cho, Shibuya-ku* ☏*03/5784–2736* ▣*MC, V* Ⓜ*Tōkyū Tōyoko private rail line, Daikanyama Station (Kita-guchi/North Exit).*

$–$$
PAN-ASIAN

✗**Monsoon Cafe** モンスーンカフェ. With several locations, Monsoon Cafe meets the demand in Tōkyō for "ethnic" food—which by local definition means spicy and primarily Southeast Asian. Complementing the eclectic Pan-Asian food are rattan furniture, brass tableware from Thailand, colorful papier-mâché parrots on gilded stands, Balinese carvings, and ceiling fans. Here, at the original Monsoon, the best seats in the house are on the balcony that runs around the four sides of the atrium-style central space. Try the satay (grilled, skewered cubes of meat) platter, steamed shrimp dumplings, or nasi goring (Indonesian fried rice). ⌧*15–4 Hachiyama-chō, Shibuya-ku* ☏*03/5489–3789* ⊕*www. monsoon-cafe.jp* ▤*AE, DC, MC, V* Ⓜ*Tōkyū Tōyoko private rail line, Daikanyama Station (Kita-guchi/North Exit).*

$$$–$$$$
ECLECTIC
Fodor's Choice
★

✕**Tableaux** タブロー. The mural in the bar depicts the fall of Pompeii, the banquettes are upholstered in red leather, and the walls are papered in antique gold. Tableaux may lay on more glitz than is necessary, but the service is cordial and professional, and the food is superb. Try Zuwaicrab-and-red-shrimp spring rolls; filet mignon with creamed potatoes, seasonal vegetables, and merlot sauce; or, for dessert, the chocolate soufflé cake. The bar is open until 1:30 AM. ⌧*Sunroser Daikanyama Bldg. B1, 11–6 Sarugaku-chō, Shibuya-ku* ☏*03/5489–2201* ⚯*Jacket and tie* ▤*AE, DC, MC, V* ⌟*No smoking* ⊘*No lunch* Ⓜ*Tōkyū Tōyoko private rail line, Daikanyama Station (Kita-guchi/North Exit).*

EBISU 恵比寿

$
JAPANESE

✕**Afuri** 阿夫利／あふり. Ramen is the quintessential Japanese fast food in a bowl: thick Chinese noodles in a savory broth, with soybean paste, diced leeks, grilled *chāshū* (pork loin), and spinach. No neighborhood in Tōkyō is without at least one ramen joint—often serving only at a counter. In Ebisu, the hands-down favorite is Afuri. Using the picture menu, choose your ramen by inserting coins into a ticket machine, find a seat, and hand over your ticket to the cooks who will prepare your ramen then and there. There's limited seating, and at lunch and dinner, the line of waiting customers extends down the street. ⌧*1–1–7 Ebisu, Shibuya-ku* ☏*03/5795–0750* ▤*No credit cards* ⊘*Closed Wed.* Ⓜ*JR Yamanote Line (Nishi-guchi/West Exit) and Hibiya subway line (Exit 1), Ebisu Station.*

GINZA 銀座

$$$–$$$$
INDIAN

✕**Ashoka** アショカ. Since 1968, Ashoka has staked out the high ground for Indian cuisine in Tōkyō—with a dining room suited to its fashionable Ginza location. The room is hushed and spacious, incense perfumes the air, the lighting is recessed, the carpets are thick, and the servers wear spiffy uniforms. The best thing to order here is the *thali*, a selection of curries, tandoori chicken, and naan served on a figured brass tray. The Goan fish curry is also excellent, as is the chicken tikka: boneless chunks marinated and cooked in the tandoor. ⌧*Ginza Inz Bldg. 1, 2F, 3–1 Nishi Ginza, Chūō-ku* ☏*03/3567–2377* ▤*AE, DC, MC, V* Ⓜ*Marunouchi and Ginza subway lines, Ginza Station (Exit C9).*

$$$$
FRENCH

✕**Gordon Ramsay at the Conrad Hotel** ゴードン・ラムゼイ. This luxurious French restaurant in the Conrad Hotel, offers breathtaking views of the Hamarikyū Gardens and Tōkyō Bay 37 floors below. There's also plenty to see inside, as the chef prepares dishes such as roasted scallops with mushroom tortellini, peas, and mint velouté with great élan in the open kitchen. Guests may even spot Ramsay himself in the kitchen during one of his frequent visits to Tōkyō. A lunch course is also available for ¥5,000. ✉ *Conrad Tōkyō 37F, 1–9–1 Higashi-Shinbashi, Minato-ku* ☎ *03/3688–8000* ⊕ *www.gordonramsay.com* ⚓ *Reservations essential* ▤ *AE, DC, MC, V* Ⓜ *Toei-Ōedo subway line, Shiodome Stationn (Exit 3).*

$$$$
JAPANESE ✕ **Kappō-Ajioka** 割烹 味岡. When prepared incorrectly, fugu, the highly poisonous puffer fish, is fatal, yet this doesn't stop people from trying it at this Tōkyō branch of the Kansai fugu ryōtei (puffer-fish restaurant). Licensed chefs prepare the fish in every way imaginable—raw, fried, stewed—using the fresh catch flown in straight from Shimonoseki, a prime fugu-fishing region. The overall flavor is subtle and somewhat nondescript—people are drawn more to the element of danger than the taste (fatalities are rare, but a few people in Japan die each year from fugu poisoning). Try the house specialty of *suppon* (Japanese turtle) and fugu nabe, fugu sashimi, or fugu *no arayaki* (grilled head and cheeks). ■ **TIP**→ **Reservations must be made two days in advance to order fugu.** ✉ *New Comparu Bldg. 6F, 7-7–12 Ginza, Chūō-ku* ☎ *03/3574–8844* ▤ *AE, MC, V* Ⓜ *Ginza, Hibiya, and Marunouchi subway lines, Ginza Station (Exit A5).*

$$$$
JAPANESE ✕ **Ōshima** 大志満. The draw at Ōshima is the *Kaga ryōri* cooking of Kanazawa, a small city on the Sea of Japan known as "Little Kyōto" for its rich craft traditions. Waitresses dress in kimonos of Kanazawa's famous Yuzen dyed silk; Kutani porcelain and Wajima lacquerware grace the exquisite table settings. Seafood at Ōshima is superb, but don't ignore the specialty of the house: a stew of duck and potatoes called *jibuni*. Kaiseki full-course meals are pricey, but there's a reasonable lunchtime set menu for ¥2,625. ✉ *Ginza Core Bldg. 9F, 5–8–20 Ginza, Chūō-ku* ☎ *03/3574–8080* ▤ *AE, DC, MC, V* Ⓜ *Ginza, Hibiya, and Marunouchi subway lines, Ginza Station (Exit A5).*

$$$–$$$$
JAPANESE ✕ **Rangetsu** らん月. Japan enjoys a special reputation for its lovingly raised, tender, marbled domestic beef. Try it, if your budget will bear the weight, at Rangetsu, in the form of this elegant Ginza restaurant's signature shabu-shabu or sukiyaki course. Call ahead to reserve a private alcove, where you can cook for yourself, or have a kaiseki meal brought to your table by kimono-clad attendants. A lunch course is available for ¥1,800 on weekends. Rangetsu is a block from the Ginza 4-chōme crossing, opposite the Matsuya Department Store. ✉ *3–5–8 Ginza, Chūō-ku* ☎ *03/3567–1021* ▤ *AE, DC, MC, V* Ⓜ *Marunouchi and Ginza subway lines, Ginza Station (Exits A9 and A10).*

$$$$
JAPANESE ✕ **Wa no Mori Sumika** 和の杜すみか. A short walk from the heart of Ginza, this respite from the haute cuisine of Ginza specializes in vegetables shipped directly from farms around Japan, reflecting a recent movement in Japan toward healthier, safer eating. There are private dining rooms with tatami seating, and sunken counter seats at the window, affording a beautiful night view of lights of Ginza and the Kabukiza theater across the street. The seasonal vegetables and fresh fish course, ¥8,400, is like taking a tour of Japan, with the best and freshest produce from around the country appearing on your plate. ✉ *Duplex Bldg. 8F, 5–13–19 Ginza, Chūō-ku* ☎ *03/3547–8383* ⚓ *Reservations essential* ▤ *AE, DC, MC, V* Ⓜ *Marunouchi and Ginza subway lines, Ginza Station (Exits A9 and A10).*

HARAJUKU 原宿

$$$$
SCANDINAVIAN

✕**Aquavit** アクアビット. One of the handful of authentic Swedish restaurants in Tōkyō, Aquavit offers a reasonably priced prix-fixe dinner (and lunch). A good appetizer to try is herring sampler, which includes pickled herring and sweet varieties that change seasonally. Good main dish choices include smoked trout with celery puree, white beech mushrooms, and apple-horseradish sauce or the venison loin served with cured ham, potato dumplings, and

lingonberry sauce. Got room for dessert? Don't pass up the scrumptious Swedish pancakes, which are served with ginger confit, fresh cream, and raspberries. Everything is served in a romantic dinning room with ultra-modern design and furniture by Fritz Hansen of Denmark. ⊠*1F Shimizu Bldg., 2–5–8 Kita-Aoyama, Minato-ku* ☎*03/5413–3300* ⊕*www. aquavit-japan.com* ⌕*Reservations recommended* ⊟*AE, DC, MC, V* Ⓜ*Chiyoda subway line, Meiji-jingū-mae Station; JR Yamanote Line, Harajuku Station (Exit 2).*

$$$$
BRAZILIAN

✕**Barbacoa Grill** バルバッコアグリル. Carnivores flock here for the great-value all-you-can-eat Brazilian grilled chicken and barbecued beef, which the efficient waiters will keep bringing to your table on skewers until you tell them to stop. Those with lighter appetites can choose the less-expensive salad buffet and *feijoada* (pork stew with black beans); both are bargains. Barbacoa has hardwood floors, lithographs of bull motifs, warm lighting, salmon-color tablecloths, and roomy seating. This popular spot is just off Omotesandō-dōri on the Harajuku 2-chōme shopping street (on the north side of Omotesandō-dōri), about 50 yards down on the left. ⊠*4–3–24 Jingū-mae, Shibuya-ku* ☎*03/3796–0571* ⊟*AE, DC, MC, V* Ⓜ*Ginza, Chiyoda, and Hanzō-mon subway lines, Omotesandō Station (Exit A2).*

$$
JAPANESE

✕**Fujimamas** フジママス. This cozy eatery is in an old converted tatami mat factory, and its location just off Omotesandō Street makes it the perfect place to have brunch before an afternoon of shopping. The Big Plate brunch includes pancakes, eggs, sausage, bacon, and roast potato. Brunch is served Saturday and national holidays, 11 AM to 4 PM, and Sunday 10 AM to 4 PM. ⊠*6–3–2 Jingū-mae, Shibuya-ku* ☎*03/5485–2283* ⊟*AE, DC, MC, V* Ⓜ*Chiyoda subway line, Meiji-jingū-mae Station (Exit 4); JR Yamanote Line, Harajuku Station (Omotesandō Exit).*

$$
SUSHI

✕**Heiroku-zushi** 平禄寿司. Ordinarily, a meal of sushi is a costly indulgence. The rock-bottom alternative is a *kaiten-zushi*, where sushi is literally served assembly-line style. The chefs inside the circular counter maintain a constant supply on the revolving belt on plates color-coded for price; just choose whatever takes your fancy as dishes pass by. Heiroku-zushi is a bustling, cheerful example of the genre, with fresh fish and no pretensions at all to decor. When you're done, the server counts up your plates and calculates your bill (¥126 for staples like tuna and squid to ¥367 for delicacies like eel and salmon roe). ⊠ *5–8–5 Jingū-mae, Shibuya-ku* ☎ *03/3498–3968* ⊟ *No credit cards* Ⓜ *Ginza, Chiyoda, and Hanzō-mon subway lines, Omotesandō Station (Exit A1).*

$$$$
FRENCH

✕ **Le Papillon de Paris** ル・パピヨン・ド・パリ. This very fashion-minded restaurant is a joint venture of L'Orangerie in Paris and couturier Mori Hanae. Muted elegance marks the dining room, with cream walls and deep brown carpets; mirrors add depth to a room that actually seats only 40. The ambitious prix-fixe menus change every two weeks; the recurring salad of sautéed sweetbreads is excellent, as is the grilled Atlantic salmon. This is a particularly good place to be on Sunday between 11 and 2:30, for the buffet brunch (¥3,650), during which you can graze through to what is arguably the best dessert tray in town; try the pear tart or the daily chocolate-cake special. ⊠ *5F Hanae Mori Bldg., 3–6–1 Kita-Aoyama, Minato-ku* ☎ *03/3407–7461* ⚐ *Reservations essential* ⊟ *AE, DC, MC, V* ⊘ *Closed Mon. No dinner Sun.* Ⓜ *Ginza, Chiyoda, and Hanzō-mon subway lines, Omotesandō Station (Exit A1).*

$$–$$$
JAPANESE

✕ **Mist** ミスト. Exercising your plastic in Tōkyō's Omotesandō Hills shopping complex can be tiring. Refuel at Mist, a 21-seat "noodle studio" inside the Tadao Ando–designed complex. The look is minimalist-chic, with counter seats, a stainless-steel kitchen, and burgundy banquettes. The food, as lovely as the space, includes homemade ramen—springy, firm, and served with a savory broth. The menu boasts two styles of ramen and three optional toppings. At lunch, gourmet ramen and one beverage will set you back $15–$17. ⊠ *4–12–10 Jingū-mae, Shibuya-ku* ☎ *03/5410–1368* ⊟ *AE, DC, MC, V* Ⓜ *Ginza, Chiyoda, and Hanzō-mon subway lines, Omotesandō Station.*

$–$$
CAFES

✕ **Montoak** モントーク. If you're into people watching, then this two-storey café on Omotesandō street in the heart of one of the most fashion-conscious areas of Tōkyō is the perfect place to relax on an afternoon. Order one of their scrumptious home made tarts or cakes, and a coffee, and watch the trendiest Tokyoites stroll by the full-length windows. ⊠ *6–1–9 Jingū-mae, Shibuya-ku* ☎ *03/5468–5928* ⊟ *AE, DC, MC, V.*

$–$$$
FRENCH

✕ **Red Pepper** レッドペッパー. This cozy bistro is a short walk down a narrow alley from Omotesandō crossing, the center of the trendy fashion shopping mecca of Tōkyō. The atmosphere is homey, and guests squeeze into tiny antique school chairs and desks topped with candles. The cuisine is constantly changing, and most dinners ignore the printed menu in favor of the daily recommendations chalked on blackboards (mostly in Japanese) propped up here and there. You might find dishes such as button mushrooms grilled in garlic and olive oil, or porcini-and-cream-sauce fettuccine. ⊠ *1F Shimizu Bldg., 3–5–25 Kita-Aoyama, Shibuya-ku* ☎ *03/3478–1264* ⊟ *AE, DC, MC, V* Ⓜ *Ginza, Chiyoda, and Hanzō-mon subway lines, Omotesandō Station.*

¢–$
JAPANESE

✕ **R Style** アールスタイル. Even in some of the swankiest restaurants, Japanese *wagashi* (sweets) aren't up to par. To sample authentic handmade wagashi while sipping green tea, head to this café. The main ingredients in wagashi are adzuki beans, rice, and other grains sweetened slightly by sugarcane—making these treats a fairly healthful dessert. These intricate morsels of edible art are almost too perfectly presented to eat—almost, but not quite. Try the *konomi* (rice dumpling with adzuki conserve) or *koyomi* (bracken dumpling with soy custard) set. ⊠*Omotesandō Hills Main Bldg. 3F, 4–12–10 Jingū-mae, Shibuya-ku* ☎*03/3423–1155* ⊟*AE, MC, V* Ⓜ*Ginza, Chiyoda, and Hanzō-mon subway lines, Omotesandō Station (Exit A2); Chiyoda subway line, Meiji-Jingū-mae Station (Exit 5).*

$$-$$$ ✗**Sakuratei** さくら亭. Tucked away between two art galleries that feature
JAPANESE   works by young Japanese artists, Sakuratei defies other conventions as well: eating here doesn't always mean you don't have to cook. At this do-it-yourself *okonomiyaki* (a kind of pancake made with egg, meat, and vegetables) restaurant, you choose ingredients and cook them on the *teppan* (grill). Okonomiyaki is generally easy to make, but flipping the pancake to cook the other side can be challenging—potentially messy but still fun. Fortunately, you're not expected to do the dishes. Okonomiyaki literally means "as you like it," so experiment with your own recipe or try the house special, *sakurayaki* (with pork, squid, and onions), or *monjayaki* (a watered-down variation of okonomiyaki from the Kanto region). ⊠*3–20–1 Jingū-mae, Shibuya-ku* ☎*03/3479–0039* ⊟*DC, MC, V* Ⓜ*Chiyoda subway line, Meiji-Jingū-mae Station (Exit 5).*

ICHIYAGA 市ヶ谷

$$ ✗**Ristorante Carmine** カルミネ. Everybody pitched in, so the story goes,
ITALIAN   when chef Carmine Cozzolino left his job at an upscale restaurant in Aoyama and opened this unpretentious neighborhood bistro in 1987: friends designed the logo and the interior, painted the walls (black and white), and hung the graphics, swapping their labor for meals. The five-course dinner (¥3,990–¥5,250) here could be the best deal in town. The menu changes weekly; specialties of the house include risotto primavera and Tuscan-style *filetto di pesce* (fish fillet) parmigiano. The wine list is well chosen, and the *torta al cioccolata* (chocolate cake) is a serious dessert. ⊠*Nishikawa Bldg. 1F, 1–19 Saiku-chō, Shinjuku-ku* ☎*03/3260–5066* ⊟*AE, MC, V* Ⓜ*Ōedo subway line, Ushigome-Kagurazaka Station (Exit 1).*

IKEBUKURO 池袋

$$-$$$ ✗**Sasashū** 笹周. This traditional-style pub is noteworthy for stocking
JAPANESE   only the finest and rarest, the Latours and Mouton-Rothschilds, of
Fodor'sChoice sake: these are the rice wines that take gold medals in the annual sake
★   competition year after year. It also serves some of the best izakaya food in town—the Japanese wouldn't dream of drinking well without eating well. Sasashū purports to be the only restaurant in Tōkyō that serves wild duck; the chefs brush the duck with sake and soy sauce and broil it over a hibachi. It's in a rambling, two-story, traditional-style building, with thick beams and tatami floors. ⊠*2–2–6 Ikebukuro, Toshima-ku* ☎*03/3971–6796* ⊟*AE, DC, V* ⊘*Closed Sun. No lunch* Ⓜ*JR Yamanote Line; Yūraku-chō, Marunouchi, and Ōedo subway lines: Ikebukuro Station (Exit 19).*

KYŌ-BASHI 京橋

$$$$
ITALIAN
✕ **Attore** アトーレ. This Italian restaurant in the elegant Hotel Seiyō Ginza is divided into two sections. The "casual" side has a bar counter, banquettes, and a see-through glass wall to the kitchen; the "formal" side has mauve wall panels and carpets, armchairs, and soft recessed lighting. On either side of the room, you'll get some of the best Italian cuisine in Tōkyō, though the menu is simpler and cheaper on the casual side. The six-course dinner (only available on the formal side) constantly changes with the seasons, but should you find eggplant and scallops baked in a shiitake mushroom and vermouth sauce on the menu, try it. ■TIP➔ Children under 7 are not allowed. ⊠*Hotel Seiyō Ginza, 1–11–2 Ginza, Chūō-ku* ☎*03/3535–1111* ⌕*Reservations essential* ⊟*AE, DC, MC, V* Ⓜ*Ginza subway line, Kyō-bashi Station (Exit 2); Yūraku-chō subway line, Ginza-Itchōme Station (Exit 7).*

$$$$
FRENCH
✕ **Chez Inno** シェ・イノ. Chef Noboru Inoue studied his craft at Maxim's in Paris and Les Frères Troisgros in Roanne; the result is brilliant, innovative French food. Try fresh lamb in wine sauce with truffles and finely chopped herbs, or lobster with caviar. The main dining room has velvet banquettes, white stucco walls, and stained-glass windows. The elegant Hotel Seiyō Ginza is nearby—making this area the locus of the very utmost in Tōkyō upscale. ⊠*Meiji Seika Honsha Bldg. 1F, 2–4–16 Kyō-bashi, Chūō-ku* ☎*03/3274–2020* ⌕*Reservations essential* ⌦*Jacket and tie* ⊟*AE, DC, MC, V* ⊘*Closed Sun.* Ⓜ*Ginza subway line, Kyō-bashi Station (Exit 2); Yūraku-chō subway line, Ginza-Itchōme Station (Exit 7).*

MEGURO 目黒

$$
THAI
★
✕ **Keawjai** ゲウチャイ. Blink and you might miss the faded sign of this little basement restaurant a minutes walk from Meguro Station. Keawjai is one of the few places in Tōkyō to specialize in the subtle complexities of Royal Thai cuisine, and despite its size—only eight tables and four banquettes—it serves a remarkable range of dishes in different regional styles. The spicy beef salad is excellent (and *really* spicy), as are the baked rice and crabmeat served in a whole pineapple, and the red-curry chicken in coconut milk with cashews. The service is friendly and unhurried. There is also a branch in Shinjuku. ⊠*Meguro Kōwa Bldg. B1, 2–14–9 Kami Ōsaki, Meguro-ku* ☎*03/5420–7727* ⊟*AE, DC, MC, V* Ⓜ*JR Yamanote and Namboku subway lines, Meguro Station (Higashi-guchi/East Exit).*

$–$$
JAPANESE
★
✕ **Tonki** とんき. Meguro, a neighborhood distinguished for almost nothing else culinary, has arguably the best tonkatsu restaurant in Tōkyō. It's a family joint, with Formica-top tables and a server who comes around to take your order while you wait the requisite 10 minutes in line. And people do wait in line, every night until the place closes at 10:45. Tonki is a success that never went conglomerate or added frills to what it does best: deep-fried pork cutlets, soup, raw-cabbage salad, rice, pickles, and tea. That's the standard course, and almost everybody orders it, with good reason. ⊠*1–1–2 Shimo-Meguro, Meguro-ku* ☎*03/3491–9928* ⊟*AE, DC, MC, V* ⊘*Closed Tues. and 3rd Mon. of*

month Ⓜ *JR Yamanote and Namboku subway lines, Meguro Station (Nishi-guchi/West Exit).*

NIBAN-CHŌ 二番町

$$ ✕**Adjanta** アジャンタ. In the mid-20th century, the owner of Adjanta
INDIAN came to Tōkyō to study electrical engineering. He ended up changing
careers and establishing what is today one of the oldest and best Indian
restaurants in town. There's no decor to speak of at this restaurant,
which stays open until 4 AM. The emphasis instead is on the variety
and intricacy of South Indian cooking—and none of its dressier rivals
can match Adjanta's menu for sheer depth. The curries are hot to begin
with, but you can order them even hotter. Try the *masala dosa* (a savory
crepe), *keema* (minced beef), or mutton curry. A small boutique in one
corner sells saris and imported Indian foodstuffs. ✉*3–11 Niban-chō,
Chiyoda-ku* ☎*03/3264–6955* ▭*AE, DC, MC, V* Ⓜ*Yūraku-chō sub-
way line, Kōji-machi Station (Exit 5).*

NIHOMBASHI 日本橋

$$ ✕**Sasashin** 笹新. Like most izakaya, Sasashin spurns the notion of decor:
JAPANESE there's a counter laden with platters of the evening's fare, a clutter of
rough wooden tables, and not much else. It's noisy, smoky, crowded—
and great fun. Like izakaya fare in general, the food is best described as
professional home cooking, and is meant mainly as ballast for the earnest
consumption of beer and sake. Try the sashimi, the grilled fish, or the
fried tofu; you really can't go wrong by just pointing your finger at anything on the counter that takes your fancy. Unlike some izakaya that stay
open into the wee hours, this one winds down around 10:30. ✉*2–20–3
Nihombashi-Ningyōchō, Chūō-ku* ☎*03/3668–2456* ⚑*Reservations not
accepted* ▭*No credit cards* ⊘*Closed Sun. and 3rd Sat. of month. No
lunch* Ⓜ*Hanzō-mon subway line, Suitengū-mae Station (Exit 7); Hibiya
and Asakusa subway lines, Ningyōchō Station (Exits A1 and A3).*

ROPPONGI 六本木

$$–$$$ ✕**Erawan** エラワン. Window tables at this sprawling Thai "brasserie"
THAI on the top floor of a popular Roppongi vertical mall afford a wonderful
view of the Tōkyō skyline, including Tōkyō Tower, at night. Black-paint-
ed wood floors, ceiling fans, Thai antiques, and rattan chairs establish
the mood, and the space is nicely broken up into large and small dining
areas and private rooms. The service is cheerful and professional. Specialties of the house include deep-fried prawn and crabmeat cakes, spicy
roast-beef salad, sirloin tips with mango sauce, and a terrific dish of stir-
fried lobster meat with cashews. For window seating, it's best to reserve
ahead. ✉*Roi Bldg. 13F, 5–5–1 Roppongi, Minato-ku* ☎*03/3404–5741*
▭*AE, DC, MC, V* Ⓜ*Hibiya subway line, Roppongi Station (Exit 3).*

$$ ✕**Ganchan** がんちゃん. The Japanese expect their yakitori joints—res-
JAPANESE taurants that specialize in bits of charcoal-broiled chicken and vegeta-
Fodor'sChoice bles—to be just like Ganchan: smoky, noisy, and cluttered. The counter
★ here seats barely 15, and you have to squeeze to get to the chairs in

back. Festival masks, paper kites and lanterns, and greeting cards from celebrity patrons adorn the walls. The cooks yell at each other, fan the grill, and serve up enormous schooners of beer. Try the *tsukune* (balls of minced chicken) and the fresh asparagus wrapped in bacon. The place stays open until 1:30 AM (midnight on Sunday). ⊠ *6–8–23 Roppongi, Minato-ku* ☎ *03/3478–0092* ⊟ *AE, MC, V* Ⓜ *Hibiya subway line, Roppongi Station (Exit 1A).*

$$–$$$$
JAPANESE
Fodor's Choice
★

✕ **Inakaya** 田舎屋. The style here is *robatayaki*, a dining experience that segues into pure theater. Inside a large U-shaped counter, two cooks in traditional garb sit on cushions behind a grill, with a cornucopia of food spread out in front of them: fresh vegetables, seafood, skewers of beef and chicken. You point to what you want, and your server shouts out the order. The cook bellows back your order, plucks your selection up out of the pit, prepares it, and hands it across on an 8-foot wooden paddle. Inakaya is open from 5 PM to 5 AM, and fills up fast after 7. If you can't get a seat here, there is now another branch on the other side of Roppongi crossing. ⊠ *Reine Bldg., 1st fl., 5–3–4 Roppongi, Minato-ku* ☎ *03/3408–5040* ⚄ *Reservations not accepted* ⊟ *AE, DC, MC, V* ⊘ *No lunch* Ⓜ *Hibiya subway line, Roppongi Station (Exit 3).*

$$$$
JAPANESE

✕ **Jidaiya** 時代屋. Entering Jidaiya, which loosely translates as "period house," is like stepping into an Edo-period tavern. Most locals order from ornately drawn strips of paper that hang from high on the walls. If you are not sure what to order, leave it up to the chef (omakase) and you will be served a selection of shabu-shabu, tempura, sushi, rice dishes, and grilled fish. The food's not so fancy, but it's filling and delicious. ⊠ *Yuni Roppongi Bldg. B1, 7–15–17 Roppongi, Minato-ku* ☎ *03/3403–3563* ⊟ *AE, DC, MC, V* Ⓜ *Hibiya subway line, Roppongi Station (Exit 2).*

¢–$
JAPANESE

✕ **Kohmen** 光麺. This lively ramen shop, like most in the city, has menus only in English, but that doesn't mean it's not authentic or tasty. The shop's known for its *tonkotsu* (pork bone) soup—the best way to order it is to yell "tonkotsu" across the counter. If you're feeling both hungry and adventurous, add *zen-bu no-say* (with the works) to your order of tonkotsu. Kohmen is open to 6 AM. ⊠ *7–14–3 Roppongi, Minato-ku* ☎ *03/6406–4565* ⊟ *No credit cards.*

$$$$
ECLECTIC

✕ **Lovenet** ラブネット. Within the 33 private theme rooms of Lovenet, you can dine and enjoy Japan's national pastime: karaoke. Go not just for the food but the entire experience. Request the intimate Morocco suite, the colorful Candy room, or the Aqua suite, where you can eat, drink, and take a dip in the hot tub while belting out '80s hits. The Italian-trained chefs prepare Mediterranean and Japanese cuisine in the form of light snacks and full-course meals, which you order via a phone intercom system. Try the duck confit with wine sauce or a salmon-roe rice bowl. The bill is calculated based on what room you use, how long you stay, and what you order. Note that there's a two-person minimum for each room. ⊠ *Hotel Ibis 3F–4F, 7–14–4 Roppongi, Minato-ku* ☎ *03/5771–5511* ⊕ *www.lovenet-jp.com* ⚄ *Reservations essential* ⊟ *AE, MC, V* Ⓜ *Ōedo and Hibiya subway lines, Roppongi Station (Exit 4A).*

2

$$-$$$$
JAPANESE
✕**Morimoto XEX** モリモトゼックス. Acclaimed chef Masaharu Morimoto's eponymous tri-level eatery features upscale Japanese cuisine with global influences. Diners can order à la carte, or opt for one of the many tasting menus. The decadent, multicourse "Steak and Ise Lobster" prix-fixe menu includes beef belly tartare with truffled egg yoke and aged soy sauce, ise lobster with leek and lobster chili sauce, and your choice of T-bone pork, beef sirloin, beef fillet, or beef Châteaubriand for a main entrée. The 13-course sushi tasting menu sticks with more traditional Japanese flavors, but is equally delicious. ⊠*7–21–19 Roppongi, Minato-ku* ☎*03/3479–0065* ⊕*www.ystable.co.jp/morimoto* ⌂ *Reservations essential* ▤ *AE, MC, V* ⊙*No lunch.*

$$-$$$
AMERICAN
✕**Roti** ロティ. Billing itself a "modern American brasserie," Roti takes pride in the creative use of simple, fresh ingredients, and a fusing of Eastern and Western elements. For an appetizer, try the falafel and char-grilled vegetables on flat bread, or shoestring french fries with white truffle oil and Parmigiano-Reggiano cheese. Don't neglect dessert: the espresso-chocolate tart is to die for. Roti stocks some 60 Californian wines, microbrewed ales from the famed Rogue brewery in Oregon, and Cuban cigars. The best seats in the house are in fact outside at one of the dozen tables around the big glass pyramid on the terrace. ⊠*Piramide Bldg. 1F, 6–6–9 Roppongi, Minato-ku* ☎*03/5785–3671* ▤*AE, MC, V* Ⓜ*Hibiya subway line, Roppongi Station (Exit 1).*

$-$$
AMERICAN
🌣
✕**Tony Roma's** トニーローマ. If your kids flee in terror when a plate of sushi is placed in front of them, you may want to take them for a taste of home at this American chain world famous for its barbecued ribs. Started in Miami, Florida, in the 1970s, this casual place—one of five in Tōkyō—serves kid-sized portions of ribs, burgers, chicken strips, and fried shrimp. ⊠*5–4–20 Roppongi, Minato-ku* ☎*03/3408–2748 www. tonyromas.jp/en/* ▤*AE, DC, MC, V* Ⓜ*Hibiya subway line, Roppongi Station (Exit 3).*

SHIBUYA 原宿

$$
CAFES
✕**Good Honest Grub** グッドオネストグラブ. This airy, laid-back restaurant has the feel of enjoying a home-cooked meal at a friend's house. Brunch is served 10:30–4:30, Saturday, Sunday, and national holidays, and includes offerings such as Greek omelets, wrap sandwiches, and perhaps the best eggs Benedict in town. Everything comes from the restaurant's own organic farm. ⊠*2–20–8 Higashi, Shibuya-ku* ☎*03/3797–9877* ⌂*Reservations not accepted for brunch* ▤*No credit cards.*

$-$$
JAPANESE
✕**Suzuran** すずらん. It's said that you can judge the quality of a Tokyo ramen restaurant by the number of people lined up out front. If that's true, Suzuran, a short walk from Shibuya station, must be one of the best in town, as people begin lining up before the restaurant opens its doors at 11:30. Expect excellent ramen, as well as *tsukemen* (wide noodles in a light, vinegary sauce) topped with boiled fish. Don't be afraid of the long line outside, it moves quickly and the ramen is worth the wait. ⊠*3–7–5 Shibuya, Shibuya-ku* ☎*03/3499–0434* ▤*No credit cards.*

$$-$$$
JAPANESE
★
✕**Tenmatsu** 天松. The best seats in the house at Tenmatsu, as in any tempura-*ya*, are at the immaculate wooden counter, where your tidbits of choice are taken straight from the oil and served immediately. You

also get to watch the chef in action. Tenmatsu's brand of good-natured professional hospitality adds to the enjoyment of the meal. Here you can rely on a set menu or order à la carte tempura delicacies like lotus root, shrimp, *unagi* (eel), and *kisu* (a small white freshwater fish). Call ahead to reserve counter seating or a full-course kaiseki dinner in a private tatami room. ✉*1–6–1 Dōgen-zaka, Shibuya-ku* ☎*03/3462–2815* ▭*DC, MC, V* Ⓜ*JR Yamanote Line, Shibuya Station (Minami-guchi/South Exit); Ginza and Hanzō-mon subway lines, Shibuya Station (Exit 3A).*

SHINAGAWA 品川

$$–$$$$ ✕**Manhattan Grill** マンハッタングリル. Only in hypereclectic Japan can
ECLECTIC   you have a French-Indonesian meal at a restaurant called the Manhattan Grill in a food court dubbed the "Foodium." Chef Wayan Surbrata, who trained at the Four Seasons Resort in Bali, has a delicate, deft touch with such dishes as spicy roast-chicken salad, and steak marinated in cinnamon and soy sauce, served with shiitake mushrooms and *gado-gado* (shrimp-flavor rice crackers). One side of the minimalist restaurant is open to the food court; the floor-to-ceiling windows on the other side don't afford much of a view. The square black-and-white ceramics set off the food especially well. ✉*Atré Shinagawa 4F, 2–18–1 Konan, Minato-ku* ☎*03/6717–0922* ▭*AE, MC, V* Ⓜ*JR Shinagawa Station (Higashi-guchi/East Exit).*

$$–$$$ ✕**T. Y. Harbor Brewery** T.Y.ハーバーブルワリーレストラン. A converted
ECLECTIC   warehouse on the waterfront houses this restaurant, a Tōkyō hot spot
★   for private parties. Chef David Chiddo refined his signature California-Thai cuisine at some of the best restaurants in Los Angeles. Don't miss his grilled mahimahi with green rice and mango salsa, or the grilled jumbo-shrimp brochettes with tabbouleh. True to its name, T. Y. Harbor brews its own beer, in a tank that reaches all the way to the 46-foot-high ceiling. The best seats in the house are on the bay-side deck, open from May to October. Reservations are a good idea on weekends. ✉*2–1–3 Higashi-Shinagawa, Shinagawa-ku* ☎*03/5479–4555* ▭*AE, DC, MC, V* Ⓜ*Tōkyō Monorail or Rinkai Line, Ten-nōz Isle Station (Exit B).*

SHINJUKU 新宿

$$ ✕**Ben's Café** ベンズカフェ. This artsy café in the student town of Taka-
CAFÉS   danobaba, is one of the few locations in Tōkyō that serve a full-English breakfast, available weekends 11:30–3. ✉*1–29–21 Takadanobaba, Shinjuku-ku* ☎*03/3202–2445* ⌔*Reservations not accepted for brunch* ▭*No credit cards.*

$$ ✕**Happy Sakaba** ハッピー酒場. (Happy Sakaba or "Happy Tavern")
JAPANESE   re-creates the atmosphere of 1950s Tōkyō, with authentic advertisements from the era gracing the wooden walls, and simple, hearty food. The menu is constantly changing, and, rather than order à la carte, most locals order the set-course meals of sashimi, fried, and grilled dishes for ¥3,500 or ¥4,000 each, the more expensive option coming with a bit more meat. Both come with all-you-can drink beer, whiskey, or shōchū (alcohol made from barley, sweet potato, or rice), and the patrons of this lively establishment often stay until closing time, around

11 on weekdays and 3 AM on weekends. ⊠*B2 Kawano Bldg., 1–26–7 Kabuki-chō, Shinjuku-ku* ☎*03/3207–5653* ⊟*AE, MC, V* ⊘*No lunch* Ⓜ*Shinjuku Station (Higashi-guchi/East Exit).*

$$$$
JAPANESE
✕**Kushinobō** 串の坊. The lively action of the cooks frying *kushi-age* (skewered meat, fish, and vegetables) coupled with good-value lunch and dinner sets make Kushinobō popular with university students, office workers, and families. For the *omakase* dinner set, the chefs choose skewers that are in season and fry them in front of you—they keep 'em coming into you call uncle. There are more than 40 different meats, seafood, and vegetables to choose from, and they're served with traditional and original sauces. Round off your meal with a selection from the extensive list of sake and shōchū—these are not bottomless, however. ⊠*1–10–5 Kabuki-chō, Shinjuku-ku* ☎*03/3232–9744* ⊟*AE, MC, V* ⊘*Closed Sun.* Ⓜ*Shinjuku Station (Higashi-guchi/East Exit).*

SHIROKANEDAI 白金台

$$$$
JAPANESE
✕**Enju** 槐樹. Happō-en, a 300-year-old-Japanese garden wrapped around a lake, is the setting for the palatial complex that houses this upscale restaurant, a shrine, and a traditional teahouse. Beautiful scenery aside, the food is what draws locals and visitors again and again. The grand exterior and pristine banquet rooms are somewhat uninviting and overly formal, but the tables overlooking the garden are a tranquil backdrop for an unforgettable meal. Among the pricey prix-fixe dinners are kaiseki, shabu-shabu, sukiyaki, and tempura, and there's also a buffet dinner. Go in the afternoon for a tour of the grounds, *sadō* (tea ceremony), and a seasonal Japanese set lunch for ¥2,625 or ¥3,675. For more casual dinning, Café Thrush, in the same complex, has an open-air terrace with a stunning view of the garden. ⊠*1–1–1 Shirokanedai, Minato-ku* ☎*03/3443–3125* ⚫*Reservations essential* ⊟*AE, DC, MC, V* Ⓜ*Mita and Namboku subway lines, Shirokanedai Station (Exit 2).*

$$
SPANISH
✕**Sabado Sabadete** サバドサバデテ. Catalan jewelry designer Mañuel Benito used to rent a bar in Aoyama on Saturday nights and cook for his friends, just for the fun of it. Word got around: eventually there wasn't room in the bar to lift a fork. Inspired by this success, Benito opened this Spanish restaurant. The highlight of every evening is still the moment when the chef, in his bright red cap, shouts out "Gohan desu yo!"—the Japanese equivalent of "Soup's on!"—and dishes out his bubbling-hot paella. Don't miss the empanadas or the *escalivada* (Spanish ratatouille with red peppers, onions, and eggplant). ⊠*2F Genteel Shirokanedai Bldg., 5–3–2 Shirokanedai, Minato-ku* ☎*03/3445–9353* ⊟*No credit cards* ⊘*Closed Sun. and Mon.* Ⓜ*Mita and Namboku subway lines, Shirokanedai Station (Exit 1).*

SHŌTŌ 松濤

$$$$
FRENCH
✕**Chez Matsuo** シェ・松尾. With its stately homes, Shōtō, a sedate sort of Beverly Hills, is the kind of area you don't expect Tōkyō to have—at least not so close to Shibuya Station. In the middle of it all is Chez Matsuo, in a lovely two-story Western-style house. The dining rooms overlook the garden, where you can dine by candlelight on spring and

autumn evenings. Owner-chef Matsuo studied as a sommelier in London and perfected his culinary finesse in Paris. His pricey French food is nouvelle; among the specialties of the house are *suprême* (breast and wing) of duck, clam-and-tomato mousse, and a fish of the day. ⊠ *1–23–15 Shōtō, Shibuya-ku* ☎ *03/3485–0566* ≜ *Reservations essential* ⊟ *AE, DC, MC, V* Ⓜ *JR Yamanote Line, Ginza and Hanzō-mon subway lines, and private rail lines: Shibuya Station (Exits 5 and 8 for Hanzō-mon, Kita-guchi/North Exit for all others).*

TORA-NO-MON 虎ノ門

$$$–$$$$ ✕ **Toh-Ka-Lin** 桃花林. Business travelers consider the Ōkura to be one
CHINESE of the best hotels in Asia. That judgment has to do with its polish, its human scale, its impeccable standards of service, and, to judge by Toh-Ka-Lin, the quality of its restaurants. The style of the cuisine here is eclectic; two stellar examples are the Peking duck and the sautéed quail wrapped in lettuce leaf. The restaurant also has a not-too-expensive midafternoon meal ($$) of assorted dim sum and other delicacies—and one of the most extensive wine lists in town. ⊠ *Hotel Ōkura Main Bldg. 6F, 2–10–4 Tora-no-mon, Minato-ku* ☎ *03/3505–6068* ⊟ *AE, DC, MC, V* Ⓜ *Hibiya subway line, Kamiya-chō Station (Exit 4B); Ginza subway line, Tora-no-mon Station (Exit 3).*

TSUKIJI 築地

$$–$$$ ✕ **Edo-Gin** 江戸銀. In an area that teems with sushi bars, this one main-
SUSHI tains its reputation as one of the best. Edo-Gin serves generous slabs of
★ fish that drape over the vinegared rice rather than perch demurely on top. The centerpiece of the main room is a huge tank where the day's ingredients swim about until they are required; it doesn't get any fresher than this. Set menus here are reasonable, especially for lunch, but a big appetite for specialties like sea urchin and *ōtoro* tuna can put a dent in your budget. ⊠ *4–5–1 Tsukiji, Chūo-ku* ☎ *03/3543–4401* ⊟ *AE, DC, MC, V* ⊗ *Closed Sun. and Jan. 1–4* Ⓜ *Hibiya subway line, Tsukiji Station (Exit 1); Ōedo subway line, Tsukiji-shijō Station (Exit A1).*

¢–$ ✕ **Takeno** たけの. Just a stone's throw from the Tōkyō fish market, Tak-
JAPANESE eno is a rough-cut neighborhood restaurant that tends to fill up at noon with the market's wholesalers and auctioneers and personnel from the nearby Asahi newspaper offices. There's nothing here but the freshest and the best—big portions of it, at very reasonable prices. Sushi and sashimi are the staples, but there's also a wonderful *tendon* bowl, with shrimp and eel tempura on rice. Prices are not posted because they vary with the costs that morning in the market. ■ TIP➔ **Reservations can only be made for large parties, or if you plan to dine before 6:30** PM. ⊠ *6–21–2 Tsukiji, Chūo-ku* ☎ *03/3541–8698* ⊟ *No credit cards* ⊗ *Closed Sun.* Ⓜ *Hibiya subway line, Tsukiji Station (Exit 1); Ōedo subway line, Tsukiji-shijō Station (Exit A1).*

CLOSE UP

The Iron Chef's Tōkyō

You never know where you'll find Masaharu Morimoto, known to millions of Americans as "Iron Chef Japan." When he's not filming television episodes for Food Network's popular *Iron Chef America*, Morimoto divides his time between his restaurants in Tōkyō, New York, Philadelphia, and Mumbai.

The time zone–traversing culinary master was born and raised in Hiroshima, Japan, where he learned the art of sushi and kaiseki (traditional Japanese haute cuisine) by training under several of his country's esteemed master chefs. After running his own restaurant in Japan for several years, he moved to New York City to explore Western cooking styles.

In 2001, he opened his first Morimoto restaurant in Philadelphia, combining Japanese and Western ingredients and preparations. In 2005, Morimoto XEX opened in Tōkyō, and in January 2006, Morimoto brought his eponymous restaurant to New York City.

Here, Morimoto shares his Tōkyō picks for where to eat, stay, and play.

Fodor's: Tell me about your restaurant in Tōkyō, Morimoto XEX.

MM: It opened in 2005 in the Roppongi Hills district. It has been changing a lot. Recently the Tōkyō Midtown project opened, and new hotels in Roppongi Hills. There are a lot of foreigners there—a lot of Americans and Europeans.

I'd say about 50% or more of my customers there are foreigners. I like to do business with Americans and Europeans. Morimoto XEX is a beautiful restaurant. It's spread over three floors. One is sushi, one is teppanyaki, and one is a lounge.

Fodor's: Are there any places you like to go out in Roppongi?

MM: I work at my restaurant late. It's open until 2 AM, and the places open are limited then. I go to karaoke and izakaya (bars with Japanese tapas). I go all over Roppongi and try different places for karaoke. For izakaya, you can go anywhere in Roppongi. They have sake and beer, and Japanese snacks like kushiyaki (grilled meat or vegetable skewers) and hiyayakko (chilled tofu with savory toppings).

Fodor's: Are there any hotels or spas you'd recommend there?

MM: I recommend the Grand Hyatt Tōkyō at Roppongi Hills. Most of the people, maybe 75%, are foreigners, and a lot of Americans. You can stay in any hotel in Tōkyō and find English speakers. At Grand Hyatt, they have a spa called Nagomi Spa & Fitness. I hear that it's nice.

Fodor's: If someone has only a day or two to explore Tōkyō, where should they go?

You have to go to Tsukiji, the fish market in the early morning and try the food from the stalls in the Tsukiji market. There are a lot of small restaurants there.

Also, try the taxi cabs. The drivers wear white hats and gloves. When you get in, the doors open and shut automatically. Most of the drivers can't speak English, so it will be an adventure. After that, you should come to Morimoto XEX for dinner. We don't do lunch, but you can come for a cocktail or have a wonderful dinner.

—Erica Duecy

2

UCHISAIWAI-CHŌ 内幸町

$$–$$$$ ✕**Heichinrou** 聘珍楼. A short walk from the Imperial Hotel, this branch
CHINESE of one of Yokohama's oldest and best Chinese restaurants commands a
★ spectacular view of the Imperial Palace grounds. Call ahead to reserve a
table by the window. The cuisine is Cantonese; pride of place goes to the
kaisen ryōri, a banquet of steamed sea bass, lobster, shrimp, scallops,
abalone, and other seafood dishes. Much of the clientele comes from
the law offices, securities firms, and foreign banks in the building. The
VIP room at Heichinrou, with its soft lighting and impeccable linens,
is a popular venue for power lunches. ⊠*28F Fukoku Seimei Bldg.,
2–2–2 Uchisaiwai-chō, Chiyoda-ku* ☎*03/3508–0555* ▤*AE, DC, MC,
V* ⊗*Closed Sun.* Ⓜ*Mita Line, Uchisaiwai-chō Station (Exit A6).*

UENO 上野

$$$$ ✕**Sasa-no-yuki** 笹の雪. In the heart of one of Tōkyō's old working-class
JAPANESE *shitamachi* (downtown) neighborhoods, Sasa-no-yuki has been serv-
ing meals based on homemade tofu for the past 315 years. The food is
inspired in part by shōjin ryōri (Buddhist vegetarian cuisine). The basic
three-course set menu includes *ankake* (bean curd in sweet soy sauce),
uzumi tofu (scrambled with rice and green tea), and *unsui* (a creamy
tofu crepe filled with sea scallops, shrimp, and minced red pepper).
For bigger appetites, there's also an eight-course banquet. There's both
tatami and table seating, and the dining room includes a view of the
Japanese garden complete with waterfall. ⊠*2–15–10 Negishi, Taitō-
ku* ☎*03/3873–1145* ▤*AE, DC, V* ⊗*Closed Mon.* Ⓜ*JR Uguisudani
Station (Kita-guchi/North Exit).*

YŪRAKU-CHŌ 有楽町

$$–$$$ ✕**Robata** 炉端. Old, funky, and more than a little cramped, Robata is
JAPANESE a bit daunting at first. But fourth-generation chef-owner Takao Inoue
Fodor'sChoice holds forth here with an inspired version of Japanese home cooking.
★ He's also a connoisseur of pottery; he serves his food on pieces acquired
at famous kilns all over the country. There's no menu; just tell Inoue-san
(who speaks some English) how much you want to spend, and leave
the rest to him. A meal at Robata—like the pottery—is simple to the
eye but subtle and fulfilling. Typical dishes include steamed fish with
vegetables, stews of beef or pork, and seafood salads. ⊠*1–3–8 Yūraku-
chō, Chiyoda-ku* ☎*03/3591–1905* ▤*No credit cards* ⊗*Closed some
Sun. each month. No lunch* Ⓜ*JR Yūraku-chō Station (Hibiya Exit);
Hibiya, Chiyoda, and Mita subway lines, Hibiya Station (Exit A4).*

$$ ✕**Shin Hinomoto** 新日の基. This izakaya is located directly under the
JAPANESE tracks of the Yamanote line, making the wooden interior shutter each
time a train passes overhead. It's a favorite with local and foreign journalists, as the Foreign Correspondents Club is just across the street,
and is actually run by a Brit, who travels down the road to Tsukiji
market every morning to buy seafood. Don't miss the fresh sashimi and
buttered scallops. ⊠*2–4–4 Yurakucho, Chiyoda-ku* ☎*03/3214 8021*
▤*No credit cards.*

WHERE TO STAY

When land prices plummeted following the collapse of the asset-inflated "bubble" economy of the late '90s, Tōkyō's developers seized the chance to construct centrally located skyscrapers. Oftentimes hotels from international brands were installed on the upper floors of these glimmering towers. This boom has complemented the spare-no-expense approach taken by many of the domestic hoteliers a decade earlier, when soaring atriums, elaborate concierge floors, and oceans of marble were all the rage. The result: Tōkyō's present luxury accommodations rival those of any big city in the world.

KNOW BEFORE YOU GO

Some useful words when checking into a hotel:

air-conditioning: *eakon*

double beds: *daburu-beddo*

king bed: *kingu saizu-no-beddo*

private baths: *o-furo*

pushed together: *kuttsukete*

queen bed: *kuīn saizu-no-beddo*

separate beds: *betsu*

showers: *shawū*

twin beds: *tsuin-heddo*

With hoteliers banking on research that says most visitors will pay well to be pampered, it begs the question: "Are there bargains to be had?" In some cases, yes, but you'll have to do your homework. Lower profile business and boutique hotels are decent bets for singles or couples who do not need a lot of space, and, in addition to hostels, exchanges, and rentals (apartments and homes), the budget-conscious traveler can utilize plenty of Japanese accommodations: *ryokan, minshuku,* "capsule" hotels, homes, and temples.

WHAT TO EXPECT

There are three things you can take for granted almost anywhere you set down your bags in Tōkyō: cleanliness, safety, and good service. Unless otherwise specified, all rooms at the hotels listed in this book have private baths and are Western-style. In listings, we always name the facilities that are available, but we don't specify whether they cost extra. When pricing accommodations, try to find out what's included and what entails an additional charge.

Assume that hotels operate on the European Plan (EP, with no meals) unless we specify that they use the Continental Plan (CP, with a Continental breakfast), Breakfast Plan (BP, with a full breakfast), Modified American Plan (MAP, with breakfast and dinner), or the Full American Plan (FAP, with all meals).

PRICES

Deluxe hotels charge a premium for good-size rooms, lots of perks, great service, and central locations. More-affordable hotels that cost less—though not *that* much less—aren't always in the most convenient places, and have disproportionately small rooms as well as fewer amenities. That said, a less-than-ideal location should be the least of your concerns. Many moderately priced accommodations are still within the central wards; some have an old-fashioned charm and personal touch the upscale places can't offer. And, wherever you're staying, Tōkyō's subway and train system—comfortable (except in rush hours), efficient, inexpensive, and safe—will get you back and forth.

WHAT IT COSTS IN YEN				
	¢	$	$$	$$$	$$$$
FOR TWO PEOPLE	under ¥10,000	¥10,000– ¥20,000	¥20,000– ¥30,000	¥30,000– ¥40,000	over ¥40,000

Price categories are assigned based on the range between the least and most expensive standard double rooms in nonholiday high season. Taxes (5%, plus 3% for bills over ¥15,000) are extra.

RESERVATIONS

The Japanese Inn Group is a nationwide association of small ryokan and family-owned tourist hotels. Because they tend to be slightly out of the way and provide few amenities, these accommodations are priced to attract budget-minded travelers. The association has the active support of JNTO.

The JNTO Tourist Information Center publishes a listing of some 700 reasonably priced accommodations in Tōkyō and throughout Japan. To be listed, properties must meet Japanese fire codes and charge less than ¥8,000 (about $76) per person without meals. For the most part, the properties charge ¥5,000–¥6,000 ($48–$57). These properties welcome foreigners. Properties include business hotels, ryokan of a very rudimentary nature, and minshuku. It's the luck of the draw whether you choose a good or less-than-good property. In most cases rooms are clean but very small. Except in business hotels, shared baths are the norm, and you are expected to have your room lights out by 10 PM. The JNTO's downtown Tōkyō office is open daily 9 to 5.

The nonprofit Welcome Inn Reservation Center can help you reserve many of the establishments on JNTO's list—and many that are not. Reservation forms are available from the JNTO office. The center must receive reservation requests at least one week before your departure to allow processing time. ■TIP→ **If you are already in Tōkyō, JNTO's Tourist Information Centers (TICs) at Narita Airport, Kansai International Airport, and downtown can make immediate reservations for you.**

Contacts Japanese Inn Group (🕾 *03/3252-1717* ⊕ *www.jpinn.com*). **JNTO Tourist Information Center** (🕾 *03/3201-3331* ⊕ *www.jnto.go.jp*). **Welcome Inn Reservation Center** (🕾 *03/6902-5081* ⊕ *www.itcj.or.jp*).

Japan Travel Agents Nippon Travel Agency (⊕ *www.nta.co.jp/english/index.htm* 🕾 *310/768-0017 in U.S.*). **JTB Sunrise Tours** (🕾 *03/5796-5454* ⊕ *www.jtbusa.com*). **IACE Travel** (🕾 *800/872-4223*).

Online Accommodations Budget Japan Hotels (⊕ *www.budgetjapanhotels.com*). **Japan Hotel.net** (⊕ *www.japanhotel.net*). **J-Reserve** (⊕ *www.j-reserve.com*). **Rakuten Travel** (⊕ *travel.rakuten.co.jp/en*).

BEST BETS FOR TŌKYŌ LODGING

Fodor's offers a selective listing of quality lodging experiences in every price range, from Tōkyō's best budget beds to its most sophisticated luxury hotels. Here, we've compiled our top recommendations by price and experience. The very best properties—in other words, those that provide a particularly remarkable experience in their price range—are designated in the listings with the Fodor's Choice logo.

Fodor'sChoice★

Claska, p. 124
Granbell Hotel Shibuya, p. 131
Park Hotel Tōkyō, p. 134
Park Hyatt Tōkyō, p. 127
The Peninsula Tōkyō, p. 122
Ryokan Mikawaya Honten, p. 117
Sumishō Hotel, p. 125

Best by Price

¢

Capsule Inn Akasaka, p. 116
Ryokan Mikawaya Honten, p. 117
Sawanoya Ryokan, p. 135
Green Plaza Shinjuku, p. 123

$

Asia Center of Japan, p. 129
Sumishō Hotel, p. 125
Ryokan Asakusa Shigetsu, p. 117
Claska, p. 124

$$

Park Hotel Tōkyō, p. 134
Granbell Hotel Shibuya, p. 131
Ginza Yoshimizu, p. 120

$$$

Hotel Century Southern Tower, p. 126
ANA InterContinental Tōkyō, p. 134

$$$$

Four Seasons Hotel Chinzan-sō, p. 130
Park Hyatt Tōkyō, p. 127
Mandarin Oriental, p. 125

Westin Tōkyō, p. 120
Grand Hyatt Tōkyō at Roppongi Hills, p. 129

Best by Experience

BEST CONCIERGE

Mandarin Oriental, p. 125
Cerulean Tower Tōkyu Hotel, p. 131
Westin Tōkyō, p. 120
Hotel Seiyō Ginza, p. 121
Asakusa View Hotel, p. 117

BEST HOTEL BARS

Grand Hyatt Tōkyō at Roppongi Hills, p. 129
The Ritz-Carlton, p. 130
Park Hyatt Tōkyō, p. 127
Conrad Tōkyō, p. 133
Granbell Hotel Shibuya, p. 131

MOST KID-FRIENDLY

Prince Hotel Shinagawa, p. 133
Asakusa View Hotel, p. 117

BEST FOR ROMANCE

Park Hyatt Tōkyō, p. 127
Four Seasons Hotel Chinzan-sō, p. 130
Grand Pacific Le Daiba, p. 120
The Ritz-Carlton, p. 130
Hotel Nikkō Tōkyō, p. 128

BEST LOCATION

Shibuya Excel Hotel Tōkyu, p. 132
Granbell Hotel Shibuya, p. 131
Royal Park Hotel, p. 121
Marunouchi Hotel, p. 124
Four Seasons Hotel Tōkyō at Marunouchi, p. 123

BEST-KEPT SECRETS

Hotel Century Southern Tower, p. 126
Claska, p. 124
The Strings by Inter-Continental Tōkyō, p. 133
Park Hotel Tōkyō, p. 134
Sumishō Hotel, p. 125

AKASAKA-MITSUKE 赤坂見附

¢ 🖭**Capsule Inn Akasaka** かぷせるイン赤坂. The Capsule Inn is a good option if you're shaking off a few drinks once the trains stop running. After changing out of your clothes (for which lockers are provided), bathing in the communal bath, and donning your yukata, you locate your accommodation, which will be one of the chambers stacked on each floor in a manner not too dissimilar from a morgue. Crawl inside the 3-foot-wide opening, lie down, stretch out (as much as the 6-foot-plus length will allow), and the next thing you know it'll be morning. Each capsule has a TV and a radio. The seventh floor has a lounge with beer, snacks, and reclining chairs from which to view a TV. **Pros:** reservations made via the Internet get a ¥500 discount; convenient location; unique experience. **Cons:** small sleeping spaces; few services; women are not allowed. ✉6–14–1 Akasaka, Minato-ku ☎03/3588–1811 ⊕www. toto-motors.co.jp/marroad/capsule ➴201 capsules ⚭In-room: no phone. In-hotel: Japanese baths, laundry facilities ☐DC, V Ⓜ Chiyoda subway line, Akasaka Station (Exit 6).

$$$–$$$$ 🖭**Grand Prince Hotel Akasaka** グランドプリンスホテル赤坂. Designed by world-renowned architect Kenzō Tange, the V-shaped Grand Prince creates a spaceship feel not too dissimilar to that of its cousin, the Shinjuku Park Tower building, which houses the Park Hyatt. Rooms from the 20th to the 30th floor offer the best views of the city, especially at night. A white-and-pale-gray color scheme accentuates the light from the wide windows that run the length of the rooms. This affords a feeling of spaciousness, though the rooms—oddly shaped because of Tange's attempt to give every accommodation a "corner" location—are a bit small compared to those in other deluxe hotels. The Tatami Suite, featuring traditional Japanese furnishings, is available for around ¥100,000. **Pros:** wonderful architecture; convenient location; salon on the premise. **Cons:** small rooms; in-room decor is a tad dated. ✉1–2 Kioi-chō, Chiyoda-ku ☎03/3234–1111 ⊕www.princehotels. co.jp/akasaka ➴693 rooms, 68 suites ⚭In-room: refrigerator, Internet. In-hotel: 8 restaurants, room service, bars, pool, laundry service, no-smoking rooms ☐AE, DC, MC, V Ⓜ Ginza and Marunouchi subway lines, Akasaka-mitsuke Station (Exit 7).

$$$–$$$$ 🖭**Hotel New Ōtani Tōkyō** ホテルニューオータニ. Opened in 1964 just prior to the Olympics and used as a setting for the 1967 James Bond film *You Only Live Twice*, the New Ōtani is a bustling complex in the center of Tōkyō. The traffic in the restaurants and shopping arcades beneath the sixth-floor lobby gives the impression of rush hour at a busy railway station. The hotel's main redeeming feature is its spectacular 10-acre Japanese garden, complete with a pond and a red-lacquer bridge. The rooms in the main building are in pleasant pastels, but they lack the outstanding views of those in the Tower, many of which overlook the garden's ponds and waterfalls. Among the many restaurants and bars is La Tour d'Argent (the only branch outside of France), Japan's first Trader Vic's, and The Bar, housed within a revolving lounge on the 40th floor that offers supreme city views. **Pros:** beautiful garden; first-rate concierge; convenient location. **Cons:** complex layout; old hotel with modern prices. ✉4–1 Kioi-chō, Chiyoda-ku ☎03/3265–1111 ⊕www.

newotani.co.jp ⟲*1,506 rooms, 27 suites* ♿*In-room: safe, refrigerator, Internet. In-hotel: 34 restaurants, room service, bars, pool, gym, laundry service, no-smoking rooms* ▤*AE, DC, MC, V* Ⓜ*Ginza and Marunouchi subway lines, Akasaka-mitsuke Station (Exit 7).*

ASAKUSA 浅草

$$–$$$ 🏨**Asakusa View Hotel** 浅草ビューホテル. Upscale Western-style accommodations are rare in Asakusa, so the Asakusa View pretty much has this end of the market to itself. Off the marble lobby, a harpist plays in the tea lounge. The communal *hinoki* (Japanese-cypress) baths on the sixth floor overlook a Japanese garden. The best of the Western-style rooms are on the 22nd and 23rd floors, with a view of the Sensō-ji pagoda and temple grounds. There's a karaoke room in the basement and the hotel's a three-minute walk from the retro amusement park, Hanayashiki; more than 100 years old, its rides have that Coney Island feel to them. **Pros:** friendly staff; affordable; located in a historic temple area. **Cons:** room interiors are generally basic; not near central Tōkyō. ✉*3–17–1 Nishi-Asakusa, Taito-ku* ☎*03/3847-1111* ⊕*www.viewhotels.co.jp/asakusa* ⟲*330 Western-style rooms, 7 Japanese-style suites* ♿*In-hotel: 4 restaurants, bars, pool, gym, Japanese baths, no-smoking rooms* ▤*AE, DC, MC, V* Ⓜ*Ginza subway line, Tawara-machi Station (Exit 3).*

$ 🏨**Ryokan Asakusa Shigetsu** 旅館浅草 指月. Just off Nakamise-dōri and ★ inside the Sensō-ji grounds, this small inn could not be better located for a visit to the temple. The best options are the rooms with futon bedding and tatami floors, though they can be cramped for more than two people; the Western rooms, plain but comfortably furnished, are less expensive. All rooms have private baths; there's also a Japanese-style wooden communal bath on the sixth floor with a view of the Sensō-ji pagoda. **Pros:** affordable rooms; located in a historic temple area; close to subway station. **Cons:** futons and tatami might not be suitable for those accustomed to Western-style beds; not convenient to central Tōkyō. ✉*1–31–11 Asakusa, Taitō-ku* ☎*03/3843-2345* ⊕*www.shigetsu.com/e/index.html* ⟲*8 Western-style rooms, 15 Japanese-style rooms* ♿*In-room: Internet. In-hotel: restaurant, Internet terminal, Japanese baths* ▤*AE, MC, V* Ⓜ*Ginza subway line, Asakusa Station (Exit 1/Kaminari-mon Exit).*

¢ 🏨**Ryokan Mikawaya Honten** 旅館三河屋本店. In the heart of Asakusa, **Fodor's Choice** this concrete ryokan's just behind the Kaminari-mon, the gateway lead- ★ ing to the Sensō-ji complex. Nearby are the Nakamise souvenir market and the Kappabashi restaurant-supply street, two popular tourist spots. The Japanese-style rooms are small for two people and lack sizable storage areas, but are very clean. Though English-challenged, the staff's attentive and very friendly. **Pros:** affordable accommodations; traditional Japanese experience; interesting shopping in the area. **Cons:** futons and tatami might not be suitable for those accustomed to Western-style beds; small rooms; staff is English-challenged. ✉*1–30–12 Asakusa, Taitō-ku* ☎*03/3844-8807* ⟲*19 Japanese-style rooms, 1 Western-style room* ▤*AE, MC, V* Ⓜ*Ginza subway line, Asakusa Station (Exit 1/ Kaminari-mon Exit).*

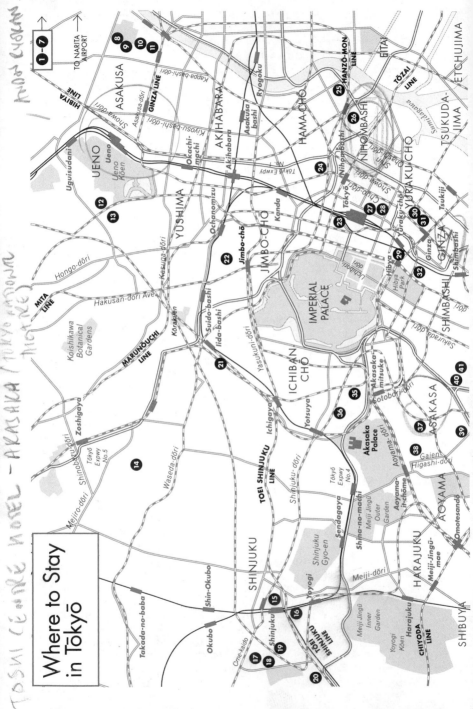

Where to Stay in Tōkyō

TOSHI CENTRE HOTEL — AKASAKA (TOKYO JMDOWN HOTEL) AKASAKA EVORAN

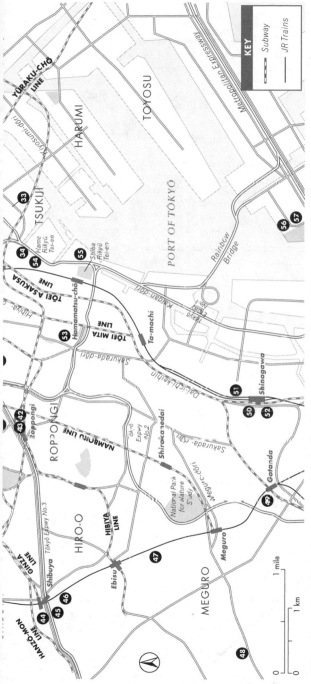

KEY

---- Subway
—— JR Trains

EBISU 恵比寿

$$$$ ⊡**Westin Tōkyō** ウェスティンホテル東京. In the Yebisu Garden Place development, the Westin provides easy access to Mitsukoshi department store, the Tōkyō Metropolitan Museum of Photography, the elegant Ebisu Garden concert hall, and the award-winning Taillevent-Robuchon restaurant (in a full-scale reproduction of a Louis XV château). The style of the hotel is updated art nouveau, with an excess of marble and bronze. The rooms are spacious—with bathrooms large enough to accommodate families—and the suites are huge by Japanese standards. The beds are the chain's famous "Heavenly Beds," which feature a special padded coil system to ensure a good night's rest. **Pros:** beds really are heavenly; large rooms; great concierge. **Cons:** pricey; Internet requires a fee. ⊠*1–4 Mita 1-chōme, Meguro-ku* ☎*03/5423–7000* ⊕*www.westin-tokyo.co.jp* ⇡*438 rooms, 22 suites* ⟐*In-room: safe, DVD, refrigerator, Internet. In-hotel: 6 restaurants, room service, bars, gym, laundry service, no-smoking rooms* ⊟*AE, DC, MC, V* Ⓜ*JR, Hibiya subway line; Ebisu Station (Higashi-guchi/East Exit).*

GINZA 銀座

$$–$$$ ⊡**Courtyard Tōkyō Ginza** コートヤード東京銀座. Recently acquired by Marriott, this hotel offers relatively reasonable prices, friendly service, and comfortable rooms, making it a good choice for the Ginza area. Though standard rooms, renovated in 2007, are small (the bathrooms are, too), they have dark-wood furniture and elegant linens covering fat mattresses. The Premium Rose rooms, located on the upper floors, are much more spacious. Restaurant options are few, but numerous trendy and traditional dining choices are just outside the front doors, including the Tsukiji fish market. **Pros:** many shopping options nearby; reasonable prices considering the area. **Cons:** small rooms; room furnishings are basic. ⊠*6–14–10 Ginza, Chūō-ku* ☎*03/3546–0111* ⊕*www.marriott.com* ⇡*197 rooms, 9 suites* ⟐*In-room: refrigerator, Internet. In-hotel: 3 restaurants, room service, bar, laundry service, no-smoking rooms* ⊟*AE, DC, MC, V* ⦿*CP* Ⓜ*Hibiya and Asakusa subway lines, Higashi-Ginza Station (Exit A1).*

$$ ⊡ **Ginza Yoshimizu** 銀座吉水. You're expected to fold up your own futon
★   at this modest traditional inn, which was inspired by owner Yoshimi Nakagawa's experience living the simple life at a commune in Woodstock, New York, in the 1970s. The money that isn't spent on service has been spent—with exquisite taste—on simple, natural appointments: wooden floors dyed pale indigo, hand-painted shōji screens, basins of Shigaraki ware in the washrooms. The two stone communal Japanese baths on the ninth floor can be reserved for a private relaxing soak for two. The inn is a few minutes' walk from the Kabuki-za and the fashionable heart of Ginza. Book early. **Pros:** many shopping options nearby; central location; opportunity to have the traditional ryokan experience. **Cons:** often fully booked; futon and tatami might not suit

2

everyone. ✉ *3–11–3 Ginza, Chūō-ku* ☎ *03/3248–4432* ⊕ *www.yoshi mizu.com* 🛏 *11 Japanese-style rooms without bath* ♿ *In-room: no phone, no TV. In-hotel: restaurant, Japanese baths, no-smoking rooms* 🍴 *AE, DC, MC, V* 🍴|*BP* Ⓜ *Hibiya subway line, Higashi-Ginza Station (Exit 3 or A2).*

$$ 🏨 **Hotel Monterey Ginza** ホテルモントレー銀座. With a somewhat cheesy, faux-stone exterior that attempts to replicate 20th-century Europe, the Monterey's a bargain in the middle of Ginza. The rooms are a tad small, but, in keeping with the theme, are outfitted with dark-wood floors, powder-white linens, and curtains tied with tassels. Flat-panel televisions and heated toilet seats are some of the few contemporary touches. The Escale restaurant is French—what else?—but all of this European stylishness isn't just for the guests; the in-house wedding chapel is busy on weekends and holidays. **Pros:** multiple shopping choices in area; central location; reasonable prices considering the area. **Cons:** rooms are a tad small; in-hotel dining options are limited. ✉ *1–10–18 Ginza, Chūō-ku* ☎ *03/3562–0111* ⊕ *www.hotelmonterey.co.jp* 🛏 *224 rooms* ♿ *In-room: refrigerator, Internet. In-hotel: 2 restaurants, room service, bar, laundry service, no-smoking rooms* 🍴 *AE, DC, MC, V* 🍴|*CP* Ⓜ *Ginza subway line, Ginza Station (Exit A13).*

$$$$ 🏨 **Hotel Seiyō Ginza** ホテル西洋銀座. The grand marble staircase, the profusion of cut flowers, the reception staff in coats and tails: all combine to create an atmosphere more like an elegant private club than a hotel. Along with this elegance, location and personalized service are the best reasons to choose the exclusive Seiyō, tucked away on a side street a few minutes from Ginza. Individually decorated rooms have walk-in closets, huge shower stalls, and a direct line to a personal secretary who takes care of your every need. The accommodations, however, are smaller than what you might expect considering the hefty room charges. **Pros:** nice lobby; many shopping options nearby; helpful staff. **Cons:** pricey; small rooms; location near a massive expressway gives the area an unappealing look. ✉ *1–11–2 Ginza, Chūō-ku* ☎ *03/3535–1111* ⊕ *www.rosewoodhotels.com* 🛏 *51 rooms, 26 suites* ♿ *In-room: safe, DVD, refrigerator, Internet. In-hotel: 3 restaurants, room service, bars, gym, laundry service, no-smoking rooms* 🍴 *AE, DC, MC, V* Ⓜ *Ginza subway line, Kyō-bashi Station (Exit 2); Yūraku-chō Line, Ginza-Itchōme Station (Exit 7).*

HAKOZAKI 箱崎

$$$–$$$$ 🏨 **Royal Park Hotel** ロイヤルパークホテル. A passageway connects this hotel to the Tōkyō City Air Terminal, where you can easily catch a bus to Narita Airport, making the Royal Park a great one-night stopover point. Guests are greeted by the comfortable, spacious, marble-clad lobby decked out in wood-panel columns, and silver-and-gold chandelier. Neutral grays and browns decorate the well-proportioned rooms. The best rooms are those on the recently renovated Executive Floors (12–14) with a view of the Sumida River, and those on floors 6–8

overlooking the hotel's delightful Japanese garden. Guests on these floors are also entitled to complimentary breakfast and evening cocktails. **Pros:** convenient airport access; nice lobby; good service. **Cons:** not located near downtown; in-room safes are not standard. ✉*2–1–1 Nihombashi, Kakigara-chō, Chūō-ku* ☎*03/3667–1111* ⊕*www.rph. co.jp* ✈*450 rooms, 9 suites* ♿*In-room: refrigerator, Internet. In-hotel: 7 restaurants, room service, bars, laundry service, no-smoking rooms* ☰*AE, DC, MC, V* Ⓜ*Hanzō-mon subway line, Suitengū-mae Station (Exit 4).*

HIBIYA 日比谷

$$$–$$$$ 🏨**Imperial Hotel** 帝国ホテル. Though not as fashionable or spanking new as its neighbor, the Peninsula, the venerable Imperial can't be beat for traditional elegance. In the heart of central Tōkyō, between the Imperial Palace and Ginza, the hotel has its finest rooms on the 30th floor of the tower, providing views of the palace grounds. The Old Imperial Bar incorporates elements from the 1923 version of the hotel, which Frank Lloyd Wright designed. The Imperial opened its doors in 1890, and from the outset the hotel has been justly proud of its Western-style facilities and personalized Japanese service. Rooms, complete with walk-in closets and flat-panel TVs, range from standard doubles to suites that are larger than many homes. Dining options are varied and superb, including the award-winning Les Saisons, which is one of Tōkyō's finest French restaurants. **Pros:** this is an old Japanese hotel with a long history; great service; large rooms; there's a salon and barbershop on the premise. **Cons:** old hotel with contemporary prices; dated interiors. ✉*1–1–1 Uchisaiwai-chō, Chiyoda-ku* ☎*03/3504–1111* ⊕*www.imperial hotel.co.jp* ✈*1,005 rooms, 54 suites* ♿*In-room: Internet. In-hotel: 13 restaurants, bars, pool, gym, no-smoking rooms* ☰*AE, DC, MC, V* Ⓜ*Hibiya subway line, Hibiya Station (Exit 5).*

$$$$ 🏨 **The Peninsula Tōkyō** ザ・ペニンシュラ東京. From the staff in caps and
Fodor'sChoice   sharp suits, often assisting guests from a Rolls-Royce shuttling to and
★   from Narita, to the shimmering gold glow emitting from the top floors, the 24-floor Peninsula Tōkyō exudes elegance and grace. The rooms feature red-lacquered elm desks, portable phones that can serve as your mobile throughout the city, and flat-screen TVs in the bathroom, which feature separate soaking tubs. Bedside panels with remote controls allow you to tweak the room's ambience from the comfort of your bed. Tall windows afford pleasant views of the downtown financial district. The view from the top-floor lounge and Peter, which offers European cuisine, make them well worth a visit. For those seeking a *kaiseki*-style tasting menu, there's Kyoto Tsuruya, which serves dishes that change with the seasons. Access to Hibiya Park, one of Tōkyō's nicest green spaces, and the upscale shopping of Ginza are within walking distance. **Pros:** first-class room interiors; wonderful spa; great service. **Cons:** high prices; breakfast options are limited. ✉*1–8–1 Yuraku-chō, Chiyoda-ku* ☎*03/6270-2888* ⊕*www.peninsula.com* ✈*267 rooms, 47 suites* ♿*In-room: safe, refrigerator, DVD, Wi-Fi. In-hotel: 3 restaurants, room service, bars, pool, spa, laundry service, no-smoking rooms* ☰*AE, DC, MC, V* Ⓜ*JR Yamanote Line, Yuraku-chō station*

(Hibiya-guchi/Hibiya Exit), Mita, Chiyoda, and Hibiya subway lines, Hibiya station (Exits A6 and A7).

HIGASHI-GOTANDA 東五反田

¢ 🏨**Ryokan Sansuisō** 山水荘. Budgeteers appreciate this basic ryokan, a two-story building near Gotanda Station and the Meguro River, where *sakura* (cherry) trees bloom each April. The proprietor will greet you with a warm smile and a bow and escort you to a small tatami room with a pay TV, a yukata, a Japanese tea set, and a rather noisy heater–air-conditioner mounted on the wall. Some rooms are stuffy, and only two have private baths, but the Sansuisō is clean, easy to find, and only 20 minutes by train from Tōkyō Station or Ginza. Multiple high-rises have recently cast a shadow over this inn (and make it a little more difficult to find), but you won't be staying here for the scenery. Since it's part of the Japanese Inn Group, the Japan National Tourist Organization (JNTO) can help you make reservations. **Pros:** affordable rooms; friendly staff. **Cons:** small accommodations; limited services; most rooms do not have an in-room bath. ✉*2–9–5 Higashi-Gotanda, Shinagawa-ku* ☎*03/3441–7475, 03/3201–3331 for JNTO* ⊕*www.sansuiso.net* ⤢*10 rooms, 2 with bath* ♿*In-hotel: Japanese baths* ▤*AE, V* Ⓜ*Asakusa subway line (Exit A3) and JR Yamanote Line (Higashi-guchi/East Exit), Gotanda Station.*

HIGASHI-SHINJUKU 東新宿

¢ 🏨**Green Plaza Shinjuku** グリーンプラザ新宿. Male budget travelers in
★ Shinjuku willing to throw claustrophobia to the wind can settle in for a night at the Green Plaza, a capsule hotel in the entertainment district of Kabuki-cho. (As with most capsule hotels, there are no accommodations for women.) Like bees in a honeycomb, patrons sleep in yellow capsules stacked in rows along the halls of each floor. Korean-style massage (on the fifth floor) is an added option not common in the capsule world. Vending machines on three floors dispense drinks, soup, and snacks. Underwear, slacks, and neckties are available for emergency purchases. The environment isn't tranquil, but it's clean, safe, and cheap. **Pros:** if you want to try a capsule hotel this is the place to do it as it's fairly priced; convenient location; public bath area offers mineral baths and saunas. **Cons:** small and limited accommodations; noisy neighborhood. ✉*1–29–3 Kabuki-chō, Shinjuku-ku* ☎*03/3207–4923* ⊕*www.hgpshinjuku.jp* ⤢*660 capsules without bath* ♿*In-room: no phone. In-hotel: restaurant, laundry service* ▤*AE, MC, V* Ⓜ*Shinjuku Station (Higashi-guchi/East Exit).*

MARUNOUCHI 丸の内

$$$$ 🏨**Four Seasons Hotel Tōkyō at Marunouchi** フォーシーズンズホテル丸の内東京. A departure from the typical large scale of most properties in the chain, this Four Seasons, set within the glistening Pacific Century Place, has the feel of a boutique hotel. The muted beige-and-bronze reception area resembles a comfortable private club, with deep-pile carpets,

plush brocade sofas, and sumptuous armchairs. Chic black-lacquer doors lead to spacious guest rooms, which actually occupy the five floors below the seventh-floor reception area. Beds have brown-leather-covered headboards that continue partway across the ceiling for a canopy effect. Design really *matters* here—but so does high-tech luxury, in touches like 42-inch plasma-screen TVs and variable lighting. **Pros:** convenient airport access; central location; helpful, English-speaking staff. **Cons:** highly priced; the only views are those of nearby Tōkyo Station, but such proximity makes catching the Narita Express a snap; in-room safe not large enough for laptop. ⊠*1–11–1 Marunouchi, Chiyoda-ku* ☎*03/5222–7222* ⊕*www. fourseasons.com/marunouchi* ⌷*48 rooms, 9 suites* ⌂*In-room: safe, refrigerator, DVD, Wi-Fi. In-hotel: restaurant, room service, bar, gym, spa, Japanese baths, laundry service, no-smoking rooms* ▤*AE, DC, MC, V* Ⓜ*JR Tōkyō Station (Yaesu South Exit).*

$$$ ⊡**Marunouchi Hotel** 丸ノ内ホテル. Convenience is one reason to choose the Marunouchi Hotel, occupying the upper 11 floors of the Marunouchi Oazo building and joining Tōkyō Station via an underground walkway. Nice, too, are the views afforded of the downstairs garden and city lights from the guest rooms, which sport high ceilings and tasteful brown and beige interiors. The Rainbow View rooms, however, are only for guests who can handle bird-shaped pillows and room interiors wrapped in bands of bright color. Among the dining selections are Daian Club, featuring tempura dishes, and the French restaurant Tōkyō John Bull, which dates back to 1924, around when the original Marunouchi Hotel opened its doors. If that's not enough, a multitude of restaurants awaits at the nearby Shin-Marunouchi Building. **Pros:** convenient airport access; central location; helpful concierge. **Cons:** breakfast choices are limited; rooms are smallish. ⊠*1–6–3 Marunouchi, Chiyoda-ku* ☎*03/3217–1111* ⊕*www.marunouchi-hotel.co.jp* ⌷*204 rooms, 1 suite* ⌂*In-room: safe, refrigerator, DVD, Internet. In-hotel: 3 restaurants, room service, bar, laundry service, no-smoking rooms* ▤*AE, DC, MC, V* Ⓜ*JR Tōkyo Station (Marunouchi North Exit).*

MEGURO 目黒

$–$$ ⊡**Claska** クラスカ. Hip, modern, and Japanese, Claska is Tōkyo's premier boutique hotel. The tiered, boxy, art deco exterior gives it a space-age, bachelor-pad feel. Room interiors are a sight to behold: hardwood floors and sleek furniture fill the Western rooms; the Japanese accommodations are lit by paper lanterns and outfitted with small cushions for tea service above a tatami floor. For meals, Kiokuh serves contemporary Japanese dishes by day and operates as a cocktail lounge staffed by DJs in the evenings. A shop sells nicely crafted eating utensils and acts as a

FodorsChoice ★

gallery space. The hotel's remote location, however, makes access a challenge, and the rooms are limited, so book well in advance. **Pros:** Japanese aesthetics in a modern setting; great staff; cool gift shop. **Cons:** it's five minutes by taxi from Meguro station; atmosphere could be seen as pretentious; often booked in advance. ⊠ *1–3–18 Chūō-chō, Meguro-ku* ☎ *03/3719–8121* ⊕ *www.claska.com* ☞ *9 Western rooms, 3 Japanese rooms, 3 weekly residence rooms* ⎮ *In-room: DVD, Internet. In-hotel: restaurant, room service, laundry service, no-smoking rooms* ⊟ *AE, DC, MC, V* Ⓜ *Tōyoko line; Gakugeidaigaku Station (Higashi-guchi/ East Exit), 5 minutes by taxi from JR Meguro station.*

NIHOMBASHI 日本橋

$$$$ 🖾 **Mandarin Oriental Tōkyō** マンダリン オリエンタル 東京. Occupying the
★ top nine floors of the glistening Nihombashi Mitsui Tower is this hotel, a blend of harmony and outright modernity. The Mandarin's amazing rooms, decorated in dark and light browns, feature large bay windows with exquisite nighttime panoramas of the city lights. The 45-inch flat-panel TVs, surround-sound systems, and iPod docking stations should please tech fans. Corner rooms have sunken marble tubs that allow you to gaze out windows while soaking. The spa devotes nine rooms to the hotel's signature body scrubs and massages. The gym and award-winning restaurants (both modern and traditional cuisines) are top-of-the-line, but guests weary from overload of superlatives might consider a short stroll toward Tōkyō Station, with its variety of tiny watering holes and *izakaya* (Japanese pubs). **Pros:** wonderful spa and concierge service; nice city views; amazing room interiors. **Cons:** pricey; one sink in the bathrooms; location is not exactly central. ⊠ *2–1–1 Nihombashi Muromachi, Chūō-ku* ☎ *03/3270–8950* ⊕ *www.mandarinoriental. com/tokyo* ☞ *157 rooms, 22 suites* ⎮ *In-room: safe, DVD, Wi-Fi. In-hotel: 4 restaurants, bars, gym, spa* ⊟ *AE, DC, MC, V* Ⓜ *Ginza and Hanzō-mon subway lines, Mitsukoshi-mae Station (Exit A7).*

NINGYŌ-CHŌ 人形町

$ 🖾 **Sumishō Hotel** 住庄ほてる. This hotel, in a down-to-earth, friendly
Fodor's Choice neighborhood, is popular with budget-minded foreign visitors who
★ prefer to stay near the small Japanese restaurants and bars of Ningyō-chō. Expect no graces here: even the biggest twin rooms are long and narrow, and the bathrooms are tiny units with low ceilings. The best accommodations are the three tatami rooms on the second floor overlooking a small Japanese garden. Full-course Japanese meals are available in the restaurant. The hotel's a bit hard to find: from Exit A5 of Ningyō-chō Station, turn right and take the first small right-hand street past the second traffic light; the Sumishō is on the left. **Pros:** nicely priced; friendly staff; great neighborhood with small restaurants and pubs that offer great food for a good price. **Cons:** small rooms and baths; location is not exactly central. ⊠ *9–14 Nihombashi-Kobunachō, Chūō-ku* ☎ *03/3661–4603* ⊕ *www.sumisho-hotel.co.jp* ☞ *72 Western-style rooms, 11 Japanese-style rooms* ⎮ *In-room: Internet. In-hotel: restaurant, Japanese baths, laundry facilities, laundry service,*

no-smoking rooms ▤*AE, DC, MC, V* Ⓜ*Hibiya and Asakusa subway lines, Ningyō-chō Station (Exit A5).*

NISHI-SHINJUKU 西新宿

\$\$–\$\$\$ ⌑**Hilton Tōkyō** ヒルトン東京. The Hilton, which is a short walk from the megalithic Tōkyō Metropolitan Government Office, is a particular favorite of Western business travelers. The lobby is on a comfortable, human scale with a copper-clad spiral staircase that reaches to the mezzanine floor and the bar-lounge. Shōji screens instead of curtains bathe the guest rooms in soft, relaxing light. LCD flat-panel TVs are standard, and executive rooms on the top seven floors feature superb views and offer private check-in, complimentary breakfast, and evening cocktails. **Pros:** affordable; convenient location; free shuttle to Shinjuku station. **Cons:** in-room Internet is not free; standard room furnishings are basic. ✉*6–6–2 Nishi-Shinjuku, Shinjuku-ku* ☎*03/3344–5111* ⊕*www.hilton. com* ⌑*677 rooms, 129 suites* ♿*In-room: safe (some), refrigerator, Internet. In-hotel: 6 restaurants, room service, bars, pool, gym, laundry service, no-smoking rooms* ▤*AE, DC, MC, V* Ⓜ*Shinjuku Station (Nishi-guchi/West Exit); Marunouchi subway line, Nishi-Shinjuku Station (Exit C8); Ōedo subway line, Tochō-mae Station (all exits).*

\$\$–\$\$\$ ⌑**Hotel Century Southern Tower** 小田急ホテルセンチュリーサザンタワー.
★ The sparse offerings at the Century (i.e., no room service, empty refrigerators) are more than compensated by the hotel's reasonable prices and wonderful location atop the 35-floor Odakyu Southern Tower, minutes by foot from Shinjuku Station. The 20th-floor lobby is understated simplicity, and basic rooms are stylishly outfitted in light-wood furnishings and sizeable writing desks suitable for the business traveler. Fusion restaurant Tribecks boasts floor-to-ceiling windows that offer views of the metropolis to go with its extensive wine list. To fill that room refrigerator, the shopping at Takashimaya Times Square is just an elevator ride away. **Pros:** affordable; convenient location; great views. **Cons:** room amenities are basic; no in-room minibar; no room service. ✉*2–2–1 Yoyogi, Shibuya-ku* ☎*03/5354–0111* ⊕*www.southerntower. co.jp* ⌑*375 rooms* ♿*In-room: safe, refrigerator, Internet. In-hotel: 3 restaurants, bar, gym, laundry service, no-smoking rooms* ▤*AE, DC, MC, V* Ⓜ*Shinjuku Station (Minami-guchi/South Exit); Ōedo and Shinjuku subway lines, Shinjuku Station (Exit A1).*

\$\$\$ ⌑**Hyatt Regency Tōkyō** ハイアットリージェンシー 東京. The Hyatt Regency, set amid Shinjuku's skyscrapers, has the trademark Hyatt atrium-style lobby: seven stories high, with open-glass elevators soaring upward and three huge chandeliers suspended from above. The rooms are spacious for the price, though unremarkable in design; the best choices are the View Rooms (10th–26th floors), which overlook Shinjuku Kōen (Shinjuku Park). Tochō-mae Station, beneath the hotel, allows swift access to the nightlife in Roppongi and Shiodome's business towers. **Pros:** friendly staff; affordable room rates; spacious rooms. **Cons:** rather bland exteriors and common areas; restaurant options are limited outside hotel. ✉*2–7–2 Nishi-Shinjuku, Shinjuku-ku* ☎*03/3348–1234* ⊕*hyattregencytokyo.com* ⌑*750 rooms, 16 suites* ♿*In-room: safe, refrigerator, Internet. In-hotel: 6 restaurants, room service, bars, pool,* *gym, laundry service, no-smoking rooms* ⊟*AE, DC, MC, V* Ⓜ*Marunouchi subway line, Nishi-Shinjuku Station (Exit C8); Ōedo subway line, Tochō-mae Station (all exits).*

$$–$$$ 🖼**Keiō Plaza Hotel Tōkyō** 京王プラザホテル. This hotel, composed of two cereal-box-shaped towers, has a reputation as a business destination that serves its guests with a classic touch. A greeter sporting a black top hat, for example, welcomes you into a lobby of generous marble and high ceilings. Equipped with spacious closets and dressing tables, the standard rooms in the south tower are large but a bit outdated. The Plaza Premier rooms in the main tower have the latest in modern furniture design—no shortage of curved wood and metal here. The Sky Pool is actually two pools, one rectangular for laps and the other circular for lounging; both afford views of Shinjuku's steel-and-concrete skyscrapers. **Pros:** nice pools; affordable nightly rates; convenient location. **Cons:** rather bland exteriors and common areas; restaurant options are limited outside hotel; can be crowded if there are conventions or large groups in residence. ⊠*2–2–1 Nishi-Shinjuku, Shinjuku-ku* ☎*03/3344–0111* ⊕*www.keioplaza.com* ⤴*1,431 rooms, 19 suites* ⚭*In-room: refrigerator, Internet. In-hotel: 13 restaurants, room service, bars, pools, gym, no-smoking rooms* ⊟*AE, DC, MC, V* Ⓜ*Shinjuku Station (Nishi-guchi/West Exit).*

$$$$ 🖼**Park Hyatt Tōkyō** パークハイアット東京. The elevator inside the sleek,
Fodor'sChoice   Kenzō Tange–designed Shinjuku Park Tower whisks you to the 41st
★   floor, where this stunning hotel—immortalized in the 2003 film *Lost in Translation*—begins with an atrium lounge enclosed on three sides by floor-to-ceiling plate-glass windows. The panorama of Shinjuku, gaudy as it can be in the daytime, spreads out in front. Check-in formalities take place at sit-down desks, reached by a pleasant walk through an extensive library. Service is efficient and personal, and the mood of the hotel is contemporary and understated to give a home-away-from-home feel. Standard rooms (measuring 484 square feet) include king-size beds with Egyptian-cotton sheets and down-feather duvets; other appointments include an in-bath TV visible from the tub, black-lacquer cabinets, and 37-inch plasma-screen TVs. The popular New York Grill, which offers 1,600 bottles of wine and a steak-and-seafood menu, provides spectacular evening panoramas. **Pros:** wonderful architecture and room interiors; great city views; top-class restaurants; airport shuttle. **Cons:** pricey; taxi is best way to get to Shinjuku station; restaurant options are limited outside hotel. ⊠*3–7–1–2 Nishi-Shinjuku, Shinjuku-ku* ☎*03/5322–1234* ⊕*tokyo.park.hyatt.com* ⤴*155 rooms, 23 suites* ⚭*In-room: safe, refrigerator, DVD, Internet. In-hotel: 4 restaurants, room service, bars, pool, gym, spa, laundry service, no-smoking rooms* ⊟*AE, DC, MC, V* Ⓜ*JR Shinjuku Station (Nishi-guchi/West Exit).*

ODAIBA お台場

A commercial and entertainment development on reclaimed land within Tōkyō Bay, Odaiba is a bit off the beaten track; although the Rinkai and Yurikamome lines serve the area Odaiba isn't convenient to the heart of the city. That said, the attractions of the area are a resort quality—with shopping, museums, amusement complexes, and a beach—an proximity to several convention centers. Note that the Hotel InterContinental is near rather than in Odaiba, though it's also accessible by the Yurikamome Line.

$$$$ ⊡**Grand Pacific Le Daiba** グランパシフィックルダイバ. A sprawling complex at the tip of a human-made peninsula in Tōkyō Bay, the Grand Pacific's a good choice for conventioneers at the nearby Tōkyō Big Site. European-inspired columns, pedestals, and flowery furnishings fill the entrance hall. The theme's carried over to the rather sizeable rooms, which are decorated in shades of gold and brown. Rooms facing Haneda Airport and the Museum of Maritime Science (which resembles a large ship) are ¥6,000 less than those overlooking the Rainbow Bridge and the flat-roofed boats ferrying passengers within the harbor. **Pros:** great views of Tōkyō Harbor; large and nicely appointed rooms; romantic setting. **Cons:** expensive room rates; isolated location. ⊠*2–6–1 Daiba, Minato-ku* ☎*03/5500–6711* ⊕*www.grandpacific.jp* ↗*795 rooms, 89 suites* ⚲*In-room: refrigerator, Internet. In-hotel: 9 restaurants, room service, bars, pool, gym, no-smoking rooms* ⊟*AE, DC, MC, V* Ⓜ*Yurikamome rail line, Daiba Station.*

$$$$ ⊡**Hotel InterContinental Tōkyō Bay** ホテルインターコンチネンタル東京ベイ. Wedged between Tōkyō Bay and an expressway, the InterContinental affords pleasant views, albeit in a slightly isolated setting. Rooms overlooking the river to the north run ¥7,000 more than those pointing to the bay. All of the rooms are large (at least 430 square feet), and the bathrooms include separate showers and tubs. Services and meeting facilities for business travelers are available on the Club InterContinental Floors (the top five floors). The surrounding area's filled with industrial complexes, offering nothing in the way of immediate entertainment options, but the sixth-floor Sunset Lounge is a relaxing place to unwind and gaze at the Rainbow Bridge and surrounding Odaiba. **Pros:** great views of the Rainbow Bridge and Tōkyō Harbor; large, nicely appointed rooms; quiet area. **Cons:** pricey; location might be too out-of-the-way for the sightseer. ⊠*1–16–2 Kaigan, Minato-ku* ☎*03/5404–2222* ⊕*www.interconti-tokyo.com* ↗*331 rooms, 8 suites* ⚲*In-room: refrigerator, Internet. In-hotel: 4 restaurants, bar, gym, laundry service* ⊟*AE, DC, MC, V* Ⓜ*Yurikamome rail line, Takeshiba Station.*

$$$–$$$$ ⊡**Hotel Nikkō Tōkyō** ホテル日航東京. Like the nearby Grand Pacific hotel, the 16-story Nikkō, whose facade follows the curve of the Tōkyō Bay shoreline, presents itself as an "urban resort" with European style. Dark-wood chairs and golden ornaments adorn the second-floor lobby, where large windows overlook the waterfront. The spacious rooms, which are decorated in yellows and beiges, include a private balcony, and select suites have Jacuzzis. The Captain's Bar serves a large selection of whisky and brandy. Access to the city center from here is cumbersome, but a boardwalk connects the hotel to a small park, an amusement area, and shopping destinations. **Pros:** great views of Tōkyō Bay; friendly staff; romantic setting. **Cons:** isolated location might not be ideal for the sightseer; room interiors are a tad bland. ⊠*1–9–1 Daiba, Minato-ku* ☎*03/5500–5500* ⊕*www.hnt.co.jp* ↗*435 rooms, 20 suites* ⚲*In-hotel: 7 restaurants, room service, bar, pool, spa, laundry service* ⊟*AE, DC, MC, V* Ⓜ*Yurikamome rail line, Daiba Station.*

ROPPONGI 六本木

¢–$
★
Asia Center of Japan アジア会館. Established mainly for Asian students and travelers on limited budgets, these accommodations have become generally popular with many international travelers for their good value and easy access (a 15-minute walk) to the nightlife of Roppongi. The "semi-doubles" here are really small singles, but twins and doubles are quite spacious for the price. Appointments are a bit spartan—off-white walls, mass-market veneer furniture—but the rooms have plenty of basic amenities like hair dryers, electric kettles, and yukatas. The Fuji restaurant offers a breakfast buffet for ¥945. **Pros:** affordable; this area is great for those who love the nightlife; in-room Internet is free. **Cons:** one restaurant; no room service; small rooms. ⊠ *8–10–32 Akasaka, Minato-ku* ☎ *03/3402–6111* ⊕ *www.asiacenter.or.jp* ⤢ *172 rooms, 1 suite* ♿ *In-room: refrigerator, Internet. In-hotel: restaurant, laundry service, no-smoking rooms* ⊟ *AE, MC, V* Ⓜ *Ginza and Hanzō-mon subway lines, Aoyama-itchōme Station (Exit 4).*

$$$$
★
Grand Hyatt Tōkyō at Roppongi Hills グランドハイアット東京. Japanese refinement and a contemporary design come together perfectly at the Grand Hyatt—a truly classy hotel that provides every imaginable convenience and comfort. A drawer in the mahogany dresser in each room, for example, has laptop cables and adaptors. The showers have two delivery systems, one through a luxurious rain-shower shower-head affixed to the ceiling. No expense has been spared on materials, from the Frette bed linens to the 20-meter red-granite pool in the spa. Rooms are huge, with high ceilings, touch-panel lighting systems, remote-control blackout blinds, and muted earth tones of brown, beige, and yellow. Guests staying in Grand Club rooms receive complimentary breakfast and evening drinks. The bar at the Oak Door steak house is very lively in the evenings. **Pros:** great spa; nice restaurants; stunning rooms; airport shuttle. **Cons:** pricey; the complicated layout of the complex can make moving around seem like a game of Chutes and Ladders. ⊠ *6–10–3 Roppongi, Minato-ku* ☎ *03/4333–1234* ⊕ *www.tokyo.grand.hyatt.com* ⤢ *361 rooms, 28 suites* ♿ *In-room: safe, refrigerator, DVD, Internet. In-hotel: 6 restaurants, room service, bars, pool, gym, spa, Japanese baths, laundry service, no-smoking rooms* ⊟ *AE, DC, MC, V* Ⓜ *Hibiya subway line, Roppongi Station Exit 1A); Ōedo subway line, Roppongi Station (Exit 3).*

$
Hotel Arca Torre ホテルアルカトーレ. This European-inspired hotel sits on a coveted location in the heart of one of Tōkyō's premier nightlife quarters, just a few minutes' walk from the Tōkyō Midtown and Roppongi Hills shopping-and-entertainment complexes. Red hanging flags and a faux-stone exterior greet you at the entry. The accommodations are ample for the price (twins are much roomier than doubles), with nice little touches like built-in hot plates for making tea and coffee, and retractable clotheslines in the bathrooms. There are, however, no closets—just some coat hooks on the wall. In keeping with the wild and wooly surroundings, adult channels are offered free of charge. **Pros:** affordable; convenient access to nightlife. **Cons:** no room service; small rooms; neighborhood's plethora of bars and clubs makes the area noisy. ⊠ *6–1–23 Roppongi, Minato-ku* ☎ *03/3404–5111* ⊕ *www.arktower.*

co.jp ⤷*77 rooms* ♿*In-room: refrigerator, Internet. In-hotel: 2 restaurants, no-smoking rooms* ▤*AE, MC, V* Ⓜ*Hibiya and Ōedo subway lines, Roppongi Station (Exit 3).*

$$$$ 🖼**The Ritz-Carlton, Tōkyō** ザ・リッツ・カールトン東京. Newly installed in
★   the top floors of the 53-story Midtown Tower, the Ritz-Carlton is the newest champ in the continually escalating battle for Tōkyō's most luxurious accommodations. Frette linens and down pillows are standard in the guest rooms, which feature relaxing chairs positioned near the windows from which to gaze at the Tōkyō skyline. The spacious marble bathrooms are equipped with double sinks, 20-inch plasmas, and deep tubs. Guests staying on the Club Level (two top floors) are presented with complimentary food and beverages. The spa has a four-lane pool, nine treatment rooms, and a hot tub overlooking Tōkyō Tower. The restaurants Forty Five (Continental fusion) and Hinokizaki (sushi) provide views of Mt. Fuji (when the weather is nice), but if romance is on your mind, the Belvedere vodka martini (¥1.8 million) at the Lobby Bar has a one-carat diamond at the bottom of the glass. **Pros:** great views of Tōkyō; romantic setting; convenient access to nightlife; stunning rooms. **Cons:** high prices; immediate area is somewhat grungy. ✉*9–7–1 Akasaka, Minato-ku* ☎*03/3423–8000* ⊕*www.ritzcarlton. com* ⤷*212 rooms, 36 suites* ♿*In-room: refrigerator, DVD, Wi-Fi. In-hotel: 2 restaurants, room service, bar, pool, spa, laundry service, no-smoking rooms, parking (paid)* ▤*AE, DC, MC, V* Ⓜ*Hibiya subway line, Roppongi Station (Exit 4); Ōedo subway line, Roppongi Station (Exit 7)*

SEKIGUCHI 関口

$$$$ 🖼**Four Seasons Hotel Chinzan-sō** フォーシーズンズホテル椿山荘. Boast-
★   ing a European flair amid a 17-acre garden setting, the elegant and isolated Four Seasons is like a sheltered haven in the busy metropolis. Modern touches in the rooms include 32-inch LCD TVs and a bedside control panel for draperies; the large bathrooms have soaking tubs and separate showers. The spectacular fifth-floor Conservatory guest rooms have bay windows overlooking private Japanese-garden terraces. The solarium pool, with its columns, tropical plants, and retractable glass roof, is straight out of Xanadu. Built on the former estate of an imperial prince, Chinzan-sō rejoices in one of the most beautiful settings in Tōkyō; in summer the gardens are famous for their fireflies. Many of the restaurants offer special seasonal menus featuring seafood delicacies from Japan's coastal regions. Since the hotel occupies a rather inconvenient section of Tōkyō, the complimentary shuttle service that connects to the subway and Tōkyō Station is very useful. **Pros:** stunning rooms; nice pool; garden views. **Cons:** expensive room rates; isolated location. ✉*2–10–8 Sekiguchi, Bunkyō-ku* ☎*03/3943–2222* ⊕*www.fourseasons. com/tokyo* ⤷*259 rooms, 44 suites* ♿*In-room: safe, refrigerator, Wi-Fi, DVD. In-hotel: 3 restaurants, room service, pool, gym, spa, Japanese baths, laundry service, no-smoking rooms* ▤*AE, DC, MC, V* Ⓜ*Yūraku-chō subway line, Edogawa-bashi Station (Exit 1A).*

SHIBA KŌEN 芝公園

$$$–$$$$ ☷**The Prince Park Tower Tōkyō** ザ・プリンス パークタワー東京. The surrounding parkland and the absence of any adjacent buildings make the Park Tower a peaceful setting. The atrium lobby is vertically impressive, with two glass elevators giving a clear look into the building's hollow core. Covering almost the entire exterior wall, the guestroom windows afford nice views of nearby Tōkyō Tower and/or Shiba Kōen (Shiba Park). Large LCD TVs and bathrooms with jetted tubs and separate full-stall showers are nice, modern touches. The relative seclusion limits restaurant choices in the immediate area, though many can be found at the nearby JR Hamamatsu-cho Station, less than 10 minutes away on foot. **Pros:** park nearby; guests have a choice of bed pillows for the large beds; there's a bowling alley and wedding chapel in the hotel. **Cons:** a tad isolated; there's an extra fee to use the spa and fitness center. ⊠*4–8–1 Shiba-kōen, Minato-ku* ☎*03/5400–1111* ⊕*www.princehotels.co.jp/parktower-e* ⇨*633 rooms, 40 suites* ⏁*In-room: refrigerator, Internet. In-hotel: 8 restaurants, room service, bars, no-smoking rooms* ▤*AE, DC, MC, V* Ⓜ*Ōedo subway line, Akabanebashi Station (Akabanebashi Exit).*

> ### BODY ART BEWARE
>
> Think twice about going to take a dip in Tōkyō if you have a tattoo. These personal expressions are strictly forbidden in many of the city's pools, fitness clubs, hot springs, and onsen because of the association between tattoos and the *yakuza* (Japanese mafia). Some places even post signs reading, PEOPLE WITH TATTOOS ARE NOT ALLOWED.

SHIBUYA 渋谷

$$$$ ☷**Cerulean Tower Tōkyū Hotel** セルリアンタワー東急ホテル. The pricey Cerulean Tower, perched on a slope above Shibuyas chaos, has a cavernous yet bustling lobby filled with plenty of attentive, English-speaking staffers. The rooms afford generous views of Tōkyō, but considering the price, the furnishings are rather plain. Some rooms include windows in the bathroom to allow for bath-time city gazing. Fans of the original Japanese *Iron Chef* TV program might want to dine at Szechwan Restaurant Chen, whose menu is directed by one of the show's combatants, Kenichi Chen. The branch of the famous Kanetanaka ryotei often features Japanese delicacies to match the season. **Pros:** friendly, attentive service; great city views; convenient location. **Cons:** pricey rates; Shibuya is one of Tōkyō's more popular (read: crowded) areas; charge to use gym and the pool (¥2,100 per day), which is off-limits to people with tattoos. ⊠*26–1 Sakuragaoka-chō, Shibuya-ku* ☎*03/3476–3000* ⊕*www.cerulean tower-hotel.com* ⇨*405 rooms, 9 suites* ⏁*In-room: refrigerator, DVD, Internet. In-hotel: 6 restaurants, room service, bars, no-smoking rooms* ▤*AE, DC, MC, V* Ⓜ*JR Shibuya Station (South Exit).*

$$ ☷**Granbell Hotel Shibuya** 渋谷グランベルホテル. Location, location, location—that's the Granbell, and with a minimalist pop-art style to boot. **Fodor'sChoice** This gray-walled boutique hotel, tucked within a cluster of restaurants ★ and shops near the West Exit of Shibuya Station, features rooms that are small but tastefully outfitted with crisp linens and curtains dotted

with a Lichtenstein-inspired mountain scene. Front doors are colored in a slick green, and bathrooms are glass-enclosed and feature overhead showers. Bar G Lounge, which is located just to the side of the reception desk, offers cocktails in the evening; Granbell House, a full restaurant, has a menu of beef and fish dishes; and the 24-hour Plate of Pie.Pop café serves beer, coffee, and, yes, plenty of pastries. **Pros:** reasonable rates; great location; funky design. **Cons:** small rooms; neighborhood can be noisy. ✉*15–17 Sakuragaoka–chō, Shibuya-ku* ☎*03/5457–2681* ⊕*www.granbellhotel.jp* ➳*52 rooms, 3 suites* ♿*In-room: safe, refrigerator, Internet. In-hotel: 2 restaurants, bar, no-smoking rooms* ▭*AE, DC, MC, V* Ⓜ*JR Shibuya Station (West Exit).*

$$$ 🏨 **Shibuya Excel Hotel Tōkyū** 渋谷エクセル東急. The key to this unremarkable but very convenient hotel, which is within the towering Mark City complex, is access: local shopping and cheap dining options are aplenty, Shinjuku is a five-minute train ride to the north, and the Narita Express departs from nearby Shibuya Station frequently each morning. The rooms, decorated in shades of beige and yellow, are plain but comfortable. North-facing rooms on the 10th floor and above (including the two "ladies-only" floors on levels 23 and 24) afford views of the Shinjuku skyline. The vibrant Estacion Cafe, above Shibuya's insanely busy "scramble intersection," serves drinks and small snacks. Perhaps equally enjoyable is the lobby vending machine, with its robot-arm dispensing soft drinks and beer. **Pros:** affordable; convenient location; friendly staff. **Cons:** uninspired rooms; crowds in the area can be intimidating. ✉*1–12–2 Dōgenzaka, Shibuya-ku* ☎*03/5457–0109* ⊕ *www.tokyuhotelsjapan.com* ➳*407 rooms, 1 suite* ♿*In-room: refrigerator, Internet. In-hotel: 3 restaurants, no-smoking rooms* ▭*AE, DC, MC, V* Ⓜ*JR Shibuya Station (Hachiko Exit).*

SHINAGAWA 品川

$$–$$$ 🏨 **Hotel Pacific Tōkyō** ホテルパシフィック東京. Just across the street from JR Shinagawa Station, the Hotel Pacific sits on grounds that were once part of an imperial-family estate. The hotel gears much of its marketing effort toward booking banquets, wedding receptions, conventions, and tour groups; the small, unremarkable rooms are quiet and comfortable, but public spaces tend to carry a lot of traffic. The Sky Lounge on the 30th floor has a fine view of Tōkyō Bay. The entire back wall of the ground-floor lounge is glass, the better to contemplate a Japanese garden, sculpted with rocks and waterfalls. **Pros:** reasonably priced rooms; good location; nice view of Tōkyō Bay. **Cons:** dated furnishings; small bathrooms. ✉*3–13–3 Takanawa, Minato-ku* ☎*03/3445–6711* ⊕*www.pacific-tokyo.com* ➳*913 rooms, 41 suites*

2

⌂ *In-room: refrigerator, Internet. In-hotel: 6 restaurants, room service, bars, pool, laundry service, no-smoking rooms* ⊟ *AE, DC, MC, V* Ⓜ *JR Yamanote Line, Shinagawa Station (Nishi-guchi/West Exit).*

$$–$$$ 🖾 **Prince Hotel Shinagawa** 品川プリンスホテル. Just a three-minute walk ☾ from JR Shinagawa Station, the Prince is a sprawling complex that's part hotel (with four towers) and part entertainment village, featuring everything from a bowling alley to tennis courts to a 10-screen movie theater. The rooms in the East Tower and the upper floors of the Main Tower (28th–37th floors) have undergone recent renovations, making them the most desirable. The kids will be right at home in the game centers and aquarium. For the parents, the Top of Shinagawa Lounge offers spectacular views of Tōkyō Bay. Be warned: the complex is swamped with families on the weekends and the layout can be confusing. There's even a wedding chapel on-site. **Pros:** affordable rates; multiple entertainment choices including a bowling alley and an IMAX theater; nice view of Tōkyō Bay from lounge. **Cons:** complicated layout; crowded on weekends. ✉ *4–10–30 Takanawa, Minato-ku* ☎ *03/3440–1111* ⊕ *www.princehotels.co.jp/shinagawa-e* 🛏 *3,679 rooms* ⌂ *In-room: refrigerator, Internet. In-hotel: 14 restaurants, bar, gym, pool, tennis courts, no-smoking rooms* ⊟ *AE, DC, MC, V* Ⓜ *JR Yamanote Line, Shinagawa Station (Nishi-guchi/West Exit).*

$$$$ 🖾 **The Strings by InterContinental Tōkyō** ストリングスホテル東京インタ ★ ーコンチネンタル. Like the Conrad up the road in Shiodome, The Strings is all about blending modernity with traditional Japanese aesthetics. From Shinagawa Station, a private elevator leads up to the hotel atrium, where a glass bridge spans a pond (often featuring an ikebana arrangement) and cut stone mixes with dark wood. High-ceilinged guest rooms include LCD TVs, high-quality linens, awesome views of the Tōkyō skyline (make sure you check it out at night), and the large bathrooms have separate showers and tubs. Prices in the hotel restaurants tend to be high, so a trip to a nearby Western steak house or coffee shop might make your wallet smile. **Pros:** great lobby; convenient location; nice view of the Tōkyō skyline. **Cons:** expensive rates; finding elevator entrance can be challenging. ✉ *2–16–1 Kōnan, Minato-ku* ☎ *03/4562–1111* ⊕ *www.intercontinental-strings.jp* 🛏 *200 rooms, 6 suites* ⌂ *In-room: refrigerator, Internet. In-hotel: 2 restaurants, room service, bars, gym* ⊟ *AE, DC, MC, V* Ⓜ *JR Yamanote Line, Shinagawa Station (Kōnan Exit).*

SHIODOME 汐留

$$$$ 🖾 **Conrad Tōkyō** コンラッド東京. The Conrad, part of the Hilton family, ★ welcomes you to the Space Age with a Japanese twist. Elevators shoot upward 28 floors in the slick, green-hue Tōkyō Shiodome Building to a lobby of dark oak paneling and bronze lattices. Straight-edge counters in shades of blue and Japanese-lantern illumination come together in the bar areas. Dining options include the French-influenced Gordon Ramsay at the Conrad Tōkyō and the adjoining brasserie, Cerise by Gordon Ramsay. The high-ceiling guest rooms allow for nice views of the bay or the city from a pair of low-back sofas. Motorized blinds and 37-inch plasma TVs with DVD players housed in lacquer boxes are thoughtful touches. Highlights in the bathrooms include dual sinks, rain-shower showerheads, and separate tubs (complete with rubber ducks). Be sure to come with plenty of Hilton points (or your best plastic)—room prices are as sky-high as the lobby entrance. **Pros:** modern design; fantastic bay view; fine restaurants. **Cons:** expensive; finding entrance to elevator is troublesome; charge to use pool and gym. ✉ *1–9–1 Higashi-Shimbashi, Minato-ku* ☎ *03/6388–8000* ⊕ *conradtokyo.co.jp* ⇢ *222 rooms, 68 suites* ♿ *In-room: safe, refrigerator, DVD, Wi-Fi. In-hotel: 4 restaurants, room service, bar, pool, gym, spa, no-smoking rooms* ☰ *AE, DC, MC, V* Ⓜ *JR Yamanote Line, Shimbashi Station (Shiodome Exit); Ōedo subway line, Shiodome Station (Exit 9).*

$$
Fodor's Choice
★

▦ **Park Hotel Tōkyō** パークホテル東京. A panorama of Tōkyō or a bay view, comfortable beds, and large bathrooms greet you in the rooms of this reasonably priced boutique hotel. As is the current trend in Tōkyō, a 10-story atrium of dark-wood paneling sits below a hexagonal skylight ceiling in the lobby. A pillow-fitting service provides advice on how you can change your sleeping habits to get a better night's sleep. If that doesn't work, take a walk to the nearby fish market in Tsukiji—the activity gets started at 5 AM. **Pros:** the guest rooms and public areas are stylish; affordable room rates; great concierge service. **Cons:** small rooms; few in-room frills. ✉ *1–7–1 Higashi Shimbashi, Minato-ku* ☎ *03/6252–1111* ⊕ *www.parkhoteltokyo.com* ⇢ *272 rooms, 1 suite* ♿ *In-room: safe, refrigerator, Internet. In-hotel: 5 restaurants, room service, bar* ☰ *AE, DC, MC, V* Ⓜ *JR Yamanote Line, Shimbashi Station Shiodome Exit); Ōedo subway line, Shiodome Station (Exit 10).*

TORA-NO-MON 虎ノ門

$$$
▦ **ANA InterContinental Tōkyō** ANAインターコンチネンタルホテル東京. The ANA typifies the ziggurat-atrium style that seems to have been a requirement for hotel architecture from the mid-1980s. The reception floor, with its two-story fountain, is clad in enough marble to have depleted an Italian quarry. In general, though, the interior designers have made skillful use of artwork and furnishings to take some of the chill off the hotel's relentless modernism. Guest rooms are sleek and spacious. The Astral Lounge on the top (37th) floor and the Executive floors provide superb views of the city and Mt. Fuji (on clear days). The open kitchen and grain-fed New Zealand beef at The Steakhouse make it a fine dining choice. The U.S. Embassy is only a short walk away. **Pros:** great concierge; wonderful city views; spacious lobby. **Cons:** there's a charge to use the pool and gym; room bathrooms are a bit small. ✉ *1–12–33 Akasaka, Minato-ku* ☎ *03/3505–1111* ⊕ *www. anaintercontinental-tokyo.jp* ⇢ *851 rooms, 16 suites* ♿ *In-room: refrigerator, Internet. In-hotel: 7 restaurants, room service, bars, pool, gym, laundry service, no-smoking rooms* ☰ *AE, DC, MC, V* Ⓜ *Ginza and Namboku subway lines, Tameike-Sannō Station (Exit 13); Namboku subway line, Roppongi-itchōme Station (Exit 3).*

$$$$
★
▦ **Hotel Ōkura Tōkyō** ホテルオークラ. Conservative dark wood in the public areas and the tiered exterior architecture at the entry help the Ōkura retain the understated sophistication of its early days in the 1960s. Amenities in the tasteful, spacious rooms include remote-

control draperies and terry robes. The odd-number rooms, 871–889 inclusive, overlook a small Japanese landscaped garden. The on-site museum houses fine antique porcelain, mother-of-pearl, and ceramics. The hotel remains a Tōkyō favorite by its Japanese clientele but given its high rates, foreign guests might want to consider the lower-priced ANA InterContinental (for its views) or the pampering of the Grand Hyatt as alternatives. **Pros:** friendly staff; one of Tōkyō's older hotels that has kept its retro design and feel intact; large rooms. **Cons:** dated furnishings; a tad pricey. ⊠ *2–10–4 Tora-no-mon, Minato-ku* ☎ *03/3582–0111* ⊕ *www.okura.com/tokyo/* 🛏 *762 rooms, 96 suites* ⚬ *In-room: safe, refrigerator, DVD, Internet. In-hotel: 10 restaurants, room service, bars, pool, gym, spa, laundry service, no-smoking rooms* ▤ *AE, DC, MC, V* Ⓜ *Hibiya subway line, Kamiya-chō Station (Exit 4B); Ginza subway line, Tora-no-mon Station (Exit 3).*

UENO 上野

c 🎌 **Ryokan Katsutarō** 旅館勝太郎. Established four decades ago, this small, simple, economical hotel is a five-minute walk from the entrance to Ueno Kōen (Ueno Park) and a 10-minute walk from the Tōkyō National Museum. The rather spacious rooms, of which the quietest are in the back, away from the main street, have traditional tatami flooring that the futon bedding is rolled out on. The largest rooms can accommodate up to five people, and the lobby includes computers with Internet access. **Pros:** a traditional and unique Japanese experience; reasonably priced room rates; free use of computers in lobby. **Cons:** rooms near the street are noisy; furnishings are dated. ⊠ *4–16–8 Ikenohata, Taitō-ku* ☎ *03/3821–9808* ⊕ *www.katsutaro.com* 🛏 *7 Japanese-style rooms, 4 with bath* ⚬ *In-room: no a/c (some), no TV (some), Internet. In-hotel: Japanese baths, laundry facilities* ▤ *AE, MC, V* Ⓜ *Chiyoda subway line, Nezu Station (Exit 2).*

YANAKA 谷中

¢–$ 🎌 **Sawanoya Ryokan** 澤の屋旅館. The Shitamachi area is known for its
★ down-to-earth friendliness, which you get in full measure at Sawanoya. This little inn's a family business: everybody pitches in to help you plan excursions and book hotels for the next leg of your journey. The inn is very popular with budget travelers, so reserve online well in advance. On occasion, the staffers, who manage to keep the facilities and rooms very clean, perform various traditional dances and ceremonies in full costume in the lobby. Japanese bathtubs are near small windows that overlook a small garden. Coffee and tea are complimentary, but the rooms don't have TVs. Smoking is not allowed on the premises. **Pros:** traditional Japanese experience; affordable room rates; friendly management. **Cons:** rooms are on the small side; it's a bit of a hike to the subway station. ⊠ *2–3–11 Yanaka, Taitō-ku* ☎ *03/3822–2251* ⊕ *www.sawanoya.com* 🛏 *12 Japanese-style rooms, 2 with bath* ⚬ *In-room: Internet. In-hotel: bicycles, Japanese baths, laundry facilities, Internet terminal* ▤ *AE, MC, V* Ⓜ *Chiyoda subway line, Nezu Station (Exit 1).*

HOSTELS

¢   🖭 **Sakura Hostel** サクラホステル浅草. Located at edge of the historic "six districts" entertainment area of Asakusa, the clean and cheap accommodations of the Sakura provide easy access to many film and performance theaters and dozens of quaint bars. Single beds in the dormitories or various private rooms (some with up to eight beds) are available. An all-you-can-eat breakfast is ¥315. **Pros:** multiple entertainment options in neighborhood; clean common areas; no curfew for those night owls. **Cons:** a little more than 10 minutes by foot from subway station; in-house meals are limited. ⊠ *2–24–2 Asakusa, Taitō-ku* ☎ *03/3847–8112* ⊕ *www.sakura-hostel.co.jp* ⤳ *162 beds* ⚷ *In-room: security lockers. In-hotel: shared kitchen, shared bathrooms, Internet cafe, laundry facilities* 🖃 *AE, DC, MC, V* Ⓜ *Asakusa or Ginza subway line, Asakusa Station (Exit A4)*.

🖭 **Tōkyō International Youth Hostel** 東京国際ユースホステル. In typical hostel style, you're required to be off the premises between 10 AM and 3 PM. Less typical is the fact that for an additional ¥1,350 over the standard rate, you can eat breakfast and dinner in the hostel cafeteria. Beds include curtains for a bit of privacy. Films are occasionally shown on a 50-inch TV in the lobby, and there's a small convenience store on-site. The set bath and shower times could be restrictive to some, and night owls might see the 11 PM curfew as a problem. The hostel's a few minutes' walk from Iidabashi Station. **Pros:** affordable room rates; good location; nice view from public areas of Tōkyō's skyline. **Cons:** overnight curfew; entrance is hard to find. ⊠ *Central Plaza Bldg., 18th fl., 1–1 Kagura-kashi, Shinjuku-ku* ☎ *03/3235–1107* ⊕ *www.tokyo-ih. jp* ⤳ *158 bunk beds* ⚷ *In-hotel: Japanese baths, Internet* 🖃 *AE, MC, V* Ⓜ *JR; Tōzai, Namboku, and Yūraku-chō subway lines: Iidabashi Station (Exit B2b)*.

¢–$ 🖭 **YMCA Asia Youth Center** YMCAアジア青少年センター. Both men and women can stay here, and all rooms are private and have private baths. Discounts are given to YMCA members, pastors, and students taking university entrance exams. Breakfast is available for ¥200. **Pros:** reasonably priced rooms; convenient access to train station; discounts for YMCA members, students taking entrance exams, and clergy. **Cons:** small rooms; hotel has a limited choice of restaurants. ⊠ *2–5–5 Sara-gaku, Chiyoda-ku* ☎ *03/3233–0611* ⊕ *ymcajapan.org/ayc* ⤳ *55 rooms* ⚷ *In-hotel: laundry facilities, Internet terminal* 🖃 *DC, MC, V* Ⓜ *JR Mita Line, Suidō-bashi Station*.

NEAR NARITA AIRPORT

Transportation between Narita Airport and Tōkyō proper takes at least an hour and a half. In heavy traffic, a limousine bus or taxi ride, which could set you back ¥30,000, can stretch to two hours or more. A sensible strategy for visitors with early-morning flights home would be to spend the night before at one of the hotels near the airport, all of which have courtesy shuttles to the departure terminals; these hotels are also a boon to visitors en route elsewhere with layovers in Narita. Many of them have soundproof rooms to block out the noise of the airplanes.

2

$-$$ ⚏**ANA Crowne Plaza Narita** ANAクラウンプラザホテル成田. With its brass-and-marble detail in the lobby, this hotel replicates the grand style of other hotels in the ANA chain. The rooms are small, but the amenities measure up, and views are of the airport or surrounding greenery. A gym, tennis court, and pool can make for good distractions during a layover. If you're flying an ANA flight bound for anywhere other than North America, you can check in at a special counter in the lobby. **Pros:** affordably priced rooms; pleasant staff, airport shuttle. **Cons:** small rooms; charge to use pool; in-house restaurants are the only nearby dining options. ✉*68 Hori-no-uchi, Narita-shi, Chiba-ken* ☎*0476/33–1311, 0120/029–501 toll-free* ⊕*www.anahotel-narita.com* ⇋*434 rooms, 8 suites* ⚏*In-room: Internet. In-hotel: 5 restaurants, room service, pool, gym, Internet terminal, no-smoking rooms* ▤*AE, DC, MC, V.*

$ ⚏**Hilton Tōkyō Narita Airport** ヒルトン成田. Given its proximity to the airport (a 10-minute drive), this C-shaped hotel is a reasonable choice for a one-night visit. The deluxe rooms on the upper floors feature funky orange blackout curtains, a work desk and ergonomic chair, kanji wall art, and a flat-screen TV. The interiors of the remaining rooms, however, are plain and very dated. The top-floor banquet facilities provide a view of the landings and takeoffs on the airport runway. The lobby-level Terrace restaurant and bar have been remodeled to include an open kitchen and designer furnishings. **Pros:** reasonably priced rooms; spacious lobby; airport shuttle. **Cons:** charge to use the pool and gym; standard rooms have dated furnishings. ✉*456 Kosuge, Narita-shi, Chiba-ken* ☎*0476/33–1121* ⊕*www.hilton.com* ⇋*548 rooms* ⚏*In-room: Internet. In-hotel: 3 restaurants, bar, pool, gym, spa, tennis court, no-smoking rooms* ▤*AE, DC, MC, V.*

¢-$ ⚏**Holiday Inn Tōbu Narita** ホリデイ・イン東武成田. The modern, Western-style accommodations at this hotel, which are a five-minute ride by shuttle bus from the airport, are some of the cheapest around. The suites are large, and banquet rooms are available. **Pros:** nicely priced rooms; large rooms; short ride to airport on shuttle. **Cons:** limited dining options in and outside the hotel; rooms in need of upgrading. ✉*320–1 Tokkō, Narita-shi, Chiba-ken* ☎*0476/32–1234* ⊕*www.holidayinntobunarita. com/eng* ⇋*494 rooms, 6 suites* ⚏*In-room: Internet. In-hotel: 2 restaurants, bar, pool, no-smoking rooms* ▤*AE, DC, MC, V.*

¢-$ ⚏**Narita Airport Rest House.** A basic business hotel without much in the way of frills, the Rest House offers the closest accommodations to the airport itself, less than five minutes away by shuttle bus. However, cleanliness in the public areas seems to have been sacrificed in favor of the low room prices. (The rooms themselves are clean.) You can also rent one of the hotel's soundproof rooms for daytime-only use from 9 AM to 5 PM for about ¥5,000. Some of the special courses at the one restaurant are supplied by an airline catering service—perhaps worth noting should you intend to eat before your flight. **Pros:** affordable rooms; close to the airport; hotel provides a shuttle to the airport. **Cons:** few dining choices outside the hotel; common areas in need of overhaul; in-room furnishings are dated. ✉*New Tōkyō International Airport, Narita-shi, Chiba-ken* ☎*0476/32–1212* ⊕*www.apo-resthouse.com/*

english ↻*129 rooms* ♿*In-hotel: restaurant, bar, Internet terminal, no-smoking rooms* ▤*AE, DC, MC, V.*

$$ 🏨**Narita Excel Hotel Tōkyu** 成田エクセル東急. Airline crews rolling their bags through the lobby are a common sight at the Excel, a hotel with reasonable prices and friendly service. The rooms on the upper floors, which are outfitted with standard water kettles and yukatas, were renovated in August 2008. The gym is adequate but transportation to and from the airport can be delayed at times. The Japanese garden and nearby Shinsho-ji temple are pleasant for walks. **Pros:** nice concierge; view of runway from bar; nice Japanese garden. **Cons:** small bathrooms; airport-shuttle service is inconsistent. ✉*31 Oyama, Narita-shi, Chiba-ken* ☎*0476/33–0109* ⊕ *www.tokyuhotelsjapan.com* ↻*710 rooms, 2 suites* ♿*In-hotel: 3 restaurants, bar, pool, tennis court, gym* ▤*AE, DC, MC, V.*

$ 🏨**Narita View Hotel.** Boxy and uninspired, the Narita View offers no view of anything in particular but can be reached by shuttle bus from the airport in about 15 minutes. The rooms, which are soundproof, are bland yet functional for a single night. The top-floor restaurant serves French dishes and offers a nice view of Tōkyō's distant lights in the evening. **Pros:** affordable rooms; nice rooftop bar; plenty of surrounding greenery; airport shuttle available. **Cons:** charge to use Internet in lobby; uninspired room furnishings. ✉*700 Kosuge, Narita-shi, Chiba-ken* ☎*0476/32–1111* ⊕*www.viewhotels.co.jp/narita* ↻*492 rooms, 4 suites* ♿*In-room: refrigerator. In-hotel: 4 restaurants, spa, no-smoking rooms* ▤*AE, DC, MC, V.*

$–$$ 🏨**Radisson Hotel Narita Airport** ラディソンホテル成田エアポート. Set on 28 spacious, green acres, this modern hotel feels somewhat like a resort, with massive indoor and outdoor pools. The standard rooms are comfortable, and those rooms in the hotel's four towers have views of the expansive property. The Junior Suites in the tower are a roomy 560 square feet and provide views of the pool and garden. Ten buses offer daily shuttle services directly to and from Tōkyō Station. **Pros:** reasonably priced rooms; high-quality bathroom toiletries by Shiseido; nice-sized rooms; airport shuttle available. **Cons:** a 15-minute drive by car to the airport; charge to use in-room Internet. ✉*650–35 Nanae, Tomisato-shi, Chiba-ken* ☎*0476/93–1234* ⊕*www.radisson.com/tokyojp_narita* ↻*488 rooms, 2 suites* ♿*In-room: refrigerator, Internet. In-hotel: 3 restaurants, room service, bar, pool, gym, laundry service, tennis court, no-smoking rooms* ▤*AE, DC, MC, V.*

NIGHTLIFE AND THE ARTS

As Tōkyō's rich cultural history entwines itself with an influx of foreign influences, Tōkyōites get the best of both worlds. An evening out can be as civilized as a night of Kabuki or as rowdy as a Roppongi nightclub. In between there are dance clubs, a swingin' jazz scene, theater, cinema, live venues, and more than enough bars to keep the social lubricant flowing past millions of tonsils nightly.

The sheer diversity of nightlife is breathtaking. Rickety street stands sit yards away from luxury hotels, and wallet-crunching hostess clubs can be found next to cheap and raucous rock bars. Whatever your style, you'll find yourself in good company if you venture out after dark.

THE ARTS

An astonishing variety of dance and music, both classical and popular, can be found in Tōkyō, alongside the must-see traditional Japanese arts of Kabuki, Nō, and Bunraku. The city is a proving ground for local talent and a magnet for orchestras and concert soloists from all over the world. Tōkyō also has modern theater—in somewhat limited choices, to be sure, unless you can follow dialogue in Japanese, but Western repertory companies can always find receptive audiences here for plays in English. And it doesn't take long for a hit show from New York or London to open. Musicals such as *Mamma Mia and Wicked* have found enormous popularity here—although you'll find the protagonists speaking Japanese.

Japan has yet to develop any real strength of its own in ballet and has only just begun to devote serious resources to opera, but for that reason touring companies like the Metropolitan, the Bolshoi, Sadler's Wells, and the Bayerische Staatsoper find Tōkyō a very compelling venue—as well they might when even seats at ¥30,000 ($335) or more sell out far in advance. One domestic company that's making a name for itself is the Asami Maki Ballet, whose dancers are known for their technical proficiency and expressiveness; the company often performs at the Tōkyō Metropolitan Festival Hall. Latin dance also has a strong following and flamenco heartthrob Joaquín Cortés visits regularly to wide acclaim and packed houses.

Tōkyō movie theaters screen a broad range of films—everything from big Asian hits to American blockbusters and Oscar nominees. The increased diversity brought by smaller distributors, and an increased appetite for Korean, Chinese, and Hong Kong cinema have helped to develop vibrant small theaters that cater to art-house fans. New multiplexes have also brought new screens to the capital, offering a more comfortable film-going experience than some of the older Japanese theaters.

INFORMATION AND TICKETS

Metropolis is a free English-language weekly magazine that has up-to-date listings of what's going on in the city; it's available at hotels, book and music stores, some restaurants and cafés, and other locations. The English-language daily newspapers *The Japan Times* and *The Daily Yomiuri* have decent entertainment features and listings in their Friday editions.

If your hotel can't help you with concert and performance bookings, call **Ticket Pia** (☎*03/5237–9999*) for assistance in English. The **Playguide Agency** (✉*Playguide Bldg., 2–6–4 Ginza, Chūō-ku* ☎*03/3561–8821* Ⓜ *Yūraku-chō subway line, Ginza Itchōme Station, Exit 4*) sells tickets to cultural events via outlets in most department stores and in other locations throughout the city; you can stop in at the main office and ask for the nearest counter, but be aware that you may not find someone who speaks English. Note that agencies normally do not have tickets for same-day performances but only for advance booking.

DANCE

Traditional Japanese dance is divided into dozens of styles, ancient of lineage and fiercely proud of their differences. In truth, only the aficionado can really tell them apart. They survive not so much as performing arts but as schools, offering dance as a cultured accomplishment to interested amateurs. At least once a year, these teachers and their students hold a recital, so that on any given evening there's very likely to be one somewhere in Tōkyō. Truly professional performances are given at the Kokuritsu Gekijō and the Shimbashi Enbujō; the most important of the classical schools, however, developed as an aspect of Kabuki, and if you attend a play at the Kabuki-za, you are almost guaranteed to see a representative example.

Ballet began to attract a Japanese following in 1920, when Anna Pavlova danced *The Dying Swan* at the old Imperial Theater. The well-known companies that come to Tōkyō from abroad, perform to full houses that are usually at the Tōkyō Metropolitan Festival Hall in Ueno. There are now about 15 professional Japanese ballet companies, including the Tōkyō Ballet and the up-and-coming Asami Maki Ballet—both of which perform at the Tōkyō Metropolitan Festival Hall—but this has yet to become an art form on which Japan has had much of an impact.

Modern dance, on the other hand, is a different story. The modern Japanese dance form known as Butō, in particular, with its contorted and expressive body movements, is acclaimed internationally and domestically. Butō performances are held periodically at a variety of event spaces and small theaters. For details, check with ticket agencies and the local English-language press.

FILM

Fortunately for film fans, Japan's distributors invariably add Japanese subtitles rather than dub their offerings. Exceptions include kids' movies and big blockbusters that are released in both versions—if there are two screenings close to each other, that's a sign that one may be dubbed. The original sound track, of course, may not be all that helpful to you if the film is Polish or Italian, but the majority of first-run foreign films here are made in the United States. Choices range from the usual Hollywood fare to independent movies, but many films take so long to open in Tōkyō that you've probably already seen them. And tickets are expensive: around ¥1,800 ($15) for general admission and ¥2,500–¥3,000 ($21–$25) for a reserved seat, called a *shitei-seki*. Slightly discounted tickets, usually ¥1,200–¥1,600 ($10–$13), can be purchased from the ticket counters found in many department stores.

Although many of the major Japanese studios struggle to compete with big-budget U.S. fare, anime remains strong and each year sees several major domestic successes. Unless your Japanese is top-notch, most domestic films will be off-limits, but if you happen to be in town during one of the many film festivals you may be able to catch a screening with English subtitles. Festival season is in the fall, with the Tōkyō International Film Festival taking over the Shibuya district in October and a slew of other more specialized festivals screening more outré fare.

First-run theaters that have new releases, both Japanese and foreign, are clustered for the most part in three areas: Shinjuku, Shibuya, and Yūraku-chō-Hibiya-Ginza. At most of them, the last showing of the evening starts at around 7. This is not the case, however, with the handful of small theaters that take special interest in classics, revivals, and serious imports. Somewhere on the premises will also be a chrome-and-marble coffee shop, a fashionable little bar, or even a decent restaurant. Most of these small theaters have a midnight show—at least on the weekends.

Bunkamura. This complex in Shibuya has two movie theaters, a concert auditorium (Orchard Hall), and a performance space (Theater Cocoon); it's the principal venue for many of Tōkyō's film festivals. ⊠*2–24–1 Dōgen-zaka, Shibuya-ku* ☎*03/3477–9999* Ⓜ*JR Yamanote Line, Ginza and Hanzō-mon subway lines, and private rail lines; Shibuya Station (Exits 5 and 8 for Hanzō-mon Line, Kita-guchi/North Exit for all others).*

Chanter Cine. A three-screen cinema complex, Chanter Cine tends to show British and American films by independent producers but also showcases fine work by filmmakers from Asia and the Middle East. ⊠*1–2–2 Yūraku-chō, Chiyoda-ku* ☎*03/3591–1511* Ⓜ*Hibiya, Chiyoda, and Mita subway lines, Hibiya Station (Exit A5).*

Cine Saison Shibuya. In addition to popular films, this theater occasionally screens recent releases by award-winning directors from such countries as Iran, China, and South Korea. ⊠*Prime Bldg., 2–29–5 Dōgen-zaka, Shibuya-ku* ☎*03/3770–1721* Ⓜ*JR Yamanote Line, Shibuya Station (Hachiko Exit).*

Haiyūza. This is primarily a repertory theater, but on the irregularly scheduled Haiyūza Talkie Nights it screens notable foreign films. ⊠*4–9–2 Roppongi, Minato-ku* ☎*03/3401–4073* Ⓜ*Hibiya subway line, Roppongi Station (Exit 4A).*

Toho Cinemas. In Roppongi Hills, this complex offers comfort, plus six screens, VIP seats, and late shows on weekends. There are plenty of bars in the area for post-movie discussions. ⊠*Keyakizaka Complex, 6–10–2 Roppongi, Minato-ku* ☎*03/5775–6090* 🎫*Regular theater ¥1,800; Premier theater ¥3,000* Ⓜ*Hibiya and Ōedo subway lines, Roppongi Station (Roppongi Hills Exit).*

MODERN THEATER

The Shingeki (Modern Theater) movement began in Japan at about the turn of the 20th century, coping at first with the lack of native repertoire by performing translations of Western dramatists from Shakespeare to Shaw. It wasn't until around 1915 that Japanese playwrights began writing for the Shingeki stage, but modern drama did not really develop a voice of its own here until after World War II.

The watershed years came around 1965, when experimental theater companies, unable to find commercial space, began taking their work to young audiences in various unusual ways: street plays and "happenings" (chaotic, often improvised public theater in temporary digs). It was during this period that surrealist playwright Kōbō Abe found his stride and director Tadashi Suzuki developed the unique system of training that now draws aspiring actors from all over the world to his "theater community" in the mountains of Toyama Prefecture. Japanese drama today is a lively art indeed; theaters small and large, in unexpected pockets all over Tōkyō, attest to its vitality.

Most of these performances, however, are in Japanese, for Japanese audiences. You're unlikely to find one with program notes in English to help you follow it. Unless it's a play you already know well, and you're curious to see how it translates, you might do well to think of some other way to spend your evenings out if you don't understand Japanese. Language is less of a barrier when you're trying to enjoy a Takarazuka show.

Cirque du Soleil. The French-Canadian acrobatic superstars are so popular in Japan that they have their own purpose-built theater on the edge of the Tokyo Disneyland complex. This permanent home doesn't appear to be stopping them from running simultaneous shows in the city. Check any major ticket vendor for current shows and locations. ✉ *1–1 Maihama, Urayasu-shi, Chiba* ☎ *05/7002–8666* *¥7,800–¥18,000* ⊕ *www.cirquedusoleil.co.jp* Ⓜ *JR Keiyo, Musashino lines, Maihama Station (South Exit).*

Takarazuka. Japan's all-female theater troupe was founded in the Ōsaka suburb of Takarazuka in 1913 and has been going strong ever since. Today it has not one but five companies, one of which has a permanent home in Tōkyō at the 2,069-seat Tōkyō Takarazuka Theater. Where else but at the Takarazuka could you see *Gone With the Wind,* sung in Japanese, with a young woman in a mustache and a frock coat playing Rhett Butler? ■**TIP→ Advance tickets are available only through the Playguide agency (☎03/3561–8821), with any remaining tickets sold at the theater box office on the second day.** ✉ *1–1–3 Yūraku-chō, Chiyoda-ku* ☎ *03/5251–2001 ¥3,500–¥11,000* Ⓜ *JR Yamanote Line, Yūraku-chō Station (Hibiya Exit); Hibiya subway line, Hibiya Station (Exit A5); Chiyoda and Mita subway line, Hibiya Station (Exit A13).*

MUSIC

Information in English about venues for traditional Japanese music (koto, shamisen, and so forth) can be hard to find; check newspaper listings, particularly the Friday editions, for concerts and school recitals. Western music poses no such problem: during the 1980s and early 1990s a considerable number of new concert halls and performance spaces sprang up all over the city, adding to what was already an excellent roster of public auditoriums.

Casals Hall. The last of the fine small auditoriums built for chamber music, before the Japanese bubble economy burst in the early '90s, was designed by architect Arata Isozaki—justly famous for the Museum of Contemporary Art in Los Angeles. In addition to chamber music, Casals draws piano, guitar, cello, and voice soloists. ✉ *1–6 Kanda Surugadai, Chiyoda-ku* ☎ *03/3294–1229* Ⓜ *JR Chūō Line and Marunouchi subway line, Ochanomizu Station (Exit 2).*

Nakano Sun Plaza. Everything from rock to Argentine tango is staged at this hall. ✉ *4–1–1 Nakano, Nakano-ku* ☎ *03/3388–1151* Ⓜ *JR and Tōzai subway lines, Nakano Station (Kita-guchi/North Exit).*

New National Theater and Tōkyō Opera City Concert Hall. With its 1,810-seat main auditorium, this venue nourishes Japan's fledgling efforts to make a name for itself in the world of opera. The Opera City Concert Hall has a massive pipe organ and hosts visiting orchestras and performers. Large-scale operatic productions such as *Carmen* draw crowds at the New National Theater's Opera House, while the Pit and Playhouse theaters showcase musicals and more intimate dramatic works. Ticket prices range from ¥1,500 to ¥21,000. The complex also includes an art gallery. ⊠*3–20–2 Nishi-Shinjuku, Shinjuku-ku* ☎*03/5353–0788, 03/5353–9999 for tickets* ⊕*www.operacity.jp* Ⓜ*Keiō Shin-sen private rail line, Hatsudai Station (Higashi-guchi/East Exit).*

NHK Hall. The home base for the Japan Broadcasting Corporation's NHK Symphony Orchestra is probably the auditorium most familiar to Japanese lovers of classical music, as performances here are routinely rebroadcast on NHK-TV, the national TV station. ⊠*2–2–1 Jinnan, Shibuya-ku* ☎*03/3465–1751* Ⓜ*JR Yamanote Line, Shibuya Station (Hachiko Exit); Ginza and Hanzō-mon subway lines, Shibuya Station (Exits 6 and 7).*

Suntory Hall. This lavishly appointed concert auditorium in the Ark Hills complex has one of the best locations for theatergoers who want to extend their evening out: there's an abundance of good restaurants and bars nearby. ⊠*1–13–1 Akasaka, Minato-ku* ☎*03/3505–1001* Ⓜ*Ginza and Namboku subway lines, Tameike-Sannō Station (Exit 13).*

Tōkyō Dome. A 55,000-seat sports arena, the dome also hosts big-name Japanese pop acts as well as the occasional international star. ⊠*1–3–61 Kōraku, Bunkyō-ku* ☎*03/5800–9999* Ⓜ*Marunouchi and Namboku subway lines, Kōraku-en Station (Exit 2); Ōedo and Mita subway lines, Kasuga Station (Exit A2); JR Suidō-bashi Station (Nishi-guchi/West Exit).*

Tōkyō Metropolitan Festival Hall *(Tōkyō Bunka Kaikan).* In the 1960s and '70s this hall was one of the city's premier showcases for orchestral music and visiting soloists. It still gets major bookings. ⊠*5–45 Ueno Kōen, Taitō-ku* ☎*03/3828–2111* Ⓜ*JR Yamanote Line, Ueno Station (Kōen-guchi/Park Exit).*

TRADITIONAL THEATER
From the enthralling beauty of Kabuki to the slow, ritualized drama of Nō or the comedic Rakugo, Japan's traditional theatrical arts are a great way to experience the Japan that once was.

KABUKI
Kabuki emerged as a popular form of entertainment by women dancing lewdly in the early 17th century; before long, the authorities banned it as a threat to public order. Eventually it cleaned up its act, and by the latter half of the 18th century it had become popular with common folks. Kabuki had music, dance, and spectacle; it had acrobatics and sword fights; it had pathos and tragedy, historical romance and social satire. It no longer had bawdy beauties, however—women have been banned from the Kabuki stage since 1629—but in recompense it developed a professional role for female impersonators, who train for years to project a seductive, dazzling femininity. It had—and still

has—superstars and quick-change artists and legions of fans, who bring their lunch to the theater, stay all day, and shout out the names of their favorite actors at the stirring moments in their favorite plays.

The Kabuki repertoire does not really grow or change, but stars like Ennosuke Ichikawa and Tamasaburo Bando have put exciting, personal stamps on their performances that continue to draw audiences young and old.

⚠Kabuki-za, the place to see a Kabuki show in Tōkyō, has been torn down because of structural concerns. It's supposed to be rebuilt and reopened in 2013.

Kokuritsu Gekijō. This theater hosts Kabuki companies based elsewhere; it also has a training program for young people who may not have one of the hereditary family connections but want to break into this closely guarded profession. Debut performances, called *kao-mise,* are worth watching to catch the stars of the next generation. Reserved seats are usually ¥1,500–¥9,000. Tickets can be reserved by phone up until the day of the performance by calling the theater box office between 10 and 5. ⊠*4–1 Hayabusa-chō, Chiyoda-ku* ☏*05/7007–9900* ⊕*www. ntj.jac.go.jp/kokuritsu* Ⓜ*Hanzō-mon subway line, Hanzō-mon Station (Exit 1).*

Shimbashi Enbujō. Dating to 1925, this theater was built for the geisha of the Shimbashi quarter to present their spring and autumn performances of traditional music and dance. It's a bigger house than the Kabuki-za, and it presents a lot of traditional dance, *kyogen* (traditional Nō-style comic skits), and conventional Japanese drama as well as Kabuki. Reserved seats commonly run ¥2,100–¥16,800, and there's no gallery. ⊠*6–18–2 Ginza, Chūō-ku* ☏*03/5565–6000* Ⓜ*Hibiya and Asakusa subway lines, Higashi-Ginza Station (Exit A6).*

NŌ

Nō is a dramatic tradition far older than Kabuki: it reached a point of formal perfection in the 14th century and survives virtually unchanged from that period. Nō developed for the most part under the patronage of the warrior class; it's dignified, ritualized, and symbolic. Many of the plays in the repertoire are drawn from classical literature or tales of the supernatural, and the texts are richly poetic. Some understanding of the plot of each play is necessary to enjoy a performance, which moves at a glacial pace. The major Nō theaters often provide synopses of the plays in English.

The principal character in a Nō play wears a carved wooden mask. Such is the skill of the actor—and the mysterious effect of the play—that the mask itself may appear expressionless until the actor "brings it to life," at which point the mask seems to convey a considerable range of emotions. The best way to enjoy Nō is in the open air, at torchlight performances called Takigi Nō, held in the courtyards of temples. The setting and the aesthetics of the drama combine to produce an eerie theatrical experience. Tickets to Takigi Nō (held outdoors in temple courtyards) sell out quickly and are normally available only through the temples.

■TIP➔ *Kyōgen* are shorter, lighter plays that are often interspersed in between Nō performances and are much more accessible than Nō. If Nō doesn't appeal to you, consider taking advantage of opportunities to see kyōgen instead.

Kanze Nō-gakudō. Founded in the 14th century, this is among the most important of the Nō family schools in Tōkyō. The current *iemoto* (head) of the school is the 26th in his line. ✉*1–16–4 Shōtō, Shibuya-ku* ☎*03/3469–5241* Ⓜ*Ginza and Hanzō-mon subway lines, Shibuya Station (Exit 3A).*

National Nō Theater. This is one of the few public halls to host Nō performances. ✉*4–18–1 Sendagaya, Shibuya-ku* ☎*03/3423–1331* Ⓜ*JR Chūō Line, Sendagaya Station (Minami-guchi/South Exit); Ōedo subway line, Kokuritsu-Kyōgijō Station (Exit A4).*

RAKUGO

A *rakugo* comedian sits on a cushion and, ingeniously using a fan as a prop for all manner of situations, relates stories that have been handed down for centuries. With different voices and facial expressions, the storyteller acts out the parts of different characters within the stories. There's generally no English interpretation, and the monologues, filled with puns and expressions in dialect, can even be difficult for the Japanese themselves. A performance of rakugo is still worth seeing, however, for a slice of traditional pop culture.

Suzumoto. Built around 1857 and later rebuilt, Suzumoto is the oldest rakugo theater in Tōkyō. It's on Chūō-dōri, a few blocks north of the Ginza Line's Ueno Hiroko-ji stop. Tickets cost ¥2,800, and performances run continually throughout the day 12:20–4:30 and 5:20–9:10. ✉*2–7–12 Ueno, Taitō-ku* ☎*03/3834–5906* Ⓜ*Ginza subway line, Ueno Hiroko-ji Station (Exit 3).*

NIGHTLIFE

Most bars and clubs in the main entertainment districts have printed price lists, often in English. Drinks generally cost ¥700–¥1,200, although some small exclusive bars and clubs will set you back a lot more. Be wary of establishments without visible price lists. Hostess clubs and small backstreet bars known as "snacks" or "pubs" can be particularly treacherous territory for the unprepared. That drink you've just ordered could set you back a reasonable ¥1,000; you might, on the other hand, have wandered unknowingly into a place that charges you ¥30,000 up front for a whole bottle—and slaps a ¥20,000 cover charge on top. If the bar has hostesses, it's often unclear what the companionship of one will cost you, or whether she is there just for conversation. Ignore the persuasive shills on the streets of Roppongi and Kabuki-chō, who will try to hook you into their establishment. There is, of course, plenty of safe ground: hotel lounges, jazz clubs, and the rapidly expanding Irish pub scene are pretty much the way they are anywhere else. But elsewhere it's best to follow the old adage: if you have to ask how much it costs, you probably can't afford it.

There are five major districts—Akasaka, Ginza, Roppongi, Shibuya, and Shinjuku—in Tōkyō that have extensive nightlife, and each has a unique atmosphere, clientele, and price level.

AKASAKA

As an ex-geisha district, Akasaka is one of the traditional Tōkyō nightspots, but until recently that was a reason not to go. It was expensive and a little dated, with plenty of hostess bars, but nothing that would draw visitors to the area. But the last couple of years have seen a massive investment in the area and many attractive but affordable shops, bars, and restaurants have given the district a new lease on life.

GINZA

Ginza is home to most of the city's greatest bartenders. The drinks won't come cheap, but they will be perfect. But be careful which door you open: this is also the area for outrageously overpriced hostess clubs where kimono-clad women pander to politicians and high-rolling businessmen. You can also now find a handful of affordable bars, but why would you come to Ginza for the cheap stuff?

ROPPONGI

Roppongi is a tale of two cities. The area developed to serve the needs of the post–World War II American occupiers, who picked the area as their base. The boisterous, crude part of Roppongi still caters to the tastes of America's servicepeople and other young visitors, but there's now another side to the area. A pair of high-end minicities have appeared in recent years: Roppongi Hills in 2003, and the Midtown complex in 2007, luring a more urbane crowd with a mix of fancy stores, restaurants, bars, hotels, and luxury apartments.

SHIBUYA

Shibuya is the heart of Tōkyō's vibrant youth culture, with shopping and nightlife geared to the teen and twentysomething crowd. The pedestrian-only Center Gai street is the place to see the latest, quirkiest Tōkyō teen fashion. Shibuya is also a delight for record shoppers, with what is said to be the highest concentration of vinyl of any square mile on the planet.

SHINJUKU

Long a favorite drinking spot for artists and businesspeople alike, Shinjuku offers everything from glamorous high-rise bars to sleazy dens. The Golden-Gai area is the haunt of writers, artists, and filmmakers. Nearby Kabuki-chō is the city's most notorious red-light district, where English-speaking touts offer myriad sordid experiences. The Ni-chōme area (near Shinjuku Gyo-en National Garden) is the center of Tōkyō's diverse and vibrant gay and lesbian scene. The compact area is deserted during the day, but each night more than 250 bars, clubs, and restaurants bring Ni-chōme to life. Thanks in part to its diminutive dimensions, Ni-chōme is said to have more gay bars per block than any other city in the world.

BARS

A971. With a plum spot on the edge of Roppongi's Midtown complex, A971 has been popular right from its opening. It has an airy, modern feel, faces a spacious patio, and often hosts house music DJs.

It's standing room only on the weekends, which means plenty of socializing, usually of the flirtatious kind. ✉ *Tokyo Midtown East, 9–7–2 Akasaka, Minato-ku* ☎ *03/5413–3210* ⊕ *www.a971. com* ⊗ *Mon.–Thurs. 10 AM–5 AM, Sun. 10 AM–midnight* Ⓜ *Hibiya, Oedo subway lines, Roppongi Station (Exit 8).*

Agave. In most Roppongi hot spots, tequila is pounded one shot at a time so it goes straight into the bloodstream. Not so at Agave: this authentic Mexican cantina treats the spirit with a little more respect, and your palate will be tempted by a choice of more than 400 tequilas and mezcals. A single shot can cost between ¥800 and ¥10,000, but most of the varieties here aren't available anywhere else in Japan, so the steep prices are worth paying. ✉ *7–15–10 Roppongi, Minato-ku* ☎ *03/3497–0229* ⊗ *Mon.–Thurs. 6:30 PM–2 AM, Fri. and Sat. 6:30 PM–4 AM* Ⓜ *Hibiya and Ōedo subway lines, Roppongi Station (Exit 3).*

Fodor's Choice
★

Donzoko. This venerable bar claims to be Shinjuku's oldest—established in 1951—and has hosted Yukio Mishima and Akira Kurosawa among many other luminaries. It also claims (along with several other bars) to have invented the popular chu-hai cocktail (shōchu with juice and soda). But for all its history, Donzoko has a young and vibrant atmosphere, with its five floors usually packed. ✉ *3–10–2 Shinjuku, Shinjuku-ku* ☎ *03/3354–7749* ⊗ *Weekdays 6 PM–1 AM; weekends 5 PM–midnight* Ⓜ *Marunouchi, Shinjuku subway lines, Shinjuku-san-chōme Station (Exit C3).*

Kamiya Bar. Tōkyō's oldest Western-style bar hasn't had a face-lift for decades, and that's part of what draws so many drinkers to this bright, noisy venue. The other major attraction is the Denki Bran, a delicious but hangover-inducing liquor (comprising gin, red wine, brandy and Curaçao) that was invented here and is now stocked by bars throughout Japan. ✉ *24F Peninsula Tokyo, 1–1–1 Asakusa, Taitō-ku* ☎ *03/3841–5400* ⊗ *Daily 11:30 AM–10 PM* Ⓜ *Asakusa, Ginza subway lines, Asakusa Station (Exit A5).*

Loof. Loof (as in "roof") may lack the sophistication of Tōkyō's other high-rise bars, but in summer it's a great spot for a brew with a view. The bar, which serves an impressive range of world beers, sits atop the nine-story Island Creation Tower building. But the real treat is the private table perched above the regular bar. It doesn't have the superlative views of a hotel high-rise bar, but there aren't many other places where you can drink at a private, open-air, rooftop table. Drinks start at ¥800. ✉ *1–22–12 Dogenzaka, Shibuya-ku* ☎ *03/3770–0008* ⊗ *Mon.–Sat. 6 PM–5 AM, Sun. 6 PM–11:30 pm* Ⓜ *JR, Ginza and Hanzō-mon subway lines, Shibuya Station (Hachiko Exit).*

Montoak. Positioned halfway down the prestigious shopping street Omotesandō-dōri, within spitting distance of such fashion giants as

CLOSE UP

The Red Lights of Kabuki-chō

Tōkyō has more than its fair share of red-light districts, but the leader of the pack is unquestionably Kabuki-chō, located just north of Shinjuku Station. The land was once a swamp, although its current name refers to an aborted post–World War II effort to bring culture to the area in the form of a landmark Kabuki theater. Nowadays, most of the entertainment is of the insalubrious kind, with strip clubs, love hotels, host and hostess clubs, and thinly disguised brothels all luridly advertising their presence.

The area's also home to throngs of Japanese and Chinese gangsters, giving rise to its image domestically as a danger zone. But in truth, Kabuki-chō poses little risk to even the solo traveler. The sheer volume of people in the area each night, combined with a prominent security-camera presence, means that crime stays mostly indoors.

Despite its sordid reputation, Kabuki-chō does offer something beyond the red lights. There are eateries galore ranging from chain diners to designer restaurants. The impressive 16th-century shrine **Hanazono Jinja** (✉ 5–17–3 Shinjuku, Shinjuku-ku ☎ 03/3209–5265

🆓 Free ☉ Daily sunrise–sunset Ⓜ Marunouchi subway line, Shinjuku-san-chōme Station [Exits B2 and B3]) hosts several events throughout the year, but comes alive with two must-see colorful festivals on its grounds. The weekend closest to May 28 brings the Hanazono shrine festival, in which portable shrines are paraded through the streets. The November Tori-no-Ichi festival (the exact days in November vary each year) is held here and at several shrines throughout Tōkyō, but Hanazono is the most famous place to buy the festival's kumade: big rakes decorated with money, mock fruit, and other items people would like to "rake in." People buy them for luck, and replace them every year.

Also here is Golden Gai, probably Tōkyō's most atmospheric drinking area. The quirky **Koma Gekijō** (Koma Stadium Theater ✉ 1–19–1 Kabuki-chō, Shinjuku-ku ☎ 03/3200–2213) is a favorite of the pension-drawing crowd, offering variety stage shows starring fading entertainers. Even if a performance here makes little sense, it should still be a memorable experience.

—Nicholas Coldicott

Gucci, Louis Vuitton, and Tod's, this hip restaurant-bar is a great place to rest after testing the limits of your credit card. With smoky floor-to-ceiling windows, cushy armchairs, and a layout so spacious you won't believe you're sitting on one of Tōkyō's toniest streets, the place attracts a hipper-than-thou clientele but never feels unwelcoming. The bar food consists of canapés, salads, cheese plates, and the like. Drinks start at ¥700. ✉ 6–1–9 Jingū-mae, Shibuya-ku ☎ 03/5468–5928 ⊕ www.mon toak.com ☉ Daily 11 AM–3 AM Ⓜ Chiyoda subway line, Meiji Jingū-mae Station (Exit 4).

★ **New York Bar.** Even before Lost in Translation introduced the Park Hyatt's signature lounge to filmgoers worldwide, New York Bar was a local Tōkyō favorite. All the style you would expect of one of the city's top hotels combined with superior views of Shinjuku's skyscrapers and neon-lighted streets make this one of the city's premier nighttime venues. The quality of the jazz on offer equals that of the view. Drinks start at ¥800, and there's a cover charge of ¥2,000 after 8 PM (7 PM on Sunday). ✉ *52F Park Hyatt Hotel, 3-7-1-2 Nishi-Shinjuku, Shinjuku-ku* ☎ *03/5322-1234* ⊗ *Sun.-Wed. 5 PM-midnight, Thurs.-Sat. 5 PM-1 AM* Ⓜ *JR Shinjuku Station (Nishi-guchi/West Exit).*

WORD OF MOUTH

"The bar at the Park Hyatt in Shinjuku has amazing views."

—W9London

Old Imperial Bar. Comfortable and sedate, this is the pride of the Imperial Hotel, decorated with elements saved from Frank Lloyd Wright's earlier version of the building—alas, long since torn down. Drinks start at ¥1,000. ✉ *Imperial Hotel, 1-1-1 Uchisaiwai-chō, Chiyoda-ku* ☎ *03/3504-1111* ⊕ *www.imperialhotel.co.jp* ⊗ *Daily 11:30 AM-midnight* Ⓜ *Hibiya Line, Hibiya Station (Exit 5).*

Fodor's Choice ★ **Peter.** Like most of Tōkyō's high-end hotels, the Peninsula has a high-rise bar. But unlike many hotel bars, especially the high-rise, five-star varieties that are dimly lit with a jazz piano and ultracomposed staff, Peter has an entrance in a rainbow of colors, eye-catching cocktails, and occasional DJs. This 24th-floor spot's decor of chrome trees and rainbow lights is defiantly anti-zeitgeist, but lots of fun. ✉ *24F Peninsula Tokyo, 1-8-1 Yuraku-chō, Chiyoda-ku* ☎ *03/6270-2763* ⊕ *www.tokyo.peninsula.com* ⊗ *Daily 11:30 AM-10 PM* Ⓜ *Hibiya Mita subway lines, Hibiya Station (Exit A6).*

Radio. Koji Ozaki is the closest thing Tōkyō has to a superstar bartender. This demure septuagenarian has been crafting cocktails for half a century, and he's known for both his perfectionism and creativity. Ozaki not only designed the bar he works behind and the glasses he serves his creations in (some of the best in the city), he also arranges the bar's flowers. ✉ *3-10-34 Minami-Aoyama, Minato-ku* ☎ *03/3402-2668* ⊕ *www.bar-radio.com* ⊗ *Mon.-Sat. 6 PM-1 AM* Ⓜ *Chiyoda, Ginza, Hanzomon subway lines, Omote-Sandō Station (Exit A4).*

Sekirei. This is simply the best place in Tōkyō to sink a cold one. The picture-perfect summertime beer garden looks like a budget buster, but it's run by the Asahi brewery and offers refreshments at a price anyone can afford. Most evenings, kimono-clad *nihon-buyō* dancers perform to the strains of shamisen music. Sekirei serves Japanese- and Western-style food to a demure after-work crowd. Drinks start at ¥700. ✉ *2-2-23 Moto-Akasaka, Minato-ku* ☎ *03/3746-7723* ⊗ *June-Sept., weekdays 4:30 PM-10:30 PM, weekends 5:30 PM-10:30 PM; dancers perform 2 or 3 times nightly at varying times* Ⓜ *JR Chūō Line, Shinanomachi Station.*

Star Bar. It's often said that Ginza has all the best bars, and Star Bar may be the best of the lot. Owner-bartender Hisashi Kishi is the Director of Technical Research for the Japan Bartenders Association, and his attention to detail is staggering. The drinks aren't cheap, but you get what you pay for. Try one of Kishi's Sidecars. ✉ *B1 1-5-13 Ginza, Chuo-ku* ☎ *03/3535-8005* ⊕ *www.starbarginza.com* ⊗ *Weekdays 6 PM-2 AM, Sat. 6 PM-midnight* Ⓜ *JR Yamanote line, Yuraku-chō Station (Kyōbashi Exit).*

Vive La Vie. Vive La Vie is exactly what a bar should be: relaxing, friendly, and stylish, with quality cocktails and good music. You can relax on the sofas here without any risk of disturbance or sit at the bar and join the locals' banter. Some weekends the bar hosts local DJs and charges an entrance fee (average ¥1,500). Drinks start at ¥700. ☒ *2–4–6 Shibuya, Shibuya-ku* ☎*03/5485–5498* ⊙ *Mon.–Thurs. 7 PM–1 AM, Fri. and Sat. 7 PM–3 AM* Ⓜ *Ginza subway line, Omotesandō Station (Exit B1).*

BEER HALLS AND PUBS

Clubhouse. Rugby is the sport of choice at this pub, but even those with no interest in watching the game will enjoy the decent food and amiable atmosphere. A good mix of locals and foreigners frequents the bar, and the place is more hospitable than many similar venues. ☒ *3F 3–7–3 Shinjuku, Shinjuku-ku* ☎*03/3359–7785* ⊙ *Daily 5 PM–12:30 AM* Ⓜ *Marunouchi subway line, Shinjuku-san-chōme Station (Exit 3).*

Ginza Lion. This bar, in business since 1899 and occupying the same stately Chūō-dōri location since 1934, is remarkably inexpensive for one of Tōkyō's toniest addresses. Ginza shoppers and office workers alike drop by for beer and ballast—anything from yakitori to spaghetti. Beers start at ¥590. ☒ *7–9–20 Ginza, Chūō-ku* ☎*03/3571–2590* ⊙ *Daily 11:30 AM–11 PM* Ⓜ *Ginza, Hibiya, and Marunouchi subway lines, Ginza Station (Exit A3).*

What the Dickens. This spacious pub is nearly always packed with a fun-seeking mix of locals and foreigners. Regular live music (funk, folk, jazz, rock, reggae—anything goes here) and other events keep the place bubbling, and a menu of traditional British grub gives it an authentic feel. ☒ *4F 1–13–3 Ebisu-Nishi, Shibuya-ku* ☎*03/3780–2099* ⊕*www. whatthedickens.jp* ⊙ *Tues. and Wed. 5 PM–1 AM, Thurs.–Sat. 5 PM–2 AM, Sun. 5 PM–midnight* Ⓜ *Hibiya subway line, Ebisu Station (Nishi-guchi/West Exit).*

DANCE CLUBS

Tōkyō's club scene isn't quite up there with the international hot spots of London or New York, but in many ways it's more enjoyable. The scene is markedly less pretentious than other cosmopolitan hubs, with the emphasis on dancing rather than preening. The crowds are enthusiastic and highly knowledgeable. And most weekends bring more than one world-renowned DJ to town.

★ **Ageha.** This massive bay-side venue has the city's best sound system and most diverse musical lineup. The cavernous Arena hosts well-known house and techno DJs, the bar plays hip-hop, a summer-only swimming-pool area has everything from reggae to break beats, and inside a chill-out tent there's usually ambient or trance music. Because of its far-flung location and enormous capacity, Ageha can be either a throbbing party or an embarrassingly empty hall, depending on the caliber of the DJ. Free buses to Ageha depart every half hour between 11 PM and 4:30 AM from the stop opposite the Shibuya police station on Roppongi-dōri, a three-minute walk from Shibuya Station (there are also return buses every half hour from 11:30 PM to 5 AM). ☒ *2–2–10 Shin-Kiba, Kōtō-ku* ☎*03/5534–1515* ⊕*www.ageha.com* ☒*Around ¥3,500* Ⓜ *Yūraku-chō subway line, Shin-Kiba Station.*

CLOSE UP

Golden Gai

Tucked away on the eastern side of Tōkyō's sordid Kabuki-chō district, Golden Gai is a ramshackle collection of more than 200 Lilliputian bars that survived the rampant construction of Japan's bubble-economy years, thanks to the passion of its patrons. In the 1980s, when the *yakuza*, Japan's crime syndicate, was torching properties to sell the land to big-thinking developers, Golden Gai's supporters took turns guarding the area each night.

Each bar occupies a few square yards, and some accommodate fewer than a dozen drinkers. With such limited space, many of the bars rely on their regulars—and give a frosty welcome and exorbitant bill to the casual visitor. And although the timeworn look of Golden Gai captures the imagination of most visitors, many of the establishments are notoriously unfriendly to foreigners. But times change, as do leases, and a new generation of owners is gradually emerging to offer the same intimate drinking experience and cold beers without the unwelcome reception.

Albatross G. When it opened in summer 2005, Albatross G quickly built a following with its friendliness and, in Golden Gai terms, affordability. The ¥300 seating charge and drinks starting at ¥600 are a marked contrast to most of its neighbors. ⊠ *2F 5th Ave., 1–1 Kabuki-chō, Shinjuku-ku* ☎ *03/3203–3699* ⊕ *www.alba-s.com* ⊗ *Daily 8 PM–5 AM* Ⓜ *Marunouchi, Shinjuku subway lines, Shinjuku-san-chōme Station (Exit B3).*

La Jetée. It should come as no surprise that French cinema is the proprietor's big passion: a film lover's paradise, La Jetée is covered in Euro-cinema posters and was named after a French movie. It struggles to seat 10 customers, but

that means intimate conversations—in Japanese, French, and sometimes English—usually about movies. If you want to discuss European cinema with Wim Wenders or sit toe-to-toe with Quentin Tarantino, this is your best bet. The music, naturally, comes exclusively from film sound tracks. The seating charge is ¥1,000. ⊠ *2F 1–1–8 Kabuki-chō, Shinjuku-ku* ☎ *03/3208–9645* ⊗ *Mon.– Sat. 7 PM–early morning* Ⓜ *Marunouchi, Shinjuku subway lines, Shinjuku-san-chōme Station (Exit B3).*

Sumire no Tenmado. Tim Burton's favorite Tōkyō bar is a tiny shrine to the gothloli (Gothic Lolita) subculture, and you'll find the director's skeletal drawings on the pitch-black walls. It's eerie but friendly, dark but fun, and even the signature cocktail—Ankoku Sumire le poison (Sumire's pitch-black poison)—is as black as the decor. ⊠ *2F 1–1–7 Kabukicho, Shinjuku-ku* ☎ *03/3209–1204* ⊕ *www.kokusyokusumire.net* ⊗ *Weekdays 4:30–11:30 PM, weekends 11:30 AM–11:30 PM* Ⓜ *Marunouchi, Shinjuku subway lines, Shinjuku-san-chōme Station (Exit B3).*

—Nicholas Coldicott

2

La Fabrique. A Continental crowd gathers at the late-night parties at this small, dressy, French restaurant-cum-club in Shibuya's Zero Gate complex. The music is predominantly house. ✉*B1F 16–9 Udagawachō, Shibuya-ku* ☎*03/5428–5100* ⊕*www.lafabrique.jp* ✉¥*3,000–*¥*3,500* ⊙*Daily 11* AM*–5* AM Ⓜ*JR Yamanote Line, Ginza and Hanzō-mon subway lines, Shibuya Station (Hachiko Exit for JR and Ginza, Exit 6 for Hanzō-mon).*

Le Baron de Paris. The Tōkyō branch of the Paris and New York club was created by superstar designer Marc Newson and is part-owned by Duran Duran's Nick Wood. As you might expect, it draws a fashionable crowd and plays host to events by trendy magazines and visiting musicians. Expect an eclectic mix of nostalgic and modern party music. Hours and prices vary greatly, so check the Web site for info. ✉*B1 3–8–40 Minami-Aoyama, Minato-ku* ☎*03/3408–3665* ⊕*www. lebaron.jp* Ⓜ*Chiyoda, Ginza, Hanzomon subway lines, Omote-Sandō Station (Exit A4).*

Super-Deluxe. This isn't quite a dance club. You could call it an experimental party space, with each night hosting a different kind of event. It's home to Pecha Kucha, a popular evening of presentations by creative types; but you might also find a techno night, underground-film screenings, a performance-art event, or anything else the imagination can conjure up. ✉*B1, 3–1–25 Nishi-Azabu, Minato-ku* ☎*03/5412–0516* ⊕*www.super-deluxe.com* ⊙*Daily 6* PM*–late* Ⓜ*Hibiya and Oedo subway lines, Roppongi Station (Exit 1C).*

★ **Warehouse 702.** Nightlife in Roppongi tends to be raucous and low-brow, so serious clubbers should head to nearby Azabu-Juban for this spacious subterranean venue with a great sound system and consistently high-quality DJs. ✉*B1, 1–4–5 Azabu-Juban, Minato-ku* ☎*03/6230–0343* ⊕*www.warehouse702.com* ✉*Around* ¥*3,500* ⊙*Wed.–Mon. 11* PM*–5* AM Ⓜ*Nanboku, Oedo subway lines, Azabu-Juban Station (Exit 7).*

Womb. Well-known techno and break-beat DJs make a point of stopping by this Shibuya überclub on their way through town. The turntable talent, including the likes of Danny Howells and Richie Hawtin, and four floors of dance and lounge space make Womb Tōkyō's most consistently rewarding club experience. ✉*2–16 Maruyama-chō, Shibuya-ku* ☎*03/5459–0039* ⊕*www.womb.co.jp* ✉*Around* ¥*3,500* ⊙*Daily 10* PM*–early morning* Ⓜ*JR Yamanote Line, Ginza and Hanzō-mon subway lines, Shibuya Station (Hachiko Exit for JR and Ginza, Exit 3A for Hanzō-mon).*

GAY BARS

Gay culture in Japan is a little different than that in the West. Most of it takes place well under the radar, which can be both a blessing and a curse; there are fewer options, but there's also less of the prejudice you might experience elsewhere. People are more likely to be baffled than offended by gay couples and some hotels may "not compute" that a same-sex couple would like a double bed, but it's a very safe city to visit and with a little digging you'll find a scene more vibrant than you—or many Tōkyōites—might expect. The city's primary queer hub is Ni-chōme in the Shinjuku district. Take the Shinjuku or Marunouchi subway line to Shinjuku-Sanchōme station (exit C7). Ni-chōme is sometimes likened to its more notorious neighbor Kabuki-chō, its name also spoken in hushed tones and accompanied by raised eyebrows. Ni-chōme, however, is more subtle in its approach. Although queer and queer-friendly establishments can be found sprinkled in other areas (Shibuya, Daikanyama Shinbashi, and Ebisu), none quite match Ni-chōme for variety or accessibility.

Advocates Cafe. Almost every great gay night out begins at this welcoming street-corner pub, where the patrons spill out onto the street. This is the perfect place to put back a few cocktails (¥700–¥900), meet new people, and get a feeling for where to go next. The crowd is mixed and very foreigner friendly. ⊠*2–18–1 Shinjuku, Shinjuku-ku* ☎*03/3358–3988* ⊕*www.advocates-cafe.com* ⊗*Mon.–Sat. 6* PM*–4* AM, *Sun. 6* PM*-1* AM.

Arty Farty. Cheap and cheesy, Arty Farty is a fun club, complete with a ministage and stripper pole. Those with aversions to Kylie or Madonna need not bother. Draft beer starts at ¥500, and the alcohol selection is comprehensive. The crowd is mixed and foreigner friendly. ⊠*2F Dai 33 Kyutei Bldg., 2–11–7 Shinjuku, Shinjuku-ku* ☎*03/5362–9720* ⊗*Sun. – Thurs. 7* PM*–3* AM, *Fri. and Sat. 7* PM*–5* AM.

Chestnut & Squirrel. The only bar on this list not in Ni-chōme, Chestnut & Squirrel (the name translates in Japanese as a certain female body part) is the place to be for lesbians on Wednesday nights in Tōkyō. The bar's cheap drinks (cocktails and most beers ¥500), friendly, unpretentious vibe, and mix of foreign and Japanese customers give it the feel of a friendly neighborhood bar. ⊠*3F O-ishi Bldg., 3–7–8 Shibuya, Shibuya-ku* ☎*No phone* ⊕*www.chestnutandsquirrel.com* ⊗*Wed. 7:30* PM*–late.*

Dragon Men. Despite the name, Tōkyō's swanky gay lounge Dragon Men also welcomes women. Remodeled in 2007, Dragon is a neondeco space that would look right at home in New York or Paris. The location could be better: it's behind a drugstore, and the outdoor tables face a ramshackle wall, but when the place is crammed on weekends with cuties of all persuasions, who's looking? ⊠*1F Stork Nagasaki, 2–11–4 Shinjuku, Shinjuku-ku* ☎*03/3341–0606* ⊗*Sun.–Thurs. 6* PM*–3* AM, *Fri. and Sat. 6* PM*–4* AM.

GB. The men-only GB has been running for two decades, and carries a whiff of the old days when things were less mainstream. Video monitors blast contemporary and classic dance hits. On weekends the place is packed with gentlemen in their twenties through fifties cruising via strategically placed mirrors. ⊠*B1 Shinjuku Plaza Bldg., 2–12–3 Shinjuku, Shinjuku-ku* ☎*03/3352–8972* ⊕*gb-tokyo.tripod.com* ⊗*Sun.–Thurs. 8* PM*–2* AM, *Fri. and Sat. 8* PM*–3* AM.

Motel #203. One of Ni-chōme's newest bars, Motel is a posh but relaxed bar for "women who love women." It's a cozy den of vintage lamps, leather sofas, and plush cushions, with no cover charge. The bar's owner is an icon in the Tōkyō lesbian scene and also runs a popular monthly dance party, called "Girlfriend," usually the last Saturday of every month at nearby Bar Hijo-guchi, or Bar Exit. Motel is women-only except Thursday, which is mixed. ⊠*203 Sunnocorpo Shinjuku Bldg., 2–7–2 Shinjuku, Shinjuku-ku* ☎*03/6383–4649* ⊕*www.bar-motel.com* ☉*Wed.–Mon. 8 PM–4 AM.*

IZAKAYA

Izakaya (literally "drinking places") are Japanese pubs that can be found throughout Tōkyō. If you're in the mood for elegant decor and sedate surroundings, look elsewhere; these drinking dens are often noisy, bright, and smoky. But for a taste of authentic Japanese-style socializing, a visit to an izakaya is a must—this is where young people start their nights out, office workers gather on their way home, and students take a break to grab a cheap meal and a drink.

Typically, izakaya have a full lineup of cocktails, a good selection of sake, draft beer, and lots of cheap, greasy Japanese and Western food; rarely does anything cost more than ¥1,000. Picture menus make ordering easy, and because most cocktails retain their Western names, communicating drink preferences shouldn't be difficult.

Tachimichiya. With its traditional Japanese dishes, wide range of sakes and shōchus, and rustic interior, Tachimichiya is a classic izakaya in all ways but one: its love of punk rock. The wall is adorned with posters of the Sex Pistols, the Ramones, and the Clash, who also provide the sound track. The theme is fun rather than overbearing, and the food alone is good enough to warrant a visit. ⊠*B1, 30–8 Sarugaku-chō, Shibuya-ku* ☎*03/5459–3431* ☉*Weekdays 6 PM–4 AM, weekends 6 PM–midnight* Ⓜ*Tōkyu Tōyoko line, Daikanyama Station.*

Takara. This high-class izakaya in the sumptuous Tōkyō International Forum is a favorite with foreigners because of its English-language menu and extensive sake list. ⊠*B1, 3–5–1 Marunouchi, Chiyoda-ku* ☎*03/5223–9888* ☉*Weekdays 11:30 AM–2:30 PM and 5:30–11 PM, weekends 11:30 AM–3:30 PM and 5:30 PM–10 PM* Ⓜ*Yūraku-chō subway line, Yūraku-chō Station (Exit A-4B).*

Watami. One of Tōkyō's big izakaya chains—with a half-dozen branches in the youth entertainment district of Shibuya alone—Watami is popular for its seriously inexpensive menu. Seating at this location ranges from a communal island bar to Western-style tables to more private areas. ⊠*4F Satose Bldg., 13–8 Udagawachō, Shibuya-ku* ☎*03/6415–6516* ☉*Sun.–Thurs. 5 PM–3 AM, Fri. and Sat. 5 PM–5 AM* Ⓜ*JR Yamanote Line, Ginza and Hanzō-mon subway lines, Shibuya Station (Hachiko Exit for JR and Ginza, Exit 6 for Hanzō-mon).*

JAZZ CLUBS

Tōkyō has one of the best jazz scenes in Asia. The clubs here attract world-class performers and innovative local acts. On any given night you can choose from more than 20 local live acts, but it'll cost you. Entrance fees start at ¥2,500 for the tiny venues and can be more than five times that for a famous act. The weekly English-language magazine *Metropolis* has listings for the major clubs. For information on jazz events at small venues, a visit to the record shop **Disk Union** (⊠*3–31–2 Shinjuku, Shinjuku-ku* ☎*03/5379–3551* Ⓜ*Marunouchi subway line, Shinjuku-san-chōme Station [Exit A1]*) is essential. The store has flyers (sometimes in English) for smaller gigs, and the staff can make recommendations.

Blue Note Tōkyō. The Blue Note isn't for everyone: prices are high, sets are short, and patrons are packed in tight, often sharing a table with strangers. But if you want to catch the legends, superstars—those of Herbie Hancock and Sly & the Family Stone caliber—and the best of the local scene, you'll have to come here. Expect to pay upward of ¥12,000 to see major acts, and put another ¥4,000–¥5,000 on the budget for food and drink. ✉6–3–16 Minami-Aoyama, Minato-ku ☎03/5485–0088 ⊙Shows usually Mon.–Sat. at 7 and 9:30, Sun. at 6:30 and 9 ⊕www.bluenote.co.jp Ⓜ Chiyoda, Ginza, and Hanzō-mon subway lines, Omotesandō Station (Exit A3).

Hot House. This could very well be the world's smallest jazz club. An evening here is like listening to live jazz in your living room with five or six other jazz lovers on your sofa. It's so small, in fact, that you can't get through the front door once the pianist is seated, so don't show up late. Live acts are trios at most, with no space for drums or amplifiers. Simple, home-style Japanese cooking helps make this a truly intimate experience. ✉B1 Liberal Takadanobaba, 2–14–8 Takadanobaba, Shinjuku-ku ☎03/3367–1233 ⊙Show times vary from 8:30 PM–early morning Ⓜ JR Takadanobaba Station (Waseda Exit).

Intro. This small basement bar features one of the best jazz experiences in Tōkyō: a Saturday "jam session" that stretches until 5 AM (¥1,000 entry fee). Other nights of the week occasionally bring unannounced live sets by musicians just dropping by, but usually it's the owner's extensive vinyl and CD collection that the regulars are listening to. Simple Japanese and Western food is available. ✉B1 NT Bldg., 2–14–8 Takadanobaba, Shinjuku-ku ☎03/3200–4396 ⊕ www.intro.co.jp ⊙Sun.–Thurs. 6:30 PM–midnight, Fri. 6:30 PM–1 AM, Sat. 5 PM–5 AM Ⓜ JR Takadanobaba Station (Waseda Exit).

Shinjuku Pit Inn. Most major jazz musicians have played at least once in this classic Tōkyō club. The veteran Shinjuku Pit stages mostly mainstream fare with the odd foray into the avant-garde. Afternoon admission is ¥1,300 weekdays, ¥2,500 weekends; evening entry is typically ¥3,000. Better-known local acts are often a little more. ✉B1 Accord Shinjuku Bldg., 2–12–4 Shinjuku, Shinjuku-ku ☎03/3354–2024 ⊙Daily, hrs vary ⊕www.pit-inn.com Ⓜ Marunouchi subway line, Shinjuku-san-chōme Station.

Fodor'sChoice ★ **Sweet Basil 139.** An upscale jazz club near Roppongi Crossing, Sweet Basil 139 (no relation to the famous New York Sweet Basil) is renowned for local and international acts that run the musical gamut from smooth jazz and fusion to classical. A large, formal dining area serves Italian dishes that are as good as the jazz, making this spot an excellent choice for a complete night out. With a spacious interior and standing room for 500 on the main floor, this is one of the largest and most accessible jazz bars in town. Prices range from ¥2,857 to ¥12,000 depending on who's headlining. ✉6–7–11 Roppongi, Minato-ku ☎03/5474–0139 ⊕stb139.co.jp ⊙Mon.–Sat. 6–11 PM; shows at 8 Ⓜ Hibiya and Ōedo subway lines, Roppongi Station (Exit 3).

CLOSE UP

All That Tōkyō Jazz

The Tōkyō jazz scene is one of the world's best, far surpassing that of Paris and New York with its number of venues playing traditional, swing, bossa nova, R & B, and free jazz. Though popular in Japan before World War II, jazz really took hold of the city after U.S. forces introduced Charlie Parker and Thelonius Monk in the late 1940s. The genre had been banned in wartime Japan as an American vice, but even at the height of the war, fans were able to listen to their favorite artists on Voice of America radio. In the 1960s Japan experienced a boom in all areas of the arts, and jazz was no exception. Since then, the Japanese scene has steadily bloomed, with several local stars—such as Sadao Watanabe in the 1960s and contemporary favorites Keiko Lee and Hiromi Uehara—gaining global attention.

Today there are more than 120 bars and clubs that host live music, plus hundreds that play recorded jazz. Shinjuku, Takadanobaba, and Kichijōji are the city's jazz enclaves. Famous international acts regularly appear at big-name clubs such as the Blue Note, but the smaller, lesser-known joints usually have more atmosphere. With such a large jazz scene, there's an incredible diversity to enjoy, from Louis Armstrong tribute acts to fully improvised free jazz—sometimes on successive nights at the same venue.

If you time your visit right, you can listen to great jazz at one of the city's more than 20 annual festivals dedicated to this adopted musical form. The festivals vary in size and coverage, but two to check out are the Tōkyō Jazz Festival and the Asagaya Jazz Street Festival.

On the last weekend in September, the **Tōkyō Jazz Festival** (☏ *03/5777–8600* ⊕ *www.tokyo-jazz.com*) takes over the Tōkyō International Forum in Marunouchi. Though the 5,000-seat hall lacks the intimacy you might seek in a jazz show, the lineup is usually an impressive mix of local talent and international stars.

The **Asagaya Festival** (☏ *03/5305–5075*), held the last weekend of October, is a predominantly mainstream affair, with venues ranging from a Shintō shrine to a Lutheran church (most venues are within walking distance of Asagaya Station). Look for festival staff at the station to help guide you (note that they may not speak English, however). Previous headliners have included the Mike Price Jazz Quintet and vocalist Masamichi Yanō. The festival gets crowded, so come early to ensure entry.

—James Catchpole

KARAOKE

In buttoned-down, socially conservative Japan, karaoke is one of the safety valves. Employees, employers, husbands, wives, teenage romancers, and good friends all drop their guard when there's a mike in hand. The phenomenon started in the 1970s when cabaret singer Daisuke Inoue made a coin-operated machine that played his songs on tape so that his fans could sing along. Unfortunately for Inoue, he neglected to patent his creation, thereby failing to cash in as karaoke became one of Japan's favorite pastimes. Nowadays it's the likely finale of any office outing, a cheap daytime activity for teens, and a surprisingly popular destination for dates.

Unlike most karaoke bars in the United States, in Japan the singing usually takes place in the seclusion of private rooms that can accommodate groups. Basic hourly charges vary but are usually less than ¥1,000. Most establishments have a large selection of English songs, stay open late, and serve inexpensive food and drink, which you order via a telephone on the wall. Finding a venue around one of the major entertainment hubs is easy—there will be plenty of young touts eager to escort you to their employer. And unlike most other touts in the city, you won't end up broke by following them.

Big Echo. One of Tōkyō's largest karaoke chains, Big Echo has dozens of locations throughout the city. Cheap hourly rates and late closing times make it popular with youngsters. The Roppongi branch is spread over three floors. ⊠ *7–14–12 Roppongi, Minato-ku* ☎ *03/5770–7700* ☏ *¥500–¥600 per hr* ☉ *Daily 6 PM–5 AM* Ⓜ *Hibiya and Ōedo subway lines, Roppongi Station (Exit 4).*

★ **Lovenet.** Despite the misleading erotic name, Lovenet is actually the fanciest karaoke box in town. Luxury theme rooms of all descriptions create a fun and classy setting for your dulcet warbling. Mediterranean and Japanese food is served. ⊠ *7–14–4 Roppongi, Minato-ku* ☎ *03/5771–5511* ☏ *From ¥2,000 per hr* ☉ *Daily 6 PM–5 AM* ⊕ *www. lovenet-jp.com* Ⓜ *Hibiya and Ōedo subway lines, Roppongi Station (Exit 4A).*

Pasela. This 10-story entertainment complex on the main Roppongi drag of Gaien-Higashi-dōri has seven floors of karaoke rooms with more than 10,000 foreign-song titles. A Mexican-theme bar and a restaurant are also on-site. ⊠ *5–16–3 Roppongi, Minato-ku* ☎ *0120/911–086* ☏ *¥400–¥1,260 per hr* ☉ *Mon.–Thurs. 5 PM–10 AM, Fri.–Sun. 2 PM–8 AM* Ⓜ *Hibiya and Ōedo subway lines, Roppongi Station (Exit 3).*

Shidax. The Shidax chain's corporate headquarters—in an excellent Shibuya location, across from Tower Records—has 130 private karaoke rooms, a café, and a restaurant. ⊠ *1–12–13 Jinnan, Shibuya ku* ☎ *03/5784–8881* ☏ *¥760 per hr* ☉ *Daily 11 AM–8 AM* Ⓜ *JR, Ginza, and Hanzō-mon subway lines, Shibuya Station (Exit 6).*

Smash Hits. If karaoke just isn't karaoke to you without drunken strangers to sing to, Smash Hits has the answer. An expat favorite, it offers thousands of English songs and a central performance stage. The cover charge gets you two drinks and no time limit. ⊠ *5–2–26 Hiro-o, Shibuya-ku* ☎ *03/3444–0432* ⊕ *www.smashhits.jp* ☏ *¥3,500* ☉ *Tues.–Sat. 7 PM–3 AM* Ⓜ *Hibiya Line, Hiro-o Station.*

LIVE HOUSES

Tōkyō has numerous small music clubs known as "live houses." These range from the very basic to miniclub venues, and they showcase the best emerging talent on the local scene. Many of the best live houses can be found in the Kichijōji, Kōenji, and Nakano areas, although they are tucked away in basements citywide. The music could be gypsy jazz one night and thrash metal the next, so it's worth doing a little research before you turn up. Cover charges vary depending on who's performing but are typically ¥3,000–¥5,000 ($25–$41).

Manda-la 2. Relaxed and intimate, this local favorite in Kichijōji attracts an eclectic group of performers. Cover charges range from ¥1,800 to ¥4,000. ⊠2–8–6 Kichijōji-Minami-cho, Musashino-shi ☎0422/42–1579 ⊙6:30 PM–varying closing times Ⓜ Keiō Inokashira private rail line, JR Chūō and JR Sōbu lines, Kichijōji Station (Kōenguchi/Park Exit, on Suehiro-dōri).

Shelter. An ever-popular, long-running venue in Shimo-Kitazawa, an area dominated by people in their late teens and early twenties, Shelter is a great place to catch promising local bands of all genres. ⊠B1F 2–6–10 Kitazawa, Setagaya-ku ☎03/3466–7430 ⊙Daily 6:30 PM, closing varies; some daytime shows on weekends Ⓜ Keiō Inokashira, Odakyū private rail lines, Shimo-Kitazawa Station (North Exit).

Showboat. A small, basic venue that's been going strong for more than a decade, Showboat attracts both amateur and semiprofessional performers. Ticket prices vary by act but are typically around ¥2,000 and often include one drink. ⊠B1 Oak Hill Kōenji, 3–17–2 Kita Kōenji, Suginami-ku ☎03/3337–5745 ⊕www.showboat.co.jp ⊙Daily 6 PM–early morning Ⓜ JR Sōbu and JR Chūō lines, Kōenji Station (Kitaguchi/North Exit).

SHOPPING

You didn't fly all the way to Tōkyō to buy European designer clothing, so shop for items that are Japanese-made for Japanese people and sold in stores that don't cater to tourists. This city is Japan's showcase. The crazy clothing styles, obscure electronics, and new games found here are capable of setting trends for the rest of the country—and perhaps the rest of Asia.

Also, don't pass up the chance to purchase Japanese crafts. Color, balance of form, and superb workmanship make these items exquisite and well worth the price you'll pay. Some can be quite expensive; for example, Japanese lacquerware carries a hefty price tag. But if you like the shiny boxes, bowls, cups, and trays and consider that quality lacquerware is made to last a lifetime, the cost is justified.

The Japanese approach to shopping can be feverish; on the weekends, some of the hipper, youth-oriented stores will have lines that wind down the street as kids wait patiently to pick up the latest trend. But shopping here can also be an exercise in elegance and refinement. Note the care taken with items after you purchase them, especially in department stores and boutiques. Goods will be wrapped, wrapped again, bagged, and sealed. Sure, the packaging can be excessive—does anybody really need three plastic bags for one croissant?—but such a focus on presentation has deep roots in Japanese culture.

This focus on presentation also influences salespeople who are invariably helpful and polite. In the larger stores they greet you with a bow when you arrive, and many of them speak at least enough English to help you find what you're looking for. There's a saying in Japan: o-kyaku-sama wa kami-sama, "the customer is a god"—and since the competition for your business is fierce, people do take it to heart.

CLOSE UP

Tōkyō Rocks!

First the bad news: Most of the biggest and best music festivals take place outside Tōkyō. But the good news is that many of them are in easy-to-get-to, often stunning countryside locations, and are well worth the trip. Most festivals take place in the summer months, and though tickets aren't cheap, they usually sell out fast. If you can't purchase tickets directly from the organizers, Ticket Pia or Lawson's convenience stores should stock them.

Fuji Rock Festival. Despite the name, Japan's most popular festival takes place far from Mt. Fuji in the picturesque ski resort of Naeba, about two hours from Tōkyō. On a good year, more than 100,000 music lovers attend this three-day event that runs, like so much in Japan, with stunning efficiency. Asian Dub Foundation and the Red Hot Chili Peppers are regular guests in a lineup of more than 200 acts across 12 stages. ✉ *Naeba Ski Resort, Niigata-ken* ⊕ *www.fujirockfestival.com* ☺ *Last weekend in July.*

Metamorphose. Japan's premier dance music festival is held annually on the Izu Peninsula, close to Mt. Fuji. The lineup has diversified slightly from its techno origins and recently saw Afrobeat pioneer Tony Allen and Japanese jazzy hip-hop DJ Nujabes on the bill.

✉ *Cycle Sports Center, Shuzenji, Shizuoka-ken* ⊕ *www.metamo.info* ☺ *4th weekend of Aug.*

Summer Sonic. This annual two-day festival takes place in a baseball stadium and convention center an hour outside of Tōkyō. The rock-centric lineup usually boasts major stars and a selection of up-and-coming acts, but the concrete and cavernous acoustics really dent the vibe. The festival also takes place in Ōsaka on the same weekend, with Saturday's Tōkyō lineup playing Ōsaka on Sunday, and vice versa. ✉ *Chiba Marine Stadium and Makuhari Messe Convention Center, Mihama-ku, Nakano, Chiba-ken* ✉ *Maishima, Ōsaka* ⊕ *www.summersonic.com* ☺ *2nd weekend in Aug.*

Tōkyō Summer Festival. One of the few festivals taking place within the city, this is one of the more eclectic programs. This is where you might catch some jazz cats from Zanzibar or a Saharan chanting troupe. The shows are spread across various venues and take place throughout July, under a different thematic banner each year. Classical and world music is the specialty. ✉ *Venues throughout Tōkyō* ⊕ *www.arion-edo.org* ☺ *July.*

—Nicholas Coldicott

Japan has been slow to embrace the use of credit cards, and even though plastic is now accepted at big retailers, some smaller shops only take cash. So when you go souvenir hunting, be prepared with a decent amount of cash; Tōkyō's low crime rates make this a low-risk proposition. The dishonor associated with theft is so strong, in fact, that it's considered bad form to conspicuously count change in front of cashiers.

Japan has an across-the-board 5% value-added tax (V.A.T.) imposed on luxury goods as well as on restaurant and hotel bills. This tax can be avoided at some duty-free shops in the city (don't forget to bring your passport). It's also waived in the duty-free shops at the international airports, but because these places tend to have higher profit margins, your tax savings there are likely to be offset by the higher markups. Stores in Tōkyō generally open at 10 or 11 AM and close at 8 or 9 PM.

SHOPPING DISTRICTS

AKIHABARA AND JIMBŌ-CHŌ

Akihabara was at one time the only place Tōkyōites would go to buy cutting-edge electronic gadgets, but the area has lost its aura of exclusivity thanks to the Internet and the big discount chains that have sprung up around the city. Still, for its sheer variety of products and foreigner-friendliness, Akihabara has the newcomers beat—and a visit remains essential to any Tōkyō shopping spree. Salesclerks speak decent English at most of the major shops (and many of the smaller ones), and the big chains offer duty-free and export items. Be sure to poke around the backstreets for smaller stores that sell used and unusual electronic goods. The area has also become the center of the *otaku* (nerd) boom, with loads of shops offering enough video games and manga (sophisticated comic books) to satisfy even the most fastidious geek. West of Akihabara, in the used-bookstore district of Jimbō-chō, you'll find pretty much whatever you're looking for in dictionaries and art books, rare and out-of-print editions (Western and Japanese), and prints. Ⓜ *For Akihabara: JR Yamanote, Keihin Tōhoku, and Sōbu lines, Akihabara Station (Electric Town Exit); Hibiya subway line, Akihabara Station. For Jimbō-chō: Hanzō-mon, Shinjuku, and Mita subway lines, Jimbō-chō Station.*

AOYAMA AND OMOTESANDŌ

You can find boutiques by many of the leading Japanese and Western designers in Aoyama, as well as elegant, but pricey, antiques shops on Kottō-dōri. Aoyama tends to be a showcase not merely of high fashion but also of the latest concepts in commercial architecture and interior design. The centerpiece of Omotesandō (a short stroll from Aoyama) is the long, wide avenue running from Aoyama-dōri to Meiji Jingū. Known as the Champs-Elysées of Tōkyō, the sidewalks are lined with cafés and designer boutiques, both foreign and domestic. There are also several antiques and souvenir shops here. Omotesandō is perfect for browsing, window-shopping, and lingering over a café au lait before strolling to your next destination. Ⓜ *Chiyoda, Ginza, and Hanzō-mon subway lines, Omotesandō Station (Exits A4, A5, B1, B2, and B3).*

ASAKUSA

While sightseeing in this area, take time to stroll through its arcades. Many of the goods sold here are the kinds of souvenirs you can find in any tourist trap, but look a little harder and you can find small backstreet shops that have been making beautiful wooden combs, delicate fans, and other items of fine traditional craftsmanship for generations. Also here are the cookware shops of Kappabashi, where you can load up on everything from sushi knives to plastic lobsters. Ⓜ *Asakusa subway line, Asakusa Station (Kaminari-mon Exit); Ginza subway line, Asakusa Station (Exit 1) and Tawara-machi Station (Exit 3).*

DAIKANYAMA
Unleash your inner fashionista in Daikanyama. Wedged between Shibuya and Ebisu, this area is a boutique heaven: shelves of funky shoes, stacks of retro T-shirts, and assortments of skate-punk wear. Ⓜ *Tōkyū Tōyoko Line, Daikanyama Station.*

GINZA
This world-renowned entertainment and shopping district dates back to the Edo period (1603–1868), when it consisted of long, willow-lined avenues. The willows have long since gone, and the streets are now lined with department stores and boutiques. The exclusive shops in this area—including flagship stores for major jewelers like Tiffany & Co., Harry Winston, and Mikimoto—sell quality merchandise at high prices. On Sunday the main strip of Chuo-dōri is closed to car traffic and umbrella-covered tables dot the pavement; it's a great place for shoppers to rest their weary feet. Ⓜ *Marunouchi, Ginza, and Hibiya subway lines, Ginza Station (Exits A1–A10); Yūraku-chō subway line, Ginza Itchōme Station; JR Yamanote Line, Yūraku-chō Station.*

HARAJUKU
The average shopper in Harajuku is under 20; a substantial percentage is under 16. Most stores focus on moderately priced clothing and accessories, with a lot of kitsch mixed in, but there are also several upscale fashion houses in the area—and more on the way. This shopping and residential area extends southeast from Harajuku Station along both sides of Omotesandō and Meiji-dōri; the shops that target the youngest consumers concentrate especially on the narrow street called Takeshita-dōri. Tōkyō's most exciting neighborhood for youth fashion and design lies along the promenade known as Kyū Shibuya-gawa Hodō, commonly referred to as Cat Street. Ⓜ *Chiyoda and Fukutoshin subway lines, Meiji Jingū-mae Station (Exits 1–5); JR Yamanote Line, Harajuku Station.*

JIYŪGAOKA
Jiyūgaoka is located at the edge of the well-to-do Meguro Ward. Big chain stores are in abundance here, but the real attractions are the boutiques offering unique bedding, crockery, and furniture items. Ⓜ *Tōkyū Tōyoko line or Oimachi lines, Jiyūgaoka Station.*

SHIBUYA
This is primarily an entertainment and retail district geared toward teenagers and young adults. The shopping scene in Shibuya caters to these groups with many reasonably priced smaller shops and a few department stores that are casual yet chic. Ⓜ *JR Yamanote Line; Tōkyū and Keiō lines; Ginza, Fukutoshin, and Hanzō-mon subway lines, Shibuya Station (Nishi-guchi/West Exit for JR, Exits 3–8 for subway lines).*

SHIMOKITAZAWA
Arguably Tōkyō's hippie bastion, the twisting streets and alleyways of Shimokitazawa boast used-clothing shops, record stores, and knick-knack outlets that generally offer low prices. Just follow the scent of patchouli oil from the station. Ⓜ *Keiō Inokashira or Odakyū lines, Shimokitazawa Station.*

SHINJUKU

Shinjuku is not without its honky-tonk and sleaze, but it also has some of the city's most popular department stores. The shopping crowd is a mix of Tōkyō youth and office ladies. Surrounding the station are several discount electronics and home-appliance outlets. Ⓜ *JR Yamanote Line; Odakyū and Keiō lines; Marunouchi, Shinjuku, Fukutoshin, and Ōedo subway lines, Shinjuku Station.*

TSUKIJI

Best known for its daily fish-market auctions (which will have a new location in 2012), Tsukiji also has a warren of streets that carry useful, everyday items that serve as a window onto the lives of the Japanese. This is a fascinating area to poke around after seeing the fish auction and before stopping in the neighborhood for a fresh-as-can-be sushi lunch. Ⓜ *Ōedo subway line, Tsukiji-shijō Station (Exit A1); Hibiya subway line, Tsukiji Station (Exit 1).*

SHOPPING STREETS AND ARCADES

Most Japanese villages have pedestrian shopping streets known as *shotengai*, and Tōkyō, a big city made up of smaller neighborhoods, is no different. But you won't find big-name retailers like pharmacies and grocery stores in these areas—Tōkyō's shotengai are thick with boutiques, accessories shops, and cafés. Just like their surrounding neighborhoods, these streets can be classy, trendy, or a bit shabby.

Ame-ya Yoko-chō Market. Everything from fresh fish to cheap import clothing is for sale at this bustling warren of side streets between Okachi-machi and Ueno stations. In the days leading up to New Years, the area turns into mosh-pit mayhem as shoppers fight for fish and snacks to serve over the holidays. The name of the market is often shortened to Ameyoko. Most shops and stalls are open daily 10–7. ✉ *Ueno 4-chōme, Taitō-ku* Ⓜ *JR Ueno Station (Hirokō-ji Exit), JR Okachi-machi Station (Exit A7).*

International Shopping Arcade. A somewhat ragtag collection of shops in Hibiya, this arcade holds a range of goods, including cameras, electronics, pearls, and kimonos. The shops are duty-free, and most of the sales staff speaks decent English. If you listen carefully you'll hear the rumble of cars passing above on the freeway that is the roof of the building. ✉ *1–7–23 Uchisaiwai-chō, Chiyoda-ku* Ⓜ *Chiyoda and Hibiya subway lines, Hibiya Station (Exit A13).*

Kyū Shibuya-gawa Hodō. With its avant-garde crafts stores, funky T-shirt shops, and hipster boutiques, this pedestrian strip serves as a showcase for Japan's au courant designers and artisans. Cat Street is the place to experience bohemian Tōkyō in all its exuberance. ✉ *Between Jingū-mae 3-chōme and Jingū-mae 6-chōme, Shibuya-ku* Ⓜ *Chiyoda and Fukutoshin subway lines, Meiji-Jingū-mae Station (Exits 4 and 5).*

Nishi-Sandō. Kimono and *yukata* (cotton kimono) fabrics, traditional accessories, swords, and festival costumes at very reasonable prices are all for sale at this Asakusa arcade. It runs east of the area's movie theaters, between Rok-ku and the Sensō-ji complex. ✉*Asakusa 2-chōme, Taitō-ku* Ⓜ*Ginza subway line, Asakusa Station (Exit 1).*

Takeshita-dōri. Teenybopper fashion is all the rage along this Harajuku mainstay, where crowds of high school kids look for the newest addition to their ever-changing, outrageous wardrobes. ✉*Jingū-mae 1-chōme, Shibuya-ku* Ⓜ*JR Harajuku Station (Takeshita-Dōri Exit).*

MALLS AND SHOPPING CENTERS

Most of these self-contained retail zones carry both foreign and Japanese brands and, like the city's department stores, house cafés, bars, and restaurants. If you don't have the time or energy to dash about Tōkyō in search of the perfect gifts, consider dropping by one of these shopping centers, where you can find a wide selection of merchandise. Most are used to dealing with foreigners.

★ **Axis.** Classy and cutting-edge housewares, fabrics, and ceramics are sold at this multistory design center on the main Roppongi drag of Gaien-Higashi-dōri. Living Motif is a home furnishings shop with exquisite foreign and Japanese goods. Savoir Vivre has an excellent selection of ceramics. The small Yoshikin sells its own brand of professional-grade cutlery. ✉*5–17–1 Roppongi, Minato-ku* ☎*03/3587–2781* ⊘*Most shops Mon.–Sat. 11–7* Ⓜ*Hibiya and Ōedo subway lines, Roppongi Station (Exit 3); Namboku subway line, Roppongi Itchōme Station (Exit 1).*

Coredo. Unlike other big stores in the Ginza and Nihombashi areas, this sparkling mall has a contemporary feel thanks to an open layout and extensive use of glass and wood. Housewares and fashion can be found here. ✉*1–4–1 Nihombashi, Chūō-ku* ☎*03/3272–4939* ⊘*Mon.–Sat. 11–9, Sun. 11–8* Ⓜ*Ginza, Tōzai, and Asakusa subway lines, Nihombashi Station (Exit B12).*

Glassarea. Virtually defining Aoyama elegance is this cobblestone shopping center, which draws well-heeled Aoyama housewives to its boutiques, restaurants, and housewares shops. ✉*5–4–41 Minami-Aoyama, Minato-ku* ☎*03/5778–4450* ⊘*Most shops daily 11–8* Ⓜ*Ginza, Chiyoda, and Hanzō-mon subway lines, Omotesandō Station (Exit B1).*

Marunouchi Building. Opened in 2003, this 37-story shopping, office, and dining complex has brought some much-needed retail dazzle to the area between Tōkyō Station and the Imperial Palace. The ground-floor Beams House shop is part of the well-respected Tōkyō fashion chain, and the second-floor Aquagirl boutique sells trendy clothes for women. ✉*2–4–1 Marunouchi, Chiyoda-ku* ☎*03/5218–5100* ⊘*Mon.–Sat. 11–9, Sun. 11–8* Ⓜ*Marunouchi subway line, Tōkyō Station (Marunouchi Building Exit); JR Yamanote Line, Tōkyō Station (Marunouchi Minami-guchi/South Exit).*

Omotesandō Hills. Architect Tadao Ando's latest adventure in concrete is Tōkyō's newest monument to shopping. The six wedge-shaped floors include some brand-name heavy hitters (Yves Saint Laurent and Harry Winston) and a wide range of smaller stores whose shelves showcase high-end shoes and bags. ✉*4–12–10 Jingū-mae, Shibuya-ku*

☎03/3497–0293 ⊙ Daily 11–9 Ⓜ Hanzō-mon, Ginza, and Chiyoda subway lines, Omotesandō Station (Exit A2).

Roppongi Hills. You could easily spend a whole day exploring the retail areas of Tōkyō's newest minicity, opened in 2003. The shops here emphasize eye-catching design and chi-chi brands. Finding a particular shop, however, can be a hassle given the building's Escher-like layout. ✉6–10–1 Roppongi, Minato-ku ☎03/6406–6000 ⊙ Most shops daily 11–9 Ⓜ Hibiya and Ōedo subway lines, Roppongi Station (Roppongi Hills Exit).

Shibuya 109. This nine-floor outlet is a teenage girl's dream. It's filled with small stores whose merchandise screams kitsch and trend. Many weekend afternoons will see dance groups and fashion shows at the first-floor entrance. ✉2–29–1 Dōgenzaka, Shibuya-ku ☎03/3477–5111 ⊙ Daily 10–9 Ⓜ JR Yamanote Line; Ginza, Fukutoshin, and Hanzō-mon subway lines: Shibuya Station (Hachiko Exit for JR, Exit 3 for subway lines).

DEPARTMENT STORES

Most Japanese depāto (department stores) are parts of conglomerates that include railways, real estate, and leisure industries. The stores themselves commonly have travel agencies, theaters, and art galleries on the premises, as well as reasonably priced and strategically placed restaurants and cafés.

A visit to a Japanese department store is not merely a shopping excursion—it's a lesson in Japanese culture. Plan to arrive just before it opens: promptly on the hour, immaculately groomed young women face the customers from inside, bow ceremoniously, and unlock the doors. As you walk through the store, all the sales assistants will be standing at attention, in postures of nearly reverent welcome. Notice the uniform angle of incline: many stores have training sessions to teach their new employees the precise and proper degree at which to bend from the waist.

On the top floor of many department stores you'll find gift packages containing Japan's best-loved brands of sake, rice crackers, and other food items. Department stores also typically devote one floor to traditional Japanese crafts, including ceramics, paintings, and lacquerware. If you're pressed for time, these are great places to pick up a variety of souvenirs.

Don't miss the depachika (food departments) on the lower levels, where you'll encounter an overwhelming selection of Japanese and Western delicacies. Though no locals in their right minds would shop here regularly for their groceries—the price tags on the imported cheeses and hams will cause your jaw to hit the floor—a brief exploration will give you a pretty good picture of what people might select for a special occasion. Many stalls have small samples out on the counter, and nobody will raise a fuss if you help yourself, even if you don't make a purchase.

Major department stores accept credit cards and provide shipping services. Some salesclerks speak English. If you're having communication difficulties, someone will eventually come to the rescue. On the first floor you'll invariably find a general information booth with useful maps of the store in English. Some department stores close one or two days a month. To be on the safe side, call ahead.

GINZA AND NIHOMBASHI AND YŪRAKU-CHŌ

FodorśChoice ★ **Matsuya.** On the fourth floor, the gleaming Matsuya houses an excellent selection of Japanese fashion, including Issey Miyake, Yohji Yamamoto, and Comme Ça Du Mode. The Louis Vuitton shops on the first and second floors are particularly popular with Tōkyō's brand-obsessed shoppers. ⊠ *3–6–1 Ginza, Chūo-ku* ☏ *03/3567–1211* ⊘ *Daily 10–8* Ⓜ *Ginza, Marunouchi, and Hibiya subway lines, Ginza Station (Exits A12 and A13).*

Matsuzakaya. The Matsuzakaya conglomerate was founded in Nagoya and still commands the loyalties of shoppers with origins in western Japan. Style-conscious Tōkyōites tend to find the sense of fashion a bit countrified. ⊠ *6–10–1 Ginza, Chūo ku* ☏ *03/3572–1111* ⊘ *Daily 10:30–7:30* Ⓜ *Ginza, Marunouchi, and Hibiya subway lines, Ginza Station (Exits A3 and A4).*

★ **Mitsukoshi.** Founded in 1673 as a dry-goods store, Mitsukoshi later played one of the leading roles in introducing Western merchandise to Japan. It has retained its image of quality and excellence, with a particularly strong representation of Western fashion designers. The store also stocks fine traditional Japanese goods—don't miss the art gallery and the crafts area on the sixth floor. With its own subway stop, bronze lions at the entrance, and an atrium sculpture of the Japanese goddess Magokoro, the remarkable Nihombashi flagship store merits a visit even if you're not planning on buying anything. ⊠ *1–4–1 Nihombashi Muro-machi, Chūo-ku* ☏ *03/3241–3311* ⊘ *Mon.–Sat. 10–8, Sun. 10–7:30* Ⓜ *Ginza and Hanzō-mon subway lines, Mitsukoshi-mae Station (Exits A3 and A5)* ⊠ *4–6–16 Ginza, Chūo-ku* ☏ *03/3562–1111* ⊘ *Daily 10–8* Ⓜ *Ginza, Marunouchi, and Hibiya subway lines, Ginza Station (Exits A6, A7, and A8).*

FodorśChoice ★ **Muji.** This chain features generically branded housewares and clothing at reasonable prices. You'll find a large selection of Bauhaus-influenced furniture, appliances, and bedding at the massive flagship branch in Yūraku-chō. If you're a bit overwhelmed by all the options, relax at the dining area that boasts—what else?—Muji meals. ⊠ *3–8–3 Marunouchi Muro-machi, Chiyoda-ku* ☏ *03/5208–8241* ⊘ *Daily 10–9* Ⓜ *JR Yamanote Line; Yūraku-chō subway line, Yūraku-chō Station (JR Kyobashi Exit, subway Exit D9).*

Takashimaya. In Japanese, *taka* means "high"—a fitting word for this store, which is beloved for its superior quality and prestige. Gift-givers all over Japan seek out this department store; a present that comes in a Takashimaya bag makes a statement regardless of what's inside. The second floor, with shops by Christian Dior, Prada, Chanel, Cartier, and many others, is one of the toniest retail spaces in a shopping district celebrated for its exclusivity. The seventh floor has a complete selection of traditional crafts, antiques, and curios. The lower-level food court carries every gastronomic delight imaginable, from Japanese crackers and green tea to Miyazaki beef and plump melons. ✉ *2–4–1 Nihombashi, Chūō-ku* 🕾 *03/3211–4111* ☉ *Daily 10–8* Ⓜ *Ginza subway line, Nihombashi Station (Exits B1 and B2)* ✉ *Takashimaya Times Sq., 5–24–2 Sendagaya, Shibuya-ku* 🕾 *03/5361–1111* ☉ *Sun.–Fri. 10–8, Sat. 10–8:30* Ⓜ *JR Yamanote Line, Shinjuku Station (Minami-guchi/South Exit).*

Wako. Wako is well-known for its high-end glassware, jewelry, and accessories, as well as having some of the handsomest, most sophisticated window displays in town. The clock atop this curved 1930s-era building is illuminated at night, making it one of Tōkyō's more recognized landmarks. ✉ *4–5–11 Ginza, Chūō-ku* 🕾 *03/3562–2111* ☉ *Mon.–Sat. 10:30–6* Ⓜ *Ginza, Marunouchi, and Hibiya subway lines, Ginza Station (Exits A9 and A10).*

IKEBUKURO AND SHIBUYA

Parco. Parco, owned by the Seibu conglomerate, is actually two vertical malls filled with small retail shops and boutiques, all in walking distance of one another in the commercial heart of Shibuya. Parco Part 1 caters to a younger crowd and stocks unbranded casual clothing, crafts fabrics, and accessories. Part 3 sells a mixture of men's and women's fashions, tableware, and household furnishings. The nearby Zero Gate complex houses the basement restaurant-nightclub La Fabrique. ✉ *15–1 Udagawa-chō, Shibuya-ku* 🕾 *03/3464–5111* ☉ *Daily 10–9* Ⓜ *Ginza, Fukutoshin, and Hanzō-mon subway lines, Shibuya Station (Exits 6 and 7).*

Seibu. Even Japanese customers have been known to get lost in this mammoth department store; the main branch is in Ikebukuro. The Shibuya branch, which still carries an impressive array of merchandise, is smaller and more manageable. Seibu has an excellent selection of household goods, from furniture to china and lacquerware, in its stand-alone Loft shops (often next door to Seibu branches, or occasionally within the department store itself). ✉ *1–28–1 Minami Ikebukuro, Toshima-ku* 🕾 *03/3981–0111* ☉ *Mon.–Sat. 10–9, Sun. 10–8* Ⓜ *JR Yamanote Line; Marunouchi, Fukutoshin, and Yūrakuchō subway lines, Ikebukuro Station (Minami-guchi/South Exit); Seibu Ikebukuro Line, Seibu Ikebukuro Station (Seibu Department Store Exit); Tōbu Tōjō Line, Tōbu Ikebukuro Station (Minami-guchi/South Exit)* ✉ *21–1 Udagawa-chō, Shibuya-ku* 🕾 *03/3462–0111* ☉ *Sun.–Wed. 10–8, Thurs.–Sat. 10–9* Ⓜ *JR Yamanote Line; Ginza and Hanzō-mon subway lines, Shibuya Station (Hachiko Exit for JR, Exits 6 and 7 for subway lines).*

SHINJUKU

Isetan. One of Tōkyō's oldest and largest department stores, Isetan is known for its mix of high-end and affordable fashions, as well as its selection of larger sizes not found in most Tōkyō stores. The basement's food selection, which includes prepared salads and dried fish, is one of the city's largest in a department store. ✉*3–14–1 Shinjuku, Shinjuku-ku* ☎*03/3352–1111* ✆*Daily 10–8* Ⓜ*JR Yamanote Line, Marunouchi subway line (Higashi-guchi/East Exit for JR, Exits B2, B3, B4, and B5 for subway line).*

Marui. Marui, easily recognized by its red-and-white logo, burst onto the department store scene in the 1980s by introducing an in-store credit card—one of the first stores in Japan to do so. Branches typically occupy separate buildings near busy train stations; there are a handful of big shops in Shinjuku with names like Marui Young, Marui City, and Marui Men. Youngsters flock to the stores in search of petite clothing, accessories, and sportswear. Marui City is the chain's main location. ✉*3–1–26 Shinjuku, Shinjuku-ku* ☎*03/3354–0101* ✆*Daily 11:30–9* Ⓜ*JR Yamanote Line, Shinjuku Station (Higashi-guchi/East Exit); Marunouchi and Fukutoshin subway lines, Shinjuku San-chōme Station (Exit B2).*

SPECIALTY STORES

ANTIQUES

From ornate *tansu* (traditional chests used to store clothing) to Meiji-era Nō masks, Tōkyō's antiques shops are stocked with fine examples of traditional Japanese craftsmanship. The two best areas for antiques are Nishi-Ogikubo (also known as Nishiogi), which is just outside of Shinjuku, and Aoyama. The elegant shops along Kottō-dōri—Aoyama's "Antiques Road"—are the places to hunt down exquisite ¥100,000 vases and other pricey items. The slapdash array of more than 60 antiques shops in Nishi-Ogikubo has an anything-goes feel. When visiting Nishi-Ogikubo, which you can reach by taking the Sōbu Line to Nishi-Ogikubo Station, your best bet is to pick up the free printed area guide available at the police box outside the train station's north exit. Even though it's mostly in Japanese, the map provides easy-to-follow directions to all stores. Dealers are evenly clustered in each of the four districts around the station, so plan on spending at least half a day in Nishi-Ogikubo if you want to see them all.

Antiquers can also find great buys at Tōkyō's flea markets, which are often held on the grounds of the city's shrines.

★ **Fuji-Torii.** An English-speaking staff, a central Omotesandō location, and antiques ranging from ceramics to swords are the big draws at this shop, in business since 1948. In particular, Fuji-Torii has an excellent selection of folding screens, lacquerware, painted glassware, and *ukiyo-e* (woodblock prints). ✉*6–1–10 Jingū-mae, Shibuya-ku* ☎*03/3400–2777* ✆*Wed.–Mon. 11–6; closed 3rd Mon. of month* Ⓜ*Chiyoda and Fukutoshin subway lines, Meiji Jingū-mae Station (Exit 4).*

Morita. This Aoyama shop carries antiques and new *mingei* (Japanese folk crafts) in addition to a large stock of textiles from throughout Asia. ✉*5–12–2 Minami-Aoyama, Minato-ku* ☎*03/3407–4466* ✆*Daily*

10–7 Ⓜ *Ginza, Chiyoda, and Hanzō-mon subway lines, Omotesandō Station (Exit B1).*

Tōgō Jinja. One of the city's biggest flea markets—where you can often find antiques and old yakuza movie posters—takes place at this shrine near Harajuku's Takeshita-dōri, on the first Sunday of the month from sunrise to sunset. ✉ *1–5 Jingū-mae, Shibuya-ku* ☎ *03/3425–7965* Ⓜ *Chiyoda and Fukutoshin subway lines, Meiji-jingū-mae Station; JR Yamanote Line, Harajuku Station (Takeshita-dōri Exit).*

Yasukuni Jinja. Every second and third Saturday of the month, from sunrise to sunset, antiques-hunters can search and explore this large flea market. It's located near the Yasukuni shrine, so when you're finished shopping, stroll over to the shrine to learn about the controversy that surrounds it. ✉ *3–1 Kudan-Kita, Chiyoda-ku* ☎ *090/8722–0437* Ⓜ *Hanzō-mon and Shinjuku subway lines, Kudanshita Station (Exit 1).*

BOOKS

If you want to read while you're in Tōkyō, it's best to bring your books and magazines with you; foreign titles are often marked up considerably. All the shops listed below are open daily.

Bookstores of Jimbō-chō. The site of one of the largest concentrations of used bookstores in the world, the Jimbō-chō area is a bibliophile's dream. In the ½-km (¼-mi) strip along Yasukuni-dōri and its side streets you can find centuries-old Japanese prints, vintage manga, and even complete sets of the *Oxford English Dictionary*. Most shops have predominately Japanese-language selections, but almost all stock some foreign titles, with a few devoting major floor space to English books. Kitazawa Shoten, recognizable by its stately entranceway, carries lots of humanities titles. Tokyo Random Walk is the retail outlet of Tuttle Publishing, which puts out books on Japanese language and culture. The large Japanese publisher Sanseidō has its flagship store here; the fifth floor sells magazines and postcards in addition to books. The stores in the area are usually open 9 or 9:30 to 5:30 or 6, and many of the smaller shops close on Sunday or Monday. Ⓜ *Mita, Shinjuku, and Hanzō-mon subway lines, Jimbō-chō Station (Exit A5).*

Kinokuniya. The mammoth Kinokuniya bookstore near the south exit of Shinjuku Station devotes most of its sixth floor to English titles, with an excellent selection of travel guides, magazines, and books on Japan. ✉ *Takashimaya Times Sq., 5–24–2 Sendagaya, Shibuya-ku* ☎ *03/5361–3300* ◷ *Daily 10–9* Ⓜ *JR Yamanote Line, Shinjuku Station (Minami-guchi/South Exit).*

Maruzen. There are English titles on the fourth floor, as well as art books; this recently relocated flagship branch of the Maruzen chain also hosts the occasional art exhibit. ✉ *1–6–4 Marunouchi, Chiyoda-ku* ☎ *03/5288–8881* ◷ *Daily 9–9* Ⓜ *JR Yamanote Line, Tōkyō Station (North Exit); Tozai subway line, Otemachi Station (Exit B2C).*

Tower Records. This branch of the U.S.-based chain carries an eclectic collection of English-language books at more reasonable prices than most bookstores in town. It also has the best selection of foreign magazines in Tōkyō. ✉ *1–22–14 Jinnan, Shibuya-ku* ☎ *03/3496–3661* ◷ *Daily*

10–11 Ⓜ *JR Yamanote Line, Hanzō-mon, Fukutoshin, and Ginza subway lines, Shibuya Station (Hachiko Exit for JR, Exit 6 for subway).*

Yaesu Book Center. English-language paperbacks, art books, and calendars are available on the seventh floor of this celebrated bookstore. ✉*2–5–1 Yaesu, Chūō-ku* ☎*03/3281–1811* ☉*Mon.–Sat. 10–9, Sun. 10–8* Ⓜ *JR Yamanote Line, Tōkyō Station (Yaesu South Exit 5).*

2

CERAMICS

The Japanese have been crafting extraordinary pottery for more than 2,000 years, but this art form really began to flourish in the 16th century with the popularity and demand for tea-ceremony utensils. Feudal lords competed for possession of the finest pieces, and distinctive styles of pottery developed in regions all over the country. Some of the more prominent styles are those of the village of Arita in Kyūshū, with painted patterns of flowers and birds; Mashiko, in Tochigi Prefecture, with its rough textures and simple, warm colors; rugged Hagi ware, from the eponymous Western Honshū city; and Kasama, in Ibaraki Prefecture, with glazes made from ash and ground rocks. Tōkyō's specialty shops and department stores carry fairly complete selections of these and other wares.

At first glance, Japanese ceramics may seem priced for a prince's table, but if you keep shopping, you can find reasonably priced items that are generally far superior in design to what is available back home. Sale items are often amazingly good bargains. Vases, sake sets, and chopstick rests all make good gifts.

Noritake. The Akasaka showroom of this internationally renowned brand carries fine china and glassware in a spacious setting. ✉*7–8–5 Akasaka, Minato-ku* ☎*03/3586–0059* ☉*Weekdays 10–6* Ⓜ*Chiyoda subway line, Akasaka Station (Exit 7).*

Savoir Vivre. In Roppongi's ultratrendy Axis Building, this store sells contemporary and antique tea sets, cups, bowls, and glassware. ✉*Axis Bldg., 3F, 5–17–1 Roppongi, Minato-ku* ☎*03/3585–7365* ☉*Daily 11–7* Ⓜ*Hibiya and Oedo subway lines, Roppongi Station (Exit 3).*

Tsutaya. *Ikebana* (flower arrangement) and *sadō* (tea ceremony) goods are the only items sold at this Kottō-dōri shop, but they come in such stunning variety that a visit is definitely worthwhile. Colorful vases in surprising shapes and traditional ceramic tea sets make for unique souvenirs. ✉*5–10–5 Minami-Aoyama, Minato-ku* ☎*03/3400–3815* ☉*Daily 10–6:30* Ⓜ*Ginza, Chiyoda, and Hanzō-mon subway lines, Omotesandō Station (Exit B3).*

CLOTHING BOUTIQUES

Japanese boutiques pay as much attention to interior design as they do to the clothing they sell; like anywhere else, it's the image that moves the merchandise. Although many mainstream Japanese designers are represented in the major upscale department stores, you may enjoy your shopping more in the elegant boutiques of Aoyama and Omotesandō—most of which are within walking distance of one another.

Bape Exclusive Aoyama. Since the late 1990s, no brand has been more coveted by Harajuku scenesters than the A Bathing Ape label (shortened to Bape) from DJ–fashion designer Nigo. At the height of the craze, hopefuls would line up outside Nigo's well-hidden boutiques for the chance to plop down ¥7,000 for a T-shirt festooned with a simian visage or a *Planet of the Apes* quote. Bape has since gone aboveground, with Nigo expanding his business empire to Singapore, Hong Kong, New York, Paris, Los Angeles, and London. Here in Tōkyō, you can see what all the fuss is about at a spacious boutique that houses the Bape Gallery on the second floor. ⊠*5–5–8 Minami-Aoyama, Minato-ku* ☎*03/3407–2145* ☉*Daily 11–7* Ⓜ*Ginza and Hanzō-mon subway lines, Omotesandō Station (Exit A5).*

★ **Comme des Garçons.** Sinuous low walls snake through Rei Kawakubo's flagship store, a minimalist labyrinth that houses the designer's signature clothes, shoes, and accessories. Staff members will do their best to ignore you, but that's no reason to stay away from one of Tōkyō's funkiest retail spaces. ⊠*5–2–1 Minami-Aoyama, Minato-ku* ☎*03/3406–3951* ☉*Daily 11–8* Ⓜ*Ginza, Chiyoda, and Hanzō-mon subway lines, Omotesandō Station (Exit A5).*

Issey Miyake. The otherworldly creations of internationally renowned designer Miyake are on display at his flagship store in Aoyama, which carries the full Paris line. ⊠*3–18–11 Minami-Aoyama, Minato-ku* ☎*03/3423–1407* ☉*Daily 11–8* Ⓜ*Ginza, Chiyoda, and Hanzō-mon subway lines, Omotesandō Station (Exit A4).*

10 Corso Como Comme des Garçons. Milanese lifestyle guru Carla Sozzani helped create this spacious boutique for designer Rei Kawakubo's Comme des Garçons lines, which include Junya Watanabe menswear and women's wear. Also on offer are Vivienne Westwood and Balenciaga brands, and the staff isn't too busy being hip to help you out. ⊠*5–3 Minami-Aoyama, Minato-ku* ☎*03/5774–7800* ☉*Daily 11–8* Ⓜ*Ginza, Chiyoda, and Hanzō-mon subway lines, Omotesandō Station (Exit A5).*

Under Cover. This stark shop houses Paris darling Jun Takahashi's cult clothing, with enormously high racks of men's and women's clothing with a tatty punk look. ⊠*5–3–18 Minami-Aoyama, Minato-ku* ☎*03/3407–1232* ☉*Daily 11–8* Ⓜ*Ginza, Chiyoda, and Hanzō-mon subway lines, Omotesandō Station (Exit A5).*

CLOTHING CHAINS

Tōkyō street fashion is often profiled in international magazines as being brash and bizarre. The chains tend to line their shelves with a little more restraint than the boutiques, but by nearly any other city's standards, the average Tōkyō store still contains plenty of eye-openers.

Beams. Daikanyama features a cluster of Beams stores that provide Japan's younger men and women with extremely hip threads. Shopping here will ensure that you or your kids will be properly attired in street-ready T-shirts and porter bags. ⊠*19–6 Sarugakuchō, Shibuya-ku* ☎*03/5428–5951* ☉*Daily 11–8* Ⓜ*Tōkyū Tōyoko line, Daikanyama Station (Komazawa-dōri Exit).*

★ **Journal Standard.** This is not a chain dedicated to outfitting copy editors and reporters in shirts and ties. In fact, this branch is frequented by young couples looking for the season's *it* fashions. ⊠*1–5–6 Jinnan, Shibuya-ku* ☎*03/5457–0700* ☉*Daily 11–8* Ⓜ*JR Yamanote Line;*

CLOSE UP

The Power of Tea

Green tea is ubiquitous in Japan. But did you know that besides being something of a national drink, it's also good for you? Green tea contains antioxidants twice as powerful as those in red wine; these help reduce high blood pressure, lower blood sugar, and fight cancer. A heightened immune system and lower cholesterol are other benefits attributed to this beverage.

Whether drinking green tea for its healing properties, good taste, or as a manner of habit, you'll have plenty of choices in Japan. Pay attention to tea varietals, which are graded by the quality and parts of the plant used, because price and quality runs the spectrum within these categories. For the very best Japanese green tea, take a trip to the Uji region of Kyōto.

Bancha (common tea). This second-harvest variety ripens between summer and fall, producing leaves larger than those of sencha and a weaker tasting tea.

Genmai (brown rice tea). This is a mixture, usually in equal parts, of green tea and roasted brown rice.

Genmaicha (popcorn tea). This is a blend of bancha and genmai teas.

Gyokuro (jewel dew). Derived from a grade of green tea called *tencha* (divine tea), the name comes from the light-green color the tea develops when brewed. Gyokuro is grown in the shade, an essential condition to develop just this type and grade.

Hōjicha (panfried tea). A panfried or oven-roasted green tea.

Kabusecha (covered tea). Similar to gyokuru, kabusecha leaves are grown in the shade, though for a shorter period, giving it a refined flavor.

Kukicha (stalk tea). A tea made from stalks by harvesting one bud and three leaves.

Matcha (rubbed tea). Most often used in the tea ceremony, matcha is a high-quality, hard-to-find powdered green tea. It has a thick, paintlike consistency when mixed with hot water. It is also a popular flavor of ice cream and other sweets in Japan.

Sencha (roasted tea). This is the green tea you are most likely to try at the local noodle or bento shop. Its leaves are grown under direct sunlight, giving it a different flavor from cousins like gyokuro.

Ginza, Fukutoshin, and Hanzō-mon subway lines, Shibuya Station (Hachiko Exit for JR, Exits 6 and 7 for subways).

Uniqlo. Uniqlo offers customers a chance to wrap themselves in simple, low-priced items from the company's own brand. The vibe of the chain fits well within the relaxed attitudes of the Jiyūgaoka area, but there are locations all over the city as well as overseas. The store focuses on simple men's and women's clothing from its own label. ✉*1–8–21 Jiyūgaoka, Meguro-ku* ☎*03/5731–8273* ☉*Daily 11–8* Ⓜ*Tōkyū Tōyoko and Oimachi lines, Jiyugaoka Station (South Exit).*

DOLLS

There are many types of traditional dolls available in Japan, and each one has its own charm. Kokeshi dolls, which date from the Edo period, are long, cylindrical, painted, and made of wood, with no arms or legs.

Daruma, papier-mâché dolls with rounded bottoms and faces, are often painted with amusing expressions. Legend has it they are modeled after a Buddhist priest who remained seated in the lotus position for so long that his arms and legs atrophied. Hakata dolls, from Kyūshū, are ceramic figurines in traditional costume, such as geisha, samurai, or festival dancers.

Beishu. Colorful and often made from precious metals, the delicate dolls handcrafted at this shop have found their way into some of Japan's larger department stores, museums, and even the Imperial Palace. ⊠ *1–23–3 Yanagibashi, Taitō-ku* ☎ *03/3834–3501* ☉ *Daily 9:30–5:30* Ⓜ *JR Sobu Line, Asakusa subway line, Asakusa-bashi Station (Exit A3).*

Kyūgetsu. In business for more than a century, Kyūgetsu sells every kind of doll imaginable. ⊠ *1–20–4 Yanagibashi, Taitō-ku* ☎ *03/5687–5176* ☉ *Daily 9:15–6* Ⓜ *Asakusa subway line, JR Sobu Line Asakusa-bashi Station (Exit A3).*

ELECTRONICS

The area around Akihabara Station has more than 200 stores with discount prices on stereos, digital cameras, computers, DVD players, and anything else that runs on electricity. The larger shops have sections or floors (or even whole annexes) of goods made for export. Products come with instructions in most major languages, and if you have a tourist visa in your passport, you can purchase them duty-free.

★ **Apple Store.** This very stylish showroom displays the newest models from Apple's line of computer products. The Genius Bar on the second floor offers consulting services should you need advice on how to resuscitate a comatose iPod or MacBook. ⊠ *3–5–12 Ginza, Chūō-ku* ☎ *03/5159–8200* ☉ *Daily 10–9* Ⓜ *Ginza, Hibiya, and Marunouchi subway lines, Ginza Station (Exit A13).*

Bic Camera. A large discount-electronics chain in the Odakyū Halc building, Bic Camera has low prices. ⊠ *1–5–1 Nishi-Shinjuku, Shinjuku-ku* ☎ *03/5326–1111* ☉ *Daily 10–9* Ⓜ *Marunouchi, Oedo, and Shinjuku subway lines; JR Yamanote Line; Keiō and Odakyū lines, Shinjuku Station (Nishi-guchi/West Exit).*

LAOX. One of the big Akihabara chains, LAOX has several locations in the area. The "Duty Free Akihabara" branch on the main Chūō-dōri strip carries a full six floors of export models. English-speaking staff members are always on call. ⊠ *1–15–3 Soto-Kanda, Chiyoda-ku* ☎ *03/3255–5301* ☉ *Daily 9–8* Ⓜ *JR Yamanote Line, Akihabara Station (Electric Town Exit).*

Softmap. One Akihabara retailer that actually benefited from the bursting of Japan's economic bubble in the early '90s is Softmap, a used-PC and -software chain with a heavy presence in Tōkyō. Most branches are open daily until 7:30 or 8. ⊠ *3–14–10 Soto-Kanda, Chiyoda-ku* ☎ *03/3253–3030* ☉ *Daily 11–8* Ⓜ *JR Yamanote Line, Akihabara Station (Electric Town Exit).*

☺ **Sony Building.** Test drive the latest Sony gadgets at this retail and entertainment space in the heart of Ginza. Kids will enjoy trying out the not-yet-released PlayStation games, while their parents fiddle with digital cameras and stereos from Japan's electronics leader. ⊠ *5–3–1*

Ginza, Chūō-ku ☎*03/3573–2371* ⊗*Daily 11–7* Ⓜ*JR Yamanote Line, Yūraku-chō Station (Ginza Exit); Ginza, Hibiya, and Marunouchi subway lines, Ginza Station (Exit B9).*

☾ **Sukiya Camera.** The cramped Nikon House branch of this two-store operation features enough Nikons—old and new, digital and film—that it could double as a museum to the brand. Plenty of lenses and flashes are available as well. ✉*4–2–13 Ginza, Chūō-ku* ☎*03/3561–6000* ⊗*Weekdays 10–7:30, weekends 10–7* Ⓜ*JR Yamanote Line, Yūraku-chō Station (Ginza Exit); Ginza, Hibiya, and Marunouchi subway lines, Ginza Station (Exit B10).*

★ **Y.K. Musen.** Welcome to a world that would truly be Maxwell Smart's dream. From pinhole cameras hidden in cigarette packs to microphones capable of picking up sound through concrete, Y.K. Musen supplies the latest and greatest in snoop technology. ✉*1–14 Soto-Kanda, Chiyoda-ku* ☎*03/3253–7219* ⊗*Daily 11–7:30* Ⓜ*JR Yamanote Line, Akihabara Station (Electric Town Exit).*

Yodobashi Camera. This discount-electronics superstore near Shinjuku Station carries a selection comparable to that of Akihabara's big boys. ✉*1–11–1 Nishi-Shinjuku, Shinjuku-ku* ☎*03/3346–1010* ⊗*Daily 9:30 AM–10 PM* Ⓜ*Marunouchi, Shinjuku, and Oedo subway lines; JR Yamanote Line; Keiō and Odakyū lines, Shinjuku Station (Nishi-guchi/West Exit).*

FOLK CRAFTS

Japanese folk crafts, called mingei—among them bamboo vases and baskets, fabrics, paper boxes, dolls, and toys—achieve a unique beauty in their simple and sturdy designs. Be aware, however, that simple does not mean cheap. Long hours of labor go into these objects, and every year there are fewer craftspeople left, producing their work in smaller and smaller quantities. Include these items in your budget ahead of time: the best—worth every cent—can be fairly expensive.

Printed fabric, whether by the yard or in the form of finished scarves, napkins, tablecloths, or pillow coverings, is another item worth purchasing in Japan. The complexity of the designs and the quality of the printing make the fabric, both silk and cotton, special. *Furoshiki*—square pieces of cloth used for wrapping, storing, and carrying things—make great wall hangings.

Bingo-ya. You may be able to complete all of your souvenir shopping in one trip to this tasteful four-floor shop, which carries traditional handicrafts—including ceramics, toys, lacquerware, Noh masks, fabrics, and lots more—from all over Japan. ✉*10–6 Wakamatsu-chō, Shinjuku-ku* ☎*03/3202–8778* ⊗*Tues.–Sun. 10–7* Ⓜ*Ōedo subway line, Wakamatsu Kawada Station (Kawada Exit).*

★ **Oriental Bazaar.** The four floors of this popular tourist destination are packed with just about anything you could want as a traditional Japanese (or Chinese or Korean) handicraft souvenir: painted screens, pottery, chopsticks, dolls, and more, all at very reasonable prices. ✉*5–9–13 Jingū-mae, Shibuya-ku* ☎*03/3400–3933* ⊗*Fri.–Wed. 10–7* Ⓜ*Chiyoda and Fukutoshin subway lines, Meiji Jingū-mae Station (Exit 4).*

FOODSTUFFS AND WARES

This hybrid category includes everything from crackers and dried sea-weed to cast-iron kettles, paper lanterns, and essential food kitsch like plastic sushi sets.

Backstreet Shops of Tsukiji. In Tsukiji, between the Central Wholesale Market and Harumi-dōri, among the many fishmongers, you can also find stores selling pickles, tea, crackers, kitchen knives, baskets, and crockery. The area is a real slice of Japanese life and one that you should check out sooner rather than later, as the Tsukiji Fish Market, in its original state, is expected to be dismantled and moved in 2012. ⊠ *Tsukiji 4-chōme, Chūō-ku* Ⓜ *Ōedo subway line, Tsukiji-shijō Station (Exit A1); Hibiya subway line, Tsukiji Station (Exit 1).*

Tea-Tsu. Some people ascribe Japanese longevity to the beneficial effects of green tea. Tea-Tsu sells a variety of leaves in attractive canisters that make unique gifts. The main Aoyama branch also sells tea sets and other ceramics. ⊠ *3–18–3 Minami-Aoyama, Minato-ku* ☎ *03/5772–2662* ⊙ *Tues.–Sun. 11–8* Ⓜ *Ginza, Chiyoda, and Hanzō-mon subway lines, Omotesandō Station (Exit A4).*

Tokiwa-dō. Come here to buy some of Tōkyō's most famous souvenirs: *kaminari okoshi* (thunder crackers), made of rice, millet, sugar, and beans. The shop is on the west side of Asakusa's Thunder God Gate, the Kaminari-mon entrance to Sensō-ji. ⊠ *1–3–2 Asakusa, Taitō-ku* ☎ *03/3841–5656* ⊙ *Daily 9–8:30* Ⓜ *Ginza subway line, Asakusa Station (Exit 1).*

Yamamoto Noriten. The Japanese are resourceful in their uses of products from the sea. Nori, the paper-thin dried seaweed used to wrap maki sushi and *onigiri* (rice balls), is the specialty here. If you plan to bring some home with you, buy unroasted nori and toast it yourself at home; the flavor will be far better than that of the preroasted sheets. ⊠ *1–6–3 Nihombashi Muro-machi, Chūō-ku* ☎ *03/3241–0261* ⊙ *Daily 9–6:30* Ⓜ *Hanzō-mon and Ginza subway lines, Mitsukoshi-mae Station (Exit A1).*

HOUSEWARES

Tōkyōites appreciate fine design, both the kind they can wear and the kind they can display in their homes. This passion is reflected in the exuberance of the city's *zakka* shops—retailers that sell small housewares. The Daikanyama and Aoyama areas positively brim with these stores, but trendy zakka can be found throughout the city.

Idee Shop. Local design giant Teruo Kurosaki's shop, located on the sixth floor of Takashimaya's Futako Tamagawa branch, carries housewares, fabrics, and ceramics by some of Japan's most celebrated young craftspeople. ⊠ *3–17–1 Tamagawa, Setagaya-ku* ☎ *03/5797–3023* ⊙ *Daily 10–9* Ⓜ *Tōkyū Denentoshi and Oimachi lines, Futako Tamagawa Station (West Exit).*

Sempre. Playful, colorful, and bright describe both the products and the space of this Kottō-dōri housewares dealer. Among the great finds here are interesting tableware, glassware, lamps, office goods, and jewelry. ⊠ *5–13–3 Minami-Aoyama, Minato-ku* ☎ *03/5464–5655* ⊙ *Mon.–Sat. 11–8, Sun. 11–7* Ⓜ *Ginza, Chiyoda, and Hanzō-mon subway lines, Omotesandō Station (Exit B3).*

Serendipity. Alessi products and other Western brands are sold at this spacious housewares store in the Coredo shopping center. ✉ *1–4–1 Nihombashi, Chūō-ku* ☎ *03/5205–0011* ⊘ *Mon.–Sat. 11–9, Sun. 11–8* Ⓜ *Ginza, Tōzai, and Asakusa subway lines, Nihombashi Station (Exit B12).*

⟳ **Tōkyū Hands.** This housewares chain is dedicated to providing the do-it-yourselfer with all the tools, fabrics, and supplies he or she may need to tackle any job. There's a selection of plastic models and rubber Godzilla action figures on the seventh floor of the Shibuya branch. ✉ *12–18 Udagawa-chō, Shibuya-ku* ☎ *03/5489–5111* ⊘ *Daily 10–8:30* Ⓜ *JR Yamanote Line; Ginza, Fukutoshin, and Hanzō-mon subway lines, Shibuya Station (Hachiko Exit for JR, Exits 6 and 7 for subway).*

JEWELRY

Japan has always been known for its craftspeople who possess the ability to create finely detailed work. Jewelry is no exception, especially when cultured pearls are used. Pearls, which have become something of a national symbol, are not inexpensive, but they are a whole lot cheaper in Japan than elsewhere.

Ginza Tanaka. From necklaces to precious metals shaped into statues, this chain of jewelry stores has crafted a reputation as one of Japan's premier jewelers since its founding in 1892. ✉ *1–7–7 Ginza, Chūō-ku* ☎ *03/5561–0491* ⊘ *Daily 10:30–7* Ⓜ *Yūraku-chō subway line, Ginza 1-Chome Station (Exit 7).*

★ **Mikimoto.** Kōkichi Mikimoto created his technique for cultured pearls in 1893. Since then his name has been associated with the best quality in the industry. Mikimoto's flagship store in Ginza is less a jewelry shop than a boutique devoted to nature's ready-made gems. ✉ *4–5–5 Ginza, Chūō-ku* ☎ *03/3535–4611* ⊘ *Daily 11–7; occasionally closed on Wed.* Ⓜ *Ginza, Hibiya, and Marunouchi subway lines, Ginza Station (Exit A9).*

Fodor'sChoice
★ **Shinjuku Watch Kan.** Standing a full seven stories, this watch emporium has just about any import brand as well as a wide selection of Casio and Seiko models that are not sold abroad. The top floor offers repair services. ✉ *3–29–11 Shinjuku, Shinjuku-ku* ☎ *03/3226–6000* ⊘ *Daily 10–9* Ⓜ *Marunouchi, Shinjuku, and Oedo subway lines; JR Yamanote Line; Keiō and Odakyū lines, Shinjuku Station (Higashi-guchi/East Exit).*

Tasaki Pearl Gallery. Tasaki sells pearls at slightly lower prices than Mikimoto. The store has several showrooms and hosts an English-language tour that demonstrates the technique of culturing pearls and explains how to maintain and care for them. ✉ *1–3–3 Akasaka, Minato-ku* ☎ *03/5561–8880* ⊘ *Weekdays 9–7, weekends 9–6* Ⓜ *Ginza subway line, Tameike-Sannō Station (Exit 9).*

KIMONOS

Traditional clothing has experienced something of a comeback among Tōkyō's youth, but most Japanese women, unless they work in traditional restaurants, now wear kimonos only on special occasions. Like tuxedos in the United States, they are often rented, not purchased outright, for social events such as weddings or graduations. Kimonos are extremely expensive and difficult to maintain. A wedding kimono, for example, can cost as much as ¥1 million ($11,000).

CLOSE UP

Shopping in Kappabashi

A wholesale-restaurant-supply district might not sound like a promising shopping destination, but Kappabashi, about a 10-minute walk west of the temples and pagodas of Asakusa, is worth a look. Ceramics, cutlery, cookware, folding lanterns, and even kimonos can all be found here, along with the kitschy plastic food models that appear in restaurant windows throughout Japan. The best strategy is to stroll up and down the 1-km (½-mi) length of Kappabashi-dōgu-machi-dōri and visit any shop that looks interesting. Most stores here emphasize function over charm, but some manage to stand out for their stylish spaces as well. Most Kappabashi shops are open until 5:30; some close on Sunday. To get here, take the Ginza subway line to Tawara-machi Station.

Kappabashi Sōshoku. Come here for *aka-chōchin* (folding red-paper lanterns) like the ones that hang in front of inexpensive bars and restaurants. ✉ *3–1–1 Matsugaya, Taitō-ku* ☎ *03/3844–1973* ⊙ *Mon.–Sat. 9:30–5:30.*

Kawahara Shōten. The brightly colored bulk packages of rice crackers, shrimp-flavored chips, and other Japanese snacks sold here make offbeat gifts. ✉ *3–9–2 Nishi-Asakusa, Taitō-ku* ☎ *03/3842–0841* ⊙ *Mon.–Sat. 9–5:30.*

☺ **Maizuru.** This perennial tourist favorite manufactures the plastic food that's displayed outside almost every Tōkyō restaurant. Ersatz sushi, noodles, and even beer cost just a few hundred yen. You can buy tiny plastic key holders and earrings, or splurge on a whole Pacific lobster, perfect in coloration and detail down to the tiniest spines on its legs. ✉ *1–5–17 Nishi-Asakusa, Taitō-ku* ☎ *03/3843–1686* ⊙ *Daily 9–6.*

Noren-no-Nishimura. This Kappabashi shop specializes in *noren*—the curtains that shops and restaurants hang to announce they're open. The curtains are typically cotton, linen, or silk, most often dyed-to-order for individual shops. Nishimura also sells premade noren of an entertaining variety—from white-on-blue landscapes to geisha and sumō wrestlers in polychromatic splendor—for home decorating. They make wonderful wall hangings and dividers. ✉ *1–10–10 Matsugaya, Taitō-ku* ☎ *03/3841–6220* ⊙ *Mon.–Sat. 10–5.*

Soi Furniture. The selection of lacquerware, ceramics, and antiques sold at this Kappabashi shop is modest, but Soi displays the items in a primitivist setting of stone walls and wooden floor planks, with up-tempo jazz in the background. ✉ *3–17–3 Matsugaya, Taitō-ku* ☎ *03/3843–9555* ⊙ *Daily 10–6.*

Most visitors, naturally unwilling to pay this much for a garment that they probably want to use as a bathrobe or a conversation piece, settle for a secondhand or antique silk kimono. You can pay as little as ¥1,000 ($8) in a flea market, but to find one in decent condition, you should expect to pay about ¥10,000 ($82). However, cotton summer kimonos, called yukata, in a wide variety of colorful and attractive designs, can be bought new for ¥7,000–¥10,000 ($58–$82).

Hayashi. This store in the Yūraku-chō International Arcade specializes in ready-made kimonos, sashes, and dyed yukata. ✉ *2–1–1 Yūraku-chō, Chiyoda-ku* ☎ *03/3501–4012* ⊙ *Mon.–Sat. 10–7, Sun. 10–6* Ⓜ *JR*

Yamanote Line, Yūraku-chō Station (Ginza Exit); Hibiya subway line, Hibiya Station (Exit A5).

Kawano Gallery. Kawano, in the high-fashion district of Omotesandō, sells kimonos and kimono fabric in a variety of patterns. ✉4–4–9 Jingū-mae, Shibuya-ku ☎03/3470–3305 ⊙Daily 11–6 Ⓜ Ginza, Chiyoda, and Hanzō-mon subway lines, Omotesandō Station (Exit A2).

Tansu-ya. This small but pleasant Ginza shop, part of a chain with locations throughout Japan and abroad, has attractive used kimonos, yukata, and other traditional clothing in many fabrics, colors, and patterns. The helpful staff can acquaint you with the somewhat complicated method of putting on the garments. ✉3–4–5 Ginza, Chūō ku ☎03/3561–8529 ⊙Daily 11–7 Ⓜ Ginza, Hibiya, and Marunouchi subway lines, Ginza Station (Exit A13).

LACQUERWARE

For its history, diversity, and fine workmanship, lacquerware rivals ceramics as the traditional Japanese craft nonpareil. One warning: lacquerware thrives on humidity. Cheaper pieces usually have plastic rather than wood underneath. Because these won't shrink and crack in dry climates, they make safer—and no less attractive—buys.

Fodor's Choice ★ Yamada Heiando. With a spacious, airy layout and lovely lacquerware goods, this fashionable Daikanyama shop is a must for souvenir hunters—and anyone else who appreciates fine design. Rice bowls, sushi trays, bento lunch boxes, hashioki (chopstick rests), and jewelry cases come in traditional blacks and reds, as well as patterns both subtle and bold. Prices are fair—many items cost less than ¥10,000—but these are the kinds of goods for which devotees of Japanese craftsmanship would be willing to pay a lot. ✉Hillside Terrace G Block # 202, 18–12 Sarugakuchō, Shibuya-ku ☎03/3464–5541 ⊙Mon.–Sat. 10:30–7, Sun. 10:30–6:30 Ⓜ Tōkyū Tōyoko line, Daikanyama Station (Komazawa-dōri Exit).

PAPER

What packs light and flat in your suitcase, won't break, doesn't cost much, and makes a great gift? The answer is traditional handmade washi (paper), which the Japanese make in thousands of colors, textures, and designs and fashion into an astonishing number of useful and decorative objects.

Items made of paper are one of the best buys in Japan. Delicate sheets of almost-transparent stationery, greeting cards, money holders, and wrapping paper are available at traditional crafts stores, stationery stores, and department stores. Small washi-covered boxes (suitable for jewelry and other keepsakes) and pencil cases are also strong candidates for gifts and personal souvenirs.

Kami-no-Takamura. Specialists in washi and other papers printed in traditional Japanese designs, this shop also carries brushes, inkstones, and other tools for calligraphy. ⊠*1–1–2 Higashi-Ikebukuro, Toshima-ku* ☎*03/3971–7111* ⊙*Daily 11–6:45* Ⓜ*JR Yamanote Line; Marunouchi and Fukutoshin subway lines, Ikebukuro Station (East Exit for JR, Exit 35 for subway).*

★ **Kyūkyodō.** Kyūkyodō has been in business since 1663—in Ginza since 1880—selling its wonderful handmade Japanese papers, paper products, incense, brushes, and other materials for calligraphy. ⊠*5–7–4 Ginza, Chūō-ku* ☎*03/3571–4429* ⊙*Mon.–Sat. 10–7:30, Sun. 11–7* Ⓜ*Ginza, Hibiya, and Marunouchi subway lines, Ginza Station (Exit A2).*

Origami Kaikan. In addition to shopping for paper goods at Yushima no Kobayahi's store, you can also tour a papermaking workshop and learn the art of origami. ⊠*1–7–14 Yushima, Bunkyō-ku* ☎*03/3811–4025* ⊙*Mon.–Sat. 9–6* Ⓜ*JR Chūō and Sōbu lines, Ochanomizu Station (West Exit); Chiyoda subway line, Yushima Station (Exit 5).*

Ozu Washi. This shop, which was opened in the 17th century, has one of the largest washi showrooms in the city and its own gallery of antique papers. ⊠*3–6–2 Nihombashi-Honchō, Chūō-ku* ☎*03/3662–1184* ⊙*Mon.–Sat. 10–7* Ⓜ*Ginza and Hanzō-mon subway lines, Mitsukoshi-mae Station (Exit A4).*

RECORD STORES

Tōkyō is perhaps the premier location in the world to purchase music. The big chains will have all the standard releases, but it is the smaller specialty stores that are the real treat: local music and wide selections of imports from around the world are usually available on both vinyl and CD.

For out-of-print editions and obscurities on vinyl, the prices can run well over ¥10,000 ($82). But collectors will find the condition of the jackets to be unmatched.

Fodor's Choice **Disk Union.** Vinyl junkies rejoice. The Shinjuku flagship of this chain
★ offers Latin, rock, and indie at 33 rpm. Other stores clustered within the nearby blocks have punk, metal, and jazz. Be sure to grab a store flyer that lists all of its branches since each usually specializes in one music genre or other. Oh, and for you digital folk: CDs are available, too. ⊠*3–31–4 Shinjuku, Shinjuku-ku* ☎*03/3352–2691* ⊙*Daily 11–9* Ⓜ*Marunouchi, Oedo, and Shinjuku subway lines; JR Yamanote Line; Keiō and Odakyū lines, Shinjuku Station (Higashi-guchi/East Exit).*

Manhattan Records. The hottest hip-hop, reggae, and R&B vinyl can be found here, and a DJ booth pumps out the jams from the center of the room. Don't expect a lot advice from the staff—no one can hear you over the throbbing tunes. ⊠*10–1 Udagawa-chō, Shibuya-ku* ☎*03/3477–7166* ⊙*Daily noon–9* Ⓜ*JR Yamanote Line; Ginza, Fukutoshin, and Hanzō-mon subway lines, Shibuya Station (Hachiko Exit for JR, Exits 6 and 7 for subway).*

SWORDS AND KNIVES

Supplying the tools of the trade to samurai and sushi chefs alike, Japanese metalworkers have played a significant role in the nation's military and culinary history. The remarkable knives on offer from the shops below are comparable in both quality and price to the best Western brands. For swords, you can pay thousands of dollars for a good-quality antique, but far more reasonably priced reproductions are available as well. Consult with your airline on how best to transport these items home.

Ichiryō-ya Hirakawa. A small, cluttered souvenir shop in the Nishi-Sandō arcade, Ichiryō-ya carries antique swords and reproductions and has some English-speaking salesclerks. ✉ *2–7–13 Asakusa, Taitō-ku* ☏ *03/3843–0051* ⊘ *Wed. and Fri.–Mon. 11–6* Ⓜ *Ginza subway line, Asakusa Station (Exit 1) or Tawara-machi Station (Exit 3).*

Kiya. Workers shape and hone blades in one corner of this Ginza shop, which carries cutlery, pocketknives, saws, and more. Scissors with handles in the shape of Japanese cranes are among the many unique gift items sold here, and custom-made knives are available on the second floor. ✉ *1–5–6 Nihombashi-Muromachi, Chūō-ku* ☏ *03/3241–0110* ⊘ *Mon.–Sat. 10–6, Sun. 11:15–5:45* Ⓜ *Ginza subway line, Mitsukoshi-mae Station (Exit A4).*

Fodor's Choice **Nippon Tōken** *(Japan Sword).* Wannabe samurai can learn how to tell ★ their *tōshin* (blades) from their *tsuka* (sword handles) with help from the English-speaking staff at this small shop, which has been open since the Meiji era (1868–1912). Items that range from a circa-1390 samurai sword to inexpensive reproductions will allow you to take a trip back in time, but make sure your wallet is ready for today's prices. ✉ *3–8–1 Toranomon, Minato-ku* ☏ *03/3434–4321* ⊘ *Weekdays 9:30–6, weekends 9:30–5* Ⓜ *Hibiya and Ginza subway lines, Tora-no-mon Station (Exit 2).*

Tōken Shibata. A tiny, threadbare shop incongruously situated near Ginza's glittering department stores, Tōken Shibata sells well-worn antique swords. ✉ *5–6–8 Ginza, Chūō-ku* ☏ *03/3573–2801* ⊘ *Mon.–Sat. 9:30–6:30* Ⓜ *Ginza, Hibiya, and Marunouchi subway lines, Ginza Station (Exit A1).*

★ **Tsubaya Hōchōten.** Tsubaya sells high-quality cutlery for professionals. Its remarkable selection is designed for every imaginable use, as the art of food presentation in Japan requires a great variety of cutting implements. The best of these carry the Traditional Craft Association seal: hand-forged tools of tempered blue steel, set in handles banded with deer horn to keep the wood from splitting. Be prepared to pay the premium for these items: a cleaver just for slicing soba can cost as much as ¥50,000. ✉ *3–7–2 Nishi-Asakusa, Taitō-ku* ☏ *03/3845–2005* ⊘ *Mon.–Sat. 9–5:45, Sun. 9–5* Ⓜ *Ginza subway line, Tawara machi Station (Exit 3).*

TOYS

☺ **Hakuhinkan.** The plethora of homegrown-character goods like Hello Kitty make this one of Japan's biggest stores for toys. But the real treat is outside, where a massive vending machine allows shoppers, or customers of one of the nearby hostess clubs, to pick up a stuffed doll or model plane after-hours. It's on Chūō-dōri, the main axis of the Ginza shopping area. ✉ *8–8–11 Ginza, Chūō-ku* ☏ *03/3571–8008* ⊘ *Daily 11–8* Ⓜ *Ginza and Asakusa subway lines, JR Yamanote Line (Ginza Exit), Shimbashi Station (Exit 1).*

☺ **Kiddy Land.** Commonly regarded as Tōkyō's best toy store, Kiddy Land also carries kitsch items that draw in Harajuku's teen brigade. ✉ *6–1–9*

Jingū-mae, Shibuya-ku ☎*03/3409–3431* ⊙*Daily 11–9* Ⓜ*JR Yamanote Line: Harajuku Station (Omotesandō Exit); Chiyoda and Fukutoshin subway lines, Meiji Jingū-mae Station (Exit 4).*

TRADITIONAL WARES

Handmade combs, towels, and cosmetics are other uniquely Japanese treasures to consider picking up while in Tōkyō.

★ **Fuji-ya.** Master textile creator Keiji Kawakami's cotton *tenugui* (teh-noo-goo-ee) hand towels are collector's items, often framed instead of used as towels. Kawakami is an expert on the hundreds of traditional towel motifs that have come down from the Edo period: geometric patterns, plants and animals, and scenes from Kabuki plays and festivals. When Kawakami feels he has made enough of one pattern of his own design, he destroys the stencil. The shop is near the corner of Dembō-in-dōri on Naka-mise-dōri. ✉*2–2–15 Asakusa, Taitō-ku* ☎*03/3841–2283* ⊙*Fri.–Wed. 10–6* Ⓜ*Ginza subway line, Asakusa Station (Exit 6).*

Hyaku-suke. This is the last place in Tōkyō to carry government-approved skin cleanser made from powdered nightingale droppings. Ladies of the Edo period—especially the geisha—swore by the cleanser. These days this 100-year-old-plus cosmetics shop sells little of the nightingale powder, but its theatrical makeup for Kabuki actors, geisha, and traditional weddings—as well as unique items like seaweed shampoo, camellia oil, and handcrafted combs and cosmetic brushes—makes it a worthy addition to your Asakusa shopping itinerary. ✉*2–2–14 Asakusa, Taitō-ku* ☎*03/3841–7058* ⊙*Wed.–Mon. 11–5* Ⓜ*Ginza subway line, Asakusa Station (Exit 6).*

Jusan-ya. A shop selling handmade boxwood combs, this business was started in 1736 by a samurai who couldn't support himself as a feudal retainer. It has been in the same family ever since. Jusan-ya is on Shinobazu-dōri, a few doors west of its intersection with Chūō-dōri in Ueno. ✉*2–12–21 Ueno, Taitō-ku* ☎*03/3831–3238* ⊙*Mon.–Sat. 10–6:30* Ⓜ*Ginza subway line, Ueno Hirokō-ji Station (Exit 3); JR Yamanote Line, Ueno Station (Shinobazu Exit).*

Naka-ya. If you want to equip yourself for Sensō-ji's annual Sanja Festival in May, this is the place to come. Best buys here are *sashiko hanten,* which are thick, woven, firemen's jackets, and *happi* coats, cotton tunics printed in bright colors with Japanese characters. Some items are available in children's sizes. ✉*2–2–12 Asakusa, Taitō-ku* ☎*03/3841–7877* ⊙*Daily 10–6:30* Ⓜ*Ginza subway line, Asakusa Station (Exit 6).*

Yono-ya. Traditional Japanese coiffures and wigs are very complicated, and they require a variety of tools to shape them properly. Tatsumi Minekawa, the current master at Yono-ya—the family line goes back 300 years—deftly crafts and decorates very fine boxwood combs. Some combs are carved with auspicious motifs, such as peonies, hollyhocks, or cranes, and all are engraved with the family benchmark. ✉*1–37–10 Asakusa, Taitō-ku* ☎*03/3844–1755* ⊙*Thurs.–Tues. 10:30–6* Ⓜ*Ginza subway line, Asakusa Station (Exit 1).*

Side Trips from Tōkyō

WORD OF MOUTH

"I fell in love with Kamakura because it's such a wonderfully quaint little town to just walk around. It was magical, and a wonderful break from the big cities."

—Hagan

"Our family still talks about the wonder of Nikkō."

—FurryTiles

"Kamakura, a city along the Yuigihama Bay about 45 minutes southwest of Tōkyō, is very artsy, and one could see how it would come alive in the warmer months. On this day the crowds were minimal, another benefit of traveling in the off-season."

—fourfortravel

Updated by
Kevin Mcgue

While there's plenty to keep you occupied in Tōkyō for days, the urge to get out and explore beyond the city limits should not be ignored. The city's a great base for numerous day trips including visits to the iconic Fuji-san (Mt. Fuji) in Fuji-Hakone-Izu National Park, one of Japan's most popular resort areas; Nikkō, a popular vacation destination for Tōkyō residents and the home of Tōshō-gū, the astonishing shrine to the first Tokugawa shōgun Ieyasu; the ancient city of Kamakura which has great historical and cultural sights; and Yokohama, a port city with an international character all its own—it's home to the country's largest Chinatown.

One caveat: the term "national park" does not quite mean what it does elsewhere in the world. In Japan, pristine grandeur is hard to come by; there are few places in this country where intrepid hikers can go to contemplate the beauty of nature for very long in solitude. If a thing's worth seeing, it's worth developing. This world view tends to fill Japan's national parks with bus caravans, ropeways and gondolas, scenic overlooks with coin-fed telescopes, signs that tell you where you may or may not walk, fried-noodle joints and vending machines, and shacks full of kitschy souvenirs. That's true of Nikkō, and it's true as well of Fuji-Hakone-Izu National Park.

ORIENTATION AND PLANNING

GETTING ORIENTED

Nikkō. Nikkō is not simply the site of the Tokugawa shrine but also of a national park, Nikkō Kokuritsu Kōen, on the heights above it. The centerpiece of the park is Chūzenji-ko, a deep lake some 21 km (13 mi) around, and the 318-foot-high Kegon Falls, Japan's most famous waterfall.

Kamakura. Kamakura is an ancient city—the birthplace, one could argue, of the samurai way of life. Minamoto no Yoritomo, the country's first shōgun, chose this site, with its rugged hills and narrow passes, as the seat of his military government. The warrior elite took much of their ideology—and their aesthetics—from Zen Buddhism, endowing splendid temples that still exist today. A walking tour of Kamakura's Zen temples and Shintō shrines is a must for anyone with a day to spend out of Tōkyō.

Yokohama. Yokohama is Japan's largest port and has an international character that rivals—if not surpasses—that of Tōkyō. Its waterfront

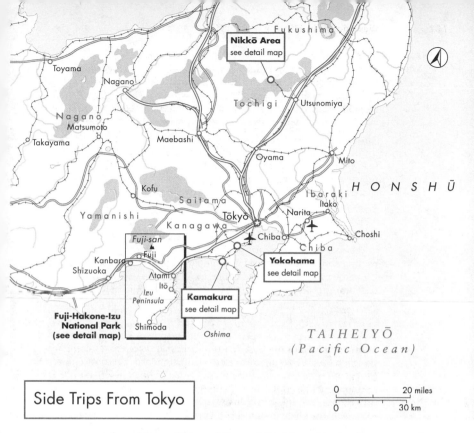

Side Trips From Tokyo

```
0              20 miles
|——————|————|
0              30 km
```

park and its ambitious Minato Mirai bay-side development project draw visitors from all over the world.

Fuji-Hakone-Izu National Park. Fuji-Hakone-Izu National Park lies southwest of Tōkyō. Its chief attraction of course, is Fuji-san. South of it, the Izu Peninsula projects out into the Pacific, with Suruga Bay to the west and Sagami Bay to the east. The beaches and rugged shoreline of Izu, its forests and highland meadows, and its numerous hot-springs inns and resorts make the region a favorite destination for the Japanese.

PLANNING

Kamakura and Yokohama are close enough to Tōkyō to provide ideal day trips, and as it's unlikely that you'll stay overnight in either city, no accommodations are listed for them. Nikkō is something of a toss-up: you can easily see Tōshō-gū and be back in Tōkyō by evening. But when the weather turns glorious in spring or autumn, why not spend some time in the national park, staying overnight at Chūzenji, and returning to the city the next day? Mt. Fuji and Hakone, on the other hand—and more especially the Izu Peninsula—are pure resort destinations. Staying overnight is an intrinsic part of the experience, and it makes little sense to go without hotel reservations confirmed in advance.

RESTAURANTS

The local specialty in Nikkō is a soybean-based concoction known as *yuba* (tofu skin); dozens of restaurants in Nikkō serve it in a variety of dishes you might not have believed possible for so prosaic an ingredient. Other local favorites are soba (buckwheat) and udon (wheat-flour) noodles—both inexpensive, filling, and tasty options for lunch.

Three things about Kamakura make it a good place to dine. It's on the ocean (properly speaking, on Sagami Bay), which means that fresh seafood is everywhere; it's a major tourist stop; and it has long been a prestigious place to live among Japan's worldly and well-to-do (many successful writers, artists, and intellectuals call Kamakura home). On a day trip from Tōkyō, you can feel confident picking a place for lunch almost at random.

Yokohama, as befits a city of more than 3 million people, lacks little in the way of food: from quick-fix lunch counters to elegant dining rooms, you'll find almost every imaginable cuisine. Your best bet is Chinatown—Japan's largest Chinese community—with more than 100 restaurants representing every regional style. If you fancy Italian, Indian, or even Scandinavian, this international port is still guaranteed to provide an eminently satisfying meal.

HOTELS

In both Nikkō and the Fuji-Hakone-Izu area, there are modern, Western-style hotels that operate in a fairly standard international style. More common, however, are the traditional *ryokan* (inns) and the Japanese-style *kankō* (literally, "sightseeing") hotels. The main difference between these lodging options is that kankō often have Western-style rooms and are situated in prime tourist locations whereas ryokans stick strictly to Japanese-style rooms and are found in less touristy locations. The undisputed pleasure of a ryokan is to return to it at the end of a hard day of sightseeing, luxuriate for an hour in a hot bath with your own garden view, put on the *yukata* (cotton kimono) provided for you (remember to close your right side first and then the left), and sit down to a catered private dinner party. There's little point to staying at a kankō, unless you want to say you've had the experience and survived. These places do most of their business with big, boisterous tour groups; the turnover is ruthless and the cost is way out of proportion to the service they provide.

The price categories listed below are for double occupancy, but you'll find that most kankō and ryokan normally quote per-person rates, which include breakfast and dinner. Remember to stipulate whether you want a Japanese or Western breakfast. If you don't want dinner at your hotel, it's usually possible to renegotiate the price, but the management will not be happy about it; the two meals are a fixture of their business. The typical ryokan takes great pride in its cuisine, usually with good reason: the evening meal is an elaborate affair of 10 or more different dishes, based on the fresh produce and specialties of the region, served to you—nay, *orchestrated*—in your room on a wonderful variety of trays and tableware designed to celebrate the season.

WHAT IT COSTS IN YEN					
	¢	$	$$	$$$	$$$$
RESTAURANTS	under ¥800	¥800–¥1,000	¥1,000–¥2,000	¥2,000–¥3,000	over ¥3,000
HOTELS	under ¥8,000	¥8,000–¥12,000	¥12,000–¥18,000	¥18,000–¥22,000	over ¥22,000

Restaurant prices are per person for a main course at dinner. Hotel price categories reflect the range of least- to most-expensive standard double rooms in nonholiday high season, based on the European Plan (with no meals) unless otherwise noted. Taxes (5%) are included.

NIKKŌ 日光

"Think nothing is splendid," asserts an old Japanese proverb, "until you have seen Nikkō." Nikkō, which means "sunlight," is a popular vacation spot for the Japanese, for good reason: its gorgeous sights include a breathtaking waterfall and one of the country's best-known shrines. In addition, Nikkō combines the rustic charm of a countryside village (complete with wild monkeys that have the run of the place) with a convenient location not far from Tōkyō.

GETTING HERE AND AROUND

By Bus and Taxi. Buses and taxis can take you from Nikkō to the village of Chūzenji and nearby Lake Chūzenji; one-way cab fare from Tōbu Nikkō Station to Chūzenji is about ¥6,000. ⚠ **There is no bus service between Tōkyō and Nikkō.** Local buses leave Tōbu Nikkō Station for Lake Chūzenji, stopping just above the entrance to Tōshō-gū, approximately every 30 minutes from 6:15 AM until 7:01 PM. The fare to Chūzenji is ¥1,100, and the ride takes about 40 minutes. The last return bus from the lake leaves at 7:39 PM, arriving back at Tōbu Nikkō Station at 9:17 PM.

By Car. It's possible, but unwise, to travel by car from Tōkyō to Nikkō. The trip will take at least three hours, and merely getting from central Tōkyō to the toll-road system can be a nightmare. Coming back, especially on a Saturday or Sunday evening, is even worse.

By Train. The limited express train of the Tōbu Railway has two direct connections from Tōkyō to Nikkō every morning, starting at 7:30 AM from Tōbu Asakusa Station, a minute's walk from the last stop on Tōkyō's Ginza subway line; there are additional trains on weekends, holidays, and in high season. The one-way fare is ¥2,620. All seats are reserved. Bookings are not accepted over the phone; they can only be bought at Asakusa station. During summer, fall, and weekends, buy tickets a few days in advance. The trip from Asakusa to the Tōbu Nikkō Station takes about two hours, which is quicker than the JR trains. If you're visiting Nikkō on a day trip, note that the last return train is at 7:43 PM, requiring a quick and easy change at Shimo-Imaichi, and arrives at Asakusa at 9:35 PM. If you have a JR Pass, use JR (Japan Railways) service, which connects Tōkyō and Nikkō, from Ueno Station. Take the Tōhoku–Honsen Line limited express to Utsunomiya (about

1½ hours) and transfer to the train for JR Nikkō Station (45 minutes). The earliest departure from Ueno is at 5:10 AM; the last connection back leaves Nikkō at 8:03 PM and brings you into Ueno at 10:48 PM. (If you're not using the JR Pass, the one-way fare will cost ¥2,520.)

More expensive but faster is the Yamabiko train on the north extension of the Shinkansen; the one-way fare, including the express surcharge, is ¥4,920. The first one leaves Tōkyō Station at 6:04 AM (or Ueno at 6:10 AM) and takes about 50 minutes to Utsunomiya; change there to the train to Nikkō Station. To return, take the 9:46 PM train from Nikkō to Utsunomiya and catch the last Yamabiko back at 10:37 PM.

VISITOR INFORMATION

You can do a lot of preplanning for your visit to Nikkō with a stop at the Japan National Tourist Organization office in Tōkyō, where the helpful English-speaking staff will ply you with pamphlets and field your questions about things to see and do. Closer to the source is the Tourist Information and Hospitality Center in Nikkō itself, about halfway up the main street of town between the railway stations and Tōshō-gū, on the left; don't expect too much in the way of help in English, but the center does have a good array of guides to local restaurants and shops, registers of inns and hotels, and mapped-out walking tours.

ESSENTIALS

Tourist Information Nikkō **Tourist Information and Hospitality Center** (☎ *0288/54–2496*).

Tours JTB Sunrise Tours (☎ *03/5796–5454* ⊕ *www.jtbusa.com*).

Train Contact Japan Railways (☎ *03/3423–0111* ⊕ *www.japanrail.com*).

EXPLORING NIKKŌ

The town of Nikkō is essentially one long avenue—Sugi Namiki (Cryptomeria Avenue)—extending for about 2 km (1 mi) from the railway stations to Tōshō-gū. You can easily walk to most places within town. Tourist inns and shops line the street, and if you have time, you might want to make this a leisurely stroll. The antiques shops along the way may turn up interesting—but expensive—pieces like armor fittings, hibachi, pottery, and dolls. The souvenir shops here sell ample selections of local wood carvings.

TŌSHŌ-GŪ AREA

The Tōshō-gu area encompasses three UNESCO World Heritage sights—Tōshō-gu Shrine, Futarasan Shrine, and Rinnōji Temple. These are known as *nisha-ichiji* (two shrines and one temple) and are Nikkō's main draw. Signs and maps clearly mark a recommended route that will allow you to see all the major sights, which are within walking distance of each other. You should plan for half a day to explore the area.

A multiple-entry ticket is the best way to see the Tōshō-gū precincts. The ¥1,000 pass gets you entrance to Rinnō-ji (Rinnō Temple), the Taiyū-in Mausoleum, and Futara-san Jinja (Futara-san Shrine); for an extra ¥300 you can also see the Sleeping Cat and Ieyasu's tomb at Taiyū-in (separate fees are charged for admission to other sights). There are two

CLOSE UP

Ieyasu's Legacy

In 1600, Ieyasu Tokugawa (1543–1616) won a battle at a place in the mountains of south-central Japan called Seki-ga-hara, that left him the undisputed ruler of the archipelago. He died 16 years later, but the Tokugawa Shōgunate would last another 252 years.

The founder of such a dynasty required a fitting resting place. Ieyasu (ee-eh-ya-su) had provided for one in his will: a mausoleum at Nikkō, in a forest of tall cedars, where a religious center had been founded more than eight centuries earlier. The year after his death, in accordance with Buddhist custom, he was given a *kaimyō*—an honorific name to bear in the afterlife. Thenceforth, he was Tōshō-Daigongen: the Great Incarnation Who Illuminates the East. The imperial court at Kyōto declared him a god, and his remains were taken in a procession of great pomp and ceremony to be enshrined at Nikkō.

The dynasty he left behind was enormously rich. Ieyasu's personal fief, on the Kantō Plain, was worth 2.5 million *koku* of rice. One koku, in monetary terms, was equivalent to the cost of keeping one retainer in the necessities of life for a year. The Shōgunate itself, however, was still an uncertainty. It had only recently taken control after more than a century of civil war. The founder's tomb had a political purpose: to inspire awe and to make manifest the power of the Tokugawas. It was Ieyasu's legacy, a statement of his family's right to rule.

Tōshō-gū was built by his grandson, the third shōgun, Iemitsu (it was Iemitsu who established the policy of national isolation, which closed the doors of Japan to the outside world for more than 200 years). The mausoleum and shrine required the labor of 15,000 people for two years (1634–36). Craftsmen and artists of the first rank were assembled from all over the country. Every surface was carved and painted and lacquered in the most intricate detail imaginable. Tōshō-gū shimmers with the reflections of 2,489,000 sheets of gold leaf. Roof beams and rafter ends with dragon heads, lions, and elephants in bas-relief; friezes of phoenixes, wild ducks, and monkeys; inlaid pillars and red-lacquer corridors: Tōshō-gū is everything a 17th-century warlord would consider gorgeous, and the inspiration is very Chinese.

3

places to purchase the multiple-entry ticket: one is at the entrance to Rinno Temple, in the corner of the parking lot, at the top of the path called the Higashi-sandō (East Approach) that begins across the highway from the Sacred Bridge; the other is at the entrance to Tōshō-gū, at the top of the broad Omote-sandō (Central Approach), which begins about 100 yards farther west.

TOP ATTRACTIONS

★ **Futara-san Jinja** 二荒山神社 *(Futara-san Shrine)*. Nikkō's holy ground is far older than the Tokugawa dynasty, in whose honor it was improved upon. Futara-san is sacred to the Shintō deities Okuni-nushi-no-Mikoto (god of the rice fields, bestower of prosperity), his consort Tagorihime-no-Mikoto, and their son Ajisukitaka-hikone-no-Mikoto. Futara-san actually has three locations: the Main Shrine at Tōshō-gū; the Chūgūshi (Middle Shrine), at Chūzenji-ko; and the Okumiya (Inner Shrine), on top of Mt. Nantai. The bronze torii at the entrance to the shrine leads to the **Chinese Gate** (Kara-mon), gilded and elaborately carved; beyond it is the **Hai-den**, the shrine's oratory. The Hai-den,

> **THE UBIQUITOUS TORII**
>
> Wondering what those gatelike structures are with two posts and two crosspieces? They are toriis and are used as gateways to Japanese Shintō temples.

too, is richly carved and decorated, with a dragon-covered ceiling. The Chinese lions on the panels at the rear are by two distinguished painters of the Kanō school. From the oratory of the Taiyū-in a connecting passage leads to the **Sanctum** (Hon-den)—the present version of which dates from 1619. Designated a National Treasure, it houses a gilded and lacquered Buddhist altar some 9 feet high, decorated with paintings of animals, birds, and flowers, in which resides the object of all this veneration: a seated wooden figure of Iemitsu himself. ✛ *Take the avenue to the left as you're standing before the stone torii at Tōshō-gū and follow it to the end* ☎*¥200, ¥1,000 multiple-entry ticket includes admission to Rinnō Temple and Taiyū-in Mausoleum* ☉ *Apr.–Oct., daily 8–5; Nov.–Mar., daily 9–4.*

★ **Rinnō-ji** 輪王寺*(Rinnō Temple).* This temple belongs to the Tendai sect of Buddhism, the head temple of which is Enryaku-ji, on Mt. Hiei near Kyōto. The main hall of Rinnō Temple, called the **Sanbutsu-dō**, is the largest single building at Tōshō-gū; it enshrines an image of Amida Nyorai, the Buddha of the Western Paradise, flanked on the right by Senju (Thousand-Armed) Kannon, the goddess of mercy, and on the left by Batō-Kannon, regarded as the protector of animals. These three images are lacquered in gold and date from the early part of the 17th century. The original Sanbutsu-dō is said to have been built in 848 by the priest Ennin (794–864), also known as Jikaku-Daishi. The present building dates from 1648.

In the southwest corner of the Rinnō Temple compound, behind the abbot's residence, is an especially fine Japanese garden called **Shōyō-en**, created in 1815 and thoughtfully designed to present a different perspective of its rocks, ponds, and flowering plants from every turn on its path. To the right of the entrance to the garden is the **Treasure Hall** (Hōmotsu-den) of Rinnō Temple, a museum with a collection of some 6,000 works of lacquerware, painting, and Buddhist sculpture. The museum is rather small, and only a few of the pieces in the collection— many of them designated National Treasures and Important Cultural Properties—are on display at any given time. ☎*Rinnō Temple ¥1,000, multiple-entry ticket includes admission to the Taiyū-in Mausoleum and Futara-san Shrine; Shōyō-en and Treasure Hall ¥400* ☉ *Apr.–Oct., daily 8–5, last entry at 4; Nov.–Mar., daily 8–4, last entry at 3.*

★ **Taiyū-in Mausoleum** 大猷院廟. This grandiose building is the resting place of the third Tokugawa shōgun, Iemitsu (1604–51), who imposed a policy of national isolation on Japan that was to last more than 200 years. Iemitsu, one suspects, had it in mind to upstage his illustrious grandfather; he marked the approach to his own tomb with no fewer

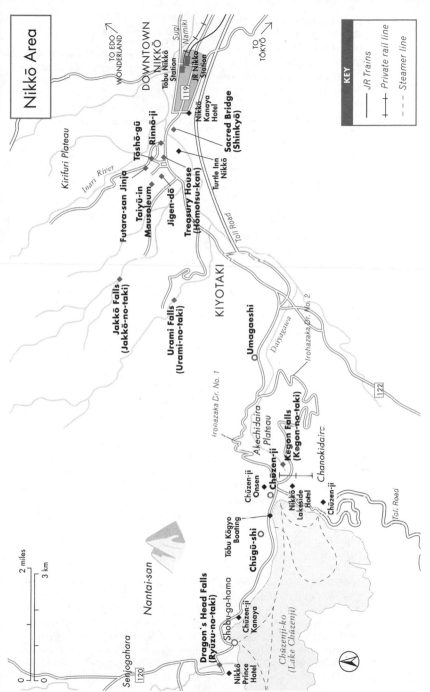

Nikkō Area

TO EDO WONDERLAND

DOWNTOWN NIKKŌ

Tōbu Nikkō Station

JR Nikkō Station

119

TO TŌKYŌ

Sugi Namiki

Nikkō Kanaya Hotel

Sacred Bridge (Shinkyō)

Tōshō-gū

Rinnō-ji

Futara-san Jinja

Taiyū-in Mausoleum

Jigen-dō

Treasury House (Hōmotsu-kan)

Turtle Inn Nikkō

Kirifuri Plateau

Inari River

Toll Road

KIYOTAKI

Jakkō Falls (Jakkō-no-taki)

Urami Falls (Urami-no-taki)

Umagaeshi

Irohazaka Dr. No. 1

Daiyagawa

Irohazaka Dr. No. 2

122

Akechi-daira Plateau

Chūzen-ji

Kegon Falls (Kegon-no-taki)

Chanokidaira

Chūzen-ji Onsen

Chūzen-ji

Nikkō Lakeside Hotel

Chūzen-ji

Tōbu Kōgyo Boating

Chūgū-shi

Nantai-san

Shōbu-ga-hama

Chūzen-ji Kanaya

Dragon's Head Falls (Ryūzu-no-taki)

Nikkō Prince Hotel

Senjogahara

120

Chūzenji-ko (Lake Chūzenji)

Toll Road

2 miles

3 km

0

0

KEY

— JR Trains

+— Private rail line

--- Steamer line

than six different decorative gates. The first is another Niō-mon—a Gate of the Deva Kings—like the one at Tōshō-gū. The dragon painted on the ceiling is by Yasunobu Kanō. A flight of stone steps leads from here to the second gate, the Niten-mon, a two-story structure protected front and back by carved and painted images of guardian gods. Beyond it, two more flights of steps lead to the middle courtyard. As you climb the last steps to Iemitsu's shrine, you'll pass a bell tower on the right and a drum tower on the left; directly ahead is the third gate, the remarkable **Yasha-mon**, so named for the figures of *yasha* (she-demons) in the four niches. This structure is also known as the Peony Gate (Botan-mon) for the carvings that decorate it.

> **SEEKING YOUR FORTUNE?**
>
> Make sure you visit **Gohōten-dō**, in the northeast corner of Rinnō Temple, behind the Sanbutsu-dō. Three of the Seven Gods of Good Fortune are enshrined here, which are derived from Chinese folk mythology. These three Buddhist deities are Daikoku-ten and Bishamon-ten, who bring wealth and good harvests, and Benzai-ten, patroness of music and the arts. You might leave Tōkyō rich and musical.

As you exit the shrine, on the west side, you come to the fifth gate: the **Kōka-mon**, built in the style of the late Ming dynasty of China. The gate is normally closed, but from here another flight of stone steps leads to the sixth and last gate—the cast copper **Inuki-mon**, inscribed with characters in Sanskrit—and Iemitsu's tomb. 🎟️ *¥1,000 multiple-entry ticket includes admission to Rinnō Temple and Futara-san Shrine* 🕐 *Apr.–Oct., daily 8–5; Nov.–Mar., daily 8–4.*

Fodor'sChoice
★ **Tōshō-gū** 東照宮. With its riot of colors and carvings, inlaid pillars, red-lacquer corridors, and extensive use of gold leaf, this 17th-century shrine to Ieyasu Tokugawa, is magnificent, astonishing, and never dull.

The west gate of Rinnō Temple brings you to Omote-sandō, which leads uphill to the stone torii of the shrine. The **Five-Story Pagoda** of Tōshō-gū—a reconstruction dating from 1818—is on the left as you approach the shrine. The 12 signs of the zodiac decorate the first story. The black-lacquer doors above each sign bear the three hollyhock leaves of the Tokugawa family crest.

From the torii a flight of stone steps brings you to the front gate of the shrine—the Omote-mon, also called the Nio-mon (Gate of the Deva Kings), with its fearsome pair of red-painted guardian gods. From here the path turns to the left. In the first group of buildings you reach on the left is the **Sacred Stable** *(Shinkyū)*. Housed here is the white horse—symbol of purity—that figures in many of the shrine's ceremonial events. Carvings of pine trees and monkeys adorn the panels over the stable. And where the path turns to the right, you'll find a granite font where visitors can purify themselves before entering the inner precincts of Tōshō-gū. The **Sutra Library** (Rinzō), just beyond the font, is a repository for some 7,000 Buddhist scriptures, kept in a huge revolving bookcase nearly 20 feet high; it's not open to the public.

As you pass under the second (bronze) torii and up the steps, you'll see a belfry and a tall bronze candelabrum on the right and a drum tower and a bronze revolving lantern on the left. The two works in bronze were presented to the shrine by the Dutch government in the mid-17th century. Behind the drum tower is the **Yakushi-dō**, which enshrines a manifestation of the Buddha as Yakushi Nyorai, the healer of illnesses. The original 17th-century building was famous for a huge India-ink painting on the ceiling of the nave, *The Roaring Dragon*, so named for the rumbling echoes it seemed to emit when visitors clapped their hands beneath it. The painting was by Yasunobu Enshin Kanō (1613–85), from a family of artists that dominated the profession for 400 years. The Kanō

THREE LITTLE MONKEYS

While in the Sacred Stable, make sure to look at the second panel from the left. The three monkeys, commonly known as "Hear no evil, Speak no evil, See no evil," have become something of a Nikkō trademark; the image has been reproduced on plaques, bags, and souvenirs. While the phrase's true origins are uncertain, scholars and legend suggest it originated from this shrine as a visual interpretation of the religious phrase, "If we do not hear, see, or speak evil, we ourselves shall be spared all evil." As for the monkeys, it's been said that a Chinese Buddhist monk introduced the image to Japan in the 8th century.

school was founded in the late 15th century and patronized by successive military governments until the fall of the Tokugawa Shōgunate in 1868. The Yakushi-dō was destroyed by fire in 1961, then rebuilt; the dragon on the ceiling now is by Nampu Katayama (1887–1980).

The centerpiece of Tōshō-gū is the **Gate of Sunlight** (Yōmei-mon), at the top of the second flight of stone steps. A designated National Treasure, it's also called the Twilight Gate (Higurashi-mon)—implying that you could gape at its richness of detail all day, until sunset. And rich it is indeed: 36 feet high and dazzling white, the gate has 12 columns, beams, and roof brackets carved with dragons, lions, clouds, peonies, Chinese sages, and demigods, painted vivid hues of red, blue, green, and gold. On one of the central columns, there are two carved tigers; the natural grain of the wood is used to show "fur." As you enter the Yōmei-mon, galleries run east and west for some 700 feet; their paneled fences are also carved and painted with nature motifs.

The portable shrines that appear in the Tōshō-gū Festival, held yearly on May 17–18, are kept in the **Shinyo-sha**, a storeroom to the left as you come through the Twilight Gate into the heart of the shrine. The paintings on the ceiling, of *tennin* (Buddhist angels) playing harps, are by Tan-yū Kanō (1602–74).

Mere mortals may not pass through the **Chinese Gate** (Kara-mon), which is the "official" entrance to the Tōshō-gū inner shrine. Like its counterpart, the Yōmei-mon, on the opposite side of the courtyard, the Kara-mon is a National Treasure—and, like the Yōmei-mon, is carved and painted in elaborate detail with dragons and other auspicious figures. The Main Hall of Tōshō-gū is enclosed by a wall of painted and carved panel screens; opposite the right-hand corner of the wall, facing the shrine, is the **Kitō-den**, a hall where annual prayers were once offered for the peace of the nation. For a very modest fee, Japanese couples can be married here in a traditional Shintō ceremony, with an ensemble of drums and reed flutes and shrine maidens to attend them.

The **Main Hall** (Hon-den) of Tōshō-gū is the ultimate purpose of the shrine. You approach it from the rows of lockers at the far end of the enclosure; here you remove and store your shoes, step up into the shrine, and follow a winding corridor to the Oratory (Hai-den)—the anteroom, resplendent in its lacquered pillars, carved friezes, and

coffered ceilings bedecked with dragons. Over the lintels are paintings by Mitsuoki Tosa (1617–91) of the 36 great poets of the Heian period, with their poems in the calligraphy of Emperor Go-Mizuno-o. Deeper yet, at the back of the Oratory, is the Inner Chamber (Nai-jin)— repository of the Sacred Mirror that represents the spirit of the deity enshrined here. To the right is a room that was reserved for members of the three principal branches of the Tokugawa family; the room on the left was for the chief abbot of Rinnō Temple, who was always chosen from the imperial line.

Behind the Inner Chamber is the Innermost Chamber (Nai-Nai-jin). No visitors come this far. Here, in the very heart of Tōshō-gū, is the gold-lacquer shrine where the spirit of Ieyasu resides—along with two other deities, whom the Tokugawas later decided were fit companions. One was Hideyoshi Toyotomi, Ieyasu's mentor and liege lord in the long wars of unification at the end of the 16th century. The other was Minamoto no Yoritomo, brilliant military tactician and founder of the earlier (12th-century) Kamakura Shōgunate (Ieyasu claimed Yoritomo for an ancestor).

■ **TIP→ Don't forget to recover your shoes when you return to the courtyard.** Between the Goma-dō and the **Kagura-den** (a hall where ceremonial dances are performed to honor the gods) is a passage to the **Gate at the Foot of the Hill** (Sakashita-mon). Above the gateway is another famous symbol of Tōshō-gū, the Sleeping Cat—a small panel said to have been carved by Hidari Jingorō (Jingorō the Left-handed), a late-16th-century master carpenter and sculptor credited with important contributions to numerous Tokugawa-period temples, shrines, and palaces. A separate admission charge (¥520) is levied to go beyond the Sleeping Cat, up the flight of 200 stone steps through a forest of cryptomeria to **Ieyasu's tomb.** The climb is worth it for the view of the Yōmei-mon and Karamon from above; the tomb itself is unimpressive. ✉ *Free; Ieyasu's tomb ¥520* ☉ *Apr.–Oct., daily 9–5; Nov.–Mar., daily 9–4.*

OFF THE BEATEN PATH

Located on the northern shore of peaceful Yunoko (Lake Yuno), these isolated hot springs were once a popular destination for 14th-century aristocrats. Today, the area is still known for its hot springs—being able to soak in an onsen all year long, even when temperatures drop below zero, will always be a major plus—but they are now controlled by separate resorts. Besides the healing and relaxing effects of the baths, visitors come for the hiking trails, fishing, camping, skiing, bird-watching, and mountain-climbing opportunities. ■**TIP→** Try to avoid the fall season, as it's peak visitor time and there are always delays. You can get to the Yumoto onsen by taking the Tōbu Operated Buses, which leave Tōbu Nikkō and JR Nikkō stations. There are one or two services an hour depending on the time of the day. A one-way trip from central Nikkō takes about 80 minutes and costs ¥1,650.

WORTH NOTING

⟳ **Edo Wonderland** 日光江戸村 *(Nikkō Edo Mura)*, a living-history theme park a short taxi ride from downtown, re-creates an 18th-century Japanese village. The complex includes sculpted gardens with waterfalls and ponds and 22 vintage buildings, where actors in traditional dress stage martial arts exhibitions, historical theatrical performances, and comedy acts. You can even observe Japanese tea ceremony rituals in gorgeous tatami-floored houses, as well as people dressed as geisha and samurai. Strolling stuffed animal characters and acrobatic ninjas keep kids happy. Nikkō Edo Mura has one large restaurant and 15 small food stalls serving period cuisine like *yakisoba* (fried soba) and *dango* (dumplings). ✉470–2 Egura, Fujiwara-chō, Shiodani-gun ☎0288/77–1777 💴¥4,500 unlimited day pass includes rides and shows ⊙ Mid-Mar.–Nov., daily 9–5; Dec.–mid-Mar., daily 9:30–4.

Jigen-dō 慈眼堂. Tenkai (1536–1643), the first abbot of Rinnō Temple, has his own place of honor at Tōshō-gū: the Jigen-dō. The hall, which was founded in 848, now holds many of Rinnō Temple's artistic treasures. To reach it, take the path opposite the south entrance to Futara-san Shrine that passes between the two subtemples called Jōgyō-dō and Hokke-dō. Connected by a corridor, these two buildings are otherwise known as the Futatsu-dō (Twin Halls) of Rinnō Temple and are designated a National Cultural Property. The path between the Twin Halls leads roughly south and west to the Jigen-dō compound; the hall itself is at the north end of the compound, to the right. At the west end sits the Go-ōden, a shrine to Prince Yoshihisa Kitashirakawa (1847–95), the last of the imperial princes to serve as abbot. Behind it are his tomb and the tombs of his 13 predecessors. 💴Free ⊙Apr.–Nov., daily 8–5; Dec.–Mar., daily 9–4.

Monument to Masasuna Matsudaira 松平正綱の杉並木寄進碑. Opposite the Sacred Bridge, at the east entrance to the grounds of Tōshō-gū, this monument pays tribute to one of the two feudal lords charged with the construction of Tōshō-gū. Matsudaira's great contribution was the planting of the wonderful cryptomeria trees (Japanese cedars) surrounding the shrine and along all the approaches to it. The project took 20 years, from 1628 to 1648, and the result was some 36 km (22 mi) of cedar-lined avenues—planted with more than 15,000 trees in all. Fire and time have taken their toll, but thousands of these trees still stand in the shrine precincts, creating a setting of solemn majesty the buildings alone could never have achieved. Thousands more line Route 119 east of Nikkō on the way to Shimo-Imaichi.

Sacred Bridge 神橋 *(Shinkyō)*. Built in 1636 for shōguns and imperial messengers visiting the shrine, the original *bridge* was destroyed in a flood; the present red-lacquer wooden structure dates to 1907. Buses leaving from either railway station at Nikkō go straight up the main street to the bridge, opposite the first of the main entrances to Tōshō-gū. Open again after a year of renovation, the bridge is free to cross, but closes at 4 or 5 PM, depending on the season. The Sacred Bridge is just to the left of a modern bridge, where the road curves and crosses the Daiya-gawa (Daiya River).

Treasury House 宝物館 *(Hōmotsu-kan)*. An unhurried visit to the precincts of Tōshō-gū should definitely include the Treasury house as it contains a collection of antiquities from its various shrines and temples. From the west gate of Rinnō Temple, turn left off Omote-sandō, just below the pagoda, onto the cedar-lined avenue to Futara-san Jinja. A minute's walk will bring you to the museum, on the left. ☞¥500 ⊙ *Apr.–Oct., daily 9–5; Nov.–Mar., daily 9–4.*

CHŪZENJI-KO (LAKE CHŪZENJI)

More than 3,900 feet above sea level, at the base of the volcano known as Nantai-san, is Lake Chūzenji, renowned for its clean waters and fresh air. People come to boat and fish on the lake and to enjoy the surrounding scenic woodlands, waterfalls, and hills.

If you're looking to sightsee, check out **Tōbu Kōgyo Boating,** which offers chartered boat rides for 60 minutes. ⊠ *2478 Chūgūshi, Nikkō, Tochigi-ken* ☎ *0288/55–0360* ☞ *Between ¥150–¥1,500 depending on route chosen* ⊙ *Dec.–Mar., daily 9:30–3:30.*

TOP ATTRACTIONS

Fodor'sChoice
★
Kegon Falls 華厳滝 *(Kegon-no-taki)*. The country's most famous falls are what draw the crowds of Japanese visitors to Chūzenji. Fed by the eastward flow of the lake, the falls drop 318 feet into a rugged gorge; an elevator (¥530) takes you to an observation platform at the bottom. The volume of water over the falls is carefully regulated, but it's especially impressive after a summer rain or a typhoon. In winter the falls do not freeze completely but form a beautiful cascade of icicles. The elevator is just a few minutes' walk east from the bus stop at Chūzenji village, downhill and off to the right at the far end of the parking lot. ⊠ *2479-2 Chūgūshi, Nikkō* ☎ *0288/55–0030* ⊙ *Daily 8–5.*

■ **NEED A BREAK?**
Take a breather at the Ryūzu-no-taki Chaya (⊠ *2485 Chūgūshi, Nikkō* ☎ *0288/55–0157* ⊙ *Daily 11–5*), a charming, but rustic, tea shop near the waterfalls. Enjoy a cup of green tea, a light meal, or Japanese sweets like rice cakes boiled with vegetables and dango (sweet dumplings) while you gaze at the falling waters.

Urami Falls 裏見滝 *(Urami-no-taki)*. "The water," wrote the great 17th-century poet Bashō, "seemed to take a flying leap and drop a hundred feet from the top of a cave into a green pool surrounded by a thousand rocks. One was supposed to inch one's way into the cave and enjoy the falls from behind." ■TIP➔The **falls and the gorge are striking—but you should make the climb only if you have good hiking shoes and are willing to get wet in the process.** ✣ *The steep climb to the cave begins at the Arasawa bus stop, with a turn to the right off the Chūzenji road.*

WORTH NOTING

Chūgū-shi 中宮祠. A subshrine of the Futara-san Shrine at Tōshō-gū, this is the major religious center on the north side of Lake Chūzenji, about

FEELING ADVENTUROUS?

If you want to avoid the hairpin turns, try the **ropeway** that runs from Akechi-daira station directly to the Akechi-daira lookout. It takes three minutes and the panoramic views of Nikkō and Kegon Falls are priceless. ✉ 709–5 Misawa, Hosoomachi, Nikkō ☎0288/55–0331 💲¥390 🕙 Apr.–Oct., daily 8:30–4; Nov.–Mar., daily 9–3.

1½ km (1 mi) west of the village. The **Treasure House** (Hōmotsu-den) contains an interesting historical collection, including swords, lacquerware, and medieval shrine palanquins. 🎫*Shrine free, Treasure House ¥300* 🕙 *Apr.–Oct., daily 8–5; Nov.–Mar., daily 9–4.*

Chūzen-ji 中禅寺 *(Chūzen Temple).* A subtemple of Rinnō Temple, at Tōshō-gū, the principal object of worship here is the **Tachi-ki Kannon,** a 17-foot-tall standing statue of the Buddhist goddess of mercy, said to have been carved more than 1,000 years ago by the priest Shōdō from the living trunk of a single Judas tree. The bus trip from Nikkō to the national park area ends at Chūzenji village, which shares its name with the temple established here in 784. ✣ *Turning left (south) as you leave the village of Chūzenji and walk about 1½ km (1 mi) along the eastern shore of the lake* 🎫*¥500* 🕙 *Apr.–Oct., daily 8–5; Mar. and Nov., daily 8–4; Dec.–Feb., daily 8–3:30.*

Dragon's Head Falls 竜頭滝 *(Ryūzu-no-taki).* If you've budgeted an extra day for Nikkō, you might want to consider a walk around the lake. A paved road along the north shore extends for about 8 km (5 mi), one-third of the whole distance, as far as the "beach" at Shōbu-ga-hama. Here, where the road branches off to the north for Senjōgahara, are the lovely cascades of Dragon's Head Falls. To the left is a steep footpath that continues around the lake to Senju-ga-hama and then to a campsite at Asegata. The path is well marked but can get rough in places. From Asegata it's less than an hour's walk back to Chūzenji village.

Jakkō Falls 寂光滝 *(Jakkō-no-taki).* Falling water is one of the special charms of the Nikkō National Park area; people going by bus or car from Tōshō-gū to Lake Chūzenji often stop off en route to see these falls, which descend in a series of seven terraced stages, forming a sheet of water about 100 feet high. About 1 km (½ mi) from the shrine precincts, at the Tamozawa bus stop, a narrow road to the right leads to an uphill walk of some 3 km (2 mi) to the falls.

Umagaeshi 馬返し. In the old days, the road became too rough for horse riding, so riders had to alight and proceed on foot; the lake is 4,165 feet above sea level. From Umagaeshi the bus climbs a one-way toll road up the pass; the old road has been widened and is used for the traffic coming down. The two roads are full of steep hairpin turns, and on a clear day the view up and down the valley is magnificent—especially from the halfway point at **Akechi-daira** (Akechi Plain), from which you can see the summit of **Nantai-san** (Mt. Nantai), reaching 8,149 feet. Hiking season lasts from May through mid-October; if you push it, you can make the ascent in about four hours. △ **Wild monkeys make their homes in these mountains, and they've learned the convenience of mooching from visitors along the route. Be careful—they have a way of not taking no for an answer. Do not give into the temptation to give them food, they will never leave you alone if you do.** ⚐ *About 10 km (6 mi) from Tōbu Station in Nikkō, or 8 km (5 mi) from Tōshō-gū.*

WHERE TO EAT

CHŪZENJI

$$–$$$ ✕ **Nantai** なんたい. The low tables, antiques, and pillows scattered on
JAPANESE tatami flooring make visitors feel like they're dining in a traditional Japanese living room. Try the Nikkō specialty, *yuba* (tofu skin), which comes with the *nabe* (hot pot) for dinner. It's the quintessential winter family meal. The seafood here is fresh and both the trout and salmon are recommended. Each meal comes with rice, pickles, and selected side dishes like soy-stewed vegetables, tempura, udon, and a dessert. ✉*2478–8 Chūgūshi, Nikkō* ☎*0288/55–0201* ▤*AE, DC, MC, V.*

NIKKŌ

$$$–$$$$ ✕ **Fujimoto** ふじもと. At what may be Nikkō's most formal Western-style
FRENCH restaurant, finer touches include plush carpets, art deco fixtures, stained and frosted glass, a thoughtful wine list, and a maître d' in black tie. The menu combines elements of French and Japanese cooking styles and ingredients; the fillet of beef in mustard sauce is particularly excellent. Fujimoto closes at 7:30, so plan on eating early. ✉*2339–1 Sannai, Nikkō* ☎*0288/53–3754* ▤*AE, DC, V* ☾*Closed Thurs.*

$$$$ ✕ **Gyōshintei** 堯心亭. This is the only restaurant in Nikkō devoted to
JAPANESE *shōjin ryōri*, the Buddhist-temple vegetarian fare that evolved centuries ago into haute cuisine. Gyōshintei is decorated in the style of a *ryōtei* (traditional inn), with all-tatami seating. It differs from a ryōtei in that it has one large, open space where many guests are served at once, rather than a number of rooms for private dining. Dinner is served until 7. ✉*2339–1 Sannai, Nikkō* ☎*0288/53–3751* ▤*AE, DC, MC, V* ☾*Closed Thurs.*

$$$–$$$$ ✕ **Masudaya** ゆば亭ますだや. Masudaya started out as a sake maker
JAPANESE more than a century ago, but for four generations now, it has been the town's best-known restaurant. The specialty is yuba, which the chefs transform, with the help of local vegetables and fresh fish, into sumptuous high cuisine. The building is traditional, with a lovely interior garden; the assembly-line-style service, however, detracts from the ambience. Masudaya serves one nine-course kaiseki-style meal; the kitchen simply stops serving when the food is gone. Meals here are prix fixe. ✉*439–2 Ishiya-machi, Nikkō* ☎*0288/54–2151* ⚖*Reservations essential* ▤*No credit cards* ☾*Closed Thurs. No dinner.*

$$$–$$$$
CONTINENTAL ✕**Meiji-no-Yakata** 明治の館. Not far from the east entrance to Rinnō Temple, Meiji-no-Yakata is an elegant 19th-century Western-style stone house, originally built as a summer retreat for an American diplomat. The food, too, is Western style; specialties of the house include fresh rainbow trout from Lake Chūzenji, roast lamb with pepper sauce, and melt-in-your-mouth filet mignon made from local Tochigi beef. High ceilings, hardwood floors, and an air of informality make this a very pleasant place to dine. The restaurant opens at 11 AM in the summer and 11:30 AM in the winter; it always closes at 7:30. ⊠*2339–1 Sannai, Nikkō* ☎*0288/53–3751* ⊟*AE, DC, MC, V* ☾*Closed Wed.*

$$–$$$
JAPANESE ✕**Sawamoto** 澤本. Charcoal-broiled *unagi* (eel) is an acquired taste, and there's no better place in Nikkō to acquire it than at this restaurant. The place is small and unpretentious, with only five plain-wood tables, and service can be lukewarm, but Sawamoto is reliable for a light lunch or dinner of unagi on a bed of rice, served in an elegant lacquered box. Eel is considered a stamina builder: just right for the weary visitor on a hot summer day. ⊠*1019 Bandu, Kami Hatsuishi-machi, Nikkō* ☎*0288/54–0163* ⊟*No credit cards* ☾*No dinner.*

WHERE TO STAY

CHŪZENJI

$$$$ 🏨 **Chūzenji Kanaya** 中禅寺金谷ホテル. A boathouse and restaurant on the lake give this branch of the Nikkō Kanaya on the road from the village to Shōbu-ga-hama the air of a private yacht club. Pastel colors decorate the simple, tasteful rooms, which have floor-to-ceiling windows overlooking the lake or grounds. **Pros:** clean; completely Western-style rooms. **Cons:** the most expensive hotel in the area. ⊠*2482 Chū-gūshi, Chūzen-ji, Nikkō, Tochigi-ken* ☎*0288/51–0001* ⊕*www.kanayahotel.co.jp/english/chuzenji/index.html* ⇆*60 rooms, 54 with bath* ⅋*In-hotel: restaurant* ⊟*AE, DC, MC, V* ꙰*MAP.*

$$–$$$ 🏨 **Nikkō Lakeside Hotel** 日光レイクサイドホテル. In the village of Chūzenji at the foot of the lake, the Nikkō Lakeside has no particular character, but the views are good and the transportation connections (to buses and excursion boats) are ideal. Prices vary considerably from weekday to weekend and season to season. **Pros:** close to the lake and hot spring baths. **Cons:** room decor is a bit dated. ⊠*2482 Chū-gūshi, Chūzen-ji, Nikkō, Tochigi-ken* ☎*0288/55–0321* ⇆*100 rooms with bath* ⅋*In-hotel: 2 restaurants, bar, tennis court, bicycles* ⊟*AE, DC, MC, V* ꙰*MAP.*

NIKKŌ

$$$–$$$$
★ 🏨 **Nikkō Kanaya Hotel** 日光金谷ホテル. This family-run operation is a little worn around the edges after a century of operation, but it still has the best location in town: across the street from Tōshō-gū. The main building is a delightful, rambling Victorian structure that has hosted royalty and other important personages—as the guest book attests—from around the world. The long driveway that winds up to the hotel at the top of the hill is just below the Sacred Bridge, on the same side of the street. The hotel is very touristy; daytime visitors browse through the old building and its gift shops. The helpful staff is better at giving area

3

information than the tourist office. Rooms vary a great deal, as do their prices. The more expensive rooms are spacious and comfortable, with wonderful high ceilings; in the annex the sound of the Daiyagawa murmuring below the Sacred Bridge lulls you to sleep. Horseback

riding and golf are available nearby. **Pros:** spacious; well-appointed. **Cons:** rooms are rather pricey. ⊠*1300 Kami Hatsuishi-machi, Nikkō, Tochigi-ken* ☎*0288/54–0001* ⊕*www.kanayahotel.co.jp/english/nikko/index.html* ⇆*77 rooms, 62 with bath* ⎈*In-hotel: 2 restaurants, bar, pool* ⊟*AE, DC, MC, V.*

¢ ☷**Turtle Inn Nikkō** タートルイン日光. This Japanese Inn Group member provides friendly, modest, cost-conscious Western- and Japanese-style accommodations with or without a private bath. Simple, cheap breakfasts and dinners are served in the dining room, but you needn't opt for these if you'd rather eat out. Rates go up about 10% in high season (late July and August). To get here, take the bus bound for Chūzenji from either railway station and get off at the Sōgo Kaikan-mae bus stop. The inn is two minutes from the bus stop and within walking distance of Tōshō-gū. **Pros:** cozy atmosphere; English-speaking staff. **Cons:** rooms are a bit on the small side. ⊠*2–16 Takumi-chō, Nikkō, Tochigi-ken* ☎*0288/53–3168* ⇆*7 Western-style rooms, 3 with bath; 5 Japanese-style rooms without bath* ⊕*www.turtle-nikko.com* ⎈*In-hotel: restaurant, Japanese baths, Internet* ⊟*AE, MC, V.*

SHŌBU-GA-HAMA

$$ ☷**Nikkō Prince Hotel** 日光プリンスホテル. On the shore of Lake Chūzenji, this hotel, part of a large Japanese chain, is within walking distance of the Dragon's Head Falls. With many of its accommodations in two-story maisonettes and rustic detached cottages, the Prince chain markets itself to families and small groups of younger excursionists. The architecture favors high ceilings and wooden beams, with lots of glass in the public areas to take advantage of the view of the lake and Mt. Nantai. **Pros:** the private cottages are very cozy. **Cons:** the hot spring baths seem a bit small for the number of guest at the hotel. ⊠*Chūgūshi, Shōbu-ga-hama, Nikkō, Tochigi-ken* ☎*0288/55–1111* ⊕*www.princehotels.co.jp* ⇆*60 rooms with bath* ⎈*In-hotel: restaurant, bar, tennis courts, pool* ⊟*AE, DC, MC, V* ⯮*MAP.*

KAMAKURA 鎌倉

Kamakura, about 40 km (25 mi) southwest of Tōkyō, is an object lesson in what happens when you set the fox to guard the henhouse.

For the aristocrats of the Heian-era Japan (794–1185), life was defined by the imperial court in Kyōto. Who in their right mind would venture elsewhere? In Kyōto there was grace and beauty and poignant affairs of the heart; everything beyond was howling wilderness. Unfortunately, it was the howling wilderness that had all the estates: the large grants of land, called *shōen*, without which there would be no income to pay for all that grace and beauty.

By the 12th century two clans—the Taira (*ta*-ee-ra) and the Minamoto, themselves both offshoots of the imperial line—had come to dominate the affairs of the Heian court and were at each other's throats in a struggle for supremacy. In 1160 the Taira won a major battle that should have secured their absolute control over Japan, but in the process they made one serious mistake: having killed the Minamoto leader Yoshitomo (1123–60), they spared his 13-year-old son, Yoritomo (1147–99), and sent him into exile. In 1180 he launched a rebellion and chose Kamakura—a superb natural fortress, surrounded on three sides by hills and guarded on the fourth by the sea—as his base of operations.

The rivalry between the two clans became an all-out war. By 1185 Yoritomo and his half brother, Yoshitsune (1159–89), had destroyed the Taira utterly, and the Minamoto were masters of all Japan. In 1192 Yoritomo forced the imperial court to name him shōgun; he was now de facto and de jure the military head of state. The emperor was left as a figurehead in Kyōto, and the little fishing village of Kamakura became—and for 141 years remained—the seat of Japan's first shōgunal government.

The Minamoto line came to an end when Yoritomo's two sons were assassinated. Power passed to the Hōjō family, who remained in control, often as regents for figurehead shōguns, for the next 100 years. In 1274 and again in 1281 Japan was invaded by the Mongol armies of China's Yuan dynasty. On both occasions typhoons—the original kamikaze (literally, "divine wind")—destroyed the Mongol fleets, but the Hōjō family was still obliged to reward the various clans that had rallied to the defense of the realm. A number of these clans were unhappy with their portions—and with Hōjō rule in general. The end came suddenly, in 1333, when two vassals assigned to put down a revolt switched sides. The Hōjō regent committed suicide, and the center of power returned to Kyōto.

Kamakura reverted to being a sleepy backwater town on the edge of the sea, but after World War II, it began to develop as a residential area for the well-to-do. Nothing secular survives from the days of the Minamoto and Hōjō; there wasn't much there to begin with. The warriors of Kamakura had little use for courtiers, or their palaces and gardened villas; the Shōgunate's name for itself, in fact, was the Bakufu—literally, the "tent government." As a religious center, however, the town presents an extraordinary legacy. Most of those temples and shrines are in settings of remarkable beauty; many are designated National Treasures. If you can afford the time for only one day trip from Tōkyō, you should probably spend it here.

GETTING HERE AND AROUND

By Bus. A bus from Kamakura Station (Sign 5) travels to most of the temples and shrines in the downtown Kamakura area, with stops at most access roads to the temples and shrines. However, you may want to walk out as far as Hōkoku-ji and take the bus back; it's easier to recognize the end of the line than any of the stops in between. You can also go by taxi to Hōkoku-ji—any cab driver knows the way—and walk the last leg in reverse.

By Tours. Bus companies in Kamakura don't conduct guided English tours. However, if your time is limited or you don't want to do a lot of walking, the Japanese tours hit the major attractions. These tours depart from Kamakura Station eight times daily, starting at 9 AM; the last tour leaves at 1 PM. Purchase tickets at the bus office to the right of the station.

■ TIP→ On the weekend the Kanagawa Student Guide Federation offers a free guide service. Students show you the city in exchange for the chance to practice their English. Arrangements must be made in advance through the Japan National Tourist Organization in Tōkyō. You'll need to be at Kamakura Station between 10 AM and noon.

Sunrise Tours runs daily English-language trips from Tōkyō to Kamakura; these tours are often combined with trips to Hakone. You can book through, and arrange to be picked up at, any of the major hotels. Check to make sure that the tour covers everything you want to see, as many include little more than a passing view of the Great Buddha in Hase. Given how easy it is to get around—most sights are within walking distance of each other, and others are short bus or train rides apart—you're better off seeing Kamakura on your own.

By Train. Traveling by train is by far the best way to get to Kamakura. Trains run from Tōkyō Station (and Shimbashi Station) every 10 to 15 minutes during the day. The trip takes 56 minutes to Kita-Kamakura and one hour to Kamakura. Take the JR Yokosuka Line from Track 1 downstairs in Tōkyō Station (Track 1 upstairs is on a different line and does not go to Kamakura). The cost is ¥780 to Kita-Kamakura, ¥890 to Kamakura (or use your JR [Japan Railways] Pass). It's now also possible to take a train from Shinjuku, Shibuya, or Ebisu to Kamakura on the Shonan-Shinjuku line, but these trains depart less frequently than those departing from Tōkyō Station. Local train service connects Kita-Kamakura, Kamakura, Hase, and Enoshima.

To return to Tōkyō from Enoshima, take a train to Shinjuku on the Odakyū Line. There are 11 express trains daily from here on week-days, between 8:38 AM and 8:45 PM; nine trains daily on weekends and national holidays, between 8:39 AM and 8:46 PM; and even more in summer. The express takes about 70 minutes and costs ¥1,220. Or you can retrace your steps to Kamakura and take the JR Yokosuka Line to Tōkyō Station.

VISITOR INFORMATION

Both Kamakura and Enoshima have their own tourist associations, although it can be problematic getting help in English over the phone. Your best bet is the Kamakura Station Tourist Information Center, which has a useful collection of brochures and maps. And since Kamakura is in Kanagawa Prefecture, visitors heading here from Yokohama can preplan their excursion at the Kanagawa Prefectural Tourist Association office in the Silk Center, on the Yamashita Park promenade.

ESSENTIALS

Tour Contacts Japan National Tourist Organization (*Tōkyō* ☎ *03/3201–3331* ⊕ *www.jnto.go.jp*). **Kanagawa Student Guide Federation** (☎ *03/3201–3331*). **Sunrise Tours** (☎ *03/5796–5454* ⊕ *www.jtbgmt.com/sunrisetour/index.aspx*).

Tourist Information Enoshima Tourist Association (☎ *0466/37–4141*). Kamakura Station Tourist Information Center (☎ *0467/22–3350*). Kamakura Tourist Association (☎ *0467/23–3050*). Kanagawa Prefectural Tourist Association (☎ *045/681–0007* ⊕ *www.kanagawa-kankou.or.jp*).

Train Contact Japan Railways (☎ *03/3423–0111* ⊕ *www.japanrail.com*).

EXPLORING KAMAKURA

There are three principal areas in Kamakura, and you can easily get from one to another by train. From Tōkyō head first to Kita-Kamakura for most of the important Zen temples, including Engaku-ji (Engaku Temple) and Kenchō-ji (Kenchō Temple). The second area is downtown Kamakura, with its shops and museums and the venerated shrine Tsuru-ga-oka Hachiman-gū. The third is Hase, a 10-minute train ride southwest from Kamakura on the Enoden Line. Hase's main attractions are the great bronze figure of the Amida Buddha, at Kōtoku-in, and the Kannon Hall of Hase-dera. There's a lot to see in Kamakura, and even to hit just the highlights will take you most of a busy day.

Numbers in the text correspond to numbers on the Kamakura map.

KITA-KAMAKURA (NORTH KAMAKURA) 北鎌倉

Hierarchies were important to the Kamakura Shōgunate. In the 14th century it established a ranking system called Go-zan (literally, "Five Mountains") for the Zen Buddhist monasteries under its official sponsorship.

TOP ATTRACTIONS

❶ ★ Engaku-ji 円覚寺 *(Engaku Temple)*. The largest of the Zen monasteries in Kamakura, Engaku-ji was founded in 1282 and ranks second in the Five Mountains hierarchy. Here, prayers were to be offered regularly for the prosperity and well-being of the government; Engaku Temple's special role was to pray for the souls of those who died resisting the Mongol invasions in 1274 and 1281. The temple complex currently holds 18, but once contained as many as 50, buildings. Often damaged in fires and earthquakes, it has been completely restored.

Engaku Temple belongs to the Rinzai sect of Zen Buddhism. Introduced into Japan from China at the beginning of the Kamakura period (1192–1333), the ideas of Zen were quickly embraced by the emerging warrior class. The samurai especially admired the Rinzai sect, with its emphasis on the ascetic life as a path to self-transcendence. The monks of Engaku Temple played an important role as advisers to the Shōgunate in matters spiritual, artistic, and political.

Among the National Treasures at Engaku Temple is the **Hall of the Holy Relic of Buddha** (Shari-den), with its remarkable Chinese-inspired thatched roof. Built in 1282, it was destroyed by fire in 1558 but rebuilt in its original form soon after, in 1563. The hall is said to enshrine a

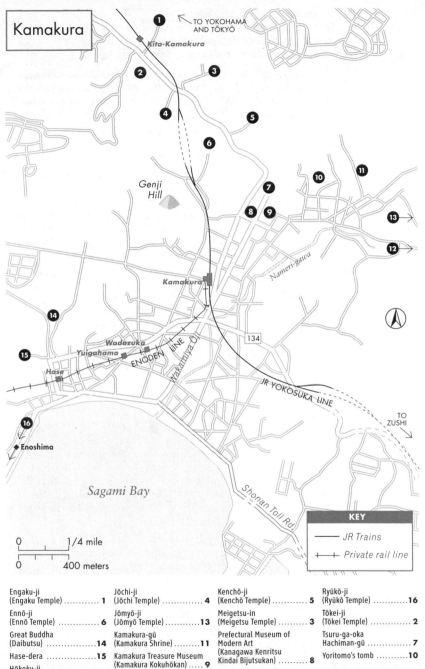

Kamakura

TO YOKOHAMA
AND TŌKYŌ

Kita-Kamakura

Genji
Hill

Kamakura

Nameri-gawa

134

Wadezuka

Yuigahama

ENODEN LINE

Wakamiya Ōji

Hase

JR YOKOSUKA LINE

TO
ZUSHI

Enoshima

Sagami Bay

Shonan Toll Rd.

0   1/4 mile

0   400 meters

KEY

—— JR Trains

+—+—+ Private rail line

tooth of the Gautama Buddha himself, but it's not on display. In fact, except for the first three days of the New Year, you won't be able to go any farther into the hall than the main gate. Such is the case, alas, with much of the Engaku Temple complex: this is still a functioning monastic center, and many of its most impressive buildings are not open to the public. The accessible National Treasure at Engaku Temple is the **Great Bell** (Kōshō), on the hilltop on the southeast side of the complex. The bell—Kamakura's most famous—was cast in 1301 and stands 8 feet tall. It's rung only on special occasions, such as New Year's Eve. Reaching the bell requires a trek up a long staircase, but once you've made it to the top you can enjoy tea and traditional Japanese sweets at a small outdoor café. The views of the entire temple grounds and surrounding cedar forest from here are tremendous.

> **TIMING TIP**
>
> If your time is limited, you may want to visit only Engaku Temple and Tōkei Temple in Kita-Kamakura before riding the train one stop to Kamakura. If not, follow the main road all the way to Tsuru-ga-oka Hachiman-gū and visit four additional temples en route.

The two buildings open to the public at Engaku Temple are the **Butsunichi-an,** which has a long ceremonial hall where you can enjoy *sado* (Japanese tea ceremony), and the **Ōbai-in.** The latter is the mausoleum of the last three regents of the Kamakura Shōgunate: Tokimune Hōjō, who led the defense of Japan against the Mongol invasions; his son Sadatoki; and his grandson Takatoki. Off to the side of the mausoleum is a quiet garden with apricot trees, which bloom in February. As you exit Kita-Kamakura Station, you'll see the stairway to Engaku Temple just in front of you. ⊠ *409 Yama-no-uchi, Kita-Kamakura* ☎ *0467/22–0478* ⊠ *Engaku Temple ¥300* ⊗ *Nov.–Mar., daily 8–4; Apr.–Oct., daily 8–5.*

❻ **Ennō-ji** 円応寺 *(Ennō Temple).* In the feudal period, Japan acquired from
★ China a belief in Enma, the lord of hell, who, with his court attendants, judged the souls of the departed and determined their destination in the afterlife. Kamakura's otherwise undistinguished Ennô-ji *(Ennō Temple)* houses some remarkable statues of these judges—as grim and merciless a court as you're ever likely to confront. To see them is enough to put you on your best behavior, at least for the rest of your excursion. Ennō Temple is a minute's walk or so from Kenchō Temple, on the opposite (south) side of the main road to Kamakura. ⊹ *A few minutes' walk along the main road to the south will bring you to Tsuru-ga-oka Hachiman-gū in downtown Kamakura.* ⊠ *1543 Yama-no-uchi, Kita-Kamakura* ☎ *0467/25–1095* ⊠ *¥200* ⊗ *Mar.–Nov., daily 9–4; Dec.–Feb., daily 9–3.*

❺ **Kenchō-ji** 建長寺 *(Kenchō Temple).* Founded in 1250, this temple was
★ the foremost of Kamakura's five great Zen temples, and it lays claim to being the oldest Zen temple in all of Japan. It was modeled on one of the great Chinese monasteries of the time and built for a distinguished Zen master who had just arrived from China. Over the centuries, fires and other disasters have taken their toll on Kenchō Temple, and although many buildings have been authentically reconstructed,

the temple complex today is half its original size. Near the Main Gate (San-mon) is a **bronze bell** cast in 1255; it's the temple's most important treasure. The Main Gate and the Lecture Hall (Hattō) are the only two structures to have survived the devastating Great Kantō Earthquake of 1923. Like Engaku Temple, Kenchō Temple is a functioning temple of the Rinzai sect, where novices train and laypeople can come to take part in Zen meditation. ⚓ *The entrance to Kenchō Temple is about halfway along the main road from Kita-Kamakura Station to Tsuruga-oka Hachiman-gū, on the left.* ✉ *8 Yama-no-uchi, Kita-Kamakura* ☎ *0467/22–0981* 💰 *¥300* 🕐 *Daily 8:30–4:30.*

❷ Tōkei-ji 東慶寺 *(Tōkei Temple).* A Zen temple of the Rinzai sect, Tōkei-ji
★ holds special significance for the study of feminism in medieval Japan. More popularly known as the Enkiri-dera, or Divorce Temple, it was founded in 1285 by the widow of the Hōjō regent Tokimune as a refuge for the victims of unhappy marriages. Under the Shōgunate, a husband of the warrior class could obtain a divorce simply by sending his wife back to her family. Not so for the wife: no matter what cruel and unusual treatment her husband meted out, she was stuck with him. If she ran away, however, and managed to reach Tōkei Temple without being caught, she could receive sanctuary at the temple and remain there as a nun. After three years (later reduced to two), she was officially declared divorced. The temple survived as a convent through the Meiji Restoration of 1868. The last abbess died in 1902; her headstone is in the cemetery behind the temple, beneath the plum trees that blossom in February. Tōkei Temple was later reestablished as a monastery.

The **Matsugaoka Treasure House** (Matsugaoka Hōzō) of Tōkei Temple displays several Kamakura-period wooden Buddhas, ink paintings, scrolls, and works of calligraphy, some of which have been designated by the government as Important Cultural Objects. The library, called the Matsugaoka Bunko, was established in memory of the great Zen scholar D. T. Suzuki (1870–1966). ⚓ *Tōkei Temple is on the southwest side of the JR tracks (the side opposite Engaku Temple), less than a five-minute walk south from the station on the main road to Kamakura (Route 21–the Kamakura Kaidō), on the right.* ✉ *1367 Yama-no-uchi, Kita-Kamakura* ☎ *0467/22–1663* 💰 *Tōkei Temple ¥100, Matsugaoka Treasure House additional ¥300* 🕐 *Tōkei Temple Apr.–Oct., daily 8:30–5; Nov.–Mar., daily 8:30–4. Matsugaoka Treasure House Mon.–Thurs. 9:30–3:30.*

WORTH NOTING

❹ Jōchi-ji 浄智寺 *(Jōchi Temple).* In the Five Mountains hierarchy, Jōchi-ji was ranked fourth. The buildings now in the temple complex are reconstructions; the Great Kantō Earthquake of 1923 destroyed the originals. The garden here is exquisite. Jōchi Temple is on the south side of the railway tracks, a few minutes' walk farther southwest of Tōkei Temple in the direction of Kamakura. ⚓ *Turn right off the main road (Route 21) and cross over a small bridge; a flight of moss-covered steps leads up to the temple.* ✉ *1402 Yama-no-uchi, Kita-Kamakura* ☎ *0467/22–3943* 💰 *¥200* 🕐 *Daily 9–4:30.*

❸ Meigetsu-in 明月院 *(Meigetsu Temple)*. This temple is also known as Ajisai-dera (the hydrangeas temple), because when the flowers bloom in June, it becomes one of the most popular places in Kamakura. The gardens transform into a sea of color—pink, white, and blue—and visitors can number in the thousands. A typical Kamakura light rain shouldn't deter you; it only showcases this incredible floral display to its best advantage. Meigetsu-in features Kamakura's largest *yagura* (a tomb cavity enclosing a mural) on which 16 images of Buddha are carved. ⊹*From Tōkei Temple walk along Route 21 toward Kamakura for about 20 minutes until you cross the railway tracks; take the immediate left turn onto the narrow side street that doubles back along the tracks. This street bends to the right and follows the course of a little stream called the Meigetsu-gawa to the temple gate.* ✉*189 Yamano-uchi, Kita-Kamakura* ☎*0467/24–3437* 💴*¥300* ⏱*Nov.–May and July–Oct., daily 9–4; June, daily 8:30–5.*

DOWNTOWN KAMAKURA

Downtown Kamakura is a good place to stop for lunch and shopping. Restaurants and shops selling local crafts, especially the carved and lacquered woodwork called Kamakura-*bori,* abound on Wakamiya Oji and the street parallel to it, Komachi-dōri.

When the first Kamakura shōgun, Minamoto no Yoritomo, learned he was about to have an heir, he had the tutelary shrine of his family moved to Kamakura from nearby Yui-ga-hama and ordered a stately avenue to be built through the center of his capital from the shrine to the sea. Along this avenue would travel the procession that brought his son—if there were a son—to be presented to the gods. Yoritomo's consort did indeed bear him a son, Yoriie (yo-*ree*-ee-eh), in 1182; Yoriie was brought in great pomp to the shrine and then consecrated to his place in the shōgunal succession. Alas, the blessing of the gods did Yoriie little good. He was barely 18 when Yoritomo died, and the regency established by his mother's family, the Hōjō, kept him virtually powerless until 1203, when he was banished and eventually assassinated. The Minamoto were never to hold power again, but Yoriie's memory lives on in the street that his father built for him: Wakamiya Ōji, "the Avenue of the Young Prince."

TOP ATTRACTIONS

⓬ Hōkoku-ji 報国寺 *(Hōkoku Temple)*. Visitors to Kamakura tend to overlook this lovely little Zen temple of the Rinzai sect that was built in 1334, but it's worth a look. Over the years it had fallen into disrepair and neglect, until an enterprising priest took over, cleaned up the gardens, and began promoting the temple for meditation sessions, calligraphy exhibitions, and tea ceremony. Behind the main hall are a thick grove of bamboo and a small tea pavilion—a restful oasis and a fine place to go for *matcha* (green tea). ⊹*The temple is about 2 km (1 mi) east on Route 204 from the main entrance to Tsuru-ga-oka Hachimangū; turn right at the traffic light by the Hōkoku Temple Iriguchi bus stop and walk about three minutes south to the gate.* ✉*2-7-4 Jōmyō-ji* ☎*0467/22–0762* 💴*¥200, tea ceremony ¥500* ⏱*Daily 9–4.*

An Ancient Soap Opera

Once a year, during the Spring Festival (early or mid-April, when the cherry trees are in bloom), the Mai-den hall at Tsuru-ga-oka Hachiman-gū is used to stage a heartrending drama about Minamoto no Yoritomo's brother, Yoshitsune. Although Yoritomo was the tactical genius behind the downfall of the Taira clan and the establishment of the Kamakura Shōgunate in the late 12th century, it was his dashing half brother who actually defeated the Taira in battle. In so doing, Yoshitsune won the admiration of many, and Yoritomo came to believe that his sibling had ambitions of his own. Despite Yoshitsune's declaration of allegiance, Yoritomo had him exiled and sent assassins to have him killed. Yoshitsune spent his life fleeing from one place to another until, at the age of 30, he was betrayed in his last refuge and took his own life.

Earlier in his exile, Yoshitsune's lover, the dancer Shizuka Gozen, had been captured and brought to Yoritomo and his wife, Masako. They commanded her to dance for them as a kind of penance. Instead she danced for Yoshitsune. Yoritomo was furious, and only Masako's influence kept him from ordering her death. When he discovered, however, that Shizuka was carrying Yoshitsune's child, he ordered that if the child were a boy, he was to be killed. A boy was born. Some versions of the legend have it that the child was slain; others say he was placed in a cradle, like Moses, and cast adrift in the reeds.

7 **Tsuru-ga-oka Hachiman-gū** 鶴岡八幡宮 *(Minamoto shrine)*. This shrine is
★ dedicated to the legendary emperor Ōjin, his wife, and his mother, from whom Minamoto no Yoritomo claimed descent. At the entrance, the small, steeply arched, vermilion **Drum Bridge** (Taiko-bashi) crosses a stream between two lotus ponds. The ponds were made to Yoritomo's specifications. His wife, Masako, suggested placing islands in each. In the larger **Genji Pond,** to the right, filled with white lotus flowers, she placed three islands. Genji was another name for clan, and three is an auspicious number. In the smaller **Heike Pond,** to the left, she put four islands. Heike (*heh*-ee-keh) was another name for the rival Taira clan, which the Minamoto had destroyed, and four—homophonous in Japanese with the word for "death"—is very unlucky indeed.

On the far side of the Drum Bridge is the **Mai-den.** This hall is the setting for a story of the Minamoto celebrated in Nō and Kabuki theater. Beyond the Mai-den, a flight of steps leads to the shrine's Main Hall (Hon-dō). To the left of these steps is a ginkgo tree that—according to legend—was witness to a murder that ended the Minamoto line in 1219. From behind this tree, a priest named Kugyō leapt out and beheaded his uncle, the 26-year-old Sanetomo, Yoritomo's second son and the last Minamoto shōgun. The priest was quickly apprehended, but Sanetomo's head was never found. Like all other Shintō shrines, the Main Hall is unadorned; the building itself, an 1828 reconstruction, is not particularly noteworthy. ✢ *To reach Tsuru-ga-oka Hachiman-gū from the east side of Kamakura Station, cross the plaza, turn left, and walk north along Wakamiya Ōji. Straight ahead is the first of three arches* *leading to the shrine, and the shrine itself is at the far end of the street* ✉*2–1–31 Yuki-no-shita* ☎*0467/22–0315* 🎟*Free* 🕙*Daily 9–4.*

⑩ **Yoritomo's tomb** 頼朝の墓. The man who put Kamakura on the map, so to speak, chose not to leave it when he died: it's only a short walk from Tsuru-ga-oka Hachiman-gū to the tomb of the man responsible for its construction, Minamoto no Yoritomo. If you've already been to Nikkō and have seen how a later dynasty of shōguns sought to glorify its own memories, you may be surprised at the simplicity of Yoritomo's tomb. To get here, cross the Drum Bridge at Tsuru-ga-oka Hachiman-gū and turn left. Leave the grounds of the shrine and walk east along the main street (Route 204) that forms the T-intersection at the end of Wakamiya Ōji. A 10-minute walk will bring you to a narrow street on the left— there's a bakery called Bergfeld (*see review below)* on the corner that leads to the tomb, about 100 yards off the street to the north and up a flight of stone steps. 🎟*Free* 🕙*Daily 9–4.*

WORTH NOTING

⑬ **Jōmyō-ji** 浄明寺 *(Jōmyō Temple).* Founded in 1188, this one of the Five Mountains Zen monasteries. Though it lacks the grandeur and scale of the Engaku and Kenchō, it still merits the status of an Important Cultural Property. This modest single story monastery belonging to the Rinzai sect is nestled inside an immaculate garden that is particularly beautiful in spring, when the cherry trees bloom. Its only distinctive features are its green roof and the statues of Shaka Nyorai and Amida Nyorai, who represent truth and enlightenment, in the main hall. ✛ *To reach it from Hōkoku-ji, cross the main street (Route 204) that brought you the mile or so from Tsuru-ga-oka Hachiman-gū, and take the first narrow street north. The monastery is about 100 yards from the corner.* ✉*3–8–31 Jōmyō-ji* ☎*0467/22–2818* 🎟*Jōmyō Temple ¥100, tea ceremony ¥500* 🕙*Daily 9–4.*

⑪ **Kamakura-gū** 鎌倉宮 *(Kamakura Shrine).* This Shintō shrine was built after the Meiji Restoration of 1868 and was dedicated to Prince Morinaga (1308–36), the first son of Emperor Go-Daigo. When Go-Daigo overthrew the Kamakura Shōgunate and restored Japan to direct imperial rule, Morinaga—who had been in the priesthood—was appointed supreme commander of his father's forces. The prince lived in turbulent times and died young: when the Ashikaga clan in turn overthrew Go-Daigo's government, Morinaga was taken into exile, held prisoner in a cave behind the present site of Kamakura Shrine, and eventually beheaded. The **Treasure House** (Hōmotsu-den), on the northwest corner of the grounds, next to the shrine's administrative office, is of interest mainly for its collection of paintings depicting the life of Prince Morinaga. ✛ *To reach Kamakura Shrine, walk from Yoritomo's tomb to Route 204, and turn left; at the next traffic light, a narrow street on the left leads off at an angle to the shrine, about five minutes' walk west* ✉*154 Nikaidō* ☎*0467/22–0318* 🎟*Kamakura Shrine free, Treasure House ¥300* 🕙*Daily 9–4.*

⑨ **Kamakura Treasure Museum** 鎌倉国宝館 *(Kamakura Kokuhōkan).* This museum was built in 1928 as a repository for many of the most important objects belonging to the shrines and temples in the area; many of these are designated Important Cultural Properties. The museum, located along the east side of the Tsuru-ga-oka Hachiman-gū shrine precincts, has an especially fine collection of devotional and portrait sculpture in wood from the Kamakura and Muromachi periods; the portrait pieces may be among the most expressive and interesting in all of classical Japanese art. ☒*2–1–1 Yuki-no-shita* ☎*0467/22–0753* ☐*¥300* ☉*Tues.–Sun. 9–4.*

8 **Prefectural Museum of Modern Art** 神奈川県立美術館 *(Kanagawa Kenritsu Kindai Bijutsukan).* On the north side of the Heike Pond at Tsuru-ga-oka Hachiman-gū, this museum houses a collection of Japanese oil paintings and watercolors, wood-block prints, and sculpture. ☒*2–1–53 Yuki-no-shita* ☎*0467/22–5000* ☐*¥800–¥1,200, depending on exhibition* ☉*Tues.–Sun. 9:30–4:30.*

> **WORD OF MOUTH**
>
> "From the Kamakura train station we boarded a local bus to Diabutsu—the Great Buddha. And great it was, an impressive 13 meter-high structure meditating in a lovely space surrounded by pine trees. Although we couldn't climb into the Buddha's ear, for a mere ¥20 each we were able to climb inside up to the Buddha's tummy (the statue is made of cypress wood with a copper patina), definitely a first for all of us!"
> —fourfortravel

HASE 長谷

TOP ATTRACTIONS

14 **Great Buddha** 大仏 *(Daibutsu).* The single biggest attraction in Hase (*"haseh"*) is the Great Buddha—sharing the honors with Mt. Fuji, perhaps, as the quintessential picture-postcard image of Japan. The statue of the compassionate Amida Buddha sits cross-legged in the temple courtyard, the drapery of his robes flowing in lines reminiscent of ancient Greece, his expression profoundly serene. The 37-foot bronze figure was cast in 1292, three centuries before Europeans reached Japan; the concept of the classical Greek lines in the Buddha's robe must have come over the Silk Route through China during the time of Alexander the Great. The casting was probably first conceived in 1180, by Minamoto no Yoritomo, who wanted a statue to rival the enormous Daibutsu in Nara. Until 1495 the Amida Buddha was housed in a wooden temple, which washed away in a great tidal wave. Since then the loving Buddha has stood exposed, facing the cold winters and hot summers, for more than five centuries.

FodorsChoice ★

■TIP→ **It may seem sacrilegious to walk inside the Great Buddha, but for ¥20 you can enter the figure from a doorway in the right side and explore (until 4:15 PM) his stomach, with a stairway that leads up to two windows in his back, offering a stunning view of the temple grounds.** ♦*To reach Kōtoku-in and the Great Buddha, take the Enoden Line from the west side of JR Kamakura Station three stops to Hase. From the east exit, turn right and walk north about 10 minutes on the main street (Route 32)* ☒*4–2–28 Hase, Hase* ☎*0467/22–0703* ☐*¥200* ☉*Apr.–Sept., daily 7–6; Oct.–Mar., daily 7–5:30.*

15 **Hase-dera** 長谷寺. The only temple in Kamakura facing the sea, this is one of the most beautiful, and saddest, places of pilgrimage in the city. On a landing partway up the stone steps that lead to the temple grounds

FodorsChoice ★

are hundreds of small stone images of Jizō, one of the bodhisattvas in the Buddhist pantheon. Jizō is the savior of children, particularly the souls of the stillborn, aborted, and miscarried; the mothers of these children dress the statues of Jizō in bright red bibs and leave them small offerings of food, heartbreakingly touching acts of prayer.

WHAT IS A BODHISATTVA?

A Bodhisattva is a being that has deferred its own ascendance into Buddhahood to guide the souls of others to salvation. It is considered a deity in Buddhism.

The **Kannon Hall** (Kannon-dō) at Hase-dera enshrines the largest carved-wood statue in Japan: the votive figure of Jūichimen Kannon, the 11-headed goddess of mercy. Standing 30 feet tall, the goddess bears a crown of 10 smaller heads, symbolizing her ability to search out in all directions for those in need of her compassion. No one knows for certain when the figure was carved. According to the temple records, a monk named Tokudo Shōnin carved two images of the Jūichimen Kannon from a huge laurel tree in 721. One was consecrated to the Hase-dera in present-day Nara Prefecture; the other was thrown into the sea in order to go wherever the sea decided that there were souls in need, and that image washed up on shore near Kamakura. Much later, in 1342, Takauji Ashikaga—the first of the 15 Ashikaga shōguns who followed the Kamakura era—had the statue covered with gold leaf.

The **Amida Hall** of Hase-dera enshrines the image of a seated Amida Buddha, who presides over the Western Paradise of the Pure Land. Minamoto no Yoritomo ordered the creation of this statue when he reached the age of 42; popular Japanese belief, adopted from China, holds that your 42nd year is particularly unlucky. Yoritomo's act of piety earned him another 11 years—he was 53 when he was thrown by a horse and died of his injuries. The Buddha is popularly known as the *yakuyoke* (good-luck) Amida, and many visitors—especially students facing entrance exams—make a point of coming here to pray. To the left of the main halls is a small restaurant where you can buy good-luck candy and admire the view of Kamakura Beach and Sagami Bay. ✢ *To reach Hase-dera from Hase Station, walk north about five minutes on the main street (Route 32) towards Kōtoku-in and the Great Buddha, and look for a signpost to the temple on a side street to the left.* ✉*3–11–2 Hase, Hase* ☎*0467/22–6300* 💴*¥300* ⊙*Mar.–Sept., daily 8–5:30; Oct.–Feb., daily 8–4:30.*

NEED A BREAK?

Kaiko-an is a spacious tearoom inside the temple grounds that offers dango (sweet rice dumplings on a stick), green tea, and sweets. Rest your feet, grab a table by the windows, and take in the breathtaking views of the ocean. ✉*3–11–2 Hase, Hase* ☎*0467/22–6300* ▭*No credit cards* ⊙*Mar.–Sept., daily 8–5:30; Oct.–Feb., daily 8–4:30*

RYŪKŌ-JI AND ENOSHIMA

⑯ Ryūkō-ji 龍口寺 *(Ryūkō Temple).* The Kamakura story would not be complete without the tale of Nichiren (1222–82), the monk who founded the only native Japanese sect of Buddhism and who is honored here.

Nichiren's rejection of both Zen and Jōdo (Pure Land) teachings brought him into conflict with the Kamakura Shōgunate, and the Hōjō regents sent him into exile on the Izu Peninsula in 1261. Later allowed to return, he continued to preach his own interpretation of the Lotus Sutra—and to assert the "blasphemy" of other Buddhist sects, a stance that finally persuaded the Hōjō regency, in 1271, to condemn him to death. The execution was to take place on a hill to the south of Hase. As the executioner swung his sword, legend has it that a lightning bolt struck the blade and snapped it in two. Taken aback, the executioner sat down to collect his wits, and a messenger was sent back to Kamakura to report the event. On his way he met another messenger, who was carrying a writ from the Hōjō regents commuting Nichiren's sentence to exile on the island of Sado-ga-shima.

THE POWER OF THE JAPANESE BLADE

In the corner of the enclosure where the Chinese Gate and Sanctum are found, an antique bronze lantern stands some 7 feet high. Legend has it that the lantern would assume the shape of a goblin at night; the deep nicks in the bronze were inflicted by swordsmen of the Edo period—on guard duty, perhaps, startled into action by a flickering shape in the dark. This proves, if not the existence of goblins, the incredible cutting power of the Japanese blade, a peerlessly forged weapon.

Followers of Nichiren built Ryūkō Temple in 1337, on the hill where he was to be executed, marking his miraculous deliverance from the headsman. There are other Nichiren temples closer to Kamakura—Myōhon-ji and Ankokuron-ji, for example. But Ryūkō not only has the typical Nichiren-style main hall, with gold tassels hanging from its roof, but also a beautiful pagoda, built in 1904. To reach it, take the Enoden Line west from Hase to Enoshima—a short, scenic ride that cuts through the hills surrounding Kamakura to the shore. ⊹ *From Enoshima Station walk about 100 yards east, keeping the train tracks on your right, and you'll come to the temple* ⊠*3–13–37 Katase, Fujisawa* ☎*0466/25–7357* ✆*Free* ☉*Daily 6–4.*

OFF THE BEATEN PATH

The Sagami Bay shore in this area has some of the closest beaches to Tōkyō, and in the hot, humid summer months it seems as though all of the city's teeming millions pour onto these beaches in search of a vacant patch of rather dirty gray sand. Pass up this mob scene and press on instead to **Enoshima** 江ノ島. The island is only 4 km (2½ mi) around, with a hill in the middle. Partway up the hill is a shrine where the local fisherfolk used to pray for a bountiful catch—before it became a tourist attraction. Once upon a time it was quite a hike up to the shrine; now there's a series of escalators, flanked by the inevitable stalls selling souvenirs and snacks. The island has several cafés and restaurants, and on clear days some of them have spectacular views of Mt. Fuji and the Izu Peninsula. To reach the causeway from Enoshima Station to the island, walk south from the station for about 3 km (2 mi), keeping the Katase-gawa (Katase River) on your right. To return to Tōkyō from Enoshima, take a train to Shinjuku on the Odakyū Line. From the island walk back across the causeway and take the second bridge over the Katase-gawa. Within five minutes you'll come to Katase-Enoshima Station. Or you can retrace your steps to Kamakura and take the JR Yokosuka Line to Tōkyō Station.

WHERE TO EAT

KITA-KAMAKURA

¢ ✕ **Bergfeld** ベルグフェルド. If you need to take a break during your
CAFE walking tour of Kamakura, you may want to stop by this quaint café and bakery. It serves German cakes and cookies that are surprisingly authentic—the baker trained in Germany. There are a few small tables outside, and cozy tables inside where you can enjoy coffee and cakes before resuming your tour. Many Japanese who visit from other parts of the country bring back the bakery's butter cookies as souvenirs. ⌧ *3–9–24 Yukinoshita, Kita-kamakura* ☎ *0467/24–2706* ▭ *No credit cards* ⊗ *Closed Tues. and the 3rd Thurs. of the month.*

$$$$ ✕ **Hachinoki Kita-Kamakura-ten** 鉢の木 北鎌倉店. Traditional shōjin ryōri
JAPANESE (the vegetarian cuisine of Zen monasteries) is served in this old Japanese
★ house on the Kamakura Kaidō (Route 21) near the entrance to Jōchi Temple. There's some table service, but most seating is in tatami rooms, with beautiful antique wood furnishings. Allow plenty of time; this is not a meal to be hurried through. Meals, which are prix fixe only, are served Tuesday to Friday 11 to 2:30, weekends 11 to 3. ⌧ *7 Yama-no-uchi, Kita-Kamakura* ☎ *0467/23–3722* ▭ *DC, V* ⊗ *Closed Mon.; July and Aug. weekends only*

$$–$$$ ✕ **Kyorai-an** 去来庵. A traditional Japanese structure houses this res-
JAPANESE taurant known for its excellent Western-style beef stew. Also on the menu are pasta dishes, rice bouillon, homemade cheesecake, and wine produced in the Kita Kamakura wine region. Half the seats are on tatami mats and half are at tables, but all look out on a peaceful patch of greenery. Kyorai-an is on the main road from Kita-Kamakura to Kamakura on the left side; it's about halfway between Meigetsu Temple and Kenchō Temple, up a winding flight of stone steps. Meals are served Monday to Thursday 11:30 to 2:30, weekends and holidays 11 to 3 and 5 to 7. ⌧ *157 Yamanouchi, Kita-Kamakura* ☎ *0467/24–9835* ⌮ *Reservations essential* ▭ *No credit cards* ⊗ *No dinner Mon.–Thurs.*

KAMAKURA

$$$–$$$$ ✕ **Ginza Isomura Kamakura-ten** ぎんざ磯むら 鎌倉店. This branch of the
JAPANESE family-style *kushiage* (freshly grilled skewers) restaurant overlooks Komachi-dōri, Kamakura's main shopping street. A place by the window is perfect for people-watching during lunchtime. Since it seats only 21, the place gets crowded during dinnertime, but if you're willing to wait you'll be rewarded with meat, fish, and seasonal vegetable kushiage that's made in front of you. ⌧ *Komachiichibankan Bldg., 2F, 2–10–1 Komachi, Kamakura* ☎ *0467/22–3792* ▭ *AE, DC, MC, V* ⊗ *Closed Wed.*

¢ ✕ **Kaisen Misaki-kō** 海鮮三崎港. This *kaiten-zushi* (sushi served on a
JAPANESE conveyor belt that lets you pick the dishes you want) restaurant on Komachi-dōri serves eye-poppingly large fish portions that hang over the edge of their plates. All the standard sushi creations, including tuna,

shrimp, and egg, are prepared here. Prices range from ¥170 to ¥500. The restaurant is on the right side of the road just as you enter Komachi-dōri from the east exit of Kamakura Station. ⊠*1–7–1 Komachi, Kamakura* ☎*0467/22–6228* ⊟*No credit cards.*

$$–$$$ ✕**T-Side** ティーサイド. Authentic, inexpensive Indian fare and a second-
INDIAN   floor location that looks down upon Kamakura's main shopping street, make this restaurant a popular choice for lunch and dinner. Curries are done well, the various *thali* (sets) are a good value, and the kitchen also serves some Nepalese dishes. T-Side is at the very top of Komachi-dōri on the left as you enter from Kamakura Station. ⊠*2–11–11 Komachi, Kamakura* ☎*0467/24–9572* ⊟*MC, V.*

HASE

$$$–$$$$ ✕**Kaiserrō** 華正楼. This establishment, in an old Japanese house, serves
CHINESE   the best Chinese food in the city. The dining-room windows look out on a small, restful garden. Make sure you plan for a stop here on your way to or from the Great Buddha at Kōtoku-in. ⊠*3–1–14 Hase, Hase* ☎*0467/22–0280* ⚐*Reservations essential* ⊟*AE, DC, MC, V.*

YOKOHAMA 横浜

In 1853, a fleet of four American warships under Commodore Matthew Perry sailed into the bay of Tōkyō (then Edo) and presented the reluctant Japanese with the demands of the U.S. government for the opening of diplomatic and commercial relations. The following year Perry returned and first set foot on Japanese soil at Yokohama—then a small fishing village on the mudflats of the bay, some 20 km (12½ mi) southwest of Tōkyō.

Two years later New York businessman Townsend Harris became America's first diplomatic representative to Japan. In 1858 he was finally able to negotiate a commercial treaty between the two countries; part of the deal designated four locations—one of them Yokohama—as treaty ports. With the agreement signed, Harris lost no time in setting up his residence in Hangaku-ji, in nearby Kanagawa, another of the designated ports. Kanagawa, however, was also one of the 53 relay stations on the Tōkaidō, the highway from Edo to the imperial court in Kyōto, and the presence of foreigners—perceived as unclean barbarians—offended the Japanese elite. Die-hard elements of the warrior class, moreover, wanted Japan to remain in isolation and were willing to give their lives to rid the country of intruders. Unable to protect foreigners in Kanagawa, in 1859 the Shōgunate created a special settlement in Yokohama for the growing community of merchants, traders, missionaries, and other assorted adventurers drawn to this exotic new land of opportunity.

The foreigners (predominantly Chinese and British, plus a few French, Americans, and Dutch) were confined here to a guarded compound about 5 square km (2 square mi)—placed, in effect, in isolation—but not for long. Within a few short years the shogunal government collapsed, and Japan began to modernize. Western ideas were welcomed, as were Western goods, and the little treaty port became Japan's principal gateway to the outside world. In 1872 Japan's first railway was built, linking Yokohama and Tōkyō. In 1889 Yokohama became a city; by then the population had grown to some 120,000. As the city prospered, so did the international community and by the early 1900s Yokohama was the busiest and most modern center of international trade in all of east Asia.

Then Yokohama came tumbling down. On September 1, 1923, the Great Kantō Earthquake devastated the city. The ensuing fires destroyed some 60,000 homes and took more than 40,000 lives. During the six years it took to rebuild the city, many foreign businesses took up quarters elsewhere, primarily in Kōbe and Ōsaka, and did not return.

Over the next 20 years Yokohama continued to grow as an industrial center—until May 29, 1945, when in a span of four hours, some 500 American B-29 bombers leveled nearly half the city and left more than half a million people homeless. When the war ended, what remained became—in effect—the center of the Allied occupation. General Douglas MacArthur set up headquarters here, briefly, before moving to Tōkyō; the entire port facility and about a quarter of the city remained in the hands of the U.S. military throughout the 1950s.

By the 1970s Yokohama was once more rising from the debris; in 1978 it surpassed Ōsaka as the nation's second-largest city, and the population is now inching up to the 3.5 million mark. Boosted by Japan's postwar economic miracle, Yokohama has extended its urban sprawl north to Tōkyō and south to Kamakura—in the process creating a whole new subcenter around the Shinkansen station at Shin-Yokohama.

The development of air travel and the competition from other ports have changed the city's role in Japan's economy. The great liners that once docked at Yokohama's piers are now but a memory, kept alive by a museum ship and the occasional visit of a luxury vessel on a Pacific cruise. Modern Yokohama thrives instead in its industrial, commercial, and service sectors—and a large percentage of its people commute to work in Tōkyō. Is Yokohama worth a visit? Not, one could argue, at the expense of Nikkō or Kamakura. But the waterfront is fun and the museums are excellent.

GETTING HERE AND AROUND

By Air. From Narita Airport, a direct limousine-bus service departs once or twice an hour between 6:45 AM and 10:20 PM for Yokohama City Air Terminal (YCAT). YCAT is a five-minute taxi ride from Yokohama Station. JR Narita Express trains going on from Tōkyō to Yokohama leave the airport every hour from 8:13 AM to 1:13 PM and 2:43 PM to 9:43 PM. The fare is ¥4,180 (¥6,730 for the first-class Green Car coaches). Or you can take the limousine-bus service from Narita to Tōkyō Station and continue on to Yokohama by train. Either way, the journey will take more than two hours—closer to three, if traffic is heavy.

The Airport Limousine Information Desk phone number provides information in English daily 9 to 6; you can also get timetables on its Web site. For information in English on Narita Express trains, call the JR Higashi-Nihon Info Line, available daily 10 to 6.

By Bus. Most of the things you'll want to see in Yokohama are within easy walking distance of a JR or subway station, but this city is so much more negotiable than Tōkyō that exploring by bus is a viable alternative. Buses, in fact, are the best way to get to Sankei-en. The city map available in the visitor centers in Yokohama has most major bus routes marked on it, and the important stops on the tourist routes are announced in English. The fixed fare is ¥210. One-day passes are also available for ¥600. Contact the Sightseeing Information Office at Yokohama Station (JR, East exit) for more information and ticket purchases.

By Subway. One subway line connects Azamino, Shin-Yokohama, Yokohama, Totsuka, and Shōnandai. The basic fare is ¥200. One-day passes are also available for ¥740. The Minato Mirai Line, a spur of the Tōkyū Tōyoko Line, runs from Yokohama Station to all the major points of interest, including Minato Mirai, Chinatown, Yamashita Park, Motomachi, and Basha-michi. The fare is ¥180–¥200, and one-day unlimited-ride passes are available for ¥450.

By Taxi. There are taxi stands at all the train stations, and you can always flag a cab on the street. ■ TIP➜ Vacant taxis show a red light in the windshield. The basic fare is ¥710 for the first 2 km (1 mi), then ¥80 for every additional 350 meters (0.2 mi). Traffic is heavy in downtown Yokohama, however, and you will often find it faster to walk.

By Tour. Teiki Yūran Bus offers a full-day (9–3:45) sightseeing bus tour that covers the major sights and includes lunch at a Chinese restaurant in Chinatown. The tour is in Japanese only, but pamphlets written in English are available at most sightseeing stops. Buy tickets (¥5,300) at the bus offices at Yokohama Station (east side) and at Kannai Station; the tour departs daily at 9:45 AM from Bus Stop 14, on the east side of Yokohama Station. A half-day tour is also available, with lunch (9:30–1:20, ¥3,000) or without (2–5:45, ¥2,300).

The sightseeing boat *Marine Shuttle* makes 40-, 60-, and 90-minute tours of the harbor and bay for ¥1,000, ¥1,600, and ¥2,200, respectively. Boarding is at the pier at Yamashita Park. Boats depart roughly every hour between 10:20 AM and 6:30 PM. Another boat, the *Marine Rouge,* runs 90-minute tours departing from the pier at 11, 1:30, and 4, and a special two-hour evening tour at 7 (¥2,800).

By Train. JR trains from Tōkyō Station leave approximately every 10 minutes, depending on the time of day. Take the Yokosuka, the Tōkaidō, or Keihin Tōhoku Line to Yokohama Station (the Yokosuka and Tōkaidō lines take 30 minutes; the Keihin Tōhoku Line takes 40 minutes and cost ¥450). From there the Keihin Tōhoku Line (Platform 3) goes on to Kannai and Ishikawa-chō, Yokohama's business and downtown areas. If you're going directly to downtown Yokohama from Tōkyō, the blue commuter trains of the Keihin Tōhoku Line are best.

The private Tōkyū Tōyoko Line, which runs from Shibuya Station in Tōkyō directly to Yokohama Station, is a good alternative if you leave from the western part of Tōkyō. ■ TIP➜ The term "private" is important because it means that the train does not belong to JR and is not a subway line. If you have a JR pass, you'll have to buy a separate ticket. Depending on which Tōkyū Tōyoko Line you catch—the Limited Express, Semi Express, or Local—the trip takes between 25 and 44 minutes and costs ¥260.

Yokohama Station is the hub that links all the train lines and connects them with the city's subway and bus services. Kannai and Ishikawa-chō are the two downtown stations, both on the Keihin Tōhoku Line; trains leave Yokohama Station every two to five minutes from Platform 3. From Sakuragi-chō, Kannai, or Ishikawa-chō, most of Yokohama's points of interest are within easy walking distance; the one notable exception is Sankei-en, which you reach via the JR Keihin Tōhoku Line to Negishi Station and then a local bus.

VISITOR INFORMATION

The Yokohama International Tourist Association arranges visits to the homes of English-speaking Japanese families. These usually last a few hours and are designed to give *gaijin* (foreigners) a glimpse into the Japanese way of life.

The Yokohama Tourist Office, in the central passageway of Yokohama Station, is open daily 9 to 7 (closed December 28–January 3). The head office of the Yokohama Convention & Visitors Bureau, open weekdays 9 to 5 (except national holidays and December 29–January 3), is in the Sangyō Bōeki Center Building, across from Yamashita Kōen.

ESSENTIALS

Airport Transportation Airport Limousine Information Desk (☎ *03/3665-7220* ⊕ *www.limousinebus.co.jp*). JR Higashi-Nihon Info Line (☎ *03/3423-0111*).

Bus Information Sightseeing Information Office (☎ *045/465-2077*).

Emergencies Ambulance or Fire (☎ *119*). Police (☎ *110*). Washinzaka Hospital (✉ *169 Yamate-chō, Naka-ku* ☎ *045/623-7688*). Yokohama Police station (✉ *2-4 Kaigan-dōri, Naka-ku* ☎ *045/623-0110*).

Tourist Information Yokohama Convention & Visitors Bureau (✉ *2 Yamashita-chō, Naka-ku* ☎ *045/221-2111*). Yokohama International Tourist Association (☎ *045/641-4759*). Yokohama Tourist Office (✉ *Yokohama Station, Nishi-ku* ☎ *045/441-7300*).

Tours Marine Shuttle (☎ *045/671-7719 Port Service reservation center*). Teiki Yūran Bus (☎ *045/465-2077*).

EXPLORING YOKOHAMA

Large as Yokohama is, the central area is very negotiable. As with any other port city, much of what it has to offer centers on the waterfront—in this case, on the west side of Tōkyō Bay. The downtown area is called Kannai (literally, "within the checkpoint"); this is where the international community was originally confined by the Shōgunate. Though the center of interest has expanded to include the waterfront and Ishikawa-chō, to the south, Kannai remains the heart of town.

Think of that heart as two adjacent areas. One is the old district of Kannai, bounded by Basha-michi on the northwest and Nippon-ōdori on the southeast, the Keihin Tōhoku Line tracks on the southwest, and the waterfront on the northeast. This area contains the business offices of modern Yokohama. The other area extends southeast from Nippon-ōdori to the Moto-machi shopping street and the International

Cemetery, bordered by Yamashita Kōen and the waterfront to the northeast; in the center is Chinatown, with Ishikawa-chō Station to the southwest. This is the most interesting part of town for tourists. ■**TIP**➜ Whether you're coming from Tōkyō, Nagoya, or Kamakura, make Ishikawa-chō Station your starting point. Take the south exit from the station and head in the direction of the waterfront.

Numbers in the text correspond to the Yokohama map.

CENTRAL YOKOHAMA 横浜市街
TOP ATTRACTIONS

9 **Basha-michi** 馬車道. Running southwest from Shinko Pier to Kannai is Basha-michi, which literally translates into "Horse-Carriage Street." The street was so named in the 19th century, when it was widened to accommodate the horse-drawn carriages of the city's new European residents. This redbrick thoroughfare and the streets parallel to it have been restored to evoke that past, with faux-antique telephone booths and imitation gas lamps. Here you'll find some of the most elegant coffee shops, patisseries, and boutiques in town. On the block northeast of Kannai Station, as you walk toward the waterfront, is **Kannai Hall** (look for the red-orange abstract sculpture in front), a handsome venue for chamber music, Nō, classical recitals, and occasional performances by such groups as the Peking Opera. If you're planning to stay late in Yokohama, you might want to check out the listings. ⊠*Naka-ku* Ⓜ*JR Line, Kannai Station; Minato Mirai Line, Basha-michi Station.*

❚ NEED A BREAK?
Japanese pâtissiers excel at making exquisite European sweets, occasionally giving them a new twist with Japanese ingredients such as sweet bean paste. The elegant **Keyuca Café and Sweets** (¢–$) is a good place to taste these skills while taking a break from your walking tour. The cappuccino is excellent, and there's a daily changing menu of bagel sandwiches and other light fare. ⊠*Queen's East B1 Floor, 2-3-2 Minato-Mirai, Nishi-ku* ☎*045/640-1361* ▭*No credit cards* ⊙*Daily 11-8.*

17 **Chinatown** 中華街 *(Chūka-gai).* The largest Chinese settlement in Japan—
★ and easily the city's most popular tourist attraction—Yokohama's Chinatown draws more than 18 million visitors a year. Its narrow streets and alleys are lined with some 350 shops selling foodstuffs, herbal medicines, cookware, toys and ornaments, and clothing and accessories. If China exports it, you'll find it here. Wonderful exotic aromas waft from the spice shops. Even better aromas drift from the quarter's 160-odd restaurants, which serve every major style of Chinese cuisine: this is the best place for lunch in Yokohama. Chinatown is a 10-minute walk southeast of Kannai Station. When you get to Yokohama Stadium, turn left and cut through the municipal park to the top of Nihon-ōdōri. Then take a right, and you'll enter Chinatown through the Gembu-mon (North Gate), which leads to the dazzling red-and-gold, 50-foot-high Zenrin-mon (Good Neighbor Gate). ⊠*Naka-ku* Ⓜ*JR Line, Ishikawa-chō Station; Minato Mirai Line, Motomachi-Chukagai Station.*

18 **Harbor View Park** 港の見える丘公園 *(Minato-no-Mieru-Oka Kōen).* The park—a major landmark in this part of the city, known, appropriately

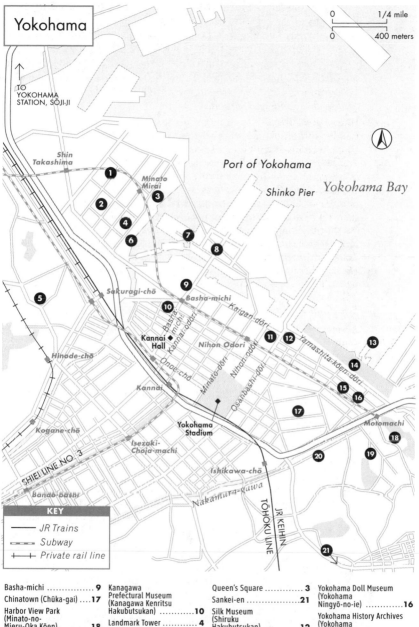

Yokohama

TO
YOKOHAMA
STATION, SŌJI-JI

Port of Yokohama

Shinko Pier   Yokohama Bay

Yokohama Bay

Shin
Takashima

Minato
Mirai

Sakuragi-chō

Basha-michi

Kaigan-dōri

Kannai
Hall

Nihon Odori

Hinode-chō

Onoe-chō

Kannai

Kogane-chō

Yokohama
Stadium

Isezaki-
Choja-machi

SHIEL LINE NO. 3

Ishikawa-chō

Bando-bashi

Nakamura-gawa

Motomachi

TŌHOKU LINE

JR KEIHIN

Yamashita-kōen-dōri

Minato-dōri

Nihon-dōri

Osanbashi-dōri

KEY

— JR Trains
═══ Subway
+—+ Private rail line

enough, as the Bluff (*yamate*)—was once the barracks of the British forces in Yokohama. Come here for spectacular nighttime views of the waterfront, the floodlit gardens of Yamashita Park, and the Bay Bridge. Foreigners were first allowed to build here in 1867, and it has been prime real estate ever since—an enclave of consulates, churches, international schools, private clubs, and palatial Western-style homes. ⊠*Naka-ku* Ⓜ*JR Line, Ishikawa-chō Station; Minato Mirai Line, Motomachi-Chukagai Station.*

⓭ **Hikawa-maru** 氷川丸. Moored on the waterfront, more or less in the middle of Yamashita Park, is the *Hikawa-maru*. It was built in 1929 by Yokohama Dock Co. and was launched on September 30, 1929. For 31 years, she shuttled passengers between Yokohama and Seattle, Washington, making a total of 238 trips. A tour of the ship evokes the time when Yokohama was a great port of call for the transpacific liners. The *Hikawa-maru* has a French restaurant, and in summer there's a beer garden on the upper deck. ⊠*Naka-ku* ☎*045/641–4361* 🎫*¥500* ☽*Apr.–June, Sept., and Oct., daily 9:30–7; July and Aug., daily 9:30–7:30; Nov.–Mar., daily 9:30–6:30* Ⓜ*JR Line, Ishikawa-chō Station; Minato Mirai Line, Motomachi-Chukagai Station.*

⓬ **Silk Museum** シルク博物館 (*Shiruku Hakubutsukan*). The museum, which pays tribute to the period at the turn of the 20th century when Japan's exports of silk were all shipped out of Yokohama, houses an extensive collection of silk fabrics and an informative exhibit on the silk-making process. People on staff are very happy to answer questions. In the same building, on the first floor, are the main offices of the Yokohama International Tourist Association and the Kanagawa Prefectural Tourist Association. The museum is at the northwestern end of the Yamashita Park promenade, on the second floor of the Silk Center Building. ⊠*1 Yamashita-chō, Naka-ku* ☎*045/641–0841* 🎫*¥500* ☽*Tues.–Sun. 9–4* Ⓜ*Minato Mirai Line, Nihon Ōdōri Station (Exit 3).*

WORTH NOTING

⓳ **International Cemetery** 外人墓地 (*Gaijin Bochi*). This Yokohama landmark is a reminder of the port city's heritage. It was established in 1854 with a grant of land from the Shōgunate; the first foreigners to be buried here were Russian sailors assassinated by xenophobes in the early days of the settlement. Most of the 4,500 graves on this hillside are English and American, and about 120 are of the Japanese wives of foreigners; the inscriptions on the crosses and headstones attest to some 40 different nationalities whose citizens lived and died in Yokohama. From Moto-machi Plaza, it's a short walk to the north end of the cemetery. ⊠*Naka-ku* Ⓜ*JR Line, Ishikawa-chō Station; Minato Mirai Line, Motomachi-Chukagai Station.*

⓾ **Kanagawa Prefectural Museum** 神奈川県立美術館 (*Kanagawa Kenritsu Hakubutsukan*). One of the few buildings in Yokohama to have survived both the Great Kantō Earthquake of 1923 and World War II, the museum is a few blocks north of Kannai Station (use Exit 8) on Bashamichi. Most exhibits here have no explanations in English, but the galleries on the third floor showcase some remarkable medieval wooden sculptures (including one of the first Kamakura shōgun, Minamoto no Yoritomo), hanging scrolls, portraits, and armor. The exhibits of prehistory and of Yokohama in the early modern period are of much less interest. ✉ *5–60 Minami Naka-dōri, Naka-ku* ☎*045/201–0926* 🖹*¥300, special exhibits ¥800* ⊘*Tues.–Sun. 9–4:30; closed last Tues. of month and the day after a national holiday* Ⓜ*JR Line, Sakuragi-chō and Kannai Stations.*

⓯ **Marine Tower** マリンタワー. For an older generation of Yokohama residents, the 348-foot-high decagonal tower, which opened in 1961, was the city's landmark structure; civic pride prevented them from admitting that it falls lamentably short of an architectural masterpiece. The tower has a navigational beacon at the 338-foot level and purports to be the tallest lighthouse in the world. At the 328-foot level, an observation gallery provides 360-degree views of the harbor and the city, and on clear days in autumn or winter, you can often see Mt. Fuji in the distance. Marine Tower is in the middle of the second block northwest from the end of Yamashita Park, on the left side of the promenade. ✉*15 Yamashita-chō, Naka-ku* ☎*045/641–7838* 🖹*¥700* ⊘*Jan. and Feb., daily 9–7; Mar.–May, Nov., and Dec., daily 9:30–9; June, July, Sept., and Oct., daily 9:30–9:30; Aug., daily 9:30 AM–10 PM* Ⓜ*JR Line, Ishikawa-chō Station; Minato Mirai Line, Motomachi-Chukagai Station.*

⓴ **Moto-machi** 元町. Within a block of Ishikawa-chō Station is the beginning of this street, which follows the course of the Nakamura-gawa (Nakamura River) to the harbor where the Japanese set up shop 100 years ago to serve the foreigners living in Kannai. The street is now lined with smart boutiques and jewelry stores that cater to fashionable young Japanese consumers. ✉*Naka-ku* Ⓜ*JR Line, Ishikawa-chō Station; Minato Mirai Line, Motomachi-Chukagai Station.*

Ⓜ **Yamashita Kōen** 山下公園 *(Yamashita Park).* This park is perhaps the only positive legacy of the Great Kantō Earthquake of 1923. The debris of the warehouses and other buildings that once stood here were swept away, and the area was made into a 17-acre oasis of green along the waterfront. The fountain, representing the Guardian of the Water, was presented to Yokohama by San Diego, California, one of its sister cities. From Harbor View Park, walk northwest through neighboring French Hill Park and cross the walkway over Moto-machi. Turn right on the other side and walk one block down toward the bay to Yamashita-Kōen-dori, the promenade along the park. ✉*Naka-ku* Ⓜ*JR Line, Ishikawa-chō Station; Minato Mirai Line, Motomachi-Chukagai Station.*

⓰ **Yokohama Doll Museum** 横浜人形の家 *(Yokohama Ningyō-no-ie).* This 🜨 museum houses a collection of some 4,000 dolls from all over the world. In Japanese tradition, dolls are less to play with than to display—either in religious folk customs or as the embodiment of some spiritual quality. Japanese visitors to this museum never seem to outgrow their affection for the Western dolls on display here, to which they tend to assign the role of timeless "ambassadors of good will" from other cultures. The museum is worth a quick visit, with or without a child in tow. It's just across from the southeast end of Yamashita Park, on the left side of the promenade. ✉*18 Yamashita-chō, Naka-ku* ☎*045/671–9361* 🖹*¥500*

🕙 *Daily 10–6; closed 3rd Mon. of month* Ⓜ *JR Line, Ishikawa-chō Station; Minato Mirai Line, Motomachi-Chukagai Station.*

⓫ **Yokohama History Archives** 横浜開港資料館 *(Yokohama Kaikō Shiryōkan)*. Within the archives, housed in what was once the British Consulate, are some 140,000 items recording the history of Yokohama since the opening of the port to international trade in the mid-19th century. Across the street is a monument to the U.S.–Japanese Friendship Treaty. To get here from the Silk Center Building, at the end of the Yamashita Park promenade, walk west to the corner of Nihon-ōdōri; the archives are on the left. ✉ *3 Nihon-ōdōri, Naka-ku* ☎ *045/201–2100* 💰 *¥200* 🕙 *Tues.–Sun. 9:30–5* Ⓜ *Minato Mirai Line, Nihon-ōdōri Station.*

AROUND YOKOHAMA
TOP ATTRACTIONS

❺ **Iseyama Kōdai Jingū** 伊勢山皇大神宮 *(Iseyama Kōdai Shrine).* A branch of the nation's revered Grand Shrines of Ise, this the most important Shintō shrine in Yokohama—but it's only worth a visit if you've seen most everything else in town. The shrine is a 10-minute walk west of Sakuragi-chō Station. ✉ *64 Miyazaki-chō, Nishi-ku* ☎ *045/241–1122* 💰 *Free* 🕙 *Daily 9–7* Ⓜ *JR Line, Sakuragi-chō Station; Minato Mirai Line, Minato Mirai Station.*

❹ **Landmark Tower** ランドマークタワー. The 70-story tower in Yokohama's
Ⓒ Minato Mirai is Japan's tallest building. The observation deck on the 69th floor has a spectacular view of the city, especially at night; you reach it via a high-speed elevator that carries you up at an ear-popping 45 KPH (28 MPH). The Yokohama Royal Park Hotel occupies the top 20 stories of the building. On the first level of the Landmark Tower is the **Mitsubishi Minato Mirai Industrial Museum,** with rocket engines, power plants, a submarine, various gadgets, and displays that simulate piloting helicopters—great fun for kids.

The Landmark Tower complex's **Dockyard Garden,** built in 1896, is a restored dry dock with stepped sides of massive stone blocks. The long, narrow floor of the dock, with its water cascade at one end, makes a wonderful year-round open-air venue for concerts and other events; in summer (July–mid-August), the beer garden installed here is a perfect refuge from the heat. ✉ *3–3–1 Minato Mirai, Nishi-ku* ☎ *045/224–9031* 💰 *Elevator to observation deck ¥1,000, museum ¥300* 🕙 *Museum Tues.–Sun. 10–5* Ⓜ *JR Line, Sakuragi-chō Station; Minato Mirai Line, Minato Mirai Station.*

❶ **Minato Mirai 21** みなとみらい21. If you want to see Yokohama urban development at its most self-assertive, then this is a must. The aim of this project, launched in the mid-1980s, was to turn some three-quarters of a square mile of waterfront property, lying east of the JR Negishi Line railroad tracks between the Yokohama and Sakuragi-chō stations, into a model "city of the future." As a hotel, business, international exhibition, and conference center, it's a smashing success. ✉ *Nishi-ku* Ⓜ *JR Line, Sakuragi-chō Station; Minato Mirai Line, Minato Mirai Station.*

㉑ **Sankei-en** 三渓園. Opened to the public in 1906, this was once the estate
★ and gardens of Tomitarō Hara (1868–1939), one of Yokohama's wealthiest men, who made his money as a silk merchant before becoming a

patron of the arts. On the extensive grounds of the estate he created is a kind of open-air museum of traditional Japanese architecture, some of which was brought here from Kamakura and the western part of the country. Especially noteworthy is **Rinshun-kaku,** a villa built for the Tokugawa clan in 1649. There's also a tea pavilion, Chōshū-kaku, built by the third Tokugawa shōgun, Iemitsu. Other buildings include a small temple transported

BLOOMIN' SEASON

Walking through Sankei-en is especially delightful in spring, when the flowering trees are at their best: plum blossoms in February and cherry blossoms in early April. In June come the irises, followed by the water lilies. In autumn the trees come back into their own with tinted golden leaves.

from Kyōto's famed Daitoku-ji and a farmhouse from the Gifu district in the Japan Alps (around Takayama). ⚓ *To reach Sankei-en, take the JR Keihin Tōhoku Line to Negishi Station and a local bus (number 54, 58, or 99) bound for Honmoku; it's a 10-minute trip to the garden. Or, go to Yokohama Station (East Exit) and take the bus (number 8 or 125) to Honmoku Sankei-en Mae. It will take about 35 minutes.* ✉*58–1 Honmoku San-no-tani, Naka-ku* ☎*045/621–0635* 💴*Inner garden ¥300, outer garden ¥300, farmhouse ¥100* 🕐*Inner garden daily 9–4, outer garden daily 9–4:30.*

WORTH NOTING

❻ Nippon-maru Memorial Park 日本丸メモリアルパーク. The centerpiece of the park, which is on the east side of Minato Mirai 21, where the Ō-oka-gawa (Ō-oka River) flows into the bay, is the *Nippon-maru,* a full-rigged three-masted ship popularly called the "Swan of the Pacific." Built in 1930, it served as a training vessel. The Nippon-maru is now retired, but it's an occasional participant in tall-ships festivals and is open for guided tours. Adjacent to the ship is the **Yokohama Maritime Museum,** a two-story collection of ship models, displays, and archival materials that celebrate the achievements of the Port of Yokohama from its earliest days to the present. ✉*2–1–1 Minato Mirai, Nishi-ku* ☎*045/221–0280* 💴*Ship and museum ¥600, ship only ¥200* 🕐*Museum closed Mon.* Ⓜ*JR Line, Sakuragi-chō Station; Minato Mirai Line, Minato Mirai Station.*

❸ Queen's Square クイーンズスクエア. The courtyard on the northeast side of the Landmark Tower connects to this huge atrium-style vertical mall with dozens of shops (mainly for clothing and accessories) and restaurants. The complex also houses the Pan Pacific Hotel Yokohama and Yokohama Minato Mirai Hall, the city's major venue for classical music. ✉*2–3–1 Minato-Mirai, Nishi-ku* ☎*045/222–5015* 🌐*www.qsy. co.jp* 🕐*Shopping 11–8, restaurants 11 AM–11 PM* Ⓜ*JR Line, Sakuragi-chō Station; Minato Mirai Line, Minato Mirai Station.*

❽ World Porters ワールドポーターズ. This shopping center, on the opposite side of Yokohama Cosmo World, is notable chiefly for its restaurants that overlook the Minato Mirai area. Try arriving at sunset; the spectacular view of twinkling lights and the Landmark Tower, the Ferris wheel, and hotels will occasionally include Mt. Fuji in the background. Walking away from the waterfront area from World Porters will lead to

Aka Renga (Redbrick Warehouses), two more shopping-and-entertainment facilities. ⊠*2–2–1 Shin-minato-chō, Naka-ku* ☎*045/222–2000* 📠*Free* ⊙*Daily 10–9, restaurants until 11* Ⓜ*JR Line, Sakuragi-chō Station; Minato Mirai Line, Minato Mirai Station.*

❼ **Yokohama Cosmo World** よこはまコスモワールド. Ths amusement park
ⓒ complex claims—among its 30 or so rides and attractions—the world's largest water-chute ride at 13 feet long and four stories high. It's west of Minato Mirai and Queen's Square, on both sides of the river. ⊠*2–8–1 Shinko, Naka-ku* ☎*045/641–6591* 📠*Park free, rides ¥300–¥700 each* ⊙*Mid-Mar.–Nov., weekdays 11–9, weekends 11–10; Dec.–mid-Mar., weekdays 11–8, weekends 11–9* Ⓜ*JR Line, Sakuragi-chō Station; Minato Mirai Line, Minato Mirai Station.*

❷ **Yokohama Museum of Art** 横浜美術館 *(Yokohama Bijutsukan)*. Designed by Kenzō Tange and housed at Minato Mirai 21, the museum has 5,000 works in its permanent collection. Vistors will see paintings by both Western and Japanese artists, including Cézanne, Picasso, Braque, Klee, Kandinsky, Ryūsei Kishida, and Taikan Yokoyama. ⊠*3–4–1 Minato Mirai, Nishi-ku* ☎*045/221–0300* 📠*¥500* ⊙*Mon.–Wed. and weekends 10–5:30, Fri. 10–7:30 (last entry)* Ⓜ*JR Line, Sakuragi-chō Station; Minato Mirai Line, Minato Mirai Station.*

OFF THE BEATEN PATH

Sōji-ji 総持寺. One of the two major centers of the Sōtō sect of Zen Buddhism, Sōji-ji, in Yokohama's Tsurumi ward, was founded in 1321. The center was moved here from Ishikawa, on the Noto Peninsula (on the Sea of Japan, north of Kanazawa), after a fire in the 19th century. There's also a Sōji-ji monastic complex at Eihei-ji in Fukui Prefecture. The Yokohama Sōji-ji is one of the largest and busiest Buddhist institutions in Japan, with more than 200 monks and novices in residence. The 14th-century patron of Sōji-ji was the emperor Go-Daigo, who overthrew the Kamakura Shōgunate; the emperor is buried here, but his mausoleum is off-limits to visitors. However, you can see the **Buddha Hall,** the **Main Hall,** and the **Treasure House.** To get to Sōji-ji, take the JR Keihin Tōhoku Line two stops from Sakuragi-chō to Tsurumi. From the station walk five minutes south (back toward Yokohama), passing Tsurumi University on your right. Look out for the stone lanterns that mark the entrance to the temple complex. ⊠*2–1–1 Tsurumi, Tsurumi-ku* ☎*045/581–6021* 📠*¥300* ⊙*Daily dawn–dusk; Treasure House Tues.–Sun. 10–4.*

WHERE TO EAT

$$$–$$$$ ✕**Aichiya** 愛知屋. One of the specialties at this seafood restaurant is fugu
SEAFOOD (blowfish). This delicacy must be treated with expert care, because the
★ fishes' organs contain a deadly toxin that must be removed before being consumed. The crabs here are also a treat. ⊠*7–156 Isezaki-chō, Naka-ku* ☎*045/251–4163* ▭*No credit cards* ⊙*Closed Mon. No lunch.*

$$$ ✕**Chano-ma** 茶の間. This stylish eatery serves modern Japanese cuisine.
JAPANESE There are bedlike seats that you can lounge on while eating and a house DJ spins tunes during dinner. While you're there, make sure you try the miso sirloin steak or grilled scallops with tasty citron sauce drizzled on top, served with a salad. It does get crowded here on the weekends, so

to avoid a long wait, try coming at lunchtime and you can take advantage of the ¥1,000 set lunch special. ✉ *Red Brick Warehouse Bldg. 2, 3F, 1–1–2 Shinkou, Naka-ku* ☎*045/650–8228* ▤*AE, DC, MC, V* Ⓜ*Basha-michi station, Minato Mirai line; Sakuragi-chi, Kannai stations, JR Negishi line.*

$$$$ ✕**Kaseirō** 華正楼. Surprisingly, Chinese food can be hit-or-miss in Japan,
CHINESE but not at Kaseirō. This elegant restaurant, with red carpets and gold-
★ tone walls, is the best of its kind in the city, serving authentic Beijing cuisine, including, of course, Peking Duck and shark-fin soup. The consistently delicious dishes, combined with the fact that both the owner and chef are from Beijing, make this restaurant a well-known favorite among locals and travelers alike. ✉*186 Yamashita-chō, Chinatown, Naka-ku* ☎*045/681–2918* ☞*Jacket and tie* ▤*AE, DC, V.*

$$$$ ✕**Motomachi Bairin** 元町梅林. The area of Motomachi is known as the
JAPANESE wealthy, posh part of Yokohama; restaurants here tend to be exclusive and expensive, though the service and quality justify the price. This restaurant is an old-style Japanese house complete with a Japanese garden and five private tatami rooms. The ¥12,000, 27-course banquet includes some traditional Japanese delicacies such as sashimi, shiitake mushrooms, and chicken in white sauce, deep-fried burdock, and broiled sea bream. ✉*1–55 Motomachi, Naka-ku* ☎*045/662–2215* ⚞*Reservations essential* ▤*No credit cards* ◷*Closed Mon.*

$$$–$$$$ ✕**Rinka-en** 隣華苑. If you visit the gardens of Sankei-en, you might
JAPANESE want to have lunch at this traditional country restaurant, which serves kaiseki-style cuisine. Meals here are prix fixe. The owner is the granddaughter of Hara Tomitaro, who donated the gardens to the city. ✉*52–1 Honmoku San-no-tani, Naka-ku* ☎*045/621–0318* ☞*Jacket and tie* ▤*No credit cards* ◷*Closed Wed. and Aug.* ⚞*Reservations essential.*

$$–$$$$ ✕**Roma Statione** ローマステーション. Opened more than 40 years ago,
ITALIAN Roma Statione, between Chinatown and Yamashita Park, remains a popular venue for Italian food. The owner, whose father studied cooking in Italy before returning home to open this spot, is also the head chef and has continued using the original recipes. The house specialty is seafood: the spaghetti *vongole* (with clam sauce) is particularly good, as is the spaghetti pescatora and the seafood pizza. An added bonus is the impressive selection of Italian wines. ✉*26 Yamashita-chō, Naka-ku* ☎*045/681–1818* ▤*No credit cards* Ⓜ*Motomachi-Chukagai station, Minato Mirai line (Exit 1).*

$$$$ ✕**Scandia** スカンディア. This Scandinavian restaurant near the Silk Cen-
SCANDINAVIAN ter and the business district is known for its smorgasbord. It's popular for business lunches as well as for dinner. Scandia stays open until midnight, later than many other restaurants in the area. Expect dishes like steak tartare, marinated herring, and fried eel, and plenty of rye bread. ✉*1–1 Kaigan-dōri, Naka-ku* ☎*045/201–2262* ▤*No credit cards.*

$$$$ ✕**Serina Romanchaya** 瀬里奈 浪漫茶屋. The hallmarks of this restaurant
STEAK are *ishiyaki* steak, which is grilled on a hot stone, and shabu-shabu—thin slices of beef cooked in boiling water at your table and dipped in one of several sauces; choose from sesame, vinegar, or soy. Fresh vegetables, noodles, and tofu are also dipped into the seasoned broth for a

filling, yet healthful meal. ✉*Shin-Kannai Bldg., B1, 4–45–1 Sumiyoshi-chō, Naka-ku* ☎*045/681–2727* ⊟*AE, DC, MC, V.*

$$$$
ITALIAN
☺ ✕**Yokohama Cheese Cafe** 横浜チーズカフェ. This is a cozy and inviting casual Italian restaurant, whose interior looks like an Italian country home. There are candles on the tables and an open kitchen where diners can watch the cooks making pizza. On the menu: 18 kinds of Napoli-style wood-fire–baked pizzas, 20 kinds of pastas, fondue, and other dishes that include—you guessed it—cheese. The set-course menus are reasonable, filling, and recommended. ✉*2–1–10 KitasaiwaiNishi-ku* ☎*045/290–5656* ⊟*DC, MC, V* Ⓜ*JR Yokohama station.*

FUJI-HAKONE-IZU NATIONAL PARK 富士箱根伊豆国立公園

Fuji-Hakone-Izu National Park, southwest of Tōkyō between Suruga and Sagami bays, is one of Japan's most popular resort areas. The region's main attraction, of course, is Mt. Fuji, a dormant volcano—it last erupted in 1707—rising to a height of 12,388 feet. The mountain is truly beautiful; utterly captivating in the ways it can change in different light and from different perspectives. Its symmetry and majesty have been immortalized by poets and artists for centuries. ■**TIP→ During spring and summer, Mt. Fuji often hides behind a blanket of clouds. Keep this in mind if seeing the mountain is an important part of your trip.**

Apart from Mt. Fuji itself, each of the three areas of the park—the Izu Peninsula, Hakone and environs, and the Five Lakes—has its own unique appeal. Izu is defined by its dramatic rugged coastline, beaches, and *onsen* (hot springs). Hakone has mountains, volcanic landscapes, and lake cruises, plus onsen of its own. The Five Lakes form a recreational area with some of the best views of Mt. Fuji. And in each of these areas there are monuments to Japan's past.

Although it's possible to make a grand tour of all three areas at one time, most people make each of them a separate excursion from Tōkyō.

Trains will serve you well in traveling to major points anywhere in the northern areas of the national-park region and down the eastern coast of the Izu Peninsula. For the west coast and central mountains of Izu, there are no train connections; unless you are intrepid enough to rent a car, the only way to get around is by bus.

VISITOR INFORMATION

Especially in summer and fall, the Fuji-Hakone-Izu National Park area is one of the most popular vacation destinations in the country, so most towns and resorts have local visitor information centers. Few of them have staff members who speak fluent English, but you can still pick up local maps and pamphlets, as well as information on low-cost inns, pensions, and guesthouses.

IZU PENINSULA

GETTING HERE AND AROUND

By Car. Having your own car makes sense only for touring the Izu Peninsula, and only then if you're prepared to cope with less-than-ideal road conditions, lots of traffic (especially on holiday weekends), and the paucity of road markers in English. It takes some effort—but exploring the peninsula *is* a lot easier by car than by public transportation. From Tōkyō take the Tōmei Expressway as far as Ōi-matsuda (about 84 km [52 mi]); then pick up Routes 255 and 135 to Atami (approximately 28 km [17 mi]). From Atami drive another 55 km (34 mi) or so down the east coast of the Izu Peninsula to Shimoda.

■TIP➔ One way to save yourself some trouble is to book a car through the Nippon or Toyota rental agency in Tōkyō and arrange to pick it up at the Shimoda branch. You can then simply take a train to Shimoda and use it as a base. From Shimoda you can drive back up the coast to Kawazu (35 minutes) and then to Shuzenji (30 minutes). It is possible to drop off the car in Tōkyō but only at specific branches, so visit your rental-car company's Web site or call them in advance.

By Tours. Once you are on the Izu Peninsula itself, sightseeing excursions by boat are available from several picturesque small ports. From Dōgashima, you can take the Dōgashima Marine short (20 minutes, ¥920) or long (45 minutes, ¥1,240) tours of Izu's rugged west coast. The Fujikyū Kōgyō company operates a daily ferry to Hatsu-shima from Atami (25 minutes, ¥2,340 round-trip) and another to the island from Itō (23 minutes, ¥1,150). Izukyū Marine offers a 40-minute tour (¥1,530) by boat from Shimoda to the coastal rock formations at Irō-zaki.

Sunrise Tours operates a tour to Hakone, including a cruise across Lake Ashi and a trip on the gondola over Ōwaku-dani (¥15,000 includes lunch and return to Tōkyō by Shinkansen; ¥12,000 includes lunch and return to Tōkyō by bus). ■TIP➔ These tours are an economical way to see the main sights all in one day and are ideal for travelers with limited time. Sunrise tours depart daily from Tōkyō's Hamamatsu-chō Bus Terminal and some major hotels.

By Train. Trains are by far the easiest and fastest ways to get to the Fuji-Hakone-Izu National Park area. The gateway stations of Atami is well served by comfortable express trains from Tōkyō, on both JR and private railway lines. These in turn connect to local trains and buses that can get you anywhere in the region you want to go. Call the JR Higashi-Nihon Info Line (10–6 daily, except December 31–January 3) for assistance in English.

The *Kodama* Shinkansen from JR Tōkyō station to Atami costs ¥3,880 and takes 51 minutes; JR Passes are valid. The JR local from Atami to Itō takes 25 minutes and costs ¥320. Itō and Atami are also served by the JR Odoriko Super Express (not a Shinkansen train) also departing from Tōkyō station; for correct platform, check the schedule display board. The Tōkyō–Itō run takes 1¾ hours and costs ¥4,190; you can also use a JR Pass. The privately owned Izukyū Railways, on which

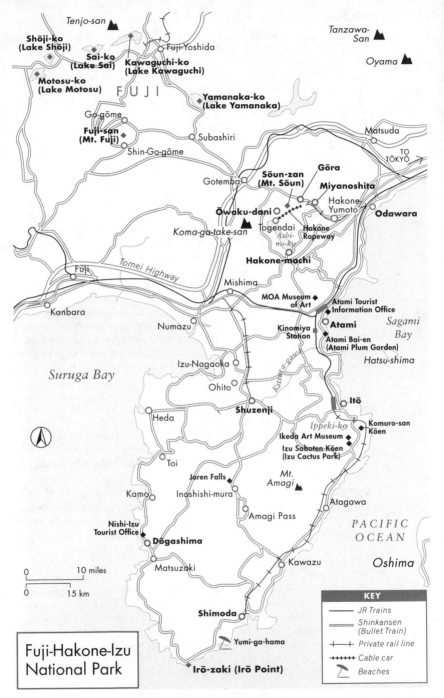

Tenjo-san

Shōji-ko
(Lake Shōji)

Sai-ko
(Lake Sai)

Kawaguchi-ko
(Lake Kawaguchi)

Fuji-Yoshida

Tanzawa-
San

Oyama

Motosu-ko
(Lake Motosu)

F U J I

Yamanaka-ko
(Lake Yamanaka)

Go-gōme

Matsuda

Fuji-san
(Mt. Fuji)

Subashiri

TO
TŌKYŌ

Shin-Go-gōme

Gotemba

Sōun-zan
(Mt. Sōun)

Gōra

Miyanoshita

Ōwaku-dani

Koma-ga-take-san

Togendai
*Ashi-
no-ko*

Hakone
Ropeway

Hakone-
Yumoto

Odawara

Hakone-machi

Fuji

Tomei Highway

Mishima

Kanbara

MOA Museum
of Art

Atami Tourist
Information Office

*Sagami
Bay*

Numazu

Kinomiya
Station

Atami

Atami Bai-en
(Atami Plum Garden)

Hatsu-shima

Izu-Nagaoka

Suruga Bay

Ohito

Katsura-kawa

Heda

Shuzenji

Itō

Ippeki-ko

Komuro-san
Kōen

Ikeda Art Museum

Izu Saboten Kōen
(Izu Cactus Park)

Toi

Mt.
Amagi

Kamo

Joren Falls

Inoshishi-mura

Amagi Pass

Atagawa

Nishi-Izu
Tourist Office

Dōgashima

*PACIFIC
OCEAN*

Oshima

Matsuzaki

Kawazu

0		10 miles
0		15 km

Shimoda

Yumi-ga-hama

Irō-zaki (Irō Point)

Fuji-Hakone-Izu
National Park

KEY	
——	JR Trains
▬▬	Shinkansen (Bullet Train)
+—+	Private rail line
++++	Cable car
⚓	Beaches

JR Passes are not valid, makes the Itō–Shimoda run in one hour for ¥1,570.

The Izu–Hakone Railway Line runs from Tōkyō to Mishima (1 hour, 36 minutes; ¥4,090), with a change at Mishima for Shuzenji (31 minutes, ¥500); this is the cheapest option if you don't have a JR Pass. With a JR Pass, a Shinkansen–Izu Line combination will save about 35 minutes and will be the cheapest option. The Tōkyō–Mishima Shinkansen leg (62 minutes) costs ¥4,400; the Mishima–Shuzenji Izu Line leg (31 minutes) costs ¥500.

ESSENTIALS

Buses from Tōkyō Fuji Kyūkō Highway Bus Reservation Center (☎*03/5376–2222*). **Keiō Highway Bus Reservation Center** (☎*03/5376–2222*). **Tōkai Bus Company** (☎*0557/36–1112 for main office, 0557/22–2511 Shimoda Information Center*).

Rental Car Contacts Nippon Rent-a-Car (☎*03/3485–7196 English operator available on weekdays 10 AM–5 PM* ⊕ *www.nipponrentacar.co.jp*). **Toyota Rent-a-Car** (☎*0070/800–0100 toll-free, 03/5954–8008 English operator available 8–8* ⊕ *www.toyota-rl-tyo.co.jp/rentacar/syasyu/info-e.html*).

Tour Contacts Dōgashima Marine (☎*0558/52–0013*). **Fujikyū Kōgyō** (☎*0557/81–0541*). **Izukyū Marine** (☎*0558/22–1151*). **Sunrise Tours** (☎*03/5796–5454* ⊕ *www.jtbgmt.com/sunrisetour*).

Tourist Information Atami Tourist Association (✉*12–1 Ginza-chō, Atami* ☎*0557/85–2222*). **Nishi-Izu Tourist Office** (✉*Dogashima, Nishi-Izu-chō, Kamogu* ☎*0558/52–1268*). **Shimoda Tourist Association** (✉*1–1 Soto-ga-oka, Shimoda-shi* ☎*0558/22–1531*).

Train Information Izukyū Corporation (☎*0557/53–1111 for main office, 0558/22–3202 Izukyū Shimoda Station*). **JR Higashi-Nihon Info Line** (☎*03/3423–0111*). **Odakyū Reservation Center** (☎*03/3481–0130*).

ATAMI 熱海
48 min southwest of Tōkyō by Kodama Shinkansen.

The gateway to the Izu Peninsula is Atami. Most Japanese travelers make it no farther into the peninsula than this town on Sagami Bay, so Atami itself has a fair number of hotels and traditional inns.

When you arrive, collect a map from the **Atami Tourist Information Office** (☎*0557/85–2222*) at the train station to guide you to the sights below.

Atami Plum Garden 熱海梅園 *(Atami Bai-en)*. The best time to visit the garden is in late January or early February, when its 850 trees bloom. If you do visit, also stop by the small shrine that's in the shadow of an enormous old camphor tree. The shrine is more than 1,000 years old and is popular spot for people who are asking the gods for help with alcoholism. The tree is more than 2,000 years old and has been designated a National Monument. It's believed that if you walk around the tree once, another year will be added to your life. Atami Bai-en is always open to the public and is 15 minutes by bus from Atami or an eight-minute walk from Kinomiya Station, the next stop south of

Atami served by local trains. ✉*1169–1 Baien-chō, Atami, Shizouka-ken* ☎*0557/85–2222* 🖨*Free.*

★ **MOA Museum of Art** MOA 美術館 *(MOA Bijutsukan).* This museum houses the private collection of the messianic religious leader Mokichi Okada. Okada (1882–1955), who founded a movement called the Sekai Kyūsei Kyō (Religion for the Salvation of the World), also acquired more than 3,000 works of art; some are from the Asuka period (6th and 7th centuries). Among these works are several particularly fine *ukiyo-e* (Edo-era wood-block prints) and ceramics. On a hill above the station and set in a garden full of old plum trees and azaleas, the museum also affords a sweeping view over Atami and the bay. ✉*26–2 Momoyama, Atami, Shizouka-ken* ☎*0557/84–2511* 🖨*¥1,600* ⊙*Fri.– Wed. 9:30–5.*

Ōyu Geyser. Located just a 15-minute walk south east from Atami Station, the geyser used to gush on schedule once every 24 hours but stopped after the Great Kantō Earthquake of 1923. Not happy with this, the local chamber of commerce rigged a pump to raise the geyser every five minutes. ✉*3 Kamijuku-cho, Atami, Shizouka-ken.*

If you have the time and the inclination for a beach picnic, it's worth taking the 25-minute high-speed ferry (round-trip ¥2,340) from the pier over to **Hatsu-shima** (☎*0557/81–0541 for ferry*). There are nine departures daily between 7:30 and 5:20. You can easily walk around the island, which is only 4 km (2½ mi) in circumference, in less than two hours. Use of the **Picnic Garden** (open daily 10–3) is free.

WHERE TO STAY

$$$$
★
🏨**Atami Taikansō** 熱海大観荘. The views of the sea must have been the inspiration for Yokoyama Taikan, the Japanese artist who once owned this villa. Now it's a traditional Japanese inn with exquisite furnishings and individualized service. The spacious rooms are classically Japanese, with floor-to-ceiling windows. The prices are high, but bear in mind that they include a multicourse dinner of great artistry, served in your room, and breakfast the next morning. There are also indoor and outdoor hot-springs baths. The inn is a 10-minute walk west from Atami Station. **Pros:** spotlessly clean rooms. **Cons:** eating dinner may take most of your evening. ✉*7–1 Hayashi-ga-oka-chō, Atami, Shizuoka-ken* ☎*0557/81–8137* ⊕*www.atami-taikanso.com* 🛏*44 Japanese-style rooms with bath* ⌂*In-hotel: restaurant, pool* ▤*AE, DC, MC, V* ¶⊚*MAP.*

$$–$$$$ 🏨**New Fujiya Hotel** ニュー富士屋ホテル. Only the top rooms have a view of the sea at this modern, inland resort hotel that's a great base for sightseeing. Service is impersonal but professional, and a foreign visitor won't fluster the staff. The hotel is a five-minute taxi ride from Atami Station. **Pros:** a number of shared hot-spring baths. **Cons:** nothing of the comfortable, at-home service of a ryokan. ✉*1–16 Ginza-chō, Atami, Shizuoka-ken* ☎*0557/81–0111* 🛏*158 Western-style rooms with bath, 158 Japanese-style rooms with bath* ⌂*In-hotel: 3 restaurants, bar, pool* ▤*AE, DC, MC, V.*

A Healing Headache

While earthquakes are an annoying, everyday fact of life in Japan, they also provide one of the country's greatest delights: thermal baths. Wherever there are volcanic mountains—and there are a lot—you're sure to find springs of hot water, called *onsen,* that are rich in all sorts of restorative minerals. Any place where lots of spas have tapped these sources is an *onsen chiiki* (hot-springs resort area). The Izu Peninsula is particularly rich in onsen. It has, in fact, one-fifth of the 2,300-odd officially recognized hot springs in Japan.

Spas take many forms, but the one plus ultra is that small secluded Japanese mountain inn with a *rotemburo* (an open-air mineral-spring pool). For guests only, these pools are usually in a screened-off nook with a panoramic view. A room in one of these inns on a weekend or in high season should be booked months in advance. (High season is late December to early January, late April to early May, the second and third weeks of August, and the second and third weeks of October.) More typical is the large resort hotel, geared mainly to groups, with one or more large indoor mineral baths of its own. Where whole towns and villages have developed to exploit a local supply of hot water, there will be several of these large hotels, an assortment of smaller inns, and probably a few modest public bathhouses, with no accommodations, where you just pay an entrance fee for a soak of whatever length you wish.

ITŌ 伊東

25 min south of Atami by JR local; 1 hr, 40 min southwest of Tōkyō via Atami by Kodama Shinkansen, then JR local.

There are some 800 thermal springs in the resort area surrounding Itō, 16 km (10 mi) south of Atami. These springs—and the beautiful, rocky, indented coastline nearby—remain the resort's major attractions, although there are plenty of interesting sights here. Some 150 hotels and inns serve the area.

Itō traces its history of associations with the West to 1604, when William Adams (1564–1620), the Englishman whose adventures served as the basis for James Clavell's novel *Shōgun,* came ashore.

Four years earlier Adams had beached his disabled Dutch vessel, *De Liefde,* on the shores of Kyūshū and became the first Englishman to set foot on Japan. The authorities, believing that he and his men were Portuguese pirates, put Adams in prison, but he was eventually befriended by the shōgun Ieyasu Tokugawa, who brought him to Edo (present-day Tōkyō) and granted him an estate. Ieyasu appointed Adams his adviser on foreign affairs. The English castaway taught mathematics, geography, gunnery, and navigation to shōgunal officials and in 1604 was ordered to build an 80-ton Western-style ship. Pleased with this venture, Ieyasu ordered the construction of a larger oceangoing vessel. These two ships were built at Itō, where Adams lived from 1605 to 1610.

This history was largely forgotten until British Commonwealth occupation forces began coming to Itō for rest and recuperation after World War II. Adams's memory was revived, and since then the Anjin Festival (the Japanese gave Adams the name *anjin,* which means "pilot") has been held in his honor every August. A monument to the Englishman stands at the mouth of the river.

WHAT TO SEE

Ikeda 20th-Century Art Museum 池田20世紀美術館 *(Ikeda 20-Seiki Bijutsukan).* The museum, which overlooks Lake Ippeki, houses works by Picasso, Dalí, Chagall, and Matisse, plus a number of wood-block prints. The museum is a 15-minute walk north west from Izu Cactus Park. ✉ *614 Totari* ☎ *0557/45–2211* 💴 *¥900* 🕐 *Thurs.–Tues. 10–4:30.*

Izu Cactus Park *(Izu Saboten Kōen).* The park consists of a series of pyramidal greenhouses that contain 5,000 kinds of cacti from around the world. At the base of Komuro-san (Mt. Komuro), the park is 20 minutes south of Itō Station by bus. ✉ *1317–13 Futo* ☎ *0557/51–5553* 💴 *¥1,800* 🕐 *Mar.–Oct., daily 9–5; Nov.–Feb., daily 9–4.*

Komuro-san Kōen 小室山公園 *(Mt. Komuro Park).* On the east side of the park there are 3,000 cherry trees of 35 varieties that bloom at various times throughout the year. You can take a cable car to the top of the mountain. The park is about 20 minutes south of Itō Station by bus. ✉ *1428 Komuro-chō, Kawana, Itō-shi* ☎ *0557/45–1444* 💴 *Free; round-trip cable car to mountain top ¥400* 🕐 *Daily 9–4.*

WHERE TO STAY

$$$–$$$$ 🏯 **Hanafubuki** 花吹雪. This traditional Japanese inn, which is located in the Jōgasaki forest, has modern, comfortable rooms, but still retains classic elements like tatami mats, screen sliding doors, and *chabudai* (low dining tables) with *zabuton* (cushion seating). The onsen are made of wood for rustic appeal. Meals are optional. **Pros:** an authentic Japanese experience. **Cons:** meals are available to nonguests, so the dining room can be a bit crowded. ✉ *1041 Yawatano Isomichi, Itō-shi, Shizuoka-ken* ☎ *0557/54–1550* ⊕ *www.hanafubuki.co.jp* 🛏 *12 Japanese-style rooms, 2 Western-style rooms, 3 family rooms* △ *In-hotel: restaurant, bar* ▭ *MC, V.*

$$$$ 🏯 **Hatoya Sun Hotel** ホテルサンハトヤ. Located along a scenic coastline, Hatoya Hotel is in the Itō onsen resort area. The hotel has an aquarium bath, which has glass walls that let guests gaze at tropical fish in an adjoining aquarium while soaking. The open-air hot springs look out onto the ocean where mountains are visible in the distance. Japanese buffet dinners are available every night. **Pros:** live entertainment at dinner. **Cons:** a lot of guests with children make this a bit noisy. ✉ *572–12 Yukawa Tateiwa, Ito[m[-shi, Shizuoka-ken* ☎ *0557/36–4126* 🛏 *187 Japanese-style rooms with bath, 3 Western-style rooms with bath, 1 mixed Western-Japanese style room* △ *In-room: refrigerator (some).* △ *In-hotel: restaurant, bar, pool, parking (free)* ▭ *DC, MC, V.*

◼ EN ROUTE   South of Itō the coastal scenery is lovely—each sweep around a headland reveals another picturesque sight of a rocky, indented shoreline. There are several spa towns en route to Shimoda. Higashi-Izu (East Izu) has numerous hot-springs resorts, of which **Atagawa** is the most fashionable. South of Atagawa is **Kawazu,** a place of relative quiet and solitude, with pools in the forested mountainside and waterfalls plunging through lush greenery.

SHIMODA 下田
1 hr south of Itō by Izu Railways.

Of all the resort towns south of Itō along Izu's eastern coast, none can match the distinction of Shimoda. Shimoda's encounter with the West began when Commodore Matthew Perry anchored his fleet of black ships off the coast here in 1853. To commemorate the event, the three-day Black Ship Festival (Kurofune Matsuri) is held here every year in mid-May. Shimoda was also the site, in 1856, of the first American consulate.

The **Shimoda Tourist Office** (☎0558/22–1531), in front of the station, has the easiest of the local English itineraries to follow. The 2½-km (1½-mi) tour covers most major sights. On request, the tourist office will also help you find local accommodations.

WHAT TO SEE
Hōfuku-ji 宝福寺. The first American consul to Japan was New York businessman Townsend Harris. Soon after his arrival in Shimoda, Harris asked the Japanese authorities to provide him with a female servant; they sent him a young girl named Okichi Saitō, who was engaged to be married. The arrangement brought her a new name, Tōjin (the Foreigner's) Okichi, much disgrace, and a tragic end. When Harris sent her away, she tried, but failed to rejoin her former lover. The shame brought upon her for working and living with a Westerner and the pain of losing the love of her life drove Okichi to drown herself in 1890. Her tale is recounted in Rei Kimura's biographical novel *Butterfly in the Wind*. Hōfuku-ji was Okichi's family temple. The museum annex displays a life-size image of her, and just behind the temple is her grave—where incense is still kept burning in her memory. The grave of her lover, Tsurumatsu, is at Tōden-ji, a temple about midway between Hōfuku-ji and Shimoda Station. ✉18–26 1-chōme ☎0558/22–0960 ☜¥300 ⊘Daily 8–5.

Ryosen-ji 了仙寺. This the temple in which the negotiations took place that led to the United States–Japan Treaty of Amity and Commerce of 1858. The **Treasure Hall** (Hōmotsu-den) contains some personal articles that belonged to Tōjin Okichi. ✉3–12–12 Shimoda ☎0558/22–2805 ☜Treasure Hall ¥500 ⊘Daily 8:30–5.

WHERE TO STAY
¢ 🏨**Pension Sakuraya** ペンション桜家. There are a few Western-style bedrooms at this family-run inn just a few minutes' walk from Shimoda's main beach, but the best lodgings are the Japanese-style corner rooms, which have nice views of the hills surrounding Shimoda. The pleasant Japanese couple who runs the pension speaks English, and cheap meals are available in the dining room. **Pros:** very homey atmosphere. **Cons:** rooms are a bit cramped. ✉2584–20 Shira-hama, Shimoda, Shizuoka-ken ☎0558/23–4470 ⇆4 Western-style rooms with bath, 5 Japanese-style rooms without bath ⊕izu-sakuraya.jp/english ♿In-hotel: restaurant, Japanese baths, laundry facilities, Internet terminal ▤AE, DC, MC, V.

$$$–$$$$ 🏨**Shimoda Prince Hotel** 下田プリンスホテル. This modern V-shaped resort hotel faces the Pacific and is steps away from a white-sand beach.

The decor is more functional than aesthetic, but the panoramic view of the ocean from the picture windows in the dining room makes this one of the best hotels in town. The Prince is just outside Shimoda, 10 minutes by taxi from the station. **Pros:** an excellent view of the sea. **Cons:** the restaurants are on the pricey side. ⊠ *1547–1 Shira-hama, Shimoda, Shizuoka-ken* ☎ *0558/22–2111* ⊕ *www.princehotels.co.jp* ⇆ *70 Western-style rooms with bath, 6 Japanese-style rooms with bath* ♿ *In-hotel: 2 restaurants, bar, tennis courts, pool* ▤ *AE, DC, MC, V.*

BATHING BEAUTIES

If you love the sun, make sure you stop at **Yumi-ga-hama** 弓ケ浜. It's one of the prettiest sandy beaches on the whole Izu Peninsula. The bus from Shimoda Station stops here before continuing to Irō-zaki, the last stop on the route.

$$–$$$$ 🛏 **Shimoda Tokyū Hotel** 下田東急ホテル. Perched just above the bay, the Shimoda Tokyū has impressive views of the Pacific from one side (where rooms cost about 10% more) and mountains from the other. Unlike at most Japanese resort hotels, the lobby here is full of character and warmth, with an airy layout and floor-to-ceiling windows overlooking the bay. Prices are significantly higher in midsummer. **Pros:** nice views of the ocean. **Cons:** restaurants quite expensive compared to Tōkyō standards. ⊠ *5–12–1 Shimoda, Shimoda, Shizuoka-ken* ☎ *0558/22–2411* ⊕ *www.tokyuhotels.co.jp* ⇆ *107 Western-style rooms with bath, 8 Japanese-style rooms with bath* ♿ *In-hotel: 3 restaurants, bar, pool* ▤ *AE, DC, MC, V.*

IRŌ-ZAKI (IRŌ POINT) 石廊崎
40 min by bus or boat from Shimoda.

If you visit Irō-zaki, the southernmost part of the Izu Peninsula, in January, you're in for a special treat: a blanket of daffodils covers the cape.

From the bus stop at the end of the line from Shimoda Station, it's a short walk to the **Irō-zaki Jungle Park** 石廊崎ジャングルパーク, with its 3,000 varieties of colorful tropical plants. Beyond the park you can walk to a lighthouse at the edge of the cliff that overlooks the sea; from here you can see the seven islands of Izu. ⊠ *546–1 Irō-zaki, Minami-Izu* ☎ *0558/65–0050* 🎟 *¥900* 🕐 *Daily 8–5.*

DŌGASHIMA 堂ヶ島
1 hr northwest of Shimoda by bus.

The sea has eroded the coastal rock formations into fantastic shapes near the little port town of Dōgashima. A **Dōgashima Marine** (☎ *0558/52–0013*) sightseeing boat from Dōgashima Pier makes 20-minute runs to see the rocks (¥920). In an excess of kindness, a recorded loudspeaker—which you can safely ignore—recites the name of every rock you pass on the trip.

The **Nishi-Izu Tourist Office** (☎ *0558/52–1268*) is near the pier, in the small building behind the bus station.

WHERE TO STAY

$$$$ ⊡**Dōgashima New Ginsui** 堂ヶ島ニュー銀水. Surrounded by its very own secluded beach, every guest room overlooks the sea at the New Ginsui, which sits atop cliffs above the water. Service is first-class, despite its popularity with tour groups. The Japanese-style rooms were given a modern makeover, and the room rate includes a seafood kaiseki dinner served in your room and a buffet breakfast. For relaxation and pampering, visit the day spa or unwind in the outdoor hot spring. In a town overflowing with upmarket hotels, this is by far the best luxury resort on Izu's west coast, and, though it's a rule that we only include Web sites if they are in English, this one is worth a thousand words. **Pros:** there's a concierge on hand. **Cons:** a bit far from sightseeing spots. ⊠*2977–1 Nishina, Nishi-Izu-chō, Shizuoka-ken* ☎*0558/52–2211* ⊕*www.dougashima-newginsui.jp* ↪*121 Japanese-style rooms with bath* ♿*In-hotel: restaurant, pools, spa, laundry service* ▤*AE, DC, MC, V* ⊙*MAP.*

SHUZENJI 修善寺

2 hrs north of Shimoda by bus, 32 min south of Mishima by Izu-Hakone Railway.

Shuzenji—a hot-springs resort in the center of the peninsula, along the valley of the Katsura-gawa (Katsura River)—enjoys a certain historical notoriety as the place where the second Kamakura shōgun, Minamoto no Yoriie, was assassinated early in the 13th century. Don't judge the town by the area around the station; most of the hotels and hot springs are 2 km (1 mi) to the west.

If you've planned a longer visit to Izu, consider spending a night at **Inoshishi-mura** いのしし村, en route by bus between Shimoda and Shuzenji. The scenery in this part of the peninsula is dramatic, and the dining specialty at the local inns is roast mountain boar. In the morning, a pleasant 15-minute walk from Inoshishi-mura brings you to **Jōren Falls** (Jōren-no-taki). Located on the upper part of the Kano River, these falls drop 82 feet into a dense forest below. This area has some nationally protected flora and fauna species and because of the cool temperature, hiking here is popular in summer.

WHERE TO STAY

¢   ⊡**Goyōkan** 五葉館. This family-run ryokan on Shuzenji's main street has rooms that look out on the Katsura-gawa, plus gorgeous stone-lined (for men) and wood-lined (for women) indoor hot springs. The staff speaks English and can make sightseeing arrangements for you. **Pros:** among the best-priced rooms in the area. **Cons:** doesn't have the cozy feel of a true ryokan. ⊠*765–2 Shuzenji-chō, Tagata-gun, Shizuoka-ken* ☎*0558/72–2066* ⊕*www.goyokan.co.jp* ↪*11 Japanese-style rooms without bath* ♿*In-room: refrigerator* ▤*AE, DC, MC, V.*

$$ ⊡**Kyorai-An Matsushiro-kan** 去来庵 松城館. Although this small family-owned inn is nothing fancy, the owners make you feel like a guest in their home. They also speak some English. Japanese meals are served in a common dining room. Room-only reservations (without meals) are accepted only on weekdays. The inn is five minutes by bus or taxi from Izu-Nagaoka Station. **Pros:** nice shared hot-spring bath. **Cons:** the decor throughout is rather dated. ⊠*55 Kona, Izunokuni, Shizuoka-ken*

☎*0559/48–0072* ⌕*14 Japanese-style rooms with bath, 2 without bath* ⌂*In-hotel: restaurant* ▭*No credit cards* ⦿❙*MAP.*

$$$$ ⊡ **Ochiairou Murakami** 落合楼村上. This traditional ryokan was built in the Shōwa period and though it has been renovated and modernized, the main wooden structure remains true to its original design. Some Japanese literary figures have stayed in this ryokan while writing their oeuvre with the natural surroundings of Yugashima as the inspiration. The rooms are spacious and comfortable, and look out into the gardens. **Pros:** there's free pickup from Yugashima bus terminal; there's a lovely garden on the grounds. **Cons:** you may have to wait for the shared baths. ✉*1887–1 Yugashima, Izu-shi, Shizuoka-ken* ☎*0558/85–0014* ⌕*15 Japanese-style rooms* ⌂*In-hotel: restaurant* ▭*AE, MC, V.*

$$$$ ⊡ **Ryokan Sanyōsō** 旅館三養荘. The former villa of the Iwasaki family,
★ founders of the Mitsubishi conglomerate, is as luxurious and beautiful a place to stay as you'll find on the Izu Peninsula. Museum-quality antiques furnish the rooms—the best of which have traditional baths made of fragrant cypress wood and overlook exquisite little private gardens (note that these high-end rooms cost as much as ¥70,000). Breakfast and dinner are served in your room and are included in the rate. The Sanyōsō is a five-minute taxi ride from Izu-Nagaoka Station. **Pros:** a truly authentic ryokan and furnishings. **Cons:** the most expensive ryokan in the area. ✉*270 Mama-no-ue, Izunokuni-shi, Shizuoka-ken* ☎*0559/47–1111* ⌕*3 Western-style, 30 Japanese-style, and 7 mixed Western-Japanese-style rooms with baths* ⌂*In-hotel: bar, Japanese baths* ▭*AE, DC, MC, V.*

HAKONE 箱根

The national park and resort area of Hakone is a popular day trip from Tōkyō and a good place for a close-up view of Mt. Fuji (assuming the mountain is not swathed in clouds, as often happens in summer). ■**TIP→ On summer weekends it often seems as though all of Tōkyō has come out to Hakone with you. Expect long lines at cable cars and traffic jams everywhere.**

TIMING

You can cover the best of Hakone in a one-day trip out of Tōkyō, but if you want to try the curative powers of the thermal waters or do some hiking, then stay overnight. Two of the best areas are around the old hot-springs resort of Miyanoshita and the western side of Koma-ga-take-san (Mt. Koma-ga-take).

GETTING HERE & AROUND

The typical Hakone route, outlined here, may sound complex, but this is in fact one excursion from Tōkyō so well defined that you really can't get lost—no more so, at least, than any of the thousands of Japanese tourists ahead of and behind you. The first leg of the journey is from Odawara or Hakone-Yumoto by train and cable car through the mountains to Tōgendai, on the north shore of Ashi-no-ko (Lake Ashi). The long way around, from Odawara to Tōgendai by bus, takes about an hour—in heavy traffic, an hour and a half. The trip over the mountains, on the other hand, will take about two hours. Credit the difference to the Hakone Tozan Tetsudō Line—possibly the slowest train you'll ever ride. Using three switchbacks to inch its way up the side of the mountain, the train takes 54 minutes to travel the 16 km (10 mi) from Odawara to Gōra (38 minutes from Hakone-Yumoto). The steeper it gets, the grander the view.

Trains do not stop at any station en route for any length of time, but they do run frequently enough to allow you to disembark, visit a sight, and catch another train.

By Bus. Within the Hakone area, buses run every 15 to 30 minutes from Hakone-machi buses to Hakone-Yumoto Station on the private Odakyū Line (40 minutes, ¥930), and Odawara Station (one hour, ¥1,150), where you can take either the Odakyū Romance Car back to Shinjuku Station or a JR Shinkansen to Tōkyō Station. The buses are covered by the Hakone Free Pass.

By Tours. Sunrise Tours operates a tour to Hakone, including a cruise across Lake Ashi and a trip on the gondola over Ōwaku-dani (¥15,000 includes lunch and return to Tōkyō by Shinkansen; ¥12,000 includes lunch and return to Tōkyō by bus). ■TIP→ These tours are an economical way to see the main sights all in one day and are ideal for travelers with limited time. Sunrise tours depart daily from Tōkyō's Hamamatsu-chō Bus Terminal and some major hotels.

ESSENTIALS

Buses from Tōkyō Fuji Kyūkō Highway Bus Reservation Center (☎ 03/5376–2222). **Keiō Highway Bus Reservation Center** (☎ 03/5376–2222). **Tōkai Bus Company** (☎ 0557/36–1112 for main office, 0558/22–2511 Shimoda Information Center).

Tour Contacts Sunrise Tours (☎ 03/5796–5454 ⊕ www.jtbgmt.com/sunrisetour).

Tourist Information Hakone-machi Tourist Association (⊠ 698 Yumoto, Hakone-machi ☎ 0460/5–8911).

TOP ATTRACTIONS

★ **Hakone Open-Air Museum** 箱根彫刻の森美術館 (*Hakone Chōkoku-no-mori Bijutsukan*). Only a few minutes' walk from the Miyanoshita Station (directions are posted in English), the museum houses an astonishing collection of 19th- and 20th-century Western and Japanese sculpture, most of it on display in a spacious, handsome garden. There are works here by Rodin, Moore, Arp, Calder, Giacometti, Takeshi Shimizu, and Kōtarō Takamura. One section of the garden is devoted to Emilio Greco. Inside are works by Picasso, Léger, and Manzo, among others. ⊠ 1121 Ni-no-taira ☎ 0460/82–1161 ⊕ www.hakone-oam. or.jp ☜ ¥1,600 ⊙ Mar.–Nov., daily 9–5; Dec.–Feb., daily 9–4.

★ **Hakone Ropeway.** At the cable-car terminus of Sōun-zan, a gondola called the Hakone Ropeway swings up over a ridge and crosses the valley called Ōwaku-dani, also known as "Great Boiling Valley," on its way to Tōgendai. The landscape here is desolate, with sulfurous billows of steam escaping through holes from some inferno deep in the earth—yet another reminder that Japan is a chain of volcanic islands. At the top of the ridge is one of the two stations where you can leave

The Road to the Shōgun

In days gone by, the town of Hakone was on the Tōkaidō, the main highway between the imperial court in Kyōto and the Shōgunate in Edo (present-day Tōkyō). The road was the only feasible passage through this mountainous country, which made it an ideal place for a checkpoint to control traffic. The Tokugawa Shōgunate built the Hakone-machi here in 1618; its most important function was to monitor the *daimyō* (feudal lords) passing through—to keep track, above all, of weapons coming into Edo, and womenfolk coming out.

When Ieyasu Tokugawa came to power, Japan had been through nearly 100 years of bloody struggle among rival coalitions of daimyō. Ieyasu emerged supreme because some of his opponents had switched sides at the last

minute, in the Battle of Sekigahara in 1600. The shōgun was justifiably paranoid about his "loyal" barons—especially those in the outlying domains—so he required the daimyō to live in Edo for periods of time every two years. When they did return to their own lands, they had to leave their wives behind in Edo, hostages to their good behavior. A noble lady coming through the Hakone Sekisho without an official pass, in short, was a case of treason.

The checkpoint served the Tokugawa dynasty well for 250 years. It was demolished only when the Shōgunate fell, in the Meiji Restoration of 1868. An exact replica, with an exhibition hall of period costumes and weapons, was built as a tourist attraction in 1965.

the gondola. From here, a ¾-km (½-mi) walking course wanders among the sulfur pits in the valley. Just below the station is a restaurant; the food here is truly terrible, but on a clear day the view of Mt. Fuji is perfect. Remember that if you get off the gondola at any stage, you—and others in the same situation—will have to wait for someone to make space on a later gondola before you can continue down to Tōgendai and Ashi-no-ko (but again, the gondolas come by every minute). ☒*1–15–1 Shiroyama, Odawara* ☎*0465/32–2205* ⊕*www.hakoneropeway.co.jp* ▧*¥970 (without Free Pass)* ☉*Mar.–Nov., daily 8:45–5:15; Dec.–Feb., daily 9:15–4:15.*

Miyanoshita 宮ノ下. The first stop on the train route from Hakone-Yumoto, this is a small but very pleasant and popular resort. As well as hot springs, this village has antiques shops along its main road and several hiking routes up the half-mi-tall Mt. Sengen. If you get to the top, you'll be rewarded with a great view of the gorge.

WORTH NOTING
Ashi-no-ko 芦ノ湖 *(Lake Ashi)*. From Ōwaku-dani, the descent by gondola to Tōgendai on the shore of Lake Ashi takes 25 minutes. There's no reason to linger at Tōgendai; it's only a terminus for buses to Hakone-Yumoto and Odawara and to the resort villages in the northern part of Hakone. Head straight for the pier, a few minutes' walk down the hill, where boats set out on the lake for Hakone-machi. Look out for the **Hakone Sightseeing Cruise** (☒*1–15–1 Shiroyama, Odawara* ☎*0465/32–6830* ⊕*www.hakone-kankosen.co.jp* ▧*¥300* ☉*Summer, 40-min intervals, winter, 50-min intervals. Mar.–Nov., daily 9:30–5;*

Dec.–Feb., daily 9:30–4). The ride is free with your Hakone Free Pass; otherwise, buy a ticket (¥970) at the office in the terminal. A few ships of conventional design ply the lake; the rest are astonishingly corny Disney knockoffs. One, for example, is rigged like a 17th-century warship. With still water and good weather, you'll get a breathtaking reflection of the mountains in the waters of the lake as you go. If a cruise is not what you're after, go exploring and fishing with hired boats from **Togendai Boat House** (☎*090/1448–1834*) or **Ashinoko Fishing Center Oba** (☎*0460/4–8984*).

> ## WHAT THE . . .?
>
> No, your eyes are not playing tricks on you. Those are in fact local entrepreneurs boiling eggs in the sulfur pits in Ōwaku-dani. Locals make a passable living selling the eggs, which turn black, to tourists at exorbitant prices. A popular myth suggests that eating one of these eggs can extend your life by seven years. What do you have to lose?

Gōra 強羅. This small town is at the end of the train line from Odawara and at the lower end of the Hakone Tozan Cablecar. It's a good jumping-off point for hiking and exploring. Ignore the little restaurants and souvenir stands here: get off the train as quickly as you can and make a dash for the cable car at the other end of the station. If you let the rest of the passengers get there before you, and perhaps a tour bus or two, you may stand 45 minutes in line.

Hakone-machi 箱根町. The main attraction here is the **Hakone Barrier** (Hakone Sekisho). The barrier was built in 1618 and served as a checkpoint to control traffic until it was demolished during the Meiji Restoration of 1868. An exact replica was built as a tourist attraction in 1965 and is only a few minutes' walk from the pier, along the lakeshore in the direction of Moto-Hakone. Last entry is 30 minutes before closing time. ✉*Ichiban-chī, Hakone-machi* ☎*0460/3–6635* ⊡*¥300* ⊗*Mar.–Nov., daily 9–5; Dec.–Feb., daily 9–4:30.*

Hakone Museum of Art (*Hakone Bijutsukan*). A sister institution to the MOA Museum of Art in Atami, Hakone Museum of Art is at the second stop of the Hakone Tozan Cablecar. The museum, which consists of two buildings set in a garden, houses a modest collection of porcelain and ceramics from China, Korea, and Japan. ✉*1300 Gōra* ☎*0460/2–2623* ⊕*www.moaart.or.jp* ⊡*¥900* ⊗*Apr.–Nov., Fri.–Wed. 9:30–4:30; Dec.–Mar., Fri.–Wed. 9:30–4.*

Sōun-zan 早雲山 (*Mt. Sōun*). The Hakone Tozan Cablecar travels from Gōra to Sōun-zan, departing every 20 minutes; it takes 10 minutes (¥410; free with the Hakone Free Pass) to get to the top. It's ideal for those wanting to spend a day hiking. There are four stops en route, and you can get off and reboard the cable car at any one of them if you've paid the full fare.

WHERE TO STAY
GŌRA

$$$$ 🏨**Gōra Tensui.** The Gōra Tensui, which opened in 2007, is unique in that it's something of a cross between a boutique hotel and a Japanese-style inn. There is no front desk; upon entering, guests remove their

Hakone Freebies

Many places in Hakone accept the Hakone Free Pass. It's valid for three days and is issued by the privately owned Odakyū Railways. The pass covers the train fare to Hakone and allows you to use any mode of transportation including the Hakone Tozan Cablecar, the Hakone Ropeway, and the Hakone Cruise Boat. In addition to transportation, Free Pass holders get discounts at museums such as the Hakone Museum of Art, restaurants, and shops. The list of participants is pretty extensive and it always changes, so it's a good idea to check out the Web site for a complete list of participating companies and terms and conditions.

The Hakone Free Pass (¥5,500) and the Fuji-Hakone Free Pass (¥7,200) can be purchased at the **Odakyū Sightseeing Service Center** (☎ 03/5321–7887 ⊕ www.odakyu-group.co.jp) inside JR Shinjuku station, near west exit, or by credit card over the phone. Allow a couple of days for delivery to your hotel. If you have a JR Pass, it's cheaper to take a Kodama Shinkansen from Tōkyō Station to Odawara and buy the Hakone Free Pass there (¥4,130) for travel within the Hakone region only.

---

shoes and socks, and sit at a counter bar with their tired feet resting in the hot-mineral-spring bath under the bar, and enjoy a tea or beer as they check in. There are Japanese rooms, Western rooms, and rooms that combine both, with raised islands of tatami on top of wood flooring. There are two shared onsen baths, one outdoors and one indoors. Some rooms have private baths on terraces with wonderful views of the mountains. **Pros:** four rooms have a private onsen on a terrace. **Cons:** no Japanese food in the restaurant. ⊠ 1320–276 Gōra, Ashigarashimo-gun Hakone-machi, Kanagawa-ken ☎ 0460/86–1411 ⊕ www.gora-tensui. com/index_english.html ⇱ 17 rooms ⚘ In-hotel: restaurant, Japanese baths ⊟ AE, MC, V.

LAKE ASHI

$$–$$$$ ★ 🖫 **Hakone Prince Hotel** 箱根プリンスホテル. The location of this resort complex is perfect, with the lake in front and the mountains of Komaga-take in back. The Hakone Prince draws both tour groups and individual travelers, and it's also a popular venue for business conferences. The main building has both twin rooms and triples; the Japanese-style Ryū-gū-den annex, which overlooks the lake and has its own thermal bath, is superb. The rustic-style cottages in the complex sleep three to four guests; these are only open mid-April to November. **Pros:** lovely quaint cottages surrounded by nature. **Cons:** a bit remote from nearby sightseeing spots. ⊠ 144 Moto-Hakone, Hakone-machi, Kanagawa-ken ☎ 0460/3–1111 ⊕ www.princehotels.co.jp ⇱ 142 Western-style rooms with bath, 116 Western-style cottages with bath ⚘ In-hotel: 2 restaurants, room service, bar, tennis courts, pools, Japanese baths ⊟ AE, DC, MC, V ⎊ CP.

MIYANOSHITA

$$–$$$$ ★ 🖫 **Fujiya Hotel** 富士屋ホテル. Built in 1878, this Western-style hotel with modern additions is showing signs of age, but that somehow adds to its charm. The Fujiya combines the best of traditional Western decor

with the exceptional service and hospitality of a fine Japanese inn. There are both Western and Japanese restaurants, and in the gardens behind the hotel is an old imperial villa that serves as a dining room. Hot-spring water is pumped right into the guest rooms. **Pros:** wonderful, friendly service. **Cons:** rooms and bath decor are rather dated. ✉*359 Miyanoshita, Hakone-machi, Kanagawa-ken* ☎*0460/2–2211* ⊕*www. fujiyahotel.co.jp* ⇆*149 Western-style rooms with bath* ⅄*In-hotel: 3 restaurants, room service, bar, golf course, pools, no-smoking rooms* ⊟*AE, DC, MC, V.*

SENGOKU

¢ 🏠**Fuji-Hakone Guest House** 富士箱根ゲストハウス. A small, family-run Japanese inn, this guesthouse has simple tatami rooms with the bare essentials. The owners, Mr. and Mrs. Takahashi, speak English and are a great help in planning trips off the beaten path. The inn is between Odawara Station and Tōgendai; take a bus from the station (Lane 4) and get off at the Senkyōro-mae stop. The family also operates the nearby Moto-Hakone Guest House, which has five Japanese-style rooms that share a typical Japanese-style bath. **Pros:** friendly staff; inexpensive rates. **Cons:** difficult to access from nearest transportation, especially at night. ✉*912 Sengoku-hara (103 Moto-Hakone for Moto-Hakone Guest House), Hakone-machi, Kanagawa-ken* ☎*0460/4–6577 for Fuji-Hakone, 0460/3–7880 for Moto-Hakone* ⇆*14 Japanese-style rooms without bath in Fuji-Hakone, 5 Japanese-style rooms without bath in Moto-Hakone* ⊟*AE, MC, V.*

¢ 🏠**Lodge Fujimien** ロッジ富士見苑. This traditional ryokan, complete with an on-site onsen, has all the trimmings of an expensive ryokan, for a fraction of the price. Spacious rooms are a little old and dark but have character in the room layout, furniture, and traditional wall hangings, and on clear days, Mt. Fuji is visible from the balcony. The restaurant serves only Japanese food, and its set meals are reasonably priced. Don't forget to book the daily dinner special in advance. Conveniently located near Minami Onsen-sou bus stop, Hakone's main sights are only a five-minute ride away. **Pros:** affordable rates; convenient location. **Cons:** its accessible location leads to occasional overcrowding. ✉*1245 Sengoku-hara, Hakone, Kanagawa-ken* ☎*0460/84–8675* ⇆*21 Japanese-style rooms with bath, 5 Western-style rooms with bath* ⅄*In-hotel: restaurant, parking (free)* ⊟*No credit cards.*

FUJI GO-KO (FUJI FIVE LAKES) 富士五湖

To the north of Mt. Fuji, the Fuji Go-ko area affords an unbeatable view of the mountain on clear days and makes the best base for a climb to the summit. With its various outdoor activities, such as skating and fishing in the winter and boating and hiking in the summer, this is a popular resort area for families and business conferences.

The five lakes are, from the east, Yamanaka-ko, Kawaguchi-ko, Sai-ko, Shōji-ko, and Motosu-ko. Yamanaka and Kawaguchi are the largest and most developed as resort areas, with Kawaguchi more or less the centerpiece of the group.

TIMING
You can visit this area on a day trip from Tōkyō, but unless you want to spend most of it on buses and trains, plan on staying overnight.

GETTING HERE & AROUND
By Bus. Direct bus service runs daily from Shinjuku Station in Tōkyō to Lake Kawaguchi every hour between 7:10 AM and 8:10 PM. Buses go from Kawaguchi-ko Station to Go-gōme (the fifth station on the climb up Mt. Fuji) in about an hour; there are eight departures a day until the climbing season (July and August) starts, when there are 15 departures or more, depending on demand. The cost is ¥1,700.

By Train. The transportation hub, as well as one of the major resort areas in the Fuji Five Lakes area, is Kawaguchi-ko. Getting there from Tōkyō requires a change of trains at Ōtsuki. The JR Chūō Line Kaiji and Azusa express trains leave Shinjuku Station for Ōtsuki on the half hour from 7 AM to 8 PM (more frequently in the morning) and take approximately one hour. At Ōtsuki, change to the private Fuji-Kyūkō Line for Kawaguchi-ko, which takes another 50 minutes. The total traveling time is about two hours, and you can use your JR Pass as far as Ōtsuki; otherwise, the fare is ¥1,280. The Ōtsuki–Kawaguchi-ko leg costs ¥1,110. Also available are two direct service rapid trains for Kawaguchi-ko that leave Tōkyō in the morning at 6:08 and 7:10 on weekdays, 6:09 and 7:12 on weekends and national holidays.

The Holiday Kaisoku Picnic-gō, available on weekends and national holidays, offers direct express service from Shinjuku, leaving at 8:10 and arriving at Kawaguchi-ko Station at 10:37. From March through August, JR puts on additional weekend express trains for Kawaguchi-ko, but be aware that on some of them only the first three cars go all the way to the lake. Coming back, you have a choice of late-afternoon departures from Kawaguchi-ko that arrive at Shinjuku in the early evening. Check the express timetables before you go; you can also call either the JR Higashi-Nihon Info Line or Fuji-kyūko Kawaguchi-ko Station for train information.

ESSENTIALS
Buses from Kawaguchi Fuji Kyūkō Lake Kawaguchi Reservation Center (☎*0555/72-2922*). **Fuji Kyūkō Gotemba Reservation Center** (☎*0550/ 82-2555*).

Buses from Tōkyō Fuji Kyūkō Highway Bus Reservation Center (☎*03/ 5376-2222*). **Keiō Highway Bus Reservation Center** (☎*03/5376-2222*). **Tōkai Bus Company** (☎*0557/36-1112 for main office, 0558/22-2511 Shimoda Information Center*).

Train Information Fuji-kyūukō Kawaguchi-ko Station (☎*0555/72-0017*). **JR Higashi-Nihon Info Line** (☎*03/3423-0111*). **Odakyū Reservation Center** (☎*03/3481-0130*).

Tourist Information Fuji-Kawaguchiko Tourist Association (✉*890 Funatsu, Kawakuchiko-machi, Minami-Tsuru-gun* ☎*0555/72-2460*).

WHAT TO SEE

Fuji-kyū Highland 富士急ハイランド.
The largest of the recreational facilities at Lake Kawaguchi, Fuji-kyū Highland has an impressive assortment of rides, roller coasters, and other amusements, but it's probably not worth a visit unless you have children in tow. In winter there's superb skating here, with Mt. Fuji for a backdrop. Fuji-kyū Highland is about 15 minutes' walk east from Kawaguchi-ko Station. ⊠ *5–6–1 Shin Nishi Hara, Fujiyoshi-da* ☎ *0555/23–2111* ✆ *Full-day "Free Pass"* ¥*4,800, entrance only* ¥*1,200* ⊙ *Weekdays 9–5, weekends 9–8.*

THE SHŌJI TRIANGLE

The Aoki-ga-hara Jukai (Sea of Trees) seems to hold a morbid fascination for the Japanese. Many people go into Aoki-ga-hara every year and never come out, some of them on purpose. If you're planning to climb Mt. Fuji from this trail, go with a guide.

3

Fuji Museum 富士博物館 *(Fuji Hakubutsukan).* One of the little oddities at Lake Kawaguchi is this museum, located on the lake's north shore, next to the Fuji Lake Hotel. The first floor holds conventional exhibits of local geology and history, but upstairs is an astonishing collection of—for want of a euphemism—phalluses (you must be 18 or older to view the exhibit). Mainly made from wood and stone and carved in every shape and size, these figures played a role in certain local fertility festivals. ⊠ *3964 Funatsu, Fujikawaguchiko-machi, Kanagawa-ken* ☎ *0555/73–2266* ✆ *1st fl.* ¥*200, 1st and 2nd fl.* ¥*500* ⊙ *Mar.–Oct., daily 9–4; Nov.–Feb., Sat.–Thurs. 9–4; closed 3rd Tues. of month.*

Kawaguchi-ko 河口湖 *(Lake Kawaguchi).* A 5- to 10-minute walk from Kawaguchi-ko Station, this is the most developed of the five lakes. It's ringed with weekend retreats and vacation lodges—many of them maintained by companies and universities for their employees. Excursion boats depart from a pier here on 30-minute tours of the lake. The promise, not always fulfilled, is to have two views of Mt. Fuji: one of the mountain itself and the other inverted in its reflection on the water.

Motosu-ko 本栖湖 *(Lake Motosu).* Lake Motosu is the farthest west of the five lakes. It's also the deepest and clearest of the Fuji Go-ko. It takes about 50 minutes to get here by bus.

Sai-ko 西湖 *(Lake Sai).* Between Lakes Shōji and Kawaguchi, Lake Sai is the third-largest lake of the Fuji Go-ko, with only moderate development. From the western shore there is an especially good view of Mt. Fuji. Near Sai-ko there are two natural caves, an ice cave and a wind cave. You can either take a bus or walk to them.

Shōji-ko 精進湖 *(Lake Shōji).* Many people consider Lake Shōji, the smallest of the lakes, to be the prettiest—not least because it still has relatively little vacation-house development.

Shōji Trail 精進湖ハイキング. This trail leads from Lake Shōji to Mt. Fuji through Aoki-ga-hara (Sea of Trees). Beware. This forest has an underlying magnetic lava field that makes compasses go haywire.

Tenjō-san 天上山 *(Mt. Tenjō).* A gondola along the shore of Lake Kawaguchi (near the pier) quickly brings you to the top of the 3,622-foot-tall mountain. From the observatory here the whole of Lake Kawaguchi lies before you, and beyond the lake is a classic view of Mt. Fuji.

Yamanaka-ko 山中湖 *(Lake Yamanaka).* The largest of the Fuji Go-ko, Lake Yamanaka) is 35 minutes by bus to the southeast of Kawaguchi. It's also the closest lake to the popular trail up Mt. Fuji that starts at Go-gōme, and many climbers use this resort area as a base.

WHERE TO STAY

KAWAGUCHI-KO

$$$–$$$$ **Fuji View Hotel** 富士ビューホテル. This hotel on Lake Kawaguchi is a little threadbare but comfortable. The terrace lounge affords fine views of the lake and of Mt. Fuji beyond. The staff speaks English and is helpful in planning excursions. Many of the guests are on group excursions and take two meals—dinner and breakfast—in the hotel, but it's possible to opt for the room rate alone. Rates are significantly higher on weekends and in August. **Pros:** comparatively inexpensive lodgings. **Cons:** rooms are rather small. ⊠*511 Katsuyama-mura, Fuji-Kawaguchiko-machi, Yamanashi-ken* ☎*0555/83–2211* ⊕*www.fuji-yahotel.co.jp* ⊅*40 Western-style rooms with bath, 30 Japanese-style rooms with bath* ⏃*In-hotel: 2 restaurants, golf course, tennis courts* ☰*AE, DC, MC, V* ⫶❙*MAP.*

YAMANAKA-KO

$$ **Hotel Mount Fuji** 富士山ホテル. This is the best resort hotel on Lake
★   Yamanaka and has all the facilities for a recreational holiday including on-site game and karaoke rooms and a nature walk on the grounds. The guest rooms are larger than those at the other hotels on the lake and are modeled after European hotels. The convenient location and large banquet halls make it a favorite among tour groups. The lounges are spacious, and they have fine views of the lake and mountain. Rates are about 20% higher on weekends. **Pros:** comfortable rooms; convenient facilities. **Cons:** one of the more expensive options in the area. ⊠*1360–83 Yamanaka, Yamanaka-ko-mura, Yamanashi-ken* ☎*0555/ 62–2111* ⊕*www.mtfuji-hotel.com* ⊅*150 Western-style rooms with bath, 1 Japanese-style room with bath* ⏃*In-hotel: 3 restaurants, pool, parking (free)* ☰*AE, DC, MC, V.*

¢   **Inn Fujitomita** 旅館ふじとみた. One of the closest lodging options to the Mt. Fuji hiking trails, this inexpensive inn is a launching point for treks around the Fuji Go-ko area. The inn might not be much to look at from the outside, but the interior is spacious and homey. The staff speaks English and can help you plan an itinerary for visiting the area sights. Meals, including vegetarian options, are available at a very low price. Shuttle service is provided from Fuji Yoshida Station and the Lake Yamanaka bus stop. **Pros:** spacious rooms; pleasant surrounding grounds. **Cons:** very crowded during climbing season. ⊠*13235 Shibokusa, Oshinomura, Minami-Tsuru-gun, Yamanashi-ken* ☎*0555/84–3359* ⊕*www.tim.hi-ho.ne.jp/innfuji* ⊅*10 Japanese-style rooms, 3 with bath* ⏃*In-room: no TV (some). In-hotel: restaurant, tennis courts, pool, laundry facilities* ☰*AE, DC, MC, V.*

FUJI-SAN (MT. FUJI) 富士山

Fodor's Choice
★

There are six routes to the summit of the 12,388-foot-high **Fuji-san,** but only two, both accessible by bus, are recommended: from Go-gōme (Fifth Station), on the north side, and from Shin-Go-gōme (New Fifth Station), on the south. The climb to the summit from Go-gōme takes five hours and is the shortest way up; the descent takes three hours. From Shin-Go-gōme the ascent is slightly longer and stonier, but the way down, via the *sunabashiri,* a volcanic sand slide, is faster. The quickest route is to ascend from Go-gōme and descend to Shin-Go-gōme via the sunabashiri.

THE CLIMB

The ultimate experience of climbing Mt. Fuji is to reach the summit just before dawn and be able to greet the extraordinary sunrise. *Go-raikō* (The Honorable Coming of the Light [here *go* means "honorable"]), as the sunrise is called, has a mystical quality because the reflection shimmers across the sky just before the sun itself appears over the horizon. Mind you, there is no guarantee of seeing it: Mt. Fuji is often cloudy, even in the early morning.

The climb is taxing but not as hard as you might think scaling Japan's highest mountain would be. That said, the air *is* thin, and it *is* humiliating to struggle for the oxygen to take another step while some 83-year-old Japanese grandmother blithely leaves you in her dust (it happens). Have no fear of losing the trail on either of the two main routes. Just follow the crowd—some 196,000 people make the climb during the official season, which is July 1 to August 26. ■TIP➔ **Outside of this season, the weather is highly unpredictable and potentially dangerous, and climbing is strongly discouraged.** In all, there are 10 stations to the top; hiking purists start at the very bottom, but if you want to save time a, you can start at the fifth station. There are stalls selling food and drinks along the way, but at exorbitant prices, so bring your own.

Also along the route are dormitory-style huts (about ¥7,000 with two meals, ¥5,000 without meals) where you can catch some sleep. A popular one is at the Hachi-gōme (Eighth Station), from which it's about a 90-minute climb to the top. ⚠ **These huts, which are open only in July and August, should be avoided at all costs. The food is vile, there's no fresh water, and the bedding is used by too many people and seldom properly aired.** Sensible folk leave the Go-gōme at midnight with good flashlights, climb through the night, and get to the summit just before dawn. Camping on the mountain is prohibited.

GETTING HERE AND AROUND

By Bus. Take one of the daily buses directly to Go-gōme from Tōkyō; they run July through August and leave from Shinjuku Station. The journey takes about 2 hours and 40 minutes from Shinjuku and costs ¥2,600. Reservations are required; book seats through the Fuji Kyūkō Highway Bus Reservation Center, the Keiō Highway Bus Reservation Center, the Japan Travel Bureau (which should have English-speaking staff), or any major travel agency.

Planning for Mt. Fuji

Beware of fickle weather around and atop the mountain. Summer days can be unbearably hot and muggy, and the nights can be a shocking contrast of freezing cold (bring numerous warm layers and be prepared to put them all on). Wear strong hiking shoes. The sun really burns at high altitudes, so wear protective clothing and a hat; gloves are a good idea, too. Bring enough food and water for the climb (remember to take your garbage down with you) and bring a flashlight in case it gets dark. Also, keep altitude sickness in mind. To avoid it, begin your ascent at a slow pace and take frequent breaks. Use a backpack to keep your hands free and as a useful tool on the way down: instead of returning to Go-gōme, descend to Shin-Go-gōme on the volcanic sand slide called the **sunabashiri**— sit down on your pack, push off, and away you go.

To return from Mt. Fuji to Tōkyō, take an hour-long bus ride from Shin-Go-gōme to Gotemba (¥1,500). From Gotemba take the JR Tōkaidō and Gotemba lines to Tōkyō Station (¥1,890), or take the JR Line from Gotemba to Matsuda (¥480) and change to the private Odakyū Line from Shin-Matsuda to Shinjuku (¥750).

ESSENTIALS

Buses from Tōkyō Fuji Kyūkō Highway Bus Reservation Center (☎ *03/ 5376–2222*). **Keiō Highway Bus Reservation Center** (☎ *03/5376–2222*). **Tōkai Bus Company** (☎ *0557/36–1112 for main office, 0558/22–2511 Shimoda Information Center*).

Nagoya, Ise-Shima, and the Kii Peninsula

WORD OF MOUTH

"We quite like Nagoya as it is a manageable size for a big city, and it has shops and goods available that we don't have in Kanazawa..It has the Nagoya Boston Museum of Fine Arts which is very good, a nice aquarium, Higashiyama zoo (so-so), nearby Edo Mura. It is a logical stop between Kyoto and Takayama as you need to change trains there anywhere between the two. "

—KimJapan

Updated
by James
Hadfield

Nagoya punches well above its weight. The present-day industries of Japan's fourth-largest city are a corollary to its *monozukuri* (art of making things) culture. This is manifested in the efficiency of Toyota's production lines, but traditional crafts including ceramics, tie-dyeing, and knife-making are still very much alive. Nagoya's GDP is greater than Switzerland's, but this economic prowess is matched by a capacity to pleasantly surprise any visitor.

Nagoya purrs along contentedly, burdened neither by a second-city complex nor by hordes of tourists, and it has an agreeable small-town atmosphere. A substantial immigrant population, by Japanese standards, includes many South Americans working in local factories and provides international flavor to the city's food and entertainment choices. Among the legacies of the city's hosting of the 2005 World Expo are a vastly improved tourism and transportation infrastructure.

On arrival, you will first notice the twin white skyscrapers sprouting from the ultramodern station, almost a city in itself. An extensive network of underground shopping malls stretches out in all directions below the wide, clean streets around Nagoya Station and in downtown Sakae. Above ground are huge department stores and international fashion boutiques. The even taller building opposite the station is the headquarters of the sales division of automaking giant Toyota, the driving force of the local economy.

Within two hours' drive of the city are the revered Grand Shrines of Ise, Japan's most important Shintō site, and to the south are the quiet fishing villages of Ise-Shima National Park. On the untamed Kii Peninsula, steep-walled gorges and forested headlands give way to pristine bays, and fine sandy beaches await in Shirahama. Inland is the remarkable mountain temple town of Kōya-san. Add to this some memorable *matsuri* (festivals), and this corner of Japan becomes far more than just another stop on the *Shinkansen*.

See the glossary at the end of this book for definitions of the common Japanese words and suffixes used in this chapter.

ORIENTATION AND PLANNING

ORIENTATION

Nagoya is on a wide plain in the main urban and industrial corridor that runs along the south side of Honshū from Tōkyō as far west as Kōbe. The mountains of the southern Japan Alps rise just north and east of the city, and to the west is the lush Kii Peninsula.

TOP REASONS TO GO

The Shrines: The Grand Shrines of Ise, rebuilt every two decades for the last 1,500 years, are the most sacred in Japan.

Shopping: Nagoya's Noritake is the world's largest porcelain maker. Seto, Tajimi, and Tokoname produce ceramics, Arimatsu tie-dyed fabrics, Gifu paper lanterns and umbrellas, and Seki samurai swords.

Japan at Work and Play: Tour the factories of Toyota, Noritake, and brewers Asahi and Kirin. See the annual sumō tournament in July or Chūnichi Dragons baseball games.

Relive Japan's Modernization: Meiji-mura holds 60 original Meiji-era buildings (1868–1912)—including the foyer of Frank Lloyd Wright's Imperial Hotel—that were reconstructed here.

Eat Fish from the Bird's Mouth: In *ukai* cormorants capture *ayu* (sweetfish), but rings around the birds' necks prevent them from swallowing their catch, which is taken by fishermen.

Nagoya. An ancient transport, business, and cultural hub, Nagoya combines the best of old and contemporary Japan. To the north, along the edge of the Gifu and Nagano mountains, are cormorant fishing and craft centers. Modern industry encroaches on the city, but it is also an essential to Nagoya's vibrancy.

Ise-Shima National Park. Many people get no farther than the shrines at Ise, but just to the south is a world of bays ringed by fishing villages and oyster farms.

Kii Peninsula. Traveling west and inland on the Kii Peninsula, time slows down, with few roads and only one coastal railway line. The peninsula rewards patient explorers with beautiful wilderness and the shrines of the Kumano Kodo pilgrimage road.

Kōya-san. Kōya-San is the headquarters of the 1,200-year-old Shingon Buddhist sect and has overnight temple accommodation. This small, isolated mountain town, dotted by 120 temples, is a calm and spiritual retreat.

PLANNING

Nagoya is between Tōkyō and Kyōto, and we recommend spending a couple of days exploring the sights. The city serves as a jumping off point for traveling south and west to Ise-Shima and the Kii Peninsula. The weather can be changeable along the coastline of Ise-Shima, and if you're heading inland on the Kii Peninsula be prepared for hilly terrain.

WHEN TO GO

Spring is the most popular season, especially early April when cherry trees bloom. Nagoya gets extremely humid in July and August, but in autumn the trees turn color under blue skies. Sea breezes make coastal areas bearable in summer. Cold winds blow into Nagoya from the ski grounds to the north during winter, but Wakayama prefecture remains mild.

CLOSE UP

Festivals

Nagoya and the surrounding cities host a wide variety of *matsuri* (festivals) throughout the year. Running the gamut from chaotic to tranquil and beautiful to bizarre, these annual events bring the culture and traditions of the area to life in ways that castles, museums, and temples cannot. We have picked out a few of the best, but whenever you visit check with the Tourist Information Center or Nagoya International Center for upcoming festivals. All these events are free.

FEBRUARY

Hadaka (Naked) Festival. For 1,200 years, thousands of men aged 42 (an unlucky age in Japan) have braved the winter cold wearing nothing but *fundoshi* (loincloths). Their goal, in an event that regularly results in serious injury to participants, is to touch the *shin otoko* (the one truly "naked man") and transmit their bad spirits to him before he reaches Kōnomiya shrine and submits to cleansing rituals. Eagerness to achieve this task often leads to dangerous stampedes, but the crowds of more than 100,000 are well protected from harm. The festival is held in the first half of February—contact Nagoya City Tourist Information Center in JR Nagoya Station for details. Kōnomiya Station is 15 minutes north of Nagoya on the Meitetsu Gifu line, and the shrine is a 10-minute walk from the station.

MARCH

Hōnen Festival. The 1,500-year-old Tagata-jinja in Komaki is home to one of Japan's infamous male fertility festivals. On March 15 large crowds gather to watch and take pictures of a 6-foot, 885-pound *owasegata* (phallus) being carried between two shrines and offered to the *kami* (god) for peace and a good harvest. The festival starts at 10 and climaxes with face-size "lucky" rice cakes being tossed into the crowd just before 4. The closest station is Tagata-jinja-mae on the Meitetsu Komaki line. Change at Inuyama if you are traveling from Nagoya. The train takes one hour.

JULY

Owari Tsushima Tennō Festival. The main feature of this charming, low-key event is five boats decorated with 365 paper lanterns (for the days of the year) arranged into a circular shape and 12 more (representing the months) hanging from a mast. The festival occurs the evening of the fourth Saturday in July. Haunting traditional music accompanies the boats as they drift lazily around the river and the lanterns and fireworks reflect in the water. Tsushima is 25 minutes west of Nagoya on the Meitetsu Bisai line. Follow the crowds west from the station to the shrine and festival area.

AUGUST

Domannaka. Dozens of troupes of up to 150 dancers each arrive from all over Japan to take over Nagoya's streets and public spaces. Started in 1999, this energetic festival has rapidly gained popularity. It mixes hip-hop beats with spiced-up traditional dance moves and colorful costumes. Domannaka takes place over a weekend in late August. The exact dates and locations change from year to year, so get the latest details from Nagoya City Tourist Information Center in JR Nagoya Station.

GETTING HERE AND AROUND

In Nagoya subways are the easiest way to get around. Outside the city the extensive rail network will take you to most places of interest, although buses may be necessary on the remote Kii Peninsula.

AIR TRAVEL

Nagoya's compact, user-friendly Chūbu International Airport (referred to locally as "Centrair") serves overseas flights and is a hub for domestic travel. Most major airlines have offices in downtown Nagoya, 45 km (28 mi) northeast of the airport. For domestic travel, Japan Airlines (JAL) and All Nippon Airways (ANA) have offices in Nagoya and fly from Nagoya to most major Japanese cities. The Meitetsu Airport Limited Express train makes the 28-minute run between Centrair and Nagoya Station for ¥1,200. This price includes a seat-reservation fee. For domestic travel, Japan Airlines (JAL) and All Nippon Airways (ANA) have offices in Nagoya, 45 km (28 mi) northeast of the airport.

BUS TRAVEL

Highway buses operated by JR and Meitetsu connect Nagoya with major cities, including Tōkyō and Kyōto. The fare is half that of the *shinkansen* trains, but the journey takes three times longer.

JR buses crisscross Nagoya, running either north–south or east–west. The basic fare is ¥200 and ¥100 for children—pay when you get on the bus. A one-day bus pass costs ¥600, and a combination bus/subway pass costs ¥850. Detailed information on bus travel can be collected at the Tourist Information Office in the center of Nagoya Station, and day- and combination-passes are available at bus terminals and subway stations.

CAR TRAVEL

The journey on the two-lane expressway from Tōkyō to Nagoya takes about five hours; from Kyōto allow 2½ hours. Major highways also connect Nagoya to Nagano, Takayama, Kanazawa, and Nara. Japanese highways are jam-prone, with holiday season tailbacks out of Tōkyō sometimes reaching 60 mi in length. Signage is confusing, so be sure to get a car with satellite navigation or a good road map.

Wide main streets make Nagoya relatively easy to navigate. Road signs in the city often point to places out of town, however, so a detailed map is advised.

TRAIN TRAVEL

Frequent bullet trains run between Tōkyō and Nagoya. The ride takes 1 hour, 52 minutes on the *Hikari* Shinkansen and 2½ hours on the slower *Kodama* Shinkansen, and costs ¥10,380. The trip west to Kyōto takes 50 minutes, and Shin-Ōsaka just over 1 hour. JR Passes are not accepted on the ultrafast *Nozomi*. Less expensive Limited Express trains proceed from Nagoya into and across the Japan Alps—to Takayama, Toyama, Matsumoto, and Nagano.

ABOUT THE RESTAURANTS

Restaurants in Nagoya and on the peninsulas are slightly less expensive than in Tōkyō. Your cheapest options are the noodle shops, *donburi* (rice bowl) chains, and *kaiten* (revolving) sushi and curry houses.

Franchised restaurants often have English alongside Japanese on their menus, but don't expect the staff to know more than a few words.

ABOUT THE HOTELS

Nagoya's lodging ranges from *ryokan* (traditional Japanese inns) and efficient business hotels to large luxury palaces. At Kōya-san, temple accommodation is a fascinating experience. Furnishings in temples are spartan but sufficient, and the food is strictly vegetarian. You may be invited to attend early-morning prayer service. In addition to holidays, hotels are busy in October owing to conferences held in Nagoya and autumn foliage outside the city. Unless otherwise noted, expect private baths, air-conditioning, and basic TV in all rooms. The large hotels in downtown Nagoya have English-speaking staff, but it's advisable to ask a tourist information center to make reservations for you outside the city.

For a short course on accommodations in Japan, see Accommodations in Travel Smart.

WHAT IT COSTS IN YEN				
	$	**$$**	**$$$**	**$$$$**
RESTAURANTS	under ¥800	¥800– ¥1,000	¥1,000– ¥2,000	¥2,000– ¥3,000	over ¥3,000
HOTELS	under ¥8,000	¥8,000– ¥12,000	¥12,000– ¥18,000	¥18,000– ¥22,000	over ¥22,000

Restaurant prices are per person for a main course, set meal, or equivalent combination of smaller dishes at dinner. Hotel prices are for a double room with private bath, excluding service and tax.

VISITOR INFORMATION

The **Nagoya International Center** 名古屋国際センター, or Kokusai Sentā, as it's locally known, is a wise stop on any Nagoya itinerary. Multilingual staff have a wealth of information on Nagoya and the surrounding area, and the center publishes a monthly newsletter, "Nagoya Calendar," which gives up-to-date advice, information, and event listings in English. It is one stop from JR Nagoya Station on the Sakura-dōri Subway Line or a seven-minute walk through the underground walkway that follows the line.

ESSENTIALS

Airline Contacts All Nippon Airways (☎ *0120/029–709* ⊕ *www.ana.co.jp*). **Japan Airlines** (☎ *052/265–3369* ⊕ *www.jal.co.jp*).

Airport Contacts Chūbu Kokusai Kūkō (Centrair) (☎ *0569/38–1195 daily 6:40 AM–10 PM* ⊕ *www.centrair.jp*). **Meitetsu Airport Limited Express** (⊠ *Meitetsu Customer Center* ☎ *052/582–5151 operators available weekdays 8–7, weekends 8–6* ⊕ *www.meitetsu.co.jp*).

Bus Contacts JR Tokai Bus (☎ *052/563–0489 daily 9–7*). **Meitetsu Highway Bus** (☎ *052/582–0489 daily 8–7*). **Nagoya City Transportation Bureau** (☎ *052/522–0111 daily 8–7* ⊕ *www.kotsu.city.nagoya.jp*).

Emergency Contacts Ambulance and Fire (☎ *119*). **Japan Helpline** (☎ *0120/46–1997*). **Police** (☎ *110*).

Visitor Information **Nagoya International Center** (⊠ *1-47-1 Nakono, Naka-mura-ku* ☎ *052/581-0100* ⊕ *www.nic-nagoya.or.jp* ☉ *Tues.–Sun. 9–7)* .

NAGOYA 名古屋

366 km (227 mi) southwest of Tōkyō, 190 km (118 mi) east of Ōsaka, 148 km (92 mi) east of Kyōto.

In 1612, shōgun Ieyasu Tokugawa established Nagoya by permitting his ninth son to build a castle here. Industry and merchant houses sprang up in the shadow of this magnificent fortress, as did pleasure quarters for samurai. Supported by taxing the rich harvests of the surrounding Nōbi plain, the Tokugawa family used the castle as its power center for the next 250 years.

After the Meiji Restoration in 1868, when Japan began trade with the West in earnest, Nagoya developed rapidly. When the harbor opened to international shipping in 1907, Nagoya's industrial growth accelerated, and by the 1930s it was supporting Japanese expansionism in China with munitions and aircraft. This choice of industry was Nagoya's downfall; very little of the city was left standing after World War II.

Less than two months after the war, ambitious and extensive recon-struction plans were laid, and Nagoya began its remarkable comeback · as an industrial metropolis. Planners laid down a grid system, with wide avenues intersecting at right angles. Hisaya-odōri, a broad avenue with a park in its 328-foot-wide median, bisects the city. At Nagoya's center is an imposing 590-foot-high television tower (useful for get-ting your bearings). Nagoya-jō is north of the tower, Atsuta Jingū to the south, Higashiyama-kōen east, and the JR station west. The Sakae subway station serves as the center of the downtown commercial area. Today Nagoya is home to 2.2 million people living in a 520-square-km (200-square-mi) area.

GETTING HERE AND AROUND

International flights from major airlines arrive at Nagoya's Chūbu International Airport, and frequent bullet trains make it easy to access Nagoya from Tōkyō and Kyōto.

All Nagoya's stations have bilingual maps, and many trains have Eng-lish announcements. The Higashiyama Line runs from the north down to JR Nagoya Station and then due east, cutting through the city center at Sakae. The Meijō Line runs in a loop, passing through the city cen-ter at downtown Sakae. A spur line, the Meitō, connects Kanayama to Nagoya Port. The Tsurumai Line runs north–south through the city, then turns from the JR station to Sakae to cross the city center. A fourth line, the Sakura-dōri, cuts through the city center from the JR station, paralleling the east–west section of the Higashiyama Line. The basic fare is ¥200. A one-day pass for Nagoya's subways costs ¥740, while a combination bus/subway pass is ¥850.

Taxis are parked at all major stations and hotels. Elsewhere it is still far easier to wave one down on the street than to call one of the Japanese-speaking reservation numbers. The initial fare is ¥500. A ride from Nagoya Station to Nagoya-jō costs about ¥1,200.

The JR trains are the easiest for jumping on and off, but they do not serve all destinations. Meitetsu and Kintetsu stations are lacking in English signage, though Meitetsu prints a handy English-language guide to their network with instructions on how to purchase tickets. You can pick up a copy at Meitetsu Nagoya Station or Chūbu International Airport.

Nagoya's subway system is user-friendly, with signs and announcements in English, and accesses almost all places of interest in the city. One-day passes cost ¥740. If you are staying a few days, consider purchasing a *Yurika* discount ticket for multiple trips. Yurika tickets can also be used on city buses and some Meitetsu trains.

The golden **Nagoya Sightseeing Route Bus**, known to locals as the *Me~guru,* provides cheap tours of the city. The service runs on a loop from Nagoya Station, via Noritake Garden, Nagoya-jō, the Tokugawa Art Museum, and Sakae. A hop-on, hop-off ticket for the day costs ¥500, and offers discounts for certain attractions.

JR Nagoya Station 名古屋駅 is like a small city, with a variety of shops in, under, and around the station complex. The main **Nagoya City Tourist Information Center** is in the station's central corridor. English-speaking staff can supply sightseeing information, subway maps, and details of upcoming events. Smaller information centers are in three other parts of the city—**Sakae, Kanayama,** and **Nagoya Port.**

ESSENTIALS

Emergency Contacts Kokusai Central Clinic (⊠ *Nagoya International Center Bldg.* ☎ *052/561–0633).* **Nagoya Medical Center** (⊠ *4–1–1 Sannomaru-ku, Naka-ku, Nagoya* ☎ *052/951–1111).*

Shipping DHL (⊠ *Nagoya Central Service Center, 2-127 Ōsu, Minato-ku, Nagoya* ⊙ *Weekdays 9–7, Sat. 9–4* ☎ *0120/39–2580* ⊕ *www.dhl.com).* **Federal Express** (⊠ *Asaikōsan 7, 1–9–57 Chitose, Atsuta-ku, Nagoya* ⊙ *Weekdays 8:30–8, Sat. 8:30–1* ☎ *0120/00–3200* ⊕ *www.fedex.com).* **Post Office** (⊠ *Central Nagoya Ekimae Bunshitsu 1-1-1 Meieki, Nakamura-ku, Nagoya* ⊙ *weekdays 9–7, Sat. 9–5, Sun. 9–12:30* ☎ *052/564–2103).*

Tour Information Nagoya Sightseeing Route Bus (☎ *052/521–8990* ⊕ *www. ncvb.or.jp/routebus/en/).*

Train Information JR Central Japan (☎ *050/3772–3910 daily 6–midnight* ⊕ *www.jr-central.co.jp).* **Kintetsu** (☎ *052/561–1604 daily 9–7).* **Meitetsu** (⊠ *Meitetsu Customer Center* ☎ *052/582–5151* ⊙ *weekdays 8–7, weekends 8–6* ⊕ *www. meitetsu.co.jp).*

Visitor Information Nagoya City Tourist Information Center (☎ *052/541–4301* ⊙ *daily 9–7).* **Sakae** (⊠ *Oasis 21 bus station and shopping center* ☎ *052/963–5252* ⊙ *daily 10–8).* **Kanayama** (⊠ *North Exit of Kanayama Station* ☎ *052/323–0161* ⊙ *daily 9–8).* **Nagoya Port** (⊠ *next to Nagoya-ko subway station* ☎ *052/654–7000* ⊙ *Tues.–Sun. 9–5).*

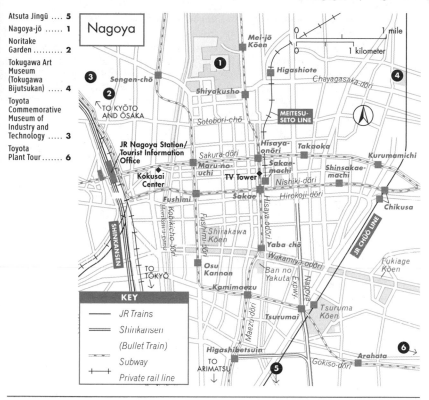

EXPLORING

TOP ATTRACTIONS

4 **Tokugawa Art Museum** 徳川美術館 *(Tokugawa Bijutsukan)*. The seldom-displayed 12th-century hand scrolls of *The Tale of Genji*, widely recognized as the world's first novel are housed here. Even when the scrolls are not available, beautiful relics of the lifestyle of the aristocratic, premodern samurai class—including swords and armor, tea-ceremony artifacts, Nō masks, clothing, and furnishings—fascinate visitors. If you're visiting specifically to see the scrolls, call the museum to make sure they are on display; if not, look for a later copy in Room 6. If you've got time, it's worth paying an additional ¥150 for entry to the adjacent **Tokugawaen** 徳川園, an attractive Japanese garden modeled in the Edo style. Tokugawa Art Museum is a 10-minute walk south of Ōzone Station, which is on the Meijō subway line and the JR Chūō Line. ✉ *1017 Tokugawa-chō, Higashi-ku* ☎ *052/935–6262* ⊕ *www.tokugawa-art-museum.jp* ✉*¥1,200* ⊗ *Museum Tues.–Sun. 10–5, garden Tues.–Sun. 9:30–5:30.*

6 **Toyota Plant Tour** トヨタ工場見学. Dropping in at an automobile factory might not be everyone's idea of holiday fun, but a Toyota Plant Tour makes all those dry books about *kaizen* (improvement) and the Japanese

Fodor'sChoice
★

post-war economic miracle come to life. The tour starts at the **Toyota Kaikan** トヨタ会館 (Toyota Exhibition Hall). After exhibits on hybrid technology, safety, and motor sports, a company bus whisks you to one of several factories in the vicinity. The main assembly shop is something to behold—a hive of modern manufacturing activity where man and machine operate as one. Workers stand or sit on specially designed equipment that moves parallel to the production line so that it never has to pause, and every employee has the authority to stop the line if a fault is identified. In a remarkable feat of logistics, cars of all shapes and sizes are produced individually rather than in batches. English guides are available at the kaikan and factory for the two- to three-hour tour.

■**TIP**➔ A reservation made at least two weeks in advance is required.

The kaikan is about 90 minutes from Nagoya Station. Take the Tsurumai subway line to Toyota-shi, then Meitetsu Bus No. 4 toward Toyota Kinen Byoin, and get off at Toyota Honsha Mae. ⊠ *Toyota Kaikan Exhibition Hall 1, Toyota-cho* ☎ *0565/23–3922* ⊕ *www.toyota.co.jp/en/about_toyota/facility/toyota_kaikan* 🎫 *Free* ⊘ *Mon.–Sat. 9:30–5 except national and summer holidays.*

WORTH NOTING

❶ **Nagoya-jō** 名古屋城. This castle is notable for its size and for the pair of gold-plated dolphins—one male, one female—mounted atop the *donjon* (principal keep). Built on land artificially raised from the flat Nagoya plain, the castle is protected by vast stone walls and two picturesque moats. The current castle is a 1959 reconstruction of the 1612 original, and an elevator whisks you between floors. Between the entrance, where you encounter a full-scale replica of the 2,673-pound female dolphin, and the top floor, which has 360-degree views of modern-day Nagoya, are five floors of exhibits. On the third floor is an evocative re-creation of Edo-era streets, complete with sound effects. Inside the east gate a traditional teahouse built of *hinoki* (Japanese cypress) stands in the **Ninomaru Tei-en** (Ninomaru Gardens), where a traditional tea ceremony costs ¥500. Nagoya-jō's east gate is one block north of the Shiyakusho (City Hall) subway station. ☎ *052/231–1700* 🎫 *¥500* ⊘ *Castle daily 9:30–4:30, garden daily 9:30–5.*

❷ **Noritake Garden** ノリタケの森. Delicate colors and intricate hand-painted designs characterize the china of Noritake, the world's largest manufacturer of porcelain. Its garden complex includes a craft center—effectively a mini-factory where workers demonstrate the 15-step manufacturing process from modeling to glazing to hand painting. You can even paint a design and transfer it to a piece of china. Workshops run 10–4 and cost ¥1,800 plus the price of shipping your piece once it has been fired (only plates can be shipped overseas). The upper floors house a small museum displaying "Old Noritake" works with art nouveau and art deco influences. Browsing is free in the "Celabo" area in the Welcome Center, which shows the diverse industrial applications of ceramics, from circuit boards to racing helmets. There's the odd bargain to be found in the outlet section of the company shop. Noritake Garden is a 15-minute walk north of JR Nagoya Station or five minutes from the Kamejima subway station. ⊠ *3–1–36 Noritake-Shinmachi, Nishi-ku* ☎ *052/561–7114 craft center, 052/561–7290 shop* ⊘ *Craft center*

CLOSE UP

Play Ball!

In Nagoya you will find Japanese sports fans just as entertaining as the action on the field. Ask Tourist Information about upcoming events and where to buy tickets.

BASEBALL

The Chūnichi Dragons play home games at the 40,500-capacity Nagoya Dome. Two leagues of six teams make up Japanese professional baseball, and the Dragons have won the Central League pennant six times and one Japan Series in 1954. In recent years the team is in a groove, reaching the Japan Series in 2004 and 2006 before finally winning it in 2007. Fans here are a bit different—they sing well-drilled songs for each of the batters on their own team, but sit in stony silence when the opposing team is at bat. The season runs from April to October, and tickets for the upper-tier "Panorama" seats start at ¥1,500, rising to ¥5,800 for those behind home plate. Other than when a big team such as the Yomiuri Giants is in town, tickets are usually available at the stadium.

SOCCER

Perennial underachievers Nagoya Grampus always seem to hang around mid-table in J-League Division One. Despite being a founder team of the J-League, and having had star players such as Gary Lineker and Dragan Stojkovic, Grampus have managed only a couple of Emperor's Cup wins. Still, remarkably loyal fans turn up in the thousands to cheer on the team. From March to December they play half their home games in Nagoya at the Mizuho Stadium, where the running track dissipates the atmosphere, and half at the futuristic 45,000-seat Toyota Stadium. Tickets on game day range in price from ¥2,200 to ¥7,000.

SUMŌ

In mid-July Nagoya's Prefectural Gymnasium, situated next to the castle, hosts one of the three sumō tournaments held outside Tōkyō in July each year. The arena holds 8,000 people, and you are almost guaranteed a good view of the dohyō (ring). Tickets, with costs starting at ¥2,800, are often available on the day of the tournament, but it's better to make advance reservations, particularly in the second half of the two-week event. The venue is a two-minute walk from Exit 7 of the Shiyakusho subway station. ✉ Aichi Prefectural Gymnasium 1–1 Ninomaru, Naka-ku ☎ 052/962–9300 ticket sales during the tournament ⊕ www.sumo.or.jp ☰ AE, DC, MC, V.

Tues.–Sun. 10–5, shop Tues.–Sun. 10–6 🖼 *Craft center and museum ¥500. Joint entrance with Toyota Commemorative Museum ¥800.*

❸ Toyota Commemorative Museum of Industry and Technology 産業技術記念館. Housed in the distinctive redbrick buildings of the company's original factory, this museum is dedicated to the rise of Nagoya's most famous company. Toyota's textile-industry origins are explored in the first of two immense halls, with an amazing selection of looms illustrating the evolution of spinning and weaving technologies over the last 200 years. The second, even larger hall focuses on the company's move into auto manufacturing. The museum's main aim is to interest today's Japanese schoolchildren in Nagoya's traditional *monozukuri* (art of making things) industrial culture, and the intimidatingly large halls are broken up into interactive display areas. In the Technoland room you can try out a wind tunnel, navigate a virtual reality maze, and use a massive lever to easily lift a 120-kg (265-lb) engine. The museum is a 20-minute walk north of JR Nagoya Station or 10 minutes from the Kamejima subway station. ✉*4–1–35 Noritake-Shinmachi, Nishi-ku* ☎*052/551–6115* ⊕*www.tcmit.org* ☯*Tues.–Sun. 9:30–5* 🏛*Museum ¥500. Joint entrance with Noritake Garden ¥800.*

❺ Atsuta Jingū 熱田神宮. A shrine has stood at the site of Atsuta Jingū for 1,700 years. After Ise, this is the country's most important Shintō shrine. The Hōmotsukan (Treasure House) holds one of the emperor's three imperial regalia—the Kusanagi-no-Tsurugi (Grass-Mowing Sword). Nestled among 1,000-year-old trees, making it easy to spot from the train, the shrine is an oasis of tradition in the midst of modern industrialism. Sixty festivals and 10 religious events are held here each year—check with the tourist office to see what's going on. From Meitetsu Nagoya Station take the Meitetsu Nagoya Line south to Jingūmae Station. The shrine is across the road from the west exit. ✉*Atsuta-ku* ☎*052/671–4151* ⊕*www.atsutajingu.or.jp/eng/* 🏛*Shrine free, Treasure Museum ¥300* ☯*Daily 9–4:30; closed last Wed. and Thurs. of month.*

OFF THE
BEATEN
PATH

Arimatsu Tie-Dyeing Village *(Arimatsu-Narumi Shibori Mura)*. Arimatsu has been producing *shibori* (tie-dyed cotton) for 400 years. The active tie-dyeing houses and traditional clay-walled buildings line a preserved stretch of the old road that connected Edo-era Tōkyō with Kyōto. At Arimatsu-Narumi Tie-Dyeing Museum (Arimatsu-Narumi Shibori Kaikan), for ¥300 you can learn about the history and techniques of the dyeing process and see demonstrations of current production. The museum sells samples of the cloth, which features striking bright white designs on the deepest indigo, as well as tie-dyed clothing and home furnishings like tablecloths. Arimatsu Station is 20 minutes south of Nagoya on the Meitetsu Nagoya Line. ✉*60–1 Hashi-higashi-minami, Arimatsu-chō, Midori-ku* ☎*052/621–0111* 🏛*Free* ☯*Thurs.–Tues. 9:30–5.*

WHERE TO EAT

Nagoya Station and Sakae have the highest concentrations of restaurants.

$$–$$$
JAPANESE

✗**Daibutsu Korokoro** 大仏ころころ. This *izakaya* (traditional) restaurant has several twists, the main one being the decor. Modern Japanese restaurants should all look like this—dark wood, discreet lighting, and a maze of private dining rooms. A 9½-foot-tall bronze Buddha is in the middle of the restaurant. If anything, the fancy trappings slightly overshadow the food, which includes decent sashimi sets and some inventive tofu dishes. The restaurant is across from the main post office, 1½ blocks north of JR Nagoya Station's Sakura-dōri exit. ✉*Kuwayama Bldg. B1, 2–45–19 Meieki, Nakamura-ku* ☎*052/581–9130* 🍴*AE, DC, MC, V.*

$$–$$$
JAPANESE
★

✗**Ibashō** いば昇. This fabulous old wooden restaurant serves a Nagoya specialty, *hitsumabushi* (chopped eel smothered in miso sauce and served on rice). Ibashō is on Motoshigechō-dōri, two blocks west from Exit 1

On the Menu

Nagoya cuisine is considered hearty, and is famous for its *aka miso* (red miso). Dishes featuring this sticky, sweet paste include *misonikomi udon*, thick noodles cooked in an earthenware pot of miso soup with chicken, egg, wood mushrooms, and green onions (you may want the chili pepper served on the side); *hitsumabushi*, chopped eel cooked in miso, and *miso katsu*, pork cutlet with miso-flavored sauce.

Other local specialties include *kishimen*, velvety smooth flat white noodles; *tebasaki*, deep-fried spicy chicken wings; and *uirō*, a sweet cake made of rice powder and sugar, eaten during the tea ceremony. The highly prized *kō-chin* is a specially fattened and uniquely tender kind of chicken.

of Sakae subway station, and a hitsumabushi set meal is ¥2,400. The restaurant closes at 8 PM and is closed Sunday and the second and third Monday of the month. ⊠ *3–13–22 Nishiki, Naka-ku* ☎ *052/951–1166* ⊟ *No credit cards.*

$$$$
JAPANESE ✕ **Kisoji** 木曽路. Come here for reasonably priced (¥4,300) *shabu-shabu*—thinly sliced beef and vegetables that you boil in broth in the center of your table and then dip into various sauces before eating. Set courses run from ¥5,000 to ¥10,000. There are Western-style tables and chairs, but waitresses wear kimonos. Kisoji is two blocks northwest of the Sakae intersection, on the corner of Nishiki-dōri and Shichiken-chō. ⊠ *3–20–15 Nishiki, Naka-ku* ☎ *052/951–3755* ⊟ *AE, DC, MC, V.*

$$
JAPANESE
★ ✕ **Mokumoku Kaze no Budō** モクモク風の葡萄. In a perfect world, all school and office canteens would be a bit more like this. For ¥2,300 (¥1,800 at lunchtime) you get all you can eat from a generously stocked buffet of healthy vegetable, fish, and meat dishes, plus drinks and dessert, all made from locally sourced produce. Picky eaters can see exactly what they're getting, and there are plenty of options for vegetarians. It is on the 7th floor of the La Chic mall in Sakae. ⊠ *La Chic, 7th fl., 3-6-1 Sakae, Naka-ku* ☎ *052/241–0909* ⊟ *AE, DC, MC, V.*

$–$$
JAPANESE ✕ **Yamamotoya Sohonke** 山本屋総本家. Nothing but *misonikomi-udon* (udon noodles in a hearty, miso-based broth with green onions and mushrooms) is served at this simple restaurant. A big, steaming bowl of this hearty, cold-chasing specialty costs just ¥976. It is halfway between the Fushimi and Yaba-chō subway stations, across the road from the eye-catching Nadya Park building. ⊠ *3–12–19 Sakae, Naka-ku* ☎ *052/241–5617* ⊟ *No credit cards.*

WHERE TO STAY

Nagoya's hotels are concentrated in three major areas: the district around JR Nagoya Station, downtown Fushimi and Sakae, and the Nagoya-jō area.

$$ 🏨 **Fushimi Mont Blanc Hotel** 伏見モンブランホテル. Centrally located and comparatively inexpensive, this business hotel is a good alternative to the luxury hotels. Refurbished in 2008, the rooms are small and simple, but not wanting in any of the standard amenities, and the restaurant serves decent Western and Japanese-style breakfasts for just ¥800. The hotel is eight minutes from Nagoya Station by taxi. **Pros:** affordable; good front desk service; less than 10 minutes' walk into central Sakae. **Cons:** rooms feel a little claustrophobic; can be noisy at times. ✉*2–2–26 Sakae, Naka-ku, Nagoya, Aichi-ken* ☎*052/232–1121* ⊕*www.montblanc-hotel.co.jp* ⌂*In-room: refrigerator, Internet. In-hotel: 2 restaurants, laundry facilities, laundry service, no-smoking rooms* ▭*AE, DC, MC, V.*

$$–$$$ 🏨**Hotel Precede Nagoya** ホテルプリシード名古屋. Bridging the divide between perfunctory business hotels and more deluxe accommodations, this hotel has garnered good reviews from Japanese travelers. The rooms are tastefully decorated in minimal dark browns, and you'll still have plenty of space after bringing in your luggage. It's a five-minute walk from central Sakae, and there is a Starbucks coffee shop on the first floor, while the French café on the second floor offers a breakfast buffet for ¥1,000. **Pros:** good value; convenient location for shoppers and party animals; spacious single rooms. **Cons:** gets booked up quickly; budget travelers will find cheaper rooms elsewhere. ✉*4-6-1 Sakae, Naka-ku,* ☎*052/263–3411* ⊕*www.hotel-precede.com* ⌂*In-room: refrigerator, Internet. In-hotel: 2 restaurants, bar, laundry service, Internet terminal, parking (paid), no-smoking rooms* ▭*AE, DC, MC, V.*

$$$$ 🏨**Nagoya Hilton** ヒルトン名古屋. Soft live music accompanies the nightly
★ dessert buffet and drifts into the cavernous lobby. Pink, green, and gold decorate the large guest rooms, complementing the light-wood furnishings and translucent *shōji* (window screens). Views from the 28th-floor Sky Lounge stretch over the city center and away to the Gifu and Suzuka mountains. The staff is multilingual, and the hotel is five minutes by taxi from Nagoya Station. **Pros:** attentive and flexible staff; convenient location; excellent restaurants. **Cons:** Internet costs extra; tiny swimming pool; some say the level of English is a bit lacking. ✉*1–3–3 Sakae, Naka-ku, Nagoya, Aichi-ken* ☎*052/212–1111* ⊕*www.hilton.com* ⤢*434 rooms, 16 suites* ⌂*In-room: safe, Internet. In-hotel: 4 restaurants, room service, tennis court, pool, gym, children's programs, laundry service, Wi-Fi, parking (paid), some pets allowed, no-smoking rooms* ▭*AE, DC, MC, V.*

$$$–$$$$ 🏨**Nagoya Kankō Hotel** 名古屋観光ホテル. The Imperial Family and pro-
Fodor's Choice fessional ballplayers are among those served by Nagoya's oldest hotel.
★ It's well located and provides the extra class and character you would expect for the price. The lobby's white-brick walls are balanced by soft-tone carpets and dark-wood furnishings. Rooms are spacious, and they look over the city center. The Kankō is five minutes by taxi from Nagoya Station. **Pros:** exceptional service; free parking; good breakfast buffet. **Cons:** plumbing could do with an overhaul; beds can be uncomfortable. ✉*1–19–30 Nishiki, Naka-ku, Nagoya, Aichi-ken* ☎*052/231–7711* ⊕*www.nagoyakankohotel.co.jp* ⤢*375 rooms, 7 suites* ⌂*In-room: safe, refrigerator, Internet. In-hotel: 5 restaurants, room service, bar, gym, laundry service, parking (free), no-smoking rooms* ▭*AE, DC, MC, V.*

$$$$ 🖵 **The Westin Nagoya Castle** ウェスティンナゴヤキャッスルホテル. Perched on the bank of the Nagoya Castle moat, this hotel is a perennial favorite among elderly travelers and has a more relaxed atmosphere than some of the other places in the city. Your room might overlook the beautiful white castle, which is illuminated at night; rooms on the other side look out over a decidedly less attractive elevated expressway. The standard rooms are spacious and conservatively decorated. A free shuttle bus leaves from JR Nagoya Highway Bus Station on the hour from 10 to 8. **Pros:** close to the castle; 1 PM check-in is perfect for sightseers; good facilities. **Cons:** inconvenient for everywhere except the castle; in a dead part of town; bathrooms feel rather clinical. ⊠*3–19 Hinokuchi-chō, Nishi-ku, Nagoya, Aichi-ken* 🕾*052/521–2121* ⊕*www.castle.co.jp/ wnc/* ⤵*195 Western-style rooms, 5 suites* ⚹*In-room: safe (some), Internet. In-hotel: 7 restaurants, room service, bars, pool, gym, spa, children's programs, laundry service, parking (free), no-smoking rooms* ▤*AE, D, DC, MC, V.*

4

NIGHTLIFE

Sakae has a high concentration of restaurants and bars. By day couples and families pack its streets, flitting between boutiques and department stores; at night the area fills with pleasure seekers of all stripes. Most of the good bars are to be found in the narrow streets to the south-west of the Sakae subway station and in the immediate vicinity of the TV tower. Anywhere designated as a "snack" establishment is best avoided unless you've got money to burn.

Close to Exit 5 of the Fushimi subway station, toward the Hilton hotel, is the **Elephant's Nest** (⊠*3–1–4 Sakae, Naka-ku* 🕾*052/232–4360*). This popular English-style pub has Guinness on tap, dart boards, and live soccer on the TV. The food, including fish-and-chips, is okay, too. It's open 5:30–1 Sunday–Thursday and until 2 on Friday and Saturday. Happy Hour is from 5:30 to 7.

The young crowd gathers at the wild, five-floor **iD Cafe** (⊠*Mitsukoshi Bldg., 3–1–15 Sakae, Naka-ku* 🕾*052/251–0382*). On weekday evenings entrance to this club costs ¥1,500, including three drinks. The price rises on weekends, as does the number of drinks.

Urbana Latina (⊠*Koasa Bldg. B1, 4–2–10 Sakae, Naka-ku* 🕾*052/252–0127*), a Brazilian restaurant-cum-bar-cum-club, has something for everyone. There is live music, always with a Latin feel, and no one stays seated for long. Opening hours are 6 PM–2 AM Tuesday–Thursday, until 3 on Friday, 4 on Saturday, and midnight on Sunday and national holidays.

Nagoya is regularly included on international DJs' tour schedules, although you might have to head out on a weekday night to catch the biggest names. Three of the city's best clubs can be found in the **Marumikankō Building** (⊠*4–3–15 Sakae, Naka-ku*), two blocks south of Hirokoji-dōri. On the third and fourth floors, the **Underground** (🕾*052/242–1388* ⊕*www.underground.co.jp*) serves up a steady diet of hip-hop and R&B without the ghetto pretensions of some of the other joints in town. In the basement, **Club JB's** (🕾*052/241–2234*

⊕*www.club-jbs.jp*) is a stronghold for house and techno. **Café Domina** (☎*052/264–3134* ⊕*www.cafe-domina.com*) leans toward more abstract and bass-heavy fare.

SOUTH GIFU-KEN

Old Japan resonates in the foothills of the Hida Sanmyaku (Hida Mountains), just north of Nagoya. Ancient customs and crafts, such as cormorant fishing and umbrella-, lantern-, pottery-, and sword-making, are still practiced, and the nation's oldest castle, Inuyama-jō, has seen it all for almost 500 years. Gifu is the main center of *ukai* (cormorant fishing). Inuyama also offers the fishing experience, and it boasts a superior castle and, in Meiji-mura, an outstanding museum.

GIFU 岐阜

30 km (18 mi) northwest of Nagoya.

Gifu's main attraction is its 1,300-year tradition of cormorant fishing. The city center spreads several blocks north from the JR and Meitetsu stations. Extensive rebuilding after World War II didn't create the prettiest place, but there is plenty going on. *Wagasa* (oiled paper umbrellas) are handmade in small family-owned shops, and *chōchin* (paper lanterns) and laquered *uchiwa* fans are also produced locally. If you are interested in seeing these items being made, ask Tourist Information for workshops that allow visitors.

GETTING HERE AND AROUND
Gifu is a quick 20-minute ride on the JR Tōkaidō Line or Meitetsu Nagoya Line from Nagoya. Gifu Park is 15 minutes by bus or 30 minutes on foot north from JR Gifu Station.

A city **Tourist Information Office** is on the second floor of the train station, just outside the ticket gates.

ESSENTIALS
Visitor Information Tourist Information Office (☎*058/262–4415* ⊙*Daily 10–7*).

WHAT TO SEE
Ukai. Fishing for cormorants, can be seen for free from the banks of the Nagara-gawa, just east of Nagara Bridge at around 7:30 PM. Or you can buy a ticket for one of approximately 130 boats, each carrying from 10 to 30 spectators. Allow two hours for an ukai outing—an hour and a half to eat and drink (bring your own food if you haven't arranged for dinner on board) and a half hour to watch the fishing. Boat trips (¥3,300) begin at around 6 PM nightly from May to October; reservations, made through Gifu City Cormorant Fishing Sightseeing Office or the Tourist Information Center, are essential. There's no fishing when there's a full moon. ☎*058/262–0104 Gifu City Cormorant Fishing Sightseeing Office, 058/262–4415 Tourist Information Office.*

Gifu-jō 岐阜城. The castle, perched dramatically on top of Mt. Kinka, overlooks the city center and Nagara River. The current building dates

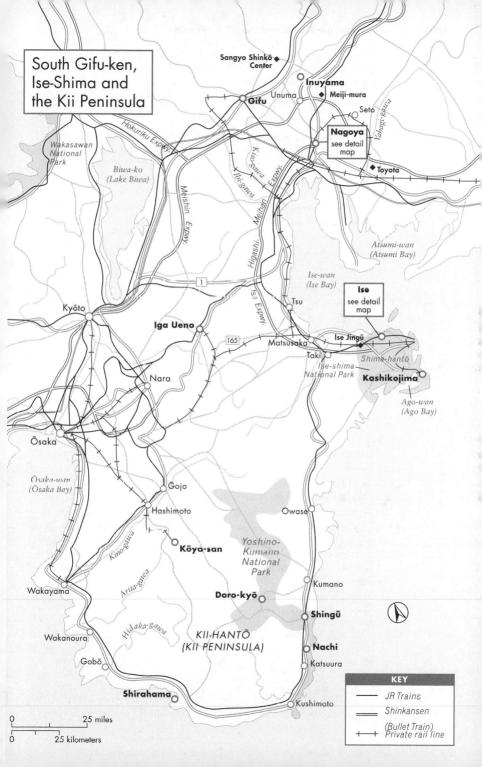

from 1951; the 16th-century structure was destroyed by an 1891 earthquake. A cable-car ride up from Gifu Park (¥600 one-way, ¥1,050 round-trip) gets you to the castle in 10 minutes, or you can walk the 2.3-km (1.5-mi) path to the 329-m summit in about an hour. Take Bus 11 (Nagara–Sagiyama) to Gifu Park (¥300). ⊠*Gifu-jō, Ōmiya-chō* ☎058/263–4853 ☜¥200 ⊙*Daily 9–5.*

☺ **Gifu City Museum of History** 岐阜市歴史博物館. In Gifu Park, five minutes' walk south of the cable-car station, is this hands-on-museum. On the second floor you can dress up in traditional clothing and play old Japanese games such as *bansugoroku* (similar to backgammon). ⊠*2–18–1 Ōmiya-chō* ☎058/265–0010 ☜¥300 ⊙*Tues.–Sun. 9–5.*

Nawa Insect Museum. Located in Gifu Park, this museum houses disturbingly large beetles, butterflies, and other bugs. ⊠*2–18 Ōmiya-chō* ☎058/263–0038 ☜¥500 ⊙*Daily 10–5, end of July–Aug; 9–6, rest of yr.*

Shōhō-ji 正法寺. Japan's third-largest Buddha resides here. This incarnation of Shaka Nyorai (Great Buddha) is 45 feet tall and constructed of pasted-together paper *sutra* (prayers) coated with clay and stucco and then lacquered and gilded; it took 38 years to complete. From Gifu Park, walk two blocks south. ⊠*8 Daibutsu-chō* ☎058/264–2760 ☜¥150 ⊙*Apr.–Nov., daily 9–5; Dec.–Mar., daily 9–4.*

OFF THE BEATEN PATH **Sangyo Shinkō Center** 産業振興センター *(Seki Swordsmith Museum)*. Seki has a 700-year-old sword-manufacturing heritage, and you'll appreciate the artistry and skill of Japanese swordsmiths at the Swordsmith Museum. Three types of metal are used to form blades forged multiple times and beaten into shape with a hammer. Demonstrations are held on January 2 and the first Sundays of March, April, June, and November. Special displays occur during the Seki Cutlery Festival the second weekend of October. Seki is 30 minutes northeast of Gifu via the Meitetsu Minomachi Line. ⊠*9–1 Minamikasuga-chō, Seki-shi* ☎0575/23–3825 ☜¥200 ⊙*Wed.–Mon. 9–4:30.*

WHERE TO EAT AND STAY

$$ ⌂ **Hotel 330 Grand Gifu** ホテル330グランデ岐阜. This tall, relatively modern hotel has larger-than-average, Western-style rooms. Take one facing Kinkazan Park for excellent views toward Gifu Castle and the Nagara River. Hotel 330 is one block north and half a block west of Gifu Station. **Pros:** more spacious than the average business hotel; close to station; 1 PM check-out available. **Cons:** more expensive than the average business hotel; often booked up well in advance. ⊠*5–8 Nagazumi-chō, Gifu-shi, Gifu-ken* ☎058/267–0330 ☎058/264–1330 ⌨119 rooms ⌂*In-room: refrigerator, Internet. In-hotel: restaurant, laundry service, parking (paid), no-smoking rooms* ▭AE, DC, MC, V.

$$$$ ⌂ **Ryokan Sugiyama** 旅館すぎ山. Across the Nagara River from the castle, Sugiyama is a tasteful blend of traditional and modern. The rooms are large, with tatami floors and elegant shōji doors—ask for one overlooking the river. The staff is polite in a mannered way, and the food (included in the room charge) features the ubiquitous ayu. The ryokan is run by the same family whose cormorant fishing masters ply the river every night, and the owner's son speaks excellent English. It

is a 15-minute taxi ride from Gifu Station or a 10-minute walk north of the ukai boat boarding area and the castle. **Pros:** good food; ideally positioned for ukai watchers. **Cons:** not cheap; decor a little threadbare in places. ✉*73–1 Nagara, Gifu-shi, Gifu-ken* ☎*058/231–0161* 🖷*058/233–5250* 📠*46 rooms* ♿*In-room: safe, refrigerator. In-hotel: Japanese bath, restaurant, parking (free)* 🚭*AE, DC, MC, V* 🍴*MAP.*

$ ✕**U no Iori U 鵜の庵　鵜.** Cormorants strut around the Japanese gar-
JAPANESE   den outside this café, where the specialty is *ayu* (sweetfish). The owner boasts of upholding the 1,300-year-old local ukai tradition, and the ayu are prepared every way imaginable. Most popular are ayu-zō*sui, a rice porridge, and ayu-no-narezushi,* a kind of reverse sushi with the ayu stuffed full of rice. It is 1½ blocks west of Ryokan Sugiyama. ✉*94–10 Naka-Ukai, Nagara, Gifu-shi* ☎*058/232–2839* 🚭*No credit cards* ☾*No dinner.*

INUYAMA 犬山

22 km (14 mi) east of Gifu, 32 km (20 mi) north of Nagoya.

Inuyama sits along the Kiso River, on the border between Aichi and Gifu prefectures. A historically strategic site, the city changed hands several times during the Edo period. You can see cormorant fishing here; tickets are available from major hotels for ¥2,500–¥2,800.

GETTING HERE AND AROUND

Access Inuyama on the Meitetsu Kakamigahara line via Gifu or on the Meitetsu Inuyama Line via Nagoya. A good way to see the Kiso-gawa is on a tame raft. To travel the hour-long, 13-km (8-mi) river trip, take the train on the Meitetsu Hiromi Line from Inuyama to Nihon-Rhine-Imawatari. Several companies, including **Kisogawa Kankō,** offer trips for a fixed rate. Call the **Tourist Information office** in the station for information on traveling the river and fishing.

ESSENTIALS

Tour Information Kisogawa Kankō (☎*0574/28–2727* 🎫 *¥3,400*).

Visitor Information Tourist Information office (☎*0568/61–6000*).

WHAT TO SEE

★   **Inuyama-jō 犬山城.** Inuyama's most famous sight is Inuyama-jō, also known as Hakutei-jō (White Emperor Castle). Built in 1537, it is the oldest of the 12 original castles in Japan. The castle is exceedingly pretty, and stands amid carefully tended grounds on a bluff overlooking the Kiso River. Climb up the creaky staircases to the top floor for a great view of the river, city, and surrounding hills. The gift shops at the foot of the castle hill are good for browsing. From Inuyama-Yūen Eki, walk southwest along the river for 15 minutes. ☎*0568/61–1711* 🎫*¥500; joint entrance with Uraku-en ¥1,200* ☾*Daily 9–5.*

Kiso-gawa 木曽川. The pretty stretch of the river that flows beneath cliff-top Inuyama-jō has been dubbed the Japanese Rhine.

Fodor'sChoice   **Meiji-mura 明治村.** Situated in attractive countryside, this expansive site—
★   considered one of Japan's best museums—has more than 60 buildings

originally constructed during the Meiji era (1868–1912), when Japan ended its policy of isolationism and swiftly industrialized. The best way to experience the exhibits is to wander about, stopping to look at things that catch your eye. There's an English pamphlet you receive upon entry to help guide you. If you get tired of walking, transport options within Meiji-mura include a tram originally from Kyōto and a steam train from Yokohama. Among the exhibits are a surprisingly beautiful octagonal wood prison from Kanazawa, a kabuki theater from Ōsaka that hosts occasional performances, and the former homes of renowned writers Sōseki Natsume, Ōgai Mori, and Lafcadio Hearn. The entrance lobby of legendary American architect Frank Lloyd Wright's Imperial Hotel, where Charlie Chaplin and Marilyn Monroe were once guests, is arguably the highlight. It opened on the day of the Great Kanto Earthquake in 1923, 11 years after the death of Emperor Meiji, and though it is not strictly a Meiji-era building, its Mayàn-influenced detailing and sense of grandeur and history are truly unique. Buses run from Inuyama Station to Meiji-mura at 6 and 36 minutes past the hour from 9 to 3. The ride takes 20 minutes and costs ¥410. ⊠ *1 Uchiyama* ☎ *0568/67–0314* ⊕ *www.meijimura.com* ⊠ *¥1,600* ⊙ *Mar.–Oct., daily 9:30–5; Nov.– Feb., daily 9:30–4.*

Jo-an Teahouse 茶室如庵. In Uraku-en, a traditional garden attached to the grounds of the Meitetsu Inuyama Hotel, sits the Jo-an Teahouse. The teahouse was constructed in Kyōto in 1618 and moved to its present site in 1971. Admission to the garden is pricey, so it's worth paying an extra ¥500 to be served green tea in the traditional style. Uraku-en is less than ½ km (¼ mi) from Inuyama-jō, behind the Meitetsu Inuyama Hotel. ⊠ *1 Gomon-saki* ☎ *0568/61–4608* ⊠ *Teahouse and gardens ¥1,000* ⊙ *Mar.–Nov., daily 9–5; Dec.–Feb., daily 9–4.*

HIKING

Tsugao-san 継鹿尾山. A hike to Tsugao-san reveals more pleasant scenery near the Inuyama-jō. Start on the paved riverside trail at the base of Inuyama-jō. Follow the trail east past the Japan Monkey Park, then north to Jakkō-in (built in 654), where the maples blaze in fall. Along the route are good views of the foothills stretching north from the banks of the Kiso-gawa. You can climb Tsugao-san or continue northeast to Ōbora Pond and southeast to Zenjino Station, where you can catch the Meitetsu Hiromi Line two stops back to Inuyama Station. The train passes through Zenjino four times an hour. From Inuyama-jō to Zenjino Station is an 8-km (5-mi) hike. Allow 2½ hours from the castle to the top of Tsugao-san; add another hour if you continue to Zenjino via Ōbora Pond.

WHERE TO STAY

$$–$$$ 🏨 **Meitetsu Inuyama Hotel** 名鉄犬山ホテル. On the south bank of the Kiso-gawa, this hotel has winning views of the river, castle, and hills. The lobby is bright and lively, and the hotel grounds, including the garden Uraku-en and hot-spring baths, are relaxing. Sunny rooms have pleasant vistas; the best face the castle, which overlooks the hotel and is illuminated in the evening. The hotel can arrange tours and is convenient for accessing local sights. **Pros:** convenient for accessing local sights; excellent on-site hot-spring baths. **Cons:** disappointing breakfast buffet; younger travelers are likely to feel a little out of place. ✉ *107–1 Kita-Koken, Inuyama, Aichi-ken* ☎ *0568/61–2211* 🖷 *0568/62–5750* 🛏 *92 Western-style rooms, 34 Japanese-style rooms* ⚭ *In-room: safe, refrigerator, Internet (some). In-hotel: 3 restaurants, room service, bar, Japanese baths, parking (free)* ▤ *AE, DC, MC, V.*

IGA UENO 伊賀上野

95 km (59 mi) southwest of Nagoya, 67 km (42 mi) east of Kyōto, 39 km (24 mi) east of Nara, 88 km (55 mi) east of Ōsaka.

This small city halfway between Nagoya and Nara has some interesting claims to fame. Noted *haiku* poet Matsuo Bashō was born here in the 1640s, and it was home to one of Japan's leading ninja schools. Iga Ueno is accessible from Nagoya, Kyōto, Nara, Ōsaka on the JR.

WHAT TO SEE

⊙ ★ **Iga-Ryū Ninja Museum** 伊賀流忍者博物館. The city makes the most of its major attraction. The Iga-Ryū school of *ninjutsu* (ninja arts) was one of the top two training centers for Japan's ancient spies and assassins in the 14th century. At the *ninja yashiki* (ninja residence), a guide dressed in ninja costume explains how they were always prepared for attack. The hidden doors and secret passages are ingenious, but it can't have been a relaxed existence. Energetic demonstrations of ninja weapons like throwing stars, swords, daggers, and sickles are fun (Dec.–Feb., weekends and holidays 11–3; Mar.–Nov., Wed.–Mon. 11–3), and for ¥200 you can try out the throwing star. Two exhibitions round out the tour. The first gives background on ninja history and techniques, and the second displays the disguises and encryption used by the Iga ninja, as well as the inventive tools that enabled them to walk on water and scale sheer walls. The museum is in Ueno Park, a 10-minute walk up the hill from Iga Ueno Station. ✉ *117–13–1 Ueno Marunouchi* ☎ *0595/23–0311* ⊕ *www.iganinja.jp/en/* 💴 ¥700 ⊙ *Daily 9–5.*

Iga Ueno-jō 伊賀上野城. This castle stands today because of one man's determination and wealth. The first castle built here was destroyed by a rainstorm in 1612, before it was completed. More than 300 years later, local resident Katsu Kawasaki financed a replica that sits atop vertiginous 98-foot stone walls—be careful when it's windy. Kawasaki also paid for the Haiku Poetry Master's Pavilion, built in memory of Japan's famous wandering poet, Matsuo Bashō, which stands near the castle in Ueno Park. ☎ *0595/21–3148* 💴 ¥500 ⊙ *Daily 9–5.*

ISE-SHIMA NATIONAL PARK 伊勢志摩国立公園

Hanging like a fin underneath central Honshū, the Ise-Shima is a scenic and sacred counterweight to Japan's overbuilt industrial corridor. Ise-Shima National Park, which holds the supremely venerated shrines of Ise Jingū, extends east from Ise to Toba (the center of the pearl industry), and south to the indented coastline and pine-clad islands near Kashikojima. The bottom hook of the peninsula, around to Goza via

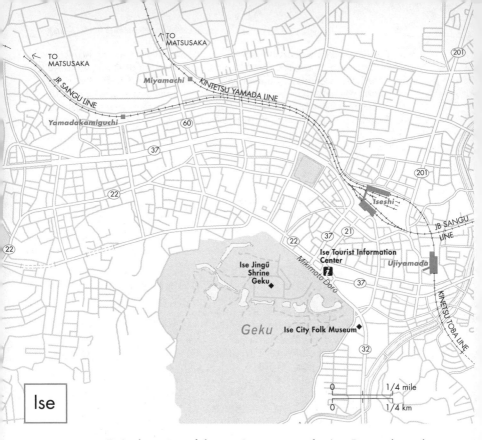

Daiō, has some of the prettiest coves on the Ago Bay, each one home to oyster nets and small groups of fishing boats.

ISE 伊勢

107 km (66 mi) south of Nagoya, 158 km (98 mi) east of Kyōto, 127 km (79 mi) east of Nara, 143 km (89 mi) east of Ōsaka .

When you step off the train, you may feel that Ise is a drab city, but hidden in two forests of towering cedar trees are the most important and impressive Shintō shrines in Japan. Indeed, the city's income comes mainly from the pilgrims who visit Gekū and Naikū, the Outer and Inner shrines, respectively. Near the Inner Shrine you'll find an array of shops hawking souvenirs to the busloads of tourists and a few spots to eat such local specialties as *Ise udon* (udon noodles with a thick broth) and *akafuku* (sweet rice cakes). The busiest times at Ise Jingū are during the Grand Festival, held October 15–17 every year, when crowds gather to see the pageantry, and on New Year's Eve and Day, when hundreds of thousands come to pray for good fortune.

GETTING HERE AND AROUND

Ise can be reached from Kyōto, Nara, and Ōsaka by JR and Kintetsu lines, with the latter's Limited Express service from Nagoya being the fastest option. The city has two stations five minutes apart, Ise-shi (JR and Kintetsu) and Uji-Yamada (Kintetsu only).from either station it's only a 10-minute walk through town to the Outer Shrine. A frequent shuttle bus makes the 6-km (4-mi) trip between Gekū and Naikū; a bus also goes directly from the Inner Shrine to Ise Station.

You can arrange a full-day tour to Ise and the Mikimoto Pearl Island at Toba from Nagoya (¥19,800) or Kyōto (¥25,300) through **JTB Sunrise Tours.**

Ise Tourist Information Center is across the street from the Outer Shrine, and has information about both Ise and the surrounding area.

ESSENTIALS

Tour Information JTB Sunrise Tours Central Japan (Nagoya) (☎ *052/211–3065* ⊕ *www.jtb-sunrisetours.jp*).

Visitor Information Ise Tourist Information Center (☎ *0596/28–3705* ⊕ *www. ise-kanko.jp/english/index.html* ⊙ *8:30–5*).

WHAT TO SEE

Fodor'sChoice
★

Ise Jingū 伊勢神宮 *(Grand Shrines of Ise).* The shrines are rebuilt every 20 years in accordance with Shintō tradition. To begin a new generational cycle, exact replicas of the previous halls are erected with new wood, using the same centuries-old methods, on adjacent sites. The old buildings are then dismantled. The main halls you see now—the 61st set—were completed in 1993 at an estimated cost of more than ¥4.5 billion. For the Japanese, importance is found in the form of the buildings; the vintage of the materials is of little concern. You cannot enter any of the buildings, but the tantalizing glimpses of the main halls that you catch while walking the grounds add to the mystique of the site.

Deep in a park of ancient Japanese cedars, **Gekū**, dating from AD 477, is dedicated to Toyouke Ō-kami, goddess of agriculture. Its buildings are simple, predating the influx of 6th-century Chinese and Korean influence. It's made from unpainted *hinoki* (cypress), with a closely cropped thatched roof. You can see very little of the exterior of Gekū—only its roof and glimpses of its walls—and none of the interior. Four fences surround the shrine, and only the imperial family and their envoys may enter.

The same is true for the even more venerated **Naikū**, 6 km (4 mi) southwest of Gekū. Naikū is where the Yata-no-Kagami (Sacred Mirror) is kept, one of the three sacred treasures of the imperial regalia. The shrine, said to date from 4 BC, also houses the spirit of the sun goddess Amaterasu, who Japanese mythology says was born of the left eye of Izanagi, one of the first two gods to inhabit the earth. According to legend, Amaterasu was the great-great-grandmother of the first mortal emperor of Japan, Jimmu. Thus, she is revered as the country's ancestral goddess-mother and guardian deity. The Inner Shrine's architecture is simple. If you did not know its origin, you might call it classically modern. The use of unpainted cypress causes Naikū to blend into the ancient forest encircling it.

Both Grand Shrines exhibit a natural harmony that the more contrived buildings in later Japanese architecture do not. You can see very little of either through the wooden fences surrounding the shrines, but the reward is in the spiritual aura surrounding Naikū and Gekū. This condition, where the inner experience is assigned more importance than the physical encounter, is very traditional Japanese. Entry to the grounds of both shrines, which are open sunrise to sunset, is free. If you are pressed for time, head for the more impressive Naikū first.

WHERE TO EAT AND STAY

$
★
🏨 **Hoshide–kan.** This 85-year-old traditional-style inn has wood-decorated tatami rooms and narrow squeaking corridors. The hosts are congenial and considerate—they provide dinner at a table for those tired of sitting on the floor, and vegetarian and macrobiotic meals if requested in advance. Hoshidekan is near the quaint Kawasaki area, 5 minutes' walk north from the Kintetsu station or 10 minutes from the JR station. Follow the main street and it's on the right just before the second set of signals. Ise will become a "bicycle town" in 2010, and if you want to explore the city on two wheels, the hotel rents them for ¥300 a day. **Pros:** foreigner friendly; good location. **Cons:** dead zone after 9 PM; at the mercy of the elements during summer and winter. ✉ *2–15–2 Kawasaki, Ise, Mie-ken* ☎ *0596/28–2377* 📠 *0596/27–2830* ➘ *10 Japanese-style rooms with shared bath* ⚑ *In-hotel: Japanese baths, restaurant, laundry facilities, Internet terminal, parking (free)* ▤ *AE, MC, V* ⦿ *MAP.*

$$–$$$
JAPANESE
✕ **Izakaya Toramaru** 虎丸. This izakaya (traditional-style) restaurant won't open on days when they aren't able to get a fresh delivery of fish, which tells you how seriously they take their food. Though there is a fairly diverse menu, the main draw here is the expertly prepared sashimi, served in haphazardly shaped pottery dishes. Ask the staff to recommend a good drink from the extensive selection of Japanese sake and shochu. Izakaya Toramaru is housed in a replica warehouse two blocks west of Hoshidekan. ✉ *2–13–6 Kawasaki, Ise-shi* ☎ *0596/22–9298* ▤ *No credit cards* ⦿ *Closed Thurs. No lunch.*

$$$$
JAPANESE
★
✕ **Restaurant Wadakin** 和田金. If you love beef, make a pilgrimage to Matsusaka, one train stop north of Ise. Wadakin claims to be the originator of Matsusaka beef's fame; the cattle are raised with loving care on the restaurant's farm out in the countryside. Sukiyaki or the chef's steak dinner will satisfy your cravings. ✉ *1878 Naka-machi, Matsusaka* ☎ *0598/21–1188* ▤ *No credit cards* ⦿ *Closed 4th Tues. of month.*

KASHIKOJIMA 賢島

25 km (16 mi) south of Toba, 145 km (90 mi) south of Nagoya.

GETTING HERE AND AROUND

Kashikojima can be reached on the Kintetsu Line from Toba or Nagoya or by bus from Toba. To take a coastal route, get off the train at Ugata and take a bus to Nakiri; then change buses for one to Goza, where frequent ferries return across the bay to Kashikojima.

The Pearl Divers

At Toba, before Kokichi Mikimoto (1858–1954) perfected a method for cultivating pearls here in 1893, Ama, or female divers (women were believed to have bigger lungs), would dive all day, bringing up a thousand oysters, but they wouldn't necessarily find a valuable pearl. Pearl oysters are now farmed, and the famous female divers are a dying breed. On the outlying islands, however, women do still dive for abalone, octopus, and edible seaweed. The **Mikimoto Pearl Museum** ミキモト真珠博物館 *(Mikimoto Shinju no Hakubutsukan)*, on Pearl Island, 500 yards southeast from Toba Station, explores the history of pearl diving in Japan. ☎ *0599/25–2028* ⊕ *www.mikimoto-pearl-museum.co.jp* ✉ *¥1,500* ⊙ *Apr.–Nov., daily 8:30–5:30; Dec. daily 9–4:30; Jan.–Mar., daily 8:30–5.*

Take one of two routes from Ise to Toba: a 45-minute bus ride from near Naikū, for ¥810, or the more scenic JR train, for ¥230. **Toba Tourist Information Center** (☎ *0599/25–2844*), outside Exit 1 of Kintetsu Toba Station, has an English map of the main attractions. Open 9–5:30.

It's possible to follow the coast from Kashikojima to the Kii Peninsula, but there is no train, and in many places the road cuts inland, making the journey long and tedious. From Kashikojima or Toba you are better off taking the Kintetsu Line back to Ise to change to the JR Sangū Line and travel to Taki, where you can take the JR Kisei Line south to the Kii Peninsula.

WHAT TO SEE

★ The jagged coastline at Ago-wan (Ago Bay), with calm waters and countless hidden coves, presents a dramatic final view of the Ise Peninsula. The best approach to Kashikojima is to catch a bus to Goza, the tip of the headland, and ride a ferry back across the bay. From the boat you'll get a close-up look at the hundreds of floating wooden rafts from which the pearl-bearing oysters are suspended.

Tucked behind a promontory, the fishing village of **Daiō** 大王 is an interesting stop on the journey around the headland. At a small fish market you can buy fresh squid, mackerel, and other seafood. Standing above the village is a 46-meter-tall lighthouse, **Daiōzaki tōdai,** open to visitors daily 9–5 for an entrance fee of ¥200. To reach this towering white structure, walk up the narrow street lined with fish stalls and pearl souvenir shops at the back of the harbor. From this lighthouse you can see **Anorizaki tōdai,** a stone lighthouse built in 1973, 11 km (7 mi) east.

WHERE TO STAY

$ ▦**Daiōsō** 大王荘. Staying at this small family-run ryokan next to the harbor in Daiō allows you to enjoy the peaceful evening after the tourists have left and witness the early-morning activity of the fishermen. A good *izakaya* (traditional-style) restaurant is attached to the ryokan. Lunch and dinner are served every day, with fresh *Ise ebi* (lobster) the main attraction. Western-style rooms are available, but try to get one of the Japanese-style tatami rooms overlooking the water. Daiō can be reached by bus from Ugata, and the harbor bus stop is just 20 meters from the ryokan. **Pros:** reasonably priced; on the harbor; good if you like fish. **Cons:** some spoken Japanese essential; Western-style rooms are drab. ⊠ *244 Namigiri, Shima, Mie-ken* ☎*0599/72–1234* 🖷*0599/72–0489* 📞*7 rooms* ᐃ *In-room: safe, refrigerator (some), Internet. In-hotel: restaurant, parking (free)* ☐*DC, MC, V* 🍴*MAP.*

$–$$ 🖳 **Ishiyama-sō** 石山荘. On tiny Yokoyama-jima in Ago-wan, this small
★   inn has painted its name in large letters on the red roof. Ishiyama-sō is a two-minute ferry ride from Kashikojima; phone the day before, and your hosts will meet you at the quay. The inn isn't fancy, but it offers rooms overlooking the sea. You'll find tea sets and *yukata* (Japanese bathrobes) in the rooms. Breakfast and dinner, included in the room rate during peak season, are served in the communal dining hall. Room-only rates are available off-season. **Pros:** idyllic setting; doesn't get much more remote than this. **Cons:** no frills; limited dining options if you don't eat in. ⊠ *Yokoyama-jima, Kashikojima, Ago-chō, Shima-gun, Mie-ken* ☎*0599/52–1527* 🖷*0599/52–1240* 📞*6 rooms* ᐃ*In-room: safe. In-hotel: Wi-Fi, Japanese baths* ☐*MC, V* 🍴*MAP.*

KII PENINSULA 紀伊半島

Beyond Ise-Shima, the Kii Peninsula has magnificent marine scenery, coastal fishing villages, beach resorts, and the temple mountain of Kōya-san. Wakayama Prefecture, which constitutes much of the Kii Peninsula, has a population of only 1 million, and life here moves at a relaxed pace. From Shingū you can reach all three great shrines of the Kumano Kodō pilgrimage route. Nearby Yoshino-Kumano National Park has pristine gorges, holy mountains, and another ancient Buddhist site at Yoshino-san, where gorgeous hillside sakura flower in early April.

SHINGŪ 新宮

138 km southwest of Taki, 231 km southwest of Nagoya.

GETTING HERE AND AROUND

You can reach Shingū by JR Limited Express from Taki or the JR Line from Nagoya. The **Shingū Tourist Association Information Center** is to the left as you exit the station.

ESSENTIALS

Visitor Information Shingū Tourist Association Information Center (☎*0735/22–2840* ⏱ *Daily 9–5:30).*

WHAT TO SEE

Shingū is home to one of the three great shrines of the Kumano Kodo, **Hayatama-taisha** 速玉大社 (daily 9–4:30). One of the few north–south roads penetrating the Kii Peninsula begins in town and continues inland to Nara by way of Doro-kyō (Doro Gorge). A drive on this winding, steep, narrow road, especially on a bus, warrants motion-sickness pills. The mossy canyon walls outside your window and the rushing water far below inspire wonder, but frequent sharp curves provide plenty of anxiety. Continue north on the road past Doro-kyō to reach **Hongū**

本宮 (daily 9–4:30), which has attractive wooden architecture and a thatched roof.

WHERE TO STAY

$$ ▦ **Shingū UI Hotel.** Better than the average business hotel, fair-size rooms and an easily accessible location make this a good option if you're staying overnight in Shingū. It's a five-minute walk from the train station. **Pros:** convenient base for day-trippers; decent service. **Cons:** perfunctory decor; showing its age. ✉ *3–12 I-no-sawa, Shingū-shi, Wakayama-ken* ☎ *0735/22–6611* 📠 *0735/22–4777* 🛏 *82 Western-style rooms* ♿ *In-room: refrigerator, Internet (some). In-hotel: 2 restaurants, laundry service, parking (free)* ▤ *AE, DC, MC, V.*

DORO-KYŌ 瀞峡

20 km (12 mi) north of Shingū.

The wide ocean views of the coastal journey to Shingū give way to gorges and mountainsides of a deep mossy green when you pass through the tunnel five minutes north of the city. Up the Kumano River, the walls of the steep-sided Doro-kyō rise above you. Farther up, sheer 150-foot cliffs tower over the Kumano-gawa.

Kumano Kyōtsu runs tours of the gorge (¥4,800) that depart from Shingū station. A bus goes as far as Shiko, and then a flat-bottomed, fan-driven boat travels upriver to Doro-hatchō and back again. Outside seats on the boats are the best. You can book a trip at the information center at Shingū station.

NACHI

13 km (8 mi) southwest of Shingū.

Nachi-no-taki 那智の滝, the highest waterfall in Japan, drops 430 feet into a rocky river. At the bus stop near the falls a large torii gate marks the start of a short path that leads to a paved clearing near the foot of the falls. A 20-minute bus ride (¥470) from Nachi Station gets you here.

A 15-minute climb up the mossy stone path opposite the souvenir shops is **Nachi Taisha** (daily 9–4:30), reputed to be 1,400 years old and perhaps the most impressive of the Kumano Kodo shrines. For ¥200 you can ride an elevator to the top of the bright red pagoda for an on-high view of the waterfall.

Next to the shrine is the 1587 Buddhist temple Seiganto-ji, starting point for a 33-temple Kannon pilgrimage through western Honshū. Many visitors walk here from a point several kilometers away on the road to Nachi Station. The temple grounds offer mountain views to the southwest.

Five miles from Kushimoto, **Shio-no-misaki** 潮岬 is Honshū's southernmost point. Stationed high above the rocky cliffs is a white lighthouse that unfortunately closes before sunset (open 9–4, ¥150). Adjacent to the lighthouse is a good spot for picnics and walking on the cliff paths.

The beach looks inviting, but sharp rocks and strong currents make swimming a bad idea.

Nachi can be reached by JR via Shingū.

SHIRAHAMA 白浜

82 km (51 mi) west of Nachi, 178 km (111 mi) south of Ōsaka.

Rounding the peninsula, 54 km (34 mi) northwest of Shio-no-misaki, Shirahama is a small headland famous for its pure white-sand beach. If you're wondering why it looks and feels so different from the other beaches, it's because this sand is imported from Australia. Hot springs are dotted along the beach and around the cape. The climate, which allows beach days even in winter, makes Shirahama an inviting base for exploring the area. While it can be intolerably busy in July and August, it is otherwise pretty laid-back. JR trains from Nachi and Ōsaka run tp Shirahama. A 17-minute bus ride from the train station gets you to the beachside town.

WHAT TO SEE

Fodor'sChoice
★

Sakino-yu Onsen 崎の湯温泉. Soak in this open-air hollow among the wave-beaten rocks facing the Pacific, where it's said that Emperors Saimei (594–661) and Mōmmu (683–707) once bathed. It's at the south end of the main beach, below Hotel Seamore. ✉¥300 ☼ *Dawn–dusk, Thurs.–Tues.*

Shirara-yu Onsen しらら湯温泉. At the north end of the beach, locals come and go all day to bathe and chat. The baths overlook the beach and ocean from the second floor of this old wooden building, and on the first floor is an open lounge area. You can rent or buy towels, but bring your own toiletries. It's a two-minute walk north of Shirara Minshuku. ✉¥300 ☼ *Daily 7–11.*

WHERE TO STAY

$–$$

🏨 **Shirara Minshuku** 南紀白浜民宿しらら. This friendly hotel right off the beach in Shirahama is a good alternative to the expensive resorts. The Japanese-style rooms are simple, and there is a natural hot-spring bath. The restaurant serves fresh local seafood in a variety of styles, including *funamori,* fresh sashimi, served on a boat. It is just across the road from the Shirarahama bus stop. **Pros:** great location; reasonably priced. **Cons:** rudimentary furnishing; 10:30 PM curfew prevents midnight dips. ✉1359 *Shirahama-chō, Nishimuro-gun, Wakayama-ken* ☎0739/42–3655 🖷0739/43–5223 ➴18 *Japanese-style rooms* ☼ *In-room: safe. In-hotel: restaurant, parking (free)* ☐*No credit cards.*

KŌYA-SAN 高野山

63 km east of Wakayama, 64 km southeast of Ōsaka.

★   This World Heritage Site is the headquarters of the Shingon sect of Buddhism, founded by Kūkai, also known as Kōbō Daishi, in AD 816.

Every year a million visitors pass through Kōya-san's **Dai-mon** 大門 *(Big Gate)* to enter the great complex of 120 temples, monasteries, schools, and graves. Traveling to Kōya-san takes you through mountain wilderness, but the town itself is sheltered and self-contained. The main buildings are imposing, while the minor temples are in a wide range of styles and colors, each offering small-scale beauty in its decor or garden. Monks, pilgrims, and tourists mingle in the main street, the sneaker-wearing, motorcycle-riding monks often appearing the least pious of all.

GETTING HERE AND AROUND

If you approach Kōya-san by cutting across the Yoshino-Kumano National Park by bus from Shingū or Hongu on Route 168, get off the bus at Gojo and backtrack one station on the JR Line to Hashimoto; then take the Nankai Line.

By rail, the last leg of the trip is a five-minute cable-car ride (¥380) from Gokuraku-bashi Station. JR Passes are not valid for the cable car. The lift deposits you at the top of 3,000-foot Kōya-san, where you can pick up a map and hop on a bus to the main attractions, which are about 2½ km (1½ mi) from the station and 4 km (2½ mi) from each other on opposite sides of town. Two buses leave the station when the cable car arrives, which is every 20 or 30 minutes. One goes to Okuno-in Cemetery, on the east end of the main road, and the other goes to the Dai-mon, to the west.

Kōya-san Tourist Association office at the intersection in the center of town can be reached by bus for ¥300.

ESSENTIALS

Visitor Information **Kōya-san Tourist Association office** (*600 Kōya-san, Kōya-chō, Ito-gun, Wakayama-ken 0736/56–2616).*

WHAT TO SEE

Okuno-in 奥の院. If time is limited, head for this memorial park, first. Many Japanese make pilgrimages to the mausoleum of Kōbō Daishi or pay their respects to their ancestors buried here. Arrive early in the morning, before the groups take over, or even better, at dusk, when it gets wonderfully spooky.

Exploring this cemetery is like peeking into a lost and mysterious realm. Incense hangs in the air, and you can almost feel the millions of prayers said here clinging to the gnarled branches of 300-year-old cedar trees reaching into the sky. The old-growth forest is a rarity in Japan, and among the trees are buried some of the country's most prominent families, their graves marked by mossy pagodas and red-robed Bodhisattvas.

You can reach Okuno-in by way of the 2½-km (1½-mi) main walkway, which is lined with more than 100,000 tombs, monuments, and statues. The lane enters the cemetery at Ichi-no-hashi-guchi; follow the main street straight east from the town center for 15 minutes to find this small bridge at the edge of the forest.

The path from Okuno-in-mae ends at the refined **Tōrō-dō** 灯籠堂 *(Lantern Hall)*, named after its 11,000 lanterns. Two fires burn in this hall; one has reportedly been alight since 1016, the other since 1088. Behind the hall is the mausoleum of Kōbō Daishi. The hall and the mausoleum altar are extremely beautiful, with subtle lighting and soft gold coloring. ⊞*Free* ⊘*Lantern Hall Apr.–Oct., daily 8–5; Nov.–Mar., daily 8:30–4:30.*

Kongōbu-ji 金剛峯寺. On the southwestern side of Kōya-san, Kongōbu-ji is the chief temple of Shingon Buddhism. It was first built in 1592 as the family temple of Hideyoshi Toyotomi, and rebuilt in 1861 to become the main temple of the Kōya-san community. The screen-door artwork and large-scale rock garden are noteworthy. ⊞*¥500* ⊘*Apr.–Oct., daily 8–5; Nov.–Mar., daily 8:30–4:30.*

Danjō Garan 壇上伽藍 *(Sacred Precinct).* The Danjō Garan boasts several outsize halls. The most striking is the **Kompon-daitō** (Great Central Pagoda). This red pagoda with an interior of brightly colored beams contains five large seated gold Buddhas. Last rebuilt in 1937, the two-story structure has an unusual style and rich vermilion color. From Kongōbu-ji walk down the temple's main stairs and take the road to the right of the parking lot in front of you; in less than five minutes you will reach Danjō Garan. ⊞ *Kompon-daitō ¥200* ⊘*Daily 8:30–5.*

Reihōkan 霊宝館 *(Treasure Hall).* Here you'll find a collection of more than 5,000 well-preserved Buddhist relics, some dating back 1,000 years. The New Wing houses themed exhibitions of sculpture, painting, and artifacts. The Old Wing (confusingly marked "Exit") has a permanent exhibition of Buddha and Bodhisattva figures and calligraphic scrolls. The museum is across the road from the Danjō Garan. ⊞*¥600* ⊘*Daily 8:30–5:30.*

WHERE TO STAY

Kōya-san has no modern hotels; however, 53 of the temples offer Japanese-style accommodations—tatami floors, futon mattresses, and traditional Japanese shared baths. You eat the same food as the priests. Dinner and breakfast is *shōjin ryōri,* vegetarian cuisine that uses locally made tofu. Prices start from ¥9,500 per person, including meals. Only a few temples accept foreign guests, so an advance reservation is advisable, especially in October, when crowds come for the autumn leaves. Arrangements can be made through Kōya-san Tourist Association, the Nankai Railway Company office in Namba Station (Ōsaka), and the Japan Travel Bureau in most Japanese cities.

$–$$ ⊞**Rengejō-in** 蓮華定院. Rengejō-in is an especially lovely temple where both the head priest and his mother speak English. For the basic price you get two meals and a simple tatami room with a TV. Pay a bit extra and you get a larger room with garden views both front and back. There is a meditation session held before dinner and a prayer service at 6 AM. From the cable-car terminus, take the bus and get off at the Ishinguchi stop. Rengejō-in is right next-door. **Pros:** excellent vegetarian food; very accommodating to foreigners. **Cons:** opposite end of town from Okuno-in; may prove a little too austere for some. ⊠*700 Kōya-san,* ☎*0736/56–2233* 🖷*0736/56–4743* 🖃*46 rooms* ⚒*In-room: safe, no phone* ⊟*No credit cards.*

The Japan Alps and the North Chūbu Coast

WORD OF MOUTH

"The town of Tsumago is absolutely delightful. You feel as though you have stepped back in time a couple of hundred years. From the main street you cannot see any power lines, all the electric lights are enclosed inside a lamp so they just have a soft glow and there is not one modern building in the main part of the village. It is all just beautiful old wooden constructions."

—Shandy

Updated by
Robert Morel

Escape from Japan's cities to this central alpine region for snow-topped mountains, coastal cliffs, open-air hot springs, and superb hiking and skiing. Many traditional villages are virtually untouched by development. Towns within the North Chūbu region (Fukui, Ishikawa, Toyama, Niigata, Nagano, and Gifu prefectures) have largely maintained their distinctive architecture. In Ogi-machi and Hida Minzoku Mura, sturdy wooden houses with thatched roofs have open-hearth fireplaces.

Famous temples such as Fukui's Zen Eihei-ji, Nagano's Zenkō-ji, and Kanazawa's Nichiren Myōryū-ji (locally called Ninja-dera or the temple of the Ninja) are symbols of the region's religious history.

Traditional arts are celebrated at annual events like Sado-ga-shima's three-day Earth Celebration, with Taiko (drum) group Kodō and the more solemn *okesa* (folk dances), and the riotous Seihakusai festival in Nanao on Noto Peninsula. Before the Tōkaidō highway was built along the Pacific coast and the Chūō train line was connected to Nagoya and Niigata, this region was extremely isolated, which led to the development of highly skilled craftsmanship. Japanese ceramics, pottery, art, and scrolls are exhibited at folklore museums, and you can watch craftspeople dye linens, paint silk for kimonos, carve wood, and hand-lacquer objects in workshops.

⇨ *See the glossary at the end of this book for definitions of the common Japanese words and suffixes used in this chapter.*

ORIENTATION AND PLANNING

ORIENTATION

The label Japan Alps does not refer to a defined political region; it's a name for the mountains in Chūbu, the Middle District. Chūbu encompasses nine prefectures in the heart of Honshū, three of which—Gifu-ken, Nagano-ken, and Yamanashi-ken—make up the central highlands. Between the Alps and the sea is a narrow coastal belt known as Hokuri-ku, comprised of Kanazawa, Fukui, and the rugged coastline of the Noto Peninsula. Heavy snowfall in winter and hot summers make this region ideal for growing rice. Niigata and Sado Island form the northeastern coast.

The Japan Alps. The Alps are divided into three ranges, the Northern Hida Mountains, the central Kiso range, and the Southern Alps of Akaishi. The northern region is the most popular for hiking and skiing and is easily accessed from Matsumoto or Nagano. The jagged

TOP REASONS TO GO

Onsen: The salty, calcium-rich waters of coastal onsen and iron- and sulfur-heavy ones in the mountains claim to benefit skin, bone, and mental health. Relaxation and rejuvenation guaranteed.

Hiking: The Japan Alps offer staggering views and a serious workout. Trails wind through peaks, and summer brings wildflowers to the highland slopes and valleys.

Skiing: The resorts around Nagano to attract outdoor enthusiasts, particularly on weekends. Shiga Kōgen, near Yudanaka, and Happō-o-ne, near Hakuba, are among the best areas.

Glimpses of Feudal Japan: Visit the former samurai quarters Kanazawa's Nagamachi section. Matsumoto castle, surrounded by merchant houses, evokes the history of a strictly hierarchical society.

Folk Art: Kanazawa is renowned for dyed silk, gilded crafts, and pottery; Matsumoto has excellent wood craftsmanship. Lacquer is a specialty of the Noto Peninsula.

snowcapped peaks interspersed with high basins reach elevations of 9,850 feet. Mostly forested, they are covered with alpine flora in the warmer months. Hot springs are scattered throughout this volcanic region.

Kanazawa and the North Chūbu Coast. Ishikawa Prefecture stretches long and narrow from north to south; thus the topographies of the Noto and the southern Kaga are significantly different. Kanazawa, as the center of the administration, economy, and culture of Kaga, has mountains and fertile plains, and is also renowned for traditional crafts. The northern part, the Noto-hantō Peninsula, has two contrasting coastlines. The Sea of Japan side is severely eroded, while the southern coast hems a becalmed bay.

PLANNING

WHEN TO GO

Temperatures vary widely from the coastal areas to the mountains. Hikers should bring warm clothes even in the summer. May, June, and September are the best months, when transportation is safe and reliable, and there aren't too many sightseers. At the height of summer, from mid-July to the end of August, the Alps and coastal regions are the getaway for those fleeing the stagnant heat of urban Japan—expect throngs of tourists and lofty prices. The skiing season peaks over Christmas and New Year's. Winter's heavy snows make driving around the Alps difficult or impossible, and only a few buses and trains run per day. Unless you've got skiing to do, and a direct train to get there, winter is not ideal.

HOW MUCH TIME?

A quick loop of the major towns and destinations—the Alps, the Noto-Hantō (Noto Peninsula), the Chūbu Coast, and Sado-ga-shima—takes over a week. To enjoy the unique scenery and culture of the region,

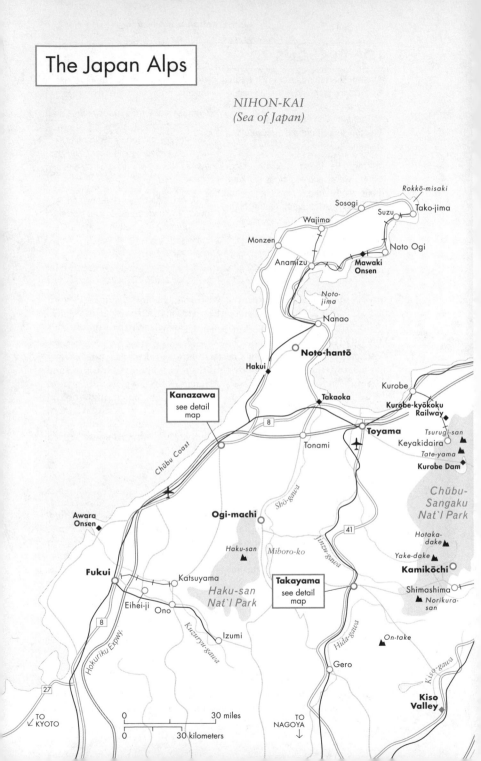

The Japan Alps

NIHON-KAI
(Sea of Japan)

Rokkō-misaki
Sosogi
Tako-jima
Suzu
Wajima
Monzen
Noto Ogi
Anamizu
Mawaki
Onsen
Noto-jima
Nanao
Noto-hantō
Hakui
Kurobe
Takaoka
Kurobe-kyōkoku Railway

Kanazawa
see detail
map

8
Tonami
Toyama
Tsurugi-san
Keyakidaira
Tate-yama
Kurobe Dam

Chūbu Coast

Chūbu-Sangaku Nat'l Park

Awara
Onsen
Ogi-machi
Shō-gawa

41
Hotaka-dake
Yake-dake
Kamikōchi

Haku-san
Miboro-ko
Jinzu-gawa

Fukui
Katsuyama
Shimashima
Norikura-san

Takayama
see detail
map

Eihei-ji
Ono
*Haku-san
Nat'l Park*
On-take

8
Izumi
Kuzuryu-gawa
Hida-gawa

Hokuriku Expwy.
Gero
Kiso-gawa

27
**Kiso
Valley**

TO
KYOTO

0   30 miles

0   30 kilometers

TO
NAGOYA

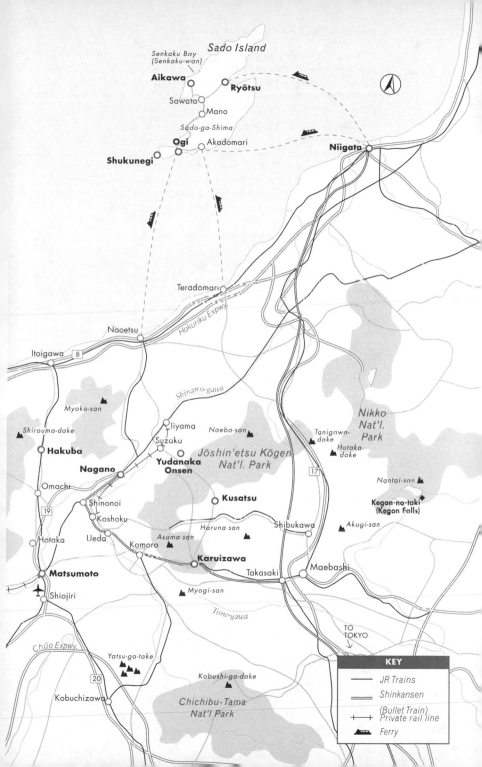

it is best to choose two or three cities as sightseeing hubs. In the Alps region, frequent trains run north and south through the mountain valleys, while cutting across the mountains east to west and visiting smaller towns requires more planning. Local tourist offices can supply you with detailed bus and train information for the surrounding area.

GETTING HERE AND AROUND

Travel in the Alps is largely restricted to the valleys and river gorges that run north and south. The only east–west route is through the mountains, between Matsumoto and Takayama. It's easier to go along the coast and through the foothills of Fukui, Ishikawa, Toyama, and Niigata, except in winter when Fukui gets hit with furious blizzards. In Noto-hantō, buses and trains can be relied on for trips to key places.

AIR TRAVEL

The major airport in the area is Komatsu Kūkō in Kanazawa, although there are daily flights from Fukuoka, Ōsaka, and Sapporo to Matsumoto and Toyama for those wanting to reach the Alps quickly. Since the opening of the airport in Wajima, you can reach the Noto Peninsula in one hour from Tōkyō. The recently opened Chūbu International Airport (Centrair) has frequent domestic and international flights.

BUS AND TRAIN TRAVEL

Whether to take the bus or the train isn't usually a choice, because there is often only one form of public transportation. Not all train lines in Nagano Prefecture are JR, so budget in additional charges if you are traveling on a rail pass.

Tōkyō–Nagano Shinkansen service has effectively shortened the distance to the Alps from the east: the trip on the Nagano Shinkansen takes only about 90 minutes. From Kyōto and Nagoya the Alps are three hours away on the Hokuriku and Takayama lines. Unless you are coming from Niigata, you will need to approach Takayama and Kanazawa from the south (connections through Maibara are the speediest) on JR.

CAR TRAVEL

To really explore the area, rent a car in Kanazawa or Toyama to make the loop of the Noto Peninsula at your own pace. Another good route is between Kanazawa and Takayama via Shirakawa-gō.

An economy-size car costs about ¥8,000 per day or ¥50,000 per week. Reserve the car in a city like Kanazawa, Nagano, or Matsumoto, or before you leave Tōkyō, Nagoya, or Kyōto—not many people speak English in rural Japan. Tollways are convenient but expensive and less scenic than the many beautiful highways in the region.

In winter certain roads through the central Japan Alps are closed. In particular, the main route between Matsumoto and Takayama via Kamikōchi is closed November–April.

RESTAURANTS

Traditional Japanese *ryōtei* specialize in seasonal delicacies while casual eateries serve delicious home-style cooking and regional dishes. Western fare is easy to come by, especially in larger cities like Kanazawa, which is famed for the local Kaga cuisine.

HOTELS

Accommodations run the gamut from Japanese-style inns to large, modern hotels. Ryokan and minshuku (guesthouses) serve traditional Japanese food, and usually highlight regional specialties. Hotels in the bigger cities have a variety of Western and Japanese restaurants. Hotels listed in this chapter have private baths, air-conditioning, telephones, and TVs unless stated otherwise. Japanese Inns mostly include two meals in the room rate. In summer, hotel reservations are advisable.

Most hotels have data ports or an Internet station, but ryokan rarely do. Hotel lobbies and areas around the stations often have free wireless access.

WHAT IT COSTS IN YEN				
	$	$$	$$$	$$$$
RESTAURANTS	under ¥800	¥800–¥1,000	¥1,000–¥2,000	¥2,000–¥3,000	over ¥3,000
HOTELS	under ¥8,000	¥8,000–¥12,000	¥12,000–¥18,000	¥18,000–¥22,000	over ¥22,000

Restaurant prices are per person for a main course, set meal, or equivalent combination of smaller dishes at dinner. Hotel prices are for a double room, excluding service and tax.

VISITOR INFORMATION

Offices of the JR Travel Information Center and Japan Travel Bureau are at major train stations. They can help you book local tours, hotel reservations, and travel tickets. You shouldn't assume English will be spoken, but usually someone speaks sufficiently well for your basic needs. Where public transportation is infrequent, such as the Noto-hantō and Sado-ga-shima, local tours are available; however, the guides speak only Japanese.

The Japan Travel Bureau runs a five-day tour from Tōkyō every Tuesday from April through October 26. The tour goes via Shirakaba-ko to Matsumoto (overnight), to Tsumago and Takayama (overnight), to Kanazawa (overnight), to Awara Onsen (overnight), and ends in Kyōto. The fare is ¥150,000, including four breakfasts and two dinners.

ESSENTIALS

Emergency Contacts Ambulance (☎119). Police (☎110). 24-hr Medical Emergency Help Line (☎0120/890–423).

Skiing Information Japan Snow (⊕ www.snowjapan.com).

Tour Contacts Japan Travel Bureau (☎03/3281–1721).

Train Information Train Route Finder (⊕ www.jorudan.co.jp/english/).

5

On the Menu

Every microregion has its specialties and unique style of preparing seafood from the Nihon-kai. Seaweed, like vitamin-rich *wakame* and *kombu*, is a common ingredient, sometimes together with tiny clams called *shijimi*, in miso soup.

In Toyama spring brings tiny purple-hued baby firefly squid (*hotaru-ika*), which are boiled in soy sauce or sake and eaten whole with a tart mustard-miso sauce. Try the seasonal *ama-ebi* (sweet shrimp) and *masu-zushi* (thinly sliced trout sushi that's been pressed flat). In winter crabs abound, including the red, long-legged *beni-zuwaigani*.

Speaking of crabs, Fukui has huge (some 28 inches leg to leg) *echizen-gani* crabs. When boiled with a little salt and dipped in rice vinegar, they're pure heaven. In both Fukui and Ishikawa, restaurants serve *echizen-soba* (home-made buckwheat noodles with mountain vegetables) with sesame oil and bean paste for dipping.

The seafood-based *Kaga-ryōri* (Kaga cuisine) is common to Kanazawa and Noto-hantō. *Tai* (sea bream) is topped with mountain fern brackens, greens, and mushrooms. At Wajima's early-morning fish market near the tip of Noto-hantō and at Kanazawa's *omi-chō* market you have your choice of everything from abalone to seaweed, and nearby restaurants will cook it for you.

In Niigata Prefecture try *noppei-jiru*, a hot (or cold) soup with *sato-imo* (a type of sweet potato) as its base, and mushrooms, salmon, and a few other local ingredients. It goes well with hot rice and grilled fish. *Wappa–meshi* is steamed rice garnished with local ingredients, especially wild vegetables, chicken, fish, and shellfish. In autumn try *kiku-no-ohitashi*, a side dish of chrysanthemum petals marinated in vinegar.

Like other prefectures on the Nihon-kai coast, Niigata has outstanding fish in winter—*buri* (yellowtail), flatfish, sole, oysters, abalone, and shrimp. A local specialty is *namban ebi*, raw shrimp dipped in soy sauce and wasabi. It's butter-tender and especially sweet on Sado-ga-shima. Also on Sado-ga-shima, take advantage of the excellent *wakame* (seaweed) dishes and *sazae-no-tsub-oyaki* (wreath shellfish) broiled in their shells with a soy or miso sauce.

The area around Matsumoto is known for its wasabi and chilled *zarusoba* (buckwheat noodles), a refreshing meal on a hot day, especially with a cold glass of locally brewed sake. Eel steamed inside rice wrapped in bamboo leaves is also popular.

Sansai soba (buckwheat noodles with mountain vegetables) and *sansai-ryōri* (wild vegetables and mushrooms in soups or tempura) are specialties in the mountainous areas of Takayama and Nagano. Local river fish like *ayu* (smelt) or *iwana* (char) are grilled on a spit with *shōyū* (soy sauce) or salt. *Hoba miso* is a dark, slightly sweet type of miso roasted on a large magnolia leaf.

Nagano is also famous for *ba sashi* (raw horse meat), *sakura nabe* (horse-meat stew cooked in an earthenware pot), and boiled baby bees. The former two are still very popular; as for the latter, even locals admit they're something of an acquired taste.

CLOSE UP

Get Your Festival On

Takayama's spring and fall festivals (April 14 and 15 and October 9 and 10) transform the usually quiet town into a rowdy, colorful party, culminating in a musical parade of intricately carved and decorated *yatai* (floats) and puppets. Flags and draperies adorn local houses, and at night the yatai are hung with lanterns. Book rooms well ahead and expect inflated prices. April's Sannō Matsuri is slightly bigger than October's Hachi-man Matsuri.

During Kanazawa's Hyaku-man-goku Matsuri (June 13–15), parades of people dressed in ancient Kaga costumes march through the city to the sound of folk music. Torchlit Nō (old-style Japanese theater) performances, ladder-top acrobatics by Kaga firemen, and singing and dancing in parks create a contagious atmosphere of merrymaking.

Of the *many* festivals on the Noto-hantō, the most impressive are Nanao's Seihakusai festival, a 400-year-old tradition where three huge 30-ton wooden *Hikiyama* (Towering Mountain) floats with unpivoted wheels, are hauled around the city streets by locals, held May 13–15, and Issaki Hōtō Matsuri, held the first Saturday of August.

5

THE JAPAN ALPS

The Japan Alps cover a region known as Shinshū, between the north and south coasts of the Chūbu Area. There are 10 peaks above 9,800 feet attracting skiers and hikers. There are many parks and forests for less strenuous nature exploring.

Roads and railways through the Japan Alps follow the valleys. This greatly lengthens trips such as the three-hour Matsumoto–Takayama ride. Route maps for Shinkansen and JR lines are at any train station or bookstore. Some routes only have a few services a day. The last train or bus may leave as early as 7 PM.

Buses are not as convenient as trains, but some scenic routes are recommended. Any bus station, always right by the train station, has maps and schedules. The local tourist-information office—also in or near the train station—will help you decipher timetables and fares.

KARUIZAWA 軽井沢

145 km (90 mi) from Tōkyō, 72 km (45 mi) from Nagano and to Kusatsu.

When Archdeacon A.C. Shaw, an English prelate, built his summer villa here in 1886 at the foot of Mt. Asama in southeastern Nagano, he sparked the interest of fashionable, affluent Tōkyōites, who soon made it their preferred summer destination. Some became patrons of the arts, which led to the opening of galleries and art museums. Pamphlets on current exhibitions are at the tourist office.

Emperor Akihito met the Empress Michiko on a tennis court here in the 1950s. Two decades later John Lennon and Yoko Ono lolled at her family's *bessō* (summer house) and the Monpei Hotel. In Kyū-Karuizawa, near the Karuizawa train station, more than 500 branches of trendy boutiques sell the same goods as their flagship stores in Tōkyō.

GETTING HERE AND AROUND

Coming from Tōkyō, Karuizawa is a nice stop en route to the hot-spring towns of Kusatsu and Yudanaka or Matsumoto and Kamikochi. The town itself is easy to explore by foot, taxi, or bicycle. Naka-Karuizawa Station, one stop (five minutes) away on the Shinano Tetsudō line, is a gateway to Shiraito and Ryūgaeshi waterfalls, the Yachō wild bird sanctuary, and hiking trails. ■TIP➔ **Karuizawa is very crowded from mid-July to the end of August. If you are visiting during this time, book your accommodation well in advance.**

Karuizawa Tourist Information Service is inside the JR station.

ESSENTIALS

Currency Exchange Hachijuni Bank (⊠ *1178 Shinkaruizawa* ☎ *0267/42–2482* ⊙ *Daily 9–3*).

Emergency Contacts Karuizawa Hospital (⊠ *2375-1 Ōzawa Nagakura* ☎ *0267/45–5111*).

Visitor Information Karuizawa Tourist Information Service (☎ *0267/42–2491* ⊕ *www.town.karuizawa.nagano.jp/html/English/index.html*).

WHAT TO SEE

Asama-san, an active volcano of more than 8,000 feet, threatens to put an end to the whole "Highlands Ginza" below.For a view of the glorious Asama-san in its entirety, head to the observation platform at **Usui-tōge** 碓氷峠 *(Usui Pass).* You can also see neighboring Myōgi-san, as well as the whole Yatsugatake, a range of eight volcanic peaks. Walk northeast along shop-filled Karuizawa Ginza street to the end, past Nite-bashi, and follow the trail through an evergreen forest to the pass. A lovely view justifies the 1½-hour walk. Two to three buses leave per hour if you want a ride back.

Hiking paths at **Shiraito-no-taki and Ryūgaeshi-no-taki** 白糸の滝と竜返しの滝 *(Shiraito and Ryūgaeshi falls)* get crowded during the tourist season, but they are a good afternoon excursion in the off-season. To get to the trailhead at Mine-no-Chaya, take the bus from Naka-Karuizawa. The ride takes about 25 minutes. From the trailhead it's about a 1½-km (1-mi) hike to Shiraito. The trail then swings southeast, and 3 km (2 mi) farther are the Ryūgaeshi Falls. For a longer hike, walk back to town via Mikasa village. It takes about an hour and 15 minutes. Or catch the bus bound for Karuizawa (10 minutes) from the parking lot.

Yachō-no-mori 野鳥の森 *(Wild Bird Forest)* is home to some 120 bird species. You can watch the birds' habitat from two observation huts along a 2½-km (1½-mi) forest course. To get to the sanctuary, take a five-minute bus ride from Naka-Karuizawa Station to Nishiku-iriguchi, and then walk up the small road for 400 meters. The narrow entrance is past the café, restaurant, and onsen on the left. Alternatively, you can bike to the sanctuary's entrance in about 15 minutes. Bikes can be rented at Naka-Karuizawa Station for ¥800 per hour or ¥2,000 a day.

WHERE TO EAT

$-$$ ✕ **Kastanie** カスターニエ. The tiled bar counter and wooden tables cov-
JAPANESE ered with red-and-white checked cloths are as inviting as the staff of this
terraced restaurant a few blocks north of the Karuizawa station. Most
dishes are seasonal, but try the grilled vegetable Veronese spaghetti
and the salmon and Camembert pizza. Meat plates include herbed,
grilled chicken (¥1,580) or sizzling rib-roast steak (¥2,630). Look for
the sign hanging from the second floor. ⊠ *Kitasakagun, Karuizawa-shi*
☎ *0267/42–3081* 🕗 *Thurs.–Tues. noon–10.*

NAGANO AND ENVIRONS 長野とその周辺

*135 mi northwest of Tōkyō, 45 mi northwest of Karuizawa, 155 mi
northeast of Nagoya.*

Nagano Prefecture is called the "Roof of Japan," home to the northern,
central, and southern Japan Alps and six national parks that offer year-
round recreational activities. Active volcanoes include Mt. Asama on
the border between Nagano and Gunma prefectures and Mt. Ontake in
Nagano Prefecture, which is a destination for religious pilgrims.

GETTING HERE AND AROUND

Nagano is 97 minutes from Tōkyō's Ueno Station by Shinkansen, 40
minutes from Karuizawa by Shinkansen, and 3 hours from Nagoya
by JR Limited Express. It's a convenient base for visiting some of the
surrounding onsen and mountains, though you can easily see the main
sights around Zenkō-ji in half a day.

ESSENTIALS

Currency Exchange and Shipping Nagano Eki-mae Post Office (⊠ *1355-5
Suehiro-cho* ✛ *In front of Nagano Station* ☎ *0279/227–0983* 🕗 *Daily 9–5).*

Visitor Information Kusatsu Information Center (⊠ *3-9 Kusatsu-machi, Kusatsu*
☎ *0279/88–3642* 🌐 *www.kusatsu-onsen.org/index.html).* **Nagano Tourist Office**
(⊠ *a692-2 Habashita, Minami* ☎ *026/226–5626* 🌐 *www.nagano-tabi.net/english).*
Yamanouchi Information Center (⊠ *Yamanouchi-machi* ☎ *0269/33–1107) .*

NAGANO 長野

Rimmed by mountains, Nagano has been a temple town since the
founding of Zenkō-ji temple in the 7th century. Before the 1998 Winter Olympics a new Shinkansen line was built connecting Tōkyō and
Nagano, and new highways were added to handle the car and bus traffic. Suddenly the fairly inaccessible Alps region was opened to visitors.
Yet as the excitement faded, a rather forlorn air descended. This lifts in
season, when people swarm the surrounding mountains.

EXPLORING

★ Nagano's unusual **Zenkō-ji** 善光寺 is the final destination each year for
millions of religious pilgrims. Since the 6th century this nonsectarian
Buddhist temple has accepted believers of all faiths and admitted wom-
en when other temples forbade it. Each morning the head priest (Tendai
sect) and head priestess (Jōdo sect) hold a joint service to pray for the
prosperity of the assembled pilgrims (usually on tour packages). Line
up outside to be blessed by the priest, who taps his rosary on each head.
You then pass the incense burner, waving the smoke over yourself for

5

good fortune and health. Inside, rub the worn wooden statue of the ancient doctor Binzuru (Pindola Bharadvaja in Sanskrit), for relief of aches and pains. A faithful disciple of Buddha, Binzuru is famous for stories of his miraculous powers and ability to fly. After the service, descend into the pitch-black tunnel in the basement to find the iron latch on the wall—seizing it is said to bring enlightenment.

It's a 3-km (2-mi) walk from the station, or you can arrange a taxi through your hotel the night before. The starting time for the morning service ranges from 5:30 to 7 AM, depending on the season, a minute later or earlier each day. From 9:30 you can hop on the Gururin-go bus for the 10-minute trip (¥100) to the temple gate. ⊠ *Motoyoshi 4–9–1* ☎ *026/234–3591* ✑ *¥500* ⊗ *Inner sanctuary daily 5:30–4:30.*

YUDANAKA ONSEN 湯田中温泉

Photographs of snow-covered white macaques cavorting in open-air thermal pools have made the Yudanaka Onsen famous. Northeast of Nagano, nine open-air hot springs are between Yudanaka Onsen and Shibu Spa Resort. The onsen where the monkeys soak is known as Jigoku-dani (Hell Valley), and is just east of Yudanaka and Shibu. Yudanaka is the last stop on the Nagano Dentetsu Line; the trip from Nagano takes 40 minutes and costs ¥1,230. Several spas string out from here. The area is not unlike Yellowstone National Park, with its bubbling, steaming, sulfurous volcanic vents and pools. Considerable development, however, including more than 100 inns and hotels, several streets, and shops, ends the comparison. The spas are the gateway to Shiga Kōgen (Shiga Heights), site of Olympic alpine skiing and the snowboarding slalom.

KUSATSU 草津

★ The highly touted hot springs at Kusatsu contain sulfur, iron, aluminum, and even trace amounts of arsenic. Just inside the border of Gunma Prefecture, the springs are reached in summer by a bus route across Shiga Kōgen from Yudanaka, or from Karuizawa. The *yu-batake* (hot-spring field) gushes 5,000 liters of boiling, sulfur-laden water per minute before it's cooled in seven long wooden boxes and sent to more than 130 ryokan in the village. The open field is beautifully lit up at night.

Netsu-no-yu 熱の湯 *(Fever Bath)* is the main and often unbearably hot public bath next door to the yu-batake. You can watch one of six daily *yumomi* shows (7 and 7:30 AM and 3, 3:35, 4, and 4:35 PM) from April to October, in which locals churn the waters with long wooden planks until the baths reach a comfortable temperature. ⊠ *414 Kusatsu-chō* ☎ *0279/88–3613* ✑ *¥500* ⊗ *Daily 7 AM–10 PM.*

For a dip in the open air, try the 5,500-square-foot milky bath at **Sai-no-kawara Dai-rotemburo** 西の河原大露天風呂 in the western end of Kusatsu village, with pleasing scenery by day and stars by night. The spa is a 15-minute walk west from the Kusatsu bus terminal. ⊠ *521–3 Kusatsu-machi* ☎ *0279/88–2600* ✑ *¥500* ⊗ *Apr.–Nov., daily 7 AM–8 PM; Dec.–Mar., daily 9 AM–8 PM.*

WHERE TO EAT AND STAY

$$ 🏨 **Nagano Sunroute Hotel** ホテルサンルート長野. A coffee table and two easy chairs are squeezed into each compact Western-style room, which is all you need if you're en route to other Alps destinations. The escalator across the street from JR Nagano Station leads to the reception area and tea lounge. Pros: convenient location next to the station. **Cons:** small rooms for the price. ✉ *1–28–3 Minami-Chitose, Nagano-shi, Nagano-ken* ☎ *026/228–2222* 📠 *026/228–2244* 🛏 *143 rooms* ♿ *In-room: Internet. In-hotel: restaurant, no-smoking rooms.*

$$$–$$$$
JAPANESE
✕ **Restaurant Sakura** さくら. A few blocks southwest of Zenkō-ji, the famous sake distiller Yoshinoya has a restaurant attached to the sake factory and warehouses. From 9 to 5 you can tour for free, ending with a sampling of fresh sake. Sakura has an open-air terrace and a glass-walled interior. The Sakura bentō for ¥1,890 holds seasonal delights like the pungent Matsutake mushroom. ✉ *941 Nishinomon-chō* ☎ *026/237–5000* ▤ *AE, MC, V* ⊗ *Closed the 4th Wed. of each month.*

$ 🏨 **Uotoshi Ryokan** 魚敏旅館. This small ryokan in the steamy bath village
★ of Yudanaka has a 24-hour, hot springs-fed *hinoki* (cypress) bathtub. The rooms are rustic and cozy and come with either a Western or Japanese breakfast. You can try Japanese archery (*kyūdō*) if the owner has free time. Dinners feature delicious mountain vegetables and Nihon-kai seafood (¥2,520–¥3,680). It's a seven-minute walk from Yudanaka Station, across the Yomase River and on the left. **Pros:** the chance to try your hand at Japanese archery is a rare treat. **Cons:** somewhat out of the way. ✉ *2563 Sano, Yamanouchi-machi, Shimo-Takai-gun, Nagano-ken* ☎ *0269/33–1215* 📠 *0269/33–0074* ⊕ *www.avis.ne.jp/~miyasaka* 🛏 *8 Japanese-style rooms without bath* ♿ *In-hotel: restaurant, Japanese baths, Internet* ▤ *AE, MC, V* ⑩*BP.*

MATSUMOTO 松本

64 km (40 mi) southwest of Nagano, 282 km (175 mi) northwest of Tōkyō, 185 km (115 mi) northeast of Nagoya.

Snowcapped peaks surround the old castle-town of Matsumoto, where the air is cool and dry on the alpine plateau. More interesting and picturesque than Nagano, this gateway to the Northern Alps is one of the best bases for exploring the area. Full of good cafés and restaurants, Matsumoto is also a center for traditional crafts including *tensan,* fabric woven from silk taken from wild silkworms; Matsumoto *shiki* or lacquerware; Azumino glass; and wood crafts. Old merchant houses stand along Nakamachi Street, south of the castle. Several influential educators, lawyers, and writers from this city have impacted Japan's sociopolitical system in the past.

Though it only takes a day to visit the main sights in town, Matsumoto's restaurants, cafés, and relaxed atmosphere make it a hard place to leave. It is worth staying a night or two to visit the outlying museums and onsen. Matsumoto is also a good base to visit Kamikōchi to the west, or the post towns of Magome and Tsumago to the south.

GETTING HERE AND AROUND

Japan Air System (JAS) has daily flights between Matsumoto and Fukuoka, Ōsaka, and Sapporo. Trains are also available: Matsumoto is 1 hour from Nagano on JR Shinonoi Line, 2 hours and 40 minutes from Tōkyō Shinjuku Station on JR Chūō Line, and 2¼ hours from Nagoya on JR Chūō Line. By highway bus it's 3¼ hours east of Takayama.

Matsumoto is very compact, so grab a map at the **Tourist Information Center** at the JR station and head for the old part of town near the Chitose-bashi Bridge at the end of Hon-machi-dōri. Alternatively, Matsumoto's Town Sneaker shuttle bus (¥100) stops at the main sights, and the tourist office can direct you to one of the many locations lending free bicycles.

ESSENTIALS

Internet **M Wing** (⊠*M Wing Bldg., 2nd fl., 18-1, Chūo 1* ☎*0263/34–3000* ⏱*9 AM–10 PM weekdays, 9–5 weekends*).

Visitor Information Tourist Information Center (⊠ *3–7 Marunoichi, Matsumoto* ☎*0263/32–2814* ⊕ *welcome.city.matsumoto.nagano.jp/*).

WHAT TO SEE

OLD TOWN

★ **Matsumoto-jō** 松本城 *(Matsumoto Castle).* Nicknamed Karasu-jō (Crow Castle) for its black walls, this castle began as a small fortress with moats in 1504. It was remodeled into its current three-turreted form from 1592 to 1614, just as Japan became a consolidated nation under a central government. The civil wars ended and the peaceful Edo era (1603–1868) began, rendering medieval castles obsolete. Its late construction explains why the 95-foot-tall *tenshukaku* (stronghold or inner tower) is the oldest surviving tower in Japan—no battles were ever fought here. Exhibits on each floor break up the challenging climb up very steep stairs to the top. If you hunker down to look through rectangular openings (broad enough to scan for potential enemies) on the sixth floor, you'll have a gorgeous view of the surrounding mountains. In the first week of June there is a *Taiko* (Japanese drums) festival and on November 3 and 4 the Matsumoto Castle Festival features a samurai parade.

In the southwest corner of the castle grounds, which bloom in spring with cherry trees, azaleas, and wisteria, the **Japan Folklore Museum** (*Nihon Minzoku Shiryōkan* ☎*0263/32–0133*) exhibits samurai wear, Edo-period agricultural implements, and explanations of Matsumoto's development. In January an ice-sculpture exhibition is held in the museum's park. The castle is a 20-minute walk from the station. ⊠*4–1 Marunouchi* ☎*0263/32–2902* 🎫*Castle and museum* ¥*600* ⏱*Daily 8:30–5.*

★ **Kaichi Primary School** 開智学校 *(Kyū Kaichi Gakkō).* Built in 1873, the former Kaichi Primary School houses more than 80,000 educational artifacts from the Meiji Restoration, when education was to become the unifying tool for the rapid modernization of postfeudal Japan. The displays in the former classrooms include wall charts (used prior to the introduction of textbooks) and 19th-century desks and writing slates.

The building was used as a school until 1960. It's bizarre style reflects the architecture of the period: a mishmash of diverse Occidental elements fashioned from Japanese materials. A big, fancy cupola sits atop the shingled roof; the white walls made of mortar are dotted with red, slatted windows; and the front door, hidden in the shadow of the blue, grandiose balcony, is protected by a skillfully carved dragon. ⊠ *2–4–12 Kaichi* ☎ *0263/32–5725* 🖃 *¥300* 🕙 *Tues.–Sun. 8:30–5.*

NEED A BREAK?

Two blocks before the Chitose-bashi bridge, which takes you from Hon-machi dōri across the river to the castle, is **Old Rock** (⊠ *2–3–20 Chūō* ☎ *0263/38–0069*), a Japanese version of a traditional British pub with roast beef for ¥1,350. Guinness, Kilkenny, Boddingtons, and Stella Artois are on draft. Open daily from 5 PM until late.

WEST OF THE STATION

Two of the city's best museums are west of the JR station. It's too far to walk, and there's no bus. You can take the Kamikōchi train (on the private Matsumoto Dentetsu Line) four stops to Oniwa Station and walk 10 minutes. The museums can be hard to find though, so the ¥2,000 taxi ride is recommended.

★ The **Japan Wood-Block Print Museum** 日本浮世絵博物館 *(Nihon Ukiyo-e Hakubutsukan)*. The museum is devoted to the lively, colorful, and widely popular *ukiyo-e* woodblock prints of Edo-period artists. Highlights include Hiroshige's scenes of the Tōkaidō (the main trading route through Honshū in feudal Japan), Hokusai's views of Mt. Fuji, and Sharaku's kabuki actors. Based on the enormous holdings of the wealthy Sakai family, the museum's 100,000 pieces (displays rotate every three months) include some of Japan's finest prints and represent the largest collection of its kind in the world. ⊠ *2206–1 Shimadachi, Koshiba* ☎ *0263/47–4440* 🖃 *¥1,050* 🕙 *Tues.–Sun. 10–5.*

Matsumoto History Village *(Matsumoto-shi Rekishi no Sato)*. Next to the Ukiyo-e Hakubutsukan is Japan's oldest palatial wooden court building and the former site of the Matsumoto District Court. Displays pertain to the history of law enforcement from the feudal period to the modern era. ⊠ *2196–01 Shimadachi, Koshiba* ☎ *0263/47–4515* 🖃 *¥400* 🕙 *Tues.–Sun. 9–4:30.*

AROUND MATSUMOTO

The local train to the Daiō horseradish farm and the Rokuzan Art Museum journeys through vibrant green fields, apple orchards, and miles of rice paddies.

Rokuzan Art Museum 碌山美術館 *(Rokuzan Bijutsukan)*. The museum displays the work of Rokuzan Ogiwara, a sculptor who was influenced by Auguste Rodin and pioneered modern sculptural styles in Japan. He is especially known for his female figures and male figures in heroic poses. This ivy-covered brick building with a stunning bell tower is in Hotaka, 10 stops north of Matsumoto Station on the JR Ōito Line. From Hotaka Station it's a 10-minute walk to the museum. ⊠ *5095–1 Ōaza-hotaka* ☎ *0263/82–2094* 🖃 *¥700* 🕙 *May–Oct., daily 9–5; Nov.–Mar., Tues.–Sun. 9–4.*

5

Daiō Wasabi Farm 大王わさび農場 *(Daiō Wasabi Nōjo)*. At the largest wasabi farm in the country, the green horseradish roots are cultivated in flat gravel beds irrigated by melted snow from the Alps. The chilly mineral water is ideal for the durable wasabi.

You should try some of the farm's products, which range from wasabi cheese to wasabi chocolate and ice cream. You can pickle your own horseradish in one of the 20-minute workshops (¥1,000). The farm is 10 stops (one on the express) north along the JR Ōito Line from Platform 6 in Matsumoto Station. To reach the farm you can rent a bike, take a 40-minute walk along a path from the train station (the station attendant will direct you), or hop in a taxi for about ¥1,300. ⊠ *1692 Hotaka* ☎ *0263/82–8112* ⊠ *Free* ⊙ *Daily 10–5:30, 4:30 in winter.*

WHERE TO EAT

$$–$$$
JAPANESE
Fodor's Choice
★

✕ **Kura** くら. For a surprisingly small number of yen you can feast in this 90-year-old Meiji-era warehouse in the center of town. Kura serves a large assortment of sushi and traditional fare: the *aji tataki* (horse-mackerel sashimi) and tempura are particularly tasty. The stoic owner expertly prepares your meal, but should his wife spot you relishing the food, you're in for some disarming hospitality—she has an arsenal of potent *ji-zake* (locally brewed sake) and a heart of gold. From the station, take a left onto Kōen-dōri. Take a left after the Parco department store, and you'll see the restaurant's whitewashed facade and curved black eaves on the left. ⊠ *1–10–22 Chūo* ☎ *0263/33–6444* ⊟ *AE, MC, V* ⊙ *Closed Wed.*

$$$
JAPANESE

✕ **Yakitori Yume-ya** 焼き鳥夢や. Adorned in retro, prewar decor, Yumeya specializes in old-style yakitori (skewered, grilled meat and vegetables). Cozy up to the narrow counter for food and drinks, or sit outside during the warmer months. Little English is spoken, but the cooks are happy to explain the menu with exaggerated gestures. ⊠ *Showa Yokocho Bldg., 1–13–11 Chūo* ☎ *0263/33–8430* ⊟ *No credit cards* ⊙ *Closed Mon.*

WHERE TO STAY

$$$

⌖ **Hotel Buena Vista** ホテルブエナビスタ. One of Matsumoto's more expensive hotels, the Buena Vista has a glowing marble lobby, a coffeehouse, a café-bar, four restaurants (two Japanese, one Chinese, one French), and a sky lounge called **Bar Fuego** that serves Italian food. Corner rooms with two large picture windows need to be requested in advance. Single rooms snugly accommodate a small double bed, while standard doubles and twins have space for a table and chairs. The hotel is four blocks southeast of Matsumoto Station. **Pros:** highest-class hotel in town. **Cons:** most expensive hotel in town. ⊠ *1–2–1 Hon-jō, Matsumoto, Nagano-ken* ☎ *0263/37–0111* 🖶 *0263/37–0666* ⊕ *www.buena-vista. co.jp* ⇆ *200 rooms* ⚐ *In-hotel: 4 restaurants, bar, no-smoking rooms* ⊟ *AE, DC, MC, V.*

$$

⌖ **Hotel New Station** ホテルニューステーション. Although good-value business hotels are often sterile, this one has a cheerful staff and a lively restaurant that serves freshwater *iwana* (char)—an area specialty. The rooms are adequate, but small. To get a "full-size" room by Western standards, request a deluxe twin. Every room has a private bath, and there are also shared Japanese baths. To reach the hotel, take a left from the station exit and walk south for two minutes. **Pros:** inexpensive; excellent staff; near the station **Cons:** small rooms. ✉ *1–1–11 Chūō, Matsumoto, Nagano-ken* ☎ *0263/35–3850* 🖷 *0263/35–3851* ⊕ *www. hotel-ns.co.jp* ⇗ *103 rooms* ♿ *In-hotel: restaurant, Japanese baths, no-smoking rooms* ▭ *AE, DC, MC, V.*

$$$$
★
🔆 **Kikunoyu** 菊の湯. A stately hot-spring ryokan built in the *honmune-zukuri* or traditional private-house style, there's a characteristic gabled roof, ornamental board above the front gable (*suzume-odōri*), and bow windows. The spacious lobby has crossbeams made from the trunk of a zelkova tree. There are three hot-spring baths: *Kikuburo* is made of Italian marble with a large carved chrysanthemum, another is made of granite, and there is an open-air bath. Ground-floor guest rooms face the garden, and some have private *hinoki* (cypress) baths. Artfully arranged meals on lacquer trays arrive in your room. A bowl of cakes called *yōkoso manjū* and buckwheat tea welcome the weary traveler upon arrival. It's a 20-minute bus ride from Matsumoto Station to **Asama Onsen,** which is northeast of the city at the foot of the Utsukushigahara highlands. **Pros:** relaxing getaway. **Cons:** not a good base for other sightseeing. ✉ *1–29–7 Asama-onsen, Matsumoto-shi, Nagano-ken* ☎ *0263/46–2300* 🖷 *0263/46–0015* ⊕ *www.kikunoyu.com/* ⇗ *17 rooms* ▭ *V* ⦿ *MAP.*

NIGHTLIFE

Eonta えおんた (✉ *Ōta 4-chōme 9–7* ☎ *0263/33–0505* ⊕ *www.getna gano.com/en/Places/Nightlife* ⊙ *Thurs.–Tues. 4 PM–midnight*) is a jazz bar that's been popular with locals since the 1970s. The owner plays songs from his 1,000-plus CDs. The corner with sofas is for those who listen only. Toasted sandwiches, light meals, and good coffee are served. It's in a quasi-dilapidated two-story building a few blocks southeast of the castle.

Off the small park north of the Hotel Buena Vista, **Half Time** (✉ *Take-uchi San-box, 2nd fl., 1–4–10 Fukashi* ☎ *0263/36–4985*) is a smaller jazz joint that has tasty cocktails and snacks from 7 PM until well into the wee hours. Owner Akira Shiohara, who is quite a trumpet player, will even join in if you ask him. Two doors down, another bar, **People's** (✉ *Washizawa Building, 2nd fl., 1–4–11 Fukashi* ☎ *0263/37–5011*), offers beer, cocktails, and Italian fare, as well as cheap Internet access (¥200 per hour).

HAKUBA 白馬

★ *40 mi north of Matsumoto, 30 mi from Nagano.*

In the northwestern part of Nagano Prefecture, **Hakuba Village** 白馬村 lies beneath the magnificent Hakuba Range, the best of the northern Japan Alps. Hakuba means "white horse," because the main peak, Mt. Shirouma-dake (9,617 foot), resembles a horse. This is an all-year resort area for trekking, skiing, and climbing around the 9,500-foot mountains among rare alpine flora, insects, and wildlife. Gondola and chair lifts carry you up to ridges with panoramic views. More than 850 lodging facilities serve the 3.7 million annual visitors. Olympic alpine runs and ski jumps await winter sports fans, and summer visitors can still find snow, especially in the Grand Snowy Gorge.

Since the main attractions of Hakuba are hiking and skiing in the mountains, plan to stay at least 2 days to take advantage of the surroundings. The ski season in Hakuba runs from December to the first week of May. The Hiking season is late-June until the end of September, though the trails can be crowded in August. In July the mountains are covered in fields of wildflowers, making for a spectacular sight.

GETTING HERE AND AROUND

Both the JR Limited Express and the JR Ōito Line run from Matsumoto to Hakuba. From Nagano the bus will take about an hour. The **Hakuba Village Office of Tourism,** to the right as you exit the train station, provides basic maps (mostly in Japanese). Near the Alpico bus terminal and Happō bus stop is the **Happō-o-ne Tourism Association.** The staff can help you reserve a hotel room, but for the peak summer and winter seasons, you should book in advance. Run by a Canadian and Japanese couple, **Evergreen Outdoor Center** offers a variety of outdoor tours year-round. It is also a good place to get information on outdoor activities in the Hakuba area.

ESSENTIALS

Tour Information Evergreen Outdoor Center (✉Wadanomori Visitor Center, 4683-2 Happō Hakuba, *Wadano* ☎0261/72–5150).

Visitor Information Hakuba Village Office of Tourism (☎ *0261/72–5000* ⊕ *www. vill.hakuba.nagano.jp/e/access/index.html*). **Happō-o-ne Tourism Association** (☎ *0261/72—3066*).

WHAT TO SEE

Happō-o-ne Ski Resort 八方尾根スキー場 *(Happō-o-ne sukiba).* Japan's first parallel jumping hills were constructed; with critical points of 393 feet and 295 feet, each has a scaffold structure for the in-run and landing slope. These ski jumps can also be used in spring and summer. The Champion and Panorama courses have starting points of an altitude of 5,510 feet, with separate courses for men (vertical drop 2,755 feet) and women (vertical drop 2,555 feet). The downhill course for super giant slalom starts lower. This ridge stretches to the east from Mt. Karamatsu (8,843 feet), with breathtaking views if the mist doesn't roll in. Even in summer a sweater or light jacket may be needed. You can reach the first cairn via three connecting gondolas (5 minutes to Happō Gondola Station, then 8 minutes by gondola for Usagidaira and an additional 10 minutes by alpine lift). From here the jewel-like Happō Pond is a 6-km (4-mi) hike. For more ambitious hikers, three more hours gets you to the top of Mt. Karamatsu-dake. It's a 5-minute bus ride from Hakuba to Happō and then a 15-minute walk through the resort of Swiss-like chalets and hotels to the gondola station. The round-trip fare is ¥2,270, and the lower gondola operates from 8 AM to 5 PM; the higher chairlift stops at 4:30 PM.

Mt. Shirouma-dake 白馬岳. Hiking at the bottom of Hakuba Grand Snowy Gorge (Daisekkei), one of Japan's largest gorges (3.5 km), which is snowy all year round, requires warm clothes even in midsummer, when temperatures can dip below freezing. More than 100 types of alpine flowers grace the nearby fields in the summer. From the trailhead at Sarukura Village heading west, it's 1 hour 45 minutes to the gorge through the forest. If you are lucky, you may see snow grouse, a protected species in Japan. For climbers who want to scale Mt. Shirouma, which takes six hours to the top (two huts are on the way for overnight stay), proper equipment is necessary. The trail southwest of Sarukura to Yarigatake—a shorter hike of three hours—leads to the highest outdoor hot spring, **Yari Onsen,** at an elevation of 6,888 feet. The onsen is part of an overnight lodge with rates from ¥8,500, which include two meals. Adequate hiking gear is necessary for the longer trails. Sarukura is a 40-minute bus ride from Hakuba Station. Equipment like snowshoes and crampons can be rented in Hakuba Village. ☎0261/72–2002 ✎¥300.

Tsugaike Natural Park 栂池自然園 *(Tsugaike Shizen-en)* is an alpine marshland with a wide variety of rare alpine flora from early June to late October and dazzling gold and crimson leaves from September to October. It is a three-hour walk to take in the entire park. Getting there requires a one-hour bus ride (early June to late October) from Hakuba Oike Station, two stops north of Hakuba Station.

WHERE TO STAY

$ 🗽**Pension Noichigo Pension** 野いちご. Located a five-minute walk (or ski) from the Happō-o-ne lift, family-run Noichigo feels more like a European pension than a Japanese inn. The rooms are simple but comfortable, and the walls of the cozy dining area are adorned with paintings and sketches by owner and "Hakuba Art Meister" Takayuki Tuno. Guests can also take colored-pencil drawing classes for a small fee. The owners are friendly and have a wealth of knowledge about the area. A hearty, four-course dinner costs an extra ¥2,000 and is well worth the cost. **Pros:** excellent location for hiking and skiing; friendly and knowledgeable owners. **Cons:** fewer luxury amenities than larger hotels. ⌂4869 *Wadano-no-mori, Wadano* ☎0261/72–4707 ⊕*www.janis.or.jp/users/noichigo/top_page_english.html* 🛏6 rooms ⌂ *In hotel: restaurant, ski storage, Internet* ⊟ *No credit cards.*

KISO VALLEY 木曾谷〔木曾路〕

★ *89 km (55 mi) south of Matsumoto.*

This deep and narrow valley is cut by the Kiso river and walled in by the central Alps to the east and the northern Alps to the west. From 1603 to 1867 the area was called Nakasendo (center highway), because it connected western Japan and Kyōto to Edo (present-day Tōkyō).

After the Tōkaidō highway was built along the Pacific coast and the Chūō train line was constructed to connect Nagoya and Niigata, the 11 old post villages, where travelers and traders once stopped to refresh themselves, became ghost towns. Two villages, Tsumago and Magome, have benefited from efforts to retain the memory of these old settlements. Beautiful houses have been restored along the sloping stone streets. Walking through these historical areas, you can almost imagine life centuries ago, when the rustic shops were stocked with regular supplies instead of the traditional crafts now offered for sale.

EN ROUTE

You can hike the **old trade route** between Magome and Tsumago. The full 310-mi post road connecting Tōkyō and Kyōto was constructed during the 8th century. This hilly three-hour trip is most commonly taken from Magome to Tsumago. At points the road becomes a dirt pathway winding through forests of cedar past small shrines and a pair of waterfalls. There's a daily baggage delivery service between the two towns (¥500 per bag) from late July to the end of August. It is available on weekends and public holidays the rest of the year. Make arrangements at tourist information offices.

To get to Takayama from here, take the two-hour bus ride from Nakatsugawa Station to Gero; transfer to a JR train for the 45-minute trip to Takayama (¥1,580; one departure per hour). Buses leave three times daily (7:21 AM and 12:05 PM with a change at Sakashita for Gero, and a direct bus at 4 PM); the fare is ¥2,300.

GETTING HERE AND AROUND

The central valley town of Nagiso is one hour south of Matsumoto on the JR Chūō Line. Tsumago is a 10-minute bus ride (¥300) from JR Nagiso Station. Magome is closer to JR Nakatsugawa Station, which is 12 minutes south on the same line. Both towns are served by buses from the Nagiso and Nakatsugawa stations, so you can take a bus to one village and return from the other. Local buses between Magome and Tsumago are infrequent.

The staff at **Magome Tourist Information Office**—in the village center along the old post road—can help you reserve a hotel room. The **Tsumago Tourist Information Office**, in the center of town, has the same services as the Magome tourist office.

ESSENTIALS

Visitor Information Magome Tourist Information Office (☎0264/59–2336 ☺Daily 9–5). **Tsumago Tourist Information Office** (☎0264/57–3123 ☺Daily 9–5).

WHERE TO STAY

$$$$
★

🏨 **Hatago Matsushiro-ya** 旅籠松代屋. This small ryokan in Tsumago has been a guesthouse since 1804. Delicately arranged dinners are served in your room. No English is spoken, so a Japanese speaker, perhaps from the tourist office, will need to make your reservation. Ten large tatami rooms share a single bath and four very clean but old-fashioned pit toilets. The ryokan is closed from Wednesday morning to Thursday morning. **Pros:** traditional setting. **Cons:** no private bath or toilets. ✉807 Azuma-terashita, Minami-Nagiso-machi, Kiso-gun, Nagano-ken ☎0264/57–3022 ➾7 Japanese-style rooms without bath ⚥In-room: no phone. In-hotel: Japanese baths ⊟No credit cards ⟦◎⟧MAP.

$$$$

🏨 **Onyado Daikichi** 御宿大吉. The windows in all six tatami rooms of this *minshuku* face the wooded valley. The chef prepares local specialties such as horse-meat sashimi, mountain vegetables, and fried grasshoppers. More familiar dishes are available as well. Owner Nobuko-san welcomes foreign guests and even speaks a little English. There are shared Japanese baths. **Pros:** lovely views; traditional setting. **Cons:**

no private bath. ✉ *Tsumago, Nagiso-machi, Kiso-gun, Nagano-ken* ☎ *0264/57–2595* 🖨 *0274/57–2203* 📞 *5 Japanese-style rooms without bath* ⚭ *In-hotel: restaurant, Japanese baths* ▤ *No credit cards* ¶ *MAP.*

KAMIKŌCHI 上高地

48 km (30 mi) west of Matsumoto, 64 km (40 mi) east of Takayama.

The incomparably scenic route from Matsumoto to Takayama winds over the mountains and through Chūbu-Sangaku National Park (Chūbu-Sangaku Kokuritsu Kōen) via Kamikōchi. Travel is only possible after the last week of April or the first week of May, when plows have removed the almost 30 feet of winter snow. If you spend the night in Kamikōchi, which is surrounded by virgin forests of birch, larch, and hemlock, consider renting a rowboat at Taishō-ike (Taishō Pond) for the spectacular view of the snow-covered peaks.

Unless you plan to do some serious hiking, Kamikōchi is best done as a day-trip from Takayama or Matsumoto. Plan to arrive in the morning, though, as it is worth spending the entire day here.

GETTING HERE AND AROUND

No cars are allowed in Kamikōchi. Take the Matsumoto Electric Railway from Matsumoto Station to Shin-Shimashima, the last stop. The ride takes 30 minutes and departs once or twice an hour. At Shin-Shimashima Station, cross the road for the bus to Naka-no-yu and Kamikōchi. There's also a bus from Matsumoto to Kamikōchi, departing only twice a day at 8:55 and 10:15 AM. The road is closed from around November until April or May. You pay ¥2,400 for both legs of the trip at the start. Up-to-date bus and road information is available at the Matsumoto and Takayama Tourist Offices.

Kamikōchi is where the trails for some of the most famed alpine ascents begin; favorite peaks are Mt. Yariga-take and Mt. Hotaka-dake. An invaluable reference is Paul Hunt's *Hiking in Japan*, since most maps are in Japanese. Planning in advance is essential; climbs range from a few days to a week, and the trails can be crowded in summer.

WHAT TO SEE

As you approach Kamikōchi, the valley opens onto a row of towering mountains: Oku-Hotaka-san is the highest, at 10,466 feet. Mae-Hotaka-san, at 10,138 feet, is on the left. To the right is 9,544-foot Nishi-Hotaka-san. The icy waters of the Azusa-gawa flow from the small Taishō Pond at the southeast entrance to the basin.

There are many hiking trails in the river valley around Kamikōchi. One easy three-hour walk east starts at **Kappa-bashi**, a small suspension bridge over the crystal-clear Azusa-gawa, a few minutes northeast of the bus terminal. Along the way is a stone sculpture of the British explorer Reverend Walter Weston, the first foreigner to ascend these mountains. Continuing on the south side of the river the trail cuts through a pasture to rejoin the river at Myōshin Bridge. Cross here to reach Myōshin-ike (Myōshin Pond). At the edge of the pond sits the small Hotaka Jinja Kappa-bashi (Water Sprite Bridge). To see the beautiful **Taishō-ike** 大正池 *(Taishō Pond)*, head southeast from Kappa-bashi for a 20-minute walk. You can rent a boat (¥800 per half hour), or continue 90 minutes farther east to **Tokusawa**, an area with camping grounds and great mountain views.

WHERE TO STAY

Hotels and ryokan close from mid-November to late April.

$$$$
Fodor's Choice
★
🏨 **Imperial Hotel** 上高地帝国ホテル. This rustic alpine lodge is owned by Tōkyō's legendary Imperial Hotel, and staff members are borrowed from that establishment for the summer. In the lounge low wooden beams support the beautifully crafted ceiling, while a central hearth warms the room. Guest rooms have sofas and gorgeous woodwork, and some have balconies. Western and Japanese restaurants are on the premises. Make reservations well in advance. You can see the red-tiled, gabled roof of the hotel from Kamikōchi's bus terminal in the center of town. **Pros:** luxurious accommodations. **Cons:** more expensive than other lodgings in the area. ✉*Azumi-kamikōchi, Matsumoto-shi, Nagano-ken* 🖀*0263/95–2006, 03/3592–8001 Nov.–Mar., 212/692–9001 in U.S.* 🖷*0263/95–2412* ⊕*www.imperialhotel.co.jp* 🛏*75 rooms* 🏠*In-hotel: 3 restaurants, bar* ⊟*AE, DC, MC, V.*

$$$–$$$$
🏨 **Taishō-ike Hotel** 大正池ホテル. This small mountain resort is perched on the rim of the brilliant-blue Taishō Pond. The lobby, restaurant, and bath have large windows with excellent views of the breathtaking landscape. Opt for the spacious Western-style rooms, with their comfortable beds and soft, puffy quilts. The Japanese rooms are not as nice as those found in a ryokan. Rooms at the back, without a view of the water, are ¥3,000–¥5,000 less. **Pros:** lovely views; comfortable rooms. **Cons:** for a Japanese-style room a small ryokan is better. ✉*Azumi-kamikōchi, Matsumoto-shi, Nagano-ken* 🖀*0263/95–2301* 🖷*0263/95–2522* 🛏*21 Western-style rooms, 6 Japanese-style rooms* 🏠*In-room: no phone. In-hotel: restaurant, Japanese baths* ⊟*MC, V* ⥮*MAP.*

TAKAYAMA 高山

Fodor's Choice
★
267 km (166 mi) north of Nagoya, 80 km (50 mi) north of Matsumoto.

Takayama, originally called Hida, is a tranquil town whose rustic charms are the result of hundreds of years of peaceful isolation in the Hida San-myaku (Hida Mountains). Downtown, shops and restaurants mingle with museums and inns along rows of traditional wood-lattice buildings. A peculiar-looking ball of cedar leaves suspended outside a storefront indicates a drinking establishment or brewery. Nicknamed "little Kyōto," Takayama has fewer crowds and wider streets, not to mention fresh mountain air and gorgeous scenery.

Takayama's hugely popular festivals, spring's Sannō Matsuri (April 14–15) and the smaller autumn Hachi-man Matsuri (October 9–10), draw hundreds of thousands of spectators for parades of floats. Hotels are booked solid during matsuri time, so if you plan to join the festivities, make reservations several months in advance.

Outside of festival time, it is easy to see all the main attractions here in a day, two at the most. Though decidedly touristy, many people like using Takayama as a hub to visit Kamikōchi and the surrounding area.

GETTING HERE AND AROUND

Takayama has connections north to Toyama by JR train (four departures daily). The ride takes about two hours (with up to an hour waiting for connections) and costs ¥1,620. From Toyama trains go east to Niigata or west to Kanazawa and the Noto-hantō, via Ogi-machi. It's easy to get to Takayama by bus from Matsumoto for ¥3,400. A highly recommended detour to Kamikōchi—available May through early November—increases the fare to ¥6,260.

Laid out in a compact grid, Takayama can be explored on foot or bicycle. Bikes at the rental shop south of the station cost ¥300 per hour.

The **Hida Tourist Information Office**, in front of the JR station, is open from April to October, daily 8:30–6:30; and from November to March, daily 8:30–5. The English-speaking staff provides maps and helps with accommodations, both in town and in the surrounding mountains.

ESSENTIALS

Visitor Information Hida Tourist Information Office (☎ *0577/32–5328* ⊕ *www.hida.jp/english*).

WHAT TO SEE

❶ Takayama Jinya 高山陣屋 *(Historical Government House)*. This rare collection of stately buildings housed the 25 officials of the Tokugawa shogunate who administered the Hida region for 176 years. Highlights include an original storehouse (1606), which held city taxes in sacks of rice, a torture chamber (curiously translated as the "law court"), and samurai barracks. Free guided tours in English are available upon request and take 30–50 minutes. In front of the house, fruit, vegetables, and local crafts are sold at the **Jinya-mae Asa-ichi**, open from April to October, daily 6–noon, and from November to February, daily 7–noon. From the JR station, head east on Hirokōji-dori for a few blocks to the old section of town. Before the bridge, which crosses the small Miya-gawa, turn right, pass another bridge, and the Takayama Jinya is on your right. ✉ *1–5 Hachiken-machi 506-0012* ☎ *0577/32–0643* 💰 *¥420* 🕙 *Apr.–Oct., daily 8:45–5; Nov.–Mar., daily 8:45–4:30.*

❷ Shōren-ji 照蓮寺. The main hall of Shōren-ji in Shiroyama Kōen (Shiroyama Park) was built in 1504. It was moved here in 1961 from its original site in Shirakawa-gō, right before the area was flooded by the Miboro Dam. Beautifully carved, allegedly from the wood of a single cedar tree, this temple is an excellent example of classic Muromachi-period architecture. The temple sits on a hill surrounded by gardens, and you can see the Takayama skyline and the park below. ✉ *Shiroyama Kōen* ☎ *0577/32–2052* 💰 *¥200* 🕙 *Apr.–Oct., daily 8–5:30; Nov.–Mar., daily 8–5.*

❸ Archaeology Museum 飛騨民俗考古館 *(Hida Minzoku Kōkokan)*. This mansion once belonged to a physician who served the local daimyō. It has mysterious eccentricities—hanging ceilings, secret windows, and hidden passages—all of which suggest ninja associations. Displays

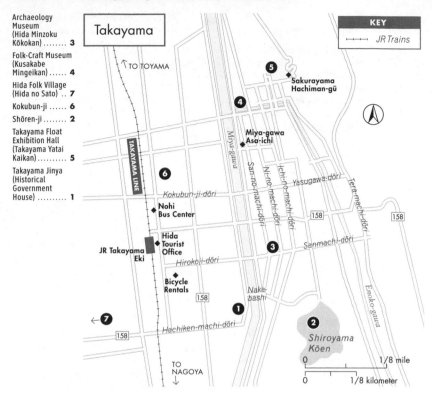

include wall hangings, weaving machines, and other Hida regional items. ⊠*82 Kamisanno-machi* ☎*0577/32–1980* ✑¥*500* ☉*Mar.– Nov., daily 8:30–5:30; Dec.–Feb., daily 9–5.*

❹ **Folk-Craft Museum** 日下部民芸館 *(Kusakabe Mingeikan)*. This musuem ★ is in a house from the 1880s that belonged to the Kusakabe family— wealthy traders of the Edo period. This national treasure served as a residence and warehouse, where the handsome interior, with heavy, polished beams and an earthy barren floor provides an appropriate setting for Hida folk crafts such as lacquered bowls and wood carvings. ⊠*1–52 Ōjin-machi* ☎*0577/32–0072* ✑¥*500* ☉*Mar.–Oct., daily 9–4:30; Nov.–Feb., Sat.–Thurs. 8:30–4:30.*

❺ **Takayama Float Exhibition Hall** 高山屋台会館 *(Takayama Matsuri Yatai* ★ *Kaikan)*. This community center displays four of the 11th-, 17th-, and 18th-century *yatai* (festival floats) used in Takayama's famous Sannō and Hachi-man festivals. More than two centuries ago Japan was ravaged by the bubonic plague, and yatai were built and paraded through the streets to appease the gods. Because this seemed to work, locals built bigger, more elaborate yatai to prevent further outbreaks. The delicately etched wooden panels, carved wooden lion-head masks for dances, and elaborate tapestries are remarkable. Technical wizardry is also involved, as each yatai contains puppets, controlled by rods and

GASSHO-ZUKURI FARMHOUSES

Gassho-zukuri means "praying hands," and refers to the sloping gable roofs made by placing wooden beams together at a steep 60-degree angle to prevent snow from piling up. In the early 18th century, there were more than 1,800 of these mountain farmhouses between Nagoya and Kanazawa. The openness of the interior was multipurpose: a central hearth sent billows of smoke upward to cure meats and dry food placed on a metal grill suspended from the ceiling; the floor space was used to make gunpowder and *washi* (Japanese paper); and the triangular alcove on top was reserved for silkworm cultivation. Stables were connected to the living space, so no one had to go outdoors during the long, cold winter months.

Perhaps most intriguing of all, the houses were built without nails. Strips of hazel branches tied the beams together, giving the joints the flexibility to sway in the wind. Although modern Japanese no longer live in gassho-zukuri houses, many of these structures have been preserved in historic village settings. These villages, developed in the 1990s, have become increasingly popular tourist destinations, especially for domestic travelers. Of the 150 or so gassho-zukuri that remain, more than half are in the Hida Folk Village in Takayama and the Shirakawa-gō Gassho-zukuri Village in Ogi-machi.

wires, that perform amazing, gymnast-like feats. ⊠*178 Sakura-machi* ☎*0577/32–5100* ☜*¥820* ☉*Mar.–Nov., daily 8:30–5; Dec.–Feb., daily 9–4:30.*

⑥ Kokubun-ji 国分寺. The city's oldest temple, dating from 1588, houses many objects of art, including a precious sword used by the Heike clan. In the Main Hall (built in 1615) sits a figure of Yakushi Nyorai, a Buddha who eases those struggling with illness. In front of the three-story pagoda is a wooden statue of another esoteric Buddhist figure, Kannon Bosatsu, who vowed to hear the voices of all people and immediately grant salvation to those who suffer. The ginkgo tree standing beside the pagoda is believed to be more than 1,200 years old. ⊠*1–83 Sowa-machi* ☎*0577/32–1395* ☜*¥300* ☉*Daily 9–4.*

⑦ Hida Folk Village *(Hida no Sato).* These traditional farmhouses, dating from the Edo era, were transplanted from all over the region, and their assembly employs ropes rather than nails. Many of the houses are A-frames with thatched roofs called *gasshō-zukuri* (praying hands). Twelve of the buildings are "private houses" displaying folk artifacts like tableware and weaving tools. Another five houses are folk-craft workshops, with demonstrations of *ichii ittōbori* (wood carving), *Hida-nuri* (Hida lacquering), and other traditional regional arts. To get to Hida Minzoku Mura, walk 1 km (½-mi) south from Takayama Station and take a right over the first bridge onto Route 158. Continue west for another ¾ km to the village. The route follows busy roads, so it's better to take a bus from Platform 6, on the left side of the bus terminal. ⊠*1–590 Kami-Okamoto-chō* ☎*0577/34–4711* ☜*¥700* ☉*Daily 8:30–5.*

Fodor's Choice
★

WHERE TO EAT AND STAY

$$$$
JAPANESE
★
✕**Kakushō** 角正. This restaurant is known for its *shōjin* ("temple food"), which includes *sansai ryōri*, light dishes of mountain vegetables soaked in a rich miso paste and served with freshwater fish grilled with salt or soy sauce. Occasionally this treat is served atop a roasted magnolia leaf and called *hōba-miso*. The owner, Sumitake-san, can translate the menu for you. From Miya-gawa, head east on the Sanmachi-dōri, crossing four side streets (including the one running along the river), walk up the hill, and take a left at the top. No English sign is out front, but a white *noren* (hanging cloth) hangs in the entrance way of this Edo-era house. You might want to steer toward the semiformal. It's directly across from a small pay parking lot. ⊠*2 Babachō-dōri* ☎*0577/32–0174* ⚞*Reservations essential* ⊟*AE, DC, MC, V.*

$$
JAPANESE
★
✕**Suzuya** 寿々や. Suzuya's recipes have been passed down over several generations. The house specialty is the superb and inexpensive *sansai-ryōri*, a time-honored mountain cuisine. Suzuya is in a traditional Hida-style house, and the dining room is intimate and wood-beamed. There's an English menu, and the staff is used to serving foreign guests. ■**TIP→ Try to go during off hours to avoid tour groups.** From the station, turn onto Kokubunji-dōri and take a right after five blocks. ⊠*24 Hanakawa* ☎*0577/32–2484* ⊟*AE, DC, MC, V.*

$$$–$$$$
🖫 **Hida Plaza Hotel** ひだホテルプラザ. This is the best international-style hotel in town. Traditional Hida ambience permeates the old wing, and beautiful wood accents the hotel's tastefully decorated restaurants. Tatami rooms are simple and elegant, and the large Western rooms have sofas. All rooms have wide-screen TVs, and many have views of the mountains. The newer wing is not as attractive, but its rooms are larger. Luxury appears in the form of mineral baths crafted of fragrant cypress wood. From the station, head north; the hotel is on the right. **Pros:** luxurious; amenity-packed. **Cons:** lacks the personal touch of many area ryokan and inns. ⊠*2–60 Hanaoka-chō, Takayama, Gifuken* ☎*0577/33–4600* ⊕*www.hida-hotelplaza.co.jp* ⇥*136 Western-style rooms, 89 Japanese-style rooms, 2 suites* ⚐*In-hotel: 4 restaurants, pool, gym, Japanese baths* ⊟*AE, DC, MC, V.*

$$
★
🖫 **Yamakyū** 山久. Cozy, antique-filled nooks with chairs and coffee tables become small lounges in this old Tera-machi minshuku. In the mineral-water baths a giant waterwheel turns hypnotically, complimented by recorded bird songs. Although there's an 11 PM curfew, dinner hours are more flexible than those of the typical minshuku, and the food, of astonishing variety, is superb. Fifteen of the rooms have private toilets. Yamakyū is east of the Enako-gawa, at the very top of San-machi dōri, a 20-minute walk from Takayama Station. **Pros:** warm, cozy atmosphere; excellent food. **Cons:** early-to-bed curfew means less freedom. ⊠*58 Tenshō-ji-machi, Takayama, Gifu-ken* ☎*0577/32–3756* ⇥*20 Japanese-style rooms without bath* ⚐*In-hotel: restaurant, Japanese baths* ⊟*No credit cards* ❑*MAP.*

NIGHTLIFE

Nightlife in sleepy Takayama revolves around locally produced beer and sake. Try one of the many small Japanese-style bars or izakaya that line the streets to the north of Kokubunji Street.

Two blocks east and one block south of City Hall is a bar popular with the foreign locals called **Red Hill** (✉ *1–4 Sowa-chō* ☎ *0577/33–8139* ☻ *Tues.–Sun. 7 PM–midnight*).

OGI-MACHI 荻町

80 km (50 mi) northwest of Takayama.

It's speculated that Ogi-machi, an Edo-era hamlet deep within Shirakawa-gō village, was originally populated by survivors of the powerful Taira family, who were nearly killed off in the 12th century by the rival Genji family. The majority of the residents living here still inhabit gasshō-zukuri houses. Their shape and materials enable the house to withstand the heavy regional snow, and in summer the straw keeps the houses cool. Household activities center on the *irori* (open hearth), which sends smoke up through the timbers and thatched roof. Meats and fish are preserved (usually on a metal shelf suspended above the hearth) by the ascending smoke, which also prevents insects and vermin from taking up residence in the straw.

Ogi-machi and the surrounding area makes for a good day trip from Kanazawa or Takayama, or as a stop on the way to either. It is also a relaxing place to spend an evening.

GETTING HERE AND AROUND

It's more convenient to drive to Ogi-machi, but it's possible to get there by public transportation. The bus to Ogi-machi departs from Nagoya at 9 AM daily, taking three hours and costing ¥3,500. You'll also find daily bus service from Ogi-machi to Kanazawa, departing at 8:40 AM and 2:40 PM. The trip also takes three hours, and costs ¥3,300, or ¥5,900 round-trip. Bus services stop from about the end of October until March or April, and it is best to reserve a seat through tourist offices in advance. From Takayama, buses go year-round four to six times daily for ¥2,400, ¥4,300 round-trip.

Many old houses function as minshuku. To stay in one, make reservations through the **Ogi-machi Tourist Office**, open daily 9–5. It's next to the Gasshō-shuraku bus stop in the center of town.

ESSENTIALS

Visitor Information Ogi-machi Tourist Office (✉ *57 Ogi-machi, Shirakawa-mura* ☎ *0576/96–1311*).

WHAT TO SEE

★ **Shirakawa-gō Gasshō-zukuri Village** 白川郷合掌造り村. Opposite Ogi-machi, on the banks of the Shō-gawa, this open-air museum has 25 traditional Gasshō-zukuri farmhouses. The houses were transplanted from four villages that fell prey to the Miboro Dam, built upriver in 1972. Over the years a colony of artisans has established itself in the village. You can watch them creating folk crafts like weaving, pottery, woodwork, and hand-dyeing in a few of the preserved houses. Many of the products are for sale. ✉ *Ogi-machi, Shirakawa mura, Ōno-gun* ☎ *0576/96–1231*.

KANAZAWA AND THE NORTH CHŪBU COAST

The center of culture and commerce in the Hokuriku region, Kanazawa ranks among Japan's best-loved cities. To the east are snow-capped mountains, including the revered (and hikeable) Haku-san. To the north stretches the clawlike peninsula of the Noto-hantō, where lush rolling hills and rice fields meet scenic coastlines. Farther north along the Nihon-kai are the hardworking industrial capitals of Toyama and Niigata, and offshore the secluded Sado Island.

KANAZAWA 金沢

225 km (140 mi) northeast of Kyōto; 257 km (160 mi) north of Nagoya; 153 km (95 mi) northwest of Takayama; 343 km (213 mi) southwest of Niigata.

Twenty-first century Kanazawa presents an extraordinary union of unblemished Old Japan and a modern, trendsetting city. More than 300 years of history have been preserved in the earthen walls and flowing canals of Nagamachi, the former samurai quarter west of downtown; the cluster of Buddhist temples in Tera-machi on the southern bank of the Saigawa River; and the wooden facades of the former geisha district, located north of the Asano-gawa river. Modern art, fashion, music, and international dining thrive in the downtown core of Kōrinbō, and in the shopping districts of Tatemachi and Katamachi. The Japan Sea provides great seafood and a somewhat dreary climate. Fortunately, cold, gray, and wet weather is offset by friendly people and only adds to the sad, romantic air of the city.

In the feudal times of the Edo period, the prime rice-growing areas around Kanazawa (known then as the province of Kaga) made the ruling Maeda clan the second wealthiest in the country. Harvests came in at more than *hyaku-man-goku* (1 million *koku*, the Edo-period unit of measurement based on how much rice would feed one person for a year). This wealth funded various cultural pursuits such as silk dyeing, ceramics, and the production of gold-leaf and lacquerware products.

This prosperity did not pass unnoticed. The fear of attack by the Edo daimyō inspired the Maeda lords to construct one of the country's most massive castles amid a mazelike network of narrow, winding lanes that make the approach difficult and an invasion nearly impossible. These defensive tactics paid off, and Kanazawa enjoyed 300 years of peace and prosperity. Nevertheless, seven fires over the centuries reduced the once-mighty Kanazawa-jō to castle walls and a single, impressive gate.

Between sightseeing, shopping, and sampling Kanazawa's many restaurants and cafés, it is worth staying here a couple of nights. Though the atmosphere of the city changes with each season, it is an excellent place to visit any time of the year.

GETTING HERE AND AROUND

The flight from Tōkyō's Haneda Kūkō to Komatsu Kūkō in Kanazawa takes one hour on Japan Airlines (JAL) or All Nippon Airlines (ANA); allow 40 minutes for the bus transfer to downtown Kanazawa, which costs ¥1,100. By train, Kanazawa is 2 hours from Kyōto; 3 hours from

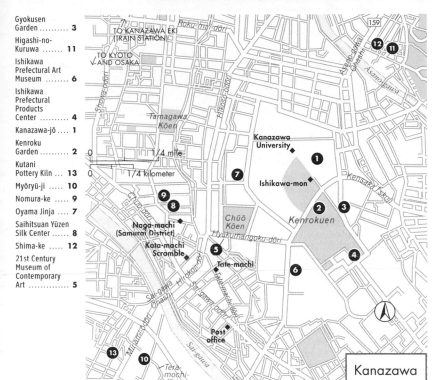

Kanazawa

Nagoya; 2½ hours from Takayama, changing trains at Toyama; and 3 hours 40 minutes from Niigata—all by JR Limited Express. Possible railway repairs between Toyama and Takayama may make the three-hour direct bus between Kanazawa and Takayama a better option; there are two daily, and the cost is ¥3,300 one way.

Ideal for tourists, the *shū-yū basu* (loop bus) departs every 15 minutes from 8:30 AM to 9 PM from Gate 0 of Kanazawa Station's east exit, and delivers you to the major tourist sites. Stops are announced in English and displayed on a digital board at the front of the bus. A single ride costs ¥200; the day pass is ¥500. You can purchase the pass from the Hokutetsu bus ticket office in front of Kanazawa Station.

Kanazawa is a good place to rent a car to explore the Noto Hanto and other parts of the Japan Sea Coast. Eki Rent-a-Car at the east exit from the train station is one reliable option.

The **Kanazawa Information Office** has two desks at the train station and staff that will help you find accommodations. An English speaker is on duty 1–6 from the **Kanazawa Goodwill Guide Network**, which offers free guide and interpreting services.

ESSENTIALS

Rental Agencies Eki Rent-a-Car (✉ *Kanazawa Station* ☎ *076/265–6659*).

Visitor Information Kanazawa Information Office (☎076/232–6200 ⊟076/ 238–6210 *Daily 9–7*).

WHAT TO SEE

❶ Kanazawa-jō 金沢城 *(Kanazawa Castle)*. The area surrounding the castle is a suitable place to start exploring Kanazawa. Recently restored, the castle's sprawling grounds and gardens make a good stop on the way to Kenrokuen Garden. Though most of the castle is a reproduction, the original **Ishikawa-mon** (Ishikawa Gate) remains intact—its thick mossy stone base is topped with curving black eaves and white lead roof tiles. The tiles could be melted down and molded into ammunition in the case of a prolonged siege. To reach the castle, take any bus (¥200) from Gate 11 at the bus terminal outside the JR station.

❷ Kenroku Garden 兼六園 *(Kenrokuen)*. Across the street from the Kanaza-
★ wa castle is the largest of the three most famous landscaped gardens in the country (the other two are Mito's Kairaku Garden and Okayama's Kōraku Garden). The Maeda lord Tsunanori began construction of Kenrokuen in 1676, and by the early 1880s it had become 25 sprawling acres of skillfully wrought bridges and fountains, ponds, and waterfalls. The garden changes with the seasons: spring brings cherry blossoms; brilliant azaleas foretell the arrival of summer; autumn paints the maples deep yellow and red; and in winter the pine trees are strung with long ropes, tied from trunk to bough, for protection against heavy snow-falls. Kenrokuen means "Garden of Six Qualities" (*ken-roku* means "integrated six"). The garden was so named because it exhibited the six superior characteristics judged necessary by the Chinese Sung Dynasty for the perfect garden: spaciousness, artistic merit, majesty, abundant water, extensive views, and seclusion. Despite the promise of its last attribute, the gardens attract a mad stampede of visitors—herded by megaphone—during cherry-blossom season (mid-April) and Golden Week (late April and early May). Early morning is the sensible time for a visit, when the grounds are peaceful and relaxing. ⊠*1 Kenroku-chō* ☎*076/221–5850* ⊑*¥300, free 3rd Sun. of month* ⊙*Mar.–mid-Oct., daily 7–6; mid-Oct.–Feb., daily 8–4:30.*

❸ Gyokusen Garden 玉泉園 *(Gyokusenen)*. This tiny, intimate garden was
Fodor'sChoice built by Kim Yeocheol, who later became Naokata Wakita when he
★ married into the ruling Kanazawa family. Yeocheol was the son of a Korean captive brought to Japan in the late 16th century. He became a wealthy merchant, using his fortune to build this quiet getaway. The garden's intimate tranquillity stems from the imaginative and subtle arrangement of moss, maple trees, and small stepping stones by the pond. Two waterfalls that gracefully form the Chinese character for *mizu* (water) feed the pond. The garden is markedly different from the bold strokes of Kenroku Garden. You can have tea here for ¥600. ☎*076/221–0181* ⊑*¥500* ⊙*Mid-Mar.–mid-Dec., Thurs.–Tues. 9–4.*

❹ Ishikawa Prefectural Products Center 石川県観光物産館 *(Ishikawa-ken Kankō Bussankan)*. Located near Gyokusen Garden, you can see dem-onstrations of Yuzen dyeing, pottery, and lacquerware production at this center. ☎*076/224–5511* ⊑*¥700, includes admission to Gyokusen Garden* ⊙*Apr.–Oct., daily 9–4:30; Nov.–Mar., Fri.–Wed. 9–4:30.*

❺ 21st-Century Museum of Contemporary Art 金沢21世紀美術館 *(21 Seiki Bijutsukan).* This circular building was created to entwine a museum's architecture with the art exhibits, and for exhibition designers to take cues from the architecture. Transparent walls and scattered galleries encourage visitors to choose their own route. Previous exhibitions have included a Gerhard Richter retrospective, a video installation by Mathew Barney, and the work of Japanese photographer Araki Nobuyoshi. It's south of Kanazawa Park, next to City Hall. ⊠*1–2–1 Hirosaka, Kanazawa, Ishikawa-ken* ☎*076/220–2801* ⊕*www.kanaz awa21.jp/en/index.html* ☞*Depends on exhibition* ⊙*Tues.–Fri. 10–6, weekends 10–8.*

❻ Ishikawa Prefectural Art Museum 石川県立美術館 *(Ishikawa Kenritsu Bijutsukan).* See the country's best permanent collection of *Kutaniyaki* (colorful overglaze-painted porcelain), dyed fabrics, and old Japanese paintings here. ⊠*2–1 Dewa-machi, southwest of Kenrokuen* ☎*076/231–7180* ☞*¥350* ⊙*Daily 9–4:30.*

❼ Oyama Jinja 尾山神社. Built in 1599, Oyama Jinja was dedicated to Lord Toshiie Maeda, the founder of the Maeda clan. The shrine's unusual three-story gate, **Shin-mon,** was completed in 1875. Previously located atop Mt. Utatsu, it's believed that the square arch containing stained-glass windows once functioned as a lighthouse, guiding ships in from the Japan Sea to the Kanaiwa port, 6 km (4 mi) northwest. You're free to walk around the shrine. To get here from the JR station, take Bus 30 or 31 from Gate 8. ⊠*11–1 Oyama-chō* ☎*076/231–7210* ☞*Free.*

❽ Saihitsuan Yūzen Silk Center 長町友禅館 (旧彩筆庵) *(Kyū-Saihitsuan).* A few houses have been carefully restored in the Samurai District, including the Saihitsuan Yūzen Silk Center, where you can watch demonstrations of Yūzen silk painting, a centuries-old technique in which intricate floral designs with delicate white outlines are meticulously painted onto silk used for kimonos. It's behind the Tōkyū Hotel, five blocks southwest of Oyama Jinja. ⊠*2–6–16 Naga-machi* ☎*076/264–2811* ☞*¥500* ⊙*Daily 9–4:30.*

❾ Nomura-ke. This elegant house in Naga-machi was rebuilt more than 100 years ago by an industrialist named Nomura. Visit the Jōdan-no-ma drawing room made of *hinoki* (cypress), with elaborate designs in rosewood and ebony. Then pass through the sliding doors, adorned with the paintings of Sasaki Senkai of the illustrious Kanō School, to a wooden veranda. Rest your feet here, and take in the stunning little garden with weathered lanterns among pine and maple trees, and various shrubs and bonsai. Stepping-stones lead to a pond dotted with moss-covered rocks and brilliant orange-flecked carp. In the upstairs tearoom you can enjoy a cup of *macha* (green tea) for ¥300 and a bird's-eye view of the gardens. ⊠*1–3–32 Naga-machi* ☎*076/221–3553* ☞*¥500* ⊙*Apr.–Sept., daily 8:30–5:30; Oct.–Mar., daily 8:30–4:30.*

Fodor's Choice
★

❿ Myōryū-ji 妙立寺. On the south side of the Sai-gawa is the intriguing and mysterious Myōryū-ji. Its popular name, Ninja-dera (Temple of the Ninja), suggests it was a clandestine training center for martial-arts masters who crept around in the dead of night armed with *shuriken* (star-shaped blades). In fact, the temple was built to provide an escape route for the daimyō in case of invasion. Ninja-dera was built by Toshitsune in 1643, when the Tokugawa shogunate was stealthily knocking off local warlords and eliminating competition. At first glance, it appears a modest yet handsome two-story structure. Inside, however, you find 29 staircases, seven levels, myriad secret passageways and trap doors, a tunnel to the castle hidden beneath the well in the kitchen, and even a *seppuku* room, where the lord could perform an emergency ritual suicide. Unfortunately (or fortunately, considering all the booby traps), visitors are not permitted to explore the hidden lair alone. You must join a Japanese tour and follow along with your English pamphlet. ✉ *1–2–12 No-machi* ☎ *076/241–0888* 💳 *¥800* ⏱ *Mar.–Nov., daily 9–4:30; Dec.–Feb., daily 9–4.*

> ## SAMURAI TOWN
>
> Behind the modern Kōrinbō 109 shopping center, Seseragi-dōri leads to **Naga-machi** 長町 (the *Samurai District*), where the Maeda clan lived. Narrow, snaking streets are lined with beautiful, golden adobe walls 8 feet high, footed with large stones and topped with black tiles.

⑪ **Higashi-no-Kuruwa** 東の郭 *(the Eastern Pleasure Quarter).* The high-class entertainment district of Edo-period Kanazawa was near the Asano-gawa. Now the pleasures are limited to viewing quaint old geisha houses recognizable by their wood-slat facades and latticed windows. Many have become tearooms, restaurants, or minshuku. If you are lucky, you might see a geisha scuttling to an appointment. Take the JR bus from Kanazawa Station (¥200) to Hachira-chō, just before the Asano-gawa Ōhashi. Cross the bridge and walk northeast into the quarter.

⑫ **Shima-ke** 志摩家. This elegant former geisha house is open to the public for tours. ✉ *1–13–21 Higashi-yama* ☎ *076/252–5675* 💳 *¥400* ⏱ *Tues.–Sun. 9–5.*

⑬ **Kutani Pottery Kiln** 九谷光仙窯 *(Kutani Kōsen Gama).* You can watch artisans making the local Kutani pottery, which is noted for its vibrant color schemes, at this spot, which was established in 1870. ✉ *5–3–3 No-machi* ☎ *076/241–0902* 💳 *Free* ⏱ *Mon.–Sat. 8:30–noon and 1–5, Sun. 8:30–noon.*

WHERE TO EAT

$$–$$$
JAPANESE

✗**Fumuroya** 不室屋. Not far from the Ōmi-Chō market, this store specializes in wheat gluten, called *ofu*, and its adjacent lunch restaurant offers a set lunch for ¥3,150 of *jibu ni*, a stew made with chicken (instead of the usual duck), ofu, and shiitake mushrooms. ✉ *2–3–1 Owari-chō* ☎ *0762/21–1377* 🍽 *Reservations essential* 💳 *V* ⏱ *Mon.–Sat. 11:30–4. Closed 2nd and 4th Mon. of each month.*

$$$
JAPANESE

✗**Itaru** いたる. Slip into Itaru for a taste of good Kaga-ryōri at a reasonable price. Although the staff speaks little English, they have English menus available to help you out. For a sampling of local cuisine, try their set course that varies seasonally. Watching the cooks behind the counter adds to the overall dining experience. Also on the menu is a good selection of local sake. ✉ *2–7–5 Katamachi 920-0981* ☎ *0762/24–4156* 💳 *No credit cards* ⏱ *Daily 5:30–11:30.*

$$$–$$$$
JAPANESE
★

✕**Kincharyō** 金茶寮. The menu changes seasonally in the showpiece restaurant of the Kanazawa Tōkyū Hotel. The lacquered, curved countertop of the sushi bar is beautiful. Superb dinner courses range from tempura sets (¥4,042–¥8,085) to mixed kaiseki (9 items cost ¥5,775). In spring your meal may include *hotaru-ika* (firefly squid) and *iidako* (baby octopus) no larger than your thumbnail. The lunch *kaiseki bentō* costs from ¥1,300 to ¥3,600. ⊠ *Kanazawa Tōkyū Hotel, 3rd fl., 2–1–1 Kōrinbo* ☏ *076/231–2411* ▭ *AE, DC, MC, V.*

¢–$
INDONESIAN
★

✕**Legian** レギャン. You might be surprised to find a funky Balinese eatery alongside the Sai-gawa. But if you try the *gado-gado* (vegetables in a spicy sauce), *nasi goreng* (Indonesian-style fried rice), or chicken *satay* (grilled on a skewer, with peanut sauce), you'll be happily surprised. Indonesian beer and mango ice cream are also available. It's open late (Monday–Thursday until 12:30 AM, Friday and Saturday until 4:30 AM), and after dinner things get interesting. From Kata-machi Scramble (the area's central intersection), turn right just before Sai-gawa bridge, and follow the narrow lane along the river. ⊠ *2–31–30 Kata-machi* ☏ *076/262–6510* ▭ *No credit cards* ⊘ *Closed Wed.*

$$$ $$$$
JAPANESE
★

✕**Miyoshian** 三芳庵. Excellent *bentō* (box lunches) and fish and vegetable dinners have been made here for nearly 100 years in the renowned Kenroku Garden. Prices are still reasonable—the Kaga kaiseki course is less than ¥3,000. In the annex matcha tea is served with Japanese pastries from Morihachi, a confectioner with a 360-year history. ⊠ *1 Kenroku chō* ☏ *076/221–0127* ▭ *AE, MC, V* ⊘ *Closed Tues.*

¢
CAFE

✕**Noda-ya** 野田屋. Slip into this little tea shop for a scoop of delicious *macha sofuto kurīmu* (green tea ice cream) or a cup of tea. You can sit in the little garden in back or on benches out front. At the far end of the Tate-machi shopping street the heavenly scent of roasting green tea leaves wafts out the door ⊠ *3 Tate-machi* ☏ *076/22–0982* ▭ *No credit cards.* ⊘ *Daily 9–8.*

$$$$
JAPANESE

✕**Sugi no I** 杉の井. This elegant restaurant in Teramachi, on the south bank of the Saigawa River close to the Sakura-bashi bridge, serves Kaga specialties like duck stew with wheat gluten called *jibu ni* and *gori no tsukuda ni*, tiny soy-simmered river fish on Kutani china, Oribe pottery, and lacquerware. There is a special ladies' course (that anyone can order) for ¥3,000. For a surcharge of ¥500 per person you can have a private room overlooking the garden. In traditional Japanese style, the meal finishes with rice, pickles, and soup; in autumn the broth is clear with herbs and a shrimp dumpling. Full-course dinners start at ¥15,000. ⊠ *3–11 Sugi no I, Kyokawa Machi* ☏ *0762/43–2288* ⚲ *Reservations essential* ▭ *AE, V.*

WHERE TO STAY

$$$$
★

▨ **APA Hotel Eki-mae** アパホテル金沢駅前. This hotel is so close to the JR station it's practically inside it. A blue ceiling with sparkling stars watches over a Seattle's Best coffee shop and a modern lobby. Inside your small yet stylish room a charming origami crane perches atop a carefully pressed bathrobe. Each room has views over Kanazawa, and the sauna and onsen are free for guests. **Pros:** directly next to JR Station; classy. **Cons:** a 30-minute walk from the sights and nightlife of Kata-machi. ⊠ *1–9–28 Hirōka, Kanazawa, Ishikawa-ken* ☏ *076/231–8111*

5

🖨*076/231–8112* ⊕*www.apahotel.com* 🛏*456 rooms* ♿*In-room: refrigerator. In-hotel: 2 restaurants, no-smoking rooms* ▤*AE, DC, MC, V.*

$$$$ ⚏**Hotel Nikkō Kanazawa.** The exotic lobby of this 30-story hotel is more
★ reminiscent of Singapore than Japan, with tropical plants, cherry-oak slatted doors, and colonial-style furniture. A winding staircase curls around a bubbling pond in the middle of the lobby and leads to a European brasserie, Garden House, which serves wonderful coffee and cake. The colorful top-floor lounge, Le Grand Chariot, has panoramic views over Kanazawa, sumptuous French cuisine, and soft piano music. Guest rooms begin at the 17th floor, and the Western-style ones are decorated with creamy pastels and blond-wood furnishings and have striking views of the sea, city, or mountains. An underground passageway connects the hotel to the JR station. The hotel charges ¥2,100 for use of the pool and gym. **Pros:** near JR Station; spacious rooms. **Cons:** it's a long walk to Katamachi's sights and nightlife. ✉*2–15–1 Honmachi, Kanazawa, Ishikawa-ken* ☎*076/234–1111* 🖨*076/234–8802* ⊕*www.jalhotels.com* 🛏*256 rooms, 4 suites* ♿*In-room: Internet. In-hotel: 4 restaurants, bars, pool, gym, laundry service, parking (fee), no-smoking rooms* ▤*AE, DC, MC, V.*

$$$–$$$$ ⚏**Kanazawa New Grand Hotel**金沢ニューグランドホテル. Stepping into this hotel's sleek black-and-cream marble lobby is a refreshing break from the dreary concrete of the main drag outside. From the sky lounge, **Dichter,** and restaurant, **Sky Restaurant Roi,** you get a great view of Oyama Shrine and the sunset. The spacious rooms, though far from new, are done in white-and-beige tones, and have sofas. Japanese-style rooms are slightly larger, but furnishings are spare. The hotel is a 15-minute walk from the station, if you head down Eki-mae-dōri and take a right on Hikoso-ōdōri. **Pros:** good location halfway between JR Station and Katamachi; restaurant serves some of the city's best contemporary French cuisine. **Cons:** few interesting places in the immediate vicinity. ✉*1–50 Takaoka-chō, Kanazawa, Ishikawa-ken* ☎*076/233–1311* 🖨*076/233–1591* ⊕*www.new-grand.co.jp* 🛏*100 Western-style rooms, 2 Japanese-style rooms, 2 suites* ♿*In-room: Internet. In-hotel: 5 restaurants, no-smoking rooms* ▤*AE, DC, MC, V.*

$$$$ ⚏**Ryokan Asadaya** 旅館浅田屋. This small ryokan, established during
★ the Meiji Restoration (1867), is the most lavish lodging in Kanazawa. The interior blends traditional elegance with innovative designs— a perfect metaphor for the age of Japan's transition into modernity. Antique furnishings and exquisite scrolls and paintings appear throughout the inn. Superb regional Kaga cuisine is served in your room or in the restaurant. **Pros:** historic property; elegant furnishings. **Cons:** expensive; a bit far from downtown. ✉*23 Jukken-machi, Kanazawa, Ishikawa-ken* ☎*076/232–2228* 🖨*076/252–4444* ⊕*www.asadaya. co.jp/asadayaryokan_e.php* 🛏*5 Japanese-style rooms* ♿*In-hotel: restaurant* ▤*AE* 🍽|*MAP.*

¢ ⚏**Yōgetsu** 陽月. In a century-old geisha house in the Eastern Pleasure Quarter, Yōgetsu is a small, stylish minshuku. The owner is a welcoming hostess and keeps a neat shared bath. The guest rooms are small and sparsely furnished, but rustic exposed beams add character. Only second-floor rooms are air-conditioned. **Pros:** quiet location; charming atmosphere. **Cons:** fewer amenities than major hotels. ✉ *1–13–22 Higashiyama, Kanazawa, Ishikawa-ken* ☎ *076/252–0497* ⌨ *5 Japanese-style rooms without bath* ♨ *In-hotel: restaurant, Japanese baths* ═ *No credit cards* ⦿*MAP.*

NIGHTLIFE

All-night fun can be found in the center of town. ■**TIP→ Be warned: these places don't take credit cards.** Free billiard tables make **Apre** (✉ *Laporto Bldg., 1–3–9 Katamachi* ☎ *076/221–0090*) a scene on weekends. When it opens at 8 PM, the tables fill up, and the action is competitive. It's tricky to find, so don't hesitate to call for directions. It's closed Monday. **Pole-Pole** (*"po-ray-po-ray"* ✉ *2–31–31 Kata-machi* ☎ *076/260–1138*) is a reggae bar run by the same jolly owner as Legian, and is just behind the restaurant. If you want to sit, arrive before midnight. The two dark cramped rooms get so full that the crowd spills out into the hallway. Pole-Pole is closed on Sunday but open until 5 AM the rest of the week.

FUKUI 福井

80 km (50 mi) southwest of Kanazawa, 177km (110 mi) north of Nagoya.

★ **Eihei-ji** 永平寺. One of the two headquarters of Sōtō Zen, Eihei-ji is 19 km (12 mi) southeast of Fukui. Founded in 1244, the extensive complex of 70 temple buildings is spread out on a hillside surrounded by hinoki and *sugi* (cedar) trees more than 100 feet tall, some as old as the original wooden structures. This temple offers a rare glimpse into the daily practice of the 200 or so monks (and a few nuns) in training. They are called *unsui* or cloud water, the traditional name for mendicant monks wandering in search of a teacher. The rigorous training remains unchanged since Dōgen started this monastery. Each monk only has one tatami mat (1 meter by 2 meters), to eat, sleep, and meditate on. The mats are lined in rows on raised platforms in a communal room. All activities, from using the bathroom to cleaning out the incense tray, are considered to be meditations, and so visitors are expected to dress modestly and explore in silence. Students of Zen or those interested in meditation can do short retreats of one to three days and lodge at the temple (for ¥8,000 a night, including two meals), with two weeks' advance notice in writing. The easiest way to get to Eihei-ji from Fukui is by train. ✉ *5–15 Shihi Eiheiji-chō, Yoshida-gun, Fukui* ☎ *0776/63–3102* ⬚¥500 ◷*Daily 5–5.*

WHERE TO STAY

¢–$ ⬚ **Hotel Akebono Bekkan** ホテルアケボノ別館. Think of this small, two-story wooden hotel as a weekend retreat—the owners can arrange training sessions in Zen meditation and classes in pottery and papermaking. The Akebono Bekkan is actually the annex of a large, modern hotel, the Riverge Akebono, so you can enjoy the best of both worlds. Both Japanese and Western breakfasts are served, but only Japanese food is available at dinner. All the small tatami rooms have private toilets, but the bath is shared. The inn is next to Sakura Bridge, a 10-minute walk from Fukui

Station. **Pros:** convenient location; benefits of a hotel with the comfort of a ryokan. **Cons:** not all rooms have baths. ✉ *3–10–12 Chūō, Fukui-shi, Fukui-ken* ☎ *0776/22–1000* 🖷 *0776/22–8023* ⊕ *www.riverge. com* 🛏 *10 Japanese-style rooms, 5 without bath* ♿ *In-hotel: restaurant, Japanese baths* 🚭 *AE, V.*

NOTO-HANTŌ (NOTO PENINSULA) 能登半島

Thought to be named after an Ainu (indigenous Japanese) word for "nose," the Noto-hantō, a national park, juts out into the Nihon-kai and shelters the bays of both Nanao and Toyama. Steep, densely forested hills line the eroded west coast, which is wind- and wave-blasted in winter and ruggedly beautiful in other seasons. The eastern shoreline is lapped by calmer waters and has stunning views of Tate-yama (Mt. Tate), the Hida Mountains, and even of some of Nagano's alpine peaks more than 105 km (70 mi) away.

A quick sightseeing circuit of the Noto-hantō, from Hakui to Nanao, can be done in six to eight hours, but to absorb the peninsula's remarkable scenery, stay two or three days, stopping in Wajima and at one of the minshuku along the coast; arrangements can be made through tourist information offices in Kanazawa, Nanao, or Wajima.

GETTING HERE AND AROUND

Nanao, on east coast of peninsula, and Wajima, on the north coast of Noto-hantō are accessible by JR Limited Express via Kanazawa. The peninsula is a good place to explore by car or bicycle. Although the interior routes can be arduous, the coastal roads are relatively flat. You can also combine train and bus trips or guided tours, which can be arranged in Kanazawa. From Anamizu the private Noto Line goes northeast to Takojima, the region's most scenic route. The line to Wajima turns inland after Hakui and misses some of the peninsula's best sights. In Wajima your best bet for a car is **Nissan Rent-a-Car** at Wajima Station. Rent bikes in Hakui from **Kato Cycle** for ¥800 per day across from Joyful Supermarket, west of the JR station.

ESSENTIALS
Bicycle Rental Katō Cycle (☎ *0767/22–0539*).

Rental Agencies Nissan Rent-a-Car (✉ *14–27 Shōwa-machi, Wajima* ☎ *0762/ 22–0177*).

Visitor Information Kanazawa Information Office (☎ *076/232–6200* 🖷 *076/ 238–6210*). **Wajima Tourist Office** (☎ *0768/22–1503* ⊗ *10–6*).

WHAT TO SEE

Hakui 羽咋. In Hakui, a 40-minute train ride from Kanazawa, you can bike along the coastal path as far as beautiful Gan-mon (Sea Gate), some 26 km (16 mi) away, where you can stop for lunch. Just north of Chirihama, a formerly popular and now unkempt beach, the scenery improves.

Myōjō-ji 妙成寺 is a less visited but well-tended temple complex a few miles north by bus from Hakui (buses leave outside the train station). The temple, founded in 1294 and belonging to the Nichiren sect of

Buddhism, has a five-story pagoda from the 1600s. A very large, colorful Buddha statue sits inside a squat wooden building. The influence of mainland Asia is visible in the gargantuan, wooden guardian deities. A recording on the bus announces where to get off for Myōjō-ji. It's a 10-minute walk to the temple from the bus stop. ⊠1 Yo Taki-danimachi ☎0767/27–1226 ☞¥500 ⊙Daily 8–5.

EN ROUTE Although you can take the inland bus directly north from Hakui to Monzen, the longer (70-minute) bus ride along the coast is recommended for its scenic value. The 16-km (10-mi) stretch between Fuku-ura and Sekinohana, known as the **Noto Seacoast** 能登金剛 (Noto-Kongō), has fantastic wind– and wave-eroded rocks, from craggy towers to partly submerged checkerboard-pattern platforms. Among the best is **Gan-mon**, a rock cut through the center by water. Gan-mon is about 45 minutes north of Hakui and is a stop on tour-bus routes.

The Zen temple complex **Sōji-ji** 總持寺 at Monzen once served as the Sōtō sect's headquarters. Though a fire destroyed most of the buildings in 1818 and the sect moved its headquarters to Yokohama in 1911, this is still an important training temple. As at Eihei-ji in Fukui, lay practitioners may stay for a few days. Strolling paths traverse the lush grounds, where you can see some spectacular red maples and an elaborately carved gate. The Sōji-ji-mae bus stop is in front of the temple; use a bus from Monzen Station to reach it. It also can be accessed from the Anamizu bus station on the Noto Chūō bus bound for Monzen (32 minutes). ⊠1–18 Monzen, Wajima-shi, Monzen-chō ☞¥400 ⊙Daily 8–5.

Only 16 km (10 mi) and one bus stop up the road from Monzen is **Wajima** 輪島. This fishing town at the tip of the peninsula is also known for its gorgeous lacquerware.

To observe the traditional lacquerware manufacturing process, visit the **Lacquerware Hall** (Wajima Shikki Kaikan). The production of a single piece involves more than 20 steps from wood preparation and linen reinforcement to the application of layers of lacquer, carefully dried and polished between coats. Wajima Shikki Kaikan is in the center of town on the north side of Route 249, just before Shin-bashi (New Bridge). From the station, turn left when you exit and walk straight (northwest) about four blocks until you hit Route 249. Turn left again—there's a Hokuriku Bank on the corner—and continue southwest along Route 249 for about four blocks. ⊠ 24–55 Kawai-machi ☎0768/22–2155 ☞¥200 ⊙Daily 8:30–5.

The **asa-ichi** 朝市, or morning market, in Wajima is held daily 8–11:30, except on the 10th and 25th of each month. You can buy seafood, fruit, vegetables, local crafts, and lacquerware from elderly women wearing indigo monpei (field pants). The smaller yū-ichi (evening market) starts around 3 PM. Almost anyone can point you in the right direction. ⊠Asa-ichi dōri, Kawai-chō ☎0768/22–7653 mornings only.

NEED A BREAK? Various sashimi and sushi teishoku (sets) are reasonably priced at **Shin-puku** (⊠ 41 Kawai-chō, Wajima-shi ☎ 0768/22–8133), a small but beautiful sushi bar a 10-minute walk from the train station. From the station, turn left as you exit and walk northwest (left) about four blocks until you hit the main road, Route 249. Then turn right and walk northeast about three blocks along Route 249. One block past the Cosmo gas station (on the left), Shin-puku is on the right, and is open daily until 10 PM.

From Wajima an hourly bus runs to **Sosogi** 曾々木, a small village 20 minutes to the northeast, passing the terraced fields of **Senmaida,** where rice paddies descend from the hills to the sea.

From Sosogi you can continue around the peninsula's northern tip by bus, from to **Rokkō-zaki** 禄剛崎 *(Cape Rokkō),* past a small lighthouse, and down to the northern terminus of the Noto Railway Line at Takojima. Unless you have a car, however, the views and scenery don't quite justify the infrequency of the public transportation.

The same hourly bus that runs between Wajima and Sosogi continues on to **Suzu** 珠洲 on the *uchi* (inside) coast. Just south of Suzu, near Ukai Station, is a dramatic offshore rock formation called *Mitsuke-jima,* a huge wedge of rock topped with lush vegetation, connected to the shore with a pebbly path popular with lovers. It is said that Kobo Daishi gave it the nickname of *Gunkan Island* or Battleship Island because it resembles a warship sailing to attack.

NEED A BREAK?

A terrific brewery and log-cabin-style restaurant called the **Heart and Beer Nihonkai Club** (✉ *92 Aza-Tatekabe, Uchiura-machi* ☎ *0768/72–8181*) is five minutes by taxi from Matsunami Station (on the Noto Line). It's operated by two beer masters from Eastern Europe in conjunction with an association that helps people with disabilities. Specials include delicious emu stew (¥1,200), raised on-site, and tasty Noto beef, along with some very good microbrewed beer (¥460). It's open from Thursday to Tuesday.

Nanao 七尾 is best known for its festivals. Seihakusai festival, a 400-year-old tradition held May 3–5, is essentially three days of nonstop partying. Huge (26-foot) 10-ton floats resembling ships called *deka-yama* (big mountains) are paraded through the streets. At midnight the floats become miniature kabuki stages for dance performances by costumed children. Since Seihakusai festival is celebrated during Golden Week, when almost everyone in Japan is on vacation, it's a wild scene. The men pulling the floats are given generous and frequent libations of beer and sake, and the crowd also suffers no shortage of refreshments.

Takaoka 高岡, the southern gateway to the Noto Peninsula has Japan's third-largest **Daibutsu** (Great Buddha), standing 53 feet high and made of bronze. Also in Takaoka, a 400-meter walk from the station, is **Zuiryū-ji,** a delightful Zen temple that doubles as a youth hostel. A sprawling park, **Kojō-kōen,** not far from the station, is particularly stunning in autumn, with its red-and-silver maples. Takaoka is mostly known for its traditions of copper-, bronze-, and iron-smithing, and remains a major bell-casting center.

WHERE TO STAY

$$ ☷ **Fukasan** 深三. Conveniently near the morning market and only one street up from the harbor, this two-story wooden minshuku is infused with the warmth of the hosts, who have furnished the interior with locally made crafts. Included in the rate are two meals. **Pros:** excellent location for visiting the morning market; traditional atmosphere. **Cons:** fewer amenities than a larger hotel. ✉ *Kawaimachi 4–4 Wajima City, Ishikawa-ken* ☎ *0768/22–9933* 🖷 *0768/22–9934* 🛏 *4 Japanese rooms* ⚘ *In-hotel: restaurant* ▭ *No credit cards* ¶◉*MAP.*

$$$$ ☷ **Mawaki Pō-re Pō-re** 真脇ポーレポーレ. This little hotel, built into a hillock, connects with the bath complex at Mawaki and has great views of the sea and surrounding hills. Breakfast is included, and the staff is kind. The Western-style rooms are done in blue and lilac; the Japanese-style rooms have shōji screens and are slightly larger and brighter but cost more. You're a minute away from the mineral baths. **Pros:** choice of Western or Japanese-style rooms. **Cons:** somewhat out of the way. ✉ *19–110 Aza-Mawaki, Noto-cho, Housu-gun, Ishikawa-ken* ☎ *0768/62–4700* 🖷 *0768/62–4702* 🛏 *5 Western-style rooms, 5 Japanese-style rooms, 1 suite* ⚘ *In-hotel: restaurant* ▭ *AE, MC, V* ¶◉*BP.*

$$$$ ☷ **Wakara Yonekyu** 和倉米久. A six-minute ride from JR Wakura Onsen station gets you to this white seven-story bay-front hotel that combines ryokan traditional touches with modern facilities. At the spacious indoor and outdoor hot-spring baths you feel the ocean spray. A complimentary cup of matcha is served in the tea ceremony room. Room rates include two meals, usually local fish and beef and sometimes snow crab. **Pros:** comforts of a hotel with hints of a ryokan. **Cons:** less traditional than the local ryokan and minshuku. ✉ *6–8–6, Kawaimachi Wajima City, Ishikawa-ken* ☎ *0768/22–4488* 🖷 *0768/22–8899* 🛏 *39 rooms* ⚘ *In-hotel: restaurant, bar* ▭ *AE, MC, V* ¶◉*MAP.*

TOYAMA 富山

18 km (11 mi) southeast of Takaoka, 61 km (38 mi) of Kanazawa, 282 km (175 mi) north of Kyōto

Busy, industrial Toyama is beautified by Toyama-jōshi Kōen (Toyama Castle Park), a spread of greenery with a reconstructed version of the original 1532 castle. **Toyama Bay** is the habitat of the glowing *hotaru ika,* or firefly squid. Their spawning grounds stretch for 15 km (9 mi) along the coast from Uozu to the right bank of Toyama City's Jouganji River and about 1.3 km from shore. From March until June, their spawning season, the females gather close to the seabed and come to the surface from dusk until midnight. From the early morning until dawn the sea magically glows from the squids' photophores, blue-white light-producing organs that attract their prey. This phenomenon has been designated a special natural monument. Sightseeing boats provide close-up views.

GETTING HERE AND AROUND

All Nippon Airways has five flights daily between Tōkyō and Toyama. Toyama is 30 minutes from Takaoka by JR local, 1 hour from Kanazawa by JR Limited Express, and three and four hours north of Kyōto and

Nagoya, respectively, by JR. Toyama has a network of streetcars that can take you to most destinations within town. Other than as a base to see some of the surrounding area, there is not much reason to linger in Toyama. It makes for a convenient overnight stop, however.

ESSENTIALS

Visitor Information Toyama Tourist Information Office (☎ *0764/32–9751*).

WHAT TO SEE

A slow open-air train called the **Kurobe-kyōkoku Railway** 黒部峡谷鉄道 operates April through November along the river of the deepest valley in Japan, Kurobe-kyōkoku (Kurobe Gorge) to Keyakidaira. On the 20-km (12½-mi), 90-minute ride the old-fashioned tram chugs past gushing springs and waterfalls, and you might even see wild monkeys or *serow,* a native type of mountain goat. One of the best views is from the 125-foot-long, 128-foot-high bridge, Atobiki-kyo. Bring a windbreaker, even in summer, as it's a cold and damp ride. Kuronagi-onsen, Kanetsuri-onsen, and Meiken-onsen, which supply water to Unazuki-onsen, and other hot springs, are along the trolley route. You can get off at any one of those springs and enjoy the spa. From June to November the Kurobe-Kyōkoku trains leave Unazuki for Keyakidaira twice hourly from 7:30 to 3:40 and cost ¥1,440 one-way. To get to Unazuki from Toyama Station, take the JR line to Uozu Station and switch to the Chitetsu line (30 minutes). A 1-km (½-mi) walk from Keyaki-daira Station leads to the precipitous cliff over the Sarutobi-kyo valley and a view of the Kurobe River.

HIKING

For experienced hikers there are some breathtaking vistas from the top of Mt. Takayama and other peaks in the area; however, adequate planning is necessary and maps in English are hard to come by.

From Keyakidaira you can proceed on foot to two rotemburo (open-air spas) nearly 100 years old: **Meiken Onsen** 名剣温泉 is a 10- to 15-minute walk; **Babadani Onsen** 祖母谷温泉, 35 to 40 minutes.

If you're a serious hiker, trails from Keyakidaira can lead you to the peak of **Shirouma-dake** *(Mt. Shirouma),* more than 9,810 feet high, in several hours. Nearby **Tate-yama** (Mt. Tate) also rewards experienced hikers with stunning views. You can also hike to Kurobe Dam and to the cable car that leads up to a tunnel through Tate-yama to Murodō. If you have several days to spare, camping gear, and a map of mountain trails and shelters, you can go as far as Hakuba in Nagano.

The **National Parks Association of Japan** 国立公園協会 in Tōkyō is a good source of help on hiking and camping around Toyama. ⊠ *Toranomon Denki Bldg., 4th fl., 2–8–1 Toranomon, Tōkyō* ✛ *From Toranomon Station on Ginza subway line, take Exit 2 and walk 2 blocks straight before taking a right. The Toranomon Denki Building will be on left in 3rd block.* ☎ *03/3502–0488.*

NIIGATA 新潟

155 mi from Toyama, 205 mi northwest of Tōkyō.
The coast between Kurobe and Niigata is flat and not so interesting. Two towns along the way, Naoetsu and Teradomari, serve as ferry ports to Ogi and Akadomari, respectively, on Sado-ga-shima. From Niigata ferries go to Sado-ga-shima and even Hokkaidō. In the skiing season people fly in to Niigata before traveling by train to the northern Alps for quick access to ski resorts.

GETTING HERE AND AROUND
Niigata is 3 hours from Toyama on the JR Hokuriku line, 1½ hours or 2 hours 15 minutes from Tōkyō by Shinkansen, and Toki local line respectively. Niigata serves as a waypoint en route to Sado-ga-shima. **Kyokushin Kōkū** (Kyokushin Aviation) has small planes that take 25 minutes to fly from Sado-ga-shima to Niigata; there are five round-trip flights a day in summer and three in winter; the one-way fare is ¥7,350.

Contact the **Niigata Kōtsū Information Center** to the left of the Ryōtsu bus terminal for a tour of Sado-ga-shima. It covers Skyline Drive, where public buses don't run. Tours, from May to November, depart daily from Ryōtsu and cost ¥6,440. You'll also find city maps, ferry schedules, and help finding a hotel there.

ESSENTIALS
Airline Contact Kyokushin Kōkū (☎ *025/273–0312 in Niigata, 0259/23–5005 in Sado).*

Visitor Information Niigata Kōtsū Information Office (☎ *025/241–7914 Daily 8:30–7).*

WHAT TO SEE
Northern Culture Museum 北方文化博物館 *(Hoppō Bunka Keikan.)* On the banks of the Agano River on the Kamabara plain the museum is a 40-minute bus ride from Niigata station. This former estate was established in the Edo period by the Itō family, which, by the 1930s, was the largest landowner in the Kaetsu area, with 3,380 hectares of paddy fields, more than 2,500 acres of forest, and 78 overseers who controlled no fewer than 2,800 tenants. The family also owned about 60 warehouses, which stored 1,800 tons of rice every autumn. Ito Mansion, built in 1887, was their home for generations until the Land Reform Act of 1946, which compelled landowners to sell off their paddy land holdings above 3 hectares. Their mansion with its valuable art collection became this museum, which has two restaurants and coffee shops. The house has 65 rooms, a special art gallery, gardens, a tearoom, and an annex for study called "Sanrakutei" where everything—pillars, furniture, and even tatami mats—is triangular or diamond-shaped. The garden is laid out in the traditional style of the Kamakura and Muromachi periods (14th–15th centuries). Its five teahouses are in different parts of the garden (two of them built later), and numerous natural rocks—mostly from Kyōto—are artistically arranged around the pond. At Niigata ask the Tourist Information Office to point you in the direction of the right bus, which takes 40 minutes. Alternatively, by taxi it

takes 25 minutes. ⊠2–15–25 Sōmi, Niigata ☎025/385–4003 ⊠¥800 🕐 Daily 9–4:30.

WHERE TO EAT AND STAY

$$–$$$
JAPANESE
★

✕**Inaka-ya** 田舎家. Their specialty, *wappa-meshi* (rice steamed in a wooden box with toppings of salmon, chicken, or crab), makes an inexpensive and excellent lunch. The *yanagi karei hitohoshi-yaki* (grilled flounder), *nodo-kuro shioyaki* (grilled local whitefish), and *buri teriyaki* (yellowtail) will make your mouth water. Inaka-ya closes between lunch and dinner from 2 to 5, and is found in the heart of Furu-machi, the local eating and drinking district. ⊠1457 Kyūban-chō, Furu-machi-dōri ☎025/223–1266 ⨼ *Reservations not accepted* ⊟ *No credit cards.*

$$–$$$
JAPANESE

✕**Marui** 丸伊. This is the place for fresh fish. For starters, order the *nami nigiri* (standard sushi set) for ¥1,400, plus a bottle of chilled sake, the local Kitayuki brand, for ¥1,260. Then glance at what your neighbors have ordered and ask for what looks good. You can't go wrong with the freshest fish, abalone, sea urchin, and squid in town. Marui closes during mid-afternoon. It's one block off the Furu-machi arcade, around the corner from Inaka-ya. ⊠8–1411 Higashibori-dōri 951-8066 ☎025/228–0101 ⊟MC, V.

$$$$

▥**Ōkura Hotel Niigata** ホテルオークラ新潟. This is a sophisticated, first-class hotel on the Shinano-gawa, ½ km from the station. Rooms overlooking Shinano-gawa have the best views. A formal French restaurant in the penthouse overlooks the city. Breakfast and lighter meals are in the Grill Room. **Pros:** the highest-class hotel in Niigata; good location. **Cons:** more expensive than other lodgings. ⊠6–53 Kawabata-chō Chuo-ku, Niigata City, Niigata-ken ☎025/224–6111, 0120/10–0120 toll-free in Japan 🖷025/224–7060 ⊕www.okura-niigata.com ⇗300 Western-style and Japanese-style rooms ♨In-hotel: 3 restaurants ⊟AE, DC, MC, V.

▥**Niigata Tōei Hotel** 新潟東映ホテル. For an inexpensive business hotel a block and a half from the station, this ranks the best. The rooms are the usual small but tidy business hotel fare but the location is a good one. The ninth floor has a Japanese steak house and a lounge that closes unusually early (9 PM). **Pros:** near Niigata Station; rooftop beer garden from June to September. **Cons:** the usual small business hotel rooms. ⊠1–6–2 Benten, Niigata ☎025/244–7101 🖷025/241–8485 ⇗133 rooms ♨In-room: Internet. In-hotel: 2 restaurants, bar ⊟AE, D, MC, V.

SADO ISLAND (SADO-GA-SHIMA) 佐渡島

84 km (52 mi) from Niigata.

Sado is known as much for its unblemished natural beauty as for its melancholy history. Revolutionary intellectuals, such as the Buddhist monk Nichiren, were banished to Sado to endure harsh exile as punishment for treason. When gold was discovered on Sado during the Edo period (1603–1868), the homeless and poverty-stricken were sent to Sado to work as forced laborers in the mines. This long history of hardship has left a tradition of soulful ballads and folk dances. Even the bamboo grown on the island is said to be the best for making *shakuhachi,* the flutes that accompany the mournful music.

May through September is the best time to visit Sado. In January and February the weather is bitterly cold, and at other times storms can prevent sea and air crossings. Although the island is Japan's fifth largest, it's still relatively small, at 530 square km (331 square mi). Two parallel mountain chains running along the north and south coasts are split by a wide plain, and it is here that the island's cities are found. Despite the more than 1 million tourists who visit the island each year (more than 10 times the number of inhabitants), the pace is slow.

Sado's usual port of entry is **Ryōtsu** 両津, the island's largest township. The town's center runs between Kamo-ko (Kamo Lake) and the coast, with most of the hotels and ryokan on the shore of the lake. Kamo-ko is connected to the sea by a small inlet running through the middle of town. Ryōtsu's Ebisu quarter has the island's largest concentration of restaurants and bars.

GETTING HERE AND AROUND

Sado Kisen has two main ferry routes, both with regular ferry and hydrofoil service. From Niigata to Ryōtsu the journey takes 2½ hours, with six or seven crossings a day; the one-way fare is ¥2,190 for ordinary second class, ¥3,100 for first class, and ¥6,210 for special class. The jetfoil (¥6,090 one-way, ¥10,990 round-trip within five days) takes one hour, with 10 or 11 crossings daily in summer, 3 in winter, and between 3 and 8 at other times of the year (depending on the weather). The bus from Bay No. 6 in front of the JR Niigata station takes 15 minutes (¥200) to reach the dock for ferries sailing to Ryōtsu.

Between Ogi and Naoetsu the hydrofoil cost is the same as the Niigata–Ryōtsu crossing, but the Naoetsu ferry terminal is a ¥150 bus ride or ¥900 taxi ride from Naoetsu Station. Depending on the season, one to three ferries sail between Teradomari (a port between Niigata and Naoetsu) and Akadomari, taking two hours. The fare is ¥1,610 for second class and ¥2,500 for first class. The port is five minutes on foot from the Teradomari bus station, and 10 minutes by bus from the JR train station (take the Teradomari-ko bus).

Frequent bus service is available between major towns on Sado-ga-shima. The 90-minute bus ride from Ryōtsu to Aikawa departs every 30 minutes and costs ¥740. Two-day weekend passes for unlimited bus travel are ¥2,000, and are available at the Ryōtsu and Ogi ports and in the towns of Sawata and Aikawa. During July and August there's a special one-day pass for ¥1,500. In hop-on, hop-off zones it is possible to flag the bus driver or get off anywhere on most routes, which is very convenient for sightseeing.

From May through November, four- and eight-hour tours of the island depart from Ryōtsu and Ogi. These buses have a magnetic attraction to souvenir shops. The best compromise is to use the tour bus for the mountain skyline drive (¥4,500) or the two-day skyline and historic-site combined tour (¥7,000), then rent a bike to explore on your own. You can make bus-tour reservations directly with the **Niigata Kōtsū Regular Sightseeing Bus Center.**

CLOSE UP

Heartbeat of Sado Island

A hawk flies overhead as the sky deepens to the indigo of the kimonos the two women are wearing. With an elegant flick, the batchi resounds against the stretched hide of the taiko drum and a rhythm begins. Soon all the members of **Kodō** 鼓童 bound onto the outdoor stage with their vibrant and distinctive blend of ensemble taiko, percussion, flute, song, and dance. The annual three-day **Earth Celebration**, held in August, kicks off.

On the second and third evenings Kodō are joined by artists they meet on tour, ranging from African and Asian drummers to a Romanian brass band, Fanfare Cio Carlia, and Carlos Nuñez, the Galician bagpipe revivalist. On stage collaborations offer surprises; cleated *geta* (Japanese clogs) were custom-made for New York tap star Tamango to dance with.

Kodō (which can mean heartbeat, child, or drum) was started in the '60s to revive Japanese folk music. About 20 core members live communally on Sado Island with their families, growing rice and vegetables organically. To play the largest ōdaiko, an 800-pound, double-headed drum, takes immense stamina; and all members train intensively.

Not only is this an opportunity to catch Kodō on their home turf, but there are fringe events, workshops, a flea market, local festivals, and a pier-side send-off when the ferry leaves. Tickets and accommodation should be booked well in advance through their Web site, ⊕ *www.kodo.or.jp.*

Give yourself at least two days to take advantage of the beauty of Sado Island. For music lovers, the Kodō Earth Celebration in mid-August is not to be missed. When choosing when to head to Sado, remember the ferry and hydrofoil are no fun in harsh winter weather.

ESSENTIALS

Ferry Contacts Sado Kisen (⊠ *353 Ryōtsu Ebisu, Sado-shi* ☎ *0259/27–5614* ⊗ *8–6).*

Tour Information Niigata Kōtsū Regular Sightseeing Bus Center (☎ *0259/ 52–3200)*

Visitor Information Sado Kisen Tourism Information (☎ *025/245–1234 in Niigata* ⊕ *www.visitsado.com/en/).*

WHAT TO SEE

The simplest way explore Sado is to take the bus from Ryōtsu west to **Aikawa.** Before gold was discovered here in 1601 it was a town of 10,000 people. The population swelled to 100,000 before the gold was exhausted. Now it's back to a tenth that size.

Aikawa's **Sado Mine** 佐渡金山 *(Sado Kinzan)* has been a tourist attraction since operations halted in the 1980s. There are about 325 km (250 mi) of underground tunnels, some running as deep as 1,969 feet. Parts of this extensive digging are open to the public. Robots illustrate how Edo-period slaves worked in the mine. The robots are quite lifelike, and they demonstrate the appalling conditions endured by the miners. The mine is a tough 40-minute uphill walk or a five-minute taxi ride (about

¥900) from the bus terminal. The return is easier. ☎0259/74–2389 ✉¥1200 🕐 Apr.–Oct., daily 8–5:10; Nov.–Mar., daily 8–sunset, last entry for tours at 3:30.

★ North of Aikawa is **Senkaku Bay** 尖閣湾 (Senkaku-wan), the most dramatic stretch of coastline on Sado-ga-shima.

Information on sightseeing boats is available from **Senkaku Bay Tourism** (Senkaku-wan Kankō ☎0259/75–2221). From the water you can look back at the fantastic, sea-eroded rock formations and 60-foot cliffs. You get off the boat at Senkaku-wan Yūen (Senkaku Bay Park), where you can picnic, stroll, and gaze at the varied rock formations offshore. From the park, return by bus from the pier to Aikawa. To reach the bay, take a 15-minute bus ride from Aikawa to Tassha for the 40-minute sightseeing cruise. The one-way cruise boat runs April–November (¥800, glass-bottom boat ¥1,000).

The most scenic drive on Sado is the **Ōsado Skyline Drive** 大佐渡スカイライン. No public buses follow this route. You must take either a tour bus from Ryōtsu or a taxi from Aikawa across the skyline drive to Chikuse (¥4,500), where you connect with a public bus either to Ryōtsu or back to Aikawa. You can do the route in reverse as well.

To reach the southwestern tip of Sado, first take a bus to Sawata from Aikawa or Ryōtsu, and then transfer to the bus for Ogi; en route you may want to stop at the town of **Mano** 真野, where the exiled emperor Juntoku (1197–1242) is buried at the **Mano Goryō** (Mano Mausoleum).

The trip from Sawata to **Ogi** 小木 takes 50 minutes, the highlight being the beautiful benten-iwa (rock formations) just past Tazawaki. Take a window seat on the right-hand side of the bus. You can use Ogi as a port for returning to Honshū by ferry (2½ hours to Naoetsu) or on the hydrofoil (1 hour).

Ogi's chief attractions are the **taraibune** たらい舟, round, tublike boats used for fishing. You can rent one (¥500 for a 30-minute paddle), and with a single oar paddle your way around the harbor. Taraibune can also be found in Shukunegi on the Sawasaki coast, where the water is dotted with rocky islets and the shore is covered with rock lilies in summer.

★ **Shukunegi** 宿根木 has become a sleepy backwater town since it stopped building small wooden ships to traverse the waters between Sado and Honshū. It has, however, retained its simple lifestyle and traditional buildings that date back more than a century. You can reach Shukunegi from Ogi on a sightseeing boat or by bus. Both take about 20 minutes; consider using the boat at least one way for the view of the cliffs that an earthquake created 250 years ago.

WHERE TO EAT AND STAY
You can make hotel reservations at the information counters of Sado Kisen ship company at Niigata Port or Ryōtsu Port.

$$–$$$ ✕**Uoharu** 魚春. At the Ferry terminal in Ogi, ask to be directed toward
JAPANESE the area clustered with restaurants. In a corner three-story building is
★ a fish shop at ground level with a restaurant upstairs. You can either

choose your fish fresh off ice or try one of the excellent lunches like the sashimi, abalone steak (*awabi*), or sea urchin (*sazae*) sets from a menu with pictures. They close at 5 PM, but accept reservations for the evening. ✉*415–1 Ogimachi* ☎*0259/86–2085* ⊕*www6.ocn. ne.jp/~uoharu* ⊟*No credit cards.*

$$$$ ▦**Sado Royal Hotel Manchō** 佐渡ロイヤルホテル万長. This is the best hotel on Sado's west coast. It caters mostly to Japanese tourists; no English is spoken, but the staff makes the few visiting Westerners feel welcome. Request a room on the sea side for the stunning ocean view. Breakfast and dinner are included in the rate. **Pros:** excellent views; friendly staff. **Cons:** no English spoken. ✉*58 Shimoto, Sado-shi, Aika-wa-orito, Niigata-ken* ☎*0259/74–3221* 📠*0259/74–3738* 🛏*90 rooms* &*In-hotel: restaurant, Japanese baths* ⊟*AE, DC, MC, V* ⦿*MAP.*

$ ▦**Sado Seaside Hotel** 佐渡シーサイドホテル. One kilometer (½ mi) from
★ Ryōtsu Port, this is more a friendly inn than a hotel. If you telephone before you catch the ferry from Niigata, the owner will meet you at the dock carrying a green Seaside Hotel flag. The rooms and shared baths are spotless. Breakfast is ¥840, and a tasty mélange of regional delicacies for dinner costs ¥1,575. **Pros:** friendly staff; good value. **Cons:** no Western-style rooms. ✉*80 Sumiyoshi, Sado-shi, Niigata-ken* ☎*0259/27–7211* 📠*0259/27–7213* ⊕*www2u.biglobe.ne.jp/~sado/ englishpage.htm* 🛏*13 Japanese-style rooms, 5 with bath* &*In-hotel: restaurant, Japanese baths, laundry service* ⊟*AE, MC, V.*

Kyōto

WORD OF MOUTH

"I walked to Sanjūsengendo, the long hall with the thousand ancient wooden statues of Kannon lined up. I liked the dusty, ancient feel of the place (seriously, the Kannons could use some attention with a feather duster). I'd put this as one of my favorite Kyōto stops, since it was so different from everything else."

—thal

"Kyōto is a wonderful city, but needs some time to truly experience it. The sights of Kyōto are quite spread out on both the eastern, western and northern extremes of the city. To truly experience it you need at least 3 full days."

—jrlaw10

Updated by
Joshua Bisker

The countless temples, shrines, and palaces that texture the city map make Kyōto's grand architecture its most famous feature abroad, but that's just part of what you'll find in this imperial city. Japan's capital for more than 1,000 years, Kyōto was the center not only for courtly affairs, but politics, religion, philosophy, art, culture, and cuisine. Essentially every one of Japan's refined cultural arts blossomed from seeds that were planted here, including the tea ceremony, kabuki theater, and Zen Buddhism.

Breathtaking sights are more abundant than blossoms on a cherry tree, but some places truly stand out. Many tourists come away most impressed by Kyōto's great temples, like Kiyomizu-dera in the city's eastern mountains and the forest-cloaked Fushimi-Inari Taisha, a mystical escape through a miles-long chain of towering vermillion gates. Visitors also flock to cultural hubs like the Museum of Traditional Crafts, showcasing the city's artisanal legacy, and Sanjusangendō, with its astonishing 1,001 golden statues of Kannon.

Kyōto residents have a fierce sense of propriety about nearly everything, ranging from good table manners to good breeding. This strict code has some notorious consequences for locals—who are not considered true Kyōto people unless they can trace their lineage back four generations—but certain benefits for visitors. The Kyōto mindset says that nothing made here should be of less than exquisite craftsmanship and stellar design. This philosophy means that whether browsing for gifts in a handkerchief shop, sightseeing at a local temple, or sitting down to a 12-course dinner, you'll encounter the best of the best. As a visitor here you're a guest of the city, and Kyōto will make sure you leave with wonderful memories.

ORIENTATION AND PLANNING

ORIENTATION

Central Kyōto is fairly compact and easily navigable. The grid-pattern layout, originally modeled on China's ancient capital Xi'an, makes this Japan's most rational urban space. The city map is not difficult to understand if you know what to look for.

Broad avenues running east–west are numbered, giving you a handy opportunity to practice your Japanese. Counting to eight—ichi, ni, san, shi, go, roku, shichi, hachi—gives you most of these main arteries: Ichijo-dōri, Nijo-dōri, Sanjo-dōri, and so on. Several important avenues don't follow this numbering system, notably Oike-dōri, running in front

TOP REASONS TO GO

Architecture: Despite modernization, about 27,000 traditional houses remain. The preservation districts include Sannen-zaka, Gion Shinbashi, and the canal street leading to Kamigamo Jinja.

Gardens: Chinese-influenced gardens symbolize paradise on earth. The *karesansui* (dry gardens) of Zen temples signifies the eternal quest for completeness; the most famous of these is at Ryōan-Jl.

Crafts: Traditional craftspeople still work here. There's no shortage of art and antiques shops, secondhand kimonos are a bargain, and ceramics, lacquerware, and woven bamboo make great souvenirs.

Live Culture: Professional dancers and performers, geisha are revered as an embodiment of culture, with their opulent kimonos; hair ornaments; and artistic skills.

Festivals: Experience one of Kyōto's many festivals including the Aoi (Hollyhock) in mid-May, the Gion in July, the Jidai (Costume) in October, the Daimon-ji in August, and Kurama in May and October.

6

of city hall, and Marutamachi-dōri and Imadegawa-dōri, on the northern and southern sides of the Imperial Palace.

Streets running north–south aren't numbered, but sights are clustered around a few main thoroughfares. Karasuma-dōri bisects Kyōto Station in the middle of the city. West of it is Horikawa-dōri (hori refers to a castle moat, and this is where you will find the fortress Nijō-jō); to the east is busy Kawaramachi-dōri. East of the Kamogawa River, the Higashiyama neighborhood holds many of the city's most popular sights, all connected by the congested Higashi-ōji-dōri. Intersections are named, and follow a helpful logic: if the sign you are approaching reads Kawaramachi-Shijō, you are walking on Kawaramachi-dōri towards Shijō-dōri.

Eastern Kyōto. Higashiyama, as eastern Kyōto is known, is chockablock with temples and shrines, among them Ginkaku-ji, Heian Jingū, and Kiyomizu-dera. Gion—a traditional shopping neighborhood by day and a geisha entertainment district by night—is also here.

Central and Southern Kyōto. Here are the hotels, the business district, and the Kiya-machi entertainment area. Central Kyōto also has one of the oldest city temples; Tō-ji, the rebuilt Imperial Palace; and Nijō-jō, the onetime Kyōto abode of the Tokugawa shōguns.

Western Kyōto. Although it doesn't have the eye-popping sights of Eastern Kyōto's, this neighborhood is well worth exploring. Among Western Kyōto's many temples and gardens are Ryōan-ji, Kinkaku-ji, and Myōshin-ji.

Arashiyama. Just outside the city is the neighborhood of Arashiyama. The exquisite villa Katsura Rikyū is in the rural hills of Arashiyama, know for its lovely temple, Tenryū-ji, and beautiful riverside parks.

Northern Kyōto. Far from the center of the city, the main attractions of northern Kyōto are the mountaintop Buddhist enclave of Enryaku-ji

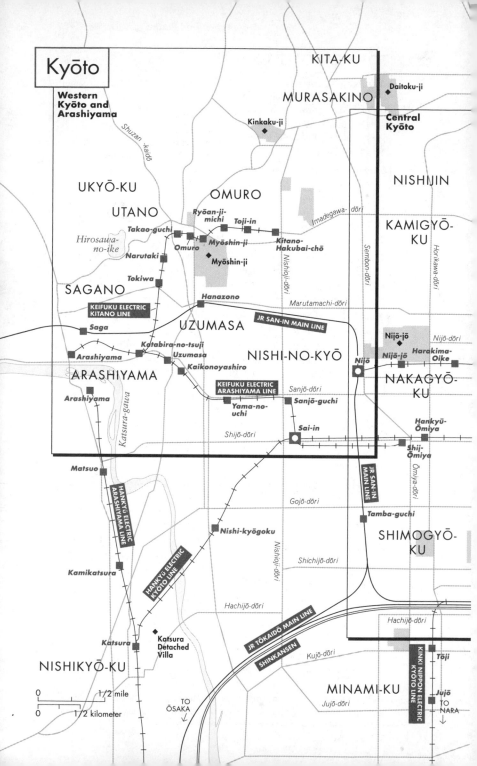

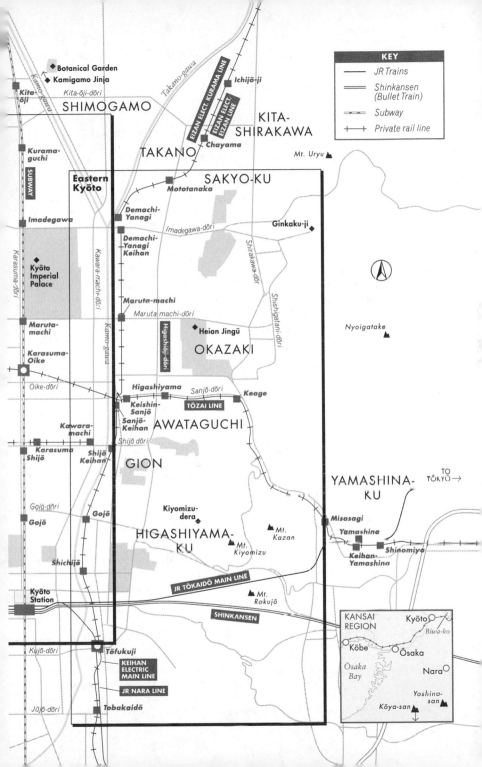

on Hiei-zan and the charming countryside of Ōhara, which also has several peaceful temples.

PLANNING

With hundreds of temples and shrines and several former imperial and shogunal residences, Kyōto has a lot to see, to say the least. Keep this in mind and don't run yourself ragged. Balance a morning at temples or museums with an afternoon in traditional shops, and a morning at the market with the rest of the day in Arashiyama or at one of the imperial villas. We highly recommended a visit to at least one of the mountaintop temple complexes, such as Enryaku-ji on Hiei-zan or Daigo-ji in central Kyōto. Remember that you must apply in advance (anywhere from one to several days) to visit attractions that require permits, such as the Imperial Palace, the imperial villas Katsura Rikyū and Shūgaku-in, and Kōinzan Saihō-ji.

WHEN TO GO

Cherry-blossom time in spring (usually the first week in April) and the glorious autumn foliage in early November are remarkable, though the city can be extremely crowded and very expensive. Except for the depths of winter and the peak of summer heat in August, Kyōto's climate is mild enough—though often rainy, especially mid-June to mid-July—to make sightseeing pleasant for most of the year. In the high season (May–October) the large numbers of visitors can make accommodations scarce.

GETTING HERE AND AROUND

Kyōto has an excellent public transportation system, so getting around the city is a snap. Buses are frequent and reliable, though the thick crowds can make them run slightly behind schedule. JR trains and five private light rails and subways service the city, and are especially useful for reaching outlying sights and making day trips to nearby cities. To get the lay of the land, newcomers should do obtain an up-to-date bus map, a tourist map, and a copy of the free monthly *Kyōto Journal* from the visitor center in Kyōto Station.

One of Kyōto's best resources, the Tourist Information Center, is on the second floor of Kyōto Station. Heading away from of the tracks, take the escalator up one flight; the information desk is opposite the donut shop courtyard. The office publishes pamphlets with descriptions of five walking tours, including maps. The tours range in length from about 40 to 80 minutes. The office is open daily 9 to 6, but closes the second and fourth Tuesday of each month.

Several private companies offer guided tours of Kyōto. The best is Kyōto-Tōkyō Private tours, run by Ian Roepke, editor of the *Kyōto Visitors Guide* and *Kyōto Journal*. The company offers half-day and full-day tours of the city. A seasoned guide who can shed insight into the mysterious world of the geisha, Peter MacIntosh of Kyōto Sights and Nights leads late-afternoon walks through the old teahouse districts. Sunrise Tours organizes half-day morning and afternoon deluxe coach tours highlighting different city attractions. Volunteer guides can be requested by calling the Utano Youth Hostel. The Kyōto International Community House can arrange home visits.

AIR TRAVEL

International and some domestic flights land at Kansai International Airport, near Ōsaka. Ōsaka's Itami Aiport handles all regional flights. To get to downtown Kyōto from Kansai, take the JR Haruka Limited Express, a train that departs every 30 minutes. The 75-minute run costs ¥3,490. From Itami, buses depart approximately every 20 minutes from 8:10 AM to 9:20 PM. The trip takes 55 to 90 minutes and costs ¥1,280 to ¥1,370, depending on the Kyōto destination. MK Taxi offers a shuttle bus from both Kansai and Itami. From KIX the cost is ¥3,000 per adult; ¥2,000 from Itami. Reserve in advance.

> ### KYŌTO QUIRKS
>
> An old saying cautions visitors to remember one thing: "Houses in Kyōto have two thresholds." This means that people may not allow you to see what is truly inside. Presenting a good outward face is extremely important within Kyōto's sense of propriety. You will never receive a cross word from the o-kami, or woman of the house, at any traditional inn or tavern, but that means it's hard to tell when you violate certain social norms. Be polite and show gratitude for any kindness offered, and you're sure to enjoy Kyōto's quirks.

6

BUS TRAVEL

Buses in Kyōto are quick, reliable, and punctual, making them an excellent form of transportation. City bus 100 is designed around the tourist route, connecting all the major sightseeing spots. Pick up route maps at the Kyōto Tourist Information Center.

Within the city the standard fare is ¥220, which you pay when leaving the bus; outside the city limits the fare varies according to distance. Several special transportation passes are available, including the following: a one-day city bus pass for ¥500, valid for use inside the inner city area; Kyōto sightseeing one-day (¥1,200) or two-day (¥2,000) passes that cover travel on city buses, the subway, and private Kyōto Line buses; and the *torafika kyō* pass, which provides ¥3,300 worth of transport via city bus or subway for ¥3,000. Passes are sold at travel agencies, main bus terminals, and information centers in Kyōto Station.

SUBWAY TRAVEL

Kyōto has a 28-station subway system. The Karasuma Line runs north to south from Kokusai Kaikan to Takeda. The Tōzai Line runs between Nijō in the west and Roku-jizō in the east. Purchase tickets at the vending machines in stations before boarding. Fares increase with distance traveled and begin at ¥210. Service runs 5:30 AM–11:30 PM.

TAXI TRAVEL

Taxis are readily available in Kyōto. Fares for smaller-size cabs start at ¥640 for the first 2 km (1 mi), with a cost of ¥100 for each additional 500 meters (.3 mi). Many taxi companies provide guided tours of the city, priced per hour or per route. Keihan Taxi has four-hour tours from ¥18,000 per car; MK Taxi runs similar tours starting at ¥18,800 for three hours. There are fixed fares for some sightseeing services that start and end at Kyōto Station. A 7½-hour tour of the city's major sights will cost in the region of ¥26,000 with any of the 17 taxi companies, including Keihan Taxi and MK Taxi.

TRAIN TRAVEL
Frequent *Shinkansen* trains run between Tōkyō and Kyōto, taking 2 hours and 40 minutes. The one-way reserved fare is ¥13,200. JR train service between Ōsaka and Kyōto costs ¥540 and takes 30 minutes; trains connecting with Shin-Osaka take 15 minutes and cost ¥1,480. Keihan and Hankyū line express trains take 40 minutes and cost between ¥390 and ¥460. They depart every 15 minutes from Ōsaka's Yodoyabashi and Umeda stations.

For travel to Kyōto's northern reaches, change from the Keihan subway line to the Eizan Railway by transferring at Imadegawa-dōri/Demachi-Yanagi station. The Eizan has two lines, the Kurama Line, running north to Kurama, and the Eizan Line, running northeast to Yase. The Hankyū Line, which runs west as far as Katsura Rikyū, connects with the subway at Karasuma Station. From Shijō-Ōmiya Station the Keifu-ku Arashiyama Line runs to western Kyōto. JR also runs to western Kyōto on the San-in Main Line.

ESSENTIALS
Emergency Contacts Daiichi Sekijūji (*Red Cross Hospital* ⊠ *Higashiyama Hon-machi, Higashiyama-ku* ☏ *075/561–1121*). **Japan Baptist Hospital** (⊠ *Kita-Shirakawa, Yamanomoto-chō, Sakyō-ku* ☏ *075/781–5191*).

Taxi Contacts Keihan Taxi (☏ *0120/113–103*). **MK Taxi** (☏ *075/702–5489* ⊕ *www.mk-group.co.jp*).

Tour Information Johnnie Hajime Hirooka (☏ *075/622–6803* ⊕ *web.kyoto-inet. or.jp/people/h-s-love*). **Kyōto International Community House** (⊠ *2–1 Torii-chō, Awata-guchi, Sakyō-ku* ☏ *075/752–3010*). **Kyōto Sights and Nights** (☏ *090/5169–1654* ⊕ *www.kyotosightsandnights.com*). **Kyōto-Tōkyō Private Tours**(⊕ *www.kyoto-tokyo-private-tours.com*). **Sunrise Tours** (☏ *075/341–1413* ⊕ *www.jtbgmt.com/sunrisetour/kyoto*). **Utano Youth Hostel**(⊠ *Utano Youth Hostel, Ukyō-ku* ☏ *075/462–2288*).

Visitor Information Kyōto Tourist Information Center (⊠ *2F JR Kyōto Station, Karasuma-dōri, Shimogyō-ku* ☏ *075/344–3300* ⊕ *www.city.kyoto.jp/koho/eng/ index.html*).

EXPLORING KYŌTO

EASTERN KYŌTO

East of the Kamogawa River, in the neighborhoods known as Higashi-yama (literally, Eastern Mountain) and Okazaki, are some of Kyōto's most dazzling shrines and temples, stretching from solemn Sanjusangen-do in the south to the elegant Ginkaku-ji in the north. The cobbled streets of the Gion district are mysterious during the day, and even more so at night. Just west of the river, taverns on the Ponto-cho Alley

CLOSE UP

Brief History of Kyōto

Although Kyōto was Japan's capital for more than 10 centuries, the real center of political power was often elsewhere, be it Kamakura (1192–1333) or Edo (1603–1868). Until 710 Japan's capital moved with the accession of each new emperor. When it was decided that this expense was too great, Nara was chosen as the permanent capital. This experiment lasted lasted 74 years, during which Buddhists rallied for, and achieved, tremendous political power. In an effort to thwart them, Emperor Kammu moved the capital to Nagaoka for a decade and then, in 794, to Kyōto.

Until the end of the 12th century, the city flourished under imperial rule. The city's nobility, known as "cloud dwellers," cultivated an extraordinary culture of refinement called miyabi. But when imperial power waned, the city saw the rise of the samurai class employed to protect the noble families' interests. Ensuing clashes between various clans led to the Gempei War (1180–85), and the samurai emerged victorious. The bushidō, or warrior spirit, found a counterpart in the minimalism of Zen Buddhism's austerity. The past luxury of miyabi was replaced with Zen's respect for frugality and discipline.

This period also brought devastating civil wars. Because the various feuding clans needed the emperor's support to claim legitimacy, Kyōto, the imperial capital, became the stage for bitter struggles. The Ōnin Civil War (1467–77) was particularly devastating for Kyōto. Two feudal lords, Yamana and Hosokawa, disputed who should succeed the reigning shōgun. Yamana camped in the western part of the city with 90,000 troops, and Hosokawa settled in the eastern part with 100,000 troops. Central Kyōto was the battlefield, and many of the city's buildings were destroyed.

Ieyasu Tokugawa, founder of the Tokugawa shogunate, eventually moved the country's political center to Edo. Kyōto remained the imperial capital, and the first three Tokugawa shōguns paid homage to the city by restoring old temples and building new villas in the early 1700s. Much of what you see in Kyōto dates from this period. When Emperor Meiji was restored to power in the late 1860s his capital and imperial court were moved to Tōkyō. Commerce flourished, though, and Kyōto continued as the center of traditional culture. What's more, the move saved the city from being bombed flat in World War II.

6

and bars and restaurants on Kiyamachi are the city's most happening neighborhoods after dark.

GETTING AROUND Subway lines crisscross Eastern Kyōto, making them a great way to get around. Maps detailing the extensive bus network are available at tourist information centers. Buses run on major roads like Shichijō-dōri, Shijō-dōri, and Higashi-ōji-dōri. The best way to explore these neighborhoods is by foot. Starting from anywhere, you can't walk 10 minutes in any direction without encountering a landmark.

TOP ATTRACTIONS

❶ **Ginkaku-ji** 銀閣寺. The Temple of the Silver Pavilion was intended to
Fodor's Choice dazzle the courtly world with its opulence, but the current structure
★ is an exercise in elegance and restraint. Yoshimasa Ashikaga spent
years constructing his retirement villa in a conspicuous homage to his
grandfather's Golden Pavilion on the opposite end of town. Carefully
sculpted gardens surround a two-story mansion that the shōgun originally intended to be wrapped in silver leaf. During construction in the
1470s, a tumultuous war and government unrest meant funds for the
audacious project dried up. What remains is a quintessentially peaceful
place. High earthen walls frame a modest compound of buildings giving
way to extensive gardens. The lovely Silver Pavilion, which stares down
at its reflection in the water, sits among the rolling moss-covered hillsides, dark pools, and an enormous dry garden, called the Sea of Sand.
To reach Ginkaku-ji from Kyōto Station, take Bus 5 to the Ginkaku-ji-
michi bus stop. ⊠ *1 Ginkaku-ji-chō, Sakyō-ku* ✉*¥500* ⊗*Mid-Mar.–
Nov., daily 8:30–5; Dec.–mid-Mar., daily 9–4:30.*

Gion Corner. Because Westerners have little opportunity to enjoy a geisha's performance in a private party setting—which requires a proper
recommendation from and probably the presence of a geisha's respected
client—a popular entertainment during the month of April is the Miyako Odori (Cherry-Blossom Dance), presented at this theater. Against
sumptuous backdrops, geisha, wearing elaborate kimonos and makeup,
enact a narrative in dance and song to the accompaniment of a *shamisen*
(a three-string instrument), flute, and drums. Before the show there is a
tea ceremony. There are also other performances in May and October,
and tickets cost between ¥2,000 and ¥7,000. ⊠*Gion Hanami-kōji,
Higashiyama-ku* ☎*075/561–1115.*

❺ **Heian Jingū** 平安神宮. The massive vermilion and white walls of Heian
Jingū are one of Kyōto's best-known landmarks. Built in the 1890s
to commemorate the 1,100th anniversary of Kyōto's founding, Heian
Jingū pays homage to the two emperors who bookend the city's era of
national prominence: Kammu, who brought the imperial throne here
in 794, and Kōmei, whose reign ending in 1866 saw the sun set on
Kyōto's days as the capital. An assertion of Kyōto's unfaded splendor,
Heian Jingū was built as a slightly smaller replica of the Imperial Palace,
destroyed in 1227. The architecture reveals China's strong influence
on the early Japanese court. The astonishing red torii gate, the biggest in Japan, and the three elaborate gardens behind the main shrine
are particularly impressive. The complex makes a wonderful backdrop
for several annual events, most famously the brazier-lighted dramas
of Takigi Nō every June 1 and 2, and the thousands of performers in
period dress for the Jidai Costume Festival on October 22. You can
get here via Bus 5, 32, 46, or 100 to Kyōto Kaikan Bijutsukan-mae,
Tozai subway to Higashiyama, or Keihan subway to Sanjo-dōri. ⊠
Okazakinishi Tennō-chō, Sakyō-ku ☎*075/371–5649* ✉*Garden ¥600*
⊗*Mid-Mar.–Aug., daily 8:30–5:30; Sept., Oct., and early Mar., daily
8:30–5; Nov.–Feb., daily 8:30–4:30.*

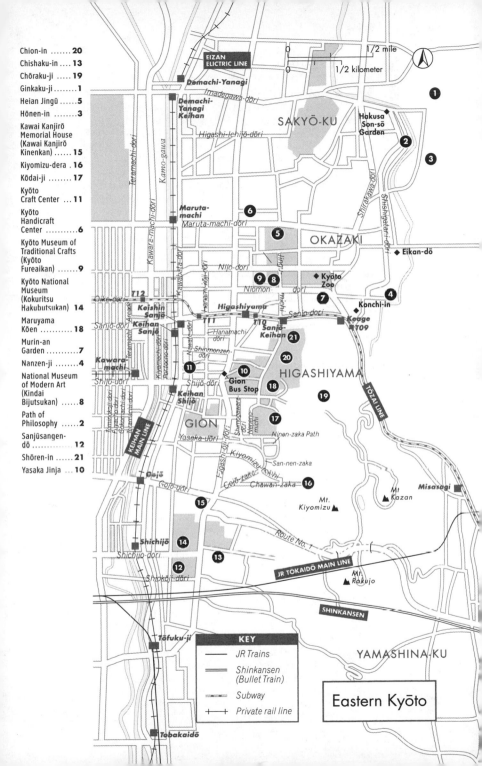

Getting to Know Gion

Japan's traditional and modern worlds intersect where Shijo-dōri crosses Hanamikoji-dōri in the district of Gion. To the south, cobblestone streets lead past wood-fronted tea houses displaying red paper lanterns, while a block northward are high-rises chock full of bars. Eastward is Yaska Jinja's commanding orange-and-white arched gate; westward are city's best department stores.

Gion remains Kyōto's center for high culture, including venues offering kabuki, noh, and bunraku puppetry theater. Perhaps more famous to foreign visitors is the floating world of geisha entertainment, brought into the spotlight recently by the film adaptation of Arthur Golen's Memoirs of a Geisha. Wandering arroundi Hanamikoji-dōri at night you're sure to see maiko-san and gekko-san, the modern equivalents of apprentice and senior geisha, on their way to appointments at exclusive tea houses behind curtained doorways.

Kiyomizu-dera 清水寺. Pilgrims have climbed Higashiyama's cobblestone streets lined with tea shops and craft vendors to this gorgeous mountainside temple for centuries. In a forest on Kyōto's eastern flank, Kiyomizu-dera's tremendous gates and pagodas are marvels to behold. The main hall's huge veranda, jutting out over the valley, has become one of the city's quintessential images. Hundreds of clean-hewn timbers support the large deck and gracefully angular cypress-shingle roof. Finding the courage to set out on a daring new adventure is often likened to "taking a leap from the veranda of Kiyomizu."

Fodor's Choice ★

The temple was founded in 780, but the buildings you see today date from 1633. Inside the towering gateway is a small shrine that is well worth exploring. Take off your shoes before descending the stairway for a metaphorical journey into the soul; in the dark passageway below the temple, quietly follow a chain of thick wooden beads to an ancient tablet carved with the Sanskrit rune for heart. (It's fine to touch the tablet.) Past the main hall, the quirky Jishu-jinja shrine is dedicated to Ōkuni Nushi-no-mikoto, a deity considered to be a powerful matchmaker. Many young people visit the shrine to seek help in finding their life partners. They try to walk between two stones placed 18 meters (59 feet) apart, with their eyes closed. It's said that love will materialize for anyone who can walk in a straight line between the two.

Farther down the path, the Sound of Feathers waterfall tumbles down in three perfect streams before a raised platform. Catch some to drink using one of the long-handled silver cups; it supposedly helps with health, longevity, and academic success. If you need more to fortify you, enjoy some noodle soup, hot tea, or cold beer from one of the old stalls below the trellised balcony. To get here, take Bus 100 or 206 to Gojō-zaka or Kiyomizu-michi, where a 10-minute uphill walk take you to the temple. ⊠ *Kiyomizu 1-chōme, Higashiyama-ku* 🎫 *¥300* ⊙ *Daily 6–6.*

NEED A BREAK?

On the road to Kiyomizu-dera, a wooden archway covered in *senja-fuda* (name cards pilgrims affix on the entryways to shrines and temples) leads to a charming courtyard teahouse, **Bunnosuke Jaya**. The specialty here is *amazake*, a nonalcoholic drink often served hot with a touch of ginger. The interior is adorned with an eclectic collection of kites and folk dolls. ⊠ *Kiyomizu 3-chō, Higashiyama-ku* ☎ *075/561–1972* ⊙ *Thurs.–Tues. 10–5:30.*

⓫ **Kyōto Craft Center** 京都クラフトセンター. Fine traditional crafts, including reasonably priced dolls, ceramics, lacquer-ware, prints, and textiles, can be found here. From Kyōto Station take Bus 206 to the Gion stop. The center is on the corner of Shijō-dōri and Higashi-ōji-dōri. ⊠ *275 Shijō-dōri, Gion-machi, Higashiyama-ku* ☎ *075/561–9660* ⊙ *Thurs.– Tues. 11–7.*

❼ **Murin-an Garden** 無隣庵庭園. In a departure from traditional Japanese
★ gardens, this garden has rolling expanses of English-style lawns that reflect the melding of Japanese and Western elements. This blending of styles is also visible in the architecture of a house that once belonged to solider and statesman Arimoto Yamagata. Backed by a sweep of hills, Murin-an has paths that meander past converging streams and a three-tier waterfall. The south side of the garden is almost always in shadow, creating wonderful contrasts. ⊠ *48 Nanzenji-kusakawa-chō, Sakyō-ku* ☎ *¥350* ⊙ *Daily 9–4:30*

❹ **Nanzen-ji** 南禅寺. Several magnificent temples share this corner of the
★ forested foothills between Heian Jingū and Ginkaku-ji. The most prominent is Nanzen-ji, with its awesome gateway. A short distance away you'll enjoy Nanzen-in's serene beauty, Kochi-in's precise garden, and Murin-an's expansive lawns.

Like Ginkaku-ji, the villa of Nanzen-ji was turned into a temple on the death of its owner, Emperor Kameyama (1249–1305). By the 14th century this had become the most powerful Zen temple in Japan, which spurred the Tendai monks to destroy it. The 15th-century Ōnin Civil War demolished the buildings again, but some were resurrected during the 16th century. Nanzen-ji has again become one of Kyōto's most important temples, in part because it's the headquarters of the Rinzai sect of Zen Buddhism.

Monks in training are still taught at the temple. You enter through the enormous 1628 San-mon (Triple Gate), the classic "gateless" gate of Zen Buddhism that symbolizes entrance into the most sacred part of the temple precincts. From the top floor of the gate you can view Kyōto spread out below. Whether or not you ascend the steep steps, give a moment to the statue of Goemon Ishikawa. In 1594 this Robin Hood–style outlaw tried but failed to kill the daimyō Hideyoshi Toyotomi. He hid in this gate until his capture, after which he was boiled in a cauldron of oil. His story is still enacted in many Kabuki plays.

Past Nanzen-ji's three-tiered gateway, quiet **Nanzen-in** (⊠ *Nanzenji-Fukuchi-chō, Sakyō-ku* ☎ *075/771–0365* ☛ *¥400* ⊙ *Daily 8:40–4)* has a peaceful garden that is well worth exploring. A curiously modern brick aquaduct cuts through the maples leading up to Emperor Kameyama's mausoleum.

6

Recognized by garden aficionados around the world as one of Japan's finest, **Konchi-in** 金地院 (✉ 86 *Fukuchi-chō, Nanzen-ji, Sakyō-ku* 🖾 *¥400* 🕙 *Mar.–Nov., daily 8:30–5; Dec.–Feb., daily 8:30–4:30*) was first established in the 15th century. It was moved inside Nanzen-ji's temple complex in 1605 and landscaped by designer Enshū Kobori several decades later. Shadow-dappled stone pathways wind past moss-covered hills to a pond hugged close by maple and cherry trees. There's a lovely temple buildings and a dry garden whose solemn rocks figure a crane and turtle symbolizing wisdom and longevity. Kochi-in is on the path leading up to Nanzen-ji, just before the main gate.

A climb to the top of this temple's pagoda affords superb views of the eastern mountains. **Eikan-dō** 永観堂(✉ 48 *Eikando-chō, Higashiyama-ku606-8437* 🖾 *Dec.–Oct. ¥500, Nov. ¥1,000* 🕙 *Dec.–Oct., daily 9–5; Nov., daily 9–9*) was built after the original temple, dating from 855, was destroyed in the 15th century. Visitors come throughout the year to see relics like the life-like Amida Buddha statue, said to have once come alive to dance with a reveling priest. The temple draws the most visitors in autumn, when people come to see the colorful foliage, and in November, when there's an excellent display of painted doors.

On your way to see these other temples and gardens, don't overlook Nanzen-ji's other attractions. The **Hōjō** (Abbots' Quarters) is a national treasure. Inside, screens with impressive 16th-century paintings divide the chambers. These wall panels of the *Twenty-Four Paragons of Filial Piety and Hermits* were created by Eitoku Kanō (1543–90) of the Kanō school—in effect the Kanō family, because the school consists of eight generations of one bloodline (Eitoku was from the fifth generation). Enshū Kobori created what's commonly known as the Leaping Tiger Garden, an excellent example of the karesansui style, attached to the Hōjō. The large rocks are grouped with clipped azaleas, maples, pines, and moss, all positioned against a plain white well behind the raked gravel expanse. The greenery effectively connects the garden with the lush forested hillside beyond. ✉ *Nanzenji-Fukuchi-chō, Sakyō-ku* 🖾 *Abbotts' Quarters ¥400, Triple Gate ¥300* 🕙 *Mar.–Nov., daily 8:40–5; Dec.–Feb., daily 8:40–4:30.*

⑫
Fodor's Choice
★

Sanjūsangen-dō 三十三間堂. One of Kyōto's most awe-inspiring spectacles, this 400-foot-long hall holds 1,000 golden statues of the many-limbed Kannon. Enthroned in the center of the hall is a 6-foot-tall version of the diety that was carved by Tankei, a sculptor of the Kamakura period (1192–1333). In the corridor behind are the 28 guardian deities who protect the Buddhist universe. Notice the frivolous-faced Garuda, a bird that feeds on dragons. In the back of the hall, explanations of the significance of Kannon's various poses. From Kyōto Station take Bus 206, 208, or 100 to the Sanjūsangen-dō-mae stop. The temple is to the south, beyond the Hyatt Regency. ✉ *657 Sanjūsangen-dō Mawari-chō, Higashiyama-ku* 🖾 *¥600* 🕙 *Apr.–mid-Nov., daily 8–5; mid-Nov.–Mar., daily 9–4.*

■
OFF THE
BEATEN
PATH

Sannen-zaka and Ninen-zaka 三年坂と二年坂. With their cobbled paths and delightful wooden buildings, these two lovely winding streets are the finest extant examples of Old Kyōto. This area is one of four historic preservation districts in the city, and the shops along the way sell snacks, souvenirs, and local crafts like pottery, dolls, and bamboo baskets. From Kiyomizu-dera turn right halfway down Kiyomizu-zaka. ✉ *Higashiyama-ku.*

🔟 **Yasaka Jinja** 八坂神社. The magnificent vermilion and white gate of Kyōto's central shrine retains an essential role in the city's fiscal good fortune: in addition to the good luck charms people flock here to buy, you will see the names of the city's biggest stores and companies adorning each glowing lantern hanging from the main hall's eaves, each of them sponsors seeking to gain financial favor. The shrine was built in the 7th century above an underground lake to ensure that the god who resides in the east—the blue water dragon—receives the fresh water needed to ensure healthy earth energy. The original enshrined Shintō deity, Susanō-no-Mikoto, later came to be associated with the Buddhist deva Gozu Ten-no, a protector against pestilence and god of prosperity. Also known as Gion Shrine, Yasaka hosts the Gion Festival, which started in 869 as a religious ritual to rid the city of a terrible plague that originated in Kyōto and swiftly spread all over Japan. From Kyōto Station take Bus 206 or 100 to the Gion bus stop; the shrine is just off Higashi-ōji-dōri. ✉ *625 Gion-machi, Kitagawa, Higashiyama-ku* 📷 *Free* 🕙 *Daily 24 hrs.*

WORTH NOTING

⓴ **Chion-in** 知恩院. The headquarters of the Jōdo sect of Buddhism, Chion-in is impressive enough to have been cast in the film *The Last Samurai* as a stand-in for Edo Castle. Everything here is on a massive scale. The imposing tiered gateway is the largest in the country, and the bell inside the temple grounds, cast in 1633, is the heaviest in all Japan, requiring 17 monks to ring it. (They don't do it every day, although you can understand why.) If you're lucky enough to be in Kyōto over New Years you can hear the progression of 108 booming gongs meant to release temple-goers from the worldly desires of the old year and welcome in the clarity of a new one (it's also nationally televised). The temple buildings are fun to explore, especially since you can take a good look at the exposed *uguisu-bari* (nightingale floor), constructed to "sing" unexpectedly in order to expose intruders. Walk underneath the corridor to examine the way the boards and nails are placed to create this inventive burglar alarm. Like most Kyōto temples, Chion-in's history includes a litany of fires and earthquakes, and most of the buildings you see date from the early 1600s. From Kyōto Station, take Bus 206 to the Gion stop. The temple is north of Maruyama Kōen. ✉ *400 Hayashi-shita-chō 3-chōme, Yamato-ōji, Higashi-hairu, Shimbashi-dōri, Higashiyama-ku* 📷 *¥400* 🕙 *Mar.–Oct., daily 9–4:30; Nov.–Feb., daily 9–4; not all buildings open to public.*

⓭ **Chishaku-in** 智積院. Paintings by Tōhaku Hasegawa and his son Kyūzo—some of the best examples of Momoyama-period—are the best reason to visit this temple. Hasegawa painted exclusively for Zen temples in his later years, with masterpieces ranging from lyrical monochrome ink creations to bolder, more colorful works like the screen paintings exhibited here. Rich in detail, the screens evoke the seasons with the images of cherry, maple, pine, and plum as well as autumn grasses. The paintings, from the 16th century, were originally created for an earlier temple on the same site. From Kyōto Station, take Bus 206 or 208 to the Higashiyama-Shichijō stop. Chishaku-in is at the end of Shichijo-dōri where it terminates at Higashi-ōji-dōri. ✉ *Hisgashiyama Shichijo, Higashiyama-ku* 🎫 *¥350* 🕙 *Daily 9–4:30.*

⑲ Chōraku-ji 長楽寺. A procession of stone lanterns lines the steep path to this tiny temple, founded by Emperor Kammu with the priest Saichō in 805. In 1185, after the Minamoto clan's defeat of the Taira clan in the momentous Genpei War, the last survivor found refuge here. Note the 11-faced statue of Kannon, evocative of the deity's Indian origins. Few tourists bother to climb to this hilltop temple, making it a tranquil place to enjoy cherry blossoms in the spring and the bird's-eye view of the city throughout the year. Flying squirrels make occasional appearances in summer. Chōraku-ji is east of Maruyama Kōen. ✉ *626 Maruyama-chō, Higashiyama-ku* 🎫 *¥400* 🕙 *Daily 9–5.*

OFF THE BEATEN PATH

Hakusasa Son-sō Garden 白沙村荘庭園. Down the hill from Ginkaku-ji, about 100 yards before the street crosses a canal, sits a century-old villa with an impeccable garden. This was once the home of painter Kansetsu Hashimoto, who created a unique style of painting that combined various Japanese periods and drew inspiration from Chinese imagery. The house contains many of Hashimoto's sketches and paintings, as well as works by both Chinese and Japanese contemporaries and an enthralling collection of Greek and Persian pottery. An exquisite stone garden and a teahouse are also open to the public. If you book at least two days in advance, it's possible to experience a complete tea ceremony. To get here from Kyōto Station, take Bus 5 to the Ginkaku-ji-michi stop and walk east along the canal. Hakusa Son-sō will be on the right. ✉ *37 Jodoji, Ishibashi-chō, Higashiyama-ku* 🎫 *¥80* 📞 *075/751–0446* 🕙 *Daily 10–5; last entry at 4:30.*

❸ Hōnen-in 法然院. Near Ginkaku-ji on the Path of Philosophy, this bamboo forest is a great place to escape from Kyōto's hustle and bustle. Flanking a flagstone pathway inside the temple' thatched gateway, two long regular mounds of sand are raked daily into shapes symbolizing the changing seasons. As you explore the surrounding green forest (if you arrive early in the morning, you can see the priests raking it clean) and stroll through the verdant garden, you may see the tombs of several notables, including novelist Junichiro Tanizaki, economist Hajime Kawakami, and artist Heihachiro Fukuda. The temple, built in 1680, is on a site chosen in the 13th century by Hōnen, founder of the populist Jōdo sect of Buddhism. In the first week of April and all of November, monks place 25 flowers before the Amida Buddha statue in the main hall, representing the 25 bodhisattvas who accompany the Buddha to receive the souls of the newly deceased. ✉ *Shishigatani-Goshonodan-chō, Sakyō-ku* 📞 *075/771–2420* 🎫 *Free* 🕙 *Daily 5–4.*

⑮ Kawai Kanjirō Memorial House 河合寛次郎記念館 *(Kawai Kanjirō Kinenkan).* The house and workshop of prolific potter Kanjirō Kawai has been transformed into a museum showcasing his distinctive works. One of the leaders of the *Mingei* (folk art) movement in the 1920s, Kawai's skill is evident in the asymmetrical vases, bowls, and pots on display in the house. Besides the fascinating workshop and enormous kiln preserved in an inner courtyard, the house itself is magnificent. It's a terrific opportunity for those who have never been inside a Japanese home. The house is a little hard to find, located in an alley just southwest of the Higashi-ōji-dōri and Gojō-dōri intersection. To get here, take Bus 100 or 206 to Gojō-zaka. Walking west on Gojō-dōri, take the first left. ⊠*569 Kanei-chō, Gojō-zaka, Higashiyama-ku* ☎*075/561–3585* ✆*¥900* ☉*Tues.–Sun. 10–5.*

⑰ Kōdai-ji 高台寺. In the heart of ancient Higashiyama's cobbled streets, the elegant Momoyama-era temples and tea houses of Kōdai-ji are set in an expansive garden of serene pools swimming with orange karp, hills of carefully tended moss, a forest of tall bamboo, and an expanse of raked gray sand. Many of the splendid paintings and friezes inside the main temples were relocated from Fushimi Castle, parts of which were used to construct Kōdai-ji in the early 1600s. The temple was a memorial to Hideyoshi Toyotomi, commissioned by his wife Nene. (The road running in front of the temple is alternately called Higashiyama-dōri or Nene-no-michi.) On the hills overlooking the main temple are teahouses designed by tea master Sen-no-Rikyū; they are identifiable by their umbrella-shaped bamboo ceilings and thatched roofs.

Evening illumination shows in April, November, and December are a great way to see the park after dark. (Avoid holiday weekends, when the place is packed.) The temple is a five-minute walk east of the Higashiyama Yasui bus stop (take number 206 or 207). ⊠*Shimogawara-chō, Higashiyama-ku* ☎*075/561–9966* ✆*¥500* ☉*Apr.–Nov., daily 9–4:30; Dec.–Mar., daily 9–4.*

❻ Kyōto Handicraft Center 京都ハンディクラフトセンター. Here you'll find seven floors filled with dolls, kimonos, pottery, swords, woodblock prints, and even pearl jewelry. The eye-popping selection and reasonable prices mean this duty-free commercial center is a great place for browsing. Regular demonstrations of traditional craft techniques make this place tourist-oriented, but don't mistake that for tourist trap. Everything is of the highest quality. To get here, take Bus 202 or 206 to Kumano Jinja-mae or Bus 5, 32, 46, or 100 to Kyōto Kaikan Bijutsukan-mae. The building is across Maruta-machi-dōri from Heian Jingū. ⊠*21 Entomi-cho Shogo-in, Sakyō-ku* ☎*075/761–5080* ☉*Daily 10–6.*

❾ Kyōto Museum of Traditional Crafts 京都伝統産業ふれあい館 *(Kyōto Fureaikan)*. Fascinating displays reveal the painstaking care taken with Kyōto's traditional crafts. Dioramas, pictures, and videos show how a wide range of crafts, from everyday items like pottery and textiles to precious objects like jewelry and kimonos. There are frequent live demonstrations, and a shop sells souvenirs. The museum faces Heian Jingū. ⊠*9–2 Seishōji-chō, Okazaki, Sakyō-ku* ☎*075/762–2670* ✆*Free* ☉*Tues.–Sun. 9–5; last entry at 4:30.*

⓮ Kyōto National Museum 京都国立博物館 *(Kokuritsu Hakubutsukan)*. The building itself is an enthralling piece of the Kyōto landscape, but its lackluster permanent collection doesn't rate as must-see. The Meiji-era brick structure holds an extensive collection of sculptures, textiles, ceramics, and metalwork, but it's nothing you won't see in other Japanese museums. It is worth checking on the temporary exhibitions, which can bring some real treasures. The museum is on the corner of Shichijo-dōri and Higashi-ōji-dōri, across from Sanjusangen-dō and Chishaku-in. From Kyōto Station take Bus 206 or 208 to the Sanjūsangen-dō-mae stop. ⊠ *527 Chayamachi, Higashiyama-ku* ☎*075/541–1151* ⊕*www. kyohaku.go.jp* ⊡*¥500* ⊗*Tues.–Sun. 9:30–5:30.*

⑱ **Maruyama Kōen** 円山公園 *(Maruyama Park).* Many people cut through this park, which lies near Yasaka Jinja and between Chion-in and Gion, when sightseeing. This is a popular venue for drinking sake outdoors during the cherry-blossom season, and vendors are usually around to supply refreshment. From Kyōto Station, take Bus 206 to the Higashi-yama stop; the park is north of Kōdai-ji. ⊠*Higashiyama-ku .*

⑧ **National Museum of Modern Art** 京都国立近代美術館 *(Kindai Bijutsukan).* This small but excellent museum is known for its collection of 20th-century Japanese paintings, emphasizing the artistic movements in the Kansai region. You'll also see ceramic treasures by Kanjirō Kawai, Rosanjin Kitaōji, Shōji Hamada, and others. There are frequent exhibitions of contemporary artists. The museum faces Heian Jingū. ⊠*Enshōji-chō, Okazaki, Sakyō-ku* ☎*075/761–4111* ⊡*¥420* ⊗*Tues.–Sun. 9:30–5.*

❷ **Path of Philosophy** 哲学の道 *(Tetsugaku-no-michi).* Cherry trees line this walkway along the canal. It has traditionally been a place for contemplative strolling since a famous scholar, Ikutarō Nishida (1870–1945), took his daily constitutional here. It offers less of an introspective environment nowadays, with crowds of tourists tramping towards the Silver Pavilion, but the quaint canal does have coffee shops and small restaurants. From Kyōto Station take Bus 5 to the Ginkaku-ji-michi bus stop. ⊠*Sakyō-ku.*

㉑ **Shōren-in** 青蓮院. Paintings by the Kanō school are on view at this tem-
★ ple, a five-minute walk north of Chion-in. Although the temple's present building dates from 1895, the sliding doors and screens inside are centuries older. They are the work of the 16th-century painter Motonobu Kanō, known for combining simple Chinese ink painting with Japanese ornamental styles. An immense camphor tree near the entrance makes the grounds a pleasant place to wander, and koto (harp) concerts are sometimes held in the evenings. From Kyōto Station take Bus 206 to the Higashiyama-Sanjō stop. ⊠*69-1 Sanjobo-chō, Awataguchi, Higashi-yama-ku* ☎ *075/561–2345* ⊡*¥500* ⊗*Daily 9–5.*

CENTRAL AND SOUTHERN KYŌTO

The two major sights in central Kyōto are the opulent Nijō Castle and the more modest Imperial Palace. The latter requires permission, and you must join a guided tour. Central Kyōto is a big shopping destination: west of the Kamo-gawa to Karasuma-dōri and on the north–south axis between Shijō-dōri and Oike-dōri, there are department stores, specialty shops, and restaurants.

The most interesting southern Kyōto sights are three religious structures: Tōfuku-ji, Fushimi-Inari Taisha, and Byōdō-in, which is actually in the tea-producing city of Uji. Both Fushimi-Inari Taisha and the temple Daigo-ji in southern Kyōto are set on mountains with trails to explore.

Buses and several subway lines service all of Central Kyōto's sights, but taxis may be more cost effective way for groups to get around. Out-of-the-way sights are best accessed by train.

The temples and shrines in Southern Kyōto are far from one another, so traveling time can eat into your day. If you visit Tōfuku-ji, consider combining it with a visit to Fushimi-Inari Taisha, farther south.

TOP ATTRACTIONS

⑨ **Byōdō-in** 平等院 *(Temple of Equality)*. South of Kyōto in Uji-shi, this
★ temple was originally the villa of a 10th-century member of the influential Fujiwara family. The **Amida-dō** is also known as the Phoenix Hall, thanks to its two protruding wings that make the building resemble the legendary bird; the hall is depicted on the ¥10 coin. Built in the 11th century by the Fujiwaras, it's considered one of Japan's most beautiful religious buildings—something of an architectural folly—where heaven is brought close to earth. Jōchō, one of Japan's most famous 11th-century sculptors, crafted a magnificent statue of Amida Buddha here; his hand mudra indicates that the Buddha rests in the highest of the nine paradises. The Aji Pond in front symbolizes the lotus lake of Amida's paradise. In the museum alongside you can see 52 small wooden *kuyo* or reverent bosatsu floating on clouds, playing celestial music.

Uji is a famous tea-producing district, and the slope up to the temple is lined with shops where you can sample the finest green tea and pick up a small package to take home. It's possible to set up a visit to a tea farm through the Kyōto Tourist Information Center. The shrines and temples surrounding the Uji River are also pleasant to explore. To get to Uji, take the JR Nara Line to Uji Station. Byōdō-in is a 12-minute walk east toward the river from the station. ⊠ *Ujirenge 116, Uji-shi* ☎ *0774/21–2861* ⊠ *¥500; additional ¥300 for Phoenix Hall* ☉ *Temple Mar.–Nov., daily 8:30–5:30; Dec.–Feb., daily 9–4:30. Phoenix Hall Mar. Nov., daily 9–5; Dec.–Feb., daily 9–4.*

■ **NEED A
BREAK?** **Opposite Byōdō-in, Taihō-an** 対鳳庵 **is an authentic tea-ceremony building set in a delightful garden. Here you can enjoy a cup of green tea with a seasonal Japanese sweet, or if you book in advance, the full tea ceremony for ¥1,500.**

⊠ **2 Ujitōgawa, Uji-shi** ☎ **0774/23–3334** ☉ **Thurs.–Tues. 10–sunset.**

⑩ **Fushimi-Inari Taisha** 伏見稲荷大社. Many visitors find Fushimi-Inari
Fodor'sChoice Taisha's thousands of red lacquered gates to be the quintessential image
★ of Japan. This is the central headquarters for 40,000 shrines nationally that do service to Inari, the god of rice, sake, and prosperity. The shrine's 10,000 torii gates, donated by the thankful, are unforgettable. They trace a path up the mountainside, broken up at irregular intervals with shrines, altars, mausoleums, and thousand upon thousand of foxes in stone and bronze. As Japan's underpinnings have shifted from agriculture to other forms of business, Inari has been adopted as a patron deity for any kind of entrepreneurial venture, and the gates in the path are donated by businesses from around the country seeking a blessing. Walking the whole circuit takes about three hours, or

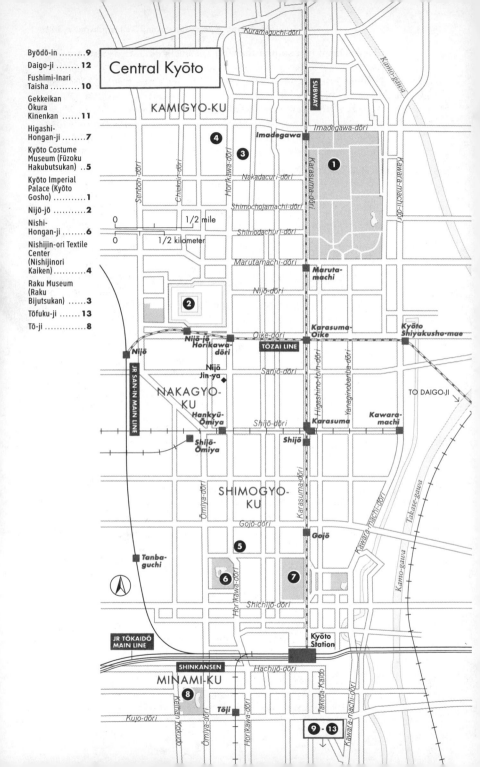

Central Kyōto

KAMIGYO-KU

Kuramaguchi-dōri

SUBWAY

Imadegawa

Imadegawa-dōri

Senbon-dōri

Chiekoin-dōri

Horikawa-dōri

Nakadacuri-dōri

Karasuma-dōri

Kawara-machi-dōri

Shimochojamachi-dōri

Shimodachuri-dōri

0   1/2 mile

0   1/2 kilometer

Marutamachi-dōri

Maruta-machi

Nijō-dōri

Nijō-jō
Horikawa-dōri

Oike-dōri

Karasuma-Oike

Kyōto Shiyakusho-mae

Nijō

JR SAN-IN MAIN LINE

TŌZAI LINE

Nijō Jin-ya

Sanjō-dōri

TO DAIGO-JI

NAKAGYO-KU

Hankyū-Ōmiya

Shijō-dōri

Karasuma

Kawara-machi

Shijō-Ōmiya

Shijō

Higashino-toin-dōri

Yanaginobanba-dōri

SHIMOGYO-KU

Ōmiya-dōri

Karasuma-dōri

Gojō-dōri

Gojō

Tanba-guchi

Shichijō-dōri

Horikawa-dōri

Kawara-machi-dōri

Tikase-gawa

Kamo-gawa

JR TŌKAIDŌ MAIN LINE

Kyōto Station

SHINKANSEN

Hachijō-dōri

MINAMI-KU

Tōji

Kujo-dōri

Ōmiya-dōri

Horikawa-dōri

Takeda-Kaido

Kawara-machi-dōri

9 - 13

a bit longer if you stop at the shops selling snacks along the way. To get here, take the JR Nara Line to Inari Station or Keihan Railway to Fushimi-Inari station. ⊠*68 Fukakusa Yabu-no-uchi-chō, Fushimi-ku* ✉*Free* ☾*Daily sunrise–sunset.*

⓫ **Gekkeikan Ōkura Kinenkan** 月桂冠大倉記念館 *(Gekkeikan Ōkura Muse-*
★ *um)*. Not far from Fushimi-Inari Taisha is a district of old white-walled sake breweries and warehouses, some dating to the early Edo era. Gekkeikan, founded in 1637, is one of the oldest breweries. The museum details the brewing process, and there's free tastings. The brewery is a five-minute walk from Chūshojima Station, on the Keihan Line, or a 10-minute walk from Momoyama Goryō-mae Station, on the Kintetsu Kyōto Line. Reservations must be made in advance. ⊠*247 Minamihama-chō, Fushimi-ku* ☎*075/623–2056* ⊕*www.gekkeikan. co.jp* ✉*¥300* ☾*Tues.–Sun. 9:30–4:30.*

❼ **Higashi-Hongan-ji** 東本願寺. Very close to Kyōto Station, this temple
★ is the first of the city's ancient sights to confronting visitors arriving by bus. Its strong walls, mighty gates, and high-roofed main hall are impressive enough to make some newcomers believe they are looking at the Imperial Palace. In the current complex, largely a reconstruction in 1895, everything is dwarfed by the cavernous main hall, the second-largest wooden structure in Japan. During construction of the temple, female devotees had their hair cut and woven into the strong thick rope needed to drag the heavy timber. A ragged section of one of these *kezuna* is on display inside the **Daishi-dō**, a double-roofed structure that is admirable for its gracefully curving lines. From Kyōto Station walk 500 yards northwest. ⊠*Shichijō-agaru, Karasuma-dōri, Shimogyō-ku* ✉*Free* ☾*Mar.–Oct., daily 5:50–5:30; Nov.–Feb., daily 6:20–4:30.*

❷ **Nijō-jō** 二条城. In the early Edo period, the first Tokugawa shōgun Ieya-
Fodor'sChoice su stripped all power from Kyōto's imperial court by consolidating a
★ new military and political center at his far-off fortress in Tōkyō. Nijō castle, begun 1603, is a grandiose and unequivocal statement of the shogunate's power. Nijō-jō's wide exterior moat and towering walls are the castle's exterior face, but one inside a second moat and defensive wall become visible. This had less to do with defense than it did with reinforcing the castle's social statement: access to the inner sanctum depended on a visitor's status within the shogunate's hierarchy, and the powers-that-be could remind anyone of their place in the system. Anyone who was permitted inside was as much a hostage as a guest, a feeling surely driven home by the castle's ingenious nightingale floors, which "sing" as you walk across them, revealing your movements at all times. (You can see how they work by looking underneath the balcony as you walk through the garden.)

The Tokugawa shōguns were rarely in Kyōto. Ieyasu stayed in the castle three times; the second shōgun stayed twice, including the time in 1626 when Emperor Gomizuno-o was granted an audience. After that, for the next 224 years, no Tokugawa shōgun visited Kyōto, and the castle started to fall into disrepair. Only when the Tokugawa shogunate was under pressure from a failing economy did the 14th shōgun, Tokugawa Iemochi (1846–66), come to Kyōto to confer with the emperor. The

15th and last Tokugawa shōgun, Yoshinobu, famously returned power to the Emperor in 1967, the central event of the Meiji Restoration. Since 1939 the castle has belonged to the city of Kyōto, and considerable restoration has taken place.

You can explore Nijō-jō at your own pace, and handy audio guides give great explanations of what you're seeing. Entry is through the impressive **Kara-mon gate**, whose sharp angles are intended to slow an attack. The path from the Kara-mon leads to the **Ni-no-maru** Palace, whose five buildings are divided into various smaller chambers. Inside the central **hall**, costumed mannequins are frozen in Tokugawa shōgunate's dying moment, returning the government to the emperor. The impressive garden was created by landscape designer Enshū Kobori shortly before Emperor Gomizuno-o's visit in 1626. Crane- and tortoise-shaped islands symbolize strength and longevity. You can get to the castle via Tōzai subway or Bus 9, 12, 50, or 101 to Nijō-jō-mae. ⊠*Horikawa Nishi-Iru, Nijō-dōri, Nakagyō-ku* ☎*075/841–0096* ☝*¥600* ☉*Daily 8:45–5; last entry at 4.*

❻ Nishi-Hongan-ji 西本願寺. Set within a sprawling compound with court-
★ yards and gardens, the graceful curves, stout lintels, and ornate gold accents of this temple are excellent examples of elegant Momoyama-era architecture. The worldwide center for the Jōdo Shinshu sect of Buddhism was founded in 1272, but what you see today dates from the early 17th century. The fascinating relics and artifacts housed within were confiscated from various palaces belonging to the deposed warlord Hideyoshi Toyotomi. As at Higashi Hongan-ji, daily rituals carried out inside the recently restored main hall are great opportunities to see daily life at the temple. Nishi-Hongan-ji is on Horikawa-dōri, a block north of Shichijō-dōri. Visits are permitted four times a day by permission from the temple office. Japanese-language tours of the Daisho-in are given throughout the year. ⊠*Shichijō-agaru, Horikawa-dōri, Shimogyō-ku* ☎*075/371–5181* ☝*Free* ☉*Mar., Apr., Sept., and Oct., daily 5:30–5:30; May–Aug., daily 5:30 AM–6 PM; Nov.–Feb., daily 6–5.*

❽ Tō-ji 東寺. Established by imperial edict in 796 and called Kyō-ō-gokoku-ji, Tō-ji was built to guard the city. It was one of the only two temples that Emperor Kammu permitted to be built in the city—he had had enough of the powerful Buddhists while in Nara. The temple was later given to the priest Kūkai (Kōbō Daishi), who founded the Shingon sect of Buddhism at the turn of the 9th century.

Fires and battles during the 16th century destroyed the temple buildings, but many were rebuilt, including in 1603 the Kon-dō (Main Hall), which blends Chinese and Japanese elements. The Kō-dō (Lecture Hall), on the other hand, has managed to survive the ravages of war since it was built in 1491. Inside this hall are 15 original statues of Buddhist gods, making up a mandala, considered masterpieces of the Heian Era (750–1150).

On the 21st of each month a market, known locally as Kōbō-san, is held. Antique kimonos, fans, and other artifacts can be found at bargain prices if you know your way around the savvy dealers. A smaller antiques market is held on the first Sunday of the month. The temple is a 10-minute walk southwest of Kyōto Station. You can walk from there, or take a Kintetsu Line subway one stop. Bus 207 also runs past Tō-ji. ✉ *1 Kujō-chō, Minami-ku* 🎫 *Free; main buildings ¥500* 🕐 *Mar. 20–Sept. 19, daily 9–5; Sept. 20–Mar. 19, daily 9–4:30.*

WORTH NOTING

Daigo-ji 醍醐寺. The main temple of this mountain enclave founded in 874 is set in the foothills, and many smaller temples stand on the ridges above. Its five-story pagoda, which dates from 951, is reputed to be the oldest existing structure in Kyōto. By the late 16th century the temple had begun to decline in importance and showed signs of neglect. Then Hideyoshi Toyotomi paid a visit one April, when the temple's famous cherry trees were in bloom. Hideyoshi ordered the temple restored. The **Sanbō-in**, with its Momoyama-period thatched roof, has bold colorful paintings of nature and Chinese village scenes; the paintings, which incorporate gold leaf, were done by the Kanō school. The intriguing garden combines elements of the *chisen-kaiyū* (stroll garden with a pond) and the *karesansui*, or dry garden. From the temple you can continue up the mountain (about an hour's hike) to several subtemples. At the top, on a clear day, it's possible to make out the Ōsaka skyline in the far distance. To reach Daigo-ji, in the southeast suburb of Yamashina, take the Tōzai subway line to Daigo Station; follow the signs for a 10-minute walk to the nearby hills. ✉ *22 Higashi Ōji-chō, Fushimi-ku* 🎫 *¥500* 🕐 *Mar.–Oct., daily 9–5; Nov.–Feb., daily 9–4.*

⑤ ★ **Kyōto Costume Museum** 風俗博物館 *(Fūzoku Hakubutsukan).* Marvel at the range of Japanese fashion, which starts in the pre-Nara era and works its way up through various historical eras to the Meiji period. The museum is one of the best of its kind, and provides an interesting perspective on Japan's history. Exhibitions, which change twice a year, use doll-size replicas to highlight a specific historical period. One room has two mannequins draped in Heian robes that can be tried on for free. From the Raku Art Museum, the Nishijin Textile Center, or Nijō-jō, take Bus 9 south on Horikawa-dōri. Disembark at the Nishi-Hongan-ji-mae bus stop. The museum is on the fifth floor of the Izutsu Building, at the intersection of Horikawa and Shin-Hanaya-chō, north of the temple on the other side of the street. ✉ *Izutsu Bldg., Shinhanayacho-Dori, Horikawa Higashiiru, Shimogyō-ku* ☎ *075/342–5345* 🎫 *¥400* 🕐 *Oct. 9–Sept. 2, Mon.–Sat. 9–5; closed Apr. 1–8, July 1–8, and Dec. 23–Jan. 6.*

① **Kyōto Imperial Palace** 京都御所 *(Kyōto Gosho).* It tops the list of must-see sights for many tourists, but the Imperial Palace leaves many underwhelmed. In fact, you are prohibited from entering any of the buildings on the rather sedate hourlong tour. The original building burned down in 1788, as did several of the replacements. The present structure dates from 1855. It's hardly palatial, though fine in its way; the ingenious cypress-bark roof is particularly attractive. And the park-like setting is very pretty.

To see the palace, you must receive permission to enter from the Imperial Household Agency. You can do on the same day with your passport at the office in the park's northwest corner, or on the Web site. Guided tours in English begin at the Seishomon entrance, inside the park. Tours

MR. MONKEY WAS NO MONKEYMAN

Hideyoshi Toyotomi was quite a man. Though most of the initial work of unifying Japan in the late 16th century was accomplished by the warrior Nobunaga Oda (he was ambushed a year after defeating the monks on Hieizan), it was Hideyoshi who completed the job. Not only did he end civil strife, he also restored the arts. For a brief time (1582–98), Japan entered one of the most colorful periods of its history. How Hideyoshi achieved his feats is not exactly known. He was brought up as a farmer's son, and his nickname was Saru-san (Mr. Monkey) because he was small and ugly. According to one legend—probably started by Hideyoshi himself—he was the son of the emperor's concubine. She had been much admired by a man to whom the emperor owed a favor, so the emperor gave the concubine to him. Unknown to either of the men, she was soon pregnant with Hideyoshi. Whatever his origins (he changed his name frequently), he brought peace to Japan after decades of civil war.

run weekdays at 10 and 2. ⊠*Kunaichō, Kyōto Gyoen-nai, Kamigyō-ku* 🕾*075/211–1215* ⊕*sankan.kunaicho.go.jp* ✉*Free* ⊗*Office weekdays 8:45–noon and 1–5.*

Kyōto Station 京都駅. Kyōto's train station, derided as an eyesore by some and hailed as a masterpiece by others, is more than just the city's central point of arrival and departure: the station houses a hotel, a theater, a department store, and dozens of shops and restaurants with great views of the city from the 16th floor. ⊠*137 Karasuma Dōri Shioko-ji sagaru, Shimogyō-ku.*

Nijō Jin-ya 二条陣屋. A short walk south of Nijō-jō is the less visited Nijō Jinya, a former merchant house built in the 17th century. The house later became an inn for traveling daimyo, or feudal lords. The house is crammed with built-in safeguards against attack, including hidden staircases, secret passageways, and hallways too narrow to allow the wielding of a sword. Fascinating hourlong tours through the warren of rooms are in Japanese; reservations are required. ⊠*137 Sembon Ōmiya-chō, Nakagyō-ku* 🕾*075/841–0972* ✉*¥500* ⊗*Tours daily 10–4.*

❹ Nishijin-ori Textile Center 西陣会館 *(Nishijinori Kaiken).* The Nishijin district, which still has some old wooden warehouses hugging the canals, hangs on to the artistic thread of traditional Japanese silk weaving. The Nishijin-ori Textile Center is a fascinating place to learn about the weaving industry. Hands-on lessons let you weave your own garment: for ¥1,800 you'll get a great souvenir and the experience is easy and fun. Reserve ahead and you can try on various different kimonos, and even rent one for a night on the town. To get here, take Bus 9, 12, 51, or 59 to the Horikawa-Imadegawa stop. ⊠*Horikawa-dōri, Imadegawa-Minami-Iru, Kamigyō-ku* 🕾*075/451–9231* ⊕*www.nishijin.or.jp* ✉*Free* ⊗*Daily 9–5.*

❸ Raku Museum 樂美術館 *(Raku Bijutsukan).* Any serious collector of tea-ceremony artifacts is likely to have a Raku bowl in his or her collection. The Raku Museum displays more than 1,000 bowls and vessels of astonishing beauty. As a potter's term in the West, *raku* refers to a low-temperature firing technique, but the word originated with this family, who made exquisite tea bowls for use in the shōgun's tea ceremonies. The museum is to the east of Horikawa-dōri, three blocks south of Imadegawa-dōri; take the Karasuma line subway to Imadegawa station or Bus 9 or 12 to Ichi-jō-modōri-bashi. ⊠ *Aburakōji, Nakadachuri-agaru, Kamigyō-ku* ☎ *075/414–0304* ☜ *¥700–¥1,000, depending on exhibition* ⊙ *Tues.–Sun. 10–4:30.*

Tōfuku-ji 東福寺. A fabulous gateway arch—the oldest Zen gateway in Japan, constructed in accordance to strict Buddhist guidelines—attracts many visitors to this expansive medieval complex. Established in 1236, this temple of the Rinzai sect of Zen Buddhism ranks as one of the most important in Kyōto, along with the Myōshin-ji and Daitoku-ji. The grand entry gate is a sight to see, both inside and out. At 22 meters tall, the gate's friezes depict scenes of the Buddha and his disciples attributed to the prominent Heian-era sculptor Teicho. Arranged around the main hall are four contrasting gardens, both dry gravel and landscaped, including a stroll garden. Autumn, with the burnished color of the maple trees, is an especially fine time for visiting. There are at least three ways to get to Tōfuku-ji, which is southeast of Kyōto Station: Bus 208 from Kyōto Station, a JR train on the Nara Line to Tōfuku-ji Station, or a Keihan Line train to Tōfuku-ji Station. From the station it's a 15-minute walk to the temple. ⊠ *Hon-machi 15-chōme, Higashiyama-ku* ☎ *075/561–0087* ⊕ *www.tofukuji.jp/english.html* ☜ *¥400* ⊙ *Daily 9–4.*

6

WESTERN KYŌTO

Western Kyōto's most iconic sights are the eye-popping golden temple at Kinkaku-ji and the rock garden at Ryōan-ji, but the city's western precincts are filled with remarkable religious architecture. The sprawling temple complexes Daitoku-ji and Myōshin-ji are well worth a visit, as is the blossom-covered Kitano Tenman-gu, which hosts a fabulous market each month.

GETTING
AROUND
The sights in the northern and western parts of this area can be reached easily using city buses. For Katsura Rikyū rail is best, and to reach Kōinzan Saihō-ji you can take Bus 29 from Karasuma Shijō.

TOP ATTRACTIONS

❺ **Kinkaku-ji** 金閣寺 *(Temple of the Golden Pavilion)*. Possibly the world's most ostentatious retirement cottage, the magnificent gold-sheathed Kinkaku-ji was built by Shōgun Yoshimitsu Ashikaga (1358–1409). He ordered it built in 1393 in anticipation of the time when he would quit politics—the following year, in fact—to manage the affairs of state through the new shōgun, his 10-year-old son. On Yoshimitsu's death, his son followed his father's wishes and converted the villa into a temple.

FodorsChoice
★

The current temple was reconstructed in the 1950s after a monk set fire to the standing structure. (His internal conflict is the focus of Yukio Mishima's 1956 famous novel Temple of the Golden Pavilion, published the year after construction had finished.) The top two stories are coated with gold leaf, as per Yoshimitsu's original vision, an especially dazzling sight when reflected in the pond's still waters. To get here, take Bus 12,

59, 101, 102, 204, or 205 to Kinkaku-ji-mae. ⊠*1 Kinkaku-ji-chō, Kita-ku* ▭*¥400* ⊙*Daily 9–5.*

❶ **Kitano Tenman-gū** 北野天満宮. In February and March, the gorgeous
★ plum blossoms that blanket this shrine make it a great place to warm your spirit during the sometimes desolate winter. The rest of the year, the shrine's biggest draw is its fabulous market. Held on the 25th of every month, the market draws vendors selling everything from gooey fried octopus balls and black soy bean tea to kimonos and woodblock prints. To get here, take Bus 50, 101, or 201 to Kitano Tenman-gū-mae. ⊠*Imakoji-agaru, Onmae-dōri, Kamigyō-ku* ▭*Shrine free; plum garden ¥500* ⊙ *Shrine Apr.–Oct., daily 5–5; Nov.–Mar, daily 5:30–5:30. Plum garden Feb.–Mar., daily 10–4.*

❾ **Myōshin-ji** 妙心寺. Surrounded by thick stone walls, this complex holds
★ some great treasures within its 47 temples. The biggest tourist draw is in the lecture hall of the main temple, with its stunning painting of a dragon stretching across the expansive ceiling. In rendering the life-like creature, the painter made clever use of a perspective to make it seem like the dragon's eyes glare at you wherever you walk. Japan's oldest bell is also at daily use in Myōshin-ji, tolling out the hour for meditation since 698. Buses 61, 62, and 63 stop at Myōshin-ji-mae; otherwise take a JR Sagano Line train to Hanazono-chō. ⊠*64 Hanazono Myōshinji-chō, Ukyō-ku* ▭*¥400 for lecture hall; ¥400 for most smaller temples* ⊙*Lecture hall and smaller temple daily 9:10–11:50 and 1–4.*

❽ **Ninna-ji** 仁和寺. With a five-tier pagoda at its center, this temple sits in a park-like setting. It's surrounded by late-blooming cherry trees that attract crowds every May. Emperor Omuro's palace stood here in the late 9th century, but the buildings you see today were constructed in the 17th century. The Hon-dō (Main Hall), moved here from the Imperial Palace, is well worth a look. Ninna-ji is a 10-minute walk west of Ryoan-ji and a 5-minute walk northwest of Myōshin-ji's north gate. Take either Bus 26 or 59 to the Omuro-ninna-ji, or a JR Sagano Line train to Hanazono-chō. ⊠ *33 Ouchi Omuro, Ukyō-ku616-8035* ▭*¥500* ⊙*Daily 9–4:30.*

❼ **Ryōan-ji** 龍安寺. The solemn stones set into the sand at Ryōan-ji's rock
★ garden has become one of Japan's quintessential images. The simple arrangement can be viewed as an oasis for contemplation or a riddle to train the mind. From any single vantage point, only 14 of the 15 stones can be seen. In the Buddhist tradition, 15 is a number that signifies completion, and it is supposed that the garden's message is that, in this world, completion is not possible. As mystical as he experience may be for some, you will be hard up to get time alone with your thoughts. The destination draws crowds by the busload. If you need a moment to yourself, head to the small restaurant on the temple grounds. Buses 50, 55, and 59 stop at Ryōan-ji-mae. ⊠*13 Goryōshita-machi, Ryōan-ji, Ukyō-ku* ▭*¥500* ⊙*Mar.–Nov., daily 8–5; Dec.–Feb., daily 8:30–4:30.*

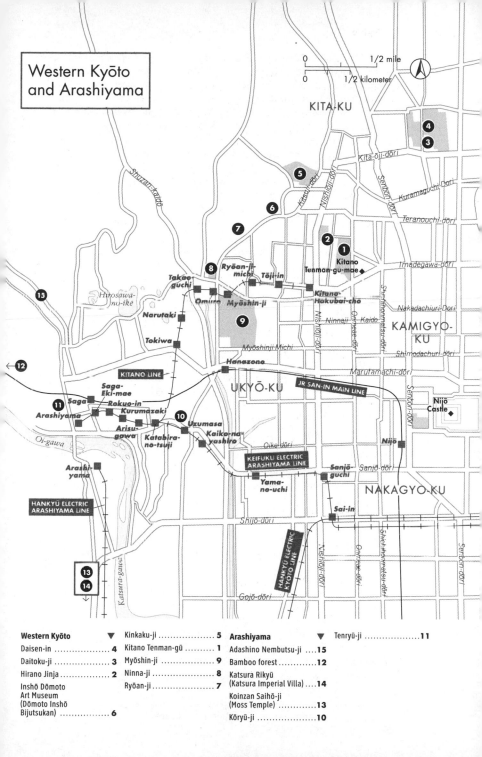

Western Kyōto and Arashiyama

KITA-KU

KAMIGYŌ-KU

UKYŌ-KU

NAKAGYŌ-KU

Kitano Tenman-gu-mae

Ryōan-ji-michi

Tōji-in

Kitano-Hakubai-chō

Ninnaji

Omuro

Myōshin-ji

Myōshinji Michi

Hanazono

KITANO LINE

JR SAN-IN MAIN LINE

Saga-Eki-mae

Rokuo-in

Kurumazaki

Uzumasa

Kaiko-na-yashiro

Katabira-no-tsuji

Arashiyama

Arisu-gawa

Saga

KEIFUKU ELECTRIC ARASHIYAMA LINE

Yama-no-uchi

Sanjō-guchi

Sanjō-dōri

Sai-in

Shijō-dōri

Gojō-dōri

HANKYŪ ELECTRIC ARASHIYAMA LINE

HANKYŪ ELECTRIC KYŌTO LINE

Arashi-yama

Ōi-gawa

Katsura-gawa

Shūzan-kaidō

Hirosawa-no-ike

Narutaki

Tokiwa

Takao-guchi

Oike-dōri

Nijō Castle

Nijō

Teranouchi-dōri

Imadegawa-dōri

Nakadachiuri-Dōri

Shimodachiuri-dōri

Marutamachi-dōri

Kita-ōji-dōri

Kuramaguchi-Dōri

Kaidō

Kitsu-dōri

Nishiōji-dōri

Nishijin-dōri

Senbon-dōri

Shichi-honmatsu-dōri

Omote-dōri

Shinmachi-dōri

Nishiōji-dōri

Nishiōji-dōri

Onmae-dōri

Shichi-honmatsu-dōri

Senbon-dōri

| 0 | | 1/2 mile |
| 0 | | 1/2 kilometer |

WORTH NOTING

3 **Daitoku-ji** 大徳寺. Two dozen temples can be found in this walled compound, a holy place for the Rinzai sect of Zen Buddhism. The original temple was founded in 1319, but fires during the Ōnin Civil War destroyed it in 1468. Most buildings you see today were built under the patronage of Hideyoshi Toyotomi in the late 16th century.

4 Several of the smaller temples are well worth exploring, **Daisen-in** 大仙院 is best known for its excellent landscape paintings by the renowned Sōami (1465–1523), as well as the famed Muromachi-era garden, attributed to Sōko Kogaku (1465–1548). Circling the building, the moody rock-and-gravel garden depicts the flow of life in the movement of a river, swirling around rocks, over a waterfall, around finally into an ocean of nothingness. Admission is ¥400, and the temple is open 9 to 5.

Ryōgen-in has five small gardens of gravel, stone, and moss. The A-Un garden includes a stone with ripples emanating from it, thought to symbolize the cycle of life, from the "a" sound said at birth to the "un" said at death, encompassing all in between. The fee for Ryōgen-in is ¥350, and the temple stays open 9 to 4:30.

Kōtō-in is famous for its long, maple-tree-lined approach and the single stone lantern central to the main garden. The fee is ¥400, and the temple stays open from 9 until 4:30 or 5.

There are several ways to get to the temple from downtown Kyōto. Take the Karasuma subway to Kita-ōji Station, where any bus going west along Kita-ōji-dōri will take you to the Daitokuji-mae stop. Buses 12, 204, and 206 make the same stop. ⊠ *53 Murasakino Daitokuji-chō, Kita-ku* ☏ *075/491–0019* 🎫*Free* 🕙 *Daily, temple hrs vary between 9 and 5.*

NEED A BREAK?

Ichiwa いち和 has been serving tea and *aburi mochi*—skewered rice-flour cakes charcoal-grilled and dipped in sweet miso sauce—since the Heian Era (750–1150). You can enjoy the treats under the eaves of a 17th-century house as you watch visitors on their way to and from Imamiya Shrine. Ichiwa is just outside the shrine, northwest of Daitoku-ji. ⊠ *69 Imamiya-chō, Murasakino, Kita-ku* ☏ *075/492–6852* 🕙 *Thurs.–Tues. 10–sunset.*

2 **Hirano Jinja** 平野神社. Near Kinkaku-ji, the gorgeous cherry blossoms at this modest shrine have been the focus of an annual spring festival since 985. The pale pink petals contrast with vermilion lanterns lining the lanes of this Heian-style complex. The shrine was brought here from Nagaoka, the country's capital after Nara and before Kyōto. The four buildings you can visit date from the 17th century. Access is via Bus 50, 52, or 100 to Kitano Tenmongu-mae. From there, the shrine is a 10-minute walk north. ⊠*Miyamoto-chō 1, Hirano, Kita-ku* 🎫*Free* 🕙*Daily 6–5.*

6 **Inshō Dōmoto Art Museum** 堂本印象美術館 *(Dōmoto Inshō Bijutsukan)*. The narrative paintings of the 20th-century artist Inshō Dōmoto, affectionately known as Inshō-san, hold wide appeal because they depict scenes from everyday life. His use of classical Japanese painting's muted color palate with a more abstract, sometimes cubist approach to figure makes his work very appealing. To get here, take Bus 12, 15, 50, 51, 55, or 59 to Ritsumeikan Daigaku-mae. ✉ *26-3 Kamiyanagi-chō, Hirano, Kita-ku* ☎ *075/463–0007* 🎫 *¥500* 🕙 *Tues.–Sun. 9:30–5.*

ARASHIYAMA

Beyond the city is the semirural hillside area of Arashiyama, which lies along and above the banks of the Ōi-gawa (the local name for the Katsura-gawa as it courses through this area). The pleasure of Arashiyama, the westernmost part of Kyōto, is the same as it has been for centuries. The gentle foothills of the mountains, covered with cherry and maple trees, are splendid. The sights are fairly spaced out, connected by a pathway that meanders along the hillside, through fields and a peaceful bamboo grove, and past several craft shops and restaurants. It's no wonder that the aristocracy of feudal Japan came here to escape famine, riots, and political intrigue.

GETTING AROUND
The easiest ways to get to Arashiyama are by the JR San-in Main Line from Kyōto Station to Saga Station, or via the Keifuku Electric Railway to Arashiyama Station (which is just south of Saga Station).

TOP ATTRACTIONS

6

🟡 Fodor's Choice ★ **Adashino Nembutsu-ji** 化野念仏寺. The most unusual feature of this temple is the cemetery, where about 8,000 stone Buddhas are packed together, a solemn sea of quiet mourners. The statues honor the vast number of nameless dead who fell victim to the tumult of pre-Edo Japan and were burned here in mass pyres. The temple's main hall, built in 1712, contains an arresting statue of Amida Buddha carved by Kamakura-era sculptor Tankei. On August 23 and 24, a ceremony called Sentō-kuyo is held here, with more than 1,000 candles lighted for the peaceful repose of ancestor spirits. Whatever time of year you visit, make sure to come in late afternoon, when the shadows beneath the statues take on animated character. ✉ *17 Adashino-chō, Toriimoto, Ukyō-ku* ☎ *075/861–2221* 🎫 *¥500* 🕙 *Mar.–Nov., daily 9–4:30; Dec.–Feb., daily 9–4.*

🟡 Fodor's Choice ★ **Katsura Rikyū** 桂離宮 *(Katsura Imperial Villa).* The setting for this villa is a perfect example of Japanese integration of nature and architecture. Here you find Japan's oldest surviving stroll garden, dating to the 17th century, with pathways that take you through an encyclopedia of famous Japanese natural sites and literary references, such as the 11th-century *Tale of Genji*. Not satisfied to create simply beautiful pictures, landscape architect Enshū Kobori focused on the rhythm within the garden: spaces open then close, are bright then dark; views are visible and then concealed.

Built in the 17th century for Prince Toshihito, brother of Emperor Go-yōzei, Katsura is in southwestern Kyōto on the banks of the Katsura-gawa, with peaceful views of Arashiyama and the Kameyama Hills. Look out at the garden from the three *shōin* (a type of house that incorporates alcoves and platforms for the display of personal possessions) and the four rustic tea arbors around the central pond, which have been strategically placed for optimal vistas. Bridges constructed from earth, stone, and wood connect five islets in the pond.

The villa is fairly remote from other historical sites—allow several hours for a visit. Special permission is required for a visit. Applications must be made in advance through the **Imperial Household Agency** (✉ *3 Kyōto Gyoen-nai, Kamigyō-ku* ☎ *075/211–1215* ⊕ *sankan.kunaicho. go.jp*). To reach the villa, take the Hankyū Railway Line from one of the Hankyū Kyōto Line stations to Katsura Station, or catch Bus 33 from Kyōto station to Katsura Rikyū mae. You can also take a taxi for about ¥800. ✉ *Katsura Rikyu Shimizu-chō, Ukyō-ku* ☎ *075/211–1215* 🎟 *Free* ☉ *Tours weekdays at 10, 11, 2, and 3; additional tours 1st and 3rd Sat. of month Dec.–Mar. and June–Sept., and every Sat. in Apr., May, Oct., and Nov.*

⓭ **Kōinzan Saihō-ji** 供隠山西芳寺 *(Moss Temple).* Entrance into this temple
Fodor'sChoice complex transports you into an extraordinary sea of green: 120 variet-
★ ies of moss create waves of greens and blues that eddy and swirl gently. You'll realize why Kōinzan Saihō-ji is also known as, Kokedera—the Moss Temple. The site was originally the villa of Prince Shōtoku (572–621). During the Tempyō era (729–749) Emperor Shōmu charged the priest Gyoki to create 49 temples in the central province, one of which was this temple. The original garden represented Jōdo, the western paradise of Buddhism.

The temple and garden, destroyed many times by fire, lay in disrepair until 1338, when the chief priest of nearby Matsuno-jinja had a revelation here. He convinced Musō Soseki, a distinguished Zen priest of Rinzen-ji, the head temple of the Rinzai sect of Zen Buddhism, to convert it from the Jōdo to the Zen sect. Soseki, an avid gardener, designed the temple garden on two levels surrounding a pond in the shape of the Chinese character for heart. Present-day visitors are grateful for his efforts.

Another interesting aspect to your temple visit is the obligatory *sha-kyō,* writing of sutras. Before viewing the garden, you enter the temple and sit at a small, lacquered writing table where you're provided with a brush, ink, and a thin sheet of paper with Chinese characters in light gray. After rubbing your ink stick on the ink stone, dip the tip of your brush in the ink and trace over the characters. A priest explains in Japanese the temple history and the sutra you are writing. If time is limited you don't have to write the entire sutra; when the priest has ended his explanation, simply place what you have written on a table before the altar and proceed to the garden. To gain admission you're supposed to send the temple a request along with a stamped, self-addressed postcard, but it's worth just asking your hotel concierge if they can call for you. It's also possible to arrange a visit through the Kyōto Tourist Information Center. To reach the temple, take the Hankyū Line train from Arashiyama to Matsuno Station; buses from JR station stop at here. ✉ *56 Jingatani-cho, Matsuo, Nishikyō-ku 615-8286* ☎ *075/391–3631* 🎟 *¥3000* ☉ *Daily 9–5.*

⓾ **Kōryū-ji** 広隆寺. One of Kyōto's oldest temples, Kōryū-ji was founded
★ in 622 by Kawakatsu Hata in memory of Prince Shōtoku (572–621). Shōtoku, known for issuing the Seventeen-Article Constitution, a set of Confucian-inspired moral dictates, was the first powerful advocate

of Buddhism after it was introduced to Japan in 552. In the **Hattō** (Lecture Hall) of the main temple stand three statues, each a National Treasure. The center of worship is the seated figure of Buddha, flanked by the figures of the Thousand-Handed Kannon and Fukukenjaku-Kannon. In the **Taishi-dō** (Prince Hall) is a wooden statue of Prince Shōtoku, thought to have been carved by him personally. Another statue of Shōtoku in this hall was probably made when he was 16 years old.

The most famous of the Buddhist images in the Reihō-den (Treasure House) is the statue of **Miroku Bosatsu,** who according to Buddhist belief is destined to appear on earth in the far-off future to save those unable to achieve enlightenment. Japan's first registered National Treasure, this rustic wooden statue is thought to date to the 6th or 7th century, carved, perhaps, by Shōtoku himself. Of all the Buddhas in Kyōto, this may be the most captivating. The epitome of serenity, the statue gently rests the fingers of its right hand against its cheek (one finger, sadly, was broken off when an ardent student clutched the statue in the late '60s).

From Kyoto Station take the JR San-in Main Line to Hanazono Station and then board Bus 61. From Shijō-Ōmiya Station, in central Kyōto, take the Keifuku Electric Arashiyama Line to Uzumasa Station. From central or western Kyōto, take Bus 61, 62, or 63 to the Uzumasa-kōryūji-mae stop. ⊠ *Mineoka-chō, Uzumasa, Ukyō-ku* ⊠ *¥600* ☉ *Mar.–Nov., daily 9–5; Dec.–Feb., daily 9–4:30.*

⓫ **Tenryū-ji** 天龍寺. For good reason is this known as the Temple of the
★ Heavenly Dragon: in the 14th century Emperor Go-Daigo, who had brought an end to the Kamakura shogunate, was forced from his throne by Takauji Ashikaga. After Go-Daigo died, Takauji had twinges of conscience. That's when Priest Musō Sōseki had a dream in which a golden dragon rose from the nearby Ōi-gawa. He told the shōgun about his dream and interpreted it to mean the spirit of Go-Daigo was not at peace. Worried about this ill omen, Takauji completed Tenryū-ji in 1339 on the same spot where Go-Daigo had his favorite villa. Apparently the late emperor's spirit was appeased. Construction took several years and was partly financed by a trading mission to China, which brought back treasures of the Ming dynasty. In the Hattō (Lecture Hall), where today's monks meditate, a huge "cloud dragon" is painted on the ceiling. The temple was often ravaged by fire, and the current buildings are as recent as 1900; the painting of the dragon was rendered by 20th-century artist Shōnen Suzuki.

The **Sōgenchi garden** of Tenryū-ji dates from the 14th century and is one of the most notable in Kyōto. Musō Soseki, an influential Zen monk and skillful garden designer, created the garden to resemble Mt. Hōrai in China. It is famed for the arrangement of vertical stones in its large pond and as one of the first gardens to use "borrowed scenery," incorporating the mountains in the distance into the design of the garden.

If you visit Tenryū-ji at lunchtime, consider purchasing a ticket for Zen cuisine served at **Shigetsu** (☎ *075/882–9725*), within the temple precinct. The ¥3,500 price includes lunch in the large dining area overlooking a garden, as well as admission to the garden itself. Here you can experience the Zen monks' philosophy of "eating to live" rather than "living to eat." Although you won't partake in the monk's daily helping of gruel, a salted plum, and pickled radishes, you will try Zen cuisine prepared for festival days. The meal includes sesame tofu served over top-quality soy sauce, a variety of fresh boiled vegetables, miso soup, and rice. The *tenzo*, a monk specially trained to prepare Zen cuisine, creates a multi-course meal that achieves the harmony of the six basic flavors—bitter, sour, sweet, salty, light, and hot—required for monks to practice Zen with the least hindrance to body and mind. The more elaborate courses cost ¥5,500 and ¥7,500. Advance reservations are required. Take the JR San-in Main Line from Kyōto Station to Saga Station or the Keifuku Electric Railway to Arashiyama Station. From Saga Station walk west; from Arashiyama Station walk north. ⊠ *68 Susuki-no-bamba-chō, Saga-Tenryū-ji, Ukyō-ku* ☎ *075/882–9725* ⊠ *Garden ¥500; Temple ¥100* ☉ *Apr.–Oct., daily 8:30–5:30; Nov.–Mar., daily 8:30–5.*

WORTH NOTING

⑫ Bamboo forest 竹林. Dense bamboo forests—with their rows upon rows of long, ringed, smooth stems—provide a feeling of composure and tranquility. The sound of wind blowing through bamboo, of stems knocking against one another and leaves rustling, is revered in Japan. Nowadays, bamboo forests are few and far between. This one, on the way to Ōkōeni Sansō from Tenryū-ji, is a delight. The forest is a short walk from the Saga-Arashiyama train station. ⊠ *Ukyō-ku.*

NORTHERN KYŌTO

The mountain Hiei-zan and the Ōhara region are the focal points in the northern suburbs of Kyōto. For several centuries Ōhara was a sleepy Kyōto backwater surrounded by mountains. Although it's now catching up with the times, it retains a feeling of Old Japan. Hiei-zan is a fount of Kyōto history. On its flanks the priest Saichō founded Enryaku-ji in the 8th century and with it the vital Tendai sect of Buddhism. It's an essential Kyōto sight, and walking on forested slopes among its 70-odd temples is a good reason to make the trek to Hiei-zan.

GETTING AROUND The sights in northern Kyōto are spread out and must be reached by a combination of train, bus, and cable car. It's best to make this a day trip to allow some time to explore Ōhara and Hiei-zan. If you're booked on a tour to the Shūgaku-in Imperial Villa on the same day, then you'll probably only have time to explore one or the other.

TOP ATTRACTIONS

Fodor's Choice ★ **Enryaku-ji.** With a view over the mountain ranges and the sound of chanting filling the air, this extensive complex of ancient temples and worship halls leaves many visitors reflecting on just how far their journey has taken them.

Enryaku-ji was established to protect the northern frontier when Emperor Kammu founded the city in the late 8th century. Because police were prohibited from entering the temple grounds, the whole mountainside became a refuge for thieves, brigands, and fugitives. To protect itself, Enryaku-ji developed its own zealous and well-trained militia, rivaling those of many feudal lords. No imperial army could manage a war without the support of Enryaku-ji, and at times Enryaku-ji's forces would slaughter monks of rival Buddhist sects. Not until the 16th century was there a force strong enough to attack the temple. Nobunaga Oda, the general who helped unify Japan and ended more than a century of civil strife, sacked the monastery in 1571. In the battle many monks were killed, and most buildings were destroyed. The structures standing today were built in the 17th century.

The **Kompon Chū-dō** hall dates from 1642 and has a stunning copper roof in the *irimoya-zukuri* layered style. Its dark, cavernous interior conveys the mysticism for which the sect is known. Giant pillars and a coffered ceiling shelter the central altar surrounded by religious images. You can kneel with worshippers on a dais above the shadowy recess containing the smaller altars, an arrangement that supposedly allows you to come face-to-face with the enshrined deities. Even if you don't see a vision of the supernatural, you can enjoy a closer look at the ornate oil lanterns hanging before the altar, each representing a stage of enlightenment. Near the main hall, a mausoleum contains the remains of Saichō, who oversaw Enryaku-ji's construction. The echoing of the monks' wooden sandals follows you as you explore Enryaku-ji's other buildings; pay particular attention to the Shaka-dō, the oldest structure in the complex.

To access the cable cars that take visitors to the base of the temple, take JR Kosei line trains to Eizan station, Keihan line trains to Hieizan Sakamoto station, or Eiden/Eizan Line from Demachiyanagi station to Yase-Yūen station. Kyōto Line buses 16, 17 and 18 also run to Yase Yūen. *Enryaku-ji ⊠4220 Sakamoto-hon-machi, Ōtsu-shi ⊕www. hieizan.or.jp ☎ ¥800, cable car ¥530 ☉ Mar.–Nov., daily 8:30–4:30; Dec.–Feb., daily 9–4.*

★ **Jikkō-in** 実光院. At this seldom-visited temple you can sit, relax, and have a taste of the tea ceremony. To enter, ring the gong on the outside of the gate. Once inside you can wander through the carefully cultivated garden with its natural waterfall, serene pond, and tiny teahouse framed against the hills. Various strains of cherry tree are planted around the lake so you can see the blossoms throughout the year. Inside the temple, the main lintel holds 36 portraits of Chinese poets by members of the Kanō school. To get here, take Kyōto Line Bus 17 or 18; the 90-minute journey from Kyōto Station costs ¥580. From the Ōhara bus stop, walk northeast for about seven minutes along the signposted road. Jikkō-in is 200 yards from Sanzen-in. *⊠187 Ohara Shorin'in-chō, Sakyō-ku ☎¥600 ☉ Daily 9–5.*

Kamigamo Jinja 上賀茂神社. One of Kyōto's oldest shrines, Kamigamo Jinja is a terrific example of rich Heian architecture. With charming bridges, sand sculptures, and vermilion gateways, Kamigamo Jinja, was built in the 8th century by the Kamo family, has always been associated with Kamo Wakeikazuchi, a god of thunder, rain, and fertility. Now the shrine is famous for its annual horserace, held on May 5, and its hollyhock festival, which started in the 6th century when people thought that the Kamigamo deities were angry at being neglected. Held

6

on May 15, it includes 500 people in Heian period costumes processing on horseback or in ox-drawn carriages. On June 30 is a purification ritual in which throngs of people cast paper effigies into the river beneath the flickering glare of charcoal braziers. The canal street that leads up to the shrine has many machiya, and some of these elongated town houses are more than 400 years old. To get to the shrine, take Bus 9 north Kamigamojinja-mae or Kamigamo Misono-bashi. Or take the subway north to Kitayama Station, from which the shrine is 20 minutes on foot northwest. ⊠*339 Motoyama, Kamigamo, Kita-ku* 🖃*Free* ⊙*Daily 9–4:30.*

★ **Sanzen-in** 三千院. This small temple of the Tendai sect was founded by the renowned priest Dengyō-Daishi (767–822). The temple is a *monzeki,* meaning the abbot has traditionally been of royal blood. The Hon-dō (Main Hall) was built by Priest Eshin (942–1017), who probably carved the temple's Amida Buddha. The Buddha is flanked by two seated attendants: the goddess of wisdom, Daiseishi, to the right; and the goddess of compassion, Kannon, to the left. Unusual for a Buddhist temple, Sanzen-in faces east, not south. Note its ceiling, on which a painting depicts the descent of Amida, accompanied by 25 bodhisattvas, to welcome the believer. Full of maple trees and moss, the gardens are serene in any season. In autumn the colors are magnificent, and the approach to the temple up a gentle slope—with the river on one side and small shops on the other—enhances the anticipation for the burnt-gold trees guarding the old, weathered temple. Snow cover in winter is also magical. Take Kyōto Line Bus 17 or 18 north for 90 minutes from Kyōto Station to Ōhara. From the Ōhara bus station walk northeast for about seven minutes along the signposted road. ⊠*500 Raigōin-chō, Ōhara, Sakyō-ku* 🖃¥*700* ⊙*Mar.–Nov., daily 8:30–4:30; Dec.–Feb., daily 8:30–4.*

WORTH NOTING

Jakkō-in 寂光院. After a devastating fire, this small monastery surrounded by a quiet garden was completely rebuilt in 2005. The temple's history goes back much further. In April 1185, after a two-year struggle, the Taira clan met its end in a naval battle against the rival Minamoto clan. Seeing that all was lost, the Taira women drowned themselves, taking with them the eight-year-old emperor Antoku. His mother, the 29-year-old Kenreimon-in, leaped into the sea, but Minamoto soldiers hauled her back on board their ship.

She here lived as a nun in solitude in a 10-foot-square cell made of brushwood and thatch for 27 years, until her death ended the Taira line. You may need to ask for directions to her mausoleum, which is higher up the hill, away from the throng of visitors and along the path by the side of the temple. When Kenreimon-in came to Jakkō-in it was far removed from Kyōto. Now Kyōto's sprawl reaches this far and beyond, but the temple, hidden in trees, is still a place of solitude. From Kyōto Station take Kyōto Line Bus 17 or 18 for a 90-minute ride and get out at the Ōhara bus stop; the fare is ¥480. Walk 20 minutes or so along the road leading to the northwest. ⊠*676 Oharakusao-chō, Sakyō-ku, Sakyō-ku* 🖃¥*600* ⊙*Mar.–Nov., daily 9–5; Dec.–Feb., daily 9–4:30.*

Miho Museum ミホミュージアム *(Miho Bijutsukan)*. The distance from Kyōto may make getting here seem daunting, but the Miho Museum is well worth the trip, thanks both to its phenomenal architecture and impressive worldly collection. Conceived by architect I. M. Pei, the building uses many of the same design elements and construction techniques employed at his extension for the Louvre in Paris. The exquisite collection consists of over 2,000 pieces, including Syrian floor mosaics, Iranian metal ornaments, Egyptian statuary, Afghani Buddha icons, and Roman frescos. Roughly 250 pieces are on display at any one time in temporary exhibitions that change seasonally. An on-site restaurant sells *bentō* (boxed meals) with organic ingredients for about ¥1,000, and a tearoom serves Japanese and Western beverages and desserts. From Kyōto Station, take the JR Tōkaidō Line to Ishiyama Station; from there the Teisan Line bus to the museum takes 50 minutes. Buses to Miho, which cost ¥800 one-way, run on the hour from 9 to 6. ⊠*300 Momodani, Shiga-ken, Shigariki* ☎*0748/82–3411* ⊕*www. miho.jp* ☜*¥1,000* ◷ *Mid-Mar.–mid-June and Sept.–mid-Dec., Tues.– Sun. 10–5; last entry at 4.*

Shūgaku-in Imperial Villa 修学院離宮 *(Shūgaku-in Rikyū)*. The focus of this compound is not the opulent villas but the sumptuous gardens. The grounds are held to be one of the great masterpieces of gardening. The manicured trees, lawns, and flowers are especially lovely thanks to the neighboring rice fields and orchards.

The Upper and Lower Villas were built in the 17th century by the Tokugawa family to entertain the emperor; the Upper Villa provides nice views of northern Kyōto. The Middle Villa was added later as a palace home for Princess Bunke, daughter of Emperor Go-mizunoo. Special permission is required to visit the villa, a few days in advance, from the **Imperial Household Agency** (⊠*3 Kyōto Gyoen, Kamigyo-ku* ☎*075/211–1215* ⊕*sankan.kunaicho.go.jp*). From Kyōto Station, Bus 5 takes about an hour. Or you can ride 20 minutes north on a Keifuku Eizan Line train from the Demachi-Yanagi terminus, which is northeast of the intersection of Imadegawa-dōri and the Kamo-gawa. ⊠*Yabusoe Shūgaku-in, Sakyō-ku* ☜*Free* ◷ *Tours in Japanese, weekdays at 9, 10, 11, 1:30, and 3; Sat. tours on 1st and 3rd Sat. of month; every Sat. Apr., May, Oct., and Nov.*

WHERE TO EAT

Attuned to subtle seasonal changes, Kyōto cuisine emphasizing freshness and contrast. From the finest ryōtei to the smallest *izakaya* (pub), the distinctive elements of gracious hospitality, subtle flavors, and attention to decor create an experience that engages all the senses. Although the finest traditional *kaiseki ryōri* is costly, this experience is highly recommended. Both elaborate establishments and casual shops usually offer set menus at lunchtime, at a considerably lower price than dinner.

If you find yourself with an unintelligible menu, ask for the *o-makase*, or chef's recommendation and you can specify your budget in some instances. The custom of dining early, from 6 PM until 8 PM, still endures in very traditional restaurants, but many restaurants are open until 10 or 11 PM. If possible, let the hotel staff make reservations for you where necessary. For more formal restaurants try to book at least two days in advance; bookings are often not accepted for the following day if called in after 4 PM. Keep in mind that not all restaurants accept credit cards.

WHAT IT COSTS IN YEN				
¢	$	$$	$$$	$$$$
At Dinner	under ¥800	¥800–¥1,000	¥1,000–¥2,000	¥2,000–¥3,000	over ¥3,000

Restaurant prices are per person for a main course, set meal, or equivalent combinations of smaller dishes.

ARASHIYAMA

$$$
SPANISH
✕**Bodegon** ボデゴン. This tile-floored Spanish restaurant in Arashiyama brings paella to a neighborhood most famous for its tofu. Nestled among the tatami-matted restaurants on the neighborhood's main drag, Bodegon combines Spanish flavors in food and wine with Kyōto hospitality. This is a great place to dine after a day of sightseeing, and you'll be happy to linger in this scenic district after the crowds thin out. ✉1 Susuki-no-bamba-chō, Saga, Tenryū-ji, Ukyō-ku ☎075/872–9652 ⊟MC, V ⊘Closed Thurs.

$$$$
JAPANESE
✕**Sagano** 嵯峨野. Amid Arashiyama's lush bamboo forests, this quiet retreat offers a fine example of *yudōfu cooking derived from the monastic tradition*. The set meal includes delicacies like *abura-age* (fried tofu with black sesame seeds). Standing in front of a backdrop of antique wood-block prints, women in kimonos prepare your meal before you eyes. If you prefer a bit more privacy, you can walk through the garden to private rooms in the back. If weather permits, choose one of the low tables in the courtyard garden. Reservations are a good idea year-round, particularly during the peak foliage season in November. ✉45 Susuki-no-bamba-chō, Saga, Tenryū-ji, Ukyō-ku ☎075/861–0277 ⊟No credit cards.

CENTRAL KYŌTO

$$
CAFÉ
☺
✕**Ask a Giraffe** アスクアジラフ. The eclectic decor and accessible menu make this longtime place an expat favorite. Sandwiches, salads, and pasta dishes are always fantastic, and the seasonal menu is full of great surprises like grilled mackerel with field greens or winter stew with fried rice. Coffees and cakes round out the selection. It's in the Shinpu-kan shopping center. ✉ Karasuma-dōri Anekōji Sagaru 586-2, Nakagyō-ku ☎075/257–8028 ⊟AE, DC, MC, V.

$$
CAFÉ
✕**Café bibliotic HELLO!** カフェビブリオテックハロー. The banana trees that mask this airy two-story town-house café are visible from several blocks away. The three lunch options change regularly and range from steak sandwiches to rice and curry dishes. Drinks like Moroccan chai or the playful seasonal smoothies (strawberry, mint and ginger anyone?)

complement desserts like mango and coconut cream or French toast with candied almonds. Browse the wall of books while you're waiting. ✉*Nijō-dōri Yanaginobana, Higashi-iru, Nakagyō-ku* ☎*075/231–8625* 🚫*No credit cards.*

$ ✗**Café Indépendants**カフェ アンデパンダン. This laid-back lunch spot
CAFÉ serves good daily specials, including curries, salads, and soups. A devoted clientele of students and artists comes for the cheap, bountiful lunch plates, the friendly service, and the convivial atmosphere. The setting is a Meiji-era building's brick and plaster basement, with funky mosaic tiles and lots of exposed masonry. It's located on the south side of Sanjo-dôri one block in from the Teramachi shopping arcade. ✉*1928 Bldg., Sanjō-dōri, Nakagyō-ku* ☎*075/255–4312.*

$ ✗**Café Sarasa** カフェさらさ. An expat favorite, this jazzy café offers an
CAFÉ exciting selection of dishes so varied and delicious you'll want to keep coming back. Try the Okinawan-style stir-fries, the Vietnamese-style pancakes, or the rice dishes with vegetables and bean curd. Whatever you choose, top it off with a soul-warming café au lait. Well deserved popularity has led to this becoming a local chain, but our favorite this branch above a bicycle shop. ✉*534 Asakuchi-chō, Tominokōji-dōri, Sanjō-agaru, Nakagyō-ku* ☎*075/212–2310* 🚫*No credit cards.*

$$$$ ✗**Cucina Il Viale** クチーナイルヴィアーレ. The signature dish in this well-
ITALIAN regarded trattoria is handmade pasta topped with a tomato sauce flavor-
★ ful enough to satisfy the most road weary traveler. The antipasti features carefully selected organic vegetables and fine Italian ham. Such entrées as tender pork steaks or grilled fish in orange-infused balsamic vinegar are excellent, and the decadent desserts are a great way to finish a meal: the litchi mousse alone is worth the visit. Lunch courses start from ¥1,575. ✉*Horikawa-dōri, Oike-sagaru 233-1, Nakagyō-ku* ☎*075/812–2366* ⌕*Reservations essential* 🚫*AE, V* 🌙*Closed Mon. No lunch Tues.*

$$$$ ✗**Giro Giro Hitoshina** 枝魯枝魯ひとしな. Quickly becoming one of
JAPANESE Kyōto's most popular restaurants, Giro Giro has a lively atmosphere,
Fodor'sChoice excellent food, and great location on the sleepy Takase-gawa River. Sit
★ at the counter surrounding the busy chefs or grab a table upstairs—both offer views of people walking along the river wishing they could trade places with you. The set menu changes monthly to showcase seasonal dishes and fresh ingredients. Giro Giro's chef defies the staid conventions of kaiseki ryōri cuisine with creations infinitely more exciting; expect dishes along the lines of mackerel in a clear broth, monkfish liver grilled on eucalyptus leaves with miso paste, tartlets enclosing scrumptious morsels of crab, and melt-in-your-mouth beef sashimi. Giro Giro is easiest to find by walking the narrow lane along the Takase-gawa; look for the glow of the massive window a few blocks north of Gojō-dōri. ✉*420-7 Namba-chō, Nishi Kiya-machi-dōri, Higashigawa, Matsubarashita, Shimogyō-ku* ☎*075/343–7070* ⌕*Reservations essential* 🚫*AE, DC, MC, V* 🌙*Closed last Mon. of month. No lunch.*

$$$$ ✗**Kerala** ケララ. Imported spices and the fresh local vegetables are the
INDIAN secret to this Indian restaurant's success. Dishes won't be as spicy as you might expect, but the spinach, lamb, and chickpea curries—not to mention the tandoori chicken—are sumptuous and flavorful. The vegetarian-friendly à la carte menu has some tasty choices like the

6

kulch (a simosa-like pouch stuffed with egg and almond). This second-story restaurant opposite the Royal Hotel has a blend of modern and traditional Indian furnishings and extremely reasonable evening set courses. ✉ *Kawaramachi-dōri Sanjō-agaru Nishigawa, Nakagyō-ku* ☎*075/251–0141* ▤*AE, DC, MC, V.*

$$$$
JAPANESE
Fodor's Choice
★

✕**Mankamerō** 萬亀楼. Since 1716 Mankamerō's specialty has been yūsoku ryōri, cuisine intended for members of the imperial court. Every step of the meal is incredibly elaborate, down to the ceremonially dressed chef who prepares your dishes using specially made utensils. A dramatic, if repellently named, course is the "dismembered fish," in which each part of a single fish is prepared and served on a series of pedestal trays. Prices reflect the aristocratic experience—up to ¥30,000 per person for the full repertoire. A wonderful *take-kago* lunch set is within reach of commoners at ¥6,350. Bamboo boxes reveal a series of steamed surprises. Mankamerō is on the west side of Inokuma-dōri north of Demizu-dōri. Look for the blue-tile roof. ✉*Inokuma-dōri, Demizu-agaru, Kamigyō-ku* ☎*075/441–5020* ⌖*Reservations essential* ▤*AE, DC, MC, V.*

$$$$
JAPANESE
Fodor's Choice
★

✕**Manzaratei Nishiki** まんざら亭. The unpretentious vibe, the sense of adventure, and the superb cuisine—Korean, French, and Italian influences feature highly in the playful menu—have made Manzaratei a local favorite. Depending on the season, the ample menu offers crab in vinegar-flavored miso, free-range chicken skewers, or spring rolls with citrusy *ponzu* dressing. The menu is in Japanese, but ask the staff for recommendations or try one of the multicourse menus. Outdoor dining in the warmer months and counter seating on both floors of the two-story town house let you mingle with other patrons; for more intimate evenings, ask for a table upstairs under the eaves. The restaurant is a block north of the intersection of Shijō-dōri and Karasuma-dōri. ✉*Karasuma Nishikikoji, 317 Nishiiru Uradeyama-chō* ☎*075/257–5748* ⌖*Reservations essential* ▤*AE, DC, MC, V* ⌚*No lunch.*

$$$$
JAPANESE

✕**Mishima-tei** 三島亭. Five generations of chefs have preserved the delicious sukiyaki recipe served here. At the street level butcher's counter, housewives line up to pay top dollar for the high-quality beef, but your feast awaits upstairs in the large tatami-matted dining room, one of the many cheerful garden rooms, or the endearing teahouse (our favorite). A kimono-clad attendant will help get you started cooking everything at your table. Sukiyaki varies between restaurants: Mishima-tei favors thin slices of beef and a platter of vegetables which you eat by dipping anything hot off the pan into cooling, flavorful raw egg before popping it into your mouth. The ¥6,000 Mini Course belies its name in terms of quantity; the Tourist Course is identical but with leaner meat. ✉*Tera-machi, Sanjō-sagaru, Higashi-Iru, Nakagyō-ku* ☎*075/221–0003* ⌖*Reservations essential* ▤*AE, DC, MC, V* ⌚*Closed Wed.*

$$$$
JAPANESE

✕**Mukadeya** 百足屋. Home-style o-banzai cooking is the specialty of this sophisticated restaurant in a refurbished town house. Bonito sashimi, simmered pumpkin, and gingery ground chicken are artfully presented on lacquer trays, feasts for the eyes that taste even better than they look. Dinner includes a rich variety of dishes, often numbering between eight and twelve courses. Unlike many traditional houses, where winding corridors lead to small interior rooms, this place's open floor plan includes a cheerful courtyard garden, making the place feel expansive and inviting. Legless chairs on the tatami matting are set comfortably around low tables. In the evening a 10% service charge is added to the bill. ✉ *381 Mukadeya-chō, Shinmachi-dōri, Nishiki-agaru, Nakagyō-ku* ☎ *075/256–9393* ✍ *Reservations essential* 💳 *AE, MC, V* ⊙ *Closed Wed.*

$$$$ **FRENCH** ✕**Ogawa** おがわ. The best in Kyōto-style nouvelle cuisine is served in this intimate spot across from the Takase-gawa canal. Dishes depend on the chef's whims as much as on what's in season, but can include buttery risotto-like rice pilaf topped with delicate sea urchin, duck meat and foie gras in bite-size portions, and hors d'oeuvres such as oyster gratin, crab-and-scallop stew, and wild mushroom tempura. The fruit and vegetable salads are exceptional, and the take-all-you-want dessert tray with tarts, tortes, and pastries is the icing on the cake. The atmosphere at the counter can be a bit stiff, so you might opt for an upstairs table instead. ✉ *Kiya-machi Oike-agaru Higashi-Iru, Nakagyo-ku* ☎ *075/256–2203* 🌐 *r-ogawa.com* ✍ *Reservations essential* 💳 *AE, DC, MC, V* ⊙ *Closed Tues.*

$$$ **JAPANESE** ✕**Oiwa** 大岩. Kura storehouses were built of thick plaster and set separate from other buildings to protect them from fire and theft: the kimono merchants that used to own this one have long since retired, and the treasure stored inside these days is fine kushikatsu cooking featuring bite-size bits of meat and vegetables skewered, battered, deep fried, and served with a variety of sauces. Usually considered a laborer's snack, kushikatsu seems an incongruous choice for Oiwa's French-trained chefs, but their interpretation offers a richness and elegance found nowhere else. Order by the skewer or ask for the set meal. There's even a menu for small children. The restaurant is along the Takase-gawa River. ✉ *Kiya-machi-dōri, Nijō-sagaru, Nakagyō-ku* ☎ *075/231–7667* 🌐 *www.kushi-oiwa.co.jp* 💳 *No credit cards* ⊙ *No lunch Wed. and weekends.*

$$$ **JAPANESE** ★ ✕**Omen** おめん. This branch of the famed noodle shop is convenient to the downtown shopping area. It's a perfect place to pop in for a delicious lunch of udon noodle soup. Add some roasted sesame for an extra kick. ✉ *Gokō-machi Shijō Agaru, Nakagyō-ku* ☎ *075/255–2125* 💳 *No credit cards* ⊙ *Closed Thurs.*

$$$$ **JAPANESE** ✕**Ōmi** 近江. This excellent steak restaurant specializes in beer-fed, hand-massaged Ōmi beef (not as well-known abroad as Kobe beef, but celebrated by Japanese gourmets). You'll be ushered through corridors to the dining room and seated around a *hori-gotatsu* (recessed grill) or at a counter in a pristine tatami room. Excellent seafood platters are also popular, as are the weekend lunches. The restaurant is in a Meiji-era town house connected to an annex of the Hotel Fujita Kyōto. A drink beside the duck pond in hotel's bar is a great way to end the evening. ✉ *Hotel Fujita Kyōto, Nijō-dōri, Kiya-machi Kado, Nakagyō-ku* ☎ *075/222–1511* ✍ *Reservations essential* 💳 *AE, DC, MC, V* ⊙ *No lunch weekdays.*

$$$$ **JAPANESE** ✕**Shinsen-en Heihachi** 神泉苑平八. Facing Nijō Castle's southern wall, this touristy restaurant is situated within the only remaining garden

6

from the original imperial palace. The 1,200-year-old Sacred Spring Garden dates from 794, when the Emperor Kammu established Kyōto as the nation's capital. Shinsen-en Heihachi's charming shrine, pond, and vermilion bridge are essentially all that remain. You can dine looking out at the pond, or, if seating is available, on a boat floating leisurely in the middle of it. Lunch courses beginning at ¥3,800 are a better buy than the ¥8,400-and-up dinners. ⊠ *Oike-dōri, Shinsenen Higashi-iru Mon-mae 167, Nakagyō-ku* ☎*075/841–0811* ▤*AE, DC, MC, V.*

$

KOREAN

Fodor'sChoice

★

✗**Somushi Tea House** 素夢子 古茶家. Dark-wood furnishings create a provocative environment for sampling the bountiful brews at Kyōto's top Korean teahouse. Unlike Japanese and Chinese teas, which pull flavor from leaves or powder, the house favorites here are brewed full of berries, spices, or herbs. The intense aromas are complemented by a menu of vegetable stews, stuffed fritters, and innovative versions of Korean staples like organic bibimbap. Reserve ahead to sample the Gozen menu, with nine bronze pots filled with royal cuisine good enough to leave you wishing you were an ancient Seoul nobleman. Seating is in a cozy private room at the back, on cushions at floor-level tables, or at a robust wooden counter with a better chance to chat with the convivial proprietors. ⊠ *Karasuma Sanjō Nishi-Iru, Mikura-chō 73, Nakagyō-ku* ☎*075/253–1456* ▤*AE, DC, MC, V* ⊘ *Closed Wed.*

$$

VIETNAMESE

✗**Tiem An Huong Viet** ティエム・アン・フォーン・ヴィェット. Tucked away in a small street, the jade colored walls and dark Vietnamese furnishings of this delightful eatery are reminiscent of a classy Hanoi café. Classics like *pho* noodle soup are excellent, and the menu is full of dishes that are great for sharing: a house favorite is *ban xeo,* a huge do-it-yourself pancake you assemble with choices of vegetables, shrimp, fragrant herbs, and spicy dipping sauce. ⊠ *Oshikōji-dōri, Higashi-ura-in, Nishi-iru 118, Nakagyō-ku* ☎*075/253–1828* ▤*No credit cards* ⊘ *Closed Tues.*

$$$$

JAPANESE

Yoshikawa 吉川. Adjacent to a well-reputed inn of the same name, Yoshikawa serves full-course kaiseki ryōri dinners. The lavish spread includes soup, vegetables, grilled or baked fish, and the light, crisp tempura that is the house specialty. Tempura dinners include 13 pieces of fried fish, meat, and vegetables. Dinner is served in a tatami room, and less elaborate but more affordable lunches are served at the counter. ⊠ *Tomino-kōji, Oike-sagaru, Nakagyō-ku* ☎*075/221–5544 or 075/221–0052* ⚐ *Reservations essential* ▤*AE, DC, MC, V* ⊘ *Closed Sun.*

$$$$

CHINESE

✗**Zezekan Pocchiri** 膳處漢 ぽっちり. Feast on Beijing-style cuisine in this Taisho-era warehouse with antique glass windows and an inner courtyard garden. The fascinating mural of ornate pocchiri clasps used by geisha-like *maiko*-san to secure their belts gives the place its name. Evening meals include a parade of small appetizers and more substantial dishes like spicy tofu stir-fries, chicken stews, and delicately flavored sea bream. For ¥11,000 you can order a meal inspired by imperial court cuisine, featuring savory Peking duck and seasonal delicacies like spiny lobster and crab stew. The detached bar stocks a good selection of Chinese aperitifs and European wines, and stays open until 11. ⊠ *Nishikikōji, Muromachi-Nishi-iru, Tenjinyamacho 283-2* ☎*075/257–5766* ⚐ *Reservations essential* ▤*AE, DC, MC, V.*

On the Menu

The experience not to miss in Kyōto is *kaiseki ryōri*, the elegant full-course meal that was originally intended to be served with the tea ceremony and later served with sake at Edo-era merchant parties. All the senses are engaged: the scent and flavor of the freshest ingredients at the peak of season; the visual delight of a continuous procession of porcelain dishes and lacquered bowls, gracefully adorned with an appropriately shaped slice of fish or vegetable; the textures of foods unknown and exotic; the sound of water in a stone basin outside in the garden. Kaiseki ryōri is often costly yet always unforgettable.

For an initiation or a reasonably priced sample, the *kaiseki bentō* (box lunch) served by many *ryōtei* (high-class Japanese restaurants) is a good place to start. Box lunches are so popular in Kyōto that restaurants compete to make their bentō unique, exquisite, and delicious.

Compared with the style of cooking elsewhere in Japan, *Kyōto-ryōri* (Kyōto cuisine) is lighter and more delicate, stressing the natural flavor of ingredients over enhancement with heavy sauces and broths. *O-banzai* (Kyōto home cooking) is served at many restaurants at reasonable cost. The freshness and quality of the ingredients is paramount, and chefs carefully handpick only the best. *Sōsaku ryōri* (creative cuisine) is becoming popular as chefs find inspiration in other cultures while retaining light and subtle flavors.

Kyōto is also the home of *shōjin ryōri*, the Zen vegetarian-style cooking best sampled on the grounds of one of the city's Zen temples, such as Tenryū-ji in Arashiyama. Local delicacies like *fu* (glutinous wheat cakes) and *yuba* (soy-milk skimmings) have found their way into the mainstream of Kyōto ryōri, but were originally devised to provide protein in the traditional Buddhist diet.

6

EASTERN KYŌTO

$
JAPANESE

✗**Gion Kappa Nawate** 祇園かっぱ縄手. In contrast to the expensive kaiseki ryōri restaurants favored by tourists, residents seek out just-plain-folks places like this one. It's a late-night *izakaya* specializing in *robata-yaki*, which is to say a casual bar-restaurant with a charcoal grill and great selection of meat, poultry, and vegetable dishes. Here it's common to order a variety of dishes to share. If there are no tables, find a seat at the long counter. The restaurant is two blocks north of Shijō-dōri in the heart of Gion. ⊠*Sueyoshi-chō, Nawate-dōri Shijō agaru, Higashiyama-ku* ☎*075/531–4048* ⊘*No lunch.*

$$$$
JAPANESE
Fodor'sChoice
★

✗**Kikunoi** 菊乃井. The care lavished on every aspect of dining is unparalleled thanks to the conscientious attention of Kikunoi's owner, world-renowned chef and authority on Kyōto cuisine, Yoshihiro Murata. A lifetime study of French and Japanese cooking, a commitment to using the finest local ingredients, and a playful creative sense make every exciting meal hum with flavor. Once seated in a private dining room, you are brought a small *sakizuke*, or appetizer, the first of up to 14 courses, each exquisitely presented and unfailingly delicious. Dishes like cedar-smoked barracuda fillets, citrus infused matsu-dake mushroom soup, or sashimi served on chrysanthemum petals keenly accord to the

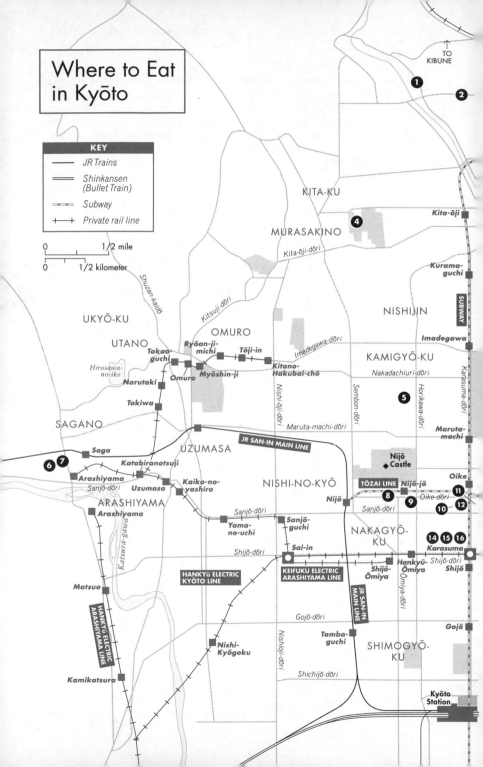

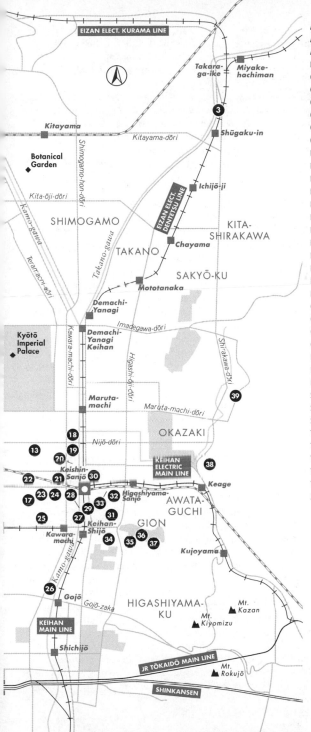

nuances of each new season. This restaurant is on the northern edge of Kōdai-ji temple. Evening courses start at ¥15,500, lunches at ¥4,200. ⊠ *Gion Maruyama Makuzugahara, Higashiyama-ku* ☎ *075/561–0015* ⊕ *www.kikunoi.jp/honten.htm* ⚔ *Reservations essential* ▭ *AE, DC, MC, V* ⊗ *No lunch Mon.*

$$$$　✕ **Kikusui** 菊水. Near Nanzen-ji temple, Kikusui serves elegant *kaiseki*
JAPANESE　*ryōri* meals with an aristocratic flair. Dine on tatami mats at low tables or at table-and-chair seating, all overlooking an elegant Japanese garden. The subtle flavors of the set menus are intended to be offset by the scenic view, where a canopy of pink-and-white cherry blossoms accents the light spring menus and fiery red and orange maples highlight the warm flavors of stews in autumn. *Kyō-no-aji*, smaller versions of kaiseki ryōri served for lunch, let you savor Kikusui's elegant setting and fine cuisine for ¥5,000. ⊠ *31 Fukui-chō, Nazen-ji, Sakyō-ku* ☎ *075/771–4101* ⚔ *Reservations essential* ▭ *AE, DC, V.*

$$$$　✕ **Kyō-machiya Suishin** 京町家すいしん. Not far from Gion Kaburenjō
JAPANESE　Theater, a black-and-white latticed storefront conceals a vegetable lover's paradise. The dining area is raised so that those seated on floor cushions are at eye level with the busy chefs in the open kitchen. Hollowed-out flooring beneath the tables and at the long bar make tatami-mat dining possible without stiff knees. For a nice primer on Kyōto's essential dishes, opt for the *Fushimi* menu or the more extensive *Goshō* menu. Suishin brings out the flavors of local organic vegetables, fish, and meats with a conspicuously restrained hand, creating flavors so light they seem to float in your mouth. Look for a lantern above the door. ⊠ *181 Zaimoku-chō, Ponto-chō, Nakagyō-ku* ☎ *075/221–8596* ▭ *AE, DC, MC, V.*

$$$$　✕ **Kyōto Gion Oishimbo** 京都祇園おいしんぼ. The menu at this restaurant
JAPANESE　in the heart of Gion hits just the right balance. Excellent preparation and
★　presentation take the simple, unpretentious *obanzai* (home-style) dishes to another level. Seishu Oishinbo, the house sake, makes everything taste even better. As is common for old houses in the neighborhood, the tatami-matted rooms on the first floor overlook a small courtyard garden. The restaurant is just off Gion's main drag. ⊠ *Gion-chō Minamigawa 570-123, Higashiyama-ku* ☎ *075/532–2285* ⚔ *Reservations essential* ▭ *AE, D, DC, MC, V.*

$$$$　✕ **Minokō** 美濃幸. Disappear behind a blue curtain off the cobbled
JAPANESE　streets of Gion into a Japanese fairy tale. Rooms connected by charming wooden passages look out onto an expansive garden, and tables are set with simple but sumptuous decorations, like grand lacquered tables and regal kimonos. The decor sets the scene perfectly for a delicious, if not overly daring, kaiseki ryōri meal. The kindly proprietors seem old enough to remember the Meiji restoration, but their attention to the quality of your meal is unfailing. Inquire about the cozy *ko-cha-shitsu*, or "small tea room" that's perfect for a romantic dinner for two. Minoko is less than a block from Yasaka Jinja's southern gate. Only minimal English is spoken, so have your concierge make the reservation for you. ⊠ *480 Kiyoi-chō, Shimogowara-dōri, Gion, Higashiyama-ku* ☎ *075/561–0328* ⚔ *Reservations essential* ▭ *DC, MC, V* ⊗ *Closed 2nd and 4th Wed. of each month.*

\$\$\$\$ ✕**Nontarō** 呑太呂. In the heart of Kyōto's busy nightlife district, Nontarō
JAPANESE has been the place for sushi for decades. Beefy chefs on impossibly tall
wooden geta sandals serve the freshest cuts of richly flavorful sushi,
mixing staples like ginger-tinged mackerel with innovative surprises
like aloe heart dabbed with horseradish. Nontaro serves its sushi in a
traditional style, which has fallen by the wayside almost everywhere
else. Each delicate roll is dropped directly onto the red-lacquer coun-
tertop for you to grab and gobble up, and running water in a narrow
channel lets you wash your hands after each go. In etiquette-over-every-
thing Kyōto, finger food feels totally scandalous. A take-out bentō box,
perfect for sightseeing or temple-hopping, is ¥6,300. ⊠*Hanamikōji
Shijō-agaru, Higashiyama-ku* ☎*075/561–3189* ⚄*Reservations essential* ▤*AE, DC, MC, V* ⊘*Closed Sun.*

\$\$\$ ✕**Omen** おめん. This branch of a Kyōto chain is perfect for an inexpen-
JAPANESE sive home-style lunch. On the Path of Philosophy between Ginkaku-ji
★ and Nanzen-ji, it's an ideal place to recharge between sights. Omen
refers to the house specialty: men means noodles, and Omen's fabulous
udon noodle soup is fantastic. Served broken down to its components—
a basket of noodles and a platter of seasonal vegetables beside a bowl
of steaming broth—it's meant to be consumed at a leisurely pace. Add
what you like to the broth, plus some roasted sesame to taste. The salted
mackerel is also excellent. The restaurant is country-style and comfortable, with a choice of counter stools, tables and chairs, or tatami mats.
Reservations are accepted only on weekdays. ⊠*74 Ishi-bashi-chō, Jōdo-
ji, Sakyō-ku* ☎*075/771–8994* ▤*No credit cards* ⊘*Closed Thurs.*

\$\$\$\$ ✕**Ponto-chō Robin** 先斗町魯ビン. An adventurous menu sets Ponto-chō
JAPANESE Robin ahead of the competition. Charcoal-colored walls, rich wooden
staircases, and a great view of the river from this 150-year-old town
house are a great setting for dishes like sea urchin in wasabi broth, grilled
river fish, and the ever-popular kami-nabe, a hot-pot made of paper and
cooked on an open flame at your table: gimmicky but mesmerizing, it's
actually pretty tasty. Seating on the riverfront deck is lovely in summer.
⊠*137-4 Wakamatsu-chō, Ponto-chō, Nakagyō ku* ☎*075/222–8200*
⚄*Reservations essential* ▤*AE, DC, MC, V* ⊙*No lunch.*

¢ ✕**Rakushō** 洛匠. This is an excellent spot to recharge while wandering
JAPANESE through the cobbled lanes of Gion. The house specialty is warabi-mochi,
★ a treat made from steamed and pounded rice that has a gelatinlike consistency. The green color and subtle spice comes from the mountain herb
yomogi. The dish is served on a mountain of golden kinako, made from
toasted soybeans, to add a delightful sweetness. Don't feel shy about
licking your bamboo spoon to enjoy the last bit. The restaurant also
serves ice creams and a variety of other Japanese treats. You'll find it on
the northern end of Higashiyama's cobbled Nene-no-michi. ⊠*Kōdai-
ji Kitamon-mae-dōri, Washio-chō, Higashiyama-ku* ☎*075/561–6892*
⚄*Reservations not accepted* ▤*No credit cards.*

\$ ✕**Ramen Santōka** らーめん山頭火. This great soup shop has all the stan-
JAPANESE dards: salt, soy, or miso ramen noodles with veggies, pork, or seaweed.
It sits in a good location with a view of a rock garden. Ramen Santōka
stays open until 2 AM, or until the soup runs out. ⊠*137 Yamato-
oji-dōri, Sanjō-sagaru Higashigawa, Daikokuchō Higashiyama-ku*
☎*075/532–1335* ▤*AE, DC, MC, V.*

6

$$$$ ✕ **Tōzentei** 陶然亭. Set among the antiques stores and kimono shops on
JAPANESE Shinmonzen-dōri, Tōzentei emphasizes to-the-letter traditional Japanese
cooking. Meals here, made with only local produce, are old school
enough to please a shōgun. Grumpy gray windows frame the counter seating at this intimate hideaway. ⊠*Nishinochō Yamato-oji-dōri
Higashi-iru, Higashiyama-ku* ☎*075/711–5136* ⚲*Reservations essential* ▭*DC, MC, V* ◔*No lunch Mon.*

$$$$ ✕ **Yagenbori** やげんぼり. Waitresses in exquisite kimonos serve posh iza-
JAPANESE kaya fare inside this 130-year-old teahouse on a cobbled corner by the
romantic Shirakawa river, just north of Shijō-dōri in Gion. The decor,
featuring original paintings by renowned woodblock revivalist Clifton
Karhu, is a feast for the eyes. The feast on the table is less exciting,
especially for those familiar with Japanese cuisine, but sashimi served
in icy tureens, delicious warm yuba tofu skin, and kamaboko fish soup
are all good. Don't miss the *hōba* miso—bean paste with mushrooms
and green onions that is wrapped in a giant oak leaf and grilled at your
table—on the à la carte menu. The excellent box lunch is a bargain
at ¥2,800. ⊠*Sueyoshi-chō, Kiridoshi-kado, Gion, Higashiyama-ku
☎075/551–3331* ▭*AE, DC, V.*

NORTHERN KYŌTO

$$$$ ✕ **Akiyama** 秋山. The refined menu at this rustic counter-seating restau-
JAPANESE rant showcases Kyōto's excellent home-style cooking. The lunch and
dinner menus often include duck meat, river eel, or fish sashimi. Inventive desserts round out the meals, like soft mochi rice paste swirled in
chocolate and roasted soybean powder. Akiyama is a few blocks east
of Kamigamo Jinja along the canal. ⊠*58 Okamoto-chō, Kamigamo,
Kita-ku* ☎*075/711–5136* ⚲*Reservations essential* ▭*AE, DC, MC,
V* ◔*Closed Wed. and last Thurs. of month.*

$$$$ ✕ **Azekura** 愛染倉. Delicious Italian fare is served here under the giant
ITALIAN wooden beams of a 300-year-old sake warehouse. The building was
★ brought here from nearby Nara by a kimono merchant a generation
ago, so it's the read deal. Entrées include lobster, roast duck, and sautéed
pork, along with an impressive selection of Italian wines. Azekura is a
perfect stop when exploring the district around the Kamigamo shrine.
⊠*30 Okamoto-chō, Kamigamo, Kita-ku* ☎*075/701–0162* ⚲*Reservations essential* ▭*No credit cards* ◔*Closed Mon.*

$$$$ ✕ **Izusen** 泉仙. Where better to try vegetarian cuisine than in the heart
JAPANESE of one of northern Kyōto's biggest temple complexes? In the garden of
★ Daiji-in, a subtemple of massive Daitoku-ji, soups and sauces bring out
the flavors of fu and yuba, wheat gluten and soy milk skin, alongside
seasonal vegetable dishes. The monastic shojin-ryōri cuisine is presented
in a series of red-lacquer bowls of diminishing sizes, one fitting inside
another as the meal goes on. Low tables in the temple garden are perfect
for soaking up the richness of the outdoors, and cheerful tatami rooms
are great for inclement weather. ⊠*4 Daitoku-ji-chō, Murasakino, Kita-
ku* ☎*075/491–6665* ▭*No credit cards.*

$$$$ ✕ **Yamabana Heihachi-Jaya** 山花 平八茶屋. Off the beaten path in the
JAPANESE northeastern corner of Kyōto, this roadside inn is well known not only
★ for its excellent full-course kaiseki ryōri dinners, duck hotpots, and

delicious boxed lunches with mountain potatoes and barley rice, but also for the sauna in which patrons relax before dining. The *kamaburo is* fashioned from thick clay and heated from beneath the floor by a pine fire. After a soothing sauna, change into a cotton kimono and retire to the large dining room or an intimate private room for an exquisitely relaxing meal. This is an unforgettable way to round off a day exploring Hiei-zan and Ōhara. ⊠ *8–1 Kawagishi-chō, Yamabana, Sakyō-ku* ☎ *075/781–5008* ⌦ *Reservations essential* ☐ *AE, DC, MC, V.*

WHERE TO STAY

No other Japanese city can compete with Kyōto for style and grace. For the ultimate experience of Kyōto hospitality, stay in a *ryokan*, a traditional Japanese inn. Though often costly, a night in a ryokan guarantees you beautiful traditional Japanese surroundings, excellent service, and elegant meals. Kyōto is a tourist city, so accommodations range from luxurious hotels to small guesthouses. Service in this city is impeccable; the information desks are well stocked, and concierges or guest-relations managers are often available in the lobby to respond to your needs.

6

WHAT IT COSTS IN YEN					
	¢	$	$$	$$$	$$$$
For 2 People	under ¥8,000	¥8,000–¥12,000	¥12,000–¥18,000	¥18,000–¥22,000	over ¥22,000

Hotel prices are for a room with private bath, including service and 5% tax.

CENTRAL KYŌTO

$$$$ ⌨ **ANA Hotel Kyōto** 京都全日空ホテル. This is not the best of the city's chain hotels, especially considering that the rooms and hallways need refurbishing. But the location, directly across from Nijō-jō Castle, is dynamite. You're close to the shopping districts, but won't be overwhelmed by constant crowds. If you can get a room facing the castle rather than an ugly high-rise, your view will be sensational. The roof garden has a great 360-degree view of the city and surrounding mountains. **Pros:** Ideal location; near shopping. **Cons:** stale decor; shabby carpeting. ⊠ *Nijō-jō-mae, Horikawa-dōri,Nakagyō-ku, Kyōto-shi* ☎ *075/231–1155* ⊕ *www.ana-hkyoto.com* ⌦ *303 rooms* ⌦ *In-room: safe, refrigerator. In-hotel: 7 restaurants, bar, pool, gym* ☐ *AE, DC, MC, V.*

$$$$ ⌨ **Hiiragiya** 柊家旅館. Join the ranks of celebrities, aristocrats, and royalty who have lodged under the holly-leaf crest of this elegant inn. Founded in 1818 to accommodate provincial lords visiting the capital, Hiiragiya is unmatched in its restrained opulence. The private hallway leading to your doorway makes every room feel like a suite. Rooms in the modern wing have luxuries like lacquerware accents, cozy sofas, and futons so cushy they might conceal box springs. The cedar baths (which will be set for you when you return from a day's adventuring) open out to private garden patios. Rooms in the older wing are just as lavish, with exquisitely sculpted wooden details, gold-leaf sliding doors, and wooden wraparound verandas with extraordinary views. Guests in this wing bathe in the large family-style baths downstairs. Tea and extravagant meals are served in your room by a kimono-clad attendant. A few blocks away the hotel's annex, Hiiragiya Bekkan, has slightly less ornate rooms and more down-to-earth prices. **Pros:** excellent location; multilingual staff; holly-infused soaps and bath oils. **Cons:** meal plans not very flexible. ⊠ *Nakahakusan-chō, Fuyachō-Anekōji-agaru, Nakagyō-ku, Kyōto-shi* ☎ *075/221–1136* ⊕ *www.hiiragiya.co.jp* ⇗ *28 rooms* ⌂ *In-room: safe, refrigerator, Internet. In-hotel: room service, laundry facilities* ▤ *AE, DC, MC, V* ¶ *MAP.*

$$$$ ⌂ **Hotel Fujita Kyōto** ホテルフジタ京都. Reasonable rates and river views make this hotel a good bargain. When you gaze down at the Kamogawa River you might even forget your room's slightly worn furnishings. The location is very central. **Pros:** near nightlife; close to the sights; quiet rooms. **Cons:** could use refurbishing; not the most multilingual staff. ⊠ *Kamogawa Nijō-ohashi TamotoNakagyō-ku, Kyōto-shi* ☎ *075/222–1511* ⊕ *www.fujita-kyoto.com* ⇗ *189 rooms* ⌂ *In-room: safe, refrigerator. In-hotel: 6 restaurants, bar* ▤ *AE, DC, MC, V.*

$$$$
Fodor'sChoice
★
☺
⌂ **Hotel Granvia Kyōto** ホテルグランヴィア京都. A fusion of ultramodern design with traditional Japanese style is what you'll find at this popular hotel above Kyōto Station. Spacious Western-style rooms have good amenities: broad desks, separate tea areas, and bathrooms with big soaking tubs. A walk between the hotel's north and south towers affords a great view from the brilliant glass walkway. The sky lounge lets you enjoy a fusion of French and Japanese cuisine and a panoramic view of the city. You'll find 15 other restaurants close at hand, including a branch of the famed Kitchō. Off-peak-season room rates drop considerably, so inquire about seasonal packages. **Pros:** good location; interesting architecture; plenty of amenities. **Cons:** charge for pool and gym; crowded area. ⊠ *Kyōto Station, Karasuma Chuo-guchi Shiokoji-sagaru Karasumadōri, Shimogyō-ku, Kyōto-shi* ☎ *075/344–8888* ⊕ *www.granvia-kyoto.co.jp/e/index.html* ⇗ *539 rooms* ⌂ *In-room: Internet. In-hotel: restaurant, pool, gym* ▤ *AE, DC, MC, V.*

$ ⌂ **Hotel Screen** ホテルスクリーン. This newcomer has already gained a foothold in this competitive market, thanks to its chic interiors. Each suite is the unique creation of a different Japanese designer. The styles range from traditional, with sliding doors painted with gold leaf, to ultra-modern, with everything in ethereal whites. One of our favorites is a sexy suite with gauzy white curtains haloing the walls and bed. If your suite isn't to your taste, the staff is happy to make a change. A rooftop bar has nice views of the city, and courtyard dining makes meals under the stars possible. **Pros:** good location; close to boutiques; pampering feel. **Cons:** restaurant service can be slow. ⊠ *640-1 Shimogoryomae-chō, Nakagyō-ku* ☎ *075/252–1113* ⊕ *www.hotelscreen.com* ⇗ *13 rooms* ⌂ *In-room: safe, refrigerator, DVD. In-hotel: restaurant, room service, bar, spa, Internet terminal, no-smoking rooms* ▤ *AE, D, DC, MC, V.*

$$$$ **Kinmata** 斤又. Only a few hundred feet from the bustling thoroughfare
★ of Shijō-dōri, stepping into this high-class ryokan is a trip back in time.
The modern age melts away as you pass under the heavy iron lamps in
the incense-tinged entranceway and through subdued wooden passages
leading to your quiet tatami room. A framed chart of ryokan guidelines from the Tokugawa shogunate speaks to the inn's long history, as
does an old photograph of the house with the current master's great-
grandfather standing in the foreground. You won't feel stifled by all the
history though; the staff is friendly, the atmosphere welcoming, and the
rooms are beautiful and decidedly unpretentious. The rate includes two
meals either in your room or in the modern dining room. **Pros:** antique
furnishings; authentic construction; great location. **Cons:** tough futons;
unofficial midnight curfew; books up fast. ✉*Gokomachi Shijō agaru,
Nakagyō-ku* ☎*075/221–1039* ⌨*3 rooms* ⚒*In-room: no TV. In-hotel:
restaurant* ☰*AE, DC, MC, V* ❢*MAP.*

¢ ⌨**K's House Kyōto** ケイズハウス京都. True, K's House bills itself first
and foremost as a backpacker hostel, but the modern architecture,
smart facilities, helpful multilingual staff, and central location make it
a great find. The cheap double rooms make it an incredibly good value
for those who have high standards but don't look for luxury. Rooms
are clean though not fancy, and big beds leave them pretty cramped.
The tradeoff is perks like free wireless connections, plentiful computer terminals, a huge communal kitchen, and lovely courtyard. It's
north of Shichijo-dōri, west of the Takase River. **Pros:** clean facilities;
great location; chance to meet fellow travelers. **Cons:** rooms are small;
spartan decor. ✉*418 Nayachō, Shichijō-agaru, Dotemachi-dōri, Shi-
mobyo-ku* ☎*075/342–2444* ⊕*kshouse.jp* ⌨*140 rooms* ⚒*In-room:
safe, no phone. In-hotel: laundry facilities, Wi-Fi, no-smoking rooms*
☰*MC, V.*

$$$$ ⌨**Kyōto Brighton Hotel** 京都ブライトンホテル. One of the city's best
Fodor's Choice hotels, the Kyōto Brighton has an elegant design sense and thorough
★ dedication to good hospitality. Glass elevators circling a large central
☾ atrium whisk you up to large rooms with separate sleeping and lounge
areas. A recent upgrade brought a PH-balancing water-purification system and Internet connections. The helpful concierge is on hand to help
you plan your sightseeing, and the excellent Hotaru restaurant is well
worth a visit; the resident chef won a challenging contest on the popular
cooking show *Iron Chef.* **Pros:** conscientious staff; great decor; tasty
restaurants. **Cons:** expensive rates. ✉*Nakadachiuri, Shin-machi-dōri,
Kamigyo-ku* ☎*075/441–4411, 800/223–6800 in U.S.* ⊕*www.brighton
hotels.co.jp* ⌨*183 rooms, 2 suites* ⚒*In-room: safe, refrigerator, Internet. In-hotel: 5 restaurants, bars, pool, spa, no-smoking rooms* ☰*AE,
DC, MC, V.*

$$$–$$$$ ⌨**Kyōto Kokusai Hotel** 京都国際ホテル. A location just across the street
☾ from Nijō-jō Castle provides excellent views from the rooftop lounge
and many of the rooms. Armchairs set before the windows in the spa-
cious rooms let you gaze down on the city as long as you wish. In the
middle of the garden's pond, a lacquer-floored platform is a stage for
performances of traditional dances. Relax with a cup of tea as you
watch, or pick from one of several decent restaurants. It's location, a

6

few yards from the Nijō-jō-mae station, is very convenient for sightseers. **Pros:** convenient access to public transportation; good facilities. **Cons:** some rooms overdue for renovation. ✉*Nijōjomae, Horikawa-dōri, Nakagyō-ku, Kyōto-shi* ☎*075/222–1111* ✆*277 rooms* ⚒*In-room: safe, refrigerator. In-hotel: 5 restaurants, bar* ▭*AE, DC, MC, V.*

$$–$$$ 🏨**Matsubaya Ryokan.** Experience traditional-style accommodations without paying through the nose at Matsubaya Ryokan. You won't find kimono-clad attendants, but you also won't find rates that won't empty your wallet. Welcoming innkeepers, pleasant rooms, and a good location facing the massive Higashi Hongan-ji temple make Matsubaya Ryokan a great find. Ask about the studio apartments on the top floor, a great place for longer stays. Recent renovations went a bit overboard in modernizing the 100-year-old property, removing some of the charm. **Pros:** friendly staff; cheap and tasty breakfast. **Cons:** bland rooms; staff speaks little English. ✉*Kamijuzuyamachi-dōri, Higashi Nito-in, Nishi-iru, Shimogyō-ku* ☎*075/351–3727* ⊕*www.matsubayainn.com* ✆*8 rooms* ⚒ *In-room: safe, refrigerator. In-hotel: laundry facilities, Internet terminal* ▭*V, MC.*

$$$–$$$$ 🏨**New Miyako Hotel** 新都ホテル**.** This gleaming white edifice with two protruding wings looks like it would be at home in any American city. The south-wing rooms have been refurbished in a thoroughly modern style, contrasting with the rather dated rooms in the other wing. On the south side of Kyōto Station, it's in a convenient spot if you're traveling by train. The friendly guest-relations manager in the bright marble lobby can help you plan your day. **Pros:** friendly staff; pleasant facilities. **Cons:** slightly stuffy rooms. ✉*17 Nishi-Kujōin-chō, Minami-ku, Kyōto-shi* ☎*075/661–7111* ⊕*www.miyakohotels.ne.jp/newmiyako* ✆*714 rooms* ⚒ *In-room: safe, refrigerator, Internet. In-hotel: 7 restaurants, bar* ▭*AE, DC, MC, V.*

$$$$ 🏨**Nishiyama Ryokan** 西山旅館**.** A central location, friendly staff, and surprisingly top-notch kaiseki dinners make this hotel a good find. It's great for travelers who want the tatami-room experience, although light sleepers should be warned that the futons are a little thin. Meals are served in a downstairs dining room. A comfortable lounge has computer terminals and ports for your laptop. Large Japanese-style baths for each sex are open late. Traditional buildings give this neighborhood a lot of charm, and it's not far from action-packed city centers like Gion or Sanjo-dōri. **Pros:** helpful concierge; flexible meal plans. **Cons:** thin futons; cramped bathrooms. ✉*Gokomachi-dōri, Nijō Sagaru , Nakagyo-ku* ☎*075/222–1166* ⊕*www.ryokan-kyoto.com* ✆*34 rooms* ⚒*In-room: safe, refrigerator. In-hotel: restaurant, laundry facilities, Internet terminal* ▭*MC, V.*

¢ 🏨**Palace Side Hotel** パレスサイドホテル**.** A great option for travelers on
★ a budget, this hotel has a good location, convenient access to public
🕐 transportation, and a very helpful multilingual concierge. It lacks the plush touches of more upscale lodgings, but it also lacks the jaw-dropping price tags. Rooms and bathrooms are comfortable, but extremely basic. Some feature paintings by local art students, drawing your eye away from the threadbare spots in the carpets. A communal kitchen is a nice touch if you're planning to stay for a few days; a discount rate

for reservations of three nights or more sweetens the pot. The hotel is on the east side of the Imperial Palace, three blocks north of Maruta-machi station. Pros: very reasonable rates; central location; massage therapists on call. Cons: lots of wear and tear; cramped bathrooms; lousy continental breakfast. ✉ *Karasuma-dōri, Shimo-dachiuri-agaru, Kamigyō-ku* ☎ *075/415–8887* ⊕ *www.palacesidehotel.co.jp* ⇱ *120 rooms* & *In-room: kitchen (some). In-hotel: restaurant, Internet terminal* ⊟ *AE, DC, MC, V.*

$$$$ 🖼 **Rihga Royal Hotel Kyōto** リーガロイヤルホテル京都. Even the smallest
☺ rooms at this well-established chain hotel are warm and inviting, with delicate shōji windows and elegant bath furnishings. The staff's painstaking attention to every detail makes you feel like a VIP. Four-person family rooms are a great option if you're traveling with kids. Kyōto's only revolving restaurant crowns the building, offering splendid views of the city, and there's also a branch of the well-known Kitchō restaurant on premises. The hotel is a five-minute walk from Kyōto Station, making it an excellent choice for those with early train connections. Pros: close to the station; deluxe rooms; excellent decor. Cons: far from the city center. ✉ *1-Taimatsuchō, Horikawa-Shiokoji, Shimogyō-ku, Kyōto-shi* ☎ *075/341–1121, 800/877–7107 in U.S.* ⊕ *www.rihga.com* ⇱ *494 rooms* & *In-room: Internet. In-hotel: 6 restaurants, bar, pool, sauna, no-smoking rooms* ⊟ *AE, DC, MC, V.*

$ 🖼 **Ryokan Hiraiwa** 旅館平岩. One of several budget lodgings near the Takase-gawa River, Ryokan Hiraiwa appeals to travelers seeking the traditional feeling of tatami-mat rooms. A nice breakfast room and friendly staff make up for the unimpressive decor. A large Japanese-style bath downstairs is great for washing away a day's travel strain, and an even larger public bath is three doors away. Pros: easy access to many sights; friendly staff. Cons: bland rooms. ✉ *314 Hayao-chō, Kaminokuchi-agaru, Ninomiyacho-dōri, Shiogyo-ku* ☎ *075/351–6748* ⊕ *www2.odn.ne.jp/hiraiwa* ⇱ *18 rooms* & *In-room: safe, refrigerator. In-hotel: restaurant* ⊟ *AE, MC, V.*

$$$$ 🖼 **Tawaraya** 俵屋. The most famous of Kyōto's traditional inns, Tawara-
Fodor'sChoice ya has been host to dignitaries, presidents, and royalty. Recent notable
★ guests have included Keanu Reeves and Steven Spielberg. Founded more than 300 years ago and currently run by the 11th generation of the Okazaki family, the hotel is known not only for its hospitality, but also for the sumptuous but subdued decor, impeccable service, and splendid gardens. Every room is unique, furnished with superb antiques from the family collection. Private baths are made from fragrant cedar. Modern comforts like air-conditioning and Internet access never intruding on the traditional aesthetics. Reservations are accepted a year in advance. Pros: excellent reputation; doting, incomparable service. Cons: extremely expensive; must reserve dinner a day in advance. ✉ *Fuyachō-Aneyakōji-agaru, Nakagyō-ku, Kyōto-shi* ☎ *075/211–5566* ⇱ *18 rooms* & *In-room: Internet. In-hotel: laundry service* ⊟ *AE, DC, V* ¶ *EP.*

$$$$ 🖼 **Yoshikawa** 吉川. This traditional inn is within walking distance of the downtown shopping area. Dating from the 1950s, it features authentic *sukiya-zukuri* style: the rooms are wrapped around a landscaped garden. Each tastefully decorated room has a cypress-wood bath. As at

most ryokan, the room rate includes two excellent meals. Guests are served kaiseki ryōri, including the specialty tempura, in their rooms. Custom meals for vegetarians and vegans available. **Pros:** excellent indoor garden; terrific meals. **Cons:** expensive rates; fixed meal times. ✉*Tomino-kōji, Oike-sagaru,Nakagyō-ku* ☎*075/221–5544 or 075/221–0052* 🛏*9 rooms* ♿*In-room: Internet. In-hotel: restaurant* ▭*AE, DC, MC, V* ⦿*MAP.*

EASTERN KYŌTO

$ 🏠**B&B Juno.** This delightful bed-and-breakfast is in a quiet residential neighborhood just north of downtown's hustle and bustle. The house itself is lovely and inviting and the atmosphere is refreshingly informal, but it's really the hospitable innkeepers, a couple with 20 years of experience, who create the inn's relaxing and enjoyable environment. (The eponymous Juno is their precocious daughter.) You can trust them for thoroughly knowledgeable sightseeing advice, as one is the longtime editor of the indispensable Kyōto Visitor's Guide. To get here from Kyōto Station, take Bus 17 to Kitashirakawa, the fourth stop after crossing the river. **Pros:** great breakfast; close to good restaurants; central location. **Cons:** books up quickly. ✉*Jōdoji Nishidachō 115-8, Sakyō-ku* ☎*No phone* ⊕ *www.gotokandk.com/casa.html* 🛏*3 rooms* ♿*In-hotel: refrigerator, Wi-Fi* ▭ *No credit cards.*

$$$$ ★ ☾   🏯**Gion Hatanaka** 祇園 畑中. A stone's throw from Yasaka Jinja, this comfortable, modern ryokan is located in the heart of Gion. It gives you easy access to many of the temples in Eastern Kyōto. The staff offers you a warm welcome, but without the stiff formality found elsewhere. Spacious tatami rooms overlook towering bamboo gardens from glassed-in balconies. Packages suit a variety of budgets, including various options for meals; inquire about rates that include dinner in nearby restaurants like Chimera downstairs or Minoko across the street. Feel like staying in? The elaborate in-room kaiseki dinners showcase an artful attention to detail. **Pros:** great location; modern facilities; relaxed vibe. **Cons:** rooms short on character; basic decor. ✉ *Yasaka Jinja, Minami-monmae, Gion, Higashiyama-ku* ☎*075/541–5315* ⊕*www.thehatanaka. co.jp* 🛏*21 rooms* ♿ *In-room: safe. In-hotel: restaurant* ▭*AE, DC, MC, V* ⦿*MAP.*

$$$–$$$$ 🏯**Hyatt Regency** ハイアットリージェンシー京都」. The central location and
Fodor's Choice ★ friendly staff make the Hyatt Regency the city's best luxury hotel. Adjacent to two of the most popuar attractions—Sanjūsangen-dō temple and its 1,000 golden statues are next door, and the Kyōto National Museum is literally across the street—the hotel is a perfect base for exploring the city's sights. In the main lobby, latticework evoking old kimono dyeing patterns frames the three well-regarded restaurants and the funky downstairs bar. Spacious rooms are accented with cheerful fabrics and look out onto the tree-shaded garden. If a day's adventuring tires you out, indulge in acupuncture or a massage in the downstairs spa. **Pros:** terrific staff; great location; extravagant continental breakfast. **Cons:** somber exterior; chain-hotel feel. ✉644-2 *Sanjūsangendo-mawari, Higashiyama-ku 605-0941* ☎*075/541–1234* ⊕*www.hyattregencykyoto.*

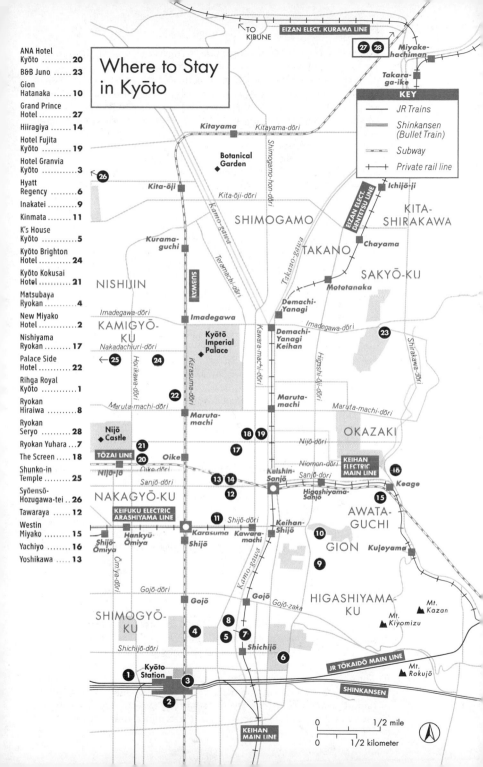

com ↩184 rooms ⚒In-room: safe, refrigerator, Internet. In-hotel: 3 restaurants, gym, spa, laundry service ▤AE, DC, MC, V ▯◗EP.

$ ▦**Ryokan Yuhara** 旅館ゆはら. Drawing many repeat visitors, the Ryokan Yuhara lets you save a few yen while exploring Kyōto. The friendliness of the staff more than compensates for the spartan amenities. Especially rewarding is a springtime stay, when the cherry trees are in full bloom along the nearby Takase-gawa. The hotel is a 15-minute walk from the hot neighborhoods of Gion and Ponto-chō. There is an 11 PM curfew. **Pros:** friendly innkeepers; family-friendly atmosphere. **Cons:** strict curfew; all shared bathrooms. ⊠188 Kagiya-chō, Shomen-agaru, Kiya-machi-dōri, Higashiyama-ku, Kyōto-shi ☎075/371–9583 ↩8 rooms with shared bath ⚒ In-room: safe. In-hotel: no-smoking room ▤ No credit cards.

$$$$ ▦**Westin Miyako Hotel** ウェティン都ホテル. Located at the foot of the mountains, the Westin Miyako feels far from the city while retaining great access to downtown (the Keage subway stop is convenient). Picturesque temples like Nanzen-ji and Chion-in are nearby, making sightseeing very easy. You can get even closer to nature by taking advantage of the hotel's walking trail, traditionally manicured gardens, and indoor and outdoor pools. Annexes hold Japanese-style rooms with the feel of traditional ryokan lodgings. **Pros:** free transfer from Kyōto Station; tasty restaurants; helpful concierge. **Cons:** far from downtown; some rooms need updating. ⊠Sanjō-Keage, Higashiyama-ku, Kyōto-shi ☎075/771–7111 ⊕www.westinmiyako-kyoto.com ↩320 rooms ⚒In-room: Internet. In-hotel: 9 restaurants, bars, pools, gym ▤AE, DC, MC, V.

$$$$ ▦**Yachiyo** 八千代. An excellent traditional ryokan, Yachio is known for its impressive garden, eager staff, and excellent meals. It's a stone's throw from Nanzen-ji temple and the Heian Jingū palace, as well as nearby attractions like the modern art museum and the city zoo. The lovely rooms—several of which are unusually expansive—are all nicely designed. The smaller rooms can be less expensive than counterparts in other upscale inns, particularly if you choose one without a private bath. The newly renovated bathrooms are terrific; one has a cedar tub as big as a twin bed. Breakfast and dinner can be served in your room or in the restaurant. **Pros:** lavish bathrooms; lots of space. **Cons:** uninspired meals; not all rooms have views. ⊠34 Nanzen-ji-fukuchi-chō, Sakyō-ku, Kyōto-shi ☎075/771–4148 ⊕www.ryokan-yachiyo.com ↩25 rooms, 20 with bath ⚒ In-room: safe. In-hotel: restaurant ▤AE, DC, MC, V ▯◗MAP.

NORTHERN KYŌTO

$$$$ ▦**Grand Prince Hotel** グランドプリンスホテル京都. Although some distance north of the city center, the deluxe Prince Hotel is regal enough to make you feel like visiting royalty. Rooms are spacious, but the rosy-hued color scheme feels slightly passé compared with other luxury hotels. The quirky architecture makes up for it, though. The doughnut-shaped building provides each room a nice view of the surrounding mountains; the interior corridors overlook a pretty garden. A teahouse beside the pond has demonstrations of the tea ceremony; ask at the helpful

CLOSE UP

Ryokan Etiquette

Upon entering, take off your shoes, as you would do in a Japanese household, and put on the slippers that are provided in the entryway. A maid, after bowing to welcome you, will escort you to your room, which will have tatami (straw mats) on the floor and will probably be partitioned off with shōji (sliding paper-paneled walls). Remove your slippers before entering your room; you should not step on the tatami with either shoes or slippers. The room will have little furniture or decoration—perhaps one small low table and cushions on the tatami, with a long, simple scroll on the wall. Often the rooms overlook a garden.

Plan to arrive in the late afternoon, as is the custom. After relaxing with a cup of green tea, have a long, hot bath. In ryokan with thermal pools you can take to the waters anytime, although the doors to the pool are usually locked from 11 PM to 6 AM. In ryokan without thermal baths or private baths in guest rooms, guests must stagger visits to the one or two public baths. Typically the maid will ask what time you would like your bath and fit you into a schedule. In Japanese baths, washing and soaking are separate functions: wash and rinse off entirely, and then get in the tub. Be sure to keep all soap out of the tub. Because other guests will be using the same bathwater after you, it is important to observe this custom. After your bath, change into a yukata, a simple cotton kimono provided in your room. Don't worry about walking around in what is essentially a robe—all other guests will be doing the same.

Dinner, which is usually included in the price, is served in your room at smaller and more personal ryokan; at larger ryokan, especially the newer ones, meals will be in the dining room. After you are finished, a maid will discreetly come in, clear away the dishes, and lay out your futon. In Japan futon means bedding, and this consists of a thin cotton mattress and a heavy, thick comforter. In summer the comforter is replaced with a thinner quilt. The small, hard pillow is filled with grain. In the morning a maid will gently wake you, clear away the futon, and bring in your Japanese-style breakfast, consisting of fish, miso soup, vegetables, and rice, although some ryokan have a Western option.

Because most ryokan staffs are small and dedicated, it is important to be considerate and understanding of their somewhat rigid schedules. Guests are expected to arrive in the late afternoon and eat around 6. Usually the doors to the inn are locked at 10, so plan for early evenings. Breakfast is served around 8, and checkout is at 10.

Not all inns are willing to accept foreign guests (though the ones listed in this chapter are amenable) because of language and cultural barriers. Also, top-level ryokan expect even new Japanese guests to have introductions and references from a respected client of the inn, which means that you, too, might need an introduction from a Japanese for very top-level ryokan. When you reserve a room, try to have a Japanese make the call for you; this will convey the idea that you understand the customs of staying in a traditional inn.

6

concierge desk on the top floor. The French-themed Beaux Sejours is the best pick of the hotel's four eateries. The Kokusai Kaikan subway station is nearby. **Pros:** excellent breakfast; responsive staff. **Cons:** far from the city's sights; dated decor. ⊠ *Takaraga-ike, Sakyō-ku, Kyōto-shi* ☏075/712–1111, 800/542–8686 *in U.S.* ⊕*www.princejapan.com* ⮑*309 rooms* ⌂*In-room: safe, refrigerator, Wi-Fi. In-hotel: 4 restaurants, bar* ▤*AE, DC, MC, V* ⦿|BP.

$$$$ ▦**Ryokan Seryō** 芹生. After a long day of sightseeing, there is nothing more relaxing than an outdoor hot spring in the mountains. Ryokan Seryō is located across from the huge Sanzen-in temple in Ōhara, north of downtown Kyōto. Since the ryokan is in the countryside, the rooms are larger than you'll find in the city. Plump futons on raised platforms and quaint balconies add charm to the guest rooms. The kaiseki dinner includes wild mountain vegetables and seasonal specialties like wild boar stew in winter. The traditional Japanese breakfast includes steamed egg custard and homemade yogurt. The hotel is a 70-minute bus ride from Kyōto Station. **Pros:** relaxed atmosphere; great food. **Cons:** far from the city; staff speaks minimal English. ⊠*22 Shorinin-chō, Ōhara, Sakyō-ku* ☏*075/744–2301* ⊕*www.seryo.co.jp* ⌂*In-room: safe. In-hotel: restaurant, no-smoking rooms* ⦿|MAP.

WESTERN KYŌTO

$ ▦**Shunko-in Temple.** Visiting Kyōto's temples gives you a taste of the city's history, but staying in one is a more intimate way of experiencing the past. The intricate woodwork, manicured stone pathways, and enigmatic gardens that characterize Shunko-in are revealed in fascinating morning tours with the American-educated vice-abbot Kawakami. He gives you a chance to examine gorgeous golden sliding-door paintings by Eigaku Kano and other artifacts from the temple's 500-year history. Rooms are comfortable but appropriately ascetic, if also a bit disappointingly western. All but two share bathrooms. A common kitchen is especially convenient for long stays. Shunko-in is a subtemple of Myoshin-ji, a sprawling temple complex in Western Kyōto. Access is via JR Sagano train line to Hanazono station, or via Bus 26 or 10 to Myoshin-ji Kitamon-mae. **Pros:** insider tour; plenty of atmosphere. **Cons:** modern rooms; books up fast. ⊠*42 Myoshinji-chō, Hanazono, Ukyo-ku* ☏*075/462–5488* ⊕*www.shunkoin.com* ⮑*6 rooms, 4 with shared bath* ⌂ *In-room: no TV* ▤ *No credit cards.*

$$$$ ▦**Syōensō-Hozugawa-tei** 松園荘保津川亭. In the mountains northwest of Kyōto, this hotel allows you to soak in your own *rotemburo* (outdoor hot tub) overlooking a private garden. If you're feeling adventurous, you can join other guests in one of the communal baths (separated by gender, of course). Though the building is nondescript, the layers of sliding paper screens of the lobby's facade and the steps bordered on one side by a gently sloping waterfall suggest Old Kyōto. Kaiseki dinners are prepared with seasonal favorites, including wild boar in winter. A great way to get here is the scenic Sagano Torokko train, which leaves from Saga Torokko Station in Arashiyama. Alternatively, you can take JR Sagano line to Kameoka station. **Pros:** healthful hot springs; mountain views. **Cons:** far from city center; expensive rates. ⊠*Yunohana-onsen,*

Kameoka City ☎*0771/22–0903* ⊕*www.syoenso.com* 🛏*56 rooms* *In-room: safe. In-hotel: restaurant* ☰*AE, MC, V* 🍴*MAP.*

NIGHTLIFE AND THE ARTS

THE ARTS

Kyōto is known for its traditional performances—particularly dance and Nō theater. All dialogue is in Japanese, but sometimes there are synopses available. From time to time world-class musicians play the intimate venues, including David Lindley, Ron Sexsmith, and Michelle Shocked. The most convenient source for information is your hotel concierge or guest-relations manager, who may even have a few tickets on hand. For further information on Kyōto's arts scene check the music and theater sections of the monthly magazine *Kansai Time Out,* at bookshops for ¥300; you can also find information on the Web site *www.kto.co.jp.* Another source is the *Kyōto Visitor's Guide,* ⊕*www.kyotoguide.com,* which devotes a few pages to "This Month's Theater." Look at the festival listings for temple and shrine performances. It's available free from the Kyōto Tourist Information Center on the ninth floor of the Kyōto Station building; the staff can also provide you with information.

GION CORNER

Some call it a tourist trap, but for others it's a comprehensive introduction to Japanese performing arts. The one-hour show combines court music and dance, ancient comic plays, Kyōto-style dance performed by *maiko* (apprentice geisha), and puppet drama. Segments are also offered on the tea ceremony, flower arranging, and koto music. Before attending a show, walk around Gion and Ponto-chō. You're likely to see beautifully dressed geisha and maiko on their way to work. It's permissible to take their picture—*"Shashin o tottemō ii desu ka?"*—but as they have strict appointments, don't delay them.

For tickets to **Gion Corner,** contact your hotel concierge or call the theater directly. The show costs ¥2,800—a bargain considering that it would usually cost 10 times as much to watch maiko and geisha perform. Two performances are held nightly at 7 and 8, March to November. No performances are offered August 16. ⊠*Gion Hanami-kōji, Higashiyama-ku* ☎*075/561–1115.*

SEASONAL DANCES

In the **Miyako Odori** in April and the **Kamo-gawa Odori** in May and October, geisha and maiko dances and songs pay tribute to the seasonal splendor of spring and fall. The stage settings are spectacular. Tickets to performances at the **Gion Kaburenjō Theater** 祇園歌舞練場 (⊠*Gion Hanami-kōji, Higashiyama-ku* ☎*075/561–1115*) cost from ¥2,000 to ¥7,000. Tickets at the **Ponto-chō Kaburenjō Theater** 先斗町歌舞伎練場 (⊠*Ponto-chō, Sanjō-sagaru, Nakagyō-ku* ☎*075/221–2025*) cost between ¥2,000 and ¥4,000.

KABUKI

Kabuki developed in the Edo era as a theatrical art with lavish costumes and sets and dynamic all-male performances. Though Kabuki is faster paced than Nō, a single performance can easily take half a day. Devotees pack bentōs to eat while watching shows. Kyōto hosts traveling Kabuki performances periodically, since most of the troupes are based in Tōkyō. Especially anticipated in Kyōto is the annual month long **Kaomise** *(Face Showing)* Kabuki Festival in December, featuring top Kabuki stars and introducing upcoming artists. Tickets range from ¥5,250 to ¥24,150 and need to be booked weeks in advance. The beautifully renovated **Minami-za** (⊠*Shijō Kamo-gawa, Higashiyama-ku* ☎*075/561–1155*), the oldest theater in Japan, hosts performances year-round.

NŌ

Kyōto is the home of Japan's most ancient form of traditional theater, Nō, which is more ritualistic and sophisticated than Kabuki. Some understanding of the plot of each play is necessary to enjoy a performance, which is generally slow-moving and solemnly chanted. The carved masks used by the main actors express a whole range of emotions, though the mask itself may appear expressionless until the actor "brings it to life." Nō performances are held year-round and range from ¥3,000 to ¥13,000. Particularly memorable are outdoor Nō performances, especially **Takigi Nō**, held outdoors by firelight on the nights of June 1 and 2 in the precincts of the Heian Jingū. For more information about performances, contact the Kyōto Tourist Information Center.

Kanze Kaikan Nō Theater. This is the older of Kyōto's Nō theaters, and it sometimes hosts Nō orientation talks. The theater does not offer programs in English. ⊠*44 Enshōji-chō, Okazaki, Sakyō-ku* ☎*075/771–6114.*

Ōe Nōgakudō 大江能楽堂. ⊠*Oshikōji-dōri, Nakagyō-ku* ☎*075/561–0622.*

Shin Kongo Nō Theater. ⊠*Karasuma-dōri, Ichijō-sagaru, Kamigyō-ku* ☎*075/441–7222.*

NIGHTLIFE

Though Kyōto's nightlife is more sedate than Ōsaka's, the areas around the old geisha quarters downtown thrive with nightclubs and bars. The Kiya-machi area along the small canal near Ponto-chō is as close to a consolidated nightlife area as you'll get in Kyōto. It's full of small watering holes with red lanterns (indicating inexpensive places) or small neon signs in front. It's also fun to walk around the Gion and Ponto-chō areas to try to catch a glimpse of a geisha or maiko stealing down an alleyway on her way to or from an appointment.

Café Independents. As its name suggests, this bar hosts a spectrum of indie rock, jazz, and blues artists, making it a good place to tap into the underground music scene. Trestle tables line the graffiti-covered walls of this basement venue with some tasty dishes on offer. ⊠ *1928 Bldg., Sanjō-dōri, Nakagyō-ku* ☎*075/255–4312.*

Le Club Jazz. You can hear live jazz, blues, and soul gigs on Tuesday, and jam sessions every night from Thursday to Monday. There's a ¥2,000 cover charge, which includes two drinks on weekends. The club is diagonally opposite Café Independents. ✉*Sanjō Arimoto Bldg.*, *2nd fl.*, *Sanjō-Gokōmachi Nishi-Iru, Kamigyō-ku* ☎*075/211–5800.*

★ **Metro.** One of the best clubs in Kansai, Metro has an extremely wide range of regular events, from salsa to reggae, as well as frequent guest appearances by famous DJs from Tōkyō and abroad. ✉*Ebisu Bldg.*, *2nd fl.*, *82 Shimotsutsumi-chō, Maruta-machi-sagaru, Kawabata-dōri, Sakyō-ku* ☎*075/752–4765* ⊕*www.metro.ne.jp.*

★ **Tadg's.** North of the Minamiz-a theater in Gion, this convivial pub entertains patrons with Irish music and sporting events on TV. Have a chat with the locals to find out what's happening around town. The menu offers classic fish-and-chips, plus Irish stew and a beef-and-Guinness pie. ✉*236 Ōtobiru 2F, Nijuichiken-chō, Yamat-ōji, Kawabata Shijō-agaru* ☎*075/525–0680* ⊕*www.tadgspub.com.*

★ **Taku Taku.** This bar is an enduring live-music venue, tending toward rock and blues, that occasionally features some stellar performers. You can find it in an old kura, or storehouse, in the backstreets southwest of the Takashimaya department store. ✉*Tominokoji- dōri, Bukkōji-sagaru, Shimogyō-ku* ☎*075/351–1321.*

Yoramu. Israeli sake aficionado Yoram has an extensive range of the delicate rice wine, from unfiltered to aged, fruity to dry, all available by the glass. A tasting set of three kinds of sake starts at ¥1,200. The dishes on the menu have all been chosen to complement the drink. The cozy bar is south of Nijō-dōri, east of Higashino-tōin-dōri. ✉*Nijō-dōri, Nakagyō-ku* ☎*075/213–1512.*

SHOPPING

Most shops slide their doors open at 10, and many shopkeepers partake of the morning ritual of sweeping and watering the entrance to welcome the first customers. Shops lock up at 6 or 7 in the evening. Stores often close sporadically once or twice a month, so it helps to call in advance if you're making a special trip. On weekends downtown can be very crowded.

A shopkeeper's traditional greeting to a customer is *o-ideyasu* (Kyōto-ben, the Kyōto dialect, for "honored to have you here"), voiced in the lilting Kyōto intonations with the required bowing of the head. When a customer makes a purchase, the shopkeeper will respond with *o-okini* ("thank you" in Kyōto-ben), a smile, and a bow. Take notice of the careful effort and adroitness with which purchases are wrapped; it's an art in itself. American Express, MasterCard, Visa, and to a lesser degree traveler's checks, are widely accepted.

SHOPPING DISTRICTS

Kyōto is compact and relatively easy to navigate. Major shops line both sides of **Shijō-dōri**, which runs east–west, and **Kawara-machi-dōri**, which runs north–south. Concentrate on Shijō-dōri between Yasaka Jinja and Karasuma Station as well as Kawara-machi-dōri between Sanjō-dōri and Shijō-dōri. Some of modern Kyōto's shopping districts are underground. **Porta,** under Kyōto Station, hosts more than 200 shops and restaurants in a sprawling subterranean arcade.

Roads leading to Kiyomizu-dera run uphill, yet you may hardly notice the steepness for all of the alluring shops that line the way. Be sure to peek in for unique gifts. Food shops offer sample morsels, and tea shops serve complimentary cups of tea. **Shin-Kyōgoku,** a covered arcade running between Teramachi-dōri and Kawara-machi-dōri, is another general-purpose shopping area with many souvenir shops.

DEPARTMENT STORES

Kyōto *depāto* (department stores) are small in comparison to their mammoth counterparts in Tōkyō and Ōsaka. They still carry a wide range of goods and are great places for one-stop souvenir shopping. Wandering around the food halls (in all but Hankyū) is a good way to build up an appetite. Prices drop dramatically during end-of-season sales. Note that all the stores close irregularly for a few days each month. You can call at the beginning of the month to find out about scheduled closures.

Daimaru mainly appeals to more expensive and conservative tastes, and is on the main Shijō-dōri shopping avenue. Its basement food hall is the best in town. ⊠ *Shijō-Karasuma, Shimogyō-ku* ☏ *075/211–8111* ⊙ *Daily 10–7:30.*

Fujii Daimaru, which is directly opposite the Teramachi mall on Shijō-dōri, is a funkier branch of the old matron Daimaru. ⊠ *Shijō-Teramachi, Shimogyō-ku* ☏ *075/211–8181* ⊙ *Daily 10–8.*

Hankyū, directly across from Takashimaya on Kawara-machi-dōri, has two revamped restaurant floors. Window displays show the type of food served, and prices are clearly marked. ⊠ *Shijō-kawara-machi, Shimogyō-ku* ☏ *075/223–2288* ⊙ *Daily 10–7:30.*

Isetan, in the Kyōto Station building, has 13 floors, including a restaurant floor, a cosmetics floor, an amusement arcade, and an art gallery. It closes periodically on Tuesday. ⊠ *Karasuma-dōri, Shimogyō-ku* ☏ *075/352–1111* ⊙ *Daily 10–7:30.*

Takashimaya, on Kawara-machi-dōri, is Japan's most established and sophisticated depāto, with designer and luxury goods at matching prices. You'll find accommodating English-speaking salespeople and a convenient money-exchange counter. The restaurant floor is rather grand, with a concierge service for diners. ⊠ *Shijō-kawara-machi, Shimogyō-ku* ☏ *075/221–8811* ⊙ *Daily 10–7:30.*

MARKETS

Contact the **Kyōto Tourist Information Center** for information about seasonal fairs from local area pottery sales to the national antiques fairs, usually held in May, June, and October. ⊠ *9F JR Kyōto Station, Kyōto International Prefectural Center, Karasuma-dōri, Shimogyō-ku* ☏ *075/344–3300* ⊕ *www.kyoto-kankou.or.jp*

Kyōto has a wonderful food market, **Nishiki-kōji**, which is north of Shijō-dōri and branches off the Teramachi-dōri covered arcade in central Kyōto. Look for delicious grilled fish dipped in soy sauce for a tasty snack or fresh Kyōto sweets. Try to avoid the market in late afternoon, when housewives come to do their daily shopping. The market is long and narrow; in a sizable crowd there's always the possibility of being pushed into the display of fresh fish. ⊠*Nishiki-kōji-dōri, Nakagyō-ku.*

TEMPLE MARKETS

Several temple markets take place in Kyōto each month. These are great places to pick up bargain kimonos or unusual souvenirs. They're also some of the best spots for people-watching. The largest and most famous temple market is the one at **Tō-ji**, which takes place on the 21st of each month. Hundreds of stalls display fans, kimonos, antiques, and trinkets, which attract many collectors. The temple also hosts a smaller antiques market on the first Sunday of the month. ⊠*1 Kujō-chō, Minami-ku.*

The vibrant flea market at **Kitano Tenman-gū** overflows into the side streets surrounding the grounds on the 25th of each month, with kimono and Japanese crafts at reasonable prices. ⊠*Imakoji-agaru, Onmae-dōri, Kamigyō-ku.*

A market specializing in homemade goods is held at **Chion-in** on the 15th of each month. To get to the Chion-in market, take Bus 206 from Kyōto Station to Hyakumanben. ⊠*400 Hayashi-shita-chō 3-chōme, Yamato-ōji, Higashi-hairu, Shimbashi-dōri, Higashiyama-ku.*

6

TRADITIONAL ITEMS AND GIFT IDEAS

ART AND ANTIQUES

Nawate-dōri between Shijō-dōri and Sanjō-dōri is noted for fine antique textiles, ceramics, and paintings. ⊠*Higashiyama-ku.*

Shinmonzen-dōri holds the key to shopping for art and antiques in Kyōto. It's an unpretentious little street of two-story wooden buildings between Higashi-ōji-dōri and Hanami-kōji-dōri, just north of Gion. What gives the street away as a treasure trove are the large credit-card signs jutting out from the shops. There are no fewer than 17 shops specializing in scrolls, *netsuke* (small carved figures to attach to Japanese clothing), lacquerware, bronze, wood-block prints, paintings, and antiques. Shop with confidence, because shopkeepers are trustworthy and goods are authentic. Pick up a copy of the pamphlet *Shinmonzen Street Shopping Guide* from your hotel or from the Kyōto Tourist Information Center. ⊠*Higashiyama-ku.*

Tera-machi-dōri between Oike-dōri and Maruta-machi is known for antiques of all kinds and tea-ceremony utensils. ⊠*Nakagyō-ku.*

BAMBOO

The Japanese wish their sons and daughters to be as strong and flexible as bamboo. Around many Japanese houses are small bamboo groves, for the deep-rooted plant withstands earthquakes. On the other hand, bamboo is so flexible it can bend into innumerable shapes. Bamboo groves used to flourish on the hillsides surrounding Kyōto, but the groves are in decline. The wood is carefully cut and dried for several months before being stripped and woven into baskets and vases. **Kagoshin** has been in operation since 1862. Basket weavers here use more than 50 varieties of bamboo in intricate designs. ✉ *Ōhashi-higashi, Sanjō-dōri, Higashiyama-ku* ☎*075/771–0209* ⊙*Mon.–Sat. 9–6.*

CERAMICS

Asahi-dō, in the heart of the pottery district near Kiyomizu-dera, specializes in Kyōto-style hand-painted porcelain, and offers the widest selection of any pottery store in the area. ✉*1–280 Kiyomizu, Higashiyama-ku* ☎*075/531–2181* ⊙*Daily 9–6.*

Tachikichi, on Shijō-dōri west of Kawara-machi, has five floors full of contemporary and antique ceramics. One floor is an art gallery that hosts exhibits of very fine ceramics by Japanese and international artists. In business since 1872, Tachikichi has an excellent reputation. ✉ *Shijō-dōri, Tominokōji, Nakagyō-ku* ☎*075/211–3143* ⊙*Thurs.–Tues. 10–7.*

DOLLS

Ningyō were first used in Japan in the purification rites associated with the Doll Festival, an annual family-oriented event on March 3. Kyōto ningyō are made with fine detail and embellishment.

Nakanishi Toku Shōten has old museum-quality dolls. The owner, Mr. Nakanishi, turned his extensive doll collection into the shop two decades ago and has since been educating customers with his vast knowledge of the doll trade. ✉*359 Moto-chō, Yamato-ōji Higashi-Iru, Furumonzen-dōri, Higashiyama-ku* ☎*075/561–7309* ⊙*Daily 10–5.*

FOLK CRAFTS

For many, the prize souvenir of a visit to Kyōto is the **shuinchō,** a booklet usually no larger than 4 by 6 inches. It's most often covered with brocade, and the blank sheets of heavyweight paper inside continuously fold out. You can find them at gift stores or at temples for as little as ¥1,000 and use them as "passports" to collect ink stamps from places you visit while in Japan. Stamps and stamp pads are ubiquitous in Japan—at sights, train stations, and some restaurants. Most ink stamping will be done for free; at temples monks will write calligraphy over the stamp for a small fee.

Kuraya Hashimoto has one of the best collections of antique and newly forged swords and will ship them for you. ✉*Nishihorikawa-dōri, Oike-agaru, southeast corner of Nijō-jō, Nakagyō-ku* ☎*075/821–2791* ⊕*www.japan-sword.com* ⊙*Thurs.–Tues. 10–6.*

At **Ryūshido** you can stock up on calligraphy and *sumi* supplies, including writing brushes, ink sticks, ink stones, paper, paperweights, and water stoppers. ✉*Nijō-agaru, Tera-machi-dōri, north of Nijō, Kamigyō-ku* ☎*075/252–4120* ⊙*Daily 10–6.*

Yamato Mingei-ten, on Kawara-mach-dōri near the BAL Building downtown, has an ever-changing selection of folk crafts, including ceramics, metalwork, paper, lacquerware, and textiles from all over Japan. ✉*Kawara-machi, Takoyakushi-agaru, Nakagyō-ku* ☎*075/221–2641* ⊙*Wed.–Mon. 10–8:30.*

INCENSE

Kungyoku-dō, on Horikawa-dōri opposite Nishi-Hongan-ji, has been dealing in fine woods, herbs, and spices for 400 years. ✉ *Horikawa-dōri, Nishihonganji-mae, Shimogyō-ku* ☎ *075/371–0162* ☉ *Daily 9–5:30, closed 1st and 3rd Sun. of month.*

KIMONOS AND ACCESSORIES

Shimmering new silk kimonos can cost more than ¥1,000,000—they are art objects, as well as couture—while equally stunning old silk kimonos can cost less than ¥3,000. You can find used kimonos at some local end-of-the-month temple markets.

Aizen Kōbō, two blocks west of the textile center on Imadegawa-dōri and a block south, specializes in the finest handwoven and hand-dyed indigo textiles. Pure Japanese indigo dye, with its famed rich color, may soften but will never fade. The shop is in a traditional weaving family home, and the friendly owners will show you their many dyed and woven goods, including garments designed by Hisako Utsuki, the owner's wife. ✉ *Ōmiya Nishi-Iru, Nakasuji-dōri, Kamigyō-ku* ☎ *075/441–0355* ⊕ *web.kyoto-inet.or.jp/people/aizen* ☉ *Mon.–Sat. 9–5:30.*

Jūsan-ya has been selling *tsugekushi* (boxwood combs) for more than 60 years. *Kanzashi,* the hair ornaments worn with kimonos, are also available. ✉ *Shinkyōgoku Higashi-Iru, Shijō-dōri, Shimogyō-ku* ☎ *075/221–2008* ☉ *Daily 10–6.*

Umbrellas protect kimonos from the scorching sun or pelting rain. Head for **Kasagen** to purchase authentic oiled-paper umbrellas. The shop has been around since 1861, and its umbrellas are guaranteed to last for years. ✉ *284 Gion-machi, Kita-gawa, Higashiyama-ku* ☎ *075/561–2832* ☉ *Daily 10–9.*

The most famous fan shop in all of Kyōto is **Miyawaki Baisen-an,** in business since 1823. It delights customers not only with its fine collection of lacquered, scented, painted, and paper fans, but also with the old-world atmosphere that emanates from the building that houses the shop. ✉ *Tominokōji Nishi-Iru, Rokkaku-dōri, Nakagyō-ku* ☎ *075/221–0181* ☉ *Daily 9–6.*

LACQUERWARE

Monju sells authentic lacquered trays, bowls, incense holders, and tea containers. Unlike the inexpensive, plastic, faux lacquerware sold at some souvenir shops, real lacquerware has a wooden base, which is then coated with natural lacquer made from the Asian sumac tree. Gold and silver powder is used in the more lavish *maki-e* lacquerware. You can even buy chopsticks with their own carrying case to use instead of the disposable ones supplied in restaurants. This shop is on Shijō-dōri in Gion. ✉ *Hanamikōji Higashi-iru, Shijō-dōri, Higashiyama-ku* ☎ *075/525–1617* ☉ *Fri.–Wed. 10:30–7:30.*

NOVELTIES

☺ **Loft** has five floors jam-packed with kitsch, from beauty products to anime merchandise. Kids and teenagers love browsing here, and you're sure to find some unusual souvenirs and gifts. ✉ *Kawara-machi-nishi, Takoyakushi-dōri, Nakagyō-ku* ☎ *075/255–6210* ☉ *Daily 11–9.*

CLOSE UP

Kyōto Crafts

Temples, shrines, and gardens can't be taken home with you. You can, however, pack up a few *omiyage* (mementos) for which this city is famous. The ancient craftspeople of Kyōto served the imperial court for more than 1,000 years, and the prefix *kyō-* before a craft is synonymous with fine craftsmanship.

Kyō-ningyō, exquisite display dolls, have been made in Kyōto since the 9th century. Constructed of wood coated with white shell paste and clothed in elaborate, miniature patterned-silk brocades, Kyōto dolls are considered the finest in Japan. Kyōto is also known for fine ceramic dolls and *Kyō-gangu*, its local varieties of folk toys.

Kyō-sensu are embellished folding fans used as accoutrements in Nō theater, tea ceremonies, and Japanese dance. They also have a practical use—to keep you cool. Unlike other Japanese crafts, which have their origin in Tang-dynasty China, the folding fan originated in Kyōto.

Kyō-shikki refers to Kyōto lacquerware, which also has its roots in the 9th century. The making of lacquerware, adopted from the Chinese, is a delicate process requiring patience and skill. Finished lacquerware products range from furniture to spoons and bowls, which are carved from cypress, cedar, or horse-chestnut wood. These pieces have a brilliant luster; some designs are decorated with gold leaf and inlaid mother-of-pearl.

Kyō-yaki is the general term applied to ceramics made in local kilns; the most popular ware is from Kyōto's Kiyomizu district. Often colorfully hand-painted in blue, red, and green on white, these elegantly shaped teacups, bowls, and vases are thrown on potters' wheels located in the Kiyomizu district and in Kiyomizu-danchi in Yamashina. Streets leading up to Kiyomizu-dera—Chawanzaka, Sannen-zaka, and Ninen-zaka—are sprinkled with kyō-yaki shops.

Kyō-yuzen is a paste-resist silk-dyeing technique developed by 17th-century dyer Yuzen Miyazaki. Fantastic designs are created on plain white silk pieces through the process of either *tegaki yuzen* (hand-painting) or *kata yuzen* (stenciling).

Nishijin-ori is the weaving of silk. *Nishijin* refers to a Kyōto district producing the best silk textiles in all Japan, which are used to make kimonos. Walk along the narrow backstreets of Nishijin and listen to the persistently rhythmic looms.

Nara

WORD OF MOUTH

"The deer running wild, searching our pockets for food was fun, the Todai-ji was impressive.The Daibutsu-den Hall has an enormous bronze Buddha but the lighting is poor and it was difficult to really appreciate it. One interesting thing was a hole in one of the pillars which supposedly confers eternal wisdom to anyone who can crawl through it. "

—joannecam

Updated by
Maruan El
Mahgiub

Nara is a place of synthesis, where Chinese art, religion, and architecture fused with Japanese language and Shintō traditions. The city was established in 710 and was then known as Heijō-Kyō (citadel of peace). Fujiwara-no-Fuhito, father-in-law of Emperor Mōmmu, was responsible for the city's creation. His grandson, the future Emperor Shōmu, later graced the new capital with its wealth of temples, pagodas, and shrines.

Buddhism had come to Japan in the 6th century. Along with *kanji* (Chinese characters) and tea, it spread throughout the archipelago. Emperor Shōmu hoped that making the new capital the center of Buddhism would unite the country and secure his position as head of an emergent nation state. The grandest of the Buddhist temples built in Nara during this era was Tōdai-ji, which Emperor Shōmu intended as a nexus for all the temples of his realm. But after 84 years the citadel of peace fell victim to the very intrigue that the Emperor had tried to suppress. In 794 the capital moved to Kyōto and Nara lost prominence, as did the Kegon sect that still manages Tōdai-ji today.

Now Nara is a provincial city whose most obvious role is a historical one, and Tōdai-ji is a monument rather than a political stronghold. Nara is a site of renewal and reinvention that has overcome typhoons, fires, and wars to remain a city of superlatives. Its position in the national consciousness as the birthplace of modern Japanese culture is well secured as it approaches its 1,300th anniversary in 2010.

⇨ *See the glossary at the end of this book for definitions of the common Japanese words and suffixes used in this chapter.*

ORIENTATION AND PLANNING

ORIENTATION

Almost at the center of the Japanese archipelago, Nara is on the Yamato plain, with Ōsaka to the west and Kyōto to the north. Much of what you'll come to Nara to see is in picturesque Nara Kōen (Nara Park), which is a short distance east of the two main stations. The commercial shopping district is south of Kintetsu Nara Station, while Sanjō-dōri, west of Nara Kōen and Nara-machi, has the two main tourist shopping areas. Hōryū-ji, Yakushi-ji, and Tōshōdai-ji, the major temples of western Nara, are all on one bus route or can be reached by JR train.

Nara Kōen. The broad and undulating Nara Kōen was created out of wasteland in 1880 and sits east of the Kasuga Mountain and the cleared slopes of Wakakusa-yama, in a dense forest. The park is home to some 1,200 tame deer, the focus of much local lore and legend.

TOP REASONS TO GO

Architecture: Nara's wealth of classical temples, pagodas, and shrines includes some of the world's oldest wooden structures. Crafted in the Chinese style, they evoke the vision of a new political order and a nation's religious and imperial odyssey.

Hospitality: The famously unaffected hospitality of Nara's citizens can best be experienced in a traditional, family-run inn.

Shopping: Locals in old wooden shops sell Nara's famous crafts: sumi (ink sticks) for calligraphy and ink painting, Nara sarashi (fine handwoven, sun-bleached linen), and akahadayaki pottery.

Local Eats: Renowned dishes include kaiseki; cha-gayu, green–tea-flavored rice porridge served with seasonal vegetables; and tangy nara-zuke, vegetables pickled in sake.

Tōdai-ji Temple Complex: The complex includes the Daibutsu-den (Hall of the Great Buddha), home to the monumental Great Buddha. The 8th-century San-gatsu-dō houses Tenpyo-era statues.

Nara-machi. This was the "new" area of Nara at the beginning of the Edo period (1600–1868). Today its lanes and alleys are still lined by old wooden houses with latticed windows and whitewashed walls. Many of these old houses have been converted into galleries, museums, and shops.

Western Nara. Hōryū-ji temple has the oldest wooden structures in the world and is considered the apotheosis of classical Japanese architecture. Tōshōdai-ji temple is where Ganjin, the first Buddhist monk to come to Japan from China, taught Japanese monks and legitimized the spread of Buddhism throughout the country.

PLANNING

WHEN TO GO

Spring (March to May) and autumn (September to November) are the best times to visit Nara. The cherry blossoms peak in late March–early April, and the turning foliage is at its brightest in late October–early November. Summer (June to August) is hot and sticky. June is when Japan's rainy season either drizzles for a few days and disappears or creates weeks of torrential downpours. There are often light snowfalls in winter (December to February).

HOW MUCH TIME?

Most visitors miss the best that Nara has to offer on hurried day trips from Kyōto, Ōsaka, or Kōbe. If time is an issue, the city is compact and well-connected enough to explore all the temples and shrines in Nara Kōen and spend a full morning or afternoon shopping and walking the streets of Nara-machi in one day. To make the most of this pleasant and relaxing city, an overnight stay is recommended. The city and park just beg to be discovered at a leisurely pace rather than packed into half-day time slot, not to mention the grand Hōryū-ji Temple on the outskirts of the city, less than 15 minutes away by train. The tranquil evening

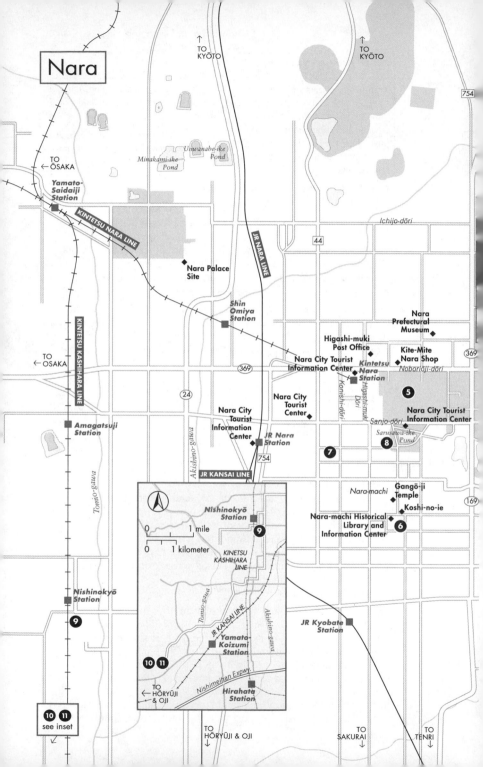

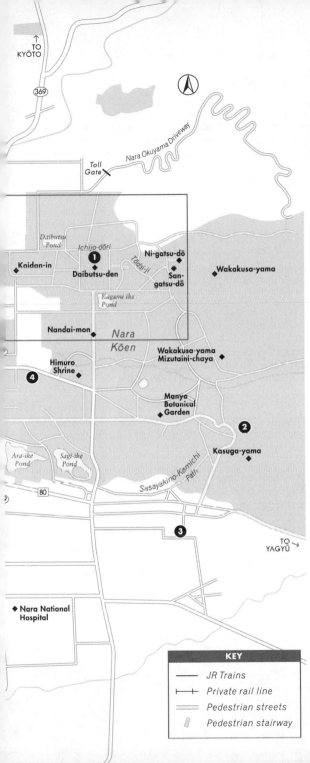

↑
TO
KYŌTO

369

Nara Okuyama Driveway

Toll
Gate

Daibutsu
Pond

Ichijo-dōri

Kaidan-in

Daibutsu-den

Tōdai-ji

Ni-gatsu-dō

San-
gatsu-dō

Wakakusa-yama

Kagami ike
Pond

Nandai-mon

Nara
Kōen

Wakakusa-yama
Mizutaini-chaya

Himuro
Shrine

Manyo
Botanical
Garden

Kasuga-yama

Ara-ike
Pond

Sagi-ike
Pond

Sasayakino-Komichi Path

80

TO
YAGYŪ →

Nara National
Hospital

KEY

—— JR Trains

├──┤ Private rail line

═══ Pedestrian streets

▌ Pedestrian stairway

atmosphere makes for a nice breather from Kyo[m]to and Ōsaka's hustle and bustle.

GETTING HERE AND AROUND

AIR TRAVEL

The nearest airports are in Ōsaka. All international and a few domestic flights use Kansai International Airport (KIX). Most domestic flights use Itami Airport. The hourly airport limousine bus from KIX takes 90 minutes and costs ¥1,800. From Itami, buses leave hourly, take 55 minutes, and cost ¥1,440.

BUS TRAVEL WITHIN NARA

Two local bus routes circle the main sites (Tōdai-ji, Kasuga Taisha, and Shin-Yakushi-ji) in the central and eastern parts of the city: Bus 1 runs counter-clockwise, and Bus 2 runs clockwise. Both stop at JR Nara Station and Kintetsu Nara Station and have a flat fare of ¥180.

Bus 97 heads west to Hōryū-ji (with stops at Tōshōdai-ji and Yakushi-ji), takes about 50 minutes and costs ¥760; you can catch it in front of either station. Pick up a bus map at the Nara City Tourist Center.

ON FOOT

With relatively flat roads, an abundance of greenery, and most of the major sights located within Nara Kōen, by far the best way to see Nara is on foot. Even the quaint, traditional streets of Nara-machi are a 10-minute walk from Nara's two central stations. For people with less time, most of the main sites can be reached by bicycle, except for those along the eastern edge of the park, such as the San-gatsu-dō, the Ni-gatsu-dō, and Kasuga Taisha.

TAXI TRAVEL

For small groups, short taxi rides within Nara city cost only slightly more than buses. Expect to pay about ¥1,000 to get to Kasuga Taisha from either of the main train stations.

TRAIN TRAVEL

From Kyōto, the best option is the private Kintetsu Railway's Limited Express trains, which leave every half hour for the 33-minute trip (¥1,110). Three JR trains from Kyōto run every hour. The express takes 45 minutes (change at Yamato-Saidai-ji); the two locals take 70 minutes. All JR trains cost ¥740 without a JR Pass.

From Ōsaka's Kintetsu Namba Station, Nara is a 31-minute ride on the hourly Limited Express (¥1,040) or 35 minutes by Ordinary Express train (¥540), which leaves every 20 minutes. The JR Line from Tennō-ji Station takes 50 minutes and costs ¥450; from JR Namba it costs ¥540 and takes 40 minutes; from Ōsaka Station it takes one hour and costs ¥780.

From Kōbe, take the JR Tōkaidō Line rapid train from San-no-miya Station to Ōsaka (around 25 minutes) and transfer to one of the trains listed above.

To get to Hōryū-ji Temple in western Nara, take a JR Main Line train from JR Nara Station. The ride to Hōryū-ji Station takes 11 minutes and costs ¥210.

VISITOR INFORMATION

The Japan Travel Bureau conducts daily bus tours to Nara. The five-hour (¥6,300) guided tour in English departs from Kyōto at 1:40. Reservations must be made one day in advance. The Student Guide Service and the YMCA Guide Service are free and leave from the JR Nara Station's Nara City Tourist Information Office and Kintetsu Nara Station. Reservations need to be made one day in advance.

The **Nara City Tourist Information Office** is on the first floor of Kintetsu Nara Station ; there's a branch at JR Nara Station. The **Nara City Tourist Information Center** has English-speaking staff on duty until 7 PM. The center is a 10-minute walk from both Kintetsu Nara Station and JR Nara Station and has free maps, sightseeing information in English, a souvenir corner, and a lounge.

ESSENTIALS

Currency Exchange Hotel Fujita Nara (⊠ *47–1 Shimo-sanjō-chō, Nara-shi, Nara-ken* ☎ *0742/23–8111* 🖷 *0742/22–0255* ⊕ *www.fujita-nara.com*).

Emergency Contacts Ambulance (☎ *119*). **Nara National Hospital** (⊠ *1 50 1 Higashi-kidera-chō, Nara-shi, Nara-ken* ☎ *0742/24–1251*). **Police** (☎ *110*).

Tour Information Japan Travel Bureau (☎ *075/341–1413*). **Student Guide Service** (⊠ *Nara City Sarusawa Tourist Information Office, 49 Nobori-ōji-chō, north side of Sarusawa-ike* ☎ *0742/26–4753*). **YMCA Guide Service** (☎ *0742/45–5920*).

Train Contacts JR Nara Station (⊠ *Sanjō-hon-chō, Nara-shi, Nara-ken* ☎ *0742/22–9821*). **Kintetsu Nara Station** (⊠ *29 Higashi-mukinaka-chō, Nara-shi, Nara-ken* ☎ *0742/24–4858* ⊕ *www.kintetsu.co.jp/foreign/english/useful/about_stations/3-4-nara.html*).

Visitor Information Nara City Tourist Information Office (⊠ *Kintetsu Nara Station, 29 Naka-machi, Higashi-muki, Nara-shi* ☎ *0742/24–4858 Daily 9-5 JR Nara Station, 1 Banchi Sanjō, Hon-machi, Nara-shi* ☎ *0742/22–9821*). **Nara City Tourist Information Center** (⊠ *23–4 Kami-sanjō-chō, Nara-shi* ☎ *0742/22–3900 Daily 9–5*).

EXPLORING NARA

NARA KŌEN 奈良公園

Nara Kōen has the city's popular tourist sites. Even so, it is wide enough to accommodate thousands of giggling school children and other Japanese tourists, yet still feel spacious and quiet. Be warned that it is home to many divine messengers of god—the tame deer seen just about everywhere. Legend has it that Takenomikazuchi-no-mikoto, one of the five gods of Kasuga Shrine, once landed atop Mt. Mikasa-yama riding a white deer. Since then these animals have been regarded as sacred messengers of Takenomikazuchi-no-mikoto and have been designated National Treasures. They very quickly convey the message that they want something to eat. *Shika-senbei* (deer crackers) are for sale throughout the park.

TOP ATTRACTIONS

❷ Kasuga Taisha 春日大社. ★ Famous for the more than 2,000 stone *manto[m]ro[m]* (lanterns) that line the major pathways, Kasuga Taisha is at once a monument to those who have paid tribute to the shrine's Shintō gods by dedicating a lantern, and to the Shintō tradition of worshipping nature. The lighting of the lanterns on three days of the year attracts large crowds that whisper with reverential excitement. February 3 is the Manto[m]ro[m] Festival, celebrating the beginning of spring, and August 14–15 is the Chugen Manto[m]ro[m] Festival, when the living show respect to their ancestors by lighting the way back to earth for them on their annual visit. As people take photographs with their mobile phones, the new messengers (men with loudspeakers) direct the well-behaved crowds. Kasuga Taisha was founded in 768 and for centuries, according to Shintō custom, the shrine was reconstructed every 20 years on its original design—not merely to renew the materials but also to purify the site. It's said that Kasuga Taisha has been rebuilt more than 50 times; its current incarnation dates from 1893. After you pass through the *torii* (orange gate), the first wooden structure you'll see is the **Hai-den** (Offering Hall); to its left is the **Naorai-den** (Entertainment Hall). To the left of Naorai-den are the four **Hon-den** (Main Shrines). They are designated as National Treasures, all built in the same Kasuga style and painted vermillion and green—a striking contrast to the dark wooden exterior of most other Nara temples.

To get to Kasuga Taisha from Nara Kōen, walk east past the Five-Story Pagoda until you reach a torii. This path will lead you to the shrine. ✉ *160 Kasuga-no-chō, Nara-shi* ☎ *0742/22–7788* 🌐 *Kasuga Shrine Museum ¥420; shrine's outer courtyard free; inner precincts with 4 Hon-den structures and gardens ¥500* ☉ *Museum daily 9–4; inner precincts Jan., Feb., and Dec., daily 7–4:30; Mar. and Nov., daily 7–5; Apr., daily 6:30–5:30; May–Sept., daily 6:30–6; Oct., daily 6:30–5:30.*

❶ Tōdai-ji Temple Complex 東大寺. ★ The temple complex was conceived by Emperor Shōmu in the 8th century as the seat of authority for Buddhist Japan. Construction was completed in 752, and even though the imperial household later left Nara, Tōdai-ji and its Great Buddha remained. An earthquake damaged it in 855, and in 1180 the temple was burned to the ground. Its reconstruction met a similar fate during the 16th-century civil wars. A century later only the central buildings were rebuilt; these are what remain today. Among the structures, the

---

DEER HUNTERS

Nara's symbolic deer have the run of the place and can be overly friendly when pursuing handouts from tourists, nibbling at bags and clothing. The deer also have little respect for traffic laws, so keep an eye open when out on the roads. Any deer that still have their antlers are of course capable of injuring humans if they feel threatened, so please act sensibly.

Behind the Ni-gatsu-dō is a lovely rest area where free water and cold tea are available 9–4. Although no food is sold, it's a quiet spot to picnic, unhindered by the antlered messengers.

GREAT WALK: NARA KŌEN

Kasuga Taisha is Nara's main shrine and one of Japan's three most important ones, along with Ise Jingu in Mie Prefecture and Izumo Taisha in Shimane. In a secluded spot at the foot of Kasuga-yama, this is reputedly where the gods first appeared in Japan. It's a 15-minute walk from the San-gatsu-dō. Beyond the lanterns of Kasuga Taisha is a refreshing 30-minute walk through a small forest that leads to Shin-Yakushi-ji temple, a treasure house of Nara-period sculpture. From Shin-Yakushi-ji it is a 30-minute walk back to central Nara Kōen, where the Five-Story Pagoda of Kōfuku-ji Temple leads you to its main hall and the magnificent statues therein. A couple of hours' strolling in the alleys of Nara-machi provides a change of pace from temple-hopping and is a good way to end the day.

Daibutsu-den is the grandest, with huge beams that seemingly converge upward toward infinity.

To get to Tōdai-ji, board Bus 2 from the front of either the JR or Kintetsu Nara station and exit at Daibutsu-den. Cross the street to the path that leads to the Tōdai-ji complex. You can walk from Kintetsu Nara Station in about 15 minutes by heading east on Noboriōji-dōri, the avenue running parallel to the station. In Nara Kōen turn left onto the pedestrians-only street, lined with souvenir stalls and restaurants, that leads to Tōdai-ji. A taxi from JR or Kintetsu Nara station costs about ¥1,000.

The following sites are close together, making this walk of about three hours, allowing for time to feed the deer.

Daibutsu-den 大仏殿 *(Hall of the Great Buddha)*. The Daibutsu-den is a rare example of monumentality in the land of the diminutive bonsai. Unfortunately the *kutsu-gata* (shoe-shaped) gilt ornaments that decorate the roof ridge of the Daibutsu-den did a lamentable job in their supposed ability to ward off fire. The current Daibutsu-den was restored in 1709 at two-thirds its original scale. At 157-feet tall and 187-feet wide, it's still considered the largest wooden structure in the world. If you want to ward off illness, follow the lead of those lighting incense at the huge bronze urn and waving it all over their bodies.

Inside the Daibutsu-den is the **Daibutsu**, a 53-foot bronze statue of the Buddha. His hand alone is the size of six tatami mats. The Daibutsu was originally commissioned by Emperor Shōmu in 743. After numerous unsuccessful castings, this figure was finally made in 749. A statue of this scale had never been cast before in Japan, and it was meant to serve as a symbol to unite the country. The Daibutsu was dedicated in 752 in a grand ceremony attended by the then-retired Emperor Shōmu, the imperial court, and 10,000 priests and nuns. The current Daibutsu is an amalgamation of work done in three eras: the 8th, 12th, and 17th centuries.

Patience may be a virtue, but here there is a fast track to enlightenment. Apparently, if you can squeeze through the hole in the pillar behind the Daibutsu you've achieved it. In a cruel irony, wisdom is thus bestowed upon children with ease while their elders struggle on. ⊠ *Tōdai-ji Temple Complex, 406-1 Zoushi-chō, Nara Kōen, Central Nara* 🖂 *¥500* ⊙ *Apr.–Sept., daily 7:30–5:30; Oct., daily 7:30–5; Nov.–Feb., daily 8–4:30; Mar., daily 8–5.*

> ### ARTS AND CRAFTS
>
> For an overview of the arts and crafts of Nara Prefecture, visit the Kite-Mite Nara Shop on your way to Nara Kōen. A brochure in English is available. **Kite-Mite Nara Shop** (⊠ *38-1 Noboriōji-chō, Nara-shi* ☎ *0742/26–8828* ⊙ *Tues.–Sun. 10–6; closed Mon.*).

Kaidan-in 戒檀院. A peaceful pebble garden in the courtyard of this small temple belies the ferocious expressions of the Four Heavenly Guardian clay statues inside. Depicted in full armor and wielding weapons, they are an arresting sight. *Kaidan* is a Buddhist word for the terrace on which monks are ordained; the Chinese Buddhist Ganjin (688–763) administered many induction ceremonies of Japanese Buddhists here. The current structure dates from 1731. Kaidan-in is in northwestern Nara Kōen, west of the Daibutsu-den. ⊠ *Tōdai-ji Temple Complex, 406-1 Zoushi-chou, Nara Kōen, Central Nara* 🖂 *¥500* ⊙ *Apr.–Sept., daily 7:30–5:30; Oct., daily 7:30–5; Nov.–Feb., daily 8–4:30; Mar., daily 8–5.*

Nandai-mon 南大門 *(Great Southern Gate).* The soaring Tōdai-ji Gate, the entrance to the temple, is supported by 18 large wooden pillars, each 62 feet high and nearly 3 feet in diameter. The original gate was destroyed in a typhoon in 962 and rebuilt in 1199. Two outer niches on either side of the gate contain fearsome wooden figures of Deva kings, who guard the great Buddha within. They are the work of master sculptor Unkei, of the Kamakura period (1185–1335). In the inner niches are a pair of stone *koma-inu* (Korean dogs), mythical guardians that ward off evil. ⊠ *Central Nara.*

Ni-gatsu-dō 二月堂 *(Second Month Temple).* Named for a ritual that begins in February and culminates in the spectacular sparks and flames of the Omizu-tori festival in March, the Ni-gatsu-dō was founded in 752. It houses important images of the Buddha that are, alas, not on display to the public. Still, its hilltop location and veranda afford a commanding view of Nara Kōen. ⊠ *Tōdai-ji Temple Complex, 406-1 Zoushi-chou, Nara Kōen, Central Nara* 🖂 *Free* ⊙ *Open 24 hrs.*

San-gatsu-dō 三月堂 *(Third Month Temple).* The San-gatsu-dō, founded in 733, is the oldest original building in the Tōdai-ji complex. It takes its name from the *sutra* (Buddhist scripture) reading ceremonies held here in the third month of the ancient lunar calendar (present-day February to April). You can sit on benches covered with tatami mats and appreciate the 1,200-year-old National Treasures that crowd the small room. The principal display is the lacquer statue of Fukūkensaku Kannon, the goddess of mercy, whose diadem is encrusted with thousands of pearls and gemstones. The two clay *bosatsu* (bodhisattva) statues on either side of her, the Gakkō (Moonlight) and the Nikkō (Sunlight), are fine examples of the *Tenpyo[m]* period (Nara period), the height of classical Japanese sculpture. The English pamphlet included with admission details all the statues in the San-gatsu-dō. ⊠ *Tōdai-ji Temple Complex, 406-1 Zoushi-chou, Nara Kōen, Central Nara* 📧 *¥500* 🕙 *Apr.–Sept., daily 7:30–5:30; Oct., daily 7:30–5; Nov.–Feb., daily 8–4:30; Mar., daily 8–5.*

NEED A BREAK?

At the foot of Wakakusa-yama and down some stone steps is **Wakakusa-yama Mizutani-chaya** 若草山水谷茶屋, a delightful old thatched-roofed farmhouse. You can order simple noodle dishes (¥650–¥750) and *matcha* whisked green tea (¥650). Alternatively, enjoy a cold beer (¥400) under the canopy of maple trees. ⊠ *30 Kasugano-chō Nara-shi* ☎ *0742/22–0627* 🕙 *Thurs.–Tues. 10–4:00 Food served 11–2.*

WORTH NOTING

⑤ Kōfuku-ji 興福寺. The Kōfuku-ji temple's Five-Story Pagoda dominates the skyline. Built in 1426, it's an exact replica of the original pagoda built here in 730 by Empress Komyo, which burned to the ground. At 164 feet it is the second-tallest in Japan, a few centimeters shorter than the pagoda at Tō-ji Temple in Kyōto. To the southwest of the Five-Story Pagoda, down a flight of steps, is the **Three-Story Pagoda.** Built in 1114, it is renowned for its graceful lines and fine proportions.

While the Five-Story Pagoda is Kōfuku-ji's most eye-catching building, the main attraction is the first-rate collection of Buddhist statues in the **Tōkondō** (Great Eastern Hall). A reconstruction dating from the 15th-century, the hall was built to speed the recovery of the ailing Empress Genshō. It is dominated by a statue of Yakushi Nyorai (Physician of the Soul) and is flanked by Four Heavenly Kings and Twelve Heavenly Generals. In contrast to the highly stylized and enlightened Yakushi Nyorai, the seated figure on the left is a statue of a mortal, Yuima Koji. A lay devotee of Buddhism, Yuima was respected for his eloquence but perhaps more revered for his belief that enlightenment could be accomplished through meditation even while mortal passions were indulged. Although Kōfuku-ji temple is no longer a religious mecca, you may see older Japanese writing on *ema* (votive plaques) left by pilgrims to ensure the happiness and safety of their families. The exquisite incense and the patina of the gold leaf on the drapery of the Yakushi Nyorai create a reflective experience.

Ironically, the architecturally contrasting concrete-and-steel **Kokuhōkan** (National Treasure House), north of Kōfuku-ji, houses the largest and most varied collection of National Treasure sculpture and other works of art. The most famous is a statue of Ashura, one of the Buddha's eight protectors, with three heads and six arms.

Kōfuku-ji is a five-minute walk west of Nara Kokuritsu Hakubutsukan (Nara National Museum) in the central part of Nara Kōen, and it's an easy 15-minute walk from the JR or Kintetsu station. ⊠ *48 Noborioji-chō, Nara-shi* ☎ *0742/22–7755* 📧 *Great Eastern Hall ¥300, National Treasure House ¥500* 🕙 *Daily 9–5.*

7

FIRE FESTIVALS AND LIGHT-UPS IN NARA

To light up doesn't mean to have a cigarette in Japan. In fact, most light-ups are at temples and shrines where, unlike most public spaces in Japan, smoking is banned. Below are the more dramatic illuminations on the Nara festival calendar.

JANUARY
Wakakusa-yama Yaki (Grass Burning Festival). On the night before the second Monday in January, 15 priests set Wakakusa-yama's dry grass afire while fireworks illuminate Kōfuku-ji's Five-Story Pagoda in one of Japan's most photographed rituals. This rite is believed to commemorate the resolution of a boundary dispute between the monks and priests of Tōdai-ji and Kōfuku-ji. The fireworks start at 5:50 and the grass fire is lit at 6.

FEBRUARY
Manto[m]ro[m] (Lantern Festival). On February 3 the 2,000 stone and 1,000 bronze lanterns at Kasuga Taisha are lighted to mark the traditional end of winter called *setsubun*. Between 6 PM and 8:30 PM.

MARCH
Shuni-e Omizutori (Water Drawing Festival). From March 1 to 14 priests circle the upper gallery of the Ni-gatsu-dō (Second Month Hall) wielding 21-foot-long *taimatsu* (bamboo torches) weighing more than 80 kg, while sparks fall on those below. Catching the embers burns out sins and wards off evil. This festival is more than 1,200 years old, a rite of repentance to the Eleven-Headed Kannon, an incarnation of the Goddess of Mercy. These evening events happen March 1–11 and 13, 7–7:20; March 12 7:30–8:15; March 14, for 5 minutes from 6:30.

JULY–OCTOBER
Light-up Promenade. Sights including Yakushi-ji, Kōfuku-ji, and Tōdai-ji are illuminated at night. July, August, September 7–10, and October 6–10.

AUGUST
To[m]ka-e. From August 1 to 15 Nara Kōen is aglow with more than 7,000 candles from 7 to 9:45.

Chu[m]gen Manto[m]ro[m] (Mid-year Lantern Festival). For more than 800 years the thousands of lanterns at Kasuga Taisha have been lit to guide ancestors back to earth on their annual pilgrimage, Obon. August 14–15, 7 to 9:30 PM.

4 **Nara National Museum** 奈良国立博物館 *(Nara Kokuritsu Hakubutsukan).* The original museum, built in 1895, houses the museum's permanent collection of sculpture from Japan, Korea, and China. The main focus is on the Nara and Heian periods. The West Wing has paintings, calligraphy, ceramics, and archaeological artifacts from Japan, some dating back to the 10th-century BC. The East Wing is used for temporary exhibitions. During the driest days of November the Shōsō-in Repository, behind the Tōdai-ji, displays some of its magnificent collection. ✉ *50 Noborioji-chō* ☎ *0742/22–7771* 🎫 *¥500* ⊗ *Tues.–Sun., daily 9:30–5; enter by 4:30.*

3 **Shin-Yakushi-ji** 新薬師寺. This temple was founded in 747 by Empress Kōmyō (701–760) in gratitude for the recovery of her sick husband, Emperor Shōmu. Only the Main Hall, which houses many fine objects from the Nara period, remains. In the center of the hall is a wooden statue of Yakushi Nyorai, the Physician of the Soul. Surrounding this statue are 12 clay images of the Twelve Divine Generals who protected Yakushi. Eleven of these figures are originals. The Generals stand in threatening poses, bearing spears, swords, and other weapons, and wear terrifying expressions. ✉*1289 Takabatake-chō* ☎*0742/22–3736* 🎫*¥600* 🕐*Daily 9–5.*

NARA-MACHI 奈良町

Nara-machi is a maze of lanes and alleys lined with old warehouses and *machiya* (traditional wooden houses) that have been converted into galleries, shops, and cafés. A lot of locals still live here, so the smell of grilled mackerel at lunchtime or roasted tea in the afternoon wafts through the air. Many of the old shops deal in Nara's renowned arts and crafts, such as akahadayaki pottery, ink, and linen. A free map, available from any Nara City Tourism Information Office, guides you to the main shops, museums, and galleries, as do English signposts. Nara-machi is a good change of pace from temple viewing.

We've noted usual hours, but stores can close irregularly. Ask at the Nara City Tourist Information Center if you'd like to check before you set out. From the southwest corner of Sarusawa-ike, with the pond notice board on your left, walk straight until you come to a main road, on the other side of which is the center of Nara-machi.

7

WHAT TO SEE

❻ Akahadayaki 赤膚焼. A potter's wheel is in the window of Akahadayaki, where beautiful ceramic candleholders (*tōkaki*) illuminate the rooms with leaf and geometric patterns. The tōkaki and ceramics at Akahadayaki are all handmade, original designs. ✉*18 Shibashinya-chō, Nara-machi* ☎*0742/23–3110* 🕐*Thurs.–Tues. 10:30–5.*

❼ Kobaien 古梅園. Nara accounts for about 90% of Japan's *sumi*-ink production, and for 400 years Kobaien has made fine ink sticks for calligraphy and ink painting. More recently, some types of sumi-ink have been used for tattooing. ✉*7 Tsubai-chō, Nara-machi* ☎*0742/23–2965* 🕐*Weekdays 9–5.*

NEED A BREAK?

Koshi-no-ie is a well-to-do merchant's house that has been thoroughly restored. It's like a quick trip through the Edo period. English pamphlets are available. ✉*44 Gango[m]-ji-chō, Nara-shi* ☎*0742/23–4820 Free* 🕐*Tues.– Sun. 9–5.*

❽ "Yū" Nakagawa 遊中川. "Yū" Nakagawa specializes in hand-woven, sun-bleached linen textiles, a Nara specialty known as *Nara Sarashi*. This shop sells *noren* (two-panel curtains put on business entranceways to show that they are open), handbags, slippers, and other linen crafts incorporating traditional Nara motifs. ✉*31–1 Ganrin-in-chō, Nara-machi* ☎*0742/22–1322* 🕐*Daily 11–6.*

WESTERN NARA 奈良西部

Hōryū-ji is home to some of the oldest wooden buildings in the world. Just east of Hōryū-ji is Chūgū-ji, with one of the finest sculptures in Japan, the 7th-century Miroku Bodhisattva. A short bus ride back toward Nara brings you to Yakushi-ji and Tōshōdai-ji temples, both religious and political centers during the Nara period. To visit all four temples in one day go to Hōryū-ji by the JR Main Line first (Chūgū-ji is a 10-minute walk from Hōryū-ji) and proceed to Tōshōdai-ji and Yakushi-ji by bus.

TOP ATTRACTIONS

⑩ Hōryū-ji 法隆寺. Hōryū-ji is the jewel in the crown of classical Japanese

Fodor's Choice architecture. In the morning, elderly locals on their way to work pray

★ in front of the temple with an intensity the younger generation usually displays toward manga and *puri-kura* (photo stickers). Founded in 607 by Prince Shōtoku (573–621), Hōryū-ji's original wooden buildings are among the world's oldest. The first gate you pass through is the **Nandai-mon,** which was rebuilt in 1438 and is thus a relatively young 500 years old. The second gate, **Chū-mon** (Middle Gate), is the 607 original. Unlike most Japanese gates, which are supported by two pillars at the ends, central pillars support this gate. Note their entasis, or swelling at the center, an architectural feature from ancient Greece that traveled as far as Japan. Such columns are found in Japan only in the 7th-century structures of Nara.

After passing through the gates, you enter the temple's western precincts. The first building on the right is the **Kon-dō** (Main Hall), a two-story reproduction of the original 7th-century hall, which displays Buddhist images and objects from as far back as the Asuka period (552–645). The Five-Story Pagoda to its left was disassembled in World War II to protect it from air raids, after which it was reconstructed with the same materials used in 607. Behind the pagoda is the **Daikō-dō** (Lecture Hall), destroyed by fire and rebuilt in 990. Inside is a statue of Yakushi Nyorai (Physician of the Soul) carved from a camphor tree.

From the Daikō-dō, walk past the Kon-dō and Chū-mon; then turn left and walk past the pond on your right. You come to two concrete buildings known as the **Daihōzō-den** (Great Treasure Hall), which display statues, sculptures, ancient Buddhist religious articles, and brocades. Of particular interest is a miniature shrine that belonged to Lady Tachibana, mother of Empress Kōmyō. The shrine is about 2½ feet high; the Buddha inside is about 20 inches tall.

Tōdai-mon (Great East Gate) opens onto Hōryū-ji's eastern grounds. The octagonal **Yumedono** (Hall of Dreams) was so named because Prince Shōtoku used to meditate in it.

To get here, take a JR Kansai Main Line train to Hōryū-ji Station (¥210). The temple is a short shuttle ride or a 15-minute walk. Alternatively, Bus 52, 60, or 97 to Hōryū-ji is a 50-minute ride from the JR Nara station or Kintetsu Nara Station (¥760). The Hōryūji-mae bus stop is in front of the temple. ⊠ *1–1 Ikaruga-chō, Hōryū-ji, Ikoma-gun, Nara-ken, Western Nara* ☎ *0745/75–2555* ⊠ *¥1,000* ⊗ *Feb. 22–Nov.*

3, daily 8–5; Nov. 4–Feb. 21, daily 8–4:30; last entry 30 min before closing.

WORTH NOTING

⑪ **Chūgū-ji** 中宮寺. Chūgū-ji was originally the home of Prince Shōtoku's mother in the 6th-century and is now a Buddhist nunnery. This temple houses an amazing wooden statue of the Miroku Bodhisattva, the Buddha of the Future. His gentle countenance has been a famous image of hope since it was carved, sometime in the Asuka period (552–645). Chūgū-ji is a few minutes' walk north of the Yumendono. ✉1–1–2 Ikaruga-chō, Hōryū-ji Kita, Ikoma-gun, Nara-ken, Western Nara ☎0745/75–2106 ☜¥500 ⊙Apr.–Sept., daily 9–4:30; Oct.–Mar., daily 9–4.

⑨ **Yakushi-ji** 薬師寺. The two pagodas
★ that tower over Yakushi-ji temple are an analogy of past and present Japan. Yakushi-ji's **East Pagoda** dates from 1285, and has such an interesting asymmetrical shape that it inspired Boston Museum of Fine Arts curator Ernest Fenollosa (1853–1908), an early Western specialist in Japanese art, to remark that it was as beautiful as "frozen music." Its simple, dark brown beams with white ends contrast starkly with its flashier, vermillion painted 20th-century neighbor, the **West Tower**, built in 1981. For many, the new goes against the "imperfect, impermanent, and incomplete" principles of the old *wabi-sabi* aesthetic; but we think the contrast dynamizes Yakushi-ji right into the 21st-century. Officially named one of the Seven Great Temples of Nara, Yakushi-ji was founded in 680 and moved to its current location in 718. From central Nara take either the Kintetsu Line train, changing at Yamato-Saidaiji to Nishinokyō, or Bus 52 or 97 to Yakushi-ji; from Hōryū-ji or Chūgū-ji, take Bus 97 to Yakushi-ji-mae. ✉457 Nishinokyō-chō, Nara-shi, Western Nara ☎0742/33–6001 ☜¥800/¥500 depending on event/season ⊙Daily 8:30–5.

SUBSTITUTE MONKEYS

So just what are those red cloth animals on pieces of rope outside houses in Nara? They are *migawarizaru* (substitute monkeys), inscribed with the phrase "*kanaianzen mubyo[m]-sokusai*" ("good health and safety for the family"). There is a monkey for every member of a household that suffers illness and accidents on behalf of its owner. The **Nara-machi Shiryōkan** 奈良町資料館 *(Nara-machi Historical Library and Information Center)* displays artifacts from the Edo period (1600–1868) to the present. It's near Gangō-ji temple. ✉12 Nishi Shinyu-chō, Nara-machi ☎0742/22–5509 ⊙Sat., Sun., and national holidays only, 10–4.

7

WHERE TO EAT

It's a sin to visit Nara and not have a *kaiseki* dinner, an aesthetically arranged 7- to 12-course set meal using the freshest ingredients. It's usually an evening meal, but most kaiseki restaurants serve mini-kaiseki at lunchtime for day-trippers. Most traditional restaurants are small and have set courses. Nara retires early, and restaurants close around 10 PM, taking last orders around 9 PM. Small restaurants and *izakaya* (after-work drinking haunts that serve an array of small dishes and drinks) are dispersed throughout the two main shopping streets, Higashi-muki

CLOSE UP

Try, Try, Try Again

Tōshōdai-ji 唐招提寺 was built in 751 for Ganjin, a Chinese priest who traveled to Japan at the invitation of Emperor Shōmu. At that time Japanese monks had never received formal instruction from a Buddhist monk. The invitation was extended by two Japanese monks who had traveled to China in search of a Buddhist willing to undertake the arduous and perilous journey to Japan.

It seemed that Ganjin would never make it to Japan. On his first journey some of his disciples betrayed him. His second journey resulted in a shipwreck. During the third trip his ship was blown off course, and on his fourth trip government officials refused him permission to leave China. Before his next attempt, he contracted an eye disease that left him blind. He persevered nonetheless, and finally reached Japan in 750. Ganjin shared his knowledge of Buddhism with his adopted country and served as a teacher to many Japanese abbots as well as Emperor Shōmu. He is also remembered for bringing the first sampling of sugar to Japan. Every June 6, to commemorate his birthday, the **Miei-dō** (Founder's Hall) in the back of the temple grounds displays a lacquer statue of Ganjin that dates from 763.

The main entrance to Tōshōdai-ji is called the Path of History, since in Nara's imperial days dignitaries and priests trod this route; today it is lined with clay-walled houses, gardens, and the occasional shop selling crafts or nara-zuke.

At the temple's entrance entastic pillars support the **Nandai-mon** (Great South Gate). Beyond the Nandai-mon is the **Kon-dō** (Main Hall), a superb example of classical Nara architecture. It is due to be under restoration until autumn 2009. Inside the hall is a lacquer statue of Vairocana Buddha, the same incarnation of Buddha that is enshrined at Tōdai-ji. The halo surrounding him was originally covered with 1,000 Buddhas; now there are 864. In back of the Kon-dō sits the **Daikō-dō** (Lecture Hall), formerly an assembly hall of the Nara Imperial Court, the only remaining example of Nara palace architecture.

Tōshōdai-ji is a 10-minute walk from the rear gate of Yakushi-ji along the Path of History. From central Nara or Hōryū-ji, take Bus 52 or 97 to the stop in front of Tōshōdai-ji. ✉ 13–46 Gojō-chō, Nara-shi, Western Nara ☎ 0742/33–7900 💴 ¥600 ⊙ Daily 8:30–5.

Dōri (a pedestrian arcade) and Konishi-dōri, close to Kintetsu Nara Station.

When ordering food, start by asking for an *osusume* (a suggestion) and go from there. Don't be embarrassed or afraid to communicate, even without Japanese, as people in Nara look after their visitors. But keep in mind that each time you eat some delicious sashimi or order tempura you add ¥600–¥900 to your bill. Learning a language can be expensive! Expect to pay about ¥750 for a large bottle of beer. Because English-speaking staff and English menus aren't givens, ask a staff member from your hotel to help make arrangements. Alternatively, stay in a *ryokan* (traditional inn), where a kaiseki dinner is included in the room rate.

⇨ *For more on Japanese cuisine, see Understanding Japan and Dining in Essentials.*

WHAT IT COSTS IN YEN				
¢	$	$$	$$$	$$$$
At Dinner	under ¥800	¥800–¥1,000	¥1,000–¥2,000	¥2,000–¥3,000	over ¥3,000

Restaurant prices are per person for a main course, set meal, or equivalent combinations of smaller dishes.

NARA KŌEN AREA

$$$$
JAPANESE
★

✕**Onjaku** 温石. Hidden down a quiet street just south of Ara-ike in Nara Kōen is this intimate restaurant serving exquisitely presented traditional kaiseki meals. Within the faded wooden walls, a common architectural motif in Nara, you can sit at a rustic counter or in one of two serene tatami rooms. Choose from one of the two set meals. ⊠*1043 Kitatemma-chō, Nara Kōen Area* ☎*0742/26–4762* ⚖*Reservations essential* ⊟*No credit cards* ☯*Lunch: noon–1; dinner: 6–7:30. Closed Tues.*

$$$$
JAPANESE

✕**Tō-no-chaya** 塔の茶屋. One of Nara's most distinctive meals is *chagayu* (green tea–flavored rice porridge). During the day Tō-no-chaya serves a light meal of this special dish, with sashimi and vegetables, plus a few sweetened rice cakes for dessert. The restaurant was named Tō-no-chaya, which means "tearoom of the pagoda," for its views of the Five-Story Pagoda of Kōfuku-ji. Bento[m]-box meals are served 11:30–4 (¥3,000). You must reserve ahead for cha-gayu in the evening. ⊠*47 Noborioji-chō, Nara Kōen Area* ☎*0742/22–4348* ⊟*No credit cards* ☯*Closed Tues.*

$$$$
JAPANESE
★

✕**Tsukihitei** 月日亭. Deep in the forest behind Kasuga Taisha, Tsukihitei has the perfect setting for kaiseki. From the walk up a wooded path to the tranquility of your own tatami room, everything is conducive to experiencing the beautiful presentation and delicate flavors—as Hellen Keller did when she dined at Tsukihitei in 1948. When reserving a table, enlist the help of a good Japanese speaker to select a set meal for you, and allow yourself to be regaled. The lunch sets cost between ¥10,000 and ¥15,000. ⊠*158 Kasugano-chō, Nara Kōen Area* ☎*0742/26–2021* ⚖*Reservations essential* ⊟*AE, DC, MC, V.*

$$$$
JAPANESE
★

✕**Uma no Me** 馬の目. In a little 1920s farmhouse just north of Ara-ike pond in Nara Kōen this delightful restaurant with dark beams and pottery-lined walls serves delicious home-style cooking. Everything is prepared from scratch. Recommended is the ¥3,500 lunch course with seasonal vegetables, tofu, and fried fish. As there is only one set meal, ordering is no problem. ⊠*1158 Takabatake-chō, Nara Kōen Area* ☎*0742/23–7784* ⚖*Reservations essential* ⊟*No credit cards* ☯*Closed Thurs.*

$$–$$$
JAPANESE

✕**Yamazakiya** 山崎屋. Pungent nara-zuke will lure you into this well-known shop and adjoining restaurant. Inside, white-capped prep cooks busily prepare packages of pickles that you can try with cha-gayu or a meal of tempura. The set menus are on display, making ordering simple. This is a good place to escape the crowds on Higashi-muki Dōri, the main shopping street. Nara Kintetsu Station and Nara Kōen are within a five-minute walk. ⊠*5 Minami-machi-chō Higashi-muki Dōri, Nara Kōen Area* ☎*0742/27–3715* ⊟*DC, MC, V* ☯*Closed Mon.*

7

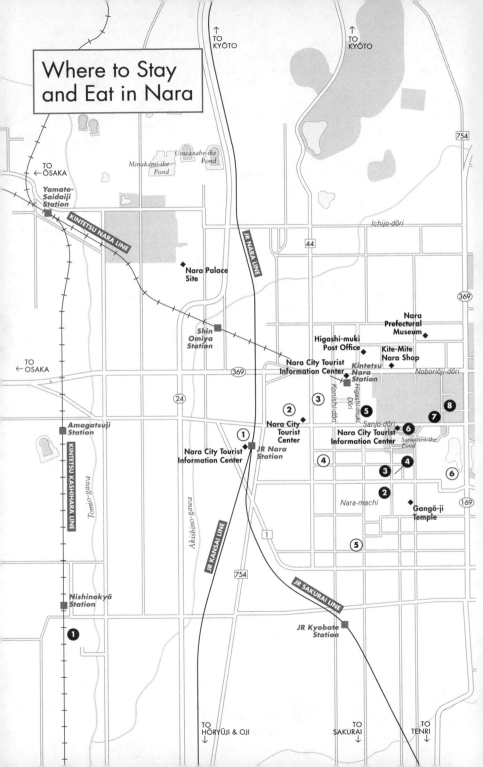

Where to Stay and Eat in Nara

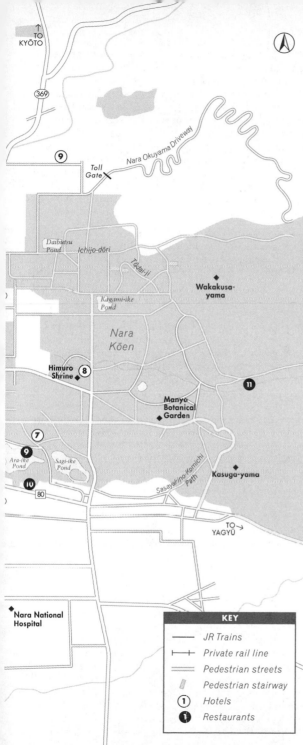

KEY

——	JR Trains
⊢—⊢	Private rail line
═══	Pedestrian streets
▱	Pedestrian stairway
①	Hotels
❶	Restaurants

\$\$\$\$
JAPANESE
★

✗**Yanagi-ja-ya** 柳茶屋. At this main branch of this Nara institution in Nara Kōen, just past the Five-Story Pagoda, you may find yourself just popping in to try some *warabi mochi* for morning or afternoon tea. Delicious morsels made from warabi (bracken fern root) are tossed in soybean flour and sweetened with brown sugar syrup. At a second branch, the unassuming exterior belies an elegant interior. You're transported to a bygone age in a secluded tatami room overlooking a garden where you'll be served simple bento[m] meals of sashimi, stewed vegetables, and tofu in black-lacquer boxes. Lunch costs ¥4,000–¥6,000. ⊠*4–48 Noborio[m]ji-chō, Nara Kōen Area* ☎*0742/22–7560* ⚲*Reservations essential* ▤*No credit cards* ◔*11–5. Closed Mon. 49 Noboriōji-chō, Nara Kōen Area* ☎*0742/22–7460* ⚲*Reservations essential* ▤*No credit cards* ◔*Closed Wed.*

NARA-MACHI

\$\$\$–\$\$\$\$
JAPANESE

✗**Harishin** はり新. Harishin's Kamitsumichi bento[m], with a selection of sashimi, tofu, fried shrimp, vegetables, and homemade plum liqueur, is a bargain for ¥2,900. Harishin is traditional and quite rustic. You sit in either a large tatami room overlooking a garden or around a large *irori* (hearth). ⊠*15 Nakashinya-chō, Nara-machi* ☎*0742/22–2669* ▤*AE, D, MC, V* ◔*Closed Mon.*

\$\$\$–\$\$\$\$
JAPANESE

✗**Hirasō** 平宗. At Hirasō you can try *kakinoha-zushi*, sushi wrapped in a persimmon leaf. What's more, you can take it away in a light wooden box wrapped with precision. Most set menus at Hirasō include *chagayu* (rice porridge flavored with green tea), which is usually made with mushrooms or seasonal vegetables. Another featured Nara delicacy is *kakisuga,* dried persimmon, dusted with *kudzu* (flour made from the East Asian kudzu vine) or arrowroot powder and cooked tempura style. Hirasō has tables and chairs, but the tatami alcoves are more intimate. It's open all day, and take-out sushi is available from 10 to 8:30. ⊠*30–1 Imamikado-chō630-8374* ☎*0742/22–0866* ▤*AE, DC, MC, V* ◔*Closed for eat-in meals on Mon.*

\$\$\$–\$\$\$\$
JAPANESE

✗**Tempura Asuka** 天ぷら飛鳥. If you choose from the selection of set meals, make sure you pick one with tempura—the house specialty. Other fare ranges from a light tempura-soba lunch to an elaborate kaiseki dinner. Lunch options start at ¥1,200. As with other less formal Nara-machi restaurants, you can sit at the counter, at a table overlooking the garden, or in a tatami room. ⊠*11 Shōnami-chō, Nara-machi* ☎*0742/26–4308* ▤*AE, DC, MC, V* ◔*Closed Mon.*

WESTERN NARA

\$\$\$–\$\$\$\$
JAPANESE

✗**Van Kio** 萬京. This large restaurant is famous for its *tamatebako* set meal. Different foods are put into beautiful paper boxes, sealed inside an earthenware bowl, and then theatrically smashed open with a wooden mallet. Apparently this custom is utilized on first dates with some success. Other specialties from the menu (in English) include the Renge set lunch, eight *obanzai* (samples) of local Japanese food arranged on spoons including *kakinoha-zushi* (sushi wrapped in a persimmon leaf). From the sumptuous dining room you look out onto a garden bordered by Japanese stone lanterns in different shapes and sizes—all for sale. It's a short walk from Yakushi-ji's south gate. ⊠*410 Rokujō-chō, Western Nara* ☎*0742/33–8942* ▤*MC, V* ◔*Closed Mon.*

WHERE TO STAY

Nara has accommodations in every style and price range. Since most people treat the city as a day-trip destination, at night the quiet streets are the domain of Nara's residents. All lodgings have air-conditioning, televisions, and communal baths unless noted otherwise. Some ryokan close on Sunday nights. Hotels in Central Nara around the main railway stations are often noisier than those closer to Nara Kōen and in Naramachi. During spring and autumn and peak holiday periods, rooms are hard to find on weekend nights. Book well in advance if you plan to travel to Nara during these times.

For a short course on accommodations in Japan, see Accommodations in Travel Smart.

WHAT IT COSTS IN YEN				
	¢	$	$$	$$$	$$$$
For 2 People	under ¥8,000	¥8,000–¥12,000	¥12,000–¥18,000	¥18,000–¥22,000	over ¥22,000

Hotel price categories are based on rack rates in high season and the European Plan (with no meals) unless otherwise noted. Tax (5%) and service charges are extra.

NARA KŌEN AREA

$$$$ ☎ **Edo-San** 江戸三. You can't get closer to the deer than this. Individual cottages, some with thatched roofs in the greenery of Nara Kōen, are what Edo-San is all about. Indulge in a kaiseki dinner served in your cottage while you gaze through a large round window out into the park. One cottage has a private bath, and there's a communal bath for other guests. The one drawback is its proximity to a noisy major road. **Pros:** located in Nara Kōen; closest neighbors are the deer. **Cons:** traffic nearby can be heard; English not spoken. ⊠*1167 Takabatake-chō, Nara-shi, Nara-ken* ☎*0742/26–2662* 🖷*0742/26–2663* ⊕*www. edosan.jp* ➪*10 Japanese-style cottages* ⚭*In-hotel: parking (no fee)* ⊟*AE, DC, MC, V* ⎟◯⎟*MAP.*

$$ ☎ **Hotel Nara Club** 奈良倶楽部. On a street of old houses with traditional gardens, this small hotel is reminiscent of a European pension. The small, plainly decorated rooms have simple, dark-wood furniture and private bathrooms. Here you're away from the hustle and bustle, while it's only a scenic 20-minute walk from Tōdai-ji. A meal plan is available. **Pros:** peaceful location; not far from main sights; home-cooked food using local produce. **Cons:** 20-40 minutes' walk from the stations; have single, twin, and family rooms, but no doubles. ⊠*21 Kita Mikado-chō, Nara-shi, Nara-ken* ☎*0742/22–3450* 🖷*0742/22–3490* ⊕*www.nara club.com* ➪*8 rooms* ⚭*In-room: Internet (some), refrigerator. In-hotel: Internet terminal, parking (no fee), no-smoking rooms* ⊟*AE, V.*

$$$$ ☎ **Kankasō** 観鹿荘. At once exquisitely refined and delightfully friendly,
★ Kankasō exemplifies the best of Japanese hospitality. Beautiful gardens surround this peaceful ryokan near Tōdai-ji, and inside, elegant ikebana arrangements adorn the alcove. Each room is decorated with scrolls and pottery. Although the building has been renovated over the centuries,

7

its 1,200-year-old central beam testifies to its longevity. The communal baths look out onto the gardens. A delicious kaiseki dinner is included, as is breakfast. **Pros:** long history of serving foreign guests; traditional Japanese building; beautifully decorated; very convenient to Nara Kōen. **Cons:** English not spoken. ✉ *10 Kasugano-chō, Nara-shi, Nara-ken* ☎ *0742/26–1128* 🖷 *0742/26–1301* ⊕ *www.kankaso.jp/* ⛵ *9 Japanese-style rooms (5 with bath)* ⚘ *In-room: safe, refrigerator (some), Internet. In-hotel: restaurant, bar, parking (paid)* ▤ *MC, V* ⦿ *MAP.*

$$$$
Fodor'sChoice
★
▦ **Nara Hotel** 奈良ホテル. No wonder the Emperor stays here. Built in 1909, when Western architecture was all the rage, the hotel has high ceilings, wide hallways, and sumptuous beds fit for, well, an emperor. The filigree-pattern light shades and silver-painted room heaters are all original. Although most rooms have a good view of the gardens or the temples, those in the new wing are not as grand as the turn-of-the-20th-century-style rooms in the old wing. Dinner is a special event in the old-fashioned Edwardian-style dining room, where French food is served. **Pros:** very spacious rooms; top-class service; imperial atmosphere . . . **Cons:** . . . but it doesn't come cheap. ✉ *1093 Takabatake-chō, Nara-shi, Nara-ken* ☎ *0742/26–3300* 🖷 *0742/23–5252* ⊕ *www.narahotel. co.jp* ⛵ *129 rooms, 3 suites* ⚘ *In-room: refrigerator, Internet. In-hotel: 2 restaurants, bar, laundry service, parking (free), no-smoking rooms* ▤ *AE, DC, MC, V.*

NARA-MACHI

$
▦ **Ryokan Seikansō** 旅館静観荘. Of the many inexpensive, small ryokans in Nara-machi, this family-run establishment is the best pick for its spotlessness and attentive service. The quiet neighborhood contributes to the inn's relaxed atmosphere. Simple rooms overlook a large central garden. It's very popular, so it's best to book far in advance. **Pros:** cheap and cheerful; great breakfasts; friendly service **Cons:** rooms are clean but getting on in years; shared bathing and toilet facilities only. ✉ *29 Higashikitsuji-chō, Nara-shi, Nara-ken* ☎ *0742/22–2670* ⛵ *9 Japanese-style rooms* ⚘ *In-room: no telephone. In-hotel: Internet, parking (free)* ▤ *AE, MC, V.*

WESTERN NARA

$$–$$$
▦ **Hotel Fujita Nara** ホテルフジタ奈良. Centrally situated between JR Nara Station and Nara Kōen, this modern hotel is often the best deal in town. Rates vary depending on the season, and drop considerably outside the April and November peak periods. The rooms are spacious and decorated in pastel tones. The pale-pink wave-shaped lighting arrangement in the atrium harks back to the '80s economic "bubble." There are two restaurants, one of which, Hanakagami, serves Japanese cuisine. **Pros:** central location; bicycle rental available. **Cons:** reasonable prices are rising steadily. ✉ *47–1 Shimo Sanjō-chō, Nara-shi, Nara-ken* ☎ *0742/23–8111* 🖷 *0742/22–0255* ⊕ *www.fujita-nara.com* ⛵ *114 rooms, 3 suites* ⚘ *In-room: refrigerator, Internet (some). In-hotel: 2 restaurants, bar, Wi-Fi, parking (paid), no-smoking rooms* ▤ *AE, DC, MC, V.*

$$$
▦ **Hotel Nikko Nara** ホテル日航奈良. Nara's largest hotel provides comfort in plush surroundings. Rooms have large windows and are generally quite bright. The thick carpets and wooden flooring in the bathrooms

of the larger twins give a feeling of solidity not always found in hotels of a similar price range. Close to downtown restaurants, the hotel is atop a shopping arcade next to Nara JR Station. The lobby, however, is on the third floor and can be difficult to find. Given its location, the rooms are remarkably quiet. All rooms have private baths, and there's a communal bath as well. **Pros:** directly connected to JR Nara Station; courteous staff. **Cons:** rooms and bathrooms are relatively small. ✉ *8–1 Sanjō-honmachi, Nara-shi, Nara-ken* ☎*0742/35–8831* 📠*0742/35–6868* ⊕*www.nikkonara.jp* 🛏*330 rooms, 1 suite* ⚙*In-room: refrigerator, Internet. In-hotel: 4 restaurants, Japanese baths, laundry service, Internet terminal, parking (paid), no-smoking rooms* 🖃*AE, D, MC, V.*

$$ 🏯**Ryokan Nanto** 旅館南都. The quietest ryokan on the city side of Nara Kōen, Nanto has airy tatami rooms of a simplicity fit for a Zen-practicing samurai. Internal dry rock gardens are throughout the mazelike collection of rooms, which makes finding the communal bath an adventure. Most rooms have toilets, some have baths, and there are large rooms for families and small groups. A Japanese breakfast is included. Ryokan Nanto is halfway between Kintetsu Nara Station and JR Nara Station. **Pros:** family-friendly; located right between the two stations. **Cons:** credit cards not accepted. ✉ *29 Kamisanjō-chō, Nara-shi, Nara-ken* ☎*0742/22–3497* 📠*0742/23–0882* ⊕*www.basho.net/nanto* 🛏*13 Japanese-style rooms, 3 with bath* ⚙*In-hotel: restaurant, parking (fee)* 🖃*No credit cards* 🍴*CP.*

$$$$ 🏯**Tsubakisō** 旅館椿荘. Friendly service and an internal garden make for a relaxed stay in this quiet mix of old and new. Rooms in the newer wing have suites with private baths, whereas rooms in the old wing share a communal bath. A *cha-gayu* (rice porridge flavored with green tea) breakfast is served in the dining room overlooking the garden. Prices include a kaiseki dinner and breakfast, and there are reduced prices for longer stays (three nights or more). Tsubakisō is down a quiet side street in central Nara, about a 10-minute walk from either of the main train stations. **Pros:** lovely garden; central yet quiet location; vegetarian meals available upon request. **Cons:** communal bathing is not for the shy. ✉ *35 Tsubai-chō, Nara-shi, Nara-ken* ☎*0742/22–5330* 📠*0742/27–3811* 🛏*7 Japanese-style rooms, 3 with bath* ⚙*In-room: refrigerator, Internet. In-hotel: Internet terminal, Wi-Fi, parking (paid)* 🖃*AE, MC, V* 🍴*MAP.*

7

Ōsaka

WORD OF MOUTH

"The Ōsaka Unlimited pass has outstanding value for the money. This pass covers travel on the Ōsakan subways (not JR line though) and free or discounted entry to museums, restaurants and other tourist locations. With a little planning and an early start, it's certainly possible to save the price of the pass twice over the two days of the pass. "

—Sydney2K

Updated by
Robert Morel

From Minami's neon-lit Dōtombori and historic Tennō-ji to the high-rise class and underground shopping labyrinths of Kita, Ōsaka is a city that pulses with its own unique rhythm. Though Ōsaka has no shortage of tourist sites, it is the city itself that is the greatest attraction. Home to some of Japan's best food, most unique fashions, and warmest locals, Ōsaka does not beg to be explored—it demands it. More than anywhere else in Japan, it rewards the whimsical turn down an interesting side street or the chat with a random stranger. People do not come here to see the city, they come to experience it.

Excluded from the formal circles of power and aristocratic culture in 16th-century Edo (Tōkyō), Ōsaka took advantage of its position and as Japan's trading center, developing its own art forms such as Bunraku puppet theater and Rakugo comic storytelling. It was in Ōsaka that feudal Japan's famed Floating World—the dining, theater, and pleasure district—was at its strongest and most inventive. Wealthy merchants and common laborers alike squandered fortunes on culinary delights, turning Ōsaka into "Japan's Kitchen," a moniker the city still has today. Though the city suffered a blow when the Meiji government canceled all of the samurai class's outstanding debts to the merchants, it was quick to recover. At the turn of the century, it had become Japan's largest and most prosperous city, a center of commerce and manufacturing.

Today Ōsaka remains Japan's iconoclastic metropolis, refusing to fit Tōkyō's norms and expectations. Unlike the often robotic hordes of Tōkyō, Ōsakans are fiercely independent. As a contrast to the neon and concrete surroundings, the people of Ōsaka are known as Japan's friendliest and most outgoing. Ask someone on the street for directions in Tōkyō and you are lucky to get so much as a glance. Ask someone in Ōsaka and you get a conversation.

⇨ *See the glossary at the end of this book for definitions of the common Japanese words and suffixes used in this chapter.*

ORIENTATION AND PLANNING

ORIENTATION

Ōsaka City is at the heart of the Kansai region (west Japan), at the mouth of the Yodo river on Ōsaka Bay. Ōsaka Prefecture is bordered by Nara Prefecture in the east, Kyōto Prefecture in the north, Hyōgo Prefecture in the northwest, and Wakayama Prefecture in the south. The main areas of the city, Kita (north) and Minami (south), are divided by two rivers: the Dojima-gawa and the Tosabori-gawa. Between Kita

TOP REASONS TO GO

The World of Tomorrow: Dōtombori buzzes with energy in the heart of Ōsaka's frenzied neonscape. Domestic robots and space shuttle parts bring high-tech to the narrow streets.

Japan's Kitchen: Ōsaka has been *nihon no daidokoro* (Japan's kitchen) since the 17th century. Now the cuisine borrows from all over the world.

Party 'til the Rising Sun: See next season's fashions previewed in Shin-sai-bashi, get down in a club, or belt out hits in a subterranean karaoke bar.

Ōsaka Aquarium: The Ōsaka Kaiyūkan is an epic voyage through the depths of the marine world. The king penguins are enchanting, and the whale shark never fails to intimidate.

Architecture: Skyscrapers share Ōsaka's 1,500-year-old skyline with 4th-century burial mounds. Minimalist master Tadao Andō redefines the Japanese cityscape from his office in downtown Ōsaka.

and Minami is Naka-no-shima, an island and the municipal center of Ōsaka. The bay area, to the west of the city center, is home to the Ōsaka Aquarium, the Suntory Museum, and Universal Studios Japan (USJ). The Shinkansen stops at Shin-Ōsaka, three stops (about five minutes) north of Ōsaka Station on the Midō-suji subway line. To the north of Shin-Ōsaka is Senri Expo Park.

Kita. Kita (north of Chūō Dōri) is Ōsaka's economic hub and contains Ōsaka's largest stations: JR Ōsaka and Hankyū Umeda. The area is crammed with shops, department stores, and restaurants. Nearby are a nightlife district, Kita-shinchi; Naka-no-shima and the Museum of Oriental Ceramics; Ōsaka-jō (Ōsaka Castle); and Ōsaka Kōen (Ōsaka Park).

Minami. Restaurants, bars, department stores, and boutiques attract Ōsaka's youth to Minami (south Chūō Dōri); theatergoers head to the National Bunraku Theater and electronics-lovers to Den Den Town. The main stations are Namba, Shin-sai-bashi and Namba Nankai. There's easy access to the Municipal Museum of Art and Sumiyoshi Taisha (Sumiyoshi Grand Shrine).

PLANNING

Ōsaka's main sights can be seen in a few days. When planning, note that most museums are closed Monday. One exception is Senri Expo Park, which closes (along with its museums) on Wednesday. Museums stay open on Monday national holidays, closing the following day instead. Likewise, Senri Expo Park stays open on Wednesday holidays, closing Thursday instead.

The city is also an excellent base from which to explore the surrounding Kansai region—Kyōto, Nara, and Kōbe are each 30 minutes away by train. Ōsaka is also the most convenient jumping-off point for a trip to the mountainside monasteries of Kōya-san, two hours away on the Nankai private rail line.

WHEN TO GO

Spring (March to May) and fall (September to November) are the best times to visit Ōsaka. The cherry blossoms flower in late March–early April, and the autumn leaves are brightest in late October–early November. Though Ōsaka's summer (June to August) is very hot and sticky, the winter is relatively balmy. This and an erratic rainy season, mostly in June, justify the extent of Ōsaka's labyrinthine underground shopping malls.

HOW-MUCH TIME?

You can see the major sights and get a glimpse of the city in a couple days. If you want to do some shopping, try the local cuisine, and get a taste of the energy that makes Ōsaka unique, plan on spending two to three nights here. Ōsaka is also an excellent base for exploring the entire Kansai area—Kyōto, Kōbe, Nara, and Wakayama.

GETTING HERE AND AROUND

AIR TRAVEL

Many international carriers fly into Kansai International Airport (KIX), either directly or with one layover. Flights from Tōkyō operate throughout the day and take 65 minutes. Japan Airlines (JAL) and All Nippon Airways (ANA) have domestic flights to major cities.

All international flights arrive at KIX, which also handles connecting domestic flights to major Japanese cities. The airport, constructed on reclaimed land in Ōsaka Bay, is easy to navigate and is an interesting sight in its own right. Exiting customs on the first floor, you will find English-language tourist information and direct access to the limousine buses that run to many downtown hotels and destinations (roughly 60 minutes depending on the destination). Frequent trains also run from KIX to Tennō-ji and Shin Ōsaka (JR Kansai Airport Express Haruka, 30 and 45 minutes), JR Kyō-bashi Station (Kansai Airport Rapid, 70 minutes), and the Nankai Namba Station (Nankai Rapid Limited Express, 30 minutes).

About 60% of domestic flights use Itami Airport, roughly 30 minutes northwest of the city. Buses from Itami Airport operate at intervals of 15 minutes to one hour (depending on your destination), daily 6 AM–9 PM, and take passengers to seven locations in Ōsaka: Shin-Ōsaka Station, Umeda, Namba (near the Nikkō and Holiday Inn hotels), Ue-hon-machi, Abeno, Sakai-higashi, and Ōsaka Business Park (near the Hotel New Otani). Buses take 25–50 minutes, depending on the destination, and cost ¥490–¥620. Schedules, with exact times and fares, are available at the information counter at the airport.

BUS TRAVEL

There are also a number of highway buses to Ōsaka from most cities in Japan. There are many bus companies, but JR Bus is one of the most popular.

SUBWAY TRAVEL

Ōsaka's subway system is extensive and efficient, running from early morning until nearly midnight at intervals of three to five minutes. Fares are between ¥200 and ¥400 and are determined by the distance traveled. Midō-suji is the main line, which runs north–south and has

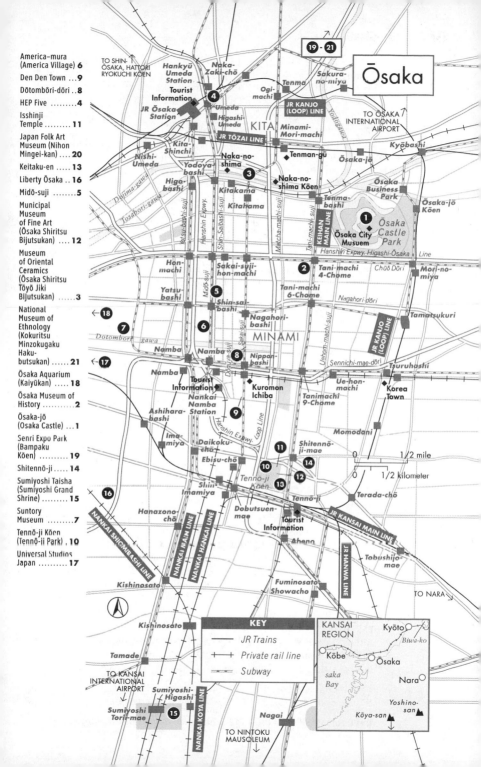

Ōsaka

stations at Shin-Ōsaka, Umeda (next to Ōsaka Station), Shin-sai-bashi, Namba, and Tennō-ji. You can purchase a one-day pass (¥850)—which provides unlimited municipal transportation on subways, the New Tram (a tram line that runs to the port area), and city buses—at the commuter ticket machines in major subway stations and at the Japan Travel Bureau office in Ōsaka Station.

The JR Loop Line (Kanjō-sen) circles the city above ground and intersects with all subway lines. Fares range from ¥120 to ¥190, or you can use your JR Pass; these trains are not included in the day-pass price.

TAXI TRAVEL
You'll have no problem hailing taxis on the street or at taxi stands. (A red light in the lower left corner of the windshield indicates availability.) The problem is Ōsaka's heavy traffic. Fares are metered at ¥550–¥640 for the first 2 km (1 mi), plus ¥90 for each additional 500 yards. Few taxi drivers speak English, so it's advisable to have your destination written in Japanese characters to show to the driver. It's not customary to tip, and many taxis now accept credit cards. Late at night, generally after midnight, there's a 20% surcharge. Expect to pay ¥1,500 for trips between Ōsaka Station and Shin-sai-bashi/Namba. Within localities, walking is recommended.

TRAIN TRAVEL
Hikari Shinkansen trains from Tōkyō Station to Shin-Ōsaka Station take about three hours and cost ¥13,950. You can use a JR Pass for the *Hikari* but not for the faster *Nozomi Shinkansen* trains, which cost ¥14,720 and are about 30-minutes faster. Shin-Ōsaka Station, on the north side of Shin-Yodo-gawa, is linked to the city center by the JR Kyoto Line and the Midō-suji subway line. On either line the ride, which takes 6–20 minutes depending on your mid-city destination, costs ¥180–¥230. Train schedules and fare information can be obtained at the Travel Service Center in Shin-Ōsaka Station. A taxi from Shin-Ōsaka Station to central Ōsaka costs ¥1,500–¥2,700.

VISITOR INFORMATION
The main visitor information center is at JR Ōsaka Station. To get there from the Midō-suji exit, turn right and walk about 50 yards. The office is beneath a pedestrian overpass, next to the city bus station. The Shin-Ōsaka center is at the JR local line exit at Shin-Ōsaka Station. For the Namba center, take Exit 24 at Namba Station in front of Starbucks; for the Tennō-ji center, take the east exit of JR Tennō-ji Station. The Universal City center is a two-minute walk from JR Universal City Station. They are all open daily 8–8 (except Universal City which opens at 9) and closed December 31–January 3.

ESSENTIALS
Airline Contacts Air Canada (☎ *0120/048–048*). **All Nippon Airways** (☎ *0120 /02–9222*). **Japan Airlines** (☎ *0120/255–931 international, 0120/25–5971 domestic*). **Northwest Airlines** (☎ *0120/120–747*).

Airport Contacts Kansai International Airport (✉ *1-Banchi, Senshu-kuko Kita, Izumisano-shi* ☎ *07/24-552-500* ⊕ *www.kansai-airport.or.jp/en/index.asp*).

Bus Contacts JR West Bus (✉ *1-3-23 Hokko, Konohana-ku* ☎ *06/6466-9990*).

Currency Exchange Mitsubishi-Tōkyō UFJ Bank (⊠ *2F Namba City, Nankai Namba Station, Minami-ku* ☏ *06/6643–6815*). **TIS** (⊠ *3-1 Umeda, Ōsaka Station, Kita-ku* ☏ *06/4797–9685*).

Emergency Contacts AMDA International Medical Center Kansai (⊠ *Yubin-kyo-dome Ōsaka Chikko, Minato-ku* ☏ *06/4395–0555*). **Sumitomo Hospital** (⊠ *2–2 Naka-no-shima 5-chōme, Kita-ku* ☏ *06/6443–1261*). **Tane General Hospital** (⊠ *1–2–31 Sakai-gawa, Nishi-ku* ☏ *06/6581–1071*). **Yodo-gawa Christian Hospital** (⊠ *9–26 Awaji, 2-chōme, Higashi, Yodo-gawa-ku* ☏ *06/6322–2250*).

Shipping FedEx Kinko's Ōsaka Station East Branch (⊠ *3–1–1 Umeda, 2F Float Ct., Kita-ku* ☏ *06/6341–7870* ⊙ *Daily 7–11*).

Tour Information Aqua Liner (☏ *06/6942–5511*). **Japan Travel Bureau Sunrise Tours** (☏ *03/5796–5454 or 075/341–1413*).

Visitor Information Ōsaka Station Tourist Information Center (⊠ *3-1-2 Umeda, JR Ōsaka Station, Kita-ku* ☏ *06/6345–2819*). **Namba Station Tourist Information Center** (⊠ *2-2-3 Namba, B1 Midō-suji Grand Bldg., Chūō-ku* ☏ *06/6211–3551*). **Tennō-ji Station Tourist Information Center** (⊠ *10–45 Hidenin-chō, 1F JR Tennō-ji Station Bldg., Tennō-ji-ku* ☏ *06/6774–3077*). **Shin-Ōsaka Tourist Information Center** (⊠ *JR Shin-Ōsaka Station, Higashi-Yodo-gawa-ku* ☏ *06/6305–3311*). **Universal City Tourist Information Center** (⊠ *6–2–61 Shimaya, Universal City Walk, Kono-hana-ku* ☏ *06/4804–3824*). **Kansai Tourist Information Center** (⊠ *1F Passenger Terminal Bldg., Kansai International Airport* ☏ *0724/56–6025*).

KITA

Culture by day and glamour by night: Kita (North of Chūō Dōri) is the place to come for the museums of Naka-no-shima, the city's deluxe department stores, and the chance to lose yourself (intentionally or not) in one of Japan's largest underground shopping labyrinths. At night take in the view from the Umeda Sky Building or the Ferris wheel at the HEP Five department store before you explore Ōsaka's upscale entertainment district, Kita-shinichi.

8

TOP ATTRACTIONS

③ Museum of Oriental Ceramics 大阪市立東洋陶磁美術館 *(Ōsaka Shiritsu Tōyō Tōji Bijutsukan)*. Located in Naka-no-shima Koen, Ōsaka's oldest park, the Museum of Oriental Ceramics houses more than 900 pieces of Chinese, Korean, and Japanese ceramics. Though only a fraction is on display at a given time, the collection is one of the finest in the world and includes 15 works designated as National Treasures or Important Cultural Properties. Those interested in art and ceramics should put this at the top of their must-see list. To get here take the Sakai-suji subway line to Kita-hama or the Midō-suji subway line to Yodoya-bashi and walk north across the Tosabori-gawa to the museum. ⊠ *1–1 Naka-no-shima, Kita-ku* ☏ *06/6223–0055* 🎫 *¥500* ⊙ *Tues.–Sun. 9:30–5; last entry at 4:30.*

FodorśChoice ★

⑱ Ōsaka Aquarium 海遊館 *(Kaiyūkan)*. This eye-catching red, gray, and blue building is Japan's best aquarium outside of Okinawa and one of the world's largest. More than 11,000 tons of water hold a multitude of sea creatures, including whale sharks, king penguins, giant spider

FodorśChoice ★

Venice of the East

When Tōkyō was but a fishing village and Kyōto a mountain hamlet, big things were happening in Ōsaka. The Ōsaka-Nara region was the center of the emerging Japanese (Yamato) nation into the 9th century, and in 645 Emperor Kōtoku (596–654) made Ōsaka his capital. He called it Naniwa, but the city's imperial ascendancy was brief. Until the 8th century capital cities were relocated upon an emperor's death. As a result, Ōsaka was the royal seat for a fleeting nine years. Despite changes in its political fortunes, Ōsaka developed as a trade center, a role its waterways had destined it to play. Exchange wasn't limited to commerce. Buddhism and Chinese characters filtered into the fledgling Japanese society through Ōsaka to Nara, and from Nara to the rest of the country.

By 1590 Hideyoshi Toyotomi (1536–98), the first *daimyo* (warlord) to unite Japan, had completed construction of Ōsaka Castle to protect his realm against the unruly clans of Kyōto. He designated Ōsaka a merchant city to consolidate his position. After Toyotomi died, Tokugawa Ieyasu's (1543–1616) forces defeated the Toyotomi legacy at the Battle of Sekigahara in 1600. Ōsaka's strategic importance was again short-lived, as Tokugawa moved the capital to Edo (now Tōkyō) in 1603. Ōsaka grew rich supplying the new capital with rice, soy sauce, and sake as Edo transformed its agricultural land into city suburbs. All copper produced in Japan was exported through Ōsaka, and the National Rice Exchange was headquartered in Dōjima, near Kita-shinchi. "70% of the nation's wealth comes from Ōsaka" was the catchphrase of the era. Some of Japan's business dynasties were founded during the economic boom of the 17th century, and they prevail today—Sumitomo, Kōnoike, and Mitsui among them.

By the end of the Genroku Era (1688–1704) Ōsaka's barons were patronizing *bunraku* puppetry and *kamigata kabuki* (comic kabuki). Chikamatsu Monzaemon (1653–1724), writer of The Forty-Seven Ronin, penned the tragedies which quickly became classics. Ihara Saikaku (1642–93) immortalized the city's merchants in the risqué Life of an Amorous Man and the The Great Mirror of Male Love. When Tōkyō became the official capital of Japan in 1868 there were fears that the "Venice of the East" would suffer. But expansion of the spinning and textile industries assured prosperity, and earned Ōsaka a new epithet—"Manchester of the East."

As a consequence of the Great Kantō Earthquake in 1923, Ōsaka became Japan's main port and by 1926 the country's largest city. Chemical and heavy industries grew during World War I, and were prime targets for American bombers during World War II. Much of Ōsaka was flattened, and more than a third of the prefecture's 4.8 million people were left homeless. During the postwar years many Ōsaka companies moved their headquarters to Tōkyō. Even so, Ōsaka was rebuilt and went on to host Asia's first World Expo in 1970. It has since fashioned itself as a city of cutting-edge technology, trendsetting, and a unique way of life. The Ōsaka City Government plans to revive the "Water City" appellation for Ōsaka, but for now the heritage of the city's waterways lives on in its place names: *bashi* (bridge), *horie* (canal), and *semba* (dockyard).

GREAT ITINERARIES

IF YOU HAVE ONE DAY:
Your first stop should be Ōsaka-jō and the surrounding park, Ōsaka-kōen. From here make your way to the Museum of Oriental Ceramics on Naka-no-shima or to the Ōsaka Aquarium on Kaigan-dōri. In the late afternoon browse the gadget stores of Den Den Town and go to the Dōguya-suji arcade for cooking utensils. For fashion, wander America-mura and Minami-horie, then head to Dōtombori-dōri for dinner. Alternatively, spend an afternoon at a *bunraku* performance to enjoy the subtleties of Japanese puppetry. Performances start at 4 PM and finish with enough time to go for a walk along Dōtombori-dōri before dinner.

IF YOU HAVE TWO DAYS:
Complete the one-day itinerary above. On the second day, head to the sights south of the city center, which can be seen in a day. Start at Tennō-ji Park, visiting the Municipal Museum of Fine Art and its collection of classical Japanese art. Northeast of the park is Shitennō-ji (commonly referred to as Tennō-ji), Japan's first temple. South of Tennō-ji is Sumiyoshi Taisha, one of Japan's three greatest shrines. To wrap up your stay, instead of heading to Dōtombori-dōri after dark, go to central Ōsaka.

crabs, jellyfish, and sea otters. You can stroll through 15 different re-created environments, including the rivers and streams of Japanese and Ecuadorian forests, the icy waters around Antarctica, the dark depths of the Japan Sea, and the volcanically active Pacific Ring of Fire. The surrounding Tempozan Harbor Village also contains the Suntory Museum, cruises around Ōsaka Bay on a reproduction of the Santa María, and various shops and restaurants. There are often street performances outside on weekends. To get here, take the Chūō subway line to Ōsaka-kō Station; the aquarium is a five-minute walk northwest from the station. ⊠*1–1–10 Kaigan-dōri, Minato-ku* ☎*06/6576–5501* ⊕*www.kaiyukan.com/eng/index.htm* 🎫*¥2,000* ⊗*Tues.–Sun. 10–8; last entry at 7.*

❶ **Ōsaka-jō** 大阪城 *(Ōsaka Castle).* Ōsaka's most visible tourist attraction
Fodor'sChoice and symbol, Ōsaka Castle exemplifies the city's ability to change with
★ the times. Originally built in the 1580s, the castle is now an impressive five-story ferro-concrete reconstruction (completed in 1931). Instead of leaving a collection of steep wooden staircases and empty rooms, Ōsaka turned its castle into an elevator-equipped museum celebrating the history of its creator, Hideyoshi Toyotomi, the chief imperial minister to unite Japan.

For those more interested in aesthetics than artifacts, the castle itself is impressive and the eighth-floor donjon offers a stunning view of Ōsaka's urban landscape. Watching the sun set behind Ōsaka's skyscrapers is reason enough for a visit. The surrounding park makes for a relaxing break from the energy of the city as well. From Ōsaka-jō Kōen-mae Station it's about a 10-minute walk up the hill to the castle. You can also take the Tani-machi subway line from Higashi-Umeda Station (just southeast of Ōsaka Station) to Tani-machi 4-chome Station. From here it's a 15-minute walk. ✉1–1 Ōsaka-jō, Chūō-ku ☎06/6941–3044 🏯Castle ¥600, garden additional ¥210 🕙Sept.–mid-July, daily 9–5, last entry at 4:30; mid-July–Aug., daily 9–8, last entry at 7:30.

WORTH NOTING

Hattori Ryokuchi Kōen 服部緑地公園. Come for the park's open-air **Museum of Old Japanese Farmhouses** (Nihon Minka Shūraku Hakubutsukan), and wander about full-size traditional rural buildings such as the giant *gassho-zukuri* (thatch-roofed) farmhouse from Gifu Prefecture. The park also has horseback-riding facilities, tennis courts, a youth hostel, and an open-air stage that hosts concerts and other events in the summer. There's even an outdoor Kabuki theater! An English-language pamphlet is available. Take the Midō-suji subway line from Umeda to Ryokuchi Kōen Station. The park is a 10-minute walk away. ✉1–1 Hattori Ryokuchi, Toyonaka-shi ☎06/6862–4946 park office, 06/6862–3137 museum 🏯Park free, museum ¥500 🕙Daily 9:30–5; last entry at 4:30.

⑳ Japan Folk Art Museum 日本民芸館 (Nihon Mingei-kan). The exhibits of "beauty from day-to-day life" at this museum in Senri Expo Park explore the diversity and intricacy of Japanese handicrafts from Hokkaidō to Okinawa. The textiles, wood crafts, and bamboo ware in simple displays evoke Japan's traditional past; they make quite a contrast to Ōsaka's modernity. ✉10–5 Bampaku Kōen, Senri Expo Park, Senri, Suita-shi ☎06/6877–1971 🏯¥700 🕙Thurs.–Tues. 10–5; last entry at 4:30.

㉑ National Museum of Ethnology 国立民族学博物館 (Kokuritsu Minzoku-gaku Hakubutsukan). The National Museum of Ethnology exhibits textiles, masks, and contraptions from around the world with sensitivity and respect. Displays on the Ainu (the original inhabitants of Hokkaidō) and other aspects of Japanese culture are particularly informative. Information sheets explaining the sections of the museum are available on request and supplement the English-language brochure included with admission. The museum is on the east side of the main road that runs north–south through Senri Expo Park. ✉Senri Expo Park, Senri, Suita-shi ☎06/6876–2151 ⊕www.minpaku.ac.jp/english/ 🏯¥420 🕙Thurs.–Tues. 10–5; last entry at 4:30.

❷ Ōsaka Museum of History 大阪歴史博物館. Informative as it is enjoyable, the Ōsaka Museum of History seeks to immerse visitors in the city's history from pre-feudal times to the early 20th century. Full of life-sized displays and hands-on activities, the museum does an excellent job of offering attractions for children and adults. There are two paths through the exhibits, a "Highlight Course" (to get a hint of Ōsaka's past in under an hour) and the "Complete Course" (for a more immersive experience). It makes an excellent stop on the way to Ōsaka Castle. To get here take the Chuo or Tanimachi subway line to Tanimachi 4-Chome station and take Exit 9 or 2. ✉1–32 Otemae, 4 chome, Chuo-ku ☎06/6946–5728 ⊕www.mus-his.city.osaka.jp 🏯¥600 🕙Mon., Wed., Thurs., and weekends 9:30–5, Fri. 9:30–8. Closed Tues.

⑲ Senri Expo Park 万博公園 (Bampaku Kōen). Originally the site of Expo '70, one of Ōsaka's defining postwar events, Senri Expo Park still draws visitors thanks to regular weekend events. This 647-acre park contains sports facilities, various gardens, and an amusement park; the National Museum of Ethnology and the Japan Folk Art Museum; and an enormous statue by Tarō Okamoto called the Tower of the Sun. Located a ways out from the city-center, the park offers an interesting look at how Ōsaka has tried to make the most of the site of a former World Expo. Unless you are particularly interested in one of the museums, or have extra time and need a break from the city, the park is easily skipped. To get to the park, take the Midō-suji subway line to Senri-Chūō Station (20 minutes from Umeda); then take the monorail to Bampaku Kōen-mae (10 minutes). ⊠*Senri, Suita-shi* ☎*06/6877–3339 for Expo Land* 🎫*Gardens ¥150–¥310 each, Expo Land ¥1,100; see separate entries for other facilities* ⊙*Thurs.–Tues. 9:30–5.*

Tenman-gū 天満宮. This 10th-century shrine is the main site of the annual **Tenjin Matsuri,** held July 24 and 25, one of the three largest and most enthusiastically celebrated festivals in Japan. Dozens of floats are paraded through the streets, and more than 100 vessels, lighted by lanterns, sail along the canals amid fireworks. The festival started as an annual procession to bestow peace and prosperity on the shrine's faithful. It is dedicated to Sugawara no Michizane, the Japanese patron of scholars. Sugawara was out of favor at court when he died in 903. Two years later plague and drought swept Japan—Sugawara was exacting revenge from the grave. To appease Sugawara's spirit he was deified as Tenjin-sama. He is enshrined at Tenman-gū. On the 5th, 15th, and 25th of each month students throughout Japan visit Tenman-gū shrines to pray for academic success. Tenman-gū is a short walk from either JR Tenman-gū Station or Minami-Mori-machi Station on the Tani-machi-suji subway line. ⊠*2–1–8 Tenjin-bashi, Kita-ku* ☎*06/6353–0025* 🎫*Free* ⊙*Apr.– Sept., daily 5:30* AM–*sunset; Oct.–Mar., daily 6* AM–*sunset.*

⑰ **Universal Studios Japan** ユニバーサルスタジオジャパン. The 140-acre 🄲 Universal Studios Japan (USJ) combines the most popular rides and shows from Universal's Hollywood and Florida movie-studio theme parks with special attractions designed specifically for Japan. Popular rides include those based on *Jurassic Park, Spider-Man,* and *E.T.* The Japan-only Snoopy attraction appeals to the local infatuation with all things cute, as do the daily Hello Kitty parades. Restaurants and food outlets abound throughout the park, and the road from JR Universal City Station is lined with the likes of Hard Rock Cafe and Bubba Gump Shrimp, local fast-food chain MOS Burger, and Ganko Sushi. Tickets are available at locations throughout the city, including branches of Lawson convenience stores and larger JR stations, as well as at USJ itself. Due to high demand on weekends and during holiday periods, tickets must be bought in advance and are not available at the gate. The park is easily reached by direct train from JR Ōsaka Station (about 20 minutes) or by changing to a shuttle train at JR Nishi-kujo Station on the Loop Line. ⊠*2–1–33 Sakurajima, Konohana-ku* ☎*06/6465–3000* ⊕*www.usj.co.jp* 🎫*¥5,800* ⊙*Daily 10–10.*

8

MINAMI

Tradition by day and neon by night, Minami is the place to come for Ōsaka history: Japan's oldest temple, a breathtaking collection of Japanese art in the Municipal Museum of Fine Art, and a mausoleum bigger than the pyramids. And then youth culture takes over when it comes to nightlife neonside: this is where future fashionistas forge the haute couture of tomorrow. Amid all this modernity are two bastions of Ōsaka tradition: the National Bunraku and Shin-Kabukiza Kabuki theaters (⇨ see the Arts, below).

TOP ATTRACTIONS

⑥ America-mura アメリカ村 *(America Village)*. Though it takes its name from the original shops that sold cheap American fashions and accessories, Ame-mura (*ah*-meh *moo*-ra), as it's called, is now a bustling district full of trendy clothing stores, record stores, bars, cafés, and clubs that cater to teenagers and young adults. Shops are densely packed, and it's virtually impossible to walk these streets on weekends. To see the variety of styles and fashions prevalent among urban youth, Ame-Mura is *the* place to go in Ōsaka. ⊠ *West side of Midō-suji, 6 blocks south of Shin-sai-bashi Station, Chūō-ku.*

⑨ Den Den Town でんでんタウン. All the latest video games, computers, cameras, phones, MP3 players, and other electronic gadgets are discounted here. Even if you are not in the market for electronics, a stroll through Den Den Town provides an interesting look at Japan's anime, video game, and computer subcultures. "Den Den" is derived from the word *denki,* which means electricity. ⊠ *2 blocks east of Namba Station, Naniwa-ku.*

⑧ Dōtombori-dōri 道頓堀通り. If you only have one night in Ōsaka,
★ Dōtombori-dōri is the place to go. Once Ōsaka's old theater district, Dōtombori-dōri is now a neon-lit pedestrian street filled with restaurants, shops, and the shouts of countless touts each proclaiming (usually falsely) that their restaurant is the only one worth visiting. Though it is becoming increasingly touristy, wandering Dōtombori-dōri and the surrounding area on a weekend evening is the essential Ōsaka experience. Stop at the recently renovated Ebisu-bashi to watch street musicians attract crowds as spiky-haired twentysomethings practice the art of nampa (the elaborate, amusing, and uniquely Japanese method of chatting people up). Stroll along the brand new riverfront walkways to avoid the crowds. Or slip into Hōzenji Yokocho Alley just two blocks south of Dōtombori-dōri to splash water on the moss-covered statues at Hōzenji Shrine or dine in any of the excellent restaurants hidden away on this quiet street. ⊠ *From Umeda, take Midō-suji subway line to Namba and walk north 2 blocks up Midō-suji. Chūō-ku.*

⑫ Municipal Museum of Fine Art 大阪市立美術館 *(Ōsaka Shiritsu Bijutsukan).* The building isn't too impressive, but the exceptional collection of 12th- to 14th-century classical Japanese art on the second floor is. Other collections include the works of Edo-period artist Kōrin Ogata, more than 3,000 examples of modern lacquerware, and a collection of Chinese paintings and artifacts. Take the Loop Line or the Midō-suji subway line to Tennō-ji Station, or the Tani-machi subway to

Shitennō-ji-mae. The museum is in Tennō-ji Kōen, southwest of Shitennō ji. ✉ *1–82 Chausuyama-chō, Tennō-ji-ku* ☏ *06/6771–4874* 🎟 *¥300 includes entry to Tennoji-Koen* ⏱ *Tues.–Sun. 9:30–5; last entry at 4:30.*

⑭ **Shitennō-ji** 四天王寺 *(Shitennō Temple).* Tennō-ji, as this temple is popularly known, is one of the most important historic sights in Ōsaka and the oldest temple in Japan. Founded in 593, architecturally it's gone through hell, having been destroyed by fire many times. The last reconstruction of the Main Hall (Kon-do), Taishi-den, and the five-story pagoda in 1965 has maintained the original design and adhered to the traditional mathematical alignment. What has managed to survive from earlier times is the 1294 stone torii that stands at the main entrance. (Torii are rarely used at Buddhist temples.)

THE MASTER OF MINIMALISM

Ōsaka native Tadao Andō is Japan's most famous architect, and a global figurehead of the minimalist movement. The Suntory Museum, his Ōsaka masterpiece, has rotating art and culture exhibitions from around the world. You can also see his work at the JR Universal City Station on the Yumesaki Line and at the cinematheque in Tennō-ji Park. The Suntory Museum

Suntory Museum ✉ *1–5–10 Kaigan-dōri, Minato-ku* ☏ *06/6577–0001* 🌐 *www.suntory.co.jp/culture/smt* 🎟 *¥1,000 gallery, ¥1,600 gallery and IMAX Theater* ⏱ *Thurs.–Tues. 10–8; last entry at 7:30.*

The founder, Umayado no Mikoto (573–621), posthumously known as Prince Shōtoku (Shōtoku Taishi), is considered one of early Japan's most enlightened rulers for his furthering of Buddhism and his political acumen. He was made regent over his aunt, Suiko, and set about instituting reforms and establishing Buddhism as the state religion. Buddhism had been introduced to Japan from China and Korea in the early 500s, but it was seen as a threat to the aristocracy, who claimed prestige and power based upon their godlike ancestry. On the 21st of every month the temple has a flea market that sells antiques and baubles; go in the morning for a feeling of Old Japan.

Three train lines will take you near Shitennō-ji. The Tani-machi-suji subway line's Shitennō-ji-mae Station is closest to the temple and the temple park. The Loop Line's Tennō-ji Station is several blocks south of the temple. The Midō-suji subway line also has a Tennō-ji stop, which is next to the JR station. ✉ *1–11–18 Shitennō-ji, Tennō-ji-ku* ☏ *06/6771–0066* 🎟 *¥300* ⏱ *Apr.–Sept., daily 8:30–4:30; Oct.–Mar., daily 8:30–4.*

OFF THE BEATEN PATH

The Korean Experience. Koreans are the largest ethnic minority in Japan, and their highest concentration is in Ōsaka. Known as *zainichi,* after decades, in some cases centuries, of "assimilation" they have only recently begun to proclaim their traditional heritage and use their Korean names. By 2004 a wave of Korean *tarento* (talent) ruled TV and cinema screens across Japan. The most popular was Bae Yong-jun, affectionately known as *Yon-sama.* You may not be able to see Yon-sama in person, but you'll get an eyeful of him from the posters outside restaurants in Tsuruhashi, Ōsaka's Korea Town. For a fun evening feasting on excellent, affordable yaki-niku (Korean-style barbeque) take the west exit of JR Turuhashi Station and step into any one of the restaurants lining the narrow street. Many also specialize in Kōbe beef, an added treat.

⑮ Sumiyoshi Taisha 住吉大社 *(Sumiyoshi Grand Shrine).* In a city of former mariners it's no surprise that locals revere Sumiyoshi Taisha, since it's dedicated to the guardian deity of sailors. According to legend, the shrine was founded by Empress Jingū in 211 to express her gratitude for her safe return from a voyage to Korea. Sumiyoshi Taisha is one of three shrines built prior to the arrival of Buddhism in Japan (the other two are Ise Jingū in Mie Prefecture and Izumo Taisha in Tottori Prefecture). According to Shintō custom, shrines were torn down and rebuilt at set intervals to the exact specifications of the original. Sumiyoshi was last replaced in 1810. Sumiyoshi is also famous for its taiko-bashi (arched bridge), given by Yodo-gimi, the consort of Hideyoshi Toyotomi, who bore him a son.

Every June 14 starting at 1 PM, a colorful rice-planting festival takes place here with traditional folk performances and processions. Sumiyoshi Matsuri, a large and lively festival, is held from July 30 to August 1. A crowd of rowdy young men carries a 2-ton portable shrine from Sumiyoshi Taisha to Yamato-gawa and back; this is followed by an all-night street bazaar. To reach the shrine, take the 20-minute ride south on the Nankai Main Line from Nankai Namba Station to Sumiyoshi Kōen Station. ⊠*2–9–89 Sumiyoshi, Sumiyoshi-ku* ☎*06/6672–0753* 🌐*Free* ⊘*Apr.–Oct., daily 6–5; Nov.–Mar., daily 6:30–5.*

⑩ Tennō-ji Kōen 天王寺公園 *(Tennō-ji Park).* The best place to get away from the noise and concrete of the city, this park contains not only the **Municipal Museum of Fine Art** and the garden of **Keitaku-en,** but also the **Tennō-ji Botanical Gardens** (Tennō-ji Shokubutsuen). Also within the park is a prehistoric burial mound, **Chausuyama Kofun,** that was the site of Tokugawa Ieyasu's camp during the siege of Ōsaka-jō in 1614–15. Visit in the morning or evening when the park is at its quietest. Take the Loop Line from Ōsaka Station to Tennō-ji Station. The park is on the left side of the road going north to Shitennō-ji. ⊠*6–74 Chausuyama-chō, Tennō-ji-ku* ☎*06/6771–8401* 🌐*¥150, park only, or ¥300 with Municipal Museum of Fine Arts* ⊘*Tues.–Sun. 9:30–4:30; last entry at 4.*

WORTH NOTING

Fujii-dera 藤井寺. An 8th-century, 1,000-handed statue of Kannon, the goddess of mercy, is this temple's main object of worship. The seated figure is the oldest Buddhist sculpture of its kind, and it's only on view on the 18th of each month. To get here, take the Midō-suji subway line to Tennō-ji Station, then transfer to the Kintetsu Minami–Ōsaka Line and take it to Fujii-dera Station. The temple is a few minutes' walk away. ⊠*1–16–21 Fujii-dera, Fujii-dera-shi* ☎*0721/938–0005* 🌐*Free* ⊘*Statue on view 18th of month.*

⑪ Isshinji Temple 一心寺. The ultramodern gate and fierce guardian statues of Isshinji Temple are a stark contrast to the nearby Shitennoji Temple.

Dating back to 1185, the temple is now known for its Okotsubutsu—a Buddha statue made of the cremated remains of more than 200,000 people laid to rest at Isshinji. Far from morbid, the statue is meant to reaffirm one's respect for the deceased and to turn them into an object of everyday worship. An Okotsubutsu is made every 10 years, the first in 1887. Though 12 Okutsubutsu have been made, due to a direct hit during World War II, only the six crafted after the war remain. To get here take the Sakisuji Subway to Ebisu Cho Station and walk east along Isshinjimae. The temple is on the right soon after passing under the expressway. ⊠ *2–8–6–9 Tennoji-ku, Tennoji-ku* 📞 *06/6774–2578* ⊕ *www.isshinji.or.jp* 🎫 *Free* ☉ *Early morning to evening.*

⑯ **Liberty Ōsaka: Osaka Human Rights Museum** リバティおおさか. In a country that often falls back on the myth of everyone living in egalitarian harmony, Liberty Ōsaka is one of the city's more unique sights. The museum delves into issues of discrimination in Japan against ethnic groups, women, the homeless, sexual minorities, and many other groups. In addition to the English audio guide, each section has a documentary video with English subtitles, and visitors are given a 30-page booklet detailing the museum's contents. The highly informed volunteer staff is happy to answer questions about the permanent and special rotation exhibits. Though less centrally located than some of Ōsaka's other sights, for anyone interested in issues of discrimination, Liberty Ōsaka is highly recommended. To get here take the JR Loop Line to Ashihara Station and walk south along the main road 600 meters. The museum will be on your right. ⊠ *3–6–36 Naniwa-Nishi, Naniwa-ku* 📞 *06/6561–5891* ⊕ *www.liberty.or.jp* 🎫 *¥500* ☉ *Tues.–Sun. 10–5, closed 4th Fri. of each month.*

⑬ **Keitaku-en** 慶沢園. Jihei Ogawa, master gardener of the late Meiji period, spent 10 years working the late Baron Sumitomo's circular garden into a masterpiece. The woods surrounding the pond are a riot of color in spring, when the cherry blossoms and azaleas bloom. Keitaku-en is adjacent to Shiritsu Bijutsukan in Tennō-ji Kōen. ⊠ *Tennō-ji-ku* 🎫 *Included in Tennō-ji Kōen admission* ☉ *Tues.–Sun. 9:30–4:30; last entry at 4.*

⑤ **Mido-suji** 御堂筋. Ōsaka's Champs Élysées, the ginko-tree-lined Midō-suji boulevard is Ōsaka's most elegant thoroughfare and home to its greatest concentration of department stores. To the east of Midō-suji is the Shin-sai-bashi-suji arcade, one of Ōsaka's best shopping and entertainment streets. If you're in town on the second Sunday in October, try to catch the annual Midō-suji Parade, with its colorful procession of floats and musicians. The Shin-sai-bashi stop (Exit 7) on the Midō-suji subway line is in the heart of the city's shopping districts. ⊠ *Chūō-ku.*

Nintoku Mausoleum 仁徳天皇陵古墳. The 4th-century mausoleum of Emperor Nintoku is in the city of Sakai, southeast of Ōsaka. The mausoleum was built on an even larger scale than that of the pyramids of Egypt—archaeologists calculate that the central mound of this site covers 1.3 million square feet. Construction took more than 20 years and required a total workforce of about 800,000 laborers. Surrounding the emperor's burial place are three moats and pine, cedar, and cypress

8

trees. You can walk around the outer moat to get an idea of the size of the mausoleum and the grounds. However, entry into the mausoleum is not allowed. From Tennō-ji Station, take the JR Hanwa Line to Mozu Station (a half-hour ride). From there the mausoleum is within a five-minute walk. ⊠ *7 Daisen-chō, Sakai-shi* ☎ *0722/41–0002.*

SHOPPING

As with everything else in Ōsaka, the city rewards shoppers with a sense of adventure. Though Ōsaka is full of shopping complexes, towering department stores, and brand-name shops, step away from the main streets and explore neighborhood shops and boutiques to find the best deals, newest electronics, and cutting-edge fashions.Ōsaka's miles of labyrinthine underground shopping complexes offer an escape from summer heat and are an experience in and of themselves. The network of tunnels and shops in underground Umeda is the most impressive (and confusing). Fortunately, signs and maps are plentiful and the information desk staff speaks English.

DESIGNER STORES

Though it is being slowly invaded by chain stores, Ōsaka's famed **America-mura** is still a good place to find hip young fashions. For original boutiques and cutting-edge styles, head to the streets of **Minami-semba** and **Minami-horie** to the west. **Evisu Tailor** (⊠ *4–10–19 Minami-semba, Chūō-ku* ☎ *06/6241–1995*) is jean designer to the stars—Madonna included. Anyone wearing a pair of handmade raw-denim Evisus is recognized by the conspicuous seagull logo on the back pockets. The main shop is in Minami-semba, a 10-minute walk north of Minami-horie.

SOZ (⊠ *2–10–70, 3F Namba ParksNaniwa-ku* ☎ *06/6641–4683*) is the brainchild of Hideki Tominaga, an Ōsaka native. He created the Mini Carpenter Block—an art toy of colorful, interlocking, plastic pieces that helps develop creativity. The Mini Carpenter Block has taken on a life of its own, with SOZ stores throughout the world and a recent exhibit at Paris's Louvre Museum. The cutest of his creations is Mr. Pen, whom you may want to buy after seeing the king penguins at the Ōsaka Aquarium. Take the Namba Parks exit from the Midosuji subway station.

There are specialized wholesale areas throughout the city, and many have a few retail shops as well. One such area is **Dōguya-suji**, just east of Nankai Namba Station and the Takashimaya department store. This street is lined with shops selling nothing but kitchen goods—all sorts of pots, pans, utensils, and glassware are piled to the rafters. Though most customers are in the restaurant trade, laypeople shop here, too. Feel free to wander around: there's no obligation to buy. A trip here could be combined with a visit to nearby **Den Den Town,** known for its electronic goods. Also in this neighborhood, east of the main entrance to Dōguya-suji, is **Kuromon Ichiba,** the famous market district where chefs select the treats—fruits, vegetables, meat, and much more—cooked up at the city's restaurants that evening.

DEPARTMENT STORES

All major Japanese *depāto* (department stores) are represented in Ōsaka. Hankyū is headquartered here. They're open 10–7, but usually close one day a month, on a Wednesday or Thursday. The food hall in the basement of Hanshin department store is the city's best. If you want to take a break from shopping, head to the roof of HEP Five, where you can ride an enormous Ferris wheel. The following are some of Ōsaka's leading depātos: **Daimaru** (⊠*1–7–1 Shin-sai-bashi-suji, Chūō-ku* ☎*06/6343–1231*). **Hankyū** (⊠*8–7 Kakuta-chō, Kita-ku* ☎*06/6361–1381*). **Hanshin** (⊠*1–13–13 Umeda, Kita-ku* ☎*06/6345–1201*). **HEP Five** (⊠*5–15 Kakuda-cho, Kita-ku* ☎*06/6342–0002* ⊠*Ferris wheel ¥500* ☻*Building and Ferris wheel daily 11–11, shops daily 11–9*). **Takashimaya** (⊠*5–1–5 Namba, Chūō-ku* ☎*06/6631–1101*).

Hilton Plaza West and East have international brands like Max Mara, Dunhill, Chanel, and Ferragamo. Herbis Ent Plaza is a local high-end shopping complex connected to the Hilton Plaza West complex. These three shopping complexes are opposite Ōsaka Station. To the east of the Hankyū Grand Building is NU Chayamachi—a collection of small boutiques, both local and foreign, and some good cafés. **Hilton Plaza East** (⊠*1–8–6 Umeda, Kita-ku* ☎*06/6348–9168*). **Hilton Plaza West** (⊠*2–2–2 Umeda, Kita-ku* ☎*06/6342–0002*). **Herbis Ent Plaza** (⊠*2–2–22 Umeda, Kita-ku* ☎*06/6343–7500*). **Namba Parks** (⊠*2–10–70 , Naniwa-ku* ☎*06/6644–7100*). **NU Chayamachi** (⊠*10–12 Chayamachi, Kita-ku* ☎*06/6373–7371*).

CRAFTS SHOPPING

At one time famous for its traditional crafts—particularly *karaki-sashimono* (ornately carved furniture), fine Naniwa Suzu-ki pewterware, and *uchihamono* (Sakai cutlery)—Ōsaka lost much of its traditional industry during World War II. The simplest way to find Ōsakan crafts is to visit one of the major department stores.

ELECTRONICS

Although some Japanese electronic goods may be cheaper in the United States than in Japan, many electronics products are released on the Japanese market 6 to 12 months before they reach the West.

Den Den Town. This district has about 300 retail shops that specialize in electronics products, as well as stores selling cameras and watches. Shops are open 10–7 daily. Take your passport, and make your purchases in stores with signs that say TAX FREE in order to qualify for a 5% discount. The area is near Ebisu-chō Station on the Sakai-suji subway line (Exit 1 or 2), and Nippon-bashi Station on the Sakai-suji and Sennichi-mae subway lines (Exit 5 or 10).

Yodobashi Camera. If you haven't the time to spend exploring Den Den Town, head to this enormous electronics department store in Umeda. Don't be put off by the name: they sell far more than just cameras. On the north side of JR Ōsaka Station, opposite the Hotel New

Hankyū, the store is impossible to miss. ⊠*1–1 Ōfuka-chō, Kita-ku* ☎*06/4802–1010* ⊙*Daily 9:30–9.*

SPORTS

BASEBALL

Kyocera Dōmu Ōsaka *(Ōsaka Dome)*. The Orix Buffaloes are the local team, but it is the Hanshin Tigers from Nishi-no-miya, between Kōbe and Ōsaka, that prompt young men to jump into the Dōtombori river in excitement. The Hanshin department store has 10% discounts when the Tigers win, and you can see their black-and-yellow colors all over the city. Ōsaka Dome looks like a spaceship and has pleasing-to-the-eye curved edges in a city dominated by the gray cube. Tickets cost as little as ¥1,600. Buy them at the gate, at branches of Lawson convenience store in the city, or by telephone from Ticket Pia. The dome is next to Ōsaka Dōmu-mae Chiyozaki subway station on Nagahori Tsurumi-ryokuchi line. ⊠*3–2–1 Chiozaki Taishō-ku* ☎*06/6363–9999 Ticket Pia.*

SOCCER

There has been a soccer boom in Japan since the World Cup was co-hosted by South Korea and Japan in 2002. Two J-League soccer teams, Gamba Ōsaka and Cerezo Ōsaka, play in Ōsaka. Tickets start at ¥1,500 for adults, and the season runs from March to November.

The Gamba Ōsaka play at **Bampaku EXPO Memorial Stadium** (⊠*5–2 Senri Bampaku Kōen, Suita-shi* ☎*06/6202–5201*) in the north of the city. Access is via the Ōsaka Monorail to Kōen Higashi-guchi Station. The Cerezo Ōsaka play at the **Nagai Stadium** (⊠*2–2–19 Nagai-Higashi, Sumiyoshi-ku* ☎*06/6692–9011*) in south Ōsaka, close to Nagai Station on the JR Hanwa Line or Midō-suji subway line.

SUMŌ

The sumō scene has become a hotbed of international rivalry as Bulgarians, Estonians, and some Russians with attitude have been edging the local talent out of the *basho* (ring). From the second Sunday through the fourth Sunday in March, one of Japan's six sumō tournaments takes place in the **Ōsaka Furitsu Taiikukaikan** *(Ōsaka Prefectural Gymnasium)*. Most seats, known as *masu-seki,* are prebooked before the tournament begins, but standing-room tickets (¥1,000) and a limited number of seats (¥3,000) are available on the day of the event. The ticket office opens at 9 AM, and you should get in line early. The stadium is a 10-minute walk from Namba Station. ⊠*3–4–36 Namba-naka, Naniwa-ku* ☎*06/6631–0120.*

WHERE TO EAT

Ōsaka has a broad range of Japanese food, from the local snack foods, *okonomiyaki* and *takoyaki* (tasty, grilled octopus in batter) to full kaiseki restaurants. The seafood from the Seto Inland Sea is always fresh, as is the tender beef used at the many Korean barbecue restaurants in Ōsaka's Korea Town, Tsuruhashi. French and Mexican foods are also popular in Ōsaka.

The department stores around Ōsaka Station are "gourmet palaces," each with several floors of restaurants. The Hankyū Grand Building and the Daimaru at JR Ōsaka Station have the best selection. Under Ōsaka Station is the Shin-Umeda Shokudokai—a maze of narrow alleys lined with *izakaya* (lively after-work drinking haunts). The beer and hot snacks comfort many an overworked salaryman on the commute home.

For some energetic dining neonside, head to Dōtombori-dōri and Soemon-chō (*so-eh-mon cho*), two areas along Dōtombori-gawa packed with restaurants and bars. Kimono clad *mama-sans* serve the city's expense-accounters at Kita-shinchi, in south Kita-ku, the city's most exclusive dining quarter.

WHAT IT COSTS IN YEN					
	¢	$	$$	$$$	$$$$
Restaurants	under ¥800	¥800–¥1,000	¥1,000–¥2,000	¥2,000–¥3,000	over ¥3,000

Restaurant prices are per person for a main course, set meal, or equivalent combinations of smaller dishes.

KITA

$$$ **✕ Bat-ten Yokatō** バッテンよかとぉ. Located in the basement of Kita-Shin-
JAPANESE ichi's Aspa Building, the hip, low-ceilinged Batsuten Yofuto serves up a wide selection of very good yakitori (skewered meat and vegetables) in a fun, cozy atmosphere. Sitting at the long bar, customers can watch the cooks work and call out requests to each other. In addition to the quality of the food, the fact that the staff is obviously having a good time makes this an excellent place to try one of the most popular foods in Japan. ✉ *1–11–24 Kita-shinchi, Chuo-ku* ☎*06/4799–7447* ⚠ *Reservations not accepted* ☰*No credit cards* ⊘ *Closed Sun.*

$$$$ **✕ Isshin** 一新. Only 16 seats grace this *kappō* restaurant to the east
JAPANESE of Kita-shinchi. Ordering the *omakase* (chef's suggestion) dispenses
★ with menu anxiety. The quality and quantity reflect Ōsaka's reputation for good food at reasonable prices. Sashimi, tempura, crab, and whatever is in season will be on the menu with a range of premium sakes to accompany them. Isshin is east of Midō-suji and Shin-midō-suji near the American consulate. Go down the street with the convenience store on your right and Isshin is about 100 yards on the left. ✉ *4–12–2 Nishi-Tenma, B1 Oshima Bldg., Kita-ku* ☎*06/4709–3020* ☰*AE, DC, MC, V.*

8

On the Menu

Ōsakans are passionate about food. Ōsakans coined the word kuidaore—to eat until you drop. They expect restaurants to use the freshest ingredients. For centuries the nearby Seto Inland Sea has allowed easy access to fresh seafood. Ōsakans continue to have discriminating palates and demand their money's worth.

Ōsakan cuisine is flavored with a soy sauce lighter in color and milder in flavor than the soy used in Tōkyō. One local delicacy is okonomiyaki, something between a pancake and an omelet, filled with cabbage, mountain yams, pork, shrimp, and other ingredients. Ōsaka-zushi (Ōsaka-style sushi), made in wooden molds, has a distinctive square shape. Unagi (eel) remains a popular local dish; grilled unagi is eaten in summer for quick energy. Fugu (blowfish) served boiled or raw is a winter delicacy.

The thick white noodles known as udon are a Japanese staple, but Ōsakans are particularly fond of kitsune udon, a local dish (now popular throughout Japan) in which the noodles are served with fried tofu known as abura-age. Another Ōsaka invention is takoyaki, griddle dumplings with octopus, green onions, and ginger smothered in a delicious sauce. Sold by street vendors in Dōtombori, these tasty snacks also appear at every festival and street market in Kansai. If you don't want to fall over, try to leave the table hara-hachi bunme, 80% full.

$$$
FRENCH
Fodor's Choice
★

✕**La Baie** ラ・ベ. The city's premier hotel restaurant serves extremely good French food. The elegant—yet relaxed—atmosphere, seasonal menus, and extensive wine list make La Baie an excellent choice for modern French cuisine. With its high ceiling, 18th-century painting, and dark-wood accents, the interior is elegant yet relaxed and the service is impeccable. The weekday lunch courses are a good way to sample some of the best French cuisine in Ōsaka. ⊠2–5–25 Umeda, Kita-ku ☎06/6343–7020 ⊟AE, DC, MC, V.

$–$$
MEXICAN

✕**Los Inkas** ロスインカス. Hugely popular with the local Latin community, Los Inkas is always busy, and the up-tempo music makes it a good place for a party. Many dishes are Peruvian, though other Latin cuisines, including Mexican, are represented. Menu highlights include ceviche mixto, shrimp, octopus, and fish marinated in lime juice and spices; and lomo saltado, beef, vegetables, and french fries sautéed together. ⊠2F Kodama Leisure Bldg., 1–14 Dōyama-chō, Kita-ku ☎06/6365–5190 ⊟No credit cards ⊙Closed Mon.

$$–$$$
JAPANESE

✕**Mimiu** 美々卯. It's the birthplace of udon-suki—thick, noodle stew with Chinese cabbage, clams, eel, yams, shiitake mushrooms, mitsuba (a three-leaved green), and other seasonal ingredients simmered in a pot over a burner at your table. Mimiu is on the 10th floor of the Hanshin department store opposite Ōsaka Station. ⊠1–13–13 Umeda, Kita-ku ☎06/6345–6648 ⚖Reservations not accepted ⊟MC, V.

$$$
JAPANESE

✕**Sakae Sushi** 栄すし. Kaiten sushi (aka "conveyor belt sushi") originated in Ōsaka, so it's worth making a stop at one of the many kaiten sushi restaurants in the city. In Kita, Sakae Sushi offers large cuts of tasty kaiten sushi at a reasonable price. The shop itself is a good representation of the standard kaiten sushi restaurant—small, unadorned, and

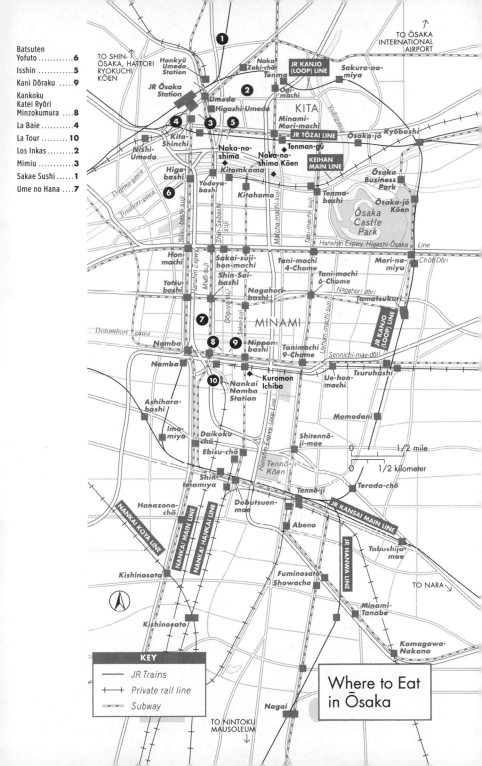

Where to Eat in Ōsaka

KEY

— JR Trains

+—+ Private rail line

═══ Subway

energetic. ✉ *5–9 Noboriyama-cho, Kita-ku* ☎*06/6313–2344* ⚑*No reservations accepted* ⊟*No credit cards.*

MINAMI

$$$–$$$$
SEAFOOD

✗ **Kani Dōraku** かに道楽. The most famous restaurant on Dōtombori-dōri—the enormous mechanical crab is a local landmark—Kani Dōraku has fine crab dishes at reasonable prices. The lunch a crab set, with large portions of crab, costs around ¥4,000; crab for dinner costs more than ¥6,000. If you prefer a quick snack, a stand outside sells crab legs (¥500 for two). An English-language menu is available. Reserve ahead on weekends. ✉*1–6–18 Dōtombori, Chūō-ku* ☎*06/6211–8975* ⊟*AE, DC, MC, V.*

$$$–$$$$
JAPANESE

✗ **Kankoku Katei Ryori Minzokumura** 韓国家庭料理民俗村. Popular with Korean celebrities, this restaurant eschews glitz for tradition. *Katei* means "home-style" in Japanese, and the Korean hot pot, teppanyaki, sumibiyaki, and seafood hot pot set menus won't break the bank. It opens early (3 PM) and closes late (4 AM). ✉*1–22 Soemon-chō, Unagi-dani, Chūō-ku* ☎*06/6212–2640* ⊟*AE, DC, MC, V.*

$$$$
FRENCH
★

✗ **La Tour** ラ・トゥア. This French restaurant in the Swissôtel Nankai Ōsaka has heavy French cutlery, Rothko lithographs, and dark-red upholstery to match its culinary aspirations. Bouillabaisse is the house specialty, accompanied by excellent service. ✉*Swissôtel Nankai Ōsaka, 1–60 Namba, 5-chōme, Chūō-ku* ☎*06/6646–5126* ⚑*Reservations essential* ⊟*AE, DC, MC, V.*

$$$$
JAPANESE

✗ **Ume no Hana** 梅の花. Healthy prix-fixe, multicourse menus of tofu-based cuisine—particularly refreshing on hot summer days—are the specialty here. This is a good spot to take a break from shopping in Shin-sai-bashi, and during the day you can order one of the cheaper lunch sets. The private dining rooms are in a traditional Japanese style with pottery and ikebana. Reserve ahead on weekends and in the evening. ✉*11F Shin-sai-bashi OPA Bldg., 1–4–3 Nishi-Shin-sai-bashi, Chūō-ku* ☎*06/6258–3766* ⊟*AE, DC, MC, V.*

WHERE TO STAY

Ōsaka is known more as a business center than as a tourist destination, so hotel facilities are usually excellent, but their features are rarely distinctive, except at the high-end of the scale. The city has modern accommodations for almost every taste. Choose accommodations based on location rather than amenities. Note that most hotels offer special rates much lower than the listed rack rates. Call hotels or check their Web sites for information on specials.

WHAT IT COSTS IN YEN				
	¢	$	$$	$$$	$$$$
For 2 People	under ¥8,000	¥8,000–¥12,000	¥12,000–¥18,000	¥18,000–¥22,000	over ¥22,000

Hotel price categories are based on the range between the least and most expensive standard double rooms in nonholiday high season, based on the European Plan (with no meals) unless otherwise noted. Taxes (5%–15%) are extra.

KITA

$$$$ ⚏ **ANA Crowne Plaza Ōsaka** 大阪全日空ホテル. One of Ōsaka's oldest deluxe hotels, the ANA overlooks Naka-no-shima Kōen. The 24-story building is a handsome white-tile structure with some unusual architectural features like great fluted columns in the lobby. There's also an enclosed courtyard with trees. The main bar is a throwback to a 1950s English gentlemen's club. Guest rooms feature shades of chocolate, tan, and cream. Each room has a trouser press, and the cups are traditional Japanese ceramics. **Pros:** centrally located. **Cons:** there are few shops and attractions directly adjacent to the hotel. ⊠*1–3–1 Dōjimahama, Kita-ku, Ōsaka* ☎*06/6347–1112* 🖷*06/6347–9208* ⊕*www. anacrowneplaza-osaka.jp/english/* ⇗*493 rooms* ⚭*In-room: safe, refrigerator, Internet. In-hotel: 5 restaurants, bar, pool, gym, parking (paid)* ▭*AE, DC, MC, V.*

$$$–$$$$ ⚏ **Hilton Ōsaka** ヒルトン大阪. Glitz and glitter lure tourists and expense-
★ accounters to the Hilton Ōsaka, across from JR Ōsaka Station in the heart of the business district. It's a typical Western-style hotel, with an orgy of marble and brass. The high-ceiling lobby is dramatic and stylish, and the hotel's arcade contains designer boutiques. The five executive floors have a lounge for complimentary continental breakfasts and evening cocktails, and the decor is 21st-century art deco with a Japanese streak. **Pros:** the Deluxe and Executive floors have some of the most stylish rooms in the city. **Cons:** other than the stylish interior there is little that sets it apart from less expensive hotels. ⊠*8–8 Umeda, 1-chōme, Kita-ku, Ōsaka* ☎*06/6347–7111* 🖷*06/6347–7001* ⊕*www. hilton.co.jp/osaka* ⇗*525 rooms* ⚭*In-room: safe (some), refrigerator, Internet. In-hotel: 7 restaurants, pool, gym, parking (paid)* ▭*AE, DC, MC, V.*

$$$$ ⚏ **Hotel New Otani Ōsaka** ホテルニューオータニ大阪. Indoor and outdoor pools, a rooftop garden, tennis courts, and a sparkling marble atrium make this amenities-rich hotel a popular choice for Japanese and Westerners. The modern rooms, large by Japanese standards, afford handsome views of Ōsaka-jō and the Neya-gawa (Neya River). Rooms have light color schemes accented with geometric patterns and Japan-inspired modern prints. The New Otani is like a minicity within Ōsaka Business Park. Spend an evening in the teppanyaki restaurant on the 18th floor enjoying Ōsaka-jō in all its floodlit glory. **Pros:** rooms facing the castle afford beautiful views; many amenities. **Cons:** not as centrally located as the Umeda or Shin-sai-bashi/Namba hotels. ⊠*4–1 Shiromi, 1-chōme, Chūo-ku, Ōsaka* ☎*06/6941–1111* 🖷*06/6941–9769* ⊕*www. osaka.newotani.co.jp* ⇗*525 rooms, 53 suites* ⚭*In-room: safe (some),*

8

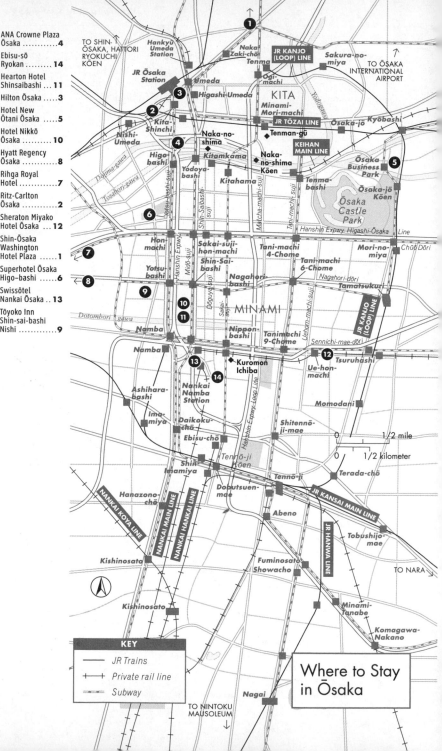

Where to Stay in Ōsaka

KEY

— JR Trains
+++ Private rail line
=== Subway

refrigerator, Internet. In-hotel: 9 restaurants, bars, tennis courts, pool, gym, bicycles, parking (paid), Internet terminal ⊟*AE, DC, MC, V.*

$$$$
★
🔲 **Rihga Royal Hotel** リーガロイヤルホテル大阪. Royal means Emperor, and the royal family stays here when visiting Ōsaka. Built in the 1930s, the Royal contains more than 20 restaurants, bars, and karaoke rooms, and no fewer than 60 shops—in addition to nearly 1,000 rooms. The West Wing has standard rooms for business travelers, the Tower Wing standard and executive floors. Each executive floor has a nature theme, so depending on your mood stay on the forest, sky, flower, or sea floors. A stay in the VIP tower means free access to the swimming club's two sun-roof pools (other guests pay ¥2,000). A shuttle bus goes to the Umeda and Yodoya-bashi stations. **Pros:** nature themes and imperial visits set it apart from similar hotels. **Cons:** less than convenient location requires taking the shuttle bus to transportation. ⊠*5–3–68 Naka-no-shima, Kita-ku, Ōsaka* ☎*06/6448–1121* 🖷*06/6448–4414* ⊕*www. rihga.com* 🛏*980 rooms, 53 suites* ♿*In-room: safe, Internet. In-hotel: 20 restaurants, bars, pools, gym, concierge* ⊟*AE, DC, MC, V.*

$$$$
Fodor'sChoice
★
🔲 **The Ritz-Carlton, Ōsaka** リッツカールトン大阪. Smaller than Ōsaka's other top hotels, the Ritz-Carlton combines a homey feel and European elegance in the city's most luxurious place to stay. King-size beds with goose-down pillows and dark-wood furnishings grace the guest rooms, and the bathrooms have plush bathrobes and towels. Stay on a Club floor for the special lounge. A rarity in Japan, the room price at the Ritz-Carlton includes use of the pool, Jacuzzi, and gym. All rooms have an IT panel through which you can connect your computer and audiovisual equipment to the flat-screen television. All this comes, you understand, at a price—the Ritz-Carlton is Ōsaka's most expensive hotel. **Pros:** luxurious to the last detail; deluxe rooms have stunning night views. **Cons:** the most expensive hotel in town. ⊠*2–5–25 Umeda, Kita-ku, Ōsaka* ☎*06/6343–7000* 🖷*06/6343–7001* ⊕*www.ritzcarlton. com* 🛏*292 rooms* ♿*In-room: Internet. In-hotel: 4 restaurants, bar, pool, gym, executive floor, parking (paid)* ⊟*AE, DC, MC, V.*

$$
🔲 **Shin-Ōsaka Washington Hotel Plaza** 新大阪ワシントンホテルプラザ. Part of a no-nonsense chain of business hotels throughout the country, the Washington is the smartest of its kind. Rooms are not large but are clean and comfortable. Among the highlights are the China Table Chinese restaurant for the food and city views, and the blend of urban groovers from Tōkyō and businessmen in the foyer. Convenient to JR Shin-Ōsaka Station, from which the Shinkansen arrives and departs. Exit 7 Shin-Ōsaka subway. **Pros:** great location if you have an early Shinkansen to catch. **Cons:** not very close to any sights or nightlife. ⊠*5–5–15 Nishi-Nakajima, Yodo-gawa-ku, Ōsaka* ☎*06/6303–8111* 🖷*06/6308–8709* ⊕*shinosaka.wh-at.com/* 🛏*190 rooms* ♿*In-room: refrigerator, Internet. In-hotel: 4 restaurants, parking (paid), no-smoking rooms* ⊟*AE, DC, MC, V.*

$
★
🔲 **Superhotel Ōsaka Higo-bashi** スーパーホテル大阪肥後橋. A member of the popular nationwide chain of business hotels, this Superhotel is in a quiet leafy neighborhood a five-minute walk south of Naka-no-shima. There are just two set prices, for singles or doubles, and they include an international buffet breakfast. That means thick slices of toast and

8

miso soup. Exit 7 Higo-bashi Station on the Yotsu-bashi line. **Pros:** located in a quiet, centrally located neighborhood; reasonably priced. **Cons:** not much of interest within walking distance. ⊠*1–20–1 Edobori, Nishi-ku, Ōsaka* ☎*06/6448–9000* 🖷*06/6448–2400* 🛏*80 rooms* ♿*In-room: no phone, Internet. In-hotel: laundry facilities, Internet terminal* ⊟*V* ⊙*CP.*

MINAMI

$ 🖼**Ebisu-sō Ryokan** えびす荘旅館. Ōsaka's only member of the inexpensive Japanese Inn Group is a partly wooden structure with 15 Japanese-style rooms. It's a very basic but quiet, no-frills operation run by two delightful old ladies who will direct you to the abundance of restaurants and cafés nearby. Close to the electrical-appliance and computer center of Den Den Town and the National Theater, Ebisu-sō Ryokan is a five-minute walk from Ebisu-chō Station (Exit A-2) on the Sakai-suji subway line. **Pros:** friendly innkeepers; excellent location. **Cons:** simple accommodations. ⊠*1–7–33 Nippon-bashi-nishi, Naniwa-ku, Ōsaka* ☎*06/6643–4861* 🛏*15 Japanese-style rooms without bath* ⊟*AE, MC, V.*

$ 🖼**Hearton Hotel Shin-sai-bashi** ハートンホテル心斎橋. For travelers on a budget, the Hearton Hotel Shin-sai-bashi offers a good location at a very reasonable price. Located in America-mura, a short walk from the Shin-sai-bashi Subway and the Midō-suji and Shin-sai-bashi shopping streets, the Hearton is perfectly situated for travelers wishing to take advantage of Ōsaka's shopping and nightlife. The rooms are small but clean and comfortable. **Pros:** well-situated for shopping and nightlife; inexpensive. **Cons:** small, simple rooms. ⊠*1–5–24 Nishi Shin-sai-bashi, Chuo-ku* ☎*06/6251–3711* ⊕*www.heartonhotel.com/hearton_hotel_shinsaibashi.htm* 🛏*302 rooms* ♿*In-room: refrigerator, Internet. In-hotel: laundry, Internet* ⊟*AE, DC, MC.*

$$$$ 🖼**Hotel Nikkō Ōsaka** ホテル日航大阪. A striking white tower in the colorful Shin-sai-bashi Station area, the Nikkō is within easy reach of Ōsaka's nightlife. Price depends on amenities, as the twin and double rooms are all the same size. Opt for a room on one of the L floors for a couple of thousand yen extra. The decor is red, black, and gray, and the rooms have plush beds with double spring mattresses. Black-and-white photographs of Midō-suji-dōri ornament the walls. From Exit 8 Shin-sai-bashi Station on the Midō-suji Line, you walk directly into the hotel. **Pros:** excellent location between the shopping and nightlife areas of Shin-sai-bashi, Namba, and America-mura. **Cons:** priced slightly higher than less centrally located hotels of the same caliber. ⊠*1–3–3 Nishi-Shin-sai-bashi, Chūo-ku, Ōsaka* ☎*06/6244–1111* 🖷*06/6245–2432* ⊕*www.hno.co.jp* 🛏*640 rooms, 5 suites* ♿*In-room: refrigerator, Internet. In-hotel: 3 restaurants, bars, parking (paid), Internet terminal* ⊟*AE, DC, MC, V.*

$$$$ 🖼**Hyatt Regency Ōsaka** ハイアットリージェンシー大阪. If Universal Studios Japan is on your itinerary, the Hyatt, in the Nankō development area, is quite convenient, and Kansai International Airport is a 45-minute bus ride away. The hotel is a 20-minute subway ride from the city center, however. Modern comforts abound: guest rooms are spacious,

especially deluxe doubles and junior suites, which are larger than the typical Japanese apartment. Some rooms on the upper floors have grand views of Ōsaka Bay. **Pros:** larger than average rooms; located near Universal Studios. **Cons:** not a convenient location for experiencing the city. ⊠*1–13 Nankō-Kita, Suminoe-ku, Ōsaka* ☎*06/6612–1234* 🖷*06/6614–7800* ⊕*www.hyattregencyosaka.com* ⤶*500 rooms, 7 suites* ☖*In-room: refrigerator, Internet. In-hotel: 11 restaurants, bars, pool, gym, spa, Internet terminal, parking (free)* ⊟*AE, DC, MC, V.*

$$$$ 🏨 **Sheraton Miyako Hotel Ōsaka** 都ホテル大阪. Renovated in 2007, the Miyako is an excellent base for exploring Ōsaka as well as taking day-trips to Kyoto and Nara. The Kintetsu Uehonmachi station next door offers quick access to Nara and Kyoto while the subway is just two stops from Namba. Ōsaka Castle and Tennō-ji are each a 15-minute walk away. Though less luxurious than some of the Umeda hotels, the Miyako is comfortable and stylish with a staff that is attentive without being obsequious. **Pros:** excellent location; great value if you book online; airport shuttle available. **Cons:** less luxurious than some of its pricier rivals. ⊠*6–1–55 Ue-hon-machi, Tennō-ji-ku, Ōsaka* ☎*06/6773–1111* 🖷*06/6773–3322* ⊕ *www.miyakohotels.ne.jp/osaka* ⤶*575 rooms, 2 suites* ☖*In-room: Internet. In-hotel: 10 restaurants, bars, pool, gym* ⊟*AE, DC, MC, V.*

$$$$ 🏨 **Swissôtel Nankai Ōsaka** スイスホテル南海大阪. With mellow contemporary art and European-style furnishings the standard rooms at this high-end hotel are some of the best in the city. The Executive Club offers additional privacy and a private lounge for breakfast, cocktails, and nightcaps. Be sure to have a drink in Tavola 36, the hotel's top-floor Italian sky lounge, complete with a DJ booth. Take the third-floor exit at Nankai Namba Station to get to the Swissôtel. **Pros:** excellent location in central Namba; connected to Nankai Namba station for easy airport access. **Cons:** one of the most expensive hotels in the area. ⊠*1–60 Namba, 5-chōme, Chūō-ku, Ōsaka* ☎*06/6646–1111* 🖷*06/6648–0331* ⊕*www.swissotel-osaka.co.jp* ⤶*535 rooms, 11 Western-style suites, 2 Japanese-style suites* ☖*In-room: Internet. In-hotel: 11 restaurants, pool, gym* ⊟*AE, DC, MC, V,*

¢–$ 🏨 **Tōyoko Inn Shin-sai-bashi Nishi** 東横イン心斎橋西. A 10-minute walk west of the Shin-sai-bashi subway station and close to the laid-back cafés of Minami Horie, the Tōyoko Inn is a good-value, comfortable business hotel. Thought has gone into the facilities for the budget traveler. Computers with free Internet access are in the foyer, and you can make free local calls from the house phone. The prices include a light breakfast of rice balls, miso soup, and coffee. **Pros:** inexpensive; located near the Minami hot spots. **Cons:** small rooms; few amenities. ⊠*1–9–22 Kita-Horie, Nishi-ku, Ōsaka* ☎*06/6536–1045* 🖷*06/6536–1046* ⊕*www.toyoko-inn.com/eng* ⤶*144 rooms* ☖*In-room: refrigerator, Internet. In-hotel: no-smoking rooms, Internet terminal* ⊟*AE, DC, V* ◎|*CP.*

8

NIGHTLIFE AND THE ARTS

THE ARTS

National Bunraku Theater. Fans of theater will not want to miss the chance to see a performance at Ōsaka's National Bunraku Theatre. Registered by UNESCO as a World Intangible Cultural Heritage in 2003, Bunraku is not your average puppet show. The meter-high puppets require three handlers, and the stories, mostly originating in Ōsaka, contain all the drama and tension (if not the swordfights) of a good Samurai drama. The National Bunraku Theatre is Japan's premier place to watch this 300-year-old art form. An "Earphone-Guide" (¥650 rental) explains the action and context in English as the play unfolds. Performances are usually twice daily (late morning, and late afternoon) on weekends. To get here take the Sennichimae or Sakai-suji subway lines to Nipponbashi Station and take exit 7. The theater is just before passing under the Hanshin Expressway. ⊠ *1–12–10 Nipponbashi, Chuo-ku* ☎*0570/07–9900* ⊕*www.ntj.jac.go.jp* ☜*¥2,300–¥5,800*

PUPPET THEATER

Ōsaka is the home of *bunraku* (puppet drama), which originated during the Heian period (794–1192). In the late 17th and early 18th centuries the local playwright Chikamatsu Monzaemon elevated bunraku to an art form. Bunraku puppets are about two-thirds human size. Three completely visible puppeteers move the puppets. At the National Bunraku Theater the story is chanted in song by the *jōruri* (chanter), with music played on a three-stringed "banjo," the *shamisen.* Try to catch a performance of *Sonezaki Shinjū* (*The Love Suicides at Sonezaki*), set where Kita-shinchi stands now.

Shōchiku-za Kabuki Theater. Ōsaka's Kabuki theater, built in 1923 as Japan's first Western-style theater, rivals Tōkyō's Kabuki-za. Technology has been cleverly incorporated into Shōchiku-za alongside traditional theater design. The house hosts Kabuki for about half the year, with major performances most months. The rest of the year it hosts musicals and other concerts. Tickets range from ¥4,000 to ¥20,000. ⊠ *1–9–19 Dōtombori, Chūō-ku* ☎*06/6214–2211, 06/6214–2200 for reservations.*

NIGHTLIFE

Ōsaka has a diverse nightlife scene. The Kita (North) area surrounds JR Umeda Station; and the Minami (South) area is between the Shinsai-bashi and Namba districts and includes part of Chūō-ku (Central Ward). Many Japanese refer to Minami as being "for kids," but there are plenty of good restaurants and drinking spots for more seasoned bon vivants. Ōsaka's hip young things hang out in America-mura, in the southern part of Chūō-ku, with its innumerable bars and clubs. Kita draws a slightly more adult crowd, including businesspeople.

BARS

Café Absinthe カフェ・アブシンス. After browsing the fashions in Minami-horie's boutiques, pop into Café Absinthe in neighboring Kita-horie for Mediterranean food and good music. Live performances usually start at around 9. The music and the crowd are very international and very laid-back. ⊠ *1–16–18 Kita-horie, Nishi-ku* ☎ *06/6534–6635.*

DANCE CLUBS

Club Karma. If you're looking for serious techno or all-night dancing, Club Karma hosts all-night drum 'n' bass/techno events on weekends and on nights before national holidays (cover from ¥2,500). On non-event nights it's a scenester bar serving good food to hip music. ⊠ *B1f Zero Bldg., 1–5–18 Sonezaki-shinchi, Kita-ku* ☎ *06/6344–6181.*

Mother Hall. Mother Hall doesn't host club events every night, but when it does they're packed. This is a large-scale club that can accommodate up to 1,500 people for trance, house, and other electronic music. ⊠ *B1 Swing Yoshimoto Bldg., 12–35 Namba, Chūō-ku* ☎ *06/4397–9061.*

Sazae. This is the city's slickest dance club, with a state of the art sound system and regular appearances by big-name international DJs. There are weekly drum 'n' bass, reggae, disco, hip-hop, and progressive house nights as well as a gay event once or twice a month. ⊠ *16–4 Chaya-machi, Kita-ku* ☎ *06/6486–3388.*

JAZZ

Blue Note. Jazz fans should head to Umeda and this high-end club where the best of the international and national jazz scenes plays two sets nightly. Tickets aren't cheap: expect to pay anywhere from ¥5,000 to ¥12,000. ⊠ *B2 Herbis Plaza Ent, 2–2–22 Umeda, Kita-ku* ☎ *06/6342–7722.*

Mr. Kelly's. This club on the ground floor of the Sun Garden Hotel regularly features a jazz trio plus a guest vocalist as well as regular touring musicians. The cover charge starts at ¥3,000 for a double-bill. ⊠ *2–4–1 Sonezaki Shinchi, Kita-ku* ☎ *06/6342–5821.*

ROCK AND ALTERNATIVE

Bears. This tiny basement, which reaches capacity with 70 people, is the city's single most interesting venue for live music. It's ground zero for the region's avant-garde musical underground, including such performers as Haco and Empty Orchestra. Events start and finish early, so get here by 6:30. There's something on every evening. ⊠ *B1 Shin-Nihon Namba Bldg., 3–14–5 Namba-naka, Naniwa-ku* ☎ *06/6649–5564.*

Club Quattro. Up-and-coming Japanese rock bands and popular Western bands play here. The sound system is excellent. ⊠ *8F Shin-sai-bashi Parco Bldg., Shin-sai-bashi-suji 1–9–1, Chūō-ku* ☎ *06/6281–8181.*

8

Kōbe

WORD OF MOUTH

"Go visit Himeji Castle. We did that from Kyōto. It is easily done in a morning, is really neat and one of the few castles left in Japan that hasn't been rebuilt. You would still have time for Kōbe in the afternoon."

—cwn

By Maruan El
Mahgiub

Kōbe resonates with a cool, hip vibe, a condition of its internationalism and its position between mountains and sea. With more than 44,000 *gaijin* (foreigners) living in the city, representing more than 120 countries, Kōbe may be Japan's most diverse city. It has great international cuisine, from Indonesian to French. It also has some of the best Japanese cuisine, specializing in Kōbe beef.

Kōbe's diversity is largely attributable to its harbor. The port was a major center for trade with China dating back to the Nara period (710–784). Kōbe's prominence increased briefly for six months in the 12th century when the capital was moved from Kyōto to Fukuhara, now western Kōbe. Japan acquiesced to opening five ports, and on January 1, 1868, international ships sailed into Kōbe's harbor. American and European sailors and traders soon settled in Kōbe, and their culture and technology spread throughout the city. Cinema and jazz made their debut in Kōbe and that legacy is ongoing. Many original residences have survived, and the European structures contrast strikingly with the old Japanese buildings and modern high-rises.

Prior to 1995, Kōbe was Japan's busiest port. But on January 17, 1995, an earthquake with a magnitude of 7.2 hit the Kōbe area, killing more than 6,400 people, injuring almost 40,000, and destroying more than 100,000 homes. Communication lines were destroyed, damaged roads prevented escape and relief, and fires raged throughout the city. Kōbe made a remarkable and quick recovery.

The city now pulses with the activity of a modern, industrialized city. The colorful skyline reflects off the night water, adding to Kōbe's reputation as a city for lovers. Don't come to Kōbe looking for traditional Japan; appreciate its urban energy, savor its international cuisine, and take advantage of its shopping.

⇨*See the glossary at the end of this book for definitions of the common Japanese words and suffixes used in this chapter.*

ORIENTATION AND PLANNING

ORIENTATION

Kōbe lies along the Seto Inland Sea in the center of Honshū, a little west of Ōsaka and several hours east of Hiroshima. Smaller than Tōkyō and Ōsaka, Kōbe is more accessible and less formidable. It is large enough, however, to keep you occupied with new attractions and events no matter how frequently you visit.

Divided into approximately 10 distinctive neighborhoods, the city extends from the business-oriented region near the harbor to the lower

TOP REASONS TO GO

The Beef: Tender, highly marbleized Kōbe beef is world famous. It's easy to find a good steak house, so don't miss out!

Night Views: Kōbe nights are famously romantic. The Ferris wheel, Akashi Bridge, the neon lights lining the ocean, and the black mountains add to the magic.

Luminarie: For two weeks before Christmas, millions of lights arch across Kōbe's streets. Commemorating the 1995 Hanshin-Awaji Earthquake the event attracts approximately 5 million visitors annually.

East Meets West: When the port opened to international trade, Western culture and entertainment flowed into the city. Jazz, international dining, and a sizeable *gaijin* population are legacies of Kōbe's history.

Nada no Sake: The sake breweries of Nada, in western Kōbe, use *miyamizu* (mineral-rich water) and Yamada Nishiki rice, grown near Mt. Rokkō. Numerous sake museums and breweries have free tastings.

slopes of Mt. Rokkō. Penned in by natural boundaries, Kōbe expanded its territory with three man-made islands in the harbor.

Downtown. San-no-miya Station, in the city center, marks the heart of Kōbe's entertainment and nightlife area. Every night passersby linger to hear musicians in a small park just north of the station. Moto-machi's stores are to the west, and most of the business district lies south of San-no-miya.

Kintano-chō. Kōbe's original European and American settlers built elegant residences, now known as *ijinkan*, on the city's northern slopes. Many of the preserved ijinkan have been turned into museums. Small boutiques, international cafés, and a few antiques shops seduce visitors to meander along Kitano-zaka and Pearl Street.

North of Kōbe. The impressive Nunobiki Falls are surprisingly accessible from downtown, just behind the Shin-Kōbe station. Rokkō-san (*san* means "mountain") is a little farther out, providing great views and cool mountain air. Arima Onsen, on the other side of Rokkō-san, is one of Japan's oldest hot-springs destinations.

PLANNING

The big attractions of Kōbe can be covered in a day or two. Hit the Great Hanshin-Awaji Earthquake Museum 阪神・淡路大震災記念人と防災未来センター and the Kōbe City Museum in the morning. Follow this with a stroll around Kitano-chō and a café stop, and wind down the day at Harborland for dinner. On a second day head up Rokkō-san and to the resort town of Arima, where you can soak in mineral hot springs and wander the quaint streets.

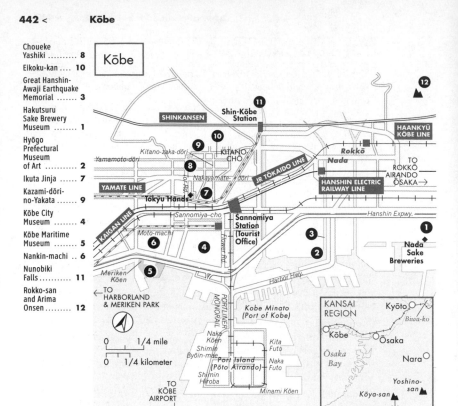

WHEN TO GO

Except for the cold days of winter and the humid days of midsummer, Kōbe enjoys a mild climate tempered by the Seto Nai-kai. Spring, especially at cherry-blossom time, and autumn are the best seasons to visit.

HOW MUCH TIME?

Although Kōbe's main sights could be covered in a day, a two-day stop in the city would not only give you enough time to see most of the sights, it would also give you enough meal times to enjoy the numerous food choices and relax into the city's laid-back rhythm. Put aside a third day for getting out of the city and into the mountains of Rokkō-san and the hot springs at the famous resort of Arima.

GETTING HERE AND AROUND

AIR TRAVEL

Kansai International Airport (KIX) is south of Ōsaka, and approximately 40 minutes from Kōbe. It handles the region's international flights and some domestic flights to and from Japan's larger cities. The Kōbe Airport, handling mainly domestic flights, is 18 minutes from JR San-no-miya Station via the Portliner (¥320 one-way).

Excellent public transport from the airports makes using taxis impractical. From Kansai International Airport, take the JR Kansai Airport

Express Haruka to Shin-Ōsaka and change to the JR Tōkaidō Line for Kōbe's JR San-no-miya Station, a 75-minute (¥3,320) trip, not including transfer times. For a quicker trip, ignore the train and take the comfortable limousine bus (70 minutes; ¥1,800), which drops you off in front of San-no-miya Station.

From Ōsaka Itami Airport, buses to San-no-miya Station leave from a stand between the airport's two terminals approximately every 20 minutes 7:45 AM–9:10 PM. The trip takes about 40 minutes (¥1,020).

SUBWAY TRAVEL

Kōbe's main subway line runs from Tanigami in the far north of the city, and passes through Shin-Kōbe and San-no-miya stations before continuing west to the outskirts of town. Another line runs along the coast from San-no-miya and links up with the main line at Shin-Nagata Station. Fares start at ¥180 and are determined by destination. The San-no-miya–Shin-Kōbe trip costs ¥200.

TRAIN TRAVEL

The Hikari *Shinkansen* runs between Tōkyō and Shin-Kōbe Station in about 3½ hours. If you don't have a JR Pass, the fare is ¥14,270. The trip between Ōsaka Station and Kōbe's San-no-miya Station takes 20 minutes on the JR Tōkaidō Line rapid train, which leaves at 15-minute intervals throughout the day; without a JR Pass the fare is ¥390. The Hankyū and Hanshin private lines run between Ōsaka and Kōbe for ¥310.

The *Shinkansen* (bullet train) stops at the Shin-Kōbe Station, just North of San-no-miya. The two are connected by the Seishin-Yamate Line that extends north from San-no-miya Station to the Shin-Kōbe station. Shin-Kōbe also connects to Arima. The City Loop bus starts at San-no-miya and circles through Meriken Park, Harborland, and Kitano before returning to San-no-miya. Taxis are easy to find at San-no-miya Station, but can also be found at any *noriba*, or taxi stand.

The **Portliner** was the first digitally driven monorail in the world, and departs from San-no-miya Station every six minutes from 6:05 AM until 11:40 PM on its loop to and around Port Island. The ride affords a close-up view of Kōbe Harbor.

Within Kōbe, Japan Rail and the Hankyū and Hanshin lines run parallel east–west and are easy to negotiate. San-no-miya and Moto-machi are the principal downtown stations. Purchase tickets from a vending machine; you surrender them upon passing through the turnstile at your destination station. Fares depend on your destination.

Three rail lines, JR, Hankyu, and Hanshin, cut straight through the city from one side to the other, and converge at San-no-miya Station. Most of the city is a 10-minute walk from a train station, making trains the most convenient way to get around.

VISITOR INFORMATION

Kōbe Tourist Information Center offers detailed maps, in English, of all the neighborhoods, with attractions and streets clearly marked. Also pick up a "Kōbe Guide" and a "Visitor's Welcome Book," which has coupons on museums, activities, and hotels. The English-speaking staff can help book rooms, find tours, and give recommendations. The Kōbe Information Center is near the west exit of JR San-no-miya; another branch is located at the JR Shin-Kōbe station. The Japan Travel Bureau can arrange for hotel reservations, train tickets, package tours, and more throughout the country.

Several voluntary guide services are available, such as Kōbe Systemized Goodwill Guides Club and Kōbe Student Guide. Guides are free, but please pay for all travel expenses, meal expenses, and building admissions.

ESSENTIALS

Airline Contacts All Nippon Airways (☎ *0120/029–222*). **Japan Airlines** (☎ *0120/25–5971*). **Skymark** (☎ *050/3116–7370*).

Airport Contacts Kōbe Airport Terminal (✉ *1 Kōbe Airport, Chuo-ku* ☎ *078/ 304–7777* ⊕ *www.kairport.co.jp/eng/index.html*).

Bus Contacts JR Bus Kanto (✉ *JR San-no-miya Station, Chuo-ku* ☎ *03/3516–1950* ⊕ *www.jrbuskanto.co.jp/bus_route_e/*).

Currency Exchange SMBC Bank Currency Exchange Corner (✉ *2nd fl., JR San-no-miya Station, Chuo-ku* ☎ *078/291–0070* ⊗ *Weekdays 11–7, weekends 9–5*).

Emergency Contacts Daimaru Depāto Pharmacy (✉ *40 Akashi-chō, Chūō-ku* ☎ *078/331–8121*). **Kōbe Kaisei Hospital** (✉ *3–11–15 Shinohara-Kita-machi, Nada-ku* ☎ *078/871–5201* ⊕ *www.kobe-kaisei.org/main.cgi?c=6:0*)

Ferry Contacts Kōbe Ferry Center (✉ *3-7 Shin Minato-chō, Chūō-ku* ☎ *078/ 327–3308*).

Shipping FedEx Kinko's (✉ *1F Makler Kōbe Bldg., 4-2-2 Kumoidori,Chūō-ku* ☎ *078/291–6731* ⊗ *Open continuously 8 am Mon.–10 pm Sat.; Sun. and holidays 8–10*).

Rental Cars Toyota Rent a Car (San-no-miya) (✉ *4–2–12 Isobe Dori, Chuo-ku* ☎ *078/222–0100* ⊕ *www.rent.toyota.co.jp/en/rental/main54.html* ⊗ *8 AM–10 PM*).

Tour Information Shi-nai Teiki Kankō Annaisho (☎ *078/231–4898*). **Systemized Goodwill Guides Club** (☎ *078/785–2898*).

Visitor Information Japan Travel Bureau (✉ *JR San-no-miya Station* ☎ *078/231–4118*). **Kōbe Information Center** (✉ *JR San-no-miya Station* ☎ *078/322–0220* ⊗ *Daily 9–7*. ✉ *Shin-Kōbe Station* ☎ *078/241–9550* ⊗ *Daily 10–6*.). **Kōbe Tourist Information Center** (✉ *At west exit of JR San-no-miya Station* ☎ *078/271–2401*).

EXPLORING KŌBE

DOWNTOWN KŌBE

In 1868, after nearly 200 years of isolation, the Kōbe port opened to the West, and Kōbe became an important gateway for cultural exchange. Confined to a small area by its natural boundaries, the city has kept its industrial harbor within the city limits. The harbor's shipping cranes project incongruously against the city's sleek skyscrapers, but the overall landscape manages to blend together beautifully. The harbor is approximately a 15-minute walk southwest of the San-no-miya area.

TOP ATTRACTIONS

❸ **Great Hanshin-Awaji Earthquake Memorial** *(Hanshin Awaji Daishinsai Kinen)*. In 1995 the Great Hanshin-Awaji Earthquake killed 6,433 people and destroyed much of the harbor and vast areas of the city. Using documentary footage and audio, an introductory film shows the frightening destruction wrought upon this modern city. A re-created post-quake display, film screenings, and high-tech exhibits convey the sorrows and memories of the event. This excellent museum has English pamphlets and electronic guides and English-speaking volunteers are on hand. It's a 10-minute walk from the south exit of JR Nada Station, one stop east of JR San-no-miya Station. ⊠ *1–5–2 Wakinohama Kaigan-dōri, Chūō-ku* ☎*078/262–5050* ⊕*www.dri.ne.jp* ☜*¥800 to both Disaster Reduction and Human Renovation museum; ¥500 each for either one* ⓥ*9:30–4:30, closed Mon.*

Fodor's Choice ★

❷ **Hyōgo Prefectural Museum of Art** 兵庫県立美術館 *(Hyōgo Kenritsu Bijutsukan)*. This striking concrete edifice was designed by acclaimed architect Tadao Andō. Andō works primarily with concrete, and is known for his use of light and water, blending indoors and outdoors and utilizing flowing geometric paths in his designs. He has innumerous works in Japan, and designed the Museum of Modern Art in Fort Worth, Texas, and the Pulitzer Foundation for the Arts building in St. Louis. The permanent exhibition features art from prominent 20th-century Japanese painters Ryōhei Koiso and Heizō Kanayama, Kōbe natives who specialized in Western techniques. The museum rotates its vast collection, displaying fantastic modern works from Japanese artists as well as sculptures by Henry Moore and Auguste Rodin. It also hosts international exhibitions. It's a 10-minute walk from the south exit of JR Nada Station, one stop east of JR San-no-miya Station. ⊠ *1–1–1 Wakinohama Kaigan-dōri, Chūō-ku* ☎*078/262 0901* ⊕*www.artm. pref.hyogo.jp* ☜*¥500* ⓥ *Daily 10–6, closed Mon.*

Fodor's Choice ★

❹ **Kōbe City Museum** 神戸市立博物館 *(Kōbe Shiritsu Hakubutsukan)*. This museum specializes in work from the 16th and 17th centuries, focusing on reciprocal cultural influences between East and West. The first floor has a variety of displays on the West's impact on Japan in the second half of the 17th century. Other exhibits document the influence of Western hairstyles for women and the arrival of electric and gas lamps. The museum also has an impressive collection of woodcuts, old maps, archaeological artifacts, and Namban-style art, namely prints, silkscreens, and paintings from the late 16th to 17th centuries, usually depicting foreigners in Japanese settings. The historical exhibits are fascinating, but it is the artwork from this period that is the real draw.

From San-no-miya Station, walk south on Flower Road to Higashi-Yuenchi Kōen. Walk through the park to the Kōbe Minato post office, across the street on the west side. Then head east along the street in front of the post office toward the Oriental Hotel. Turn left at the

★

9

corner in front of the hotel, and the City Museum is in the old Bank of Tōkyō building at the end of the block. ✉*24 Kyō-machi, Chūō-ku* ☎*078/391–0035* ✉*¥200; more for special exhibitions* ⊙*Tues.– Sun. 9:30–5.*

Harborland & Meriken Park ハーバーランドとメリケンパーク. A trip to Kōbe is incomplete without a waterside visit. Within Meriken Park broken slabs of thick concrete and crooked lightposts are preserved as part of the Port of Kōbe Earthquake Memorial Park. Across the grassy park the Kōbe Maritime Museum's roofline of white metal poles, designed like the billowing sails of a tallship, contrast beautifully with the crimson Port Tower. The top of the tower provides a 360-degree view of Kōbe. A walkway connects to **Mosaic**, Harborland's outdoor shopping mall. You can eat dinner at any of the restaurants on the waterfront. The nighttime view is stunning, with Port Tower and the Maritime Museum lighted up. Nearby, a small Ferris wheel rotates lazily, the colors of its flashing lights bouncing off the sides of nearby ships. Meriken Park and Harborland are a 10-minute walk south of Moto-machi station.

> **SAKELICIOUS!**
>
> **Hakutsuru Sake Brewery Museum** 白鶴酒造資料館. Nada, one of Kōbe's westernmost neighborhoods, is home to a number of museums and breweries—many offering free sake tasting! The best is the Hakutsuru Sake Brewery Museum. At the door is a sake barrel of immense proportions. Traditional tools and devices, videos in English, and life-size figures of traditionally clad brewers demonstrate the sake-brewing process. The tour ends with free tasting. It's a five-minute walk south from Hanshin Sumiyoshi Station. ✉*4–5–5 Sumiyoshiminami-machi, Higashinada-ku* ☎*078/822–8907* ✉*Free* ⊙*Tues.–Sun. 9:30–4:30.*

WORTH NOTING

❼ Ikuta Jinja 生田神社. Legend has it that this shrine was founded by Empress Jingū in the 3rd century, making it one of Japan's oldest. An impressive orange torii, rebuilt after the 1995 earthquake, stands amid the bustle of modern Kōbe, welcoming tourists and religious observers alike. Every year two Noh plays, *Ebira* and *Ikuta Atsumori*, at Ikuta's Autumn Festival (Akimatsuri) retell parts of the 12th-century *Genpei* war. It's around the corner from Tokyu Hands, about 450 yards west of San-no-miya Station. ✉*1–2–1 Shimoyamate-dōri, Chūō-ku.*

❺ Kōbe Maritime Museum & Kawasaki Good Times World 神戸海洋博物館 *(Kōbe Kaiyō Hakubutsukan)*. The Maritime Museum is the stunning building with a billowing roofline of metal-pipe sails. It showcases detailed ship models, opening with a 9-meter model of the HMS *Rodney,* the British flagship that led a 12-ship flotilla into Kōbe Harbor on January 1, 1868. A model of the *Oshoro Maru,* one of Japan's earliest sailing ships, is adorned with pearls, rubies, gold, and silver. There are also displays of modern tankers. **Kawasaki Good Times World** is also inside the museum. High-tech displays and interactive models showcase the Kawasaki company's products, from Jet Skis to the Shinkansen bullet train, and its history. Visitors can ride a helicopter flight simulator and see a robot work at a Rubik's cube. Admission is included in the fee for the Kōbe Maritime Museum. ⊠ *2 Meriken Kōen, Hatoba-chō, Chūō-ku* ☎ *078/327–8983* 🏷 *¥500 for museum, ¥600 for Port Tower, or ¥800 for both* ☉ *Tues.–Sun. 10–5.*

 Nankin-machi 南京町. If you're heading to Meriken Park or Harborland, consider a short stop in Kōbe's Chinatown. The area was originally a center for Chinese immigrants to Kōbe, though it is now mostly popular with Japanese tourists for souvenirs and food. It's a lot more Japan-like than one would expect China to be. To find Nankin-machi from Moto-machi Station, walk on the port side and enter the neighborhood through the large fake-marble gate.

The Islands. Three man-made islands rest in the middle of the harbor. Rokkō Island is home to numerous foreign companies, a number of shopping plazas, and the Sheraton hotel, and is where foreigners now tend to settle. Port Island features conference centers, an amusement park, and the Portopia Hotel. Port Island is linked with downtown by a fully computerized monorail—with no human conductor—that extends south to the Kōbe airport.

KITANO-CHŌ

Wealthy foreigners, including Americans, English, and Germans, settled in the Kitano area in the late 19th century, bringing Western-style domestic architecture. Their homes are referred to in Kōbe as *ijinkan,* and the district is extremely popular with Japanese tourists, who enjoy the rare opportunity to see old-fashioned Western houses. Some residences are still inhabited by Westerners, but more than a dozen 19th-century ijinkan in Kitano-chō are open to the public. A few of them are worth exploring, but seeing them all can be repetitious. The curious mélange of Japanese and Western Victorian and Gothic architecture makes for a good neighborhood walk. The streets are littered with small boutiques, cafés, and a few antiques shops. Try **Nanae** for antiques and the **Bistrot Café de Paris** for a bite of French cuisine.

To get to Kitano-chō, walk 15 minutes north along Kitano-zaka-dōri from San-no-miya Station or 10 minutes west along Kitano-dōri from Shin-Kōbe Station. Yamamoto-dōri (nicknamed Ijinkan-dōri) is Kitano's main east–west street, and the ijinkan are on the small side streets ascending the hill. Tourist information centers offer detailed area maps with all attractions marked in English.

TOP ATTRACTIONS

 Choueke Yashiki シュウエケ邸 *(Choueke ["choo-eh-keh"] Mansion).*
★ This ijinkan should be your first priority. Built in 1889, this is the only currently inhabited house open to the public. It's chock-full of Namban woodblock prints, most dating 1861–62, and memorabilia from East and West. Mrs. Choueke is on hand to show you her treasures. ⊠ *3–17 Yamamoto-dōri, also known as Ijinkan-dōri, Chūō-ku* ☎ *078/221–3209* 🏷 *¥500* ☉ *Wed.–Mon. 9–5.*

Eikoku-kan 英国館 ("eh-ee-ko koo-kan," English House). This typical old-fashioned Western house was constructed in 1907 by an Englishman named Baker and served as a makeshift hospital during World

War II. Now it's a house museum by day and an English pub by night. Antique baroque and Victorian furnishings dominate the interior, there are several downstairs bars, and, as if belonging to a decadent member of the royal family, a bottle of champagne rests in the bathtub. A classic black Jaguar in the driveway and an enormous moose head on the wall complete the English atmosphere. ✉2–3–16 *Kitano-dōri, Chūō-ku* ☎078/241–2338 ☑¥700 ⊙*Museum: daily 9–5; pub: 5 PM–1 AM.*

❾ **Kazami dori-no-Yakata** 風見鶏の館 *(Weathercock House).* More elaborate than any other Kōbe ijinkan, this one, built by a German trader in 1910, stands out strikingly in red brick at the north end of Kitano-chō. It is listed as an Important Cultural Property. (Japan is fond of titles that evoke great importance!) The interior reflects various traditional German architectural styles, including that of a medieval castle. Its architecture makes this the most famous ijinkan, but the interiors are spartan, with few additional attractions. ✉*3–13–3 Kitano-cho, Chūō-ku* ☎*078/242–3223* ☑*¥300* ⊙ *Apr.–Nov, daily 9–6; Dec.–Mar, daily 9–5; closed 1st Tues. of Mar., June, Sept., and Dec.*

NORTH OF KŌBE

Thanks to Kōbe's mountain backdrop, hiking is a popular local pastime. From Shin-Kōbe Station it's a short climb to the Nunobiki Falls. For a good mountain day hike, try going up Rokkō-san; from Hankyū Kōbe Line Rokkō Station you can take a bus or taxi to Rokkō Cable-Shita cable-car station ("Shita" means down or bottom). From there you can either hike all the way up the mountain or take the cable car partway. You may see wild boar—harmless unless provoked—in the forested mountains.

TOP ATTRACTIONS

⓫ **Nunobiki Falls** 布引の滝 *(Nunobiki-no-taki).* In the bustle of this modern city, you wouldn't think that one of Japan's most impressive waterfalls would be just behind the train station. Nunobiki Falls has four gushing cascades in the forests of Mt. Rokkō. References to their beauty have appeared in Japanese literature since the 10th century. They are a 20-minute walk from behind the Shin-Kōbe station. After the falls you can pick up the Shin-Kōbe Ropeway, which stops just above the falls before continuing on to the Nunobiki Herb Park. The stopping point provides a beautiful view of the city, especially at night. Follow the signs to the falls from the station or ask directions from the Ropeway staff. ✉*Chūō-ku*651-0058.

⓬ **Rokkō-san and Arima Onsen** 六甲山と有馬温泉. Three cable cars scale Mt. Rokkō, providing spectacular views of the city. For convenience, take the Shin-Kōbe Ropeway up to the Nunobiki Herb Park. It departs just east of the Shin-Kōbe station. Time the trip so you'll descend soon after dusk, when the city lights shine against the black sea.

The Rokkō cable also has staggering views of lush forests. On the mountain are various recreational areas, including the oldest golf course in Japan, designed in 1903 by the English merchant Arthur H. Gloom, and the summer houses of Kōbe's wealthier residents.

To get to Rokkō-san, take the Hankyū Kōbe Line from Hankyū San-no-miya Station to Hankyū Rokkō Station (¥180). From there take a taxi or a bus to Rokkō Cable-shita Station. A funicular railway travels up the mountain to Rokkō-sanjō Station (¥570). You can return to Kōbe by cable car or by rail. Take the Kōbe Dentetsu to Tanigami Station and change for the subway back to San-no-miya (¥900).

The Japanese were already enjoying the thermal waters at **Arima Onsen** before the 7th century. Arima is on the north slope of Rokkō-san and consists of a maze of tiny streets and traditional houses. Some 30 ryokan use the thermal waters' reputed curative powers to attract guests. Although the water gushes up freely from springs, some ryokan charge as much as ¥10,000 for use of their baths. Go instead to the public bath, **Arima Onsen Kaikan,** in the center of the village near the bus terminal. Here ¥520 gets you a soak in the steaming waters. Arima Onsen Kaikan is open daily 8 AM–10 PM (closed the first and third Tuesday of the month). Take the subway north from JR Shin-Kōbe Station, transferring at Tanigami and ending at Arima (¥900).

> **DISAPPEARING DOLLS**
>
> If you make it to Arima, the *Arima ningyo fude* (Arima doll brush) makes a nice souvenir. Made for calligraphy, the brushes have handles wrapped in colorful silk thread, and a little doll pops out of the handle when writing. The doll disappears when the brush is laid down. Legend has it that long ago Emperor Kōtoku greatly desired a son. After he visited Arima Springs his wish was granted and a son was born. Made for more than 1,300 years, the dolls symbolize the birth of Prince Arima. The brushes are hand-made locally, and their beautiful designs make them popular gift items.

SHOPPING

9

SHOPPING AREAS

Kōbe's historic shopping area is known as **Moto-machi.** It extends west for 2 km (1 mi) from JR Moto-machi Station. Much of the district is under a covered arcade, which starts opposite the Daimaru department store and runs just north of Nankin-machi. Moto-machi is more of a functional shopping area, selling housewares (including antiques), imported foods, and electronics, with restaurants scattered between.

Nearly connected to the Moto-machi arcade, the **San-no-miya Center Gai** arcade extends from the department store Sogo to the Moto-machi area for 1 km (½ mi). Because it's next to San-no-miya Station, this is a good stop for a bite to eat. Center Gai has a hipper vibe than the Moto-machi district. Next to Sogo is a branch of the Loft department store, home to crafts and lifestyle accessories spread over four floors. The building also houses a branch of the Kinokuniya bookstore, which has a small English-language selection.

Piazza Kōbe and **Motokō Town** are two names for one long shopping district full of used goods running under the JR train tracks from San-no-miya to Moto-machi.

SPECIALTY STORES

Nanae is a darling and inexpensive antiques shop in Kitano-chō with a large collection of high-quality used *yukata* (lightweight summer kimonos) that shoppers can try on and a collection of ceramics and other antiques. Nanae, the owner, enjoys explaining the history behind the pieces. ✉*Kurata Bldg. 1F, 2–14–26 Yamamoto-dōri, Chūō-ku* ☎*078/222–8565* ⊙*Daily 10:30–7.*

> **BOUTIQUE ROW**
>
> Kōbe's trendy crowd shops in the exclusive stores on **Tor Road**, which stretches north–south on a tree-lined slope into Kitano-chō. Fashionable boutiques selling Japanese designer brands and imported goods alternate with chic cafés and restaurants. The side streets are fun to poke about.

Naniwa-ya sells excellent Japanese lacquerware at reasonable prices, and has been in operation since before World War I. ✉*3–8 Moto-machi-dōri, 4-chōme, Moto-machi* ☎*078/341–6367* ⊙*Thurs.–Tues. 11–6.*

Sakae-ya has traditional Japanese dolls, from Oshie (three-dimensional pictures made of silk) to kimekomi dolls (animals representing the zodiac calendar) to the traditional samurai and kimono-clad ladies. The tiny shop is packed with cloth for doll-making, cupboards for hiding doll-making supplies, and, of course, dolls. ✉*8–5 Moto-machi-dōri, 5-chōme, Moto-machi* ☎*078/341–1307* ⊙*Tues.–Sun. 10–5:30.*

Santica Town is an underground shopping mall with 120 shops and 30 restaurants. It extends for several blocks beneath Flower Road south from San-no-miya Station. It's closed the third Wednesday of the month. ✉*1–10–1 San-no-miya, Chūō-ku, Kōbe-shi, Hyōgo-ken* ⊙*Daily 10–8.*

Tasaki Shinju, the main shop of this pearl company, not only sells pearls but also exhibits astounding works of "pearl" art, including a model of the "Akashi Pearl Bridge" and a rooster with an impossibly long pearl tail. ✉*Tasaki Bldg., 6–3–2 Minatojima, Naka-machi, Port Island* ☎*078/303–7667* ⊙*Daily 9–6.*

WHERE TO EAT

Kōbe is the place to find international cuisine, especially dishes from Southeast Asia. Excellent restaurants are found practically anywhere, but are especially prevalent north of San-no-miya Station and in the Kitano area.

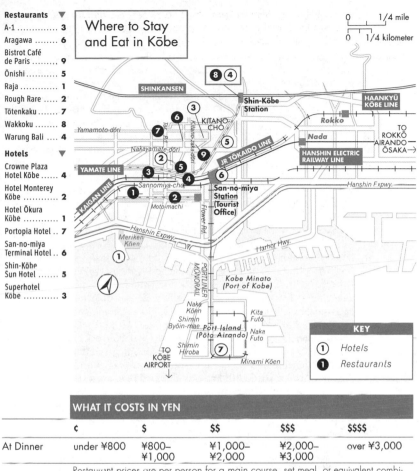

Where to Stay and Eat in Kōbe

WHAT IT COSTS IN YEN					
	¢	$	$$	$$$	$$$$
At Dinner	under ¥800	¥800–¥1,000	¥1,000–¥2,000	¥2,000–¥3,000	over ¥3,000

Restaurant prices are per person for a main course, set meal, or equivalent combinations of smaller dishes.

$$$$ **×A-1.** A-1 has a relaxed atmosphere and serves thick slices of Kōbe
STEAK beef. The *teppanyaki* (broiled on a hot plate) steak is cooked in a spice, wine, and soy marinade and served with charcoal-grilled vegetables and crisp garlic potatoes. Their "small" is enough to fill you up, and costs ¥5,400. Four shops are about town, but the main one is conveniently north of Hankyū San-no-miya Station, across from the B-Kōbe hotel. ⊠ *Lighthouse Bldg., ground floor, 2–2–9 Shimoyamate-dōri, Chūō-ku* ☎ *078/331–8676* ☐ *AE, MC, DC, V.*

$$$$ **×Aragawa** あら皮. Japan's first steak house is famed for its superb hand-
STEAK fed Kōbe beef from one farm in the nearby city of Sanda. The melt-in-
Fodor'sChoice your-mouth *sumiyaki* (charcoal-broiled) steak is worth its weight in
★ yen and only served with mustard and pepper. (Don't even think about asking for other condiments.) The dining room's dark-wood paneling and lovely chandelier give it a European air. Be prepared to spend over

¥28,000 for your main course. ⊠*2–15–18 Nakayamate-dōri, Chūō-ku* ☎*078/221–8547* ⊟*AE, DC, MC, V* ◎*Closed Sun.*

$$$–$$$$
FRENCH

✕**Bistrot Café de Paris** ビストロカフェドパリ. This lively café offers delectable French cuisine and features a popular outdoor terrace—a true rarity in Japan at a prime location. The menu ranges from couscous to bouillabaisse. Midway up the hill on Kitano-zaka, it's great for people-watching and is a good stop while cruising the Kitano district. Lunch sets start at around ¥1,000, dinners around ¥3,000. ⊠*1–7–21 Yamamoto-dōri, Chūō-ku* ☎*078/241–9448* ⊟ AE, MC, V.

$$$$
STEAK
★

✕**Ōnishi** 大西. Ōnishi has a well-deserved reputation, both with Japanese locals and longtime foreign residents, for serving fine Kōbe beef. Steaks are cooked by master chefs in the middle of an enormous counter–hot plate around which diners sit. Baseball players and sumō wrestlers are among the celebrity patrons. ⊠ *Kitanofenikusu Bldg. 3F, 1–17–6 Nakayamate-dōri, Chūō-ku* ☎*078/332–4029* ⊟*No credit cards* ◎*Tues.–Sat. 6 PM–3 AM, Sun. 6 PM–10 PM*

$$
INDIAN
★

✕**Raja** ラジャ. Raja's mellow ambience is matched by delicious Indian food, reputedly made by the first Indian chef in Kōbe. Among their home-style Indian food of spicy curries and samosas, vegetarians can find something *mecha oishii* (very delicious). Raja attributes the excellence of their tandoori chicken to using the highest grade charcoal available in Japan. It's located on the west end of Chinatown, near Moto-machi. Dinner sets start from ¥3,200. ⊠*Sanotatsu Bldg., basement, 2–7–4 Sakae-machi, Chūō-ku* ☎*078/332–5253* ⊟*AE, DC, V.*

$–$$
CONTEMPORARY

✕**Rough Rare** ラフレア. This funky, laid-back, two-story café attracts a young, stylish clientele. A DJ booth is upstairs, and the tables are cleared away for dancing on weekends. Pasta, burgers, salads, and *omuraisu* (a Japanese omelet filled with ketchup-flavored rice) are served. The food isn't gourmet, but the restaurant is just plain cool. ⊠*18–2 Akashi-chō, near Daimaru department store, Chūō-ku* ☎*078/333–0808* ⊟*No credit cards.*

$$$$
CHINESE

✕**Tōtenkaku** 東天閣. This Chinese restaurant has been famous among Kōbe residents since 1945 for its Peking duck, flown in fresh from China. Built at the turn of the 20th century, Tōtenkaku is in one of Kōbe's *ijinkan*, the F. Bishop House. With tall ceilings, red carpets, luxurious curtains, and artwork from China, the building itself is worth the proverbial cost of admission. You can keep the price down by ordering one of the Chinese noodle specialties to fill you up, or by going at lunchtime, when you can have a set meal for just ¥2,100. ⊠*3–14–18 Yamamoto-dōri, Chūō-ku* ☎*078/231–1351* ⊟*AE, DC, MC, V.*

REARED ON BEER

Around the world, **Kōbe beef** is legendary for its succulence and taste. Cows receive daily massages, and in summer they ingest a diet of sake and beer mash. They are descended from an ancient line of *wagyu* (Japanese cows) known to be genetically predisposed to higher marbling. True Kōbe beef comes from only 262 farms in the Tajima region of Hyogo Prefecture (of which Kōbe is the capital), each of which raise an average of five animals. The best beef restaurants are mostly in the central Chūō-ku district, and Kōbe beef is on the menu at the top hotels.

$$$$ ✕**Wakkoku** 和黒. Wakkoku is a swank but affordable restaurant in the
STEAK shopping plaza underneath the Oriental hotel. The beef is sliced thin
and cooked before you on a teppanyaki grill along with fresh vegetables and served with pepper, mustard, and soy sauce for dipping. The
food is delicious. Wakkoku uses three-year-old cows that have never
been bred, which assures their highest-quality beef of unbelievable tenderness. Lunch sets start at ¥2,940 and go up to ¥5,040. The pricier
option uses the highest-quality meat, a small but noticeable difference.
⊠ *Kitano-chō, 1-chōme, Chūō-ku* ☎ *078/262–2838* ⊟ *AE, DC, V.*

$$–$$$ ✕**Warung Bali** ワルン・バリ. The dulcet sounds of the gamelan drift about
INDONESIAN Warung Bali, a tasty Indonesian restaurant serving Balinese food. The
tempeh goring and tofu with peanut sauce are simply amazing. Owner
and chef Made Widjaja is on hand to do more than inspire Japanese
to eat *nasi campur* with their hands; he speaks fluent English and can
custom-make dishes, a relief for vegetarians dining in Japan. ⊠ *Ōnaga
Bldg., 1st fl., 2–4–5 Kitanagasa Dōri, Chūō-ku* ☎ *078/321–6080* ⊟ *No
credit cards.*

WHERE TO STAY

Kōbe is an industrialized city that caters to business travelers. There
are many comfortable, well-situated business hotels. Unless otherwise
noted, all hotel rooms have air-conditioning, private bathrooms, and
televisions.

WHAT IT COSTS IN YEN				
¢	$	$$	$$$	$$$$
For 2 People	under ¥8,000	¥8,000–¥12,000	¥12,000–¥18,000	¥18,000–¥22,000	over ¥22,000

Hotel price categories are for two people and based on rack rates in high season
and the European Plan (with no meals) unless otherwise noted.

9

$$$$ 🏨 **Crowne Plaza Hotel Kōbe.** The tallest building in Kōbe, this stunning
Fodor's Choice luxury hotel stands out prominently at night, a brightly lighted needle-
★ thin tower jutting into the sky. The entire hotel is sumptuous, spacious,
and chic. Guest rooms have pastel fabrics and are furnished with a
desk, a coffee table, and two reading chairs. Corner rooms on higher
floors have superb views over Kōbe. Beneath the lobby are five floors of
shops and restaurants including Wakkoku. It is a five-minute walk from
Kitano-cho, the Shin-Kōbe Ropeway is just outside, and several hiking
trails, including one to Nunobiki Falls, pass very close to the hotel. It's
directly connected to Shin-Kōbe Station, where the Shinkansen arrives
and is three minutes from downtown by subway. **Pros:** nice views of the
city; only a few steps away from the bullet train station. **Cons:** slightly
outside central Kōbe. ⊠ *Kitano-chō, 1-chōme, Chūō-ku, Kōbe-shi,
Hyōgo-ken* ☎ *078/291–1121* 🖷 *078/291–1151* ⊕ *www.ichotelsgroup.
com/h/d/cp/1/en/hotel/osakb* 🛏 *592 rooms (including 12 suites)* 🛆 *In-
room: Internet (no fee). In-hotel: 7 restaurants, room service, bar, pool,
gym* ⊟ *AE, DC, MC, V.*

$$$$ ⌂**Hotel Monterey Kōbe** ホテルモントレー神戸. With its Mediterranean-style courtyard fountains and European furnishings, the Hotel Monterey takes you off Kōbe's busy streets and into modern Italy. It was modeled after a monastery in Florence. The rooms are beautiful and spacious, with terra-cotta floors and tiled bathrooms. The hotel is in a fantastic location, just east of Ikuta Jinja in the heart of San-no-miya. Pros: Italian styling; large rooms; great location. Cons: not a very Japanese experience. ✉ *2–11–13 Shimoyamate-dōri, Chūō-ku, Kōbe-shi, Hyōgo-ken* ☎*078/392–7111* 🖷*078/322–2899* ✇*164 rooms* &*In-room: Internet (no fee). In-hotel: restaurant, Wi-Fi, parking (paid)* ▭*AE, DC, MC, V.*

$$$$
★ ⌂**Hotel Okura Kōbe** ホテルオークラ神戸. A 35-story hotel on the wharf in Meriken Kōen, this is one of the city's best. Beautifully furnished, the hotel lives up to the Okura chain's reputation for excellence. Rooms were by David Hicks, who has designed interiors for the British royal family. The hotel has a well-equipped health club and stunning views of the bay from the beautiful French Emerald Restaurant on the 35th floor. Pros: high-level customer service; choice of Western or Japanese rooms; great views. Cons: the extras and restaurant meals are pricey. ✉*Meriken Kōen, 2–1 Hatoba-chō, Chūō-ku, Kōbe-shi, Hyōgo-ken* ☎*078/333–0111* 🖷*078/333–6673* ⊕*www.kobe.hotelokura.co.jp* ✇*457 Western-style rooms, 5 Japanese-style rooms, 12 suites* &*In-room: Internet, refrigerator. In-hotel: 5 restaurants, room service, bar, pools, gym* ▭*AE, DC, MC, V.*

$$$$ ⌂**Portopia Hotel** ポートピアホテル. A huge hotel with every facility imaginable, rooms here overlook the port, and the restaurants and lounges on the top floors have panoramic views of Rokkō-san and Ōsaka Bay. Ask for a room in the south wing if you want a balcony and ocean view. The Portopia suffers from being on man-made Port Island and can be reached only by the Portliner monorail or by taxi, but it is very convenient to the new Kōbe Airport. Its subpar location is somewhat countered by the fact that everything from food—Chinese, Japanese, and French—to clothing is available inside the hotel. Pros: lots of facilities. Cons: a little dated; not very convenient for downtown sightseeing. ✉*6–10–1 Minatojima Naka-machi, Chūō-ku, Kōbe-shi, Hyōgo-ken* ☎*078/302–1111* 🖷*078/302–6877* ⊕*www.portopia.co.jp* ✇*745 rooms* &*In-room: Internet, refrigerator. In-hotel: 10 restaurants, room service, bar, tennis court, pools, gym* ▭*AE, DC, MC, V.*

$$$ ⌂**San-no-miya Terminal Hotel** 三宮ターミナルホテル. In the terminal building above JR San-no-miya Station, this hotel is extremely convenient, particularly if you need to catch an early train. The rooms are large for the price, but the hotel doesn't have much in the way of facilities. Shops and restaurants abound in the station complex, however. Pros: great location for access to public transportation. Cons: basic facilities (. . . but Kōbe is just outside your door). ✉*8–1–2 Kumoi-dōri, Chūō-ku, Kōbe-shi, Hyōgo-ken* ☎*078/291–0001* 🖷*078/291–0020* ⊕*www.sth-hotel.co.jp* ✇*190 rooms* &*In-room: Wi-Fi, refrigerator* ▭*AE, DC, MC, V.*

$ ⌂**Shin-Kōbe Sun Hotel** 新神戸サンホテル. This old-fashioned business hotel was built in the early boom years after World War II. The rooms are a little tired, but the hotel has a nice, large, Japanese-style public bath, the staff is very friendly, and the building is quiet. Served 7–9, breakfast (Japanese or Western) is included in the bill. The hotel is a 10-minute walk from the San-no-miya station, halfway up the hill toward the JR Shin-Kōbe station. Pros: good public bathing facilities. Cons: the rooms have seen better days. ⊠2–1–9 *Nunobiki-chō, Chūō-ku, Kōbe-shi, Hyōgo-ken* ☎078/272–1080 ⊟078/272–1080 ⟋159 *rooms* ⟋*In-room: refrigerator, Wi-Fi. In-hotel: Japanese baths, no-smoking rooms* ⊟*AE, DC, MC, V* ⫧CP.

¢ ⊞**Superhotel Kōbe.** This business hotel features rooms built according to a formula, with just two set prices for singles and doubles. The bathrooms are tiny, and don't expect stunning interior design. But you get a functional space with a comfortable bed in central Kōbe, halfway between the city's two main train stations, San-no-miya and Shin-Kōbe. Pros: bargain price for a central location. Cons: small rooms; semi-double rather than double beds. ⊠2–1–11 *Kanō-chō, Chūō-ku, Kōbe-shi, Hyōgo-ken* ☎078/261–9000 ⊟078/261–9090 ⟋87 *rooms* ⟋*In-room: no phone, Internet* ⊟*MC, V.*

NIGHTLIFE

Kōbe's compactness is an advantage—virtually all the best bars are within walking distance of each other. Kōbe is regarded as the center of Japan's thriving jazz scene.

Booze Up Bar. Entering Booze Up feels like stepping onto the retro set of a Quentin Tarantino movie. Soul and funk LPs are artfully blended one to the other on dual turntables. Tasty pizzas and pastas are served up alongside good cocktails. Can ya dig it? Just northwest of Tokyu Hands. ⊠2–15–3 *Shimoyamate-dōri* ☎078/322–2873.

Polo Dog. Polo Dog is regularly packed with foreigners, both longtime residents and travelers passing through, and usually has live music on weekends, when it gets loud. The bar serves burgers, salads, and excellent garlic french fries. It's arrayed with '50s and '60s Americana and known for having the cheapest drinks in town ⊠ *K. Bldg., 2nd fl., 1 3 21 San-no-miya-chō, Chuo-ku One street south of Center Gai, near Flower Rd.* ☎078/331–3945.

Sone. The city's most famous jazz club, in existence since 1961, Sone is run by the Sone family. Four sets of live music are played every night, starting at 6:50, and the action often centers on a piano trio with rotating guest vocalists. The musicians are a mix of Japanese and visiting foreigners. Spacious and relaxed, Sone serves pizza, pasta, and salads. There's a cover charge of ¥900. ⊠1–24–10 *Nakayamate-dōri* ☎078/221–2055.

Western Honshū

10

WORD OF MOUTH

"The Itsukushima Jinja Shrine was different than all the rest we visited on our trip as it was built out over water so as to not defile the sacred island. We were able to see the Torii both at high tide when it seemed to float and at low tide when you could walk under it and watch the local people digging for clams. . . . Miyajima was a real highlight of our trip. Don't miss it."

—joannecam

Updated by
John Malloy
Quinn

Like disparate siblings born of a set of common genes, the two coasts of Western Honshū have distinctly different personalities. Taken together, however, they embody the ancient and modern—those two seemingly bipolar time frames that exist in a more profound juxtaposition in Japan than perhaps in any other country in the world.

While the southern coast, or San-yō, has basically gone along with Japan's full-steam-ahead efforts to set the pace for the developed world, you can still encounter pockets of dramatic Old World charm among the modern and shockingly new. On the other hand, thanks to its remoteness, the San-in coast, on the north side of the rugged Chūgoku San-chi, or Central Mountains, has been largely left off the "Things to Exploit" list, yet you may be surprised to learn that everything you'd likely want in a city can be found up there, concentrated in and around lovely Matsue.

Happily, neither coast is short on history, religious significance, scenic beauty, or culinary delights. Hiroshima survived one of history's most horrible events to become a lively, famously friendly, forward-looking city. Kurashiki has a remarkably preserved old-style district that can whisk you back to Edo times with a stroll down willow-draped canals and stylishly tiled warehouses. Hagi is a scenic bayside town that for 500 years has been the center of Hagi-yaki ceramics, coveted light-colored and smooth-textured earthenware glazed with mysteriously translucent milky colors.

⇨ *See the glossary at the end of this book for definitions of the common Japanese words and suffixes used in this chapter.*

ORIENTATION AND PLANNING

ORIENTATION

Western Honshū is bisected by a chain of rugged mountains called the Chūgoku San-chi. Although they are certainly attractive in all seasons, they run (seemingly endlessly) east–west, and this makes going north–south a difficult proposition. Also, keep in mind that travel along the north coast, or San-in, is incredibly slow—by local trains that still plod from village to village—so if you are pressed for time to get to Hagi or Tsuwano, use Yamaguchi as your base; for Matsue, Kurashiki and Okayama work best.

San-yō. San-yō comprises the sunny southern coastline of Western Honshū, and the major cities are Okayama and Hiroshima. If you go to Hiroshima expecting to see a city dressed in a state of perpetual mourning, you will be surprised. While you can indeed easily verify what misery man has wrought, you can also see that it was certainly

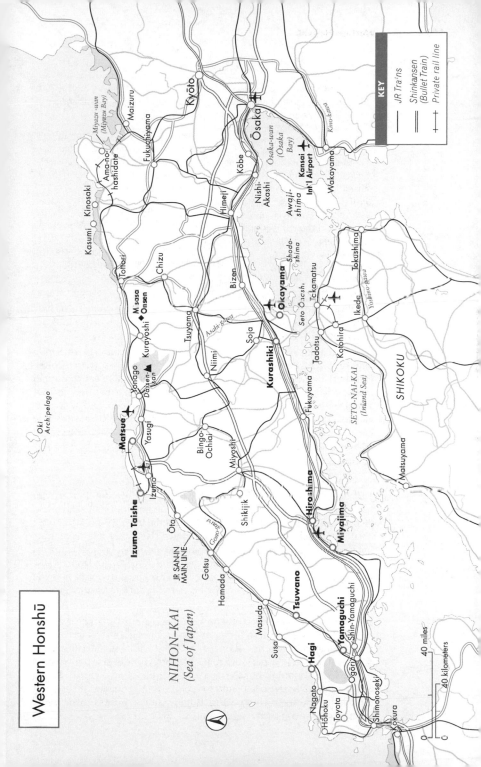

TOP REASONS TO GO

Photogenic Icons: Beside Miyajima, the Ō-torii rises from the Inland Sea. An hour from Matsue is the austere Izumo Taisha, a Shintō shrine reputed to ensure marital happiness.

Fabulous Seafood: Great seafood abounds: oysters in Hiroshima (*kaki*); anago (conger eel) in Miyajima; *uni-don* (sea urchin over rice) in Hagi; *mamakari* (a sardine-like fish) in Kurashiki and Okayama; and little black shijimi clams in Matsue.

Lessons of the Past: Although Atomic-Bomb Dome in Hiroshima is held in great reverence, the city has embraced the future with its energetic multinational vibe.

Gardens: Okayama is home to one of Japan's top three gardens, the spacious and dazzling Kōrakuen, which surrounds the stunning black U-jō, or "Crow Castle."

The People: The people here are among the friendliest and most unhurried in Japan. Foreigners may garner stares, but locals go above and beyond to help puzzled tourists.

not the end for this amazing city. Though the entire stretch is heavily populated, industrialized, and congested, bright spots worth a look are Kurashiki, Okayama, and Miyajima, near Hiroshima.

San-in. Remote as it is, a trip through the surreal landscape of San-in may come closest to providing the best of what Japan has to offer. Hagi and Tsuwano can make you feel absolutely giddy that you found them—and also make you never want to leave. Matsue, though considerably larger than it used to be, can still enchant and weave its magic, as it did for Lafcadio Hearn, the Greek-Irish writer who came here 116 years ago and made a living by telling the rest of the world all about it.

PLANNING

Travel along San-yō is easy, and the weather is usually mild. If you seek adventure along San-in, you'll need time for slow trains, layovers, incomplete or changeable information, and the like. It is possible to get from Yamaguchi up to Matsue in a harried day, but you'll have more fun if you take a couple of days or more. Slow down a bit, and enjoy the mellow pace in the mysterious realms of Hagi and Tsuwano. Sure, these towns are a genuine pain to get to, but they also hold treasures that you won't find anywhere else, precisely because they are so hard to get to.

WHEN TO GO

The San-yō is the sunniest region in Japan, and almost anytime is a good time to visit. The northern shore, or San-in, does get a stronger dose of winter than the southern one but is rewarded with a wonderfully long, delightful spring. Like most of Japan, Western Honshū gets oppressively muggy by midsummer, but the wind off the Nihon-kai cools the San-in coast. Summer festivals and autumn colors are spectacular throughout the region, and these always attract many tourists; reserve well ahead if you are traveling then.

GETTING HERE AND AROUND

AIR TRAVEL

Hiroshima Kūkō is the region's major airport, with many daily flights to Haneda Kūkō in Tōkyō and direct daily flights to Kagoshima, Okinawa, Sendai, and Sapporo. Other airports in Western Honshū—at Izumo, Tottori, and Yonago—have daily flights to Tōkyō. JAS and ANA fly out of Iwami Airport, which serves Hagi, Tsuwano, and Masuda, to Tōkyō and Ōsaka.

Seven daily flights connect Hiroshima and Tōkyō's Haneda Kūkō, and there are flights to Kagoshima, on Kyūshū, and to Sapporo, on Hokkaidō. There are also many flights to Singapore, Hong Kong, Seoul, and other regional hubs.

BOAT AND FERRY TRAVEL

Hiroshima is a ferry hub. Seto Nai-kai Kisen Company runs eight boats daily to Miyajima (¥1,460 one-way, ¥2,800 round-trip). Two important connections are to and from Matsuyama on Shikoku: 16 hydrofoil ferries a day take one hour (¥6,000), and 12 regular ferries a day take three hours (¥4,340 first class, ¥2,170 second class); and one ferry a day makes the three hour trip to and from Beppu on Kyūshū (¥8,500).

BUS TRAVEL

In the major cities local buses or streetcars are a good way to get around. You won't likely need highway buses, except for making the one-hour run between Yamaguchi and Hagi (knocking three hours off the train-travel time). Two companies operate bus routes: JR and Bōchō bus lines. Japan Rail Passes are only valid for use on the JR buses. During peak travel times, call ahead and reserve seats for these buses. Local tourist information offices will help reserve tickets for non-Japanese speakers.

CAR TRAVEL

All the major cities and most of the towns listed here will have at least a basic choice of car-rental outlets. If you know a little Japanese, can handle both middle-of-nowhere navigation and hectic urban traffic situations, you might consider renting a car and exploring Western Honshū at your own pace—but you'll also need a good Japanese map atlas or GPS in your car.

TRAIN TRAVEL

By far the easiest way to travel to Western Honshū and along its southern shore is by Shinkansen from Tōkyō, Kyōto, and Ōsaka. Major Shinkansen stops are Okayama, Hiroshima, and Shin-Yamaguchi. It takes approximately four hours on the Shinkansen to travel to Hiroshima from Tōkyō, less than half that from Ōsaka.

JR express trains run along the San-yō and San-in coasts, making a loop beginning and ending in Kyōto. Crossing from one coast to the other in Western Honshū requires traveling fairly slowly through the mountains. Several train lines link the cities on the northern Nihon-kai coast to Okayama, Hiroshima, and Shin-Yamaguchi on the southern coast. From Shin-Yamaguchi you can visit Hagi (a bus is highly recommended for this) and take trains up to Tsuwano or Matsue. From there, a train can get you down to Kurashiki and Okayama City for a grand loop of the whole region.

10

The JR San-in Main Line from Shimonoseki to Kyōto is the second-longest in Japan, at 680 km (422 mi). It has the most stations of any line in Japan, and to a tourist pressed for time or without proper planning and consideration, this could make for exasperating travel. Note that only two Limited Express trains a day cover the entire Shimonoseki–Kyōto route in either direction. Local trains and buses run between major towns on the San-in coast, but still nowhere near as often or as quickly as in San-yō.

It is always advisable to reserve seats on the popular routes between big cities and to holiday destinations during peak season. Most stations now have tourist offices with English-speakers that can help with this.

RESTAURANTS

Western Honshū is one of the best regions to sample local Japanese seafood, with regional specialties from the Nihon-kai (Japan Sea) and Seto Nai-kai (Inland Sea). The oysters in Hiroshima, sea eel on Miyajima, and sashimi and sushi on the San-in coast are all superb. Matsue's location means that a variety of both freshwater and saltwater fish are available. Most reasonably priced restaurants have a visual display of the menu in the window, if not photos on the menu pages. If you cannot order in Japanese and no English is spoken, after you secure a table, lead the waiter to the window display and point. If you're adventurous, it is always fun to ask, "Osusume?" which means, "(What do you) recommend?"

HOTELS

Accommodations cover a broad spectrum, from pensions and *minshuku* (private residences that rent rooms) to large, modern resort hotels that have little character but all the facilities of an international hotel. Large city and resort hotels have Western and Japanese restaurants. In summer or on holiday weekends hotel reservations are necessary. Unless otherwise noted, rooms have private baths, air-conditioning, and basic TV service.

⇨ *For a short course on accommodations in Japan, see Accommodations in Travel Smart.*

WHAT IT COSTS IN YEN					
	¢	$	$$	$$$	$$$$
RESTAURANTS	under ¥800	¥800–¥1,000	¥1,000–¥2,000	¥2,000–¥3,000	over ¥3,000
HOTELS	under ¥8,000	¥8,000–¥12,000	¥12,000–¥18,000	¥18,000–¥22,000	over ¥22,000

Restaurant prices are per person for a main course, set meal, or equivalent combinations of smaller dishes. Hotel prices are for a double room with private bath, excluding service and tax.

VISITOR INFORMATION

Most major towns and nowadays even the small ones have tourist information centers that offer free maps and brochures. They can also help you secure accommodations. Except for the internationally known places, though, you should not assume that extensive English is spoken.

ESSENTIALS

Boat and Ferry Information Seto Nai-kai Kisen Company (✉ *12–23 Uji-nakaigan, 1-chōme, Minami-ku, Hiroshima* ☎ *002/253–1212* 🖷 *082/505–0134*).

Emergency Contacts Ambulance (☎ *119*). **Police** (☎ *110*).

THE SAN-YŌ REGION 山陽地方

San-yō means "sunny side of the mountain range," and the southern region along the Inland Sea is celebrated for its mild, clear climate. Although it's highly developed, to say the least, and you can't see or appreciate much of its beauty from the train or the highway, it's wonderfully easy to stop and get a closer look at it. Major sights of scenic and historic note heading westward are Okayama City, Kurashiki, Hiroshima, and Miayajima. Shin-Yamaguchi is a great place to hop off the Shinkansen if you are heading to the well-hidden towns of Hagi and Tsuwano, and with a nice mineral bath at Yuda Onsen only a short taxi or train ride or long walk away, nearby Yamaguchi City makes a perfect place to base or branch out from.

HIROSHIMA 広島

342 km (213 mi) west of Shin-Ōsaka, 864 km (537 mi) from Tōkyō.

On August 6, 1945, at 8:15 AM, a massive chunk of metal known as "Little Boy" fell from an American plane, and the sky ignited and glowed for an instant. In that brief moment, however, it became as hot as the surface of the sun in Hiroshima, until then a rather ordinary workaday city in wartime Japan. Half the city was leveled by the resulting blast, and the rest was set ablaze. Rain impregnated with radioactive fallout then fell, killing many that the fire and 1,000-MPH shock wave had not. By the end of this mind-boggling disaster, more than 140,000 people died.

In modern Hiroshima's Peace Memorial Park, the monuments to that day abound, but only one original site bears witness to that enormous release of atomic energy 60 years ago: the A-Bomb Dome. Its gloomy shadows are now surrounded by a vibrant, rebuilt city. As if to show just how earnestly Hiroshima has redefined itself, only a short walk to the east is Nagarekawa-chō, the city's most raucous nightlife district.

10

GETTING HERE AND AROUND

The streetcar (tram) is an easy form of transport in Hiroshima. Enter the middle door and take a ticket from the automatic dispenser. Pay the driver at the front door when you leave. All fares within city limits are ¥150. A one-day pass is ¥600, available for purchase at the platform outside JR Hiroshima Station. There are seven streetcar lines; four either depart from the JR station or make it their terminus. Stops are announced by a recording, and each stop has a sign in *rōmaji* (romanized Japanese) posted on the platform. Buses also joust with the traffic on Hiroshima's hectic streets; the basic fare is ¥200. Information in English can be gathered at any of the Hiroshima Tourist Info Centers.

Taxis can be hailed throughout the city. The fare for the first 1½ km (1 mi) is ¥570 for small taxis, ¥620 for larger ones, then ¥70 for every 300 meters (335 yards).

Two excellent, English-speaking **Tourist Information Offices** are in JR Hiroshima Station: the south exit office, on the first floor, is the main one; the other is on the first floor at the Shinkansen (north) exit. The main tourist office, the **Rest House In Peace Memorial Park** is in the Peace Memorial Park, next to the Motoyasu fork of the river, between the Children's Peace Memorial and the Flame of Peace. Also in the park, in the southwest corner between the Ōta River and the Peace Memorial Museum, is the **International Conference Center Hiroshima**, which offers ample useful English information.

ESSENTIALS
Currency Exchange Hiroshima Bank (⊠ *1–3–8 Kamiya-chō, Naka-ku* ☎ *082/ 247–5151*).

Internet Futaba @ Café GIGA (⊠ *Hiroshima Eki-Mae, 2–22 Matsubara-cho, Minami-ku* ☎ *082/568–4792*).

Shipping Higashi-machi Post Office (*Outside Hiroshima Station's south exit 9–5*).

Visitor Information International Conference Center Hiroshima (☎ *082/ 242–7777* ⊙ *May–Nov., daily 9–7; Dec.–Apr., daily 10–6*). **Rest House In Peace Memorial Park** (☎ *082/247–6738* ⊙ *Apr.–Sept., daily 9:30–6; Oct.– Mar., daily 8:30–5*). **Tourist Information Offices** (☎ *082/261–1877, south exit; 082/263–6822, north exit* ⊙ *Daily 9–5:30*). **Rest House In Peace Memorial Park** (☎ *082/247–6738* ⊙ *Apr.–Sept., daily 9:30–6; Oct.–Mar., daily 8:30–5*).

WHAT TO SEE
The **Peace Memorial Park** 平和祈念公園 (*Heiwa Kinen Kōen*) contains the key World War II sites in Hiroshima. It's situated in the northern point of the triangle formed by two of Hiroshima's rivers, the Ōta-gawa (also called Hon-kawa) and Motoyasu-gawa. From Hiroshima Station it's a 20-minute walk southwest, or take Streetcar 2 or 6 to the Gembaku-Dōmu-mae stop and cross over Motoyasu-gawa on the Aioi-bashi. The park entrance is in the middle of the bridge, and between there and Peace Memorial Museum are statues and monuments. Head straight for the museum (a 10-minute walk from the bridge); you can linger at the monuments on your way back. A less dramatic approach from Hiroshima Station is to take the Hiroshima Bus Company's red-and-white Bus 24 to Heiwa Kōen, only a two-minute walk to the museum, or to take Streetcar 1 to Chūden-mae for a five-minute walk to the museum.

①
Fodor's Choice
★

The **A-Bomb Dome** 原爆ドーム (*Gembaku Dōmu*) is a poignant symbol of man's self-destructiveness. It was the city's old Industrial Promotion Hall, and it stands in stark contrast to the new Hiroshima, which hums along close by. Despite being directly below the bomb blast, the building did not collapse into rubble like the rest of the city. Eerie, twisted, and charred, the sturdy domed structure of iron and concrete has stood darkly brooding next to the river, basically untouched since that horrible morning. A visit to A-Bomb Dome is a sobering reminder of nuclear destruction, and at dusk the sad old building's foreboding,

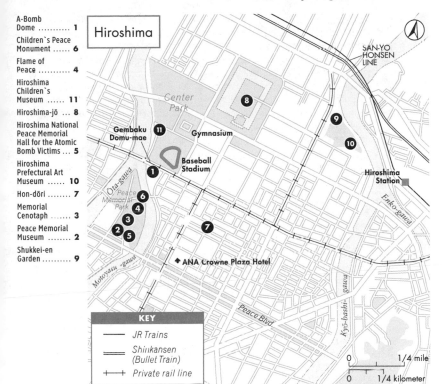

Hiroshima

Center Park

Gembaku Domu-mae ⑪

Gymnasium

⑧

⑨

⑩

SAN-YO HONSEN LINE

Hiroshima Station

Baseball Stadium

① Ota-gawa

Peace Memorial Park

⑥

④

③

② ⑤

⑦

Enko-gawa

Motoyasu-gawa

♦ ANA Crowne Plaza Hotel

Peace Blvd.

Kyo-bashi-gawa

KEY

——— JR Trains

=== Shinkansen (Bullet Train)

+—+ Private rail line

0 ___ 1/4 mile

0 ___ 1/4 kilometer

derelict appearance can be emotionally overwhelming. The site is just outside the official northeast boundary of Peace Memorial Park. Take Streetcar 2 or 6 from Hiroshima Station to the Gembaku-Dōmu-mae stop. ⊠ *Heiwa Kinen Kōen.*

❷ A visit to the **Peace Memorial Museum** 平和祈念資料館 *(Heiwa Kinen Shiryōkan)* may be too intense an experience for some. Displays of models, charred fragments of clothing, melted ceramic tiles, lunch boxes, watches, and shocking photographs, tell Hiroshima's story of death and destruction. The heat-ray-photographed human shadow permanently imprinted on granite steps can take you well beyond sadness, and the Dalí-esque watch forever stopped at 8:15 is chilling. Most exhibits have brief explanations in English, and more detailed information is on audiocassettes, which you can rent for ¥150. ⊠ *Heiwa Kinen Kōen* ☎ 082/241–4004 ☞ ¥50 ⊘ *Apr.–July, daily 9–5:30; Aug. 1–15, daily 8:30–6:30; Aug. 16–Nov., daily 8:30–5:30; Dec.–Mar., daily 9–4:30.*

❸ The **Memorial Cenotaph** 原爆死没者慰霊碑 *(Gembaku Shibotsusha Irei-hi),* designed by Japanese architect Kenzō Tange, resembles the primitive A-frame houses of Japan's earliest inhabitants. Buried inside is a chest containing the names of those who died in the destruction and aftermath of the atomic bomb. On the exterior is the inscription (translated), REST IN PEACE, FOR THE ERROR SHALL NOT BE REPEATED. The cenotaph

10

1,000 Paper Cranes

Pause before the **Children's Peace Monument** 原爆の子像 *(Genbaku-no-ko-zō)* before leaving the park. Many consider this the most profound memorial in Peace Memorial Park. The figure is of a Sadako, a young girl who at age 10 developed leukemia as a result of exposure to the atomic radiation that lingered long after the blast. She believed that if she could fold 1,000 paper *senbazuru* (cranes)—a Japanese symbol of good fortune and longevity—her illness would be cured. She died before finishing the thousand, and it is said that her schoolmates finished the job for her. Her story has become a folktale of sorts, and it inspired a nationwide paper crane–folding effort among schoolchildren that continues to this day. The colorful chains of paper cranes—delivered daily from schools all over the world—are visually and emotionally striking. ⊠ *Heiwa Kinen Kōen.*

stands before the north side of the Heiwa Kinen Shiryōkan. ⊠ *Heiwa Kinen Kōen.*

❹ The **Flame of Peace** 平和の灯 *(Heiwa no Tomoshibi)* burns behind the Memorial Cenotaph. The flame will be extinguished only when all atomic weapons are banished. In the meantime, every August 6, the citizens of Hiroshima float paper lanterns down the city's rivers for the repose of the souls of the atomic-bomb victims. ⊠ *Heiwa Kinen Kōen.*

❺ The **Hiroshima National Peace Memorial Hall for the Atomic Bomb Victims** 原爆死没者追悼平和祈念館 *(Kokuritsu Hiroshima Hibakusha Tsuitō Heiwa Kinen-kan)* recounts the stories of known victims of the atomic devastation. In addition to the extensive archives of names, a collection of victims' photos lends immediacy to one of the most shocking moments in history. Heartbreaking first-hand accounts and memoirs of survivors are available for viewing. ⊠ *1–6 Nakajima-chō, Heiwa Kinen Kōen, Hiroshima* ☎ *082/543–6271* 🖷 *082/543–6273* 🎫 *Free* ☉ *Apr.–July, daily 9–6; Aug. 1–15, daily 8:30–7; Aug. 16–Nov., daily 8:30–6; Dec.–Mar., daily 9–5.*

❼ Around **Hon-dōri** 本通り, Hiroshima's central district, are hundreds of shopkeepers. Take the tram that runs from the main station to stop T-31 (Hon-dōri), or simply walk east across the north bridge out of Peace Park. The big department stores are at the east end of the arcade, near the Hatchobori streetcar stop: Sogō (closed Tuesday) is open 10–8; Fukuya (closed Wednesday) and Tenmaya (closed Thursday) are open from 10 to 7:30; and Mitsukoshi (closed Monday) is open 10–7. Many restaurants, including a big, gorgeous Andersen's, a popular bakery chain (one block down on the right from T-31) and a range of modern hotels are also found here. ⊠ *Hon-dōri.*

❽ **Hiroshima-jō** 広島城 was originally built by Terumoto Mōri on the Ōtagawa delta in 1589. He named the surrounding flatlands *Hiro-Shima,* meaning "wide island," and it stuck. The Imperial Japanese Army used the castle as headquarters in World War II, and with its significant depot of munitions it was one of the targets of the bomb. It was destroyed in the blast. In 1958 the five-story donjon was rebuilt to its original specifications. Unlike many castles in Japan, it has lots of brown wood paneling that gives it a warm appearance, and it stands in intriguing contrast to the modern city that has evolved around it. Inside are exhibits from Japan's feudal Edo Period (17th–19th centuries). It's a 15-minute walk north from the A-Bomb Dome. ✉21–1 Moto-machi, Naka-ku ☎082/221–7512 ✆Castle and museum ¥360 ☾Apr.–Sept., daily 9–5:30; Oct.–Mar., daily 9–4:30.

⑨ The garden laid out in 1630 by Lord Naga-akira Asano, **Shukkei-en** 縮景園 (literally, shrunken scenery garden), resembles one once found around a famed lake in Hangzhou, China, which the *daimyō* wanted to re-create for leisurely strolls. The water is dotted with tiny rocky islets sprouting gnarled pine trees. Small bridges cross above lots of colorful carp, a fish venerated for its long and vigorous life. Shukkei-en is east of Hiroshima-jō castle on the banks of the Kyō-bashi-gawa. Return to the JR station on Streetcar 9; at the end of the line transfer to Streetcar 1, 2, or 6. If you purchase a combined ticket (¥600) for the garden and the Prefectural Art Museum, you must visit the museum first and enter the garden from the museum. ✉2–11 Kamiya-chō, Naka-ku ☎082/221–3620 ✆¥250 ☾Apr.–Sept., daily 9–6; Oct.–Mar., daily 9–5.

⑩ Hiroshima Prefectural Art Museum (*Hirosohima Kenritsu Bijutsukan*), next to the Shukkei Garden, is a visual treat. Standouts include two particularly surrealistic pieces: a typically fantastical piece by Salvador Dalí called *Dream of Venus;* and Ikuo Hirayama's much closer-to-home *Holocaust at Hiroshima.* Hirayama, who became one of Japan's most acclaimed artists, was a junior-high-school student at the time the A-bomb was dropped. ✉2–22 Kaminobori-cho, Naka-ku ☎082/221–6246 ✆¥500; museum and park ¥600 ☾Tues.–Sun. 9–5, Sat. until 7.

⑪ The hands-on **Hiroshima Children's Museum** 広島子供文化科学館 (*Kodomo Bunka Kagakukan*) is a good diversion for the kids. The joyful noise of excited children alleviates the somber mood of Peace Memorial Park. Kids get a kick out conducting their own hands-on science "experiments." To get here, leave the park via Aioi-bashi at the North Entrance and walk north and east, keeping the river on your left and the baseball stadium on your right. A planetarium is next door. ✉5–83 Moto-machi, Naka-ku ☎082/222–5346 ✆Center free, planetarium ¥500; kids ¥250 ☾Tues.–Sun. 9–5.

10

WHERE TO EAT

$$–$$$
JAPANESE

✕**Hiroshima Station** 広島駅. If you don't have enough time to go out on the town for lunch or dinner, try the beer garden–restaurant area in the station's basement or the restaurants on the second and sixth floors of the Asse Department Store. You'll find restaurants of all types, from in-and-out cheapies to elegant eateries—many are branches of famous establishments elsewhere in the city. Enter the Asse complex from the south exit of the JR Hiroshima station. ✉JR Hiroshima Station Bldg., 9–1 Matsubara-chō, Higashi-ku ☎082/248–2391 ☾Daily 10–9.

$$$$
SEAFOOD
★

✕**Kakifune Kanawa** (*Kanawa Oyster Boat*). Hiroshima is known for its oysters, and Kanawa, on a barge moored on the Motoyasu-gawa, near Peace Memorial Park, gets its oysters from a particularly salty area of the Inland Sea. It's believed that these waters impart the firm flesh and sweet, robust taste that loyal customers love to splurge on. It's not cheap, but the oysters are worth every yen. An English menu makes it all very easy, and dining is on tatami mats, with relaxing river views. ✉*3–1 Ohashi, Ohte-machi, moored on river at Heiwa-Ohashi, Naka-ku* ☎*082/241–7416* ▤*AE, DC, MC, V* ☻*Mon.–Sat. 11–2, 5–9.*

$–$$　✕**Okonomi Mura** お好み村 *(Village of Okonomiyaki).* In this enclave 20
JAPANESE　shops serve *okonomi-yaki,* literally, "as you like it grilled." Okonomi-yaki is best described as an everything omelet, topped with bits of shrimp, pork, squid, or chicken, cabbage, and bean sprouts. Different areas of Japan make different okonomi-yaki; in Hiroshima the ingredients are layered rather than mixed, and they throw in lots of fried noodles. Seating in these shops, which are generally open late, is either at a wide counter in front of a grill or at a table with its own grill. This complex is near the Hon-dōri shopping area, just west of Chūō-dōri. ✉*Shintenchi Plaza, 5–13 Shintenchi, 2nd–4th fls., Naka-ku* ▤*No credit cards.*

$$$–$$$$　✕**Suishin** 酔心. Famous for its *kamameshi,* or rice casseroles, this res-
JAPANESE　taurant serves the freshest fish from the Seto Nai-kai—fugu, or puffer-fish, oysters, and eel, to name but a few. If you prefer your fish cooked, try the rockfish grilled with soy sauce. Suishin has an English-language menu, and a simple set-up with only a counter bar and four tables. ✉*6–7 Tate-machi, Naka-ku* ☎*082/247–4411* ▤*AE, DC, MC, V* ☻*Closed Wed.*

WHERE TO STAY

$$$$　▦**ANA Crowne Plaza Hotel Hiroshima** ANA クラウンプラザホテル広島.
★　This reliable and popular hotel was renovated in 2007 and remains one of the very best in town. The Peace Park and the nightlife of Nagarekawa are only a short walk away. The Unkai restaurant, on the fifth floor, has good Japanese food and looks over a garden of dwarf trees, rocks, and a pond with colorful carp. **Pros:** free Internet access in rooms and lobby. **Cons:** bring your own laptop as on-site rentals are expensive. ✉*7–20 Naka-machi, Naka-ku, Hiroshima, Hiroshima-ken* ☎*082/241–1111* 📠*082/241–9123* ➷*430 Western-style rooms, 1 royal suite* ☌*In-room: Internet. In-hotel: 6 restaurants, pool, gym, Wi-Fi* ▤*AE, DC, MC, V.*

$$　▦**Comfort Hotel Hiroshima** コンフォートホテル広島. This affordable hotel stands near Peace Memorial Park, and it's also just a short walk from the happening nightspots. Rooms, though standard, are comfortable, and guests have free Internet access in the lobby and free Wi-Fi in the rooms. **Pros:** free Western and Japanese buffet breakfast; 10-minute walk to Peace Park and Hondori shopping street. **Cons:** tiny bath-rooms; thin walls transmit some noise. ✉*3–17 Komachi , Naka-ku, Hiroshima, Hiroshima-ken* ☎*082/541–5555* 📠*082/541–0096* ➷*282 Western-style rooms* ☌ *In-room: Wi-Fi. In-hotel: Internet terminal* ▤*AE, DC, MC, V.*

$$$–$$$$　▦**Hotel Granvia Hiroshima** ホテルグランヴィア広島. Connected by walk-ways to Hiroshima's JR station, this nice, relaxing hotel is convenient and welcoming to weary travelers. The Japanese restaurant Seto-uchi on the second floor offers a sampling of good traditional fare, and the expansive multilevel lobby is great for people-watching. **Pros:** convenient for train access; helpful staff; good food; free Internet. **Cons:** far from the action; spartan room furnishings and tight spaces; lack of English. ✉ *1–5 Matsubara-cho, Minami-ku, Hiroshima, Hiroshima-ken* ☎ *082/262-1111* 📠 *082/262-4050* 🛏 *400 rooms, 4 suites* ♿ *In-hotel: 5 restaurants, bar* ⊟*AE, DC, MC, V* ⑩*EP, MAP.*

TOURS

A number of sightseeing tours are available, including tours of Hiroshima and cruises on the Seto Nai-kai, in particular to Miyajima, the island with the famous tidal-basin torii.

To arrange for a sightseeing taxi ahead of time, telephone the **Hiroshima Station Tourist Information Center** (☎ *082/261-1877*). A two-hour tour runs approximately ¥8,400. Because these taxi drivers are not guides, you should rent an audio guide that describes key sights in English. These special taxis can be picked up from a special depot in front of Hiroshima Station at the Shinkansen entrance.

A 4-hour, 40-minute tour of the city's major sights operated by **Hiroshima Bus Company** (☎ *082/545-7950* 📠 *082/545-7963*) costs ¥3,500. Tours leave at 9 AM and 2 PM. An eight-hour tour of both the city and Miyajima costs ¥9,470, and includes lunch. It leaves at 9:30 AM. You depart from in front of Hiroshima Station's Shinkansen entrance. All tours are in Japanese, but the sights are gaijin-friendly.

Hiroshima Peace Culture Foundation International Relations and Cooperation Division (☎ *082/242-8879* 📠 *082/242-7452*) has a home-visit program. To make arrangements, go the day before you wish to visit a Japanese home to the International Center on the ground floor of the International Conference Center in Peace Memorial Park. Although not required, bringing an inexpensive gift such as flowers or treats from your home country helps to ensure a successful visit.

MIYAJIMA 宮島

Miyajima's majestic orange Ō-torii, or big gate, is made of several stout, rot-resistant camphor-tree trunks, and is famed for the illusion it gives of "floating" over the water. The torii is one of Japan's most enduring scenic attractions, but most of the time it actually presides over brownish tidal sand flats, so you will want to time your visit for when the tide is in. Ferry offices and hotels can give you a tidal forecast—don't forget to ask.

Behind the sea-gate is the elegant shrine Itsukushima Jinja. For a few hundred yen you can walk the labyrinthine wooden boardwalks out over the tidal basin and pick your spots to snap those perfect photos.

To get to the shrine and to see the torii, go right from the pier on the path that leads through the village, which is crowded with restaurants, hotels, and souvenir shops. As you pass through the park, expect to be greeted by herds of fearless deer. Don't show or let them smell any food, or else you'll become too popular; they do have little horns, and they are known to head-butt those who disappoint them!

10

GETTING HERE AND AROUND

The easiest, least expensive way to get to Miyajima is to take the train on the JR San-yō Line from Hiroshima Station to Miyajima-guchi Station. From Miyajima-guchi Station, a three-minute walk takes you to the pier where ferries depart for Miyajima. The train takes about 25 minutes (¥400) and departs from Hiroshima every 15–20 minutes. The first train leaves Hiroshima at 5:55 AM; the last ferry returns from Miyajima at 10:05 PM. There are two boats, but the JR Rail Pass is only valid on the JR-operated boat (¥340 round trip without Rail Pass). Allow a minimum of three hours for the major sights of Miyajima, or just one hour to get photos of Ō-torii and the shrine.

Inside the ferry terminal (common to both lines), tucked in the entrance to a novelty and snack shop, is the English-speaking **Miyajima Tourist Association.**

ESSENTIALS

Visitor Information Miyajima Tourist Association (☎ *0829/44–2011* ☉ *Daily 9–7*).

WHAT TO SEE

★ **Ō-torii** 大鳥居 stands nearly 50 feet tall at the entrance to the cove where the ancient Shintō shrine is. This, the 18th version, was built in 1875, and has become one of the nation's most recognizable symbols. Hotels and ferry operators have tide charts so you can maximize your photo opportunities; otherwise you may gasp in surprise to find the mythic gate suspended over drab sand flats.

If you stay overnight on the island, and if the weather cooperates, you're guaranteed to get some photos to die for, because the gate is lit up in spectacular fashion and looks hallucinatory set against the black night air and calm reflecting water. The nearby five-story pagoda and the shrine are also illuminated.

Itsukushima Jinja 厳島神社 was founded in 593 and dedicated to the three daughters of Susano-o-no-Mikoto, the Shintō god of the moon—also of the oceans, moon-tugged as they are. The shrine has been continually repaired and rebuilt, and the present structure is a 16th-century copy of 12th-century buildings. The orange woodwork next to the glaring white walls is surprisingly attractive, especially when complemented by a blue sky and sea. The deck has the best frontal views of the torii. 🖭 *¥300* ☉ *Mar.–Oct., daily 6:30–6; Nov.–Feb., daily 6:30–5:30.*

Atop a small hill overlooking Itsukushima Jinja, **Go-jū-no-tō** 五重の塔 *(Five-Storied Pagoda)* is lacquered in bright orange, like the shrine and gate, and dates from 1407. At night, it's extra gorgeous—you'll want a roll of high-speed film or a steady hand for digital photos.

Many people spend only half a day on Miyajima, but if you have more time, take a stroll through **Momijidani Kōen** 紅葉谷公園 *(Red Maple Valley Park)*, inland from Itsukushima Jinja. A steeply priced cable car goes a mile up, stopping nearly at the summit of **Misen-dake** (Mt. Misen). It's a short hike from the upper terminus to the top of the mountain, where you can look out over Seto Nai-kai and all the way to Hiroshima. 🖭 *Cable car ¥900 one-way, ¥1,800 round-trip; park free.*

WHERE TO STAY

$$$$ ⌂ **Iwasō Ryokan** 岩惣. For traditional elegance, it's easy to like this venerable Japanese inn. The rooms in the newer wing are nice enough, but the older rooms have more character. Two quaint cottages on the grounds have suites decorated with antiques. Prices vary widely according to the size of your room, its view, and the kaiseki dinner you select, so be sure to get it all ironed out when you make reservations. Breakfast and dinner are included in the rates, and can be made Western style. Nonguests can also enjoy the food. **Pros:** the oldest and most famous lodging on the island; everyone important has stayed here; delicious 12-course meals. **Cons:** sure, you'll feel just like the royalty that signed their guest book—until you get the bill; onsen may be a bit too hot and stuffy for some. ✉*345 Miyajima-chō, Hiroshima, Hiroshima-ken* ☎*0829/44–2233* 🖷*0829/44–2230* ⬳*38 Japanese-style rooms, 33 with bath* ⚒*In-hotel: restaurant, Japanese baths* ▤*AE, DC, V* ⎮⊙⎮*EP, MAP.*

$$$$ ⌂ **Ryokan Jukei-sō** 聚景荘. This charming and relatively modernized
★ hillside ryokan has been around for more than a century. It also has the best views available anywhere on the island. Every room is blessed with a panorama of Ō-torii, the shrine, and the pagodas—and all are backed by the sea, lush trees, or mountains. The friendly English-speaking owners provide excellent service and food. It's off the quiet east side of the bay, and getting here is a nice stroll—or ask the Tourist Info Office inside the ferry terminal to call for you, and a van will pick you up. A private (no extra charge) outdoor bath on a sheltered overhanging corner has great views, so don't forget to reserve your 30-minute slot of pure Zen when you check in. Down in the basement there are more baths, separated by sex and open 24 hours. While soaking you can stare at what is probably the most impressive noncommercial aquarium you'll ever see. **Pros:** great views, inside and out; quiet hillside retreat; unobtrusive, respectful service. **Cons:** a bit boring if peace and quiet isn't your thing. ✉*50 Miyajima-chō, Hiroshima, Hiroshima-ken* ☎*0829/44–0300* 🖷*0829/44–0388* ⬳*13 Japanese-style rooms* ⚒*In-hotel: restaurant, Japanese baths* ▤*AE, DC, MC, V* ⎮⊙⎮*EP, MAP.*

YAMAGUCHI 山口

146 km (91 mi) west of Hiroshima.

Convenient access to the Shinkansen at nearby Shin-Yamaguchi (which itself has no notable attractions), unbeatable connections to territory's most remote hinterlands, and some disarmingly nice hospitality and local charm make Yamaguchi City a logical base for striking out for Hagi and Tsuwano—especially if accommodations are fully booked in those romantic hideaways. This capital city has a rare and well-preserved five-story pagoda, a somewhat famous park, a decent shopping mall that isn't wall-to-wall people, and a lot of lush greenery descending from the mountains. Perhaps most enticing of all are the countless healing sulfurous baths of Yuda Onsen, only a short ¥500 cab ride or one train-stop away.

10

GETTING HERE AND AROUND

The Shinkansen at Shin-Yamaguchi will get you here. Should you need a map of Yamaguchi, restaurant or hotel recommendations and assistance, or useful onward travel information, head to the English-speaking **Tourist Information Office** on the second floor of the JR Yamaguchi Station. Shin-Yamaguchi also has a helpful English-speaking **Tourist Information Office** on the second floor by the station's north (Shinkansen) exit.

ESSENTIALS

Currency Exchange Yamaguchi Bank (⊠ *JR Yamagcuhi Station Bldg., 2-5-5 Yamaguchi-chi, Yamaguchi-ken* ☏ *083/922-1750).*

Visitor Information Tourist Information Office (☏ *083/933-0090* ⏱ *Apr.-Nov., daily 9-6; Dec.-Mar., daily 8:30-5:30).* **Shin-Yamaguchi Tourist Information Office** (☏ *083/972-6373* ⏱ *Daily 9-6).*

WHERE TO EAT AND STAY

$$ 🏨**Sunroute International Hotel Yamaguchi** サンルート国際ホテル山口. The staff handles your every request with grace. Rooms are adequate, the views of those gorgeous green mountains are good, and the price is right. It's on a right-hand corner a few blocks up the big street heading straight from the station exit. **Pros:** quiet, yet not too far from sights and shops; top-notch attentive staff. **Cons:** business-hotel style rooms; not much doing in these parts, especially if you're alone. ⊠ *1–1 Nakagawara-chō, Yamaguchi-shi, Yamaguchi-ken* ☏ *083/923–3610* 🖷 *083/923–2379* 🛏 *80 Western-style rooms, 1 Western-style suite* ⚒ *In-hotel: restaurant, bar* ☰ *AE, DC, MC, V.*

$$-$$$ ✕**Tojima-zushi** とじま寿司. A favorite with locals for a nice night out, this
JAPANESE   simple but intimate spot has invigorating and delicious, fresh sushi. A few minutes' walk from the station's exit is a covered shopping arcade. Turn right, then take the next cross street to the left and look for the sign up above, a few doors down on the left. ☏ *083/922–1835* ☰ *No credit cards* ⏱ *Wed.–Mon. 11:30–2:30 and 5–10:30.*

THE SAN-IN REGION 山陰地方

If you are looking for adventure in a "real Japan" setting, you have come to the right place. Though the endless narrow ridges of steep mountains can make access from the south difficult, slow, and expensive, this hard fact of geography has kept the entire north stretch of Western Honshū delightfully isolated. Any effort to explore it pays off in dividends of great scenery, precious local crafts, tasty seafood, rich history, and genuinely welcoming people.

HAGI 萩

117 km (73 mi) north of Yamaguchi.

Hagi is virtually surrounded by two branches of the Abu-gawa—the river's south channel, Hashimoto-gawa, and the river's northeast fork, Matsumoto-gawa. Rising in great semi-circles behind the sleepy town are symmetrical waves of shadowy mountains, while before it stretches a sparkling blue sea.

Hagi is rich with history, and owing to its remoteness retains the atmosphere of a traditional castle town—though, unfortunately, its castle was a casualty of the Meiji Restoration. Turning away from feudalism to support the new order, the city was of critical importance in the 1865 to 1867 movement to restore power to the emperor. Japan's first prime minister, Hirobumi Ito (1841–1909), was a Hagi native.

Hagi is also famous for Hagi-yaki, a type of earthenware with soft colors and milky, translucent glazes ranging from beige to pink. The esteemed local ceramics industry began in the 16th century when a Mōri general brought home captive Korean potters (perhaps his consolation for a failed invasion) to create pottery for their new masters. The visually soothing Hagi-yaki is second only to Raku-yaki as the most coveted pottery in Japan, and it does not come cheaply, except during the annual price-friendly Hagi-yaki Festival every May 1–5.

GETTING HERE AND AROUND

The fastest way to Hagi is by JR Bus (Rail Pass accepted), crossing the mountains in just 1 hour for ¥1,680 from Yamaguchi City. The bus departs from the front of the train station. A JR bus also leaves from the Shinkansen exit of Shin-Yamaguchi for an 80-minute ride for ¥1,970. Buses run one per hour between 6 AM and 7 PM. Some buses stop at Hagi Station, the Hagi Bus Center, or Higashi-Hagi Station; all stop at the last two. Return buses follow the same plan. The ideal way to explore Hagi is by bicycle, and you can rent a bike for ¥1,000 per day near the stations or shopping arcades. A local bus system (red bus) loops around town for ¥100 a ride or ¥500 for a full day.

City information is available from English-speaking staff at the **Hagi City Tourist Bureau** next to Hagi Station. For local information at Higashi-Hagi Station, try **Hagi Tourist Office** in the building to the left of the station, on the left side of the shopping arcade. The **City Tourist Office** is downtown in Hagi City Hall.

ESSENTIALS

Currency Exchange Yamaguchi Bank (✉ 16–1 Higashi Tamachi, Hagi shi, Yamaguchi-ken ☎ 0838/22–0380).

Visitor Information City Tourist Office (✉ 495–4 Emukai, Hagi-shi ☎ 0838/25–3131 ☉ Mon.–Sat. 9–5). **Hagi City Tourist Bureau** (☎ 0838/25–1750 ☉ Daily 9–5:45). **Hagi Tourist Office** (☎ 0838/22–7599 🖶 0838/24–2202).

WHAT TO SEE

If you've just arrived by bus, you won't be impressed by the run-down buildings around the Hagi Bus Center. That's okay—there's no need to linger here. Head three short blocks north, then left onto Tamachi Mall, and then west through the quaint older sections of town for 15 minutes to see the park and castle ruins. If you need to make a Tourist Info stop first, head south two blocks and then west two more, to Hagi City Hall.

Tamachi Mall 田町モール is the busiest street in Hagi, with some 130 shops selling local products from Yamaguchi Prefecture. The shopping mood is addictive, the wares gorgeous, and the shopkeepers friendly, so your money can go quickly. Tamachi Mall is six blocks southwest from

10

the dated, Jetson's-style Hagi Grand Hotel, across the Matsumoto-gawa from Higashi-Hagi Station. ⊠*Central Hagi.*

Shizuki Kōen 指月公園, bounded on three sides by the sea, is at Hagi's westernmost end. This large, lovely park contains the Hagi-jō ruins and Hana-no-e Teahouse. Hagi-jō was one of many castles destroyed by the Meiji government around 1874 for being an embarrassing symbol of backward ways. The dramatic seaside location, with its stupendous mountain backdrop, must have made the castle a truly superb sight in its day, but alas, we can only imagine, since the walls and moats are all that remain.

★ The **Hana-no-e Teahouse** is a bare-bones oasis of Zen, set amid meditative gardens and judiciously pruned greenery. The attendants make the classic, slightly bitter *matcha* (¥500) tea for you while you reflect upon the transient nature of life—or consider where you'd like to go next. **Mōri House,** south of the park, is a long narrow building once home to samurai foot soldiers in the late 18th century. The rooms are sparse and placed one next to the other. This arrangement allowed the soldiers to leap into rank-and-file assembly just outside at a moment's notice. ⊠*Ō-aza Horiuchi* ☎*0838/25–1826* ⊠*¥210, includes admission to Hagi-jō grounds, Hana-no-e Teahouse, and Mōri House* ⊙*Apr.–Oct., daily 8–6:30; Nov.–Feb., daily 8:30–4:30; Mar., daily 8:30–6.*

Stop in at **Jō-zan Gama** 城山窯 (*Jō-zan Kiln*), near Shizuki Kōen, perhaps the best place to browse through and purchase magnificent pottery. Usually you are welcome to enter the studios and see the kilns across the street. Classes for a chance to make your own may be available. Bicycles can be rented here as well. ⊠*Hagi-jō-ato, Horiuchi* ☎*0838/25–1666* ⊙*Daily 8–5.*

WHERE TO EAT

$$$–$$$$
JAPANESE
Fodor's Choice
★

✕**Chiyo** 千代. A *tsubaki* course, at ¥3,150, includes squid and scallops cooked before you with butter on a sizzling-hot river stone, and such goodies as *fugu* (blowfish)—as sashimi or cooked tempura-style—stuffed with foie gras. Zingy homemade pickles reset your palate for each successive treat. Women beautifully dressed in formal wear serve you in a classically elegant manner, and off to the right of the intimate 10-seat counter are views of a mossy green and flowery window garden. ⊠*20–4 Imafuruhagi-machi* ☎*0838/22–1128* ⊟*AE, DC, MC, V* ⊙*Closed Mon. No dinner Sun.*

SAMURAI LIVING

Horiuchi 堀内 is the old samurai section of town. From Shizuki Kōen, cross the canal (on the middle bridge) to the east side, and head toward downtown. The tomb of **Tenjū-in** is a memorial to Terumoto Mōri, who in the early 16th century founded the tenacious clan that ruled the Chōshu area for 13 generations. Next you come to the **Outer Gate of Mōri**; the **Toida Masuda House Walls** are on your right as you head south. Dating from the 18th century, these are the longest mud walls in the area. At the next chance, turn right and head west to the ancient, wooden **Fukuhara Gate.**

$-$$
JAPANESE

✕**Fujita-ya**藤田屋. Colorful local characters come to this casual restaurant for beer and sake and seiro-*soba* (thin buckwheat noodles served in steaming hot baskets), and hot tempura served on fragrant handmade cypress trays. ✉*59 Kumagaya-cho* ☎*0838/22–1086* ▤*No credit cards* ⊙*Closed 2nd and 4th Wed. of month.*

$$$-$$$$
JAPANESE

✕**Nakamura** 中村. Set-menu courses at this reliable and popular traditional restaurant typically offer a variety of fish, mountain vegetables, miso soup, and steamed rice. Nakamura has tatami and Western seating but no English-language menu. You can select your food from the tempting window display. ✉*56 Furuhagi-machi* ☎*0838/22–6619* ⚑*Reservations not accepted* ▤*No credit cards* ⊙*Daily 11–2 and 5–8.*

WHERE TO STAY

$$$-$$$$

🏨**Hagi Tanaka Hotel** 萩たなかホテル. It's one station north of town and behind the marina. Enticingly close to the hypnotic Mt. Kasa, its baths tap an onsen, and delectable morsels from the bay are served for dinner in your room. You won't have to tear yourself away from the views until you line up for the buffet breakfast (either Japanese or Western) in the morning. Guest rooms are all Japanese style, and face either the bay or the mountains. Don't expect any English—but then, you already know how to eat and relax, right? **Pros:** wonderful hot spring baths; great local cuisine; clean, new rooms still embody fine old traditions. **Cons:** not much English spoken here; remote location. ✉*707–10 Koshigahama, Hagi, Yamaguchi-ken* ☎*0838/25–0001* 🖷*0838/24–1111* ⚑*92 Japanese-style rooms* ⚒*In-hotel: bar, Japanese baths* ▤*AE, DC, MC, V.*

$$$$

🏨**Hokumon Yashiki** 北門屋敷. An elegant ryokan built upon the ruins of an old Mōri clan estate, with fine touches of understated luxury, the Hokumon Yashiki pampers you in a style the ruling elite were surely accustomed to in the good old days. The inn overlooks a garden in the samurai section of town, near the castle grounds. Meals are served in your room. **Pros:** top-notch hospitality; one of the most conspicuously traditional inns in the world. **Cons:** nothing lively for miles around. ✉*210–12 Horiuchi, Hagi-shi, Yamaguchi-ken* ☎*0838/22–7251* 🖷*0838/25–8144* ⚑*42 Japanese-style rooms without bath, 5 Western-style rooms* ⚒*In-hotel: Japanese baths* ▤*No credit cards* ⊙|MAP.*

$

🏨**Urban City Hotel Hasegawa** ビジネスホテル長谷川. If you want a cheap, decent place to crash near the Hagi Bus Center, this business hotel is adequate—and right across the street. **Pros:** convenient to the old part of town; cheap. **Cons:** feels like you're staying in a ghost town; rooms are as minimalist as can be. ✉*17 Karahi-machi, Hagi, Yamaguchi-ken* ☎*0838/22–0450* 🖷*0838/22–4884* ⚑*18 rooms, 6 Japanese style* ⚒*In-hotel: restaurant, bar* ▤*AE, DC, MC, V.*

10

TSUWANO 津和野

93 km (58 mi) northeast of Hagi; 50 km (31 mi) northeast of Yamaguchi; 63 km (39 mi) northeast of Shin-Yamaguchi.

Fodor'sChoice
★

This hauntingly beautiful town, tucked into a narrow north–south valley at the foot of conical Aono-yama and its attendant dormant volcanic mountain friends, may be the most picturesque hamlet in all Japan. If you catch it on a clear day, the view from the old castle ruins simply takes your breath away. Even when it's cloudy, the mist hangs romantically among the trees and ridges. The stucco-and-tile walls hearken back to ancient times, like those in Hagi and Kurashiki, and the clear, carp-filled streams running beside the streets can induce even tired, jaded travelers to take a leisurely stroll or bike ride backward through time. It's easy to see how a gifted spirit and intellect could soar here. The towering Japanese literary figure Ōgai Mori, novelist and poet, was born (in 1862) and lived here, until, at the age of 12, he went off and enrolled at Tōkyō University's preparatory program in medicine.

GETTING HERE AND AROUND

Tsuwano can be reached by train: it's 2 hours 23 minutes northeast of Hagi by JR (¥1,620); 1 hour 13 minutes northeast of Yamaguchi by JR Yamaguchi Line (¥950); or 1 hour northeast of Shin-Yamaguchi by JR Super Oki Express (¥2,770). Though JR trains from Yamaguchi are quick and easy, JR train routes from Hagi to Tsuwano involve a change and long layovers in Masuda. You can also take a bus from Hagi's **Bōchō Bus Center** directly to Tsuwano, which takes around two hours (¥2,080).

In Tsuwano all sights are within easy walking distance. You can rent a bicycle from one of the four shops near the station plaza (two hours ¥500; all day ¥800).

Tsuwano's **Tourist Information Office** is inside the Photograph Gallery to the right of the railway station. It has free brochures, and staff members will help you reserve accommodations. As with most places in town, little English is spoken here.

ESSENTIALS

Bus Contacts Bōchō Bus Center (☎ 0856/72–0272).

Visitor Information Tourist Information Office (☎ 0856/72–1771 ⊙ Daily 9–5).

WHAT TO SEE

The **Taikodani Inari Jinja** 太鼓谷稲荷神社 *(Taiko Valley Inari Shrine)* is one of the five most revered Inari shrines in Japan. Inari shrines are connected with the fox, a Shintō symbol of luck and cleverness. People come to pray for good fortune in business and health. A series of 1,174 red wooden gates are suspended above steps that climb up the western side of the valley to the shrine, and the journey is a nice hike. From the station, follow the stream-side Tono-machi-dōri past the Katorikku Kyōkai (Catholic church), but before crossing the river turn right onto the small lane. The lane leads to the tunnel-like approach through the gates to the structure high on a cliffside. The shrine is nothing astounding, but the views out over the valley are. You can also take a bus that approaches by a back road; the Tourist Information Office can help with this. **Yasaka Jinja** is another shrine on the site, where every July 20 and 27 sees the Heron Dance Festival.

Tsuwano-jō (Tsuwano Castle) was another casualty of the Meiji Restoration in the late 19th century, but from the derelict ruins (⊙ Daily 10–5) there is an awesome panoramic view of the dormant volcanic cone of

Aono-yama to the east, surrounding similar peaks, and the entire valley stretching out below. To get up here you can hike a marked trail that leads from Taikodani Inari Jinja or take a chairlift from below the Inari shrine for ¥450 round-trip. The chairlift takes only 5 minutes, and from the top it's about a 15-minute hike to the castle foundations.

The **Old House of Ōgai Mori** 森鴎外 旧宅 / 森鴎外記念館 is spartan, but perhaps worth a visit if only to commemorate the achievements of this gifted genius who called Tsuwano his home. Ōgai Mori (1862–1922), son of the head physician to the *daimyō* (lord) of Shimane, became a doctor at the young age of 19, and who, in spite of courting trouble for his outspoken criticism of Japan's backward ways compared to the West, went on to become the author of such acclaimed novels as *The Wild Geese* and *Vita Sexualis*. He was also a prominent figure in the fledgling government behind the Meiji Restoration. From Tsuwano Station it's a 12-block walk south along the main road, or take the bus and get off at Ōgai Kyūkyo-mae. ☎*0856/72–3210* ☒*¥600* ☻*Tues.– Sun. 9–5.*

> ### BATHING AND THE VOLCANO
>
> Tsuwano puts its geothermal gifts to good use at the spa at **Nagomi-no-Sato**. Inside and out, the tubs have great views of the surrounding gumdrop-shaped volcanic peaks. It's west of everything else in town, across the river from the Washibara Hachiman-gū (a shrine where traditional horseback archery contests are held the second Sunday of April every year), but still not too far to get to by rented bike. ☒ *257-Ō-aza Washibara* ☎*0856/72–4122, 0120/26–4753 toll-free* ☒*¥500* ☻*Hot springs daily 10–8 except 2nd and 4th Thurs. of month; restaurant daily 10–10, except 1st and 3rd Thurs.*

OFF THE BEATEN PATH

Otometōge Maria Seidō 乙女峠マリア聖堂. Between 1868 and 1870, in an effort to disperse Christian strongholds and cause them extreme hardship—in the hope that the believers would recant their faith—the Tokugawa shogunate sent 153 Christians from Nagasaki to Tsuwano, where they were imprisoned and tortured. Many gave in, but 36 died for their faith. Otometōge Maria Seidō (St. Mary's Chapel at the Pass of the Virgin) was built in 1948 to commemorate the plight of the 36 martyrs, which is portrayed in the stained-glass windows. The chapel is a 1-km (½-mi) walk from Tsuwano Station. Go right out of the station, make another right at the first street (which leads to Yōmei-ji), and just after crossing the tracks turn right again and walk up the hill. Every May 3 a procession begins at the church in town and ends in the chapel courtyard, where a large outdoor mass is celebrated.

WHERE TO EAT AND STAY

$$
JAPANESE

✕**Aoki** あおき. An old-fashioned, rustic-decor sushi restaurant with a few tables on tatami mats and a long bar counter with stools, Aoki has a cheerful staff and reasonable prices. It's also within easy walking distance of Tsuwano Station. Try the *jyo-nigiri* (deluxe sushi set); it will likely include a slice or two of tasty, chewy koi, or local carp. That and a frosty mug of beer set you back only ¥1,900. They stay open until 10 PM. ☒*Takaoka-dōri, Ushioro-da, Tsuwano-cho, Kanoashi-gun, Shimane-ken* ☎*0856/72–0444* ▭*No credit cards* ☻*Closed Thurs.*

10

$$
Fodor'sChoice
★ Tsuwano Lodge 津和野ロッジ. Relax and revel in style at this lodge tucked among the rice paddies and bamboo groves along the way to the Washibara Hachiman-gū shrine. The owners are friendly (but don't speak much English), the rooms are basic but tasteful, and the food is diverse, healthy, and prepared with flair. Perhaps best of all, there's a rooftop *rotemburo* (outside bath) full of sulfur- and calcium-laden water that's good for the skin, hair, and nails. **Pros:** roof-top bath; fantastic, multicourse meal is a great value; frog-song lullabies in season. **Cons:** rustic and isolated, in an already quite remote place. ⊠*Rte. 345, Washibara, Kanoashi-gun, Shimane-ken, Tsuwano-chō* ☎*0856/72–1683* 🖷*0856/72–2880* ⌨*8 Japanese-style rooms without baths* &*In-hotel: restaurant, Japanese baths* ≡*No credit cards* ¶◎*EP, MAP.*

$$ Wakasagi-no-Yado 民宿若さぎの宿. Despite their limited English, the family that runs this small but satisfactory inn is eager to help overseas tourists and will meet you at Tsuwano Station, only an eight-minute walk away. Typical of *minshuku*, there's a common bath. A Japanese or Western breakfast is served and included in the rates. **Pros:** nice location; heartwarming hospitality; bicycles for rent on-site. **Cons:** small, spartan rooms; no private bathrooms. ⊠*Mōri-mura, Kanoashi-gun, Tsuwano-chōShimane-ken* ☎🖷*0856/72–1146* ⌨*7 Japanese-style rooms without bath* &*In-hotel: Japanese baths* ≡*No credit cards* ◎*BP.*

$$$–$$$$
JAPANESE
Fodor'sChoice
★ ✕Yūki 遊亀. Carp dishes—yes, carp—and delectable mountain vegetables maintain Yūki's highly venerated reputation. They have ayu, or river smelt, and other things, but for only ¥2,800 you can get the Tsuwano *teishoku*, or gourmet carp course, which offers a smattering of everything a fat and happy carp can become: there's chewy carp sashimi (with a wonderful lemony-mustard-thyme dipping sauce), tender deep-fried carp, carp steeped so long in soy sauce, sake, and brown sugar that it is dense and even slightly dry but very delicious, and carp boiled in a tangy miso soup until it's almost flaky. This is bona-fide stamina food, and tastes way better than you might think—these are not like the carp you and your uncles pulled out of those old muddy ponds! The dining room is chock-full of old farm and country-life implements, and there's even a stream burbling at your feet. Come early, as they close at around 7 PM. ⊠*271-4 Ro, Ushioro-da, Tsuwano-cho, Kanoashi-gun, Shimane-ken* ☎*0856/72–0162* ≡*No credit cards* ◐*Closed Thurs.*

IZUMO TAISHA

37 km (23 mi) west of Matsue.

Oldest of all Japan's Shintō shrines, this site has been of tremendous cultural significance—second only to the great shrine at Ise—since the 6th century. The main building was last rebuilt in 1744. In ancient days it was the largest wooden building in the country, but since the 13th century, each time it was rebuilt, it was scaled to half its former size, and it is now *only* 24 meters tall. The original must have been a humbling thing to stand in front of! Nature has arrayed a shrine of its own to compliment the ornate but somehow subdued structures: a lofty ridge of forested peaks rises behind, a boulevard of fragrant ancient pines lines the approach, and lush green lawns flank both sides. Pilgrims come here primarily to pray for success in courtship and marriage.

GETTING HERE AND AROUND

The easiest way is to go from Matsue Shinji-ko Onsen. Buses run often between it and Matsue station for ¥200. It takes one hour on the Ichibata Dentetsu (electric railway, ¥790), from Matsue Shinji-ko Onsen Station. After about 50 minutes you'll need to change trains at Kawato Station for the final 10-minute leg to Izumo Taisha-mae Station. You can also get there by taking the JR train from Matsue Station to JR Izumo-shi Station, then transferring to the Ichibata Bus for a 30-minute ride, ¥490, to Izumo Taisha Seimon stop.

WHAT TO SEE

Although **Izumo Taisha** is Japan's oldest Shintō shrine, the *hon-den* (main building) dates from 1744 and most of the other were buildings from 1688 onward. The newest were built in 1874. The architectural style, with its saddled crests and ornamental roof fixtures resembling crossed swords, is said to be unique to the Izumo region, but some similarities with the main Shintō shrine of Ise Jingū on the Kii Peninsula can be noted. The taisha is dedicated to a male god, Ōkuninushi, the creator of the land and god of marriage and fortune. Instead of clapping twice, as at other shrines, you should clap four times—twice for yourself, and twice for your current or future partner. According to folklore, if you successfully throw a 5-yen coin so that it sticks up into the sacred hanging strands of the enormously thick 5-ton, 25 foot-long twisted straw rope, or *shimenawa*, suspended above the entrance to the main building, you will be doubly assured of good luck in marriage. As you will undoubtedly see, it is almost impossible to do without some kind of cheating—which may say something about the difficulties of marriage.

Two rectangular buildings on either side of the compound are believed to house the visiting millions of Shintō gods during the 10th lunar month of each year. In the rest of Japan the lunar October is referred to as Kannazuki, "month without gods," while in Izumo, October is called Kamiarizuki, "month with gods." The shrine is a five-minute walk north, to the right along the main street, from Izumo Taisha-mae Station. ⊠ *Izumo Taisha, Izumo-shi* ☎ 0853/53-2298 ☜ *Free* ⊗ *Daily 8:30–5:30.*

MATSUE 松江

Fodor's Choice ★ *194 km (121 mi) northeast of Tsuwano, 172 km (107 mi) northwest of Kurashiki.*

Matsue is a city blessed with so much overwhelming beauty and good food that you will wonder what to look at, what to eat, and what to do first. It's where the lake named Shinji-ko empties into the lagoon called Naka-umi, which connects directly with the Sea of Japan. This makes Matsue a seafood lover's paradise; specialties include both kinds of eel, all kinds of shrimp, shellfish, carp, sea bass, smelt, whitebait, and the famous black shijimi clams from Shinji-ko. The water also provides the city with a lovely network of canals.

10

Matsue also attracts and holds onto some of the country's most welcoming and interesting people, both foreign and native. This remote realm is a traveler's favorite, and once you've come here you'll surely be back—it's that kind of place. In the 1890s, the famed journalist-novelist Lafcadio Hearn came here and promptly fell in love, first with the place, and then with a local woman—a samurai's daughter, no less. In true journalistic fashion he proceeded to let the entire world know about it.

GETTING HERE AND AROUND

Japan Rail can get you to Matsu from Tsuwano (2 hours 34 minutes northeast by JR Super Oki Express, ¥5,870) or Kurashiki, Okayama (2 hours 17 minutes northwest by JR Yakumo Limited Express, ¥5,550). Most sights in Matsue are within walking distance of each other. Where they are not, the buses fill in. The bus station faces the train station.

The **Matsue Tourist Information Office** is outside JR Matsue Station and open daily 9–6. You can collect free maps and brochures. The Shimane Tourist Association offers a substantial discount of 30%–50% for foreigners at nine of its tourist attractions; the current list includes the castle and four museums. You need only present your passport or foreigner's registration card at the entrance to these places.

ESSENTIALS

Currency Exchange San-in Godo Bank (✉10 Sakana-chō, Matsue, Shimane ☎0120/31–5180). **Shimane Bank** (✉2–35 Tōhon-chō ☎085/224–4000).

Internet Café Diner Sign (✉494–1 Asahi-machi ☎0120/31–5180).

Visitor Information Matsue Tourist Information Office (✉665 Asahi-machi ☎0852/21–4034 🖷0852/27–2598).

WHAT TO SEE

★ Start a tour of Matsue at the enchanting and shadowy **Matsue-jō** 松江城 and walk in the castle park, **Shiroyama Kōen,** under aromatic pines. Constructed of exactly such wood, the castle was completed in 1611. Not only did it survive the Meiji upheavals intact, it was, amazingly, never ransacked during the civil war–type turbulence of the Tokugawa shogunate. Perhaps it's the properties of the wood, or the angles, or the mysterious tricks of light and shadows, but this castle truly feels *alive* and is a certified must-see sight of the region.

Built by the daimyō of Izumo, Yoshiharu Horio, for protection, Matsue-jō's donjon (main tower), at 98 feet, is the second-tallest among originals still standing in Japan. Crouching as it does below and behind the surrounding lofty pines, Matsue-jō is at best slightly spooky at all times. Despite its foreboding aspect, the castle seems to beckon you inside for a peek. By all means, obey the call! This is a fabulously preserved walk-in time capsule, with six interior levels belied by a tricky facade that suggests only five. The lower floors display an appropriately macabre collection of samurai swords and armor. The long climb to the castle's uppermost floor is definitely worth it for the view encompasses the city, Lake Shinji, the Shimane Peninsula, and—if weather conditions permit—the distant mystical snowy peak of Daisen.

The castle and park are a 1-km stroll northwest from Matsue Station, or take the Lakeline Bus from Terminal 7 in front of the station and get off at Ōtemae; the fare is ¥150. ☎*0852/21–4030* ✉*¥550* ☉*Apr.– Sept., daily 8:30–6; Oct.–Mar., daily 8:30–4:30.*

Meimei-an Teahouse 明々庵, built in 1779, is one of Japan's best-preserved teahouses. For ¥400 you can contemplate the mysteries of Matsue-jō, and for ¥400 more, you get tea and a sweet. To get here, leave Shiroyama Kōen, the castle park, at its east exit and follow the moat going north; at the top of the park a road leads to the right, northwest of the castle. The teahouse is a short climb up this road. ✉*Kitahori-cho* ☎*0852/21–9863* ✉*¥400; ¥800 with tea* ☉*Daily 9–5.*

Samurai Residence 武家屋敷 *(Buke Yashiki)*, built in 1730, belonged to the well-to-do Shiomi family, chief retainers to the daimyō. Note the separate servant quarters, a shed for the palanquin, and slats in the walls to allow cooling breezes to flow through the rooms. Buke Yashiki is on the main road at the base of the side street on which Meimei-an Teahouse is located (keep the castle moat on your left). ✉*305 Kitahori-cho* ☎*0852/22–2243* ✉*¥300* ☉*Apr.–Sept., daily 8:30–6; Oct.–Mar., daily 8:30–4:30.*

The **Lafcadio Hearn Residence** 小泉八雲旧宅 *(Koizumi Yakumo Kyūkyo)*, next to the Tanabe Bijutsukan, has remained unchanged since the famous writer left Matsue in 1891. Born of an Irish father and a Greek mother, Lafcadio Hearn (1850–1904) spent his early years in Europe and moved to the United States to become a journalist. In 1890 he traveled to Yokohama, Japan and made his way to Matsue, where he began teaching. There he met and married a samurai's daughter named Setsu Koizumi. He later took posts in Kumamoto, Kōbe, and Tōkyō. Disdainful of the materialism of the West, he was destined to be a lifelong Japanophile and resident. He became a Japanese citizen, taking the name Yakumo Koizumi. His most famous works were *Glimpses of Unfamiliar Japan* (1894) and *Japan: An Attempt at Interpretation* (1904). ☎*0852/23–0714* ✉*¥350* ☉*Daily 9–5; Dec.–Feb., 10–4:40.*

The **Lafcadio Hearn Memorial Hall** 小泉八雲記念館 *(Koizumi Yakumo Kinenkan)* has a good collection of the author's manuscripts and other artifacts that reflect his life in Japan. It's adjacent to Koizumi Yakumo Kyūkyo. Two minutes from the Memorial Hall is the Hearn Kyūkyo bus stop, where a bus goes back to the center of town and the station. ☎*0852/21–2147* ✉*¥300* ☉*Apr.–Sept., daily 8:30–6:30; Oct.–Mar., daily 8:30–5.*

When dusk rolls around, you'll want to position yourself well. You won't get a better sunset than the one seen every night over **Shinji-ko** 宍道湖. As locals do, you can watch it from Shinji-ko Ohashi, the town's westernmost bridge, but the best spot is south of the bridge, along the road, down near water level in **Shirakata Kōen**, the narrow lakeside park just west of the NHK Building and the hospital. This is a great place to kick back and enjoy some tasty local microbrews and portable sushi. A very popular *Yūhi*, or sunset, spot is the patio of the Prefectural Art Museum, visible and adjacent to the park above.

10

Matsue English Garden 松江イングリツシユ　ガーデン is of the same scale, arrangement, and style of a traditional English garden. There's an outdoor rest area, fountain plaza, sunken garden, indoor garden, "white" garden, pergola, cloister courtyard, landscape garden, rose terrace, and laburnum arch. If you've covered everything else, try this place—it's quite stunning, and it was put together in only five years by a jovial English gardener named Keith Gott. The garden is out on the lakeshore northwest of town, at Nishi-Hamasada. It's one stop (5 minutes; get off at English Garden-mae Station) west of Matsue Shinji-ko Onsen Station by the Ichibata Railway, so it can be seen on the way to or from Izumo Taisha. ✉*369 Nishi-Hamadasa-chō* ☎*0852/36–3030* 🖅*Free* ⊙*Apr.–Sept., daily 9–5; Oct.–Mar., daily 9–4.*

WHERE TO EAT

$$–$$$
JAPANESE
Fodor's Choice
★

✕**Kawakyō** 川京. This is the best place to try the seven famous delicacies from Shinji-ko: *suzuki* (or *hosho-yaki*), sea bass wrapped in *washi* (paper) and steam-baked over hot coals; *unagi* (freshwater eel) split, broiled, and basted in sweet soy sauce; *shirao,* a small whitefish often served as sashimi or cooked in vinegar-miso; *amasagi* (smelt), teriyaki-grilled or cooked in tempura; *shijimi,* small black-shelled clams served in miso or other soup; *koi,* string-bound, washi-wrapped, steam-baked carp; and *moroge-ebi,* steamed shrimp. Especially good is the hosho-yaki. The staff is very outgoing, as is the regular crowd. Don't forget to request one of the delicious *ji-zake* (locally made sake) samplers. Reservations are a good idea. Kawakyō is in the block just east of the middle (Matsue Ōhashi) bridge, a block north of the river. ✉*65 Suetsugu Honmachi, Matsue-shi, Shimane-ken* ☎*0852/22–1312* 🖃*No credit cards* ⊙*Mon.–Sat. 6–10:30. No lunch.*

$
JAPANESE

✕**Ōhashi** 大橋. If you're pressed for time but want to grab a decent lunch, try some warigo soba, a local buckwheat noodle specialty. Ōhashi is right inside the Shamine department store next to the station and has a filling, healthy Yakumo Gozen set course for ¥1,000. ✉*472-2 Asahimachi* ☎*0852/26–6551* 🖃*No credit cards* ⊙*Daily 10:30–8.*

$–$$
JAPANESE

✕**Yakumo-an** 八雲庵. A colorful garden surrounds the dining area at this traditional house that serves good soba. Recommended dishes include the *sanshurui soba* (three kinds of soba) for ¥750. Take the top dish and, leaving the garnishes in, pour the broth into it, then dunk the noodles as you go. Drink the leftover broth, too; it's full of B vitamins and good for your metabolism. ✉*Just west of Tanabe Bijutsukan, north of castle* ☎*0852/22–2400* 🖃*No credit cards* ⊙*Daily 9–4:30.*

WHERE TO STAY

$$$$
★

🖬**Naniwa Issui** なにわ一水. A swanky ryokan near the Matsue Shinji-ko Onsen Station (for easy Izumo Taisha access), Naniwa Issui is envied for its amazing views out over the big lake—and for its onsen. The seven mind-blowing super-deluxe rooms on the fourth floor have private rotemburos to soak in out on the balconies—and the newest, largest big-screen entertainment centers available. Naniwa offers impeccable service and fabulous Matsue seafood cuisine. In season, the delightful lounge-side garden becomes a beer and cocktail patio. **Pros:** unbeatable access to everything this city and region has to offer; private balcony onsen put you in the lap of luxury. **Cons:** you'll need take taxis or walk 7–10 minutes to the JR Matsue Shinji-ko bus stop. ⊠*63 Chidori-chō, Matsue, Shimane-ken* ☎*0852/21–4132* 🖷*0852/21–4162* ⇨*29 Japanese-style rooms* ♿*In-hotel: restaurant, Japanese baths* ⊟*DC, MC, V* ⅃⊙⅃*MAP.*

$–$$ 🖭**Ryokan Terazuya** 旅館寺津屋. The same family has maintained a tradition of heart-warming hospitality at this charming riverside ryokan since 1893. Rooms are cozy but air-conditioned, and the location is perfect for watching sunsets. The food is superb and of an astounding variety—virtually all the local seafood and vegetable specialties, both raw and cooked, are served. English is spoken, and your kind hosts may even demonstrate sushi-making and tea ceremony. Pros: high level of hospitality will inspire a deeper appreciation of Japan; station pick-up service. Cons: don't expect to practice your Nihongo as the master will insist on using his excellent English; no private baths. ⊠*60–3 Tenjin-machi, Matsue, Shimane-ken* ☎*0852/21–3480* 🖷*0852/21–3422* ⇨*9 Japanese-style rooms without baths* ♿*In-hotel: Japanese baths* ⊟*No credit cards* ⅃⊙⅃*EP, MAP.*

OKAYAMA 岡山

733 km (455 mi) west of Tōkyō, 188 km (117 mi) southeast of Matsue.

The city of Okayama claims to have the most sunny days in Japan, and the disposition of the locals tends to reflect this. A beautiful black castle is set amid a spacious and luxuriant garden, justly rated among Japan's top three.

GETTING HERE AND AROUND

The JR Shinkansen will whisk you away from Tōkyō to Okayama in 3 hours 17 minutes (¥16,860), or from Matsu, you can reach the city in 2 hours 27 minutes by JR Yakumo Express (¥5,870).

Hop on one of the frequent streetcars plying Momotaro-dōri, the main boulevard heading east from the Shinkansen station (¥100) to get around town. To get to the castle, park, and museums ride three stops east and walk southeast. For ¥520 you can buy a combined park-castle admission ticket.

The Shinkansen station makes Okayama an attractive base for visiting the historic charms of Kurashiki—only an 11-minute local JR train hop to the west.

Should you need a map of Okayama or city information, head to the **Tourist Information Office** on the first floor near the east exit of the JR station.

ESSENTIALS

Currency Exchange Chūgoku Bank (⊠*1-15-20 Marunouchi, Okayama* ☎*086/223-3111*).

Visitor Information Tourist Information Office (☎*086/222-2912* ⊙*Daily 9–6*).

10

WHAT TO SEE

★ **Kōraku Garden** 後楽園 *(Kōrakuen)* is one of the country's finest gardens (and officially listed as one of the top three), with charming tea arbors, green lawns, ponds, and hills that were created three centuries ago on the banks of the Asahi-gawa. Gardens in Japan, whether dry, wet, or a combination of both, are constructed with many elements in mind, but the goal is always to engender feelings of peace and tranquillity. They are a form of visual meditation, so to speak. Kōrakuen scores high in all relevant areas. The maple, apricot, and cherry trees give the 28-acre park plenty of flowers and shade. The riverside setting, with Okayama-jō in the background, is delightful. The garden's popularity increases in peak season (April through August), but this is perhaps the largest park in Japan, so you won't feel hemmed in by crowds. Bus 20 (¥160) from Platform 2 in front of the JR station goes directly to Kōrakuen. ⊠*1–5 Kōrakuen* ☎*086/272–1148* 🎫*¥350* ◷*Apr.–Sept., daily 7:30–6; Oct.–May , daily 8–5.*

Painted an unexpectedly attractive shadowy black, and set off dramatically by lead tiles and contrasting white vertical-slat shutters, **Okayama-jō** 岡山城 is known locally as U-jō ("Crow Castle"). Though the castle was built in the 16th century, only the "moon-viewing" outlying tower survived World War II. A ferroconcrete replica was painstakingly constructed to scale in 1966. The middle floors now house objects that represent the region's history, including a collection of armor and swords and a palanquin you can climb into to have your photo taken. Unlike many other castles with great views, this one has an elevator to take you up the six floors. A five-minute walk across the bridge brings you from the south exit of Kōrakuen to the castle. Boats are for rent on the river below. ⊠*2–3–1 Marunouchi700-0823* ☎*086/225–2096* 🎫*¥300* ◷*Daily 9–5.*

The **Museum of Oriental Art** 岡山市立オリエント美術館 *(Orient Bijutsukan)* has on display at least 2,000 items from its impressive collection. Special exhibitions vary, but they generally show how Middle Eastern art reached ancient Japan via the Silk Road, and items range from Persian glass goblets and ornate mirrors to early stringed instruments. To reach the museum from the JR station, take the streetcar (¥140) bound for Higashiyama directly north for 10 minutes. The museum is across Asahi-gawa from Kōrakuen (about a 10-minute walk). ☎*086/232–3636* 🎫*¥300* ◷*Tues.–Sun. 9–5.*

WHERE TO EAT AND STAY

$$$$ 🏨**Hotel Granvia Okayama** ホテルグランヴィア岡山. This large, luxurious hotel makes a comfortable base for exploring the area. Bright white marble and classy-looking wood dominate the lobby. The bilingual staff is cheerful and welcoming. The spacious rooms have the sheen of opulence. It's conveniently connected to the JR Okayama station—stay on the second (Shinkansen) level and follow the signs toward the south end. **Pros:** best location in town; large, posh rooms; nice breakfast included. **Cons:** pool and other amenities cost extra; be careful with the touchy in-room bar—don't move a thing unless you mean to buy it. ⊠*1–5 Ekimoto-chō, Okayama-shi, Okayama-ken* ☎*086/234–7000* 🖷*086/234–7099*

₪323 *Western-style rooms, 3 Western-style suites, 2 Japanese-style suites* ᕧ *In-hotel: 7 restaurants, bar* ▭*AE, DC, MC, V.*

$$$–$$$$
JAPANESE
✕**Musashi** 武蔵. You'll find healthy, vegetable-laden Okayama-style cuisine at this delightful eatery. For lunch we recommend the unbeatable *bara-zushi teishoku,* or bits and pieces of sushi with vegetables set, a feast for only ¥1,000 yen. Musashi is a few minutes' walk straight out along the boulevard from the east exit of JR Okayama Station, on the left just past Tully's Coffee Shop. ✉*1–7–18 Nodaya-chō* ☎*086/222–3893* ▭*AE, DC, MC, V* ☉*Mon.–Sat. 10:30–2:30 and 5–10:30.*

KURASHIKI 倉敷

★ *749 km (465 mi) west of Tōkyō or 196 km (122 mi) west of Shin-Ōsaka.*

From the 17th through the 19th centuries, this vital shipping port supplied Ōsaka with cotton, textiles, sugar, reeds, and rice. Today Kurashiki thrives on income from tourism. If your view were limited to what you see just outside the station, you'd be forgiven for thinking Kurashiki is just another over industrialized modern Japanese city. We strongly recommend, however, venturing 10 minutes on foot southeast of the station to Bikan Chiku, a neighborhood of canals, bridges, shops, restaurants, ryokans, and museums.

You can see most of Kurashiki's sights in a day, but it's worth staying longer, perhaps in a splendid old ryokan, to fully appreciate the time-machine aspect of the place. The Bikan district is artfully lit up at night, and a stroll down the willow-draped canals after a sumptuous meal can be an unforgettably romantic journey.

The white-stucco walls of old warehouses are accented smartly with charred pine-plank paneling and leaden-gray, burnt-brown, and carbon-black tiles crisscrossed with raised diagonals or squares of stark white mortar. These structures follow the willow-shaded canals and cobblestone streets linked by graceful stone bridges.

Note that virtually the entire town shuts down on Monday.

GETTING HERE AND AROUND
Kurashiki is 3 hours 28 minutes west of Tōkyō or 1 hour west of Shin-Ōsaka by the Shinkansen and San-yō line. In town, you can stroll leisurely through the streets taking in the scenery.

Kurashiki Tourist Information Office, on the right outside the second-floor south exit from the JR station, has knowledgeable locals who provide useful maps and information. Another office is in the Bikan district, at the first bend of the canal, on the right a block past the Ōhara Museum of Art, just across the bridge from the Ryokan Tsurugata. They sell tickets for the 20-minute canal-boat tours (summer only) for ¥300, and provide information on the museums located around the Bikan area.

ESSENTIALS
Visitor Information Kurashiki Tourist Information Office (☎*086/426–8681, main branch; 086/422–0542, Bikan branch* ☉*Apr.–Oct., daily 9–6; Nov.–Mar., daily 9–5:15).*

10

WHAT TO SEE

★ **Ōhara Art Museum** 大原美術館 *(Ōhara Bijutsukan)*, in the old town, is a museum not to be missed. In 1930, noted art collector and founder Magosaburo Ōhara built this Parthenon-style building to house a collection of Western art with works by El Greco, Corot, Manet, Monet, Rodin, Gauguin, Picasso, Toulouse-Lautrec, and many others. They were shrewdly acquired for him by his friend Kojima Torajiro, a talented Western-style artist whom he dispatched to Europe for purchases. The museum is wonderfully compact and can be appreciated in a single morning or an afternoon. Two wings exhibit Japanese paintings, tapestries, wood-block prints, and pottery—including works by Shōji Hamada and Bernard Leach—as well as modern and ancient Asian art, much of it also brought home from trips made by Torajiro at Ōhara's behest. ✉*1–15–Chūō* ☎*086/422–0005* ☞*¥1,000* ☉*Tues.–Sun. 9–5.*

WHERE TO EAT

$$–$$$
JAPANESE
✗**Hamayoshi** 浜吉. Three tables and a counter make up this intimate restaurant specializing in fish from the Seto Nai-kai. Sushi is one option; another is *mamakari,* a kind of vinegared sashimi sliced from a small fish caught in the Inland Sea. Other delicacies are *shako-ebi,* or mantis-shrimp, and lightly grilled *anago,* or sea eel. No English is spoken, but the owner will help you order and instruct you on how to enjoy the chef's delicacies. Hamayoshi is on the main street leading from the station, just before the Kurashiki Kokusai Hotel. ✉*Achi 2–19–30* ☎*086/421–3430* ⊟*No credit cards* ☉*Tues.–Sun. 11:30–2, 5–10; closed Mon.*

$$$–$$$$
STEAK
✗**Kiyū-tei** 亀遊亭. For the best reasonably priced grilled steak in town, come to this attractive Kurashiki-style restaurant. The entrance to the restaurant is through a nearly hidden courtyard behind a gate across the street from the entrance to the Ōhara Museum. ✉*1–2–20 Chūō* ☎*086/422–5140* ⊟*AE, DC, MC, V* ☉*Tues.–Sun. 11–9; closed Mon.*

$
JAPANESE
✗**KuShuKuShu (9494)** くしゅくしゅ. Feeling a bit restless? Want to get out of the ryokan or hotel? Want something different to eat but are afraid that there is no nightlife in old Bikan-Chiku town? You'll be happy to be wrong, and happy to find this lively little hideaway. Cool music and loud laughter can be heard from here when all else on the streets is locked up tight. Unwind to an eclectic mix of traditional white stucco, black wooden beams, bright lights, and jazz. Scores of tasty à la carte snacks, such as grilled meats or cheese and salami plates, and low-priced beer and sake add to the fun. It's tucked along the east side of the covered Ebisu-dōri shopping arcade halfway between the station and Kanryu-ji. ✉*Achi 2–16–41* ☎*086/421–0949* ⊟*No credit cards* ☉*No lunch.*

WHERE TO STAY

$$–$$$
🏨**Kurashiki Kokusai Hotel** 倉敷国際ホテル. The town's oldest Western-style hotel welcomes guests with a black-tile lobby and dramatic Japanese wood-block prints. Ask for a room in the newer annex at the back of the building overlooking the garden. Rooms are dated but large. The location of the Kokusai is ideal—just around the corner from Bikan Chiku and the Ōhara Museum, a 10-minute walk on the main road leading southeast from the station. **Pros:** location is near the

good stuff; welcoming, capable staff. Cons: not right on the old canals; rooms, though large, are dated. ✉ *1–1–44 Chūō, Kurashiki, Okayama-ken* ☎*086/422–5141* 🖨*086/422–5192* 🛏*106 Western-style rooms, 4 Japanese-style rooms* ♿*In-hotel: restaurant, bar, parking (no fee)* ▤*AE, DC, MC, V.*

$$$$ 🏨**Ryokan Kurashiki** 旅館倉敷. Refurbished in a newly polished old-style splendor, this is perhaps the most luxurious place to submit to the ritual of pleasures sought by wealthy Japanese at a traditional ryokan more than 300 years ago. Limited English is spoken, but for navigation of the deeper intricacies, you'll want a command of Japanese. Pros: great food in great quantities; lots of antiques and period pieces. Cons: remodeled rooms have less personality, style, and space; now priced beyond reach. ✉*4–1 Hon-machi, Kurashiki, Okayama-ken* ☎*086/422–0730* 🖨*086/422–0990* 🛏*5 rooms with bath* ♿*In-hotel: restaurant, Japanese baths* ▤*AE, DC, MC, V* ❑*MAP.*

$$$–$$$$ 🏨**Ryokan Tsurugata** 旅館鶴形. Treat yourself to a stay—or perhaps just a fantastic dinner—at this charming ryokan built in 1774. Rooms are intimate and secluded, but it's best to come for the fabulous, filling, traditional dinners that incorporate the best local delicacies, from fish to fruit. The suite overlooking the 400-year-old garden is especially captivating. The same friendly and hospitable folks who run the Kurashiki Kokusai Hotel own and manage the Ryokan Tsurugata, so some English is spoken and foreigners are welcome and pampered. You'll need patience and advance planning when requesting reservations, since the number of available rooms is limited and the demand is high. The hotel is across the bridge from the Ōhara Art Museum. Pros: best local value for this type of accommodation; steeped in tradition. Cons: ancient tradition means a slower pace than Westerners are used to. ✉*1–3–15 Chūō, Kurashiki, Okayama-ken* ☎*086/424–1635* 🖨*086/424–1650* 🛏*11 Japanese-style rooms, 3 with private bath* ♿*In-hotel: Japanese baths* ▤*AE, DC, MC, V* ❑*MAP.*

¢ 🏨**Tōyoko Inn Kurashiki Station South Exit** 東横イン倉敷駅南口. One of Kurashiki's newest and most popular hotels, this place, with a sunny lobby, offers great value and convenience only minutes away from the station's south exit. Pros: location; free breakfast; free Internet. Cons: perhaps a bit too modern given the location; it's a shame to stay anywhere but Bikan Chiku in Kurashiki. ✉*2–10–20 Achi, Kurashiki, Okayama-ken* ☎*086/430–1045* 🖨*086/430–1046* 🛏*154 Western-style rooms* ♿*In-room: Internet. In-hotel: Wi-Fi* ▤*AE, DC, MC, V* ❑*CP.*

10

Shikoku

WORD OF MOUTH

"I really liked Matsuyama on Shikoku Island. There's a famous hot spring there, but what I really liked was its laid-back feel, plus there's an area of densely packed restaurants and bars for some nice nightlife."

—bkkmei

"Matsuyama was lovely and the fast ferry from Miyajima was a highlight of our trip."

—moxie

Updated by
Joshua Bisker

Leave modernized Japan behind: cross the sea to rushing rivers, sky-high mountains, historic villages, funky cities, local craftworks, brilliant summer festivals, and a thousand terrific sights found only on Shikoku. Child-rearing and small scale, back-breaking agriculture dominate life below the factory-ridden northern coast, but you'll find diverse cuisines, festivals, special products, and even various dialects of Japanese thanks to a long history outside the country's mainstream.

If you didn't know Shikoku's key products were textiles, fish, lumber, and ships, you'd swear they were grizzled old farmers and tiny, adorable children. Every autumn, country people in their sixties, seventies, eighties, and even nineties toil through the harvest, while herds of school children bobble through their rice fields in matching yellow hats. In summer, white-robed *o-hemro-san* stand out against the green: pilgrims walking Shikoku's famous pilgrimage path, an 88-temple circuit established by the Buddhist saint Kōbō Daishi in the 8th century. You probably won't have the spare months it takes to circumnavigate it, but you can ease a pilgrim's burden by offering *o-settai,* a few coins or some other charity, as he walks the road to enlightenment.

Shikoku's simple lifestyle may feel exotic to a traveler, but from the local perspective it's visitors who appear exotic and strange. Meeting foreigners still verges on the fantastical for people here, and outside Shikoku's four major cities you may be treated more like a celebrity (or a space alien) than a faceless tourist. Connecting with people will be more personal here than in Tōkyō or Kansai, and every encounter can be an adventure: locals on Shikoku will actually shout out loud when they see you—Ah! Gaijin-san!—and welcome you into their towns.

ORIENTATION AND PLANNING

ORIENTATION

Shikoku has four prefectures—Kagawa in the northeast, Tokushima below it, Ehime in the west, and Kōchi along the entire bottom shore. This chapter is arranged as an itinerary beginning in Kagawa's Takamatsu and moving through Tokushima to the central Iya valley, south to Kōchi, and finally north towards Ehime's Matsuyama. The reverse loop is just as practicable. The advantage of finishing around Matsuyama is the easy access by bus or bicycle to Hiroshima, or by ferry to Hiroshima, Kyūshū, Kōbe, or Ōsaka—perfect for a direct link to Kansai Airport if it's time to go home.

TOP REASONS TO GO

11

Get Off The Concrete: Discover Shikoku's natural charms by rafting, hiking, walking, and swimming. Best of all, bicycle across the Seto Inland Sea on bridges to Honshū!

Get Your Hands Dirty: Try a martial art, make soba noodles, dye fabrics, and learn a two-step in time for the summer dances.

Get Down, Get Funky: Festivals mark every weekend between April and October leading up to the biggest in the nation—the summer dance festivals Yosakoi and Awa Odori.

Get Personal: You might be the first foreigner this old farmer has ever spoken with. He might make your day with a good photo, a great story, and some juicy, hand-picked mikans.

Get Real: You'll hear that Shikoku is "the real Japan," with its time-forgotten towns like Uchiko and Nishi-Iya, unique landmarks like Dōgo Onsen and Kompira-san, and acres of rice.

Takamatsu and Eastern Shikoku. In Kagawa and Tokushima prefectures natural spectacles like the giant whirlpools in Tokushima and artistic attractions like Takamatsu's Noguchi Garden Museum springboard you to small towns and craft workshops nearby.

Kōchi and Central Shikoku. The mile-high mountains of central Shikoku have escaped global homogenization and heavy industry. Visit two great escapes: the forest paradise of Iya—gorges and tiny villages best explored on a rafting trip down the vibrant Yoshino river—and the rowdy, fun-loving Kōchi City on the sun-kissed southern sea.

Matsuyama and Western Shikoku. Matsuyama mixes small-town character with an exciting urban landscape. Come for Japan's best eating, fashion, and in-city sights outside of Honshū. See the superb clifftop castle and dreamlike Dōgo Onsen, the oldest exploited hot spring in Japan, and venture into the surrounding mountain villages.

PLANNING

Your trip will almost certainly start at one of the island's northern cities: coming from Kansai your most likely access is via Takamatsu or Tokushima in eastern Shikoku; from Hiroshima or Western Honshū it's Matsuyama in the west. In both cases you'll want to move through the island's central mountains before gaining the other coast. This circuit is perfect if you want to get off the beaten path without finding yourself totally off the map.

Because Shikoku's rewards lie off the beaten path, exploring involves the challenges of a road less traveled. Disabled access is sorely limited, public transportation imperfect, and English competence minimal. On the other hand, locals here will be more excited to socialize with you here than anywhere else in the country. Avoid scaring them off with too much English: "Hello, what's your name?" is the best way to begin integrating with people, and kids may be better in-roads than their shy parents. They'll be tickled to finally use the English they're studying in school.

Use the cities for access to small towns and natural getaways, and tailor the route to suit your aims and schedule. If you'll only have a few days, decide what's most important to you: is it tasting the distinct flavors Shikoku's remote cities, seeing the unique cultural attractions not found anywhere else in the world, or exploring the secluded forests of Iya and the rough-edged back mountain towns of Ehime?

WHEN TO GO

Shikoku's unspoiled scenery offers some perfect locations to bask in the fleeting glories of springtime cherry blossoms and autumn foliage. Summer is festival time throughout the country, but Shikoku has the best of the bunch: the epic dance festivals **Yosakoi** よさこい in Kōchi, held August 9–12, and Tokushima's **Awa Odori** 阿波踊り, August 12–15.

GETTING HERE AND AROUND

Trains and buses are the easiest ways to travel, though in rural areas they can be infrequent and irregular. Missing a train doesn't always mean just waiting for the next one: the next one might not come until October. Check schedules and find out when renting a car will save you time and money. Ask Tourist Information Centers (not JR ticket windows) to help you plan. Driving is a fantastic way to explore the countryside, but be ready for challenging mountain roads.

AIR TRAVEL

All Nippon Airways (ANA) and Japan Airlines (JAL) provide domestic flights to and from Shikoku's four major cities: Takamatsu, Kōchi, Matsuyama, and Tokushima. International connections through Seoul and Taipei are rarely cost-effective; use bus or ferry connections to airports in Tōkyō or Ōsaka.

BOAT TRAVEL

Cities and small ports offer ferry connections to Tōkyō, Ōsaka, Kōbe, Western Honshū, and Kyūshū. The Japan Cycling Association has a great Web sites compiling Shikoku's various ferry routes. Use the respective ferry companies' sites to check timetables; reservations are rarely necessary if you don't have a vehicle. International ferry routes link Matsuyama to Korea and Russia.

BUS TRAVEL

Short-range and overnight buses connect Shikoku's four capitals to a number of cities on Honshū and with each other—useful when no direct train route exists, like between Matsuyama and Kōchi or Tokushima. Buses also provide access to far-off coastal points and mountains.

CAR TRAVEL

Shikoku's narrow roads present challenges, but having your own transportation provides a priceless escape into the island's mountainous interior and secluded small towns. The easiest rental-car service is **ToCoo** トクー, with branch connections in all of Shikoku's airports and cities. Make reservations through the English Web site. (You must have an international driving permit). ToCoo Tourist information centers have good maps illustrating Shikoku's major roads and highways, and getting around is pretty straightforward.

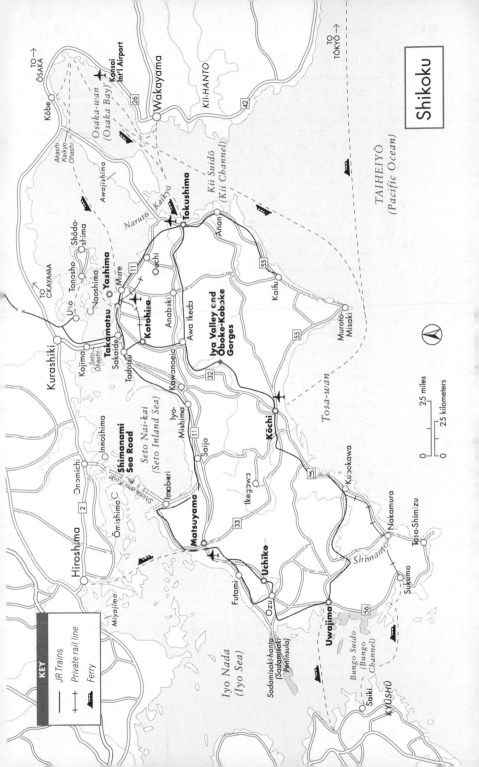

Shikoku

CLOSE UP

On the Menu

Every corner of Shikoku has a special dish, cuisine, or crop. Ehime is famous for *mikan*—clementines—and between November and March you can't walk a country mile without a farmer handing you a bag. Ehime is also the nation's main cultivator of *tai*, or red snapper; tai-meshi is rice that's cooked with chunks of the fish, usually in a flaming tin pot. Kagawa-ken's *sanuki-udon* is widely thought to be the nation's best, and Tokushima-ken's delicious *Iya-soba*, made from the valley's hearty strand of buckwheat flour, is even tastier if you've pounded the dough yourself at a *soba dojo*. Sand-grown at Naruto are the best *satsumaimo*, purple Japanese sweet potatoes, and *imo-taki* are popular across the island in autumn: potato baking parties for watching the full moon. The most renowned cuisine styles are in Kōchi: tosa-ryōri and sawachi-ryōri, different ways of serving enormous amounts of delicious fish, particularly slices of lightly seared *katsuo*.

■ **TIP→Get off the highways!** Don't miss out on seeing some of the "Real Japan" you came here for. Fishing towns and rice-farming villages contour the island, and although highway travel will save you a little time, you'll never see what life is like outside of the city. Try the rewarding, easily navigable numbered prefectural routes (you'll save on the exorbitant tolls). Get directions at the information centers and enjoy that countryside. Shikoku's hidden corners are awaiting with adventure.

TRAIN TRAVEL

Shikoku is belted around by a single rail track with branches going off to the interior. Since it is just the single track in most places, expect irregular schedules and long waits for local trains as express ones hurtle by. The JR Pass is good on all normal and express trains. A ¥15,700 Shikoku Free Kippu is good for three days of unlimited train use.

RESTAURANTS

Three of Shikoku's four main cities—Takamatsu, Kōchi, and Matsuyama—specialize in a variety of cuisines at very reasonable prices. In smaller towns expect places to close at 8 PM.

HOTELS

Accommodations on Shikoku range from *ryokan* and *minshuku* in old homes to international hotels and lavish onsen resorts. Unless otherwise noted, all hotel rooms have private baths, phones, and air-conditioning. Large city and resort hotels serve Western and Japanese food. Reservations are essential during major festivals, and Japanese holiday periods.

⇨ *For a short course on accommodations in Japan, see Accommodations in Travel Smart.*

11

WHAT IT COSTS IN YEN				
¢	$	$$	$$$	$$$$
RESTAURANTS under ¥800	¥800–¥1,000	¥1,000–¥2,000	¥2,000–¥3,000	over ¥3,000
HOTELS under ¥8,000	¥8,000–¥12,000	¥12,000–¥18,000	¥18,000–¥22,000	over ¥22,000

Restaurant prices are per person for a main course, set meal, or equivalent combinations of smaller dishes. Hotel prices are for a double room with private bath, excluding service and tax.

VISITOR INFORMATION

Tourist information centers in Shikoku's main cities might have the only skilled English speakers you meet on the island. Use them for advice, transportation info, reservations, recommendations, maps, and local news. Ask a lot of questions: desk staff won't make suggestions unless prodded, but they are great resources for scenic driving routes and events information. Community festivals are happening all the time—a one-horse town over those mountains may be celebrating its 400th annual lantern festival tomorrow night, but you'll never know unless you ask. Information centers are listed throughout the chapter.

A nationwide toll-free **English-language hotline** for assistance or travel information is available from yellow, blue, or green public phones (not red phones); insert a ¥10 coin, which will be returned.

ESSENTIALS

Airline Information All Nippon Airways (ANA) (☏ 800/235-9262 in U.S. and Canada, 0120/02-9222 in Japan ⊕ www.anaskyweb.com). **Japan Airlines (JAL)** (☏ 800/525-3663 in U.S. and Canada, 0120/255-971 in Japan ⊕ www.jal.co.jp).

Car Rental ToCoo (⊕ www2.tocoo.jp).

Emergency Contact Ambulance (☏ 119). **Police** (☏ 110).

Train Information JR Pass (⊕ www.japanrailpass.net).

Visitor Information English-language hotline (☏ 0120/444-800 or 0088/224-800 ⊙ Daily 9-5).

TAKAMATSU AND EASTERN SHIKOKU

TAKAMATSU 高松

71 km (44 mi) south of Okayama.

Coming to Shikoku almost certainly means a trip through cosmopolitan Takamatsu, a city whose urban verve doesn't compromise the relaxed down-home atmosphere; a short walk down the city's wide, sunlit boulevards brings you to funky shops, artsy cafés, an exciting nightlife, a bevy of dazzling cultural sights, and a friendly local population not afraid to share it all with you.

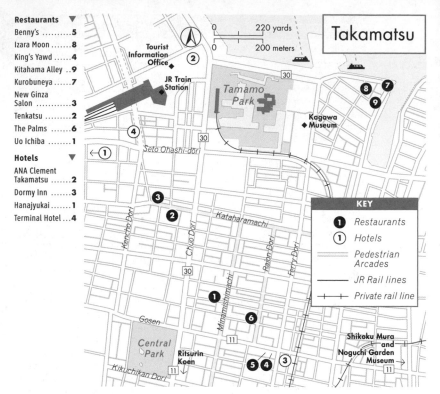

GETTING HERE AND AROUND

It takes one hour to get here from Okayama by JR. Buses from Tōkyō are 10 hours; Nagoya 7 hours; Ōsaka, 4 hours; Kyōto or Shin-Kōbe 3 hours 30 minutes; Sannomiya 2 hours 25 minutes; Matsuyama 2 hours 30 minutes; Kōchi 2 hours; and Tokushima 1 hour 30 minutes. Ferries from Ōsaka and Kōbe arrive in 2 hours 20 minutes.

You're most likely to set off exploring from Takamatsu's northern tip, where the JR station, bus platforms, and ferry port bracket a wide piazza around the Clement Hotel. At the northwest corner of the grassy, highly missable **Tamamo castle park**, continue straight along the park's edge towards the **Kagawa Museum** and **Kitahama Alley**, or turn left down broad Chūō Dōri to hit the city. Ten minutes will bring you to the covered Hyogo-Machi shopping arcade and within easy striking distance of the city's other sights. The city's biggest draw, the 120-acre **Ritsurin Garden**, is 20 minutes farther south.

The east-lying districts Yashima and Mure are home to two more captivating attractions: the historical preserve **Shikoku Mura** and the **Isamu Noguchi Garden Museum,** a superb sculpture park in a studio of the late master. Just outside of the main city, both sites are easy to access by car or local train.

A squat **Information Office** in front of the JR station is the place for maps, time tables, and travel advice. Some staff speak English quite well, so use them to help plan your next move. If you need more multilingual help or local events info, try **IPAL**, a cultural exchange office in the central Chūō-kōen. Ask for their city map, better than the standard one, the latest *Kagawa Journal* events newsletter, and a **Kagawa Welcome Card**, great for discounts on sights. You can print the card off their Web site, too.

> **RIDE-N-SEEK**
>
> Why let walking from sight to sight eat up your whole day? Take advantage of the cheap bicycle rental available from an underground garage near the JR station. For ¥100 the whole city will open up to you. Explore some out of the way spots, like the two skinny piers and cute lighthouses off the sunport north of the station, perfect for watching the sunset.

ESSENTIALS

Visitor Information Kagawa Welcome Card (⊕*www.21kagawa.com/visitor/index2.htm).* **Information Office** (☎*087/851–2009).* **IPAL** (☎ *087/837–5908* ⊕ *www. i-pal.or.jp* ☉ *Tues. Sun. 9–6).*

WHAT TO SEE

Takamatsu's number one attraction, the great garden park **Ritsurin-kōen** 栗林公園, is a breathtaking, peaceful retreat from the world around. Though not on the list of Japan's three best gardens, Ritsurin-kōen offers a more intimate and immersive experience than any traditional garden in the country. You'll want a few hours to explore, and although you get a handy trail map as you enter, remember to walk your own path while you explore. Just around the next bend are great surprises: an embankment of irises in full bloom in June; a thousand turtles surfacing in a pond to say hello; a sea of ferns surrounding the thatch-roofed teahouse where your bowl of bitter matcha induces your afternoon's meditation. This secluded haven was once the summer estate of nobility, and though the ancient clans have crumbled with time, the park has lost none of its magic or beauty. ☎*087/833–7411* ☎*¥400* ☉ *May–Sept., daily 5:30–6; Oct.–Apr., daily 7–5.*

☺ Just south of the decaying castle park, the **Kagawa Museum** *(Kagawa-ken Rekishi Hakubutsukan)* emphasizes interactive learning with hands-on exhibits—everything from sword-making to woodblock-printing to producing (and playing with) Japanese toys—and an engaging permanent collection. You won't need a lick of Japanese to enjoy walking in a Neolithic hut, crawling with a magnifying glass on the giant photo map of Kagawa, or dressing up in full samurai armor and lush ceremonial kimonos. The museum staff will help you don the costumes and even take a Polaroid for you, and it's all included in the entry fee. ⊠*5–5 Tamamo-chō* ☎*087/822–0002* ⊕*www.pref.kagawa.jp/kmuseum* ☎*¥400* ☉ *Tues.–Sun. 9–4:30, Fri. until 7.*

★ Bamboo groves conceal a trove of ancient treasures at the mountainside park **Shikoku Mura.** Dozens of historical buildings and bridges from around Shikoku have been brought to this expansive forest park and lovingly restored. English information boards provide a surprisingly interesting history for each location, and a web of well-kept pathways lets you wander freely without feeling either too shepherded or too lost. Take a break at the **Shikoku Mura Gallery** 四国村ギャラリー, nestled on the hillside above an ancient sugar mill. Designed by Tadao Ando, the gallery has a collection with works by Picasso, Chagall, Monet, and literary notable Natsume Soseki. Access is by Kotoden train: take the Shido line 20 minutes to Yashima station and walk five minutes to the park. Going by car, take Route 11 toward Tokushima and turn left at the first McDonalds on the right. ✉*91 Yashima-Nakamachi-chō Takamatsu* ☎*087/843–3111* ⊕*www.shikokumura.or.jp* ✉*¥800* ⊗*Apr.–Oct., daily 8:30–5; Nov.–Mar., daily 8:30–4:30.*

NEED A BREAK?

Locals take fierce pride in Kagawa's local culinary specialty *sanuki udon,* and people travel distances beguiling good sense to partake at **Waraya** わら家 ($$$), a restored riverside house at the base of Shikoku Mura. Stop here for lunch and enjoy the rustic waterwheel. Remember: people say the noodles taste better if you slurp them loudly and although quiet eating isn't rude *per se,* why would you forgo the extra flavor? If you're with a party of three or more, don't pass up the family size noodle barrel for the most fun for your buck. ✉ *91 Yashima-Nakamachi,* ⊗ *Weekdays, 10–6:30, weekends 10–9.*

Fodor'sChoice
★

Isamu Noguchi Garden Museum イサムノグチ庭園博物館. A wonderland of sculpture both playful and profound, the installations and extensive outdoor facility embrace you with the nuances of Noguchi's creativity. The sensitivity and expressiveness of the Japanese-American sculptor are so potent here in his former studio and home that you'll feel as if he's giving the tour himself. The site holds hundreds of his works in stone and other media, although the emphasis tends away from the paper sculpture with which Noguchi is most often associated abroad. Officially visitation requires at least two weeks' advance reservation by mail or fax, but they're not as strict as they sound. A phone call ahead will usually get you admitted. The museum is a 10-minute taxi ride from Yashima Station, or go two stops farther on the Kotoden Shido line to Yakuri before hopping a cab. ✉*3–5–19 Mure, Mure-chō* ☎*087/870–1500* 🖷*087/845–0505* ⊕*www.isamunoguchi.or.jp/* ✉*¥2,100* ⊗*Tues., Thurs., and Sat. at 10, 1, and 3 by appointment.*

WHERE TO EAT

Dozens of great restaurants and stores are scattered along the central Marugame-machi arcade and the side streets lacing it to Raion Dōri. The city's late bedtime makes it easy to move from a meal to nightlife spot before finding a second dinner later on.

$
JAMAICAN

✗**King's Yawd** キングズヤード. King's Yawd will spice your night up with a lip-smacking jerk chicken platter, tropical cocktail, and if you're lucky, a Jamaican movie night (projected onto the red and yellow walls) or a live-music event or dance party under the giant Haile Selassie tapestry. King's Yawd becomes a popular nightspot late into almost every evening, but usually without getting too loud to enjoy yourself. On the south side of Kawara-machi dōri near Marugamemachi look out for the glowing Jamaican flag. ⊠*4th fl. of Kawara-machi Bldg., 1–9–9 Kawaramachi-dōri* ☎*087/837–2660* ◷*Closed Sun.*

$$
JAPANESE
★

✕**New Ginza Salon** ギンザサロン. This lovely little bistro compliments a swanky-chic decor with cuisine so unpretentiously good that you'll imagine whatever today's special is has always been your favorite dish. The New Ginza excels at using very standard Japanese kitchen ingredients in dishes that soar above the tired tastes of standard kitchen fare. The antique tables and plush chairs create a perfect setting for their delicious lunch plates, colorful dinner menu, and excellent handmade pastries. Don't worry about the Japanese-only menu—decide on fish, chicken, or meat and order one of the day's three prix-fix sets. ⊠*2–4–11 Hyōgo-machi* ☎*087/823–7065* ◷*Daily 11 AM–1 AM.*

$$
HAWAIIAN

✕**The Palms.** On cushy divans under the cheesy beach-dioramas, Hawaiian food and imported beer might not transport you to Oahu, but it's a great start to a Takamatsu night. Strike up conversation with the affable proprietor Kengo and his super-friendly regulars, or strum the in-house ukulele at the bar. ⊠*2–9–7 Kawaramachi, on the 2nd fl.* ☎*087/862–3444* ◷*Thurs.–Tues. 3 PM midnight.*

$$–$$$
JAPANESE

✕**Tenkatsu** 天勝. Find your favorite fish in the pool at Tenkatsu and it will be on your plate a minute later. Forgo the tatami tables to sit close to the action at the big black countertop. This interior design doesn't overwhelm, but the food makes up for it. Plastic displays and a picture menu help you choose the dish (choosing the fish is rather more intuitive). Nabe pots in autumn and winter are house favorites. ⊠*Nishizumi Hiroba, Hyōgo-machi* ☎*087/821–5380* ▭*AE, DC, MC, V.*

$$$
JAPANESE

✕**Uo Ichiba** 魚市場. The simmering energy of a cantina thrives in this upscale three-floor restaurant. Flags and banners hang above tanks full of eels and fish waiting to be selected for your plate, and the chefs do a dazzling job preparing the freshest, most sumptuous seafood. Other Japanese fare is also top-notch. Dinner is lively, but the set menus at lunch are considerably cheaper. Located just across from Kawaroku Hotel off Marugame-machi arcade. ⊠*9–5 Hyakken-machi* ☎*087/826–2056.*

WHERE TO STAY

$$$$

▦**ANA Hotel Clement Takamatsu** 全日空ホテルクレメント高松. This branch of the upscale ANA hotel chain was built to be Takamatsu's premier Western-style hotel. Although its bright rooms and plush facilities don't fail to impress, other lodgings like the Terminal Hotel and Dormy Inn offer cozier, competitively classy Western rooms at a fraction of the cost. If you're inclined to indulge in Takamatsu's luxury, you'll have a more memorable, exciting time at the Hanajyukai. **Pros:** great city access; spacious rooms. **Cons:** small bang for your buck; no onsen or bath; bland skybar. ⊠*1–1 Hamamo-chō* ☎*087/811–1111* 📠*087/800–2222* ⊕*www.anahotels.com/eng/index.html* ⇖*500 rooms* ▭*AE, DC, MC, V.*

$
★

▦**Dormy Inn** ドーミーイン. This branch of the national chain feels almost too good to be true. The excellent central location, plush rooms, and great in-hotel amenities—particularly the rooftop bath—seem like they should be going for twice the rate. Doors opened in June 2008, and facilities are fresh and modern. The terrific onsen on the top floor gets bonus points for the excellent and affordable in-house massage service:

KITAHAMA ALLEY

The wharf-side warehouses of Kitahama Alley escaped the wrecking ball and now house an enclave of funky interior shops, hipster craft workspaces, several great restaurants, a few on-again-off-again cafés and a large gallery space. Because this grassroots venture is the work of a younger cohort of entrepreneurs, English speakers are easy to find. What's more challenging is finding the place itself: the salt-blasted wooden buildings look so derelict you might pass by without a thought. Follow the coastline past Tamamo Kōen until a canal cuts back toward the city and you're there. Poke into stores like **Depot**, selling great house and kitchen items, and **Peekabooya**, selling baby clothes more fashionable than anything in your own wardrobe. For eating, try second-floor **Juke Joint Kurobuneya** (☎ *087/826–3636* ⏱ *6* PM*–3* AM, *closed Mon.*) with good Mexican fare next to Japanese izakaya staples, and the trendied-up Japanese dishes and a helpful picture menu at **Izara Moon** (☎ *087/811–4531* ⏱ *11* AM*–1* AM, *closed Tues.*).

¥2,000 for 20 minutes, 7 PM–midnight, with room-service massage at no extra charge. **Pros:** great value; great location; newly opened. **Cons:** no in-room cots for a third body; garish inn-room robes. ✉ *1–10–10 Kawaramachi* ☎ *087/832–5489* ⊕ *www.hotespa.net* ✍ *in-takamatsu@ dormy-hotels.com* ⚴ *In-room: refrigerator, DVD, Internet. In-hotel: restaurant, laundry facilities, hot spring* ▭ *V.*

$$$–$$$$
★   ⊡ **Hanajyukai.** Overlook city and sea from a flower-covered mountainside at ryokan Hanajyukai. The friendly staff will give you the royal treatment in your smart tatami rooms with an exquisite in-room dinner service and beautiful kimonos. The scenic rooftop spa rooms will melt your travel stress away. Reservations are best made by e-mail. It's a 10-minute taxi ride from the city center. **Pros:** friendly staff; new tatami in all rooms in 2008; optional breakfast and dinner can cut down the cost. **Cons:** away from downtown; harsh Western rooms face the cliff side; little-to-no English help. ✉ *3–5–10 Nishitakara-chō* ☎ *087/861–5580* 🖷 *087/834–9912* ⊕ *www.hanajyukai.co.jp* ✍ *hana@ hanajyukai.co.jp* ⚲ *48 Japanese-style rooms* ⚴ *In-hotel: restaurant, laundry facilities, no-smoking rooms* ▭ *AE, DC, MC, V* 🍴 *MAP.*

$ ⊡ **Terminal Hotel.** A stylish full renovation in the summer of 2008 has bumped the Terminal Hotel up the ranks of Takamatsu's most fashionable places to stay. The window dressings and wallpaper make it chic; thick piled carpets and plush bedspreads make it comfortable. **Pros:** close to the station; great furnishings; English Web site where you can make reservations. **Cons:** no double rooms; large beds take up most of the floor space. ✉ *10–17 Nishinomaruchō* ☎ *087/822–3731* ⊕ *www. webterminal.co.jp* ⚴ *In-room: Internet. In-hotel: Internet terminal, no-smoking rooms* ▭ *AE, MC, V.*

NIGHTLIFE

Avalanche アバランチ. Avalanche can shut totally for weeks at a time only to burst to life with electrifying hip-hop, house, and DJ events, often featuring big name tickets from Tōkyō or Ōsaka. On the fifth floor of the Kawaramachi Building. ✉ *5th fl. of Kawara-machi Bldg., 1–9–9 Kawaramachi-dōri* ☎ *087/862–1655* ⊘ *Closed Sun.*

Benny's ベニーズ. For a change of pace and music, head to Benny's. Sofas encourage mingling with the friendly clientele, and if there's no local band tonight then pick up an instrument and jam down. Benny will accompany you on blues harmonica if you ask him. All drinks are ¥500. It's located in the Kawaramachi Building. ✉ *6th fl. of Kawara-machi Bldg., 1–9–9 Kawaramachi-dōri* ☎ *090/2891–6481* ⊘ *8:30* PM– *3* AM. *Closed Sun.*

KOTOHIRA 琴平

45 km (28 mi) from Takamatsu.

GETTING HERE AND AROUND

Partake in a centuries-long story of pilgrimage when you climb the sacred mountain Kompira-san in the town of Kotohira, smack in the middle of Shikoku. Kotohira is 1 hour from Takamatsu by JR or Kotoden train. JR lines run south 40 minutes to Awa Ikeda for easy access to Iya or Kōchi; otherwise, a change at Tadōtsu gives access to Matsuyama. The easy access is a blessing since the town dies after nightfall and you'll prefer to lodge elsewhere. Ditch your bags in coin lockers and pick up a map at the local information center located smack between the JR and Kotoden stations before heading to the mountain.

ESSENTIALS

Visitor Information Information Center (☎ *087/775–3500* ⊘ *Daily 9:30–8*).

WHAT TO SEE

The first half of your climb up the sacred mountain is a chaotic mix of vendors' wares and tourists' chatter. But the final half of the ascent is filled with the rewards of pilgrimage: the echo of your footsteps, a splash of blue sea through a break in the trees, a hummed *konnichiwa* from above you on the trail. The stairways leading up the mountain Kompira-san are famous—785 steps to the impressive main shrine and 583 more to the final lookout—and finishing the climb, breathless at the summit, you will see why this path to enlightenment is so well worn.

On the way down you may want to rest at the **Shōin** (¥400), an Edo-period hall with artifacts and screens painted by Ōkyo Maruyama. When you reach the bottom, congratulate yourself with a tour through the **Kinryō Sake Museum and Brewery** 金陵の郷, marked by an enormous sake bottle fountaining into the street in front of the temple stairs. Sample the wares for ¥100 a shot.

TOKUSHIMA 徳島

70 km (43 mi) from Takamatsu and from Awa Ikeda.

Tokushima has a treasure trove of fabulous sights and unique local attractions. Most visitors stay near the city's center or in Naruto, a nearby peninsula famous for giant whirlpools that churn and thunder in the rocky straights below the cliffs. Nearby, the ambitious **Ōtsuka Museum** attracts huge crowds for its bizarre and breathtaking archive of

SIDE TRIP: NAOSHIMA

The museums and installation projects have brought this classic Shikoku backwater back from the brink. The island's art projects attract thousands of visitors every year, and you too can enjoy busing or bicycling to the three big installation sights or staying a night in the project itself. It's an easy side trip from Takamatsu.

GETTING HERE AND AROUND

Ferries between Takamatsu and Miyanoura port on Naoshima take 50 minutes–1 hour, cost ¥510, and leave several times daily. High-speed 25-minute boats (¥1,200) depart once a day. On weekends and holidays between March and November an additional high-speed service is available. A Naoshima bus schedule with a map and route recommendations is available on the Naoshima tourist Web site (www.naoshima.net) and from the Information Center at Takamatsu's JR station (087/892–2299). Bringing your own transportation across on the ferry will save time and stress.

WHAT TO SEE

Be forewarned, the project isn't for everybody. Works are, with very few exceptions, large-scale installation pieces, and the aesthetic is not emotional or sublime but provocative. A set of Monet water lily paintings at the **Chichū Art Museum** 地中美術館 departs from this norm; more representative is the traditional Shintō shrine in which glass elements juxtapose with wooden ones. Many visitors are fascinated by the idiosyncratic art; others come away feeling that the **Art House Projects** 家プロジェクト and **Benesse Art Site** ベネッセアートサイト lack substance or depth. Look through Naoshima's Web sites to see if the island does speak to you; if you're keen to see

the contrast between modern architecture and rural countryside, then make the trip. Information is available at **Honmura Lounge and Archive** 本村ラウンジ＆アーカイブ.

WHERE TO STAY

The Benesse House Art Project has a variety of accommodations for those wanting to spend the night. Doubles on the museum sight, the park, and the beach range from ¥30,000 to ¥70,000. More affordable and delightfully surreal are the Mongolian-style yurts built on the southern beach, running ¥4,200 per person. Ask the Takamatsu information desk to call for you.

ESSENTIALS

Art House Project (☎ 087/892–2030 ✉ ¥1,000 for 6 sights or ¥400 per sight ⊘ Tues.–Sun. 10–4:30).

Benesse Art House (☎ 087/892–2030 ✉ ¥1,000 ⊘ Daily 8–9, last admission 8 ⊕ www.naoshima-is.co.jp/english/concept/art/benesse_house.html).

Chichū Art Museum (☎ 087/892–3755 ✉ ¥2000 ⊘ Mar.–Sept., Tues.–Sun. 10–6, last admission 5; Oct.–Feb., Tues.–Sun. 10–5, last admission 4).

Honmura Lounge and Archive (☎ 087/840–8272)

the world's art. In surrounding hamlets you can try your hand at local crafts like **indigo-dyeing, paper-making** as they've done it for centuries. Back in the city proper you'll learn to dance the **Awa Odori,** either in a special performance hall or with the million others dancing the streets every summer during the **Awa Odori Festival.** Tokushima's major sights can be covered in a well-planned day or two, giving you plenty of time in the mountains and gorges of **Iya** after moving on.

GETTING HERE AND AROUND

Tokushima is accessible by JR train: 1 hour 15 minutes from Taka-matsu; 1 hour 30 minutes from Awa Ikeda; 2 hours 25 minutes from Kōchi; 3 hours 40 minutes from Matsuyama; 3 hours 20 minutes from Shin-Ōsaka; 1 hour 30 minutes from Okayama. Highway and JR Buses are also an option. Highway Buses depart from Takamatsu (1 hour 30 minutes); Kōchi (2 hours 40 minutes); Matsuyama (3 hours 10 min-utes); Kōbe (2 hours); Kyōto, Ōsaka, or Kansai Airport (3 hours); or overnight from Tōkyō. By JR Bus it's 2 hours 25 minutes from Ōsaka, Kōbe or Shin-Kōbe. The ferry arrives from Tōkyō (18 hours) and Wakayam (2 hours).

Buses leave Tokushima for Naruto on the hour between 9 and 3, taking 63 minutes and costing ¥690; the return has more varied times, so check the schedule. The boat quay at Naruto Kan-kōkō is a few stops before the end of the line, about an eight-minute walk from uzu-no-michi. There are also trains to Naruto Station; catch a bus or taxi from there to the coast. Going by car from Tokushima takes roughly a half hour.

Before hitting the town, head up by glass elevator to the sixth floor of the Clement Tower station building to **TOPIA**, the best tourist informa-tion center in western Japan. The city employs a native English speaker there nearly full time who can provide bus schedules, train times, tide calendars (necessary for seeing the whirlpools at their best), and a good battle plan for tackling it all.

■TIP➜Tokushima's best sights are far from the city center and not well serviced by public transportation. Hiring your own car to access the craft centers and whirlpools makes for a better, easier time.

ESSENTIALS

Visitor Information TOPIA (☎ *088/656-3033* ⊕ *www.topia.ne.jp/e_index.htm* ✆ *Daily 10-6*).

WHAT TO SEE

The thunderous roar of **giant whirlpools** fills the cliffs around the Naruto Kaikyō (the Naruto Straits), splitting the peaceful sky and green moun-tainsides asunder with a chaos of furious, frothing sea. See the whirl-pools from a glass-bottomed gantry 45 meters above the water or, better still, from the deck of a tour boat down in the belly of the beast.

The walkway, called **uzu-no-michi,** gives a great view of the pools and the seacoast, but you'll wish you had chosen the boats. There are a few companies with different-size vessels and marginally different prices (¥1,500–¥2,500). All the rides are exhilarating. Two of the best boat tours are Wonder Naruto and Aqua Eddy. Which you select will depend on what time you arrive, and what time the pools reach their active peak on that day. The whirlpools are formed when the pull of changing tides forces a huge volume of seawater through the narrow, rocky bottleneck. The tide calendar will let you know what time to see the pools at their best on any given day; the straights will froth furiously for a good hour on each end of the peak.

★ From uzu-no-michi a boardwalk rings the high coastline; walk south for 10 minutes and you'll come to the **Ōtsuka Museum of Art** 大塚美術館, a surreal and ambitious exhibition space collecting Western art from all over the world . . . sort of. Over a thousand great works of art have been precisely reproduced on ceramic tiles and arranged throughout the enormous facility by era and location. More than a Greatest Hits of Art, you'll find well-known and obscure works on display. Surround yourself with a room full of Rubens altars, stand alone in the Sistine Chapel or before Picasso's *Guernica,* wander through replicated French churches, Greek tombs, a banquet hall from Pompeii, and countless other sights you'd thought were one-of-a-kind. Indeed, these pieces are unique, and seeing them can be confounding, as you feel moved by the power of a thousand stunning pictures of pictures. It is a unique and enlightening experience. ✉ *65-1 Aza Tosadomari-ura Fukuike, Naruto-chō* ☎ *088/687–3737* 🌐 *www.o-museum.or.jp* 🎫 *¥3,150* ⏲ *Tues.–Sun. 9:30–5; last entry at 4.*

At Ai-no-Yakata, **The House of Indigo,** try the ancient craft of dyeing cloth in cauldrons of blue-black, pungent indigo. Someone at the desk will show you a price chart for items—cotton handkerchiefs are only ¥500, silk scarves close to ¥2,000. Towels come out splendidly, but you have to ask for the separate price chart (the word is *ta-o-ru*). It's fun, and you'll be delighted with what you make. Snoop around the 400-year-old craft center when you're finished. One of the proprietors performs daily on the *shaku-hachi,* a thick bodied wooden flute, and he'll play anytime you ask. From Tokushima Station hop a 20-minute bus to Higashi Nakatomi. Walk down the hill behind you and follow the indigo signs. ✉ *Aizumi-chō, Tokumei Aza Maesunishi* ☎ *088/692–6317* 🎫 *¥300* ⏲ *Daily 9–5.*

Trek out to the Awagami **Hall of Awa Handmade Paper** 阿波和紙伝統産業会館 *(Awa Washi Dentō)* to make your own postcards and browse their phenomenal gift shop; it goes from sheets of softer-than-silk wrapping paper to peerless fans and parasols. It's also something of a pain to get to by train. It's one hour to Awa-Yamakawa Station, then walk 15 minutes to the hall. *136 Kawahigashi* ☎ *0883/42–6120* 🌐 *www.awagami.or.jp/en/* 🎫 *¥300* ⏲ *Tues.–Sun. 9–5.*

WHERE TO EAT

Tokushima is well served by slick bars and restaurants; the two best are easily Wine and its upstairs neighbor Shanghai Fang. Although Tokushima has a thriving nightlife, it's not welcoming: there's a divide between ex-pats and locals, and the foreigner-friendly places feel grubby and cheap. Get the partying out of your system in Takamatsu.

$$–$$$ CHINESE ✕ **Chinese Kitchen Shanghai Fang** 上海ファング. Perhaps you'll take the tall, skinny private room beneath the stairwell, the sumptuously secluded loveseat beside the door, a thick dark-wood table on flagstones, or

Dancing the Shikoku

11

The Awa Odori Festival happens every summer over Ōbon, festival of the dead, and if you miss it you can still get a dose at the **Awa Odori Kaikan** 阿波踊り会館. *Odori* means "dance," and at the Kaikan silk-robed professionals perform the famous local step nightly. But shine your shoes: when the troupe leader starts talking to the audience, he's looking for volunteers. Everyone will be thrilled to see you try, so stand up! They'll give you some fragmented English directions and thankfully, it's a very easy dance. The first volunteering round is for men, the second for women; each has different steps to learn. You might get a prize for participating, and one special award goes to the biggest fool on the floor—this honor is a staple of the festival, and it's not always the foreigners who win.

The best show is at 8 PM. Arrive early and browse the gift shop or treat yourself to a ropeway ride up the mountain for a lovely view of the city. *20 Shinmachibashi, 2-chōme* ☎ *088/611-1611* ✉ *Afternoon dance ¥500, evening dance ¥700. Ropeway ¥1,000 round-trip* ☉ *Gift shop daily 9–6. Performances at 2, 3, 4, and 8; also at 11 on weekends. Closed 2nd and 4th Wed. of month.*

one of the sunken floor tables ringed by water and rocks upstairs. Shanghai Fang's funky mixture of hidden tables and cozy private dining rooms will make you stay all night, even though their ¥3,000 course won't knock your socks off. Still it's delicious and includes unlimited drinks for two hours. ✉ *12–1 Konya-machi, 4th fl.* ☎ *088/624–5838* ☉ *Daily 5:30–12:30.*

$$-$$$
JAPANESE ✗**Wine** 和いん. Excellent Japanese cuisine balances the traditional with the experimental, and the funky décor is as good a reason to come as the food. Across three floors and dozens of differently crafted environs you'll find cushioned corner nooks, normal sit-down tables, latticed-in private chambers, and other one-of-a-kind settings to relish in your meal. The friendly staff will help you decipher the Japanese menu. But you can't go wrong with the ¥3,500 set course: seven wide-ranging dishes include staples like seasonal sashimi and vegetables, and a three-hour all-you-can-drink (two hours on Friday). ✉ *12–1 Konya-machi, 1st fl.* ☎ *088/657–7477* ☉ *Daily 5:30–12:30.*

$
★
JAPANESE ✗**YRG.** The secret favorite of Tokushima's burgeoning young-and-cool demographic and those expats that stay aloof from the binge drinking scene downtown, YRG's laid-back atmosphere and hip but unpretentious decor make it the best lunch or dinner spot in Tokushima. The English speaking proprietor Takao decides the set menus daily, aiming for nutritionally balanced yet provocative comfort food: it's home-cooking *plus*. Drink menus are inside kids books from a dozen countries on shelves and tables. Wireless is available. Coming out of the JR station you'll see two smaller streets and one major one branch off to the left; take the middle street and walk two minutes to just before it terminates. ✉ *1-33–4 Terashima Honchō Higashi* ☎ *088/656–7889* ☉ *Sun.–Wed. 11–10; Fri. and Sat. 11–midnight.*

WHERE TO STAY

For lodging the expensive resorts like Grand Hotel Kairakuen and the Washington Hotel feel old and worn-out, and don't deal well with non-Japanese-speaking guests. Better choices exist among the newer business hotels by the station.

$$ **Agnes Hotel** アグネスホテル. The friendly atmosphere amongst staff and patrons could have to do with the delicious French pastries served downstairs, all baked on premises with high-quality imported ingredients and seasonal fruits, but surely the root is the Agnes's proprietor Takashi, gregarious in English and Japanese and dying to make your stay enjoyable. Walking out of the station, take the second of two narrow streets that branch out to the right. **Pros:** a minute away from the station; bilingual manager; terrific pastries. **Cons:** no doubles; spartan decor. ⊠ *1–28 Terashima Honchō Nishi* ☎*088/626–2222* ⊕*www.agneshotel.jp* ✉ *takashi-okomoto@ agneshotel.jp* ✈*76 rooms* ⅗*In-hotel: Internet* ▤*AE, DC, MC, V.*

> ### SAIL TOKUSHIMA
>
> Although Tokushima best serves you as a hub for accessing its surroundings, it's a charming city in its own right. Take advantage of the half-hour river tours running from Ryokokubashi near the Toyoko Inn. Weekdays, tours run on the hour from 1 to 5, but weekends (and likely any other time) the adorable old men running it will take you any time you show up. Write your name in the book and drop ¥100 in the box on the pier before boarding.

$$ **Hotel Sunroute** ホテルサンルート. Luxurious but affordable, this hotel comes with good English assistance, great city access—it's located across from the JR station—and excellent amenities. The Sunroute is preferred by several international tour groups and most expats with visiting relatives. Doubles are spacious with queen-size beds and corner twins are huge. The only downside comes when you need your mid-day nap; the hotel blasts music out from the front facade from mid-morning until early evening, and some guests request room changes to escape. **Pros:** nice bathrooms, international clientele. **Cons:** that music! ⊠ *1–5–1 Motomachi* ☎*088/653–8111* ⊕*www.sunroute-tokushima.com* ✈*177 rooms* ⅗*In-room: refrigerator, DVD player, Internet. In-hotel: hot spring, laundry service, no-smoking rooms* ▤*AE, DC, MC, V.*

$$$$ **Renaissance Resort Naruto** ルネッサンスリゾート鳴門. Stretching along the sandy beaches at Naruto, this new Renaissance Resort is peerless for comfort, service, luxury, and access to the sights and surroundings of Naruto. Pick your favorite room from a variety of Western and Japanese arrangements with unique character; the Resort's Japanese Web site has pictures of every room. Ask to be beachside and the sound of the surf will lull you to sleep. In daylight you'll forgo swimming in the rough waves, but there's a fun restaurant on the dunes. **Pros:** sumptuous rooms and facilities; great access to Naruto. **Cons:** far from city center; no swimming on the beach. ⊠ *16–45 Oge Tosadomariura* ☎*088/687–2580* 🖷*088/687–2211* ⊕*www.renaissance-naruto.com* ✈*208 rooms* ⅗*In-room: refrigerator, DVD. In-hotel: restaurant, pool, laundry facilities* ▤*AE, D, MC, V.*

$ **Toyoko Inn** 東急イン. Clean, fresh facilities and easy city access make for a relaxing stay at Shikoku's newest branch of this comfortable chain hotel, opened in October 2008. Rooms are nice but not inspirational, and sport Ethernet jacks. Walking out of the station, follow the big road that branches off diagonally to the left. **Pros:** two-minute walk from the station; close to YRG. **Cons:** rooms could be bigger. ⊠*1–5 Ryogokuhonchō* ☎*088/657–1045* ⊕*www.toyoko-inn.com* ☜*139 rooms* ♿*In-room: safe, refrigerator, Internet. In-hotel: no-smoking rooms* ⊟*AE, DC, V.*

NIGHTLIFE

Bourbon Street. An expat run bar in the maze of drinking holes downtown, Bourbon Street gets its name for the frequent Jazz shows (often highlighting the soaring voice of Vivian, the proprietress). October 2008 marked the 1st anniversary, and some aesthetic changes are in the works in the coming year, but the great drink selection and comradely atmosphere are sure to stick around. ⊠*1–73–1 Sakae-Machi; Toku Bldg., 1st fl.* ☎*088/626–5758* ◷*Daily 8 PM–3 AM.*

CENTRAL SHIKOKU

IYA VALLEY AND ŌBOKE-KOBOKE GORGES
祖谷と大歩危小歩危

Fodor'sChoice
★ *25 km (16 mi) from Awa-Ikeda; 105 km (65 mi) from Tokushima; 135 km (84 mi) from Matsuyama.*

At the exact center of Shikoku the old roads yield a hidden paradise. The roaring river Yoshino-gawa cuts through tall verdant mountains and the gray stone gorges **Ōboke** and **Koboke,** while over the next ridge, ancient **vine bridges** sway high above the thundering turquoise spray. Dive into the wilderness or relax in the area's fabulous hot springs and spend the night in a luxurious spa hotel. Trek deeper into the **Iya Valley** and hike the sloping sides of Mt. Tsurugi, or try your hand at making delicious **Iya soba,** tōfu, or a number of local crafts.

GETTING HERE AND AROUND

The Yoshino-gawa is an amazing river, and it's easy to access and enjoy. Express trains go to **Awa-Ikeda** in northern Tokushima-ken, where local trains run south to **Ōboke Station.** Once there, local buses can bring you to the sights: ask Chiiori house for up-to-date bus tables and advice on getting around.

A car is the best way to see the valley. The closest rentals are in Awa Ikeda, but coming from any of Shikoku's big northern cities shouldn't take more than a couple of hours, even on the prefectural roads. Make for Awa Ikeda (get off at the Ikeda Interchange from the expressway) and follow Route 32 south alongside the Yoshino River to Ōboke station. Coming north from Kōchi, go toward Ōtoyo or the Ōtoyo Interchange and take Route 32 north.

WHAT TO SEE

Fodor'sChoice
★ If you have time for nothing else in the region, hitting the wild river and rocky gorges should be your top priority. Doing it couldn't be more hassle-free thanks to rafting and canyoning trips run by **Happy Raft**

ハッピーラフト, the friendliest adventure-tour group on the planet, touring the best river in the country. The international staff are fun-loving but safety-conscious, and they'll show you the river in a way that's great for first-timers and veterans alike. Half-day trips start at ¥7,000 but you'll wish you had done the full day for ¥13,500. Spend a morning or day here wet and happy before moving on through Iya, or try a longer combination rafting-and-canyoning trip; you can even overnight at the inexpensive Happy Guest House in between.

South of Ōboke station on the 32 and just inside the Kōchi border, find Happy Raft on the other side of the river just behind Tosa-Iwahara station, between the train tracks and the water. ✉ *10–4 Iwahara Ōtoyochō Nagaoka-gun* ☎*088/775–0500* ⊕*www.happyraft.com/en.*

Chiiori House ちいおりプロジェクト. Chiiori began when popular anthropologist and Japanese-culture patron Alex Kerr stumbled upon the abandoned house during his college years and bought it on the spot. The taxing restoration has involved help from two communities: Chiiori's neighbors in Iya; and an international network of preservationists, tourists, and volunteers. Countless hands have contributed to the effort, especially regarding the quintessential, beautiful thatched roof. New thatch is harvested every November, and it's taken years to stockpile enough try rethatching the whole house. The Herculean undertaking is planned for autumn 2010, and more volunteer hands may be sought out to help. But helping hands, or simply friendly faces, are ever welcome: call the house to arrange your stay. If the futons are all booked, a daytime visit is still rewarding and the house managers can suggest nearby alternatives and contact tour guides or taiken centers for you. ✉ *209 Higashi-Iya Aza-Tsurui, Tokushima-ken* ☎*088/388–5290* ⊕*www.chiiori.org.*

Iya's most famous features are the three vine bridges, **Kazura-Bashi** かずら橋, that span the gorges, one 20 minutes from Ōboke station and a pair near Mt. Tsurugi. The bridges date back 800 years, to the aftermath of the momentous Gempei War, when the defeated Taira clan fled to these valleys after losing the throne to the rival Minamoto clan. If the refugees were attacked, they could cut the bridges' vines at a moment's notice. These days, thin steel wires reinforce the precarious planks, and fresh vines are restrung every three years, but it still feels death-defying to cross the boards over the rivers. From Route 32 or Route 45 follow the signs to Kazura-bashi. Skip the ¥500 lot next to the big tourist center and park for free right next to the bridge. The tall waterfall down the path is free, and the bridge is ¥500.

WHERE TO STAY

$ ⓣ **Chiiori House** ちいおりハウス. This 300-year-old thatched-roof house ☽ hidden among the cedars and maples high in the mountains is so capti-★ vatingly serene that visitors arrive looking like they've found an entrance to Narnia. Whether it's the down-to-earth volunteer caretakers or the smoky warmth of the traditional irori-style open hearth that you'll eat around, the cooperative (and entirely optional) gardening and housework, or even just the mist that envelops the house at daybreak, a visit to Chiiori will leave your spirit warmed and rejuvenated. For a suggested donation of ¥3,800 a night, this secret escape is too good to pass up.

Make Like Indiana Jones

11

If a day or two spent rafting, canyoning, and bridge walking (with a night in a hot spring) leaves you wanting more, grab your bullwhip and fedora and head farther into the valley. Mt. Tsurugi, the "Fūfu-Bashi" (so-called "husband and wife" vine bridges), and a handful of onsen-hotels and craft workshops await you. Driving there is not complicated per se—follow signs toward Higashi-Iya and Tsurugi-san—but the narrow mountain roads are challenging, and you'll want someone to mark the way for you on a map. The *taiken*, literally *experiences*, offered by local artisans are unique activities. Making delicious buckwheat soba noodles is rewarding, especially since this region is famous for its hearty strand of buckwheat, but making tofu or hiring a local sherpa to climb Tsurugi-san with you are great fun, too. For a full listing of these taiken, check ⊕ *iya.jp/takumi/e.htm*. For logistical help, turn to the good folks at Chiiori House. But remember, the trouble with hidden paradises is that they're *hidden*. A car, some basic Japanese ability and some gusto will help you get the most out of being here.

■**TIP**➜ If the futons are all booked, a daytime visit is still rewarding (and free) and the house managers can suggest nearby alternatives and contact tour guides or taiken centers for you. **Pros:** traditional hearth-side meals; secluded location; farm-lodge experience. **Cons:** cold in winter; roads can be nerve-wracking; all amenities self-serve. ✉*209 Higashi-Iya Aza-Tsurui, Tokushima-ken* ☎*088/388–5290* ⊕*www.chiiori.org.*

$$$ **Hikyō-no-yu** 秘境の湯. Along Route 45, this onsen resort looms down from a bluff. The hotel's separate bath annex is what you're here for: ¥1,000 (plus a few hundred extra for a towel) lets you access the sumptuous outdoor bath and indoor spa, and even a skin-cleansing salt-rub sauna. The restaurant also impresses; each table is a traditional raised hearth where fresh river fish and mountain vegetables are cooked in front of you. The hotel itself is pretty flavorless. **Pros:** great baths; clean facilities; sumptuous *irori*-style restaurant. **Cons:** nowhere near the undeveloped interior of the valley; low on personality. ✉*401 Oi-no-Uchi Nishiyamamura, Miyoshi, Tokushima-ken* ☎*0883/87–2300* 🖷*0883/87–2313* ➦*8 Western-style room, 15 Japanese-style rooms* ⑂*In-hotel: restaurant, hot spring* ▤*AE, D, MC, V* ⦿|*MAP.*

$$$-$$$$ ▥**Iya Bijin** 祖谷美人. Private onsen bathtubs on each room's balcony give breathtaking views into the unspoiled valley below. Follow ★ Route 45 as it curves right and transforms back into the old Route 32; make a left just after the decrepit pink Kazurabashi Hotel and the lush Iya Bijin will come up on your right. **Pros:** luxurious Japanese-style rooms; unbeatable views; in-room onsen baths. **Cons:** cash only; no English assistance; low room-count. ✉*9–3 Nishiiya Yamason Zentoku, Miyoshi City* ☎*088/387–2009* ⊕ *iyabijin.jp* ➦*8* ⑂*In-room: refrigerator, safe* ▤*No credit cards.*

KŌCHI 高知

170 km (105 mi) from Takamatsu; 175 km (108 mi) from Tokushima; 155 km (96 mi) from Matsuyama; 110km (68 mi) from Nakamura, near the southern Ehime border.

Kōchi has earned a reputation for being different. The locals are rough-talking, boisterous, and social, and their spirited city has an attitude far from the Japanese mainstream. The famous **Yosakoi Dance Festival,** one of Japan's most popular summer events, is an explosion of parades and performances that fills the city for days. For weeks before and after, the streets shake with excitement, making summer the best time to visit. Kōchi smacks of a brash, square-shouldered gumption simply not found anywhere else in Japan, and it richly rewards a short swagger through.

GETTING HERE AND AROUND

Kōchi is 2 hours 10 minutes from Takamatsu, 2 hours from Tokushima, 4 hours from Matsuyama, 3 hours 30 minutes from Ōsaka, or 2 hours from Nakamura near the Ehime border by train. By bus it is 2 hours 30 minutes from Matsuyama.

The **Tourist Information Booth** at Kōchi station has few regular English speakers, but they'll put a great effort into helping you anyway. They also lend bicycles free of charge from 10 to 5 any day of the week, but the city center at **Harimaya-bashi** is only a 10-minute walk south. Streetcars go from the station to just about anywhere you want to go for ¥180, and the tram lines are easily navigable. A taxi ride from Kōchi Station to Harimaya-bashi runs about ¥550. There you are in striking distance to half the city's best attractions. Other hot spots lie farther out: a compact but cultured **Art Museum** and the green mountain **Godai-san,** home to a large **temple** and a breathtaking **botanical garden.**

ESSENTIALS

Visitor Information Tourist Information Booth (☎ *088/882–7777* ⊕ *www. attaka.or.jp/foreign/english/index.html* ☯ *Daily 9–9).*

WHAT TO SEE

DOWNTOWN

Harimaya-bashi 播磨屋橋 is the bridge at the center of Kōchi's best-known story, retold in a Yosakoi song, about the Buddhist priest espied here buying a hairpin for a lover, thus breaking his vow of celibacy for an affair that ended in tragedy. The arched red bridge still spans a canal downtown; see what's for sale there these days, or else try shopping in the twisting, tunneled arcades and the shops and side streets that sprout off from them. Locals come out to dine, chat, and dance (yes, dance) in parks and at outdoor cafés until the wee hours. Even in this, Kōchi is a world apart from the general Japanese stigma against eating, lounging, and horsing around in public. When the stores and bars finally close, there's always a ramen cart on a corner brimming with commerce, so pull up a stool and dig in! Kōchi people won't pay you a lot of mind until you start talking to them, but many are multilingual, affable, and easy to engage.

★ The best place to mingle with the locals is at their two popular markets. Kōchi goes for culinary treasure over material stuff, and while the busy, hivelike **Hirome-ichiba** ひろめ市場 has interesting pottery, jewelry, and photographs, everyone's really here for the food. This exciting maze of minirestaurants and food counters has enough strange, delicious foods that you couldn't try everything in a year. Displays, pictures, and abundant people traffic will help you ask for what you want, and you can always point to someone else's plate across the broad wooden tables. Open daily 11–11, it's at the western end of the main arcade, close to the castle. Look for the mass of bicycles hemming in a squat coffee stand beside the entrance, a big orange-and-green sign above the hangar-bay door, and a large crowd of well-fed locals.

Nichiyō-ichi market 日曜市 offers a mile of bizarre fruits and vegetables (some looking like they're from other planets), tasty walking-food, local crafts, and kitsch, and an army of fellow browsers. It's not the place for good souvenir shopping, but why not try some *yuzu-an* in a pastry pocket? A Kōchi specialty replaces red-bean *anko* in normal desserts with a paste made from sour yellow yuzu fruit grown in the prefecture. Nichiyō-ichi runs along broad, palm-lined Ōtetsuji-dōri, parallel to the arcade and just north of it, and goes from Harimaya-bashi right up to the gates of the castle, early morning to mid-afternoon every Sunday.

★ Go west through the markets and arcades downtown to find the barrel-chested body of **Kōchi Castle** 高知城. Kōchi-jō has a slightly different feel from other Japanese castles, more rough-hewn and well lived-in. The view from the topmost watchtower is splendid, and walking up the enormous steps or through the daimyō's receiving chambers is like being transported to the Edo period. From the station, hop a green Yosakoi Gurarin bus for a short ¥100 ride. Walking from Harimaya-bashi should take 15 minutes. ✉ *1–2–1 Marunouchi* ☎ *088/872–2776* ◙ ¥400 ⊙ *Daily 9–5; last entry at 4:30.*

Ⓒ The playful, modern **Yokoyama Memorial Manga Museum** 横山隆一 記念まんが館 *(Yokoyama Ryūichi Kinen Mangakan)* celebrates the life and work of Japan's first great cartoonist, Ryūichi Yokoyama. Many people here don't remember his name either, but his most popular character, Fuku-chan, is still widely loved. The Mangakan offers a window into a talented creator's life and work, and it's a lot of fun: the cartoons inspire and delight, and no language skill is required to enjoy most of the visual humor. Look through World War II propaganda cartoons (from the other side), interactive print stations, dioramas, model railroads, and tons of comic strips. ✉ *On 3rd–5th flrs. of Cul-Port, Kōchi Culture Plaza; 2–1 Kutanda* ☎ *088/883–5029* ◙ ¥400 ⊙ *Tues.–Sun. 9–7.*

OUTSIDE THE CITY CENTER

Ⓒ The city's best attraction lies away from downtown Kōchi. The **Makino**
FodorsChoice **Botanical Garden** *(Makino Shokubutsuen)*, an Eden-like valley of flow-
★ ers and trees hidden atop the mountain Godaisan. Different trails for each season show off the best nature has to offer. Hours disappear as you walk through the azaleas, camellias, chrysanthemums, and thousands of other plants in this huge and lovingly tended landscape

(don't miss the giant ferns, so big you can actually sit in them). You're encouraged to leave the paths and explore on your own—for "to commune with nature we need to make ourselves free and jump into her," wrote botanist Tomitaro Makino, for whom the garden was planted. You'll find more of his quotes, recollections, philosophy, and drawings in a fascinating museum inside the park. *4200–6 Godaisan, Kōchi* ☎*088/882–2601* ✉*¥500* ☼*Tues.–Sun. 9–5.*

The prefecture may be known for its great surfing and swimming beaches, but the city's **Katsurahama** 桂浜 is not one of them. Rocks and breakers prohibit any fun in the water, and the pebbly sand isn't comfortable for picnicking, but the view from a cliff-top shrine is great (moon-watching from this spot is depicted in many ukiyo-e prints). Katsurahama is best known for the giant statue of **Sakamoto Ryōma** 坂本竜馬, Kōchi's local-born historic hero, staring grimly out to sea from his big black pedestal.

Ryōma was a radical and a revolutionary during the turbulent times before the Meiji Restoration, and the political changes he instigated were big enough to get him killed; at the **Sakamoto Ryōma Memorial Museum** (Sakamoto Ryōma Kinenkan), jutting fabulously over the sand and surf, you can see the blood-splashed screen from the room where he was assassinated, and learn about his life and politics. You'll finally know who the cowboyish samurai is plastered on every street corner in Kōchi. One stop before Katsurahama on an orange Kenkotsu bus, the trip takes 40 minutes. ✉*830 Urado-Shiroyama* ☎*088/841–0001* ⊕*www.kōchi-bunkazaidan. or.jp/~ryoma/english1.htm* ✉*¥400* ☼*Daily 9–5.*

OFF THE
BEATEN
PATH

Muroto Point 室戸岬 *(Muroto Misaki).* A surreal coastline of rocks, steep precipices, and surf awaits you at far-off cape Misaki. The road east follows a rugged shoreline cut by inlets and indentations along a rockscape out of Dr. Seuss, where the Pacific Black Current has shaped enormous terraces going down to the sea. It's about a 2½-hour drive along the coast road out to the cape, or a long bus ride to the black-sand beaches at Murotomisaki-mae. A concrete promenade lets you walk the farthest tip of sea-sculpted land.

WHERE TO EAT

¢–$

JAPANESE

✕**Faust** ファースト. This delightful café-restaurant is just off the arcades' main drag. Sit outdoors and people-watch on the cobbled lane or head indoors to the fancy, intimate third floor. The first floor is dinerlike, the second acceptable, but sitting in the literati-chic upper level and getting to order from the same cheap, delicious menu is having your cake and eating it, too. The cake, incidentally, is excellent. ✉*1–2–22 Hon-machi* ☎*088/873–4111.*

¢–$

JAPANESE

★

✕**Myōjin-Suisam** 明神水産. Inside Hirome-ichiba, just follow your nose, but don't leave without trying the *katsuo tataki,* Kōchi's regional fish specialty. Look for the orange flames erupting from this stall's window. Fresh cuts of katsuo are seared to perfection by a cook perilously close to being engulfed by the flames that he's feeding with big handfuls of straw. Most katsuo for Kōchi come from the port town **Kure** to the southwest, and this shop belongs to the captain of Kure's largest fishing vessel. The fish is served on beds of rice or drizzled with citrusy Pons sauce, and you'll never get enough of it. ⊠*Inside Hirome-ichiba 2–3–1 Obiya-machi Arcade* ☎*088/822–5287* ☯*Daily 11–11.*

$$–$$$
JAPANESE ✗**Tosahan** 土佐藩. If you want to see Kōchi's refined side, try a *Tosa Ryōri* course at Tosahan. Dark-wood beams, tatami floors, and red-paper lanterns create a rich atmosphere. A picture menu and displays make ordering easy. Katsuo is the specialty, along with *nabe* hot pots, and anything you get will be more or less perfect. Look for the giant backlit poster of Ryōma, Kōchi's claim-to-fame samurai, glowering at you a few blocks into Obiya-machi arcade. ⊠*1–2–2 Obiya-machi Arcade* ☎*088/821–0002* ⊟*AE, DC, MC, V.*

$$$–$$$$
JAPANESE ✗**Tosa Ryōri Tsukasa** 土佐料理 司高知本店. Set courses range from bento-box to jaw-dropping sashimi feasts: *sawachi ryōri*, lavish fish platters that are a Kōchi specialty. The staff recommend the katsuo—in Japanese it's *sasuga Kōchi*, "just as you'd expect in Kōchi"—but consider the *shabu-shabu* meat and veggie sets, which your servers will teach you to cook on a special table in your private tatami room. Be careful with seating; the main area on the first floor is a bland cafeteria, so indicate that you want an upstairs tatami room instead. ⊠*1–2–15 Harimaya-chō* ☎*088/873–4351* ⊟*AE, DC, MC, V.*

WHERE TO STAY

$$$ ▦**Hotel Shin-Hankyū** 新阪急ホテル. This Western-style luxury chain hotel feels almost out of place in gruff Kōchi city, which can either mean a missed opportunity to experience Kōchi hospitality or a relaxing escape from the verve of the streets and nightlife. It is spacious and modern, with a lovely cake-and-tea shop on the ground floor and slightly expensive restaurants on the second. Rooms are pleasant and roomy, and the staff is extremely helpful to foreign guests. **Pros:** friendly staff helpful with city orientation; close to city center. **Cons:** slightly twee next to the down-to-earth city. ⊠*4–2–50 Hon-machi* ☎*088/873–1111* ▦*088/873–1145* ⊕ *hotel.newhankyu.co.jp/kochi-e/index.html* ⇗*238 Western-style rooms with 4 doubles, 4 Japanese-style rooms* ♿*In-hotel: 4 restaurants, bar, pool, gym, no-smoking rooms* ⊟*AE, DC, MC, V.*

$$$$ ▦**Jyōseikan** 城西館. "Fit for a king" is an expression we take for grant-ed, but watch yourself—Jyōseikan is where the Emperor stays when the royal family comes to Kōchi. A monumental, somewhat dated exterior gives way to a grand interior with spacious bedrooms (some strangely decorated), exquisite tatami suites, and a sauna and bath with wonder-ful prospects of the city and castle. Two stops west of Harimaya-bashi by tram. **Pros:** spacious tatami rooms; close to the castle and Sunday market. **Cons:** easy to get lost walking back at night; no English-capable staff. ⊠*2–5–34 Kami-machi, Kōchi-shi, Kōchi-ken* ☎*088/875–0111* ▦*088/824–0557* ⊕*www.ryokan.or.jp/shikoku/details/kochi/e-jyosei-kan.html* ⇗*72 Japanese-style rooms* ♿*In-hotel: restaurant* ⊟*AE, DC, MC, V.*

$ ▦**7Days Hotel/7Days Hotel Plus** セブンデイズホテル/セブンデイズホテルプラス. The 7Days and its slightly plusher annex are primarily business hotels but stand out from the pack for their pampered, comfortable feel. 7Days Plus has only one double room, but twins are spacious and clean. Slight-ly removed from the nightlife center at Ōtetsuji-dōri, hidden behind Harimaya-bashi. **Pros:** spacious rooms; nice digs. **Cons:** mostly twins available; away from entertainment. ✉2–13–6 and 2–13–17 Harimaya-chō, Kōchi City,Kōchi Prefecture ☎088/884–7100 or 088/884–7111 ⊕www.7dayshotel.com ⤳134 rooms ♿In-room: refrigerator, safe. In-hotel: parking ▤AE, DC, MC, V.

$$ 🏨**Washington Hotel** ワシントンホテル. The location on Ōtetsuji-dōri puts you right by the castle, on top of the Sunday market, and in the best spot to get home from a night out feasting and rollicking your way through town. There's a small restaurant inside for the unadventurous. The Washington is cozy without being exceptional, and the rooms are good sized. Fifteen minutes from the JR station. **Pros:** in the heart of the city; easy for non-Japanese speakers. **Cons:** unexciting rooms; lobby feels stale. ✉1–8–25 Ōtetsuji ☎088/823–6111 🖷088/825–2737 ⤳172 rooms ♿In-hotel: restaurant ▤AE, V.

MATSUYAMA AND WESTERN SHIKOKU

MATSUYAMA 松山

160 km (100 mi) from Takamatsu; 120 km (75 mi) from Awa-Ikeda; 195 km (120 mi) from Tokushima; 155 km (95 mi) from Kōchi; 75 km (46 mi) from Hiroshima (hydrofoil); 160 km (100 mi) to Ōita (ferry).

Shikoku's largest city, Matsuyama prides itself on a great history, friendly disposition, fantastic cultural attractions, and a love for fine food, intense fashion, and haiku. You'll be quickly captivated by the sights and feel of the city, and you can join in the fun; bathe at Dōgo Onsen, Japan's oldest hot spring, hit the fashion avenue downtown, or go restaurant crawling through the best spots on the island. Denizens say it's *sumi-yasui*, easy living here, and you'll find Matsuyama is one of the most rewarding stops along your route.

GETTING HERE AND AROUND

By train Matsuyama is 2 hours 10 minutes from Takamatsu; 1 hour 30 minutes from Awa-Ikeda; 3 hours from Tokushima; 3 hours from Kōchi. By bus it is about 3 hours to Kōchi or Tokushima. By hydrofoil it takes 1 hour 30 minutes to Hiroshima or by ferry: 3 hours. The ferry will take you 6 hours to Oita, overnight to Beppu, Ōsaka, and Kōbe and longer onto Seoul and Vladivostok.

■TIP➜**The Orange Ferry that runs overnight between Ōsaka's Ferry Terminal and Toyo port in Ehime feels like a floating luxury hotel, with chandeliers, a simulated hot-spring bath, cotton yukata, and a nice cafeteria.** Boats each way depart 10:30 PM and arrive at 6 AM. Berths in an eight-person room go for ¥6,700; a private cabin is ¥10,700 per person. Tell the clerk that you're going to Matsuyama when purchasing the ticket and he'll flag you for the appropriate bus to Matsuyama station. For the reverse trip, make a reservation for the bus that leaves Matsuyama station for Toyo at 8 PM.

Matsuyama is easy to get around in, served by a good tram network and an enormous central landmark, **Matsuyama Castle** and the moat surrounding it. Orientation is not difficult, though it's a large and not particularly well-organized city; the hastiness with which sections have been developed—and the antiquity of other areas—has left many grimy sectors and dead zones, but for visitors the action is concentrated around a few locations.

No. 5 trams run from the JR station to Dōgo Onsen, and most of the city's best spots are on the way. Hand the conductor ¥150 when you exit at the huge orange facade of the now-defunct Laforet, a Tōkyō-based department store. The stop is **Ōkaidō-mae** on the street Ichiban-chō, in front of the city's busy arcades and the restaurant mile surrounding them. Uphill across from the arcades, a five-minute walk past the Starbucks and through one of Matsuyama's cutest shopping streets (the work of several recent years of public works and private investment) will bring you to Matsuyama Castle's ropeway. It's especially nice at night thanks to waist-high streetlights and tall fishbowl lampposts.

If you need help, the **City Tourist Information Office** has maps and brochures, but no English support. For real assistance with anything head to the **Ehime Prefectural International Center.** EPIC is a peerless resource for advice on the city and region. The desk staff will bend over backwards to help you with event info, transport tips, hotel reservations, and even rental bikes (for a refundable ¥1,000 deposit). It's next to the Kenmin Bunka Kaikain, or People's Cultural Hall, off the #5 tram's Minami-machi stop.

ESSENTIALS

Visitor Information City Tourist Information Office (✉ *Matsuyama Station* ☎ *089/931–3914*). **Ehime Prefectural International Center (EPIC)** (✉ *1–1 Dōgo Ichiman* ☎ *089/917–5678* ⊕ *www.epic.or.jp/english/index.html*).

WHAT TO SEE

★ **Dōgo Onsen** 道後温泉. Mention Matsuyama to anyone and Dōgo Onsen will be the first place they recommend. It has been the city's number one attraction since time began for this nation. Dōgo is the oldest hot spring in Japan, with a history stretching back almost 3,000 years. Japan's first written text mentions it as a favorite of gods, emperors, and peasants alike, and it's still in daily use by locals and tourists. The main wooden building at present-day Dōgo dates from 1894 and looks like a fairy-tale castle; the only thing that's changed significantly is the view.

You want the ¥800 course for a bath with some frills. Head upstairs and you'll get a basket with towels and a lightweight *yukata* robe. Staff will point you to the Kami-no-Yu, or the Water of the Gods. The gods apparently liked it simple; the great granite tub is plainer than the modern multibath complexes, but the water feels terrific. Come wash away your cares and concerns.

■TIP➔**Remember your onsen procedure: go into the bathroom with your teeny prop towel, and wash and rinse yourself (and rinse your towel!) before getting into the bath. Don't worry much about bathing faux pas like dropping your towel in the water. On laid-back Shikoku, and especially at Dōgo, no one is too fussy. Even tattoos are usually no problem.**

After you bathe, don the soft yukata and relax upstairs. Your ticket includes green tea and *sembei* crackers, served in a serene public tatami room. Relaxing in this second-story terrace is one of the great joys

A Shopping Tour

Matsuyama is the fashion capital of Shikoku, and a stroll down its main shopping arcades, **Ōkaidō and Gintengai,** will leave you reeling from the getups, ranging from gorgeous to grotesque. Nowhere else outside of Tōkyō does fad-fashion get this high a priority. Ōkaidō begins at the Starbucks on Ichiban-chō and goes south for a kilometer until turning right into the Gintengai; Gintengai empties out by a large Takashimaya department store and the city bus and tram terminal, **Shi-eki** (a block north to Kinokuniya with English books on the fourth floor). Follow the tram lines a few blocks past a Mr. Donut to find Ladkey's, terrific Indian food with good lunch specials but a temperamental owner. A block farther to Matsuyama's best lunch place, Amitie, across from the castle moat and **Ehime Museum of Art** 愛媛県立美術館. The tram stop here is Bijutsukan-mae.

Ōkaidō, **Gintengai,** and Shi-eki complete a square adjacent the moat. Inside is Chifunemachi, bursting with clothing stores, cafés, and other shops.

You won't stumble on any hidden temples or ancient ruins, but there's plenty of good shopping and city life. Walk a square of the same area on the *other* side of Ōkaidō after dark and you'll hit a staggering number of great restaurants. The two best streets to follow both run parallel to the main arcade. For the first, head into **Ōkaidō** from Laforet and go left at the first stoplight (this is Niban-chō), then make a right to find foody heaven. No spot on the strip is terribly expensive, and each place has a lot of character and great food. A few blocks farther east, the main artery Yasaka-dōri demarcates the restaurant miles from the red-light district; lots of great places to eat and drink line both sides. Places for late-night coffees and deserts have multiplied recently; newcomer **Un Patit Peu** is on Niban-chō between Ōkaidō and Yasaka-dōri, in the opposite direction from the old town favorite **Sakura**; on the other side of Ōkaidō and one block past the red London bus hair salon. The pink, cherry-blossom beer is better in someone else's glass but the coffees and cakes are wonderful.

of coming to Dōgo. Stay as long as you like, sipping free tea refills, or explore the upstairs quarters where writer Sōseki Natsume stayed and worked during his time in Matsuyama. (Dōgo was about the only thing he liked about the city, although Matsuyama inexplicably claims him as a favorite son.) The baths are open 6:30 AM to 11 PM. ⊠ *5–6 Yunomachi, Dōgo* ☎ *089/921–5141* ☒ *¥400–¥1,500* ⊗ *Daily 6–10; last entry 9:00.*

Ehime Museum of Art 愛媛県立美術館. The modern building at the city's center could have a bigger permanent collection, but the selection of recent Japanese art is terrific and the traveling exhibition spaces are extensive. ⊠ *Horinouchi* ☎ *089/932–0010* ☒ *¥300* ⊗ *9:40–6. Closed Mon. and Dec. 29–Jan. 3.*

Ishiteji 石手寺. Ishiteji is like an ancient, Buddhist-theme amusement park. With more fun things to see and do than at any other holy site, it's without a doubt the best temple on Shikoku. As sprawling and unkempt as the city around it, its surprises are, like the temple cats, too numerous to count. Ghastly statues and lovely bridges wait in the

11

forest, a scrambling rock pathway leads up the back of the mountain, and two spooky caves are yours to explore (even most locals don't know about them). The obvious draws are wonderful, too—a pagoda and huge temple buildings, painted panels, and golden statues, a giant mandala on the stairway to the main shrine, a wood-carved Kami with a sword you can heft, a huge bronze bell to ring for a hundred yen, a cauldron of ash to light incense in. Pass a stone dragon at the entrance and a strip of *omiyage* merchants and you'll see a table for making origami cranes; they'll be added to the heavy, colorful bunches hanging around pillars everywhere, and in return you can take home a white placard on which the monks have written a sutra. Don't miss the cave behind the main temple building. The darkness is not total, but it feels impossibly long, and when you finally emerge on the other side—past startling wooden statues and 88 stone Buddhas (one for each temple on the pilgrimage)—you'll be confronted by a 100-foot statue of the Kobo Daishi striding across the mountains. Remember those huge sandals you saw at the gate? They're his. Don't miss Ishiteji's regular festival, held on the 20th day of every month. ⊠*Ishite 2 9–11* ☎*089/977–0870* 🖫*Free* 🕙*Shops and caves close4–5.*

Itami Juzō Memorial Museum. Alongside Akira Kurosawa and Hayao Miyazaki, the late Juzō Itami is regarded as one of Japan's most innovative and captivating directors. His films are known for their affectionate and absurdist look at mundane scenes of Japanese life. Each film starred his wife Nobuko Miyamoto as an everywoman lead counterpointed by an off-the-wall supporting role, sometimes Itami himself. Best-known films include almost-a-Western Tampopo, centering on a bedraggled ramen-shop owner trying to make the perfect soup, and Osōshiki, the story of an idiosyncratic family coming together for a funeral. If you haven't seen them, they're musts for any Japan tourist; if you have, then you'll love the museum, curated by Miyamoto herself, showcasing video clips and objects from Itami's life. Tobe-bound buses from Shieki take 20 minutes to Amayama-bashi; backtrack two minutes to the museum. ⊠*1 6 10 Higashi Ishii* ☎*089/969–1313* ⊕*itami-kinenkan.jp* 🖫*¥800* 🕙*Daily 9–5. Closed Mon.*

OFF THE BEATEN PATH

Twin Stadiums. Watch Ehime's minor-league baseball team, the Mandarin Pirates, at **Botchan Stadium** 坊ちゃんスタジアム for an affordable taste of Japan's baseball mania. Even more fun are the high-school games: Japan is nuts for high-school baseball, and Ehime's teams have been national competitors the last few years, so home games are boisterous and well attended. Get schedules and information at EPIC. Next door, Japan's finest martial-arts stadium stands out like a black-roofed fortress: watch or try a class in any number of arts, any time of day at the **Ehime Ken-Budōkan** 愛媛県武道館.

Matsuyama Castle 松山城. Large, well-kept, and mighty, Matsuyama-jō is one of the cooler castles in Japan. Inside you can watch footage of the post–World War II reconstruction; the hand labor is astonishing, from the shaping and joining of wood to the stamping out of straw wattle for the walls. There are no concrete, no rebar, and only enough nails to hold down the floorboards. Dark-wood passageways carry the smell of old smoke, from the numerous fires the castle has suffered. For daytime visits, ride the ropeway up and wander around with a delightful wax-paper parasol. Hit the lovely garden just west of the castle, and exit from there to Ichiban-chō, a few blocks west of Laforet. ⊠ *5 Maru-no-uchi, Matsuyama-shi* ☎*089/921–4873* 🎫*Castle ¥500. Ropeway ¥500 round-trip, or a ¥1,000 comprehensive ticket* ⏰*Tues.–Sun. 9–4:30.*

WHERE TO EAT

$$–$$$
ECLECTIC
★
✕**Amitie** アミティエ. The alleys and side streets east off Ōkaidō offer an endless number of great dinner spots, but for lunch this is our favorite. Cuisine and presentation are excellent without being snooty, the interior is funky without being crass or grimy. Sit upstairs and strike up conversation with your neighbors; the convivial hosts and softly worn wooden interior engender affability. Amitie is outside Bijutsukan-mae tram stop, across the moat from the Art Museum. ⊠ *Minami Horibata-chō 6-23* ☎*089/998–2811* ⏰*Daily 11:30–2, lunch; 2–4:30 tea time; 5:30–9, dinner.*

$$
INDIAN
✕**Ladkey's** ラルキー. Mr. Ladkey's mood can change at the drop of a turban, but the quality of the Pakistani/Indian food here is always superb. The ¥3,200, two-hour all-you-can-eat-and-drink course is a closely kept secret of Matsuyama's expat population. A picture menu helps you order. Lunch sets come with salads and choice of naan or saffron rice. Between Shieki and the Museum. ⊠ *5–9 Hanazono-chō* ☎*089/948–0885* ⏰*Daily 11–2:30 and 5–9:30.*

$
THAI
✕**Mirai Kanai** ミライ・カナイ. A laid-back international clientele, extensive list of cocktails, nightly Thai-food themed specials, and a low-key attitude about almost everything will make you think you've found a portal to Chiang Mai. It's one block down a side street just across from the castle ropeway entrance. ⊠ *2–5–1 Kiyo-chō* ☎*089/934–0108* ⏰*6 PM–midnight.*

$$$
JAPANESE
✕**Taihei Sushi** 大平寿司. At this totally unremarkable counter with totally sumptuous sushi dinner times are crowded and fun. A ¥2,500 or ¥3,500 fixed course gets you 8 to 10 different kinds of sushi, with soup. There's zero English ability in-house but folks are friendly; if you're unsated, start pointing to what looks good. Look for the purple-and-white polka dot curtain on Yasaka-dōri, north of Sanbanchō. ⊠ *2–6–19 Sanbanchō* ☎*089/934–0007* ⏰*Mon.–Sat. 5 PM–2:30 AM.*

$$
ECLECTIC
✕**Tipitina's.** Funky and unpretentious decor, the friendly bilingual staff and a menu of delicious share-me-sized dishes will endear you to this second floor izaka-cum-bistro. Avail yourself of the computer and the free ice cream, self-serve by the faux-cowhide door. On a Yasaka-dōri corner one block north of Sanbanchō. ⊠ *2–6–18 Sanbanchō* ☎*089/921–7011* ⏰*6 PM–2 AM.*

$
ECLECTIC
✕**Travelers** 旅人のカフェ. A block off the beaten track, Travelers feels a world away. It's the perfect place to relax and recoup your energy away from the city buzz over a Vietnamese-inspired sandwich or bowl of green curry. The Cha tea is an extreme comfort-drink, though the spiked Cha Cocktail isn't as good as the Irish Coffee: you'll want to curl up inside its cup and go to sleep. Where the Ōkaidō branches right into Gintengai, go left instead and straight for two blocks. ⊠ *2–4–5 Minato-machi* ☎*089/933–5722* ⏰*6 PM–midnight.*

$ ✕**Un Petit Peu** アン・プチ・プー. Delicious hand-made custards and crepes
CAFE across two cute floors with corner views of Matsuyama's busy night
scene make this comfy coffee-and-pastry shop a perfect part of any
evening out. It's been so popular with such a wide demographic that
construction began on a second location only five months after the
opening in May 2008. In the ineffable Japanese accent, "An Poochi
Poo," on the corner of Nibanchō and Yasaka-dōri. ⊠ *1–10–9 Nibanchō*
☎*089/931–8550* ⊗ *Mon.–Sat. 3–3*

WHERE TO STAY

$$$$ 🖵**ANA Hotel Matsuyama** 松山全日空ホテル. The biggest international hotel downtown, the ANA is just next to Laforet on Ichiban-chō.
Ask for a room on the 11th or 12th floor that overlooks the Bansu-
iso Mansion, an imitation French château floodlighted at night. The
hotel has shopping arcades, several restaurants, and a rooftop beer
garden. **Pros:** next to city center; easy access to sights. **Cons:** not good
with foreign tourists; no English speaking staff. ⊠*3–2–1 Ichiban-chō*
☎*089/933–5511* 🖶*089/921–6053* 📞*327 rooms* ♿*In-hotel: 4 restaurants, bar* ▤*AE, DC, V.*

$ 🖵**Hotel Checkin Matsuyama** チェックイン松山. This hotel is at the epicen-
ter of restaurants and nightlife in downtown Matsuyama. Rooms are
surprisingly luxurious though a little bit dated. An English interpreter
is, theoretically, on hand at all times. **Pros:** prime location; parking; convenient shopping and going out. **Cons:** lower floors can be a bit noisy
from the street; far from Dōgo. ⊠ *2–7–3 Sanbanchō* ☎*089/998–7000*
⊕*www.checkin.co.jp* 📞*270 rooms* ♿*In-room: refrigerator, safe,
Internet. In-hotel: hot spring, laundry facilities, gym* ▤*MC, V.*

$ 🖵**Hotel Patio Dōgo** ホテルパティオドウゴ. Even after staying here it's
hard to believe a hotel this nice and in this excellent location can be
so affordable. Literally next door to the main building at Dōgo Ons-
en, you couldn't ask for better access to the baths and the city. Ask
for an A-class room for a view of the onsen. **Pros:** nice bathrooms;
May 2008 renovation; excellent location. **Cons:** C rooms cramped; far
from nightlife. ⊠*Dōgo Onsen Honkanmae, Dōgo* ☎*089/941–4128*
⊕*www.patio-dogo.co.jp* 📞*101 rooms* ♿*In-room: refrigerator, Wi-
Fi. In-hotel: restaurant, laundry service, no-smoking rooms* ▤ *AE,
DC, MC, V.*

$ 🖵**JAL City Matsuyama** JALシティ松山. Overlooking the moat and castle
just east of the JR station, this western-style hotel has comfortable
rooms and great city access. **Pros:** friendly staff; good city and tram
access. **Cons:** unexciting rooms; far from both Dōgo and downtown.
⊠*1–10–10 Ōhtemachi* ☎*089/913–2580* ⊕*matsuyama.jalcity.co.jp*
📞*120 rooms* ♿*In-room: DVD, refrigerator, Internet. In-hotel: 2 restaurants* ▤*AE, DC, MC, V.*

$ 🖵**Oyado Hina** お宿ひな. The owners of Yume Kura are building a
more affordable alternative to visitors seeking luxury accommodation in Dōgo. Twin rooms begin at ¥11,000 and invoke the same
ambitious design and amenities aesthetic as their luxury counterpart.
Set to open in late 2009. **Pros:** close to Dōgo; fashionable facilities.
Cons: minimal English-language support. ⊠*6–50 Dōgo Tako-chō,*

Dōgo ☎*089/931–1180* 📞*132 rooms* ⚓*In-room: Internet* 🖥 *AE, DC, MC, V.*

$ 📺**Yume Kura** 夢蔵. A high-class ryokan looking out upon Dōgo Onsen from just behind it, two-year-old Yume Kura delivers the royal treatment in a great location. Rooms are extremely spacious with elevated views gazing down onto Dōgo and the city; you can even enjoy them from the balcony in your own wooden onsen bath, with waters drawn from the same spring as Dōgo. Rooms are twin style with mostly wooden floors. An extra futon can be put out on the tatami section for a third person. Meals are in rooms in the restaurant downstairs. **Pros:** location; volcanic spring bathtubs, memory foam beds; bath-gear baskets to carry to Dōgo Onsen. **Cons:** no double beds; no in-room dinner service; meals not optional. ✉*Dōgo Yutsuki-chō, Dōgo* ☎*089–931–1180* 🌐*www. yume-kura.jp* 📞*6 rooms* ⚓*In-room: DVD, refrigerator. In-hotel: restaurant* 🖥*AE, DC, MC, V.*

NIGHTLIFE

Indie's Kashimashi. Don't be fooled by the underwhelming first-floor café: head downstairs to the chic bar floor underneath this popular early-to-late nightspot to see what the buzz is all about. No English menu may render the delicious Italian kitchen upstairs inaccessible but wine and excellent cocktails make up for it. Cakes and pastries arrive daily from an off-site bakery. On Yasaka-dōri between Nibanchō and Sanbanchō. ✉*2–1–1 Nibanchō790-0002* ☎*089/913–0769* 🕐*Mon.–Thurs. 6* PM*– 3* AM*, Fri. and Sat. 6–4, Sun., 6–1.*

Salon Kitty. These compact quarters host some of Japan's biggest-name bands in intimate shows at great prices. Tastes lean towards rock and J-punk; recent guests include Bump of Chicken and the Cro-Magnons, bands that can easily sell out the Japan Budokan. Call to find out who's coming up. ✉*138 Kawahara-chō* ☎*089/945–0020.*

UCHIKO 内子

50 km (30 mi) south of Matsuyama.

Walking the cobbled hills of Uchiko feels like traveling back in time. Go straight out of the station and follow a wooden sign pointing left to the old shopping street **Yokaichi** よか市, where the only change in centuries has been the height of plants against the beige-orange walls. You won't need more than a morning to poke through the fun shops, full of good, cheap *omiyage*: straw pinwheels, tea leaves, sour *tsukemono*, and local sake. The highlight is a waxworks, where an old man and his sons hand-make distinctive candles (the smaller ones are as surprisingly inexpensive as the larger are surprisingly costly).

There are a few sights—old merchant houses and an impressive turn-of-the-century kabuki theater, **Uchiko Za** 内子座, notable for hosting a performance by the famous Kodō Taiko group every October—but Uchiko is more of a meandering town. A path between houses reveals a hillside of peach trees and wildflowers; open doorways lead to secluded gardens with men playing *shōgi*, or the occasional restaurant. One thing is not to be missed, however; at the very end of the road you'll crest a final hill and see a mountainous statue of the **sleeping Buddha** ねはんさん reclining across the lap of enlightenment. It's the last thing you'd expect to find in this sleepy town—especially since it isn't marked on a single tourist map or guidebook anywhere else.

UWAJIMA 宇和島

90 km (56 mi) south of Matsuyama, 130 km (80 mi) west of Kōchi.

Uwajima's claims to fame are its sumō-style bullfights and a notorious **sex museum** with displays that would make Jenna Jameson blush.

The **tourist information office** across from the station (opposite the bull statue) is open 9–5, and can lend you a bike (stickers with Uwajima's demon-bull are ¥50 and great souvenirs). ✉ *3-24 Nishiki-machi* ☎ *089/522-3934.*

The museum is located at a Shinto fertility shrine, **Taga Jinja** 多賀神社, not far from the station. It's easy to zip past the entrance, but once there you can tell you've arrived. No, that's no giant squid. Just beyond is the museum, called **Deko Boko Jindou** 凸凹人道, literally a place honoring "things that poke out, things that go in." The three-floor collection is astonishing. What is that samurai doing with his . . .? It's best to leave the kids at the castle for this one (it's up the arcade and to the right). ✉ *1340 Deko* ☎ *089/522-3444* 💴 *¥800* ⏱ *Daily 8–5.*

Uwajima's other attraction is the **tōgyū** 闘牛, a sport in which two bulls lock horns and push, à la sumō, for control of the ring. The bullfights date back 400 years, and if you can make it during one of the six annual tournaments you'll have a great time (January 2, the third Sunday in March, the first Sunday in April, July 24, August 14, and the second Sunday in November). The stadium is at the foot of Maruyama, a 30-minute walk from Uwajima Station. ✉ *1 Akebono-chō* ☎ *089/524-1111* 💴 *¥3,000.*

THE SHIMANAMI SEA ROAD しまなみ街道

Beginning in Imabari, 45 km (28 mi) north of Matsuyama.

Your Shikoku excursion will begin and end with trips over the water, and the best way to come or go from Western Honshū is the **Shimanami Kaidō**: 10 long bridges create an unbroken thoroughfare between Imabari (just north of Matsuyama) and Onomichi (just east of Hiroshima), across islands in the Seto Nai-kai, Japan's inland sea. Most of these places were inaccessible before the bridges were completed in 1999, so the scenery is unspoiled: fishing villages, kaki orchards, seaweed pastures, pearl farms, and a stretch of sparkling sea. Driving, busing, and ferrying from Imabari to Hiroshima are all delightful, and going across even part of the way with a rental bike is unforgettable.

Ⓒ

Fodor's Choice

★

Biking the Shimanami Kaidō is a safe, exciting experience that anyone with a reasonable level of fitness can accomplish. The bridges were built with cyclists in mind: a separate cycling track runs along each one, so you won't deal with car traffic for almost the entire ride. The cycling isn't strenuous, so don't get discouraged by the first big corkscrew pathway up from Imabari to the Kurushima Ōhashi, or the unattractive hills on the first island, Ōshima. After that it's clear sailing.

Biking straight to Onomichi takes about six hours, but you don't have to cycle the whole way: leave the bikes on any of the islands' rental stations and ferry the rest of the way across. Your hotel can send your luggage ahead. For renting bikes, try Imabari's

Sunrise Itoyama (⊠ *2–8–1 Sunaba-chō, Imabari-shi* ☎ *089/841–3196*). Rental bikes are ¥500 a day plus a ¥1,000 refundable deposit. The shop is open from May to September, daily 8–8. Between October and March it's 8–5.

The shop workers won't speak much English, so it's best to go through Imabari's helpful International Organization, **ICIEA** ⊠ *1–1–16 Kitahorai-chō, Imabari-shi, Ehime-ken* ☎ *089/834–5763* ⊕ *iciea.imabari-cc.ac.jp/* ⊘ *Weekdays 8:30–5:15.*

★ On the third island from Imabari, **Ōmishima**, stands the **Ōyamazumi Jinja** 大山祇神社, 1,200 years a shrine to battle. In the 8th century victorious warriors started leaving their weaponry here as thanks for divine favor. The museum holds more than two-thirds of the nation's designated national treasures in swords, spears, breastplates, and helmets. ⊠ *3327 Miya-ura, Ōshima-chō* ☎ *089/782–0032* ✏¥*1,000* ⊘ *Daily 8:30–4:30.*

Kyūshū

WORD OF MOUTH

"Get beyond Tōkyō-Kyōto-Tōkyō. Prices drop when you get off of the well beaten path, especially for lodging . . . There is a lot of beautiful country in Japan and the people are a bit more relaxed outside of the megacities. Go to Kyūshū."

— mrwunrfl

Updated by
John Malloy
Quinn

Kyūshū's landscape couldn't be more varied, with active yet accessible volcanoes, numerous thermal spas, endless fields of rice and famous potatoes, forested mountains capped by winter snows, busy harbors along lively seacoasts, and pleasant seaside retreats.

Kyūshū has been inhabited and favored for human settlement for more than 10,000 years, and ruins and artifacts thousands of years old suggest that the region was the most important gateway for human contact between Japan and the rest of Asia. The most rapid anthropological changes occurred from about 300 BC to AD 300, when rice became widely cultivated and complex pottery and tools began to appear, thus conveniently framing the Yayoi Period. Continuous trade with China brought prosperity and culture, and advanced ceramics were introduced—and then produced—by Korean masters that were employed and enslaved by the local fiefdoms of the 16th and 17th centuries.

It was also through Kyūshū that Western knowledge, weapons, religion, and cooking methods first made their way into Japan. In the mid-1500s Nagasaki saw the arrival of fleets of enterprising and courageous European merchants and missionaries, and the resulting frenzy of trade in ideas and goods continued unabated until the Tokugawa Shōgunate slammed the door shut on the whole show in the early 1600s. What brought things to a halt was a plague of panic induced by an alarming new phenomenon: Christianity. The Portuguese and other Catholics not afraid to preach to the natives were expelled and permanently barred. The Dutch, however, were considered more money-minded, and therefore less threatening, and were permitted to stay—under scrutiny and isolation. They were rounded up and housed within the enclave of Dejima, a man-made island in Nagasaki Harbor, where they were encouraged to keep bringing in coveted goods but were constantly guarded and watched. For the next 200 years, this profitable little arrangement would be the only form of contact the West would have with Japan until the arrival of Perry's forceful "Black Ship."

Today Kyūshū is a fascinating mix of old and new, nature and culture. Much of the remote and rugged interior—such as that surrounding Mt. Aso's fuming cone—is still an isolated wilderness, yet the amenities of modern life are well supplied in cities and coastal resorts.

⇨ *See the glossary at the end of this book for definitions of the common Japanese words and suffixes used in this chapter.*

TOP REASONS TO GO

Diverse Cities: Fukuoka has free-wheeling nightlife, Nagasaki radiates old-world charm, Kumamoto's castle contrasts with traffic-heavy streets, and Kagoshima's palm trees calm travelers.

Gastronomy Domain: Find the sought-after Hakata ramen in Fukuoka. Nagasaki has *chanpon* (seafood and vegetable noodle soup), and Kagoshima has *kurobuta tonkatsu* (breaded pork cutlet).

Inside the Volcano: Mt. Aso, in the center of the island, is notoriously active, as is Sakura-jima, across the bay from Kagoshima. Hot springs are found throughout Kyūshū.

Into the Wild: With its lava flows, outlying islands, rugged mountains, and national parks, Kyūshū is an adventurer's dream. Most trails require only good shoes, water, and some time.

Remote Access: A high-speed train links Kumamoto with Kagoshima in an hour, and in another hour, you can be on the hot sand of Ibusuki's beaches.

12

ORIENTATION AND PLANNING

ORIENTATION

Situated perfectly as the gateway to the continent of Asia, Kyūshū is quite close to the Korean Peninsula. It's considerably west and a little south of Tōkyō. A good route starts with a flight or Shinkansen run into Hakata/Fukuoka in the north, moves down to Nagasaki on the west coast by express train, winds eastward by bus or train to the central city of Kumamoto, with a possible side trip to Aso-san (Mt. Aso), and a jaunt south to the city of Kagoshima via the fancy high-speed train, then farther south by local train to the thermal spa resort area of Ibusuki, famous for its hot sand baths, where you can be heat-treated on the picturesque, breezy beach. This R&R can be addictive, so if time and finances permit, go back up through Kumamoto to the tony hot-springs resort of Yufuin.

Fukuoka. With one of the most convenient airports in the world, you can be downtown in six minutes by subway. Fabulous dining, ultramodern shopping, and nicely humming nightlife are among the joys that this vibrant city has to offer.

Nagasaki. Consistently rated by the Japanese a favorite destinations, Nagasaki has maintained its rich and colorful international past even in the face of the devastation brought on by the plutonium bomb that ended World War II. Today you'll still see the spirit of entrepreneurship that helped the city rebuild itself.

Kumamoto. The Herculean effort to restore Kumamoto's massive 17th-century castle was completed just in time for its 400-year anniversary in 2007. Impressive and menacing, its black facade and angular aspects give it the appearance of a sinister hideout. Suizen-ji Jōju-en, a luxurious garden, is another highlight.

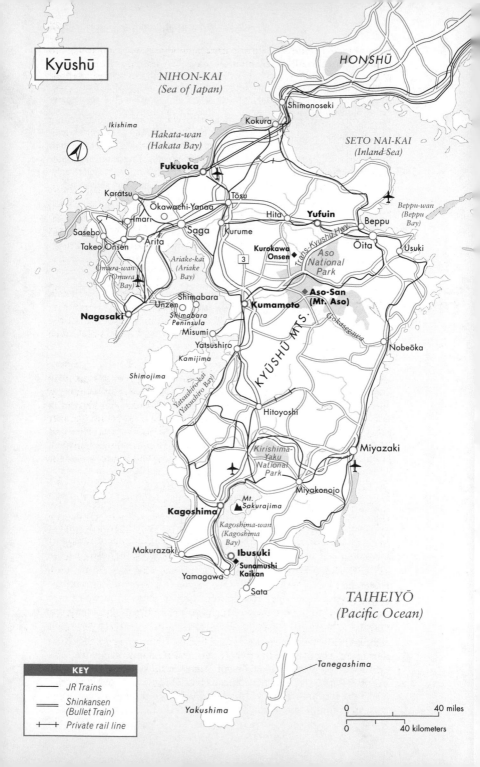

Kagoshima. The mild climate and easygoing vibe draw comparisons to Naples, Italy, but locals fear that one day, the smoking, rumbling cone of Sakura-jima out in the bay will make Pompeii a more apt analogy. Famous hot-sand baths and remote beaches are found along the southern reaches of the prefecture.

Aso-san (Mt. Aso). Aso National Park contains lakes, fields, and this chain of five volcanic peaks situated inside the largest caldera in the world. Naka-dake is the only active one, but the whole thing has roared to life countless times in recorded history. Earth is still very much under construction here.

Yufuin. Yufuin is a delightful and popular upscale hot-springs resort beneath the dramatic twin-peaked mountain known as Yufu-dake. Galleries, microbreweries, museums, and trendy eateries are scattered among the charming inns. You won't find much of the tacky edge that can put people off of the region's other spa-town, Beppu.

PLANNING

Travel in Kyūshū is pretty easy. Between May and October, pack rain gear, since fierce wind and rain render umbrellas useless. As for attire, businesses and restaurants are casual throughout Kyūshū. In all the big cities, you can find people who can speak and understand some English.

WHEN TO GO

In early spring it's pleasantly warm, and the greenery is at its best. May and June usher in heavy rains, and July and August are intensely muggy. September is summery, but watch for typhoons, which can blow in at any time until late October. Autumn colors, appearing in late October or early November, are nice, particularly in the north. In January and February the mountains of central Kyūshū receive a little snowfall, and that's when the Siberian cranes show up for the gentle winter the region enjoys.

GETTING HERE AND AROUND

Travel in Kyūshū is for the most part straightforward, with trains providing the bulk of the transport. Highway buses are useful for certain routes. Frequent and inexpensive ferries ply the bays and ports, linking Kyūshu with offshore islands. During holiday seasons you'll want to reserve seats on express trains, but with most buses and ferries turning up 20 minutes prior to departure you should get on board with no trouble.

AIR TRAVEL

Air routes link Kyūshū's major cities with Tōkyō and Ōsaka. Fukuoka, Nagasaki, and Kagoshima have the most frequent and useful daily connections and offer some international flights. When using domestic carriers like ANA you need not enter and return from the same city: it's easy to fly into Fukuoka and out of Kagoshima, for example.

BUS TRAVEL

Buses make useful connections around Kyūshū, and if you don't have a JR Rail Pass, they are often much cheaper than the trains. For example, the bus between Nagasaki and Kumamoto is half the price and takes about the same time; plus you don't have to make any changes or wait for connections, as you do with trains. A highway bus makes a trip between Kumamoto to Yufuin, either direct or with a stopover at the Aso-san crater.

CAR TRAVEL

Car rental is a good idea in Kyūshū if you have lots of time and if you explore the more out-of-the-way places such as Aso-san. All the major rental outfits have offices in the big cities near the JR stations. The roads in Kyūshū are sometimes wider than in other regions, but don't expect them to be any less jammed with speeding trucks or lumbering tour buses!

TRAIN TRAVEL

High-speed train service now links Kumamoto with Kagoshima, via a quick and easy change in Yatsushiro. The new Tsubame (Swallow) train is chic, posh, spacious, and uncrowded. Express trains making the popular run between Fukuoka and Nagasaki are jammed on weekends and holidays, so book at least a day ahead.

RESTAURANTS

Fresh fish is served everywhere on Kyūshū. Appetites are on the hearty side here, so there's lots of meat, too. Local specialties abound and are often reasonably priced. In the bigger cities like Fukuoka, Nagasaki, Kumamoto, and Kagoshima—and along the stylish new streets of Yufuin—you'll find plenty of Western-style restaurants.

HOTELS

You can find the usual American hotel chains, with all the familiar extras, in places like Fukuoka and Nagasaki. The rural areas surrounding Aso and Kagoshima have snug little inns with views of the surrounding peaks. In Yufuin nearly all hotels and *ryokan* offer soothing thermal mineral water baths. Unless otherwise noted, all hotel rooms have private baths, basic television service, and air-conditioning. Reservations are essential during the long national holidays, particularly Golden Week (late April–early May), Ōbon (mid-August), and New Year's (first week of January) when Japanese tourists flock to the island.

WHAT IT COSTS IN YEN					
	¢	$	$$	$$$	$$$$
RESTAURANTS	under ¥800	¥800–¥1,000	¥1,000–¥2,000	¥2,000–¥3,000	over ¥3,000
HOTELS	under ¥8,000	¥8,000–¥12,000	¥12,000–¥18,000	¥18,000–¥22,000	over ¥22,000

Restaurant prices are per person for a main course, set meal, or equivalent combinations of smaller dishes. Hotel prices are for a double room, excluding 5% tax and tip.

CLOSE UP

12

On the Menu

The most celebrated dish in Fukuoka is *tonkotsu ramen*, a strongly flavored pork-bone-based soup with extra-thin noodles, scallions, and strips of roasted pork. Usually it gets heaps of garlic, chili pepper, and other toppings. Wherever you are on Kyūshū, ramen can never be too far, and it's always good.

Popular in Nagasaki, *shippoku* consists of elaborately prepared dishes that blend the flavors of Asia and Europe. Served Chinese style on a revolving round tabletop and perfect for large groups, shippoku is not a solitary affair. Another Nagasaki favorite, *chanpon*, consists of Chinese-style noodles, vegetables, and shellfish in a thick soup. *Sara* udon has the chanpon ingredients fried crispy instead of boiled.

Ba-sashi (raw horse meat) is a Kumamoto specialty. If you are hungry enough to eat a horse, all you need to know is that it tastes better than beef, and you feel the power *instantly*. Perhaps an easier-to-swallow delicacy

is *karashi renkon*, slices of lotus root stuffed with mustard and/or cayenne and deep-fried. Compared to the subdued flavors of most Japanese cuisine, these dishes attest to the region's bolder palate.

In Kagoshima, don't pass up a chance to try the famed *kurobuta tonkatsu*, or breaded fried pork cutlet from locally bred black pigs. There's also *satsuma-age*, a fried-fish cake stuffed with ingredients like garlic, cheese, meat, potato, or burdock root. *Imo-jōchū*, a much-loved local spirit distilled from sweet potatoes, helps wash down these goodies—or start a fire. Fair warning: the hangovers from this stuff can take you every bit as low as the night before was high and then some!

In Yufuin trendy European-style cafés and eateries of all price ranges crowd the streets. Many people also dine in their hot-spring lodgings, where the culinary focus is usually fresh game and vegetables.

VISITOR INFORMATION

Every major city has tourist information offices near shopping, sightseeing, and eating areas, and one or more near the high-speed train exit of each JR train station. Generally, one English speaker is on duty during peak travel hours. The bigger hotels usually have front desk employees who speak and understand some English; they are good sources for information on local sights and restaurant recommendations. For the full range of brochures, detailed travel and connection questions, and timetables, see the tourist info offices.

ESSENTIALS
Airline Contacts All Nippon Airways (☎ *0120/029–222*). **Japan Airlines** (☎ *0120/25–5971*). **Skymark** (☎ *050/3116–7370*).

Consulates U.S. Consulate (✉ *2–5–26 Ōhori, Chūō-ku, Fukuoka* ☎ *092/751–9331*).

Emergency Services Ambulance (☎ *119*). **Police** (☎ *110*).

FUKUOKA 福岡

1,175 km (730 mi) west of Tōkyō or 622 km (386 mi) west of Shin-Ōsaka.

Fukuoka is a good base to begin exploring Kūshū. To get a sense of the city, walk along the meandering Naka-gawa river. The stunning Canal City shopping complex, a 15-minute walk west of Hakata Station, is full of great people-watching, shops, and dining. You'll find a bit of everything, from global coffee and fast food outlets to famous local ramen.

For night owls, there's plenty happening in the west-central downtown alleys in an area known as Tenjin at truly astounding hours. Friday nights only begin at midnight, usually with a huge and hearty bowl of *tonkotsu* (pork-bone soup) ramen—often referred to as "Hakata ramen"—a rich, tasty staple that locals seem to depend on for their legendary all-night stamina.

The Naka-gawa divides the city. Everything west of the river is known as Fukuoka, while everything east—including the station and airport—is referred to as Hakata, so trains or planes might say to or from Hakata rather than Fukuoka. But don't be confused: Hakata is just a ku, or district, of the whole place, which is still Fukuoka.

GETTING HERE AND AROUND

Fukuoka Airport is Kyūshū's main airport. It's just two stops away—only six minutes—from Fukuoka's Hakata train station on the Kūkō subway line. All Nippon Airways (ANA), Japan Airlines (JAL), and Skymark Airlines (SKY) fly the 1½-hour route to Fukuoka Airport from Tōkyō's Haneda Airport. JAL also flies once daily (1¾ hours) between Tōkyō's Narita International Airport and Fukuoka Airport. ANA and JAL have 12 direct flights (1¼ hours) between Ōsaka and Fukuoka.

The **Kyūshū Kyūkō Bus Company** makes the two-hour trip between Fukuoka's Tenjin Bus Center and Nagasaki. Frequent buses make the four-hour trip between Fukuoka (departing from Hakata Kōtsū Bus Center and Tenjin Bus Center) and Kagoshima.

JR Shinkansen trains travel between Tōkyō and Hakata Station in Fukuoka (5½ hours) via Ōsaka and Hiroshima. The regular fare is ¥22 and there are 15 daily runs. Regular JR express trains also travel this route, but take at least twice as long.

After World War II Fukuoka was rebuilt with wide, tree-lined avenues arranged on an easy-to-navigate Western-style grid. The subway system connects the downtown attractions with a convenient extension to the international airport. The two major transportation hubs are Hakata Station and Tenjin Station. Tenjin, in the heart of downtown Fukuoka, is the terminal for both subway lines. The Kūkō Line runs to Hakata Station and on to Fukuoka (Hakata) Airport, and the Hakozaki Line runs out toward the bay. Fares start at ¥200.

A low-cost bus (¥100) operates in the city center. Most city buses leave from **Hakata Kōtsū Bus Center** across the street from Hakata Station, and from Tenjin Bus Center.

Sightseeing buses leave from **Tenjin Bus Center** and from Hakata Kōtsū Bus Center. Very few tours are given in English, so ask at your hotel or the tourist information office for the recommended ones. A four-hour tour costs approximately ¥2,400.

The **Fukuoka International Association** has an English-speaking staff, and English-language newspapers and periodicals are available for visitors

CURRENCY EXCHANGES

In Fukuoka, outside the West Exit from Hakata Statiion, there are a number of major banks that exchange currency. In the area around Tenjin station there are a few big ones at the intersection of Watanabe-dōri and Meiji-dōri.

12

to read.**Fukuoka Station Information** offers information on travel, sightseeing, and accommodations.

ESSENTIALS

Airport Information Fukuoka Airport (☎ *092/483–7003*).

Bus Contacts Kyūshū Kyūkō Bus Company (☎ *092/734-2500 or 092/771-2961*).

Bus Depots Hakata Kōtsū Bus Center (☎ *092/431-1171* 🚌 *¥100*). **Tenjin Bus Center** (☎ *092/734-2500 or 092/771-2961*).

Hospital Contacts Fukuoka Nakagawa Hospital (✉ *17–17 Mukaishin-machi, 2-chōme, Minami-ku* ☎ *092/565-3531*).

Internet Kinkos (✉ *Taihaku-Center Bldg., 1F, 2-19-24 Hakata-ekimae, , in front of Hakata Station, Hakata-ku, Fukuoka* ☎ *092/473-2677* 🕐 *Open 24 hrs* ✉ *Humming Bird Bldg., 1F, Fukuoka JPN Tenjin-minami, 1–22-7 Imaizumi, Chūō-ku, Fukuoka* ☎ *092/722-4222* 🕐 *8AM-10 PM.*).

Media Fukuoka International Association (✉ *Rainbow Plaza, IMS Bldg. [locals call it "Eemuzu Biru"], 8th fl., 1–7-11 Tenjin, Chūō-ku* ☎ *092/733-2220* 🕐 *Daily 10-8; closed 3rd Tues. of each month*).

Visitor Information Fukuoka Station Information (✉ *JR Fukuoka Station, 1 F, Central Gate* ☎ *092/731-5221* 🕐 *Daily 8-8*).

WHAT TO SEE

The monk Eisai (1141–1215) returned from a long stint in China to introduce Zen Buddhism to Japan and, so the story goes, planted the first tea-bush seeds. Nowadays most tea is grown in other regions such as Shizuoka, but you can still buy the green tea from this region, with its legendary hue and flavor, in stores as far away as Tōkyō. Esai also established Japan's first Zen temple, **Shōfuku-ji** 正福寺, which the inscription on the main gate by Emperor Gotoba commemorates. In Zen tradition, the grounds and structure reflect the calm, austere nature of this deeply meditative philosophy. The bronze bell in the belfry was designated an Important Cultural Property by the Japanese government. The temple is a 15-minute walk northwest from Hakata Station, or a five-minute Nishitetsu bus ride from the station to the nearby Oku-no-dō stop (you can pick up the bus on the main road in front of Hakata Station's west exit). ⊠*6–1 Gokushō-machi, Hakata-ku* ☎*092/291–0775* ⊡*Free* ⊙*Daily 9–5.*

The lake at **Ōhori Kōen** 大濠公園 was once part of an impressive moat surrounding Fukuoka's castle. A leisurely 1-mi path follows the perimeter of the lake. In early April the pink and white flowers of the park's 2,600 cherry trees present a dazzling display. Within the park is the **Fukuoka City Art Museum** 福岡市美術館, which houses a few notable works by Dalí, Miró, Chagall, and Warhol. Across from it is a traditional Japanese garden. From Hakata Station, take the subway to Ōhori Kōen Station; it's a 20-minute ride. ⊠*Chūō-ku* ☎*092/714–6051* ⊡*Park free, museum ¥200, garden ¥240* ⊙*Museum and garden, Tues.–Sun. 9–4:45.*

To see where the hipsters do their fair share of serious shopping or to while away the hours people-watching, go for a stroll around the astounding **Canal City** キャナルシティ. Restaurants range from upscale dining to takeout, and there are countless cafés, shops, hotels, and a huge cinema in the area. At one end is a zigzagging water-lined patio-scape where folks go to see and be seen. At the other end is a futuristic half-dome structure ingeniously tiered with balconies lined with shops and cafés, and it's all done up in an eye-catching palette of salmon pinks and pastel blues. The tantalizing sightlines, liberal use of glass, open space, and clever angles make it seems as though you can see into, over, and under everything else in the structure. To experience this M.C. Escher–esque structure yourself follow the street leading from the west exit of Hakata Station; it's a 15-minute walk. ⊠*1–2 Sumiyoshi, Hakata-ku* ☎*092/282–2525* ⊕*www.canalcity.co.jp/.*

WHERE TO EAT

$$$
JAPANESE

✕**Bassin** バサン. Inside the fancy Plaza Hotel Tenjin, Bassin (locals pronounce it "Bah-san") has wooden counters and furniture set off against cream-color walls and art deco lamps. Try the garden salad with seaweed dressing or the marinated tofu. Unique dishes include grilled chicken in a burdock-root sauce, and stewed snapping-turtle meat with summer vegetables. More elaborate Japanese courses run ¥3,500–¥7,000. ⊠*1–9–63 Daimyō, Chūō-ku* ☎*092/739–3210* ⊟*AE, DC, MC, V.*

¢
JAPANESE

✕**Deko** デコ. Deko has no English menu, but the daily special, or *teishoku*, is a reliable choice. The central low tables of this boisterous bar are Japanese style; regular tables and chairs are in the back. The salmon-and-basil spring rolls are an excellent appetizer. It's between the Hakata train station and Yakuin subway station on Sumiyoshi-dōri. ⊠*1–24–22 Takasago, Rasa Bldg., B1, Chūō-ku* ☎*092/526–7070* ⊟*AE, DC, MC, V.*

¢
JAPANESE
★

✕**Hōrin** 鳳凛. To prepare for a big night in Tenjin, this is a convenient, delicious, and inexpensive place to grab some tonkotsu ramen beforehand. For less than ¥800 you can dive into a big bowl of thin noodles in a steamy pork-based soup garnished with sliced pork, chopped onions, slivers of ginger, and whatever other toppings you choose. The most recommended and popular topping is the sliced *kikurage* ("tree jellyfish" or black mushrooms)—high in protein, full of B vitamins, and said to boost the immune system. It's on a corner, just off the south side of Kōkutai-dōri, two blocks west of Haruyoshi Bridge, on the way to all-night fun in the Tenjin district. ⊠*3–21–15 Haruyoshi, Chūō-ku* ☎*092/738–5811* ⊟*No credit cards.*

¢ ✕**Ichi-ran** 一蘭. Folks in Fukuoka wait in long lines to get their fix of
JAPANESE distinctive extra-thin noodles swimming in a rectangular black box of
★ pork-bone broth topped with tasty slices of *char-shū*, or roasted pork, *negi* (green onions), and sprinkles of *tōgarashi* (red pepper). Additional toppings such as *kikurage*, extra pork, or boiled eggs can be added for ¥100 each. The clerk gives you an order form (with English), and you indicate exactly how you like it, from the amount of shredded garlic to the fat content (locals go for more fat to get that sweet flavor they adore). You then buy a ticket from the machine inside the door. The clerk will help you if you are new to this gig. Hang onto it until you are seated in back at a private cubicle with a curtain that conceals all but the smells of the intoxicating substance you are about to receive. You place your ticket and order form on the counter below the curtain, and moments later the goods appear. The noodles taste best when ordered slightly chewy, and the soup is flavorful even with a light fat content. There are several branches, including one in the basement of the Hakata Station complex (and even some in Tōkyō), but the best one is in Canal City. ⊠*1–2–22 B1F, Sumiyoshi, Hakata-ku* ☎*092/263–2201* ⊟*No credit cards.*

WHERE TO STAY

$$ 📷 **Canal City Fukuoka Washington Hotel** キャナルシテイ福岡ワシントンホテル. This is no ordinary Washington Hotel; it's a full snazzy class above the others members of the chain. It's in Canal City, and the rooms have views of either the sci-fi half-dome end of the mall or out over the city. The lobby has free Internet, and hundreds of shops and eateries are steps away. **Pros:** great value; located almost as conveniently as the Hyatt but much cheaper; flat-screen TVs. **Cons:** limited English; some really small rooms; carpets could use some sprucing up. ⊠*1–2–20 Sumiyoshi, Hakata-ku, Fukuoka, Fukuoka-ken* ☎*092/282–8800* 🖷*092/282–0757* ⇥*423 rooms* ⚅*In-room: refrigerator. In-hotel: 2 restaurants, laundry facilities, Internet terminal, no-smoking rooms* ⊟*AE, DC, MC, V.*

$$$$ 📷 **Fukuoka Grand Hyatt Hotel** 福岡グランドハイアットホテル. Far and
★ away the best digs in town, the Grand Hyatt overlooks—or rather, looks into—the Canal City entertainment complex. Those craving extravagance tempered with sophistication won't be disappointed. Mauve accents, green lighting, huge white stone pillars, and blonde wood panels set the relaxing mood of the lobby, which descends into a lounge with one of the most arresting views in the world. Beyond an invisible and immense wall of glass, a fountain plays, and on the other side of it is the concave hemisphere of Canal City's Urban Theater. The hotel's opulent rooms peer out over either a view of the mall's interior or the Naka River and the rest of town. **Pros:** the coolest spot to base yourself, bar none; feels like you're in a space movie. **Cons:** there have been reports of indifferent service, tricky charges, and facility glitches; could use

better sound proofing. ✉*1–2–82 Sumiyoshi, Canal City, Hakata-ku, Fukuoka, Fukuoka-ken* ☎*092/282–1234* 🖶*092/282–2817* ⊕*www. fukuoka.grand.hyatt.com* 💻*370 rooms, 14 suites* ♿*In-room: Internet. In-hotel: 4 restaurants, bars, pool, gym, no-smoking rooms* ☐*AE, DC, MC, V.*

$$$–$$$$ 🖥️**Hakata Excel Hotel Tōkyū** 博多エクセルホテル東急. This is an upscale, Western-style hotel located near the Nakasu Kawabata Station (on the way into town from the airport or five minutes out from Hakata Station; use Exit 1). Rooms have free satellite TV, and you're just one minute from the subway and 10 from Canal City. Some rooms are reserved for women only. **Pros:** great location; free breakfast. **Cons:** perhaps a bit bland and businesslike for some. ✉*4-6-7 Nakasu, Hakata-ku, Fukuoka, Fukuoka-ken* ☎*092/262–0109* 🖶*092/262–5578* ⊕*www. tokyuhotels.co.jp/en* 💻*176 rooms, 2 suites* ♿*In-room: refrigerator, Internet. In-hotel: 2 restaurants, bar, no-smoking rooms, Internet terminal* ☐*AE, DC, MC, V.*

$ 🖥️**Tōyoko Inn Hakata Nishinakasu** 東横イン博多西中洲. This Western-style hotel is a nice inexpensive choice for those staying downtown around the Naka-gawa. The lobby has a sunny lounge area with good views of the street for people-watching while you sip your coffee or surf the Internet for free. It's only one block west of the Haruyoshi Bridge along Kōkutai-dōri, on the right (north) side of the street. **Pros:** 5 minutes to Hakata Station and Naka River; nice, free toiletries set. **Cons:** rooms are adequate but not overly large; small "unit" bathrooms. ✉*1–16–1 Nakasu, Chūō-ku, Fukuoka, Fukuoka-ken* ☎*092/739–1045* 🖶*092/739–1046* ⊕*www.toyoko-inn.com* 💻*260 rooms* ♿*In-room: refrigerator, Internet. In-hotel: restaurant, laundry, Internet terminal, Wi-Fi* ☐*AE, DC, MC, V.*

NIGHTLIFE

Fukuoka seems forever in the throes of an ongoing party—perhaps in a heroic endeavor to put off the inevitable hangover—but the surest places for memorable nightlife action are the Nakasu and Tenjin areas, which run along the Naka-gawa. Nakasu is on the east side of the river; Tenjin is on the west.

To be seen with the in crowd, be sure to drop by the bar and café known as **Propeller Drive** プロペラドライブ (✉*1–13–30 Imaizumi, Chūō-ku* ☎*092/715–6322*). It's open late every night, and you are practically guaranteed to see some of the prettiest and most stylishly dressed women in the world—Hakata Bi-jin—as well as a few confident guys who are invigorated rather than intimidated by this. It's fancy, but there's no cover charge. All three floors have white stucco walls, and the second floor has a wonderful overhang with tables where you can sit and enjoy the lovely view. Countless intricately framed mirrors reflect the light of crystal chandeliers. The signature cocktail is a gem called the Love Swallow, a rum-based drink built around a single strawberry frozen in a perfect sphere of ice. Teetotalers will be pleased with the mango lassi, and a snack you won't want to miss is the pasta with bacon in a creamed-spinach sauce.

SHOPPING

Fukuoka is known for two traditional folk crafts: Hakata *ningyō* (dolls) and Hakata obi (kimono sashes). Made of fired clay, hand-painted with bright colors and distinctive expressions, Hakata ningyō represent children, women, samurai, and geisha. The obi are made of a local silk that has a slightly coarse texture; bags and purses made of this silk make excellent souvenirs.

Kyūshū has a rich ceramics tradition. Though not as colorful or exotic as Hagi-yaki, the shops and kilns of Arita and other towns of Saga Prefecture, in particular, continue to produce fine pottery, especially a delicate-looking but surprisingly tough type of porcelain.

The seventh floor of the department store **Iwataya** 岩田屋 (✉2–11–1 *Tenjin, Chūō-ku* ☎092/721–1111) carries the most complete selection of local merchandise, including Hakata dolls, silk, and ceramics. From the Tenjin subway station, take Exit W-5 and follow the street straight for two blocks. Traditional Edo-style restaurants and shops selling quaint souvenirs line the **Kawabata Shopping Arcade** 川端商店街 *(Kawabata Shōtengaii)* stretching along the Naka-gawa from the Nakasu-Kawabata subway station to Canal City.

NAGASAKI 長崎

154 km (96 mi) southwest of Fukuoka (Hakata Station).

Blessed with a breathtaking location, Nagasaki is strung together on a long series of hillocks in a scenic valley that follows the arms of the Urakami River down into a gentle harbor. Unlike Hiroshima the city was left with no suitably intact reminders of the atomic bombing, and perhaps for this reason, there were apparently no compunctions about rebuilding the town right up to the edge of a tiny ground-zero circle with a stark steel monument at its center. Still, relatively new as it all may be, everything here exudes flavors of Nagasaki's international history, from the city's lively and compact Chinatown to the European-style mansions and Catholic churches on the hillsides.

In the mid-16th century, Portuguese missionaries, including Saint Francis Xavier, came ashore to preach throughout Kyūshū. This new and altruistic religion—coinciding with the arrival of firearms—threatened to spread like an epidemic through the impoverished and restive masses of the feudal system, and in 1597, to give bite to a new decree by Chief Minister Toyotomi to stifle worship, 26 followers were publicly crucified in Nagasaki, an act that brought condemnation from the world. This cruel and shocking display was followed not long after by Tokugawa's nationwide edict making the practice of Christianity a capital offense.

All foreigners were expelled except the Dutch, who, considered to be lacking overt propensities to convert anything but profits on trades, were sequestered on the island, Dejima. Of the local population, only merchants and prostitutes were allowed direct interactions with them. The Dutch took over the considerable trade brokering between China and Japan formerly done by the Portuguese. Though the rest of Japan was strangled by isolation and starved for foreign goodies, Nagasaki continued to prosper by making use of this tiny but important off-shore loophole in the Tokugawa anti-trade policy out in the harbor. This arrangement lasted until 1859, when insular Japan was forced to open up to the outside world.

Once other ports became popular, the city lost much of its special status. Centuries later, Mitsubishi decided to concentrate its arms manufacturing and shipbuilding capabilities here; the industrial presence and bad weather over the primarily target of Kokura in northern Kyūshū made Nagasaki the target for the second atomic bomb drop in 1945.

The city isn't small, but as it lies in a long winding valley that you experience it in small, manageable increments. Similarities with San Francisco are frequently touted, and the comparison is not far off—although the posters advertising whale-bacon and manga remind you of where you are.

GETTING HERE AND AROUND

Nagasaki Airport is approximately one hour by bus or car from Nagasaki. A regular shuttle bus travels between Nagasaki Airport and Nagasaki Station and costs ¥1,200. All Nippon Airways and Japan Airlines fly daily from Haneda Airport in Tōkyō to Nagasaki Airport (1¾ hours). From Ōsaka the flights are about 1¼ hours.

The **Kyūshū Kyūkō Bus Company** (☎092/734–2500) runs buses between Fukuoka's Tenjin Bus Center and **Nagasaki Bus Terminal**; the trip takes two hours. The **Nagasaki Ken-ei Bus Company** can get you to Unzen (¥1,900), a string of hot springs on the Shimabara Peninsula, in two hours, and direct to Kumamoto in three hours for ¥3,600.

The JR Kamome Express train costs ¥4,710 and takes 1 hour 51 minutes from Fukuoka's Hakata Station to **Nagasaki Station**. To get to Kumamoto from Nagasaki, take the JR Kamome to Tosu (two hours) and switch to the Tsubame Relay (one hour). Note that unless you have a free ride with a RailPass, at ¥6,770, it's going to be nearly double the cost of the bus.

Nagasaki is small enough to cover on foot; otherwise, the streetcar system is the most convenient mode of transportation. Stops are posted in English, and lines extend to every attraction in town. You can purchase a one-day streetcar pass (¥500) at tourist offices and major hotels. Otherwise, pay ¥100 as you get off the streetcar at any stop. If you wish to transfer from one streetcar to another, get a *norikae kippu* (transfer ticket) from the driver of the first one. Local buses are not as convenient, and the routes, timetables, and fares are complicated.

While most of the interesting sights, restaurants, and shopping areas are south of Nagasaki Station, the Peace Park and the Atomic Bomb Museum are to the north, about 10–15 minutes by streetcar or taxi.

One-hour **cruises** of Nagasaki Harbor depart from Nagasaki-kō (Nagasaki Port) at 10:30, noon, 1:30, and 3; the cost is ¥1,300.

The **City Tourist Information Center** provides English assistance, maps, and brochures. The **Nagasaki Prefectural Tourist Information Center** is across the street from Nagasaki Station. Use the pedestrian bridge on the second floor of the station to reach it. English travel information for the entire prefecture, including maps and bus schedules.

ESSENTIALS

Airport Information Nagasaki Airport (⊠ *Mishima-machi, Omura-city, Nagasaki* ☎ *0120/029–222, 03/5435–0750*).

Bus Contacts Kyūshū Kyūkō Bus Company (☎ *092/734–2500*). **Nagasaki Ken-ei Bus Company** (☎ *095/823–6155*).

Bus Depot Nagasaki Bus Terminal (⊠ *3–1 Daikoku-machi* ☎ *095/826–6221*).

Hospital Contacts Nagasaki University Hospital (⊠ *7–1 Sakamoto-machi, 1-chōme* ☎ *095/847–2111*).

Train Station Nagasaki Station (⊠ *1–1 Onoue-machi, Nagasaki-shi* ☎ *095/826–4336*).

Tour Information Cruises (☎ *095/824–0088* ☞ *¥1,300*).

Visitor Information City Tourist Information Center (⊠ *Inside Nagasaki Station, 1–1 Onoue-machi* ☎ *095/823–3631* ⊕ *www1.city.nagasaki.nagasaki.jp Daily 8–8*). **Nagasaki Prefectural Tourist Information Center** (⊠ *Nagasaki Ken-ei Bus Terminal Bldg., 2nd fl., 3–1 Daikoku-machi* ☎ *095/828–7875* ⊕ *www.nagasaki-tabinet. com* ⊗ *Daily 9–5:45*).

WHAT TO SEE

❶ Heiwa Kōen 平和公園 *(Peace Park)* was built on the grounds of an old prison that was destroyed in the atomic blast. In the middle is a large statue of a godlike man sitting with one arm stretched to the sky and one to the land. A short distance down the hill, **Hypocenter Kōen** 原爆落下中心地 marks the bomb's "hypocenter." A solitary pillar was erected to mark the exact epicenter, and there is curiously little distance separating this from anything else. Traffic rumbles by not far below, and apartment buildings and a hotel or two look down from the hill directly behind. In contrast to the looming Hiroshima dome, when you came upon the spot you might not immediately recognize its significance. But as you get closer the significance of the solemn pillar becomes starkly clear. From Nagasaki Station, take either Streetcar 1 or 3 for the 10-minute ride to the Matsuya-machi stop. ☞ *Free* ⊗ *Park never closes.*

❷ The spiral staircase of the **Atomic Bomb Museum** 原爆資料館 *(Genbaku Shiryōkan)* takes you down into a dark, depressing collection of video loops, dioramas, and exhibits that demonstrate the devastating effects of the bomb that was detonated here. English audio tours are available, though what you see is already too much to handle. The continuous, unblinking film footage is absolutely nauseating at several points, and a melted and blasted wall clock, as surreal as any Dalí painting, sears its way into your conscience. Out in the brightly lighted hallway, across from life-size mock-ups of the two atomic bombs, is a strange exhibit under a caption that reads "Japan's Wartime Aggression in the Pacific," which has a perfunctory list of conflicts, and includes

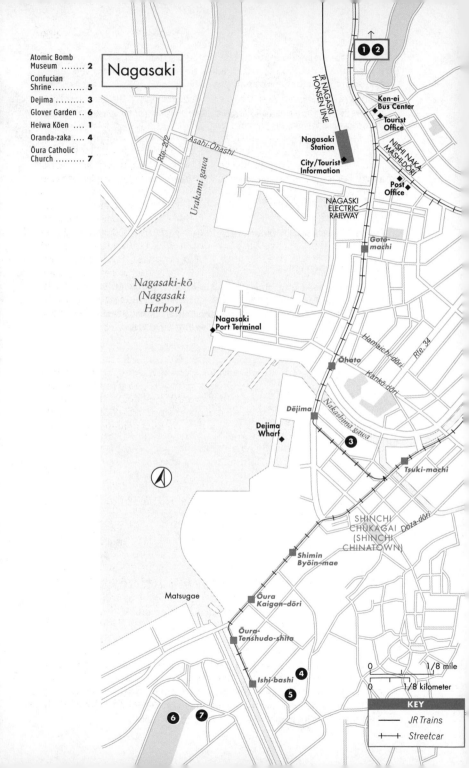

Nagasaki

JR NAGASKI HONSEN LINE

Rte. 202

Asahi-Ōhashi

Urakami gawa

Ken-ei Bus Center
Tourist Office

NISHI NAKA MASHI-DŌRI

Nagasaki Station

City/Tourist Information

Post Office

NAGASKI ELECTRIC RAILWAY

Gotō-machi

Nagasaki-kō
(Nagasaki Harbor)

Nagasaki Port Terminal

Hamaichi-dōri

Rte. 34

Ōhato

Kankō-dōri

Dējima

Nakashima gawa

Dejima Wharf

Tsuki-machi

SHINCHI CHŪKAGAI
(SHINCHI CHINATOWN)

Dōza-dōri

Shimin Byōin-mae

Matsugae

Ōura Kaigan–dōri

Ōura-Tenshudo-shita

Ishi-bashi

0   1/8 mile
0   1/8 kilometer

KEY

— JR Trains

+ + + Streetcar

CLOSE UP

August 9, 1945

On August 9, 1945, two days after the blast at Hiroshima, Nagasaki fell victim to a second atomic bomb because of bad weather. The plane, named *Bock's Car,* was supposed to drop the Fat Man, a new and experimental plutonium bomb, on the war industry complexes in Kokura. A delay in hooking up with *Bock's Car's* B-29 escorts meant that when they reached Kokura, bad weather had rolled in and blocked their view. So they headed over to the secondary target, Nagasaki and its vital ship yards, and dropped the bomb there.

More powerful than the uranium bomb dropped on Hiroshima, the Fat Man's core of plutonium, surrounded by TNT, imploded. The runaway fission chain reaction released the heat- and light-wave radiation of a small sun over the target, which in turn delivered a blast pressure of tons per square inch. Virtually nothing with in miles of the blast was left standing, or even recognizable. Nagasaki's hilly topography and conformity to undulating river valley floors had made it a less desirable target, but it did help save a number of residential areas from total destruction. Meanwhile, 6.7 square km (2.59 square mi) were obliterated, 74,884 people were killed in the blast or died shortly thereafter, and another 74,909 were injured. The effects of radioactivity caused the deaths of an estimated 70,000 others within five years.

12

an odd picture of Chinese peasant women training with pistols—though there's no mention of the atrocity that Tōkyō's Yasukuni Shrine calls "The Nanjing Strategy." To get to the museum, take Streetcar 1 from Nagasaki Station to the Hamaguchi stop. ✉ *7–8 Hirano-machi* ☎ *095/844–1231* ⊕ *www1.city.nagasaki.nagasaki.jp/na-bomb/museum* 🖂 *¥200, audio guide ¥150* 🕑 *Sept.–Apr., daily 8:30–5:30; May–Aug., daily 8:30–6:30.*

❸ When the government deported foreigners from Japan in the mid-17th century, Dutch traders were the only Westerners allowed to remain—but they were relegated to and confined on the artificial island of **Dejima** 出島 in Nagasaki Harbor. Here you can see a 450-year-old mix of Dutch housing styles that is popular among Japanese tourists. Take Streetcar 1 to the Dejima stop. ✉ *6–3 Dejima-machi* ☎ *095/821–7200* 🖂 *¥500* 🕑 *Daily 8–6.*

❹ **Oranda-zaka** オランダ坂 *(Holland Slope)* is a good place to wander on the way to Chinatown and Glover Garden. It's a cobblestone incline with restored wooden houses originally built by Dutch residents in the late 19th century. Many have become shops and tearooms in summer. To get here, follow the street on the southeast side of the Confucian Shrine.

❺ The bright red **Confucian Shrine** 孔子廟 *(Kōshi-byō)* was built in 1893 by the Chinese residents of Nagasaki. The small museum displays artifacts on loan from Beijing's Palace Museum of Historical Treasures and National Museum of Chinese History. The closest streetcar stop is Ishi-bashi; look for the signs leading to the shrine. ☎ *095/824–4022* 🖂 *¥525* 🕑 *Daily 8:30–5.*

6 **Glover Garden** グラバー邸 contains an impressive assortment of 19th-century Western houses. Wooden verandas, Greco-Roman porticos and arches, and other random elements of European architecture adorn these houses, which arc often crowned with Japanese-style roofs. The main attraction is the former mansion (1863) of Thomas Glover, a prominent Scottish merchant who introduced steam locomotives and industrialized coal-mining to Japan. Escalators whisk you up the steep hillside to the gardens, where you can admire the views of Nagasaki and the harbor. Take Streetcar 5 to Ōura Tenshudo-shita and follow the signs. ☎095/822–8223 ☜¥600 ☉Apr. 24–May 6, July 19–Oct. 9, daily 8–9:30; Dec. 19–31, 8–8, all other dates, 8–6.

Fodor'sChoice
★

7 **Ōura Catholic Church** 大浦天主堂 (Ōura Tenshu-dō) survived the bomb that leveled much of the city farther up the valley. It was constructed in 1865 to commemorate the death of 26 Christians crucified in 1597, victims of Toyotomi's gruesome message of religious intolerance. It's the oldest Gothic-style building in Japan. Below the entrance to Glover Garden, the church is a five-minute walk from the Ōura Tenshu-dō-shita streetcar stop. ✉5–3 Minami Yamate-machi, Dejima-machi ☎095/823–2628 ☜¥300 ☉ Daily 8–6.

WHERE TO EAT

$$–$$$
CONTEMPORARY

✗**Dejima Wharf** 出島ワーフ. Warm nights draw crowds to the outdoor terraces of this trendy two-story wooden complex on the pier next to Nagasaki Port. You'll find a sprawl of tantalizing seafood restaurants downstairs; a quiet pub serving pasta dishes, pizza, and cocktails at the north end of the second floor; and a family restaurant with burgers and Japanese noodle and rice dishes on the south end of the second floor. ✉Dejima Wharf ☎095/828–3939 ☐AE, DC, MC, V.

$$$$
JAPANESE

✗**Kagetsu** 花月. This quiet hilltop retreat is Nagasaki's most prestigious restaurant. Dishes are served as kaiseki (Kyōto-style multicourse meals) or shippoku, an elaborate course blending Asian and European elements. Lunch runs from ¥5,200 to ¥11,000; dinners start at ¥11,000. The interior wooden beams date to 1618, when Kagetsu was reputedly a high-class brothel. According to another local legend, Meiji Restoration leader Ryōma Sakamoto once took a chunk out of a wooden pillar with his sword during a brawl, leaving a still visible gash. ✉2–1 Maruyama-chō ☎095/822–0191 ☐DC, MC, V.

$–$$
CHINESE
★

✗**Kairakuen** 会楽園. This ornate Chinese restaurant is a local favorite, and it's easy to see, smell, and taste why. It serves the best chanpon—Nagasaki's signature dish of Chinese-style noodles, vegetable, and pork-based broth—in town. The reasonable price is an added bonus. Mama-san speaks English if given the chance, and Papa-san sits like Buddha and watches over the customers. It's just inside the entrance to Chinatown, on the left. Take the streetcar to Tsukimachi and walk a couple of blocks south. ✉10–16 Shinchi-machi ☎095/822–4261 ☐MC, V.

$
ITALIAN

✗**Karuda** カルダ. Authentic pizza and pasta are the mainstays at this Italian restaurant in the Shian-bashi entertainment quarter (east of Chinatown). From rustic wooden tables upstairs you watch the narrow streets below. Takeout is also available. From the Shian-bashi tram stop, head two blocks north into the arcade and another two blocks east. ⊠ *1–20 Kajiya-machi* ☎ *095/826–1302* ⊟ *No credit cards.*

WHERE TO STAY

12

$$ 🏨 **Holiday Inn Nagasaki** ホリデイイン長崎. For value and location—with a dash of style and sophistication—this is the place. Leather chairs, vintage sofas, antique telephones, and dark oil paintings in the lobby are reminiscent of an old European drawing room. Free international newspapers are at the entrance, and the hotel staff provides advice in perfect English. Rooms are spacious, with rare king-size beds. Look for the familiar sign on Kankō-dōri, the busy, main strip of downtown Nagasaki, at the Shian-bashi tram stop. **Pros:** in the thick of things; comfortable and stylish; friendly, capable staff. **Cons:** some single rooms have no view; room service only available from 5 to 10 PM. ⊠ *6–24 Dōza-machi, Nagasaki-shi, Nagasaki-ken* ☎ *095/828–1234* 🖷 *095/828–0178* ⊕ *www.ichotelsgroup. com* ➳ *87 rooms, 6 suites* ⚙ *In-room: refrigerator. In-hotel: restaurant, room service, bar, no-smoking rooms* ⊟ *AE, DC, MC, V.*

$$$$ 🏨 **Hotel New Nagasaki** ホテルニュー長崎. Glossy marble and massive
★ slabs of granite dominate this popular and upscale hotel. Standard twin rooms are large and comfortable, with enough space for a couple of easy chairs and a table. Light colors, pastel carpets, and tasteful gold accents keep things looking chic. It's unbeatably convenient, right next to Nagasaki Station and the always lively Amu Plaza shopping center. **Pros:** you can't get closer to the station; great shopping and more next door. **Cons:** a bit too lively and beehive-like for solitude seekers. ⊠ *14–5 Daikoku-machi, Nagasaki-shi, Nagasaki-ken* ☎ *095/826–8000* 🖷 *095/823–2000* ⊕ *www.newnaga.com* ➳ *130 rooms* ⚙ *In-room: Internet. In-hotel: 3 restaurants, pool, gym* ⊟ *AE, DC, MC, V.*

$$ 🏨 **Hotel WingPort** ホテルウィングポート. Computer rentals and in-room Internet access make the WingPort popular with business travelers. Guest quarters are nice but small—unless you splurge for the super or deluxe twins. The hotel is a two-minute walk from Nagasaki Station, across the pedestrian bridge on the narrow road past the convenience store. **Pros:** spacious rooms; clean; location. **Cons:** light sleepers beware—noises travel well here. ⊠ *9–2 Daikoku-machi, Nagasaki-shi, Nagasaki-ken* ☎ *095/833–2800* 🖷 *095/833–2801* ➳ *200 rooms* ⚙ *In-room: Internet. In-hotel: restaurant* ⊟ *AE, DC, MC, V.*

$$$$ 🏨 **Sakamoto-ya** 坂本屋. Established in 1895, this wooden ryokan is the oldest lodging in town, and it seems to have changed very little over time. It's small and has extremely personalized service and fragrant Japanese *hinoki* (cypress) bathtubs. The cost of the rooms varies according to size and location, but charges always include breakfast and dinner. The restaurant specializes in *shippoku*, which takes its name from Chinese kanji meaning dinner table, available for ¥3,500. **Pros:** private aromatic wooden bathtubs; private gardens. **Cons:** baths are not hot springs (but are nice!); no Internet access. ⊠ *2–13 Kanaya-machi, Nagasaki-shi, Nagasaki-ken* ☎ *095/826–8211* 🖷 *095/825–5944* ➳ *14 Japanese-style rooms* ⚙ *In-hotel: restaurant, Japanese baths* ⊟ *AE, DC, MC, V* ⦿ *MAP.*

SHOPPING

Castella sponge cake, the popular souvenir of Nagasaki, was introduced by the Portuguese in the mid-16th century. The original recipe called for just eggs, flour, and sugar, but it's been tinkered with over time. Every sweet shop and souvenir store in town has its own specially flavored recipe, but you're advised to stick with the good old plain version—a delightful treat with coffee or tea and raspberries.

The bakery **Fukusaya** 福砂屋 (⊠ *3–1 Funadaiku-machi* ☎ *095/821–2938*) has been in business since the Meiji period. When you say "castella" in Nagasaki, most people think of this shop and its distinctive yellow packaging. There's a branch on the first floor of the New Nagasaki Hotel, next to Nagasaki Station.

Not far from Dejima, **Hamano-machi** 浜野町 is the major shopping district in downtown Nagasaki. This covered arcade stretches over four blocks and contains numerous department stores, cake shops, cafés, pharmacies, and fashion boutiques.

Everyone converges at **Amu Plaza (Amu Puraza)** アムプラーザ as the sun sets. Towering over Nagasaki Station, this is where the newest shops and restaurants are, and a multi-theater movie complex is inside. It's thoroughly modern, and a striking contrast to the city's old-fashioned style.

KUMAMOTO 熊本

118 km (73 mi) south of Fukuoka (Hakata).

Kumamoto is situated nearly midway along the curve of the west coast of Kyūshū. From here you can go to Nagasaki to the west, Fukuoka to the north, Aso-san to the east, Kagoshima to the south on the new high-speed train line.

The town has many sights of its own, including the nationally famous Suizen-ji Garden, but the most renowned is the castle once deemed impregnable. Kiyomasa Katō ushered in the 17th century with the construction of a mighty fortress that was even bigger than the current replica, and he and his son held sway here until the 1630s. The Hosokawa clan then took over, and for the next few centuries Kumamoto was a center of the Tokugawa governmental authority. In 1877, the real "Last Samurai," Saigō Takamori, brought his army of rebels here to battle untested Meiji government conscripts holed up inside. Things were looking grim. Then Takamori ordered his starving men to butcher their horses for raw and ready food. Strengthened, they did breach the castle 53 days into the siege, but reinforcements forced them to backpedal as much of the castle and compound were destroyed in a huge conflagration. It may have been the first time raw horseflesh (ba-sashi) was eaten in Japan, but locals continue to devour it to help their stamina.

A number of notable folks had homes which can still be seen in town, including the writers Lafcadio Hearn and Sōseki Natsume, both of whom lived here for brief periods while teaching English.

GETTING HERE AND AROUND

The Kyūshū Sankō bus makes the 50-minute run from **Kumamoto Airport** to JR Kumamoto Station for ¥670. Flights on ANA, JAL, and Sky Net Asia (SNA) connect Tōkyō's Haneda Airport with Kumamoto Airport (1¾ hours). ANA and JAL fly the hour-long route from Ōsaka's Itami Airport eight times a day.

12

The Nagasaki Ken-ei Bus (from Nagasaki Ken-ei Bus Terminal) costs ¥3,600 and takes three hours to **Kumamoto City Kōtsū Center.** Kyūshū-Sankō buses leaving from Kumamoto City Kōtsū Center take 3 hours 15 minutes to Kagoshima, via change at Hotoyoshi for ¥3,650. There's also a bus route linking the onsen paradise of Yufuin and Kumamoto in 4½ hours for ¥3,450, and from April to October a trip via Aso-san (90-minute-stop for Aso sightseeing) can be done for ¥5,800 in about six hours. Call Kyūshy[m]-Sankō at 096/354–4845 for reservations (recommended).

A sightseeing bus, also operated by **Kyūshū Sankō,** makes a four-hour scenic trip (¥3,790) that starts at Fugen-dake and Shimabara, then ferries across Ariake Bay to Kumamoto-kō (Kumamoto Port) before ending the journey at Kumamoto City Kōtsū Center.

The JR Tsubame or Ariake Express from Fukuoka's Hakata Station stops at **Kumamoto Station** and takes 1¼ hours, ¥3,740. From Nagasaki, take JR to Tosu and change to the train for Kumamoto (3 hours, ¥ 6,170).

In most Japanese cities the hive of activity is around the station. However, very little of interest surrounds JR Kumamoto Station; the bulk of the town's attractions are to the northeast, squeezed in between the Tsuboi and Shira rivers. Most of what constitutes downtown huddles around the old castle, up there.

This is one spread-out city, and buses get stuck in all the traffic, so your best bet is to hop a streetcar. Tram lines (Nos. 2 and 3) connect the major areas of the city. The fare is a flat ¥150; pay as you get off. From the Kumamoto Eki-mae streetcar stop in front of the train station it's a 10-minute ride downtown. One-day travel passes, good for use on streetcars and city buses, are available for ¥500 from the City Tourist Information Office. There is also Castle Loop Bus that connects a string of sights around the castle with a stop across from the main train station and runs every 30 minutes from 8:30 to 5 daily. Tickets (¥130 single stop, or ¥300 for the day) can be bought at the tourist office in the station or at the Kotsu Center Bus Terminal near the castle.

The **City Tourist Information Office** can provide maps and information in English. The city's Web site, Visit Kumamoto, also has good descriptions of major sights.

ESSENTIALS

Airport Information Kumamoto Airport (✉ *1802–2 Oyatsu, Mashiki-machi, Kumamoto 096/232-2311).*

Bus Contacts Kyū-Sankō buses (☎ *096/355–2525).* **Kyūshū Sankō** (☎ *096/ 325–0100).*

CLOSE UP

In the Footsteps of the "Last Samurai"

As Tom Cruise publicly noted about his film *The Last Samurai,* it was not the character he portrayed, Nathan Algren, who was the true hero of the story, but rather the samurai he'd come to admire—his captor, Katsumoto, played by Ken Watanabe. The character Katsumoto was based on an enigmatic man from Kagoshima named Saigō Takamori, a central figure in the effort to restore the Emperor, who turned away when he felt betrayed by his cause. A physically and mentally imposing man influenced strongly by the conscience-honing philosophies of Confucianism and Zen, Takamori understood that dramatic changes would be necessary to ensure the success of Japan's transition from feudal state to modern society. Among them was the need for a trained, tested, and respected army. To

further this end, he devised a scheme to provoke a war with the "hermit kingdom" of Korea. So audacious was his plan—it involved his own sacrifice to bring it off—that although it gained a high degree of secret support unknown to him, officially he was rebuked for it. He withdrew to the hills to school a band of disgruntled out-of-work samurai into making a last stand for a dying lifestyle, a movement that evolved into the historic Satsuma Rebellion. With the unlikely exception of the character of Algren, the movie provided the fairly accurate basis of events. Key battles were in Kumamoto—in that castle's long history, it was Takamori that led the only successful siege—and Kagoshima, where it all came to a dreadful end in late 1877.

Bus Depot Kumamoto City Kōtsū Center (✉ *3–10 Sakura-machi* ☎ *096/ 354–6411*).

Hospital Contacts Kumamoto Chūō Hospital (✉ *96 Tamukae* ☎ *096/370– 3111*).

Internet Hotel New Ōtani Kumamoto (✉ *1–13–1 Kasuga* ☎ *096/326–1111 10 minutes for ¥100*).

Train Station Kumamoto Station (✉ *3–15–1 Kasuga* ☎ *096/211–2406*).

Visitor Information City Tourist Information Office (✉ *JR Kumamoto Station, 3–15–1 Kasuga* ☎ *096/352–3743* ⊙ *Daily 8:30–7*). Visit Kumamoto (⊕ *www. visitkumamoto.com*).

WHAT TO SEE

★ Towering, ominous **Kumamoto Castle** 熊本城 *(Kumamoto-jō)* was completed in 1607, designed and built by Kiyomasa Katō (1562–1611), the area's feudal lord or *daimyō.* Gracefully curved white-edged roofs rest atop the mysterious black keep. The wide stone base has *mushagaeshi,* concave walls with stout platform overhangs, situated under slanted windows perfect for unleashing rock falls, one of many clever features to prevent intrusion. Although some sources claim that the castle was never successfully attacked, it did suffer a fatal blow during the Battle of Seinen, when rebellious samurai led by Saigō Takamori went up against

12

government troops stationed inside. The fighting raged for more than seven blood-drenched weeks during the Satsuma Rebellion of 1877. Most accounts report that Takamori and his rebels breached, sacked, and burned the castle before running off to regroup in Kagoshima. The top floor of the reconstructed castle commands an excellent view of Kumamoto, and exhibits include samurai weapons and armor arrayed to evoke images of the fearless warriors charging into battle. To get here, board Streetcar 2, get off at the Kumamoto-jō-mae stop, and walk up the tree-lined slope. Volunteer guides conduct tours in English. ☎096/352–5900 ☜¥500; ¥640 *for combined admission to castle and Hosokawa Mansion, purchase ticket at castle* ⊗*Apr.–Oct., daily 8:30–5:30; Nov.–Mar., daily 8:30–4:30.*

The **Hosokawa Mansion** 旧細川刑部邸 *(Kyū-Hosokawa Gyōbu-tei)* was built in 1646 for the Hosokawa family, who took power at the behest of Tokugawa in 1611—and whose local lineage produced Japan's still popular former "reformist" Prime Minister Morihiro Hosokawa (served 1993–94). ⊠*3–1 Furukyō-machi* ☎096/352–6522 ☜¥300; ¥640 *for combined admission to mansion and Kumamoto Castle; purchase ticket at castle* ⊗*Apr.–Oct., daily 8:30–5:30; Nov.–Mar., daily 8:30–4:30.*

Created in the mid-17th century, **Suizen-ji Jōju-en** 水前寺成趣園 *(Suijzen-ji Garden)* was originally part of the sprawling villa of the ruling Hosokawa family. An undulating hummock of lush green grass representing Japan—there's even a Fuji-san-like cone in about the right place—is beside a pond surrounded by a network of stone bridges. The garden is dotted with impeccably trimmed bushes and trees. A tiny old teahouse gives welcome respite from the sun's glare and tour-bus groups' clatter. Also on the grounds is Izumi Jinja (Izumi Shrine), which houses the tombs of several eminent Hosokawa clan members. To get to the garden, take Streetcar 2 or 3 east from the castle to the Suizen-ji Jōju-en-mae stop. ⊠*8–1 Suizenji-koen* ☎096/383-0074 ☜¥400 ⊗*Mar.–Nov., daily 7:30–6; Dec.–Feb., daily 8:30–5.*

WHERE TO EAT

$ × **Aoyagi** 青柳. When you enter, you'll be greeted by elegant women
JAPANESE dressed in full kimono. But don't just stand there, there's serious work to be done! The extensive menu includes regional favorites—*ba-sashi* (raw horse meat) and *karashi renkon* (lotus root stuffed with fiery chili and mustard powder, sliced and fried tempura-style)—in addition to various types of sushi and tofu dishes. You can relax in a booth, or sit at the counter and admire the skilled chefs. It's tucked behind the Daiei department store, not far from the Shi-yakusho-mae streetcar stop. ⊠*1–2–10 Shimotori-chō* ☎096/353-0311 ⊗*Daily 11:30–10* ▤*AE, DC, V.*

$$$$ × **Loire** ロワール. Deluxe French dishes are served with flourish and flash
FRENCH at this elegant, spacious restaurant on the 11th floor of the Kumamoto Castle Hotel. Windows provide a dramatic view of the castle, which is flooded in pale-green light at night. Slices of smoked black pig with fresh fruit make a wonderful hors d'oeuvre, and the lamb chops and sea bass are both superb. Sumptuous desserts start at only ¥630. Choose

between fixed courses, or order things à la carte. ✉️*4–2 Jōtō-machi* 📞*096/326–3311* 🚇*AE, DC, MC, V.*

$$$–$$$$ ✗**Suganoya** 菅乃屋. When in Kumamoto, do as the locals do—eat some
FRENCH   *ba-sashi!* What do you think gave the Last Samurai that legendary
★   stamina during that castle siege? If you order the Nishiki Set (¥6,300),
you can get it served in all its forms: there's a starter of raw tidbits
with garlic, ginger, and assorted dunking sauces; or a finale of hari-hari
nabe, a soup of thinly sliced delicately flavored meat (horse, of course!)
and vegetables cooked in a folded-paper vessel that doesn't burn. Sit at
the bar for a delightful atmosphere of friendly frenzy, or kick back at
one of the secluded tables. ✉️*2–12 Jō-tō-machi, Lion Parking Biru 2F*
📞*096/355–3558* 🕐*Daily 11:30–2 and 4:30–10* 🚇*AE, DC, V.*

WHERE TO STAY

$$$ 🏨**Hotel New Ōtani Kumamoto** ホテルニューオータニ熊本. It's not as over-
the-top as its big-city counterparts, but it's endowed with the same
crisp service and all the amenities. Weary travelers will be happy to
know it's just to the left (north) of Kumamoto Station. The small bright
lobby does interesting things with color, space, and geometry. **Pros:**
unlike everything else in town, it's close to the station; Internet access
in lobby. **Cons:** it's close to the station, all right—but nothing else is.
✉️*1–13–1 Kasuga, Kumamoto-shi, Kumamoto-ken* 📞*096/326–1111*
📠*096/326–0800* 🌐*www.newotani.co.jp/en* 🛏️*130 rooms* ⚃*In-hotel:*
4 restaurants, room service, bar 🚇*AE, DC, MC, V.*

$$$–$$$$ 🏨**Kumamoto Hotel Castle** 熊本ホテルキャッスル. Just across from the
★   castle, things here are dark-wooded and traditional enough to be mys-
terious, but the service is excellent and modern. They'll even help you
plan out a timetable for a journey to Aso-san, continue to check into it
while you get yourself ready, and then be forthright enough to tell you
that persistent cloud cover and showers are likely to make your arduous
day-trip a dubious adventure, and suggest alternative local activities.
Rooms come in an amazing variety of layouts, all with ornate puffy fur-
nishings in luscious creamy colors, and now that the castle restoration is
finished, you'll get a great view. **Pros:** great staff; great location. **Cons:**
confusing lobby arrangement makes an intimidating first impression.
✉️*4–2 Jōtō-machi, Kumamoto-shi, Kumamoto-ken* 📞*096/326–3311*
📠*096/326–3324* 🛏️*185 rooms* ⚃*In-hotel: 5 restaurants, bars* 🚇*AE,*
DC, MC, V.

$ 🏨**Tōyoko Inn Karashima Kōen** 東横イン唐島公園. This adequate but inex-
pensive hotel offers a rare bonus: a free in-room movie channel in the
otherwise basic Western-style rooms. There's also a simple but tasty com-
plimentary Japanese breakfast—*onigiri* (rice balls wrapped in seaweed),
miso soup, and coffee—in the lobby. To get here, take the streetcar to
Karashima-chō. **Pros:** free Internet access in lobby; laundry facilities.
Cons: late check-in (4 PM); rooms are a bit small and sparse. ✉️*1–24*
Kōyaima-machi, Kumamoto-shi, Kumamoto-ken 📞*096/322–1045*
📠*096/322–2045* 🌐*www.toyoko-inn.com/e_hotel/00077/index.html*
🛏️*153 rooms* ⚃*In-hotel: restaurant, laundry facilities, no-smoking*
rooms, Wi-Fi 🚇*AE, DC, MC, V* 🍴*CP.*

SHOPPING

Kumamoto's most famous product is *Higo zōgan*, or Higo inlay. A unique form of metalwork originally employed in the decoration of swords, scabbards, and gunstocks of the Hosokawa clan, it consists of black steel delicately inlaid with silver and gold, and it is now used to make fashionable jewelry that does not come cheap; a simple pendant can run ¥8,000, and prices for large pieces reach ¥700,000 and more. Other local products include gold paper lanterns, dolls, tops, and fine cutlery.

Dentō Kōgei-kan (*Kumamoto Traditional Crafts Center* ⊠ *3–35 Chiba-jō* ☎ *096/324–4930*), open Tuesday–Sunday, October–June 9–5, July–September 9–6, is the best place to buy *zōgan* and regional handicrafts. It's in a redbrick building across from the Akazu-mon entrance to the castle.

ASO-SAN 阿蘇山 (MT. ASO)

Aso-san comprises the world's largest caldera—128 km (80 mi) in circumference, from 11 to 15 mi wide in places—formed after a massive lava-dome collapse around 100,000 years ago. Inside the crater are seven settlements and herds of cows and horses. The emerald-green grasses that nourish them thrive in the fertile volcanic soil. The crater area, officially named the Aso-Kujū (Mt. Aso National Park), contains five volcanic cones; one is the still-active Naka-dake, and it sticks up out of the side of the taller Taka-dake just east of the crater's center. There's no mistaking the sulfurous stench of the mighty belches that gust freely from its mouth.

GETTING HERE AND AROUND

Kyūshū Sankō buses make frequent runs between Kumamoto City Kōtsū Center, the Aso Nishi cable-car station at Asosan-jō, and Kurokawa Onsen. The Kyūshū bus continues from Kurokawa Onsen to Yufuin and Beppu.

The JR Hōhi Line runs between Kumamoto Station and **JR Aso Station** (¥1,680, express; ¥1,080, local) and also connects Aso to Kagoshima (¥7,400). From JR Aso Station you must board a **Kyūshū Sankō** bus (40 minutes; ¥540 one-way) to get to Aso-San Nishi Station. Buses run every 1–2 hours starting at 8:30; the last bus down is at 7:44. From there you can walk 30 minutes to the crater or take the **Aso Nishi Cable Car** (4 mins) to the terminus at Kako Nishi (West Crater). Aso-san makes an excellent stopover on the way to Yufuin from Kumamoto. The JR Odan Line also connects JR Aso Station to Yufuin via change in Oita (¥4,850).

If you start early, you can make Aso-san a day trip. You have until 9 for the last Kumamoto-bound train, but the last bus back from the ropeway to distant Aso Station is at 5. If you want to spend more time in the park, spend the night in one of the many mountain pensions clustered in the southern half.

Stop by the **Aso Station Information Center** to get your bearings and check conditions. The mountain's emissions occasionally take the lives of tourists, and park officials will shut things down when the alarm is raised.

ESSENTIALS

Bus Contacts Kyūshū Bus Co. (☎ *096/325–0100*).

Cable Car Contact Aso Nishi Cable Car (operated by Kyūshū Sangyō Bus Co.) (✉ *Furubōchū, Aso-chō* ☎ *0967/34–0411* ¥*1,000 round-trip;* ¥*500, one-way*).

Train Station JR Aso Station (✉ *Kurokawa, Aso-chō* ☎ *0967/34–0101*).

Visitor Information Aso Station Information Center (✉ *Inside JR Aso Station* ☎ *0967/34–0751* ⊙ *Thurs.–Tues. 9–5*).

WHAT TO SEE

Fodor'sChoice
★
The view from the top of 5,000-foot **Naka-dake** 中岳 is reason enough to visit Mt. Aso National Park. Inside the crater, a churning ash-gray lake bubbles and spits scalding, reeking steam. Naka-dake's rim is a 30-minute walk from the bottom of the **Aso Nishi Cable Car** at Asosan-jō; the cable car takes you up in four minutes. You can skirt around some of the lip, but the northern reaches have been out of bounds since 1997, when toxic fumes seeped out and killed two tourists. If rumbling turns to shaking, and steam and smoke turn to sizeable ash-fall, know where the bunker-like shelters are located. These were built after a dozen people perished in a sudden eruption some 50 years ago.

Kusasenri 草千里, a 35-minute ride from the JR Aso Station on the Kyūshū Sankō bus line, is a bowl-shaped meadow where cows and horses graze on the lush grass and wade in shallow marshes. If you have time, hike along an easy trail that goes 5½ km (3½ mi) around the base of Kijima-dake. It takes an hour or so, and provides excellent views of the otherworldly terrain. You could also march the 3 km (2 mi) straight across the rugged lava plain to the foot of Naka-dake. ■TIP→ **For several trails of other lengths and difficulty in the area, pick up the "Aso Trekking Route Map" at the information center in JR Aso Station.**

The **Aso Volcano Museum** 阿蘇火山博物館 *(Aso Kazan Hakubutsukan)* is across from the Kusasenri parking lot and rest area. Want to see what's happening inside the volcano? Two heat-impervious cameras were inserted into the most active part of the volcano, and museum visitors can watch what's being recorded in there. Another display explains that Japan sits on the busiest tectonic plate junction in the world and that these fault lines are visible from space. ✉ *Kusasenri Aso-cho* ☎ *0967/34–2111* ✍ ¥*840* ⊙ *Daily 9–5.*

WHERE TO STAY

There are more than 50 lodging outfits in and around Aso National Park to choose from.

$$ ☷ **Pension Angelica** ペンションアンジェリカ. The main appeal of this manor in the woods is the hospitality of the Tatsuji family. White lacy bedspreads decorate the bright guest rooms, which have tall windows

overlooking flower bushes. The kitchen creates culinary wonders, from fresh bread to Mediterranean dishes. At craft time, you can learn to make *washi* (Japanese paper) or clay figurines. From Kumamoto, take the JR Hōhi Line to Tateno and switch to the Minami Aso Tetsudō Line. Get off at Takamori and call the pension, which will have someone pick you up; the hosts ask that you get there before dinner, served at 6:30. **Pros:** heartwarming hosts; homemade bread; fresh air and quiet. **Cons:** have to hustle to get there early; long way to go if your stay is short. ⊠*1–1800 Shirakawa, Minami-aso-mura, Aso-gun, Kumamoto-ken* ☎🖷*0967/62–2223* ⊕*www.pensionangelica.com/* ⏎*7 rooms, 2 with bath* ♿*In-hotel: restaurant, bar, Japanese baths, no-smoking rooms* 🞏*No credit cards* ⦿*MAP.*

$$$ 🖈**Yamaguchi Ryokan** 山口旅館. From the outdoor baths of this rustic lodge you can watch mineral water meander down the rocky cliffs of the green mountainside. Don't be shy—mixed bathing is often practiced here. Two meals are included, and dinner is served in your Japanese-style room. The lobby has a raftered ceiling and a toasty old-fashioned furnace. It's a cozy place to enjoy a cup of coffee or tea. From Kumamoto, take the JR Hōhi Line to Tateno and switch to the Minami Aso Tetsudo Line. **Pros:** about as isolated as one can get in this country; awe-inspiring baths and falls; rated by some as Best Outdoor Baths in Japan; indoor baths are great, too. **Cons:** about as isolated as one can get in this country; food not as stunning as the baths. ⊠*2331 Kawayō, Aso-gun, Minami-Aso-mura, Kumamoto-ken* ☎*0967/67–0006* 🖷*0967/67–1694* ⏎*35 Japanese-style rooms* 🞏*AE, DC, MC, V* ⦿*MAP.*

KAGOSHIMA 鹿児島

171 km (106 mi) south of Kumamoto, 289 km (180 mi) south of Hakata/Fukuoka.

Kagoshima is a laid-back, flowery, palm-lined southern getaway on the Satsuma Peninsula with mild weather, outgoing people, and a smoking volcano out in the bay. Ancient relics believed to date back to 9,000 BC indicate that humans have been in the area a very long time. It became a center of trade with Korea and China, and was an important fortress town from the mid-16th century until the Meiji Restoration. This is where Saigō Takamori and his rebel followers (reduced to a few hundred from 40,000) made their last stand against the new Emperor on September 24, 1877, chased here after having sacked Kumamoto Castle. Facing 300,000 well-supplied troops, they had no chance, and Takamori was injured in the fight. Rather than face capture, he ordered one of his own men to cut off his head. Reviled and vilified during the rush to modernization, he was posthumously pardoned and honored as a national hero.

Today, the area is famous for growing the world's smallest mandarin oranges (only an inch across) and the largest white daikon radishes—grown in the rich volcanic soil, these can span 3 feet and weigh in at more than 100 lbs. There's also *kurobuta*, a special breed of black pig that locals convert into breaded, fried cutlets called *tonkatsu (ton is pork; katsu, katsu-retsu means cutlet).*

GETTING HERE AND AROUND

The flight between Tōkyō's Haneda Airport and **Kagoshima Airport** takes 1¾ hours. From Ōsaka the flight takes about 1 hour. The **Airport Limousine** picks up passengers every 10 minutes (until 9 PM) at Bus Stop No. 2 outside the Kagoshima Airport. From downtown, catch it in the terminal in the Nangoku Nissei Building, across the street from the

> **MALL BREAK**
>
> The lively Amu Plaza complex attached to the Chūo Station will keep you busy with shopping and food opportunities, and, if you get bored, there's a cineplex. A giant Ferris wheel is on top, for one of the best views in town!

East (Sakura-jima) Exit from JR Kagoshima **Chūō** Station. The 40-minute trip costs ¥1,200.

Frequent buses make the four-hour trip for ¥5,300 from Fukuoka (departing from Hakata Kōtsū Bus Center and Tenjin Bus Center) to **Kagoshima Chūō Station.** Trains to the same station arrive on the JR Tsubame and Relay Tsubame Limited Express lines from Fukuokata's Hakata station and Kumamoto via Shin-Yatsushiro.

For the past hundred years the easiest way to get around Kagoshima has been by streetcar. A ¥160 fare will take you anywhere on the trusty old network. One-day travel passes for unlimited rides on streetcars and buses cost ¥600. You can buy one at the Kagoshima-Chūō Station Tourist Information Center, or on a streetcar or bus. Buses get around, but are run by five competing outfits on a complicated system.

JR Kyūshū Bus runs a 6 hour, 10 minute–tour of the area for ¥4,000. It departs from Chūō Station Bus Stop East–9 at 8:50 AM and includes the city and the volcano; however, guides speak only Japanese.

The **Kagoshima-Chūō Station Tourist Information Center** is on the second floor of the station's Sakura-jima Exit. An English-speaking person is on hand to arm you with maps and info or help you make hotel reservations.

ESSENTIALS

Airport Information Kagoshima Airport (☎ *099/558–4686*).

Airport Transfer Airport Limousine (☎ *099/247–2341*).

Bus and Train Station Kagoshima Chūō Station (✉ *1–1 Chūō-chō* ☎ *099/256–1585*).

Tour Information JR Kyūshū Bus (☎ *099/247–5244*).

Visitor Information Kagoshima-Chūō Station Tourist Information Center (✉ *1–1 Chūō-cho* ☎ *099/253–2500* ☉ *Daily 8:30–7*).

WHAT TO SEE

★ Across Kinkō Bay rises **Sakura-jima** 桜島, and you can often see it spewing thick plumes of dust and smoke. Its last big eruption was in 1955, but the far side of the cone sometimes lets loose with explosive burps that light the night sky red and cover the town in a blanket of ash. There are scattered lodgings and hot springs, as well as winding paths up to old lava plateaus with great views over the crater or back toward town.

A **24-hour ferry** connects **Kagoshima Port** (✉ *4–1 Shin-machi, Hon-kō* ☎ *099/223–7271*) with **Sakura-jima Port** (✉ *61–4 Yokoyama-chō, Sakura-jima* ☎ *099/293–2525*), at the foot of the volcano itself. There are four to six ferries per hour, with fewer connections after 9 PM. The one-way fare is ¥150, and the trip takes only 10–15 minutes. To get to the pier from Kagoshima Chūō Station, take Bus East–4 or 5 for the short ¥180 ride.

12

OFF THE
BEATEN
PATH

Ibusuki Tennen Sunamushi Onsen (and Sand-Bath Center Saraku) 指宿天然砂むし温泉と砂楽 is a laid-back seaside resort on the southern tip of the Satsuma Peninsula that may provide your one chance to try a therapeutic hot-sand bath. Exit Ibusuki Station and follow the signs to the NATURAL HOT SAND BATHING SPOT, a 15–20 minute walk or five-minute cab ride to the beach. You buy your ticket and rent a *yukata,* or cotton robe—the small towel is yours to keep—on the second floor of the main "Saraku" Sand Bath Hall, and then go down into the locker rooms (separate sexes) to remove your clothes and change into the robe before heading to the beach. Stand in line and wait for an assistant to call you over. They'll scoop a place for you and show how to wrap your head and neck in the towel. They will then bury you in hot, mildly sulfur-smelling sand with their shovels. It'll get squirmy, but stay in the Zen zone for at least 10 minutes. Fifteen will give you a full charge—if you can take it! Aside from giving you a powerful dose of joint-penetrating heat, the stimulating, sweaty experience is also guaranteed to cleanse your pores and soften your skin. It's a highly scenic one-hour trip south of Kagoshima on the Ibusuki Nanohana local train line. ✉ *5–25–18 Yū-no-hama, Ibusuki-shi* ☎ *0993/23–3900* 💰 *¥1,000, including towel and robe rental* ⊘ *Daily 8:30–noon and 1–8:30.*

WHERE TO EAT AND STAY

$$
Fodor'sChoice
★

🏨 **Furusato Kankō Hotel** ふるさと観光ホテル. This hotel is on Sakura-jima, and the *rotemburo* (outdoor bath) offers amazing views. There's even a thermal-water lap pool. Two meals are included in the rate. Every room has a view of the water; five have miniature gardens. There's even a Zen room for meditation. A free shuttle (15 minutes) runs every half hour between the hotel and the Sakura-jima ferry port. **Pros:** spectacular ocean-side baths; great for a romantic hideaway. **Cons:** you won't want to re-enter the rat race after a dose of this place's magic. ✉ *1076–1 Furusato-machi, Kagoshima-shi, Kagoshima-ken* ☎ *099/221–3111* 🖷 *099/221–2345* 🛏 *38 Japanese-style rooms* ⌂ *In-hotel: restaurant, bar, pool* ☰ *AE, DC, MC, V* ⏀ *MAP.*

$$$
JAPANESE
★

✗ **Kumaso-tei** 熊襲亭. Enjoy the best of Satsuma specialties in a maze of private and semiprivate Japanese-style rooms. There's an English photo menu, and deluxe set meals range from ¥3,360 to ¥10,500. Highlights include *kibinago* (raw herring), *satsuma-age* (fish cakes filled with potato or gobo, burdock root), *kurobuta-tonkatsu* (breaded, fried pork cutlets from locally bred black pigs). From the Tenmonkan-dōri streetcar stop, walk four blocks north through the covered arcade and turn left; the restaurant will be on the right. ✉ *6–10 Higashi Sengoku-cho* ☎ *099/222–6356* ☰ *AE, DC, MC, V* ⊘ *Daily 11–2:30, 5–9:30.*

$$$–$$$$ ⊡ **Shirōyama Kanko Hotel** 城山観光ホテル. Also called Castle Park Hotel in brochures, the hotel is on Shirō-yama, site of Takamori's last stand. High enough to provide enviable views but not too far away to be inconvenient, this hotel is famous for its rotemburo baths and fantastic views of both the town and the volcano. It's a 10-minute taxi ride from the JR Kagoshima Chūō Station. **Pros:** panoramic views; great baths; free Wi-Fi. **Cons:** nothing but relaxation happening here; it'll be hard to give it up when the time comes. ✉ *1–41 Shinshoin-cho, Kagoshima-shi, Kagoshima-ken* ☎ *099/224–2211* 🖷 *099/224–2222* 🛏 *365 Western rooms* ♨ *In-hotel: 6 restaurants, bar* ☰ *AE, DC, MC, V* ⦿ *EP.*

$–$$ ⊡ **Sun Days Inn Kagoshima** サンデイズイン鹿児島. This sleek business hotel offers excellent value, style, and convenience. You're within five minutes by taxi from the Kagoshima Chūō train station, Tenmon-kan nightlife district, and the Sakura-jima ferry port. Deluxe "DX" rooms with lounge furniture cost ¥25,000. **Pros:** spanking-new and clean; top value for the yen. **Cons:** could use a nice bath to compete with its rivals; meals in the restaurant are a bit small for Westerners. ✉ *9–8 Yamanokuchi-chō, Kagoshima-shi, Kagoshima-ken* ☎ *099/227–5151* 🖷 *099/227–4667* 🛏 *351 Western-style rooms* ♨ *In-hotel: restaurant, bar, no-smoking rooms* ☰ *AE, MC, V.*

YUFUIN 湯布院

★ *135 km (84 mi) southeast of Hakata/Fukuoka.*

Southwest of the majestic twin peaks of Yufu-dake, this tranquil village resembles a checkered quilt. Forests nestle up to clusters of galleries, eclectic cafés, local crafts shops, and rustic lodgings. Most of the year, Yufuin is a relatively peaceful area, but things heat up in July and August with the arrival of national music and film festivals.

Yufuin has suffered from fewer of the pitfalls of modern tourism than the nearby and over-developed Beppu. But it wasn't an accident. City planners and investors went to Europe and came back with ideas about how to set up a quaint and lovely spa town—and how *not to*. The town has blossomed into a quieter, more sedate getaway than its garish counterpart to the east. Relatively unadorned natural baths with great views can be found here, as can a thriving arts-and-crafts industry and fantastic food.

GETTING HERE AND AROUND

The closest airport is **Ōita Airport.** The flight to Ōita Airport from Tōkyō's Haneda Airport takes 1½ hours; the flight from Ōsaka's Itami Airport takes one hour. From the airport to Yufuin, buses run six times daily (8–8, ¥1,500, 55 minutes).

The *Kujūgō,* run by **Kyūshū Ōdan Teiki Kankō Bus** travels between Kumamoto and Beppu three times times daily (8:40 AM, 9:50 AM, and 2:30 PM), stopping in Yufuin along the way. The one-way fare from Kumamoto to Yufuin (3¾ hours) is ¥5,800.

JR Yufuin-no-Mori Express trains run three times daily between Fuku-oka's Hakata Station and **Yufuin Station;** they take 2 hours 10 minutes and cost ¥4,440.

To enjoy the best of Yufuin in a day, start by picking up an English map at **Yufuin Tourist Information Office.** For more detailed information, visit the **Yufuin Tourist Center,** a five-minute walk from the station. Bicycles can be rented from either office.

ESSENTIALS

Airport Information Ōita Airport (⊠ *13 Shimobaru, Aki-machi, Higashi Kunisaki-shi* ☎ *0978/67–1174*).

Airport Transfer Ōita Kōtsu Bus Company (☎ *097/534–7455*).

Bus Contacts Kyūshū Ōdan Teiki Kankō Bus (☎ *096/355–2525*).

Train Station Yufuin Station (⊠ *8–2 Kawakita* ☎ *0977/84–2021*).

Visitor Information Yufuin Tourist Information Office (⊠ *In Yufuin Station, 8–2 Kawakita* ☎ *0977/84–2446* ☉ *Daily 9–7*). **Yufuin Tourist Center** (⊠ *2863 Kawakami* ☎ *0977/85–4464* ☉ *Daily 9–6*).

WHAT TO SEE

From Yufuin Station, take the five-minute taxi ride north to **Kūsō-no-Mori** 空想の森—a collection of art galleries along the foot of Yufu-dake.

Work your way back south toward the train station via the **Yu-no-tsu** neighborhood, a long shopping street lined with traditional Japa-nese wooden buildings, where you can mill in and out of artsy craft shops and souvenir stalls, or relax in one of the many coffee shops or tearooms.

In winter steam rises from the surface of **Kinrin-ko** 金麟湖 *(Lake Kinrin)*, a thermal lake in the east end of town. Warm up with a dip in one of the many bathhouses along its shores.

On most days an artist is painting at the large wooden table in the cen-ter of the **Yutaka Isozaki Gallery** 由夛加磯崎ギャラリー. Small cards with inspirational messages and illustrations such as persimmons and wild-flowers make original souvenirs (¥300–¥2,000). For a unique memento of old Japan you can sift through clothing made from antique kimonos at the rear of the gallery or piles of antique cotton and silk textiles in **Folk Art Gallery Itoguruma,** the little shop to the right of the entrance. ⊠ *1266–21 Kawakami* ☎ *0977/85–4750* ☉ *Daily 9–6*.

WHERE TO EAT AND STAY

$$$$
JAPANESE
★

✕ **Budōya** 葡萄屋. Part of the pricey Yufuin Tamanoyu hotel, which was until 1975 a lodging for Zen Buddhist monks, this restaurant retains an air of solemnity. The first level has stone floors, thick wooden tables, and windows overlooking a thicket of wildflowers and tall grass. Upstairs, rooms have tatami floors and bamboo-mat ceilings. For a splurge, try the *amiyaki* course (¥8,820), with tender charcoal-grilled beef, sea-sonal vegetables, and homemade *kabosu* (lime) sherbet. ⊠ *Yunotsubo,*

12

Yufuin-cho, Yufu-shi ☎*0977/84–2158* ▭*AE, DC, MC, V* ◷*Daily noon–2:30 and 5–8:30.*

$$$–$$$$
FRENCH

✕**Moustache** レストランムスタシュ. Started by a Japanese chef who wanted to create a European atmosphere in the shadow of Yufu-dake, Moustache is a café and restaurant with a flair for hearty, country French–style fare. Food can be ordered in set courses or à la carte. The *masu*, or sea trout, is highly recommended. ✉*1264–7 Kawakami, Yufuin-cho, Yufu-shi* ☎*0977/84–5155* ▭*AE, DC, MC, V* ◷*11:30–9:30; closed Mon.*

$$$–$$$$

🛏**Onyado Yufu Ryōchiku** 御宿由布両築. In winter, when not submerged in the mineral waters here, you can toast yourself by the burning coals in the *irori* (sunken hearth) in the lobby of this 1925 inn. Breakfast and dinner are included and are served in your room. The inn is among the shops and galleries near the thermally heated Lake Kinrin, which gives off steam much of the year. **Pros:** charming, tranquil atmosphere; locks on mineral bath doors mean they can be made private. **Cons:** no Internet; not much except bathing going on. ✉*1097–1 Kawakami, Ōita-gun, Ōita-ken, Yufuin-chō, Yufuin-shi* ☎*0977/85–2526* 🖷*0977/85–4466* ⇆*8 Japanese-style rooms without bath, 2 houses with bath* ▭*MC, V* �*MAP.*

$$$–$$$$

🛏**Pension Momotaro** ペンション桃太郎. The owners of this interesting and very rustic pension make every effort to make you feel at home; they'll even take you to the station when you depart. Both Western-style and Japanese-style rooms are available in the main building, and four charming A-frame cottages are on the premises—each with hot spring water piped into the bath and shower. Rates include two meals, which can include duck, pheasant, and river smelt. **Pros:** funky little shacks; private baths inside; open-air bath with views of Yufu-dake. **Cons:** cottages like tents in a yard; might be too much like "camp" for some. ✉*1839–1 Kawakami, Ōita-ken, Yufuin-chō, Yufuin-shi* ☎*0977/85–2187* 🖷*0977/85–4002* ⇆*6 Western-style rooms, 4 Japanese-style rooms, 4 chalets* ⚲*In-hotel: restaurant* ▭*No credit cards* ⟨𐃓⟩*MAP.*

Okinawa

THE KINGDOM OF RYŪKYŪ

WORD OF MOUTH

"Okinawans are very proud, and rightly so, of their culture—the music, traditional dance, glassware and pottery, all aspects of their culture which is so different and distinct from Japan or China. They're also proud of the gorgeous beaches and landscapes (hopefully you'll be lucky enough to travel north on the island and escape some of the city and bases—the sights are incredibly peaceful and beautiful up there.) . . . be aware and appreciative of the astounding progress the island has made in 60 years—from a burned out wasteland in Naha, to their modern buildings and monorail."

—ChgoGal

Updated by
Joshua Bisker

You'll swear you've hit an entirely different country: let the tropical climate get you ready for sun-kissed beaches and crystal blue waters, deserted islands ringed by rainbow-hued coral reefs, verdant jungle trails leading to ancient time-frozen hamlets, and funky port-towns full of laid-back, fun-loving islanders: it's all here welcoming you to Okinawa, Japan's most unique and exciting destination.

Okinawa is a far leap from the Japanese main in every sense. True, the archipelago is literally closer to Taiwan than to any of Japan's main islands, and farther from Tōkyō than Seoul is, but deeper distinctions of culture and history are what really set the islands apart. When people here tell you that Okinawa isn't Japan, they're not just being figurative; Okinawa's indigenous population comprises an ethnic group independent from the mainland Japanese, and local pride lays much heavier with Okinawa's bygone Ryūkyū Kingdom than it ever will with the Empire of the Rising Sun. Island culture today forms an identity around its Ryūkyū roots but also reflects the centuries of cross-cultural influence brought to Okinawa on successive tides of imperialism. Ships have plied from ancient Polynesia, Ming China, Edo Japan, and most recently war-time America bearing the ravages of conquest and the joys of new tradition (snake-skin instruments, the stir-fry, salarymen, and Spam). Okinawa's melting pot is sharply different from mainland Japan's commercial culture of appropriation and pastiche, touching every element of island life and lending flavor to the music, language, cuisine, architecture, arts, and lifestyle that define the archipelago.

The Okinawan archipelago spans about 700 km of ocean, reaching from south of Kyūshū's Kagoshima prefecture to just east of Taiwan. Of the hundreds of islands only a handful are inhabited, and even the settled ones sport more jungle and beach than they do road and city. Over 90% of the population, numbering about 1.3 million, lives on Okinawa Hontō, the largest and most developed island of the chain, most in the capital city Naha. Hontō is notorious for also housing the bulk of the Japan's American military presence, though unless you're here visiting a friend in uniform your focus will be the island's beaches, moving war memorials, natural escapes, and arresting historical attractions.

Island hopping outside of Okinawa Hontō means traveling among several disparate clusters of islands; Okinawa Prefecture is a conflation of smaller archipelagos gerrymandered together, not a steady string of pearls. Traverse the long distances by plane and use ferries to get from one nearby island to another; on the islands themselves you'll enjoy the most freedom with your own transportation, but whether a bicycle or an automobile is more appropriate depends on the size of the island. With limited time to spend in Okinawa, we recommend you choose one of the three main island groups to explore instead of trying to cram it all in. Many travelers make the mistake of staying put on Hontō, but

TOP REASONS TO GO

Hit the Waves: Surfers and diving pros will argue about which beaches are the best, but virtually anywhere you go in Okinawa you'll find sparkling sand, clear water, and a lot of time for R&R.

Secret History: Moving memorials tell a captivating story of the chaos that ravaged this idyllic landscape during World War II's fierce final battle.

Getting Wild: Snorkeling, diving, trekking, sailing, fishing, whale-watching, and kayaking are in your reach in

Japan's most pristine and enticing natural vistas.

Local Flavors: Okinawa's food, music, art, and local spirit combine powerful influences from all over Asia and funky homegrown flavors.

Dazzling Reefs: Cresting an underwater ridgeback that divides some of the globe's deepest currents, Okinawa's abundant reefs are home to varied marine life thriving in clear, warm seas.

13

while its sights are terrific, you'll find more great fun, diverse adventure, and welcoming islander hospitality as you get farther afield from the mainland. Okinawa rewards a traveler's intrepid spirit, so cast away your map and head out into the wild blue yonder.

ORIENTATION AND PLANNING

GETTING ORIENTED

Okinawa Hontō. Naha's Kokusai-dōri avenue and Shuri castle are a great introduction to the area. More captivating are the war memorials and Ryūkyū monuments on the southern peninsula, and the diving and snorkeling spots, active artisan workshops, and jungle hiking trails to the north.

Kerama Islands. Dazzling coral reefs, white beaches, and verdant scenery are only a stone's throw away from Naha's port. Though close to Okinawa's mainland, infrequent ferry times make planning ahead essential, but the vivid blue ocean makes it well worth the hassle.

Miyako Islands. A short flight from Naha, Miyako Island and its neighbors are supplied with support for diving tours with giant manta-rays, good beach-side accommodation, and a whole lot of R&R time.

Yaeyama Islands. Only an hour flight from the capital, hip Ishigaki City is a great launch point for the island's surrounding sights and offers great access the time-forgotten villages on Taketomi and the reefs and leaves of untamed Iriomote—and the perfect mixture of developed getaways and seriously off-the-map adventure.

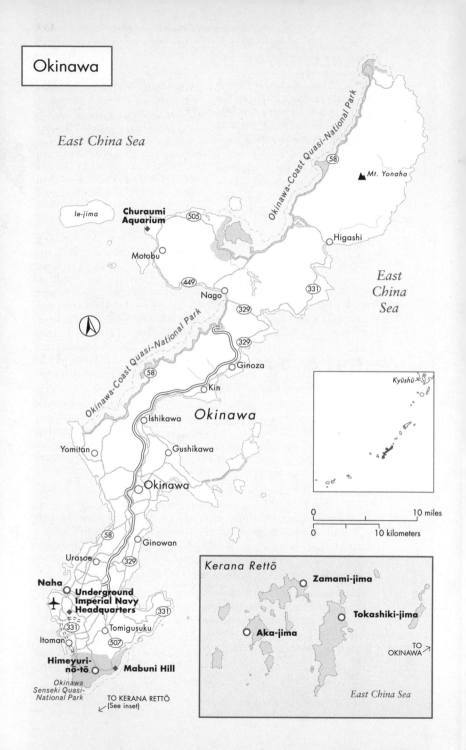

Okinawa

East China Sea

Okinawa-Coast Quasi-National Park

▲ Mt. Yonaha

58

Ie-jima

Churaumi Aquarium

505

Higashi

Motobu

East China Sea

449

Nago

329

331

329

Okinawa-Coast Quasi-National Park

Ginoza

58

Kin

Okinawa

Ishikawa

Yomitan

Gushikawa

Okinawa

58

Ginowan

Urasoe

329

Naha

Underground Imperial Navy Headquarters

331

Tomigusuku

507

Itoman

Himeyuri-nō-tō

◆ **Mabuni Hill**

Okinawa Senseki Quasi-National Park

TO KERANA RETTŌ (See inset)

Kyūshū

0   10 miles
0   10 kilometers

Kerana Rettō

Zamami-jima

Tokashiki-jima

Aka-jima

TO OKINAWA

East China Sea

PLANNING

WHEN TO GO

Okinawa enjoys winters most folks dream about but temperatures can be extreme in summer months. Waters are warm and swimmable year-round, but you probably want to come between October and March during the off-season. Thanks to mainland Japan's fairly inflexible vacation system, prices drop and crowds thin out just when the weather turns ideal. The exception is whale-watching season in February, when tourists will make the hustle from Tōkyō to Okinawa's Miyako Islands in order to see the spectacle. Try to avoid the rainy season, late May to early July. Arriving to Okinawa in August you'll be mocked by locals for not having gone to Hokkaido instead.

13

GETTING HERE AND AROUND

Naha is the most common entry point to Okinawa, with flights taking roughly two hours and departing regularly from most places in Japan and several nearby international hubs. Most odysseys through Okinawa begin here before moving farther into the archipelago, but there's no reason not to start farther out and work your way back: flights connect directly to Miyako Airport from Ōsaka-Itami and Tōkyō-Haneda, and to Ishigaki from Ōsaka-Kansai, Kōbe, and Tōkyō-Haneda. Flying from Naha to either one takes around an hour. Travel agents anywhere in the country can arrange tickets for you. Buying seven days in advance and shopping for morning flights garner substantial discounts. From within the prefecture, Okinawa Tourist storefronts are your best resource for tickets and information on getting around.

Public transport leaves a lot to be desired. Naha is serviced by a handy monorail running from the airport through the city and terminating at Shuri castle, taking less than an hour end-to-end with trains running about every ten minutes. Outside the city things are less promising. The story is the same on each of the islands: yes, buses link to urban centers and popular tourist destinations, but schedules are inconvenient, hard to decipher, and confining. Budget for rental cars to get the most of your time on the larger islands.

RESTAURANTS

Okinawa's culinary history doesn't have a corollary to the haute cuisine of Kyōto or Tōkyō. A similar aristocratic tradition hasn't prevailed here, and prized local ingredients like soba, pork, and mozuku seaweed aren't necessarily expensive or hard to produce. This isn't to say that Okinawan cuisine falls short on rare delicacies or delicious cooking but simply that great, true-blue Okinawan food can be had on the cheap, anywhere. Greasy-spoon joints will have fare as traditional and as tasty as the fancy gourmet establishments, so go enjoy!

■TIP→**One effect of the American military presence has been to increase English language proficiency throughout Okinawa. Most restaurants and hotels will have some English speaking staff, so feel confident about going into anywhere for a meal or to inquire about a stay.**

On the Menu

Okinawa's famously long-lived and hearty population has made the Okinawa Diet into a buzzword among Slow Food enthusiasts and others interested in healthy eating. Islanders aren't sure where the secret of their longevity lies, but do your best to try it all: is it in the knobbly, green bitter gōya; delicious tofu-like fu; salty mozuku seaweed; abundant tropical fruits like pineapple, mango, and papaya; conscientious consumption of every single little part of the pig; everything goes champlu stir-fry dishes; alien-looking fish, and crustaceans, sometimes still wriggling; delicious white sōki-soba noodles, tastiest in a hot pork-stock soup with soft soki rib meat lining the bowl; Thai rice or the blindingly potent awamori liquor it's distilled into; aromatic, atomic koregusu hot sauce, made from red chilis pickled in awamori; cloying kokutō black sugar; savory umi-budo sea grapes; purple beni-imo potatoes; or a mix of it all?

HOTELS

Lodgings range from no-frills beach shacks to shockingly lavish resorts. As you get farther from Naha things begin to look decidedly more local, and with a few exceptions, you won't find anything suggesting "luxury" among the outlying islands. We recommend the smaller-scale accommodations in Okinawa, especially on Hontō, where the nicest resorts line the grubbiest beaches along an over-developed central coast twinkling with electric lights—probably not what you came here for. Find unspoiled scenery, friendly service, interesting locals and tourists, and knowledgeable recommendations for local tours at smaller, local-run hotels and inns.

⇨ *For a short course on accommodations in Japan, see Accommodations in Travel Smart.*

WHAT IT COSTS IN YEN					
	¢	$	$$	$$$	$$$$
RESTAURANTS	under ¥800	¥800–¥1,000	¥1,000–¥2,000	¥2,000–¥3,000	over ¥3,000
HOTELS	under ¥8,000	¥8,000–¥12,000	¥12,000–¥18,000	¥18,000–¥22,000	over ¥22,000

Restaurant prices are per person for a main course, set meal, or equivalent combinations of smaller dishes. Hotel prices are for a double room with private bath, excluding service and 5% tax.

ESSENTIALS

Visitor Information Okinawa Prefectural Government Tourism and Resort Bureau (✉ *1–2–2 Izumizaki, Naha* ☎ *098/866–2764*). **Naha Airport Information Desk** (☎ *098/857–6884*). **Okinawa Tourist Information Office** (✉ *Kokusai-dōri* ☎ *098/868–4887*).

WHO'S WHO?

Encoded into islander speech are delineations for who comes from where. Ethnic Ryūkyū are shimanchu—written with the Chinese-Japanese ideographs to literally mean island-people and pronounced in Okinawa's dialect. Ethnic Japanese by contrast are yamatochu, reflecting Japan's archaic name, Yamato. Everyone else in the world? Naichu, or mainlanders. These systems are all relative, however. More obscure islands hold denizens of Okinawa's capital Naha to be naichu, while on the bigger landmasses they differentiate between yamanchu and uminchu, mountain folks and sea people. Make friends by asking who comes from where: shimanchu desu ka? By the time you go home, Okinawa's beach life may make you a dedicated uminchu, but for the moment be happy with what you are: tabinchu means traveler.

13

OKINAWA HONTŌ 沖縄本島

By air: 2½ hrs from Tōkyō, 2 hrs from Ōsaka and Western Honshū. Weekly or daily connections with most major domestic airports.

Arriving from the Japanese mainland onto Okinawa Hontō brings a fresh wave of culture shock. The exciting urban landscape of Naha, the bizarre American-esque strip malls, chain diners, mammoth resorts, and funky dive shops all grafted seamlessly over the place's laid-back, tropical vibe will feel to you like Japan and Thailand are having a custody battle for this island's shores.

Naha's sights make for a great day or two, and some great bars and restaurants offer a good scene after dark. But rather than indulging too much in Naha's nightlife, take advantage of the early daylight to drive out to Hontō's other sights. To the south, moving war memorials tell the valuable story of Okinawa's tragic history in World War II. North of Naha, small towns sprawling up the coast are cut at intervals by bloated resort areas and some great treasures: active artisan enclaves, sweet diving spots, and the phenomenal Churaumi Aquarium. Beyond, the road opens out to the lush, empty northern peninsula. Scenic overviews, rocky karsts, mangrove forests, and waterfalls make for a great daytrip. You can see everything in about three or four days: a two-night stay in Naha lets you spend one in the city and one circling the southern peninsula, a following night near a beach up north lets you hit the sights along the coast getting there, and a day in the northernmost natural parks gets you back to Naha for a night out before the flight or ferry to your next destination.

NAHA 那覇

Orchids growing in the airport lounges are the first sign you've come to a very different sort of place. Okinawa's provocative capital city Naha is the center of commerce, tourism, and youthful enterprise in the region. People here are less scrubbed-clean looking and more laid-back than elsewhere in Japan, and you'll probably have an easy time feeling

Legend of the Shii-sā

The ceramic gargoyles protecting doorways and adorning rooftops throughout the islands have quite a history. It's remembered that during the reign of one of the ancient Ryūkyū kings a terrible dragon was terrorizing Naha, destroying settlements and devouring townsfolk. When the king went to the seaside, a local shaman and his boy confronted him with advice they had received in dreams. The boy took hold of a pendant the king wore around his neck, a lionlike figurine that had been a gift from a Chinese emissary. Held aloft toward the dragon, the figure cracked forth a ferocious roar, so powerful it toppled boulders from the heavens to pin the dragon to the shallow sea bed, where it died and became part of the islands, now a park near Naha.

These days shii-sā lions are Okinawa's most iconic image. Homes and businesses display them on either side of their entranceways, the open mouthed one scaring off evil spirits, the closed mouth partner keeping in good spirits. These good luck totems are popular souvenirs and come in myriad shapes and descriptions; which style you display will depend on the character of your home.

---

relaxed and energized by the city's verve as you tour the sights. Naha's appeal has a short half-life, however, and you may quickly tire of the students on school trips swarming the sidewalks, the chintzy souvenir shops and arcades, shore-leave marines shouldering into bars, and noisy teen moped-gangs dominating street traffic, helmet straps flapping worryingly in the wind. Enjoy the wonderful sights before moving out to explore the rest of the island.

GETTING HERE AND AROUND

JTA and **ANK**, regional arms of Japan Airlines and All Nippon Airways fly to Naha from most major Japanese destinations, with tickets usually running between 20,000 and 30,000, but discounts for booking in advance can bring the price as low as ¥9,000. Ferries between Naha and Kansai, Tōkyō and southern Kyūshū run fares expensive enough to make flying worthwhile, especially in light of the time you save: compare a two-hour flight from Tōkyō versus a four day boat ride with at best a ¥10,000 difference in price. Naha also has flights to Miyako, Ishigaki, and Yonaguni further out in the archipelago.

Getting to the city is easy thanks to the clean, convenient monorail. The line begins at the airport, Naha Kūko, and weaves through the city before terminating at the castle Shuri-jō. Shopping, accommodations, and activities are all centered around the bustling avenue Kokusai-dōri in the middle of town. Depending on which end your hotel is closest to, you'll get off at the Kenchō-mae, Miebashi, or Makishi stations. Everything you need is in within walking distance or a few monorail stops away. Trains run about every 10 minutes from 6 AM until about 11:30 PM, and fares are ¥130–¥260 per trip.

When it's time to leave the city, ask your hotel for the closest rental car place; Naha is denser with these than with noodle shops. Local businesses like **Arpo Rentals** are good for motorbikes and may have cheaper

PLANNING YOUR TIME

A journey to the tropics means relaxation is top priority, so plan well to avoid the travel stresses Okinawa can throw at you. Two factors make getting around challenging: it's easy to forget just how vast an area the prefecture covers; and you're competing with "Okinawa Time," the entrenched "What me worry?" philosophy. Minimize tension and maximize your fun by choosing one or two places to explore instead of trying to see it all—but don't spend your whole vacation on Hontō. The farther you get from the beaten track, the more richly rewarding your time here will be.

Follow up a day devoted to Naha's sights with another day each for the northern and southern sights of Hontō. After that, pick an island chain and head out. Adventure activities like scuba diving, sea kayaking, trekking, and snorkeling are readily available. Remember, though, that these sports take up energy and time, so if you plan to try a range of activities consider lingering around one locale for a few days rather than pinballing across the archipelago.

We recommend Ishigaki-jima and its neighbors Iriomote-jima and Taketomi-jima for a week away from it all; you'll find reliable guides servicing the entire gamut of adventure activities through the region's diverse natural environments and sights ranging from homey city to rainforest-like wilderness. The area has remained largely sheltered from the tourist industry, so this frontier is yours to claim.

13

cars than the big chains like **Toyota Rent-a-Car**, but these are more convenient if you want to drop your car off somewhere else on the island, and the cars are often in better shape.

Before you leave the airport, equip yourself with good local maps, time schedules, and service information at the **Tourist Information Center** in the main lobby of the airport. In the city, step into **Okinawa Tourist**, a sponsored chain of tourist information offices with branches in every city on the archipelago. The main branch on the right hand side of Kokusai-dōri just north of the Kenchō-Mae monorail stop is the most helpful, with a second-floor office specializing in English communications and fielding calls from overseas.

ESSENTIALS
Airline Information ANK (☏ *0120/02-9222*). JTA (☏ *0120/25-5971* ⊕ *www. japanair.com*).

Car Rental Japaren (☏ *098/861-3900*). **Kūko Rent-a-Car** (☏ *098/859-1111*). **Nippon** (☏ *098/868-4554*). **Orion Rent-A-Car** (☏ *098/867-0082*). **Toyota** (☏ *098/ 857-0100*).

Visitor Information Tourist Information Center (*Naha Airport*). **Okinawa Tourist** (⊠ *Okie Ōdōri at Ichiba-dōri* ☏ *098/868-4887*).

WHAT TO SEE
★ **Shuri-jō** 首里城. The sprawling, grandiose seat of the ancient Ryūkyū Kingdom is as reminiscent of Beijing's Forbidden City as Kyōto's Imperial Palace and deserves an afternoon of exploration. A marvel for the eyes from the bright red walls and roof tiles to the massive gray and

white walls ringing the vast stone courtyard, the original 15th-century castle was once part of an even more extensive property, but was mostly leveled during World War II when the Japanese Imperial Army made the complex its local headquarters. After reconstruction in 1992, Shuri-jō was named a UNESCO world heritage sight. A 10-minute walk from Shuri station, the last stop on the monorail; follow the signs from the station. ⊠ *1–2 Kinjo-chō, Shuri* ☎ *098/886–2020* ⊠ *¥800* ☉ *Daily 8:30–7:30.*

Kokusai-dōri 国際通り. You're sure to get caught up in the buzzing, infectious beat of Kokusai-dōri, Naha's central hub for commerce, nightlife, restaurants, souvenirs, and people-watching. A day's wander or a night's crawl through Kokusai will give an eye-popping introduction to Okinawa's varied demographics, from the crew-cut military personnel to teenie-boppers out clubbing, the street musicians to octogenarians on shopping trips. The shlock shops can be overwhelming, but those selling everything from high-proof snake-liquor to pickled pig's ears carry an irresistible charm. Ceramic shiisa figurines depicting the fantastic lion creature of Okinawan legend seem to come in every shape and size, although more distinctive statures can be found in remoter locations.

■**TIP→Bypass Kokusai-dōri's Starbucks for any of the Blue Sky ice-cream shops that pop up along the strip—a soft-serve swirl of vanilla and purple Beni-Imo potato at an outdoor patio chair is the finest way to beat the heat.**

★ **Kōsetsu Ichiba Market** 那覇公設市場. Two covered shopping arcades snake out from Kokusai-dōri, filled with shops specializing less in trinkets and more in snack-foods and produce. Sample deep-fried ball doughnuts, leaf-wrapped mochi, and tropical fruit drinks on your way to the expansive market await you at the first big intersection. Passing between outdoor fruit stalls into an unassuming doorway leads you to a carnival of delightful and grotesque butchers' counters, fish mongers, and pickle-sellers. Smoked pigs' faces stare ghoulishly down from racks displaying every other part of the animal (including some things you likely never thought anyone could eat), displays rivaled only by multicolor shellfish, neon eels, and giant crustaceans so shockingly exotic they seem like they were pinched from Churami Aquarium.

Tsuboya Pottery District 壺屋焼. More than 300 years of ceramic tradition are celebrated in this area behind Kokusai-dōri's main drag. In more than 20 workshops around these hills Master Craftsman and Living Cultural Asset plaques hang on the walls between various examples of Okinawa's distinctive pottery, on sale ranging from cheap to affordable to absurd. The famous Japanese potter Shōji Hamada came here in the 1920s and '30s and left with the inspiration for his notable works, but you may be more inspired by what you find in the nearby pottery museum than what you see on sale—a lot of the dishes and lion statues can be kitchey and unimpressive, although the bits of broken pottery whimsically accenting walls and doorways in Gaudi-esque embellishment are a lot of fun. Some workshops have doors or windows open to visitors, but you'll have a better view of it all one-hour's drive north of Naha at the pottery collective **Yachimun no Sato.**

The small but heartful **Tsuboya Pottery Museum** (*Tsuboya Yakimono Hakubutsukan* ✉*1–9–32 Tsuboya* ☎*098/862–3761*) has exhibits illustrating the history of the region's earthenware production, including representative pieces from all periods, and a reproduction of a traditional Okinawan house, showing Tsubo-yaki tableware and kitchen utensils. Next to the museum is an intact 19th-century climbing kiln, called a *nobori-gama*. Recent attention to providing more detailed English explanations has made the experience more exciting and informative. To get to the pottery district, walk through Heiwa-dōri, the left-hand arcade, until it empties out into Yachimun-dōri. ✉*Tsuboya 1–9–32,* ☎*098/862–3761* ⊕*www.edu.city.naha.okinawa.jp/tsuboya.*

Chindami Kōgei ちんだみ工芸. You can't spend a day in Okinawa without hearing the entrancing, energetic sound of the sanshin, Okinawa's banjo-like string instrument. A fretless lacquered neck with three strings on a body traditionally made from snake skin wrapped around a tight drum produces a sound at once upbeat and melancholic—and wholly otherworldly if you've grown up anywhere but here. Music is one of the most celebrated parts of Okinawa's culture, and you might easily fall in love with the mesmerizing sanshin. So don't leave Naha without taking a peek into one of the most highly regarded sanshin-maker's shops in the country. Higa-san will give you a free, good lesson for as long as you have time for, and several ranks of beginner-oriented sets let you choose a good arrangement if you want to take one home (they all include a great instructional DVD). If you don't have a solid idea of what Okinawan music can really sound like at its best, ask to hear some Kadeharu Rinsho, a master of traditionally inspired songs, or something by modern folk-pop group Begin (they're kind of Okinawa's Beatles), or just go out drinking later into the night than you're used to. Chindami Kōgei is on the side street off Kokusai-dōri abutting the south side of the JAL City Hotel. ✉*Makishi 1–2–18* ☎*098/869–2055* ⊕*www.chindami.com* ☾*Daily 10–8.*

WHERE TO EAT

$$$
JAPANESE

✕**Hateruma** 波照間. A lively izakaya-style restaurant with Okinawan food on the helpful picture menu and full live music and dance shows most nights of the week at 7, 8, and 9. On Kokusai-dōri a few blocks south of the Starbucks. ✉*Makishi 1–2–30* ☎*098/863–8859* ♿*Reservations recommended* ☾*11 AM–midnight.*

$–$$
ECLECTIC

✕**Helios Pub** ヘリオスパブ. This microbrewery and pub serves up four tasty home brews along with hearty snacks like tender oxtails stewed in black beer, a goya champlu omelet with rice, and herb-seasoned bratwurst sausages. Wood floors and thick roof beams, brick pillars, and hanging sheaves of barley don't exactly scream, "Okinawa," but it's a great place for a hearty comfortable meal. Two blocks south of Starbucks on Kokusai-dōri. ✉*1–2–25 Makishi* ☎*098/863–7227* ⊟*D, MC, V.*

$
CAFE

✕**Mafali Cafe** マファリカフェ. Hidden in a second floor north behind the Makishi station monorail tracks on Kokusai-dōri is a laid-back oasis of good food, great music, and chill staff and clientele. A decent drink selection is backed by a surprisingly varied food menu, with curry soups, alligator steaks, duck stir-fry, and taco-rice. Coffee and cake sets

13

are a great excuse to get out of the weather in the daytime, and most weekend nights have live shows or DJs—depending on what you're looking for, it's probably even more fun as a night spot than as a lunch café. ⊠ *Makishi 1–1–3, 2F* ☎*098/894–4031* ◷ *Sun.–Tues. and Thurs. 6 PM–3 AM. Fri. and Sat. 6 PM–5 AM. Closed Wed.*

¢ ✕**Mutsumi** むつみ. This greasy spoon counter place has been serving
JAPANESE some of the best Okinawan fare on the island since 1958, with endearing hand-drawn renderings on the walls serving as a handy picture menu. Everything is twice as big and three times as filling as it looks, with soup and rice included. Walking north on Kokusai-dōri two blocks past Starbucks, make a left onto the cobbled street just before the Mitsukoshi department store main entrance; it's the unassuming place on your left. ⊠ *Makishi 2–1–16* ☎*098/867–0862* ◷ *Daily 11 AM– midnight.*

$$$$ ✕**Sam's Anchor Inn** サムズアンカーイン. You wouldn't think that the
CONTINENTAL cheesy samurai-pose chef's portrait and sailor-suited waitresses would
★ speak to getting an authentically high-quality meal, but Sam's Anchor Inn—and its two siblings, Sam's Maui and Sam's By-the-Sea, at intervals along Kokusai-dōri—offer a great Japanese steak-house experience in a rollicking, fun atmosphere. The dinner-show experience combines with steak or seafood platters for a fun meal; it can be packed on weekends. ⊠*3–3–18 Kumoji, 2F* ☎*098/862–9090* ▭*AE, MC, V.*

WHERE TO STAY

$ ⛾**Hotel Royal Orion** ホテルロイヤルオリオン. You couldn't ask for a better place to find this reasonable, classy Western hotel. Just north of the Makishi monorail station where Kokusai-dōri gets suddenly quieter, nine floors of clean, sturdy accommodation are a perfect place to stay a night on your way through Naha. Standard twin rooms actually have cozy semi-double beds with decor erring towards boring; more deluxe rooms have opulent bathrooms and big desks. **Pros:** great location; good rates; helpful tour desk. **Cons:** still close to noisy Kokusai-dōri; no Internet. ⊠*Asato 1–2–21,* ☎*098/866–5533* ⊕*www.royal-orion. co.jp* ⫘*209 rooms* ⟁*In-room: safe, refrigerator. In-hotel: 3 restaurants* ▭ *AE, DC, MC, V*

$–$$ ⛾**Hotel Sun Palace** ホテルサンパレス. Earth-toned tiles and rounded-balconies overflowing with tropical flowers welcome you to this appealing riverside hotel. Attractive rooms make for a pleasant stay at a reasonable price, and the city and harbor views are great. From the Kenchō-mae monorail station, cross the bridge spanning the Kumoji River, then turn right. **Pros:** good location; near but not overwhelmed by the city. **Cons:** showing some wear and tear; no Internet. ⊠*2–5–1 Kumoji, Naha* ☎*098/863–4181* ⊕*www.palace-okinawa.com* ☎*098/861–1313* ⫘*67 Western-style rooms, 8 Japanese-style rooms* ⟁*In-room: Internet. In-hotel: restaurant* ▭*D, MC, V.*

¢ ⛾**Hyper Hotel Naha** ハイパーホテル那覇. It's far from the city center and the rooms are nothing fancy, but if you're here to zip through Naha's sights before striking farther out into the islands then the budget-friendly Hyper Hotel might be perfect for you. Beds are wider than in most business hotels, and desks are in each room with plans to install wireless Internet hubs on each floor by 2009. Family rooms have a raised bed.

Smack between Kokusai-dōri and the airport, with 10-minute taxi rides going either way. **Pros:** budget-friendly; clean, easy access in and out of the city. **Cons:** inconvenient for Naha's center; small rooms. ⊠*5–11–1 Kanagusuku, Naha* ☎*098/840–1000* 🖷*098/858–1001* 🛏*89 rooms* ♿*In-hotel: restaurant, laundry service, Internet* ▤*MC, V* ⦿❙*CP.*

$$$$ 🏨 **Okinawa Harbor View Hotel** 沖縄ハーバービューホテル. One of Naha's finest, this spiffy ANA-operated hotel caters to the higher-end market, from the pool's careful nighttime lighting scheme to the dark woods of the lobby. Rooms are distinctive and elegant, with cream walls and pastel furnishings. The restaurants' meals start at ¥2,000, and you can head to the rooftop bar for a cocktail. The nearest monorail stop is the Asahibashi Station; from there head southeast on Tsubokawa-dōri to the third major intersection, then turn left. **Pros:** elegant facilities; spacious rooms. **Cons:** far from Kokusai-dōri; pricey. ⊠*2–46 Izumizaki, Naha* ☎*098/853–2110* 🖷*098/835–9696* ⊕*www.harborview.co.jp* 🛏*352 rooms* ♿*In-hotel: 4 restaurants, bar, pool, laundry service* ▤*AE, D, V.*

$ 🏨 **Station Hotel Makishi** ステーションホテル牧志. Right where Kokusai-dōri quiets down you'll find a stark white-tiled lobby leading up to improbably spacious, accommodating guest rooms at this high-rise, Western-style hotel. The prices and location are perfect for spending a few nights in town, with great access to Kokusai-dōri and within sight of a central monorail station. **Pros:** large rooms; good rates; massage chairs in the pricier rooms. **Cons:** no double beds; ghastly lobby floor. ⊠*Asato 1-2-2590*2-0067 ☎*098/862–8001* ⊕*www.hotel-makishi. com* 🛏*79* ♿ *In-room: safe, refrigerator, Internet. In-hotel: restaurant; laundry facilities* ▤ *AE, DC, MC, V.*

NIGHTLIFE

American Idol. In Matsuyama, Naha's only foreigner-run karaoke bar is the perfect place to work out all the do-the-hop inspiration that sweaty sea-air and '50s impersonation groups will send pumping through you by the end of the night. With a huge English song list, great drink selection, and wide white marble countertops, where better to become a karaoke star than in this far corner of Japan? ⊠*Matsuyama 1–14–19, Matsumachi Peatsuti Bldg. 4F* ☎*098/868–1888* ⊘*Daily 7 PM–5 AM.*

Club Cielo. This is an upscale, rooftop, strut-your-stuff dance club. Patrons are allowed entrance only between 9 PM and midnight, but the party never stops. Cover charges range from ¥1,500 to ¥2,000. Club Cielo is in the Best Denki Building on Kokusai-dōri, diagonally across from the Palette Kumoji shopping center. ⊠*1–1–1 Matsuo, 6F* ☎*098/861–9955.*

Kento's Live House. In Naha's admittedly seedier area, Matsuyama, Kento's Live House has been going strong for decades with mostly '50s and '60s cover bands in great getups rocking a stage so warmly neoned out it feels like the whole bar is inside a Wurlitzer jukebox: there's a whole lotta shakin' goin' on. Most nights have performances with entry ¥1,500–¥2,500. It's a famous spot, so anyone can point you the way. Walking from Kokusai-dōri, follow Ichigin-dōri north until you get to the bustling Matsuyama intersection and hang a left at the Lawson. ✉ *Matsuyama 1–14–19, Matsumachi Peatsuti Bldg. BF* ☎ *098/868–1268* ☺ *Daily* 6 PM–3 AM.

Rehab. Best of Naha's foreigner hang-out bars, and easily the most fun place in town to relax for a few drinks at the end of your night, Rehab and its owner Paul Patry are institutions in Naha's nightlife. Come in to hear stories from Norwegian ship captains on leave, multi-lingual local businessmen, the convivial bar-maids or Paul himself, the most gregarious person within city limits. Paul is also a great resource for arranging sailing cruises, reef walking, diving, kayaking, and more. ✉ *Makishi 2–4–14, Kakazu Bldg. 3A* ☎ *098/864–0646* ✎ *okinawarehab@gmail. com* ☺ *Daily 7–2.*

Rock in Okinawa. This venue hosts live rock shows nearly every night of the year. It's open from 7 PM to 7 AM nightly, and the cover charge is generally ¥1,000 to ¥2,000. Rock in Okinawa is on Kokusai-dōri, near the Heiwa-dōri arcade and the Kokusai shopping center. ✉ *3–11–2 Makishi* ☎ *098/861–6394.*

SOUTH OF NAHA

Two great attractions draw visitors to Okinawa's southern spur. The culture park **Okinawa World** is an interactive trip through the islands' Ryūkyū past, with restored houses, a cool cave, and traditional performances. More than the ancient Ryūkyū culture, however, it is Okinawa's history during World War II that will resonate most with visitors. Several deeply moving museums trace Okinawa's tragic story. Caught between American and Japanese militaries during the last months of the war, Okinawa suffered an astronomical toll in life and resources. Like Hiroshima's **Atomic Dome** these sights are important not only to local history, but also for their message teaching the value of peace to all inheritors of the post-war world.

GETTING HERE AND AROUND
Buses route past the sights, but infrequent schedules will rush you or leave you bored. It's an easy drive from the city though—every sight is on Route 331—and renting a car is highly advisable. Bus schedules change year to year; check the Okinawa Tourist Office for schedules if you don't want to rent.

WHAT TO SEE
Himeyuri Peace Museum ひめゆり平和祈念資料館. The most moving sight tells the story of 240 students from a girls' high school near Naha. Mobilized as field nurses in the war's final months, the girls' hellish experience tending to wounded Japanese soldiers in hidden caves near the city are retold in an intensely poignant series of dioramas, textual explanations, and displays. Photographs and journals at the recently renovated museum show the girls' innocence and hope before the war, providing a moving counterpoint to the artifacts and diaries that highlight the ghastly conditions they endured during the fighting. Portrait photos of each girl taken drive home the waste and finality of the war's tragic effects. The museum is very clear about its message, stating, "we must continue to tell our stories of a war filled with insanity and

The Battle of Okinawa

By late March 1945, American forces had increased their tactical position in the Pacific and began the assault on Okinawa, a pivotal stepping-stone to attacking the Japanese mainland. The initial bombardment was so fierce it disfigured the very topography of the island, a 90-day Typhoon of Steel that destroyed homes, farms, and infrastructure across the island. Japan's strategy was to drag out the conflict here for as long as possible by forcing a war of attrition. Every sector of Okinawa's civilian population was mobilized into the front lines of the fighting. Astronomical losses during the bombardment and in the awful land-war that followed were made worse after the military began falling back. Of those who did not succumb to starvation, disease, or despair-driven suicide, many fell victim to retreating Japanese troops. The final battle of WWII claimed roughly 240,000 lives—more than half of them civilian losses—over a third of Okinawa's population. The memorials commemorating these events and the memorials to peace left in their wake are an important part of Okinawa's cultural legacy.

13

brutality, now that the post-war generations, who have no idea what war is, have formed the majority of the population . . . threats to peace in both domestic and international politics cannot be ignored." It's 60 minutes from Naha via bus No. 32 or 89 (¥550), with a change in Itoman to bus No. 82 (¥270). Buses depart hourly and continue on to the Peace Memorial. ✉ *671–1 Aza-Ihara, Itoman, Okinawa* ☎*098/997-2100* ⊕*www.himeyuri.or.jp* ⊠¥300 ⊗*Daily 9–5.*

Okinawa Peace Memorial Museum 沖縄県立平和公園. Several monuments including a memorial flame and long walls inscribed with every name of the thousands of lives lost in the fighting dot the rolling, peaceful green hills around this excellent, sophisticated museum complex. Inside, several exhibits designed specifically for children provide a rare opportunity to focus on global issues education, while other areas explore and document the various facets of the momentous Battle of Okinawa. Interesting exhibits highlighting each side's tactical perspective and the progress of the fighting are offset by more personal displays of what life was like on the ground during the chaos and testimonies of survivors (unfortunately, only a few of these are translated). A diorama showing what life in American-occupied postwar Okinawa offers further insight into local history. It is 80 minutes from Naha via bus; change from 89 to 82 at Itoman Terminal. The total cost is ¥900. ✉ *614–1 Aza-Mibuni, Itoman City, Okinawa,* ☎*098/997-3844* ⊕*www.peace-museum.pref. okinawa.jp* ⊠¥300 ⊗*Daily 9–5.*

NORTH OF NAHA

WHAT TO SEE

Yachimun no Sato Potters Village やちむんの里. This enclave of potters studios, workshops, and giant kilns (and the occasional glass-blower's forge) meanders charmingly through a woodsy jumble of dirt lanes and old Ryūkyū houses. You can see artisans at work crafting bowls, dishes, and sculptures in any number of distinctive styles as you wander around the tiny village. Most studios are run by a master potter with a staff of in-house apprentices. Masters are generally locals, but workbenches and wheels are manned by people from all over the country who come to study, so the place has lots of creative energy and a diversity of skilled linguists. It's great for sightseeing or gift-shopping. Pieces here are made to be sold. Most studios have adjoining shops, and many offer shipping options. An hour north of Naha in Yomitan Village past Kadena base; turn left onto Route 12 from Route 58 and follow signs. ✉ *Yomitanson, Yachimun no Sato* ☎ *098/958–1020.*

✪ ★ **Churaumi Aquarium** 美ら海水族館. The most impressive aquarium in Japan with the biggest salt-water tank in the world is a wonderland for the eyes. A pioneering coral-breeding experiment has tons of information about the fragile tropical ecosystem, while tanks hold dangerous sharks, freaky deep-water species, and myriad other wondrous inhabitants of the sea. The star attraction is the 10-meter-deep tank big enough to give free play space for three majestic whale sharks, a dozen giant, graceful mantas, and schools of fish big and small from the nutrient-rich pacific. The first tank deep enough to allow the whale sharks to feed in their natural, vertical position, viewing them from below is a breathtaking experience. ■**TIP**➔**In addition to the Aquarium, Ocean Expo Park also houses a great Oceanic Culture Museum and Traditional Okinawa Village Arboretum.**

Take bus No. 20, 111, or 120 from Naha Terminal to Nago (¥1,740; 140 minutes), and change to the No. 65, 66, or 70 (¥790, 60 minutes). Driving is faster: take the expressway one hour to Nago and continue on Route 58, 449, or 114 another hour to Ocean Expo Park. ✉ *424 Ishikawa, Motobu-chō, Kunigami-gun* ☎ *0980/48–3748* ⊕ *www.kaiyouhaku.com* ✑ ¥*1,800* ◷ *Mar.–Sept., daily 8:30–7; Oct.–Feb., daily 8:30–5:30.*

Ryūkyū Mura 琉球村. A cultural park showcasing traditional Okinawa's roots, with reconstructed architecture, music lessons and foods, frequent variety performances, and a terrifying show featuring the poisonous Habu viper. It's most fun in the high season with lots of other visitors. ✉ *1130 Yamada, Onna Village* ☎ *098/965–1234* ⊕ *www.ryukyumura.co.jp* ✑ ¥*840* ◷ *Daily 9–5.*

Kongou Sekirinzan Boulder Park 金剛石林山. This great nature preserve lets you wander through the eerie land-before-time rock formations and gorgeous limestone spires of Japan's only tropical karst. Of the three trails, the longer "Strange and Big Rock Course" marked in yellow is nowhere near as challenging or time consuming as the park rangers make it out to be, and with its varied terrain more reminiscent of Papua New Guinea or Indonesia, the hour you'll spend trail-walking will be highly rewarding. It's all the way up Route 58 just before the road ends, about an hour from Nago. After leaving the karst continue 10 minutes to Hedo Misaki, Okinawa's northernmost tip, for more other-worldly cliffs and rock formations and a great scenic lookout before coming back down the coast. ✉ *973 Hedo, Kunigami Village*

☎0980/41–8111 ⊕*www.sekirinzan.com* 💷¥800 ⊘*Apr.–Sept., daily 9–5; Oct.–Mar., daily 9–4.*

OUTDOOR ACTIVITIES

Island Club Okinawa. Snorkeling is the perfect way to enjoy the water and see some of the wonderland waiting for you underneath the tropical waves. Tours by the Island Club are very English friendly and extremely reasonable (¥3,000–¥6,000 with options for sea kayaking) and timed to not eat up your entire day. ⊠*Onna-son 590–1, Yamada* ☎098/963–0177 ⊕*www.okinawa123.jp.*

Natural Blue Diving Company. Seeing the breathtaking whale-sharks feeding at the Churaumi Aquarium is one thing, but swimming with them is out of this world. Okinawa Hontō's best English-language oriented diving tour company is perfect for veterans and beginners alike. The bilingual diving instructor Yasu excels at providing a safe, exciting introduction to first-time divers, and his preferred locations—including a dazzling underwater cave, vibrant coral reefs and, yes, whale-shark feeding grounds (don't worry, they aren't dangerous)—are sure to wow even the most experienced diver. Competitively priced packages range from $80 to $140. Reservations essential, no credit cards. ⊠*1279–25 Yomitan-son 904-0304* ☎090/9497–7374 ⊕*www.natural-blue.net.*

WHERE TO STAY

$ ⌨ **Lue on the Beach** オン・ザ・ビーチ・ルー. The strip of noisy resorts on polluted beaches may have dashes your hopes for a quiet stay near the sand and surf, but this bungalow hideaway just south of the Churaumi Aquarium is the perfect antidote to bothersome big-business resorts. Rooms are spacious and most face the beach. The restaurant on the sandy deck is relaxing and intimate, and grill-it-yourself sets are especially fun for families or groups. The water is great for swimming and the beach is silent and dark at night, a wonderful break from the tourism-tainted beaches just south of here. This is a perfect spot to spend a night after circling the northern scenery on either side of a trip to the Aquarium. **Pros:** great location; isolated beach; good restaurant. **Cons:** slim menu; no double beds; spartan rooms. ⊠*2626 1 Motobu 905-0225* ☎0980/47–3535 ⊕*www.luenet.com* ⟿*12 rooms, 12 condos* ♿*In-room: refrigerator. In-hotel: restaurant, Internet* 🗖 *AE, DC, MC, V.*

KERAMA ISLANDS 慶良間諸島

35 km (22 mi) west of Naha by ferry.

The Kerama Islands have many pristine beaches, and divers rate the coral and clear water off their coasts highly. Three main islands are in the group: Tokashiki, Zamami, and Aka-jima, plus many more small uninhabited islets. You can experience the best of the Keramas in a day trip or two from Naha. Eating and drinking establishments are scattered over the three main islands, so you won't lack for sustenance.

GETTING HERE AND AROUND

From Naha's Tomari Port you can catch ferries to all three main islands. The Ferry Kerama reaches Tokashiki-jima in 70 minutes. The fare is ¥1,360, and there are generally two departures daily. Call **Tokashiki-son Renrakusho** to confirm schedules.

To get to Zamami-jima you have two choices: the high-speed *Queen Zamami* ferry reaches the island in 55 minutes, stopping at Aka-jima along the way. The fare is ¥2,750 per person, and there are two or three departures daily. The slower *Zamami-maru* ferry reaches the island in two hours, and makes one run daily, also via Aka-jima. The fare is ¥1,860. Call **Zamami-son Renrakusho** for schedules.

Once you're on one of the islands, you can rent bicycles or scooters from vendors at the piers. Bicycles rent for about ¥500 per hour, scooters ¥3,000 per day. Zamami-jima also has a car-rental agency, **Zamami Rent-a-Car,** extending from the jetty at the east end of the village. Prices range from ¥3,000 an hour to ¥8,000 a day. You can also walk to many places of interest.

At Zamami's harbor you can duck into the **tourist information office** in the cluster of buildings to the left of the ferry exit for information in English on boat tours, bike rentals, and diving outfitters. **Fathoms Diving,** run by an American expat, former U.S. Marine Richard Ruth, offers guided diving tours from Naha out to the Keramas.

ESSENTIALS

Car Rental Zamami Rent-a-Car (☎ *098/987–3250).*

Ferry Information Tokashiki-son Renrakusho (☎ *098/868–7541).* Zamami-son Renrakusho (☎ *098/868–4567).*

Visitor Information Tourist Information Office (✉ *Zamami-jima* ☎ *098/987–2277* ⏱ *Daily 8:30–5).*

Tour Information Fathoms Diving (☎ *090/8766–0868 mobile).*

TOKASHIKI-JIMA 渡嘉敷島

The largest of the Kerama Islands, and the closest one to Okinawa Hontō, Tokashiki-jima gets the most tourist traffic from Naha. Two lovely beaches with clean, white sand are on the west side: Tokashiki Beach, in the center of the coast, and Aharen Beach, toward the south.

ZAMAMI-JIMA 座間味島

SNORKELING

For great snorkeling, try **Furuzamami Beach** (a short walk south of the harbor and village. In summer there are snorkel rentals and showers. There's also a restaurant, and shuttle buses run to and from the pier and other beaches.

WHALE-WATCHING

On Zamami-jima, late January through March is prime whale-watching season, and during those months you can join two-hour boat tours for ¥5,000. From land, the north shore gives you the best chance of seeing whale tails and fin-slapping humpback antics—bring your best binoculars.

Weather permitting, the **Zamami Whale Watching Association** (☏098/987–2277) sends out boats from Zamami port daily at 10:30 AM.

13

AKA-JIMA 阿嘉島

Aka-jima doesn't get much traffic, but those who make it here won't say that's a bad thing!

Beautiful and quiet **Nishibama Beach**, near the northern tip of the island, offers good snorkeling and diving, with equipment rental locations. From the pier, walk over the hill to the east. The gently sloping beach west of the pier is also pretty and has places to eat and rent snorkel gear.

MIYAKO ISLANDS 宮古諸島

300 km (186 mi) southwest of Okinawa Hontō.

Some intensive beach therapy can be engaged in here. In the southwest corner of the main island, Miyako-jima, is Maehama, perhaps Japan's finest beach, and across the bridge on the adjacent tiny island of Kurima-jima lies the gorgeous, secluded beach Nagama-hama. Throughout the Miyako islands you can find bright white sand and emerald, turquoise, and cobalt waters. If you're traveling to Miyako-jima in July or August, or during a Japanese holiday, book your lodging ahead of time.

GETTING HERE AND AROUND

Japan TransOcean Air (JTA) and **ANK** fly from Naha (45 minutes, 11 flights daily) and Ishigaki-jima (another Okinawan island) to Miyako-shotō. From the airport to Hirara a taxi costs about ¥1,300.

Ferries from Naha reach Miyako-jima in 8¼ hours; a one-way ticket costs about ¥5,000. Some ferries go on to Ishigaki-jima, an additional five-hour, ¥2,700 trip. All trips are overnighters, and require at least two weeks' advance booking. From Hirara Port ferries make day trips to nearby Irabu-jima, Shimoji-jima, Tarama-jima, and Minna-jima. Tickets can be bought in the Hirara ferry terminal. Boats generally leave every half hour for the 10-minute trip to Irabu-jima (¥410). Boats to the other islands depart less often.

Buses on Miyako-jima depart from two terminals in Hirara and travel the coastal roads around the island. Buses to the north of the island and Ikema-jima (35 minutes from Hirara) depart from the Yachiyo bus station, a few blocks north of the central post office along Route 83. Buses heading south to Maehama (25 minutes from Hirara) and Cape Higashi-henna (50 minutes from Hirara) depart from the Miyako Kyōei terminal, about a kilometer east of the downtown post office on

McCrum-dōri. Buses run every couple of hours from morning to early evening.

Taxi use on Miyako-jima is convenient and reasonable. A taxi for the 10-km (6-mi) trip to Maehama Beach should cost ¥5,000 or less. **Miyako Taxi** has English-speaking drivers. For car rentals, reserving in advance is essential. **Nippon Rent-a-Car** will pick you up at the airport or ferry terminal. Rates average

> **CAUTION**
>
> Although following the coastal roads is straightforward enough, driving in the interior of Miyako-jima requires time and patience, and should not be attempted after dark. Signage is confusing, and the endless sugarcane fields look identical.

¥5,500–¥6,000 per day. Perhaps the best option for getting around the island is by scooter (¥3,000–¥4,000 per day) or motorbike (¥6,500 per day). Nippon Rent-a-Car also rents motorbikes, and you can arrange for one to be dropped at your hotel.

Whether you arrive by plane or ferry, stop in at the **Tourist Information Desk** in Hirara for help on travel, tour, and lodging arrangements.

ESSENTIALS

Airline Information ANK (☎0120/02-9222). JTA (☎0120/25-5971 ⊕www. japanair.com).

Car Rental Nippon Rent-a-Car (☎0980/72-0919, 0120/17-0919 toll-free).

Taxi Information Miyako Taxi (☎0980/72-4123).

Visitor Information Tourist Information Desk (⊠Hirara ☎0980/72-0899 airport, 098/073-1881 ferry ⊗Daily 9-5).

HIRARA 平良

On the main island of Miyako-jima, sprawling, unremarkable Hirara, population 48,000, doesn't have much to see but offers plenty of budget accommodations.

DIVING AND SNORKELING

The Goodfellas Club (☎0980/73-5483) on Route 390 just east of Route 192 in south Hirara offers diving trips in the waters around Miyako-jima. You can rent or buy snorkeling equipment at one of the many shops in Hirara or near the beaches.

BEACHES

Boraga Beach 保良泉ビーチ. Here, on the southern shore of the island, a swimming pool filled with water from a cold natural spring is next to some picturesque stretches of sand. Snorkel gear and kayak rental are arranged through the pool complex, which includes a refreshment stand.

Fodor'sChoice **Maehama Beach** 前浜ビーチ. Maehama, or as you may see on local signs, ★ Yonaha Maehama, is regarded by many as Japan's best beach, and it lives up to its reputation. White sand stretches for miles on a smooth, shallow shelf extending far into the warm, clear water. Eventually the sand gives way to forests and canyons of coral that provide shelter and

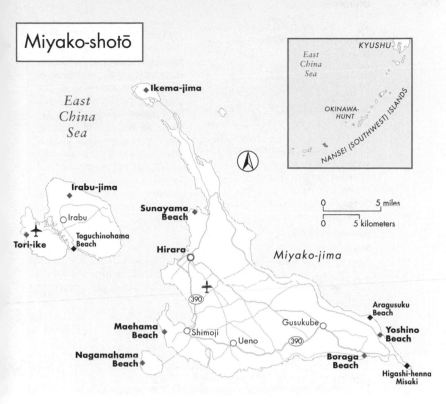

Miyako-shotō

East China Sea

Ikema-jima

KYUSHU

East China Sea

OKINAWA-HUNT

NANSEI (SOUTHWEST) ISLANDS

Irabu-jima

Sunayama Beach

Irabu

Toguchinohama Beach

Tori-ike

Hirara

Miyako-jima

0   5 miles
0   5 kilometers

390

Maehama Beach

Shimoji

Ueno

Gusukube

390

Aragusuku Beach

Yoshino Beach

Nagamahama Beach

Boraga Beach

Higashi-henna Misaki

playgrounds for beautiful, luminescent aquatic creatures. A tiny slice of Maehama can keep you entertained all day, but it actually stretches for 7 km (4.4 mi). At the Tokyu Resort are water-sports equipment rentals and a marina. The beach is 25 minutes from Hirara via bus.

Nagamahama Beach 長間浜ビーチ. A lovely and often deserted beach on the west side of tiny Kurima-jima, Nagamahama can be reached via the bridge just southeast of Maehama. This is a fantastic place to spend the day snorkeling and picnicking on the fine white sand.

Sunayama Beach 砂山ビーチ. This beach has an enormous sand dune (*suna-yama* means "sand mountain"), out of which juts a marvelously rugged natural stone arch. The snorkeling is as good as at Maehama, and the beach is only a few kilometers (15 minutes by bus) north of Hirara.

Higashi-henna Misaki 東平安名岬 *(Cape Higashi-henna)*. If you're in the southern corner of Miyako-jima and you have a couple of hours to spare, take a leisurely walk out to see Cape Higashi-henna's surreal landscape. A twisty, narrow road atop a spine of rock leads through a thatch of green grass out to a lonely, perfectly lovely lighthouse. The 2-km (1.2-mi) peninsula retains an impressive, end-of-the-earth feeling; and in spring the ground is covered with trumpet lilies. The transparent water is too shallow and the shore is too rocky for safe snorkeling, but the multicolor coral can be viewed from above. Allow about one hour to walk from the Bora bus stop at Boraga Beach. If you rent a scooter in Hiraga, you can ride to the end of the road next to the lighthouse. **Yoshino Beach** 吉野ビーチ. The water here is said to have the highest concentration of colorful fish in all of Miyako-shotō; needless to say, it's an awesome spot to snorkel. The beach is just north of Higashi-henna-misaki. Aragusuku Beach, just north of Yoshino Beach, is nearly identical.

Ikema-jima 池間島. Connected to the northwestern corner of Miyako-jima by a bridge, this small island, ringed by a scenic coastal road, has fine views above and below the sea. A distinctive rock formation shaped like a whale tail poised to slap the water lies offshore (and is prominent in postcards). The island is 35 minutes by bus from Hirara.

Irabu-jima 伊良部島. This small, rural island, only a 15-minute boat ride (¥410) from Hirara port, has two more gorgeous and secluded beaches: **Toguchi-no-hama** and **Sawada-no-hama**.

OF JETS AND CAVERNS

Tōri-ike 通り池. Travel even farther, across one of the several small bridges from Irabu-jima to Shimoji-jima, and proceed to its west side, beyond the oversize runway where All Nippon Airways sometimes trains its jumbo-jet pilots to take off and land the unbelievably noisy things, and you can check out Tori-ike, a deep, mysteriously dark cenote connected by underwater caverns to the sea. It's a justly celebrated spot for diving.

WHERE TO EAT

$
ASIAN
✗**Chūzan** 中山. This simple tavern serves inexpensive Okinawa favorites such as gōya champur; Korean-style *bibimbap,* a delicious, tangy, healthy dish of kimchi, bean sprouts, spinach, and other vegetables stirred into rice; and a plate of *katsuo* (bonito) sashimi big enough for two or three people. A couple of blocks east from the port, it's on the left side of McCrum-dōri before it meets Route 83. ⊠*McCrum-dōri, Hirara, Miyako-jima* ☎*0980/73–1959* ▭*No credit cards* ⊙*No lunch.*

¢–$
JAPANESE
★
✗**Gōya** 郷家. The wooden walls of this rustic establishment are full of alcoves holding treasures and knickknacks from dolls to farm implements to ancient jugs full of fresh awamori (rice liquor). Partially enclosed tatami-style rooms offer intimate dining and drinking experiences, while the beer hall–style area in front of the stage makes socializing easy. There's live music nightly, and cheap, filling, delicious food. Tasty gōya chips, rafute (bacon slow-cooked in a mix of awamori, soy sauce, brown sugar, and ginger root), and garlicky *gyoza* (fried meat dumplings) should be accompanied by large mugs of icy cold Orion beer. Gōya is 10 minutes from downtown Hirara by taxi. ⊠*570–2 Nishizato, Rte. 78 just past Rte. 390, Hirara, Miyako-jima* ☎*0980/74–2358* ▭*No credit cards* ⊙*Closed Wed. No lunch.*

WHERE TO STAY

$$$$
▭**Hotel Atoll Emerald** ホテルアトールエメラルド. Every room at this contemporary high-rise hotel next to the pier has ocean views. The Atoll Emerald is the nicest and most convenient hotel in downtown Hirara. The rooms are large, and each has a big picture window, and corner

deluxe rooms enjoy two of them. Suites are enormous, with L-shaped sectional sofas. **Pros:** friendly staff; nearly every room has a sea view; great access to town, beach and port. **Cons:** close to the city; no standard doubles. ✉*108–7 Shimozato, Hirara, Miyako-jima* 🕿*0980/73–9800* 🖷*098/073–0303* ⊕*www.atollemerald.jp* 📠*133 Western-style rooms, 4 Japanese-style rooms, 4 Western-style suites* ♿*In-hotel: 4 restaurants, bar, pool, laundry facilities* ▤*AE, D, MC, V.*

$–$$ 🖵**Miyako Central Hotel** ミヤコセントラルホテル. On Route 78, a few blocks from the pier, this tidy, narrow, eight-story hotel caters to the economically minded. You can get a spartan room or a spacious deluxe twin at an affordable price. It's within walking distance of downtown, near the bus depot, ferry port, dive outfits, and car-rental agencies. Several nightspots are also within walking distance. **Pros:** nice price; good location; clean rooms. **Cons:** rooms views lack scenery; cheaper rooms slightly bland. ✉*225 Nishizato, Hirara, Miyako-jima* 🕿*0980/73–2002* 🖷*0980/73–5884* ⊕*www.cosmos.ne.jp/~mcentral* 📠*62 rooms* ♿*In-hotel: restaurant* ▤*AE, V.*

$$$$ 🖵**Miyakojima Tōkyū Resort** 宮古島東急リゾート. One of Okinawa's finest
Fodor'sChoice   kept resorts regally situated on Japan's finest beach, the Miyakojima
★   Tōkyū Resort delivers everything you could want from a tropical vacation. Rooms are spacious and beautiful (newer ones are in the Coral Wing), and most have superb views over one of the most incredible beach scenes in the world. Significant discounts can be had by booking air-hotel packages through any major travel agency. **Pros:** clean, magnificent rooms; friendly staff. **Cons:** pricey; can fill up in the high season. ✉*914 Yonaha, Shimoji-chō, Miyako-jima,* 🕿*0980/76–2109* 🖷*0980/76–6781* ⊕*www.tokyuhotels.co.jp* 📠*205 Western-style rooms, 40 Japanese-style rooms, 3 Western-style suites* ♿*In-hotel: 5 restaurants, bar, tennis courts, pools, diving, water sports, bicycles, laundry service* ▤*AE, D, MC, V* 🍴*BP.*

NIGHTLIFE

Miyako-jima has a notoriously hard-drinking nightlife. A common boast is that Miyako-jima has more bars per person than in any other part of the country, which, given the Japanese fondness for drinking, likely means that Miyako-jima has one of the highest concentration of bars in the world. Countless nightspots adorn Hirara, especially in the blocks just east of the piers.

Bar Alchemist (✉*215–3 Shimozato, Hirara* 🕿*090/4582–4278*) is a good vibes bar with a piano, a telescope, and an endearing, eccentric owner. It's a couple of blocks south of the ferry terminal on the seafront road, upstairs above the A Dish restaurant. It's closed on Monday, but other nights you might find live music.

South Park (✉*638 Shimozato, Hirara* 🕿*0980/73–7980*) bills itself as an "American shot bar." Cocktails are only ¥700, and shots begin at ¥600. South Park is a bit of a hike east of the piers, near where Route 243 crosses Route 190. From the post office downtown, walk south five blocks then east for two blocks. It's closed Monday; the rest of the week it opens at 6 PM.

13

YAEYAMA-SHOTŌ 八重山諸島

430 km (267 mi) southwest of Okinawa Hontō.

This is Japan's final frontier. For a country so famous for its high-tech urban centers and overdeveloped, concreted natural vistas, Japan's furthest islands are a dramatic incongruity. The difference is like day and night, even between Ishigaki-jima, the most developed island, and Okinawa Hontō. Ishigaki sports a tiny, funky port city, a few beaches and very, very little else. The picturesque sandy lanes of its neighbor Taketomi-jima have more lion-shaped shiisa statues than actual people. You're unlikely to make it to Yonaguni-jima, Japan's farthest shore, to dive to the bizarre Atlantis-like ruins deep underwater or hack through its primordial wilderness, but the more easily accessible Iriomote-jima promises plenty of adventure: practically the entire island is protected national parkland, from the lush jungles and mangrove-lined rivers to the glittering, shimmering coral under the waves.

ISHIGAKI-JIMA 石垣島

1 hr by plane from Naha.

A day of beachside R&R and a night in Ishigaki City's fun bars and a cheap restaurants may be all it takes to make you want to move in. You wouldn't be alone: most of Ishigaki's people are either escapees seeking asylum from Japan's business-driven culture or descendants of islanders repatriating themselves into their forebears' country.

GETTING HERE AND AROUND

Both **JTA** and **ANK** airlines make the 55-minute flight from Naha to Ishigaki-jima. Late night arrivals may miss the last bus to the city, but a taxi-ride won't cost more than ¥1,000. From Ishigaki city, ferries connect to the surrounding islands. Only far-off Yonaguni requires another flight.

Ishigaki City is small and walkable; pick up a map at your hotel or the bus center across from the port, where you'll also find pamphlets on attractions and vital ferry and bus schedules. Getting around the island by car and motor-scooter is a snap—there's really no traffic and only a few roads—and rental places litter the town like sandal shops. Try **Ai-Ai** caddy-corner to the post office for bicycles, scooters and motorcycles.

ESSENTIALS

Airline Information ANK (☎ *0120/02–9222*). **JTA** (☎ *0120/25–5971* ⊕ *www.japanair.com*).

Bicycle Rental Ai-Ai (☎ *0980/83–9530*).

Car Rental Toyota (☎ *0980/82–0100*) and **Nippon Rent-a-Car** (☎ *0980/82–3629*). **Nissan Rent-a-Car** (☎ *0980/83–0024*).

WHAT TO SEE

Yonehara Beach 米原キャンプ場. The most idyllic beach on Ishigaki has great swimming and snorkeling off a hundred-meter long stretch of clean, sparkling sand. Beach access involves walking through the Yonehara Campground, but as there are rarely any tents up even in the high

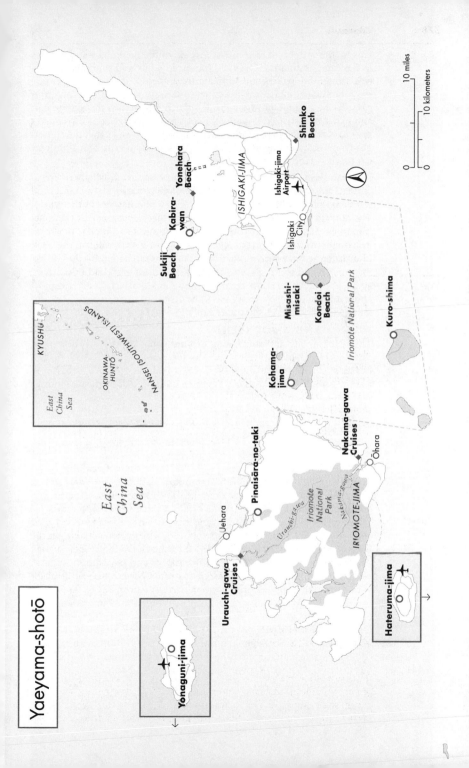

Yaeyama-shotō

East China Sea

KYUSHU

OKINAWA-HONTŌ

NANSEI (SOUTHWEST) ISLANDS

East China Sea

Yonaguni-jima

Jehara

Urauchi-gawa Cruises

Pinaisāra-no-taki

Urauchi-gawa

Iriomote National Park

IRIOMOTE-JIMA

Nakama-gawa

Nakama-gawa Cruises

Ōhara

Haterima-jima

Kohama-jima

Misashi-misaki

Kondoi Beach

Iriomote National Park

Kuro-shima

Sukiji Beach

Kabira-wan

Yonehara Beach

ISHIGAKI-JIMA

Shimko Beach

Ishigaki-jima Airport

Ishigaki City

10 miles

10 kilometers

season, the water will be more or less all yours. Behind a stand of trees in the campground the Orange House rents fins and snorkels; at low-tide the sea life will beautiful if alarmingly close up, and in high-tide the rainbow-colored coral and alien-looking sea life are amazing. You can use the Orange House's shower when you return the equipment, and plates of tasty Okinawan yaki-soba will recharge you. If you can't bear to leave, rent a tent and a barbeque set there and catch the sunset. Yonehara is about one hour from Ishigaki-shi by bus or a half-hour by car on the island's northern shore.

Taketomi Island 竹富島. The 10-minute ferry trip from Ishigaki City to quaint Taketomi's terra cotta–roofed Ryūkyū cottages, sleepy lanes, and empty bright beaches feels like a journey to another age of the world. The cute little town is easily navigable by bicycle; ask one of the touts standing at the pier when you show up. Another fun option is the "old-fashioned" tour—meander between the narrow rock walls in the back of a water buffalo–drawn cart and you'll be serenaded by the plonking sanshin and soaring voice of the cart's skilled grandfatherly driver; again, ask when you show up at the port. Kondoi Beach コンドイビーチ, about 15 minutes cycle away from the center of town, has good swimming with shower and changing facilities.

DIVING AND SNORKELING

The scuba-diving and snorkeling around Ishigaki-jima is superb; you can find plenty of outfitters, such as **Tom Sawyer** (☎0980/83–4677), based in downtown Ishigaki-shi. Trips include the coral reefs near Kabira-wan, Yonehara, and Cape Hirakubo. Lunch-inclusive outings cost around ¥12,000.

WHERE TO EAT AND STAY

$
JAPANESE
☾
★

✕**Buku Buku Cha-Ya Tea Shop** ぶくぶく茶屋. Two blocks up from Ishigaki's city's main intersection and set back into an inviting wooden storefront, Buku Buku Tea Shop would be famous just for its kitchen, were it not for the rare traditional tea that really steals the show. Great lunch and dinner sets usually begin from a standard base like the *don-buri*—a rice bowl with stir-fried meat or vegetables served on top—but dishes are tweaked and specialized with locally grown vegetables and innovative styles of rice preparation and rare strains of rice to bowl over your palette. Tea is delightful by itself, too, when you try making it the Ryūkyū way. A wooden bowl holds thick black tea made from baked rice grains, but this isn't what you drink: with a big bamboo whisk, you'll whip it into a thick cloud of foam to spoon onto the drink of your choice; sharing one drink among friends so everyone looks equally foolish with a splash of foam on his nose is highly encouraged, and the drinks are delicious. ✉ *238 Ōkawa, Ishigaki-shi* ☎*0980/87–8033* ☾ *Daily 11:30–midnight.*

$$
JAPANESE
Fodor'sChoice
★

✕**Usagi-Ya** うさぎや. Ishigaki's finest example of Okinawan izakaya cooking, where many small dishes add up to a sensational, weird meal—be sure to try something with delicious fu, a soft tofulike bean paste if the crunchy pig's ears are too much for you, and curry favor with the staff by washing it down with golden Orion beer (pronounced oh-ree-yon), Okinawa's proud local brew, or awamori, fierce island-made liquor distilled from rice. Food and drink here is terrific, but even better is the nightly floor show. From about 8 until the mood dies, staff armed with guitars and snakeskin sanshin banjos will go through every song in the archipelago's catalog, the moving traditional pieces balanced with rock-pop hits. Join in wherever the feeling hits you; Okinawan songs are built to involve boisterous shouting and clapping from the audience, so don't be shy! After the show, see how far you can get on one of the instruments. Just off of Ishigaki's main drag next to Shima-Soba. ✉ *Nakamura Heights 1F, 1-1 Ishigaki* ☎*0980/88–5014* ⊙ *Daily 5–late.*

13

$ Chisun Resort Ishigaki チサンリゾート石垣. A member of the up-scale Solaris resort group, the Chisun Ishigaki is pretty down to earth while being luxurious enough to let you really relax and enjoy your stay. Located at Ishigaki's one major intersection downtown within striking distance of everything. Rooms are plush and the staff are helpful and friendly. A great choice for maintaining a bit of luxury without going over the top. **Pros:** gorgeous wood flooring; excellent decoration sense; big beds. **Cons:** no doubles; only one suite. ✉*1 Tonoshiro907-0004* ☎*0980/82–6161* 📠*83* ⚲*In-room: refrigerator, safe, Internet. In-hotel: restaurant, Japanese bath, coin laundry* ▭*AE, DC, MC, V.*

¢–$ Hyper Hotel Ishigaki ハイパーホテル石垣. Big beds, fluffy duvets and a great location—it's a block east of the ferry dock—make Hyper Hotel a great choice despite the silly name and slightly grubby trimming. If you've come this far, you're probably not out for luxury anyway, and the prices are unbeatable for comfy-enough Western-style rooms. Families or groups will love the ¥1,000 rate for adding a third person in the room. **Pros:** price; location; basic amenities covered. **Cons:** showing some age; gruff staff. ✉*1–2–3 Yashima-chō, Ishigaki-shi* ☎*0980/82–2000* 📠*0980/82–3933* ⊕*www.hyper-ishigaki.co.jp* ⇆*94 rooms* ⚲*In-hotel: laundry facilities* ▭*MC, V* ▯*CP.*

IRIOMOTE-JIMA 西表島

31 km (19 mi) west of Ishigaki-jima, 50 min by ferry.

Surging brown rivers, dense green forests, and crystal blue seas are Iriomote's essential draws, and there's a surprising amount of helpful infrastructure in place to help you get the most fun out of it all. Skilled guides and tour companies make it easy and safe to explore the wilds of this pocket of primordial wilderness, and a few extremely nice lodging options let you enjoy some refined relaxation while you do. You'll want at least two nights—preferably three or four—to get the most out of Iriomote's varied environs, depending on what you want to try. It's all a blast. Returning even to two-horse Ishigaki after a few days jungle-trekking, sea-kayaking, sailing, snorkeling, scuba diving, or river cruising will feel like re-emerging into civilization.

GETTING HERE AND AROUND

Ferries from Ishigaki-jima connect to two ports on Iriomote, southeastern Ohara and northern Uehara, in just under an hour. You want to head for Uehara, but in heavy storm weather boats may not con-

CLOSE UP

Pottery

Walking through stalls of nearly identical terra-cotta shiisa statues in the Tsuboya district, you may think that Okinawa's pottery tradition is a newfangled tourist gimmick: don't be fooled. Stop into Kiyomasa Tōki for a look at 320 years of unbroken tradition. Kiyomasa Tōki was begun by a mandate from the old Shuri Emperor to a distant forbear of the kiln's current master, Takashi Kobashikawa, himself a government-designated Master of Traditional Crafts. "The pots shapes change generation to generation with the hands of the individual potters," says Takashi, but the freewheeling geometrics and whimsical fish pattern in a unique red-and-blue glaze were perfected generations ago and are lovingly celebrated in new pieces with every firing. Bearing left out of the Heiwa-dōri arcade, go 200 meters until a small incline leads you up to the red-and-black sign. Mugs and tankards are around ¥4,000, cup and saucer sets from around ¥5,000; larger bowls and platters scale from affordable to astronomical. Take home a keepsake and you'll be in good company: during the G8 summit Okinawa hosted in 2008, the dignitaries that dined at Shuri-Jō ate on plates made by Kiyomasa Tōki and each received one as a gift from the city. Wrapping and shipping service available.

tinue past Ohara. There are between 9 and 12 departures daily each way for ¥2,300.

The long road ringing Iriomote's northern half terminates in the west at Shirohara and the east in Funaura, and although infrequent buses connect them, all tour companies will take care of transporting you to and from your hotel or port of call at the time of your excursion. Rental scooters and cars are available, but there aren't really a lot of places to go; rely on your tour guides to get you around, and center your meals around your lodging. The post-office ATM may be working, but its in your best interest to bring enough cash for your entire stay.

HIKING

Simamariasibi. Trekking tours through Iriomote's *Predator*-like jungle is fun and exotic, especially with a tour guide so thoroughly knowledgeable about the island's trails and conscientious about his customer's safety and enjoyment. Nagasawa-san moved to Iriomote from Tōkyō more than a decade ago with a background in ecology and environmental engineering. He learned the ins and outs of Iriomote's riddled interior by going boar-hunting with local men during the winter off-seasons, and focuses his tours away from the regular, frequented tour spots to really let you feel immersed in nature. Along the way he'll point out a surprising amount of information about the jungle and reveal some very special overlooks and locations. Nagasawa-san offers a variety of trekking packages to suit every level of conditioning and interest amongst customers, ranging from ¥8,000 up and including lunch and transportation, all detailed on his Web site. ⊠ *972 Taketomi-chō, Iriomote* ☎ *0980/84–8408* ⊕ *www.simamariasibi.com/.*

DIVING

Waterman Tours. If burly diving instructor Tokoku-san's beach-bum appearance doesn't immediately inspire confidence, his experienced, skilled instructional manner will win you over in no time. Twenty years teaching diving courses in the U.S., Mexico, New Caledonia, and here on Iriomote give him a sensitivity to people's different learning styles when approaching diving for the first time. His guidance will put you at ease, and his courses through reefs and rocks will thrill you. ⊠ *538-1 Uehara, Iriomote,* ☎*0980/85–6005* ✆*from ¥12,000.*

Good Outdoor. The best English language skills of all the dive shops on Iriomote, along with a great and very experienced staff make Good Outdoor a terrific choice for first timers. ☎*0980/84-8116* ⊕*www9. plala.or.jp/g-o-d* ✆*From ¥12,000.*

KAYAKING

Mansaku Tour Service. Sea kayaking is a terrific way to experience some of the best of what Iriomote has to offer. Tours set off where the road ends at Shirahama; from there it's into the waves. After navigating some shore points and smaller straights and islets, you'll weave in and out of the mangrove rivers and waterfalls dotting the coast. You won't really hit the open ocean, but the scenery is wonderful and it's tiring enough if you are not accustomed to it. Your guide Mansaku-san is decently conversant in English and skilled at creating a fun atmosphere during the trip. If the weather is good you can snorkel off the kayaks into the crystal-clear bay. Longer camping tours and lure-fishing are available as well. ⊠*10-75 Uehara #201, Taketomi* ☎*0980/85–6222* ⊕*www. cosmos.ne.jp/mansaku/* ✆*Sea-kayak and snorkeling from ¥10,500 for a full-day tour.*

BOAT TOURS

Urauchi-gawa Cruises. If you go with your guide at Shimamariashibi, take one of the boat tours up Iriomote's Amazon. The river is the sole reason many day-trippers come to the island, with boats navigating excitingly up the broad, coffee-colored water through mangroves and ferns to an impressive waterfall, all for ¥1,500. Allow three hours for the round-trip. Kayak rentals can also be negotiated from the boat operators if you want to go it yourself. The first boats depart at 9 AM and the last depart at 4 PM. Since this is the most popular activity for visitors to Iriomote-jima, you'll find plenty of boats as well as frequent buses to Urauchibashi, the mouth of the river, if you arrive at Uehara port in the early part of the day.

WHERE TO STAY

$$ 🏨**Hotel Irifune** ホテル入船. This hotel in the main village of Sonai, on Yonaguni's north coast, is nothing to rave about, but the management offers guided dive expeditions, and at ¥14,000 for two in a Western-style room with private bath, including meals, the price is right. Also, there are a few Japanese-style rooms with shared bath, and these run ¥12,000 for two. **Pros:** knowledgeable staff; clean rooms; diving instructors on site. **Cons:** can be empty in the off-season ⊠ *59-6 Aza Yonaguni, Sonai* ☎*0980/87–2311* ✆*8 Western-style rooms, 3 Japanese-style rooms without bath* ⊟*No credit cards* ⊙*MAP.*

13

$ ⚇ **Nilaina Resort and Yacht Holiday** ニライナリゾート. The most modern
★   and high-class building on the island is also the most traditional, with
ancient joinery techniques connecting lintels and posts along the expansive decks of this hilltop resort. But you'll probably be thinking more
about the view standing upon it. Whether it's the rolling pastures, the
mountains framing them or the sea stretching to infinity, Nilaina has a
perfect location to take advantage of it all. Rooms could be more spacious, and there are only four of them, but they're wooden and smartly
built, with excellent details like fancy full baths and subtle lighting
touches. Snorkling and kayaking tours are possible, and diving and
sailing tours can be arranged on Nilaina's private boat. **Pros:** diverse
customer base; friendly staff; new facilities. **Cons:** pricey; no doubles.
✉*10–425 Uehaea* ☎*9080/85–6400* ⊕*www.nilaina.com* ⤺*4 rooms*
&*In-room: full bath. In-hotel: restaurant, bar* ▭ *AE, DC, MC, V.*

$ ⚇ **Pension Hoshinosuna** ペンション星の砂. The price could be double for
what the hotel offers: bright rooms mostly facing the ocean, excellent breakfast and dinner in the dining room, and a facade backing
onto a clean beach with good swimming and gorgeous sunset views.
Close to Uehara port, with diving, snorkeling and sailing plans. **Pros:**
great access; diverse clientele; good value. **Cons:** rooms aren't plush;
no doubles. ✉*289–1 Uehara* ☎*0980/85–6448* ⊕*www.hoshinosuna.
ne.jp* ⤺*11 rooms* & *In-room: safe, refrigerator. In-hotel: restaurant*
▭ *AE, DC, MC, V.*

Tōhoku

WORD OF MOUTH

"We loved Kakunodate and Lake Tazawa. They are both at altitude so would be a little cooler in July. Lots of people also do the Sendai to Matsushima area. Aomori and the Oriase stream is nice, and along with Lake Towadako is cooler in the mountains with a lot of ryokan in the area. Lots of area to explore in Northern Tōhoku."

—hawaiiantraveler

Updated by
John Malloy
Quinn

Tōhoku translates as "east-north," and a visit can do more than shift your physical coordinates. Though the Shinkansen has made getting up here easier, it is still a world away from the crowded south. In Tōhoku, the mountain villages are more remote, the forests more untamed, and the people more reserved—but don't be fooled, they are quite friendly if you show them you appreciate the pace, look, and feel of things.

Wild as the northeastern territory can be, Sendai sets things in balance, right on the doorstep of the great wilderness. This attractive modern city of a million, with wide, shady boulevards, covered walkways, and shopping complexes, puts on perhaps the country's biggest festival, Tanabata, every summer in early August, in honor of an ancient legend of star-crossed lovers. It attracts more than 3 million people, and it caters to them surprisingly well.

Beyond Sendai you won't find another city as large or lively until you hit Sapporo in Hokkaidō, and the countryside looms all around. In comfort and convenience, you can ride the Akita Shinkansen to places like Lake Tazawa, Japan's deepest lake—a powder-blue reflection of sky that sits nestled in a caldera surrounded by virgin stands of beech trees draped in sweet-smelling vines, and steep hills studded with blue-green pines preside over all. Samurai history lives on virtually everywhere in the region, but especially in the well-preserved dwellings and warehouses that now play host to curious tourists in Kakunodate, a town also famous for its hundreds of lovely, ancient *shidare-zakura,* or danglingbranch cherry trees.

Tōhoku cherishes its forever-frontier status, and has plenty of low-key cities and timeless small towns full of folks who work hard in the cool summers and somehow bide their time through the fierce winters. Many ski areas collect neck-high powder snow, making for great skiing and snowboarding. There are also broad, bountiful plains that stretch between mountains and ocean, and they yield a bounty of treats, from the sweetest apples and tastiest tomatoes to the perfect rice and purest water that go into some of the best dry, crisp, or karakuchi, sake in the land. As a bonus, you're sure never to be far from an *onsen,* or hot spring—there seems to be one in each and every municipality!

⇨ *See the glossary at the end of this book for definitions of the common Japanese words and suffixes used in this chapter.*

TOP REASONS TO GO

Lakes: Japan's two deepest lakes, Tazawa-ko and Towada-ko, are sky-blue and never freeze. Towada-ko has some trout, but Tazawa-ko's water is too acidic for a large fish population.

Coastal Beauty: Matsu-shima Bay's 250 islands near Sendai are beautiful, but the coast is postcard-pretty virtually anywhere, especially the mountains from Akita City to Atsumi Onsen.

Seafood and Vegetables: The freshest seafood you'll ever eat is presented in many ways, all of them tasty. *Sansai* (wild mountain vegetables) are a specialty of the region.

Country Life: Tōhoku claims some of the cleanest water in the country, which helps produce high-quality rice, noodles, apples, cherries, tomatoes, and beef and dairy cattle.

Mountain Adventures: The many fine mountain playgrounds are made all the more appealing by the relative absence of people using them.

14

ORIENTATION AND PLANNING

ORIENTATION

Tōhoku, like the rest of Honshū, is riven by a series of dramatic chains of densely forested mountains. Not only their rugged beauty will take your breath away, they can make travel difficult. If you allow for this, you won't be overly frustrated. Tōhoku is comprised of six prefectures, and stretches from the more developed and increasingly urbanized corridor of Fukushima, just a short train ride from Tōkyō, to the remote and rugged Aomori, the northernmost tip of Honshū, within easy striking distance of Hokkaidō. This broad swath of territory encompasses mountain ranges, primitive forests, stunning seacoasts, well-preserved feudal villages, sacred glaciated peaks and secluded temples, relaxing hot springs, and bottomless lakes in the craters of volcanoes.

Sendai. Sendai has made itself into a fun-loving, livable, navigable, stylish haven of great shopping, friendly people, and fine eateries. Every year Sendai hosts the immense and colorful Tanabata Matsuri, a four-night, three-day festival that swells the town to three times its normal size.

Northern Tōhoku. By branching out from the Shinkansen hub of Morioka, you'll come across traditional iron-ware teakettles, grand old castles, lovingly preserved samurai houses, sparkling lakes, and huge national parks with mountains to climb, hiking trails for all abilities, large virgin forests, and hot springs galore.

West Coast Tōhoku. Mountains give way to fertile plains that extend to the Sea of Japan. While you will find an occasional castle, everywhere you explore, you'll encounter the best food, local women nationally celebrated for their legendary fairness, mountains often buried in powder snow, and countless onsen.

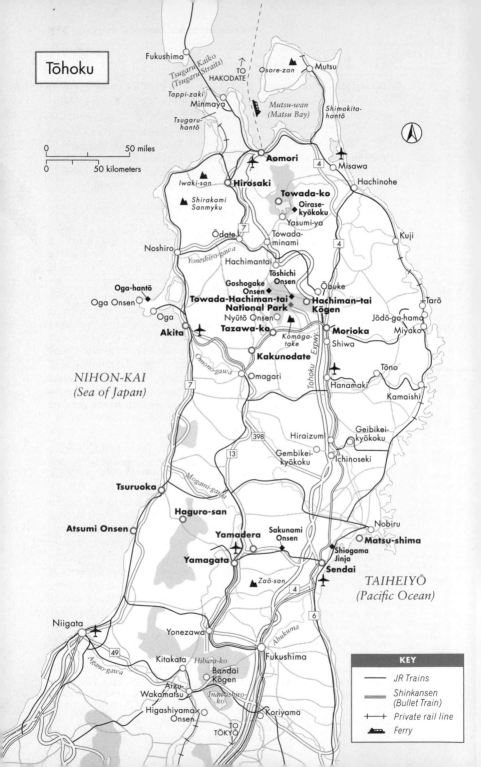

PLANNING

To enjoy Tōhoku to the fullest, travel lightly, tack on a day or two for the unexpected, and bring something for cooler and wetter turns in the weather. You won't find many speakers of English or other Western languages, so it pays to drop into the tourist information offices (located within nearly every major train station) as soon as you arrive. Usually, someone will speak English, and you'll save yourself a lot of frustration later. One of the best features of the region is the incredible friendliness of those who live here, and even if they can't say much in reply, they will be eager to help.

WHEN TO GO

In the north and west, where winters are most severe, transportation slows down significantly, even grinding to a halt during prolonged sieges of snowfall. Along the Pacific and around Sendai, however, things are decidedly milder. Fall colors in the region are fantastic, and spring brings spectacular blossoms of cherry and other fruit trees. Summer is cooler with less humidity and rainfall than in most of Japan.

It would be a hectic rush, but festival freaks could conceivably see all of Tōhoku's big summer festivals in a single whirlwind visit, starting with Hirosaki's Neputa Matsuri (August 1–7), Aomori's Nebuta Matsuri (August 3–7), Akita's Kantō Matsuri (August 5–7), Yamagata's Hana-gasa Festival (August 5–7, and the granddaddy of them all, Sendai's Tanabata Matsuri (August 6–8). Things do get fully booked well ahead, so secure arrangements as soon as plans allow. Don't be caught unaware—this includes train tickets, especially for reserved seats on Shinkansen, which usually are sold out up to a month before the date of travel.

GETTING HERE AND AROUND

Most of the island's trains and buses ply north–south routes on either side of the mountains. Though trains are a viable means of getting around up here, in some cases a bus will save time. The most important travel routes fan out from Sendai and Morioka in the east, and from Akita City and Tsuruoka on the Japan Sea coast in the west. Routes are often highly scenic, but there are also many tunnels and occasional boring stretches where the road or track cuts away from the coast or into a steep ravine. A journey in Tōhoku is all about life at a different pace, so expect those out-of-the-way places to be hard to reach. In winter, prepare for frequent delays or closings due to heavy snows or high winds.

BUS TRAVEL

Buses take over where trains do not run, and in most instances they depart from JR train stations. From Morioka to Hirosaki, highway buses (JR Buses accept Rail Passes) are more convenient (and twice as fast) for getting to Akita than trains. From Tsuruoka to Yamagata, it's the same story (but it's a private bus line, not JR, and one of the terminals is in a modern shopping mall). Most buses pick you up or leave you near the station. Note: Overhead space is so severely limited that nothing bigger than a briefcase or handbag will fit. Fortunately, it is perfectly safe to store your bigger bags below.

14

CAR TRAVEL

Driving in Tōhoku may be a good way for getting to the remote spots but presents much of the same problems as driving in other parts of Japan, and then some: absence of proper signage (especially in English), inclement weather, following tour buses on narrow, winding roads, and getting nearly run off the highways by big trucks driven by daredevils. Furthermore, gas, tolls, and car rentals make driving expensive, and it's also considerably slower to drive than ride on the Shinkansen. The approximate driving times from Tōkyō (assuming you can clear the metropolitan area in two hours) are 5 hours to Fukushima, 6 hours to Sendai, 8–10 hours to Morioka, and 10–11 hours to Aomori.

All major towns have car-rental agencies. Hertz is the one most frequently represented. Other car-rental companies are usually limited to Toyota or Nissan Rent-A-Car. These outfits usually have offices near major train stations, and even smaller ones. All you need is a valid International Driver's License (available from AAA in the U.S.) and your home state or country's license. ■TIP→Note that maps are not provided by car-rental agencies; be sure to obtain bilingual maps in Tōkyō or Sendai.

TRAIN TRAVEL

The most efficient way to get to Tōhoku from Tōkyō is on the Tōhoku Shinkansen trains, all of which the JR Pass covers. The Hayate, which makes the fewest stops, and the slower Yamabiko Shinkansen run to Sendai, Morioka, and Hachinohe; the Tsubasa runs to Yamagata; and the Komachi goes to Akita. North of Hachinohe, conventional trains continue on to Aomori (an additional 70 minutes). Shinkansen lines don't go farther north than the west-coast city of Akita, and Hachinohe, on the northeast coast. From Yamagata City train and bus routes extend to Tsuruoka and beyond.

Elsewhere in Tōhoku, JR local trains are slower and less frequent (every two hours rather than every hour during the day) when they cross the region's mountainous spine. Most railways are owned by Japan Railways, and many buses are, too, so a JR Rail Pass will be a worthwhile purchase. Be aware that most trains stop running before midnight. Overhead racks are adequate for small packs, but you should stow larger items in spaces at the ends of cars. In Japan no one is ever likely to touch your bags, even if left unattended.

DISCOUNTS AND DEALS

Northern Tōhoku (Aomori, Iwate, and Akita prefectures) has an excellent way for foreigners staying in Japan one year or less to see the sights of the prefecture: the Northern Tōhoku Welcome Card gets you discounts on public buses (50%), at hotels (10%), and at museums (discount varies). The card is available upon presentation of your passport after filling out a short application form. Inquire at the JNTO office in Tōkyō, the information office at Aomori Airport, JR Aomori Station, or Hrosaki Station. The list of facilities offering the discount is limited, and they have blackout periods for high seasons. For complete information in English, visit the Northern Tōhoku Welcome Card Web site.

RESTAURANTS

Tōhoku's a great place for fresh food, whether from the fields, mountains, forests, or seas. Restaurants range from local sake shacks to upscale sushi bars and steak houses, and dress may be street-casual to office attire, but rarely will it be formal. Menus may not always be in English, but nearly every shop will have its window displays full of plastic representations of the menu. Remember this before you take off your shoes and wiggle your knees across the tatami mats to wedge them under that low table-top. In the cities credit cards work well enough, but out in the countryside few if any places will accept them.

HOTELS

Hotels in Tōhoku run the gamut from minuscule to behemoth, and often reflect local character. No matter the size or place, reserve in advance for the busy summer season. Many hotels in the larger cities have the standard amenities, and, as is common in Japan, provide free toothbrushes, hair articles, robes, slippers, plentiful towels, hair dryers, and more. Most larger Western-type lodgings offer a choice of Japanese or Western breakfast (and sometimes room style, as well), and though it is not always included in the rates, breakfast is seldom more than ¥1,500 per person, or ¥1,800 ¥2,000 for buffet. Casual clothes are usually fine, but as in most Asian countries, short pants on men are not nearly as widely seen as in the West.

14

WHAT IT COSTS IN YEN					
	¢	$	$$	$$$	$$$$
RESTAURANTS	under ¥800	¥800–¥1,000	¥1,000–¥2,000	¥2,000–¥3,000	over ¥3,000
HOTELS	under ¥8,000	¥8,000–¥12,000	¥12,000–¥18,000	¥18,000–¥22,000	over ¥22,000

Restaurant prices are per person for a main course, set meal, or equivalent combinations of smaller dishes. Hotel prices are for a double room with private bath, excluding service and 5% tax.

VISITOR INFORMATION

Individual towns have offices that provide local information. The largest and most helpful tourist centers, which provide information on all of Tōhoku, are at the Sendai and Morioka stations. In Tōkyō each prefecture has an information center with English brochures and maps. In summer the local Japan Travel Bureau at the train station in each major tourist area, or at major hotels, can make arrangements for scenic bus tours. The offices in Tōkyō, Kyōto, and Sendai arrange tours, some in English.

ESSENTIALS

Airline Contacts All Nippon Airways (☎ *0120/029–222*). **Japan Airlines** (☎ *0120/ 25-5971*).

Discounts Northern Tōhoku Welcome Card (⊕ *www.northern-tohoku.gr.jp/ welcome*).

Emergency Contacts Ambulance (☎ *119*). **Police** (☎ *110*).

On the Menu

Visitors seeking culinary excellence and diversity will not be disappointed in Tōhoku. Restaurants in the region serve the freshest assortment of seafood, in sushi, sashimi, grilled, broiled, and boiled versions, as well as a bounty of seaweed and generous offerings of wild mountain vegetables (*sansai*) and mushrooms (*kinoko*) in season. *Hinaijidori*, or special local chicken, is a year-round treat and so is the marbled, exquisitely tender beef known as Yonezawa-gyū—very expensive, but well worth it!

In Sendai, don't be afraid to try the local delicacy—grilled or braised beef tongue, *gyū-tan*, which tastes like a juicy and less chewy version of well-seasoned beef jerky. In Morioka, try the *reimen*, or cold, chewy ramen-type

egg noodles served in a big bowl with a slice of beef, a helping of kimchi, half a boiled egg, slices of cucumber, and a large wedge of watermelon. In Akita they are fond of *inaniwa* udon noodles that are flatter, whiter, and tenderer than the usual. In Kakunodate they mix sakura, or cherry blossoms, into the flour, and the result is mildly sweet noodles, as edible as they are pink! Don't miss the truly unique *kiritampo*, or hot pot made with chicken, local vegetables, and distinctive tubular rice cakes that have been formed and cooked onto sticks of bamboo or cedar. Yamagata has its distinctive rounded, chewy soba and incomparable beef. The local sake is uniformly excellent throughout the region, thanks to the quality rice and water.

Rental Agency Hertz Domestic Reservation Center (☎ *0120/48–9882 toll-free in Japan* ⊕ *www.hertz.com*).

Visitor Information Japan Travel Bureau (☎ *022/221–4422*). **JNTO Tourist Information Center in Tōkyo** (*TIC* ✉ *Tōkyō Kotsu Kaikan, 2–10–1 Yurakucho, Chiyoda-ku* ☎ *03/3201–3331* Ⓜ *Yūraku-chō Line, Yūraku-chō station [Exit A-4B]*). **Prefecture Information Offices in Tōkyō** (☎ *03/3211–1775 for Akita* ☎ *03/5276–1788 for Aomori* ☎ *03/3524–8282 for Iwate* ☎ *03/3504–8713 for Yamagata*).

SENDAI 仙台

352 km (219 mi) north of Tōkyō.

Sendai is Tōhoku's largest city, and its one million residents enjoy its big-city feel. Meanwhile, they can relax in knowing it's as safe and easy-going as a small town. Devastated by World War II, Sendai has since become a thoroughly modern and well-planned city, with wide boulevards and a surprising amount and variety of greenery. It's the economic and educational capital of the region, hosting a broad range of industries and universities. In recent decades the city has become a magnet for international students, teachers, and workers, and this has helped foster Sendai's energetic and affable atmosphere.

The city's origins can largely be traced to the story of the "one-eyed dragon," local warlord Date Masamune (1567–1636). Affectionately nicknamed for both his one working eye (he was blinded in the other during a childhood bout with smallpox) and his valor in battle, Masamune established a dynasty in Sendai that maintained its position as one of the three most powerful *daimyō* (feudal lord) families during the shōgun period. In later life, his talents expanded: he engineered a canal linking two rivers, improving the transport of rice; and in an effort to further trade with Europe, he dispatched an emissary to Rome and The Vatican.

EXPLORING SENDAI

A convenient entry point for striking out into the region, Sendai has its noteworthy sights and is a fun place to spend a day or two poking around, shopping, and enjoying good restaurants. Walkers and people-watchers will love Sendai; it seems as if the whole city is within a quick stroll. Thousands of shops, bars, restaurants, and cafés line glittering arcades that stretch in all directions. Spiffy hotels and glitzy department stores are well located. Not far from the station, and slicing cleanly through the downtown entertainment area, are three broad avenues: Aoba-dōri, Hirose dōri, and Jōzen-ji-dori. There's also Chūō-dōri shopping street, and all of these conveniently intersect and are linked by the wide shopping arcade of Ichiban-chō.

GETTING HERE AND AROUND
Sendai Airport is well-connected, with numerous daily flights to and from every major airport in Japan, and destinations in Asia and the Pacific as well.

The **Tōhoku Kyūkō Express night bus** (☎*03/3529–0321 in Tōkyō, 022/ 262–7031 in Sendai*) from Tōkyō to Sendai is inexpensive (¥6,210) and takes approximately six hours. Five departures leave Tōkyō Station (Yaesu-guchi side) between 11 PM and midnight. The bus from Sendai departs from the train station at 11 PM and arrives in Tōkyō at 5 AM. Reservations are required for all buses.

From Tōkyō, the *Hayate* Shinkansen rockets to Sendai in just 1 hour 40 minutes, for ¥10,790. To use city buses, consult the bus and subway information office, near the subway station in front of the JR station. Here you can pick up English-language brochures with bus departure points, stops, and fares for the major sights. Sendai Loople, a limited-access bus, stops at Zuihō-den (20 minutes from the station) and Aoba Castle (30 minutes) and returns to the station in about an hour. A full-day pass costs ¥600, and single stops are ¥250; buses depart from the west exit of JR Sendai Station (Platform 15-3) every half hour from 9 to 4. At present, the Sendai subway runs roughly north–south only, and its stations are far from the most interesting sights. It's really only of use to resident commuters.

The **Sendai City Tourist Information Center** (☎*022/222–4069* ◷*Daily 8:30–8*) on the second floor of Sendai JR Station has English-speakers who will gladly recommend hotels and restaurants. They also provide essential maps with walking and bus routes, as well as an Internet facility with coin-operated, multilingual terminals (17 languages; 15 minutes for ¥100). **Sendai International Center** (☎*022/265–2450 hotline,*

14

CLOSE UP

Tanabata Matsuri (Tanabata Festival)

Tōhoku's Tanabata festival, one of the largest in Japan, is held every year from August 6 to 8 (heralded by massive fireworks over the river the night of the 5th), when Sendai's population triples. The festival is believed to have evolved from a Chinese legend of a weaver girl (the star Vega in her afterlife) and her cowherd boyfriend (the star Altair, in his). As lovers tend to do, they slowly went mad, and began to spend their time idly, living as if in a dream. The jealous ruler became irate and banished them to the far sides of his kingdom (the Milky Way). But he relented, perhaps remembering some foolish love affair of his own, and allowed them to meet on one day a year: the seventh day of the seventh month.

Why the people here celebrate this quintessentially cosmic love story on the sixth day of the eighth month is probably more closely linked with a need to give restive subjects time off to party in a time of great heat. Whatever the background, the festival creates a great reservoir of energy. Colorful streamers flutter from every perch in town. To walk along the arcades with the endless streamers brushing down against your face, neck, and shoulders—as you bump against and smile back at other enraptured souls also seduced by the whole grand pageant—is to feel glad to be alive and in Sendai at such a wonderful time.

From 5 PM the evening of the 6th, parades, dances, events, and demonstrations of festival spirit are held nightly through the 8th, along a short stretch of Jōzen-ji-dōri between Kotodai Park and Bansui-dōri. The tourist information office in Sendai Station can help with more details, also contained in countless pamphlets.

022/265-2471 *general assistance*) is across the street from the Sendai Municipal Museum. The office operates an English-language hotline to deal with questions about the city and prefecture.

ESSENTIALS

Bus Contacts Tōhoku Kyūkō Express (☎ *03/3529-0321 in Tōkyō, 022/262-7031 in Sendai*).

Currency Exchange Sendai Chūo Post Office (✉ *1-7 Kitamemachi, Aoba-ku, Sendai* ☎ *022/223-8241*).

Emergency Contacts Sendai City Hospital (✉ *3-1 Shimizukōji, Wakabayashi-ku, Sendai, Miyagi-ken* ☎ *022/266-7111*).

Visitor Information Sendai City Tourist Information Center (☎ *022/222-4069* ⊙ *Daily 8:30-8*). **Sendai International Center** (☎ *022/265-2450 hotline, 022/265-2471 general assistance*).

WHAT TO SEE

Views of the city and ruined stone walls await those who hike or take a bus up Aoba-yama to **Aoba Castle** 青葉城 *(Aoba-jō)*. A restored guardhouse and ruins are all that remain today. The Date dynasty kept its residence here for nearly three centuries after beginning construction of the once grand castle around 1600. Sadly, it was all pulled down during the Meiji Restoration. **Gokoku Jinja** (Gokoku Shrine) is now the main feature of the area. Near the observation terrace is a statue of the city's founder and favorite ruler, Masamune Date, mounted on a horse. In clear weather the Pacific Ocean can be seen far off to the right. Take a bus from Stop No. 9 in front of JR Sendai Station, or ride the Sendai Loople tourist bus (daily pass ¥600, one ride ¥250) to get here. You'll want the Sendai-joshi stop. ✉ *1 Kawauchi, Aoba-ku, Sendai* ☎ *022/214–8259* ✆ *Free* ☉ *Daily dawn–dusk.*

The **Sendai City Museum** 仙台市博物館 *(Sendai-shi Hakubutsukan)*, at the foot of the hill beneath Aoba Castle, displays cultural artifacts, including pottery, paintings, and armor relating to the history of the Date family and the city, and hosts special exhibitions. ✉ *26 Kawauchi, Aoba-ku, Sendai* ☎ *022/225–3074* ✆ *¥400* ☉ *Tues.–Sun. 9–4:45, last entry at 4:15; closed the day following national holidays.*

Not your ordinary cold gray slab of stone memorial, **Zuihō-den** 瑞鳳殿, the grand mausoleum of Masamune Date, the most revered ruler of ancient Sendai, was made in the showy style of the Momoyama period (16th century), where figures of people, birds, and flowers are carved and inlaid in natural colors. Looking like the world's fanciest one-story pagoda, there is so much gold leaf that in the right light it practically glows. Having burned during the firebombing in 1945, Zuihō-den was reconstructed in a five-year period beginning in 1974. During the excavation, Masamune Date's well-preserved remains were found and have been re-interred in what appears to be a perfect replica of the original hall. To get here, take Bus 11 from JR Sendai Station to the Otamaya-bashi stop (20 minutes), or take the Loople Bus (¥250) to the Zuihō-den stop. The mausoleum is a short walk up the hill. From Aoba Castle it's a 30-minute walk down Aoba-yama and across the Hirose-gawa (Hirose River). ✉ *23-2 Otamayashita, Aoba-ku, Sendai* ☎ *022/262–6250* ✆ *¥550* ☉ *Feb.–Nov., daily 9–4:30; Dec. and Jan., daily 9–4.*

Ōsaki Hachiman-gu 大崎八幡宮 was one of the few structures World War II left standing in Sendai. Built in Yonezawa in 1527, the shrine pleased Masamune Date so much that he had it brought to Sendai in 1607. Nestled among trees, it is an elegant structure, with bright-metal ornamentation over subdued black lacquer. The main building has been designated a National Treasure. It's in the northwest section of the city, about 10 minutes from downtown (or Aoba-yama) by taxi and 15 minutes from the Zuihō-den area. You can also take the 30-minute ride on Bus 15 from JR Sendai Station for ¥220. ✉ *4–6–1 Hachiman, Aoba-ku, Sendai* ☎ *022/234–3606* ✆ *Free* ☉ *Daily dawn–dusk.*

For a bit of garden Zen, go to **Rinnō-ji** 輪王寺 *(Rinnō Temple)*. This is a quintessentially Japanese garden, with stream, lotus-pond, gnarled pines, azalea bushes, irises, and bamboo. In June the garden is a blaze of color, but with so many visitors then it's not as tranquil. It's a 20-minute walk from **Ōsaki Hachiman Jinja**, northwest of the city center. Use Bus 24 if you are coming directly from JR Sendai Station. ✉ *1–14–1 Kitayama, Aoba-ku, Sendai* ☎ *022/234–5327* ✆ *¥300* ☉ *Daily 8–5.*

14

Visitors who want to see the sights from on high can do so from the observatory deck on the top floor of the 30-story **SS (Sendai Sumitomo) 30 Building** (✉*4–6–1 Chūō, Aoba-ku, Sendai* ☎*022/267–4465* 💷*Free* ◷*Daily 7* AM*–1* AM).

WHERE TO EAT

Sendai has hundreds of great restaurants, but the highest concentrations are found along the parallel streets Ichiban-chō, Inari-kōji, and Kokubun-chō. Most places display their menus in their windows, along with the prices. Also, within the JR station is the underground mall called Restaurant Avenue, which includes small branches of established restaurants.

$$
JAPANESE
✕**Aji Tasuke** 味太助. This small shop is a local institution that serves excellent and inexpensive Japanese meals. A ¥1,450 *shokuji* (meal) gets you the full set of grilled beef tongue and pickled cabbage, oxtail soup, and a bowl of barley mixed with rice. From the Ichiban-chō exit of Mitsukoshi department store turn left, walk to the first narrow street, turn right, then go left at the next corner; Aji Tasuke is 50 yards ahead on the left, next to a small shrine. ✉*4–4–13 Ichiban-chō, Aoba-ku, Sendai* ☎*022/225–4641* 🚫*No credit cards* ◷*Closed Tues.*

$–$$
SEAFOOD
✕**Beko Masamune** べこ政宗. Fancy a taste of the local delicacy? For ¥1,400 you get the cow's-tongue set: grilled and seasoned with miso, soy sauce, or salt; a tasty bowl of oxtail soup; and a healthy mix of steamed rice and barley. Substitute skewers of chicken or sirloin for the tongue if you're less adventurous. Earthen walls, dark passages, and intimate lighting conjure up a romantic setting. It's a few minutes' walk from the station, at the entrance of the Clis Road/ Hapina Nakakacho (Chūō-dōri) arcade, on the second floor—look for the red sign with the black cow's head. ✉*1–8–32 Chūō, Aoba-ku* ☎*022/217–1124* 🚫*MC, V* ◷*Daily 11:30–2 and 5–11:30.*

$$$–$$$$
SEAFOOD
✕**Gintanabe Bekkan** 銀たなべ別館. A favorite with locals, this establishment prepares a variety of delicious fresh fish with great variety. The sashimi *moriawase* (assorted sashimi) at ¥4,000 is an excellent selection for two people. From the Ichiban-chō exit of Mitsukoshi department store, turn left, take a right at the first narrow street, walk two short blocks, then turn left and walk 50 yards. It's the restaurant with the tub-shaped fish tank. ✉*2–9–36 Kokubun-chō, Aoba-ku, Sendai* ☎*022/227–3478* 🚫*AE, DC, MC, V* ◷*No lunch.*

$–$$
SEAFOOD
✕**Go Shu In Sen** 御酒印船. A good place for cheap seafood, you can't beat their lunch sets. For ¥770 you get the grilled fish of the day, and just ¥1,350 buys you *unaju*, or eel grilled in sweet soy sauce on rice. Go Shu In Sen is in the basement of the Shonai Bank Building, a couple of minutes from the JR station, on Aoba-dōri, near where it meets Atago Kamisugi-dōri. ✉*3–1–24 Chuo, Aoba-kū* ☎*022/225–6868* 🚫*AE, V* ◷*Daily 11:30–11.*

$$$–$$$$
JAPANESE
✕**Jirai-ya** 地雷也. A curtain next to a big red paper lantern leads to this inviting Sendai gem where *kinki* (deepwater white fish) are paired with tempura-style fresh local vegetables. Try *kinoko-jiru* (mushroom soup), a local dish popular in autumn. It's just off Ichiban-chō, near Hirose-

dōri. ⊠*2–1–15 Kokubun-chō* ☎*022/261–2164* ⊟*MC, V* ⊘*Closed Sun.*

WHERE TO STAY

$ 🖵 **Comfort Hotel Sendai East** コンフオートホテル仙台東口. A three-minute walk east from JR Sendai Station, this very Western-looking rectangular hotel is one of the newest in town. The business-ready and functional rooms come at an unbeatable price, with lots of parking nearby. From the station, walk east past the east bus terminal, and turn at the first left. It's in the third block, on the left, across from the MiniStop convenience store. **Pros:** decent rooms; free Internet; coin laundry. **Cons:** a bit spartan. ⊠*1–345 Nakake-chō, Miyagino-ku, Sendai, Miyagi-ken* ☎*022/792–8711* 🖷*022/792–8712* 🖳*202 rooms with bath* ♿ *In-room: Internet. In-hotel: laundry; Internet terminal* ⊟*AE, DC, MC, V* 🍴*BP.*

$$$$ **Hotel Metropolitan Sendai** ホテルメトロポリタン仙台. This upscale hotel adjacent to the railway station offers great value for its price range, and the service makes you feel like this could be your town if you only stayed a bit longer. Enjoy reasonably large Western-style guest rooms. The restaurants are all good (the Japanese one on the second floor, where the breakfast buffet is also served, has a fabulous glass-front view for people-watching), and simpler fare is available in the coffee shop. **Pros:** unbeatably convenient; 20% off with JR Rail Pass. **Cons:** a bit noisy and busy. ⊠*1–1–1 Chūō, Aoba-ku, Sendai, Miyagi-ken* ☎*022/268–2525* 🖷*022/268–2521* ⊕*www.s-metro.stbl.co.jp/english/index.html* 🖳*300 rooms with bath* ♿ *In-hotel: 5 restaurants, bar, pool, gym* ⊟*AE, DC, MC, V* 🍴*EP.*

$ 🖵 **Hotel Shōwa** ホテル昭和. Tucked inside one of the best shopping arcades in town, only a five-minute walk from JR Sendai Station, this business hotel is convenient for sightseeing and getting to the best downtown restaurants. The simple, clean rooms are reasonably priced. From the station, walk to the Chūō-dōri arcade and turn left. In the second block on the right, take one flight up to the hotel entrance. **Pros:** hotel entrance is literally in the shopping arcade. **Cons:** perhaps too close to the action for some. ⊠*2–6–8 Chūō, Aoba-ku, Sendai, Miyagi-ken* ☎*022/224–1211* 🖷*022/224–1214* 🖳*117 rooms with bath* ⊟*AE, DC, MC, V.*

$$$–$$$$ 🖵 **Sendai Kokusai Hotel** 仙台国際ホテル. The outside may be blockish, unimaginative concrete, but inside lurks one of Sendai's most stylish hotels. The Kokusai stands next to the SS 30 complex, and is a short walk from the station or downtown. Choose between swanky French, Chinese, or Japanese restaurants on the fifth floor, and a British-style pub on the first. **Pros:** minutes from JR and subway. **Cons:** tiny rooms. ⊠*4–6–1 Chūō, Aoba-ku, Sendai, Miyagi-ken* ☎*022/268–1112* 🖷*022/268–1113* ⊕*www.tobu-skh.co.jp/english/english.htm* 🖳*234 rooms with bath* ♿ *In-hotel: 6 restaurants, bars* ⊟*AE, DC, MC, V* 🍴*EP.*

14

SHOPPING

Sendai is the unofficial capital of the Tōhoku region, and you can find many of the regional crafts here, including kabazaiku cherry-bark items and *washi* (handmade paper), which are made outside Miyagi Prefecture. Heading west out of the station, follow the elevated walkways across the busy street below to where the shopping begins in earnest.

The best variety of shops may be found along the popular and chic CLIS Road arcade or the Sun Mall Ichiban-chō (which it intersects after a few blocks heading west), but if you are pressed for time, drop down into the shopping center that lies beneath Sendai Station. **Shimanuki** (⊠*B1F, Sendai Station, 1–1–1 Chūō, Aoba-ku, Sendai* ☎*022/267–4021*) is tops for folk crafts and snacks from around Tōhoku. Open daily 10:30–7:30. Their main store (⊠*3–1–17 Ichiban-chō* ☎*022/223–2370*) is also open daily 10:30–7:30.

The Asaichi, or Farmer's Market, is an east–west alley positioned midway in the big block that sits roughly between JR Sendai Station's west exit and the SS 30 Sumitomo Sendai Building. It's busy from early morning to night, and you'll be able to see, hear, smell, and taste it all.

SIDE TRIPS FROM SENDAI

MATSU-SHIMA 松島

Matsu-shima and its bay are the most popular coastal resort destinations in Tōhoku. Matsu-shima owes this distinction to the Japanese infatuation with oddly shaped rocks, which the bay has in abundance. Hordes come to see the 250 small, pine-clad islands scattered about the bay. Long ago it was such a sublime and tranquil scene that it was fondly written of by the 17th-century haiku poet Bashō. Overpopularity and a bit of pollution aside, the bay is still beautiful, and it makes for a worthwhile side trip from Sendai.

GETTING HERE AND AROUND

If you can avoid weekends or holidays and obtain a good vantage point—consider renting a bicycle from one of the shops and pedaling up into the hills—you can indeed feel your cares float away, and the islands themselves may seem to bob and sway on the gentle breeze-driven swells. The key sights are within easy walking distance of each other. To get here, take the JR from Sendai (25 minutes northeast, ¥400). For maps and info, visit the **tourist office** at the end of the Matsu-shima Kaigan Pier. Many restaurants are in the area, but they are overpriced and often full of pushy tour-bus groups. This makes returning to Sendai a good option. However, if you fancy a stay, the hotels listed below have good food.

ESSENTIALS

Visitor Information Matsu-shima Town Office (☎*022/354–2263*).

WHAT TO SEE

Just to the right as you step off the boat on the pier in Matsu-shima is the small temple of **Godai-dō** 五大堂. Constructed in 1609 at the behest of Masamune Date, the temple is on a tiny islet connected to the shore by two small arched bridges. Animals are carved in the timbers beneath the temple roof and among the complex supporting beams.

Zuigan-ji 瑞巌寺, Matsu-shima's main temple, dates from 828, but the present structure was rebuilt to meet Masamune Date's tastes in 1609. Zuigan-ji is perhaps the most representative Zen temple in the Tōhoku region. The main hall is a large wooden structure with elaborately carved wood panels and paintings (now faded) of some of Date's favorite totems: flowers, birds, and trees. The relaxing—outside of holidays—temple grounds are full of trees, including two plum trees brought back from Korea in 1592 by Masamune Date after a failed military venture. The natural caves surrounding the temple are filled with Buddhist statues that novices carved from the rock face as part of their training. Zuigan-ji is down the street from Godai-dō, across Route 45 and the central park. ☎022/354–2023 ⬛¥700 ⊗Apr.–Sept., daily 8:30–5; Oct.–Mar., daily 9–4.

14

From Godai-dō it's a short walk across the 250-yard pedestrian bridge near the Matsu-shima Century Hotel to the islet of **Fukurajima** 福浦島. For the ¥200 toll you can walk away from the crowds to enjoy a picnic in the park with views across the bay.

WHERE TO STAY

$$ 🏨**Folkloro Matsu-shima Hotel** フォルクローロ松島ホテル. This reasonably priced and popular hotel is a 10-minute walk from the station. There is no dinner restaurant, but you can enjoy your breakfast on a terrace overlooking the bay. When you come out of the (Matsu-shima Kaigan) station, make a right, go under the tracks, then turn right again and climb the hill—it's on the left. For ¥3,000 more, the larger "family" rooms is a good splurge—a few of them have nice ocean views. **Pros:** a good price for this popular tourist area; 10% off with Rail Pass. **Cons:** only breakfast served; not flashy compared to other hotels. ✉17 Sanjukari, Matsu-shima Aza, Matsu-shima-chō, Miyagi-ken ☎022/353–3535 🖷022/353–3588 ⬢29 Western-style rooms with bath ⛋In-hotel: 2 restaurants, pool ▤AE, DC, MC, V.

$$$$ 🏨**Hotel Ichinobō** ホテル一の坊. This posh, expensive resort hotel with the feel of a family-run ryokan has a gorgeous garden that stays illuminated up at night. All the large, bright rooms overlook the bay, as do the delightfully relaxing Tea Room, the public baths, and the well-heated outdoor pool on the fifth floor. **Pros:** luxurious touches from top to bottom; friendly, helpful staff. **Cons:** price keeps many away. ✉1–4 Takagi Aza Hama, Matsu-shima-chō, Miyagi-ken ☎022/353–3333 🖷022/353–3339 ⬢20 Western-style rooms with bath, 104 Japanese-style rooms with bath ⛋In-hotel: restaurant, pool ▤AE, DC, MC, V ❣❘EP.

$$$$ 🏨**Matsu-shima Century Hotel** 松島センチュリーホテル. This hotel sits on the island-studded bay. The communal hot-spring bath has perhaps the best view of all, but the one from the coffee shop is not bad, either. Many rooms are lavish, especially the Japanese ones; some even have

sea-view balconies. Indulge in the oysters, in season. **Pros:** great views abound; free pick-up from station after call. **Cons:** price may be too high for some; a bit far from station. ✉ *8 Senzui, Matsu-shima Aza, Matsu-shima-chō, Miyagi-ken* 📞*022/354–4111* 🖨*022/354–4191* 🛏*192 Western-style and Japanese-style rooms with bath* ⚴ *In-hotel: 2 restaurants, pool* ▤ *AE, DC, MC, V.*

YAMADERA 山寺

49 km (30 mi) west of Sendai.

If you'd like to see one of Japan's most revered—and scenic—temple complexes, come up here on an easy day trip from Sendai on the JR Senzan Line (¥820), or from Yamagata City on the same line (¥230). Once you leave the station, you'll find a tourist information office near the bridge, but no English is spoken. 📞*023/695–2816* 🎫*¥300* 🕑 *Daily 8–5.*

WHAT TO SEE

If you are expecting just another mundane temple, you will certainly be surprised. Yamadera is like something conjured out of the ethereal mists of an ancient Japanese charcoal painting. Built in the year 860, Yamadera's ambitious complex of temples is perched high on the upper slopes of **Hōju-san** 宝珠山 *(Mt. Hōju)*, with divine vistas. Belonging to the Tendai Buddhists, who believe in the existence of "Buddha-nature" within all living things, Yamadera attracts a steady stream of pilgrims. To get here, walk through the village from the station, cross the bridge, and turn right. Just inside the entrance is **Kompon Chū-dō,** the temple where the sacred Flame of Belief has burned constantly for 1,100 years.

Near Kompon Chū-dō is a statue of the Japanese poet **Matsuo Bashō** (1644–94), whose pithy and colorful haiku related his extensive wanderings throughout Japan. During a visit to the temple, he wrote, "Stillness . . . the sound of cicadas sinks into the rocks" and buried the poem on the spot.

The path continues up a lot of steps—nearly 1,100 of them, well-tended though they be. At the summit is **Oku-no-in,** the hall dedicated to the temple founder, Jikaku Daishi. But if you've come this far, keep going. Of all the temples hanging out over the valley, the view from **Godai-dō** is the best. The path becomes crowded in summer and slippery in winter. Allow one to one and a half hours for a leisurely climb up and a careful tramp down. On the way back to the station, pick up refreshments at the shop to the right of the bridge, where you can sit and see the river.

EN ROUTE

Sakunami Onsen 作並温泉 is a relaxing hot-spring stop off the train between Yamadera and Sendai. It's only 42 minutes (¥570) from Sendai Station, close enough to be an alternative spot to spend the night.

WHERE TO STAY

$$$$ 🏨 **Iwamatsu Ryokan** 岩松旅館. Situated along a waterfall, this ryokan has rooms that look out on trees and the stream. The original *rotemburo*—or open-air bath—has mixed-sex bathing. At dinner local specialties are served. Expect some spit-roasted and salted river smelt, or

ayu—an algae-eating fish with skin and flesh so sweet that a bucket of them smells like a ripe watermelon—and tasty *sansai,* or mountain vegetables, such as fern bracken, baby bamboo, and any number of types of mushrooms. The breakfast buffet has a large selection of Japanese and Western foods. The inn has shuttle-bus service from JR Sakunami Station and regular bus service from JR Sendai Station. **Pros:** storied 180-year history; traditional comfort in remote setting. **Cons:** nonaficionados may not appreciate its simple charms; no Western rooms; little English spoken. ✉*16 Sakunami Motoki, Aoba-ku, Sendai-shi, Miyagiken* ☎*022/395–2211* 🖷*022/395–2020* 🛏*102 Japanese-style rooms with bath* ♿*In-hotel: restaurant* ▤*AE, MC, V* ❖*MAP.*

YAMAGATA 山形

14

63 km (39 mi) west of Sendai, 120 km (75 mi) from Tsuruoka.

Yamagata, or Mountain Terrain, is the capital of the prefecture of the same name (and the Sister City of Boulder, Colorado). It's a community of a quarter-million souls who enjoy one of the most visually stunning locations in Japan. Everywhere you look there are arrayed lovely mountains, a play of light and shadow shifting across their sculpted flanks and lofty summits. Connoisseurs of soba and mountain vegetables will be delighted, as will fans of sweet, perfectly marbled beef. Yamagata Prefecture is the only prefecture to be 100% thermal—having at least one onsen, or hot spring, in each of its 44 municipalities.

GETTING HERE AND AROUND

The train is your best bet for getting to Yamagata. The JR Senzan Line from Sendai takes 1 hour (¥1,110); by Tsubasa Shinkansen it's 2½ hours from Tōkyō (¥11,300). If you're coming from Akita or Atsumi Onsen, you can take the non-JR bus via Tsuruoka (2 hours 7 minutes, ¥2150). Yamagata is easy to get around in and not very large. Walking is the way to go unless you need to head further afield.

You can pick up free maps and brochures from the **Yamagata Tourist Information Office** opposite the ticket turnstiles inside Yamagata JR Station.

ESSENTIALS

Currency Exchange Yamagata Bank (✉*3–1–2 Nanoka-machi* ☎*023/623–1221*).

Emergency Contacts Yamagata City Hospital (✉*1–3–26 Nanoka-machi, Yamagata* ☎*023/625-5555*).

Tourist Information Yamagata Tourist Information Office (☎*023/631–7865 Daily 9–5:30*).

EXPLORING YAMAGATA

At the **Hana-gasa Festival** (August 5–7), some 10,000 dancers from the region dance through the streets in traditional costume and *hana-gasa,* hats so named for the safflowers (locally called *benibana*) decorating them. It's based on an old ritual to promote fertility and ensure a rich harvest. Floats are interspersed among the dancers, and stalls provide food and refreshments.

Hands-On Ceramics

If you're interested in pottery, go to **Hirashimizu** 平清水 on the outskirts Yamagatan. This small enclave of traditional buildings and farmhouses is a step back in time. About six pottery families each specialize in a particular style. Two of them, the Shichiemon and Heikichi, offer pottery lessons, and participants can have the results fired and glazed and, two to four weeks later, mailed back home. The best-known pottery is that of the Seiryū-gama (Seiryū kiln). Their works have been exhibited in America and Europe, so the prices are high. The potteries are generally open daily 9–3, but may honor irregular holidays, so check with the tourist information office at the train station. From Bus Stop 5, in front of JR Yamagata Station, board the bus bound for Geijutsu Kōka Daigaku (Tōhoku University of Art and Design; whose bijitsu-kan, or Art Museum, has not only good art but great panoramic views of the mountains) for an 11-minute ride (¥210); a taxi is about ¥2,000.

Most people come to Yamagata for the snows that blanket **Zaō-san** 蔵王山 *(Mt. Zaō)*. Nearly 1.5 million alpine enthusiasts ski its 14 slopes between December and April, but in summer hikers walk among the colored rocks around **Zaō Okama,** a mineral-tinted (often a copper-oxide green, but color varies) caldera lake nearly a quarter-mile across. A cable-car lift rises from **Zaō Onsen,** the mountain's resort town, climbing 1,562 feet from the base lodge; another makes the final ascent, an additional 1,083 feet. Each ride takes 7 minutes and costs ¥1,400, ¥2,500 for the return, and a total of ¥5,000 if you ride the whole way up and down. Even nonskiers make the wintertime trip to see the *juhyō,* a forest of snowy monsters caused by heavy snowfall sticking to the conifers, which the wind will shape and reshape into fantastic creatures all winter long. Zaō Onsen is 19 km (12 mi) from Yamagata Station, a 40-minute bus trip (buses hourly, ¥860). English info can be obtained from the Zaō Onsen Info Office. ☎023/694–9328 ⊙ *Daily 9–5.*

WHERE TO EAT

$$–$$$ ✕**Mimasu** 三枡. The highlights are good sushi, tempura, and *donburi*—
JAPANESE bowls with cutlets, tempura, and chicken on top of rice. Lunch specials include *danjurō bentō,* a filling medley of tasty seasonal vegetables and fish. Mimasu is a 15-minute walk from the station, or a short walk from the Yamagata Washington Hotel. ⊠2–3–7 *Nanoka-machi* ☎023/632–1252 ⊙*Closed 2nd Wed. of month* ⊟*AE, DC, MC, V.*

$–$$ ✕**Mitsuya** 三津屋. A short walk from the station will put you in front of
JAPANESE some fine and slightly chewy Yamagata soba, or buckwheat, noodles. Everything is good, but in summer try the hiyashi-dori soba (with cold chicken). Head south (right) from the east exit, and keep to the street that follows along the tracks until you can cross over them and turn to the right. Then it's just a hop to the traditional black-wood and white-stucco building on the left. ⊠1–1–75 *Uwa-machi, Yamagata-shi* ☎023/644–4973 ⊙ *Wed.–Mon. 11–8* ⊟*No credit cards.*

$$$–$$$$ ✕**Sagorō** 佐五郎. If you have never indulged in some strictly top-end
JAPANESE sukiyaki, shabu-shabu, or steak—or if you have and want to feel that
★

way again—Sagorō will serve you a full dose of some excellent Yonezawa beef. This will not only inebriate you for the entire evening, but you will gush for days about its impossible tenderness, its impeccable marbling of such ineffably sweet fat, and so on. Although most dishes are pricey, a simple plate of *shōga-yaki* (beef sauteed in ginger sauce; ¥1,785), *oshinko moriawase* (pickled vegetables; ¥735), rice, and soup can make for a fairly reasonable meal. Go three blocks east from the station. Turn left. Look for the meat shop and you'll see the black bull on the sign above the street next to it. Take the stairs up one flight to heaven. ✉*1–6–10 Kasumi-chō* ☎*023/631–3560* 🕐*Mon.–Sat. 11:30–2 and 5–9* 🚫*No credit cards.*

¢–$ ╳**Shōjiya** 庄司屋. Yamagata is famous for soba, and this is one of the
JAPANESE best places to try it. For lunch or a light dinner, try the simple *kake* soba (served in a hot broth; ¥650), tempura soba (¥1,440), or *nameko* soba (with mushrooms; ¥990). Point to the picture menu if you have to. It's a 10-minute walk from the JR station. Go south, or right, from the east exit, and turn left at the first track-crossing you come to. Mitsuya is the equally good soba shop in the other direction, across the tracks. ✉*14–28 Saiwai-chō* ☎*023/622–1380* 🚫*No credit cards* 🕐*Tues.– Sun., 11–4 and 5:30–8; closed Mon.*

WHERE TO STAY

$$$ 🏨**Hotel Metropolitan Yamagata** ホテルメトロポリタン山形. Yamagata's best—and best-located—hotel is on your right as you exit the east side of the station. The decor is snappy and stylish, with lots of wood paneling and old-fashioned chairs. The staff is breezily efficient. The Mogami-tei restaurant on the second floor is widely famous for its quality beef—shabu-shabu style is the best. Higher-floor rooms have views you won't want to turn away from. To top things off, you're within walking distance of the best downtown restaurants. **Pros:** central location to beat all; nice views out front. **Cons:** lots of distractions with the busy station next door. ✉*1–1–1 Kasumi-chō, Yamagata, Yamagata-ken* ☎*023/628–1111* 📠*012/628–1166* 🌐*www.jrhotel group.com/eng/hotel/* 🛏*116 rooms with bath* ⚐*In-hotel: 3 restaurants* 🚫*AE, DC, V.*

$$ 🏨**Ryokan Sendaiya** 旅館仙台屋. Only a 13-minute walk from the station, near a park and a shrine, this four-story wooden building is a member of the ever-reliable, always reasonable Japan Inn Group, and has been impressing folks in the know for years now. There's a coin laundry for guests and large communal alkaline hot-spring baths (but none in the rooms). The meals are decent and cheap: ¥840 for Japanese or Western breakfast; ¥2,100 for dinner (Japanese only). Exit the east side of the station, and turn left (north). When you pass the NHK Building, turn right, and make the next left. It's on the left, about the middle of the block. **Pros:** great winter atmosphere; nice onsen; Internet facilites. **Cons:** a bit quiet and subdued compared to modern places. ✉*10–26 Kinomi-chō, Yamagata, Yamagata-ken* ☎*023/642–0913* 📠*023/642–0939* 🛏*17 rooms, without bath* ⚐*In-hotel: laundry facilities, Internet terminal* 🚫*V.*

$$ 🏨**Yamagata Washington Hotel** 山形ワシントンホテル. This downtown Yamagata business hotel is on a busy street full of shops and bars and

14

practically right across from the large-windowed Tully's Coffee Shop, perhaps the best people-watching, upscale java-stop in town. Rooms are on the third to the eighth floors, which makes it quieter than you might think they'd be. It's a long walk or short taxi ride from the station. **Pros:** cheap; clean; good location. **Cons:** run-of-the-mill rooms. ✉ *1–4–31 Nanoka-machi, Yamagata, Yamagata-ken* ☎ *023/625–1111* 🏠 *023/624–1512* 📞 *227 rooms with bath* ⚼ *In-hotel: 2 restaurants* 🗏 *AE, DC, MC, V.*

NORTHERN TŌHOKU 北東北

MORIOKA 盛岡

184 km (114 mi) from Sendai, 535 km (332 mi) from Tōkyō.

Morioka is a busy commercial and industrial city ringed by mountains. Though it's not a particularly scenic destination, three rivers pass through, so there's lots of greenery. A nice, expansive park surrounds a ruined castle, and an ancient cherry tree has proven it belongs here by rooting itself into the crack of a huge granite slab in front of the district courthouse. But the city's major attraction is Nambu-tetsu, a special type of cast iron forged into functional and highly ornamental wares. The most popular are heavy iron kettles. They are expensive, because they're specially tempered not to rust. As tea connoisseurs know, once conditioned, these pots soften the water by leaching out unwanted minerals and chemicals while adding the taste and health benefits of elemental iron. They will go on doing it forever, too, if properly cared for. Many locals are still using kettles from centuries past. Dozens of shops throughout the city sell Nambu-tetsu, but the main shopping streets are Saien-dōri and Ō-dōri, which pass right by Iwate Kōen (Iwate Park).

GETTING HERE AND AROUND

Morioka (whose Hanamaki Airport is 50 minutes by bus, ¥1260, from downtown) has 2–3 flights daily from Ōsaka Airports (1 hour 30 minutes, ¥31,000–¥33,000) by JAL. There are also flights to Nagoya, Fukuoka, and Sapporo's Chitose Airport.

To get to downtown Morioka from the JR Morioka Station, take the convenient loop bus, called Denden-mushi, that goes to the shopping area on the far side of the river past the park, departing every 10–15 minutes between the hours of 9–7, from Bus Stop 15 or 16 in front of JR Morioka Station (¥100 for one ride, ¥300 for the day pass).

The **Northern Tōhoku Tourist Information Center** is on the second floor of JR Morioka Station, and the English-speaking staff has maps and other information on the three prefectures of Iwate, Akita, and Aomori. The office can help arrange accommodations from ritzy city splurges to rustic bath retreats. From mid-April to late-November (check with Tourist Info Office for the exact schedule), the **Iwate Kankō Bus Company** runs a morning and afternoon half-day tour of Morioka with Japanese-speaking guides. The 10:30–12:55 tour costs ¥2,000, and the 1:45–5 tour costs ¥2,500. All departures are from JR Morioka Station.

ESSENTIALS

Currency Exchange Bank of Iwate (✉*1–2–3 Chūo-dōri, Morioka, Iwate* ☎*019/623–1111*).

Emergency Contacts Iwate Medical College Hospital (✉*Uchimaru 19–1, Morioka-shi, Iwate-ken* ☎*019/ 651–5111*).

Tour Information Iwate Kankō Bus Company (☎*019/651–3355*).

Visitor Information Northern Tōhoku Tourist Information Center (☎*019/ 625–2090 Daily 9–5:30*).

HORSING AROUND

If you happen to be in town on the second Saturday in June, a small festival called **Chagu-chagu Umako**—named for the noise the big horses' bells make—features 100 locally bred and gaily decorated Nambu-koma horses brought from nearby Takizawa Village to parade around in front of the station. The horses clomp through the streets between 9:30 and 1:30 that day only.

WHAT TO SEE

Iwate Kōen 岩手公園 *(Iwate Park)* is large enough to get lost in, with varied landscapes, an astonishing variety of artfully placed flowers and trees, shady groves, streams, and colors in every season. It's a good place for a romantic walk. In 1597 the 26th Lord of Nambu had a fine castle built here, but all that remains is ruined walls. To reach the park from JR Morioka Station, cross Kai-un-bashi and walk straight down the middle of the three roads that meet there.

At the **Kamasada Iron Casting Studio** 釜足南部鉄器, Nobuho Miya is the affable and patient resident master caster. He speaks good English and will gladly take your order. Samples of all wares including traditional iron tea kettles are displayed, and catalogs are for the taking. Your piece will be produced in two months' time and can be shipped anywhere. To get there, go half a block down the tiny street that extends in front of the venerable and well-known Azuma-ya soba restaurant *(➪ Where to Eat)*. ✉*2–5 Konya-chō Morioka, Iwate-ken* ☎*019/622–3911* 🖷*019/622–3912* ✐*kamasada@mac.ne.jp* ☉*Daily 10–5, but if your time is limited, call, fax, or e-mail ahead. He is sometimes pouring a cast in his foundry out back.*

Have a look around **Kōgensha** 光原社, which specializes in quality folk crafts like lacquerware, kites, dyed fabrics, and pottery. The main shop is composed of several small buildings around a courtyard. You can walk through the courtyard to a *kissaten* (coffee shop) and farther on to the river. Along the wall to the left are poems by famous local poet Kenji Miyazawa. To get to Kōgensha from Morioka Station, walk left to the stoplight in front of the Hotel Metropolitan Morioka, turn right, and cross the river on Asahi-bashi. Take the first left into a funky little street that leads to the main shop, 50 yards down on the left. There's also a branch shop across the street that sells basketry and wooden bowls. ✉*2–18 Zaimoku-chō* ☎*019/622–2894* ☉*Daily 10–6; closed 15th of each month and several days in mid-Aug.*

WHERE TO EAT

$$–$$$
JAPANESE
★

✕**Azuma-ya** 東屋. Hearty soba comes from plentiful northern Japanese buckwheat grain, and Azuma-ya is easily Morioka's most famous place to eat these healthy noodles. The second level is devoted to the courageous and hearty of appetite, where *wanko* soba courses—you can attack and devour all the soba you desire—start at ¥2,600. Down on the first floor, delicious tempura soba is only ¥1,200. The *maneki-neko* (decorative beckoning cats) are mascots to keep customers coming back, and they seem to be doing their job. Azuma-ya is near the bus center, along the small street across the busy road from the Nakasan department store, on the other side of the river from Iwata Park; it's 10 minutes from the train station by taxi. ✉*1–8–3 Naka-no-hashi-dōri* ☎*019/622–2252* ▭*No credit cards* ☉*Has irregular holidays, so check before going.*

$$$–$$$$
SEAFOOD
✕**Ban-ya Nagasawa** 番屋ながさわ. Everyone in town recommends this restaurant for *buri,* or yellowtail, and grilled shellfish such as scallops and abalone. You'll be eating hand-picked mushrooms in fall and wild vegetables in spring, and drinking excellent, local sake with friendly regulars. To reach Banya Nagasawa from the train station, follow Ō-dori to the Iwate Bank and turn right at the statue of Takuboku Ishikawa. The restaurant is 2½ blocks ahead on the right, across from the Hotel New Carina. From the station you could also follow Saien-dōri to the Saien police box and turn left; the restaurant will be on your left. ✉*1–11–23 Saien* ☎*019/622–6152* ▭*MC, V* ☉*Mon.–Sat.11–8; closed Sun. and mid-Aug.*

$$–$$$
JAPANESE
✕**Daido-En** 大同苑. Reimen are clear, slippery noodles made from flour, starch, and water. They came from Korea and are frequently combined with spicy kimchee. Here, the reimen is spicy, all right, and it comes with half a boiled egg, green onions, cucumber pickles, a slice or two of meat, and a fat wedge of watermelon. Quality local beef is available for at-table yaki-niku grilling, too. It's in the entertainment district, halfway between the station (three blocks) and Iwate Park. ✉*2–6–19 Saien* ☎*019/654–5588* ▭*No credit cards* ☉*Open daily 11–3* AM.

WHERE TO STAY

$$$
▦**Hotel Metropolitan Morioka** ホテルメトロポリタン盛岡. Just to the left of the station plaza, this hotel was renovated in 2008 and has clean rooms and good service. Guests can use the Central Fitness Club facilities for ¥525, including a 25-meter pool, weight machines, a sauna, and a Jacuzzi. **Pros:** central location; very good value. **Cons:** lost some of its prerenovation quirkiness. ✉*1–44 Morioka, Eki-mae-dōri Morioka, Iwate-ken* ☎*019/625–1211* 🖷*019/625–1210* ⊕*www.jrhotelgroup. com/eng/hotel/* ⇱*184 Western-style rooms* ⚒*In-hotel: 2 restaurants, bar* ▭*AE, DC, MC, V.*

$$$–$$$$
▦**Morioka Grand Hotel** 盛岡グランドホテル. This pleasingly secluded hotel is near the top of a wooded hill with a breezy lookout over the rolling green hills that surround the otherwise ordinary-looking city. The staff is extremely polite and attentive, and the very large corner double and deluxe twin rooms have enough space to toss a Frisbee in. Some bathrooms are set up like a royal chamber. Virtually the entire front of the structure is glass, and the elegant breakfast and lunch lounge and wine bar and steak house have equally distracting views and reasonable prices. It's a ¥1,000, 10-minute taxi ride up from the station, and a 20- to 30-minute walk down to the action in town if you don't mind meandering around some jungly switchbacks and wending your way

along the easy-flowing Nakatsu River. **Pros:** tranquillity reigns; great views. **Cons:** a bit far from the action; the attached wedding chapel may strike some as strange and tacky. ⊠*1–10 Atagoshita, Morioka, Iwate-ken* ☎*019/625–2111* 🖷*019/625–1003* ⊕*www.j-hotel.or.jp/ hotel/MORIOKAGRANDHOTEL/en/index.html* ⇦*27 total rooms: 5 Japanese-style, 14 twins, 7 doubles, 1 suite* ⅗*In-hotel: 2 restaurants, bar* 🖃*AE, DC, V.*

$$ ⚇**Ryokan Kumagai** 旅館熊ヶ井. This place is very welcoming to foreigners, and is a member of the affordable Japanese Inn Group. Expect basic tatami rooms. There's a small dining area that serves optional Japanese and Western breakfasts and Japanese dinners. It's traditional old-style, so no rooms have private baths. Located between the station and the center city, the inn is an 8-minute walk from JR Morioka Station—cross the river at Kozukata-bashi and turn right at the second traffic signal, and the ryokan is on the right. **Pros:** friendly; festive though basic atmosphere. **Cons:** a bit rustic. ⊠*3–2–5 Ōsawakawara, Morioka, Iwate-ken* ☎*019/651–3020* 🖷*019/626–0096* ⇦*11 Japanese-style rooms without bath* ⅗*In-hotel: restaurant, Japanese baths* 🖃*AE, MC, V* ⚇*MAP.*

TAZAWA-KO AND KAKUNODATE 田沢湖と角館

The lake area of Tazawa-ko (Lake Tazawa) and the traditional town of Kakunodate are good side trips into Tōhoku's wilder interior, approachable from either Morioka or the west-coast city of Akita. For a little thermal relaxation in a very rustic setting, forge on to the old spa town of Nyūtō Onsen, just north of Lake Tazawa.

TAZAWA-KO 田沢湖

★ *40 km (25 mi) west of Morioka, 87 km (54 mi) east of Akita.*

GETTING HERE AND AROUND

A 15-minute bus ride (¥350) from the JR Tazawa-ko Station gets you to the Tazawa-ko-han center on the eastern lakeshore. A very small and shallow swimming area is a short distance to the northwest along the road. A 30-minute bus ride from JR Tazawa-ko Station via Tazawa-ko-han goes up to Tazawa-ko Kōgen, or Plateau, for ¥580. The journey offers spectacular views of the lake. You can rent your own paddleboat or rowboat, and a motorboat takes 40-minute cruises on the lake from late April to November (¥1,170). You'll want sunscreen and a hat or sunshade. There's also regular bus service around the lake (sometimes only halfway around in winter), and bicycles are available for rent (¥500 a day; ¥300 for 2 hours, usually sufficient for the loop) at the Tazawa-ko-han bus terminal and at many lodgings in the area.

The **Tazawa-ko Tourist Information Office** to the left of the JR Tazawa-ko Station has maps and bus schedules; it's open daily 8:30–5:30.

ESSENTIALS

Visitor Information Tazawa-ko Tourist Information Office (☎*0187/43–2111*).

WHAT TO SEE

The clear waters and forested slopes of **Tazawa-ko** (Lake Tazawa), Japan's deepest lake, create a mystical quality that appeals so much to the Japanese. According to legend, the great beauty from Akita, Takko Hime, sleeps in the water's deep disguised as a dragon. The lake never freezes over in winter because Takko Hime and her dragon husband churn the water with their passionate lovemaking. The scientific reason is this: Tazawa-ko has been measured to a depth of 426 meters (1,397 feet), and its profundity is what prevents it from turning over or freezing. Though clear enough to allow you to see a startling 90 meters (300 feet) or more down into it, the mineral-blue water is too acidic to support anything but a few hardy fish. A scenic 20-km-long (12-mi-long) two-lane road rings the crater lake, and a great afternoon activity is to cycle completely around it in a refreshing, leisurely loop.

Near the bus stop and roadhouse there may be some traffic, but it is generally sporadic; once you get away from there the road and the exhilarating mountain air are all yours. In summer, the perfume rising from the vines that line the shady road is intoxicating. Halfway around, there is a good place to stop for ice cream or a drink. The road traverses twisty, leaf-strewn flats and gently sloping grades through mixed forest. You'll see several spots where indicator posts set in the lake show depths of 345 meters (1,132 feet) or more, and, surprisingly, some of them are only a couple of yards from the lake's edge. Clearly, all around you here is perched precariously on the lip of a flooded, cliff-walled abyss. In winter, the Tazawa area is a popular powder-skiing destination, and the gleaming deep blue of the mesmerizing lake steals the show in every view from the lifts or trails.

Nyūtō Onsen 乳頭温泉, accessible by bus from Tazawa-ko, are small, unspoiled, mountain hot-spring spas in some of the few traditional spa villages left in Tōhoku. Most of these villages have only one inn, and you'll have to take your meals there. It's advisable to arrange accommodations before you arrive if you plan to stay the night, and the Tazawa-ko tourist info office can help arrange this.

Komaga-take 駒ケ岳 (*Mt. Komaga*) stands a few miles east of Lake Tazawa. At 1,637 meters or a mile high, it's the highest mountain in the area, and one of the easiest to climb. Between June and October a bus from Tazawa-ko Station runs up to the eighth station, from where it takes an hour to hike to the summit. If you hike after rainshowers in June or July, you can walk through a landscape of alpine wildflowers.

KAKUNODATE 角館

★ *19 km (12 mi) southwest of Tazawa-ko; 59 km (37 mi) from Morioka; 69 km (43 mi) from Akita City.*

The little samurai town of Kakunodate was founded in 1620 by Yoshikatsu Ashina, the local lord, who chose it for its defensible position and reliable water sources. It has remained an outpost of traditional Japan, and it is consistently regarded as one of the very best places for seeing cherry blossoms in the spring. The whole town is full of *shidare-zakura*, or weeping cherry trees, and their pink flowers grace the dark-wood gates, walls, and roofs of ancient samurai houses.

Along the banks of Hinokinai-gawa (Hinokinai River), these living jewel factories dangle a 2-km-long (1¼-mi-long) pink curtain.

GETTING HERE AND AROUND
Kakunodate can be reached from Tazawa-ko on JR Komachi Shinkansen (¥1760) or JR Tazawako Line (¥320). From Morioka take the JR Komachi Shinkansen (¥2,770) or the JR Tazawako Line (¥1,110). Akita City is 43 minutes away on the Komachi Shinkansen (¥2,940) or accessible ¥1,280 by JR Ou and Tazawako Lines (¥1,280).

The **Kakunodate Tourist Information Center** is in an old *kura*-style (warehouse-like) building, adjacent to the tea shop by the station, and the English-speaking staff have maps and information about the samurai houses and walks in town, and can recommend nearby lunch or dinner options.

> **BARK SHOPPING**
>
> Shops in Kakunodate are the best places in Tōhoku to pick up the locally made kaba-zaiku, or cherry-bark veneer items—everything from warmly translucent maroon lampshades to tiny, intricate business-card holders. If you're looking to score great and unique souvenirs and crafts, this is an important tip to remember, since anything you're likely to find in the hokey souvenir shops in the big cities will be overpriced and fake.

14

ESSENTIALS
Visitor Information Kakunodate Tourist Information Center (☎ *0187/54–2700* ⊙ *Daily 9–6*).

WHAT TO SEE
Several well-preserved samurai houses date from the founding of the town. The most renowned and interesting is **Aoyagi-ke** 青柳家 *(Aoyagi Manor)*, with its sod roof. Part of this intricate, rambling estate is still lived in. Inside the old kura or warehouses that have been turned into museums are all kinds of historical artifacts to pore over, such as farm implements, old bicycles, and samurai battle armor and accoutrements of siege warfare. The cherry tree in the garden is nearly three centuries old. It's a 15-minute walk northwest from the station. ✉ *26 Higashi Katsuraku-chō* ☎ *0187/54–3257* 🎫 *¥500* ⊙ *Apr.–Nov., daily 8:30–5; Dec.–Mar., daily 9–4.*

Denshō House 伝承館 *(Denshōkan)*, a hall in front of a cluster of samurai houses, serves as a museum and a workshop for the local cherry-bark veneer handicrafts that became the new source of income for samurai when they suddenly found themselves fresh out of jobs. There are more varieties of this auburn wood, with its warm glow and eye-riddled surface, than you might think. Don't be put off by the imposing exterior of the Denshō House—go right on in and watch master craftsmen at work, or relax over coffee upstairs. You can buy what they make here, often at better prices than in the shops on the street. The Satake-Kita family armor and heavily Kyōto-influenced ancient heirlooms are exhibited in adjacent parts of the building. You can also learn about life in old-time winters, with displays of plaited-maple sleighs and some truly inventive and adaptive tools and togs for fighting snow. ✉ *10–1e Shimo-chō,*

Omote-machi ☎0187/54–1700 ✉¥300 ⊘*Apr.–Nov., daily 9–4:30; Dec.–Mar., daily 9–4. Closed Dec. 28–Jan. 4.*

WHERE TO STAY

$$ 🏨**Forukurōro (Folklore) Kakunodate** フォルクローロ角館. This inexpensive and very friendly small hotel has bright, clean rooms with private baths. Deluxe twins have a sofa and additional space. A simple buffet breakfast and unbeatable convenience are included in a low-price night here. An attached soba shop is to the right on the first floor. The hotel is the first building on your left outside the station exit. **Pros:** nice and new; great place to chill between Shink-stops. **Cons:** nothing doing after dusk. ✉*14 Nakasugasawa, Iwaze-aza, Kakunodate-machi, Akita-ken* ☎*0187/53–2070* 🖷*0187/53–2118* ⇌*26 rooms with bath* ▤*MC, V* ❢❶*CP.*

TOWADA–HACHIMAN-TAI NATIONAL PARK

158 km (98 mi) northwest of Morioka.

GETTING HERE AND AROUND

The fastest way to Towada-ko is by one of the three daily buses directly from Morioka Station (2 hours 15 minutes, ¥2,420). The last stop on the bus is Hachiman-tai Kankō Hotel. There's also bus service from Morioka to Matsukawa, Tōshichi, and Goshogake Onsen. Local buses run along a network that links all the main spots, but note that service is frequently suspended during winter storms. See the Northern Tōhoku Tourist Information Office for more info on routes, schedules, activities, and places to stay in Towado-Hachimantai National Park.

WHAT TO SEE

For walking among the splendid and vast virgin beech, pine, and cedar forests covering the verdant valleys and mountainsides deep in the heart of Tōhoku, you could not pick a better destination than **Towada-Hachiman-tai National Park** 十和田八幡平国立公園. The mountains afford sweeping panoramas over the park's gorges and valleys, crystal-clear lakes like Towada-ko, gnarled and windswept trees, and volcanic mountain cones. The park straddles Aomori, Iwate, and Akita prefectures, and sprawls over 330 square mi. Hot springs and tiny villages lost in time are secreted away here, and the fresh tree-scented air promotes a feeling of true wilderness. Fall foliage can be spectacular, but this draws boisterous crowds.

Two hours 10 minutes by bus from Morioka Station, **Hachiman-tai Kōgen** 八幡平 *(Hachiman Plateau)*, situated roughly between Lakes Tozawa and Towada, is a hummock of scantily covered geological activity suspended between volcano tops, and the geysers and mudboils remind you of all that goes on beneath us. But remember, there are always wonderful onsen for relaxing and recharging near such geo-thermally active places!

Though remote and rustic, intrepid travelers will find some truly unique onsen resorts to soak in and linger at among the wilds. One of the most visited resting spots is **Goshōgake Spa** 後生掛温泉, 2 hours 10 minutes from Tazawa-ko bus station, three buses daily, late April–late October.

You can hike the 2-km (1.2-mi) nature trail, and then be steamed, boiled, or braised—try the old-fashioned "steaming-box" baths where only your head protrudes—in a wide assortment of mineral baths situated among the bubbling mud and vaporous swamps.

Hachiman-numa 八幡沼 *(Hachiman Marsh)*, formerly the crater lake of a collapsed shield volcano, is worth a visit. There's a paved road around the rim, and in July and August, the wildflowers are abloom. From the Hachiman-tai-chōjō bus stop off the Aspite Line, it's a 20-minute walk up the path.

Tōshichi Onsen 藤七温泉, a year-round spa town—elevation 4,593 feet at the foot of Mokko-san, off the Aspite Line, before Goshogake if coming from Morioka—is a popular spring skiing resort. On the north side of Tōshichi is **Hōraikyō**, a natural garden with dwarf pine trees and alpine plants scattered among strange rock formations. In early October, the autumn colors are fantastic.

Thanks to famous colors and a rumbling fleet of packed tour buses, the area around **Towada-ko** 十和田湖 *(Lake Towada)* is almost too popular in autumn. The lake fills a volcanic crater to a depth of 334 meters (1,096 feet), making it the third-deepest in Japan, and is held aloft like a giant goblet 400 meters above the surrounding topography, giving it a dramatic illusory aspect. There are boat tours, and near Yasumiya Village facilities include a campsite. The lake borders remote reaches of Aomori and Akita prefectures, and it's not nearly as convenient or unhurried as Tazawa-ko. The town of Towada-minami (Towada South) is 20 minutes north of Hachiman-tai on the JR Hanawa Line. From here buses leave on the hour to Lake Towada; the bus fare is ¥1,110.

At the village resort of **Yasumi-ya** 休屋—the word *yasumi* means "holiday"—pleasure boats run across the lake to the village of Nenokuchi. The one-hour trip costs ¥1,320. Boats run every 30 minutes from mid-April to early November, and then less frequently until January 31, then not at all, due to extreme cold.

An excellent choice for a walk—if a bit crowded—is to the **Oirase-kyōkoku** 奥入瀬峡谷 (Oirase [oh-*ee*-ra-seh] Gorge), northeast of the lake at Nenokuchi. The carefully tended trail to the gorge follows the stream for a total of 9 km (5½ mi; about 2 hours 40 minutes). A two-lane road parallels the river, and you can catch buses at intervals of about 2 km (1¼ mi). Buses go north to Aomori and south to Nenokuchi and Yasumi-ya. Though very popular with tour groups, especially in fall, this does take you through one of the most pristine areas of Tōhoku. Be prepared for cold mist or rain, take a map of the river and bus stops, and find out the bus schedule before you start out.

WHERE TO STAY

$$$$ 🏨 **Towada Kankō Hotel** 十和田観光ホテル. This hotel makes a good base for enjoying the lake, since it's one that is not usually overrun by tour buses. Western-style rooms have comfortable beds and a separate tatami area. Elaborate, traditional, kaiseki-style Japanese dinners are served in your room, and include local pickles, stews made with kiritampo, or grilled tubes of pressed rice, and fish or chicken, mushrooms, and wild vegetables. Japanese breakfast is served in the dining room. **Pros:**

stylish and authentic, yet not over-the-top. **Cons:** remote; not much to do for big-city types. ✉ *Towada-ko, Yasumi-ya, Aomori-ken* ☎*0176/75–2111* 🖷*0176/75–2327* ⇆*72 rooms with bath* ♿*In-hotel: restaurant, bar* ▤*AE, DC, MC, V* �“⚏*MAP.*

HIROSAKI 弘前

★ *230 km (143 mi) northwest of Morioka.*

Hirosaki is one of Northern Tōhoku's most attractive cities. It's most famous for its sweet apples, and its only real cultural attraction is a small but photogenic, reconstructed castle. The town has a very appealing, easy-going nature, and this is suitably reflected in a local slang word, *azumashii*, or "a feeling of coziness." Perhaps owing to latitude and topography, there also a blue-tinged component to the light that is reminiscent of Santa Fe or Taos, New Mexico.

FOLLOW THE PARADE

In the first week of August Hirosaki outdoes itself with the **Neputa Festival** ねぷた祭り. Each night, following various routes, internally illuminated fan-shaped floats brightly painted with mythological scenes and characters (borrowed from Chinese legends) parade through town. The festival is thought to have its origins in the preparation, 400 or more years ago, for some horrible battle, as a big send-off to the warriors. In any case, the blood-quickening thrum of the humongous drums will get you celebrating without the swordplay.

GETTING HERE AND AROUND

From Morioka, you can take the JR express highway bus 2 hours 15 minutes northwest (¥2,700), or if you're in Aomori, take the Aomori Shinkansen and then the JR trains via Hachinohe (2 hours 8 minutes, ¥7,090).

Hirosaki is compact and walkable, but finding your bearings in this ancient castle town can prove difficult, for the streets were designed to disorient invaders before they could get to the battlements. So, by all means, pick up a map at the **Hirosaki City Tourist Information Center** before setting out. It's on the right side of the train station as you exit.

ESSENTIALS

Currency Exchange Aomori Bank (✉ *6–1 Fujimi-chō, Hirosaki-shi* ☎*017/223–6321*).

Visitor Information Hirosaki City Tourist Information Center (✉ *2–11 Omote-chō, Hirosaki, Aomori-ken* ☎*0172/32–0524 Jan. 4–Mar., daily 8–5; Apr.–Dec. 28, daily 8:45–6*).

WHAT TO SEE

Hirosaki Castle 弘前城 *(Hirosaki-jō)* is situated atop a high stone base, and guarded by deep moats over which a red wooden bridge crosses in a picturesque curve. The original castle, completed in 1611, was set ablaze 16 years later by a lightning bolt. The present castle, of a smaller scale, dates back to 1810. When the more than 5,000 *somei-yoshino* cherry trees blossom, or when the maples turn, the setting is even more gorgeous. A snow-lantern festival with illuminated ice sculptures is held in early February. The castle is a 30-minute walk from the station on the northwest side of town, across the river. Take the ¥100 bus from the No. 2 stop and get off at the Shiyaku-sho-mae, or City Hall stop. ⊠*2–1 Shimo-Shirogane-chō, Hirosaki, Aomori-ken* ☎*0172/33–8733* ⌨*Grounds free, castle ¥300* ☉*Grounds daily 7 AM–9 PM; castle Apr.–Nov., daily 9–5.*

The **Hirosaki Sightseeing Information Center** (⊠*2–1 Shimo-Shirogane-chō, Hirosaki Koen Mae, Hirosaki, Aomori-ken* ☎*0172/26–3600* 🖳*0172/26–3601* ☉*Daily 8:45–6*), south of the castle grounds, displays local industry, crafts, and regional art (free) and provides tourist information.

On the northeast corner of the castle grounds, **Tsugaru-han Neputa Mura (Tsugaru Peninsula Neputa Village)** exhibits the giant drums and floats used in the Neputa Festival. If you miss the real thing, come here to see the 40-foot fan-shaped floats as they sleep off their hangovers from the mad mid-summer revelry. In the workshop you can paint your own traditional kite, paper-and-frame goldfish, and *kokeshi* (traditional wooden dolls) to take home as souvenirs. ☎*0172/39–1511* ⌨*¥500* ☉*Apr.–Nov., daily 9–5; Dec.–Mar., daily 9–4.*

SHAMISEN

Literally meaning "three-tastes-strings," and sometimes called jamisen if preceded by a suffix such as Tsugaru (Tōhoku dialect), the shamisen is similar to the American banjo in sound and playing manner. The sound-amplification board is traditionally made of tightly stretched dog or cat skin. It is usually played with a comblike plectrum made of tortoise shell or ivory. In Tōhoku (as well as in southern Japan), styles are bent to suit local moods and ears. The shamisen has recently been exposed to young Japanese audiences—and to Westerners—by bands like the Yoshida Brothers, who forgo tradition and play the instrument with the ferocity of a rock guitar.

WHERE TO EAT

$$$
JAPANESE
✕**Anzu** 杏. Performances of live Tsugaru-jamisen—the shamisen is a Japanese banjo—and the odd, wailing Tsugaru vocals are the main attraction at this Japanese restaurant. Jams take place evenings at 7, 9, and 10:30. Arrive an hour early to sit on cushions on the floor, in local style, and enjoy a menu of seasonal vegetables, sashimi, grilled scallops, grilled fish and rice, and soup for a reasonable ¥3,000. ⊠*44–1 Oyakata, Hirosaki, Aomori* ☎*0172/32–6684* ☉*Mon.–Sat. 5–11* ⎙*No credit cards.*

$$–$$$
JAPANESE
✕**Kikufuji** 菊富士. Tasty, healthy, and authentic dishes from the region are Kikufuji's specialty, from delicious vegetable stews like *kenoshiru* to the freshest seafood. The scallops brought in from the Mutsu Bay coast are superb, so try the *hotate-no-sugate-yaki,* or scallops grilled in the shell. Many *teishoku,* or meal-set assortments, cover all the bases. Excellent dry, cold local varieties of sake are also available. It's a short taxi ride from JR Hirosaki Station, or a long walk out along the main NW–SE diagonal, near the stream-crossing, and not far from the tall, freaky sci-fi building that is the new Naka-san department store. ⊠*1 Sakamoto-chō, Hirosaki, Aomori* ☎*0172/36–3300* 🖳*0172/36–3319* ☉*Daily 11–10* ⎙*No credit cards.*

14

$$$
JAPANESE

✕**Yamauta** 山唄. Hirosaki's most interesting eatery serves sashimi, grilled fish, yakitori, and other grilled meat for ¥380–¥2,700 and has live shamisen music every hour. The restaurant gets its musical character from its owner, Yamazato Senri; he was once national shamisen champion and now uses the premises as a school for aspiring artists. A five-minute walk past the Best Western Hotel New City Hirosaki from the train station. ✉*1–2–4 Ō-machi* ☎*0172/36–1835* ◷*Daily 5–11, closed 1st and 3rd Sun. of month* ▭*No credit cards.*

WHERE TO STAY

$$–$$$

▦**Best Western Hotel New City Hirosaki** ベストウエスタンホテル ニューシテイ弘前. This modern hotel is on the left next to the JR Hirosaki Station, and the lively coffee shop on the first floor is terrific for people-watching. Elegant hotel restaurants serve teppanyaki and French fare. In the building next door is a ritzy boutique mall with a private fitness center where the in-crowd goes (you can't access it, but windows allow you to watch the fashionistas sweat it out). **Pros:** well-situated; great prices. **Cons:** a bit impersonal. ✉*1–1–2 Ō-machi, Hirosaki, Aomori-ken* ☎*0172/37–0700* ☎*0172/37–1229* ⊕*www.tokyuhotels. co.jp/en* ⇆*141 rooms with bath* ⚐*In-hotel: 2 restaurants, bar* ▭*AE, DC, MC, V.*

$$$$

▦**Hotel New Castle** ホテルニューキャッスル. This decent business hotel sits on a hill a block and a half from Hirosaki Castle. The restaurants serve formal Japanese meals. It's a 15-minute walk or short taxi ride northwest of the station. **Pros:** close to the quaint, photogenic castle (and the park's spectacular cherry blossoms in season). **Cons:** small roms; sparce decor. ✉*24–1 Kamisayashi-machi, Hirosaki, Aomori-ken* ☎*0172/36–1211* ☎*0172/36–1210* ⇆*52 Western-style rooms, 2 suites, 4 Japanese-style rooms* ⚐*In-hotel: 2 restaurants* ▭*AE, DC, MC, V.*

AOMORI 青森

37 km (23 mi) from Hirosaki.

Aomori is not as busy as it once was, before the train tunnel linked Honshū and Hokkaidō, and there's not experience—except for extraordinary weather. Over 35 feet of snowfall annually is typical. Year-round, you can enjoy delicious seafood, fruit, and vegetables, and come every summer, they cut loose to throw the decidedly wild Nebuta Matsuri festival, a frenzied, utterly unaccountable period when normal gets thrown to the wind.

GETTING HERE AND AROUND

Aomori Airport has six daily flights from Tōkyō's Haneda Airport by JAS (JAL affiliate) and six by All Nippon Airways: 1 hour 15 minutes, ¥25,500 one-way, ¥42,900 round-trip. Aomori also has two JAL flights from Nagoya, four to six from Ōsaka, and two from Sapporo's Chitose Airport.

By train it's 31 minutes (¥1,660) by JR express or 49 minutes (¥650) by JR local train from Hirosaki; or 2 hours 14 minutes (¥7,090) by JR express from Morioka.

The **Aomori City Tourist Information Center** is on the south end of Aomori Station. English maps and brochures for the city and prefecture are available, and you can apply for the discount Tōhoku Welcome Card if you haven't done so online (*beginning of chapter).*

ESSENTIALS

Airport Information Aomori Airport (⊠ *1-5 Kotani, Ōtaniaza, Ōaza , Aomori-shi, Aomori-ken* ☎ *017/739-2121).*

Currency Exchange Aomori Bank (⊠ *1-9-30 Hashimoto, Aomori-shi* ☎ *017/777-1111).*

Visitor InformationAomori City Tourist Information Center (⊠ *JR Aomori Station, 1-1-1 Yamagawa, Aomori-shi, Aomori-ken* ☎ *017/723-4670* ⊘ *Daily 8-5:30).*

14

WHAT TO SEE

Aomori's main event is its **Nebuta Festival** ねぶた祭り (August 2–7), not to be confused with Hirosaki's Neputa Festival (residents of each locale tend to get annoyed when they are). Both are held in early August, and both have large, illuminated floats of gigantic samurai figures paraded through the streets at night. Aomori's festival is one of Japan's largest, and is said to celebrate the euphoria of post-battle victory, and is thus encouraged to be noisier and livelier than you may have been exposed to in other Japanese festivals. Dancers, called *heneto,* run alongside the floats, dancing crazily, and you're encouraged to join in. Brace yourself, and enjoy!

If you can't visit during the Nebuta Festival, head to the **Nebuta-no-Sato, or Nebuta Village Museum,** in the southeast part of town, where glowing papier-mache sculptures painted with the fierce countenances of warriors used in Aomori's festival are displayed. To get here, take the JR bus bound for Lake Towada from Bus Stop 8 or 9 (30 minutes, ¥450), just outside the train station. ☎ *017/738-1230* ☞¥630 ⊘ *July–Sept., daily 9–8 (closed during Nebuta Festival in early Aug.); mid-Apr.–June, Oct., and Nov., daily 9–5:30.*

Many people arriving in town will be tempted to head to the pyramid-shaped ASPAM building, but as locals will tell you, it's a waste of ¥800, the shops are no good, and well, there's something better on offer: the **Auga** market complex, where fish, shellfish, preserved seaweed, smoked fish, and fish eggs—in short, all manner of marine organisms—are hawked by hundreds of shopkeepers in 87 stores. It's one block east of JR Aomori Station, in the basement level of a modern building with distinctive crimson pillars, across from the Aomori Grand Hotel. ⊘ *Daily 5 AM–6:30 PM.*

WHERE TO EAT AND STAY

$$$–$$$$
SEAFOOD

✕**Hide-zushi** 秀寿司. You're in a major seafood city, and if you want some of the best available from that cold, clean water, then this is the place to get it. Excellent service, bright surroundings, and sea urchin, salmon roe, scallops, squid, tuna, and crab await your whetted appetite. ⊠ *1–5 Tsutsumi-machi, Aomori-shi, Aomori-ken* ☎ *017/722-8888* ▭*AE, MC, V* ⊘ *Closed Sun.*

$$–$$$ ✕**Nishimura** 西村. It'd be hard to walk out of this Japanese restaurant
JAPANESE   hungry: the *danna* course (¥3,000), for example, includes abalone and
sea-urchin soup, seaweed and fish, a mixed hot pot, and fried eggplant.
From JR Aomori Station, walk east one block on Shinmachi-dōri, and
then take the first left. Nishimura is on your right after two blocks.
⊠*1–5–19 Yasukata Aomori-shi, Aomori-ken* ☎*017/773–2880* ▭*AE,
MC, V* ◷*Mon.–Sat. 11–2 and 4:30–10.*

$$ ⌂**Aomori Grand Hotel** 青森グランドホテル. The rates are good and it's
only one block southeast of the train station, just past the bus depot
and tourist information office. The lounge for morning coffee has
comfortable armchairs, and the Belle View Restaurant and Sky Bar
on the 12th floor, where most of the interior decorating budget seems
to have been spent, can provide an enjoyable afternoon or evening of
relaxing and watching the harborscape and new bridge. Rooms are
comfortable, though without much flourish. **Pros:** good value; great
location; tasty food; opulent bar with great views. **Cons:** not much
local color; a bit sterile. ⊠*1–1–23 Shin-machi, Aomori-shi, Aomori-
ken* ☎*017/723–1011* ⌨*017/734–0505* ⬎*138 Western-style rooms,
2 Japanese-style suites, 1 Western suite* ⚒*In-hotel: 3 restaurants, bar*
▭*AE, DC, MC, V.*

$$–$$$ ⌂**Hotel JAL City Aomori** ホテルジャルシテイ青森. Opened in 1996, this
nine-story upscale art deco–style hotel curves around the corner as if
it belonged in 1960s Miami Beach. The lobby is dominated by stone
floors and walls and a gallery-like lighting scheme. The rooms are bright
and spacious. La Sera restaurant is good for buffets, brunches, and its
pleasant pub. Only a six-minute walk east of the station, the hotel is on
the corner of ASPAM-dōri. **Pros:** cool, chic digs in unremarkable city.
Cons: not much doing outside unless it's festival time. ⊠*4–12 Yasukata,
2-chōme, Aomori-shi, Aomori-ken* ☎*017/732–2580* ⌨*017/735–2584*
⬎*165 Western rooms, 2 suites* ⚒*In-hotel: 2 restaurants, bar, gym, spa*
▭*AE, DC, MC, V* ⎮◎⎮*EP.*

TŌHOKU WEST COAST

AKITA 秋田

*186 km (116 mi) from Aomori City; 148 km (92 mi) from Hirosaki;
663 km (412 mi) from Tōkyō.*

In the scenic, faraway realm of Akita, the peaks of the Dewa Sanchi
(Dewa Range), marked by Mt. Taihei, march off to the east, and the
Sea of Japan lies at the edge of the fertile plains that extend to the west.
The region's history began in 733, during the turbulent Nara Period,
with the establishment of Dewa-no-saku, a fortress built on a hill in
Takashimizu by the powerful Yamato clan. The area, set up to guard
trade routes, soon gained strategic importance, and during the Heian
era, soldiers and their families began spreading outward. The Ando and
Satake families each built major bastions in the Yuwa and Kawabe dis-
tricts after the Battle of Sekigahara some 400 years ago. These munici-
palities, now merged, are considered to be the foundations of modern

Akita City. Today the prefectural capital (population 320,000) is a lively, likeable city full of delicious food from the mountains, plain, rivers, and sea.

The countryside is devoted to producing what locals feel is the best rice in Japan, and they certainly do make good sake with it. Additionally, the fruits and vegetables grown here are unbelievably cheap and flavorful. The combination of climate, pure water, and healthy food is said to make the women of Akita the fairest in the land—a matter of prefectural, even national, pride. In the Japanese media, "scientific" studies have been trotted out since the 19th century as proof of the Akita bii-jin (Akita beauty) phenomenon.

> ### BIG BAMBOO
>
> The **Kantō Festival** (August 3–6) celebrates ancient fertility rites with young men balancing 36-foot-long bamboo poles (*kantō*) hung with as many as 46 lighted paper lanterns on its eight crossbars—and weighing up to 110 pounds—against a special pouched strap on their waist, hip, back, or shoulder. The lanterns represent sacks full of rice, and a bountiful harvest is fervently prayed for and celebrated in anticipation of its arrival.

14

GETTING HERE AND AROUND

ANA and JAL fly to **Akita Airport** four to six times daily from Tōkyō's Haneda Airport in 65 minutes for ¥22,900, and twice daily from Ōsaka's Kansai Airport. They also fly from the Nagoya and Fukuoka Airports.

If you're traveling regionally by train, take the 2 hours 31 minutes (¥5,450) trip on the JR Kamoshika Express from Aomori City or the 2 hours (¥4,330) ride from Hirosaki by JR Kamoshika Limited Express (3–4 trains daily). From Tōkyō the JR Komachi Shinkansen will spirit you off to Akita in 3 hours 52 minutes (¥16,810).

The **Akita City Tourist Information Center** is on the second floor just across from the exit from the Shinkansen tracks at the station, and supplies many colorful English-language pamphlets and lots of friendly advice.

ESSENTIALS

Airport Information Akita Airport (⊠ *Terminal Bldg., 48-3 Aza Yamagomori Yuwatsubakigaw, Akita* ☎ *018/881–3177*).

Currency Exchange Hokuto Bank (⊠ *41 Nakamichi, Akita-shi* ☎ *018/833–4211*). **Central Post Office** (⊠ *41 Nakamichi, Hodono, Akita-shi* ☎ *018/862–3504*).

Tourist Information Akita City Tourist Information Center (⊠ *JR Akita Station, 7-1-2 Naka-dōriAkita City, Akita-ken* ☎ *018/832–7941* ⊙ *Daily 9:30–5*).

WHAT TO SEE

Senshū Kōen 千秋公園 *(Senshū Park)* was the site of the now-ruined Kubota Castle, this large, shady respite from the sun is a pleasant haven of green leaves and strolling paths, with cherry blossoms and azaleas adding color in season. Large koi and goldfish swim lazily about the streams, ponds, and moats, while ducks come and go. A reconstructed **former castle tower** with an elevated lookout floor stands in the northwest corner of the park. In clear weather you can see all the way to the seacoast and distant ponderous hump of Oga Peninsula to the west and the stunning series of blue-green mountain ridges parading endlessly to the east. The park is a 10-minute walk west of the train station on Hiroko-ji-dōri. ⊠*Senshu Koen Akita-shi, Akita-ken* ☎*018/832–5893* 🖭*¥100 for castle tower* ☉*Castle tower daily 9–4:30.*

Under the distinctive copper-covered Japanese palace–style roof of the **Hirano Masakichi Museum of Fine Art** 平野政吉美術館 *(Hirano Masakichi Bijutsukan)* is an impressive and varied collection of some 600 works, including 48 paintings by Tsuguji Fujita (1886–1968) and an excellent selection of Western art (93 masterpieces are here), with works by Toulouse-Lautrec and Picasso and a fantastic array of Goya etchings. The most eye-catching is Fujita's enormous Annual *Events in Akita.* Fujita took just 15 days to complete the painting of three local festivals merged into a single scene, rendered on one of the world's largest canvases at the time, measuring 11 feet by 66 feet. The interior galleries provide an airy and minimalist aesthetic that allows the art to speak for itself. ⊠*3–7 Meitoku-chō, Akita-shi, Akita-ken* ☎*018/833–5809* 🖭*¥610* ☉*Early Jan.–Apr. and Oct.–late Dec., Tues.–Sun. 10–5; May–Sept., Tues.–Sun. 10–5:30; last entry 30 min before closing.*

The avenue known as **Kawabata-dōri** 川反通り is where people come in the evening to sample the regional hot-pot dishes *shottsuru-nabe* (a salty fermented sandfish stew) and kiritampo-nabe, drink *ji-zake* (locally brewed sake), and to enjoy the lively bars. It's six blocks west of the Atorion Building, across the Asahi-gawa (Asahi River) and slightly south.

EN ROUTE

As you approach the flat rice-growing plains that surround and supply Akita, the train goes through Hirosaki and past the 5,331-foot **Iwaki-san** 岩木山 *(Mt. Iwaki),* presiding over the countryside. If you fancy seeing the view from on top, a bus from Hirosaki (many daily, 50 minutes, ¥950) travels to Dake Onsen, at the foot of the mountain, and from there a sightseeing bus travels up the Iwaki Skyline toll road (open late April–late October) to the Hachigōme, or Eighth Station, for ¥1,000. The final ascent, with a 360-degree view from a mile up, is by cable car, for ¥750. There are four buses daily; the first goes up at 8:40 and the last comes down at 3:55.

South of Mt. Iwaki, straddling Aomori Prefecture's border with Akita, are the **Shirakami Sanmyaku** 白神山脈 *(Shirakami Mountains),* site of the world's largest virgin beech forest. This is on UNESCO's list of World Heritage Sites. In keeping with the goal of preservation, access is provided by just a few tiny roads. The area is truly pristine and great for hiking.

WHERE TO EAT

$$$–$$$$
JAPANESE

✕**Dai-ichi Kaikan** 第一会館. The third-floor restaurant of this complex specializes in Akita cuisine such as kiritampo-nabe: ¥2,000 for the hot pot alone or ¥3,500 for the full-course set. The *inaniwa gozen* is a tray with noodles, chicken, dried ray, seaweed, wild vegetables, noodles, and *tsukemono* (pickled vegetables). Don't be squeamish, even if you have never seen some of the ingredients before. ⊠*5–1–17 Ō-machi* ☎*018/823–4141* ▭*MC, V* ☉*Daily 5–11.*

$$–$$$
JAPANESE
★
✕ **Shukitei-Hinaiya** 酒季亭比内や. This restaurant is named after the local breed of chicken that goes into *Hinai-jidōri* kiritampo-nabe, a hot pot made with kiritampo, or rice that's cooked, pasted onto sticks (usually cedar or bamboo), then grilled over a charcoal fire. The rice is then simmered in a pot with chicken and broth, seasonal vegetables, burdock root, green onions, and mushrooms (¥1,800). To get to Hinaiya, in the heart of the Kawabata entertainment district, walk one block from the river on Suzuran-dōri; it's on the second floor. Noisy, fun-loving Hinaiya is conducive to partying, and even the fish swimming in the big tank seem oblivious to their fate. ⊠*4–2–2 Ō-machi, Akita-shi, Akita-ken* 🕿*018/823–1718* ▤*DC, MC, V.* ◷*Daily 5–11:30.*

WHERE TO STAY

$$$–$$$$
🛏 **Akita Castle Hotel** 秋田キャッスルホテル. Opposite the moat and a 10-minute walk west from the train station, this hotel has the best location in town and highly polished service. The dancing fluorescent jellyfish in the arty display in the glassy center of the lobby will catch your eye. The Western-style doubles are spacious, and the three Japanese-style rooms are huge. Both the bar and the French restaurant overlook the moats of Senshū Kōen and the distant mountains. Japanese and Chinese restaurants have this same enviable vantage. While in summer the dense trees block views of the castle buildings behind them, the tranquil shades of green soothe the soul. **Pros:** good location; nice ambience. **Cons:** some rooms could use renovation. ⊠*1–3–5 Naka-dōri, Akita-shi, Akita-ken* 🕿*018/834–1141* 🖷*018/834–5588* 📶*179 Western-style rooms with bath, 3 Japanese-style rooms with bath* ⟨In-hotel: 4 restaurants, bar* ▤*AE, DC, MC, V.*

$$–$$$
🛏 **Akita View Hotel** 秋田ビューホテル. The largest hotel in town, with an enormous lobby and a five-lane swimming pool, the Akita View is on the right side of Seibu department store. You're right in the thick of all the shops that line the arcade extending from the station, and many restaurants are nearby. A three-minute walk east will bring you to JR Akita Station, and a 10-minute walk will take you to the edge of the entertainment district. **Pros:** exciting location; big city feel; great staff. **Cons:** rooms are on the small side; fee for Internet use. ⊠*2–6–1 Naka-dōri, Akita-shi, Akita-ken* 🕿*018/832–1111* 🖷*018/832–0037* 📶*192 rooms with bath* ⟨In-hotel: 3 restaurants, bar, pool, gym, Internet* ▤*AE, DC, MC, V.*

$$$
🛏 **Hotel Metropolitan Akita** メトロポリタンホテル秋田. This terra-cotta-color hotel is just outside the west side of JR Akita Station and is perfect for shopping, people-watching, or exploring sights. The lobby is small, but you're right next to some fine street-side coffee and snack shops, and rooms here offer good value—deluxe versions have great views and an extra 12 square feet for an additional ¥1,000 (single) or ¥3,000 (twin). Breakfast is only ¥1,260, served in a sunny café on the third floor. **Pros:** perfect location; 10% off for Rail Pass holders. **Cons:** impersonal, chain hotel feel at times. ⊠*7–2–1 Naka-dōri, Akita-shi, Akita-ken* 🕿*018/831–2222* 🖷*018/831–2290* 📶*123 Western-style rooms* ⟨In-hotel: 3 restaurants* ▤*AE, DC, MC, V.*

14

TSURUOKA AND DEWA-SANZAN 鶴岡と出羽三山

132 km (82 mi) south of Akita, 32 km (20 mi) from Atsumi Onsen

South of Akita along the Nihon-kai coast are small fishing villages where nets hang to dry only inches from train windows, vast plains of rice fields lead to faraway hills, rushing rivers and clear streams are full of fish, and, closer to Atsumi Onsen, you will be confronted with lofty forested mountains coming down to the endless crashing waves. Along the way is the town of **Tsuruoka** 鶴岡, once a castle stronghold of the Sakai family, which serves as a (bus) gateway to Yamagata City and the three mountains of Dewa-Sanzan that are held sacred by the *yama-bushi,* the popular name given to members of the ascetic and nature-loving Shugendō sect of "mountain warrior" Buddhists.

GETTING HERE AND AROUND

Tsuruoka is 1½ hours south of Akita by JR Uetsu Line (¥2,210), or 31 minutes from Atsumi Onsen (¥480). It's easiest to get to the base of Haguro by bus (55 minutes), either from Bus Stop 2, in front of JR Tsuruoka Station, or from Stop 5, at Shō-Kō (Shō-nai Kō-tsu) Mall (it's not a JR bus); there are four departures in winter and at least hourly departures in summer. A fare of ¥700 will take you from the station to the Haguro Center village at the entrance to the peak itself. Most buses from Tsuruoka to Haguro Center continue to the summit, Haguro-san-chō, which is not much farther, but the fare jumps to ¥990 (it covers a toll charge on a private road).

The **Tsuruoka Tourist Information Office** is just to the right from the station exit. They might not speak much English, and most pamphlets about Dewa Sanzan are in Japanese, but they can help with bus schedules and lodging arrangements.

ESSENTIALS

Visitor Information Tsuruoka Tourist Information Office (☎ *0235/25–7678* ☉ *Daily 10–5*).

WHAT TO SEE

The climb up **Haguro-san** 羽黒山 *(Mt. Haguro)* begins in Haguro Center, at the red **Zaishin Gate** (Zaishin-mon), then goes up 2,446 or so stone steps to the summit. The strenuous ascent cuts through ancient cedar trees that rise to dominate the sky. You'll pass an aged 14th-century five-story pagoda sitting alone in the forest. A teashop, open from April through November, is situated at a perfect stop to take in the view. The trail is just over a mile, or 1.7 km in all, and it may take you an hour to reach the 414-meter (1,400-foot) summit with its thatch-roof shrine **Dewa Sanzan Jinja.** You may happen upon one of the mysterious ceremonies held there—the initiation ritual of a *yamabushi* (a "mountain warrior" who seeks power from ascetic practices and close bonds to nature) lasts nine grueling days, and it is said that if an apprentice wants to complete his training he must first prove that he can engage and destroy an imaginary demon. Seventeen to 19 buses a day (¥700) take 40 minutes to Haguro Center from JR Tsuroka Station; many of the buses go all the way to the summit in another 15 minutes for an extra ¥330. It is possible to stay overnight on the mountain at the temple-lodge of Sai-kan, which is attached by a long stairway to the Dewa-Sanzan Jinja.

Haguro-san is the only mountain with year-round access, but if you want to visit the other holy peaks, buses leave JR Tsuruoka Station at 6 and 7 AM in summer for the 90-minute trip (¥1,650) to the Ga-san Hachigome (8th Station) stop, from where you can hike three hours past the glaciers and wildflowers to the 1,984-meter (6,500-foot) summit of Ga-san, or Moon-mountain. From the top you can see the whole gorgeous gallery of mountains that is Yamagata, including one called Dewa-Fuji (after Mt. Fuji) for its shape, and to the Sea of Japan to the west.

The last of the trio of peaks, Yudono-san, is 1,504 meters (5,000 feet) high, and is generally the last on pilgrims' rounds. You can descend on foot in a few hours from Ga-san but it involves some exertion, kanji-sign navigational ability, and slippery metal ladders, and you'll want to talk with the tourist info folks about current conditions. Buses make the 80-minute (¥1,490) run between Tsuruoka and Sen-in-zawa, a trailhead for a short climb to the summit, where you must make a small monetary donation and be purified in a secret ritual that you are forbidden to photograph or tell anyone about. Once cleansed, don't miss the last bus back down to Tsuruoka, which leaves promptly at 4:30.

In summer only, Shōnai Kōtsū buses also depart from Yamagata Bus Terminal (confer with the Tourist Information Office), with stops at all three sacred mountains.

Note that many of the bus companies conducting the trips to the mountains and towns in this area are not affiliated with JR, but they are generally not expensive.

WHERE TO EAT AND STAY

Spending the night around Tsuruoka, you can stay in town or up on Haguro-san, or best of all make your way to Atsumi Onsen *(below)*. If you're hanging around Tsuruoka, here are some places in town.

$$–$$$
JAPANESE ✕ **Kanazawa-ya** 金沢屋. An excellent place to eat soba, Kanazawa-ya offers *tenzaru* (tempura served with cold soba noodles) and *kamo nan-ban soba* (sliced duck breast boiled with soba in hot, savory broth) that are delicious. From the station, walk straight to the corner of Marica and Mister Donut, then turn left, and walk past the highway. Kanaza-wa-ya is on the left. ✉ *3–48 Daihōji-machi, Tsuruoka* ☎ *0235/24–7208* 🚫 *No credit cards* 🕐 *Tues.–Mon., 11–3 and 5–8; closed Wed.*

$$ ⛩ **Sai-kan** 出羽三山神社斉館. This temple lodge connected to Dewa Sanzan Jinja by a long stairway allows you to enjoy the shrine and scenery at the summit after most tourists have gone. The cedar-lined approach is more than majestic, but inside, this shukubo, or Buddhist monks' lodging, is spartan. The large tatami-mat rooms can be separated by *fusuma* (sliding paper doors on wood frames) to create smaller guest rooms. Two vegetarian meals of local goodies are served daily. The place is a madhouse at festival times, but because Sai-kan can handle 300 guests, one more person can probably flop down a futon and squeeze in. **Pros:** great healthy food; tranquil Zen garden. **Cons:** 10-minute walk to bus stop; long bus ride (53 minutes) from Tsuruoka. ✉ *Tōge, Haguro-machi, Higashi Tagawa-gun, Yamagata-ken*

☎*0235/62–2357* 📠*0235/62–2352* 🛏*300 futons* ⚲*In-room: no a/c, no phone, no TV* ▭*No credit cards* ◎*MAP.*

$$ 🎫**Tōkyō Dai-ichi Hotel Tsuruoka** 東京第一ホテル鶴岡. The rooms and views are pleasant, and an open-air bathhouse and sauna for guests are on the roof. The hotel connects to a shopping mall, and the travel connections are unbeatably convenient. It's a three-minute walk from JR Tsuruoka Station and next to the Shōnai Kōtsū Mall and the bus terminal from which buses depart for Haguro-san and Yamagata City (¥2,150, 2 hours 7 minutes). **Pros:** best location in town; fantastic roof-bath. **Cons:** austere decor is uninspiring. ✉*2–10 Nishiki-machi, Tsuruoka-shi, Yamagata-ken* ☎*0235/24–7611* 📠*0235/24–7621* ⊕*www.tdh-tsuruoka.co.jp* 🛏*124 rooms with bath, 1 suite* ⚲*In-hotel: 4 restaurants, bar, Japanese baths* ▭*AE, DC, MC, V.*

ATSUMI ONSEN 熱海温泉

32 km (20 mi) south of Tsuruoka.

Whether you have just climbed one or the whole trio of Dewa's holy mountains, or come a long way by buses and trains, the idea of a long soak in some truly fine mineral waters while listening to a rushing river or pounding surf may sound good to you. We have found a place that is so special that even if you have no interest other than reaching the ultimate Zen moment of pure relaxation, it would still be well worth your while to drop everything, wherever you are, and come here immediately. From Tsuruoka the JR Uetsu Line will whisk you to relaxation in about half an hour (¥480).

Densely forested mountains rear up from the wave-battered seacoast and range themselves at staggering angles along and behind a lovely river valley. As you lean as far back as possible to take it all in, you will be forgiven for blinking and wondering if you dreamed your way into another world. People come here not only to look around in awe but also to soak in and drink the famous regenerative waters. There are many choices, but there is hardly a better place, nor any more luxurious, than at the Tachibana-ya.

$$$$ 🎫**Tachibana-ya** たちばなや. Come in, take off your shoes, and sit back
★ while they pour you some tea and deliver the briefing. Your expansive room is stuffed with simple elegance, and the exquisite bath is equipped with a *hinoki,* or cedar-cypress bathtub. The faucets dispense naturally sweet and curative waters, raised from the same submerged vaults that fill the greenstone indoor and outdoor baths down below. In front, the large expanse of glass behind the shoji screens looks out upon a river valley steep and lushly green, and the only decisions you need make during your stay are how many hours you'd like to soak before and after whatever time you would like your banquets served to you by your room's very own personal attendant. All of this and more soul repair is just a short ¥1,000 taxi ride or 10-minute ¥200 bus ride from JR Atsumi Onsen Station. **Pros:** this will surely be the highlight of your entire trip. **Cons:** price be cursed, but you won't want to leave! ✉*Atsumi 3-chōme, Oaza, Nishitagawa-gun, Yamagata-ken* ☎*0235/43–2211*

Hokkaidō

WORD OF MOUTH

"Hokkaidō is very new as far as Japanese culture goes. It's a great place to BE. To relax, and breathe fresh air."

—TokachiM

"Linda had a whole hairy crab with a crab onigiri while I had the crab ramen with some edamame and an umeboshi onigiri. I could not believe the bill as it came out to only 2,260 yen ($22.60 US). The crab alone would have cost much more back home."

—Hawaiintraveler

Updated
by Amanda
Harlow

Hokkaidō is Japan untamed. Wild mountains, virgin forests, sapphire lakes, and surf-beaten shores keep cities and towns at bay. Hokkaidō, as a distinct part of Japan, was born during the Meiji Restoration (1868–1912), when the Japanese government settled its border regions to ward off economic and political interests of Russia and Europe. Until then the large northern island had been left to the Ainu people, hunter-gatherers who traded with the Japanese and the Russians, and who believed in natural spirit worship.

Then the Meiji Emperor decided to colonize the north. In the 1870s, after studying American and European agriculture, city design, and mining, his government sent 63 foreign experts to harness Hokkaidō resources, and introduced a soldier-farmer system to spur mainlanders north to clear the land and settle. Hokkaidō was ripe with natural resources—coal and gold, herring shoals, and fertile land conducive to dairy farming, potato growing, horse breeding, and even cold-climate, hardy rice farming. The legacy lives on—small holdings with silos and red- or blue-roof barns dot the rolling farmland and wide landscapes give stretches of Hokkaidō an American flavor.

On the losing end of the 19th-century Japanese colonization were the Ainu, who died in the thousands from previously unencountered diseases, forced labor, and conflict with the Japanese. Forced name changes and intermarriage threatened a whole way of life. Thanks to political and cultural activism in recent decades, the Ainu people have clawed their way back to a grudging level of official and public acceptance.

Hokkaidō's Japanese people—who call themselves *Dosanko* after the region's draft horses—are open-minded and individualistic. They readily come to the rescue of foreign travelers with a warmth and directness that make up for language problems. Even now Japanese seeking an alternative way of life head north to Hokkaidō to start new lives as farmers, artists, outdoor adventure guides, and guesthouse owners.

Because Hokkaidō consists more of countryside than of culture-rich cities, the number of foreigners who visit has traditionally been small, although many Japanese visitors are attracted to this unusual, less traditional-looking area of the country. Many locally promoted attractions—flower fields and dairy farms—may be of less interest to people from Western countries than mountain scenery, wildlife, and volcanically active areas. Visitors from other Asian countries and Australian skiers are a common sight.

This is also one of Japan's more politically active borders. In 2006 a Russian patrol boat shot a Nemuro fisherman dead and fined his captain for poaching and border incursion. All over Hokkaidō, signboards and petitions support Japan's claim to the southern four of the Kuril Islands,

TOP REASONS TO GO

The Beer: Beer is king in Hokkaidō, with the Sapporo Beer brewery and local microbreweries in Otaru and Hakodate. Sapporo hosts the Beer Garden Festival in July.

The Slopes: Deep powder snow and uncrowded lift lines are hallmarks of Hokkaidō's ski resorts at Niseko, Rusutsu, and Furano.

The Valley of Hell: Sulfur-spewing springs at Noboribetsu, Tōya, Akan, and Shiretoko burst forth into vents and craters. Check out the ash-flow from the eruption of Tōya's Mt. Usu.

The Last Frontier: Salmon-fishing bears and red-crested cranes, alpine flowers, and vast forests hold modern Japan at bay. The vistas of mountains and plains are best viewed on foot or bike.

Winter Wonderland: Frigid winter nights are brightened by festivals. Out east, icebreakers cut through Arctic ice floes and passengers spy seals and eagles.

which Russia snatched up in the final days of World War II. The Russian business presence is noticeable in Hokkaidō's eastern fishing ports, used-car export yards, and adult entertainment districts.

It's easy to romanticize Japan's northernmost island as largely uncharted territory. But Hokkaidō's big-city dwellers compare the latest fashions while drinking cappuccinos in American coffee-shop chains, and the countryside is crisscrossed by road and rail networks. Beyond the cities, though, small-town life in Hokkaidō is still quiet (often owing to economic stagnation), and for the adventurous visitor wild beauty and open spaces abound. The island is a geological wonderland: lava-seared mountains hide deeply carved ravines; hot springs, gushers, and steaming mud pools boil out of the ground; and crystal-clear lakes fill the seemingly bottomless cones of volcanoes. Half of Hokkaidō is covered in forest. Wild, rugged coastlines hold back the sea, and all around the prefecture islands surface offshore. The remnants of Hokkaidō's bear population, believed to number about 2,000, still roam the forests, snagging rabbits and scooping up fish from mountain streams. Hokkaidō's native crane, the *tanchō-zuru,* is especially magnificent, with a red-cap head and a white body trimmed with black feathers. Look for it in the marshes of Kushiro, on the Pacific coast.

⇨ *See the glossary at the end of this book for definitions of the common Japanese words and suffixes used in this chapter.*

ORIENTATION AND PLANNING

ORIENTATION

Hokkaidō is Japan's northernmost island. Mountains topping 6,500 feet were formed, and are still formed, by volcanic activity. The island is dotted with deep caldera lakes and pockets of rich farmland. Summers are cooler and less humid, winters colder and snowier than elsewhere in Japan.

Hakodate. Gateway to Hokkaidō for train travelers, this bustling port and tourist city has 19th-century clapboard buildings built for early foreign residents, rattling streetcars, and the best public fish market in the region.

Sapporo. Hokkaidō's capital is modern, green, clean, and easy to navigate. At its heart is Ōdōri Park, which hosts the Snow Festival in February and the Beer Festival in July. City specialties include barbecued lamb, crabs, and potatoes, and the Susukino nightlife area is a blaze of neon and noise.

Otaru and Niseko. A historic harbor town, Otaru is now popular for its short canal, cafés, shops, and restaurants, and its artists crafting glass in small studios. Niseko has the best powder snow for skiers and snowboarders from December to April, and adventure sports such as river rafting and mountain biking in summer.

Shikotsu-Tōya National Park. Soaring mountains and deep lakes offer an escape into nature two hours from Sapporo. At Tōya Onsen in the south the mountains visitors hike the recently solidified ash flows that engulfed a village, while at Shikotsu, campers, hikers, and fishing enthusiasts relax around one of Japan's deepest, prettiest lakes.

Eastern Hokkaidō. Bears and eagles on the Shiretoko Peninsula have world protection status with UNESCO, and the red-crested *tancho* cranes stalk the Kushiro wetlands in the south. Farther north, Ainu people at Lake Akan share their culture through song and dance; Arctic ice flows grip the eastern shores in January and February.

Central and Northern Hokkaidō. At the Daisetsu Mountains, in Hokkaidō's center, cable cars lift visitors to flower-filled plateaus, and hiking trails promise panoramic views. Small guesthouses provide lamb barbecues, beer, and hot springs. To the far north are Rebun and Rishiri islands, wild places with short summers, rare flowers, and creamy *uni* sea urchin.

PLANNING

Hokkaidō's expansiveness is daunting. The main sights—calderas, remote onsen, craggy coasts, dramatic mountains—are everywhere. Rather than rushing to see everything, consider balancing the natural with the urban, the inland with the coastal, and figure in the seasonal appropriateness of sights, activities, and available access.

WHEN TO GO

Hokkaidō has Japan's most dramatic seasons. Festivals are ample in summer and winter. May and early summer bring lilacs and alpine flowers. The best time to visit is in late April and early May when the cherry trees in Hokkaidō offer up the last *sakura* (cherry blossoms) in Japan. Glorious weather from May to October lures Japanese drowning in the muggy air of Honshū. Hotel rooms become more difficult to book in summer, and the scenic areas are crowded with tour groups and Japanese families. Late September brings brief but spectacular golden

CLOSE UP

15

Of Slopes and Powder

Up to 40 feet of powder snow makes Hokkaidō the best skiing and snowboarding destination in Japan. Although only Niseko, two hours from Sapporo, has skiing above the tree line and runs are short by North American standards, there is great variety with so many areas within easy reach by public transport. The most spacious areas are Niseko and Rusutsu, two hours west of Sapporo; Kokusai and Kiroro, one hour west of Sapporo; and Furano, Tomamu, and Sahoro, two hours east of Sapporo. Trails are well groomed, lift lines outside the Christmas–New Year's peak season are short, and backcountry exploring wondrous.

Many ski schools (notably Kiroro, Rusutsu, Furano, and Kokusai) and the adventure-tour companies in Niseko have English-speaking guides and teachers. A day's lift pass averages ¥4,500, but ski packages that include bus transportation are a better option and often include lunch and/or hotspring tickets. Hotels and sports shops in Sapporo have discount lift coupons, too. All *su-ki-jō* have beginner courses, and if you are downtown in Sapporo, a taxi can get you to Mount Moiwa in 20 minutes. "Expert" courses are not as hard as in other countries. The biggest danger to novices would likely be mountaintop temperatures reaching minus 15°C (5°F).

Reservations for short ski tours to Hokkaidō from Tōkyō or Ōsaka should be made a week in advance. Reliable domestic delivery companies forward equipment to hotels, but Hokkaidō trains, taxis, and rental cars are fitted to transport winter gear. Equipment and wear can be rented at the resorts, but call ahead to check availability of larger boot sizes.

foliage, reaching a peak in early October. The crisp fall gives way to chilly drizzle in November and early December. Winter makes travel more difficult (some minor roads and attractions are closed), and especially on the east coast the weather is frigid. It's no less beautiful a time, however, with snow covering everything in mounds of white and ice floes crowding the Ohotsuku-kai. If you're here during the second week in February, don't miss the dazzling Snow Festival in Sapporo.

HOW MUCH TIME?

You'll need at least a week to experience Hokkaidō, with a day or two in Sapporo and then a stay in either Hakodate or one of the national parks. Distances are large and a train or road trip across the island takes most of a day. Flying into a regional airport cuts down on unnecessary travel. Hire cars and make hotel reservations in advance; outside Sapporo and Hakodate people who speak enough English to do bookings are hard to find. Check on access for each destination when planning a winter trip.

GETTING HERE AND AROUND

The best way to explore Hokkaidō is by train and car. Most car-rental companies allow different pick-up and drop-off locations and will meet customers at trains, ferries, and local flights.

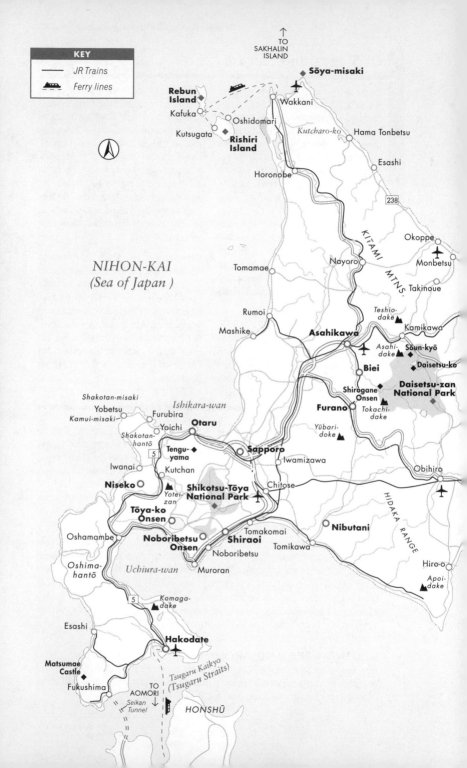

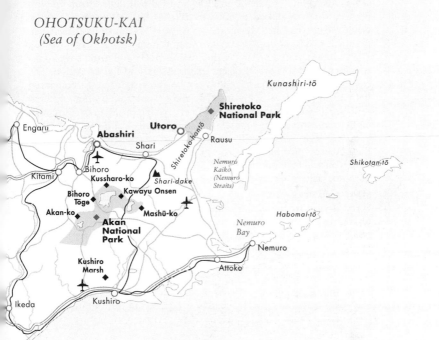

Hokkaidō

OHOTSUKU-KAI
(Sea of Okhotsk)

Kunashiri-tō

Shiretoko
National Park

Utoro

Shiretoko-hantō

Engaru

Abashiri

Shari

Rausu

Nemuro
Kaikō
(Nemuro
Straits)

Shikotan-tō

Kitami

Bihoro

Kussharo-ko

Shari-dake

Bihoro
Tōge

Kawayu Onsen

Akan-ko

Mashū-ko

Akan
National
Park

Habomai-tō

Nemuro
Bay

Nemuro

Kushiro
Marsh

Attoko

Ikeda

Kushiro

TAIHEIYŌ
(Pacific Ocean)

0   20 miles

0   20 kilometers

AIR TRAVEL

Domestic carriers Japan Airlines, All Nippon Airways, and the budget carriers Air Do and SkyMark connect major Japanese airports with Sapporo (New Chitose), Asahikawa, Hakodate, Abashiri (Memambetsu), and Kushiro. Flying across Hokkaidō is a good way to cross the distances, particularly eastern and northern regions. In winter sudden changes in weather can divert or cancel flights, so plan adequate time for connections.

Japan Airlines (JAL), Japan Air System (JAS), and All Nippon Airways (ANA) link Hokkaidō to Honshū by direct flights from Tōkyō's Haneda Kūkō to Hakodate, Sapporo (New Chitose Airport), Asahikawa Airport, Abashiri (Memambetsu Airport), Nemuro (Nakashibetsu Airport), and Kushiro Airport. Two flights a day depart from Tōkyō's Narita International Airport. Other major cities on Honshū have flights to Sapporo, as do several places in the Asian and Pacific region. The cost by air from Tōkyō to Sapporo can be as low as ¥12,000, compared with ¥22,430 by train. Fly-stay packages from Tōkyō offer excellent deals for short trips. Some air travelers arriving in Japan on European flights can, with a change of planes at Tōkyō, fly at no extra charge to Sapporo. If you're flying from overseas to Sapporo via Tōkyō, book the domestic portion when you buy your international ticket; otherwise, you will fork out for what is, per mile, one of the most expensive domestic tickets in the world.

BOAT AND FERRY TRAVEL

Ferry services from Honshū connecting to Tomakomai, Hakodate, and Otaru are a leisurely way to arrive, while around Hokkaidō boats connect the islands of Rebun and Rishiri to the northern tip of Japan. In the far east they offer the best bear-viewing off the Shiretoko Peninsula.

The ferries are the cheapest way to travel to Hokkaidō on paper, but for only a few thousand yen more you can fly and get to the northern island in just over an hour from most places on the mainland. If slow travel is your style there are ferries from Niigata into Otaru and services on the Pacific side, (Nagoya, Oarai, Sendai and Aomori) connect to Hakodate and Tomakomai.

First class is usually double second-class prices and the extra buys you privacy and comfort as most regular passengers stretch out on communal carpeted areas. Out of the summer holiday season the ferries are mostly used by long distance truck drivers with cargos of livestock, timber, and foodstuffs.

Most useful, if you don't mind a 24-hour journey, is Shōsen Mitsui's Pacific Story package. This is a bus/ferry/bus service which connects Tōkyō to Sapporo for only ¥9,900 (excluding July 18 to August 31), departing Tōkyō mid-afternoon and reaching Sapporo the following afternoon. Check the English Web site for info and reserve tickets at the Tōkyō or Shinjuku Highway Bus terminals. Tickets can also be bought for the Oarai to Tomakomai section only, and economy tickets range from ¥8,500 to ¥14,000 depending on the season.

Other ferry services for Hokkaidō are Shin Nihon-kai Ferry's Niigata to Otaru ¥6,200; Taiheiyō Ferry's Sendai to Tomakomai 14-hour service for ¥8,000 and the mammoth 39-hour Nagoya-Sendai-Tomakomai costing only ¥10,500; Kawasaki Kinkai Kisen's Hachinohe to Tomakomai in nine hours for ¥5,000; and Seikan Ferry's service that crosses between Aomori and Hakodate in four hours and costs ¥1,800.

BUS TRAVEL

Buses cover most of the major routes through the scenic areas, and all the excursions in this chapter may be accomplished by bus. There's no English-language telephone service for buses in Hokkaidō. Plaza i in Sapporo will supply bus-route and schedule information and make telephone bookings if required.

CAR TRAVEL

Driving in Hokkaidō has been made easy, despite mountain bends and snow, by wide roads and English signage that helps guide you to wilder places. Toll highways link only Sapporo with Oshamambe, Asahikawa, and Obihiro. Otherwise, two-lane roads are the norm, and farm vehicles can slow travel.

Hokkaidō is the best place in Japan for driving. Most major companies have offices at Chitose Airport, in major cities, and in smaller centers in tourist areas. JR Hokkaidō arranges very good value train/car/stay packages, although reservations can only be made in English at major stations such as Sapporo and Hakodate. Telephone reservations in English depend on staff availability. Car rental, depending on the season, can cost as little as ¥6,000 per day. August is peak holiday driving season, so book early.

The staffs at local offices do not speak English. Reservations are best made through the ToCoo Web site for Mazda, Nissan, Toyota, MMC, and J-Net. Japanese are cautious drivers, though a combination of wide straight roads, light traffic, treacherous weather conditions, and Honshū visitors' unfamiliarity with all of the above gives Hokkaidō the worst traffic fatality figures in Japan. Beware of speed traps: in apparently rural areas a hidden village can dictate urban speed limits of 50 to 60 KPH. Most signage is in English. When booking, request an English navigation system.

TRAIN TRAVEL

Japan Railways Hokkaidō helps visitors enjoy the big country in comfort, with a three- or five-day Hokkaidō Rail Pass and good English-language information at major stations. Although there are no *Shinkasen* yet, super express trains connect Sapporo south to Hakodate (and on to Honshū), and north and east to Asahikawa, Kushiro, Abashiri, and Wakkanai. Three days cost ¥14,000 and five days ¥18,000; Green superior cars cost ¥6,000 extra. Train and car packages are available.

The train journey from Tōkyō to Sapporo can take as little as 10 hours. This trip involves a combination of the Shinkansen train to Morioka (2½ hours), the northernmost point on the Tōhoku Shinkansen Line, and a change to an express train for the remaining journey to Hakodate (4 hours, 20 minutes) and then on to Sapporo (3¼ hours). The JR Pass covers this route (the cost is ¥22,430 without the pass). The Hokutosei sleeper train provides greater comfort and eliminates the need to change trains, but the voyage takes 17 hours. The fare is ¥23,520 (¥9,450 for

15

JR Pass holders). Forget about local trains from Tōkyō, the combined travel time to Sapporo is 30 hours, not including the required overnight stop in Aomori. Travelers with more time than cash would do better on the ferry.

RESTAURANTS

Eat at local Japanese restaurants for Hokkaidō's regional food, which includes delicious seafood and lamb. Many reasonably priced restaurants have a visual display of their menu in the window. If you cannot order in Japanese and no English is spoken, lead the waiter to the window display and point. Outside the cities there may not be many dining choice in the evening, and while large hot spring hotels often have huge buffet dinners, the smaller guest houses excel in food that is locally caught, raised, and picked.

HOTELS

Accommodations that are easily booked in English tend to be modern, characterless hotels built for Japanese tour groups. Gorgeous lobbies and cookie-cutter rooms are the norm. Room air-conditioning is unusual, except in large hotels, but the cool Hokkaidō summers render it unnecessary. More attractive and comfortable hotels are appearing as younger Japanese seek out lodging with more personality. Guesthouses or pensions are a cheaper and friendlier option, with welcoming owners who strive to impress with the catch of the day or wild vegetables on the dinner menu. Most guesthouses have Western-style beds. Although booking in Japanese is the norm, simple English faxes or e-mails via a Web site can work, too. Dinner reservations at guesthouses are required. Youth hostels are also a good option; in the towns and cities they are usually clean and modern, and in the national parks, although older, they are excellent touring bases.

Outside Sapporo and Hokkaidō's other commercial cities, hot-spring hotels charge on a per-person basis including two meals, excluding service and tax. In those cases, the rates listed below are for two people with two meals each, and the Modified American Plan (MAP) is noted in the service information. If you don't want dinner, you can often renegotiate the price; remember, though, that hot spring hotels and guesthouses are your best bet for dinner in remote areas.

WHAT IT COSTS IN YEN				
¢	$	$$	$$$	$$$$
RESTAURANTS under ¥800	¥800–¥1,000	¥1,000–¥2,000	¥2,000–¥3,000	over ¥3,000
HOTELS under ¥8,000	¥8,000–¥12,000	¥12,000–¥18,000	¥18,000–¥22,000	over ¥22,000

Restaurant prices are per person for a main course, set meal, or equivalent combinations of smaller dishes. Hotel prices are for a double room, excluding service and 5% tax.

On the Menu

Hokkaidō is known for its seafood—the prefecture's name means "the Road to the Northern Sea." *Shake* (salmon), *ika* (squid), *uni* (sea urchin), *nishin* (herring), and *kai* (shellfish) are abundant, but the real treat is the fat, sweet scallop, *kai-bashira*, collected from northernmost Wakkanai. The other great favorite is crab, which comes in three varieties: *ke-gani* (hairy crab), *taraba-gani* (king crab), and Nemuro's celebrated *hana-saki-gani* (spiny king crab).

Jingisukan is thinly sliced mutton cooked on a dome-shaped griddle. The name comes from the griddle's resemblance to helmets worn by Mongolian cavalry under Genghis Khan. Vegetables—usually onions, green peppers, and cabbage—are added to the sizzling mutton, and the whole mix is dipped in a tangy brown sauce. Ramen is extremely popular and inexpensive. Local residents favor miso ramen, which uses a less delicate variety of fermented soybean paste than miso soup. Ramen with *shio* (salt) or *shōyu* (soy sauce) soup base is also widely available.

EMERGENCIES

Traveler emergencies are most likely to happen when driving, hiking, or engaging in winter sports in Hokkaidō. Driving conditions in November and early December are hazardous; locals are quick to aid stranded drivers, and many carry chains and winch cables in their vehicles. Distances between gas stations in rural areas can be long. In spring and fall hikers should heed bear warning signs at trailheads, and solo travelers should inform guesthouse staff about their hiking plans and sign in at trailhead visitor books. Beyond major cities English is not widely spoken, but police and other emergency service staffs are generally unfazed by a foreign face.

BANKS AND EXCHANGE SERVICES

Outside major cities there are no exchange services. Hokkaidō towns are small, and local banks are not user-friendly for foreign visitors. Sapporo, Hakodate, Asahikawa, and Kushiro have banks with exchange counters and automatic teller machines. Credit card use is not widespread, apart from large hotels and gas stations.

Banks in Sapporo are concentrated on Eki-mae Dōri, the wide main street linking the station and the Ōdōri shopping area. Banking hours are weekdays 10–3.

VISITOR INFORMATION

The Japan National Tourist Organization's Tourist Information Center (TIC) in Tōkyō has free Hokkaidō maps and brochures. It's the best place for travel information in English.

To really get out into Hokkaidō and see its wild side, join a hiking tour with **Japan Adventures.** The Hokkaidō Bush Pig, New Zealander Leon Roode, runs two- to seven-day camping and hiking trips for the novice and the hard-core hiker.

ESSENTIALS
Airline Information Air Do (☎011/200–7333). **Air Hokkaidō and Air Nippon** (☎0120/029–222). **Hokkaidō Air System** (☎0120/511–283). **Japan Airlines** (☎0120/255–931 international, 0120/255–971, 011/232–3690 domestic). **Japan Air System** (☎0120/711–283 international, 0120/511–283 domestic). **SkyMark** (☎050/3116–7370 Japanese only ⊕ www.skymark.co.jp/ja/).

Boat and Ferry Contacts Kawasaki Kinkai Kisen (☎03/3502–4838, Japanese-only). **Seikan Ferry** (☎017/782–3671, Japanese-only). **Shin Nihonkai Ferry** (☎03/3543–5500, Japanese-only). **Shōsen Mitsui** (☎03/3844–1950, Tōkyō-Japanese only, 029/267–4133, Ōrai-Japanese only ⊕ www.sunflower.co.jp/ferry/). **Taiheiyō Ferry** (☎052/582–8611, Japanese-only).

Consulate Contact U.S. Consulate (✉ Kita 1-jō, Nishi 28, Chūō-ku, Maruyama Park, Sapporo ☎011/641–1115).

Currency Exchange The Hokkaidō Bank Money Exchange Plaza (✉ Ōdōri, Nishi 4, Sapporo ☎011/233–1167 ⊙ Weekdays 10–7, Sat. 10–5).

Emergency Contacts Ambulance (☎119). **Police** (☎110).

Hostel Contact Hokkaidō Youth Hostel Association (☎011/825–3389 ✍ hokkaido@youthhostel.or.jp ⊕ www.youthhostel.or.jp/English).

Rental Agencies JR Hokkaidō–Rent-a-Car (☎011/742–8211). **Nippon Rent-a-Car** (☎03/3485–7196). **ToCoo Car Rental** (☎03/5333–0246 ⊕ www2.tocoo.jp/). **Toyota Rent-a-Car** (☎0123/40–0100 English ⊕ www.toyotarentacar.net/english).

Road Conditions Hokkaidō Traffic Information (☎011/281–6511).

Tour information Japan Adventures. (☎090/8275–5012 Leon direct ⊕ www.japan-adventures.com).

Train Information Japan Railway Information Line (☎03/3423–0111). **JR Hokkaidō Twinkle Plazas at main stations** (☎011/209–5030 ⊕ www.jrhokkaido.co.jp/global/).

Visitor Information Tourist Information Center (TIC) (✉ Tōkyō International Forum Bldg., Fl. B-1, 3–5–1 Marunōchi, Chiyoda-ku, Tōkyō ☎03/3201–3331).

HAKODATE 函館

160 km (99 mi) from Aomori, 318 km (198 mi) south of Sapporo.

Facing out on two bays, Hakodate is a 19th-century port town, with clapboard buildings on sloping streets, a dockside tourist zone, streetcars, and fresh fish on every menu. In the downtown historic quarter, a mountain rises 1,100 feet above the city on the southern point of the narrow peninsula. Russians, Americans, Chinese, and Europeans have all left their mark; this was one of the first three Japanese ports the Meiji government opened up to international trade in 1859.

EXPLORING HAKODATE

The main sights around the foot of Mount Hakodate can be done in a day, but the city is best appreciated with an overnight stay for the illumination in the historic area, the night views from either the mountain or the fort tower, and the fish market at dawn. City transport is easy to navigate and English information is readily available. Evening departure trains from Tōkyō arrive here at dawn—perfect for fish market breakfasts.

GETTING HERE AND AROUND

Hakodate is 3 hours south of Sapporo by express train and 2½ hrs north of Aomori by JR Rapid via the Seikan Tunnel.

Streetcars cost ¥200–¥250, and municipal buses cost ¥200–¥260. The sightseeing area is hilly, so save foot power by using a one- or two-day bus and streetcar pass (¥1,000/1,700), and borrow an audio walking guide (deposit ¥500) from the tourist center.

For sightseeing, hotel, and travel information in English stop at the **Hakodate City Tourist Information Center** inside the station building.

ESSENTIALS

Car Rental Mazda Car Rental (Hakodate Airport) (☎0138/59–0002; 03/5286–0712 English inquiries ⊕ www.car-rental.europcar.com/).

Currency Exchange Hokuyō Bank (⊠15–7 Wakamatsu-chō ☎0138/23–8511 ⊙9–3).

Visitor Information Hakodate City Tourist Information Center (⊠12–14 Wakamatsu-chō 040-0063 ☎0138/23–5440 ⊙Apr.–Oct., daily 9–7, and Nov.–Mar., daily 9–5).

WHAT TO SEE

Hakodate History Plaza 函館歴史プラザ *(Hakodate Puraza).* On the cobbled waterfront of Moto-machi, redbrick warehouses now bustle with 21st-century tourism: shops, restaurants, bars, harbor boat trips, street entertainers, and glass-blowing studios. In December it offers a giant Canadian Christmas tree and nightly fireworks. This is a good place to wind down, although most bars close at 10:30 PM. The Plaza is a 1.5-km (1 mi) walk from Hakodate Station. ⊠14–16 Suehiro-cho, about 750 feet northwest of Jūji-gai streetcar stop ☎0138/23–0350.

Hakodate Russian Orthodox Church 函館ハリストス正教会 *(Harisutosu Sei Kyōkai).* A green Byzantine dome and tower rise above this beautiful white church. The present building dates from 1916, and donations help with the upkeep of Hakodate's most exotic attraction. The Episcopal and Catholic churches are on either side. ⊠3–13 Moto-machi ☎0138/23–7387.

Morning Market 朝市 *(Asa-ichi).* Bright red crabs wave giant claws from old fishing boats filled with water, squid dart furiously around restaurant tanks, and samples of dried octopus parts are piled high—it's all at Hokkaidō's largest public fish market one block from Hakodate Station. It opens at dawn; if you can face it, try a fish-on-rice breakfast. Asa-ichi, which also has a fruit and vegetable section, stays active until mid-afternoon. ⊠Asa-ichi, Wakamatsu-chō.

The Moto-machi Historic Area. Overlooking the western bay at the foot of Mount Hakodate is a 2-square-kilometer area of wide, sloping streets lined with the 19th-century churches, consulates, shops, and homes of the Japanese and foreigners who first opened up this part of Japan to commerce. Only the main historic buildings have English information, but many others have been converted into shops and cafés. Return here at night when the illuminated buildings, particularly in winter, show why Hakodate is a favorite Japanese romantic movie and TV drama location.

The most interesting historic buildings and museums, namely the arch-Victorian **Old Public Hall**, with the Emperor's Toilet; the **British Consulate**, a nice place for tea and scones; and the **Museum of Northern Peoples**. They can be visited with combined tickets. Get off the streetcar at Suehiro-chō stop and start at the museum, then walk 10 minutes up the Motoizaka Slope to the other two. ✉*¥300 for 1 site, ¥500 for 2, ¥720 for all 3* ⊙ *Apr.–Oct., daily 9–7, Nov.–Mar., daily 9–5.*

NEED A BREAK? More than 100 kimono-clad dolls watch guests with their coffees, teas, and traditional desserts in the tiny, two-room **Kitchen and Cafe Hana** (✉ *2–21 Funami-chō* ☎ *0138/24–4700*), in a house near the gates of the Old Public Hall. Shoes off at the door, please.

WHERE TO EAT

¢–$ ✕**Hakodate Beer Hall** 函館ビアホール. This seaside hall in Hakodate His-
SEAFOOD   tory Plaza serves seafood specialties such as squid, octopus, and tofu *shabu shabu* (cooked tableside by dipping into boiling water and then into a sauce) for ¥1,300 and three local brews (wheat beer, ale, and the slightly more bitter "alt" beer). Its spaciousness and conviviality are typical of Hokkaidō, and although it's in a tourist complex, locals like the wide range of Hokkaidō's seasonal specialties. ✉ *5–22 Ote-machi* ☎ *0138/23–8000* ▭ *AE, V.*

$–$$ ✕**Michi-no-iie** 道乃家食堂. What do squid eyes taste like? Imagine the
JAPANESE   dog's chew toy, all slimy and gristly, add in an exploding juice ball, and you have the eye-light of the *ika-sashi ika-sumi don* set at ¥1,800. Your squid is pulled flapping from the tank and returns minutes later sliced, with squid-ink black rice, delicious slivers of still-twitching flesh, soup, pickles, and two big black eyes. Wash it down with gray-squid ice cream for dessert. Luckily, the restaurant has plenty of other seafood, and a picture menu for easy selection. It's on the Morning Market's closest corner to the station, first restaurant on the right in the eating alleyway. ✉ *Donburi Yokochō Ichiba, Asa-ichi* ☎ *0138/22–6086* ▭ *No credit cards.*

WHERE TO STAY

$$$–$$$$ ▦**Hakodate Kokusai Hotel** 函館国際ホテル. This bustling modern hotel
occupies three buildings a short walk from the station, the Morning Market area, and the History Plaza warehouses. Standard rooms in pastel shades have views of the ugly waterside highway or—much better—the city. If you're coming from Sapporo, check with Japan Rail about rail-hotel combination packages for good deals at this hotel. **Pros:** walking distance from station fish market and waterfront History

Plaza. **Cons:** modern box hotel; tour group central. ⊠*5–10 Ohtemachi* ☎*0138/23–5151* 🖷*0138/23–0239* ⊕*www.hakodate.ne.jp/kokusai hotel* 🖙*304 Western-style rooms, 6 Japanese-style rooms* ⚒*In-hotel: 4 restaurants, room service, bars, laundry service, parking (free)* ⊟*AE, MC, V.*

$$$ 🖺**Pension Kokian** ペンション古稀庵. A 100-year-old former seaweed shop with a modern annex behind the waterfront warehouses has small Western motel–style rooms, each with sink units and shared bathrooms. The traditional restaurant in the old building prepares the best of the morning's catch. **Pros:** excellent location near the waterfront warehouses; attractive main building. **Cons:** no lounge to relax in; really a restaurant with rooms upstairs. ⊠*13–2 Suehiro-chō, Hakodate* ☎*0138/26–5753* 🖷*0138/22–2710* 🖙*17 Western-style rooms* ⚒*In-room: no a/c. In-hotel: restaurant, bar* ⊟*AE, DC, V.*

¢–$ 🖺**Pension Puppy Tail** ペンションパピーテール. Decoupage decorations
★ and garlands of silk flowers overwhelm and so does the family's welcoming manner. The owner, Fukui-san, speaks English and can pick guests up from the station. Breakfast (¥1,000) and dinner (¥2,000) should be reserved the day before. Faxed reservations are best. The kitschy name? The Fukui family thought their red setter's tail looked like the Hakodate part of the Hokkaidō map. Rooms in the newer annex have private bathrooms. It's a 10-minute walk north of the station on Route 5. **Pros:** genuine family welcome; walking distance to station. **Cons:** from the station it's the opposite direction to the sights; some rooms very small. ⊠*30–16 Wakamatsu-chō, Hakodate* ☎*0138/23–5858* 🖷*0138/26–8239* ⊕*www.p-puppytail.com* 🖙*6 Western-style rooms, 13 Japanese-style rooms* ⚒*In-hotel: restaurant, Japanese baths* ⊟*No credit cards.*

SAPPORO 札幌

318 km (297 mi) north of Hakodate.

Modern, open-hearted Sapporo is a good planning base for any trip to Hokkaidō's wilder regions, with plenty of English-language information and transport connections. Hokkaidō's capital is also worth a few days' stay for its major snow (February), dance (June), and beer (July and August) festivals.

With 1.8 million inhabitants, it's four times larger than Asahikawa, the prefecture's next-largest city, but the downtown area can be crossed on foot in 25 minutes. Centered on the 11-block-long Ōdori Kōen (park), an ideal people-watching place, it has wide streets and sidewalks and bustling shopping complexes. There is limited sightseeing, but there's enough to fill a day or two at a holiday's start or finish. Products from all over Hokkaidō can be found, and the dining-out standards are high.

EXPLORING SAPPORO

The name *Sapporo* is derived from a combination of Ainu words meaning "a river running along a reed-filled plain." In 1870 the governor of Hokkaidō visited President Grant in the United States and requested that American advisers visit Hokkaidō to help design the capital on the site of an Ainu village. As a result, Sapporo was built on a grid system with wide avenues and parks. Today, the downtown area has uncluttered streets and English signs. It's distinctly lacking in pre-Meiji historic sights.

GETTING HERE AND AROUND

The two domestic airlines—Japan Air System (JAS) and All Nippon Airways (ANA)—have local companies connecting Sapporo with Hakodate, Kushiro, Wakkanai, and the smaller Memambetsu, Naka-Shibetsu, and Ohotsuku-Mombetsu airports in eastern Hokkaidō. Hokkaidō Air System is part of JAS. Air Hokkaidō and Air Nippon are part of ANA. There's also daily service between Wakkanai and both Rebun and Rishiri islands.

No nonstop flights go from the United States to Hokkaidō. Passengers arriving in Japan on international flights with All Nippon Airways (ANA) and Japan Airlines (JAL) can get domestic discounted connections to Sapporo's New Chitose Airport Shin-Chitose Kūkō, Hokkaidō's main airport. The Hokkaidō-based Air Do and budget start-up SkyMark often have the least expensive flights between Tōkyō and Sapporo.

More than 30 domestic routes link Chitose, 40 km (25 mi) south of the city, to the rest of Japan, and flights from Chitose to other parts of Asia are increasing. Some local flights also depart from Okudama Airport, 5 km (3 mi) north of downtown.

Japan Railways (JR) runs every 20 minutes or so between the airport terminal and downtown Sapporo. ■TIP➔ Don't make the mistake of getting off at the suburban Shin-Sapporo station, 10 minutes before Sapporo station itself. If you are heading directly east from the airport, change at Minami Chitose to pick up the Kushiro-bound train. The trip into Sapporo is usually made by rapid-transit train (¥1,040, 40 minutes). Hokuto Bus and Chūō Bus run shuttle buses (¥820) that connect the airport with downtown hotels and Sapporo Station, twice every an hour. The trip takes about 70 minutes but can be slower in winter.

Sapporo is easy to navigate. Eki-mae Dōri (Station Road) runs south of the station, crossed east–west by Ōdōri Kōen (park), then continues south through the shopping district to the nightlife area Susukino and beyond to Nakajima Park. Addresses use the cardinal points: north, south, east, and west are *kita, minami, higashi,* and *nishi,* respectively.

Downtown sights are easily covered on foot in a few hours, using Ōdōri Subway Station as the center point. In winter underground shopping malls linking the subway station with both Susukino and the TV Tower become bustling thoroughfares.

Two circular bus routes connect many of the main sites. The Factory Line—bus stops are confusingly marked "Sapporo Walk"—connects downtown shops, the train station, the fish market, the Sapporo Factory, and the Sapporo Beer Garden. The Sansaku or Stroller Bus (May to October only) connects downtown with Maruyama Park and Ōkurayama Jump Hill. Rides on both cost ¥200 each time or ¥750 for a day pass. Tickets are available on the buses or from Chūō Bus counter at the JR station or bus terminal.

Most of Sapporo's subway signs include English. There are three lines: the Namboku Line, the Tōzai Line, and the Tohō Line. They cross at Ōdōri Station.

> **BOOK SMARTS**
>
> Outside Sapporo, finding English-language books is difficult, so you may want to browse in the expansive Kinokuniya near the west exit of Sapporo station first; foreign magazines are on the first floor near the escalators, and fiction, nonfiction, and English-language teaching books are on the second floor. The children's section also has many Japanese titles in translation. ✉ *Kita-5 jō, Nishi 6, Sapporo station, Sapporo* ☎ *011/231-2131* ⊙ *Daily 10–9.*

The basic fare, covering a distance of about three stations, is ¥200. A one-day open ticket (*ichi-nichi-ken*) for ¥1,000 provides unlimited subway (¥800 for the subway alone), bus, and streetcar access. Tickets are available at subway stations and the machines have English instructions. There are also prepaid cards (¥1,000, ¥3,000, ¥5,000, and ¥10,000 at vending machines) for multiday travel.

Public transportation makes renting a car for Sapporo sightseeing unnecessary, but it's a good place to rent for setting out into the southern and western national parks. Trips farther north and east are best made by train; rent a car at the destination. In Sapporo major car companies are clustered around Sapporo Station.

Taxi meters start at ¥550 or ¥600, depending on the company. An average fare, such as from the JR station to Susukino, runs about ¥800 ($7). In winter most taxies are fitted with ski and board roof-racks, and drivers are adept at stowing even the bulkiest winter gear.

ESSENTIALS

Car Rental Honda (✉ *1–2, Nishi 2, Kita 10, Sapporo Station* ☎ *011/737–5353* ⊕ *www.hondarent.com/English/* ⊙ *Daily 8–8*). **Toyota Rent-a-Car** (✉ *Sapporo Station east, Higashi 2–1, Kita 5, Kita-ku* ☎ *011/281–0111* ⊕ *www.toyotarentacar. net* ⊙ *Daily 8–8*).

Emergency Contacts Hokkaidō University Hospital (✉ *Kita 14-jō Nishi 5, Sapporo* ☎ *011/716–1161*).

Internet ComicLand Internet Cafe (✉ *Ōdōri Nishi 4, near Exit 10 from Ōdōri subway station, Sapporo* ☎ *011/200–3003* ⊙ *Until 3 AM*). **Sapporo Main Post Office** (✉ *Kita-6 jō, Higashi 1, 2 blocks from Sapporo Station, Sapporo* ☎ *011/251–3957* ⊙ *Daily 9–5, but 24-hr window for registered mail*).

Shipping DHL (✉ *Nishi 6, Kita-5 jō, Chūō-ku, Sapporo* ☎ *011/894–8315*).

15

Tour Information Nippon Travel Agency (☎ *011/207–5533*). **Nextage Inc.** (☎ *011/210–7255* ⊕ *www11.ocn. ne.jp/~nextage*). **Skybus** (⊕ *www.sky bus-jp.com*).

Visitor Information Hokkaidō-Sapporo Food and Tourism Information Center (✉ *Sapporo Station, Western Concourse, North Exit* ✉ *North Ticket Gate, Ōdōri Subway Station, Ōdōri* ☎ *011/213–5088* ⊙ *Daily 8:30–8*).

WHAT TO SEE
DOWNTOWN SAPPORO

❸ **Ōdōri Kōen** 大通公園 *(Ōdōri Park)*. This 345-foot-wide green belt bisects the city center. In summer everyone buys soy sauce or butter-covered corn and potatoes from food vendors and sits down to watch the street performers, skateboarders, and each other. The Sapporo Beer Festival lasts three weeks in July, when every block becomes an outdoor beer garden and thousands of drinkers enjoy open-air stage shows. Sapporo Snow Festival is one week in February, when volunteers create blockwide life-like snow sculptures and 2 million marveling visitors slip and slide around. ✉ *Nishi 11-chome bus or subway stop Ōdōri*.

❹ **Tanuki Mall** 狸小路 *(Tanuki Kōji)*. A *tanuki* is a raccoon dog, which is known in Japanese mythology for its cunning and libidinous nature. The Tanuki Kōji covered arcade got its name because the area used to be frequented by prostitutes. Now a different breed of merchant is eager to lighten the wallets of passersby. The arcade is crowded with small shops selling clothing, footwear, electronics, records, and Ainu-inspired souvenirs of Hokkaidō. Tanuki Kōji has considerably lower prices than the area's department stores. It's also the place to find Hokkaidō specialties from melon confections to dried salmon and seaweed. ✉ *Minami 3-jō, extending from Nishi 1 to 7, Chūō-ku*.

❷ **Clock Tower** 時計台 *(Tokeidai)*. For millions of Japanese, this little white-clapboard Russian-style meeting house defines Sapporo; it is used as the city's symbol on souvenir packaging. Now almost lost among the modern office blocks, it was the 1878 drill hall for the pioneer students of Sapporo Agricultural College (now Hokkaidō University). Inside are photographs and documents of city history and a clock from Boston. More entertainment is had outside, watching tourists backing up at a busy intersection to fit everything into the camera frame. ✉ *Kita 1-jō Nishi 2, Chūō-ku* ☎ *¥200* ⊙ *Tues.–Sat. 9–5*.

❶ **Botanical Gardens** 北大植物園 *(Shokubutsu-en)*. With more than 5,000 plant varieties, the gardens are a cool summer retreat, both for their green space and their shade. Nonplant highlights include a small Ainu

FOUND IN TRANSLATION

Sapporo International Communication Plaza 札幌国際プラザ *(Sapporo Kokusai Kōryū Puraza)* is the best place for travel, nightlife, restaurant, and travel suggestions in Hokkaidō and for meeting people who speak English. You can have something translated from Japanese into English. The salon with books, newspapers, and brochures in English is meant for informal socializing. Pick up a free copy of *What's On in Sapporo* at the salon information counter. The Clock Tower faces the building. ✉ *3rd fl., Kita 1-jō, Nishi 3, Chūō-ku, Ōdōri* ☎ *011/221–2105* ⊕ *www.plaza-sapporo.or.jp* ⊙ *Mon.–Sat. 9–5:30.*

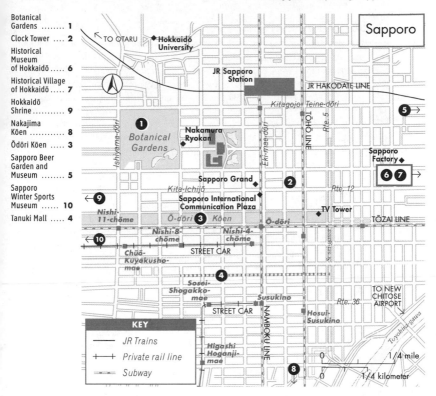

Museum with a grisly but fascinating 13-minute film of an Ainu bear-killing ceremony in Asahikawa in 1935, and a large taxidermied husky dog shares a room with bears and an Ezo wolf. This glassy-eyed hound is—or, was—Tarō, one of the canine survivors of the abandoned 1958 Antarctic expedition, a story brought to non-Japanese audiences in the Disney movie *Eight Below*. After his ordeal, Taro retired to Hokkaidō University and died in 1970. ⊠ *Kita 3-jō, Nishi 8, Chūō-ku* 🚆 *May–Oct., gardens and greenhouse ¥400; Nov.–Apr., gardens free, greenhouse ¥110 ⏲ Apr.–Sept., daily 9–4; Oct.–Nov., daily 9–3:30; Dec.–Mar., weekdays 9–5.*

❽ **Nakajima Kōen** 中島公園 *(Nakajima Park)*. This green escape is a 10-minute walk beyond Susukino's lights and contains **Hōheikan,** a white-and-blue Russian-influenced 19th-century imperial guesthouse, **Hassō-an Teahouse,** a simple, empty 17th-century teahouse in the Japanese garden on the right as you enter the park's northern side, a boating lake, and the concert hall Kitara, home of the Pacific Music Festival, started in 1990 by Leonard Bernstein.

ELSEWHERE IN SAPPORO

❼ **Historical Village of Hokkaidō** 北海道開拓の村 *(Kaitaku-no-mura).* Step out of your shoes and into the 19th century at the herring-fleet dormitory where 60 fishermen appear to have just folded up their futons

CLOSE UP

Sapporo Festivals

One of Japan's best-known annual events, held for a week beginning February 5 or 6, is the **Sapporo Snow Festival.** More than 300 lifelike ice sculptures as large as 130 feet high by 50 feet deep by 80 feet wide are created each year. Memorable statues include baseball star Matsui, cavorting whales, dinosaurs, and the Taj Mahal.

The festival began in 1950 with six statues commissioned by the local government to entertain Sapporo citizens depressed by the war and the long winter nights. Now the event is so large that the sculptures are spread around three different sections of the city: Ōdōri Kōen, Susukino and the suburban Tsudome site. You'll also find ice slides for children. Everyone looks on as international teams of amateur and professional ice sculptors hired by major local businesses have four days to sculpt their creations. Although statues are roped off, taking photographs is no problem. The festival attracts more than 2 million visitors each year, so book your stay well in advance.

During the **Yosakoi Festival** every June, Sapporo's streets stage Japan's version of Carnival. More than 40,000 performers go wild in brightly colored costumes and face paint as they run, jump, and chant their way through the city streets. Dance teams wave flags and snap *naruko* (wooden clappers) in the wake of giant trucks mounted with powerful sound systems and *taiko* drummers in loincloths. Ticketed seats are available in the stands along the route in Ōdōri Kōen and at an outdoor stage, but they aren't necessary. Most people just perch wherever they can get a vantage point. Dance teams also perform in Susukino at night. A boisterous Japanese take on hip-hop crossed with aerobics, Yosakoi is far more exciting than the traditional *bon ōdōri* community dancing.

The Yosakoi Festival is based on the Kōchi Festival in Shikoku. Dancers perform to music based on *sōran*, a Hokkaidō fisherman's folk song. Yosakoi usually starts the second week of June, and the main events take place over a long weekend.

and left for a day's work, or the village clinic where Dr. Kondō seems to have vanished, leaving his scary-looking birthing table and books behind. It's easy to spend a few hours walking in and out of 60 homes, shops, farms, and offices brought from all over Hokkaidō in a park museum that shows how ordinary people lived and worked. A ride down main street in a horse-drawn trolley (summer) or sleigh (winter) costs ¥200. ■TIP➡ **Ask for the excellent, free, blue-colored English guide at the ticket counter.** The village is about 10 km (6 mi) outside Sapporo; easiest access is via an hour bus ride (¥260) from Sapporo Station on a Japan Rail Bus or a 10-minute taxi ride from Shin-Sapporo Station. ✉ *1–50–1 Konopporo, Atsubetsu-chō, Atsubetsu-ku* ☎ *011/898–2692* ☞ *¥830* ⊙ *Tues.–Sun. 9:30–4:30.*

⑥ Historical Museum of Hokkaidō 開拓記念館 *(Kaitaku Kinenkan).* From mammoth molars on through Ainu and samurai-farmers, to bulky 1950s home electronics, the history of Hokkaidō is meticulously exhibited in glass-case and map displays, which are dry compared to the people's history in the Historical Village 10 minutes away. But this is a thorough overview of how Meiji Japan realized it had a northern island

CLOSE UP

The Beer

Sapporo means beer to drinkers around the world, and what would a visit to the city of the same name be without a little beer research?

Head to Sapporo Beer Museum, 2 km (1 mi) northeast of Sapporo Station for a cursory history lesson in the redbrick former factory, and then to the neighboring Biergarten, where waiters in a cavernous noisy hall will rush to get a glass of the golden brew into your hands. Raise your glass—*Kampai!*

If you are in town in July and early August, join Sapporo Beer and other companies at the Sapporo Beer Garden festival in Ōdōri Park in the city center: every night for three weeks hundreds of revelers sit out under the trees with beer kegs and snacks, while musicians provide distraction on outdoor stages. The faithful can do the factory tour and tasting at Hokkaidō Brewery at Eniwa, near New Chitose Airport, where guides (Japanese-language only) show the brewing process.

Brewmaster Seibei Nakagawa spent two years at the Berliner Brauerai studying German know-how and returned ready to put it all into practice. The first brewery was at the current Sapporo Factory shopping mall, and Sapporo Reisi (cold) Beer, with a red-and-black label bearing the red star symbol of the Kaitakushi, first went on sale in 1877.

Toriaezu biiru! (First, beer!) is chorused at parties, beer-hall barbecues, and campsite cookouts. Sapporo Beer dominates the market, but microbreweries offer interesting alternatives. Look for local brews *ji-biiru*, particularly Otaru (factory tour available), Hakodate, and Taisetsu.

15

rich in coal, fish, and agricultural opportunities. The village and museum are linked by a free shuttle bus on Sundays, and the public bus from Sapporo stops at the museum first. ⊠*Konoppoto 53–2, Atsubetsu-chō, Atsubetsu-ku* ☎*011/898–0456* ☜¥*450* ☉*Tues.–Sat. 9:30–4:30.*

❾ Hokkaidō Shrine 北海道神宮 *(Hokkaidō Jingū).* Wash your hands and mouth at the stone basin first, then step up the gray stone steps. This 1871 Shintō shrine houses three gods deemed helpful in Hokkaidō's development: the gods of land and nature, of land development, and of healing. Sapporo families bring babies, children, anxious students, young engaged couples, and even cars to Shintō ceremonies. In May this is Sapporo's main *hanami* (cherry blossom) venue. It's a 15-minute walk from Maruyama Subway Station and shares the park with the zoo. ⊠*474 Miyagaoka, Maruyama Kōen, Chūō-ku.*

❺ Sapporo Beer Garden and Museum 札幌ビール園と博物館 *(Sapporo Biiruen).* Redbrick buildings overshadowed by a giant shopping mall make up the public face of Sapporo's most famous export. The original brewery buildings are at another nearby mall, Sapporo Factory, and now brewing takes place way out of town near Chitose Airport. At the north-of-downtown site a small museum with mostly Japanese-only information shows the development of bottle and label designs, and beer-poster pin-up ladies over the ages. For ¥100 for one kind or ¥400 for three, visitors can taste the brews: Black Label is most popular, Classic is only available in Hokkaidō, and the original brew of Kaitakushi uses local hops.

In the evening the cavernous Sapporo Biergarten is filled with the cries of *"Kampai!"*—"Bottoms up!"—as serious drinkers tackle the *tabe-nomi-hodai* (all you can eat and drink) feast of lamb barbecue and beer (¥3,570 per head). Recent menu additions include fish and vegetable dishes.

Free tours of Hokkaidō Brewery, a 20-minute local train ride from Chitose Airport, are available all year. Tours (which are only in Japanese, but there is English signage) last 60 minutes and start at 9, 10, and 11 AM and 1, 2, and 3 PM. Visitors receive a free beer at the tour's end. No reservations are necessary except for large groups.

To get to the Sapporo Beer Garden and Museum, take a 15-minute Sapporo Walk circular bus from the station or Ōdōri area (the same bus also stops at Sapporo Factory mall) or a ¥1,000 taxi ride. Hokkaidō Brewery is served by Chūō Bus and trains stopping at Sapporo Beer Teien Station on the Chitose–Sapporo line. ⊠*Sapporo Beer Garden and Museum, Kita 7-jō, Higashi 9, Higashi-ku* ☎*011/731–4368 museum, 011/742–1531 restaurant* ⊕*www.sapporobeer.jp* ☜*Free* ⊙*Museum Sept.–May, daily 9–5; June–Aug., daily 8:40–6, last entry 80 min before closing; beer garden May–Sept., daily 11–9:30; Oct.–Apr., daily 11–8:45* ⊠*Hokkaidō Brewery, 542–1 Toiso, Eniwa City* ☎*0123/32–5811* ☜*Free* ⊙*Daily 9–11:45 and 1–3:50, no tours on weekends Nov.–Apr. and public holidays.*

🔟 **Sapporo Winter Sports Museum** 札幌ウィンタースポーツミュージアム. Leap off a ski jump into the freezing air and land like a pro—or not. A realistic simulator has visitors comparing jump distances and style in the museum with a body-on approach at the base of the Olympic Ōkura Jump. The 1972 Winter Oympics and other Japanese sporting successes in skating, curling, and many forms of skiing are celebrated with displays interesting even to nonsporting types. Outside the museum, take the chair lift to the top of the real jump 300 meters above the city with a chilling view of what jumpers face before take-off. Take a 15-minute bus ride from Maruyama Bus Terminal, City Bus Nishi 14 (¥200). ⊠*1274 Miyanomori, Chūō-ku* ☎*011/641–1972* ☜*¥600* ⊙*May–Oct., daily 9–6; Nov.–Apr., daily 9:30–5.*

WHERE TO EAT

The greatest concentration of restaurants for nighttime dining is in the entertainment district of Susukino; good daytime choices are in the downtown department stores and the shopping complex around the JR station. Hokkaidō is known for its ramen, and Sapporo for its miso ramen. The city has more than 1,000 ramen shops, so it's not hard to find a noodle lunch. To track down the current ramen star look for the lines of enthusiastic youths outside otherwise unassuming restaurants; young Japanese use their mobile phones and the Internet to research the newest hot spot.

Soup curry—curry with more sauce than content—is currently touted domestically as a Sapporo creation, but the curry restaurants run by Indian and Nepali ex-pats in the city are a better bet.

$$$–$$$$
JAPANESE

✗**Daruma** だるま. Below the sign with a roly-poly red doll, this 40-year-old establishment serves the freshest lamb barbecue *jingisu-kan* (¥700 a plate). At the end of the meal you're given hot tea to mix with the dipping sauce remaining from your meat. You drink the tea and sauce together: it's delicious! Be sure to wear your least favorite clothes and don a paper bib. ⊠*Crystal Bldg., Minami 5, Nishi 4, Chūō-ku* ☎*011/552–6013* ⚄*Reservations not accepted* ▭*No credit cards* ☽*Closed Mon.* ⊠*Noguchi Bldg., Minami 6, Nishi 4, Susukino* ☎*011/533–8929* ⚄*Reservations not accepted* ▭*No credit cards* ☽*Closed Tues.*

$$$–$$$$
JAPANESE
★

✗**Kani Honke** かに本家. This crab-eating haven serves raw, steamed, boiled, and baked crustaceans from the Hokkaidō (or Russian) seas. The waitress will tell you whether the *ke-gani* (hairy crab), *taraba* (king crab), or *zuwai-kani* (snow crab) is in season. The menu is in English and has photographs, so it's easy to choose from the set dinners, which start at ¥2,000. Wooden beams, tatami mats, and traditional decorations provide an authentic setting for the feast. There are two restaurants, one near the station and the other in Susukino. ⊠*Station branch, Kita 3, Nishi 2* ☎*011/222–0018* ⊠*Susukino, Minami 6, Nishi 4* ☎*011/551–0018* ▭*AE, DC, MC, V.*

¢–$
JAPANESE

✗**Keyaki** けやき. It's a mystery why some ramen restaurants are famous and millions are not. This ordinary-looking 10-stools-at-the-plastic-counter joint in Susukino has had lines of faithful outside for more than six years (a lifetime in ramen shop terms) and is still chopping, boiling, and serving it's six item menu: miso, *chā-shū* (pork slice), *negi* (long onion), butter corn, *karai* (spicy), and *nin-niku* (garlic). There's even a branch in the Ramen Museum in Yokohama. At the original shop you order while standing in line outside, pay when you claim a counter spot, and then wait for the cook to hand down the steaming bowl (topped generously with vegetables) from the raised and hidden kitchen. Ahhh. Maybe you'll deduce the secret of good ramen. ⊠*Minami 6, Nishi 3, Susukino* ☎*011/552–4601* ▭*No credit cards* ☽*Daily 11–11.*

$$$–$$$$
JAPANESE
★

✗**Sushi-zen** すし善. Hokkaidō sushi is famed throughout Japan, and this is the best in Hokkaidō. It's the place locals take guests when they want to impress them with a pure sushi experience. Sushi-zen operates three restaurants and a delivery service. To taste the best at bargain prices, visit the Maruyama branch the third Wednesday of every month when the trainee chefs' sushi is available for ¥200 apiece. ⊠*Kita 1, Nishi 27, Maruyama, Chūō-ku* ☎*011/644–0071* ⊠*109 Bldg., Minami 4, Nishi 5, Chūō-ku* ☎*011/521–0070* ⊠*Minami 7, Nishi 4, Chūō-ku* ☎*011/531–0069* ▭*AE, DC, MC, V* ☽*Closed Wed.*

WHERE TO STAY

$

▦**Hotel Maki** ぺんしょん まき. Need a "Welcome back!" after sightseeing? Help with booking hotels ahead? The Inada family does their best with simple English. Hotel Maki is a change of style from the sterility of big-city hotels. Half the big tatami-mat rooms have private baths, and all have toilets and washbasins. There's also a general bath. The hotel is a favorite with out-of-town baseball and ski teams, who wolf down the extensive Japanese-style breakfast available for ¥900. It's in a quiet area five streetcar stops from Susukino. Simple English faxed reservations are best. **Pros:** genuine family welcome; home cooking. **Cons:** 15 minutes from downtown, in a residential area; 10 minutes from Horohira subway stop. ⊠*1–20, Minami 13, Nishi 7, Chūō-ku, Sapporo* ☎*011/521–1930* 🖷*011/531–6747* 🛏*15 Japanese-style rooms* ⚘*In-room: no a/c. In-hotel: restaurant, Japanese baths* ⊟*No credit cards* ⵔ*MAP.*

$$$–$$$$
★   ⊡**Hotel Ōkura** ホテルオークラ. In the shopping heart of the city, one block from the Ōdōri subway station, the Ōkura gets the balance between style and the personal connection just right. Public areas are small, so the staff gets to know you quickly, although upstairs the rooms are spacious. Artful lighting, interior blinds, and a color scheme of browns and creams set a Japanese mood missing in many large hotels. Toh-Ka-Lin, the hotel's Cantonese restaurant, offers a good, inexpensive lunch set for couples (¥3,700), and at the afternoon tea at Kanshouan you get your own cake stand full of goodies (¥3,600). Twenty-four-hour advance reservations are essential for the tea. **Pros:** close to shopping; near public transportation; personal attention for a city hotel. **Cons:** limited public seating areas. ⊠*Nishi 5, Minami 1, Chūō-ku, Sapporo* ☎*011/221–2333* 🖷*011/221–0819* ⊕*www.okura.com/sapporo/index. html* 🛏*147 Western-style rooms* ⚘*In-room: Internet. In-hotel: 3 restaurants, bar, no-smoking rooms* ⊟*AE, DC, MC, V.*

$$$$
★   ⊡**JR Tower Hotel Nikko Sapporo** JRタワーホテル日航札幌. Sapporo's skyscraper over the station puts the city at your feet from small, modern rooms with cream and brown furnishings and throw pillows. Corner-room prices buy more space. Guests get a discount at the 22nd-floor super spa, where deep pools and big windows let you soak naked with a view and hope that no office worker has a telescope. **Pros:** inside the station complex; city views. **Cons:** small, standard rooms; restaurants are crowded with nonguests. ⊠*Sapporo Station JR Tower, Kita 5, Nishi 2, Chūō-ku, Sapporo* ☎*0120/58–2586 or 011/251–2222* 🖷*011/251–6370* ⊕*www.nikkohotels.com* 🛏*350 Western-style rooms* ⚘*In-room: Internet. In-hotel: 3 restaurants, bar* ⊟*AE, DC, MC, V.*

$$$
⊡**Nakamuraya Ryokan** 中村屋旅館. The small, family-run hotel is on a tree-lined street between government buildings near the botanical gardens. A large paper parasol decorates the lobby. Popular multi-box lunches and dinner-in-your-room service help foreign guests enjoy quintessential Japanese hospitality, although anyone with multiple bags may find the storage space limited. All six tatami rooms have small private bathrooms, and the large communal bath is a welcome comfort in winter. Now housed in a modern building, Nakamuraya Ryokan has been a business since 1898: the little boy in the sepia photograph in the lobby is the current owner's father. Basic English is spoken. **Pros:** welcoming environment; foreign-guest friendly; quiet location. **Cons:** limited storage space; 10 minutes walk to station and shopping area. ⊠*Kita 3-jō, Nishi 7, Chūō-ku, Sapporo* ☎*011/241–2111* 🖷*011/241–2118* 🛏*29*

BARS 101

Bars come in several kinds: clubs stocked with hostesses who make small talk (¥5,000 and up per hour, proving that talk is *not* cheap); *sunakku* bars (the word sounds like "snack," which translates into fewer hostesses and expensive *ōdoburu*, or hors d'oeuvres); izakaya, for both Japanese and Western food and drink; bars with entertainment, either karaoke or live music; and "soapland" and *herusu* (health) massage parlors, which are generally off-limits to non-Japanese without an introduction. Signs that say NO CHARGE only mean that there's no charge to be seated; beware of hidden extras. Many bars add on charges for peanuts, female companionship, song, cold water, hand towels, etc. The term "free drink" refers to an all-you-can-drink special that costs money.

Japanese-style rooms ☆*In-room: refrigerator. In-hotel: restaurant, Japanese baths, Wi-Fi* 🖃*AF, MC, V* 🍴|*MAP.*

$$$$ 🏨**Sapporo Grand Hotel** 札幌グランドホテル. Classic European style with
★ white-gloved bellhops, first-rate service, and modern conveniences like room refrigerators tastefully hidden away in wooden cabinets, Sapporo's grand old hotel has welcomed guests since 1934. In the heart of downtown, the three buildings (Main, Annex, and East) almost fill a city block. Rooms in the older Main Building feel like gentlemen's-club chambers, with striped wall paper and small armchairs, and rooms in the restyled East Wing exhibit more modern flair. Standard rooms are average size, and closet space is limited. Specify when booking for requirements such as in-room broadband, room windows that open, or a double bed. In the Memorial Library check out photographs of VIP guests and mementos of their stays, like Margaret Thatcher's thank-you letter and the 1955 lunch menu for the visiting New York Yankees. **Pros:** useful halfway point between station and park; traditional, high-end service. **Cons:** small windows in main building; long walk from some rooms to public areas; you need to know what amenities you want when booking. ✉*Kita 1-jō, Nishi 4, Chūō-ku, Sapporo* 🕾*011/261–3311* 🖷*011/231–0388* 🌐*www.mitsuikanko.co.jp/sgh* ⬅*560 Western-style rooms* ☆*In-room: safe, refrigerator, Internet (some). In-hotel: 8 restaurants, room service, bars, no-smoking rooms* 🖃*AE, DC, MC, V.*

NIGHTLIFE

★ **Susukino** すすきの, Sapporo's entertainment district, is seven by seven mind-boggling blocks of neon and noise with more than 4,000 bars, nightclubs, and restaurants. Bars stay open late, some until 5 AM, though restaurants often close before midnight. Susukino mainly extends south of Route 36, although there are bars in the streets just north of the main road, too. The seedier alleys are mostly west of Station-mae-dōri, but all of Susukino is safe.

Start the evening perched on a bar stool looking out at the heart of the Susukino main intersection at **St. John's Wood** (⊠ *Keiai Bldg. 1F, Minami 4-jo, Nishi 4, Susukino* ☎011/271–0085 ⊕*www.sjw.k-ai.jp* ⊗*Daily 5 PM–2 AM, until 5 AM weekends*). Can it call itself an Irish bar with no Guinness or Kilkenny in sight? This friendly, pay-at-the-counter style bar serves beer, mint juleps, whiskeys, malts, and . . . haggis, fish-and-chips, and onion rings.

At **Saloon Maco** (⊠*Asano Bldg., 2nd fl., Minami 3-jō, Nishi 4, Ōdōri* ☎011/222–4828), Stetson-wearing Japanese staff (and drinkers) sing country and pop karaoke, fortified by a no-time-limit *nomi-hodai* (all-you-can-drink plan) for ¥2,000. Pasta and salad dishes go for under ¥1,000. Look behind the JRA Building to find this bar.

Brian Brew (⊠*FA-S3 Bldg., Minami 3-jō, Nishi 3* ☎011/219–3556 ⊗*Daily 11:30 AM–1 AM*) can claim to be an Irish pub, with Guinness and Kilkenny, and it has foods for expats such as fish-and-chips and meat pies. It's open for lunch, and sporting events are shown on big screen TVs.

Willie sings the blues at a casual basement bar (Thursday to Saturday) at **Blues Alley** (⊠*Miyako Bldg. B1, Minami 3-jo, Nishi 3, Susukino* ☎011/231–6166 ⊗*Daily 6 PM–3 AM*). Hang out with a drink and keep the hand steady for a game of darts or pool in a bar where nobody is going to be put out by foreign customers. You'll have to look for it; it's hidden behind the Kentucky Fried Chicken at the Susukino intersection.

British rock and roll is played in five nightly sets (first at 9.30 PM) by bar owner Kazuaki and his band at **Brits Beat Club** (⊠*Green Bldg. No. 4, 2nd fl., Minami 5-jō, Nishi 3, Susukino* ☎011/531–8808 ⊕*www.brits. jp*). The small bar serves cheap Brit fare, such as fish-and-chips and cottage pie, while the band plays everything from Beatles to Blur. There's a steep ¥2,100 cover charge, and the bar is open nightly 8–4. Cheap and popular with young, foreign English teachers is **Locotonte** (⊠*Susukino Kaikan Bldg., 4th fl. Minami 7-jō, Nishi 4, Susukino* ☎011/553–3728). Friday night DJs make you sweat (¥2,000 men; ¥1,500 women) on a small dance floor to hip-hop and house music.

On Susukino's main street across from the Toyokawainari shrine one of Sapporo's veteran pick-up joints, **Rad Brothers** (⊠*Minami 7-jō, Nishi 3064-0807* ☎011/561–3601), can get packed, especially if a U.S. aircraft carrier is making a port call in Otaru.

OTARU AND NISEKO 小樽とニセコ

West of Sapporo, Meiji-era stone warehouses line a canal lighted at night by glowing lamps and filled by day with rickshaw runners and sightseeers. Otaru is a small, touristy port city facing the Japan Sea. Its herring-fishing heyday between the 1870s and 1930s created the riches that built the banks, warehouses, and grand houses that give the city its historical visage.

The Niseko area lies over the mountains and extends into the hinterland, where the perfect cone-shaped Mount Yōtei is surrounded by farms that grow fruit, potatoes, pumpkins, and corn; villages; and hot springs. In winter this is one of Japan's leading ski areas, and from May to October outdoors enthusiasts enjoy river rafting and hiking. Niseko is best experienced by car over two or three days. Adventure tours should be booked in advance.

OTARU 小樽

★ *40 km (25 mi) west of Sapporo.*

Otaru nets its wealth in tourists these days, rather than herring, but the canal where barges used to land the shimmering silver catch is still the center of action for the thousands of domestic and Asian visitors reeled in by images of a romantic weekend retreat. Gaijin from countries with 19th-century stone buildings may be less impressed by the tourist strip along the canal, but rent a bike or walk away from the main drag and you can explore quaint neighborhoods and interesting buildings. The Otaru Snow Gleaming Festival (February 9–18), when thousands of snow lanterns light up the canal area and old buildings, is beginning to rival the bigger Sapporo Snow Festival with its quieter, local atmosphere.

15

GETTING HERE AND AROUND

Otaru is an easy day trip from Sapporo. Trains run every 20 minutes and take about 40 minutes (sit on the right facing forward for the best coast views); the ¥1,500 Sapporo–Otaru Welcome Pass from JR Hokkaidō permits one day travel on Sapporo subways and the JR train to and from Otaru.

Otaru makes a good base for touring around Hokkaidō by car. **Toyota Car Rental** is near Otaru Station. **Nippon Rentacar** is downtown. Neither agency has an English-speaking staff, so ask the tourist office or your hotel to help with reservations.

While you're in town explore by bike; **JR Rent Cycle,** just to the right of the station exit, offers pedal (¥1,000/2 hours) or electric (¥1,200/2 hours) powered rentals.

The **Otaru Tourist Office** is to the left of the ticket gates inside the station. It has room availability lists for hotels. English is basic, but they try hard. The **Unga Plaza Tourist Office,** by the canal, has city information and leaflets for further travel. From the station, walk down the main street for eight blocks; the office is in the stone buildings on the left before the canal.

ESSENTIALS

Bike Rental JR Rent Cycle (☎ *0134/24–6300*).

Car Rental Nippon Rentacar (☎ *0134/32–0919* ⊘ *Daily 8:30 AM–7 PM*). **Toyota Car Rental** (☎ *0134/27–0100* ⊘ *Daily 8–8*).

Visitor information Otaru Tourist Office (☎ *0134/29–1333* ⊘ *Daily 9––6*). **Unga Plaza Tourist Office** (✉ *Ironai 2-1-20* ☎ *0134/33–1661*).

THE HOUSE THAT HERRING BUILT

Aoyama Villa 旧青山別邸 *(Aoyama Bettei)*. Gorgeous, gold-painted sliding doors and dark lacquered floors testify to the huge wealth of fishing millionaires, the Aoyamas. Teenage daughter Masae came home from a trip with another rich family in Honshū with big ideas about how her family could spend its fortune, and in 1917 her father commissioned the chief imperial carpenter and a team of top craftsmen to create a home and garden of sumptuousness rare in Hokkaidō. The modern annex also has a good restaurant serving herring-on-rice lunches. Take bus No. 3 from the station to the Shukutsu 3-chōme bus stop, then walk up the hill for about half a mile. ✉ *3–63 Shukutsu* ☎ *0134/24–0024* ✉ *¥1,000* ⏱ *Apr.– Oct., daily 9–6; Nov.–Mar., daily 9–5.*

WHAT TO SEE

The Canal and Sakai-machi Street Historic District. The canal sandwiched between a contemporary shopping area and a busy port eight blocks downhill from the station. Former banks and trading homes have been converted into glass and clothing stores. Don't miss the music box collection and the musical steam clock at Marchen Square on the eastern end of the Sakai-machi district. Hoards of bus tours descend on the strip, but for some quiet time, dive into one of the cool, dark stone buildings to escape 21st-century Japan. A one-day pass (¥750) on the replica trolley is a useful energy-saver; and sun-burned rickshaw runners offer tours (starting at ¥3,000 for two people).

In the port you'll see Russian, Chinese, and Korean (North as well as South) ships loaded up with used cars, bicycles, and refrigerators; ferries heading off to Niigata; and sightseeing boats in summer. The Russian presence is quite noticeable. Sightseeing boats leave the dock just beyond the Chuo Bridge for a 25-minute, ¥550 trip to the Otaru Aquarium and Herring Mansion area. Boats also go for an hour beyond this area along the mineral-stained cliff coastline.

🅒 **Otaru Canal Glass Factory** 小樽運河工藝館. Blow your own beer mug in the heat of the sandblasting room, shot through with the color of your choice (beer glasses ¥2,310 and tumblers ¥1,890). Nineteenth-century Otaru craftsmen made glass buoys and gas lamps for the fishing fleets. Ten minutes is all you need to make your drinking vessel. Reservations in advance are necessary; creations are ready the next day after cooling or can be shipped both domestically and internationally for a ¥2,000 extra charge. Children over 10 are welcome to try their hand in the furnace room. ✉ *Ironai 2–1–19* ☎ *0134/29–1112* 🌐 *www.otaru-glass. com/english/index* ✉ *Free to factory shop* ⏱ *Oct.–Mar., daily 9:30–6; Apr.–Sept., daily 9–7.*

★ **Herring Mansion** 鰊御殿 *(Nishin Goten)*. Herring fishermen ate, slept, and dreamt of riches in this 1897 working base of a fishery boss and his crew. On display are kitchen appliances, nets, and mislaid personal items of the men who toiled. Photographs of the Otaru coastline lined with ships and beaches piled high with fish reveal how the herring heydays brought riches to some and put a serious dent in the Pacific fish stocks. ⊠*3–228 Shukutsu* ☎*0134/22–1038* ⊡*¥200* ⊗*Apr.–Nov., daily 9–5.*

WHERE TO EAT

¢

CAFÉ

✕**Kita-no Ice Cream** 北のアイスクリーム. Beer ice cream anyone? Maybe you'd prefer sake ice cream? Or squid, cherry-blossom, or pumpkin? This Otaru institution serves up 20 varieties from a shop in an 1892 warehouse in an alleyway one block from the canal. ⊠*Ironai 1-chōme* ☎*0134/23–8983* ▭*No credit cards.*

$$$

JAPANESE

✕**Kita Togorashi** 北とうがらし. There's lamb barbecue heaven among all the sushi joints in Otaru at the easiest to find branch of a famous Genghis Khan restaurant. Plates of fresh, succulent lamb cost ¥700, and you cook them yourself on a dome-shaped griddle with side orders of bean sprouts (moyashi) and leeks (negi). Along the canal, look for the tiny dive on the corner of the food court complex opposite the group photo–spot. ⊠ *1–1 Denuki Ironai* ☎*0134/33–0015* ⚔*No reservations accepted* ▭*No credit cards.*

$$–$$$

SUSHI

✕**Masazushi** 政寿司. This is sushi central in Otaru with this morning's catch of herring, tuna, abalone or salmon perched on quality vinegared rice. A good quick lunch is the basic nine-piece and soup Hamanasu set (¥1,500) with seasonal changes, and staff check your wasabi (horse-radish) tolerance levels when taking the order. The restaurant is quiet and removed from the daytrip crowds during the day, and in the evening this is where local business leaders hold court in private rooms. There's also a canal-area branch called **Zen-an** ぜん庵, which often has a 30-minute wait. There are English menus and some English-speaking staff. ⊠ *1–1–1Hanazono, Sushi-ya* ☎*0134/23–0011* ▭*MC, V* ⊗ *Closed Wed.* ⊠*Zen-an 1–2–1 Ironai, Canal Area* ☎*0134/22–0011* ⊗ *Closed Thurs.*

¢–$

JAPANESE

✕**Takeda** たけだ. Crab legs dripping juice and darkly gleaming red salmon eggs piled high on a bowl of rice are just two of Otaru's famous rawfish options at this small family restaurant in the middle of the noisy fish market, just up the steps to the left of the station. The *Omakase-don* at ¥2,500 somehow gets eight kinds of fish into one bowl, although anyone hoping to still manage some sightseeing after lunch may prefer crab soup (¥200) and one portion of fish (¥400). There is no English spoken, but menus have plenty of pictures to choose from and point to. ⊠ *3–10–16 Inaho, Sankaku Market, Otaru Station* ▭*No credit cards.* ⊗ *Daily 7–4.*

WHERE TO STAY

$$$–$$$$

★

▦**Authent Hotel** オーセントホテル. A former department store was reborn as an elegant city-center hotel in the heart of the downtown shopping area. The lobby's cream upholstery and yellow walls are echoed in the rooms, which have larger than usual bathrooms. Kaio is a small *teppanyaki* restaurant, and the 11th-floor piano bar has city views from the curved front of the building. **Pros:** in the town center; sunset views from the piano bar. **Cons:** less expensive rooms are boxlike; crowded with tour groups. ⊠*15–1, Inaho 2, Otaru* ☎*0134/24–8100*

15

🏠*0134/27–8118* ⊕*www.authent.co.jp* ➴*190 Western-style rooms, 5 Japanese-style rooms* ♿*In-hotel: 3 restaurants, bars, Japanese baths, no-smoking rooms, Internet (some)* ▤*AE, DC, MC, V.*

$–$$ 🔲**Hotel Furukawa** ふる川. Dark wooden beams, shadowy corridors, and antiques transform a modern canal-side building into a comfortable, old-fashioned Japanese inn—a rarity in Otaru. The traditionally clad staff bows low on the raised straw matting in the reception area, and the first-floor restaurant has an outdoor terrace for sunset drinks with a canal view. The charm of the public areas is slightly marred by the small, faintly tobacco-smelling rooms that look out over the canal (and the road) or back to the city, but the eighth-floor Japanese bathroom has a one-person-sized whisky barrel perfect for outdoor soaking. **Pros:** Old-Japan atmosphere; by the canal. **Cons:** tobacco smells in some rooms; overlooks main road. ✉*1–2–15 Ironai* 🕾*0134/29–2345* ⊕*www.otaru-furukawa.com/index.html* ➴*43 Western-style rooms, 1 Japanese-style room, 2 suites* ♿*In-hotel: restaurant, Internet terminal (free)* ▤*AE, MC, V* 🍽*EP.*

$$$–$$$$ 🔲**Otaru Hilton** 小樽ヒルトン. Overlooking Otaru Marina, 18 floors of
★ hotel sit atop the huge WingBay shopping complex giving easy access to outlet clothes bargains, movie theaters, a hot spring, and even a Ferris Wheel. Inside is reliable, familiar franchised service with English speakers on staff. Western-style rooms in gold, blue, and brown have large twin or double beds, and luckily most overlook the marina out front and not the unattractive railway sidings behind. It's 2 km (1 mi) from the historic district, but a trolley bus stop is just outside. It's a five-minute walk from Otaru Chikko Station, one stop before Otaru city station. The on-site Marina Restaurant is a favorite with local foodies. Early booking and a best-rate guarantee can produce competitive rates, depending on the season. **Pros:** reliable service; handy shopping without leaving the building. **Cons:** out-of-the-way location; shopping mall atmosphere beyond the doors. ✉*11–3 Otaru Chikkō, Otaru* 🕾*0134/21–3111, 0120/48–9852 toll-free* 🏠*0134/21–3322* ⊕*www.hilton.com* ➴*289 Western-style rooms* ♿ *In-room: safe, Internet. In-hotel: 3 restaurants, bars, no-smoking rooms, Internet* ▤*AE, DC, MC, V.*

NISEKO ニセコ

★　*73 km (45 mi) southwest of Otaru.*

For the best skiing in Hokkaidō, head for Niseko. This is boomsville for Australian leisure developers, with foreign-owned holiday homes and apartments shooting up everywhere, particularly in Hirafu village. Direct flights between Chitose and Cairns, Australia from November to April have revitalized Niseko, which had its heyday with Japanese skiers in the 1970s.

Between the skiing and boarding on Mt. Annupuri and the conical Mt. Yōtei is a gentle landscape of hot springs, dairy and vegetable farms, artists' workshops, and hiking trails. The Japanese love the outdoor farm and nature attractions, but for most Western visitors the adventure-sport opportunities are the real reason to come. Outdoor-adventure companies run by Australian and Canadian expats offer year-round thrills, including rafting (best from April to May), backcountry skiing, mountain biking, and bungee jumping.

Niseko is developing into a major self-catering vacation destination, meaning visitors provide their own food in exchange to access to a full kitchen. With most companies staffed by English-speaking ex-pats, this offers an unusual-in-Japan stay opportunity. The Niseko area is hands-down the best place to discover the Hokkaidō countryside, and it's easy to find an English-speaking guide.

GETTING HERE AND AROUND
Niseko is really a collection of villages near the town of Kutchan, a 2½-hour drive from New Chitose Airport. From November to May public buses go from the airport to the Niseko ski resorts almost hourly. In July and August Chūō Bus Company has two buses a day. The one-way trip costs ¥2,300.

From Sapporo you can drive to the Niseko area in two hours, up and over Nakayama Pass. Trains from Sapporo to Kutchan depart hourly; the trip takes two hours and costs ¥1,790. You may have to switch trains in Otaru. From Kutchan seven trains a day go to the Hirafu and Niseko villages at the heart of the scenic area. Hotels and pensions pick up guests at these two stations. Travelers with no pick up arranged should go to Niseko station because Hirafu is tiny and deserted once the train has gone (although there is a one-person hot spring bath carved out of a tree trunk in a little building on the platform). In ski season there are shuttle buses connecting Kutchan, the villages, and the lift stations. Out of season public transport is limited and car-hires make sense. **Nippon Rental Car** and **Mazda Rent-A-Car 9–5** are both a five-minute walk from Niseko station. Down the street in front of Kutchan Station (three blocks and on the left) is the excellent **Machi-no-eki – PLAT**, run by the Kutchan Tourist Association, which has information, Internet access, hotel booking help, and event listings. In Niseko go to the **Niseko Welcome Center** for accommodation help, tourist information, and essential heaters while waiting for the bus. It's next to the bus arrival/departure area at the top of Hirafu village, near the Hotel Niseko Alpen.

Niseko is developing into a major self-catering holiday destination, and with most companies staffed by English-speaking ex-pats this offers an opportunity that is unusual in Japan. Outside of the ski season the houses available provide a good base for driving tours of south Hokkaidō. The main self-catering companies are the **Niseko Company, Hokkaidō Tracks,** and **Niseko Management Service.**

ESSENTIALS
Car Rental Mazda Rent-A-Car 9–5 (✉ 74–4 Aza-Honchō ☎ 0136/44–1188 ☯ Daily 9–5). **Nippon Rental Car** (✉ 247–7 Aza-Soga, Niseko-cho ☎ 0136/43–2929 ☯ Apr.–Oct., daily 9–6, Nov.–Mar., daily 9–5).

Self-Catering Companies The Niseko Company (☎ 0136/21–7272 ⊕ www. thenisekocompany.com). **Hokkaidō Tracks** (☎ 0136/23–3503 ⊕ www.hokkaido tracks.com). **Niseko Management Service** (☎ 0136/21–7788 ⊕ www.niseko management.com).

15

Skiing Information Niseko United (⊕ www.niseko.ne.jp). Niseko Grand Hirafu(⊕ www.grand-hirafu.jp). Snow Japan (⊕ www.snowjapan.com).

Visitor Information Machi-no-eki -PLAT (✉ Minami 1-jō, Nishi 4-chōme, Kutchan-chō ☎ 0136/22-1121 ⊕ www.niseko.co.jp/). Niseko Welcome Center (✉ 204 Aza-Yamada, Hirafu, Niseko Grand Hirafu, parking area, Hirafu-Zaka St., Hirafu ☉ 10-6).

HIKING

Head for **Yōtei-zan** 羊蹄山 *(Mt. Yōtei)*. Climbing this Fuji look-alike takes four hours. Two trails lead up the mountain: the more challenging **Hirafu Course** and the easier but still arduous **Makkari Course**. Regardless of your approach, you'll find wildflowers in summer, and elderly Japanese chomping on bamboo shoots that grow wild on the hills. A hut at the top provides crude lodging. To get to the trails, take the bus from JR Kutchan Station 20 minutes to Yōtei To-zan-guchi (hiking trail entrance) for the Hirafu Course or 40 minutes to the Yōtei Shinzan Kōen stop for the Makkari Course.

SKIING

From November to May skiers and snowboarders enjoy 61 courses covering 47 km (30 mi) of powder in the Niseko area. There are five ski resorts, but the big three are Grand Hirafu, Higashiyama, and Annupuri. You can ski them all with a Niseko All-Mountain Pass costing ¥4,800 for one day or ¥8,800 for two days. Only the very top is above the tree line, and reaching Hirafu's big, off-trail bowl entails a 30-minute trek above the top chairlift. Nondrivers coming from Sapporo can buy package ski tours, including lunch and transportation by bus, for about ¥4,500. You can book tours at almost any city hotel. If you're driving to Niseko, check Sapporo convenience stores for discount lift tickets.

Annupuri Resort (☎ 0136/58-2080) has wide, gently sloping runs that are kind to beginners and shaky intermediates. Day passes cost ¥4,400. **Higashiyama Resort** (☎ 0136/44-1111), based at the Hilton Niseko Village, has a super-fast cable car that takes you to beautifully designed forested courses. You descend through the trees to the mountain base. Day passes cost ¥4,000. **Grand Hirafu** (☎ 0136/22-0109) is the largest of the Niseko ski resorts, with 34 courses, 27% of which are classed "expert." The longest run is more than 5 km (3 mi) long. A day pass costs ¥4,900.

OUTFITTERS

Niseko Adventure Centre (☎ 0136/23-2093 ⊕ www.nac-web.com) arranges river trips, mountain biking, and winter sport outings, and has an indoor rock-climbing wall at its village-center base. **Scott Adventures** (☎ 0136/21-3333 ⊕ www.sas-net.com) has rafting trips popular with school groups. The company also arranges hot-air ballooning, fishing, snowshoeing, and dogsled riding with a team of huskies.

WHERE TO EAT

$-$$　✕ **Izakaya Bang Bang** 居酒屋ばんばん. *Yakitori* (sizzling meats on wood
JAPANESE　skewers) and other Hokkaidō favorites, such as salmon and herring, keep company with menu imports like spare ribs and tacos. Your dining

neighbors could become tomorrow's skiing or adventure-tour buddies, and your pension's staff may enjoy their evenings off here. In Hirafu Village, Izakaya Bang Bang is definitely the place to be. English translations are on the menu. ✉*188–27 Aza Yamada, Hirafu* ☎*0136/22–4292* ⊕*www.niseko.or.jp/bangbang* ⊟*MC, V* ⊘*Closed Wed. No lunch.*

¢–$ ✗**Jo-Jo's.** Platters overflow with power food for adventurers—juicy
AMERICAN hamburgers and generous salads, followed by home-baked cakes smothered in cream. A spacious laid-back restaurant on the second floor of the Niseko Adventure Center, it's all soaring beams and big windows looking out to Yōtei-zan and is busy all day with adventure guides and their nervous or elated customers. It's on the right, off the main road arriving in Hirafu village from Kutchan. ✉*53–79 Aza Yamada, Hirafu* ☎*0136/23–2093.*

WHERE TO STAY

$ 🏨**Grand Papa** ぐらんぱぱ. In keeping with Niseko's wishful claim to be the St. Moritz of Asia, this Alpine-style pension at the bottom of Hirafu village has lots of dark wood and red carpeting. The owners are exceptionally friendly. Nikawara-san is a woodcut artist and alpenhorn player, Yoko used to be a British Airways flight attendant, and son Kohei is a ski instructor. Rooms are simple, and only three have private bathrooms. Everyone heads to Yukou hot spring (¥600) just minutes away on foot; the truly exhausted use the pension's shared public bath. After a dinner of Swiss cheese fondue, retire to Grand Papa's snug bar. **Pros:** friendly family owners; casual atmosphere; home-cooking. **Cons:** stairs, stairs, stairs—there's no elevator; limited rooms with baths; far from the lifts. ✉*163 Hirafu, Niseko* ☎*0136/23–2244* 📠*0136/23–2255* ⊕*www.niseko-grandpapa.com* 🛏*17 Western-style rooms, 3 with bath; 2 Japanese-style rooms without bath* &*In-hotel: restaurant, bar, bicycles, Internet* ⊟*MC, V* ⦿*BP.*

$$$–$$$$ 🏨**Hotel Niseko Alpen** ホテル ニセコ アルペン. Smack-dab at the base of Grand Hirafu ski slopes is a modern hotel with English speakers to help plan a Niseko stay. The rooms are disappointingly like airport sleepover places, but nobody comes to Niseko to sit in a hotel room. The hotel hot springs have an outdoor pool with views of Yōtei-zan, and guests with any energy left after skiing, rafting, hiking, or mountain biking can use the 25-meter indoor pool or the stone-bed sauna. Front-desk staff can supply special modems for in-room broadband Internet connection. **Pros:** ski-in ski-out; close to village life; 20 steps from the bus terminal; onsen views. **Cons:** bland rooms; public areas crowded with skiers during the day in-season. ✉*Yamada 204, Kutchan* ☎*0136/22–1105* 📠*0136/23–2202* ⊕*www.grand-hirafu.jp* 🛏*72 Western-style rooms, 39 combination rooms* & *In room: refrigerator, Internet. In-hotel: 2 restaurants, pool, spa, parking (free)* ⊟*AE, DC, MC, V* ⦿*EP, MAP.*

$$$$ 🏨**Hilton Niseko Village** ヒルトンニセコビレッジ. Reopened as a Hilton in 2008, this resort hotel has wonderful views either to Mount Yōtei or the Higashiyama ski area year round. From the deep, plushy sofas chairs in the lobby around a huge "hanging" gas-flame fire to the comfortable, but not huge, brown-and-white rooms, this hotel is a class act. It has three deluxe floors, and these guests get a range of benefits from free

15

in-room Internet to a 24-hour fitness center. In winter guests can ski-in, ski-out to the Niseko cable car and take a nine-minute ride to powder heaven. The staff speaks English and Korean. **Pros:** awesome views; 10-person tenpanyaki counter; ski valet and horseback riding available; great service. **Cons:** a 20-minute shuttle bus ride to aprés-ski life in Hirafu village; standard rooms small for the price. ⊠*Higashiyama Onsen, Niseko-chō, Abuta-gun* ☎*0136/44–1111* ⊕*www.hilton.com/ worldwideresorts* ⇨*506* ♿*In-room: safe, refrigerator, Internet, Wi-Fi (some). In-hotel: 5 restaurants, room service, 3 bars, golf course, tennis courts, gym, spa, children's programs (seasonal), laundry service, Internet terminal, no-smoking rooms* ▤*AE, DC, MC, V.*

SHIKOTSU-TŌYA NATIONAL PARK 支笏洞爺国立公園

Mountains, forests, caldera lakes, hot-spring resorts, and volcanoes are virtually in Sapporo's backyard. Less than an hour from Sapporo, Route 230 passes the large hot-spring village Jōzankei, then the mountains close in, the road climbs to Nakayama Pass at 2,742 feet. On a clear day the view from the top is classic Hokkaidō—farmland with the stately Mount Yōtei in its midst, and on the horizon to the south Lake Tōya's volcanic crater and Noboribetsu hot springs, where the earth steams, rumbles, and erupts.

TŌYA-KO 洞爺湖

★ *179 km (111 mi) southwest of Sapporo.*

World leaders met here for the G8 Summit in 2008, but Tōya's most notable activity is still its most recent volcanic events. At lunchtime on March 28, 2000, Usu-zan volcano exploded for the first time in 23 years and shot a 10,500-foot-high cloud of ash and smoke into the skies over the quiet resort town of Lake Tōya. About 16,000 farmers, hoteliers, and townspeople evacuated. Earth tremors cracked open the north–south expressway and ash flows engulfed the outskirts of the town. Lake Tōya exploded into the headlines. Amazingly, by July everyone came back, cleaned up their town, and reopened for business with still smoking craters in their midst.

GETTING HERE AND AROUND

Usu-zan is one of several peaks on Lake Tōya's crater, a huge volcanic rim that dominates the landscape. Route 230 from Sapporo drops over the northern edge, and Route 453 from Lake Shikotsu and Noboribetsu and roads from the coast come in from the south. Volcanic activity is centered around the small town of Tōya-ko Onsen, and a few kilometers around the lake at Shōwa Shin-zan. A road rings the water, dotted with campsites and hot springs, and pleasure boats go out to three small islands where deer beg for snacks.

Direct buses from Sapporo to Tōya-ko Onsen via Nakayama Tōge take 2½ hours (¥2,700). **Jōtetsu Bus** runs between Sapporo and Tōya-ko Onsen; reservations are necessary. **Dōnan Bus** makes the Sapporo to Tōya-ko

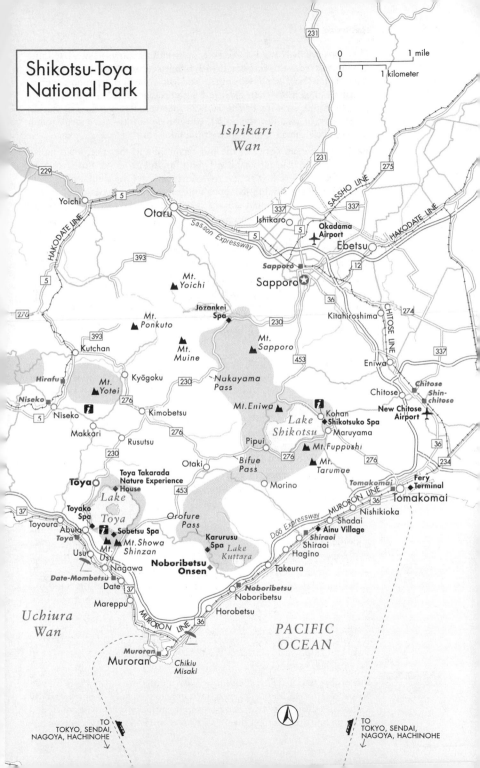

Onsen trip daily. Tōya-ko Onsen is on the JR Sapporo–Hakodate Line. Disembark from the train at JR Tōya Station for a 15-minute bus ride to the lake. There is a ¥100 shuttle bus four times a day round the lake, nonstop takes more than an hour. Sightseeing boats leave the pier for the 20-minute crossing to the islands. Bike rentals near the bus station cost ¥900 for two hours and ¥1,200 for three, the latter just enough time to cycle the circumference of the lake.

Tourist Information, between the bus terminal and the lake, has English speaking staff, and although officially unable to make hotel reservations, the Web site has access to online booking for some hotels. **Tōya Guide Center** provides English-speaking guides for year-round excursions such as Canadian canoeing on the lake, walking the volcano, deer spotting, and waterfall walking.

ESSENTIALS

Bus Information Jōtetsu Bus (☎011/572–3131). Dōnan Bus (☎011/261–3601).

Tour Information Tōya Guide Center (✉402 Tōya-chō, Tōya-ko Onsen ☎0142/82–5002 ⊕www.toya-guide.com/).

Visitor Information Tourist Information (✉Tōya-ko Onsen 144 Tōyako-chō, Abuta-gun ☎0142/75–2446 ⊕www.laketoya.com).

WHAT TO SEE

Tōya-ko Onsen 洞爺湖温泉. Fireworks enjoyed over sake from a rooftop hot spring after a gargantuan dinner—this is why thousands of Japanese come to the one-street town year-round. From April 28 to October 31 the 30-minute, nightly fireworks are the highlight of any stay. A waterside walk in front of the wall of hotels is quiet before the bus groups arrive late afternoon.

☾ **Nishiyama Crater Trail** 西山火口群散策路. A brand-new fire station, a
★ school, and houses stand at crazy angles amid the solidified ash flows where the 2000 eruption reached the edges of Tōya-ko Onsen. Walkways wind up into the still steaming hills. Although hardly as exciting as Hawaiian lava-flow hikes, it's an impressive scene of what can happen when you live next to a volcano. Buses from Tōya Station to the onsen stop at the trailhead. The trail is accessible from the coast or from the lakeside above the village. ✉3–4–5 Takashaga-dōri, between Abuta and Tōya-ko ⌧Free ⊙Apr.–Nov., daily.

☾ **Volcanic Science Museum and Visitor Center** 洞爺湖ビジターセンター 火山科学館 (Abuta Kazan Kagaku-kan). Rumbling soundtracks and shaking floors re-create the 1977 and 2000 eruptions in a small, official information center. Though there's a good explanation of the science and the geography, the museum is less useful in describing the impact on residents' lives. It's left of the bus terminal. ✉142–5 Toyako-Onsen, Toyako-chō ☎0142/75–2555 ⊕www.toyako-vc.jp ⌧¥600 ⊙Daily 9–5.

Shōwa Shin-zan 昭和新山. Beginning with an earthquake in 1943, Shōwa Shin-zan rose suddenly from a farmer's wheat field. Kept secret by authorities during the war as a potentially unlucky symbol, it continued growing to its present height of 1,319 feet in 1945, and its name means "new mountain of the Shōwa era." It is privately owned by the family of the village postmaster who monitored its growth. A cable-car ride (¥1,450) up the eastern flank of Mount Usu (734 meters) provides great views of Shōwa Shin-zan, Lake Tōya, and the sea in Funka (Eruption) Bay. Whatever you do, avoid the Bear Ranch at the base, a depressing tourist attraction and a disgrace in a region that won World Heritage status for its efforts to preserve the bears' habitat.

WHERE TO EAT AND STAY

$$-$$$
CONTINENTAL
✕ **Biyōtei** びようてい. A European-style restaurant amid a garden in the heart of the village, Biyōtei has a stone floor, low beams, log table legs, and sepia family photos of the 60-plus years in business. The menu is in English, and the sizzling hamburger platters are the best choices. ⊠ *38 Rte. 2, Tōya-ko Onsen* ☎ *0142/75–2311* ▤ *MC, V.*

$-$$
🛏 **Lakeside Inn Kawanami** 洞爺かわなみ. Lake and firework show views are available from almost all rooms at this family-run hotel. It's a 15-minute walk along the shoreline from the village. English-speaking owners Kazuhiko and Emiko ensure friendly, personal service in the rambling complex that they are busy modernizing. Rooms have no private baths, but guests can use the small hot springs round-the-clock. The inn provides pick-up service from the Higashi-machi bus stop in the village. **Pros:** peaceful getaway from the resort village; English-speaking owners; friendly service. **Cons:** old buildings being upgraded; no lake views from small hot spring; no private baths. ⊠ *53 Tokako Onsen, Sobetsu-cho, Usu-gun* ☎ *0142/75-2715* ⊕ *www2.ocn.ne.jp/~kawanami/* ⤳ *50 Japanese-style rooms* ⴸ *In-room: no a/c (some), refrigerator. In-hotel: restaurant, bar, spa, hot spring, laundry facilities, Internet terminal, no-smoking rooms* ▤ *AE, DC, MC, V MAP.*

$$$$
Fodor'sChoice
★
🛏 **The Windsor Hotel** ウインザーホテル. Visible for miles around—the hotel looks like a giant luxury cruise ship perched on the rim of the Tōya volcano—the Windsor is the best hotel in Hokkaidō for location and service. This is where world leaders infamously dined on a luxurious eight-course meal after discussing the global food crisis. The blue rooms have views of the lake and Tōya-ko Onsen's volcanic activity, while the rust-color rooms look out to the sea. It's a vast hotel, but bars and restaurants are personal in scale. Unusual in Japan, the Windsor asks guests to refrain from smoking in all restaurants and most rooms. Foreign staff speak English, French, and Japanese. **Pros:** top service; top views; chance to spot Asian celebs on private holidays. **Cons:** top prices; some restaurants known to claim being "fully booked" during quiet season. ⊠ *Shimizu, Tōya-ko Onsen Abuta-chō* ☎ *0120/29–0500 or 0142/73–1111* 📠 *0142/73–1210* ⊕ *www.windsor-hotels.co.jp* ⤳ *395 Western-style rooms, 3 Japanese-style rooms* ⴸ *In-room: Wi-Fi. In-hotel: 14 restaurants, bars, golf courses, tennis courts, pool, gym, spa, bicycles, Japanese baths, airport shuttle, Internet terminal* ▤ *AE, D, DC, MC, V.*

15

NOBORIBETSU ONSEN 登別温泉

53 km (32 mi) east of Tōya-ko, 100 km (62 mi) south of Sapporo.

GRRR! A bright red, 32-foot-tall, concrete demon brandishing a club points the way from the highway interchange to Noboribetsu Onsen, Hokkaidō's most famous spa. The town claims that some 34,300 gallons of geothermally heated water are pumped out every hour, making it the most prodigious hot spring in Asia.

Don't come here expecting a quaint little hot-spring town; this is the height of garish Japanese tourism. The natural beauty of the steep-sided, wooden valley is dominated by ugly, mammoth hotels and tatty town buildings housing souvenir shops. Buses swing in every evening with hundreds of visitors for a boisterous one-night stay. At the top of the town a cobbled street leads to the Valley of Hell entrance, where the landscape is still dramatically scarred by nature, not Japanese architects. If you are coming from Sapporo, you can get more for your yen if you arrange a tour through your hotel, Japan Railways, or the Plaza i tourist office.

GETTING HERE AND AROUND

Noboribetsu City is one hour south of Sapporo by JR Limited Express. From the JR station in there, a shuttle bus serves Noboribetsu Onsen. Don't confuse Noboribetsu Onsen with Noboribetsu, an industrial city that is 13 minutes by bus from its namesake spa town.

Dōnan Bus travels from Sapporo to Noboribetsu Onsen; the trip takes 1 hour 20 minutes (¥1,900; reservations advised). From June to late October three buses per day make the 1¼-hour run between Tōya-ko Onsen and Noboribetsu Onsen; only one bus runs per day the rest of the year (¥1,530; reservations necessary). Heavy snows keep the road closed until spring.

ESSENTIALS

Bus Contact Dōnan Bus (☎ 011/261–3601).

WHAT TO SEE

☺ **Valley of Hell** 地獄谷 *(Jigokudani).* In this volcanic crater that looks like
★ a bow-shaped valley, boiling water spurts out of thousands of holes, sounding like the heartbeat of the earth itself. With its strong sulfur smell, though, you might describe it differently. Whereas hot springs elsewhere in Japan—Unzen on Kyūshū is a notable example—were used to dispose of zealous foreign missionaries during periods of xenophobia, these natural cauldrons were favored by suicidal natives. Moms shouldn't worry, though; the walkways to photo-op points have handrails and are very safe. Local maps detail several short hikes around the area. Even if the town itself disappoints, the Valley of Hell is worth a stop. Admission is free.

WHERE TO EAT AND STAY

$ ✕**Dosanko-Tei** どさんこ亭. One of the few restaurants open during the
JAPANESE day, this family-owned establishment serves up fish and meat dishes with pickles, miso soup, and rice. The sign in the window reads, "Spoken English," but you'll probably be taken outside to point at the plastic displays in the window. Inside, farm implements and crafts adorn the

walls. It's on the main street; look for the orange lanterns outside. ✉49 *Noboribetsu-onsen 059-0551* ☎*0143/84–2393* ▭*No credit cards.*

$–$$ 🏨 **Dai-ichi Takimoto-kan** 第一滝本館. Contemplate Hell while soaking the soul in one of the 12 different pools as more than 1,000 guests a night tuck in at this prime example of Japanese mass-tourism. It's like a giant youth hostel, and it's always busy, recently with tour groups from Taiwan and Hong Kong. Some of the rooms are a bit worn, but you come here to sit in the sumptuous waters anyway. The hotel now allows swimsuits in some of the outside baths in response to requests from shier foreign customers. Daily shuttle bus from Sapporo. Nonguests can bathe for ¥2,000 (¥3,000 on weekends). **Pros:** hot water to ease every known condition; crab crazy buffets. **Cons:** mass tourism; noisy with groups. ✉*55 Noboribetsu Onsen, Noboribetsu* ☎*0143/84–2111* 🖷*0143/84–2202* ⊕*www.takimotokan.co.jp* ⤴*393 Western-style rooms, 8 Japanese-style rooms* ⚿*In-hotel: 3 restaurants, room service, bars, pool, laundry service, Internet terminal (paid), Wi-Fi (free)* ▭*AE, DC, MC, V* ⦿*MAP.*

$$$$ 🏨 **Ryotei Hanayuraya** 旅亭花ゆら. This is most foreigners' idea of a peaceful hot-spring hotel: floor-to-ceiling lobby windows look out on a small canyon and river, and the hotel hot springs on the top floor bubble gently among rocks and trees. Spend a little more and enjoy your own, private, one-person cypress wood bath on your balcony, followed by a traditional dinner delivered to the door. This relatively small, modern hotel is unvisited by the tour groups; it is connected to a larger hotel, so you can use its bar and souvenir shop. No English speakers are on staff but reservations can be made in English through the hotel group's Web site. Guests can reserve seats on a free shuttle bus from Sapporo. **Pros:** peaceful, dignified environment. **Cons:** 10 minutes walk from Hell Valley; no English spoken. ✉*100 Noboribetsu Onsen, Noboribetsu* ☎*0143/84–2322* 🖷*0143/84–2035* ⊕*www.tohoresort. com* ⤴*58 rooms* ⚿*In-hotel: restaurant, safe, refrigerator, spa* ▭*AE, DC, MC, V* ⦿*MAP.*

NIBUTANI 二風谷

★ *40 km (24 mi) east of Tomakomai, 115 km (71 mi) southeast of Sapporo.*

Nibutani is one of the last places in Hokkaidō with a sizable Ainu population, or at least part Ainu, as few pure-blooded Ainu are left. The tiny village, which is nothing more than some scattered homes along a main road, has two museums and a handful of souvenir shops. It's a very long daytrip from Sapporo, and if you have toured Native people's centers in North America it may feel like more of the same, but it is where you can find the best, non-touristy collection of Ainu art and artifacts in Hokkaidō.

GETTING HERE AND AROUND
Nibutani is hard to reach by public transport. It involves an early train from Sapporo, a change, and then a local bus—all costing about ¥6,000 round-trip. The Tourist Office in Sapporo has information on the current public transport connections if this is your only option. Otherwise,

15

Hokkaidō's First Inhabitants

Once upon a time in *Ainumosir* (human being peaceful land), *aynu* (human beings) lived in *kotan* (villages), raising their families on a diet of *ohaw* (salmon, meat, or plants) and *sayo* (millet and other grains). They honored the god *Okikurmikamu*, and told *yukar* (epic poems) to remember the interwoven lives of human and the spirit world, particularly of bears and owls. Sometimes they traded kelp, salmon, and herring with the *sisam*, the neighbors north or south.

Around the 15th century life changed. The southern *sisam*—the Japanese—began arriving in greater numbers and building trading posts along the far south coast. As the Japanese moved north and solidified their presence on the island, the *aynu*—regarded as "hairy people"—became forced laborers.

In 1869 the new Meiji Government lumped Ainu together with Japanese as "commoners," and the Ainu language and lifestyle were outlawed. Along with intermarriages, this nearly obliterated the culture. The Hokkaidō Former Aborigine Protection Law sliced up land ownership, and many Ainu lost out to *wajin*, the Japanese immigrants.

But the Ainu have fought back. By the 1980s Ainu were calling for basic human rights, drawing support from indigenous groups in other countries. The United Nations made 1993 the Year of Indigenous Peoples, which bolstered their efforts, and a victory was achieved in 1994 when leading activist Shigeru Kayano of Nibutani was elected the first Ainu to Japan's House of Councilors. In May 1997 the national government passed belated legislation acknowledging the existence of Ainu and requiring the local and national governments to respect their dignity as a distinct race by promoting Ainu culture and traditions. The act stopped short of designating Ainu as an indigenous ethnic group, due to concerns about aboriginal rights to land and natural resources.

Visitors to Hokkaidō may find it hard to recognize full-blooded Ainu outside the tourist centers of Shiraoi, Nibutani, and Akan. Some 24,000 people declare themselves Ainu. Most Japanese have little knowledge or interest in Ainu affairs, beyond buying cute wooden carvings as souvenirs. Otherwise well-informed, worldly Japanese hosts may be surprised, and a little embarrassed, by foreigners' interest in Ainu. Kayano's death in 2006 was hardly noted by the national media.

Today, Ainu tourist parks are being revamped as cultural centers. Ainu language is taught at 14 locations, and Shiro Kayano is continuing his father's monthly Ainu radio broadcasts (FM- Pipaushi).

The **Foundation for Research and Promotion of Ainu Culture** アイヌ文化振興・研究 (*FRPAC Presto 1.7 (7th fl.) Kita-1-jō, Nishi 7-chōme, Sapporo* ☎ *011/271–4171* ⊕ *www. frpac.or.jp*) has English-language information. The best places to learn more about Ainu culture and politics are the Nibutani Ainu Culture Museum and Kayano Shigeru Nibutani Archive; Poroto Kotan and Ainu Museum, Shiraoi; and at Akan Ainu Kotan cultural performances.

you're better off renting a car for the day. *See Sapporo Essentials for car rental information.*

WHAT TO SEE

FodorsChoice **Nibutani Ainu Culture Museum** 二風谷アイヌ文化博物館 *(Nibutani Ainu*
★ *Bunka Hakubutsukan).* This museum is an excellent resource for information about the Ainu, and it's sadly unknown to many Japanese. Ainu artifacts, such as shoes of salmon skin, water containers made from animal bladders, and heavy blue-and-black embroidered coats are displayed, as well as implements used in *iyomante,* an Ainu ritual that sent the spirit of the bear back to the nonhuman world. There is an hour long movie in English and translated books on sale. A selection of videos lets you listen to eerie traditional Ainu chants and songs. ⊠*Off Rte. 237, Nibutani 55, Biratori-chō* ☎*0145/72–2892* 💴¥*400, ¥700 joint ticket with Kayano Shigeru Nibutani Ainu Archive* ⊗*Mid-Jan.– mid-Dec., Tues.–Sun. 9:30–4:30.*

Kayano Shigeru Nibutani Ainu Archive 萱野茂 二風谷アイヌ資料館 *(Kayano Shigeru Nibutani Shiyō-kan).* This museum puts a spotlight on artifacts, particularly Ainu clothing and items used in sacred rites collected by the late prominent Ainu activist and Nibutani resident Shigeru Kayano. Until his death in 2006, Kayano traveled extensively, and the archive contains presents to the Ainu from other indigenous peoples. The museum is across the main road from the Culture Museum. ⊠*Nibutani 54, Biratori-chō* ☎*0145/72–3215* 💴¥*400, ¥700 joint ticket with Nibutani Ainu Culture Museum* ⊗*Mid-Jan.–mid-Dec., Tues.–Sun. 9:30–4:30.*

15

CENTRAL HOKKAIDŌ

Breathtaking and often snowy Daisetsu-zan is Japan's largest national park and home to Mount Asahi-dake, Hokkaidō's highest peak, at 7,311 feet. Roads in the region skirt through farmland and flower fields to circle the mountains north and south, and cable cars lift visitors onto mountain plateaus with steaming volcanic vents, alpine flower meadows, and awe-inspiring views. Allow at least two days for reaching the area and enjoying its grandeur. Asahikawa is the largest city and the transport gateway to the park. Staying places are Biei and Furano for gentle countryside and Sōun-kyō Gorge and Asahidake for mountain grandeur.

DAISETSU-ZAN NATIONAL PARK 大雪山国立公園

FodorsChoice *50 km (31 mi) east of Asahikawa.*
★
GETTING HERE AND AROUND

Sōun-kyō village and canyon are 90 minutes northeast of Asahikawa by car on Route 39. The highway skirts the northern side of the park, and Sōun-kyō is the access point for the park. You can catch a bus directly to Sōun-kyō Onsen (¥1,900) from in front of Asahikawa's JR station. If you are using a JR Pass, you can save money and time by taking the train to Kamikawa Station and transferring to the Dōhoku Bus for the 30-minute run to Sōun-kyō. Bicycles can be rented for ¥1,000 a day in the village at the Northern Hotel, and a short cycling trail along the old road by the river is a peaceful way to enjoy the gorge. Rock falls have closed the road 3 km (2 mi) from the onsen. From July to September a ¥390 bus ride connects the village with the Daisetsu dam and lake.

The **Sōun-kyō tourist office**, in the bus terminal, provides hiking maps and information on sightseeing and lodging. English is spoken here.

ESSENTIALS
Visitor Information The Sōun-kyō tourist office (☎ 0165/85–3350).

WHAT TO SEE

The geographical center of Hokkaidō and the largest of Japan's national parks, **Daisetsu-zan National Park** 大雪山国立公園 contains the very essence of rugged Hokkaidō: vast plains, soaring mountain peaks, hidden gorges, cascading waterfalls, wildflowers, forests, hiking trails, wilderness, and onsen. Daisetsu-zan, which means great snow mountains, refers to the park's five major peaks, whose altitudes approach 6,560 feet. Their presence dominates the area and channels human access into the park: only a few roads pass through. The rest dead-end in formidable terrain.

★ **Sōun-kyō** 層雲峡 *(Sōn-kyō Gorge).* As you follow the main route through the park, the first place to go is this 24-km (15-mi) ravine extending into the park from its northeast entrance. For an 8-km (5-mi) stretch, sheer cliff walls rise on both sides of the canyon as the road winds into the mountains. In winter and early spring forbidding stone spires loom as if in judgment; in other seasons they thrust through glorious foliage. Sōun-kyō Onsen is at the halfway point of the ravine.

Sōun-kyō Onsen village tries hard to be attractive. In summer, the pedestrianized main street is full of flower planters, and the guesthouses and souvenir shops do their best to add charm to what is basically a modern and concrete Alpine village–wannabee. Activities take placc in resort hotels, not in the village, and during the day most people are hiking through the park. From Late January to March the frozen river is illuminated for the Ice Waterfall Festival.

HIKING

☾ **Kuro-dake** 黒岳. Technology helps even the most reluctant up the moun-
★ tains: a cable car and chair lift (¥2,200 round-trip) rise up the side of the gorge above the village to 4,264 feet. Hikers trudge on one more hour to the top of Kuro-dake, 2,244 feet higher. From here numerous well-marked trails lead either across volcanic gravel or low shrub plateaus. Crimson foliage sets the slopes ablaze in September. Between June and mid-October the cable car starts at 6 AM, and experienced hikers can cross the range to Asahi-dake and take its cable car down to Asahi-dake Onsen in one long day. But Daisetsu's beauty is best enjoyed slowly, and you may encounter deer, foxes, and bears. While most trails are busy during the summer months, care should be taken on quieter mid-week or early-season visits when bear cubs—and bear mamas—are around.

On the park's west side two **spa towns** serve as summer hiking centers and winter ski resorts. **Shirogane Onsen**, at 2,461 feet, has had especially good skiing since its mountain, Tokachi-dake, erupted in 1962, creating a superb ski bowl. It erupted again in 1988. At **Asahi-dake Onsen** you can take a cable car (¥2,800 round-trip) up Asahi-dake to an altitude of 5,250 feet, and hike for two hours to the 7,513-foot summit. In late spring and early summer the slopes are carpeted with alpine flowers. Serious skiers come for Japan's longest ski season.

WHERE TO EAT AND STAY

You have no option but to lodge at **Sōun-kyō Onsen** 層雲峡温泉 if you want to stay in the northern part of the park. Rates tend to be 20% lower in winter. Because Sōun-kyō's hotels are almost exclusively ryokan, where meals are included, other dining opportunities in town are limited. A list of hotels and onsen is on the English page of *www.sounkyo.net.*

$$–$$$ ⌕**Chōyōtei** 朝陽亭. Perched on a bluff halfway up the side of the gorge, this hotel has the best views of any in the park. Unfortunately, the hotel is also an eyesore, and spoils some of Sōun-kyō's beauty. It's full of tour groups, and nobody will notice your arrival or departure. On the upside the hotel has sumptuous baths. Rooms facing the gorge merit the price, but rooms at the back have parking lot vistas. **Pros:** service and food quality like other large hotels; big baths. **Cons:** public areas make you feel like you're in a Japanese resort town. ⌂*Sōun-kyō Onsen, Kamikawa* ☎*0165/85–3241* ⌕*5 Western-style rooms, 257 Japanese-style rooms* ⌕*In-hotel: 3 restaurants, bar* ⊟*AE, DC, MC, V* ⊜*MAP.*

¢   ⌕**Sōun-kyō Youth Hostel** 層雲峡ユースホステル. Between the big hotels—but at a fraction of the price and with a more personal welcome—this 40-year-old hostel is a good base for mountain hiking. Dorm rooms have eight wide bunk beds, and there are tatami or bunk-bed family rooms. There are small Japanese baths and you can rent mountain boots. The hostel is closed from October to May. **Pros:** foreigner friendly; hiking conditions news provided; discounted use of the big hotel onsens. **Cons:** early morning bustle among hikers prevents sleeping in. ⌂*Sōun-kyo Onsen, Kamikawa* ☎*0165/85–3418* ⌕*0165/85–3186* ⌕*12 rooms* ⌕*In-room: no phone, no TV. In-hotel: restaurant, Japanese baths, Internet terminal (paid), Wi-Fi (free)* ⊟*No credit cards.*

$$–$$$ ⌕**Yamanoue** 山の上. This modern guesthouse is in the center of the village's flower-filled pedestrian area. The owner is a keen fisherman, so dinners can include freshwater fish, plus a wild mushroom soup served from a giant cauldron in the dining room. Sake liqueurs made from fruits such as mountain grapes may enhance (or hinder) the next day's hiking power. There are clean tatami rooms with shared washing areas, and use of the hot spring next door is free. No English is spoken, but faxed reservations in simple English are okay. **Pros:** in village center; expansive dinners. **Cons:** guests have to use hot springs next door. ⌂*Sōun-kyō Onsen, Kamikawa* ☎*0165/85–3206* ⌕*0165/85–3207* ⊕*www.tabi-hokkaido.co.jp/p.yamanoue* ⌕*14 Japanese-style rooms without bath* ⌕*In-hotel: restaurant, Japanese baths* ⊟*MC, V* ⊜*MAP.*

15

ASAHIKAWA 旭川

136 km (84 mi) northwest of Sapporo.

Asahikawa, Hokkaidō's second-largest city, is the principal entrance to Daisetsu-zan National Park. Cosmopolitan it is not; daytime life centers around a pedestrian shopping area and at night the entertainment district is raucously full of men from the farming hinterland. Travelers pass through its station, bus terminal, or airport on their way to more beautiful places, but a small Ainu museum and a winter festival in February are worthwhile if the schedule dictates a one-night stay.

GETTING HERE AND AROUND

Trains leave Sapporo for Asahikawa twice an hour and the journey takes about 1 hour, 30 minutes. The Hokkaidō Expressway also connects the two cities and takes just under two hours to drive. Domestic airlines from Haneda (Tōkyō), Ōsaka and Nagoya fly into Asahikawa Airport, 10 km from the city center, making it a good entry point for a holiday in central and eastern Hokkaidō. There are car rentals at the airport and station.

ESSENTIALS

Currency Exchange Hokkaidō Bank (⊠ *2-jo-dori, 9-chōme* ☎ *0166/26–0141*).

Rental Agencies Toyota Car Rental (⊠ *9–396–2 Miyashita-dori, Asahikawa, Station area* ☎ *0166/23–0100* ⊕ *rent.toyota.co.jp/top.asp*).

Visitor Information Asahikawa Tourism (⊠ *Okuno Bldg. 5F, 3-jo, 7-chōme* ⊕ *www. asahikawa-tourism.com/index.html*).

WHAT TO SEE

Kawamura Kaneto Ainu Memorial Hall 川村兼人アイヌ記念館 *(Kawamura Kaneto Ainu Kinen-kan)*. This slightly ramshackle, dusty museum in the suburbs, is owned by a genuine Ainu, a man named Kaneto Kawamura, whose family has lived in the Asahikawa area for seven generations. There's no English information, but photographs of his family and Ainu ceremonies, a small collection of artifacts, and a traditional house hold some interest. To get here, take Bus 24 (¥170) from Platform 14, which is two blocks north of the JR station, and get off at Ainu Kinenkan-mae. ⊠ *11 Hokumon-chō* ☎ *0166/51–2461* ⊠¥*500* ☉ *July and Aug., daily 8–6; Sept.–June, daily 9–5.*

WHERE TO EAT AND STAY

Far from the sea and from Hokkaidō's breadbaskets, Asahikawa is not known for its cuisine, with two notable exceptions: ramen and *tonkatsu* (breaded, deep-fried pork cutlet). Asahikawa ramen features a distinctively salty pork broth prized by ramen connoisseurs. Several noodle shops pepper the area around the station.

$–$$
JAPANESE ✕**Takada-ya** 高田屋. *Tonkatsu* and soba noodles, tempura and noodles, and curry with noodles are served at this traditionally decorated restaurant favored by shoppers and business people alike. At lunchtime there's a no-smoking rule to allow full appreciation of the soba. Diners are seated in booths and entertained with quiet jazz, and free *ban-cha* (roasted green tea) is served with all meals. It's on the main street three blocks from the station, opposite the Okuno department store. No

English is spoken, but the menu has pictures. ⊠*3-jō, 8-chōme, Heiwa-dōri* ⊟*No credit cards.*

$$ ⊡**Washington Hotel** ワシントンホテル. Anyone forced to stay the night in Asahikawa can make do at this bright, busy hotel with small motel-type rooms located across the street from the station. The first-floor restaurant Bonjour is a popular lunch spot for Asahikawa ladies for its pasta and salad sets. In the evening the 12th-floor Japanese restaurant Ginza is used for business dinners by local companies. Make reservations in English through the Web site. **Pros:** at the station; near restaurants. **Cons:** small, characterless rooms. ⊠*7 Miyashita-dōri, Asahikawa* ☎*0166/23–7111* 🖷*0166/26–6767* ⊕*www.wh-rsv.com* ⇨*260 Western-style rooms* ♿*In-hotel: 2 restaurants, no-smoking rooms* ⊟*AE, MC, V* ⍾*CP.*

BIEI AND FURANO 美瑛と富良野

15

Biei: 23 km (15 mi) east of Asahikawa. Furano: 31 km (19 mi) farther south.

Flower fields and small farms at the base of the Daisetsu-zan mountain range attract thousands of domestic and East Asian visitors hoping to get a taste of the simple country life. Although Western visitors may not be so wowed with lavender farms and potato fields, or the art galleries and cutesy coffee shops that dot the region, it makes an attractive stop-over area while driving to central or east Hokkaidō between late May and September. Biei is a small modern village with neighboring rolling hills and a patchwork of crop fields (potato, corn, soba, sunflowers) to cycle around; Furano is a small town famous throughout Japan for its lavender farms and as the setting for a 1970s TV hit drama about city dwellers making a new life in a farming community. There is also a large ski resort.

GETTING HERE AND AROUND

Trains from Asahikawa depart every hour and reach Biei in 30 minutes and Furano in 70 minutes. In July and August there are special trains, sightseeing buses, and bus or train packages from Sapporo, which combine Biei and Furano flowers with a popular zoo at Asahikawa. Check with JR Hokkaidō and Chuo Bus for details. Outside Furano station, flower farm information, shuttles buses, and help with hotel searches are available at the **Furano Tourist Association.**

ESSENTIALS

Visitor Information Furano Tourist Association (⊠*1–26 Hinode-machi, Furano-shi* ☎*0167/23–3388* ⊕*www.furano.ne.jp/kankou/* ☯*Daily 9–5*).

WHAT TO SEE

Farm Tomita ファーム富田Lavender is the leading souvenir from Hokkaidō as well as the most popular tourist brochure image, and this is where it all started! The Tomita family started these lavender fields in 1903. Now thousands of visitors come to see fields of lavender, poppies, cosmos, herbs and marigolds. Irodori (Color Roads) is the field with flowers planted in seven strips, each a different color. Lavender peak season is early July to early August, and during this time the Lavender Batake

Station—seven minutes closer than Nakafurano Station—is open. JR Hokkaidō and Chūō Bus offer packages for one-day visits in summer. ⊠*Hokusei, Nakafurano-chō* ☎*0167/39–3939* ⊕*www.farm-tomita. co.jp/* ☑*Free* ☉*Daily 8:30–5.*

WHERE TO STAY

$$$$ ⊡**Auberge Hermitage** オーベルジュ エルミタージュ. A manor house overlooking Biei's rolling fields and the Daisetsu mountains has local fresh produce on the menu, and a TV ban ensures nothing but quiet. The Western-style rooms are simple for this price range, but the Jacuzzi with mountain views and the personal service make up for it. Macrobiotic and vegetarian guests are particularly welcome to join the chef in the kitchen. Pick-up from Biei Station 15 minutes away. English spoken. **Pros:** fresh local veggies; quiet; views of flowers and mountains. **Cons:** rooms lack luxurious touches; no TV. ⊠*San ai midori, Biei* ☎*0166/92–0991* ⊕*en.hermitage-web.com/* ☞*5 rooms, 2 cottages* ♿*In-room: refrigerator, no TV, Wi-Fi. In-hotel: restaurant, no kids under 12, no smoking rooms* ▤*MC, V* ⊺◎⊺*MAP.*

EASTERN HOKKAIDŌ 道東

Bears and eagles rule the mountains of Shiretoko National Park. Farther inland are the mysterious lakes of the Akan National Park, where Ainu people hold on to their pre-Japanese culture with spirit worship, music, and dance. South, around Kushiro, are the vast wetland breeding grounds of the striking *tanchō-zuru* (red-crested crane). On the eastern coast flowers carpet the land in the short summer, while in winter creaking ice floes nudge against the shore, providing a temporary home to seals and seabirds. Unfortunately, the ice is getting thinner and the viewing season shorter—this is the front line of global warming.

Japan's last frontier is also a hotbed of international politics. Japan and Russia are engaged in bitter disputes over islands and fishing and mineral rights. Russian sailors hang around fishing ports and bars in small towns, and signboards across the region proclaim, "Return the Northern Territories!" This is Japan's campaign to reclaim islands, some just kilometers off its eastern shore, that were lost after World War II.

There are regional airports in Kushiro and Memanbetsu, and express trains reach Abashiri and Kushiro. The largest city is Kushiro, which is famous for its morning fish market, but more beautiful touring bases include Akan Onsen and Abashiri, and the small fishing town of Utoro, halfway up the Shieroko Peninsula, is Japan's easternmost outpost.

ABASHIRI 網走

517 km (321 mi) east of Sapporo.

A good touring base for eastern Hokkaidō, Abashiri is a small town in the shadow of Tento-zan. On the town outskirts are shallow coastal lakes with flowers and seabirds. Bicycles can be rented for slow sightseeing. The whaling fleet sets out from here on "research" trips ("research" is the official word, common parlance would call it "hunting") under

Japan's interpretation of IWC rules, which keeps Japan at loggerheads with conservationists. Winters are harsh: visitors bundle up for boat tours through the *ryūhyō* (ice floes) that jam up on its shores and stretch out to sea as far as the eye can see.

GETTING HERE AND AROUND

The significant distance from Sapporo to Abashiri makes it advisable to take one of the four daily so-called express trains out. This is a five-hour plus trip with almost walking speeds thru the northern Daisetsu mountain area and a deadend turn at Engaru when all passengers stand and turn the seats to face forwards.

Abashiri has enough sights for a day, or more you set out to cycle the 27 km (17 mi) lakeside cycling road. There are seven buses a day from the station, circling the sights on Tento-zan and a day pass costs ¥900. Be careful if you arrive on the morning train from Sapporo that gets in at 12:46 PM because you'll only have eight minutes to run for bus stop Number 2, or face a two-hour wait for the next bus. Tourist office staff will keep bags for ¥300 per item. After doing Abashiri's sights, rent a car or go by bus to the Shiretoko, Akan, or Kushiro Marsh areas.

Some staff members at the **Abashiri Tourist Office,** adjoining the JR station, speak English. This is where to find information about transportation and lodging in the area. At the station, inside the JR Hokkaidō car rental office you'll find **Bicycle – Ekimae Rental** where you can rent a bike for ¥500 an hour, June to September.

ESSENTIALS

Bicycle Rental Bicycle – Ekimae Rental (☎0152/43-6197).

Visitor Information Abashiri Tourist Office (☎0152/43–4261 ⊕www?s.big lobe.ne.jp/~abushirl/).

WHAT TO SEE

Aurora Terminal オーロラ号. Ice-floe sailing with bird and seal spotting is possible late January to April from boats leaving Aurora Terminal at the east end of the port. The *Aurora 1* and the *Aurora 2* let you inspect the ryūhyō at close range for ¥3,000. Travel agencies in Tōkyō and Sapporo and JR Hokkaidō offer ice-floe/hot-spring package tours that always include this boat trip. ☎0152/43–6000.

Hokkaidō Museum of Northern Peoples 北方民族博物館 *(Hoppō Minzoku Hakubutsukan)*. Hokkaidō is the most southerly point of the northern community of the Ainu. This museum's exhibits link indigenous people, such as the Ainu, Inuits, and Sami (or Lapps). Displays compare and contrast the kitchen implements, clothes, and hunting snares and nets of various cultures from northern Japan, the neighboring Russian island of Sakhalin, and the northern parts of America and Eurasia. English information is limited, but Hokkaidō items have blue tags. Look out for the alienlike fish-skin suit. The museum is 5 km (3 mi)—a 10-minute drive—from JR Abashiri Station on Tento-zan. ☎0152/45–3888 ☜¥450 ⊙*Tues.–Sun. 9:30–4:30.*

Prison Museum 網走監獄博物館 *(Abashiri Kangokuku Hakbutsukan)*. Spartan cells line the central corridors in five wooden prison blocks, showing how the convicts who built much of early Hokkaidō lived out their years. Used between 1912 and 1984, the prison is now a park museum with the blocks, watch towers, and farm buildings preserved. Only the most heinous criminals were banished to this forbidding northern outpost, the Alcatraz of Japan. English information is entertainingly lost in translation, but anguished-looking mannequins illustrate the grimness of life behind bars. ✉ *1–1 Yobito* ☎ *0152/45–2411* ⊕ *www.kangoku.jp/world* ✉ *¥1,050* ⊙ *Apr.–Oct., daily 8–6; Nov.–Mar., daily 9–5.*

WHERE TO EAT AND STAY

¢–$
CAFÉ

✗ **Bangaichi Café** 番外地カフェ. This small windowless café above a mainstreet shop looks unpromising from its stair entrance, but inside is a cocoon of peace with sofas, warm lighting, and jazz. The menu includes hemp and raisin scones, fresh-brewed coffee, cheese on toast, and parfaits. ✉ *2nd fl., Honma Bldg., West 2, South 4, Abashiri* ☎ *0152/43–7110* ⊟ *No credit cards* ⊙ *Daily 7–7*

$–$$
JAPANESE

✗ **Nakazushi** 中鮨. Rotarian Kanio Nakano presides over the Ohotsuku-kai's freshest catch in a small restaurant near the Abashiri Central Hotel run for more than 40 years by the same family. Depending on the season, Nakano-san has salmon roe on rice, sea urchin, and the plump, juicy Abashiri scallop. *Tsuchi-kujira* (Baird's beaked whale) is sometimes on the menu. Although Nakano-san doesn't speak English, he's aware of the whale-meat debate and can make substitutions if you let him know your no-whale preference through gestures. ✉ *Minami 2-jō Nishi 2, Abashiri* ☎ *0152/43–3447* ⊟ *No credit cards.*

$$$–$$$$
★

🏨 **Hotel Abashiri-ko-so** ホテル網走湖荘. Waterbirds and mist drift by the windows of the big but friendly hotel on the shore of Lake Abashiri, a few kilometers from town. It has the usual noise of Japanese resort hotels—game corners, tour groups, and karaoke rooms. But beyond the doors you can enjoy the peace of a lakeside walk, then a hot spring, and finally retire to your room and relax over a multicourse crab dinner. The combination rooms have raised beds and tatami sitting areas. The hotel has even has a barbershop for guests' dogs. Reservations can be made in English via the Web site. **Pros:** lakeside; ideal for birdwatching. **Cons:** out of town; used by tour groups. ✉ *Abashiri Kohan Onsen, Abashiri* ☎ *0152/48–2245* 🖷 *0152/48–2828* ⊕ *www.abashirikoso.com* 🛏 *37 Western-style rooms, 20 Japanese-style rooms, 100 combination rooms* ⚘ *In-hotel: 3 restaurants, bars* ⊟ *AE, MC, V* ⛄ *MAP.*

$$–$$$

🏨 **Abashiri Central Hotel** 網走セントラルホテル. Luxury awaits you at this downtown hotel, which seems a world away from small-town Abashiri. Rooms in yellows and blues overlook a main road out front or parking at the back. Fish from the local icy waters are a specialty of the Grand Glacier restaurant, which serves Japanese, Chinese, and French food. The weekday lunch buffet is only ¥1,200. English speakers are on staff. **Pros:** town center; foreigner friendly service. **Cons:** could be anywhere in the world; boring views. ✉ *7, Minami 2-jo, Nishi 3, Abashiri* ☎ *0152/44–5151* 🖷 *0152/43–5177* ⊕ *www.abashirich.com* 🛏 *94 Western-style rooms, 2 Japanese-style rooms* ⚘ *In-room: Internet, Wi-Fi. In-hotel: restaurant, bar.*

SHIRETOKO NATIONAL PARK 知床国立公園

★ *50 km (31 mi) east of Abashiri.*

GETTING HERE AND AROUND

From Sapporo to Abashiri it's a five-hour express train, then a local train to Shari, and finally a 55-minute bus ride to Utoro. With connections the trip takes seven hours. Depending on the season, about seven daily bus connections go from Shari to Utoro. Buses from Abashiri and the airports in Kushiro and Membanbetsu also connect to Utoro. Kushiro and Abashiri have several car-rental companies, and Shari has only one (Nippon Rent a Car). Coming from Kushiro it's a two-hour drive to the non-touristy fishing village of Rausu on the south side of the peninsula, and then a 30-minute drive over the Shiretoko Pass (closed November–April) to Utoro.

From Sapporo the twice-daily Eagle Liner bus takes seven hours (¥15,000 round-trip), departing Sapporo Chūō Bus terminal at 9 AM and 11:15 PM. Reservations with Chūō Bus are necessary and can be made at the terminal behind the TV Tower in Sapporo, where the bus departs. Utoro and Rausu are also connected by four buses daily.

The village of Utoro is the center of visitor activity. It's a simple working fishing village, with a hotel zone built on a bluff above the center. From the end of April to the end of October one-hour shuttle-bus trips link the town with the Nature Center and Shiretoko Five Lakes. They run three times a day and cost ¥900. Beyond here, the 12-km (7-mi) dirt road to Kamuiwaka is open to shuttle buses July 13 to September 20. In winter the roads beyond Utoro are closed. Be careful of wildlife when driving, Shiretoko is full of grazing deer who favor cleared roadside verges.

Apart from hiking, a boat is the best way to see the wildest parts. Late April to October, several boat companies in Utoro harbor offer one- to three-hour trips (¥3,000–¥8,000) out along the peninsula, beneath soaring 600-foot cliffs to the tip of the cape. Early-morning and late-afternoon trips on a small boat offer the best chances to see bears come down to the beaches and the river outlets to forage for food. On the Rausu side, boats head out into the Nemuro Straits toward Russia's Kunashiri island and summer is the best time for whale-watching. A stay of at least one night is recommended for hiking, hot springs, wildlife spotting, and silence. We recommend **Ever Green Nature Cruises** out of Rausu and Gojira-Iwa and **CafeFox Cruises** out of Utoro.

Utoro-Shiretoko Michi-no-eki, a two-minute walk from the bus terminal on the waterfront. On the Rausu side, information can be found at the **Rausu Visitor Center.** Don't forget to check out the hourly 8-meter-high geyser in the woods out back.

ESSENTIALS

Boat Tours Ever Green Nature Cruises (0153/87–4002 ✎ captain-h@e-shiretoko.com ⊕ www.e-shiretoko.com). **Gojira-Iwa** (⊕ www.gojiraiwa.com/). **CafeFox Cruises** (0152/24–2680 ⊕ www.hitcolour.com/cafefox/cruise).

Bus Contacts Chūō Bus (Eagle Liner) (☎ 011/231–0500, Japanese only).

15

Tour Information Shiretoko Nature Office (*0152/22–5041)*. Shiretoko Naturalist's Association (Shinra) (☎*0152/22–5522* ⊕ *www.shinra.or.jp/)*.

Visitor Information Utoro-Shiretoko Michi-no-eki (✉*186-Banchi 8, Utoro Nishi* ☎*0152/23–3131* ☉ *Daily 8–7)*. Rausu Visitor Center (✉*Yunosawa, Rausu* ☎*0153/87–2828)*.

WHAT TO SEE

The spectacular **Shiretoko National Park** 知床国立公園 on the Shiretoko Peninsula is worlds away from modern Japan and rewards visitors who have the time to make it there: brown bears hook salmon out of tumbling rivers; Blackiston's fish owls and Steller's sea eagles glide the skies; and a steaming hot river tumbles to the sea. However, with the UNESCO designation came mass tourism. The Japanese bid to control and preserve has resulted in high metal fences, strict rules, and limited shuttle-bus access to the last few kilometers of peninsula road—which can give an unwelcome Jurassic Park feel to the visit.

Most tour buses whisk their captives in and out in 24 hours—with an overnight stay in a big hotel in Utoro's hotel zone and quick photo-stops at Shiretoko Five Lakes, the nature center, and maybe a boat tour. Time your sightseeing at these places during the noon–1 PM tour lunch break or late in the day, and head for the places off the tour route. The magic of Shiretoko is found just beyond the bus park hordes. We and acquaintances have seen bear on the road near the Nature Center—they are out there for sure. Shiretoko is lovely but local weather, even in summer, is fickle. A Shiretoko stay (and hiking plans) can be marred by mists and rain.

If you visit outside the summer crush—June and September are good times—Shiretoko is a remarkable, untouched pocket of wilderness in a heavily industrialized and technologically advanced nation. Read *Audrey Hepburn's Neck* (1996, Simon & Schuster), a novel by Alan Brown, for a tale of a 20th-century childhood on Shiretoko.

☺ **Kamuiwakka Onsen** カムイワッカ温泉. *Kamui* means "spirit" or "god"
Fodor's Choice in the Ainu language, and there's something wondrous, almost other-
★ worldly, about this tumbling hot river on the north shore under Iō-zan (Mt. Iō). Water rushes down the mountain through a series of falls and pools, creating a rotemburo with an ocean view. The pools are free—just strip and hop in. It's best to wear shoes if you want to scramble up over slippery rocks to the pools higher upstream. Strict access rules have put this place almost out of reach except from one month in summer. Bear and park-patrol activity is high, so if you plan to hike the 12 km (7 mi) along the road from Five Lakes to Kamuiwakka, tred carefully.

Shiretoko Go-ko 知床五湖 *(Five Lakes)*. Twenty minutes east of Utoro by car—and on every tour bus route in the region—a collection of small lakes hides in the forest on a precipice above the ocean. It takes just over an hour to walk round all five on boardwalk paths. Most tour groups only reach the first two, and the others are sometimes closed due to the presence of bears. The lakes are pretty but not essential viewing if you are on a tight schedule. Better to make time for a boat trip.

Shiretoko National Park Nature Center. Crowds from buses swarm the center for a big screen film show, souvenir shopping, and a restaurant, but you might be more interested in latest information about the animal and plant sightings. The 2-km trail behind the center offers a peaceful trek to the Furepe Waterfall where the day visitors hardly venture. Bears have been spotted on this trail in the early morning. The Nature Center is 3 km (2 mi) from Utoro, at the junction of the roads leading to Iwaobetsu and the Shiretoko Pass/Rausu. ⊠ *531 Iwaobetsu, Shari-cho, Utoro* ☎ *0152/24–2114* ⊕ *www.shiretoko.or.jp/* ⊗ *Apr. 18–Oct. 20, daily 8–5:40; Oct. 21–Apr. 19, daily 9–4.*

Mt. Rausu 羅臼岳. Snow-covered from October to June and towering 5,448 feet along the spine of the peninsula, Mt. Rausu provides the real getaway from the crowds. The most accessible trailhead is 5 km (3 mi) east of Utoro behind the Hotel Chi-no-hate; you walk 1 hour 20 minutes to a 1,920-foot rocky outcrop, then another two hours to the top. From there trails head west (two hours) along the peninsula to meet the Utoro-Rausu highway at Shiretoko Pass or over the ridge and down to Rausu (three hours). Finally there is a much more difficult train for serious hikers only; it's eight hours along the ridge to the 5,127-foot Mt. Iō and then down to Kamuiwakka Onsen. Check weather conditions before hiking, sign the trailhead books, and fix a bear bell to your backpack.

Aching muscles can be soaked in open-air hot springs waiting at the end of the hike: **Iwaobetsu Onsen** 岩尾別温泉, just below the Hotel Chi-no-hate car park, has four steaming rocky pools in a forest with no changing hut and a strong likelihood of sitting naked with strangers. Near the trailhead and campsite on the Rausu side look for **Kuma-no-yu** 熊ノ湯, two boiling pools areas for men and women separated by some unfortunate concrete and rusty pipes, but fenced in for privacy.

WHERE TO EAT

$ ✕**Shiretoko Station of the Journey.** This bustling village eatery serves
JAPANESE steaming crab curry, golden sea urchin on rice, and anything else they can make out of this morning's catch. They often give free crab legs to suck on while you wait. It's by the entrance to the harbor; picture menus are available for easy ordering. ⊠ *172 Utoro Nishi, Shari-chō* ☎ *0152/24–2910* ⊟ *No credit cards.*

WHERE TO STAY

$$ ⌂**Iruka (Dolphin) Hotel** いるか小テル. Owned by diver/wildlife photographer this hotel guesthouse sits waterside in Utoro. Vast fish dinners are served in the bright modern dining room and on the wooden deck overlooking Utoro Bay. Guests can use the tiny outdoor hot spring. Yamamoto-san speaks some English and is qualified to take guests diving under the ice floes in winter. From the small tatami rooms at dusk, keep an eye out for local foxes that curl up on the hoods of the still-warm cars in the car park. It's the bright yellow, first house in the village as you arrive from Abashiri, but you'll need to double back to get into the tiny entrance road. **Pros:** personal welcome; great food; nature spotting advice. **Cons:** slow to respond to e-mail reservation enquiries; small

15

rooms. ⊠*5 Utoro-Nishi, Shari-chō,* ☎*015/24–2888* 🖷*0152/24–2788* ⊕*www.iruka-hotel.com* ⇌*13 rooms* ♿*In-hotel: diving* ❘⊙❘*MAP.*

$ 🖪**Iwaobetsu Youth Hostel** 岩尾別ユースホステル. It is old and unlovely outside, but inside is an efficient working hostel with wood floors and worn furnishings. Hikers and bikers sit down to salmon roe and rice dinners, then attend the evening meeting fortified with Mountain Grape wine. A little English is spoken, and the staff can rent mountain bikes and arrange sea-kayaking tours (¥8,000 for three hours). It's by the river, 4 km (2½ mi) out of Utoro on the road to the Five Lakes, where deer graze in the car park and bears are tempted by the nearby salmon hatchery. The road opposite the hostel leads to Chi-no-hate, Iwaobetsu, and Mount Rausu. **Pros:** national park peace just outside the front door; deer and bear-spotting chances. **Cons:** old building; out of town; bring your own sheet if you are bed bug fodder. ⊠*Aza Iwaobetsu, Utoro* ☎*015/24–2311* 🖷*0152/24–2312* ⊕*www.youthhostel.or.jp.*

$$$–$$$$ 🖪**Shiretoko Daiichi Hotel** 知床第一ホテル. Beneath vast sunset ceiling murals replica antique furniture stands toe-deep in plush carpets decorated with regional flowers—this is a Japanese hotel stay at its most luxurious. At the very top of Utoro's hotel area, the hot-spring sunset views are sensational. Mountain-facing windows look over the small vegetable fields around Utoro, where bear and deer can be spotted helping themselves at dusk. Hotel guests do the same at over-the-top buffets. English-speakers are on duty in the evening at the tour desk. Reserve in English through the Web site. **Pros:** luxury; best place for sunset view; pig-out dining. **Cons:** Hokkaidō's nature can seem a world away; tour group frenzy in the lobby. ⊠*306 Utoro Onsen, Shari-chō* ☎*0152/24–2334* 🖷*0152/24–2261* ⊕*www.shiretoko-1.co.jp/* ⇌*238 rooms, 178 Japanese-style, 41 Western-style, 19 combination* ♿ *In-hotel: 3 restaurants, bars, no-smoking rooms, Internet terminal* ▤*AE, DC, MC, V* ❘⊙❘*MAP.*

AKAN NATIONAL PARK 阿寒国立公園

58 km (36 mi) southeast of Abashiri.

Volcanoes rise from primeval forests, and lakeside beaches bubble with hot springs in this national park that is unfairly out-shone by its neighbors Daisetsu and Shiretoko. In Akan's northern forests, strange, cylindrical algae bob to the surface of Lake Akan. Ainu men pluck and blow eerie music from traditional instruments while women dancers duck and weave in honor of the red-crested white cranes that fly in every winter to breed on the wetland on the park's southern border. In summer it's a hiker's heaven of trails and hot springs; in winter the lakes freeze over and ice festivals spill out onto the frozen expanses.

GETTING HERE AND AROUND

There are about six buses (¥2,650, 90 minutes) a day to Akan-ko from Kushiro airport and station. You can also catch a bus from Akan-ko to Abashiri if you change buses in Bihoro. One bus a day also connects Akan to Sounkyou. Akan Bus Co. has escorted (Japanese only) bus tours (May to end of October) that depart from Kushiro Station for Lake Akan, the crane watching areas, Lake Mashu, and Kawayu

Onsen. On the Web site look at the route map under "Sightseeing Bus." Reservations required.

ESSENTIALS

Bus Contacts Akan Bus (☎*0154/ 37–2221* ⊕ *www.akanbus.co.jp*).

WHAT TO SEE

★ **Akan-ko** 阿寒湖 *(Lake Akan)*. Chugging tour boats with noisy Japanese commentaries and even speedboats disturb the waters below smoking volcanoes Me-Akan and O-Akan (Mr. and Mrs. Akan). But out on Churui Island silence is green among Lake Akan's strangest inhabitants, *marimo*, as they nestle peacefully in display tanks. These rare spherical colonies of green algae that may be as small as a Ping-Pong ball or as large as a soccer ball (the latter taking up to 500 years to form).

SMELT FISHING
Lake Akan in winter is dotted with ice holes. Fishermen crouch in sub-zero temperatures to hook *wakasagi* (pond smelt) from the depths. Visitors can slide across the lake and try their luck, fortified with *ama-sake*, a delicious—but alcoholic—drink made from sweetened brown rice. The successful can head back to the shore where stallholders are on hand to mince the catch for a raw meal or fry or grill it. Grilled wakasagi often appears on the winter menus of Hokkaidō izakayas. *Wakasagi* fishing costs ¥800 for adults and ¥400 for kids. The gear includes a chair and your own personal ice hole.

15

The only other areas marimo can be found are in Yamanaka-ko (Lake Yamanaka), near Fuji-san, and in a few lakes in North America, Siberia, and Switzerland. These strange algae act much like submarines, bobbing to the lake surface when bright sunshine increases their photosynthesis but staying submerged in inclement weather, when light levels drop.

Enjoy the lake from a canoe with the help of the **Akan Adventure Center,** which offers two- or eight-person Canadian canoes for a 45-minute beginner course (¥2,100), a 90-minute adventure course (¥5,300), or for the strong-of-arm the 2½-hour Yaitai Island course (¥8,400). Reserve one day in advance by calling 0154/67–2081, or e-mailing in simple English via www.akan.co.jp. The center is in Akan Kohan, near the Ainu village and next to Pension Yamaguchi on the north end of the town street.

Akan-kohan 阿寒湖畔. The small town on the lakeshore is a major stop on regional bus tours, with giant hotels blocking off the lake from the main road running through the town. Kitschy souvenir shops sell endless rows of carved bears made by Ainu residents and bottles containing *marimo* that may never grow. At the northern end of the town is the Ainu village, one cobbled street lined by shops and restaurants, with the Culture Performance Center and a small museum at the top. May to October there are excellent 30-minute, traditional dance performances five times a day, and the 9 PM show features *yukara,* chanted epic poems. Performances cost ¥1,100.

★ **Kushiro Marsh** *(Kushiro Shitsugen)*. Graceful red-crested cranes preen and breed in protected Kushiro Marsh, which constitutes 60% of Japan's marshland. These rare cranes, whose feathers were thought to bring good luck, were ruthlessly hunted at the beginning of the 20th century and were even believed extinct until a handful of survivors were discovered in 1924. They have slowly regenerated and now number about 650. The crane—long-legged, long-billed, with a white body trimmed in black and a scarlet cap on its head—is a symbol of long life and happiness. Legends hold that the birds live 1,000 years, and they have made it to a rather impressive 80 years of age in captivity. They pair for life, making them the symbol of an ideal couple, and they are frequently cited in Japanese wedding speeches.

November to March is the best season for wild-crane watching, because this is when the birds fly in from Russia, China, and Korea and gather at feeding stations such as Tsurumidai, off Route 53. In summer the birds that stay retreat deep into the swamps to raise their chicks and can only be spotted with binoculars. The **Akan International Crane Center** (Akan Kokusai Tsuru Centa) and the adjoining Tanchō-no-Sato, **Crane Home** (⊠ *23–40 Akan-chō* ☎ *0154/66–4011*) are both about one hour south of Lake Akan, near the Tanchō-zuru bus stop on the Akan-kohan–Kushiro bus route. Here you can watch a feeding and visit the center's units for egg hatching, chick rearing, and bird medical care.

Canoe paddlers on the Kushiro River have a chance to see cranes and other birds: rental companies are at Lake Toro, off Route 391, and by the Norroko-go, a slow, sightseeing train from Kushiro (July and August only). The marshland comprises 183 square kilometers, and viewing areas with wooden walkways and observation towers are located off routes 53 and 359.

WHERE TO EAT AND STAY

$$$$ ⬚**Lake Spa Takada** レイクスパ たかだ. This is a small European-style hotel on the lakeside by the boat dock. It's fronted by a wooden deck of flower planters and garden umbrellas—a good spot to sit back and watch resort life. Rooms are small and quiet. Dinners in the Western-style dining room are impressive spreads with Lake Akan trout, venison, and seasonal vegetables. At the roof's small outdoor hot spring you look out over the lake. English is spoken and the owners have family living in Australia, so bushman hats are on sale in the lobby shop. **Pros:** lakeside, village center, good dinners. **Cons:** small onsen. ⊠ *1–6–11 Akan-ko Onsen, Akan-chō* ☎ *0154/67–4157*   *0154/67–4158* ⊕ *www.lakes pa-takada.com/* ⟳ *10 rooms, 7 Japanese-style, 3 Western-style* ⊟ *AE, MC, V* ¶◎¶*MAP.*

$ ⬚**Minshuku Yamaguchi** 民宿山口. The mynah bird, Tarō, may screech a welcome as you enter this small home. This is like staying with elderly relatives. While the Yamaguchis don't speak English, they proudly welcome foreign guests to their slightly faded rooms and mineral-stained shared baths. Look for the impressive flower display out front, just past the Ainu village end of the town. **Pros:** cheap; friendly. **Cons:** faded rooms; thin walls; old, shared baths; no lake views. ⊠ *5–3–2 Akan-ko Onsen, Akan-chō* ☎ *0154/67–2555* ⟳ *10 Japanese-style rooms without bath* ♿ *In-room: no phone. In-hotel: restaurant, Japanese baths, no elevator* ⊟ *No credit cards* ¶◎¶*MAP.*

NORTHERN HOKKAIDŌ 道北

Travelers with more time should trek north to Sōya-misaki, Japan's northernmost point, and the stark beauty of the Rebun and Rishiri islands. Wakkanai, the transport center, is a working fishing town. It serves as the jumping off point to the islands and to the coastal grasslands to the south. The best season is late May to early September.

THE NORTHERN CAPE

Wakkanai is 396 km (246 mi) north of Sapporo.

Japan's northernmost point is windy and empty. In the short summer season tiny alpine flowers bloom in coastal grasslands and on rocky outcrops overlooking the sea. In winter the Arctic ice floes lock the land for months of darkness. This is only a place to come when you've already seen Daisetsu and Shiretoko. Long-term residents and repeat visitors come this far north for the hiking, the flowers, and the peace found in such edge-of-the-world places.

15

GETTING HERE AND AROUND

From June through August, Air Nippon flies from Shin-Chitose Airport directly to Rishiri Airport (45 minutes) on Rishiri-tō. At other times there are flights to Wakkanai from Okadama airport in Sapporo (1hour), and then bus and ferry connections to the islands.

Heart Land Ferry has boats that make the daily two-hour crossing to Rebun-tō and the one-hour, 40-minute crossing to Rishiri-tō. In summer there are four or five daily ferries, in winter two. Fares to Rebun are ¥4,080 for first class and ¥2,400 second class. Fares to Rishiri are ¥3,660 and ¥2,180. A ferry between the two islands costs ¥880.

ESSENTIALS
Ferry Information Heart Land Ferry (☎ *0162/23–3780*).

WHAT TO SEE
Rebun Island 礼文島 *(Rebun-tō)* is the older of two Nihon-kai islands created by an upward thrust of the earth's crust. Along the east coast there are numerous fishing villages where fleets of *uni* boats fish just offshore; prickly sea urchins are spotted through bottomless boxes held over the side of the boat and then raked in.

On the west coast is an eight-hour hiking trail, and cliffs stave off the surging waters of the Nihon-kai. Inland, more than 300 species of wild alpine flowers blanket the mountain meadows in such profusion in mid-June that each step seems to crush a dozen of the delicate blossoms, including the white-pointed *usuyo-kiso,* which is found only on Rebun. Its name roughly translates as "dusting of snow."

★ **Rishiri Island** 利尻島 *(Rishiri-tō).* The island is the result of a submarine volcano whose cone now towers 5,640 feet out of the water. The scenery is wilder than on Rebun-tō, and though it's a larger island Rishiri-tō has fewer inhabitants. The rugged terrain makes it hard to support life and figures for hardier climbing. The intermediate **Kutsugata Course** (four hours to the top), on the west side of the island, takes you past patches of wildflowers, including the buttercuplike *botan kimbai* and the vibrant purple *hakusan chidori,* and numerous bird species.

Sōya-misaki 宗谷岬 *(Cape Sōya).* This is the end of Japan. Behind lies a world of sushi, cherry blossoms, and bowing—ahead across frigid waters is Russia's Sakhalin Island. This lonely but significant spot is the site of several monuments marking the end of Japan's territory, as well as a memorial to the Korean airliner downed by the Soviet military north of here in 1982. A public bus makes the hour-long run between Wakkanai and Cape Sōya six times a day.

WHERE TO STAY

$$$ 🏨 **Pension Ūnii** ペンションうーにー. This sky-blue building is at the top of the cliffs above Rebun's ferry terminal. Rooms have private bathrooms, and the two meals included in the rate feature the absolute freshest ingredients. Gargantuan dinners alternate between Western- and Japanese-style, although the switch from cutlery to chopsticks may be your only clue as to which is which. **Pros:** good views; sea urchin at every meal. **Cons:** no English spoken; steep climb up from the harbor. ✉ *Kafuka-Irifune, Rebun-chō* ☎ *0163/86–1541* 📞 *9 Western-style rooms, 1 Japanese-style room* ♿ *In-hotel: restaurant* ▤ *No credit cards* ‖⊘‖ *MAP.*

UNDERSTANDING JAPAN

KANPAI!

Whether you're out with friends, clients, or belting out a tune at the local karaoke bar, you're sure to have a drink at least once during your stay. Things may look a little different, even before you start knocking back a few, so take note of the liquors of this island nation. And remember, shout *Kanpai!* (sounds like "kaan-pie") instead of *Cheers!* when you raise your glass.

Beverage of the Samurai

Sake, pronounced *sa*-kay, is Japan's number one alcoholic beverage. There are more than 2,000 different brands of sake produced throughout Japan. Like other kinds of wine, sake comes in sweet (*amakuchi*) and dry (*karakuchi*) varieties; these are graded *tokkyū* (superior class), *ikkyū* (first class), and *nikkyū* (second class) and are priced accordingly. (Connoisseurs say this ranking is for tax purposes, and is not necessarily a true indication of quality.)

Best drunk at room temperature (*nuru-kan*) so as not to alter the flavor, sake is also served heated (*atsukan*) or with ice (*rokku de*). It's poured from *tokkuri* (small ceramic vessels) into tiny cups called *choko*. The diminutive size of these cups shouldn't mislead you into thinking you can't drink too much. The custom of making sure that your companion's cup never runs dry often leads the novice astray.

Junmaishu is the term for pure rice wine, a blend of rice, yeast, and water to which no extra alcohol has been added. Junmaishu sake has the strongest and most distinctive flavor, compared with various other methods of brewing, and is preferred by the sake *tsū*, as connoisseurs are known.

Apart from *nomiya* (bars) and restaurants, the place to sample sake is the izakaya, a drinking establishment that usually serves dozens of different kinds of sake, including a selection of *jizake*, the kind produced in limited quantities by small regional breweries throughout the country.

Heavenly Spirits

Shōchū is made from grain and particularly associated with the southern island of Kyūshū. It's served either on the rocks or mixed with water and can be hot or cold. Sometimes a wedge of lemon or a small pickled apricot-like fruit, known as *umeboshi*, is added as well. It can also be mixed with club soda and served cold.

Havin' a Biiru

Japan has four large breweries: Asahi, Kirin, Sapporo, and Suntory. Asahi and Kirin are the two heavyweights, constantly battling for the coveted title of "Japan's No. 1 Brewery," but many beer fans rate Suntory's Malts brand and Sapporo's Yebisu brand as the tastiest brews in the land. Although the popularity of microbreweries is on the rise, locally produced brews can still be hard to find.

JAPANESE GARDENS

Many of the principles that influence Japanese garden design come from religion. Shintoism, Taoism, and Buddhism, the three major religious influences in Japan, all stress the contemplation and re-creation of nature as part of the process of achieving understanding and enlightenment.

From Shintoism, Japan's ancient religion, comes *genus loci* (the spirit of place) and the search for the divine presence in remarkable natural features: special mountains, trees, rocks, and so forth. You can see the Taoist influence in islands, which act as a symbolic heaven for souls who achieve perfect harmony. Here sea turtles and cranes—creatures commonly represented in gardens—serve these enlightened souls.

Buddhist gardens function as settings for meditation, the goal of which is enlightenment. Shōgun and samurai were strongly drawn to Zen Buddhism, so Zen gardens evolved as spaces to use almost exclusively for meditation and growth. The classic example is the *karesansui* (dry landscape) consisting of meticulously placed rocks and raked gravel.

The first garden designers in Japan were temple priests. Later, tea masters created gardens to refine the tea ceremony experience. A major contribution of the tea masters was the *roji*, the path or dewy ground that leads through the garden to the teahouse. The stroll along the roji prepares participants for the tea ceremony emotionally and mentally.

Gradually gardens moved out of the exclusive realm to which only nobles, *daimyō*, (feudal lords), wealthy merchants, and poets had access, and the increasingly affluent middle class began to demand professional designers. In the process, aesthetic concerns came to override those of religion.

In addition to genus loci, karesansui style, and the roji mentioned above, here are a few terms that will help you more fully experience Japanese gardens.

Change and movement. Change is highlighted in Japanese gardens with careful attention to the seasonal variations that plants undergo: from cherry blossoms in spring to summer greenery to autumn leaf coloring to winter snow clinging to the garden's bare bones. A water element, real or abstract, often represents movement, as with the use of raked gravel or a stone "stream."

Mie gakure. The "reveal-and-hide" principle dictates that from no point should all of a garden be visible, that there is always mystery and incompleteness; viewers move through a garden to contemplate its changing perspectives.

Miniaturized landscapes. The depiction of celebrated natural and literary sites has been a frequent design technique in Japanese gardens—Fuji-san, represented by a truncated cone of stones; Ama-no-Hashidate, the famous spit of land, by a stone bridge; or a mighty forest by a lone tree.

Shakkei. "Borrowed landscape" extends the garden's boundaries by integrating a nearby mountain, grove of trees, or a sweeping temple roofline, and framing and capturing the view by echoing it with elements of similar shape or color inside the garden.

Symbolism. Abstract concepts and mythological legends are part of the garden vocabulary. The use of boulders in a streambed can represent life's surmountable difficulties, a pine tree can stand for stability, or islands in a pond for a faraway paradise.

THE TEA CEREMONY

The tea ceremony is a precisely choreographed program that started more than 1,000 years ago with Zen monks. The ritual begins as the server prepares a cup of tea for the first guest. This process involves a strictly determined series of movements and actions, which include cleansing each of the utensils to be used. One by one, the participants slurp up their bowl of tea, then eat a sweet confectionary served with it. Finally, comments about the beauty of the bowls used are exchanged. The entire ritual involves contemplating the beauty in the smallest actions, focusing on their meaning in the midst of the uncertainty of life.

The architecture of a traditional teahouse is also consistent. There are two entrances: a service entrance for the host and server and a low door that requires that guests enter on their knees, in order to be humbled. Tearooms often have tatami flooring and a flower arrangement or artwork in the alcove for contemplation and comment. The three best-known schools of tea ceremonies are the Ura Senke, the Omote Senke, and the Musha Kōji, each with its own styles, emphases, and masters.

Most of your tea experiences will be geared toward the uninitiated: the tea ceremony is a rite that requires methodical initiation by education. If you don't go for instruction before your trip, keep two things in mind: first, be in the right frame of mind when you enter the room. Though the tea ceremony is a pleasant event, some people take it quite seriously, and boisterous behavior is frowned upon. Instead, make conversation appropriate to a mood of serenity. Second, be sure to sit quietly through the serving and drinking—controlled slurping is expected—and openly appreciate the tools and cups afterward, commenting on their elegance and simplicity. This appreciation is the ritual's important final step. Above all, pay close attention to the perfect elements of the ceremony, from the art at the entryway and the kimono of the server to the quality of the utensils.

■ TIP➜ **Want to experience this ancient and highly ritualized art form firsthand? Stop by the Hotel Ōkura Tōkyō in the heart of Roppongi (➪ Where to Stay in Chapter 1), where one-hour and full-day sessions are available.** ☎03/3582-0111 ⊕www. okura.com/tokyo/info/teaceremony.html ⊗Mon.–Sat. 11–4

—David Miles

POTTERY AND LACQUERWARE

Pottery

Ranging from clean, flawlessly decorated porcelain to rustic, spirited "mugs," Japanese ceramics maintain a strong following worldwide. The form has significantly influenced methods in the West. The popularity of raku firing techniques, adapted from those of the Japanese pottery clan of the same name, is one example. Japanese ceramic styles are regionally defined. Arita *yaki* (ceramic ware from Arita on Kyūshū), Tobe yaki, Kutani yaki, and Kyōto's Kyō yaki and Kiyomizu yaki are all porcelain ware. True to the nature of porcelain—a delicate, fine-particled, clay body—these styles are either elaborately decorated or covered with images. Stoneware decoration tends to have an earthier but no less refined appeal, befitting the rougher texture of the clay body. Mashiko yaki's brown, black, and white glazes are often applied in splatters. Celebrated potter Shōji Hamada (1894–1978) worked in Mashiko.

Other regional potters use glazes on stoneware for texture and color—mottled, crusty Tokoname yaki; speckled, earthtone Shigaraki yaki made near Kyōto; and the pasty white or blue-white Hagi yaki come to life with the surface and depth of their rustic glazes. Bizen yaki, another stoneware, has no liquid glaze applied to its surfaces. Instead, pots are buried in ash, wrapped in straw, or colored in the firing process by the potters' manipulations of kiln conditions.

Unless your mind is set on the idea of kiln-hopping in pottery towns like Hagi, Bizen, and Arita, you can find these wares in department stores. If you do go on a pilgrimage, call local kilns and tourist organizations to verify that what you want to see will be open and to ask about yearly pottery sales. Reading: *Inside Japanese Ceramics* (Weatherhill, 1999) by Richard L. Wilson.

Lacquerware

Japanese lacquerware had its origins in the Jōmon period (8,000–300 BC), but as early as the Nara period (AD 710–84) most of the techniques we recognize today were being used. For example, *maki-e* (literally, "sprinkled picture") refers to several different techniques that use gold or silver powder in areas coated with liquid lacquer.

The production of lacquerware starts with draining, evaporating, and filtering the sap from lacquer trees. Successive layers of lacquer are carefully painted on basketry, wood, bamboo, woven textiles, metal, and even paper. The lacquer strengthens the object, making it durable for eating, carrying, or protecting fragile objects, such as fans. Lacquerware can be mirrorlike if polished; often the many layers contain inlays of mother-of-pearl or precious metals inserted between coats, creating a complicated design of exquisite beauty and delicacy.

The best places to see lacquerware are Hōryū-ji in Nara—the temple has a beautiful display—and Wajima in Ishikawa. For a taste of what is available closer to Tōkyō—along with a range of other unique crafts from Japan—head to Bingoya Folk Craft Shop, just past Shinjuku on the Oedo subway line.

Another option is the Japan Folk Crafts Museum, which is two stops from Shibuya on the Keio Inokashira line at Komada-Todaimae station. Not only is this a must-see for fans of Japanese folk craft, it is also the best museum in the Shibuya area, featuring pottery, textiles, and lacquerware.

–David Miles and Barbara Blechman

BATHING: AN IMMERSION COURSE

Japanese cultural phenomena often confound first-time visitors, but few rituals are as opaque as those surrounding bathing. Baths in Japan are as much about pleasure and relaxation as they are about washing and cleansing. Traditionally, communal bathhouses served as centers for social gatherings, and even though most modern houses and apartments have bathtubs, many Japanese still prefer the pleasures of communal bathing—either at onsen while on vacation or in public bathhouses closer to home.

Japanese bathtubs are deep enough to sit in upright with (very hot) water up to your neck. It's not just the size of the tub that will surprise you; the procedures for using them are quite different from those in West. You wash yourself in a special area outside the tub first. The tubs are for soaking, not washing—soap must not get into the bathwater.

Many hotels in major cities have only Western-style reclining bathtubs, so to indulge in the pleasure of a Japanese bath you need to stay in a Japanese-style inn or find a *sen-tō* (public bathhouse). The latter are clean but disappearing fast. Modern versions of the sentō include saunas, steam rooms, and even a restaurant. Japanese bath towels, typically called *ta-o-ru,* are available for a fee at onsen and bathhouses. No larger than a hand towel, they have three functions: covering your privates, washing before and scrubbing while you bathe (if desired), and drying off (wring them out hard and they dry

you quite well). If you want a larger towel to dry off, you have to bring one along.

You may feel apprehensive about bathing (and bathing *properly*) in an o-furo, but if you're well versed in bathing etiquette, you should soon feel at ease. And once you've experienced a variety of public baths—from the standard bathhouses to idyllic outdoor hot springs—you may find yourself a devotee of this ancient custom.

The first challenge in bathing is acknowledging that your Japanese bath mates will stare at your body. Take solace in the fact that their apparent voyeurism most likely stems from curiosity.

When you enter the bathing room, help yourself to two towels, soap, and shampoo (often included in the entry fee), and grab a bucket and a stool. At one of the shower stations around the edge of the room, use the handheld showers, your soap, and one of your towels to wash yourself thoroughly. A head-to-toe twice-over will impress onlookers. After rinsing, you may enter the public bath. You can use your one dry towel to cover yourself, or you can place it on your head (as many of your bath mates will do) while soaking. The water in the bath is as hot as the body can endure, and the reward for making it past the initial shock of the heat is the pleasure of a lengthy soak in water that is never tepid. All you need to do is lean back, relax, and experience the pleasures of purification.

–David Miles

FILMS AND LITERATURE

Films

Akira Kurosawa, Japan's best-known filmmaker, began directing in 1943. His film *Rashōmon* (1950), a 12th-century murder mystery told by four different and untrustworthy narrators, sparked world interest in Japanese cinema. Among his classic-period films are *Seven Samurai* (1954), *The Hidden Fortress* (1958) (also the inspiration for Star Wars), *Yōjimbō* (1961), *Red Beard* (1965), *Dersu Uzala* (1975), and *Kagemusha* (1980). The life-affirming *Ikiru* (1952) deals with an office worker dying of cancer. *The Bad Sleep Well* (1960), meanwhile, portrays a nightmare of (then) contemporary Japanese corporate corruption. Two of Kurosawa's most honored films were adapted from Shakespeare plays: *Throne of Blood* (1957), based on *Macbeth*, and *Ran* (1985), based on *King Lear*. Many of Kurosawa's films star the irrepressible Toshiro Mifune, whose intense character is constantly exploding against a rigid social structure.

Other seminal samurai pics, known as jidai-geki, include Teinosuke Kinugasa's *Gate of Hell* (1953), which vividly re-creates medieval Japan and won an Oscar for best foreign film, and *The Samurai Trilogy* (1954), directed by Hiroshi Inagaki, which follows the adventures of a legendary 16th-century samurai hero, Musashi Miyamoto. The tale of Zatōichi, a blind swordsman who wanders from town to town seeking work as a masseur but instead always finds himself at the center of bloody intrigue, has been made into some 25 movies over the past five decades.

A new group of filmmakers came to the forefront in postwar Japan including Kon Ichikawa, Hiroshi Teshigahara, and Shōhei Imamura. Ichikawa directed two powerful antiwar movies, *The Burmese Harp* (1956) and *Fires on the Plain* (1959). Teshigahara is renowned for the allegorical *Woman in the Dunes* (1964), based on a novel by Kōbō Abe.

The Ballad of Narayama (1983), about the death of the elderly, and *Black Rain* (1989), which deals with the atomic bombing of Hiroshima, are two powerful films by Imamura.

Other Japanese filmmakers worth checking out are Jūzō Itami, Masayuki Suo, Kitano Takeshi, and Iwai Shunji. Itami won international recognition for *Tampopo* (1986), a highly original comedy about food. His other films include *A Taxing Woman* (1987), which pokes fun at the Japanese tax system, and *Mimbō* (1992), which dissects the world of Japanese gangsters. Suo's *Shall We Dance?* (1996) is a bittersweet comedy about a married businessman who escapes his daily routine by taking ballroom dancing lessons. (A U.S. version in 2004 starred Richard Gere, Susan Sarandon, and Jennifer Lopez). Iwai Shunji's *Love Letter* (1995) is a touching story about a girl who receives a lost letter from her boyfriend after he has died.

Akin to the samurai films are Japanese gangster flicks. Though they date back to such Kurosawa classics as *Drunken Angel* (1948) and *Stray Dog* (1949), an edgy gangster genre emerged in the 1990s led by Beat Takeshi Kitano. His films *Fireworks* (1997) and *Zatōichi* (2003) have won awards at the Venice Film Festival. There are many Japanese gangster films, including a whole exploitative subset that mixes extreme violence with basically soft-core porn.

Those interested in Japanese animated or anime movies, should start with the Academy Award–winning picture *Spirited Away* (2002) by Hayao Miyazaki. Other modern anime pioneers include Tezuka Osamu, Mamoru Oshii, and Katsuhiro Otomo.

Recently, Japanese horror has also enjoyed international popularity. Focusing more on anticipation and psychological horror than blood-spurting special effects—though some can be quite gruesome, such as the hair-raising *Audition*

(1999), directed by cult favorite Takashi Miike—Japanese horror tends to leave an eerie feeling that's hard to get rid of. Many involve unseen, unstoppable, or difficult-to-understand threats, like ghosts, poltergeists, and inalterable, tragic destiny. The horror hits, *Ringu* (1998) and *Ju-on: The Grudge* (2003) and their American remakes *The Ring* (2002) and *The Ring Two* (2005) and *The Grudge* (2004) and *The Grudge 2* (2006) are representative of this genre. Not quite your classic horror film but nonetheless horrifying international audiences was Kinji Fukasaku's *Battle Royale* (2000), where kidnapped teenagers brutally killed one another in order to get off a deserted island where they were placed by an overly paranoid government.

Japan has also been the subject of numerous Western movies. For a look at wartime Japan, Steven Spielberg's *Empire of the Sun* (1987) explores the Japanese occupation of China and the Japanese treatment of the Western colonists they replace. The classic *Bridge on the River Kwai* (1957) also explores Japan's treatment of British prisoners of war. Clint Eastwood's *Flag of Our Fathers* and *Letters from Iwo Jima*, both released in 2006, examine the Battle of Iwo Jima from the American and Japanese perspectives, respectively.

First-time visitors to Tōkyō will likely empathize with Sofia Coppola's *Lost in Translation* (2003), about the alienation experienced by an American visitor to Tōkyō. It is a compelling and accurate view of life in contemporary Tōkyō.

Literature

Fiction and Poetry. The great classic of Japanese fiction is the *Tale of Genji*, written by Murasaki Shikibu, a woman of the imperial court around 1000 AD. Genji, or the Shining Prince, has long been taken as the archetype of male behavior. From the same period, Japanese literature's golden age, *The Pillow Book of Sei Shōnagon* is the stylish and stylized diary of a woman's courtly life.

For a selection of Edo-period ghost stories, try Akinari Ueda's *Ugetsu Monogatari: Tales of Moonlight and Rain,* translated by Leon Zolbrod. The racy prose of late-17th-century Saikaku Ihara is translated in various books, including *Some Final Words of Advice* and *Five Women Who Loved Love.*

Modern Japanese fiction is widely available in translation. One of the best-known writers among Westerners is Yukio Mishima, author of *The Sea of Fertility* trilogy and *The Temple of The Golden Pavilion.* His books often deal with the effects of postwar Westernization on Japanese culture. Two superb prose stylists are Junichirō Tanizaki, author of *The Makioka Sisters, Some Prefer Nettles,* and the racy 1920s *Quicksand*; and Nobel Prize–winner Yasunari Kawabata, whose superbly written novels include *Snow Country* and *The Sound of the Mountain.* Kawabata's *Thousand Cranes,* which uses the tea ceremony as a vehicle, is an elegant page-turner. Jirō Osaragi's *The Journey* is a lucid, entertaining rendering of the clash of tradition and modernity in postwar Japan. Also look for Natsume Sōseki's charming *Botchan* and delightful *I Am a Cat.*

Other novelists and works of note are Kōbō Abe, whose *Woman in the Dunes* is a 1960s landmark, and Shūsaku Endō, who brutally and breathlessly treated the early clash of Japan with Christianity in *The Samurai.* Seichō Matsumoto's *Inspector Imanishi Investigates* is a superb detective novel with enlightening details of Japanese life. For a fictional retelling of the nuclear devastation of Hiroshima read Ibuse Masuji's classic novel *Black Rain.*

The "new breed" of Japanese novelists are no less interesting. Haruki Murakami's *Wild Sheep Chase* is a collection of often bizarre and humorous stories, and *Hard Boiled Wonderland and the End of the World* paints a vivid and fantastical picture of the frenetic changes of modern

Japan. Murakami's *The Wind-up Bird Chronicle*, a dense and daring novel, juxtaposes the banality of modern suburbia with the harsh realities of 20th-century Japanese history. Along with Murakami's books, Banana Yoshimoto's *Kitchen* and other novels are probably the most fun you'll have with any Japanese fiction. Kōno Taeko's *Toddler-Hunting* and Yūko Tsushima's *The Shooting Gallery* are as engrossing and well crafted as they are frank about the burdens of tradition on Japanese women today. Nobel Prize–winner Kenzaburō Ōe's writing similarly explores deeply personal issues, among them his compelling relationship with his disabled son. His most important works are *A Personal Matter* and *Silent Scream*.

The flip side to these serious books is the emergence of cell-phone novels. Many stories (which often center on teen angst) are written by those in their teens and early twenties, or those who are very fast at texting. Five out of the ten best selling novels in Japan in 2007 were originally cell-phone novels and some have been made into films!

For books by Westerners, there's a host of titles. The emotional realities of Japan life for foreigners are engagingly rendered in *The Broken Bridge: Fiction from Expatriates in Literary Japan*, edited by Suzanne Kamata. The enormously popular tale *Memoirs of a Geisha*, by Arthur Golden, recounts the dramatic life of a geisha in the decades surrounding World War II. For a humorous and absorbing account of the Gaijin condition, try Will Ferguson's *Hokkaido Highway Blues: Hitchhiking Japan*.

Haiku, the 5-7-5-syllable form that the monk Matsuo Bashō honed in the 17th century, is the flagship of Japanese poetry. Bashō's *Narrow Road to the Deep North* is a wistful prose-and-poem travelogue that is available in a few translations. But there are many more forms and authors worth exploring. Three volumes of translations by Kenneth Rexroth include numerous authors' work from the last 1,000 years: *One Hundred Poems from the Japanese*, *100 More Poems from the Japanese*, and *Women Poets of Japan* (translated with Akiko Atsumi). *Ink Dark Moon*, translated by Jane Hirshfield with Mariko Aratani, presents the remarkable poems of Ono no Komachi and Izumi Shikibu, two of Japan's earliest women poets. The Zen poems of Ryōkan represent the sacred current in Japanese poetry; look for *Dew Drops on a Lotus Leaf*. Other poets to look for are Issa, Buson, and Bonchō. Two fine small volumes that link their haiku with those of other poets, including Bashō, are *The Monkey's Raincoat* and the beautifully illustrated *A Net of Fireflies*.

History and Society. Fourteen hundred years of history are a lot to take in when going on a vacation, but good survey makes the task much easier: read George Sansom's *Japan: A Short Cultural History*.

Yamamoto Tsunetomo's *Hagakure* (*The Book of the Samurai*) is an 18th-century guide of sorts to the principles and ethics of the "Way of the Samurai," written by a Kyūshū samurai. Dr. Junichi Saga's *Memories of Silk and Straw: A Self-Portrait of Small-Town Japan* is his 1970s collection of interviews with local old-timers in his hometown outside Tōkyō. Saga's father illustrated the accounts. Few books get so close to the realities of everyday life in early modern rural Japan.

John Hersey's *Hiroshima* records the stories of survivors, and is essential reading. George Feifer's *Tennozan: The Battle of Okinawa and the Atomic Bomb* recounts the grueling final battle of World War II. John W. Dower is an important historian about Japan whose best known books are *War Without Mercy: Race and Power in the Pacific War*, followed by *Embracing Defeat: Japan in the Wake of World War II*, which won the Pulitzer Prize.

Or pick up any book by Japanese writer Saburo Ienaga, who died in 2002 at age

89. He had long court battles with the Japanese government, arguing that government textbooks distorted Japan's responsibility for bringing on World War II and euphemizing atrocities. He was in large part the catalyst for forcing the Japanese government to finally apologize for the 1937 Nanking massacre in the early 1980s, and later in the 1990s to acknowledge imprisoning Chinese and Korean women as sex-slaves to the Japanese Army and the existence of Unit 731, responsible for the deaths of thousands of prisoners in biochemical experiments. One of his major books is *The Pacific War: World War II and the Japanese, 1931–1945.*

Karel van Wolferens *The Enigma of Japanese Power* is an enlightening book on the Japanese sociopolitical system, especially for diplomats and businesspeople intending to work with the Japanese. Alex Kerr's *Lost Japan* examines the directions of Japanese society past and present. This book was the first by a foreigner ever to win Japan's Shinchō Gakugei literature prize. Elizabeth Bumiller's 1995 *The Secrets of Mariko* intimately recounts a very poignant year in the life of a Japanese woman and her family.

Art and Architecture. A wealth of literature exists on Japanese art. Much of the early writing has not withstood the test of time, but R. Paine and Alexander Soper's *Art and Architecture of Japan* remains a good place to start. A more recent survey, though narrower in scope, is Joan Stanley-Smith's *Japanese Art.*

The multivolume *Japan Arts Library* covers most of the styles and personalities of the Japanese arts. The series has volumes on castles, teahouses, screen painting, and wood-block prints. A more detailed look at the architecture of Tōkyō is Edward Seidensticker's *Low City, High City.* Kazuo Nishi and Kazuo Hozumi's *What Is Japanese Architecture?* treats the history of Japanese architecture and uses examples of buildings you will see on your travels.

Religion. Anyone wanting to read a Zen Buddhist text should try *The Platform Sutra of the Sixth Patriarch*, one of the Zen classics, written by an ancient Chinese head of the sect and translated by Philip B. Yampolsky. Another Buddhist text of great importance is the *Lotus Sutra*; it has been translated by Leon Hurvitz as *The Scripture of the Lotus Blossom of the Fine Dharma: The Lotus Sutra.* Stuart D. Picken has written books on both major Japanese religions: *Shintō: Japan's Spiritual Roots* and *Buddhism: Japan's Cultural Identity.*

Travel Narratives. Three travel narratives stand out as introductions to Japanese history, culture, and people. Donald Richie's classic *The Inland Sea* recalls his journey and encounters on the fabled Seto Nai-kai. Leila Philip's year working in a Kyūshū pottery village became the eloquent *Road Through Miyama.* Peter Carey's *Wrong About Japan* follows the author and his 12-year-old son on their journey through Japan and the world of manga and anime.

Language. There's an overwhelming number of books and courses available for studying Japanese. *Japanese for Busy People* uses conversational situations (rather than grammatical principles) as a means of introducing the Japanese language. With it you will also learn the two syllabaries, *hiragana* and *katakana,* and rudimentary *kanji* characters.

JAPAN AT A GLANCE

FAST FACTS

Capital: Tōkyō

National anthem: *Kimigayo (The Emperor's Reign)*

Type of government: Constitutional monarchy with a parliamentary government

Administrative divisions: 47 prefectures

Independence: 660 BC (traditional founding)

Constitution: May 3, 1947

Legal system: Modeled after European civil law system with English-American influence; judicial review of legislative acts in the Supreme Court

Suffrage: 20 years of age; universal

Legislature: Bicameral Diet or Kokkai with House of Councillors (242 seats, members elected for six-year terms, half reelected every three years, 146 members in multiseat constituencies and 98 by proportional representation); House of Representatives (480 seats, members elected for four-year terms, 300 in single-seat constituencies, 180 members by proportional representation in 11 regional blocs)

Population: 127.3 million

Population density: 343 people per square km (880 people per square mi)

Median age: Female: 45.7, male: 42.1

Life expectancy: Female: 85.6; male: 78.7

Literacy: 99%

Language: Japanese

Ethnic groups: Japanese 99%; other (Korean, Chinese, Brazilian, Filipino) 1%

Religion: Shintō and Buddhist 84%; other 16%

GEOGRAPHY AND ENVIRONMENT

Land area: 374,744 square km (144,689 square mi), slightly smaller than California

Coastline: 29,751 km (18,486 mi)

Terrain: Mostly rugged and mountainous

Islands: Bonin Islands (Ogasawara-gunto), Daitō-shotō, Minami-jima, Okino-torishima, Ryūkyū Islands (Nansei-shoto), and Volcano Islands (Kazan-retto)

Natural resources: Fish, mineral resources

Natural hazards: Japan has about 1,500 earthquakes (mostly tremors) every year; tsunamis; typhoons; volcanoes

Environmental issues: Air pollution from power-plant emissions results in acid rain; acidification of lakes and reservoirs degrading water quality and threatening aquatic life; Japan is one of the largest consumers of fish and tropical timber, contributing to the depletion of these resources in Asia and elsewhere

ECONOMY

Currency: Yen

Exchange rate: 108 yen

GDP: $4.3 trillion

Per capita income: 4.1 million yen ($37,670)

Inflation: 0.0%

Unemployment: 3.9%

Work force: 66.7 million; services 70%; industry 28%; agriculture 5%

Major industries: Chemicals, electronic equipment, machine tools, motor vehicles, processed foods, ships, steel and nonferrous metals, textiles

Agricultural products: Dairy products, eggs, fish, fruit, pork, poultry, rice, sugar beets, vegetables

Exports: $676.9 billion

Major export products: Chemicals, motor vehicles, electrical machinery, semiconductors

Export partners: U.S. 20.4%; China 15.3%; South Korea 7.6%; Taiwan 6.3%; Hong Kong 5.4%

Imports: $572.4 billion

Major import products: Chemicals, foodstuffs, fuels, machinery and equipment, raw materials, textiles

Import partners: China 20.5%; U.S. 11.6%; Saudi Arabia 5.7%; UAE 5.2%; Australia 5%; South Korea 4.4%; Indonesia 4.2%

POLITICAL CLIMATE

Japan has more than 10,000 political parties, mostly small, regional bodies without mass appeal. The Liberal Democratic party (LDP) has held the majority in the legislature since 1955, when the party was formed, with a brief ouster in the 1990s. The LDP is considered a conservative party and has supported close ties with the United States, especially concerning security. The Democratic Party of Japan and New Komeito form the largest opposition groups. Economically, deregulation and growth in the free market are important policy issues. Japan's aging population is also becoming a crucible for politicians, as they balance a dwindling labor force and increasing pensions and benefits for the elderly.

DID YOU KNOW?

■ Japanese engineers have built a car that can go 11,193 mi on one gallon of fuel, a world record. The car performs best at 15 mph and engineers are adapting the technology for commercial production. Japan is also home to the world's first environmentally friendly rental-car company. Kobe-Eco-Car in Kobe has rented electric vehicles, compressed-natural-gas vehicles, and hybrid cars since it was founded in 1998.

■ With an average life expectancy of 78.7 years for men and 85.6 years for women, the Japanese live longer than anyone else on the planet.

■ To take any of the 2,200 daily trips on the East Japan Railway is to ride the world's busiest train system. It carries 16 million passengers over 4,684 mi of track, stopping at a dizzying 1,707 stations.

■ The largest sumō wrestling champion in the history of the sport isn't Japanese, but American. Chad Rowan, born in Hawaii, reached the top ranking of yokozuna, in 1983. He was 6 feet 8 inches and 501 pounds.

■ The Japanese prime minister earns an annual salary of 69.3 million yen ($676,000), the highest of any prime minister in the world.

■ Japan's Yomiuri Shimbun has more readers than any other newspaper on earth. Its combined morning and evening circulation is 14.3 million, 10 times more than that of the New York Times.

■ Japan is the third-largest consumer of cigarettes. The Japanese smoke about 325 billion cigarettes each year, about 100 billion less than Americans and more than a trillion less than the Chinese.

■ Japan has the highest density of robots in the world.

CHRONOLOGY

10,000 BC–300 AD Neolithic Jōmon hunting-and-fishing culture leaves richly decorated pottery.

AD 300 Yayoi culture displays knowledge of farming and metallurgy imported from Korea.

after 300 The Yamato tribe consolidates power in the rich Kansai plain and expands westward, forming the kind of military aristocratic society that will dominate Japan's history.

ca. 500 Yamato leaders, claiming to be descended from the sun goddess, Amaterasu, take the title of emperor.

538–52 Buddhism is introduced to the Yamato court from China by way of Korea, and complements the indigenous Shintō religion.

593–622 Prince Shōtoku encourages the Japanese to embrace Chinese culture and has Buddhist temple Hōryū-ji built at Nara in 607 (its existing buildings are among the world's oldest surviving wooden structures).

NARA PERIOD

710–784 Japan has first permanent capital at Nara; great age of Buddhist sculpture, piety, and poetry.

FUJIWARA OR HEIAN (PEACE) PERIOD

794–1160 The capital is moved from Nara to Heian-kyō (now Kyōto), where the Fujiwara family dominates the imperial court. Lady Murasaki's novel *The Tale of Genji*, written circa 1020, describes the elegance and political maneuvering of court life.

KAMAKURA PERIOD

1185–1335 Feudalism enters, with military and economic power in the provinces and the emperor a powerless, ceremonial figurehead in Kyōto. Samurai warriors welcome Zen, a new sect of Buddhism from China.

1192 After a war with the Taira family, Yoritomo of the Minamoto family becomes the first shōgun; he places his capital in Kamakura.

1274 and 1281 The fleets sent by Chinese emperor Kublai Khan to invade Japan are destroyed by typhoons, praised in Japanese history as kamikaze, or divine wind.

ASHIKAGA PERIOD

1336–1568 The Ashikaga family assumes the title of shōgun and settles in Kyōto. The Zen aesthetic flourishes in painting, landscape gardening, and tea ceremony. Nō theater emerges. The Silver Pavilion, or Ginkaku-ji, in Kyōto, built in 1483, is the quintessential example of Zen-inspired architecture. The period is marked by constant warfare but also by increased trade with the mainland. Ōsaka develops into an important commercial city, and trade guilds appear.

1467–77 The Ōnin Wars initiate a 100-year period of civil war.

1543 Portuguese sailors, the first Europeans to reach Japan, initiate trade relations with the lords of western Japan and introduce the musket, which changes Japanese warfare.

1549–51 St. Francis Xavier, the first Jesuit missionary, introduces Christianity.

MOMOYAMA PERIOD OF NATIONAL UNIFICATION

1568–1600 Two generals, Nobunaga Oda and Hideyoshi Toyotomi, are the central figures of this period. Nobunaga builds a military base from which Hideyoshi unifies Japan.

1592 and 1597 Hideyoshi invades Korea. He brings back Korean potters, who rapidly develop a Japanese ceramics industry.

TOKUGAWA PERIOD

1600–1868 Ieyasu Tokugawa becomes shōgun after the battle of Sekigahara. The military capital is established at Edo (now Tōkyō), spurring phenomenal economic and cultural growth. A hierarchical order of four social classes—warriors, farmers, artisans, then merchants—is rigorously enforced. The merchant class, however, is increasingly prosperous and effects a transition from a rice to a money economy. Merchants patronize new, popular forms of art: Kabuki, haiku, and the ukiyo-e school of painting. The latter part of this era is beautifully illustrated in the wood-block prints of the artist Hokusai (1760–1849).

1618 Japanese Christians who refuse to renounce their foreign religion are persecuted.

1637–38 Japanese Christians are massacred in the Shimabara uprising. Japan is closed to the outside world except for a Dutch trading post in Nagasaki harbor.

1853 U.S. commodore Matthew Perry reopens Japan to foreign trade.

MEIJI PERIOD

1868–1912 Opponents of the weakened Tokugawa Shogunate support Emperor Meiji and overthrow the last shōgun. The emperor is "restored" (with little actual power), and the imperial capital is moved to Edo, which is renamed Tōkyō (Eastern Capital). Japan is modernized along Western lines, with a constitution proclaimed in 1889; a system of compulsory education and a surge of industrialization follow, formally known as the Meiji Restoration.

1902–05 Japan defeats Russia in the Russo-Japanese War and achieves world-power status.

1910 Japan annexes Korea.

TAISHO PERIOD

1914–18 Japan joins the Allies in World War I.

1923 The Great Kantō Earthquake devastates much of Tōkyō and Yokohama, killing 142,807 people, destroying more than 400,000 buildings, and leaving at least 2 million people homeless.

SHOWA PERIOD

1931 As a sign of growing militarism in the country, Japan seizes the Chinese province of Manchuria.

1937 Following years of increasing military and diplomatic activity in northern China, open warfare breaks out (and lasts until 1945); Chinese Nationalists and Communists both fight Japan.

1939–45 Japan, having signed anti-Communist treaties with Nazi Germany and Italy (1936 and 1937), invades and occupies French Indochina.

1941 The Japanese attack on Pearl Harbor on December 7 brings the United States into war against Japan in the Pacific.

1942 Japan's empire extends to Indochina, Burma, Malaya, the Philippines, and Indonesia. Japan bombs Darwin, Australia. U.S. defeat of Japanese forces at Midway turns the tide of the Pacific war.

1945 Tōkyō and 50 other Japanese cities are devastated by U.S. bombing raids. The United States drops atomic bombs on Hiroshima and Nagasaki in August, precipitating Japanese surrender.

1945–52 The American occupation under General Douglas MacArthur disarms Japan and encourages the establishment of a democratic government. Emperor Hirohito retains his position.

1953 After the Korean War, Japan begins a period of great economic growth.

1964 Tōkyō hosts the Summer Olympic games.

late 1960s Japan develops into one of the major industrial nations in the world.

mid-1970s Production of electronics, cars, cameras, and computers places Japan at the heart of the emerging "Pacific Rim" economic sphere and threatens to spark a trade war with the industrial nations of Europe and the United States.

1989 Emperor Hirohito dies.

HEISEI PERIOD

1990 Coronation of Emperor Akihito. Prince Fumihito marries Kiko Kawashima.

1991 Mount Unzen erupts for the second time since 1792, killing 38 people.

1992 The Diet approves use of Japanese military forces under United Nations auspices.

1993 Crown Prince Naruhito marries Masako Owada.

1995 A massive earthquake strikes Kōbe and environs. Approximately 5,500 people are killed and 35,000 injured; more than 100,000 buildings are destroyed.

Members of a fringe religious organization, the Aum Shinri Kyō, carry out a series of poison-gas attacks on the transportation networks of Tōkyō and Yokohama, undermining, in a society that is a model of decorum and mutual respect, confidence in personal safety.

1997 The deregulation of rice prices and the appearance of discount gasoline stations mark a turn in the Japanese economy toward genuine privatization.

1998 The Japanese economy is crippled from slumps throughout Asia. Banks merge or go bankrupt, and Japanese consumers spend less and less.

1999 Japanese toys, films, and other accoutrements of pop culture find themselves in the international spotlight like never before. The economy, however, continues to suffer as politicians debate economic measures that foreign economists have been recommending for years. Small businesses are most affected, and the attitude of the average Japanese is grim.

A nuclear accident 112 km (70 mi) northeast of Tōkyō injures few but raises many questions about Japan's vast nuclear-power industry.

2001 In support of the U.S. war against terrorism in Afghanistan, the Japanese government extends noncombat military activities abroad for the first time since World War II by sending support ships to the Indian Ocean under a reinterpretation of the existing post-1945, pacifist constitution. Asian leaders express concern for the first Japanese military presence abroad since 1945.

2002 North Korea admits to the kidnapping of 11 Japanese civilians in the 1970s and '80s for use as language teachers. Japan negotiates the return of several of its citizens.

2003 Prime Minister Koizumi sends Japanese combat troops to Iraq in the first deployment of Japanese troops since World War II.

2006 The Bank of Japan (BOJ) raises interest rates for the first time in six years, from 0% to 0.25%, marking an end to a decade of economic stagnation. The decision brings Japan's monetary policy in line with those of the United States and Europe, where central bankers contain inflation by raising rates.

Shinzo Abe is elected as the country's youngest postwar prime minister and the first to be born after World War II.

2007 Less than a year after being elected to the post, Shinzo Abe abruptly resigns as prime minister. Yasuo Fukuda, the longest-lasting chief cabinet secretary, assumes the post.

Long absent from Japanese textbooks, the government decides to acknowledge the country's role in forcing a mass suicide by civilians in Okinawa during the final months of World War II.

2008 A censure motion against Prime Minister Fukuda passes in the Diet's upper house, the first of its kind against a prime minister in Japanese history. Fukuda survives a few more months but resigns exactly 365 days after he took office for failure to pass key bills and reach consensus with the opposing political party, the Democratic Party of Japan. Former foreign minister Taro Aso takes over as premier in late September.

The Japanese government officially accepts the Ainu population in Hokkaido as "an indigenous people." With its own distinct language and culture, the Ainu have been living in northern Japan for centuries but had yet to be recognized as such.

ABOUT JAPANESE

Japanese sounds and spellings differ in principle from those of the West. We build words letter by letter, and one letter can sound different depending where it appears in a word. For example, we see *ta* as two letters, and *ta* could be pronounced three ways, as in *tat, tall,* and *tale.* For the Japanese, *ta* is one character, and it is pronounced one way: *tah.*

The *hiragana* and *katakana* (tables of sounds) are the rough equivalents of our alphabet. There are four types of syllables within these tables: the single vowels *a, i, u, e,* and *o,* in that order; vowel-consonant pairs like *ka, ni, hu,* or *ro;* the single consonant *n,* which punctuates the upbeats of the word for bullet train, *Shinkansen (shee-n-ka-n-se-n);* and compounds like *kya, chu,* and *ryo.* Remember that these compounds are one syllable. Thus Tōkyō, the capital city, has only two syllables—*tō* and *kyō*—not three. Likewise pronounce Kyōto *kyō-to,* not *kee-oh-to.*

Japanese vowels are pronounced as follows: *a*–ah, *i*–ee, *u*–oo, *e*–eh, *o*–oh. The Japanese *r* is rolled so that it sounds like a bounced *d.*

No diphthongs. Paired vowels in Japanese words are not slurred together, as in our words *coin, brain,* or *stein.* The Japanese separate them, as in *mae (ma*-eh), which means in front of; *kōen (ko*-en), which means park; *byōin (byo*-een), which means hospital; and *tokei* (to-*keh*-ee), which means clock or watch.

Macrons. Many Japanese words, when rendered in *rōmaji* (roman letters), require macrons over vowels to indicate correct pronunciation, as in Tōkyō. When you see these macrons, double the length of the vowel, as if you're saying it twice: *to-o-kyo-o.* Likewise, when you see double consonants, as in the city name Nikkō, linger on the Ks—as in "bookkeeper"—and on the O.

Emphasis. Some books state that the Japanese emphasize all syllables in their words equally. This is not true. Take the words *sayōnara* and *Hiroshima.* Americans are likely to stress the downbeats: sa-yo-*na*-ra and *hi*-ro-*shi*-ma. The Japanese actually emphasize the second beat in each case: sa-*yō*-na-ra (note the macron) and hi-*ro*-shi-ma. Metaphorically speaking, the Japanese don't so much stress syllables as pause over them or race past them: Emphasis is more a question of speed than weight. In the vocabulary below, we indicate emphasis by italicizing the syllable that you should stress.

Three interesting pronunciations are in the vocabulary below. The word *desu* roughly means "is." It looks like it has two syllables, but the Japanese race past the final *u* and just say "dess." Likewise, some verbs end in -*masu,* which is pronounced "mahss." Similarly, the character *shi* is often quickly pronounced "sh," as in the phrase meaning "pleased to meet you:" ha-ji-me-*mash(i)*-te. Just like *desu* and -*masu,* what look like two syllables, in this case *ma* and *shi,* are pronounced *mahsh.*

Hyphens. Throughout *Fodor's Tōkyō,* we have hyphenated certain words to help you recognize meaningful patterns. This isn't conventional; it is practical. For example, *Eki-mae-dōri,* which literally means "Station Front Avenue," turns into a blur when rendered Ekimaedōri. And you'll run across a number of sight names that end in -*jingū* or -*jinja* or -*taisha*. You'll soon catch on to their meaning: Shintō shrine.

Structure. From the point of view of English grammar, Japanese sentences are structured back to front, ie. subject-object-verb instead of subject-verb-object as in English. An English speaker would say "I am going to Tōkyō," which in Japanese would translate literally as "Tōkyō to going."

Note: placing an "o" before words like *tera* (*otera*) and *shiro* (*oshiro*) makes the word honorific. It is not essential, but it is polite.

ESSENTIAL PHRASES

BASICS

Yes/No	*ha-i*/*ii*-e	はい / いいえ
Please	o-ne-*gai* shi-masu	お願いします
Thank you (very much)	(*dō*-mo) a-*ri*-ga-tō go-*zai*-ma su	(どうも) ありがとう ございます
You're welcome	*dō* i-ta-shi-ma-shi-te	どういたしまして
Excuse me	su-mi-ma-*sen*	すみません
Sorry	go-men na-*sai*	ごめんなさい
Good morning	o-*ha*-yō *go*-zai-ma-su	おはようございます
Good day/afternoon	kon-*ni*-chi-wa	こんにちは
Good evening	kom-*ban*-wa	こんばんは
Good night	o-*ya*-su-mi na-*sai*	おやすみなさい
Good-bye	sa-*yō*-na-ra	さようなら
Mr./Mrs./Miss	-san	～さん
Pleased to meet you	*ha*-ji-me-*mashi*-te	はじめまして
How do you do?	*dō*-zo yo-*ro*-shi-ku	どうぞよろしく

NUMBERS

The first reading is used for reading numbers, as in telephone numbers, and the second is often used for counting things.

1	*i*-chi / hi-*to*- 一 / 一つ tsu	10	jū / tō	十
2	ni / fu-*ta*-tsu 二 / 二つ	11	*jū*-i-chi	十一
3	san / *mit*-tsu 三 / 三つ	12	*jū*-ni	十二
4	yon (shi) / 四 / 四つ *yot*-tsu	13	*jū*-san	十三
5	go / i-*tsu*-tsu 五 / 五つ	14	*jū*-yon	十四
6	*ro*-ku / *mut*- 六 / 六つ tsu	15	*jū*-go	十五
7	*na*-na / 七 / 七つ *na*-na-tsu	16	*jū*-ro-ku	十六
8	*ha*-chi / *yat*- 八 / 八つ tsu	17	*jū*-shi-chi	十七
9	kyū / *ko*-ko- 九 / 九つ no-*tsu*	18	*jū*-ha-chi	十八

19	*jū*-kyū	十九	70	na-na-jū	七十
20	*ni*-jū	二十	80	*ha*-chi-jū	八十
21	*ni*-jū-i-chi	二十一	90	kyū-jū	九十
30	*san*-jū	三十	100	*hya*-ku	百
40	*yon*-jū	四十	1000	sen	千
50	*go*-jū	五十	10,000	*i*-chi-man	一万
60	*ro*-ku-jū	六十	100,000	*jū*- man	十万

DAYS OF THE WEEK

Sunday	*ni*-chi yō-bi	日曜日
Monday	*ge*-tsu yō-bi	月曜日
Tuesday	*ka* yō-bi	火曜日
Wednesday	*su*-i yū-bi	水曜日
Thursday	*mo*-ku yō-bi	木曜日
Friday	*kin* yō-bi	金曜日
Saturday	*dō* yō-bi	土曜日
Weekday	hei-ji-tsu	平日
Weekend	shū-ma-tsu	週末

MONTHS

January	*i*-chi *ga*-tsu	一月
February	*ni* ga-tsu	二月
March	*san* ga-tsu	三月
April	*shi* ga-tsu	四月
May	*go* ga-tsu	五月
June	*ro*-ku *ga*-tsu	六月
July	*shi*-chi *ga*-tsu	七月
August	*ha*-chi *ga*-tsu	八月
September	*ku* ga-su	九月
October	*jū* ga-tsu	十月
November	*jū*-i-chi *ga*-tsu	十一月
December	*jū*-ni *ga*-tsu	十二月

USEFUL EXPRESSIONS, QUESTIONS, AND ANSWERS

Do you speak English?	*ei*-go ga wa-*ka*-ri-ma-su *ka*	英語がわかりますか。
I don't speak Japanese.	*ni*-hon-go ga wa-*ka*-ri-ma-*sen*	日本語がわかりません。
I don't understand.	wa-*ka*-ri-ma-*sen*	わかりません。
I understand.	wa-*ka*-ri-ma-shi-*ta*	わかりました。
I don't know.	*shi*-ri-ma-*sen*	知りません。
I'm American (British).	wa-*ta*-shi wa a-*me*-ri-ka (i-*gi*-ri-su) jin *desu*	私はアメリカ（イギリス）人です。
What's your name?	o-*na*-ma-e wa *nan* desu *ka*	お名前はなんですか。
My name is.	.to *mo*-shi-*ma*-su	〜と申します。
What time is it?	i-ma *nan*-ji desu ka	今何時ですか。
How?	*dō* yat-te	どうやって。
When?	*i*-tsu	いつ。
Yesterday/today/tomorrow	ki-*nō*/kyō/*ashi*-ta	昨日 / 今日 / 明日
This morning	*ke*-sa	けさ
This afternoon	*kyō* no *go*-go	今日の午後
Tonight	*kom*-ban	今晩
Excuse me, what?	su-*mi*-ma-*sen*, *nan* desu *ka*	すみません、何ですか。
What is this/that?	*ko*-re/*so*-re wa *nan* desu *ka*	これ / それは何ですか。
Why?	*na*-ze desu *ka*	なぜですか。
Who?	*da*-re desu *ka*	だれですか。
I am lost.	*mi*-chi ni ma-yo-i-*mashi*-ta	道に迷いました。
Where is [place]	[place] wa *do*-ko desu *ka*	はどこですか
.. train station?	e-ki	駅
... subway station?	chi-*ka*-te-tsu-no eki	地下鉄の駅
... bus stop?	*ba*-su *no*-ri-*ba*	バス乗り場
... taxi stand?	*ta*-ku-shi-i *no*-ri-*ba*	タクシー乗り場

... airport?	kū-kō	空港
... post office?	*yū*-bin-*kyo*-ku	郵便局
... bank?	*gin*-kō	銀行
... the [name] hotel?	[name] ho-*te*-ru	ホテル
... elevator?	e-re-bē-tā	エレベーター
Where are the restrooms?	*to*-i-re wa *do*-ko desu *ka*	トイレはどこですか。
Here/there/over there	*ko*-ko/*so*-ko/*a*-so-ko	ここ / そこ / あそこ
Left/right	hi-*da*-ri/*mi*-gi	左 / 右
Straight ahead	mas-*su*-gu	まっすぐ
Is it near (far)?	chi-*ka*-i (*tō*-i) desu *ka*	近い（遠い）ですか。
Are there any rooms?	*he*-ya *ga* a-ri-masu *ka*	部屋がありますか。
I'd like [item]	[item] *ga* ho-*shi*-i no desu ga	がほしいのですが。
... newspaper	*shim*-bun	新聞
... stamp	*kit*-te	切手
... key	*ka*-gi	鍵
I'd like to buy [item]	[item] o kai-*ta*-i no desu ga	を買いたいのですが。
... a ticket to [destination]	[destination] *ma*-de no *kip*-pu	までの切符
Map	*chi*-zu	地図
How much is it?	i-*ku*-ra desu *ka*	いくらですか。
It's expensive (cheap).	ta-*ka*-i (ya-*su*-i) de su *ne*	高い（安い）ですね。
A little (a lot)	su-*ko*-shi (*ta*-ku-san)	少し（たくさん）
More/less	*mot*-to o-ku/ su-ku-na-ku	もっと多く / 少なく
Enough/too much	*jū*-bun/ō-su-*gi*-ru	十分 / 多すぎる
I'd like to exchange	*ryō*-ga e shi-*te* i-*ta*-da-ke-masu *ka*	両替して いただけますか。
... dollars to yen	*do*-ru o *en* ni	ドルを円に
.... pounds to yen	*pon*-do o *en* ni	ポンドを円に
How do you say... in Japanese?	ni-*hon*-go de.wa *dō* i-i-masu *ka*	日本語で. はどう言いますか。

I am ill/sick.	wa-*ta*-shi wa *byō*-ki desu	私は病気です。
Please call a doctor.	*i*-sha o *yon*-de ku-da-*sa*-i	医者を呼んでください。
Please call the police.	*ke*-i-sa-tsu o *yon*-de ku-da-*sa*-i	警察を呼んでください。
Help!	*ta*-su-*ke*-te	助けて!

USEFUL WORDS

Airport	Kūkō	空港
Bay	Wan	湾
Beach	-hama	浜
Behind	Ushiro	後ろ
Bridge	hashi or -bashi	橋
Bullet train, literally "new trunk line"	Shinkansen	新幹線
Castle	shiro or -jō	城
Cherry blossoms	Sakura	桜
City or municipality	-shi	市
Department store	depāto (deh-pah-to)	デパート
District	-gun	郡
East	Higashi	東
Exit	deguchi or -guchi	出口
Festival	Matsuri	祭
Feudal lord	Daimyō	大名
Foreigner	Gaijin	外人
Garden	Niwa	庭
Gate	mon or torii	門 / 鳥居
Gorge	Kyōkoku	峡谷
Hill	Oka	丘
Hot-spring spa	Onsen	温泉
In front of	Mae	前
Island	shima or -jima/-tō	島

	Rōmaji	ローマ字
Japanese words rendered in roman letters	Rōmaji	ローマ字
Lake	mizumi or -ko	湖
Main road	kaidō or kōdō	街道 / 公道
Morning market	asa-ichi	朝市
Mountain	yama or −san	山
Museum	Hakubutsukan	博物館
North	Kita	北
Park	Kōen	公園
Peninsula	hantō	半島
Plateau	Kōgen	高原
Pond	ike or -ike	池
Prefecture	-ken/-fu	県 / 府
Pub	Izakaya	居酒屋
River	kawa or -gawa	川 / 河
Sea	umi or -nada	海
Section or ward	-ku	区
Shop	mise or -ya	店 / 屋
Shrine	jinja or -gu	神社 / 宮
South	Minami	南
Street	michi or -dō	道
Subway	Chikatetsu	地下鉄
Temple	tera or -ji/-in	寺 / 院
Town	Machi	町
Train	Densha	電車
Train station	Eki	駅
Valley	Tani	谷
West	Nishi	西

MENU GUIDE

RESTAURANTS

BASICS AND USEFUL EXPRESSIONS

A bottle of	*ip*-pon	一本
A glass/cup of	*ip*-pai	一杯
Ashtray	*ha*-i-*za*-ra	灰皿
Bill/check	kan-*jō*	勘定
Bread	Pan	パン
Breakfast	*chō*-sho-ku	朝食
Butter	ba-*tā*	バター
Cheers!	kam-*pai*	乾杯!
Chopsticks	*ha*-shi	箸
Cocktail	*ka*-ku-*te*-ru	カクテル
Does that include dinner?	*Yū*-sho-ku *ga* tsu-ki- *ma-su-ka*	夕食が付きますか。
Excuse me!	su-mi-ma-*sen*	すみません。
Fork	*fō*-ku	フォーク
I am diabetic.	wa-ta-*shi* wa tō-*nyō*-byō de su	私は糖尿病です。
I am dieting.	*da*-i-et-to *chū* desu	ダイエット中です。
I am a vegetarian.	*saisho*-ku shu-*gi*-sha/ beji-*tari*-an de-su	菜食主義者 / ベジタリアンです。
I cannot eat [item]	[item] wa *ta*-be-ra- re-ma-*sen*	は食べられません。
I'd like to order.	*chū*-mon o shi-*tai* desu	注文をしたいです。
I'd like [item]	[item] o o-ne-*gai*-shi-ma su	をお願いします。
I'm hungry.	o-na-ka ga *su*-i-te i-*ma* su	お腹が空いています。
I'm thirsty.	*no*-do ga ka-*wa*-i-te i-*ma* su	喉が渇いています。
It's tasty (not good)	o-i-shi-i (ma-*zu*-i) desu	おいしい(まずい)です。
Knife	*na*-i-fu	ナイフ
Lunch	*chū*-sho-ku	昼食
Menu	me-nyū	メニュー
Napkin	*na*-pu-*kin*	ナプキン

Pepper	ko-*shō*	こしょう
Plate	*sa*-ra	皿
Please give me [item]	[item] o ku-da-*sa*-i	をください。
Salt	*shi*-o	塩
Set menu	*te*-i-sho-ku	定食
Spoon	su-*pūn*	スプーン
Sugar	sa-tō	砂糖
Wine list	*wa*-i-n *ri*-su-to	ワインリスト
What do you recommend?	o-su-su-me *ryō*-ri wa *nan* desu *ka*	おすすめ料理は何ですか。

MEAT DISHES

gyōza	Minced pork spiced with ginger and garlic in a Chinese wrapper and fried or steamed.	ギョウザ
hambāgu	Hamburger pattie served with sauce.	ハンバーグ
hayashi raisu	Beef flavored with tomato and brown sauce with onions and peas over rice.	ハヤシライス
kara-age	Chicken deep-fried without batter	から揚げ
Karē-raisu	Curried rice. A thick curry gravy typically containing beef is poured over white rice.	カレーライス
katsu-karē	Curried rice with tonkatsu.	カツカレー
niku-jaga	Beef and potatoes stewed together with soy sauce.	肉じゃが
okonomi-yaki	Sometimes called a Japanese pancake, this is made from a batter of flour, egg, cabbage, and meat or seafood, griddle-cooked then sprinkled with green onions and a special sauce.	お好み焼き

oyako-domburi (oyako-don)	Literally, "mother and child bowl"—cooked chicken and egg in broth over rice.	親子どんぶり（親子丼）
rōru kyabetsu	Rolled cabbage; beef or pork rolled in cabbage and cooked.	ロールキャベツ
shabu-shabu	Extremely thin slices of beef are plunged for an instant into boiling water flavored with soup stock and then dipped into a thin sauce and eaten.	しゃぶしゃぶ
shōga-yaki	Pork cooked with ginger	しょうが焼き
Shūmai	Shrimp or pork wrapped in a light dough and steamed (originally Chinese).	シュウマイ
subuta	Sweet and sour pork, originally a Chinese dish.	酢豚
sukiyaki	Thinly sliced beef, green onions, mushrooms, thin noodles, and cubes of tofu are simmered in a large iron pan in front of you. These ingredients are cooked in a mixture of soy sauce, mirin (cooking wine), and a little sugar. You are given a saucer of raw egg to cool the suki-yaki morsels before eating. Using chopsticks, you help yourself to anything on your side of the pan and dip it into the egg and then eat. Best enjoyed in a group.	すき焼き
sutēki	Steak	ステーキ
tanin-domburi (tannin-don)	Literally, "strangers in a bowl"—similar to oyako-domburi, but with beef instead of chicken.	他人どんぶり（他人丼）
tonkatsu	Breaded deep-fried pork cutlets	トンカツ

yaki-niku	Thinly sliced meat is marinated then barbecued over an open fire at the table.	焼き肉
yaki-tori	Pieces of chicken (white meat, liver, skin, etc.) threaded on skewers with green onions and marinated in sweet soy sauce and grilled.	焼き鳥

SEAFOOD DISHES

age-zakana	Deep-fried fish	揚げ魚
aji	Horse mackerel	あじ
ama-ebi	Sweet shrimp	甘えび
asari no sakamushi	Clams steamed with rice wine	あさりの酒蒸し
buri	Yellowtail	ぶり
dojo no yanagawa-nabe	Loach cooked with burdock root and egg in an earthen dish. Considered a delicacy.	どじょうの柳川鍋
ebi furai	Deep-fried breaded prawns	海老フライ
ika	Squid	イカ
iwashi	Sardines	いわし
karei furai	Deep-fried breaded flounder	かれいフライ
katsuo no tataki	Bonito cooked slightly on the surface. Eaten with chopped ginger and scallions and thin soy sauce.	かつおのたたき
maguro	Tuna	まぐろ
nizakana	Soy-simmered fish	煮魚
saba no miso-ni	Mackerel stewed with soybean paste	さばの味噌煮
samma	Saury pike	さんま

sashimi	Very fresh raw fish served sliced thin on a bed of white radish with a saucer of soy sauce and horse-radish. Eaten by lightly dipping fish into soy sauce mixed with horseradish.	刺身
sawara	Spanish mackerel	さわら
shake / sāmon	Salmon	しゃけ / サーモン
shimesaba	Mackerel marinated in vinegar.	しめさば
shio-yaki	Fish sprinkled with salt and broiled until crisp.	塩焼き
tako	Octopus	たこ
ten-jū	Deep-fried prawns served over rice with sauce	天重
teri-yaki	Fish basted in soy sauce and broiled	照り焼き
una-jū	Eel marinated in a slightly sweet soy sauce is char-coal-broiled and served over rice. Considered a delicacy.	うな重
yaki-zakana	Broiled fish	焼き魚

SUSHI

aji	Horse mackerel	あじ
ama-ebi	Sweet shrimp	甘えび
anago	Conger eel	あなご
aoyagi	Round clam	あおやぎ
chirashi zushi	In chirashi zushi, a variety of seafood is arranged on the top of the rice and served in a bowl	ちらし寿司
ebi	Shrimp	えび
futo-maki	Big roll with egg and pick-led vegetables	太巻き
hamachi	Yellowtail	はまち
hirame	Flounder	ひらめ

hotate-gai	Scallop	ほたて貝
ika	Squid	いか
ikura	Salmon roe	いくら
kani	Crab	かに
kappa-maki	Cucumber roll	かっぱ巻き
kariforunia-maki	California roll, containing crabmeat and avocado. This was invented in the U.S. but was reexported to Japan and is gaining popularity there.	カリフォルニア巻き
kazunoko	Herring roe	数の子
kohada	Gizzard (shad)	こはだ
maguro	Tuna	まぐろ
maki zushi	Raw fish and vegetables or other morsels are rolled in sushi rice and wrapped in dried seaweed. Some popular varieties are listed here.	巻き寿司
miru-gai	Giant clam	みる貝
nigiri zushi	The rice is formed into a bite-sized cake and topped with various raw or cooked fish. The various types are usually named after the fish, but not all are fish. Nigiri zushi is eaten by picking up the cakes with chopsticks or the fingers, lightly dipping the fish side in soy sauce, and eating.	にぎり寿司
saba	Mackerel	さば
shake / sāmon	Salmon	しゃけ / サーモン
shinko-maki	Shinko roll (shinko is a type of pickle)	新香巻き

sushi	Basically, sushi is rice, fish, and vegetables. The rice is delicately seasoned with vinegar, salt, and sugar. There are basically three types of sushi: nigiri, chirashi, and maki.	寿司
tai	Red snapper	たい
tako	Octopus	たこ
tamago	Egg	玉子
tekka-maki	Tuna roll	鉄火巻き
toro	Fatty tuna	とろ
uni	Sea urchin on rice wrapped with seaweed	うに

VEGETABLE DISHES

aemono	Vegetables dressed with sauces	和えもの
daigaku imo	Fried yams in a sweet syrup	大学いも
gobō	Burdock root	ごぼう
hōrenso	Spinach	ほうれん草
kabocha	Pumpkin	かぼちゃ
kimpira gobō	Carrots and burdock root, fried with soy sauce	きんぴらごぼう
kyūri	Cucumber	きゅうり
negi	Green onions	ねぎ
nimono	Vegetables simmered in a soy- and sake-based sauce	煮物
oden	Often sold by street vendors at festivals and in parks, etc., this is vegetables, octopus, or eggs simmered in a soy fish stock	おでん
o-hitashi	Boiled vegetables with soy sauce and dried shaved bonito or sesame seeds	おひたし
renkon	Lotus root	れんこん
satoimo	Taro root	さといも

su-no-mono	Vegetables seasoned with vinegar	酢の物
takenoko	Bamboo shoots	タケノコ
tempura	Vegetables, shrimp, or fish deep-fried in a light batter. Eaten by dipping into a thin sauce with grated white radish.	天ぷら
Tsukemono	Japanese pickles. Made from white radish, eggplant or other vegetables. Considered essential to the Japanese meal.	漬け物
yasai itame	Stir-fried vegetables	野菜炒め
yasai sarada	Vegetable salad	野菜サラダ

EGG DISHES

bēkon-eggu	Bacon and eggs	ベーコンエッグ
chawan mushi	Vegetables, shrimp, etc., steamed in egg custard	茶碗蒸し
hamu-eggu	Ham and eggs	ハムエッグ
medama-yaki	Fried eggs, sunny-side up	目玉焼き
omuraisu	Omelet with rice inside, often eaten with ketchup	オムライス
omuretsu	Omelet	オムレツ
sukuramburu eggu	Scrambled eggs	スクランブルエッグ
yude tamago	Boiled eggs	ゆで卵

TOFU DISHES

Tofu, also called bean curd, is a white, high-protein food with the consistency of soft gelatin.

agedashi dōfu	Deep fried plain tofu garnished with spring onions, dipped in hot broth.	揚げだし豆腐
hiya-yakko	Cold tofu with soy sauce and grated ginger.	冷やっこ
mābō dōfu	Tofu and ground pork in a spicy red sauce. Originally a Chinese dish.	マーボー豆腐

tofu no dengaku	Tofu broiled on skewers and flavored with miso.	豆腐の田楽
yu-dōfu	Boiled tofu	湯豆腐

RICE DISHES

chāhan	Fried rice; includes vegetables and pork.	チャーハン（炒飯）
chimaki	Sticky rice wrapped in bamboo skin.	ちまき
gohan	Steamed white rice	ご飯
okayu	Rice porridge	お粥
onigiri	Triangular balls of rice with fish or vegetables inside and wrapped in a type of seaweed.	おにぎり
pan	Bread; usually rolls with a meal.	パン

SOUPS

miso shiru	Miso soup. A thin broth containing tofu, mushrooms, or other morsels in a soup flavored with miso or soy-bean paste. The morsels are taken out of the bowl and the soup is drunk straight from the bowl without a spoon.	みそ汁
suimono	Clear broth soup, often including fish and tofu.	吸い物
tonjiru	Pork soup with vegetables.	豚汁

NOODLES

hiyamugi	Similar to sōmen, but thicker.	ひやむぎ
rāmen	Chinese noodles in broth, often with chāshū or roast pork. Broth is soy sauce, miso, or salt flavored.	ラーメン

soba	Buckwheat noodles. Served in a broth like udon or, during the summer, cold on a bamboo mesh (called zaru soba).	そば
sōmen	Very thin wheat noodles, usually served cold with a tsuyu or thin sauce. Eaten in summer.	そうめん
supagetti	Spaghetti. There are many interesting variations on this dish, notably spaghetti in soup, often with seafood.	スパゲッティ
udon	Wide flour noodles in broth. Can be lunch in a light broth or a full dinner called nabe-yaki udon when meat, chicken, egg, and vegetables are added and cooked in a pot.	うどん
yaki-soba	Noodles fried with beef and cabbage, garnished with pickled ginger and vegetables.	焼きそば

FRUIT

āmondo	Almonds	アーモンド
Apurikotto / anzu	Apricot	アプリコット / あんず
banana	Banana	バナナ
budō	Grapes	ぶどう
gurēpufurūtsu	Grapefruit	グレープフルーツ
rēzun / hoshi-budō	Raisins	レーズン / 干しブドウ
ichigo	Strawberries	いちご
ichijiku	Figs	いちじく
kaki	Persimmon	柿
kiiui	Kiwi	キーウイ
kokonattsu	Coconut	ココナッツ

kuri	Chestnuts	栗
kurumi	Walnuts	くるみ
mango	Mango	マンゴ
meron	Melon	メロン
mikan	Tangerine (mandarin orange)	みかん
momo	Peach	桃
nashi	Pear	梨
orenji	Orange	オレンジ
painappuru	Pineapple	パイナップル
papaiya	Papaya	パパイヤ
piinattsu	Peanuts	ピーナッツ
purūn	Prunes	プルーン
remon	Lemon	レモン
ringo	Apple	リンゴ
cherii / sakurambo	Cherry	チェリー / さくらんぼ
Suika	Watermelon	西瓜

DESSERT

aisukuriimu	Ice cream	アイスクリーム
appuru pai	Apple pie	アップルパイ
kēki	Cake	ケーキ
kōhii zerii	Coffee-flavored gelatin	コーヒーゼリー
kurēpu	Crepes	クレープ
purin	Caramel pudding	プリン
shābetto	Sherbert	シャーベット
wagashi	Japanese sweets	和菓子
yōkan	Sweet bean paste jelly	ようかん

DRINKS

ALCOHOLIC

| bābon | Bourbon | バーボン |
| biiru | Beer | ビール |

burandē	Brandy	ブランデー
chūhai	Shōchū mixed with soda water and flavored with lemon juice or other flavors.	チューハイ
kakuteru	Cocktail	カクテル
nama biiru	Draft beer	生ビール
nihonshu (sake)	Sake, a wine brewed from rice.	日本酒 (酒)
atsukan	warmed sake	熱燗
hiya	cold sake	冷や
sake	Rice wine	酒
shampan	Champagne	シャンパン
shōchū	Spirit distilled from potatoes	焼酎
sukocchi	Scotch	スコッチ
uisukii	Whisky	ウイスキー
wain	Wine	ワイン
aka	Red	赤
shiro	White	白
roze	Rose	ロゼ

NONALCOHOLIC

aisu kōhii	Iced coffee	アイスコーヒ
aisu tii	Iced tea	アイスティー
gyū-nyū/miruku	Milk	牛乳 / ミルク
jasumin cha	Jasmine tea	ジャスミン茶
jūsu	Juice, but can also mean any soft drink.	ジュース
kō-cha	Black tea	紅茶
kōhii	Coffee	コーヒー
kokoa	Hot chocolate	ココア
kōra	Coca-Cola	コーラ
miruku sēki	Milk shake	ミルクセーキ

miruku tii	Tea with milk	ミルクティー
nihon cha	Japanese green tea	日本茶
remon sukasshu	Carbonated lemon soft drink	レモンスカッシュ
remon tii	Tea with lemon	レモンティー
remonēdo	Lemonade	レモネード
ūron cha	Oolong tea	ウーロン茶

Travel Smart Japan

WORD OF MOUTH

"On our first trip to Japan our plane arrived 5 hours late on a Friday night. The train we were supposed to take had stopped running. One kind Japanese gentleman on his way home to see his family for the weekend spent 45 minutes with us trying to get us to where we were supposed to be. That is why we keep going back to Japan."

—Vonk17

www.fodors.com/forums

GETTING HERE & AROUND

■ AIR TRAVEL

Flying time to Japan is 13¾ hours from New York, 12¾ hours from Chicago, and 9½ hours from Los Angeles. Japan Airlines' GPS systems allow a more direct routing, which reduces its flight times by about 30 minutes. Your trip east, because of tailwinds, can be about 45 minutes shorter.

You can fly nonstop to Tokyo from Chicago, Detroit, New York, Los Angeles, San Francisco, Portland (OR), Seattle, Minneapolis, and Washington, D.C. You can also fly nonstop to Ōsaka from Chicago, Detroit, Pittsburgh, and San Francisco. Because of the distance, fares to Japan tend to be expensive, usually around $1,200 for a seat in coach.

Both of Japan's major carriers offer reduced prices for flights within the country, which are real cost- and time-savers if your trip includes destinations such as Kyūshū or Hokkaidō, though tickets must be booked outside Japan and there are restrictions on use in peak times. JAL offers the Yōkoso Japan Airpass; ANA has the Visit Japan Fare. Cathay Pacific offers a pass that includes 18 cities throughout Asia.

All domestic flights in Japan are no-smoking.

Airline Security Issues Transportation Security Administration (⊕ *www.tsa.gov*) has answers for almost every question that might come up.

Air Pass Information Visit Japan Fare (☎ *800/235–9262 All Nippon Airways in U.S.* ⊕ *www.anaskyweb.com*). **All Asia Pass** (☎ *800/233–2742 Cathay Pacific* ⊕ *www. cathay-usa.com*). **Yōkoso Japan Airpass** (☎ *800/525–3663 Japan Airlines* ⊕ *www.jal. co.jp*).

TRAVEL TIMES FROM TŌKYŌ			
To	By Air	By Car or Bus	By Train
Ōsaka	1¼ hours	7–8 hours	2½ hours
Hiroshima	1½ hours	10 hours	5 hours
Kyōto	1¼ hour	7 hours	2½ hours
Fukuoka	2 hours	14 hours	6 hours
Sapporo	1½ hours	15 hours	10 hours
Naha (Okinawa)	3 hours	NA	NA

■TIP➔ Ask the local tourist board about hotel and local transportation packages that include tickets to major museum exhibits or other special events.

AIRPORTS

The major gateway to Japan is Tōkyō's Narita Airport (NRT), 80 km (50 mi) northeast of the city. International flights also use Kansai International Airport (KIX) outside Ōsaka to serve the Kansai region, which includes Kōbe, Kyōto, Nara, and Ōsaka. In 2005 Centrair Airport (NGO) near Nagoya opened to take even more of the strain off Narita. Fares are generally cheapest into Narita, however. A few international flights use Fukuoka Airport, on the island of Kyūshū; these include Continental flights from Guam, JAL from Honolulu, and flights from other Asian destinations. Shin-Chitose Airport, outside Sapporo on the northern island of Hokkaidō, handles some international flights, mostly to Asian destinations such as Seoul and Shanghai. Most domestic flights to and from Tōkyō are out of Haneda Airport.

Tōkyō Narita's Terminal 2 has two adjoining wings, north and south. When you arrive, your first task should be to convert your money into yen; you need it for transportation into Tōkyō. In both wings ATMs and money-exchange counters are in the wall between the customs inspection area and the arrival lobby. Both terminals have a Japan National Tourist Organization tourist information center, where you can get free maps, brochures, and other visitor information. Directly across from the customs-area exits at both terminals are the ticket counters for airport limousine buses to Tōkyō.

If you have a flight delay at Narita, take a local Keisei line train into Narita town 15 minutes away, where a traditional shopping street and the beautiful Narita-san Shinsho-ji Temple are a peaceful escape from airport noise.

If you plan to skip Tōkyō and center your trip on Kyōto or central or western Honshū, Kansai International Airport (KIX) is the airport to use. Built on reclaimed land in Ōsaka Bay, it's laid out vertically. The first floor is for international arrivals; the second floor is for domestic departures and arrivals; the third floor has shops and restaurants; and the fourth floor is for international departures. A small tourist information center on the first floor of the passenger terminal building is open daily 9–5. Major carriers are Air Canada, Japan Airlines, and Northwest Airlines. The trip from KIX to Kyōto takes 75 minutes by JR train; to Ōsaka it takes 45–70 minutes.

Airport Information Centrair (Chubu) Airport (NGO) (0569/38–1195 www. centrair.jp). **Fukuoka Airport (FUK)** (092/483–7007 www.fuk-ab.co.jp). **Haneda Airport (HND)** (03/5757–8111 www.tokyo-airport-bldg.co.jp). **Kansai International Airport (KIX)** (0724/55–2500 www.kansai-airport.or.jp). **Narita Airport (NRT)** (0476/34–5000 www. narita-airport.jp). **New Chitose Airport (CTS)** (0123/23–0111 www.new-chitose-air port.jp).

GROUND TRANSPORTATION
Narita Airport is famously inconvenient for accessing the country it serves, and everyone has to head into Tōkyō first. It takes about 90 minutes—a time very dependent on city traffic—and costs

around $20. If you are arriving with a Japan Rail Pass and staying in Tōkyō for a few days, it is best to pay for the transfer into the city and activate the Rail Pass for travel beyond Tōkyō.

Directly across from the customs-area exits at both terminals are the ticket counters for buses to Tōkyō. Buses leave from platforms just outside terminal exits, exactly on schedule; the departure time is on the ticket. The Friendly Airport Limousine offers the only shuttle-bus service from Narita to Tōkyō.

Japan Railways trains stop at both Narita Airport terminals. The fastest and most comfortable is the Narita Limited Express (NEX), which makes 23 runs a day in each direction. Trains from the airport go directly to the central Tōkyō station in just under an hour, then continue to Yokohama and Ōfuna. Daily departures begin at 7:43 AM; the last train is at 9:43 PM. The one-way fare is ¥2,940 (¥4,980 for the first-class Green Car and ¥5,380 per person for a private compartment that seats four). All seats are reserved, and you'll need to reserve one for yourself in advance, as this train fills quickly.

The Keisei Skyliner train runs every 20–30 minutes between the airport terminals and Keisei-Ueno station. The trip takes 57 minutes and costs ¥1,920 ($17). The first Skyliner leaves Narita for Ueno at 9:21 AM, the last at 9:59 PM. There's also an early train from the airport, called the Morning Liner, which leaves at 7:49 AM and costs ¥1,400. From Ueno to Narita the first Skyliner is at 6:32 AM, the last at 5:21 PM.

Contacts Airport Transport Service Co. (03/3665–7232 in Tōkyō, 0476/32–8080 for Terminal 1, 0476/34–6311 for Terminal 2). **IAE Co** (0476/32–7954 for Terminal 1, 0476/34–6886 for Terminal 2). **Japan Railways** (03/3423–0111 for JR East InfoLine Weekdays 10–6). **Keisei Railway** (03/3831–0131 for Ueno information counter, 0476/32–8505 at Narita Airport).

TRAVEL TIMES FROM TŌKYŌ

FROM NARITA	TO	FARES	TIMES	NOTES
Friendly Airport Limousine (buses)	Various $$$$ hotels in Tōkyō & JR Tōkyō and Shinjuku train stations	¥2,400–¥3,800 ($21–$35)	Every hour until 11:30 PM	70–90 min, can be longer in traffic
Friendly Airport Limousine (buses)	Tōkyō City Air Terminal (TCAT)	¥2,900 ($26)	Every 10–20 min from 6:55 AM to 11 PM	
Narita Limited Express (NEX)	Central Tōkyō station, then continue to Yoko-hama and Ōfuna	One-way fare ¥2,940; Green Car ¥4,980; private compartment (four people) ¥5,380 per person	Daily departures begin at 7:43 AM; the last train is at 9:43 PM	All seats are reserved
Kaisoku (rapid train on JR's Narita Line)	Tōkyō station, by way of Chiba	¥1,280; ¥2,210 Green Car	16 departures daily, starting at 7 AM	Trip takes 1 hour 27 min
Keisei Skyliner train	Keisei-Ueno station	¥1,920 ($17)	Every 20–30 min, 9:21 AM–9:59 PM	All seats are reserved
Taxi	Central Tōkyō	¥20,000 (about $180) or more		

TRANSFERS BETWEEN AIRPORTS

Transfer between Narita and Haneda, the international and domestic airports, is easiest by the Friendly Limousine Bus, which should take 75 minutes and costs $30. Train transfers involve two changes.

Contacts Friendly Airport Limousine (☎ *03/3665–7220* ⊕ *www.limousinebus.co.jp*).

FLIGHTS

Japan Airlines (JAL) and United Airlines are the major carriers between North America and Narita Airport in Tōkyō; Northwest, American Airlines, Delta Airlines, and All Nippon Airways (ANA) also link North American cities with Tōkyō. Most of these airlines also fly into and out of Japan's number two other international airports, Kansai International Airport, located south of Ōsaka and Centrair, near Nagoya.

Airline Contacts All Nippon Airways (☎ *800/235–9262, 0120/02–9222 in Japan for domestic flights, 0120/02–9333 in Japan* for international flights ⊕ *www.anasky web.com*). **American** (☎ *800/433–7300, 0120/00–0860 in Japan* ⊕ *www.aa.com*). **Delta Airlines** (☎ *800/221–1212 for U.S. reservations, 800/241–4141 for international reservations* ⊕ *www.delta.com*). **Japan Airlines** (☎ *800/525–3663, 0120/25–5931 international in Japan, 0120/25–5971 domestic in Japan* ⊕ *www.jal.co.jp*). **Northwest** (☎ *800/447–4747, 03/3533–6000, 0120/12–0747 in Japan* ⊕ *www.nwa.com*). **United** (☎ *800/241–6522, 0120/11–4466 in Japan* ⊕ *www.united.com*).

▌ BOAT TRAVEL

Ferries connect most of the islands of Japan. Some of the more popular routes are from Tōkyō to Tomakomai or Kushiro in Hokkaidō; from Tōkyō to Shikoku; and from Tōkyō or Ōsaka to Kyūshū. You can purchase ferry tickets in advance from travel agencies or before boarding. The ferries are inexpensive and are a pleasant, if slow, way of traveling. Private cabins are available, but it's more fun to travel in the economy class, where everyone sleeps on the carpeted floor in one large room. Passengers eat, drink, and enjoy themselves in a convivial atmosphere. *There is little English information for local ferries, apart from three companies serving the Inland Sea between Ōsaka/Kōbe and Kyūshū. For information on local ferries, see the Essentials sections for individual towns within each chapter.*

Information Hankyu Ferry (⊕ *www.han9f. co.jp*). **Kansai Ferry** (⊕ *www.kanki.co.jp*). **Meimon Taiyo Ferry** (⊕ *www.cityline.co.jp*).

❙ BUS TRAVEL

Japan Railways (JR) offers a number of long-distance buses that are comfortable and inexpensive. You can use Japan Rail Passes (⇨ *By Train, below*) on some, but not all, of these buses. Routes and schedules are constantly changing, but tourist information offices will have up-to-date details. It's now possible to travel from Ōsaka to Tōkyō for as little as ¥5,000 one-way. Buses are generally modern and very comfortable, though overnight journeys are best avoided. Nearly all are now no-smoking. Foreign travelers are not often seen on these buses, and they remain one of the country's best-kept travel secrets. Japan Rail Passes are not accepted by private bus companies. City buses outside of Tōkyō are quite convenient, but be sure of your route and destination, because the bus driver probably won't speak English.

Local buses have a set cost, anywhere from ¥100 to ¥200, depending on the route and municipality, in which case you board at the front of the bus and pay as you get on. On other buses cost is determined by the distance you travel. You take a ticket when you board at the rear door of the bus; it bears the number of the stop at which you boarded. Your fare depends on your destination and is indicated by a board at the front of the

bus. Japan Railways also runs buses in some areas that have limited rail service. Remember, these buses are covered by the JR Pass, even if some JR reservation clerks tell you otherwise. Bus schedules can be hard to fathom if you don't read Japanese, however, so it's best to ask for help at a tourist information office. The Nihon Bus Association and the personal Web site Japan Buses has information about routes and which companies have English Web information.

Reservations are not always essential, except at peak holiday times and on the most popular routes, like Tōkyō–Ōsaka.

Bus Information JR Kantō Bus (☎ *03/3516–1950* ⊕ *www.jrbuskanto. co.jp*). Nihon Bus Association (⊕ *www. bus.or.jp/e/index.html*). Nishinihon JR Bus (☎ *06/6466–9990* ⊕ *www.nishinihonjrbus. co.jp*).

❙ CAR TRAVEL

You need an international driving permit (IDP) to drive in Japan. IDPs are available from the American Automobile Association. These international permits, valid only in conjunction with your regular driver's license, are universally recognized; having one may save you a problem with local authorities. By law, car seats must be installed if the driver is traveling with a child under six.

Major roads in Japan are sufficiently marked in roman type, and on country roads there's usually someone to ask for help. However, it's a good idea to have a detailed map with town names written in *kanji* (Japanese characters) and *romaji* (romanized Japanese).

Car travel along the Tōkyō–Kyōto–Hiroshima corridor and in other built-up areas of Japan is not as convenient as the trains. Roads are congested, gas is expensive (about ¥250 per liter), and highway tolls are exorbitant (tolls between Tōkyō and Kyōto amount to ¥10,550). In major cities, with the exception of main arteries,

English signs are few and far between, one-way streets often lead you off the track, and parking is often hard to find.

That said, a car can be the best means for exploring cities outside the metropolitan areas and the rural parts of Japan, especially Kyūshū and Hokkaidō. Consider taking a train to those areas where exploring the countryside will be most interesting and renting a car locally for a day or even half a day. Book ahead in holiday seasons. Rates in Tōkyō begin at ¥6,300 a day and ¥37,800 a week, including tax, for an economy car with unlimited mileage.

Local Agencies Japan Railways Group (⊕ www.japanrail.com). **ToCoo!** (☎ 03/5333–0246 www2.tocoo.jp).

Major Agencies Avis (☎ 800/331–1084 ⊕ www.avis.com). **Budget** (☎ 800/472–3325 ⊕ www.budget.com). **Hertz** (☎ 800/654–3001 ⊕ www.hertz.com). **National Car Rental** (☎ 800/227–7368 ⊕ www.nationalcar.com).

GASOLINE

Gas stations are plentiful along Japan's toll roads, and prices are fairly uniform across the country. Credit cards are accepted everywhere and are even encouraged—there are discounts for them at some places. Self-service stations have recently become legal, so if you pump your own gas you may get a small discount. Often you pay after putting in the gas, but there are also machines where you put money in first and then use the receipt to get change back. Staff will offer to take away trash and clean car windows. Tipping is not customary.

PARKING

There is little on-street parking in Japan. Parking is usually in staffed parking lots or in parking towers within buildings. Expect to pay upward of $3 per hour. Parking regulations are strictly enforced, and illegally parked vehicles are towed away. Recovery fees start at $300 and increase hourly.

ROAD CONDITIONS

Roads in Japan are often narrower than those in the United States, but they're well maintained in general. Driving in cities can be troublesome, as there are many narrow, one-way streets and little in the way of English road signs except on major arteries. Japanese drivers stick to the speed limit, but widely ignore bans on mobile phone use and dash-board televisions, and ignore rules on baby seats. Wild boars are not uncommon in rural districts, and have been known to block roads and ram into cars in the mountainous city of Kōbe and in Kyūshū, especially at night. From December to April northern areas are snow covered.

ROADSIDE EMERGENCIES

Emergency telephones along highways can be used to contact the authorities. A nonprofit service, JHelp.com, offers a free, 24-hour emergency assistance hotline. Car-rental agencies generally offer roadside assistance services. Mobile phones are now so widespread that local drivers can call for help from the middle of nowhere.

Emergency Services Police (☎ 110). **Fire** (☎ 119). **JHelp.com** (☎ 0570/00–0911).

RULES OF THE ROAD

In Japan people drive on the left. Speed limits vary, but generally the limit is 80 KPH (50 MPH) on highways, 40 KPH (25 MPH) in cities. Penalties for speeding are severe. By law, car seats must be installed if the driver is traveling with a child under six, while the driver and all passengers in cars must wear seat belts at all times. Driving while using hand-held phones is illegal.

Many smaller streets lack sidewalks, so cars, bicycles, and pedestrians share the same space. Motorbikes with engines under 50 cc are allowed to travel against automobile traffic on one-way roads. Fortunately, considering the narrowness of the streets and the volume of traffic, most Japanese drivers are technically skilled. They may not allow quite as much distance between cars as you're used to. Be prepared for sudden lane changes by other drivers. When waiting at intersections after dark, many drivers, as a courtesy to other drivers, turn off their main headlights to prevent glare.

2006 saw a nationwide crackdown on drunk driving, following a spate of horrific, headlining-grabbing accidents, so it's wisest to avoid alcohol entirely if you plan to drive.

■ CRUISE SHIP TRAVEL

Nagasaki, Ōsaka, and Kōbe are among the Japanese ports welcoming foreign cruise ships. Japanese are not big cruise-takers, although domestic ferry companies connect many of the islands.

Cruise Lines Crystal Cruises (☎ 310/785–9300 or 800/446–6620 ⊕ www. crystalcruises.com). **Princess Cruises** (☎ 661/753–0000 or 800/774–6237 ⊕ www. princess.com).

■ TRAIN TRAVEL

Riding Japanese trains is one of the pleasures of travel in the country. Efficient and convenient, trains run frequently and on schedule. The Shinkansen (bullet train), one of the fastest trains in the world, connects major cities north and south of Tōkyō. It is only slightly less expensive than flying, but is in many ways more convenient because train stations are more centrally located than airports (and, if you have a Japan Rail Pass, it's extremely affordable).

Other trains, though not as fast as the Shinkansen, are just as convenient and substantially cheaper. There are three types of train services: *futsū* (local service), *tokkyū* (limited express service), and *kyūkō* (express service). Both the tokkyū and the kyūkō offer a first-class compartment known as the Green Car. Smoking is allowed only in designated carriages on long-distance and Shinkansen trains.

Local and commuter trains are entirely no-smoking.

Because there are no porters or carts at train stations, it's a good idea to travel light when getting around by train. Savvy travelers often have their main luggage sent ahead to a hotel that they plan to reach later in their wanderings. It's also good to know that every train station, however small, has luggage lockers, which cost about ¥300 for 24 hours.

If you plan to travel by rail, get a Japan Rail Pass, which offers unlimited travel on Japan Railways (JR) trains. You can purchase one-, two-, or three-week passes. A one-week pass is less expensive than a regular round-trip ticket from Tōkyō to Kyōto on the Shinkansen. You must obtain a rail pass voucher prior to departure for Japan (you cannot buy them in Japan), and the pass must be used within three months of purchase. The pass is available only to people with tourist visas, as opposed to business, student, and diplomatic visas.

When you arrive in Japan, you must exchange your voucher for the Japan Rail Pass. You can do this at the Japan Railways desk in the arrivals hall at Narita Airport or at JR stations in major cities. When you make this exchange, you determine the day that you want the rail pass to begin, and, accordingly, when it ends. You do not have to begin travel on the day you make the exchange; instead, pick the starting date to maximize use. The Japan Rail Pass allows you to travel on all JR-operated trains (which cover most destinations in Japan) but not lines owned by other companies.

The JR Pass is also valid on buses operated by Japan Railways (⇨ *By Bus, above*). You can make seat reservations without paying a fee on all trains that have reserved-seat coaches, usually long-distance trains. The Japan Rail Pass does not cover the cost of sleeping compartments on overnight trains (called blue trains), nor does it cover the newest and fastest of the Shinkansen trains, the *Nozomi,* which make only one or two stops on longer runs. The pass covers only the *Hikari* Shinkansen, which make a few more stops than the Nozomi, and the *Kodama* Shinkansen, which stop at every station along the Shinkansen routes.

Japan Rail Passes are available in coach class and first class (Green Car), and as the difference in price between the two is relatively small, it's worth the splurge for first class, for real luxury, especially on the Shinkansen. A one-week pass costs ¥28,300 coach class, ¥37,800 first class; a two-week pass costs ¥45,100 coach class, ¥61,200 first class; and a three-week pass costs ¥57,700 coach class, ¥79,600 first class. Travelers under 18 pay lower rates. The pass pays for itself after one Tōkyō–Kyōto round-trip Shinkansen ride. Contact a travel agent or Japan Airlines to purchase the pass.

Many travelers assume that rail passes guarantee them seats on the trains they wish to ride. Not so. If you're using a rail pass, there's no need to buy individual tickets, but you should book seats ahead. You can reserve up to two weeks in advance or just minutes before the train departs. If you fail to make a train, there's no penalty, and you can reserve again.

Seat reservations for any JR route may be made at any JR station except those in the tiniest villages. The reservation windows or offices, *midori-no-madoguchi,* have green signs in English and green-stripe windows. If you're traveling without a Japan Rail Pass, there's a surcharge of approximately ¥500 (depending upon distance traveled) for seat reservations, and if you miss the train you'll have to pay for another reservation. When making your seat reservation you may request a no-smoking or smoking car. Your reservation ticket shows the date and departure time of your train as well as your car and seat number. Notice the markings painted on the platform or on little signs above the platform; ask someone which markings correspond to car numbers. If you

don't have a reservation, ask which cars are unreserved. Unreserved tickets can be purchased at regular ticket windows. There are no reservations made on local service trains. For traveling short distances, tickets are usually sold at vending machines. A platform ticket is required if you go through the wicket gate onto the platform to meet someone coming off a train. The charge is ¥140 (the tickets are ¥130 in Tōkyō and Ōsaka).

Most clerks at train stations know a few basic words of English and can read roman script. Moreover, they are invariably helpful in plotting your route. The complete railway timetable is a mammoth book written only in Japanese; however, you can get an English-language train schedule from the Japan National Tourist Organization (JNTO ⇨ *Visitor Information, above*) that covers the Shinkansen and a few of the major JR Limited Express trains. JNTO's booklet *The Tourist's Handbook* provides helpful information about purchasing tickets in Japan.

Information Japan Railways Group (✉*1 Rockefeller Plaza, Suite 1410, New York, NY* ☎*212/332–8686* ⊕ *www.japanrail.com*).

Buying a Pass Japan Rail Pass (⊕*www. japanrailpass.net*).

Train Information JR Hotline (☎*03/3423–0111*) is an English-language information service, open weekdays 10–6.

ESSENTIALS

■ ACCOMMODATIONS

Overnight accommodations in Japan run from luxury hotels to *ryokan* (traditional inns) to youth hostels and even capsules. Western-style rooms with Western-style bathrooms are widely available in large cities, but in smaller, out-of-the-way towns it may be necessary to stay in a Japanese-style room—an experience that can only enhance your stay.

Outside cities and major towns, most lodgings quote prices on a per-person basis with two meals, exclusive of service and tax. If you do not want dinner at your hotel, it is usually possible to renegotiate the price. Stipulate, too, whether you wish to have Japanese or Western breakfasts, if any. When you make reservations at a noncity hotel, you are usually expected to take breakfast and dinner at the hotel—this is the rate quoted to you unless you specify otherwise. In this guide, properties are assigned price categories based on the range between their least and most expensive standard double rooms at high season (excluding holidays).

A top-notch agent planning your trip to Japan will make sure you have all the necessary domestic travel arrangements reserved in advance and check ahead for reservations for sumō tournaments, geisha shows or the one-day-a-month temple opening. And when things don't work out the way you'd hoped, it's nice to have an agent to put things right.

Japan Hotel.net, J-Reserve, Rakuten Travel, and Tabiplaza, an off-shoot of Nippon Travel Agency, offer a wide range of accommodations from big city luxury to out-of-the-way family guesthouses. Budget Japan Hotels offers big discounts on cheaper rooms at major hotels.

■TIP→ Assume that hotels operate on the European Plan (**EP**, no meals) unless we specify that they use the Breakfast Plan (**BP**, with full breakfast), Continental Plan (**CP**, continental breakfast), Full American Plan (**FAP**, all meals), or Modified American Plan (**MAP**, breakfast and dinner) or are all-inclusive (**AI**, all meals and most activities).

Online Accommodations Budget Japan Hotels (⊕ *www.budgetjapanhotels.com*). Japan Hotel.net (⊕ *www.japanhotel.net*). J-Reserve (⊕ *www.j-reserve.com*). Rakuten Travel (⊕ *www.travel.rakuten.co.jp/en/*). Tabiplaza (⊕ *www.tabiplaza.net/japanhotels/*).

Japan Travel Agents Nippon Travel Agency (⊠ *Shimbashi Ekimae Bldg., Number 1, Shimbashi, Minato-ku, Tōkyō* ⊕ *www.nta. co.jp/english/index.asp* ⊠ *1025 W. 190th St., Suite 300, Gardena, CA* ☎ *310/768-0017*). JTB Sunrise Tours (⊠ *2-3-11 Higashi-Shinagawa, Shinagawa-ku, Tōkyō* ☎ *03/5796-5454* ⊕ *www.jtbusa.com*). IACE Travel (⊠ *Kounan Okamoto Bldg., 3F, Kounan, Minato-ku, Tōkyō* ☎ *03/5282-1522* ⊕ *www.iace-usa.com* ⊠ *18 E. 41st St., New York* ☎ *800/872-4223*).

APARTMENT & HOUSE RENTALS

In addition to the agents listed below, English-language newspapers and magazines such as the *Hiragana Times*, *Kansai Time Out* or *Metropolis*, or the *City-Source English Telephone Directory* may be helpful in locating a rental property. Note that renting apartments or houses in Japan is not a common way to spend a vacation, and weekly studio-apartment rentals may be fully booked by local business travelers.

The range of online booking services for Japan is expanding, although most of the accommodation booked this way is large and impersonal and staff in the hotel may not speak any English. Also check the location carefully to avoid incurring unforeseen extra costs and hassles in trying to reach the sights from a suburban hotel.

Contacts Sakura House—Apartments (☎ *03/5330-5250 www.sakura-house.com*). Weekly Mansion Tokyo (*www.wmt-tokyo. com*). The Mansions (☎ *03/5414-7070 or 03/5575-3232*).

Rental Listings Metropolis (☎ 03/3423–6932 ⊕ www.metropolis.co.jp). Kansai Time Out (☎ 078/232–4517 ⊕ www.kto.co.jp).

Exchange Clubs Home For Exchange (⊕ www.homeforexchange.com); $59 for a 1-year online listing.

HOME VISITS

Through the home visit system travelers can get a sense of domestic life in Japan by visiting a local family in their home. The program is voluntary on the homeowner's part, and there's no charge for a visit. The system is active in many cities throughout the country, including Tōkyō, Yokohama, Nagoya, Kyōto, Ōsaka, Hiroshima, Nagasaki, and Sapporo. To make a reservation, apply in writing for a home visit at least a day in advance to the local tourist information office of the place you are visiting. Contact the Japan National Tourist Organization (⇨ *Visitor Information, above*) before leaving for Japan for more information on the program.

HOSTELS

Hostels in Japan run about ¥2,000–¥3,000 per night for members, usually ¥1,000 more for nonmembers. The quality of hostels varies a lot, though the bad ones are never truly terrible, and the good ones offer memorable experiences, particularly in the national parks, where staff are knowledgeable about hiking and wildlife. Most offer private rooms for couples or families, though you should call ahead to be sure. Note that hostels tend to be crowded during school holidays, when university students are traveling around the country, and at other times they may be busy accommodating retiree hiking groups. Booking ahead is pretty essential.

Information Hostelling International—USA (☎ 301/495–1240 ⊕ www.hiusa.org). Japan Youth Hostels, Inc. (✉ Kanda Amerex Bldg., 9th fl., 3–1–16 Misaki-chō, Chiyoda-ku, Tōkyō ☎ 03/3288–1417). Check www.jyh.or.jp/english/index.html for regional Web sites.

HOTELS

Full-service, first-class hotels in Japan resemble their counterparts all over the world, and because many of the staff members speak English, these are the easiest places for foreigners to stay. They are also among the most expensive, tending to fall into the $$$ and $$$$ categories. Most major Western hotel chains, including Hilton, Hyatt, and Sheraton, have built hotels across Japan.

Business hotels are a reasonable alternative. These are clean, impersonal, and functional. All have Western-style rooms that vary from small to minuscule; service is minimal. However, every room has a private bathroom, albeit cramped, with tub and handheld shower, television (no English-language channels), telephone, and a hot-water thermos. Business hotels are often conveniently near the railway station. The staff may not speak English, but the rates fall into the $ and $$ categories.

Finding smaller, more personal hotels or guesthouses when you have no Japanese-language skills is hard, but it's worth doing an Internet search (using the word "pension" or "minshuku" for your destination, because enterprising owners of some smaller hotels have English Web sites.

Some useful words when checking into a hotel: air-conditioning, *eakon;* private baths, *o-furo;* showers, *shawā;* double beds, *daburubeddo;* twin beds *tsuinbeddo;* separate beds, *betsu;* pushed

LOCAL DO'S & TABOOS

CUSTOMS OF THE COUNTRY

In the United States being direct, efficient, and succinct are highly valued traits. In Japan this style is often frowned upon. Most Japanese do not use first names casually, so use last names with the honorific –*san* after the name in social situations. Make sure you don't express anger or aggression. These traits are equated with losing face in Japan, something you do not want to happen. Also stick to neutral subjects in conversations; private lives are kept private. There is no "fashionably late" in Japan, so be on time. Eating in public and overt physical affection is also frowned on by older Japanese.

GREETINGS

Japanese of all ages and backgrounds bow in greeting each other (even on the telephone!), and foreign visitors who at least bob the head will get a smile of recognition. However, Japanese know all about handshaking now, and the visitor's head may crash with an outstretched hand.

SIGHTSEEING

There's no strict dress code for visiting temples and shrines, but you will feel out of place in shorts or outfits with modest skin coverage. Casual clothes, including jeans, are fine for sightseeing. Remember to remove your shoes when entering temples. There are usually slippers by the entrance for you to change into.

OUT ON THE TOWN

Men are expected to wear a jacket and tie at more expensive restaurants and nightclubs. Women should wear a dress or skirt. If you've been invited out to dinner, either in a private home or restaurant, it's customary to bring a small token for your host. If you are in a home, remember to remove your shoes and put on the slippers that are usually waiting for you. When eating, it's okay to ask for a fork if you're not comfortable with chopsticks. If you do use chopsticks, do not use the end of the chopstick that has been in your mouth to pick up food from communal dishes. And never leave you're chopsticks sticking straight up in your food. This is a big no-no. Rest them on the edge of your bowl or plate instead.

Drinking is something of a national pastime in Japan. If you're not up to the task, never refuse a drink (it's considered very rude). Instead, sip away, making sure you're glass is half full. Whatever you do, do not pour your own glass. Companions traditionally pour drinks for each other and pouring your own is pointing out that your companions are not attentive. In the same vein, if you see an empty glass, fill it.

DOING BUSINESS

Make sure you allow adequate time for travel—being late for a business function is not appreciated. Wear conservative-color clothing and bring along *meishi* (business cards). Meishi are mandatory in Japan, and it is expected that when you bow upon meeting people you will also hand them a card, presented using both hands; only English is okay, but if you have one side in Japanese and one in English, your business associates will be very impressed. Remember to use last names with the honorific –*san* when addressing people. Also, hierarchy matters to the Japanese, so make sure your job title and/or rank is indicated on your card. You may see your associates putting the cards on the table in front of them, this is so they can remember your name easily. Follow suit; never shove the cards you have just received in your pocket or bag.

It's not customary for Japanese business people to bring their spouses along to dinners, so never assume it's okay to bring yours. If you want to bring your spouse along, ask in a way that eliminates a direct refusal.

If you are a woman traveling on business in Japan, it's good to note that many Japanese women still don't have careers, and Japanese businessmen may not know how to interact with a Western businesswoman. Be patient, and if need be, gently remind them to treat you the same as they would a man.

together, *kuttsukerareta;* queen bed, *kuīn saizun-no-beddo;* king bed, *kingu saizu-no-beddo.*

All hotels listed have private bath unless otherwise noted.

Contacts Hankyu-Hanshin-Dai-ichi Hotels (☎ *03/3501–4411 Tōkyō* ⊕ *www.hankyu-hotel. com*). **New Otani Hotels** (☎ *03/3265–1111* ⊕ *www.newotani.co.jp*). **Prince Hotels** (☎ *03/5986–8686* ⊕ *www.princejapan.com*). **Tōkyū Hotels** (☎ *03/3462–0109* ⊕ *www. tokyuhotels.com*). **Washington Hotels** (☎ *03/3433–4253* ⊕ *www.wh-rsv.com*).

INEXPENSIVE ACCOMMODATIONS

JNTO publishes a listing of some 700 accommodations that are reasonably priced. To be listed, properties must meet Japanese fire codes and charge less than ¥8,000 (about $70) per person without meals. For the most part, the properties charge ¥5,000–¥6,000 ($44–$54). These properties welcome foreigners (many Japanese hotels and ryokan do not like to have foreign guests because they might not be familiar with traditional-inn etiquette). Properties include business hotels, *ryokan* of a very rudimentary nature, *minshuku* (Japanese bed-and-breakfasts), and pensions. It's the luck of the draw whether you choose a good or less-than-good property. In most cases rooms are clean but very small. Except in business hotels, shared baths are the norm, and you are expected to have your room lights out by 10 PM.

Many establishments on the list of reasonably priced accommodations—and many that are not on the list—can be reserved through the nonprofit organization **Welcome Inn Reservation Center.** Reservation forms are available from your nearest JNTO office *(⇨ Visitor Information, above).* The Japanese Inn Group, which provides reasonable accommodations for foreign visitors, can be reserved through this same service. The center must receive reservation requests at least one week before your departure to allow processing

time. If you are already in Japan, the Tourist Information Centers (TICs) at Narita Airport and Kansai International Airport and in downtown Tōkyō and Kyōto can make immediate reservations for you at these Welcome Inns. Telephone reservations are not accepted.

Contacts Japanese Inn Group (☎ *03/3252–1717* ⊕ *www.jpinn.com*). **Welcome Inn Reservation Center** (✉ *Tōkyō Kotsu Kaikakan Bldg., 10th fl., 2–10–1 Yurakuchō, Chiyoda-ku, Tōkyō* ✉ *Kyōto Tourist Information, Kyōto Station* ⊕ *www.itcj.jp* ⊙ *Closed 2nd and 4th Tues.*).

MINSHUKU

Minshuku are private homes that accept guests and are similar to bed-and-breakfasts. Usually they cost about ¥6,000 (about $54) per person, including two meals. Although in a ryokan you need not lift a finger, don't be surprised if you are expected to lay out and put away your own bedding in a minshuku. Meals are often served in communal dining rooms at fixed times. Minshuku vary in size and atmosphere; some are private homes that take in only a few guests, while others are more like no-frills inns. Some of your most memorable stays could be at minshuku, as they offer a chance to become acquainted with a Japanese family and their hospitality.

Contacts Japan Minshuku Center (☎ *03/5858–0103* ⊕ *www.minshuku.jp*).

RYOKAN

If you want to sample the Japanese way, spend at least one night in a ryokan (inn). Usually small, one- or two-story wooden structures with a garden or scenic view, they provide traditional Japanese accommodations: simple rooms in which bedding is rolled out onto the floor at night.

Ryokan vary in price and quality. Some older, long-established inns cost as much as ¥80,000 ($700) per person, whereas humbler places that are more like bed-and-breakfasts are as low as ¥6,000 ($54).

Prices are per person and include the cost of breakfast, dinner, and tax. Some inns allow you to stay without having dinner and lower the cost accordingly. However, this is not recommended, because the service and meals are part of the ryokan experience. It is important to follow Japanese customs in all ryokan. *For more information, see the Ryokan Etiquette box in Chapter 6.*

Contacts Japan Ryokan Association (☎ *03/3231-5310* ⊕ *www.ryokan.or.jp*).

TEMPLES

You can also arrange accommodations in Buddhist temples, known as *shukubo*. JNTO has lists of temples that accept guests and you can arrange for your stay here as well. A stay at a temple generally costs ¥3,000–¥9,000 ($27–$80) per night, including two meals. Some temples offer instruction in meditation or allow you to observe their religious practices, while others simply offer a room. The Japanese-style rooms are very simple, and range from beautiful, quiet havens to not-so-comfortable, basic cubicles. For specific information on temple lodging in the Kii Mountain range in southern Japan, try contacting the Shukubo Temple Lodging Cooperative.

Contacts JNTO (⇨ Visitor Information, below). **Shukubo Temple Lodging Cooperative** (☎ *03/3231-5310* ⊕ *www.shukubo.jp*).

BUSINESS SERVICES AND FACILITIES

FedEx Kinko's offices throughout Japan will help with business services, and the Japan Convention Service can arrange interpretation and conference planning. The Japan National Tourist Office has extensive contacts for business travelers. Major hotels have business centers.

Contacts FedEx Kinko's (⊕ *www.english. fedexkinkos.co.jp*). **Japan Convention Service** (⊕ *www.jcs-pco.com*). **Japan External Trade Organization** (✉ *Ark Mori Bldg., 6F 12–32,*

Akasaka 1-chōme, Minato-ku, Tōkyō ⊕ *www. jetro.go.jp*).

COMMUNICATIONS

INTERNET

Phone jacks are the same in Japan as in the United States. Many hotels have ADSL or Ethernet connections for high-speed Internet access. Ethernet cables are usually available to buy at hotels if you don't bring your own. Wireless Internet access (Wi-Fi) is increasingly available for free at certain coffee shops and in many hotel lobbies across the country. There are Internet cafés in many cities, often doubling as manga libraries where you can rent a relaxation room with massage chair, computer, and desk.

Contacts Cybercafes (⊕ *www.cybercafes. com*) lists more than 4,000 Internet cafés worldwide.

PHONES

The good news is that you can now make a direct-dial telephone call from virtually any point on earth. The bad news? You can't always do so cheaply. Calling from a hotel is almost always the most expensive option; hotels usually add huge surcharges to all calls, particularly international ones. Calling cards usually keep costs to a minimum, but only if you purchase them locally.

The country code for Japan is 81. When dialing a Japanese number from outside Japan, drop the initial "0" from the local area code.

CALLING WITHIN JAPAN

Public telephones are a dying species in cell-phone-happy Japan. But there are usually public telephones near convenience stores, stations, and of course in hotel lobbies. Phones accept ¥100 coins as well as prepaid telephone cards. Domestic long-distance rates are reduced as much as 50% after 9 PM (40% after 7 PM). Telephone cards, sold in vending machines, hotels, and a variety of stores, are tremendously convenient.

Operator assistance at 104 is in Japanese only. Weekdays 9–5 (except national holidays) English-speaking operators can help you at the toll-free NTT Information Customer Service Centre.

Contacts Directory Assistance (☎104). **NTT Information Customer Service Centre** (☎0120/36–4463).

CALLING OUTSIDE JAPAN

Many gray, multicolor, and green phones have gold plates indicating, in English, that they can be used for international calls. Three Japanese companies provide international service: KDDI (001), Japan Telecom (0041), and IDC (0061). Dial the company code + country code + city/area code and number of your party. Telephone credit cards are especially convenient for international calls. For operator assistance in English on long-distance calls, dial 0051.

The country code for the United States is 1.

Access Codes Japan has several telephone companies for international calls, so make a note of all the possible access code numbers to use to connect to your U.S. server before departure. **AT&T Direct** (☎800/222–0300). **MCI WorldPhone** (☎800/444–4444). **Sprint International Access** (☎800/877–4646).

CALLING CARDS

Telephone cards for ¥1,000 ($9) can be bought at station kiosks or convenience stores and can be used in virtually all public telephones. For international calls, look for phones that accept KDDI prepaid cards valued between ¥1,000 and ¥7,000. Cards are available from convenience stores.

MOBILE PHONES

Japan is the world leader in mobile-phone technology, but overseas visitors cannot easily use their handsets in Japan because it is a non-GSM country. Best to rent a phone from one of the many outlets at Narita, Kansai, and Nagoya airports. Softbank sells 3G SIM cards so you can use your own number in Japan. Most

company rental rates start at ¥525 ($5) a day, excluding insurance. Check the airport Web sites for the current companies. Phones can be ordered online or by fax, or rented for same-day use.

Contacts G-call (⊕ www.g-call.com). **JALABC Rental Phone** (⊕ www.rental-mobile.com/en/domestic/). **Softbank** (⊕ www.softbank-rental.jp).

∎ CUSTOMS AND DUTIES

Japan has strict regulations about bringing firearms, pornography, and narcotics into the country. Anyone caught with drugs is liable to be detained, refused reentry into Japan, and deported. Certain fresh fruits, vegetables, plants, and animals are also illegal. Nonresidents are allowed to bring in duty-free: (1) 400 cigarettes or 100 cigars or 500 grams of tobacco; (2) three 760-ml bottles of alcohol; (3) 2 ounces of perfume; (4) other goods up to ¥200,000 value.

Getting through customs at a Japanese airport goes more smoothly if you are well dressed, clean-shaven, and as conventional-looking as possible. Visitors arriving off flights from other Asian countries are particularly scrutinized for narcotics.

Japan Information Ministry of Finance, Customs and Tariff Bureau (☎03/3581–4111 ⊕ www.customs.go.jp).

U.S. Information U.S. Customs and Border Protection (⊕ www.cbp.gov).

∎ DAY TOURS AND GUIDES

The Japan Guide Association will introduce you to English-speaking guides. You need to negotiate your own itinerary and price with the guide. Assume that the fee will be ¥25,000–¥30,000 for a full eight-hour day. The Japan National Tourist Organization can also put you in touch with various local volunteer groups that conduct tours in English; you need only to pay for the guide's travel expenses, admission fees to cultural sites, and meals if you eat together.

The Japan National Tourist Organization (JNTO) sponsors a Good-Will Guide program in which local citizens volunteer to show visitors around; this is a great way to meet Japanese people. These are not professional guides; they usually volunteer both because they enjoy welcoming foreigners to their town and because they want to practice their English. The services of Good-Will Guides are free, but you should pay for their travel costs, their admission fees, and any meals you eat with them while you are together. To participate in this program, make arrangements for a Good-Will Guide in advance through JNTO in the United States or through the tourist office in the area where you want the guide to meet you. The program operates in 75 towns and cities, including Tōkyō, Kyōto, Nara, Nagoya, Ōsaka, and Hiroshima.

Goodwill Guides is a network of volunteer guides who take foreigners on tours for free. You are only required to pay their expenses while they are with you, including a meal if you eat together. Bookings can be done through their Web site.

Contacts Goodwill Guides (⊕ *www.jnto.go.jp/ eng/arrange/essential/list_volunteerGuides_a-n.html*). **Japan Guide Association** (☎ *03/3213-2706* ⊕ *www.jga21c.or.jp*). **Japan National Tourist Organization** (☎ *03/3201-3331* ⊕ *www.jnto.go.jp*).

▌ EATING OUT

The restaurants we list are the cream of the crop in each price category. Food, like many other things in Japan, can be expensive. Eating at hotels and famous restaurants is costly; however, you can eat well and reasonably at standard restaurants that may not have signs in English. Many less expensive restaurants have plastic replicas of the dishes they serve displayed in their front windows, so you can always point to what you want to eat if the language barrier is insurmountable. A good place to look for moderately priced dining spots is in the restaurant concourse of department stores, usually on the bottom floor.

In general, Japanese restaurants are very clean (standards of hygiene are very high). Tap water is safe, and most hotels have Western-style restrooms, although restaurants may have Japanese-style toilets, with bowls recessed into the floor, over which you must squat.

If you're in a hurry, a visit to one branch of the MOS Burger, Freshness Burger, or First Kitchen will fit the bill. These nationwide chains offer familiar hamburgers, but they also have local variations. Yoshinoya is another popular chain, serving grilled salmon, rice and miso soup for breakfast (until 10), and then hearty portions of rice and beef for the rest of the day.

Local and regional specialties are discussed at the beginning of each chapter in this book; for more general information on dining in Japan, see Understanding Japan at the end of this book. For information on food-related health issues, see Health below.

MEALS AND MEALTIMES

Office workers eat lunch from noon to 1 PM, so eat later to avoid crowds. Many restaurants have lunchtime specials until 2:30 PM aimed at housewives, and some close their doors between 3 and 5 PM. Note that many restaurants in rural towns are closed by 9.

Unless otherwise noted, the restaurants listed in this guide are open daily for lunch and dinner.

PAYING

Beyond major hotels and smart city dining, credit cards may not be accepted, so check before ordering.

RESERVATIONS

For upmarket, evening dining in major cities ask hotel staff to make reservations—not only will this guarantee a table, but it gives the management time to locate an English menu or staff with some language skills.

▮ ELECTRICITY

The electrical current in Japan is 100 volts, 50 cycles alternating current (AC) in eastern Japan, and 100 volts, 60 cycles in western Japan; the United States runs on 110-volt, 60-cycle AC current. Wall outlets in Japan accept plugs with two flat prongs, as in the United States, but do not accept U.S. three-prong plugs.

Consider making a small investment in a universal adapter, which has several types of plugs in one lightweight, compact unit. Most laptops and mobile phone chargers are dual voltage (i.e., they operate equally well on 110 and 220 volts), so require only an adapter. These days the same is true of small appliances such as hair dryers. Always check labels and manufacturers' instructions to be sure. Don't use 110-volt outlets marked FOR SHAVERS ONLY for high-wattage appliances such as hair dryers.

Contacts Steve Kropla's Help for World Travelers (⊕ www.kropla.com) has information on electrical and telephone plugs around the world. **Walkabout Travel Gear** (⊕ www. walkabouttravelgear.com) has a good coverage of electricity under "adapters."

▮ EMERGENCIES

Assistance in English is available 24 hours a day on the toll-free Japan Helpline.

The following embassies and consulates are open weekdays, with one- to two-hour closings for lunch. Call for exact hours.

Contacts U.S. Embassy and Consulate (✉ 1–10–5 Akasaka, Minato-ku, Toranomon ☎ 03/322–4500 ⊕ tokyo.usembassy.gov/ Ⓜ Namboku Line, Tameike-Sannō station [Exit 13]).

General Emergency Contacts Ambulance and Fire (☎ 119). **Japan Helpline** (☎ 0120/46–1997 or 0570/00–0911). **Police** (☎ 110).

▮ HEALTH

Japan is a safe, clean country for travelers with good drinking water and no major water- or insect-borne diseases. Drugs and medications are widely available at drug stores, although the brand names and use instructions will be in Japanese, so if on regular medication, take along enough supplies to cover the trip. Condoms are sold widely, but they may not have the brands you're used to. Speak with your physician and/or check the CDC or World Health Organization Web sites for health alerts, particularly if you're pregnant or traveling with children or have a chronic illness.

SPECIFIC ISSUES IN JAPAN

Japan is basically a safe country for travelers. The greatest danger is the possibility of being caught up in an earthquake and its resulting tsunami. Earthquake information is broadcast (in Japanese) as news flashes on television within minutes, and during major disasters national broadcaster N.H.K. broadcasts information in English on radio and television. Minor tremors occur every month, and sometimes train services are temporarily halted. Check emergency routes at hotels and higher ground if staying near coastal areas.

General Information and Warnings U.S. Department of State (⊕ www.travel.state. gov). Tap water is safe everywhere in Japan. Medical treatment varies from highly skilled and professional at major hospitals to somewhat less advanced in small neighborhood clinics. At larger hospitals you have a good chance of encountering English-speaking doctors who have been partly educated in the West.

Mosquitoes can be a minor irritation during the rainy season, though you are never at risk of contracting anything serious like malaria. If you're staying in a *ryokan* or any place without air-conditioning, anti-mosquito coils or an electric-powered spray will be provided. Dehydration and heatstroke could be concerns if you spend a long time outside during the summer months, but isotonic sports drinks are readily available from the nation's ubiquitous vending machines.

OVER-THE-COUNTER REMEDIES

It may be difficult to buy the standard over-the-counter remedies you're used to, so it's best to bring with you any medications (in their proper packaging) you may need. Medication can only be bought at pharmacies in Japan, but every neighborhood seems to have at least one. Ask for the *yakyoku*. Pharmacists in Japan are usually able to manage at least a few words of English, and certainly are able to read some, so have a pen and some paper ready, just in case. In Japanese, aspirin is *asupirin* and Tylenol is *Tairenōru*. Following national regulations, Japanese drugs contain less potent ingredients than foreign brands, so the effects can be disappointing; check advised dosages carefully.

▌ HOURS OF OPERATION

General business hours in Japan are weekdays 9–5. Many offices also open at least half the day on Saturday, but are generally closed on Sunday.

Banks are open weekdays from 9 to at least 3, some now staying open until 4 or 5. As with shops, there's a trend toward longer and later opening hours.

Gas stations follow usual shop hours, though 24-hour stations can be found near major highways.

Museums generally close on Monday and the day following national holidays. They are also closed the day following special exhibits and during the week-long New Year's celebrations.

Department stores are usually open 10–7, but close one day a week, varying from store to store. Other stores are open from 10 or 11 to 7 or 8. There's a trend toward longer and later opening hours in major cities, and 24-hour convenience stores, many of which now have ATM facilities, can be found across the entire country.

HOLIDAYS

As elsewhere, peak times for travel in Japan tend to fall around holiday periods. You want to avoid traveling during the few days before and after New Year's; during Golden Week, which follows Greenery Day (April 29); and in mid-July and mid-August, at the time of Ōbon festivals, when many Japanese return to their hometowns (Ōbon festivals are celebrated July or August 13–16, depending on the location). Note that when a holiday falls on a Sunday, the following Monday is a holiday.

Japan's national holidays are January 1 (*Ganjitsu*, New Year's Day); the second Monday in January (*Senjin-no-hi*, Coming of Age Day); February 11 (*Kenkoku Kinenbi*, National Foundation Day); March 20 or 21 (*Shunbun-no-hi*, Vernal Equinox); April 29 (*Midori-no-hi*, Greenery Day); May 3 (*Kempō Kinen-bi*, Constitution Day); May 5 (*Kodomo-no-hi*, Children's Day); the third Monday in July (*Umi-no-hi*, Marine Day); the third Monday in September (*Keirō-no-hi*, Respect for the Aged Day); September 23 or 24 (*Shūbun-no-hi*, Autumnal Equinox); the second Monday in October (*Taiiku-no-hi*, Sports Day); November 3 (*Bunka-no-hi*, Culture Day); November 23 (*Kinrō Kansha-no-hi*, Labor Thanksgiving Day); December 23 (*Tennō Tanjōbi*, Emperor's Birthday).

MAIL

The Japanese postal service is very efficient. Air mail between Japan and the United States takes between five and eight days. Surface mail can take anywhere from four to eight weeks. Express service is also available through post offices.

Although there are numerous post offices in every city, it's probably best to use the central post office near the main train station, because the workers speak English and can handle foreign mail. Some of the smaller post offices are not equipped to send packages. Post offices are open weekdays 9–5 and Saturday 9–noon. Some central post offices have longer hours, such as the one in Tōkyō, near Tōkyō Eki (train station), which is open 24 hours year-round. Most hotels and many convenience stores also sell stamps.

The Japanese postal service has implemented the use of three-numeral-plus-four postal codes, but its policy is similar to that in the United States regarding ZIP-plus-fours; that is, addresses with the three-numeral code will still arrive at their destination, albeit perhaps one or two days later. Mail to rural towns may take longer.

It costs ¥110 (98¢) to send a letter by air to North America. An airmail postcard costs ¥70 (63¢). Aerograms cost ¥90 (81¢).

To get mail, have parcels and letters sent "poste restante" to the central post office in major cities; unclaimed mail is returned after 30 days.

SHIPPING PACKAGES

FedEx has drop-off locations at branches of Kinko's in all major cities. A 1-kg/2.20-lb package from central Tōkyō to Washington, DC, would cost about ¥7,200 ($64), and take two days to be delivered. The Japanese postal service is very efficient, and domestic mail rarely goes astray. To ship a 5-kg/11.02-lb parcel to the United States costs ¥10,150 ($91) if sent by airmail, ¥7,300 ($65) by SAL

(economy airmail), and ¥4,000 ($36) by sea. Allow a week for airmail, 2 to 3 weeks for SAL, and up to 6 weeks for packages sent by sea. Large shops usually ship domestically, but not overseas.

Express Services FedEx (☎ *0120/00–320 toll-free, 043/298–1919* ⊕ *www.fedex.com/ jp_english).*

MONEY

Japan is expensive, but there are ways to cut costs. This requires, to some extent, an adventurous spirit and the courage to stray from the standard tourist paths. One good way to hold down expenses is to avoid taxis (they tend to get stuck in traffic anyway) and try the inexpensive, efficient subway and bus systems; instead of going to a restaurant with menus in English and Western-style food, go to places where you can rely on your good old index finger to point to the dish you want, and try food that the Japanese eat.

ITEM	AVERAGE COST
Cup of Coffee	¥250–¥600
Glass of Wine	¥500
Glass of Beer	¥300–¥600
Sandwich	¥300
One-Mile Taxi Ride in Capital City	¥660
Museum Admission	¥1,000

Prices throughout this guide are given for adults. Substantially reduced fees are almost always available for children, students, and senior citizens.

■ TIP→ Banks never have every foreign currency on hand, and it may take as long as a week to order. If you're planning to exchange funds before leaving home, don't wait until the last minute.

ATMS AND BANKS

Your own bank will probably charge a fee for using ATMs abroad; the foreign bank you use may also charge a fee. Nevertheless, you'll usually get a better rate of exchange at an ATM than you will at a currency-exchange office or even when changing money in a bank. And extracting funds as you need them is a safer option than carrying around a large amount of cash.

■ TIP➔ PIN numbers with more than four digits are not recognized at ATMs in many countries. If yours has five or more, remember to change it before you leave.

ATMs at many Japanese banks do not accept foreign-issue cash or credit cards. Citibank has centrally located branches in most major Japanese cities and ATMs that are open 24 hours. UFJ and Shinsei banks are members of the Plus network, as are some convenience store cash machines. Post offices have ATMs that accept Visa, MasterCard, American Express, Diners Club, and Cirrus cards. Elsewhere, especially in more rural areas, it's difficult to find suitable ATMs. PIN numbers in Japan are comprised of four digits. In Japanese an ATM is commonly referred to by its English acronym, while PIN is *anshō bangō*. Because of a spate of ATM crimes allegedly involving "foreigners" asking for help, Japanese bank customers may react badly to requests for assistance. Instead, contact bank staff by using the phone next to the ATM. Many machines also have English on-screen instructions.

CREDIT CARDS

Throughout this guide, the following abbreviations are used: **AE**, American Express; **D**, Discover; **DC**, Diners Club; **MC**, MasterCard; and **V**, Visa.

It's a good idea to inform your credit-card company before you travel, especially if you're going abroad and don't travel internationally very often. Otherwise, the credit-card company might put a hold on your card owing to unusual activity—not a good thing halfway through your trip.

Record all your credit-card numbers—as well as the phone numbers to call if your cards are lost or stolen—in a safe place, so you're prepared should something go wrong. Both MasterCard and Visa have general numbers you can call (collect if you're abroad) if your card is lost, but you're better off calling the number of your issuing bank, since Master-Card and Visa usually just transfer you to your bank; your bank's number is usually printed on your card.

If you plan to use your credit card for cash advances, you'll need to apply for a PIN at least two weeks before your trip. Although it's usually cheaper (and safer) to use a credit card abroad for large purchases (so you can cancel payments or be reimbursed if there's a problem), note that some credit-card companies *and* the banks that issue them add substantial percentages to all foreign transactions, whether they're in a foreign currency or not. Check on these fees before leaving home, so there won't be any surprises when you get the bill.

■ TIP➔ Before you charge something, ask the merchant whether or not he or she plans to do a dynamic currency conversion (DCC). In such a transaction the credit-card processor (shop, restaurant, or hotel, not Visa or Master-Card) converts the currency and charges you in dollars. In most cases you'll pay the merchant a 3% fee for this service in addition to any credit-card company and issuing-bank foreign-transaction surcharges.

Dynamic currency conversion programs are becoming increasingly widespread. Merchants who participate in them are supposed to ask whether you want to be charged in dollars or the local currency, but they don't always do so. And even if they do offer you a choice, they may well avoid mentioning the additional surcharges. The good news is that you *do* have a choice. And if this practice really gets your goat, you can avoid it entirely thanks to American Express; with its cards, DCC simply isn't an option.

MasterCard and Visa are the most widely accepted credit cards in Japan. When you use a credit card you'll be asked if you intend to pay in one installment as most locals do, say *hai-ikkai* (Yes, one time) just to fit in, even if you plan differently once you get home. Many vendors don't accept American Express. Cash is still king in Japan, and older Japanese consider it shameful to use a card.

Reporting Lost Cards American Express (☎ 0120/02–0120 for Japan office ⊕ www.americanexpress.com). **Diners Club** (☎ 0120/07—4024 for Japan office ⊕ www.dinersclub.com). **MasterCard** (☎ 00531/11–3886 Japan office ⊕ www.mastercard.com). **Visa** (☎ 0120/13–3173 for Japan office ⊕ www.visa.com).

CURRENCY & EXCHANGE

The unit of currency in Japan is the yen (¥). There are bills of ¥10,000, ¥5,000, ¥2,000, and ¥1,000. Coins are ¥500, ¥100, ¥50, ¥10, ¥5, and ¥1. Japanese currency floats on the international monetary exchange, so changes can be dramatic.

At this writing the exchange rate was ¥108 for U.S.$1.

■ TIP→ Even if a currency-exchange booth has a sign promising no commission, rest assured that there's some kind of huge, hidden fee. And as for rates, you're almost always better off getting foreign currency at an ATM or exchanging money at a bank.

▌RESTROOMS

The most hygienic restrooms are found in hotels and department stores, and are usually clearly marked with international symbols. You may encounter Japanese-style toilets, with bowls recessed into the floor, over which you squat facing the top. This may take some getting used to, but it's completely sanitary as you don't come into direct contact with the facility. If you can't face a squat, check out the last cubical in the row because it may be a Western-style toilet.

In many homes and Japanese-style public places, there will be a pair of slippers at the entrance to the restroom. Change into these before entering the room, and change back when you exit.

Many public toilets don't have toilet paper, though there are dispensers where packets can be purchased for ¥50 (45¢) or so. Many locals accept the free tissue packets that are handed out as advertisements in the center of town for this reason. Similarly, paper towel dispensers and hand dryers are not always installed, so a small handkerchief is useful for drying your hands.

Find a Loo The Bathroom Diaries (⊕ www. thebathroomdiaries.com) is flush with unsanitized info on restrooms the world over—each one located, reviewed, and rated.

PACKING

Pack light, because porters can be hard to find and storage space in hotel rooms may be tiny. What you pack depends more on the time of year than on any dress code. For travel in the cities, pack as you would for any American or European city. At more expensive restaurants and nightclubs men usually need to wear a jacket and tie. Wear conservative-color clothing at business meetings. Casual clothes are fine for sightseeing. Jeans are as popular in Japan as they are in the United States, and are perfectly acceptable for informal dining and sightseeing.

Although there are no strict dress codes for visiting temples and shrines, you will be out of place in shorts or immodest outfits. For sightseeing leave sandals and open-toe shoes behind; you'll need sturdy walking shoes for the gravel pathways that surround temples and fill parks. Make sure to bring comfortable clothing that isn't too tight to wear in traditional Japanese restaurants, where you may need to sit on tatami-matted floors. For beach and mountain resorts pack informal clothes for both day and evening wear. Central and southern Japan are hot and humid June to September, so pack cotton clothing. Winter daytime temperatures in northern Japan hover around freezing, so gloves and hats are necessary, and clip-on shoe spikes can be bought locally.

Japanese do not wear shoes in private homes or in any temples or traditional inns. Having shoes you can quickly slip in and out of is a decided advantage. Take wool socks (checking first for holes!) to help you through those shoeless occasions during the winter.

All lodgings provide a thermos of hot water and bags of green tea in every room. For coffee you can call room service, buy very sweet coffee in a can from a vending machine, or purchase packets of instant coffee at local convenience stores. If you're staying in a Japanese inn, they probably won't have coffee.

Sunglasses, sunscreen lotions, and hats are readily available, and these days they're not much more expensive in Japan. It's a good idea to carry a couple of plastic bags to protect your camera and clothes during sudden cloudbursts.

Take along small gift items, such as scarves or perfume sachets, to thank hosts (on both business and pleasure trips), whether you've been invited to their home or out to a restaurant.

PASSPORTS

Hotels in Japan require foreign guests to show passports at check in, but police are unlikely to ask foreign visitors for on-the-spot identification, although crime crackdowns on nightlife areas of big cities and political tensions with North Korea or Russia can alter local circumstances in some areas.

U.S. Passport Information U.S. Department of State (☎ 877/487-2778 ⊕ travel.state.gov/ passport).

U.S. Passport and Visa Expediters A. **Briggs Passport & Visa Expediters** (☎ 800/806-0581 or 202/464-3000 ⊕ www. abriggs.com). **American Passport Express** (☎ 800/455-5166 or 603/559-9888 ⊕ www. americanpassport.com). **Passport Express**

(☎ 800/362-8196 or 401/272-4612 ⊕ www. passportexpress.com). **Travel Document Systems** (☎ 800/874-5100 or 202/638-3800 ⊕ www.traveldocs.com).

▌SAFETY

Even in its major cities Japan is a very safe country, with one of the lowest crime rates in the world. You should, however, keep an eye out for pickpockets and avoid unlit roads at night like anywhere else. The greatest danger is the possibility of being caught up in an earthquake and its resulting tsunami. Earthquake information is broadcast (in Japanese) as news flashes on television within minutes, and during major disasters national broadcaster N.H.K. broadcasts information in English on radio and television. Minor tremors occur every month, and sometimes train services are temporarily halted. Check emergency routes at hotels and higher ground if staying near coastal areas.

▌TIP→ **Distribute your cash, credit cards, IDs, and other valuables between a deep front pocket, an inside jacket or vest pocket, and a hidden money pouch. Don't reach for the money pouch once you're in public.**

▌TAXES

A 5% national consumption tax is added to all hotel bills. Another 3% local tax is added to the bill if it exceeds ¥15,000 (about $134). You may save money by paying for your hotel meals separately rather than charging them to your bill.

At first-class, full-service, and luxury hotels, a 10% service charge is added to the bill in place of individual tipping. At more expensive ryokan, where individualized maid service is offered, the service charge is usually 15%. At business hotels, minshuku, youth hostels, and economy inns, no service charge is added to the bill.

There's an across-the-board, nonrefundable 5% consumption tax levied on all sales, which is included in the ticket price. Authorized tax-free shops will knock the tax off purchases over ¥10,000 if you show your passport and a valid tourist visa. A large sign is displayed at such shops. A 5% tax is also added to all restaurant bills. Another 3% local tax is added to the bill if it exceeds ¥7,500 (about $67). At more expensive restaurants a 10%–15% service charge is added to the bill. Tipping is not customary.

∎ TIME

All of Japan is in the same time zone, which is 14 hours ahead of New York, and 17 hours ahead of San Francisco. Daylight saving time is not observed, although government officials are now pushing to introduce the concept over the next several years.

∎ TOURS

Tōkyō and Kyōto feature on almost every tour of Japan, while Hiroshima, Nara, and Nikkō being the normal secondary destinations. Read brochures carefully and try to see through the inevitable pictures of cherry trees and geisha—to check whether what is planned fits your idea of a holiday. Is it temple after temple? Does the tour include experiences such as sushi and sumō—or are they only pricey options? Is the domestic travel by bullet train, plane, or bus? Japan can be quite a culture shock, so resist the temptation to pack in too much, and go for tours that include half days of freedom, because just stepping outside the hotel into the local streets is likely to provide some unimagined sights and experiences.

Along with the usual destinations, General also goes to the Inland Sea, some ancient onsen towns and World Heritage sites; Kintetsu promises to get you closer to the world of geisha in Kyōto. IACE and Nippon Express Travel USA have tours that look to modern Japan by taking in the Tōkyō Anime Festival and the Comic Market (side trip to techie-paradise Akihabra) and architecture old and new. Even the big companies try to get visitors off the beaten track: Explorient goes to the Kisō Valley near Nagoya.

Japan is daunting for first-time visitors and anyone without Japanese-language skills, so a package tour is a great way to get into the country and find your feet. However, beware of expensive optional tours such as tea ceremonies, Kabuki tours, and night views. Local tourist offices can probably tell you how to have the same experience more economically.

Recommended Companies Exlororient Travel Services (☎800/785–1233 ⊕www.explorient.com). **General** (☎800/221–2216 ⊕www.generaltours.com). **IACE** (☎866/735–4223 ⊕www.iace-asia.com). **JALPAK International** (☎800/525–3663 ⊕www.jalpak.com). **Kintetsu** (☎800/422–381 ⊕www.kintetsu.com). **Nippon Express Travel USA** (☎212/319–9021 New York, 415/412–1822 San Francisco ⊕www.nipponexpresstravel.us./jp/index.htm).

SPECIAL-INTEREST TOURS

ART

Japan is overflowing with art—from pottery and painting to the precise skills of flower arranging and calligraphy. Many tours include museums and art galleries, but only some get you right into the artists' studios with English-language help to understand their skills and the chance to try your hand.

Contacts Absolute Travel (☎800/736–8187 ⊕www.absolutetravel.com). **Smithsonian Journeys** (☎877/338–8687 ⊕www.smithsonianjourneys.org).

BIKING

Most airlines accommodate bikes as luggage, provided they're dismantled and boxed.

Biking is popular in Japan, but local bike-rental shops may not have frames large enough for non-Japanese bikers.

Contacts One Life Japan (☎03/3231–5310 or 03/3361–1338 ⊕www.onelifejapan.com/).

DIVING

Okinawa, Kyūshū, and the islands and peninsular south of Tōkyō are all popular diving areas. If you are a novice diver, make sure that a dive leader's "English spoken" means real communication skills. Dive Japan has lists of dive services and locations.

Contacts Dive Japan (⊕ *www.divejapan.com*).

ECOTOURS

Whales, monkeys, bears, and cranes— Japan does have fauna and flora to appreciate slowly, but English-language tours are limited. Naturalist Mark Brazil, who writes extensively about wild Japan, leads ecotours through Zegrahm Eco Expeditions.

Contacts Zegrahm Eco Expeditions (☎ 800/628–8747 ⊕ *www.zeco.com*).

GOLF

Japan's love affair with golf does not make it any easier for non-Japanese-speaking visitors to reserve a game unless introduced by a club member. Japan Golf Tours takes guided groups from the United States, and Golf in Japan, put together by golfing expats, helpfully lists more than 2,000 courses that welcome foreign golfers.

Contacts Golf in Japan (⊕ *www. golf-in-japan.com*). **Japan Golf Tours** (☎ 827/277–6841 ⊕ *www.japan-golf-tours. com*).

HIKING

Japan has well-marked trails, bus-train connections to trailheads, and hidden sights to be discovered. Millions of Japanese are avid and well-equipped hikers. English information is growing, so check local tourist offices for details. Visit Outdoor Japan's Web site for all outdoor activities. Hike Japan, run by an experienced British hiker, has a range of tours in all seasons.

Contacts Hike Japan (⊕ *www.hikejapan.com*). **Outdoor Japan** (⊕ *www.outdoorjapan.com/*).

LANGUAGE PROGRAMS

No better way to learn the language than to immerse yourself by studying Japanese in Japan, with classes, a homestay, and cultural tours on which to put the new-found skills into action. The Japanese Embassy information and culture section (JICC) Web site has good links to schools and procedures for study abroad programs.

Contacts Japan Information and Culture Center (JICC) (☎ 877/338–8687 ⊕ *www. us.emb-japan.go.jp*). **World Link Education** (☎ 800/621–3085 ⊕ *www.wle-japan.com*).

WINTER SPORTS

Japanese ski areas are smaller than those in North America and Europe, but excellent powder and après-ski features like hot springs are pulling in Australian and Asian visitors. Resorts in Nagano and Hokkaidō are most popular. Boarding is cooler than skiing for young Japanese. Ski Japan's Web site has tours, information, and weather reports.

Contacts Ski Japan (⊕ *www.skijapanguide. com*).

∎ TIPPING

Tipping is not common in Japan. It's not necessary to tip taxi drivers, or at hair salons, barbershops, bars, or nightclubs. A chauffeur for a hired car usually receives a tip of ¥500 ($4.50) for a half-day excursion and ¥1,000 ($9) for a full-day trip. Porters charge fees of ¥250–¥300 (about $2.50) per bag at railroad stations and ¥200 ($1.80) per piece at airports. It's not customary to tip employees of hotels, even porters, unless a special service has been rendered. In such cases, a gratuity of ¥2,000–¥3,000 ($18–$26) should be placed in an envelope and handed to the staff member discreetly.

VISITOR INFORMATION

The Japan National Tourist Organization (JNTO) has offices in Tōkyō and Kyōto. Away from the main offices, the JNTO-affiliated International Tourism Center of Japan also has more than 140 counters/offices nationwide. Look for the sign showing a red question mark and the word "information" at train stations and city centers. Needing help on the move? For recorded information 24 hours a day, call the Teletourist service.

Japan National Tourist Organization (JNTO) Contacts Japan: (✉2-10-1 *Yūrakuchō, 1-chōme, Chiyoda-ku, Tōkyō* ☎03/3502-1461). **United States:** (✉1 *Rockefeller Plaza, Suite 1250, New York, NY* ☎212/757-5640 ✉401 N. Michigan Ave., Suite 770, Chicago, IL ☎312/222-0874 ✉1 Daniel Burnham Ct., San Francisco, CA ☎415/292-5686 ✉515 S. Figueroa St., Suite 1470, Los Angeles, CA ☎213/623-1952 ⊕ www.jnto.go.jp).

Teletourist Service Tōkyō (☎03/3201-2911).

Tourist Information Centers (TIC) Tōkyō International Forum B1 (✉3-5-1 *Marunouchi, Chiyoda-ku, Tōkyō* ☎03/3201-3331 ✉Main Terminal Bldg., Narita Airport, Chiba Prefecture ☎0476/34-6251 ✉2F, JR Kyōto Station Bldg., Hachijō-guchi, Minami-ku, Kyōto ☎075/343-6655 ✉Kansai International Airport, Ōsaka ☎0724/56-6025).

ONLINE TRAVEL TOOLS

Online cultural resources and travel-planning tools abound for travelers to Japan. Aside from the expected information about regions, hotels, and festivals, Web Japan has off-beat info such as the location of bargain-filled ¥100 shops in Tokyo and buildings designed by famous architects. Another good source for all-Japan information and regional sights and events is Japan-guide.com.

Urban Rail, maintains a useful subway navigator, which includes the subway systems in Tōkyō and the surrounding areas. The Metropolitan Government Web site is an excellent source of information on sightseeing and current events in Tōkyō.

Check out the Web sites of Japan's three major English-language daily newspapers: the *Asahi Shimbun, Daily Yomiuri,* and the *Japan Times.* Expats share insider knowledge on the magazine sites *Metropolis* and *Tokyo Journal.* Both have up-to-date arts, events, and dining listings. In the Kansai region, *Kansai Time Out* is definitely worth a look.

Avoid being lost in translation with the help of Japanese-Online, a series of online language lessons that will help you pick up a bit of Japanese before your trip. (The site also, inexplicably, includes a sampling of typical Japanese junior-high-school math problems.) Order Japan's tastiest with confidence by checking translations on the Tokyo Food Page.

The Web site, the Japanese Garden, has photographic tours of more than 20 famous gardens and explanations about their history and design elements. Keep an eye on Mount Fuji with the 24-hour live camera at Mt. Fuji Live. The Japan Sumō Association's Web site sets you straight with everything from the moves, the rankings, and even translated interviews with the wrestlers; tournament ticket information (but not booking) is also available. The Kabuki-za Theater in Tōkyō has history, stories, and sounds of the ancient art form (with good information about costumes and makeup) at its Web site. Japan has a good share of places designated by UNESCO. Check them out at Web Japan, a site sponsored by the Ministry of Foreign Affairs, which includes some quirky J-trends info such as massage chairs and beauty products for middle-aged men.

All About Japan Japan-guide.com (⊕ www. japan-guide.com). **Web Japan** (⊕ web-jpn.org).

Transportation Hitachi's "Hyperdia-timetable" (⊕ www.hyperdia.com). **Jorudan's "Japanese Transport Guide"** (⊕ www.jorudan.co.jp/english). **Metropolitan Government** (⊕ www.metro.tokyo.jp). **Urban Rail** (⊕ www.urbanrail.net).

English-Language Media Sources Asahi Shimbun (⊕ *www.asahi.com/english*). Daily Yomiuri (⊕ *www.yomiuri.co.jp/dy*). Japan Times (⊕ *www.japantimes.co.jp*). Metropolis (⊕ *www.metropolis.co.jp*). Tōkyō Journal (⊕ *www.tokyo.to*). Kansai Time Out (⊕ *www.japanfile.com*).

Learn Japanese Japanese-Online (⊕ *www.japanese-online.com*). Tokyo Food Page (⊕ *www.bento.com/tokyofood.html*). Japanese CultureThe Japanese Garden (*learn.bowdoin.edu/japanesegardens/*). **Mt. Fuji Live** (⊕ *live-fuji.jp/fuji/livee.htm*). The Japan Sumō Association (⊕ *www.sumo.or.jp/eng*). The **Kabuki-za Theater** (⊕ *www.shochiku.co.jp/play/kabukiza/theater*).

Currency Conversion Google (⊕ *www.google.com*). Oanda.com (⊕ *www.oanda.com*). XE.com (⊕ *www.xe.com*).

Time Zones Timeanddate.com (⊕ *www.timeanddate.com/worldclock*).

Weather Japan Meteorological Agency (⊕ *www.jma.go.jp/jma/indexe.html*).

INDEX

Photo Credits

NOTES

NOTES

NOTES

NOTES

NOTES

NOTES

NOTES

NOTES

NOTES

NOTES

NOTES

ABOUT OUR WRITERS

Joshua Bisker moved to Japan after completing a degree in English at Oberlin College. He loves surprising Japanese speakers with his thick country accent, proudly gained from three years in the rice fields, mikan groves, towel factories, and schoolrooms of Ehime prefecture on Shikoku. He has recently returned to New York. Josh updated the Kyōto, Shikoku, and Okinawa chapters.

When he's not hitting the pavement for the entertainment business newspaper Variety or his online column, Sake-Drenched Postcards, **Brett Bull** can be found working away behind a drafting table at a Japanese construction company, his occupation since arriving in Tōkyō from California eight years ago. He contributed to the Experience Japan and the Exploring Tōkyō and Tōkyō Where to Stay sections.

Nicholas Coldicott arrived in Japan in 1998 intending to stay for a year. Almost a decade later he spends his time exploring the city's nightlife as the drink columnist for the Japan Times. In his spare time he plays funk and soul 45s in bars, clubs, festivals, and ski resort cafeterias. He revised the Tōkyō Nightlife and the Arts section.

Maruan El Mahgiub came to Japan from England in 2003. Having travelled to almost every prefecture in Japan, he is now paying his dues working as a *sarariman* for Japan's largest travel company. He updated the Nara and Kōbe chapters.

James Hadfield lived in Nagoya for 3½ years before moving to Tōkyō, where he works as a freelance writer and editor. He updated the Nagoya chapter.

Hokkaidō updater **Amanda Harlow** left the south of England and settled in Japan in 1993, eventually stopping in Hokkaidō, where she works proofreading, teaching, and narrating government videos about clearing snow from roads.

Born in Washington state, **Misha Janette** moved to Japan in 2004 to study at Tōkyō's Bunka Fashion College. A regular fashion columnist for The Japan Times, JCReport.com, and Kyodo News agency, Misha is also a stylist for magazines and celebrities and makes TV appearances as a fashion critic. She updated the shopping section in the Tōkyō chapter.

Currently based in New York, **Kaya Laterman** has lived on-and-off in Japan for over 15 years. She has worked as a reporter for numerous wire services and newspapers and now translates Japanese manga into English. She updated the Travel Smart, Understanding Japan, and front matter sections.

Kevin Mcgue moved to Tōkyō in 2000, having spent time in Hungary and the Czech Republic. He writes on Japanese music, fashion and business for Metropolis, J@pan Inc, and a number of other magazines published both inside and outside Japan. He has also worked as a filmmaker and Tōkyō location scout for foreign film crews. He updated the Where to Eat section in the Tōkyō chapter and the Side Trips from Tōkyō chapter.

Japan Alps and Osaka updater **Robert Morel** lived in Western and Central Japan for four years, and has crossed the country both by train and bicycle. He now lives in a charmingly neglected neighborhood in Tōkyō where he teaches and writes.

John Malloy Quinn got his B.A. and M.A. in English at University of Colorado at Boulder, and has spent 16 of the last 21 years in various parts of Japan. He currently lives in the Setagaya district of Tōkyō, and teaches at Meiji and Tokai Universities. He's searched the world, from Ngapali Beach to Apollo Bay, and Machu Picchu to Mt. Everest, but he always finds something special among the romantic mists of Tsuwano or the towering cypress of Koya-san. John updated the Tōhoku, Western Honshū, and Kyūshū chapters.